श्रीमद्वाल्मीकीय रामायणम्

VAALMEEKI RAAMAAYANA

अयोध्या काण्ड

ayodhya kaanda

आनो भद्रा: क्रतवो यन्तु विश्वत:

Let noble thoughts come to us from all over the GLOBE

श्रीमद्वाल्मीकीय रामायणम्
VAALMEEKI RAAMAAYANA

अयोध्या काण्ड
ayodhya kaanda

by

L. Swaminathan

Sanskrit text edited by Smt. Shantha Srinivasam
English Translation by L. Swaminathan

Motilal Banarsidass Publications

MOTILAL BANARSIDASS
PUBLICATIONS
4741/23, Ansari Road, Daryaganj, New Delhi - 110002 (India)
Email: mlbd@mlbd.com | sales@mlbd.com | exports@mlbd.com
Website: www.mlbd.com

Vaalmeeki Raamaayana
Ayodhya Kaanda
by
L. Swaminathan

First Edition Published in 2023

Published in India by Motilal Banarsidass Publications

ISBN : 978-93-91759-68-1 (PB)

Printed and bound in India

SALUTATION

TO
THE RAMCO GROUP OF INDUSTRIES
founded by

Sri P.A.C. Ramasamy Raja of Rajapalayam

who was a man of Dharma
who tried to live by RAAMA's VALUES.

We offer our thanks to
Sri PR Raamasubrahmaneya Rajha, Chairman,
RAMCO GROUP

Who has been source of inspiration and support in
our studies on Vaalmeeki Raamaayana
for over two decades.

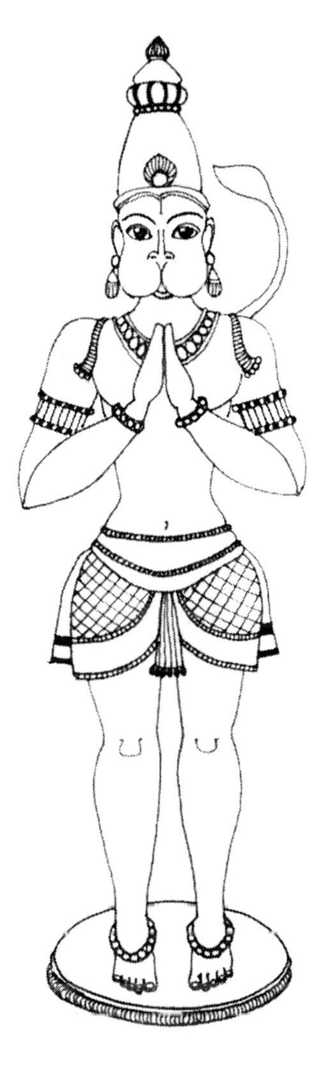

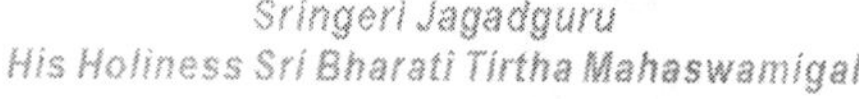

Sringeri Jagadguru
His Holiness Sri Bharati Tirtha Mahaswamigal

Sri Sharadamba, Sringeri

।। श्री शृङ्गेरी श्रीजगद्गुरुमहासंस्थानम् ।।

श्रीमत्परमहंसपरिव्राजकाचार्यवर्य पदवाक्यप्रमाणपारावारपारीण यम
नियमासनप्राणायामप्रत्याहारधारणाध्यानसमाध्यष्टाङ्गयोगानुष्ठाननिष्ठ
तपश्चक्रवर्त्यनाद्यविच्छिन्न श्रीशफराचार्यगुरुपरम्पराप्राप्त
षड्दर्शनस्थापनाचार्य व्याख्यानसिंहासनाधीश्वर सकलनिगम
ागमसारहृदय सांख्यत्रयप्रतिपादक वैदिकमार्गप्रवर्तक
सर्वतन्त्रस्वतन्त्रादिराजधानी विद्यानगरमहाराजधानी
कर्णाटकसिंहासनप्रतिष्ठापनाचार्य श्रीमद्राजाधिराजगुरुभूमण्डलाचार्य
ऋष्यशृङ्गपुरवराधीश्वर तुङ्गभद्रातीरवासि
श्रीमद्विद्याशफरपादपद्माराधक श्रीजगद्गुरु
श्रीमदभिनवविद्यातीर्थस्वामिगुरुकरकमलसन्जात

।। श्री जगद्गुरु शृङ्गेरी श्रीमद्भारतीतीर्थमहास्वामिभिः ।।

अस्मदत्यन्त प्रियशिष्य लोकानाथार्यतनूज स्वामिनाथार्यविषये
नारायणस्मरणपुरस्सरं विरचिता आशिषस्समुल्लसन्तु ।
मपरित्राणाय साधूनां विनाशाय च दुष्कृताम् ।
धर्मसंस्थापनार्थाय सम्भवामि युगे युगे ।।

इति भगवान् प्रतिजज्ञे । तदनुसारं त्रेतायुगे विश्वामि
त्रादिसाधुपरित्राणाय रावणादिदुष्कृतां विनाशाय च
स भगवान् श्रीरामचन्द्रात्मना अवततार । तस्य भगवतः
श्रीरामचन्द्रस्य पवित्रं चरित्रं आदिकविः महर्षिर्वाल्मीकिः
चतुर्विंशतिसहस्रसंमितैः श्लोकैः श्रीमद्रामायणे उपनिबबन्ध।
तदेव च आदिकाव्यमिति प्रसिद्धिमगमत् । तच्च सर्वेषां सनातनधम
र्नुयायिनां अतितरामुपादेयमास्ते । तत्रत्यस्य एकैकस्यापि
श्लोकस्य महिमातिशयो विद्यते । तस्य च श्रीमद्रामायणस्य
प्रायस्सर्वास्वपि भाषासु अनुवादा
व्यधायिषत । रामायणगतां रामकथामाश्रित्य बहवः कवयः
काव्यनाटकादीनि विरचय्य कृतार्था बभूवुः ।

भवानस्मद्गुरुचरणानामव्याजकृपापात्रतां प्राप्य
श्रीमद्रामायणं महत्या श्रद्धया अभ्यस्य
प्रतिश्लोकमाङ्ग्लभाषया अन्ववादीत् । अनेकभागात्मकः
स ग्रन्थः प्रकाशितः आस्तिकानामादरपात्रभूत् । अधुना
पुनः श्रीमद्रामायणगतान् कतिपयान् सारभूतान्
श्लोकानुपादाय आङ्ग्लानुवादं व्यधासीत् ।
सम्पूर्णग्रन्थावलोकनाक्षमाः एतद्ग्रन्थावलोकनेनैव
रामकथां सुखमवबोद्धुं पारयन्ति । भवदीयोऽयं परिश्रमः
श्लाघ्यतरो वर्तते ।

डीशारदाचन्द्रमौलीश्वरयोरसीमया कृपया ग्रन्थोऽयं न
चिरादेव प्रकाशितो भूत्वा सहृदयहृदयाह्लादको भूयात्
भवांश्च श्रेयःपरम्परया समेधतामित्याशास्महे ।

शृङ्गगिरिः इति नारायणस्मरणम्

पार्थिवप्रोष्ठपदकृष्णद्वादशी
भार्गववासरः ०१.०१.२०२३

SRIMUKHAM
from
Shri JAGADGURU SRINGERI SHRIMAD BHARATHEE THEERTHA MAHAA SWAAMIGAL

May these blessings offered, after invoking the benign Presence of Lord NAARAAYANA, shower Luminescence, in the endevour of our most devoted disciple Sri. Swaminathan, the son of Sri (Dr. P.S.) Lokanathan.

"To save and protect the good, to destroy evil forces to establish Dharma, I am born (in the world, time and again) Yuga after Yuga."

Thus, The Lord declared.

As a consequence, in Thretha Yuga, for protecting good people like Vishwaamithra and to destroy evil persons like Raavana, the Lord descended (on earth) as incarnation in the form of Ramachandra.

The first amongst poets, the great sage VAALMEEKI, composed to holy story of Lord Ramachandra, in Srimad Raamaayana in 24,000 slokas.

This became renowned as the first composition of its kind.

This is accepted as The Foremost by followers of Sanaathana Dharma.

In this great work, each sloka excels the other in grandeur.

Translation of Srimad Raamaayana have been rendered in almost all languages.

Many great poets have found fulfillment by authoring poetic works, Drama and Dance, based on the story of Sri Raama in Srimad Raamaayana.

Having obtained Grace under the (Lotus) feet of our Guru (Sri Sri Abhinava Vidya Theertha Maha Sannidhaanam), having thus become worthy of his compassion and blessings, you have carefully translated each verse in English.

This exposition of this great epic in many chapters, has become repository for pious people.

Now again, you have given elevating expression and translation to some selective slokas from Raamaayana.

Those who are impatient to go through the entire epic will obtain enjoyment of the history of Raama be beholding this (four new) book.

Your effort is praiseworthy.

With unlimited grace of Sri Shaaradaamba and Sri Chandramouleeswarar, may this book that is to be released soon, bring enjoyment to the heat of good people.

We pray and bless you for your well being and prosperity.

Sringagiri — By grace of Naaraayana

Baargava Vaasara
(01.01.2023)

Dr. M. B. Athreya, Ph.D. (Harvard)
Padma Bhushan (GoI), Bhishma Pitamah of HRD (NHRDN & NDIM),
Icon of Costing Profession (ICMA),
Dharma Pracharak (Sringeri)
A-28, Chittaranjan Park, New Delhi - 110 019
Tel: +91-11-40573252; Email: athreyamb@gmail.com

FOREWORD

It is an act of *bhakti*, faith, to hear the Ramayana. Ram *Katha* is an old Indian tradition. I have heard it, in the 1950s, as a school boy, in my village Pattamadai in Tirunelveli District, Tamil Nadu. We would trek a few miles to neighbouring villages to hear different *Kathakars*.

Reading the Ramayana is a part of *praarthana*, prayer. The Sundara Kanda is frequently read. Millions in India recite the *Ramcharitha Manas*. Kavi Goswami Tulasidas made it accessible to the common people of North India, in Mythili. Similarly, Kamban in Tamil, and local poets in other states have brought Ramayana to their people. Ramayana is read, heard, played and danced in many other countries, in their own languages.

Valmiki Ramayana in Sanskrit is the original source. To translate Ramayana, as Respected Swaminathan ji has done is a *tapasya*. He has been at it for at least the last thirty years! He began at the age of 70, after a career as Manager, and later, Entrepreneur in the Chemical industry. He will, *Bhagavad Krupa*, celebrate his century next year. He has translated the entire epic into English. He has also written a dozen other books, drawing from the Ramayana, for different audiences. He has not stopped writing. Just recently he has finished a book of Ramayana stories for "Boys and Girls". He has in mind, The Autobiography of Rama. Swaminathan ji was inspired by the *Acharyas* of the Sringeri Sarada *Peetam*, one of the four *Peetas* founded by Adi Shankara, the others being in Badrinath, Dwaraka and Puri. He could not have done this without the grace of Sri Rama, Himself; *ashirvads* of his elders; and the total support of his family and friends. He has shown exceptional discipline, commitment, faith and sheer physical and mental stamina. He has not just run a marathon, but completed a Triathlon! My humble *namaskars* to him.

Writing a Foreword to Ramayana is a *sowbhagyam*. Earlier Forewords to Swaminathan ji's books have been written by Sringeri Sankaracharya, our Jagadguru; and also by stalwarts like Padma Vibhushan Dr. Karan Singh; and Padma Vibhushan Shri E. Sreedharan, known as the Metro Man, and now a Trustee of the new Ram Mandir at Ayodhya. Who am I to write a Foreword, in front of them? I do so, primarily because of the pressing invitation of the author.

This Foreword is not for the whole of Ramayana. It is specifically for the Ayodhya Kanda. After the serenity of Bala Kanda, this Kanda is the start of the trials and tribulations, which will bring out the *Avatara Purusha* in Rama. It also starts auspiciously in the first six chapters, with preparations for Rama's much awaited coronation. But, then disaster strikes. It comes in the person of Manthara. She manages to poison the mind of Kaikeyi, who is tempted at her son Bharata becoming the King of Ayodhya. Kaikeyi is cursed by Dasaratha, and severely criticised by Bharata, himself. Rama, the victim, is the only person who shows no animosity towards her. One more evidence of his being a "*maryada purushottama*".

I have been a lifelong student of Management and Philosophy. Not just Management in Organisations. But, also, equally importantly, if not more, Management in life. *Sanatana Dharma* is a most comprehensive philosophy, applicable in all situations. There are many insights on both these aspects of Philosophy and Management from the Ayodhya Kanda. It begins with a description of Rama's outstanding qualities. Let us imbibe as many of them as possible, and inculcate the same in all our children, biological or otherwise. Even a great Emperor like Dasaratha does not unilaterally decide on the coronation of Rama. He can. But, he will not. He takes the advice of *Rajaguru* Vasishtha and his *mantris*. This is an important element and demonstration of his *Raja Dharma*. With their approval, preparations start for Rama's *Rajyabhishekam*. It is a big event. Needs great Project Management! Since it is a generational shift, and it is vital for the people of Ayodhya that the new King succeeds, an auspicious date and time are chosen for a *shubha aarambham*. As personal preparation for his *yogyata* for the new, big role, Rama observes certain procedures and *pratigyas*.

Alas, even Rama is not exempt from the vagaries of *dasha*. As Kalidasa says in the Meghadhootam "*Neechaih gacchati; upari, cha; dashaa; chakra nemi kramena*! --- "One's fate goes down; and also, up; like the spokes of a wheel". --- Rama's *uccha dasha* now goes down. The *nimittam*, instrument, is Mantara, Kaikeyi's maid. She puts into her Mistress's mind the idea that her son Bharata should become the new King. Not Rama. Should we hate Mantara? We may, as the first reaction. But, she shows loyalty. Also, Rama has so much to do, during the next fourteen years, for *dharma samsthapanam*, in Dandakaranya, Kishkinda, and Lanka. That is the Mission of his *avatar*!

Once Mantara has succeeded, Kaikeyi evolves her *yukti*, strategy, to banish Rama. An intelligent and creative woman. She pretends and acts out deep sorrow. Dasaratha was a great king. But, he also had his human weaknesses. Especially, of a male. In particular, *Kaama*. He tries to pacify Kaikeyi. She insists on Dasaratha delivering on the two boons that he had granted her. He could not have imagined such a severe price. Kaikeyi demands that Rama be banished; and Bharata crowned. Preposterous. Even though he was a besotted husband, Dasaratha now curses Kaikeyi.

Dasaratha, naturally, does not have the heart to call Rama himself to break this terrible news. That will not deter Kaikeyi. She sends Sumantara to bring Rama. On hearing Sumantara, Rama as a dutiful son, immediately goes to king Dasaratha's palace. There, again, it is Kaikeyi who breaks the news of exile to Rama. What does Rama do? Does he talk back to Kaikeyi? Argue with his father? Even abuse him? No. He accepts the command and promises his total compliance. This has a predictable chain reaction. First, the mother Kausalya is shattered. Yesterday preparations for coronation. Today, to the forest! Not for 14 days, or even 14 months; but 14 years! At age 16. Forests full of dangers. *Rakshasas*, wild animals, natural hazards. Does Rama have second thoughts? No way. He reiterates his vow. He talks of *dasha* and *prarabdham*. He is so persuasive that he gets Kausalya's *ashirvads*. As per his *prakriti*, Lakshmana is angry. Even at Rama. Again, Rama pacifies him. Refuses to use this as another pretext to wriggle out of his commitment. An awesome example of "*Pran jaye; vachan na jaye*!".

Next is the turn of Sita. She does not contest Rama's *pratigya*. But, she does not take his advice to stay back in Ayodhya and look after the elders. She insists that her role is to be with her *patidev*. Rama relents. In his *manusha janma*, he could not foresee her abduction by Ravana.

Sumitra, the mother herself advises her own son, Lakshmana, to go to the *aranya*, with his *jyeshtha brata*. What a contrast to Kaikeyi! Rama agrees. He has won on his commitment to *vanavas*. Preparations begin. A different kind of preparation. This time it is for *vanavas*. Not coronation. A demonstration of *samatva*, equanimity. As the Gita says "*Yogah samatva ucchyate*". --- What is the preparation? Not that of a royal Prince. But, of a *vanavasi*. Rama does *daana dharmam* of his jewels and other possessions. – Discarding. Not, acquiring.

Having made the decision for *vanavas*, Rama goes to take leave of Dasharatha. The father faints. What a cruel twist of fate! Instead of ascending the *Simhasan*, his eldest, dear son is going to *aranya*! Also his own guilt in being the cause of it. Naturally, Sumitra is sad and worried. Even she, normally, calm and soft, is angered enough to criticise Kaikeyi. Nothing stops Rama from leaving Ayodhya. He, Sita and Lakshmana wear austere clothing, made of tree barks. Rama says a *praarthana* for the *sowkhyam* of his mother Kausalya, and takes leave of her.

The royal family has been tackled. A tough job. But, managed. Rama still has to deal with the *praja*. They want to go with him! There is, naturally, disappointment, anger and chaos in Ayodhya *nagar*. Their enthusiastic expectation of the coronation of their dear Rama has been dashed. Dasharatha and Kausalya are crying. Sumitra tries to console her *didi*, Kausalya. On reaching the banks of the river, Rama persuades the people to return home. The women continue to cry at Rama's departure. The ideal relationship between citizens and rulers. The seeds of Rama Rajya.

The two brothers meet the boatman Guha on the banks of Ganga. They have a beautiful exchange of words and feelings. Guha says that he and Rama are both boatmen. He takes people across the river. But, Rama takes them across the samsara. What profound native wisdom and humility!

The next few cantos deal with the turmoil in the palace. Dasaratha dies. Bharata is called back. He gives severe feedback to his mother Kaikeyi. He does not want to be king. He would like to bring back Rama. How noble! Ayodhya was offered to him on a platter. All obstacles cleared. Dasaratha dead. Rama and Lakshmana away in *vanavasam*. May not even survive and come back. But Bharata rejects it. History is replete with examples of how ambitious princes will kill their own siblings and elders, to ascend the throne. But, *Sanatana Dharma* does not advocate that.

Bharata departs. With the army. Why the army? Can it be misunderstood? Lakshmana did. But, Rama knew Bharata will not attack them. Bharata meets Guha. They have another uplifting dialogue about Rama and Lakshmana. Guha, who may have been initially suspicious of Bharata, admires him for his nobility in wanting to bring back Rama. He takes Bharata to *Bharadwaja* Muni's ashram, where Rama had made his first stop. The Muni offers Bharata hospitality fit for a king. Bharata proceeds to *Chitrakoot*. Finds Rama. The prime concern in Rama's mind is the welfare of the people of Ayodhya. Bharata breaks the news of Dasaratha death. Rama does not blast Kaikeyi. Neither does he regret his *vanavasam*. He and Lakshmana simply perform the last rites for their deceased father.

Bharata begs Rama to come back. Rama will not disobey his father's command. Another temptation brushed aside. The very brother for whom the *Simhasan* was robbed by his mother is genuinely offering it back to Rama, to whom it rightfully belongs. Instead, Rama, as the *jyeshta*, "Commands" Bharata to go back and rule the Ayodya Kingdom. At this point, Rishi Jabali criticises Rama for being weak and throwing away great opportunities. He is a Charvaka, Hedonist, and atheist. Rama loses his temper, uncharacteristically, and severely condemns Jabali and his philosophy.

Despite Rama's command, Bharata cannot bring himself to sit on the *simhasan*. He finds a creative solution. He wants Rama's *padaraksha*, sandals. On return to Ayodhya, he performs the famous *Paduka Patta Abhishekam*. He rules in the name of Rama. He follows the guidance on Good Governance given by Rama, in their famous *samvadam*. Rama and Bharata are two fine examples of a Raja Rishi.

Meantime, in the *aranya*, Rama's work begins. The sages brief him about the atrocities and obstacles created by Khara and other *rakshasas*. *Rishipatni* Anasuya talks about dharma and virtuousness. She also bestows her ornaments on Sita. Rama proceeds to *Dandakaranya*. The Ayodhya Kanda ends here.

Rama's conduct in this Kanda may lead some to ask – Does Rama have no feelings? Does he not get angry, sad, frustrated, jealous, cheated, vengeful etc. Of course, he will have feelings as a *manushya*. They arise in our *manas*, mind. Rama uses his strong *buddhi*, intellect, to manage those feelings. He avoids the two *vairies*, internal enemies – *Kama* and *Krodha*. He is a model of Self Management. He is a *Sthitapragya*. — "*Yasya pragya prathistitha*" — He whose Consciousness is firmly rooted.

He upholds *dharma* at every step. It is worth reiterating that he is the only one who has not criticised Kaikeyi. She and Sumitra are *maatru samaan* – his mothers, like Kausalya. He resolves *dharma sankats*, by choosing to follow the higher of any two clashing *dharmas*. He understands Kausalya's grief, but Dasarata's boon to Kaikeyi, and its honouring take precedence. He appreciates Bharata's love, humility, sincerity, respect, etc., but obeying his father's command is vital. There are many such instances in the rest of *Valmiki Ramayana*. Hence the tribute – "*Ramo vigrahavan dharma*" --- "Rama is the very embodiment of ethics/virtue".

Swaminathan ji has given us a lucid translation of the whole of *Valmiki Ramayana*, including this volume on Ayodhya Kanda. Let us all benefit from his *tapasya*. May I suggest the following actions --- First, read a few *slokas* a day, both the Sanskrit and English versions. Some of us can read the *devanagari lipi*, but not fully understand. The translation is a great help. It will, gradually, deepen your understanding of Sanskrit. Overcome any phobia. "Practice makes perfect". – If you don't know *devanagari*, just read the English version. Whichever version you choose, read it with your family. As many of them, as possible. Second, discuss the meanings and lessons of what you have read daily. Clarify. Internalise. Third, go back to particular cantos and *slokas* which are pregnant with lessons on *dharma*, management of *dharma sankats*, handling of one's feelings, differences, conflicts, etc. Fourth, share your learning with colleagues and friends. Persuade some of them to start reading. Compare notes. Benefit, mutually. Fifth, give this and other volumes as presents on birthdays, anniversaries, weddings, competitions etc. Sixth, start your own short Rama *Katha* sessions for your children and those in the neighbourhood. Seventh, start writing your own simple articles, on your learning, for English, Hindi and regional language newspapers and magazines. Eighth, donate copies to local libraries. Ninth, send copies to your relatives abroad and to their local Hindu temples and community halls.

The publishers of these Valmiki Ramayana volumes may, please, make them available for easy purchase in Ayodhya, Kashi, Ujjain and other pilgrimage sites. I hope an electronic edition will be made available, globally. The product is half. Good Marketing is the other half. This faithful, accessible translation of Valmiki Ramayana is a precious offering. It deserves the best Marketing. My prarthanas for its nation-wide and world-wide acceptance.

New Delhi
January 2023

Dr. Mrityunjay Athreya
Management Mentor

AYODHYA KAANDA

An Introduction by L. Swaminathan

The Second Book (kkanda) of Vaalmeeki Raamaayana, the Ayodhya Kaanda consists of 4357 slokas (stanzas) in 119 sargams (Chapters). Momentous events take place in this long Kaanda. King Dhasharatha is a happy man. His four sons Raama, Lakshmana, Bharatha and Shathrugna are all married and well settled. As he is very old, a thought occurs to him that he should crown his eldest son Raama as Crown Prince to take on the responsibility of ruling over the vast kingdom. Being a democratic ruler, he seeks the opinion of the VIP-s and citizens. They are all so happy that with one voice they affirm king's idea and they all want Raama as their ruler. Dhasharatha asks his chief priest and counselor of Ikshwaaku kings, Sage Vasishta, to fix a date and time for Raama's coronation forthwith, although his other two sons Bharatha and Shathrugna are away at Kekeya kingdom, enjoying their holiday with Bharatha's maternal uncle and grandfather. The city of Ayodhya is gay with preparations for Raama's coronation.

Now this woman Manthara, a hunchback who is a confidante and mentor of Kaikeyi the youngest of the three queens of Dhasharatha and the mother of Bharatha, "Works" upon Kaikeyi poisons her mind, tells her how she would be reduced to a slave if Kowsalya's son Raama is crowned as successor. Her own son Bharatha must be crowned and Raama must be banished.

And this evil genius has a strategy by which this can be achieved. She reminds Kaikeyi about the two boons she had received long, long ago, during a battle in a war between Dheva-s and Asura-s, when she had saved the life of her husband Dhasharatha. And Kaikeyi had kept her options open and had not used these two boons at that time or ever since. Manthara reminds Kaikeyi that the time for fulfillment of these two boons is 'Here and Now'. Manthara presses Kaikeyi to demand from her husband immediately the two boons; the two boons must be given effect to this way and this way only. Raama should be banished and her own son Bharatha to be crowned instead.

King Dhasharatha is shocked. But being an Ikshwaaku king cannot but honour Kaikeyi 's demands through the two boons he had offered her long ago. An Ikshwaaku king never breaks a promise or commitment even after long years and even if it is detrimental to his interests. And Kaikeyi is adamant. Raama must go. Bharatha must take over. No other way.

In spite of advice from elders and ministers like Vasishta, Sumanthra and Sidhaartha, Kaikeyi refuses to give up her demands. And so Raama along with Seetha and Lakshmana leave for forest on 14 years exile. The King, unable to bear all this, unable to bear the separation from Raama dies. The kingdom is now without a ruler. Raama and Lakshmana on exile. Bharatha and Shathrugna at Kekeya kingdom on holiday.

Urgent summons are sent out to Bharatha to return to Ayodhya from his holiday.

Bharatha is shocked, devastated on hearing the news of his father's death and the reason why he died so suddenly. Bharatha cannot tolerate the "Crime" committed by his mother Kaikey4 ostensibly for his welfare. As far as he is concerned, it is Raama and Raama who is and is fit to be, ruler of the kingdom after his father. And after 13 days of Funeral Rituals for his father Dhasharatha, he takes a huge Army with him to go to forest, meet Raama there, crown him there itself and bring back Raama to Ayodhya as a king worthy of Ikshwaaku royalty.

Bharatha leaves with his ministers, mothers, VIP-s, Commanders of Army, technical men, singers and other ordinary citizens to bring back Raama to Ayodhya cutting back his exile. On the banks of river Ganges he gets some news from Guha about his brother Raama. Then at Bharadhwaaja's hermitage where he and his Army are treated to very great hospitality and feasting, he hears from the Sage about Raama 's abode at Chithrbkoot, not very far from there.

Bharatha meets Raama. Begs him to return. But Raama is firm. He will go through with his 14 years exile as per his father 's command. And he tells Bharatha that he also is "Bound" by his father's command equally in as much as he is to rule over Ayodhya during his exile. Rama affirms that both he and his brother Bharatha are bound to honour the two boons.

Bharatha realises that nothing can change Raama as he is devoted to Truth, Dharma and father's command. And as a compromise, agrees to get back to Ayodhya and rule over thekingdom on condition that he will Rule Only as A Caretaker Ruler and Agent of Raama. And as token of Raama 's authority, he takes Raama 's Sandals with him back to Ayodhya.

Bharatha establishes a caretaker capital not far from Ayodhya, an obscure town called Nandhigram. As far as he is concerned, only Raama can occupy the throne at their official capital Ayodhya. NOT he:

And Bharatha rules the kingdom gloriously for 14 years, drawing inspiration - from Raama 's 'Sandals which he honours by placing on the throne and worshipping it daily.

And Raama continues his exile. Goes to Dhandaka forest.

(From now on, the entire Raamaayana is about Raaina and Raama. Poet Vaalmeeki takes leave of Ayodhya. It is all about Raama 's life during his 14 years exile.)

Guru Parampara

H.H. (S.S.) Narasimha Bharati
(1879-1912) (33)

H.H. Chandrasekhara Bharati
(1912-1954) (34)

H.H. Abhinava Vidyatirtha
(1954-1989) (35)

H.H. Sri Bharati Tirtha
(1989 -) (36)

Contents

AYODHYA KAANDA

Chapter 1

Raama's Qualities Described

(Leaving his parents, Bharatha the son of king Dhascharatha through his third wife Kaikeyi, goes on a holiday to his maternal grandfather's place, accompanied by his brother Schathrugna. King Dhascharatha decides to appoint Raama as crown prince- Yuva Raaja at Ayodhya)

❍ ❍ ❍

१. गच्छता मातुलकुलं भरतेन तदाऽनघः ।
शत्रुघ्नो नित्शत्रुघ्नो नीतः प्रीतिपुरस्कृतः ॥

1. During his visit to his maternal (grandfather's place and) home, Bharatha affectionately took along (with him) the sinless brother Schathrugna, the destroyer of *eternal enemies (like passion, greed etc.: Schathru Enemy; Gna-destroyer).

(Readers may note that in one word -*Nithyaschathrugna- Vaalmeeki describes the greatness of this Schathrugna).

❍ ❍ ❍

२. स तत्र न्यवसद्भ्रात्रा सह सत्कारसत्कृतः ।
मातुलेनाश्वपतिना पुत्रस्नेहेन लालितः ॥

2. There, (Bharatha), who was accompanied by his brother (Schathrugna), was pampered like a son by his uncle Aschwapathi (Yudhaajith), who extended his fine hospitality to him and he stayed there.

❍ ❍ ❍

३. तत्रापि निवसन्तौ तौ तर्प्यमाणौ च कामत: ।
भ्रातरौ स्मरतां वीरौ वृद्धं दशरथं नृपम् ।।

3. Staying there, these two brave brothers, (Bharatha & Schathrugna), enjoyed all pleasures to their satisfaction, although they were always thinking (and worrying) about their aged (father) King Dhascharatha (who was back h ome at Ayodhya).

❍ ❍ ❍

४. राजाऽपि तौ महाभागौ सस्मार प्रोषितौ सुतौ ।
उभौ भरतशत्रुघ्नौ महेन्द्रवरुणोपमौ ।।

4. And the king (Dhascharatha) also, was always thinking about his two most illustrious sons, Bharatha & Schathrugna, who were like Lord Indhra and Varuna, when they were living away (from him).

❍ ❍ ❍

५. सर्व एव तु तस्येष्टाश्चत्वार: पुरुषर्षभा: ।
स्वशरीराद्विनिर्वृत्ताश्चत्वार इव बाहव: ।।

5. Indeed all the four noble sons (Raama, Lakshmana, Bharatha & Schathrugna) who were 'Bulls' amongst men, were like four limbs of his body, most cherished.

❍ ❍ ❍

६. तेषामपि महातेजा रामो रतिकर: पितु: ।
स्वयंभूरिव भूतानां बभूव गुणवत्तर: ।।

6. And amongst them, Raama was like God Bramma to living beings. Possessing foremost qualities, he gave immense pleasure to his most brilliant father.

❍ ❍ ❍

७. स हि देवैरुदीर्णस्य रावणस्य वधार्थिभि: ।
अर्थितो मानुषे लोके जज्ञे विष्णु: सनातन: ।।

7. (Indeed) He, (Raama), was none other than God

Vishnu, who descended on this world of human beings in response to the prayers of Dheva-s who sought destruction of the terrible (Demon) Raavana.

❍ ❍ ❍

८. कौसल्या शुशुभे तेन पुत्रेणामिततेजसा ।
यथा च देवी देवानामदितिर्वज्रपाणिना ॥

8. (In the following stanzas, Raama's qualities are described).

Through her son (Raama) of boundless power and brilliance, (his mother) Kowsalya shone in splendor, like lady Adhithi (the mother of) Indhra, the wielder of Vajra, (the lord) of Dheva-s.

❍ ❍ ❍

९. स हि रूपोपपन्नश्च वीर्यवाननसूयक: ।
भूमावनुपम: सूनुर्गुणैर्दशरथोपम: ॥

9. In this world, in qualities, this son was like (his father) Dhaschartha; None was comparable to him; Was endowed with beauty; very brave: yet never spiteful (or jealous).

❍ ❍ ❍

१०. स तु नित्यं प्रशान्तात्मा मृदुपूर्वं च भाषते ।
उच्यमानोऽपि परुषं नोत्तरं प्रतिपद्यते ॥

10. Had a tranquil mind, a composed mind; Was tender & soft in speech; never raised his voice even when harshly spoken to.

❍ ❍ ❍

११. कथञ्चिदुपकारेण कृतेनैकेन तुष्यति ।
न स्मरत्यपकाराणां शतमप्यात्मवत्तया ॥

11. He was easily satisfied even by a (small) and single service rendered to him in any way; Being noble

minded he never remembered (or harboured ill will) even when hundreds of disservice was done to him.

❍ ❍ ❍

१२. शीलवृद्धैर्ज्ञानवृद्धैर्वयोवृद्धैश्च सज्जनैः ।
कथयन्नास्त वै नित्यमस्त्रयोग्यान्तरेष्वपि ॥

12. Everyday, after performing military exercises, he would be only with elders old with age who were good men, who were men of wisdom, who were of high moral character and he will be discussing with them.

❍ ❍ ❍

१३. बुद्धिमान् मधुराभाषी पूर्वभाषी प्रियंवदः ।
वीर्यवान्न च वीर्येण महता स्वेन विस्मितः ॥

13. He was a man of wisdom; spoke sweetly; sweet tongued; spoke majestically; was very brave; Yet, was never arrogant of his bravery.

❍ ❍ ❍

१४. न चानृतकथो विद्वान् वृद्धानांप्रतिपूजकः ।
अनुरक्तः प्रजाभिश्च प्रजाश्चाप्यनुरज्जते ॥

14. (No flippancy) No falsehood in his talk; Man of learning; respected elders; charmed all citizens; (Therefore) was endeared by all citizens.

❍ ❍ ❍

१५. सानुक्रोशो जितक्रोधो ब्राह्मणप्रतिपूजकः ।
दीनानुकम्पी धर्मज्ञो नित्यं प्रग्रहवाञ्छुचिः ॥

15. Always compassionate; Controlled anger; Honoured Braamin (scholars); Compassionate to the downtrodden; He knew Dharma; Took hold of his responsibilities; (never shirked from duty): He was very pure.

❍ ❍ ❍

१६. कुलोचितमतिः क्षात्रं धर्मं स्वं बहुमन्यते ।
मन्यते परया कीर्त्या महत्स्वर्गफलं ततः ॥

16. He was worthy of his race; Firmly believed that by good renown (in this world, by deeds performed here) there will be fruits of heavenly bliss; Therefore regarded Kshathriya Dharma with great esteem. (Took affairs of royalty seriously).

❍ ❍ ❍

१७. नाश्रेयसि रतो यश्च न विरुद्धकथारुचिः ।
उत्तरोत्तरयुक्तौ च वक्ता वाचस्पतिर्यथा ॥

17. Never indulged in inferior acts; Never indulged in perverse logic; (A superb conversationalist) who met arguments with proper rejoinders; Such a man was he, who was like Vaachaspathy, the Lord of Letters (& speech).

❍ ❍ ❍

१८. अरोगस्तरुणो वाग्मी वपुष्मान्देशकालवित् ।
लोके पुरुषसारज्ञः साधुरेको विनिर्मितः ॥

18. A healthy man; Progressive man; Knew proper time & place (for anything). He knew the 'inner' mind of his citizens. (Could feel the 'pulse' of his subjects); He was unique; Was righteous; Master of speech; Most celebrated and most handsome in the world.

❍ ❍ ❍

१९. स तु श्रेष्ठैर्गुणैर्युक्तः प्रजानां पार्थिवात्मजः ।
बहिश्चर इव प्राणो बभूव गुणवत्तरः ॥

19. This (Raama the) Son of Emperor was endowed with foremost qualities, splendid qualities; For his citizens, he was like their own life appearing in an outside body.

❍ ❍ ❍

२०. सम्यग्विद्याव्रतस्नातो यथावत्साङ्गवेदवित् ।
इष्वस्त्रे च पितु: श्रेष्ठो बभूव भरताग्रज: ।।

20. This (Raama) the elder brother of Bharatha, had undergone rigorous training in all faculties and completed Vows: (He was 'bathed' in vows and learning); He knew Vedha-s and its ancillaries thoroughly; Master of Arms-Archery; he was better than even his father (Dhascharatha).

❍ ❍ ❍

२१. कल्याणाभिजन: साधुरदीन: सत्यवागृजु: ।
वृद्धैरभिविनीतश्च द्विजैर्धर्मार्थदर्शिभि: ।।

21. Virtuous; Born with noble qualities; very straight; a man of word & Truth; well educated by elderly braamins who were expounders of Dharma-Artha Shaashra.

❍ ❍ ❍

२२. धर्मकामार्थतत्त्वज्ञ: स्मृतिमान् प्रतिभानवान् ।
लौकिके समयाचारे कृतकल्पो विशारद: ।।

22. A man of (Immaculate) memory; Had presence of mind; Knew the essence (codes) of Dharma, Artha & Kaama: In worldly and mundane affairs was well versed; knew customs.

(Dharma- Duties, Moral code etc.: Artha- Wealth, substance etc.: Kaama- Pleasures, love, fine arts etc.).

❍ ❍ ❍

२३. निभृत: संवृताकारो गुप्तमन्त्र: सहायवान् ।
अमोघक्रोधहर्षश्च त्यागसंयमकालवित् ।।

23. He was modest; Could conceal his feelings; who would not reveal his options; who had support (of vast number of friends); His smile was never wasted, nor was his anger; He knew the time when to give and when to receive.(Master of Income & Expenditure).

❍ ❍ ❍

२४. दृढभक्तिः स्थिरप्रज्ञो नासद्ग्राही न दुर्वचाः ।
निस्तन्द्रिरप्रमत्तश्च स्वदोषपरदोषवित् ।।

24. A man of faith; firm in devotion; had a sharp intellect; shunned bad men; never used improper words; never lazy; ever vigilant; ever conscious of his own failings and those of others.

❍ ❍ ❍

२५. शास्त्रज्ञश्च कृतज्ञश्च पुरुषान्तरकोविदः ।
यः प्रग्रहानुग्रहयोर्यथान्यायं विचक्षणः ।।

25. A knower of Shaasthra; A man of gratitude; Clear sighted in understanding other man's mind (& feelings); had the ability to form and foster friendships (after deliberation); Such a man was he.

❍ ❍ ❍

२६. सत्संग्रहप्रग्रहणे स्थानविन्निग्रहस्य च ।
आयकर्मण्युपायज्ञः संदृष्टव्ययकर्मवित् ।।

26. Receptive to ideas of good men and discarding (ideas of the bad); had knowledge about local places (and their customs); He knew the art of collecting revenue. And the art of spending judiciously.

❍ ❍ ❍

२७. श्रैष्ठ्यं शास्त्रसमूहेषु प्राप्तो व्यामिश्रकेषु च ।
अर्थधर्मौ च संगृह्य सुखतन्त्रो न चालसः ।।

27. Had obtained great eminence in (knowledge of) diverse Shaasthra-s and associated subjects. He was never lazy, spending his time in happy pursuit of Artha (Mundane) and Dharma (Moral).

❍ ❍ ❍

२८. वैहारिकाणां शिल्पानां विज्ञाताऽर्थविभागवित् ।
आरोहे विनये चैव यूक्तो वारणवाजिनाम् ।।

28. He knew the finer aspects of Sport & Pastime; Sculpture; He was master in Budget (Distributed funds properly); Expert in riding horses and elephants, making them obey (his command).

❍ ❍ ❍

२९. धनुर्वेदविदां श्रेष्ठो लोकेऽतिरथसंमत: ।
अभियाता प्रहर्ता च सेनानयविशारद: ।।

29. He was foremost amongst men well versed in Dhanur Vedha (Science of War-Arms); A foremost warrior, accepted as such by all in the world; He 'sought' (enemies &) destroyed them; Master in deploying various divisions of the Army.

❍ ❍ ❍

३०. अप्रधृष्यश्च संग्रामे क्रुद्धैरपि सुरासुरै: ।।

30. Even by angry (warriors like) Dheva-s and Asura-s (of celestial world) he could never be bruised in a war.

❍ ❍ ❍

३१. अनसूयो जितक्रोधो न दृप्तो न च मत्सरी ।
न चावमन्ता भूतानां न च कालवशानुग: ।।

31. He was free from jealousy; never arrogant; he treated none with contempt; had (subdued) conquered his anger; never selfish; never overwhelmed by situations (bad times).

❍ ❍ ❍

३२. एवं श्रेष्ठैर्गुणैर्युक्त: प्रजानां पार्थिवात्मज: ।
संमतस्त्रिषु लोकेषु वसुधाया: क्षमागुणै: ।।
बुद्ध्या बृहस्पतेस्तुल्यो वीर्येणापि शचीपते: ।।

32. Endowed with such foremost qualities, this (Raama) the son of the emperor, was esteemed by all the citizens of all the three worlds. Like mother Earth he was equal in qualities of endurance; In wisdom, was

equal to Brihaspathi; In bravery was equal to (Indhra) the husband of Sachi.

❍ ❍ ❍

३३. तथा सर्वप्रजाकान्तैः प्रीतिसञ्जननैः पितुः ।
गुणैर्विरुरुचे रामो दीप्तः सूर्य इवांशुभिः ।।

33. Just as Sun shines brilliantly with his rays, Raama shone before his father, with qualities that captivated all citizens and which brought joy to all citizens.

❍ ❍ ❍

३४. तमेवं गुणसंपन्नमप्रधृष्यपराक्रमम् ।
लोकपालोपमं नाथमकामयत मेदिनी ।।

34. Endowed with such qualities and possessing invincible valour, the Earth desired that (Raama) who was comparable to Lokpaals must be the Lord (of the world): (The Lokpaals are the mystical, celestial protectors of the worlds).

❍ ❍ ❍

३५. एतैस्तु बहुभिर्युक्तं गुणैरनुपमैः सुतम् ।
दृष्ट्वा दशरथो राजा चक्रे चिन्तां परंतपः ।।

35. Perceiving that his son was endowed with such and many other incomparable qualities, the tormentor of enemies Dhascharatha, began to contemplate.

❍ ❍ ❍

३६. अथ राज्ञो बभूवैवं वृद्धस्य चिरजीविनः ।
प्रीतिरेषा कथं रामो राजा स्यान्मयि जीवति ।।

36. To this very old king who had seen lot of life, such (a thought) arose: = Even as I am alive, Raama could be 'King' (Crown prince): Why not? This is desirable =.

३७. एषा ह्यस्य परा प्रीतिर्हृदि संपरिवर्तते ।
कदा नाम सुतं द्रक्ष्याम्यभिषिक्तमहं प्रियम् ॥

37. This foremost desire was engulfed in his heart: = When am I going to see this beloved son (Raama) anointed.

❍ ❍ ❍

३८. वृद्धिकामो हि लोकस्य सर्वभूतानुकम्पनः ।
मत्तः प्रियतरो लोके पर्जन्य इव वृष्टिमान् ॥

38. Like lord of Rain bringing rain, he, who is compassionate to all living beings of the world, and who desires prosperity (for all) is more beloved in the world than myself.

❍ ❍ ❍

३९. यमशक्रसमो वीर्ये बृहस्पतिसमो मतौ ।
महीधरसमो धृत्यां मत्तश्च गुणवत्तरः ॥

39. In valour he is equal to Lord Indhra and Yama; Equal to Brihaspathi in intellect: Is equal to God Vishnu in (offering) protection; He is superior to me in qualities.

❍ ❍ ❍

४०. महीमहमिमां कृत्स्नामधितिष्ठन्तमात्मजम् ।
अनेन वयसा दृष्ट्वा यथा स्वर्गमवाप्नुयाम् ॥

40. Old as I am, I should obtain (go to) Heaven, only after seeing this son (Raama) well established (as ruler) of all this earth. =.

❍ ❍ ❍

४१. इत्येतैर्विविधैस्तैस्तैरन्यपार्थिवदुर्लभैः ।
शिष्टैरपरिमेयैश्च लोके लोकोत्तरैर्गुणैः ॥

41. With such noble and diverse qualities rare to be seen in any other king in the world or any one else in the world, (Qualities) that are most eminent, and limitless.

❍ ❍ ❍

४२. तं समीक्ष्य महाराजो युक्तं समुदितैः शुभैः ।
निश्चित्य सचिवैः सार्धं युवराजममन्यत ॥

42. ...seeing him who was endowed with such lofty and eminent qualities, Emperor (Dhascharatha) decided (to discuss) with his ministers to consider him (for appointment as) Crown Prince.

❍ ❍ ❍

४३. दिव्यन्तरिक्षे भूमौ च घोरमुत्पातजं भयम् ।
सञ्चचक्षे च मेधावी शरीरे चात्मनो जराम् ॥

43. (Observing &) Reflecting upon the gruesome fear caused by (evil) portends in heaven, sky and earth, this learned (king Dhascharatha) pondered (over this and) over the decaying body of his (due to his old age).

❍ ❍ ❍

४४. पूर्णचन्द्राननस्याथ शोकापनुदमात्मनः ।
लोके रामस्य बुबुधे संप्रियत्वं महात्मनः ॥

44. Then to relieve his fear and anxiety, (Dhascharatha) considered this most satisfying (honour) for the great soul Raama whose face was like moon ..... .

❍ ❍ ❍

४५. आत्मनश्च प्रजानां च श्रेयसे च प्रियेण च ।
योक्तुकामस्स धर्मात्मा भक्त्या त्वरितवान्नृपः ॥

45. ....for the welfare of citizens of the world, this man of Dharma, king (Dhascharatha) was desirous of making (him crown prince) without delay, and out of his attachment and love towards him (as well).

❍ ❍ ❍

४६. नाना नगरवास्तव्यान् पृथग्जानपदानपि ।
समानिनाय मेदिन्याः प्रधानान्पृथिवीपतीन् ॥

46. Leaving out people living in far away cities and towns,

(the king) asked such of those important men and lords (living nearby) to assemble before him. (to be brought to Ayodhya).

❍ ❍ ❍

४७. न तु केकयराजानं जनकं वा नराधिपम् ।
त्वरया चानयामास पश्चात्तौ श्रोष्यतः प्रियम् ।।

47. He did not invite King of Kekeya (his father-in-law) and father of Kaikeyi). Nor (did he invite) King Janaka (the father-in-law of his son Raama) because of the urgency (& lack of time). Of course these two would (be pleased to) hear the good news later.

❍ ❍ ❍

४८. तान्वेश्म नानाभरणैर्यथार्हं प्रतिपूजितान् ।
ददर्शालंकृतो राजा प्रजापतिरिव प्रजाः ।।

48. Decorating himself properly with various ornaments, the king saw and appeared before these men who came to his palace to honour him; he appeared like God Bramma before his subjects.

❍ ❍ ❍

४९. अथोपविष्टे नृपतौ तस्मिन्परबलार्दने ।
ततः प्रविविशुः शेषा राजानो लोकसम्मताः ।।

49. And when this emperor (Dhascharatha) who could check the enemy army, sat down (on throne) the other renowned rulers of the world entered (the council hall).

❍ ❍ ❍

५०. अथ राज्ञा वितीर्णेषु विविधेष्वासनेषु च ।
राजानमेवाभिमुखा निषेदुर्नियता नृपाः ।।

50. These devoted 'rulers' faced the king who personally directed them and they sat in various well furnished seats (as per protocol).

❍ ❍ ❍

५१. स लब्धमानैर्विनयान्वितैर्नृपैः
पुरालयैर्जानपदैश्च मानवैः ।
उपोपविष्टैर्नृपतिर्वृतो बभौ
सहस्रचक्षुर्भगवानिवामरैः ॥

51. The King appeared (at that time) like the thousand eyed Lord (Indhra) before celestials, when he was amidst these devoted 'Rulers' who had occupied appropriate seats and when he was surrounded by men from cities & villages.

❍ ❍ ❍

Chapter 2

Dhascharatha Seeks Counsel Regarding Raama's Coronation

(Even though it is his divine right to chose, king Dhascharatha being a democratic ruler who does not want to 'thrust' his son Raama on the throne, calls an assembly & discusses with them).

❍ ❍ ❍

१. ततः परिषदं सर्वामामन्त्र्य वसुधाधिपः ।
हितमुद्धर्षणं चैवमुवाच प्रथितं वचः ॥

1. Welcoming such an assembly, the lord of earth (Dhascharatha), spoke pleasant and salutary words to all of them, revealing his intentions.

❍ ❍ ❍

२. दुन्दुभिस्वनकल्पेन गम्भीरेणानुनादिना ।
स्वरेण महता राजा जीमूत इव नादयन् ॥

2. The king (spoke) with a powerful deep voice that was

like thunder of the clouds, sound reverberating like Dhundhubi (drums) ......

❍ ❍ ❍

३. राजलक्षणयुक्तेन कान्तेनानुपमेन च ।
उवाच रसयुक्तेन स्वरेण नृपतिर्नृपान् ।।

3. ....the king said to the 'kings' there with a voice of incomparable (tone) with (words) endowed with qualities of royalty, pleasing, and relished (by all there).

❍ ❍ ❍

४. विदितं भवतामेतद्यथा मे राज्यमुत्तमम् ।
पूर्वकैर्मम राजेन्द्रैः सुतवत्परिपालितम् ।।

4. You are aware that this foremost kingdom of mine has been ruled and protected by my royal forefathers, like (father protecting) a son.

❍ ❍ ❍

५. सोऽहमिक्ष्वाकुभिः सर्वैर्नरेन्द्रैः परिपालितम् ।
श्रेयसा योक्तुकामोऽस्मि सुखार्हमखिलं जगत् ।।

5. Ruled (and fostered) by all the Ikshwaaku kings (before me), such as I am, am desirous (to see) this kingdom which deserves to be (happy and) prosperous, most prosperous in all the world.

❍ ❍ ❍

६. मयाऽप्याचरितं पूर्वैः पन्थानमनुगच्छता ।
प्रजा नित्यमनिद्रेण यथाशक्त्यभिरक्षिताः ।।

6. Following diligently the eternal path followed by my forefathers, the citizens were protected by me also, even without sleep & rest, to the best of my ability.

❍ ❍ ❍

७. इदं शरीरं कृत्स्नस्य लोकस्य चरता हितम् ।
पाण्डुरस्यातपत्रस्य छायायां जरितं मया ।।

7. By the salutary service rendered by me to all the world like (giving solace under) the shade of a white umbrella, this body of mine has become decayed.

❍ ❍ ❍

८. प्राप्य वर्षसहस्राणि बहून्यायूंषि जीवतः ।
जीर्णस्यास्य शरीरस्य विश्रान्तिमभिरोचये ।।

8. Having lived a life of many thousand years, I wish to give rest to this body which is worn out.

❍ ❍ ❍

९. राजप्रभावजुष्टां हि दुर्वहामजितेन्द्रियैः ।
परिश्रान्तोऽस्मि लोकस्य गुर्वीं धर्मधुरं वहन् ।।

9. In this world, having shouldered the hard to bear, noble and heavy burden of (Royal) Dharma, serving on the seat of royal power with unsubdued passion (& zeal), I am (now really) tired.

❍ ❍ ❍

१०. सोऽहं विश्रममिच्छामि पुत्रं कृत्वा प्रजाहिते ।
सन्निकृष्टानिमान्सर्वाननुमान्य द्विजर्षभान् ।।

10. Such as I am, with the consent of all these Braamins who have assembled here, I desire to seek retirement after appointing my son (as Crown prince) for welfare of citizens.

❍ ❍ ❍

११. अनुजातो हि मां सर्वैर्गुणैर्ज्येष्ठो ममात्मजः ।
पुरन्दरसमो वीर्येरागः परपुरञ्जयः ।।

11. Raama is my eldest son: In bravery is comparable to Lord Indhra; he is destroyer of enemies' fortress; In all qualities he takes after me.

❍ ❍ ❍

१२. तं चन्द्रमिव पुष्येण युक्तं धर्मभृतां वरम् ।
यौवराज्ये नियोक्ताऽस्मि प्रीतः पुरुषपुङ्गवम् ।।

12. He is like full moon associated with star Pushya, Is foremost amongst men devoted to Dharma; a tiger of men!; I am desirous of appointing him as Yuvaraaja (Crown prince- king designate).

❍ ❍ ❍

१३. अनुरूपः स वै नाथो लक्ष्मीवांलक्ष्मणाग्रजः ।
त्रैलोक्यमपि नाथेन येन स्यान्नाथवत्तरम् ।।

13. This elder brother of Lakshmana, (this Raama), is a man of splendour; If three worlds can shine with a single lord who will be foremost lord, verily he is such a lord.

❍ ❍ ❍

१४. अनेन श्रेयसा सद्यः संयोज्यैवमिमां महीम् ।
गतक्लेशो भविष्यामि सुते तस्मिन्निवेश्य वै ।।

14. Handing over this earth to this son thus, now, freed from worries, I am going (to live) 'binding' myself in spiritual bliss.

❍ ❍ ❍

१५. यदीदं मेऽनुरूपार्थं मया साधु सुमन्त्रितम् ।
भवन्तो मेऽनुमन्यन्तां कथं वा करवाण्यहम् ।।

15. This has been well deliberated by me; If my (idea) is in conformity (with yours) you must give me your approval; If not (please advise me) what else should I do.

❍ ❍ ❍

१६. यद्यप्येषा मम प्रीतिर्हिमन्यद्विचिन्त्यताम् ।
अन्या मध्यस्थचिन्ता हि विमर्दाभ्यधिकोदया ।।

16. This is my desire; But if there is any other good (alternative) may you deliberate; Only when a matter is

examined by others who are 'neutral', great prosperity results by such an examination.

❍ ❍ ❍

१७. इति ब्रुवन्तं मुदिताः प्रत्यनन्दन्नृपा नृपम् ।
वृष्टिमन्तं महामेघं नर्दन्त इव बर्हिणः ॥

17. Pleased like peacocks shrieking with joy at the (sight of) clouds during rain, the kings (gathered there) extolled king (Dhascharatha) when he spoke thus.

❍ ❍ ❍

१८. स्निग्धोऽनुनादी सञ्जज्ञे तत्र हर्षसमीरितः ।
जनौघोद्घुष्टसन्नादो विमानं कम्पयन्निव ॥

18. The intense (but endearing) sound emanating from the voices of the people shouting together out of joy, reverberated the Palace of many-storeys, making it 'tremble' (so to speak).

❍ ❍ ❍

१९. तस्य धर्मार्थविदुषो भावमाज्ञाय सर्वशः ।
ब्राह्मणा बलमुख्याश्च पौरजानपदैः सह ॥

19. The citizens from towns & villages, the learned braamins, the chiefs of army who knew the mind of the king, who all knew Dharma & Artha, ... in every way.....

❍ ❍ ❍

२०. समेत्य मन्त्रयित्वा तु समतां गतबुद्धयः ।
ऊचुश्च मनसा ज्ञात्वा वृद्धं दशरथं वचः ॥

20. ... they all together examined this, and came to the same conclusion; They addressed the old king Dhascharatha with these words, having deliberated this in their minds (individually also).

❍ ❍ ❍

२१. अनेकवर्षसाहस्रो वृद्धस्त्वमसि पार्थिव ।
स रामं युवराजानमभिषिञ्चस्व पार्थिवम् ।।

21. Oh King! (Ruling for) over many thousand years, you are old (& tired). You may anoint Raama as YuvaRaaja to rule the kingdom.

❍ ❍ ❍

२२. इच्छामो हि महाबाहुं रघुवीरं महाबलम् ।
गजेन महताऽऽयान्तं रामं छत्रावृताननम् ।।

22. We are all desirous of seeing the mightily strong, long limbed and brave Raama the Raghu, coming out (in procession) on a mighty elephant, his face protected by royal umbrella.

❍ ❍ ❍

२३. इति तद्वचनं श्रुत्वा राजा तेषां मनःप्रियम् ।
अजानन्निव जिज्ञासुरिदं वचनमब्रवीत् ।।

23. Hearing such sweet words from them, king (Dhascharatha) addressed them thus, feigning ignorance, as though seeking enlightenment (from them in this matter).

(King Dhascharatha is an old 'Fox': Having 'goaded' his subjects to accept Raama and knowing fully well they all want Raama, he pretends as if he is not quite clear as to whether they really want Raama. He is surprised at the quick response; So he says).

❍ ❍ ❍

२४. श्रुत्वैव वचनं यन्मे राघवं पतिमिच्छथ ।
राजानः संशयोऽयं मे किमिदं ब्रूत तत्त्वतः ।।

24. Oh kings! How is it that (the moment) you heard my words, you all desired to make (Raama) the Raaghava your lord and king; This (raises) some doubt in me. Tell me truthfully .....

❍ ❍ ❍

२५. कथं नु मयि धर्मेण पृथिवीमनुशासति ।
भवन्तो द्रष्टुमिच्छन्ति युवराजं ममात्मजम् ।।

25. .....How come, even while I am ruling over the land with norms of (royal) Dharma, you wish to see my son YuvaRaaja.

(Dhascharatha was not prepared for such a quick vote of confidence).

❍ ❍ ❍

२६. ते तमूचुर्महात्मानं पौरजानपदैः सह ।
बहवो नृप कल्याणा गुणाः पुत्रस्य सन्ति ते ।।

26. (In the next 30 stanzas, they all extol Raama and assure the king that Raama is worthy enough to be their lord).

Enjoined by citizens from cities & villages, they all addressed the great soul (Dhascharatha): Oh King! Many good and auspicious qualities are found in your son.

❍ ❍ ❍

२७. गुणान् गुणवतो देव
देवकल्पस्य धीमतः ।
प्रियानानन्दनान् कृत्स्नान्
प्रवक्ष्यामोऽद्य ताञ्छृणु ।।

27. Oh Lord! We shall describe all the qualities, entirely, about this wise (Raama) who is like a celestial, who is endowed with qualities that are pleasing and which bring joy (to all): (Please) Listen.

❍ ❍ ❍

२८. दिव्यैर्गुणैः शक्रसमो रामः सत्यपराक्रमः ।
इक्ष्वाकुभ्योऽपि सर्वेभ्यो ह्यतिरिक्तो विशां पते ।।

28. Oh (Dhascharatha the) lord of earth! Verily Raama is truly brave; by his divine qualities, he is equal to

Schakra (Indhra): And in the lineage of Ikshwaaku-s, he stands foremost.

❍ ❍ ❍

२९. रामः सत्पुरुषो लोके सत्यधर्मपरायणः ।
साक्षाद्रामाद्विनिर्वृत्तो धर्मश्चापि श्रिया सह ॥

29. Verily Raama is embodiment of goodness (Truly a good man); Resolute in following Truth & Dharma; (Indeed it appears) in this world, the very Dharma has come forth along with Raama in splendour. (Dharma itself manifests in Raama, is hallowed by him).

❍ ❍ ❍

३०. प्रजासुखत्वे चन्द्रस्य वसुधायाः क्षमागुणैः ।
बुद्ध्या बृहस्पतेस्तुल्यो वीर्येसाक्षाच्छचीपतेः ॥

30. Verily he is like moon bringing joy to citizens; he is like mother Earth in endurance; In intelligence like Brihaspathi; And in valour like (Lord Indhra) the husband of Sachi.

❍ ❍ ❍

३१. धर्मज्ञः सत्यसन्धश्च शीलवाननसूयकः ।
क्षान्तः सान्त्वयिता श्लक्ष्णः कृतज्ञो विजितेन्द्रियः ॥
मृदुश्च स्थिरचित्तश्च सदा भव्योऽनसूयकः ॥

31. A knower of Dharma; A man of word, Truth; A man of good conduct; free from jealousy; very indulgent (even to sinners); Very gentle and conciliatory; tender; soft (spoken): A man of gratitude. One who has conquered senses (passions, wrath etc.); Man of composure; very righteous and free from envy.

❍ ❍ ❍

३२. प्रियवादी च भूतानां सत्यवादी च राघवः ।
बहुश्रुतानां वृद्धानां ब्राह्मणानामुपासिता ॥

32. This (Raama) the Raaghava, always speaks sweetly but ever speaks truth before all living beings; well versed in Schruthi-s (Fundamental Holy Texts); Ever worships (serves) elderly braamins.

❍ ❍ ❍

३३. तेनास्येहातुला कीर्तिर्यशस्तेजश्च वर्धते ।
देवासुरमनुष्याणां सर्वास्त्रेषु विशारद : ।।

33. In all weapons he is an expert even amongst Dheva-s, Asura-s, and men. Therefore, in this world, his brilliance, renown and fame is unequalled.

❍ ❍ ❍

३४. सम्यग्विद्याव्रतस्नातो यथावत् साङ्गवेदवित् ।
गान्धर्वेच भुवि श्रेष्ठो बभूव भरताग्रजः ।।

34. This (Raama the) brother of Bharatha, is 'bathed' thoroughly in knowledge, vows; He is well versed in Saanga Vedha (The supplementary to Vedha-s): And he is foremost in (Science and art of) Ghandharva Vedha (of music, dance, painting etc.).

❍ ❍ ❍

३५. कल्याणाभिजनः साधुरदीनात्मा महाद्युतिः ।
द्विजैरभिविनीतश्च श्रेष्ठैर्धर्मार्थनैपुणैः ।।

35. He is virtuous: Born with auspicious qualities: (never gives way) never depressed; most majestic; He is well trained by foremost Braamins who are experts in Dharma & Artha.

❍ ❍ ❍

३६. यदा व्रजति संग्रामं ग्रामार्थेनगरस्य वा ।
गत्वा सौमित्रिसहितो नाविजित्य निवर्तते ।।

36. Going out (to settle) affairs of villages or towns, this (Raama) who is (ever) with Lakshmana, never returns without 'conquest' after a hostile encounter.

❍ ❍ ❍

३७. संग्रामात्पुनरागम्य कुञ्जरेण रथेन वा ।
पौरान् स्वजनवन्नित्यं कुशलं परिपृच्छति ॥

37. Mounted on a chariot or an elephant, when he comes back after an encounter (with enemy), he always enquires every one of us (successively) about the welfare of citizens as though they are his own (relatives).....

❍ ❍ ❍

३८. पुत्रेष्वग्निषु दारेषु प्रेष्यशिष्यगणेषु च ।
निखिलेनानुपूर्व्याच्च पिता पुत्रानिवौरसान् ॥

38. ....(He enquires) about their children, about their fire and other rituals, about their wives, about their servants, disciples, all about them, like a father towards son born to him.

❍ ❍ ❍

३९. शुश्रूषन्ते च वः शिष्याः कच्चित्कर्मसु दंशिताः ।
इति नः पुरुषव्याघ्रः सदा रामोऽभिभाषते ॥

39. This 'Tiger' of men, this Raama, speaks to us like this:= Do your disciples perform their duties diligently at all times and serve you.?=.

❍ ❍ ❍

४०. व्यसनेषु मनुष्याणां भृशं भवति दुःखितः ।
उत्सवेषु च सर्वेषु पितेव परितुष्यति ॥

40. When grief afflicts citizens, he becomes very sad; In all their (joys and) festivities he rejoices like a father.

❍ ❍ ❍

४१. सत्यवादी महेष्वासो वृद्धसेवी जितेन्द्रियः ।
स्मितपूर्वाभिभाषी च धर्मं सर्वात्मना श्रितः ॥

41. Following Dharma with all his soul, he ever speaks truth; A great wielder of bow Serves elders; sports a

smile as he speaks; Has control over his senses (passions etc.).

❍ ❍ ❍

४२. सम्यग्योक्ता श्रेयसां च न विगृह्यकथारुचिः ।
उत्तरोत्तरयुक्तौ च वक्ता वाचस्पतिर्यथा ॥

42. Perfectly able to bring prosperity: Will never give room for inimical conversation: (An excellent conversationalist) who gives (proper) rejoinders: In speech he is like Vaachaspathi.

❍ ❍ ❍

४३. सुभ्रूरायतताम्राक्षः साक्षाद्विष्णुरिव स्वयम् ।
रामो लोकाभिरामोऽयं शौर्यवीर्यपराक्रमैः ॥

43. Has beautiful eyebrows; long eyes with reddish hue; Most valorous, brave, most heroic; delights the worlds (Endeared by all in the world); He is as if God Vishnu is in human form as Raama.

❍ ❍ ❍

४४. प्रजापालनतत्त्वज्ञो न रागोपहतेन्द्रियः ।
शक्तस्त्रैलोक्यमप्येष भोक्तुं किं नु महीमिमाम् ॥

44. He has knowledge of essence of ruling over his subjects; never indulges in activities afflicted by passion; He is capable of ruling Three Worlds; (When that is so) What is (there in ruling) this Earth!

❍ ❍ ❍

४५ नास्य क्रोधः प्रसादश्च निरर्थोऽस्ति कदाचन ।
हन्त्येव नियमाद्वध्यान् यत्रैष परिकुप्यति ॥

45. His anger or favour is never wasted; And when he gets angry justifiably he will offer punishment to one who deserves punishment.

४६. युनक्त्यर्थैः प्रहृष्टश्च तमसौ यत्र तुष्यति ।।

46. When he is pleased with one, with great joy he enjoins him with wealth.

❍ ❍ ❍

४७. शान्तैः सर्वप्रजाकान्तैः प्रीतिसंजननैर्नृणाम् ।
गुणैर्विरुरुचे रामो दीप्तः सूर्य इवांशुभिः ।।

47. Like Sun illuminating the world with its rays, Raama shines with his tranquil qualities that bring forth happiness to men, and which captivate the hearts of all citizens.

❍ ❍ ❍

४८. तमेवं गुणसंपन्नं रामं सत्यपराक्रमम् ।
लोकपालोपमं नाथमकामयत मेदिनी ।।

48. Endowed as he is with such qualities and being truly valiant, the Earth desired this Raama who is comparable to Lokpaals (the Mythical guardians of Universe), as its lord.

❍ ❍ ❍

४९. वत्सः श्रेयसि जातस्ते दिष्ट्याऽसौ तव राघव ।
दिष्ट्या पुत्रगुणैर्युक्तो मारीच इव काश्यपः ।।

49. Oh (Dhascharatha the) Raaghava! By our good fortune this (Raama) is born to you, by your own fortune & distinction (as well): He is endowed with noble qualities of a son just like Kaaschyapa the son of Mareechi.

❍ ❍ ❍

५०. बलमारोग्यमायुश्च रामस्य विदितात्मनः ।
देवासुरमनुष्येषु सगन्धर्वोरगेषु च ।।

50. Strength, good health, long life for Raama who has perceived "Self",....the Dheva-s, Asura-s, Ghandharva-s, Uraga-s and men .....

५१. आशंसते जनः सर्वोराष्ट्रे पुरवरे तथा ।
आभ्यन्तरश्च बाह्यश्च पौरजानपदो जनः ।।

51. .....all the citizens residing in cities and lands, and living in inner apartments (of houses and mansions), and other folks living in other places are (all) praying for. (Every one prays for Raama).

❍ ❍ ❍

५२. स्त्रियो वृद्धास्तरुण्यश्च सायंप्रातः समाहिताः ।
सर्वान्देवान्नमस्यन्ति रामस्यार्थेयशस्विनः ।।
५३. तेषामभिमतं देव त्वत्प्रसादात्समृद्ध्यताम् ।।

52 & 53.

The women folk young & old, are all enjoined, morning and evening, in worship of all Deities and (they all) prostrate, for the welfare of the famous Raama Oh Lord (Dhascharatha) By your grace their wishes must be fulfilled.

❍ ❍ ❍

५४. राममिन्दीवरश्यामं सर्वशत्रुनिबर्हणम् ।
पश्यामो यौवराज्यस्थं तव राजोत्तमात्मजम् ।।

54. We all wish to see your most noble royal son Raama who is radiant like blue lotus, who is destroyer of all enemies, appointed as crown prince.

❍ ❍ ❍

५५. तं देवदेवोपममात्मजं ते
सर्वस्य लोकस्य हिते निविष्टम् ।
हिताय नः क्षिप्रगुदारजुष्टं
मुदाऽभिषेक्तुं वरद त्वमर्हसि ।।

55. Oh benefactor! As he possesses exalted virtues and is ever concerned with welfare of the World and as he is like lord of Dhevas, you should, without delay, anoint your son with great joy, for our welfare.

❍ ❍ ❍

Chapter 3

Preparation for (Royal) Coronation

(Having obtained such a vote of confidence from citizens, Dhascharatha prepares Coronation of Raama).

❍ ❍ ❍

१. तेषामञ्जलिपद्मानि प्रगृहीतानि सर्वशः ।
प्रतिगृह्याब्रवीद्राजा तेभ्यः प्रियहितं वचः ॥

1. Accepting their most welcome benediction with his hands cupped in Anjali, king (Dhascharatha) replied with words pleasing in every way.

❍ ❍ ❍

२. अहोऽस्मि परमप्रीतः प्रभावश्चातुलो मम ।
यन्मे ज्येष्ठं प्रियं पुत्रं यौवराज्यस्थमिच्छथ ॥

2. (All of) You desire that my eldest son should be crown prince: By this (acclamation) my glory is beyond measure; Ah! I am very pleased.

❍ ❍ ❍

३. इति प्रत्यर्च्य तान्राजा ब्राह्मणानिदमब्रवीत् ।
वसिष्ठं वामदेवं च तेषामेवोपश्रृण्वताम् ॥

3. After returning the greetings of these braamins, the king, even while they were listening, addressed Vasishta & Vaamadheva.

❍ ❍ ❍

४. चैत्रः श्रीमानयं मासः पुण्यः पुष्पितकाननः ।
यौवराज्याय रामस्य सर्वमेवोपकल्प्यताम् ॥

4. This is the month of Chithra (April-May) when flowers blossom on trees; Eminently holy (auspicious); Let

preparations be made for Raama's coronation as crown prince.

❍ ❍ ❍

५. राज्ञस्तूपरते वाक्ये जनघोषो महानभूत् ।
शनैस्तस्मिन्प्रशान्ते च जनघोषे नराधिपः ॥
वसिष्ठं मुनिशार्दूलं राजा वचनमब्रवीत् ॥

5. (Some commentators are surprised that Dhascharatha did not consult Vasishta and ministers; he took up the issue directly with citizens & VIP-s about Raama's choice as crown prince).

The king had not completed his speech when a loud roar was heard from the multitude (gathered there). When this tumult of the people had subsided a little, the lord of men (King Dhascharatha) addressed Vasishta who was a 'Lion' amongst Muni-s, the following words.

❍ ❍ ❍

६. अभिषेकाय रामस्य यत्कर्म सपरिच्छदम् ।
तदद्य भगवन्सर्वमाज्ञापयितुमर्हसि ॥

6. Oh Lord (Vasishta)! May you give orders so that steps may be taken now to provide various necessities for Raama's coronation.

❍ ❍ ❍

७. तच्छ्रुत्वा भूमिपालस्य वसिष्ठो द्विजसत्तमः ।
आदिदेशाग्रतोराज्ञः स्थितान्युक्तान्कृताञ्जलीन् ॥

7. (As traditional chief Priest, Vasishta takes over arrangements).

Hearing thus from the ruler of Earth, the noble Braamin Vasishta commanded (various) secretaries who were standing there before the king in Anjali (in reverence).

❍ ❍ ❍

८. सुवर्णादीनि रत्नानि बलीन्सर्वौषधीरपि ।
शुक्लमाल्यांश्च लाजांश्च पृथक् च मधुसर्पिषी ।।

8. (Stanzas 8 to 20 describe the preparation for coronation). Golden things; gems; ritual offerings; herbal twigs (for Fire Rituals), white flowers and garlands; puffed Rice; sweet things like honeys, sugar; ... one by one (Item by item) .....

❍ ❍ ❍

९. अहतानि च वासांसि रथं सर्वायुधान्यपि ।
चतुरङ्गबलं चैव गजं च शुभलक्षणम् ।।

9. Garments without blemish; chariots; All weapons; Armed forces drawn from various services; pleasant looking elephants ......

❍ ❍ ❍

१०. चामरव्यजने चोभे ध्वजं छत्रं च पाण्डुरम् ।
शतं च शातकुम्भानां कुम्भानामग्निवर्चसाम् ।।

10. .... masts & banners; two whisk fans; white umbrella; hundreds of golden pots, shining like fire ......

❍ ❍ ❍

११. हिरण्यश्रृङ्गमृषभं समग्रं व्याघ्रचर्म च ।
यच्चान्यत्किंचिदेष्टव्यं तत्सर्वमुपकल्प्यताम् ।।

11. ..... Bull with golden horn; Blemishless tiger skins; all other necessities that are needed should be got ready (said Vasishta) .....

❍ ❍ ❍

१२. उपस्थापयत प्रातरग्न्यगारं महीपतेः ।।

12. ..... and brought to the Royal Sacrificial Hall (of Ceremonies) before morning ......

❍ ❍ ❍

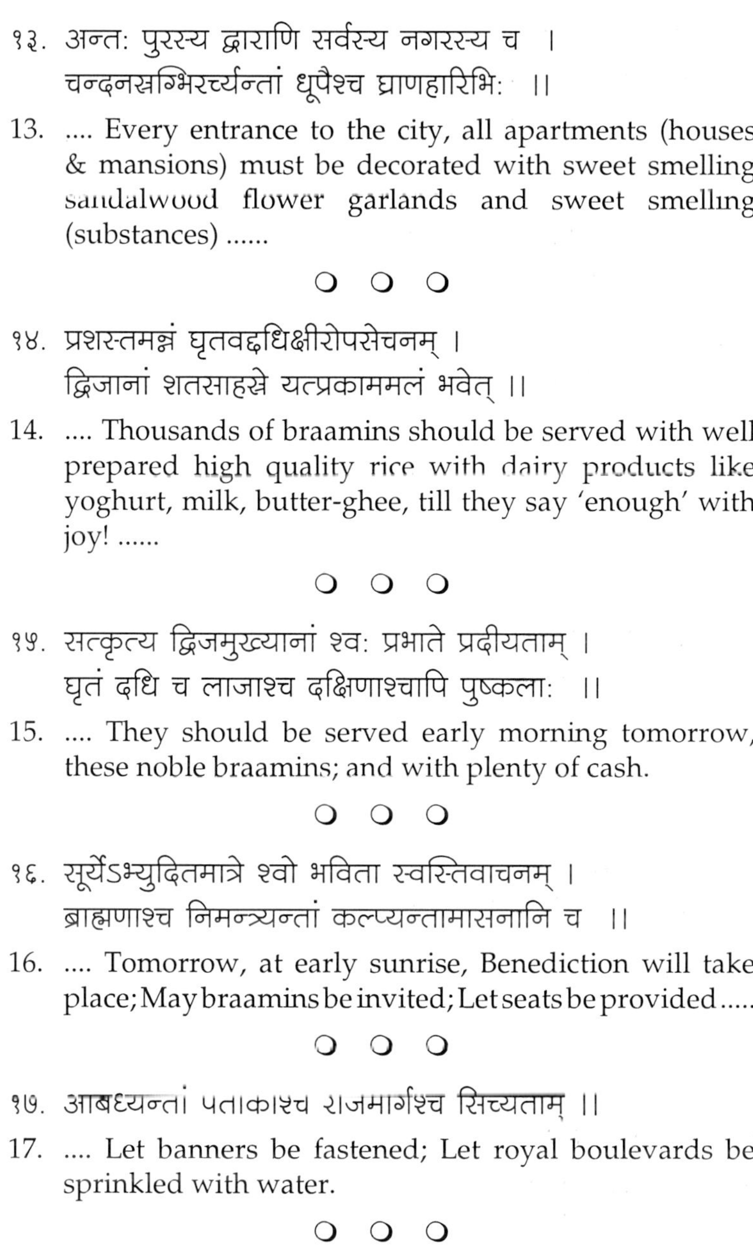

१३. अन्त: पुरस्य द्वाराणि सर्वस्य नगरस्य च ।
चन्दनस्रग्भिरर्च्यन्तां धूपैश्च घ्राणहारिभि: ।।

13. .... Every entrance to the city, all apartments (houses & mansions) must be decorated with sweet smelling sandalwood flower garlands and sweet smelling (substances) ......

❍ ❍ ❍

१४. प्रशस्तमन्नं घृतवद्दधिक्षीरोपसेचनम् ।
द्विजानां शतसाहस्रे यत्प्रकाममलं भवेत् ।।

14. .... Thousands of braamins should be served with well prepared high quality rice with dairy products like yoghurt, milk, butter-ghee, till they say 'enough' with joy! ......

❍ ❍ ❍

१५. सत्कृत्य द्विजमुख्यानां श्व: प्रभाते प्रदीयताम् ।
घृतं दधि च लाजाश्च दक्षिणाश्चापि पुष्कला: ।।

15. .... They should be served early morning tomorrow, these noble braamins; and with plenty of cash.

❍ ❍ ❍

१६. सूर्येऽभ्युदितमात्रे श्वो भविता स्वस्तिवाचनम् ।
ब्राह्मणाश्च निमन्त्र्यन्तां कल्प्यन्तामासनानि च ।।

16. .... Tomorrow, at early sunrise, Benediction will take place; May braamins be invited; Let seats be provided .....

❍ ❍ ❍

१७. आबध्यन्तां पताकाश्च राजमार्गश्च सिच्यताम् ।।

17. .... Let banners be fastened; Let royal boulevards be sprinkled with water.

❍ ❍ ❍

१८. सर्वे च तालावचरा गणिकाश्च स्वलङ्कृता: ।
कक्ष्यां द्वितीयामासाद्य तिष्ठन्तु नृपवेश्मन: ।।

18. .... Let all drummers, courtesans dressed up nicely, station themselves in the second segment (Enclosure) of the palace.

❍ ❍ ❍

१९. देवायतनचैत्येषु सान्नभक्ष्याः सदक्षिणाः ।
उपस्थापयितव्याः स्युर्माल्ययोग्याः पृथक् पृथक् ॥

19. ... In all temples, public places, vendors offering various eats, men of charity, flower vendors, should all station themselves separately in their respective places.

❍ ❍ ❍

२०. दीर्घासिबद्धा योधाश्च सन्नद्धा मृष्टवाससः ।
महाराजाङ्गणं सर्वे प्रविशन्तु महोदयम् ॥

4. .... All warriors must wear their clean uniforms with armoured vests and carry long swords and stand (in attention) at the entrance of king's palace during the great ceremony.

❍ ❍ ❍

२१. एवं व्यादिश्य विप्रौ तौ क्रियास्तत्र विनिष्ठितौ ।
चक्रतुश्चैव यच्छेषं पार्थिवाय निवेद्य च ॥

21. ..... The two Braamins (Vasishta & Vaamadheva) appointed (by the king) gave instructions thus and informed the king and they completed (also) whatever that remained (to be done).

❍ ❍ ❍

२२. कृतमित्येव चाब्रूतामभिगम्य जगत्पतिम् ।
यथोक्तवचनं प्रीतौ हर्षयुक्तौ द्विजर्षभौ ॥

22. These two noble Braamins who were very happy and who were dear (to the king), came back to the king and told him:= As per your instructions all have been done.=.

❍ ❍ ❍

२३. ततः सुमन्त्रं द्युतिमान्राजा वचनमब्रवीत् ।
रामः कृतात्मा भवता शीघ्रमानीयतामिति ॥

23. The majestic king who had a disciplined mind, then addressed Sumanthra these words = May Raama be brought by you at once.=

❍ ❍ ❍

२४. स तथेति प्रतिज्ञाय सुमन्त्रो राजशासनात् ।
रामं तत्रानयांचक्रे रथेन रथिनां वरम् ॥

24. On hearing king's command, Sumanthra (who was king's minister, charioteer & friend) resolved (saying): = I will do as you say = Then he brought Raama, who was a foremost charioteer, in a chariot.

❍ ❍ ❍

२५. अथ तत्र समासीनास्तदा दशरथं नृपम् ।
प्राच्योदीच्याः प्रतीच्याश्च दाक्षिणात्याश्च भूमिपाः ॥

२६. म्लेच्छाचार्यश्च ये चान्ये वनशैलान्तवासिनः ।
उपासांचक्रिरे सर्वे तं देवा इव वासवम् ॥

25 & 26.

Then, there, the chieftains of earth from eastern, western, southern regions assembled there...(to await arrival of) Dhascharatha, ... Mlecha lords residents of forests and mountains, and all common folks, awaited (his arrival) like Dheva-s (awaiting) Vaasava (Lord Indhra).

❍ ❍ ❍

२७. तेषां मध्ये स राजर्षिर्मरुतामिव वासवः ।
प्रासादस्थो रथगतं ददर्शायान्तमात्मजम् ॥

27. Then this royal sage (Dhascharatha) standing at his palace before all of them like Lord Indhra before celestials, saw his son coming on in a chariot .....

❍ ❍ ❍

२८. गन्धर्वराजप्रतिमं लोके विख्यातपौरुषम् ।
दीर्घबाहुं महासत्वं मत्तमातङ्गगामिनम् ।।

28. (Raama) appeared like a Ghandharva king; Most celebrated in valour in the world; he had long and powerful limbs; possessed the strides of an elephant......

❍ ❍ ❍

२९. चन्द्रकान्ताननं राममतीव प्रियदर्शनम् ।
रूपौदार्यगुणैः पुंसां दृष्टिचित्तापहारिणम् ।।

29. ... His face bright like the moon; very lovely to look at; He possessed lofty qualities; He could captivate the mind (& heart) and the 'sight' of men. (Such a) Raama .....

❍ ❍ ❍

३०. घर्माभितप्ताः पर्जन्यं ह्लादयन्तमिव प्रजाः ।
न ततर्प समायान्तं पश्यमानो नराधिपः ।।

30. ... who was coming, this king (Dhascaratha) saw (& beheld) like rain gladdening citizens tormented by heat and draught; (Yet he) Was not (entirely) satisfied (He was worried).

❍ ❍ ❍

३१. अवतार्य सुमन्त्रस्तं राघवं स्यन्दनोत्तमात् ।
पितुः समीपं गच्छन्तं प्राञ्जलिः पृष्ठतोऽन्वगात् ।।

31. (Helping) Raama the Raaghava alight from the foremost chariot, Sumanthra followed (Raama) as he was walking up to his father's proximity with arms cupped in Anjali.

❍ ❍ ❍

३२. स तं कैलासश्रृङ्गाभं प्रासादं रघुपुङ्गवः ।
आरुरोह नृपं द्रष्टुं सह सूतेन राघवः ।।

32. This (Raama) the Raaghava who was 'tiger' amongst Raghus, who (wished to) see his father, climbed (the staircase of) the palace that was like mountain peaks of Kailaash, along with charioteer (Sumanthra).

❍ ❍ ❍

३३. स प्राञ्जलिरभिप्रेत्य प्रणतः पितुरन्तिके ।
नाम स्वं श्रावयन् रामो ववन्दे चरणौ पितुः ॥

33. Raama (presenting himself) before his father approached him with reverence, his hands cupped in Anjali and prostrated at his feet: Then he announced himself by name (as per protocol).

❍ ❍ ❍

३४. तं दृष्ट्वा प्रणतं पार्श्वे कृताञ्जलिपुटं नृपः ।
गृह्याञ्जलौ समाकृष्य सस्वजे प्रियमात्मजम् ॥

34. The king, on seeing his beloved son near him standing in reverence with Anjali, clasped his hands and drew them out and then hugged him.

❍ ❍ ❍

३५. तस्मै चाभ्युदितं सम्यग्मणिकाञ्चनभूषितम् ।
दिदेश राजा रुचिरं रामाय परमासनम् ॥

35. The king then directed his son to a lovely elevated (Royal) foremost seat studded with (gem) stones, well done up in gold.

❍ ❍ ❍

३६. तदासनवरं प्राप्य व्यदीपयत राघवः ।
स्वयैव प्रभया मेरुमुदये विमलो रविः ॥

36. The blemishless (Raama) the Raaghava, sitting on the grand seat, shone by his brilliance, like Sun at sunrise (over) Meru mountain.

❍ ❍ ❍

३७. तेन विभ्राजता तत्र सा सभाऽपि व्यरोचत ।
विमलग्रहनक्षत्रा शारदी द्यौरिवेन्दुना ॥

37. The Assembly hall itself shone then by the (presence of) the most radiant (Raama) like sky adorned with blemishless stars, shining by the moon.

❍ ❍ ❍

३८. तं पश्यमानो नृपतिस्तुतोष प्रियमात्मजम् ।
अलंकृतमिवात्मानमादर्शतलसंस्थितम् ॥

38. The king was mightily pleased to see his dear son fully decorated and appearing to him like his own image in a mirror.

❍ ❍ ❍

३९. स तं सस्मितमाभाष्य पुत्रं पुत्रवतां वरः ।
उवाचेदं वचो राजा देवेन्द्रमिव काश्यपः ॥

39. Foremost amongst those who are (blessed) with sons, this king spoke the following words to his son (Raama) with a smile, just like Kaaschyapa to Indhra.

❍ ❍ ❍

४०. ज्येष्ठायां मे धर्मपत्न्यां सदृश्यां सदृशः सुतः ।
उत्पन्नस्त्वं गुणश्रेष्ठो मम रामात्मजः प्रियः ॥

40. Oh Raama! Possessing such noble qualities, you, my beloved son, was born to my eldest and most worthy and devoted wife (Kowsalya).

❍ ❍ ❍

४१. यतस्त्वया प्रजाश्चेमाः स्वगुणैरनुरञ्जिताः ।
तस्मात्त्वं पुष्ययोगेन यौवराज्यमवाप्नुहि ॥

41. All these citizens here are charmed by you with your inborn qualities: Therefore from the day of Pushya star, you will (become and) obtain (the title of) crown prince.

४२. कामतस्त्वं प्रकृत्यैव विनीतो गुणवानसि ।
गुणवत्यपि तु स्नेहात्पुत्र वक्ष्यामि ते हितम् ।।

42. By nature you are a man of (great) merit; Well behaved; Oh my son! Yet, although endowed with (noble) qualities, I will now tell you of my own accord, what is salutary, because of my attachment.

❍ ❍ ❍

४३. भूयो विनयमास्थाय भव नित्यं जितेन्द्रियः ।
कामक्रोधसमुत्थानि त्यजेथा व्यसनानि च ।।

43. (Dhascharatha gives advice to his son, the future king).

Greatly steadfast in (Self) Discipline, you must ever be, controlling your senses (of passion, wrath, etc.); The (Eightfold) Suffering arising out of passion and wrath must be abandoned...

(Drink, Women, Gambling, Indiscriminate hunting, Gossip, Excessive Punishment, Excessive Taxes, Excessive Expenditure etc.).

❍ ❍ ❍

४४. परोक्षया वर्तमानो वृत्त्या प्रत्यक्षया तथा ।
अमात्यप्रभृतीः सर्वाः प्रकृतीश्चानुरञ्जय ।।

44. Following the (Righteous) path of good conduct in both visible & non visible, you should always please ministers and all the people.

(The visible: Helping people with food, clothing etc.: Non visible: like removing fear from people).

❍ ❍ ❍

४५. कोष्ठागारायुधागारैः कृत्वा सन्निचयान् बहून् ।
तुष्टानुरक्तप्रकृतिर्यः पालयति मेदिनीम् ।।

45. Making granaries full with grains and vaults full with armaments, if one rules the land, earning gratitude of happy citizens .....

❍ ❍ ❍

४६. तस्य नन्दन्ति मित्राणि लब्ध्वाऽमृतमिवामराः ।
तस्मात्त्वमपि चात्मानं नियम्यैवं समाचर ॥

46. ... then his friends (& friendly chiefs of other territories) will rejoice, just as Dheva-s (when they obtained) Nectar: Therefore you must conduct yourself in such a manner.

❍ ❍ ❍

४७. तच्छ्रुत्वा सुहृदस्तस्य रामस्य प्रियकारिणः ।
त्वरिताः शीघ्रमभ्येत्य कौसल्यायै न्यवेदयन् ॥

47. Hearing all this, Raama's friends and well wishers at once rushed out (of the Hall) and went to (his mother) Kowsalya and informed her (about the happy event).

❍ ❍ ❍

४८. सा हिरण्यं च गाश्चैव रत्नानि विविधानि च ।
व्यादिदेश प्रियाख्येभ्यः कौसल्या प्रमदोत्तमा ॥

48. The foremost (virtuous) lady Kowsalya, at once gave (as gifts) various gems, stones and gold to those who brought her the happy tidings.

(It is surprising that Dhascharatha had not consulted nor even informed Kowsalya about Raama's coronation).

❍ ❍ ❍

४९. अथाभिवाद्य राजानं रथमारुह्य राघवः ।
ययौ स्वं द्युतिमद्वेश्म जनौघैः प्रतिपूजितः ॥

49. Then (Raama) the Raaghava who was honoured by the multitude of people gathered there, bowed to the king and then left for his beautiful palace riding on a chariot.

❍ ❍ ❍

५०. ते चापि पौरा नृपतेर्वचस्त –
च्छ्रुत्वा तदा लाभमिवेष्टमाशु ।
नरेन्द्रमामन्त्र्य गृहाणि गत्वा
देवान् समानर्चुरभिप्रहृष्टाः ॥

50. All the citizens who had listened to the speech of their king, took leave of the king who was like one who obtained whatever he wanted. They then went back to their abode at once and began to propitiate the Deities with great joy.....

❍ ❍ ❍

Chapter 4

Fixing Date & Time for Coronation

(Dhascharatha again talks to his son: Date & Time Fixed for Coronation).

❍ ❍ ❍

१. गतेष्वथ नृपो भूयः पौरेषु सह मन्त्रिभिः ।
मन्त्रयित्वा ततश्चक्रे निश्चयज्ञः सुनिश्चयम् ॥

1. A man of conviction (a man who knew consequences of his decisions), this king (Dhascharatha) reflected upon this good decision along with his ministers after the citizens had left.

❍ ❍ ❍

२. श्व एव पुष्यो भविता श्वोऽभिषिच्यन्तु मे सुतम् ।
रामो राजीवताम्राक्षो युवराज इति प्रभुः ॥

2. (Dhascharatha thought): Tomorrow morning, in the star of Pushya, they will anoint my son; From tomorrow itself the lotus eyed Raama will become lord as YuvaRaaja.

❍ ❍ ❍

३. अथान्तर्गृहमाविश्य राजा दशरथस्तदा ।
सूतमामन्त्रयामास रामं पुनरिहानय ॥

3. Then retiring to the inner apartments (of palace) King Dhascharatha commanded charioteer (Sumanthra) thus:= Get Raama over here again.=

❍ ❍ ❍

४. प्रतिगृह्य स तद्वाक्यं सूतः पुनरुपाययौ ।
रामस्य भवनं शीघ्रं राममानयितुं पुनः ।।

4. Obeying his words (of command), the charioteer left at once for Raama's palace again to bring Raama.

❍ ❍ ❍

५. द्वाःस्थैरावेदितं तस्य रामायागमनं पुनः ।
श्रुत्वैव चापि रामस्तं प्राप्तं शङ्कान्वितोऽभवत् ।।

5. His arrival was announced to Raama by the guards; Hearing this, Raama became apprehensive about him who had come there again (and about the purpose of his visit).

❍ ❍ ❍

६. प्रवेश्य चैनं त्वरितं रामो वचनमब्रवीत् ।
यदागमनकृत्यं ते भूयस्तद्ब्रूह्यशेषतः ।।

6. (Inviting him) to enter, Raama said these words to him;= Please tell me all, without leaving out anything, about the purpose of your visit again (here).=

❍ ❍ ❍

७. तमुवाच ततः सूतो राजा त्वां द्रष्टुमिच्छति ।
श्रुत्वा प्रमाणं तत्र त्वं गमनायेतराय वा ।।

7. Then the charioteer said this to him= The King desires to see you. After hearing this (command of your father) whether to go or not,.... about that, you are the authority=

(Poet Vaalmeeki says that the old Sumanthra was rather vexed that Raama should ask him about his father's purpose. Of course Raama leaves at once)

❍ ❍ ❍

८. इति सूतवच: श्रुत्वा रामोऽथ त्वरयान्वित: ।
प्रययौ राजभवनं पुनर्द्रष्टुं नरेश्वरम् ।।

8. Hearing the charioteer's words, Raama making haste, at once (started) and reached king's palace to see the king again.

❍ ❍ ❍

९. तं श्रुत्वा समनुप्राप्तं रामं दशरथो नृप: ।
प्रवेशयामास गृहं विवक्षु: प्रियमुत्तमम् ।।

9. Hearing that Raama was approaching him, king Dhascharatha asked him to enter his apartment, to tell him about the foremost happy (event).

❍ ❍ ❍

१०. प्रविशन्नेव च श्रीमान्राघवो भवनं पितु: ।
ददर्श पितरं दूरात्प्रणिपत्य कृताञ्जलि: ।।

10. And the resplendent Raama the Raaghava (clasping his hands) in Anjali even from a distance, entered his father's abode: He bowed to his father and looked (at his father for his command).

❍ ❍ ❍

११. प्रणमन्तं समुत्थाप्य परिष्वज्य स भूमिप: ।
प्रदिश्य चास्मै रुचिरमासनं पुनरब्रवीत् ।।

11. Lifting him up who was prostrating before him, this king embraced him and directed him to a lovely seat once again and said:

❍ ❍ ❍

१२. राम वृद्धोऽस्मि दीर्घायुर्भुक्ता भोगा मयेप्सिता: ।
अन्नवद्भि: क्रतुशतैस्तथेष्टं भूरिदक्षिणै: ।।

12. Oh Raama! I am old (having seen) long years. Many pleasures desired by me have been enjoyed by me. Likewise, I have satisfied myself with hundreds of

ceremonial sacrifices with offerings of foods and many gifts (gold etc.).

❍ ❍ ❍

१३. जातमिष्टमपत्यं मे त्वमद्यानुपमं भुवि ।
दत्तमिष्टमधीतं च मया पुरुषसत्तम ॥

13. Now therefore, in this world, this, which is incomparable, this, which I had sought, this, which was offered (as a boon) was (bestowed upon me and) enjoyed by me: Oh noble man (Raama): You thus became my beloved son. (Dhascharatha tells Raama only through the mighty yaaga he was born to him after long years, being childless).

❍ ❍ ❍

१४. अनुभूतानि चेष्टानि मया वीरसुखान्यपि ।
देवर्षिपितृविप्राणामनृणोऽस्मि तथाऽऽत्मनः ॥

14. All the desirable healthy pleasures obtained through bravery have been enjoyed by me: Likewise (my debt), my duty to Dheva-s, Rishi-s, and braamins have been discharged.

❍ ❍ ❍

१५. न किञ्चिन्मम कर्तव्यं तवान्यत्राभिषेचनात् ।
अतो यत्त्वामहं ब्रूयां तन्मे त्वं कर्तुमर्हसि ॥

15. Apart from crowning you, nothing else remain to be done by me; therefore you are (now) bound to do what I am going to tell you, for me (for my sake).

❍ ❍ ❍

१६. अद्य प्रकृतयः सर्वास्त्वामिच्छन्ति नराधिपम् ।
अतस्त्वां युवराजानमभिषेक्ष्यामि पुत्रक ॥

16. Oh my son (Raama)! All the citizens desire you to be (their) king; Therefore I am going to anoint you as crown prince, now.

❍ ❍ ❍

१७. अपि चाद्याशुभान्राम स्वप्ने पश्यामि दारुणान् ।
सनिर्घाता महोल्का च पततीह महास्वना ॥

17. Oh Raama! Yet: In my dreams I see a mighty meteor falling down here with thunder and mighty sound, a dreadful ill omen.

❍ ❍ ❍

१८. अवष्टब्धं च मे राम नक्षत्रं दारुणैर्ग्रहैः ।
आवेदयन्ति दैवज्ञाः सूर्याङ्गारकराहुभिः ॥

18. Oh Raama! Astrologers tell me that my (Birth) Star is afflicted by a cruel combination of stars of Sun, Mars and Raahu.

❍ ❍ ❍

१९. प्रायेण च निमित्तानामीदृशानां समुद्भवे ।
राजा हि मृत्युमाप्नोति घोरां वाऽऽपदमृच्छति ॥

19. (Indians have faith in astrology, no wonder) On account of such ill omen arising, a king faces terrible disaster or even death. Or perhaps he may lose faculty of mind & senses.

❍ ❍ ❍

२०. तद्यावदेव मे चेतो न विमुञ्चति राघव ।
तावदेवाभिषिञ्चस्व चला हि प्राणिनां मतिः ॥

20. Oh (Raama) the Raaghava! Before my faculty of mind & soul leaves me, you be crowned. Men's mind (& resolutions) are unsteady (fickle).

❍ ❍ ❍

२१. अद्य चन्द्रोऽभ्युपगतः पुष्यात्पूर्वं पुनर्वसुम् ।
श्वः पुष्ययोगं नियतं वक्ष्यन्ते दैवचिन्तकाः ॥

21. Today moon is 'on' the Star of Punarvasu, preceding star Pushya: Astrologers (opine and) tell me that tomorrow of the auspicious Pushya star is appropriate.

❍ ❍ ❍

२२. तत्र पुष्येऽभिषिक्तस्त्वं मनस्त्वरयतीव माम् ।
श्वस्त्वाऽहमभिषेक्ष्यामि यौवराज्ये परन्तप ।।

22. Oh (Raama) the tormentor of enemy! On the day of Pushya star you must be anointed: My mind longs for this only. I am going to anoint you tomorrow in duties of YuvaRaaja.

❍ ❍ ❍

२३. तस्मात्त्वयाऽद्य व्रतिना निशेयं नियतात्मना ।
सह वध्वोपवस्तव्या दर्भप्रस्तरशायिना ।।

23. Therefore, along with your wife Seetha, this night should be spent in vow of celibacy by you, lying down on a mattress of Dharbha grass with your mind directed (to Gods) in prayer.

❍ ❍ ❍

२४. सुहृदश्चाप्रमत्तास्त्वां रक्षन्त्वद्य समन्ततः ।
भवन्ति बहुविघ्नानि कार्याण्येवंविधानि हि ।।

24. Such auspicious events are confronted with obstacles. Therefore your friends should protect you with vigilance at this time in every way.

❍ ❍ ❍

२५. विप्रोषितश्च भरतो यावदेव पुरादितः ।
तावदेवाभिषेकस्ते प्राप्तकालो मतो मम ।।

25. (Your brother) Bharatha also is now away from (our) capital: but the auspicious time is now. Because of this (reason) your coronation has my approval (now itself).

❍ ❍ ❍

२६. कामं खलु सतां वृत्ते भ्राता ते भरतः स्थितः ।
ज्येष्ठानुवर्ती धर्मात्मा सानुक्रोशो जितेन्द्रियः ।।

26. And there is this surely: Your brother Bharatha follows the conduct of the virtuous; (He is firm in virtue):

Obedient to elders; has controlled his senses: Very compassionate; A noble soul, man of Dharma.

❍ ❍ ❍

२७. किं तु चित्तं मनुष्याणामनित्यमिति मे मतिः ।
सतां च धर्मनित्यानां कृतशोभि च राघव ।।

27. Oh (Raama) the Raaghava! (But) The minds of even good men who are steadfast in Dharma is uncertain (unsteady) at the good fortune (of others). This is well known to me.

(No wonder some commentators have felt that it was indiscreet on the part of Dhascharatha to anoint Raama when his two sons Bharatha & Schathrugna were far away. Of course there would be no Raamaayana if Raama had been anointed when Bharatha was around. The World knows that Bharatha would have been the happiest man to see his beloved brother Raama crowned.)

❍ ❍ ❍

२८. इत्युक्तः सोऽभ्यनुज्ञातः श्वो भाविन्यभिषेचने ।
व्रजेति रामः पितरमभिवाद्याभ्ययाद्गृहम् ।।

28. Having thus been told about the coronation fixed for the next day, Raama who was given leave to go, went back to his palace after bowing to his father who had said: =You may return= (to your abode).

❍ ❍ ❍

२९. प्रविश्य चात्मनो वेश्म राज्ञोद्दिष्टेऽभिषेचने ।
तस्मिन् क्षणे स निर्गम्य मातुरन्तःपुरं ययौ ।।

29. After being enlightened by the king about the impending coronation and after he had returned to his palace, (Raama) came out and went to his mother (Kowsalya's) palace.

❍ ❍ ❍

३०. तत्र तां प्रवणामेव मातरं क्षौमवासिनीम् ।
वाग्यतां देवतागारे ददर्शायाचतीं श्रियम् ।।

30. There, at her prayer hall, he saw his mother clad in a robe of silk, praying to Schree (Goddess Lakshmi) with deep devotion, uttering chants.

❍ ❍ ❍

३१. प्रागेव चागता तत्र सुमित्रा लक्ष्मणस्तथा ।
सीता चानायिता श्रुत्वा प्रियं रामाभिषेचनम् ।।

31. Hearing the good news about Raama's coronation, Sumithra (the second queen of Dhascharatha and mother of Lakshmana and Schathrugna) was brought (invited) there; And Seetha and Lakshmana had reached earlier.

(Readers may note that the third queen Kaikeyi was not there!)

❍ ❍ ❍

३२. तस्मिन्काले हि कौसल्या तस्थावामीलितेक्षणा ।
सुमित्रयाऽन्वास्यमाना सीतया लक्ष्मणेन च ।।

32. At that time, Kowsalya who was assisted by Sumithra, Seetha and Lakshmana (in prayers), was (seen) with her eyes closed in (meditation).

❍ ❍ ❍

३३. श्रुत्वा पुष्येण पुत्रस्य यौवराज्याभिषेचनम् ।
प्राणायामेन पुरुषं ध्यायमाना जनार्दनम् ।।

33. Hearing about his son's coronation as crown prince on the day of Pushya star, she was meditating upon The Purusha, The Janaardhana (God Vishnu), controlling her breath.

❍ ❍ ❍

३४. तथा सनियमामेव सोऽभिगम्याभिवाद्य च ।
उवाच वचनं रामो हर्षयंस्तामनिन्दिताम् ।।

34. Then approaching her who was blameless and who was in meditation, this Raama bowed to her and said these words.

❍ ❍ ❍

३५. अम्ब पित्रा नियुक्तोऽस्मि प्रजापालनकर्मणि ।
भविता श्वोऽभिषेको मे यथा मे शासनं पितुः ।।

35. Oh Mother! I have been entrusted with the task of protecting (ruling) the citizens by my father; By the command of my father, the coronation for me is going to take place tomorrow.

❍ ❍ ❍

३६. सीतयाऽप्युपवस्तव्या रजनीयं मया सह ।
एवमृत्विगुपाध्यायैः सह मामुक्तवान्पिता ।।

36. Father who was with Rithviks and Upaadhyaya-s, told me further; that this night should be spent by me and (Seetha the) Vaidhehi. (in Dheeksha-Vows).

❍ ❍ ❍

३७. यानि यान्यत्र योग्यानि श्वो भाविन्यभिषेचने ।
तानि मे मङ्गलान्यद्य वैदेह्याश्चैव कारय ।।

37. Whatever auspicious things are to be done in lieu of tomorrow's coronation, all those may be done for me & (Seetha the) Vaidhehi.

❍ ❍ ❍

३८. एतच्छ्रुत्वा तु कौसल्या चिरकालाभिकाङ्क्षितम् ।
हर्षबाष्पकलं वाक्यमिदं राममभाषत ।।

38. Hearing these words which she was looking forward to for a long time, Kowsalya addressed Raama with tears of joy.

❍ ❍ ❍

३९. वत्स राम चिरं जीव हतास्ते परिपन्थिनः ।
ज्ञातीन्मे त्वं श्रिया युक्तः सुमित्रायाश्च नन्दय ।।

39. Oh my son Raama! May you live long. May your antagonists be destroyed. Endowed with resplendency, you shall gladden me & Sumithra.and relatives.
(Here again, no mention about Kaikeyi)

❍ ❍ ❍

४0. कल्याणे बत नक्षत्रे मयि जातोऽसि पुत्रक ।
येन त्वया दशरथो गुणैराराधितः पिता ॥

40. Your father king Dhascharatha has been well served by you, by your good qualities; Oh son! You were born to me as on auspicious (day of) the stars. Ah!

❍ ❍ ❍

४१. अमोघं बत मे क्षान्तं पुरुषे पुष्करेक्षणे ।
येयमिक्ष्वाकुराज्यश्रीः पुत्र त्वां संश्रयिष्यति ॥

41. Oh son! Ah! This glorious Mother (we call as) our Ikshwaaku kingdom will 'cling' to you. My prayers to (Lord Vishnu) the lotus eyed God, has not been in vain.

❍ ❍ ❍

४२. इत्येवमुक्तो मात्रेदं रामो भ्रातरमब्रवीत् ।
प्राञ्जलिं प्रह्वमासीनमभिवीक्ष्य स्मयन्निव ॥

42. When told thus by his mother, Raama looked at his devoted brother Lakshmana who was seated with his arms in Anjali and he said this with a smile.

❍ ❍ ❍

४३. लक्ष्मणेमां मया सार्धं प्रशाधि त्वं वसुंधराम् ।
द्विितीयं मेऽन्तरात्मानं त्वामियं श्रीरुपस्थिता ॥

43. Oh Lakshmana! This resplendent (kingdom) belongs to you (also) who are my very soul (in another body), and who are my "double": You rule the Earth along with me.

❍ ❍ ❍

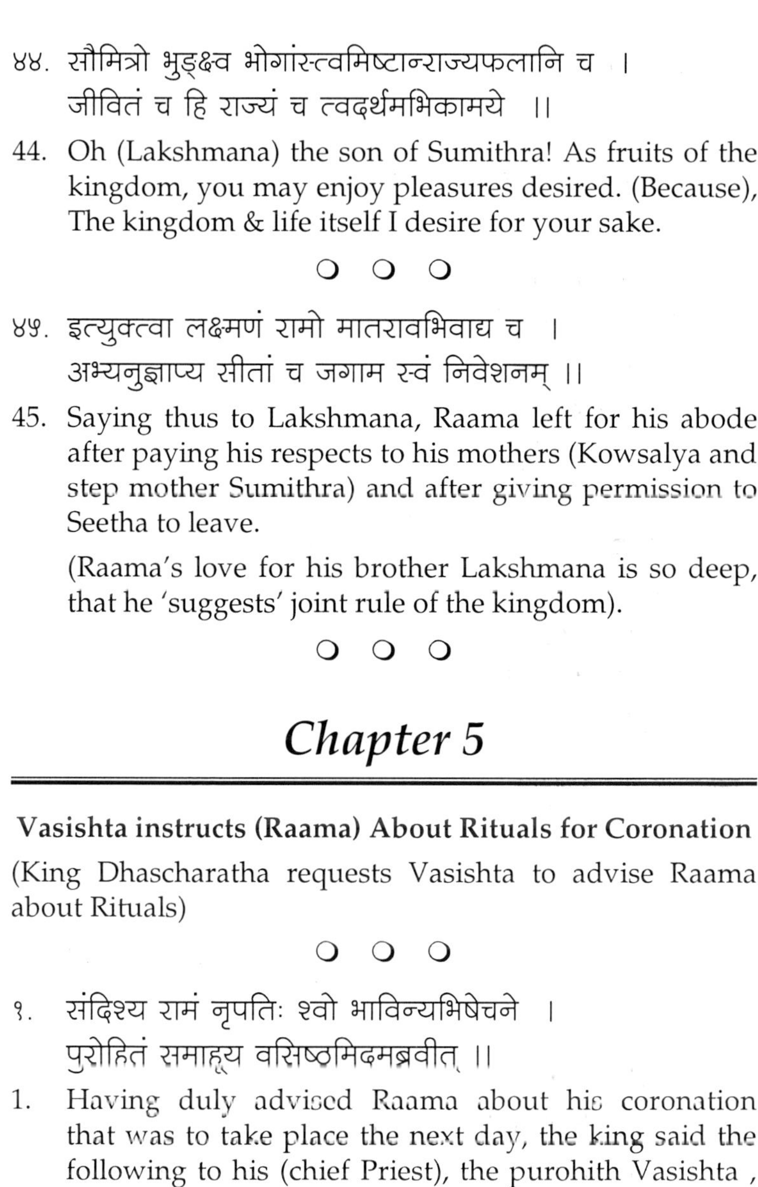

४४. सौमित्रो भुङ्क्ष्व भोगांस्त्वमिष्टान्राज्यफलानि च ।
जीवितं च हि राज्यं च त्वदर्थमभिकामये ॥

44. Oh (Lakshmana) the son of Sumithra! As fruits of the kingdom, you may enjoy pleasures desired. (Because), The kingdom & life itself I desire for your sake.

❍ ❍ ❍

४५. इत्युक्त्वा लक्ष्मणं रामो मातरावभिवाद्य च ।
अभ्यनुज्ञाप्य सीतां च जगाम स्वं निवेशनम् ॥

45. Saying thus to Lakshmana, Raama left for his abode after paying his respects to his mothers (Kowsalya and step mother Sumithra) and after giving permission to Seetha to leave.

(Raama's love for his brother Lakshmana is so deep, that he 'suggests' joint rule of the kingdom).

❍ ❍ ❍

Chapter 5

Vasishta instructs (Raama) About Rituals for Coronation

(King Dhascharatha requests Vasishta to advise Raama about Rituals)

❍ ❍ ❍

१. संदिश्य रामं नृपतिः श्वो भाविन्यभिषेचने ।
पुरोहितं समाहूय वसिष्ठमिदमब्रवीत् ॥

1. Having duly advised Raama about his coronation that was to take place the next day, the king said the following to his (chief Priest), the purohith Vasishta , after inviting him.

❍ ❍ ❍

२. गच्छोपवासं काकुत्स्थं कारयाद्य तपोधन ।
श्रीयशोराज्यलाभाय वध्वा सह यतव्रतम् ॥

2. (Oh Vasishta) for whom wealth is penance! (Please) perform (Rituals) and make (Raama) the Kaakuthsa, who is with his wife, to observe total abstinence & to comply with 'Vows'. (Please) Go now, (do all this) for the sake of glory, kingdom, and prosperity.

❍ ❍ ❍

३. तथेति च स राजानमुक्त्वा वेदविदां वरः ।
स्वयं वसिष्ठो भगवान्ययौ रामनिवेशनम् ॥

3. This foremost amongst those knowing Vedha, this Lord Vasishta said:= So be it.= Then he himself went to Raama's place.

❍ ❍ ❍

४. उपवासयितुं रामं मन्त्रविन्मन्त्रपारगः ।
ब्राह्मं रथवरं युक्तमास्थाय सुधृतव्रतः ॥

4. (Vasishta) Who was master of chants & prayers, who was a wise counsellor, who was resolute in vows, mounted on a chariot that was fit for a braamin (of his stature) ...which was waiting (for him and he went) to advise Raama to keep his vows ......

❍ ❍ ❍

५. स रामभवनं प्राप्य पाण्डुराभ्रघनप्रभम् ।
तिस्रः कक्ष्या रथेनैव विवेश मुनिसत्तमः ॥

5. Crossed the three large enclosures (Courtyards of Raama's palace). This foremost Muni reached Raama's palace which was like white cloud (in the sky).

❍ ❍ ❍

६. तमागतमृषिं रामस्त्वरन्निव ससम्भ्रमः ।
मानयिष्यन्स मानार्हं निश्चक्राम निवेशनात् ॥

6. And Raama excitedly got up from his seat exhibiting his reverence and went out (to greet) the Rishi (Vasishta) who was coming there and who deserved to be honoured.

❍ ❍ ❍

७. अभ्येत्य त्वरमाणश्च रथाभ्याशं मनीषिणः ।
ततोऽवतारयामास परिगृह्य रथात्स्वयम् ।।

7. Rushing forth from there, (Raama) reached the proximity of this great man's chariot and (extending his hand) clasped him by hand and alighted him himself.

❍ ❍ ❍

८. स चैनं प्रश्रितं दृष्ट्वा संभाष्याभिप्रसाद्य च ।
प्रियार्हं हर्षयन्राममित्युवाच पुरोहितः ।।

8. This (family) Priest (Vasishta), seeing this Raama who was dear to him so courteous, blessed him after conversing with him (after exchanging pleasantries); He then said happily:

❍ ❍ ❍

९. प्रसन्नस्ते पिता राम यौवराज्यमवाप्स्यसि ।
उपवासं भवानद्य करोतु सह सीतया ।।

9. Oh Raama! Your father is tranquil (very happy) as you are going to obtain (the title of) crown prince. Along with Seetha you should observe total abstinence-vows .....

❍ ❍ ❍

१०. प्रातस्त्वामभिषेक्ता हि यौवराज्ये नराधिपः ।
पिता दशरथः प्रीत्या ययातिं नहुषो यथा ।।

10. like (King) Nahusha towards (son) Yayaathi, your father king Dhascharatha will anoint you as crown prince tomorrow, happily.

❍ ❍ ❍

११. इत्युक्त्वा स तदा राममुपवासं यतव्रतम् ।
मन्त्रवत्कारयामास वैदेह्या सहितं मुनिः ।।

11. Saying thus, the Muni performed the (Pre-coronation) vows and abstinence as per norms of religious code,

upon Raama who was with (his wife Seetha the) Vaidhehi.

❍ ❍ ❍

१२. ततो यथावद्रामेण स राज्ञो गुरुरर्चितः ।
अभ्यनुज्ञाप्य काकुत्स्थं ययौ रामनिवेशनात् ।।

12. This teacher of the king, (this Vasishta) was duly worshipped by Raama: Then after taking leave of (Raama the) Kaakuthsa, left Raama's abode.

❍ ❍ ❍

१३. सुहृद्भिस्तत्र रामोऽपि सुखासीनः प्रियंवदैः ।
सभाजितो विवेशाथताननुज्ञाप्य सर्वशः ।।

13. After conversing with his affable (sweet speaking) friends and pleasing them in every way, Raama took leave of them and went (re-entered the inner apartments of his palace).

❍ ❍ ❍

१४. हृष्टनारीनरयुतं रामवेश्म तदा बभौ ।
यथा मत्तद्विजगणं प्रफुल्लनलिनं सरः ।।

14. Like a lake with beautiful flowers & intoxicated birds, Raama's palace shone with plenty of ladies and men in merriment.

❍ ❍ ❍

१५. स राजभवनप्रख्यात्तस्माद्रामनिवेशनात् ।
निःसृत्य ददृशे मार्गं वसिष्ठो जनसंवृतम् ।।

15. Coming out of Raama's abode that was like an emperor's palace, this Vasishta saw the entire route full with multitude of men.

❍ ❍ ❍

१६. बृन्दं बृन्दमयोध्यायां राजमार्गाः समन्ततः ।
बभूवुरतिसंबाधाः कुतूहलजनैर्वृताः ।।

16. The royal boulevards of Ayodhya and all the bye lanes were filled with groups and groups of people who were curious (to witness the festivities) and it was very crowded.

❍ ❍ ❍

१७. जनबृन्दोर्मिसङ्घर्षहर्षस्वनवतस्तदा ।
बभूव राजमार्गस्य सागरस्येव निस्वनः ।।

17. Because of the 'embrocation' of the crowd and because of the loud laughter (and talks), the sound emanating from royal boulevards was like those of turbulent ocean.

❍ ❍ ❍

१८. सिक्तसंमृष्टरथ्या सा तदाऽथ वनमालिनी ।
आसीदयोध्या नगरी समुच्छ्रितगृहध्वजा ।।

18. At that time, this Ayodhya city was cleansed with water sprinkled (on roads etc.): Arches with garlands of flowers: Banners raised high on house tops.

❍ ❍ ❍

१९. तदा ह्ययोध्यानिलयः सस्त्रीबालाखिलो जनः ।
रामाभिषेकमाकाङ्क्षन्नाकाङ्क्षदुदयं रवेः ।।

19. All the citizens living in Ayodhya including girls and children were keenly looking forward to Raama's coronation and were awaiting sunrise.

❍ ❍ ❍

२०. प्रजालङ्कारभूतं च जनस्यानन्दवर्धनम् ।
उत्सुकोऽभूज्जनो द्रष्टुं तमयोध्यामहोत्सवम् ।।

20. The citizens were anxiously looking forward to witness this grand spectacle at Ayodhya which was well decorated by citizens and which brought joy to all people.

❍ ❍ ❍

२१. एवं तं जनसंबाधं राजमार्गं पुरोहितः ।
व्यूहन्निव जनौघं तं शनै राजकुलं ययौ ।।

21. Wading through the multitude slowly along the royal boulevard that was crowded with people, the purohith (Vasishta) reached king (Dhascharatha's) palace.

❍ ❍ ❍

२२. शुभ्राभ्रशिखरप्रख्यं प्रासादमधिरुह्य सः ।
समीयाय नरेन्द्रेण शक्रेणेव बृहस्पतिः ।।

22. Climbing (the steps of) the palace that was like white clouds over (mountain) peaks, (Vasishta) appeared before king like Brihaspathi before Lord Indhra.

❍ ❍ ❍

२३. तमागतमभिप्रेक्ष्य हित्वा राजासनं नृपः ।
पप्रच्छ स च तस्मै तत्कृतमित्यभ्यवेदयत् ।।

23. When he saw (Vasishta) coming, King (Dhascharatha) got up from the throne and asked him: (Vasishta) informed him: =(All)That, has been done =

❍ ❍ ❍

२४. तेन चैव तदा तुल्यं सहासीनाः सभासदः ।
आसनेभ्यः समुत्तस्थुः पूजयन्तः पुरोहितम् ।।

24. Then all the men in the assembly who were seated there got up from their seats, thus honouring the Purohith (Vasishta) who was (worthy of and) equal to (the King).

❍ ❍ ❍

२५. गुरुणा त्वभ्यनुज्ञातो मनुजौघं विसृज्य तम् ।
विवेशान्तःपुरं राजा सिंहो गिरिगुहामिव ।।

25. After being given leave by his teacher (Vasishta) the king gave permission to the crowd of men to leave and entered the inner apartments of his palace, like a lion going to its cave.

❍ ❍ ❍

२६. तदग्र्यवेषप्रमदाजनाकुलं
महेन्द्रवेश्मप्रतिमं निवेशनम् ।
विदीपयंश्चारु विवेश पार्थिवः
शशीव तारागणसङ्कुलं नभः ।।

26. At the beautiful palace which was like Lord Indhra's abode (in heaven) and which was full with most wonderfully decorated girls, the king shone like moon in star studded night.

❍ ❍ ❍

Chapter 6

(Raama) Observes Vows

(Raama prepares himself for coronation; Ayodhya is colorful & gay)

❍ ❍ ❍

१. गते पुरोहिते रामः स्नातो नियतमानसः ।
सह पत्न्या विशालाक्ष्या नारायणमुपागमत् ।।

1. After Purohith (Vasishta) had left, Raama took (Holy) bath: With his mind steadfast in Prayers, he prayed to (God Vishnu the) Naaraayana, along with his wife (Seetha) whose eyes were wide.

❍ ❍ ❍

२. प्रगृह्य शिरसा पात्रीं हविषो विधिवत्ततः ।
महते दैवतायाज्यं जुहाव ज्वलितेऽनले ।।

2. Carrying the vessel containing Havis (Oblation) on his head, he then offered the oblation mixed with ghee (melted butter oil) in the burning fire as per norms, to the great God.

❍ ❍ ❍

३. शेषं च हविषस्तस्य प्राश्याशास्यात्मनः प्रियम् ।
ध्यायन्नारायणं देवं स्वास्तीर्णे कुशसंस्तरे ॥

3. Partaking the balance (part of) Havis, he meditated upon the Lord, Naaraayana (God Vishnu), seeking His welfare: Then on the bed of Dharbha grass which he himself spread out ......

❍ ❍ ❍

४. वाग्यतः सह वैदेह्या भूत्वा नियतमानसः ।
श्रीमत्यायतने विष्णोः शिश्ये नरवरात्मजः ॥

4. he lay: This (Raama) the son of the emperor, along with (Seetha the) Vaidhehi uttered prayer with utter devotion to Vishnu to obtain prosperity, (lying down) at that resting place.

❍ ❍ ❍

५. एकयामावशिष्टायां रात्र्यां प्रतिविबुध्य सः ।
अलङ्कारविधिं कृत्स्नं कारयामास वेश्मनः ॥

5. Getting up at night before the last part of the night was over (One Yaama of the night), he got everything done like (cleaning and) decoration of his place (of worship).

❍ ❍ ❍

६. तत्र श्रृण्वन्सुखा वाचः सूतमागधवन्दिनाम् ।
पूर्वां सन्ध्यामुपासीनो जजाप यतमानसः ॥

6. Hearing the sweet strains of music from (professional) singers and bards of Sootha-s, Maagada-s, and Vandhitha-s, he meditated upon the Deity Sandhya (Deity of early morning rituals): And with great devotion recited (Chants).

❍ ❍ ❍

७. तुष्टाव प्रणतश्चैव शिरसा मधुसूदनम् ।
वमलक्षौमसंवीतो वाचयामास च द्विजान् ॥

7. Draped in white robes and bowing with his head down, he 'pleased' (God Vishnu the) Madhusoodhana (by extolling him): And Braamins began to recite Hymns (which he heard)

○ ○ ○

८. तेषां पुण्याहघोषोऽथ गम्भीरमधुरस्तदा ।
अयोध्यां पूरयामास तूर्यघोषानुनादितः ॥

8. At that time, the entire Ayodhya was full with reverberating sounds of Thoorya (a musical instrument), along with their holy renderings that were loud and sweet.

○ ○ ○

९. कृतोपवासं तु तदा वैदेह्या सह राघवम् ।
अयोध्यानिलयः श्रुत्वा सर्वः प्रमुदितो जनः ॥

9. All the citizens of Ayodhya having heard of the (successful) completion of Raama's (Pre-coronation) vows along with (Seetha the) Vaidhehi, greatly rejoiced.

○ ○ ○

१०. ततः पौरजनः सर्वः श्रुत्वा रामाभिषेचनम् ।
प्रभातां रजनीं दृष्ट्वा चक्रे शोभयितुं पुरीम् ॥

10. All the citizens hearing about (and thinking about) Raama's coronation and observing that night had passed away, began to decorate the city.

○ ○ ○

११. सिताभ्रशिखराभेषु देवतायतनेषु च ।
चतुष्पथेषु रथ्यासु चैत्येष्वट्टालकेषु च ॥

11. In the temples which were like peaks towering over white clouds, in the roads, in the four cross roads, in the religious and sacrificial halls, in the market place ....

○ ○ ○

१२. नानापण्यसमृद्धेषु वणिजामापणेषु च ।
कुटुम्बिनां समृद्धेषु श्रीमत्सु भवनेषु च ॥

12. .... in shops where traders had heaped up various items (of merchandise), in the houses of rich and prosperous families ....

❍ ❍ ❍

१३. सभासु चैव सर्वासु वृक्षेष्वालक्षितेषु च ।
ध्वजाः समुच्छ्रिताः साधु पताकाश्चाभवंस्तदा ॥

13. ...... In various council halls, in huge tall trees: (In all these), lovely banners with ensigns (emblems) were erected.

❍ ❍ ❍

१४. नटनर्तकसङ्घानां गायकानां च गायताम् ।
मनःकर्णसुखा वाचः शुश्रुवुश्च ततस्ततः ॥

14. There were hosts of bards & singers, dancers, musicians (singing to accompaniment of Instruments), and they heard the music that pleased the ears and hearts ....

❍ ❍ ❍

१५. रामाभिषेकयुक्ताश्च कथाश्चक्रुर्मिथो जनाः ।
रामाभिषेके संप्राप्ते चत्वरेषु गृहेषु च ॥

15. ...... As Raama's coronation approached, the people in homes and in streets and in corners of roads, talked about Raama's coronation ......

❍ ❍ ❍

१६. बाला अपि क्रीडमाना गृहद्वारेषु सङ्घशः ॥

16. ...... In the entrance of houses crowds gathered: even playing children; (Total involvement of citizens during the festival)

❍ ❍ ❍

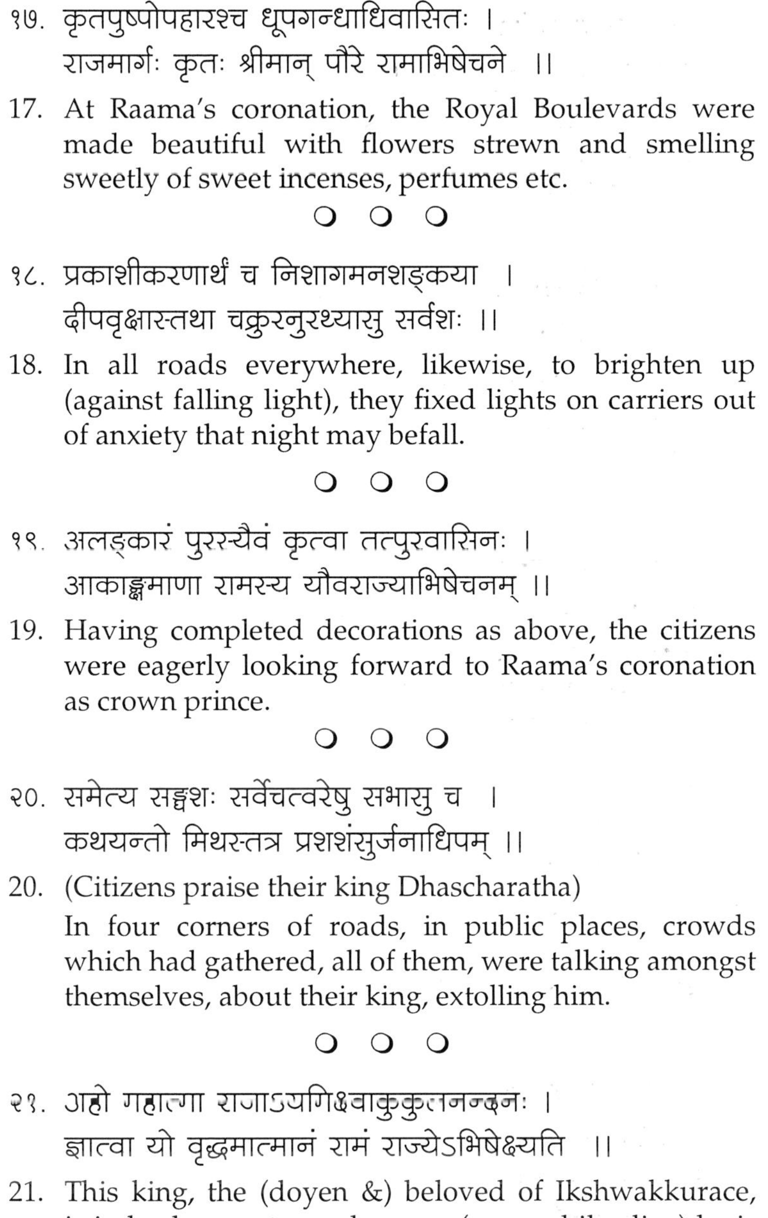

१७. कृतपुष्पोपहारश्च धूपगन्धाधिवासितः ।
राजमार्गः कृतः श्रीमान् पौरे रामाभिषेचने ॥

17. At Raama's coronation, the Royal Boulevards were made beautiful with flowers strewn and smelling sweetly of sweet incenses, perfumes etc.

❍ ❍ ❍

१८. प्रकाशीकरणार्थं च निशागमनशङ्कया ।
दीपवृक्षास्तथा चक्रुरनुरथ्यासु सर्वशः ॥

18. In all roads everywhere, likewise, to brighten up (against falling light), they fixed lights on carriers out of anxiety that night may befall.

❍ ❍ ❍

१९. अलङ्कारं पुरस्यैवं कृत्वा तत्पुरवासिनः ।
आकाङ्क्षमाणा रामस्य यौवराज्याभिषेचनम् ॥

19. Having completed decorations as above, the citizens were eagerly looking forward to Raama's coronation as crown prince.

❍ ❍ ❍

२०. समेत्य सङ्घशः सर्वेचत्वरेषु सभासु च ।
कथयन्तो मिथस्तत्र प्रशशंसुर्जनाधिपम् ॥

20. (Citizens praise their king Dhascharatha)

In four corners of roads, in public places, crowds which had gathered, all of them, were talking amongst themselves, about their king, extolling him.

❍ ❍ ❍

२१. अहो महात्मा राजाऽयमिक्ष्वाकुकुलनन्दनः ।
ज्ञात्वा यो वृद्धमात्मानं रामं राज्येऽभिषेक्ष्यति ॥

21. This king, the (doyen &) beloved of Ikshwakkurace, is indeed a great man because (even while alive) he is anointing Raama, realising he is old.

❍ ❍ ❍

२२. सर्वेह्यनुगृहीताः स्मो यन्नो रामो महीपतिः ।
चिराय भविता गोप्ता दृष्टलोकपरावरः ॥

22. Blessed indeed are we all that Raama the lord of earth who knows the tradition of the world, will be our protector for a long time.

❍ ❍ ❍

२३. अनुद्धतमना विद्वान्धर्मात्मा भ्रातृवत्सलः ।
यथा च भ्रातृषु स्निग्धस्तथास्मास्वपि राघवः ॥

23. (Raama the) Raaghava is a wise and humble man; Noble soul, man of Dharma; Affectionate to his brothers; And likewise, he is attached to us like (he is dear to) his brothers.

❍ ❍ ❍

२४. चिरं जीवतु धर्मात्मा राजा दशरथोऽनघः ।
यत्प्रसादेनाभिषिक्तं रामं द्रक्ष्यामहे वयम् ॥

24. May this blemishless and noble soul king Dhascharatha by whose grace we are going to see (our) Raama crowned, live long.

❍ ❍ ❍

२५. एवंविधं कथयतां पौराणां शुश्रुवुस्तदा ।
दिग्भ्योऽपि श्रुतवृत्तान्ताः प्राप्ता जानपदा जनाः ॥

25. Citizens from villages came from all directions hearing the news (of Raama's coronation): And they heard such conversations of the residents of the city at that time.

❍ ❍ ❍

२६. ते तु दिग्भ्यः पुरीं प्राप्ता द्रष्टुं रामाभिषेचनम् ।
रामस्य पूरयामासुः पुरीं जानपदा जनाः ॥

26. They came to the city from all directions to witness Raama's coronation. The villagers crowded the city.

❍ ❍ ❍

२७. जनौघैस्तैर्विसर्पद्भिः शुश्रुवे तत्र निस्वनः ।
पर्वसूदीर्णवेगस्य सागरस्येव निस्वनः ॥

27. The sound emanating from the mass of people creeping along (to the city) was like roar of torrential (waves) of ocean during season (of high tide).

❍ ❍ ❍

२८. ततस्तदिन्द्रक्षयसन्निभं पुरं
दिदृक्षुभिर्जानपदैरुपागतैः ।
समन्ततः सस्वनमाकुलं बभौ
समुद्रयादोभिरिवार्णवोदकम् ॥

28. When the (multitude of) village folks arrived to witness (the coronation) this city that was like Lord Indhra's capital, shone: With reverberating sounds, it was full everywhere (with people), like ocean waters full with marine life.

❍ ❍ ❍

Chapter 7

(Hunchback) Manthara Bemoans

(Now enters Manthara, the hunchback in the high drama; She was close to queen Kaikeyi, being her mentor & adviser, a confidante. She 'poisons' the mind of Kaikeyi. Poisons her mind to such an extent that not only her own son Bharatha should be crowned, but see to it that Raama, the son of Kowsalya the eldest queen of her husband, should be banished from the kingdom. Poet Vaalmeeki is in his elements as he unfolds the drama and brings out the character of this evil genius Manthara.)

❍ ❍ ❍

१. ज्ञातिदासी यतोजाता कैकेय्यास्तु सहोषिता ।
प्रासादं चन्द्रसङ्काशमारुरोह यदृच्छया ।।

1. A woman who did not know her antecedents, who was always with Kaikeyi, who was her family maid, unexpectedly came to the Royal palace which was like the moon ......

❍ ❍ ❍

२. सिक्तराजपथां रम्यां प्रकीर्णकुसुमोत्कराम् ।
अयोध्यां मन्थरा तस्मात्प्रासादादन्ववैक्षत ।।

2. This (Hunchback who was) Manthara, (viewing) from the palace, saw Ayodhya strewn with heaps of flowers, the royal boulevards sprinkled with (and cleaned with) water, and beautiful ......

❍ ❍ ❍

३. पताकाभिर्वराहाभिर्ध्वजैश्च समलंकृताम् ।
सिक्तां चन्दनतोयैश्च शिरःस्नातजनैर्युताम् ।।

3. (Manthara saw Ayodhya like this;stanzas 3 to 6)
With costly masts and banners, well decorated; men anointing themselves with sandal paste after taking head baths; (roads) watered.

❍ ❍ ❍

४. माल्यमोदकहस्तैश्च द्विजेन्द्रैरभिनादिताम् ।
शुक्लदेवगृहद्वारां सर्ववादित्रनिस्वनाम् ।।

4. with sounds of recitations from braamins who were carrying pots and garlands in their hand; The gates of places of worship shining white; with sounds from various (musical) instruments ......

❍ ❍ ❍

५. संप्रहृष्टजनाकीर्णां ब्रह्मघोषाभिनादिताम् ।
प्रहृष्टवरहस्त्यश्वां संप्रणर्दितगोवृषाम् ।।

5. Full of people who were all exhilarated with joy; reverberating with sounds of Brammam (Vedhas); lots of gay elephants and well bred horses; cows & bulls (surging forth happily) making sounds ......

❍ ❍ ❍

६. प्रहृष्टमुदितैः पौरैरुच्छ्रितध्वजमालिनीम् ।
अयोध्यां मन्थरा दृष्ट्वा परं विस्मयमागता ॥

6. Citizens exhilarated, joyous; Huge flower arches raised high up; Seeing all this Manthara was amazed (& bewildered).

❍ ❍ ❍

७. सा हर्षोत्फुल्लनयनां पाण्डुरक्षौमवासिनीम् ।
अविदूरे स्थितां दृष्ट्वा धात्रीं पप्रच्छ मन्थरा ॥

7. This Manthara asked her benefactress (her 'foster' mother) whose eyes were dilated by joy, even as she was standing near her dressed up in white garment.

❍ ❍ ❍

८. उत्तमेनाभिसंयुक्ता हर्षेणार्थपरा सती ।
राममाता धनं किं नु जनेभ्यः संप्रयच्छति ॥

8. (Manthara asks Kaikeyi)
How come the tight fisted ('miserly' Kowsalya) the mother of Raama, looking happy, is handing out money in plenty to citizens?

❍ ❍ ❍

९. अतिमात्रं प्रहर्षोऽयं किं जनस्य च शंस मे ।
कारयिष्यति किं वाऽपि संप्रहृष्टो महीपतिः ॥

9. This exhilaration of people is immense; Why so? What has the king (in mind) to do (all this) in great joy: Tell me.

❍ ❍ ❍

१०. विदीर्यमाणा हर्षेण धात्री तु परया मुदा ।
आचचक्षेऽथ कुब्जायै भूयसीं राघवश्रियम् ।।

10. (Manthara feigns ignorance, as though she does not know about Raama's coronation when every one knows).

The foster mother (benefactress Kaikeyi) who was 'overflowing' with joy told this hunchback about (Raama the) Raaghava's grand coronation, thus, with joy.

❍ ❍ ❍

११. श्वः पुष्येण जितक्रोधं यौवराज्येन राघवम् ।
राजा दशरथो राममभिषेचयिताऽनघम् ।।

11. Tomorrow, on the star of Pushya, king Dhascharatha is going to crown the sinless Raama, the Raaghava who has conquered wrath, as crown prince.

❍ ❍ ❍

१२. धात्र्यास्तु वचनं श्रुत्वा कुब्जा क्षिप्रममर्षिता ।
कैलासशिखराकारात् प्रासादादवरोहत ।।

12. The Hunchback (Manthara) hearing thus from foster mother (Kaikeyi) became angry and got down from the balcony of the palace which was like peaks of Himaalayas.

❍ ❍ ❍

१३. सा दह्यमाना कोपेन मन्थरा पापदर्शिनी ।
शयानामेत्य कैकेयीमिदं वचनमब्रवीत् ।।

13. Burnt up (consumed) by wrath, this wicked Manthara went near Kaikeyi who was resting (on couch) and said the following:

❍ ❍ ❍

१४. उत्तिष्ठ मूढे किं शेषे भयं त्वामभिवर्तते ।
उपप्लुतमघौघेन किमात्मानं न बुध्यसे ।।

14. (Manthara begins to 'work' on Kaikeyi)
You fool! A (great) calamity awaits you; How come you are not even aware of the danger that awaits you? Why are you resting (& relaxing at a time like this): Get up.

❍ ❍ ❍

१५. अनिष्टे सुभगाकारे सौभाग्येन विकत्थसे ।
चलं हि तव सौभाग्यं नद्याः स्रोत इवोष्णगे ॥

15. (Oh Kaikeyi) who is most enchanting to your beloved (husband)! You boast that you have the good fortune (to be the most beloved amongst your husband's other queens); Oh You unfavoured and (unwanted) woman! Your fortune is like the current of a river in (dry) summer.

❍ ❍ ❍

१६. एवमुक्ता तु कैकेयी रुष्टया परुषं वचः ।
कुब्जया पापदर्शिन्या विषादमगमत्परम् ॥

16. Hearing such harsh words from the malevolent hunchback who was in rage, Kaikeyi became despondent (and disappointed with her).

❍ ❍ ❍

१७. कैकेयी त्वब्रवीत्कुब्जां कच्चित्क्षेमं न मन्थरे ।
विषण्णवदनां हि त्वां लक्षये भृशदुःखिताम् ॥

17. Yet she, this Kaikeyi addressed the hunchback:= Oh Manthara! I see your face is downcast with utter grief. All is well (with you), Is it not? (or am I wrong).–

❍ ❍ ❍

१८. मन्थरा तु वचः श्रुत्वा कैकेय्या मधुराक्षरम् ।
उवाच क्रोधसंयुक्ता वाक्यं वाक्यविशारदा ॥

18. The angry (Manthara the) hunchback who was very clever (cunning) in speech, hearing such sweet words from Kaikeyi, then replied with these words.

❍ ❍ ❍

१९. सा विषण्णतरा भूत्वा कुब्जा तस्या हितैषिणी ।
विषादयन्ती प्रोवाच भेदयन्ती च राघवम् ।।

19. This hunchback who was interested in her welfare became very dejected and replied to her, to cause her despair and to bring harm and injury upon Raama.

❍ ❍ ❍

२०. अक्षय्यं सुमहद्देवि प्रवृत्तं त्वद्विनाशनम् ।
रामं दशरथो राजा यौवराज्येऽभिषेक्ष्यति ।।

20. King Dhascharatha is going to crown Raama as YuvaRaaja: Oh Lady (Kaikeyi)! This event that is to take place is going to bring eternal, great, ruin to you.

❍ ❍ ❍

२१. साऽस्म्यगाधे भये मग्ना दुःखशोकसमन्विता ।
दह्यमानाऽनलेनेव त्वद्धितार्थमिहागता ।।

21. Engulfed by unfathomable fear, deeply afflicted by grief and sorrow, I came here for your sake as though I am burnt by fire.

❍ ❍ ❍

२२. तव दुःखेन कैकेयि मम दुःखं महद्भवेत् ।
त्वद्वृद्धौ मम वृद्धिश्च भवेदेव न संशयः ।।

22. Oh Kaikeyi! If there is suffering for you, it will be great suffering for me as well; And in your prosperity there is prosperity for me. No doubt at all.

❍ ❍ ❍

२३. नराधिपकुले जाता महिषी त्वं महीपतेः ।
उग्रत्वं राजधर्माणां कथं देवि न बुध्यसे ।।

23. Oh Lady (Kaikeyi)! You are born in royal family; you are consort of the emperor: (And yet) how is it you do not understand (ramifications) and acrimony of politics (of Royal Dharma)?

❍ ❍ ❍

२४. धर्मवादी शठो भर्ता श्लक्ष्णवादी च दारुणः ।
शुद्धभावे न जानीषे तेनैवमतिसन्धिता ।।

24. Your husband speaks of Dharma (but) is a cheat: Speaks sweetly, but most cruel (in deeds); Oh Kaikeyi of pure conduct! You do not understand you are being cheated by him.

❍ ❍ ❍

२५. उपस्थितः प्रयुञ्जानस्त्वयि सान्त्वमनर्थकम् ।
अर्थेनैवाद्य ते भर्ता कौसल्यां योजयिष्यति ।।

25. Your husband merely talking (sweet) soothing words to you, is now enjoining (and bestowing) Kowsalya with wealth (fortune), treating you worthless.

❍ ❍ ❍

२६. अपवाह्य स दुष्टात्मा भरतं तव वन्धुषु ।
काल्ये स्थापयिता रामं राज्ये निहतकण्टके ।।

26. The evil minded (husband of yours), having sent away (your son) Bharatha to your (father and your) relatives, is now going to install Raama tomorrow morning in this kingdom (as YuvaRaaja) without any hindrance.

❍ ❍ ❍

२७. शत्रुः पतिप्रवादेन मात्रेव हितकाम्यया ।
आशीविष इवाङ्केन बाले परिहृतस्त्वया ।।

27. Oh child (Kaikeyi)! A snake that he is, this enemy who is called a husband by you, was taken on your lap like a mother who ever desires welfare (for a son).

❍ ❍ ❍

२८. यथा हि कुर्यात् सर्पोवा शत्रुर्वा प्रत्युपेक्षितः ।
राज्ञा दशरथेनाद्य सपुत्रा त्वं तथा कृता ।।

28. Like what a neglected enemy or a serpent would do (to a careless person), likewise you, along with your son (Bharatha), has been done for by king Dhascharatha.

❍ ❍ ❍

२९. पापेनानृतसान्त्वेन बाले नित्यसुखोचिते ।
रामं स्थापयता राज्ये सानुबन्धा हता ह्यसि ॥

29. Oh child (Kaikeyi) who ever deserves to be in comfort! By this sinner who spoke untruth to you although sweetly (cunningly), you are indeed destroyed along with your relatives, as he is installing Raama in the kingdom (as his successor).

❍ ❍ ❍

३०. सा प्राप्तकालं कैकेयि क्षिप्रं कुरु हितं तव ।
त्रायस्व पुत्रमात्मानं मां च विस्मयदर्शने ॥

30. Oh Kaikeyi who has (lovely) stunning look! You must act at once at (this) proper time for your welfare: (and thus) save me, yourself and your son (from calamity).

❍ ❍ ❍

३१. मन्थराया वचः श्रुत्वा शयाना सा शुभानना ।
उत्तस्थौ हर्षसम्पूर्णा चन्द्रलेखेव शारदी ॥

31. (But the first reaction of Kaikeyi to the news of his step son Raama's coronation was one of great joy & satisfaction. Kaikeyi loved Raama as much as his own son Bharatha. But Manthara works upon her, finally convinces her that Raama's prosperity is her doom).

Hearing Manthara's words while reclining in her couch, (Kaikeyi) was filed with joy, her face glowed like moon in autumn: She got up.

❍ ❍ ❍

३२. अतीव सा तु संहृष्टा कैकेयी विस्मयान्विता ।
एकमाभरणं दत्त्वा कुब्जायै प्रमदोत्तमा ॥

३३. कैकेयी मन्थरां दृष्ट्वा पुनरेवाब्रवीदिदम् ।।

32. & 33

The noble lady, this Kaikeyi who was wonderstruck (at such a good fortune having come by his step son Raama) became extremely exhilarated and gave an ornament to this hunchback: And looking at Manthara, again addressed her thus.

❍ ❍ ❍

३४. इदं हि मन्थरे मह्यमाख्यासि परमं प्रियम् ।
एतन्मे प्रियमाख्यात्र्याः किं वा भूयः करोमि ते ।।

34. Oh Manthara! You are telling me a very good news: To you who told me such good news, I will do whatever more (you desire).

❍ ❍ ❍

३५. रामे वा भरते वाऽहं विशेषं नोपलक्षये ।
तस्मात्तुष्टाऽस्मि यद्राजा रामं राज्येऽभिषेक्ष्यति ।।

35. The king is going to anoint Raama in the kingdom. Therefore I am very pleased. Because I make no distinction between (my stepson) Raama and (my own son) Bharatha.

❍ ❍ ❍

३६. न मे परं किञ्चिदितस्त्वया पुनः
प्रियं प्रियार्हेसुवचं वचः परम् ।
तथा ह्यवोचस्त्वमतः प्रियोत्तरं
परं तरं ते प्रददामि तं वृणु ।।

36. (This news) To me is most happy: There cannot be anything better than that conveyed by you, hereafter; Such, you have spoken: Therefore, you, who deserve (my love, may) ask for anything else that will please you most and I will give that to you.

(So happy is Kaikeyi, that she even presents a fine

ornament to this evil genius hunchback Manthara. But this Manthara has her way; as we shall see in following chapters.)

❍ ❍ ❍

Chapter 8

(Manthara) Disturbs Kaikeyi's Mind

(Manthara the hunchback 'works' on Kaikeyi further; To change her mind, to instill hatred for Raama & Dhascharatha in her. Poet Vaalmeeki's masterly rendering.)

❍ ❍ ❍

१. मन्थरा त्वभ्यसूयैनामुत्सृज्याभरणं च तत् ।
उवाचेदं ततो वाक्यं कोपदुःखसमन्विता ॥

1. At this, Manthara then became (so dejected and) overpowered (stricken) with wrath and grief that she threw down the ornament (Kaikeyi had presented to her on hearing the good news about Raama). Then she said this to her:

❍ ❍ ❍

२. हर्षं किमिदमस्थाने कृतवत्यसि बालिशे ।
शोकसागरमध्यस्थमात्मानं नावबुध्यसे ॥

2. Oh childish (Kaikeyi)! You are not aware that you are submerged in ocean of grief: What is this! You have obtained happiness at the wrong time.

❍ ❍ ❍

३. मनसा प्रहसामि त्वां देवि दुःखार्दिता सती ।
यच्छोचितव्ये हृष्टाऽसि प्राप्येदं व्यसनं महत् ॥

3. Oh Lady: At a time when great calamity has befallen and when you should be aggrieved, you are joyous.

Because of this I deride and mock you with all my mind (and heart) even as I am tormented by sorrow.

❍ ❍ ❍

४. शोचामि दुर्मतित्वं ते का हि प्राज्ञा प्रहर्षयेत् ।
अरेः सपत्नीपुत्रस्य वृद्धिं मृत्योरिवागताम् ।।

4. Who (in her right mind) if she is intelligent (enough) will be happy at the arrival of prosperity to a co-wife's son who is verily 'death' to her. I grieve at your stupidity.

❍ ❍ ❍

५. भरतादेव रामस्य राज्यसाधारणाद्भयम् ।
तद्विचिन्त्य विषण्णाऽस्मि भयं भीताद्धि जायते ।।

5. Fear is caused by the Feared: There is fear for Raama from Bharatha who is equal in royal status. I grieve thinking about this.

❍ ❍ ❍

६. लक्ष्मणो हि महेष्वासो रामं सर्वात्मना गतः ।
शत्रुघ्नश्चापि भरतं काकुत्स्थं लक्ष्मणो यथा ।।

6. And the great wielder of bow, this Lakshmana, follows Raama in every way. Like Lakshmana to Raama so is Schathrugna to Bharatha.

❍ ❍ ❍

७. प्रत्यासन्नक्रमेणापि भरतस्यैव भामिनि ।
राज्यक्रमो विप्रकृष्टस्तयोस्तावत् कनीयसोः ।।

7. Oh passionate (Kaikeyi)! In the matter of royal succession, (right to rule), for (your son) Bharatha and his two younger brothers (Lakshmana & Schathrugna), their rank is very (low and) remote.

(In effect Manthara enlightens Kaikeyi that only Raama's sons will take over after king Raama passes away.)

❍ ❍ ❍

८. विदुषः क्षत्रचारित्रे प्राज्ञस्य प्राप्तकारिणः ।
भयात् प्रवेपे रामस्य चिन्तयन्ती तवात्मजम् ।।

8. I tremble when I think about the harm and fear to your son (Bharatha) from Raama who is learned, who is astute in political matters (the Kshathriya Dharma), and who is (clever enough) to do things at proper time.

❍ ❍ ❍

९. सुभगा खलु कौसल्या यस्याः पुत्रोऽभिषेक्ष्यते ।
यौवराज्येन महता श्वः पुष्येण द्विजोत्तमैः ।।

9. She, whose son is going to be anointed as the mighty crown prince tomorrow on the Pushya star by braamins, that (woman) Kowsalya indeed is the most fortunate (one, not you).

❍ ❍ ❍

१०. प्राप्तां सुमहतीं प्रीतिं प्रतीतां तां हतद्विषम् ।
उपस्थास्यसि कौसल्यां दासीवत्त्वं कृताञ्जलिः ।।

10. With folded arms (in Anjali), like a slave, you are going to serve Kowsalya who will be most powerful, having eliminated opposition and having obtained affection (from Dhascharatha) and honoured.

❍ ❍ ❍

११. एवं च त्वं सहास्माभिस्तस्याः प्रेष्या भविष्यसि ।
पुत्रश्च तव रामस्य प्रेष्यभावं गमिष्यति ।।

11. Then, along with us, you are going to be her servant; and your son (Bharatha) will also obtain the state of servitude before Raama.

❍ ❍ ❍

१२. हृष्टाः खलु भविष्यन्ति रामस्य परमाः स्त्रियः ।
अप्रहृष्टा भविष्यन्ति स्नुषास्ते भरतक्षये ।।

12. (Even) Distantly related ladies of Raama will be thrilled

with joy; and the noble women close to you will become most unhappy when Bharatha wanes away.

❍ ❍ ❍

१३. तां दृष्ट्वा परमप्रीतां ब्रुवन्तीं मन्थरां ततः ।
रामस्यैव गुणान्देवी कैकेयी प्रशशंस ह ॥

13. (Thus Manthara sows the seed of hatred & fear in Kaikeyi.)

Hearing such unpalatable words from Manthara, queen Kaikeyi narrated Raama's (noble) qualities only.

(Kaikeyi is still not convinced; still loves Raama; has no fear at all)

❍ ❍ ❍

१४. धर्मज्ञो गुरुभिर्दान्तः कृतज्ञः सत्यवाक्छुचिः ।
रामो राज्ञः सुतो ज्येष्ठो यौवराज्यमतोऽर्हति ॥

14. Raama knows Dharma: has been taught by elders; he is a man of gratitude; he is pure; a man of word; he is eldest son of king; therefore he deserves to be crown prince.

❍ ❍ ❍

१५. भ्रातॄन् भृत्यांश्च दीर्घायुः पितृवत् पालयिष्यति ।
संतप्यसे कथं कुब्जे श्रुत्वा रामाभिषेचनम् ॥

15. He will protect his brothers and dependents like a father till his long life (is over). Oh Hunchback! Why are you aggrieved hearing Raama's coronation?

❍ ❍ ❍

१६. भरतश्चापि रामस्य ध्रुवं वर्षशतात् परम् ।
पितृपैतामहं राज्यमवाप्स्यति नरर्षभः ॥

16. After hundreds of years (of rule), after Raama, the noble amongst men (the'Bull' amongst men, my son) Bharatha will surely obtain the kingdom of his forefathers.

(So much faith Kaikeyi has in Raama that her son will be asked to take over from Raama; perhaps Raama may even abdicate in favour of Bharatha before his life is over.)

❍ ❍ ❍

१७. सा त्वमभ्युदये प्राप्ते वर्तमाने च मन्थरे ।
भविष्यति च कल्याणे किमर्थं परितप्यसे ॥

17. Oh Manthara ! When this event that is to take place tomorrow morning as per norms and is auspicious and will be prosperous (for all), why are you alone in torment?

❍ ❍ ❍

१८. यथा मे भरतो मान्यस्तथा भूयोऽपि राघवः ।
कौसल्यातोऽतिरिक्तं च सोऽनुशुश्रूषते हि माम् ॥

18. (Surely my son) Bharatha is worthy of my esteem; but (Raama) the Raaghava is more to me! Because he serves me more than (he serves even his mother) Kowsalya.

❍ ❍ ❍

१९. राज्यं च यदि रामस्य भरतस्यापि तत्तथा ।
मन्यते हि यथाऽऽत्मानं तुा भ्रातृंश्च राघवः ॥

19. And (Raama) the Raaghava considers his brothers (as dearly) as his own (life). Therefore even if the kingdom belongs to Raama (ruled by him), that will be like Bharatha's (as well).

❍ ❍ ❍

२०. कैकेयीवचनं श्रुत्वा मन्थरा भृशदुःखिता ।
दीर्घमुष्णं विनिश्वस्य कैकेयीकिदमब्रवीत् ॥

20. (Thus Kaikeyi tried to pacify Manthara: But Manthara is too clever: She continues to 'work' on Kaikeyi.)

Hearing Kaikeyi's words, Manthara became even more sad; and breathing hard and (emitting) hot (breath), told Kaikeyi thus:

❍ ❍ ❍

२१. अनर्थदर्शिनी मौर्ख्याद्दात्मानं नावबुध्यसे ।
शोकव्यसनविस्तीर्णेमज्जन्तं दुःखसागरे ॥

21. Submerged in the ocean of sorrow that is full of pain and suffering, you do not understand (what I am telling you), out of your stupidity, as you are having an 'Eye' only for worthless things (of life).

❍ ❍ ❍

२२. भविता राघवो राजा राघवस्य च यः सुतः ।
राजवंशात्तु भरतः कैकेयि परिहास्यते ॥

22. Oh Kaikeyi! Raama will become king; And whoever is Raama's son, he (alone) will be (future king). And (your son) Bharatha will be eliminated from royal line of succession.

❍ ❍ ❍

२३. न हिं राज्ञः सुताः सर्वेराज्ये तिष्ठन्ति भामिनि ।
स्थाप्यमानेषु सर्वेषु सुमहाननयो भवेत् ।

23. Oh passionate woman (Kaikeyi)! All sons of a king are not installed (as ruler) in kingdom: If all of them (get this right to) rule, and are installed, great (grave) mismanagement will be there.

❍ ❍ ❍

२४. तस्माज्येष्ठे हि कैकेयि राज्यतन्त्राणि पार्थिवाः ।
स्थापयन्त्यनवद्याङ्गि गुणवत्स्वितरेषु च ॥

24. Oh Kaikeyi with faultless limbs! That is why king appoints only the foremost from amongst those possessing (noble) qualities in affairs of the kingdom.

❍ ❍ ❍

२५. असावत्यन्तनिर्भग्नस्तव पुत्रो भविष्यति ।
अनाथवत्सुखेभ्यश्च राजवंशाच्च वत्सले ॥

25. Oh beloved (Kaikeyi)! And this son of yours, having no support will be absolutely disinherited from royal line of succession and from the (inherent) pleasures (of the kingdom).

❍ ❍ ❍

२६. साऽहं त्वदर्थेसंप्राप्ता त्वं तु मां नावबुध्यसे ।
सपत्निवृद्धौ या मे त्वं प्रदेयं दातुमिच्छसि ॥

26. I came here (only) for your welfare; You fail to understand me in this matter: (And the irony is) that you who are (after all) a mere co-wife, desire to offer gifts to me!

❍ ❍ ❍

२७. ध्रुवं तु भरतं रामः प्राप्य राज्यमकण्टकम् ।
देशान्तरं नाययिता लोकान्तरमथापि वा ॥

27. And Raama after obtaining the kingdom, will drive away Bharatha to another kingdom or even to another world (of death), to be free from worries. Surely.

❍ ❍ ❍

२८. बाल एव हि मातुल्यं भरतो नायितस्त्वया ।
सन्निकर्षाच्च सौहार्दं जायते स्थावरेष्वपि ॥

28. Bharatha is (but) a boy: He has been sent to his uncle's place by you: Affection develops only when one is near (in proximity), even in respect of inanimate objects.

❍ ❍ ❍

२९. भरतस्याप्यनुवशः शत्रुघ्नोऽपि समागतः ।
लक्ष्मणो हि यथा रामं तथाऽसौ भरतं गतः ॥

29. What Lakshmana is to Raama, Schathrugna is to Bharatha: (attached and) obedient: And (Schathrugna) has gone along with Bharatha.

❍ ❍ ❍

३०. श्रूयते हि द्रुमः कश्चिच्छेत्तव्यो वनजीविभिः ।
सन्निकर्षादिषीकाभिर्मोचितः परमाद्भयात् ।।

30. It is (said and) heard that a (big) tree about to be felled by forest men, escapes (felling) and from great fear (of destruction), when it is surrounded by cane trees (wild grass).

❍ ❍ ❍

३१. गोप्ता हि रामं सौमित्रिर्लक्ष्मणं चापि राघवः ।
अश्विनोरिव सौभ्रात्रं तयोर्लोकेषु विश्रुतम् ।।

31. The son of Sumithra (this Lakshmana), protects Raama; and (Raama) the Raaghava (likewise) protects Lakshmana. It is well known in the world that their brotherhood is like the (twin) Ashwinis,

❍ ❍ ❍

३२. तस्मान्न लक्ष्मणे रामः पापं किञ्चित्करिष्यति ।
रामस्तु भरते पापं कुर्यादेव न संशयः ।।

32. Therefore Raama will not cause harm to Lakshmana, not even a trifle. But in Bharatha's case Raama will surely cause (harm). No doubt about it.

❍ ❍ ❍

३३. तस्माद्राजगृहादेव वनं गच्छतु ते सुतः ।
एतद्धि रोचते मह्यं भृशं चापि हितं तव ।।

33. Therefore (I suggest) that your son (Bharatha) may go to forest from his Royal palace! This (appears) to me as desirable. What else will be better or good for you!

❍ ❍ ❍

३४. एवं ते ज्ञातिपक्षस्य श्रेयश्चैव भविष्यति ।
यदि चेद्भरतो धर्मात्पित्र्यं राज्यमवाप्स्यति ।।

34. (On the contrary) As such, if (your son) Bharatha obtains this kingdom of his forefathers by norms of Dharma, there will be fortune for you and your relatives.

❍ ❍ ❍

३५. स ते सुखोचितो बालो रामस्य सहजो रिपुः ।
समृद्धार्थस्य नष्टार्थोजीविष्यति कथं वशे ॥

35. Your son is used to comforts; how can he, losing his (position and) substance, live along, when he is the brother and enemy to Raama whose (power and) substance has increased. (as king designate).

❍ ❍ ❍

३६. अभिद्रुतमिवारण्ये सिंहेन गजयूथपम् ।
प्रच्छाद्यमानं रामेण भरतं त्रातुमर्हसि ॥

36. Like a chief elephant of a herd (of elephants) before a lion in forest, you must (protect and) save Bharatha who is wrapped up and attacked by Raama (the lion).

❍ ❍ ❍

३७. दर्पान्निराकृता पूर्वं त्वया सौभाग्यवत्तया ।
राममाता सपत्नी ते कथं वैरं न धारयेत् ॥

37. Previously, (and on many occasions), (Kowsalya) the mother of Raama, your co-wife, has been spurned by you because of your arrogance out of your good fortune (as being the most beloved of your husband amongst you all). Will she not 'bear' revenge (and enmity) upon you (now that her son Raama is crown prince)?

❍ ❍ ❍

३८. यदा हि रामः पृथिवीमवाप्स्यति
प्रभूतरत्नाकरशैलपत्तनाम् ।
तदा गमिष्यस्यशुभं पराभवं
सहैव दीना भरतेन भामिनि ॥

38. Oh passionate (Kaikeyi)! The moment Raama receives the kingdom along with the oceans, mountains and cities (and all), you, along with Bharatha, will become feeble and obtain most unpleasant humiliation.

❍ ❍ ❍

३९. यदा हि रामः पृथिवीमवाप्स्यति
ध्रुवं प्रनष्टो भरतो भविष्यति ।
अतो हि संचिन्तय राज्यमात्मजे
परस्य चैवाद्य विवासकारणम् ॥

39. If Raama obtains the kingdom, Bharatha is sure to be ruined. Therefore You Must Think (about ways and means) To Get The Kingdom For Your Son and For the Other One, (for this Raama) Banishment, Now Itself.

(Note: This evil genius, the hunchback Manthara who was Kaikeyi's family maid, eventually succeeds to poison the mind of Kaikeyi and she also shows the way as to how Raama can be got rid of and her own Bharatha crowned instead. Poet Vaalmeeki describes all this beautifully in the following chapters.)

❍ ❍ ❍

Chapter 9

Strategy to Send Raama to Forest: Kaikeyi Enters House of Sorrow

(Kaikeyi is completely 'converted' by this evil genius: Strategy being worked out to send Raama to forest so that her son Bharatha may be crowned instead.)

❍ ❍ ❍

१. एवमुक्ता तु कैकेयी क्रोधेन ज्वलितानना ।
दीर्घमुष्णं च निश्वस्य मन्थरामिदमब्रवीत् ॥

1. When told thus (by Manthara) Kaikeyi's face was 'burning' with anger: Breathing hard, emitting hot breath, she said this:

❍ ❍ ❍

२. अद्य राममितः क्षिप्रं वनं प्रस्थापयाम्यहम् ।
यौवराज्येन भरतं क्षिप्रमेवाभिषेचये ॥

2. I myself will send Raama from here to forest today: And I will crown Bharatha as YuvaRaaja.

(Being a passionate and impulsive woman, Kaikeyi's outburst is understandable. But quickly realises her limitations. So asks Manthara for the ways & means to achieve this.)

❍ ❍ ❍

३. इदं त्विदानीं संपश्य केनोपायेन मन्थरे ।
भरतः प्राप्नुयाद्राज्यं न तु रामः कथश्चन ॥

3. Oh Manthara! How and by what means Raama will be denied (the Crown) now. There after Bharatha should obtain the kingdom: Show me (the way) in this matter.

❍ ❍ ❍

४. एवमुक्ता तया देव्या मन्थरा पापदर्शिनी ।
रामार्थमुपहिंसन्ती कैकेयीमिदमब्रवीत् ॥

4. When she heard this from the lady (Kaikeyi), the sinful Manthara who was bent on doing harm to Raama, then addressed Kaikeyi.

❍ ❍ ❍

५. हन्तेदानीं प्रवक्ष्यामि कैकेयि श्रूयतां च मे ।
यथा ते भरतो राज्यं पुत्रः प्राप्स्यति केवलम् ॥

5. (The evil genius shows the way: Not only she has made Kaikeyi accept her evil advice, she has also a fool proof strategy.)

Oh Kaikeyi! Wonderful! I shall explain now how your son Bharatha can obtain sole possession of the kingdom. May you listen.

❍ ❍ ❍

६. किं न स्मरसि कैकेयि स्मरन्ती वा निगूहसे ।
यद्धुच्यमानमात्मार्थं मत्तस्त्वं श्रोतुमिच्छसि ।।

6. Oh Kaikeyi! Have you forgotten or remembering this you have chosen to forget! (Dont you recall): You now wish to hear from me the (very same) secret that was told by you to me (long ago).

❍ ❍ ❍

७. मयोच्यमानं यदि ते श्रोतुं छन्दो विलासिनि ।
श्रूयतामभिधास्यामि श्रुत्वा चापि विमृश्यताम् ।।

7. Oh playful (Kaikeyi)! Anyway, as it is your wish, what was spoken (to me by you long ago) you may hear that from me (now) After hearing this, may you deliberate (on future course of action).

❍ ❍ ❍

८. श्रुत्वेदं वचनं तस्या मन्थरायास्तु कैकयी ।
किंचिदुत्थाय शयनात्स्वास्तीर्णादिदमब्रवीत् ।।

8. The moment Kaikeyi heard this spoken by Manthara, she got up a little from the couch she was resting on and said this.

❍ ❍ ❍

९. कथय त्वं ममोपायं केनोपायेन मन्थरे ।
भरतः प्राप्नुयाद्राज्यं न तु रामः कथंचन ।।

9. Oh Manthara! By what means Raama will somehow be denied (the crown) and Bharatha will obtain the kingdom? You tell me the means.

❍ ❍ ❍

१०. एवमुक्ता तु कैकेय्या मन्थरा पापदर्शिनी ।
रामार्थमुपहिंसन्ती कुब्जा वचनमब्रवीत् ।।

10. When she was told thus by Kaikeyi, the sinful

(malevolent) hunchback Manthara who was bent on doing harm to Raama said the following words.

❍ ❍ ❍

११. तव दैवासुरे युद्धे सह राजर्षिभिः पतिः ।
अगच्छत् त्वामुपादाय देवराजस्य साह्यकृत् ॥

11. (And Manthara recalls an incident in Kaikeyi's life long ago.)

(Long ago) In a war between Dheva-s and Asura-s, your husband (Dhascharatha), in order to help the Lord of Dheva-s (Indhra), took you along with (other) royal sages.

❍ ❍ ❍

१२. दिशमास्थाय कैकेयि दक्षिणां दण्डकान् प्रति ।
वैजयन्तमिति ख्यातं पुरं यत्र तिमिध्वजः ॥

12. Oh Kaikeyi! In southern region of Dhandaka (forests), he went to the renowned place called Vaijayantha where there was this demon Thimidhwaja.

❍ ❍ ❍

१३. स शम्बर इति ख्यातः शतमायो महासुरः ।
ददौ शक्रस्य संग्रामं देवसङ्घैरनिर्जितः ॥

13. A great Asura, renowned by the name of Schambara who was invincible before entire multitude of Dheva-s and who was expert in magical warfare, offered a battle to Lord Indhra.

❍ ❍ ❍

१४. तस्मिन् महति संग्रामे पुरुषान् क्षतविक्षतान् ।
रात्रौ प्रसुप्तान् घ्नन्ति स्म तरसाऽपास्य राक्षसाः ॥

14. In the great war, the Raakshasa-s (& Asura-s), in utter disregard (to war conventions), came with their full strength at night, and mauled them, killed them while they were sleeping.

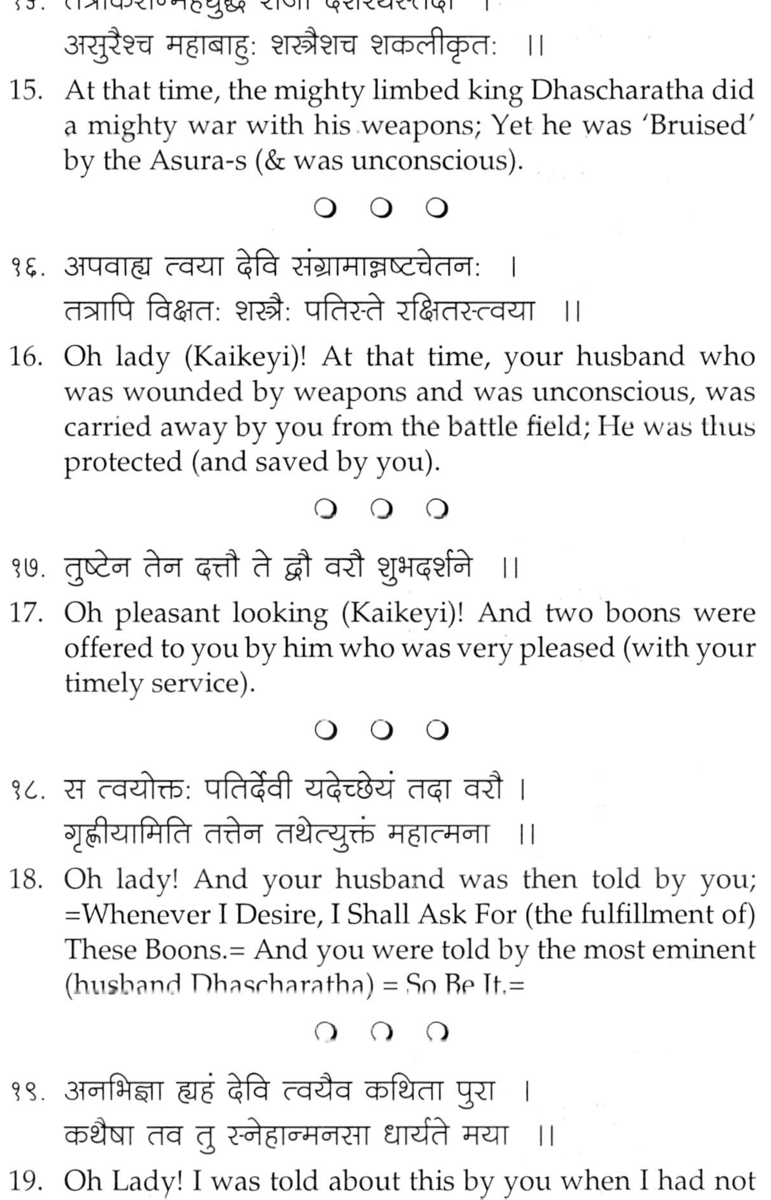

१५. तत्राकरोन्महद्युद्धं राजा दशरथस्तदा ।
असुरैश्च महाबाहुः शस्त्रैशच शकलीकृतः ॥

15. At that time, the mighty limbed king Dhascharatha did a mighty war with his weapons; Yet he was 'Bruised' by the Asura-s (& was unconscious).

❍ ❍ ❍

१६. अपवाह्य त्वया देवि संग्रामान्नष्टचेतनः ।
तत्रापि विक्षतः शस्त्रैः पतिस्ते रक्षितस्त्वया ॥

16. Oh lady (Kaikeyi)! At that time, your husband who was wounded by weapons and was unconscious, was carried away by you from the battle field; He was thus protected (and saved by you).

❍ ❍ ❍

१७. तुष्टेन तेन दत्तौ ते द्वौ वरौ शुभदर्शने ॥

17. Oh pleasant looking (Kaikeyi)! And two boons were offered to you by him who was very pleased (with your timely service).

❍ ❍ ❍

१८. स त्वयोक्तः पतिर्देवी यदेच्छेयं तदा वरौ ।
गृह्णीयामिति तत्तेन तथेत्युक्तं महात्मना ॥

18. Oh lady! And your husband was then told by you; =Whenever I Desire, I Shall Ask For (the fulfillment of) These Boons.= And you were told by the most eminent (husband Dhascharatha) = So Be It.=

❍ ❍ ❍

१९. अनभिज्ञा ह्यहं देवि त्वयैव कथिता पुरा ।
कथैषा तव तु स्नेहान्मनसा धार्यते मया ॥

19. Oh Lady! I was told about this by you when I had not known (about this incident): Out of my friendship (& love) for you, this incident was retained in my memory.

❍ ❍ ❍

२०. रामाभिषेकसंभारान्निगृह्य विनिवर्तय ।
तौ वरौ याच भर्तारं भरतस्याभिषेचनम् ।।
प्रव्राजनं च रामस्य त्वं वर्षाणि चतुर्दश ।।

20. (And Manthara comes up with her Trump Card-or Cards.)

You Ask For These Two Boons Now: Raama's Exile For 14 Years and The Crowning Of Bharatha. You Must Restrain Your Husband And Stop Preparations That Are Going On For Raama's Coronation:

❍ ❍ ❍

२१. चतुर्दश हि वर्षाणि रामे प्रव्राजिते वनम् ।
प्रजाभावगतस्नेहः स्थिरः पुत्रो भविष्यति ।।

21. When Raama is exiled to the forest for 14 years, your son (Bharatha) will firmly establish himself (on throne) having obtained the citizens' affection, (loyalty during his rule).

❍ ❍ ❍

२२. क्रोधागारं प्रविश्याद्य क्रुद्धेवाश्वपतेः सुते ।
शेष्वानन्तर्हितायां त्वं भूमौ मलिनवासिनी ।।

22. Oh Kaikeyi, the daughter of Aschwapathi! You now enter the House of Mourning (& sorrow in the palace) as though you are angry (and in utter grief) and lie down on bare (unconcealed) uncovered floor, in dirty robes.

❍ ❍ ❍

२३. मा स्मैनं प्रत्युदीक्षेथा मा चैनमभिभाषथाः ।
रुदन्ती चापि तं दृष्ट्वा जगत्यां शोकलालसा ।।

23. (And lying down) On bare earth, consumed by grief and crying even on seeing him, you should turn your face away from (your husband) And you should not talk to him.

❍ ❍ ❍

२४. दयिता त्वं सदा भर्तुरत्र मे नास्ति संशयः ।
त्वत्कृते स महाराजो विशेदपि हुताशनम् ।।

24. You are ever the most beloved of your husband: And this Emperor (Dhascharatha, your husband) will even jump into fire for your sake No doubt about it.

❍ ❍ ❍

२५. न त्वां क्रोधयितुं शक्तो न क्रुद्धां प्रत्युदीक्षितुम् ।
तव प्रियार्थं राजा हि प्राणानपि परित्यजेत् ।।

25. The king cannot bear to behold you in anger (& sorrow); He will never get angry with you; he will even give up life for the sake of your love.

❍ ❍ ❍

२६. न ह्यतिक्रमितुं शक्तस्तव वाक्यं महीपतिः ।
मन्दस्वभावे बुध्यस्व सौभाग्यबलमात्मनः ।।

26. Oh soft hearted (Kaikeyi)! You must realise the power of your good fortune, (the power of) your husband's love for you And so the king will never go against your word. (He will surely honour boons given to you long ago).

❍ ❍ ❍

२७. मणिमुक्तासुवर्णानि रत्नानि विविधानि च ।
दद्याद्दशरथो राजा मा स्म तेषु मनः कृथाः ।।

27. King Dhascharatha will offer many wonderful gems, pearls, and golden ornaments (to console you): You must have no 'mind' for all these. (Be firm, dont be 'cheated' by cheap gifts, says Manthara).

❍ ❍ ❍

२८. यौ तौ दैवासुरे युद्धे वरौ दशरथोऽददात् ।
तौ स्मारय महाभागे सोऽर्थो मा त्वामतिक्रमेत् ।।

28. Oh most illustrious (Kaikeyi)! This event (of Coronation) will not take place against your (wishes): You must

remind Dhascharatha about the two boons he gave you during the Dheva Asura war.

❍ ❍ ❍

२९. यदा तु ते वरं दद्यात्स्वयमुत्थाप्य राघवः ।
व्यवस्थाप्य महाराजं त्वमिमं वृणुया वरम् ।।

29. And (your husband Dhascharatha the) Raaghava will himself lift you up (from the floor) and offer (& fulfill) the boons. You should direct the great king in this matter (of honouring his boons). and you ask for (the fulfillment of) boons thus:

❍ ❍ ❍

३०. रामं प्रव्राजयारण्ये नव वर्षाणि पञ्च च ।
भरतः क्रियतां राजा पृथिव्यां पार्थिवर्षभः ।।

30. You exile Raama for 14 years in forest; And may Bharatha be made king and shine in the world as foremost ruler (as 'Bull' amongst rulers).

❍ ❍ ❍

३१. चतुर्दश हि वर्षाणि रामे प्रव्राजिते वनम् ।
रूढश्च कृतमूलश्च शेषं स्थास्यति ते सुतः ।।

31. (Manthara assures Kaikeyi)

When Raama goes away to forest for 14 years, your son (Bharatha) with firm roots, would have well established himself. And even after that: (after 14 years, no one will talk about Raama says Manthara).

❍ ❍ ❍

३२. रामप्रव्राजनं चैव देवि याचस्व तं वरम् ।
एवं सेत्स्यन्ति पुत्रस्य सर्वार्थास्तव भामिनि ।।

32. Oh passionate (Kaikeyi)! You must surely solicit the exile of Raama: Then all benefits will (follow), accrue to your son, likewise.

❍ ❍ ❍

३३. एवं प्रव्राजितश्चैव रामोऽरामो भविष्यति ।
भरतश्च हतामित्रस्तव राजा भविष्यति ॥

33. When Raama is exiled thus, he will become 'Araama' (A non delighter): And your son Bharatha will become king without enemies.

(Manthara says that Raama, as his name suggests, is Delighter: But after 14 years as a hermit in forest he would have no charm and will be A-Raama, non delighter. Who will care for Raama!)

❍ ❍ ❍

३४. येन कालेन रामश्च वनात्प्रत्यागमिष्यति ।
तेन कालेन पुत्रस्ते कृतमूलो भविष्यति ।
संगृहीतमनुष्यश्च सुहृद्भिः सार्धमात्मवान् ॥

34. By the time Raama returns from forest, by that time your son (Bharatha) would have become self reliant along with his friends, with firm roots (as king). He will have hold on the citizens.

❍ ❍ ❍

३५. प्राप्तकालं तु ते मन्ये राजानं वीतसाध्वसा ।
आमाभिषेकसङ्कल्पान्निगृह्य विनिवर्तय ॥

35. I consider this as the right time for you (to act): Discarding your timidity, coercing him, you must (make him) stop preparations of Raama's anointing ceremony (immediately).

❍ ❍ ❍

३६. अनर्थमर्थरूपेण ग्राहिता सा ततस्तया ।
हृष्टा प्रतीता कैकेयी मन्थरामिदमब्रवीत् ॥

36. (Thus Manthara 'prepares' Kaikeyi)

Made to accept evil as good, Kaikeyi who was (now) convinced, then addressed Manthara thus with joy .....

❍ ❍ ❍

३७. सा हि वाक्येन कुब्जायाः किशोरीवोत्पथं गता ।
कैकेयी विस्मयं प्राप्ता परं परमदर्शना ।।

37. ...... like an (immature) young girl, this beautiful Kaikeyi was wonderstruck by words (of evil advice) from the hunchback Manthara. (Kaikeyi said) ......

❍ ❍ ❍

३८. कुब्जे त्वां नाभिजानामि श्रेष्ठां श्रेष्ठाभिधायिनीम् ।
पृथिव्यामसि कुब्जानामुत्तमा बुद्धिनिश्चये ।।

38. Oh Hunchback: You are indeed foremost amongst hunchbacks in the world, in sharpness of mind (particularly). I had not known you as foremost amongst those who express what is most salutary.

❍ ❍ ❍

३९. त्वमेव तु ममार्थेषु नित्ययुक्ता हितैषिणी ।
नाहं समवबुद्ध्येयं कुब्जे राज्ञश्चिकीर्षितम् ।।

39. I had not realised the true designs of the king in this matter. Oh Hunchback! You are the only one in my affairs who are ever a devoted, (true) well wisher.

❍ ❍ ❍

४०. सन्ति दुःसंस्थिताः कुब्जा वक्राः परमदारुणाः ।
त्वं पद्ममिव वातेन सन्नता प्रियदर्शना ।।

40. It is said that hunchbacks are very cruel, crooked and of improper conduct. Possessing the most desired character (of doing good) you are indeed most pleasing like lotus, although you are bent, (a hunch back)!

❍ ❍ ❍

४१. उरस्तेऽभिनिविष्टं वै यावत्स्कन्धं समुन्नतम् ।
अधस्ताच्चोदरं शातं सुनाभमिव लज्जितम् ।।

41. Your chest which is big and goes right upto your shoulders, is pretty! And below, your pretty waist is very slender, as though out of modesty!

❍ ❍ ❍

४२. परिपूर्णं च जघनं सुपीनौ च पयोधरौ ।
विमलेन्दुसमं वक्त्रमहो राजसि मन्थरे ।।

42. Oh Manthara! Ah! How becoming are you! Your back (buttocks) is broad; Your breasts are wholesome: Your face is like spotless moon!

❍ ❍ ❍

४३. जघनं तव निर्घुष्टं रशनादामशोभितम् ।
जङ्घे भृशमुपन्यस्ते पादौ चाप्यायतावुभौ ।।

43. Your waist shines with a sparingly sized girdle; Your thighs are well rounded. Your feet long and slender.

❍ ❍ ❍

४४. त्वमायताभ्यां सक्थिभ्यां मन्थरे क्षौमवासिनी ।
अग्रतो मम गच्छन्ती राजहंसीव राजसे ।।

44. Oh Manthara! You appear before me as a bright royal swan even as you are draped in white linen around your long thighs!

❍ ❍ ❍

४५. आसन्याः शम्बरे मायाः सहस्रमसुराधिपे ।
सर्वास्त्वयि निविष्टास्ता भूयश्चान्याः सहस्रशः ।।

45. You possess all the thousands of black magic found with lord of Asura-s, (demon) Schambara and also many others (in art of magic).

❍ ❍ ❍

४६. तवेदं स्थगु यद्दीर्घं रथघोणमिवायतम् ।
मतयः क्षत्रविद्याश्च मायाश्चात्र वसन्ति ।।

46. (It seems) that your knowledge, political wisdom and cunning (magic) are all hidden in your (deformity): That is why (your hunch) is long and fulsome like the beam of chariot.

❍ ❍ ❍

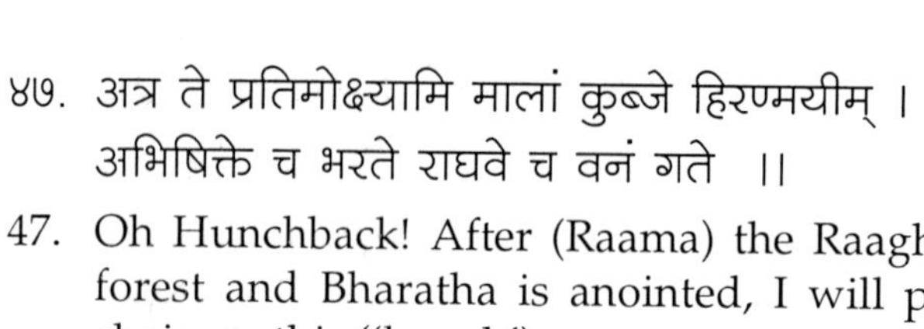

४७. अत्र ते प्रतिमोक्ष्यामि मालां कुब्जे हिरण्मयीम् ।
अभिषिक्ते च भरते राघवे च वनं गते ॥

47. Oh Hunchback! After (Raama) the Raaghava goes to forest and Bharatha is anointed, I will put a golden chain on this ('hunch').

❍ ❍ ❍

४८. जात्येन च सुवर्णेन सुनिष्टप्तेन मन्थरे ।
लब्धार्था च प्रतीता च लेपयिष्यामि ते स्थगु ॥

48. With (my) object fulfilled and happy, I will anoint your hunchback body with quality golden (sandal paste) free from impurities.

❍ ❍ ❍

४९. मुखे च तिलकं चित्रं जातरूपमयं शुभम् ।
कारयिष्यामि ते कुब्जे शुभान्याभरणानि च ॥

49. Oh Hunchback! I will anoint your face with most wonderful and lovely golden cosmetics; I will put on you lovely ornaments.

❍ ❍ ❍

५०. परिधाय शुभे वस्त्रे देवतेव चरिष्यसि ॥

50. Wearing lovely dress you will 'roam' about like a celestial.

❍ ❍ ❍

५१. चन्द्रमाह्वयमानेन मुखेनाप्रतिमानना ।
गमिष्यसि गतिं मुख्यां गर्हयन्ती द्विषज्जनम् ॥

51. With a face incomparable, putting to shame even the brilliancy of the moon, you will obtain great status, treating unfriendly people with contempt.

❍ ❍ ❍

५२. तवापि कुब्जाः कुब्जायाः सर्वाभरणभूषिताः ।
पादौ परिचरिष्यन्ति यथैव त्वं सदा मम ॥

52. As you serve me so will you, a hunchback, be served by many ornamented hunchbacks at all times, at your feet (at your command).

❍ ❍ ❍

५३. इति प्रशस्यमाना सा कैकेयीमिदमब्रवीत् ।
शयानां शयने शुभ्रे वेद्यामग्निशिखामिव ॥

53. When she was extolled thus, (Manthara) addressed Kaikeyi who was resting in a splendid couch that was like fire on a ritual Fire mound, with following words.

(Readers may note that from stanzas 40 to 52, Kaikeyi 'flatters' her mentor and maid, this evil minded genius Manthara: Everyone knows a hunchback is far from beautiful, yet Kaikeyi praises her 'beauty'. This Manthara must have been taunted for her ugliness and perhaps Kaikeyi offers her something this hunchback has never received in all her life - 'Praise' for her" beauty" Flattery!)

❍ ❍ ❍

५४. गतोदके सेतुबन्धो न कल्याणि विधीयते ।
उत्तिष्ठ कुरु कल्याणं राजानमनुदर्शय ॥

54. Oh Auspicious (Lady Kaikeyi)! No purpose is served in putting up a dam after flood has gone away (and done its havoc): Get up: Do this good deed: Await the king (your husband Dhascharatha).

❍ ❍ ❍

५५ तथा प्रोत्साहिता देवी गत्वा मन्थरया सह ।
क्रोधागारं विशालाक्षी सौभाग्यमदगर्विता ॥

55. Then the wide eyed lady (Kaikeyi), encouraged thus (by Manthara), went to The House of Sorrow (in palace), along with Manthara, in arrogance, because of her (impending) good fortune ......

❍ ❍ ❍

५६. अनेकशतसाहस्रं मुक्ताहारं वराङ्गना ।
अवमुच्य महार्हाणि शुभान्याभरणानि च ।।

56. ..... casting away the pearl necklace that was worth many thousands and also many lovely costly ornaments, this most lovely ......

❍ ❍ ❍

५७. ततो हेमोपमा तत्र कुब्जावाक्यवशं गता ।
संविश्य भूमौ कैकेयी मन्थरामिदमब्रवीत् ।।

57. ...... lady Kaikeyi who was under her subjugation, by the words of this hunchback, lay on the floor that was plain as mountain snow: She then addressed Manthara thus

❍ ❍ ❍

५८. इह वा मां मृतां कुब्जे नृपायावेदयिष्यसि ।
वनं वा राघवे प्राप्ते भरतः प्राप्स्यति क्षितिम् ।।

58. When Raama goes to forest, Bharatha will obtain kingdom; If not, Oh Hunchback! You are going to announce to the king that I am dead here itself.

❍ ❍ ❍

५९. न सुवर्णेन मे ह्यर्थोन रत्नैर्न च भोजनैः ।
एष मे जीवितस्यान्तो रामो यद्यभिषिच्यते ।।

59. I will not be satisfied with gold; nor gems; nor good foods; If Raama is crowned, this will be the end of my life.

❍ ❍ ❍

६०. अथो पुनस्तां महिषीं महीक्षितो वचोभिरत्यर्थमहापराक्रमैः ।
उवाच कुब्जा भरतस्य मातरं हितं वचो राममुपेत्य चाहितम् ।।

60. (Thus Kaikeyi resolved when she lay in the House of Sorrow without ornaments, in ragged clothes, lying on bare floor.)

With ruin of Raama in view, then the hunchback spoke the following: once again to the mother of Bharatha,(to this Kaikeyi) the wife of king Dhascharatha, with soothing words (but) generating intense zeal (and wrath on Kaikeyi).

❍ ❍ ❍

६१. प्रपत्स्यते राज्यमिदं हि राघवो यदि ध्रुवं त्वं यतस्व च तप्स्यसे।
अतो हि कल्याणि यतस्व तत्तथा यथा सुतस्ते
भरतोऽभिषेक्ष्यते ॥

61. Oh auspicious (Kaikeyi)! If Raama obtains kingdom, you and your son will surely suffer; therefore make such effort that your son Bharatha will be crowned.

❍ ❍ ❍

६२. तथाऽतिविद्धा महिषी तु कुब्जया समाहता वागिषुभिर्मुहुर्मुहुः ।
निधाय हस्तौहृदयेऽतिविस्मिता शशंस कुब्जां कुपितां
पुनः पुनः ॥

62. Having been struck by words of arrows from the hunchback repeatedly and having been 'wounded' by her thus, queen (Kaikeyi) who became greatly bewildered, told this hunchback who was in wrath, once again, with her two arms placed on her chest.

❍ ❍ ❍

६३. यमस्य वा मां विषयं गतामितो निशाम्य कुब्जे
प्रतिवेदयिष्यसि ।
वनं गते वा सुचिराय राघवे समृद्धकामो भरतो भविष्यति ॥

63. Oh Hunchback (Manthara)! If Raama goes away to forest for a long time, Bharatha would have his desire fulfilled: If not, you will see me departed to the House of Death from here. You (will be the first one to) announce this.

❍ ❍ ❍

६४. अहं हि नैवास्तरणानि न स्रजो न चन्दनं

नाञ्जनपान भोजनम् ।

न किञ्चिदिच्छामि न चेह जीवितम् न चेदितो गच्छति

राघवो वनम् ।।

64. If (Raama the) Raaghava does not go to forest from here, I will desire nothing else: No beds for me; no garlands; no sandal paste; no cosmetics, no drinks, no food. Nor life in the world.

❍ ❍ ❍

६५. अथैतदुक्त्वा वचनं सुदारुणं

निधाय सर्वाभरणानि भामिनी ।

असंवृतामास्तरणेन मेदिनीं

तदाऽधिशिश्ये पतितेव किन्नरी ।।

65. After speaking such harsh words, this passionate (Kaikeyi) discarded all ornaments and like a Kinnara woman fallen down (from heaven), she lay on plain floor that was not covered by any mattress or carpets.

❍ ❍ ❍

६६. उदीर्णसंरम्भतमोवृतानना

तथाऽवमुक्तोत्तममाल्यभूषणा ।

नरेन्द्रपत्नी विमना बभूव सा

तमोवृता द्यौरिव मग्नतारका ।।

66. Her face completely covered (and darkened) by intense wrath, losing all her honour (& self respect), this consort of the king, (this Kaikeyi) who had discarded and 'stripped' herself of foremost ornaments and chains, shone like the sky covered by darkness without stars.

(Note: Thus the course of Raamaayana took a different turn. She was a slave of queen Kaikeyi, this Manthara the hunchback. Yet she had worked her way up to be her mentor and confidante. She was no ordinary woman. A evil genius. Kaikeyi loved her stepson Raama as much if not more than her own son Bharatha. Yet, step by step, she convinces Kaikeyi that with Raama around, she and her son have no future in the kingdom And she remembers the two unfulfilled Boons that were given to Kaikeyi by her husband Dhascharatha long ago. She tells Kaikeyi that she must exercise her options now & this way only: Exile for Raama and Rule of Kingdom for Bharatha. Her loyalty to Kaikeyi is unquestionable; but she must have had some vested interests. Perhaps entertained the idea of wielding Political power through Bharatha, son of her 'foster mother' Kaikeyi Or perhaps she wanted to take revenge on Society which must have treated her with contempt because of her ugliness (& crookedness). After all in one stanza-stanza 40-Vaalmeeki has indicated this in an oblique way.)

❍ ❍ ❍

Chapter 10

(Dhascharatha) Tries to Pacify Kaikeyi

(King Dhascharatha visits his favourite wife Kaikeyi to convey personally the happy news of Raama's coronation: He is aghast that she considers this as a calamity for her. He tries to pacify her)

❍ ❍ ❍

१. विदर्शिता यदा देवी कुब्जया पापया भृशम् ।
तदा शेते स्म सा भूमौ दिग्धविद्धेव किन्नरी ॥

1. Blinded' by the sinful hunchback totally, lady (Kaikeyi) lay on the bare floor like a kinnara bird struck by a poisonous arrow.

❍ ❍ ❍

२. निश्चित्य मनसा कृत्यं सा सम्यगिति भामिनी ।
मन्थरायै शनैः सर्वमाचचक्षे विचक्षणा ॥

2. Deciding in her mind as to what she should do, passionate (Kaikeyi) who was very clever, told Manthara slowly = Everything is Okay = (I will do according to plan).

❍ ❍ ❍

३. सा दीना निश्चयं कृत्वा मन्थरावाक्यमोहिता ।
नागकन्येव निश्वस्य दीर्घमुष्णं च भामिनी ।
मुहूर्तं चिन्तयामास मार्गमात्मसुखावहम् ॥

3. Completely swayed (& stupefied) by Manthara's words (of evil advice), this passionate (Kaikeyi), having decided (thus) was (somewhat) worried. Like a female cobra, was breathing hard and (emitting) hot (breath). And she began to think about the strategy which will bring her comfort (& success to her boons when Dhascharatha came to visit her).

❍ ❍ ❍

४. सा सुहृच्चार्थकामा च तन्निशम्य सुनिश्चयम् ।
बभूव परमप्रीता सिद्धिं प्राप्येव मन्थरा ॥

4. And the selfish Manthara who loved her, hearing about (Kaikeyi's) decision (to go through with her scheme), became so happy that she (thought) the task was already accomplished.

❍ ❍ ❍

५. अथ सा रुषिता देवी सम्यक् कृत्वा सुनिश्चयम् ।
संविवेशाबला भूमौ निवेश्य भ्रुकुटीं मुखे ॥

5. Having firmly resolved, lady Kaikeyi) lay on bare floor like an ordinary woman in wrath, drawing her eye brows close on her face.

६. ततश्चित्राणि माल्यानि दिव्यान्याभरणानि च ।
अपविद्धानि कैकेय्या तानि भूमिं प्रपेदिरे ।।

6. At that time (in the House of Sorrow), various exquisite and costly jewels and necklaces were scattered on the floor, having been cast away by Kaikeyi.(from her body)

❍ ❍ ❍

७. तया तान्यपविद्धानि माल्यान्याभरणानि च ।
अशोभयन्त वसुधां नक्षत्राणि यथा नभः ।।

7. And the jewels and necklaces that were cast away by her, made the floor glitter, like stars in the sky.

❍ ❍ ❍

८. क्रोधागारे निपतिता सा बभौ मलिनाम्बरा ।
एकवेणीं दृढं बध्वा गतसत्त्वेव किन्नरी ।।

8. Dressed in dirty clothes with her hair tied in one bunch, lying on the floor at the House of Wrath (& sorrow), she appeared like a (celestial) Kinnari girl bereft of any goodness.

❍ ❍ ❍

९. आज्ञाप्य तु महाराजो राघवस्याभिषेचनम् ।
उपस्थानमनुज्ञाप्य प्रविवेश निवेशनम् ।।

9. And king (Dhascharatha) having given orders for (Raama the) Raaghava's coronation, entered the palace after dismissing the assembly.

❍ ❍ ❍

१०. अद्य रामाभिषेको वै प्रसिद्ध इति जज्ञिवान् ।
प्रियार्हां प्रियमाख्यातुं विवेशान्तःपुरं वशी ।।

10. (But Dhascharatha does not find his beloved Kaikeyi at her lovely apartment of the palace)

Observing that (the news of) Raama's Coronation

had become known (to all) only then, the ruler (Dhascharatha) entered the inner apartments (of the palace) to announce the good (news,personally) to (Kaikeyi) who deserved his love.

❍ ❍ ❍

११. स कैकेय्या गृहं श्रेष्ठं प्रविवेश महायशाः ।
पाण्डुराभ्रमिवाकाशं राहुयुक्तं निशाकरः ।।

11. (Stanzas 11 to 15 the scene described)

The most famous (Dhascharatha) entered the (beautiful and) foremost palace of Kaikeyi that was like moon shining in the sky covered by white clouds and Raahu....

❍ ❍ ❍

१२. शुकबर्हिणसंयुक्तं क्रौञ्चहंसरुतायुतम् ।
वादित्ररवसंघुष्टं कुब्जावामनिकायुतम् ।।

12. ...... (At the palace of Kaikeyi) There were plenty of peacocks and parrots; sound emanating from Krauncha birds; Musical strains from various instruments: Full of hunchbacks & midgets (attendants) .....

❍ ❍ ❍

१३. लतागृहैश्चित्रगृहैश्चम्पकाशोकशोभितैः ।
दान्तराजतसौवर्णवेदिकाभिः समायुतम् ।।

13. ...... Tall Champaka trees, Asoka trees, around; House gardens and rooms full of paintings; The pavilion studded with works of ivory, silver, gold ......

❍ ❍ ❍

१४. नित्यपुष्पफलैर्वृक्षैर्वापीभिश्चोपशोभितम् ।
दान्तराजतसौवर्णैः संवृतं परमासनैः ।।

14. ...... there were trees that blossomed throughout (the year) with flowers & fruits. Furniture done up in gold, silver, ivory.. with lovely ponds around ......

❍ ❍ ❍

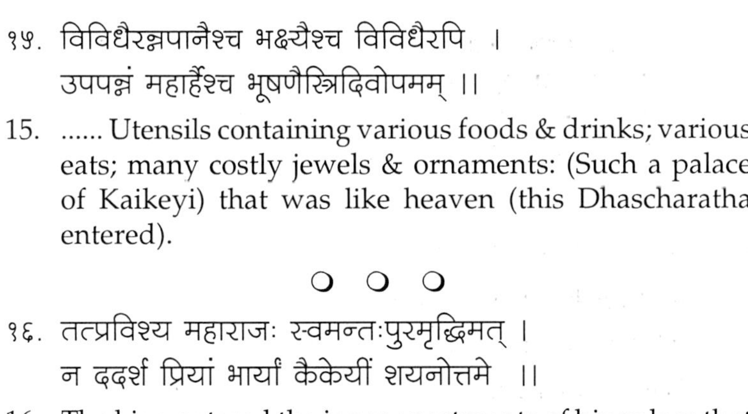

१५. विविधैरन्नपानैश्च भक्ष्यैश्च विविधैरपि ।
उपपन्नं महार्हैश्च भूषणैस्त्रिदिवोपमम् ।।

15. ...... Utensils containing various foods & drinks; various eats; many costly jewels & ornaments: (Such a palace of Kaikeyi) that was like heaven (this Dhascharatha entered).

❍ ❍ ❍

१६. तत्प्रविश्य महाराजः स्वमन्तःपुरमृद्धिमत् ।
न ददर्श प्रियां भार्यां कैकेयीं शयनोत्तमे ।।

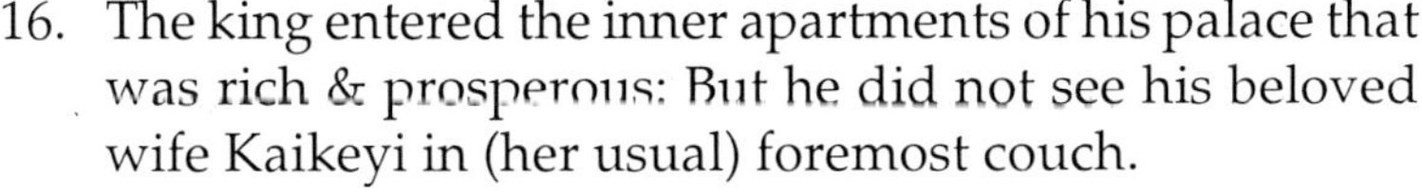

16. The king entered the inner apartments of his palace that was rich & prosperous: But he did not see his beloved wife Kaikeyi in (her usual) foremost couch.

❍ ❍ ❍

१७. स कामबलसंयुक्तो रत्यर्थी मनुजाधिपः ।
अपश्यन्दयितां भार्यां पप्रच्छ विषसाद च ।।

17. The lord of men (Dhascharatha), unable to see (find) his dear wife whom he loved with passion, became very sad; And he asked for his amorous (Kaikeyi).

❍ ❍ ❍

१८. न हि तस्य पुरा देवी तां वेलामत्यवर्तत ।
न च राजा गृहं शून्यं प्रविवेश कदाचन ।।

18. Because, never had the king entered the palace (finding it) empty; Never before his lady (Kaikeyi) was not present there at that time (to receive him).

❍ ❍ ❍

१९. ततो गृहगतो राजा कैकेयीं पर्यपृच्छत ।
यथापुरमविज्ञाय स्वार्थलिप्सुमपण्डिताम् ।।

19. Thinking Kaikeyi (as usual) was 'foolish', ignorant and was selfish, king (Dhascharatha) who had entered the (inner apartments of) palace, asked about her as usual.

❍ ❍ ❍

२०. प्रतिहारी त्वथोवाच संत्रस्ता सुकृताञ्जलिः ।
देव देवी भृशं क्रुद्धा क्रोधागारमभिद्रुता ।।

20. Trembling before him, the door keeper with her hands in Anjali spoke: = Oh Lord (my king)! Lady (Kaikeyi) in great wrath has gone away to The House of Wrath.=

❍ ❍ ❍

२१. प्रतिहार्या वचः श्रुत्वा राजा परमदुर्मनाः ।
विषसाद पुनर्भूयो लुलितव्याकुलेन्द्रियः ।।

21. Hearing the words of the door keeper, the king became even more disheartened, was agitated, shaken up, downcast.

❍ ❍ ❍

२२. तत्र तां पतितां भूमौ शयानामतथोचिताम् ।
प्रतप्त इव दुःखेन सोऽपश्यज्जगतीपतिः ।।

22. (Dhascharatha) the ruler of earth, saw her, (saw his most beloved Kaikeyi) there, lying on bare floor, as never before, tormented by great sorrow.

❍ ❍ ❍

२३. स वृद्धस्तरुणीं भार्यां प्राणेभ्योऽपि गरीयसीम् ।
अपापः पापसङ्कल्पां ददर्श धरणीतले ।।

23. (Scene described: Stanzas 23 to 25)

This old sinless (king) to whom his wife (Kaikeyi) was more precious than his life, saw her who was bent on evil, (saw this) very young (Kaikeyi) lying on bare floor.....

❍ ❍ ❍

२४. लतामिव विनिष्कृत्तां पतितां देवतामिव ।
किन्नरीमिव निर्धूतां च्युतामप्सरसं यथा ।।

24. ...... like a cut out creeper, like a celestial lady thrown out (from heaven), like a stricken kinnara bird, like an expelled Apsara maiden ......

❍ ❍ ❍

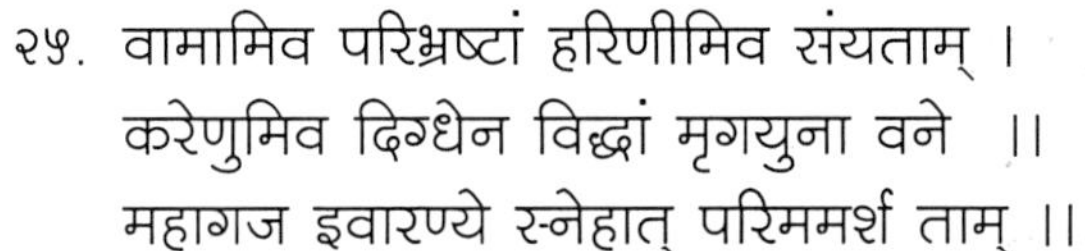

२५. वामामिव परिभ्रष्टां हरिणीमिव संयताम् ।
करेणुमिव दिग्धेन विद्धां मृगयुना वने ॥
महागज इवारण्ये स्नेहात् परिममर्श ताम् ॥

25. ...... like a woman abandoned (by society), like deer in captivity, like a female elephant hit by poisoned arrow by a hunter in forest. He affectionately stroked her.

❍ ❍ ❍

२६. परिमृज्य च पाणिभ्यामभिसन्त्रस्तचेतनः ।
कामी कमलपत्राक्षीमुवाच वनितामिदम् ॥

26. This passionate (king) embraced her whose eyes were like lotus, with both hands. His mind totally agitated, he said these words:

❍ ❍ ❍

२७. न तेऽहमभिजानामि क्रोधमात्मनि संश्रितम् ।
देवि केनाभिशप्तासि केन वा त्वं विमानिता ॥

27. Oh lady (Kaikeyi)! I do not know (the cause of your) anger that is afflicting you. Have you been falsely accused by any one? Have you been insulted by any one?

❍ ❍ ❍

२८. यदर्थं मम दुःखाय शेषे कल्याणि पांसुषु ॥

28. Oh Auspicious (Kaikeyi)! Why are you lying in dust making me miserable.

❍ ❍ ❍

२९. भूमौ शेषे किमर्थं त्वं मयि कल्याणचेतसि ।
भूतोपहतचित्तेव मम चित्तप्रमाथिनी ॥

29. When I am very happy and in splendour, why are you lying on the floor as though possessed by evil spirits, making my mind agitated and numb.

❍ ❍ ❍

३०. सन्ति मे कुशला वैद्यास्त्वभितुष्टाश्च सर्वशः ।
सुखितां त्वां करिष्यन्ति व्याधिमाचक्ष्व भामिनि ॥

30. I have with me (at my command) pleasant and able doctors, everywhere. Oh passionate (Kaikeyi)! Tell me about your ailment. They will (cure you and) make you comfortable.

❍ ❍ ❍

३१. कस्य वा विप्रियं कार्यं केन वा विप्रियं कृतम् ।
कः प्रियं लभतामद्य को वा सुमहदप्रियम् ॥

31. Has transgression been done upon you by any one? Do you want me to cause injury upon any one? (Now tell me): Now, who should be favoured and who should obtain great harm?

❍ ❍ ❍

३२. मा रोदीर्मा च कार्षीस्त्वं देहसंपरिशोषणम् ।
अवध्यो वध्यतां को वा वध्यः को वा विमुच्यताम् ॥

32. (Dhaschaaratha is so much infatuated, that he loses his composure. he is even prepared to offer punishment to a non sinner).

Do not cry. Dont allow your body to wither away (in grief); Which one who does not deserve (punishment of) death, must be put to death? Or who must be let off who deserves (punishment of) death.

❍ ❍ ❍

३३. दरिद्रः को भवत्वाढ्यो द्रव्यवान् वाऽप्यकिञ्चनः ।
अहं चैव मदीयाश्च सर्वेतव वशानुगाः ॥

33. (You know very well) Me and my (friends & folks) are all devoted to you (and follow you at your will and pleasure): Which poor man must be made wealthy: And which rich man must be reduced to poverty (by me).

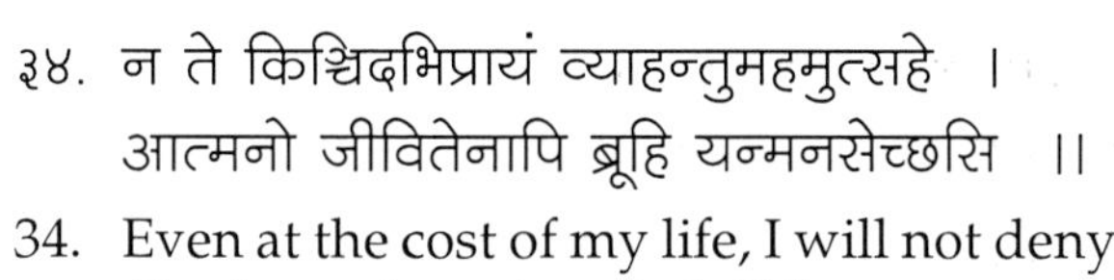
३४. न ते किञ्चिदभिप्रायं व्याहन्तुमहमुत्सहे ।
आत्मनो जीवितेनापि ब्रूहि यन्मनसेच्छसि ।।

34. Even at the cost of my life, I will not deny you anything (that) you have in mind. Whatever you desire in your mind, tell me that.

❍ ❍ ❍

३५. बलमात्मनि जानन्ती न मां शङ्कितुमर्हसि ।
करिष्यामि तव प्रीतिं सुकृतेनापि ते शपे ।।

35. Knowing the power of my (attachment) to you, you should have no doubts: I will fulfill your desires. I vow by all the good deeds.

❍ ❍ ❍

३६. यावदावर्तते चक्रं तावती मे वसुन्धरा ।।

36. Wherever the Sun makes his rounds, the entire Earth is (under) my (control).... (Readers may note a parallel of early 20th. Century The Sun never sets upon the British Empire!).

❍ ❍ ❍

३७. प्राचीनाः सिन्धुसौवीराः सौराष्ट्रा दक्षिणापथाः ।
वङ्गाङ्गमगधा मत्स्याः समृद्धाः काशिकोसलाः ।।

37. Whether in east, or south regions; In Sindh and Sowveera regions; Sowraashtra, Vanga and Anga territories, Mathsya, Kaashi, Kowsala... All... (are in my control, says Emperor Dhascharatha).

❍ ❍ ❍

३८. तत्र जात बहुद्रव्यं धनधान्यमजाविकम् ।
ततो वृणीष्व कैकेयि यद्यत्त्वं मनसेच्छसि ।।

38. Oh Kaikeyi! In these (kingdoms) are found many exquisite products, food grains, produce, and herds of goats, cows: Whatever you desire in your mind, ask (and it will be yours).

❍ ❍ ❍

३९. किमायासेन ते भीरु उत्तिष्ठोत्तिष्ठ शोभने ।
तत्त्वं मे ब्रूहि कैकेयि यतस्ते भयमागतम् ।।
तत्ते व्यपनयिष्यामि नीहारमिव रश्मिवान् ।।

39. Oh timid (Kaikeyi)! Tell me what causes fear in you; I will destroy (this), like Sun upon snow. Oh pretty Kaikeyi! Get up. Get up why this weariness in you?

○ ○ ○

४०. तथोक्ता सा समाश्वस्ता वक्तुकामा तदप्रियम् ।
परिपीडयितुं भूयो भर्तारमुपचक्रमे ।।

40. When told thus, (Kaikeyi) who was desirous of speaking about this most unpleasant (design of hers), began to torment her husband even more when she was somewhat comforted (by her husband's assurance).

(Note: When a person is in passion he loses his composure. Here we find the great king Dhascharatha telling his beloved wife that he would do anything for her, even put to death an innocent man for her sake!)

○ ○ ○

Chapter 11

(Kaikeyi) Demands the Two Boons

(Kaikeyi demands her 'pound of flesh': She wishes to exercise her options of using the two boons given to her, now, and this way only; Raama to go on Exile & Kingdom for Bharatha.)

१. तं मन्मथशरैर्विद्धं कामवेगवशानुगम् ।
उवाच पृथिवीपालं कैकेयी दारुणं वचः ।।

1. Kaikeyi said the following most cruel words to the

emperor (her husband Dhascharatha) who was struck by arrows of love (Manmatha) and who was under her subjugation due to the intensity of his passion towards her.

❍ ❍ ❍

२. नास्मि विप्रकृता देव केनचिन्नावमानिता ।
अभिप्रायस्तु मे कश्चित्तमिच्छामि त्वया कृतम् ।।

2. Oh Lord (Dhascharatha)! I have not been disrespected (by any one): I have not been insulted by any one. There is one desire in me that I desire, which can be satisfied by you.

❍ ❍ ❍

३. प्रतिज्ञां प्रतिजानीष्व यदि त्वं कर्तुमिच्छसि ।
अथ तद्व्याहरिष्यामि यदभिप्रार्थितं मया ।।

3. If you desire to fulfill this, first you promise to give your assent (to do what I seek): Then (only) I will (disclose and utter) what I have in mind.

❍ ❍ ❍

४. तामुवाच महातेजाः कैकेयीमीषदुत्स्मितः ।
कामी हस्तेन संगृह्य मूर्धजेषु शुचिस्मिताम् ।।

4. (Kaikeyi is very clever: She wants her husband to give her an open promise.)

The most brilliant (Dhascharatha) who was passionate, smiling somewhat, gently stroked Kaikeyi on her hair with his hands and said thus to her who was (now somewhat) smiling cheerfully.

❍ ❍ ❍

५. अवलिप्ते न जानासि त्वत्तः प्रियतरो मम ।
मनुजो मनुजव्याघ्राद्रामादन्यो न विद्यते ।।

5. Oh proud Kaikeyi! You know (very well) that none is

dearer to me than you. And no man is dearer to me than that 'tiger' of men Raama.

❍ ❍ ❍

६. तेनाजय्येन मुख्येन राघवेण महात्मना ।
शपे ते जीवनार्हेण ब्रूहि यन्मनसेच्छसि ॥

6. I swear by that (Raama the) Raaghava who is invincible, who is a great soul, who is foremost, and who sustains my very life. What you desire in your mind, Tell Me That.

❍ ❍ ❍

७. यं मुहूर्तमपश्यंस्तु न जीवेयमहं ध्रुवम् ।
तेन रामेण कैकेयि शपे ते वचनक्रियाम् ॥

7. If I dont see him even for a moment, surely I will lose my life: On such a Raama, Oh Kaikeyi, I swear to fulfill your command*.

❍ ❍ ❍

८. आत्मना वाऽऽत्मजैश्चान्यैर्वृणे यं मनुजर्षभम् ।
तेन रामेण कैकेयि शपे ते वचनक्रियाम् ॥

8. He who is 'bull' amongst men, whom I cherish more than my life and more than all my other sons and all others, on that Raama I Swear, Oh Kaikeyi, that I will fulfill your word*.

(*Poet uses word= Vachana kriya)

❍ ❍ ❍

९. भद्रे हृदयमप्येतदनुमृश्योद्धरस्व माम् ।
एतत्समीक्ष्य कैकेयि ब्रूहि यत्साधु मन्यसे ॥

9. Oh blemishless (Kaikeyi)! Reflect (consider) that such is my heart, straight and proper. Put away (this grief): Consider this and so tell me what you have in mind, Oh Kaikeyi.

❍ ❍ ❍

१०. बलमात्मनि पश्यन्ती न मां शङ्कितुमर्हसि ।
करिष्यामि तव प्रीतिं सुकृतेनापि ते शपे ।।

10. You who can 'see' the power (of my attachment) towards you, should not have any apprehensions over me. I will fulfill your wish. I swear by my good deeds also.

❍ ❍ ❍

११. सा तदर्थमना देवी तमभिप्रायमागतम् ।
निर्मध्यस्थाच्च हर्षाच्च बभाषे दुर्वचं वचः ।।

11. This selfish lady (Kaikeyi) on seeing him coming round to her purpose, (thought of) speaking to him with pleasant words although they were hard to utter (in view of the matter) being unfair (one sided).

❍ ❍ ❍

१२. तेन वाक्येन संहृष्टा तमभिप्रायमात्मनः ।
व्याजहार महाघोरमभ्यागतमिवान्तकम् ।।

12. Pleased by his words (of assurance) and (realising that) he had come around to fulfill her thinking (of satisfying her wish), (Kaikeyi) uttered the most gruesome words, (leading one to) Death.

❍ ❍ ❍

१३. यथा क्रमेण शपसि वरं मम ददासि च ।
तच्छृण्वन्तु त्रयस्त्रिंशद्देवाः सेन्द्रपुरोगमाः ।।

13. You are swearing. As a consequence of which what boon you offer me, that, may the 33 Dheva-s and their Lord Indhra hear

❍ ❍ ❍

१४. चन्द्रादित्यौ नभश्चैव ग्रहा रात्र्यहनी दिशः ।
जगच्च पृथिवी चेयं गन्धर्वाश्च सराक्षसाः ।।

14. ...... (May these also be witness to Dhascharatha's oath):

Sun & Moon: The Sky also: The Constellations Lord of Day & Night: Lords of All Directions: Entire World: Earth: Ghandharva-s & Raakshasa-s.

❍ ❍ ❍

१५. निशाचराणि भूतानि गृहेषु गृहदेवताः ।
यानि चान्यानि भूतानि जानीयुर्भाषितं तव ॥

15. Let the ghosts which roam about at night around houses; Let fairies and other celestial bodies whoever they may be, know about your words (of oath, your commitment to me).

❍ ❍ ❍

१६. सत्यसन्धो महातेजा धर्मज्ञः सुसमाहितः ।
वरं मम ददात्येष तन्मे श्रृण्वन्तु देवताः ॥

16. This man of truth, the knower of Dharma, the most brilliant man of composure and steadfastness, (this my beloved husband King Dhascharatha), is offering me boons: Oh Deities: Hear (Ye all) this, for my sake!

❍ ❍ ❍

१७. इति देवी महेष्वासं परिगृह्याभिशस्य च ।
ततः परमुवाचेदं वरदं काममोहितम् ॥

17. This lady (Kaikeyi thus) bound him who was a mighty warrior, who was stricken with passion (over her), who had offered her boons (long, long ago), Taking a firm 'hold' on him thus, she then said the following most important (part).

❍ ❍ ❍

१८. स्मर राजन् पुरावृत्तं तस्मिन्दैवासुरे रणे ।
तत्र चाच्यावयच्छत्रुस्तव जीवितमन्तरा ॥

18. (Kaikeyi now puts forth her demands: She reminds Dhascharatha of an incident long ago)
Oh king (my husband Dhascharatha)! (Please) Recollect

about an incident that happened during Dheva-Asura war. During this (war) the enemy (almost) extinguished your life.

❍ ❍ ❍

१९. तत्र चापि मया देव यत्त्वं समभिरक्षितः ।
जाग्रत्या यतमानायास्ततो मे प्रददौ वरौ ।।

19. Oh Lord! At that time, you were protected by me. Therefore you gave me two Boons, for (having served you) with great care, self control (& vigil).

❍ ❍ ❍

२०. तौ तु दत्तौ वरौ देव निक्षिप्तौ मृगयाम्यहम् ।
तवैव पृथिवीपाल सकाशे सत्यसङ्गर ।।

20. Oh lord, the ruler of earth who keeps his word! What was then offered by you (committed by you) and 'entrusted'* with you, those two boons I seek now.

(*Word used is - Nikshiptha- Deposited, pledged with you)

❍ ❍ ❍

२१. तत्प्रतिश्रुत्य धर्मेण न चेद्दास्यसि मे वरम् ।
अद्यैव हि प्रहास्यामि जीवितं त्वद्विमानिता ।।

21. If you (now) deny me these two Boons which were promised by (and as per) Dharma, then I shall give up my life now itself (as) being 'insulted' by you. Surely.

❍ ❍ ❍

२२. वाङ्मात्रेण तदा राजा कैकेय्या स्ववशीकृतः ।
प्रचस्कन्द विनाशाय पाशं मृग इवात्मनः ।।

22. Like a deer (falling into) a net for its destruction, this (Dhascharatha) the king bound himself at the hands of Kaikeyi by mere words (of Assurance) and (thus) "perished".

❍ ❍ ❍

२३. ततः परमुवाचेदं वरदं काममोहितम् ।
वरौ यौ मे त्वया देव तदा दत्तौ महीपते ॥

23. Then she spoke the most important part to him who was seized by passion over her and who had given her the boons. Oh my Lord, the two Boons given to me by you ......

❍ ❍ ❍

२४. तौ तावदहमद्यैव वक्ष्यामि श्रृणु मे वचः ॥

24. ...... these I am now asking you: Listen to my words:

❍ ❍ ❍

२५. अभिषेकसमारम्भो राघवस्योपकल्पितः ।
अनेनैवाभिषेकेण भरतो मेऽभिषिच्यताम् ॥

25. (Preparations are going on and) Materials are being collected for Raama's Coronation: With these same (Coronation) materials, my (son) Bharatha must be crowned (forthwith).

❍ ❍ ❍

२६. यो द्वितीयो वरो देव दत्तः प्रीतेन मे त्वया ।
तदा दैवासुरे युद्धे तस्य कालोऽयमागतः ॥

26. Oh Lord! The second boon that was offered by you in joy during the Dheva-Asura war, the time (for utilising that boon) has come.

❍ ❍ ❍

२७. नव पञ्च च वर्षाणि दण्डकारण्यमाश्रितः ।
चीराजिनजटाधारी रामो भवतु तापसः ॥

27. Let Raama sporting "tufted hair locks", wearing bark and deer skin material, live in Dhandaka forest for 9 plus 5 (14) years as a hermit.

❍ ❍ ❍

२८. भरतो भजतामद्य यौवराज्यमकण्टकम् ।
एष मे परमः कामो दत्तमेव वरं वृणे ॥
अद्य चैव हि पश्येयं प्रयान्तं राघवं वनम् ॥

28. I am (only) asking for the boons now that were offered already (to me by you). I must see Raama leaving for forest today itself. This, is my foremost wish. And let Bharatha become YuvaRaaja without hindrance.

❍ ❍ ❍

२९. स राजराजो भव सत्यसङ्गरः
कुलं च शीलं च हि रक्ष जन्म च ।
परत्र वासे हि वदन्त्यनुत्तमं
तपोधनाः सत्यवचो हितं नृणाम् ॥

29. As you are king of Kings, you must be true (to your promise): You must protect the honour of your family, your birth, your good conduct. Sages say that for mortals, honouring one's word alone will be the foremost and most salutary (means) to reach heaven.

(Thus, Kaikeyi, instigated by Manthara 'Binds' Dhascharatha the man of Dharma. And a king never breaks a promise, even after many, many years, even if it is against his own good. And Dhascharatha was no ordinary king: An Ikshwaaku king).

❍ ❍ ❍

Chapter 12

Dhaschaaratha Curses Kaikeyi

(Dhascharatha is stunned by Kaikeyi's demands: Could not believe that his most beloved wife could be so cruel. He curses her.)

❍ ❍ ❍

१. ततः श्रुत्वा महाराजः कैकेय्या दारुणं वचः ।
चिन्तामभिसमापेदे मुहूर्तं प्रतताप च ।।

1. Hearing the most cruel words of Kaikeyi, the emperor went into (a state of) anxiety: For a muhoortha, (about 48 minutes), was (consumed by) torment.

❍ ❍ ❍

२. किं नु मे यदि वा स्वप्नश्चित्तमोहोऽपि वा मम ।
अनुभूतोपसर्गोवा मानसो वाऽप्युपद्रवः ।
इति संचिन्त्य तद्राजा नाध्यगच्छत्तदा सुखम् ।।

2. (Dhascharatha imagines!): Is this a dream for me; Or perhaps, is it mental aberration: Or a calamity caused by nature. Or (caused by) an accident. Thus the king pondered but could not obtain any solace* (*Poet uses word- Sukham-).

❍ ❍ ❍

३. प्रतिलंभ्य ततस्संज्ञां कैकेयीवाक्यताडितः ।
व्यथितो विक्लबश्चैव व्याघ्रीं दृष्ट्वा यथा मृगः ।।

3. Then regaining his composure (somewhat) after he was wounded (thus) by the (most) cruel words of Kaikeyi, he was frightened like a deer when it sees a tiger....he was agitated ......

❍ ❍ ❍

४. असंवृतायामासीनो जगत्यां दीर्घमुच्छ्वसन् ।
मण्डले पन्नगो रुद्धो मन्त्रैरिव महाविषः ।।

4. ...... and sat on the bare floor, sighing deeply, (hissing) like a poisonous Cobra bound by Magic within circle......

❍ ❍ ❍

५. अहो धिगिति सामर्षो वाचमुक्त्वा नराधिपः ।
मोहमापेदिवान्भूयः शोकोपहतचेतनः ।।

5. ...... he was enraged, and was saying words like: "Ah!

Fie!" The lord of men (Dhascharatha) whose mind was engulfed by grief, once again lost his consciousness.

❍ ❍ ❍

६. चिरेण तु नृपः संज्ञां प्रतिलभ्य सुदुःखितः ।
कैकेयीमब्रवीत्क्रुद्धः प्रदहन्निव चक्षुषा ॥

6. Regaining his consciousness after a long time, in great wrath, the king who appeared as though he would burn up Kaikeyi with his eyes, spoke to her in great anguish.

❍ ❍ ❍

७. नृशंसे दुष्टचारित्रे कुलस्यास्य विनाशिनि ।
किं कृतं तव रामेण पापे पापं मयाऽपि वा ॥

7. (Now Dhascharatha goes on a tirade against this Kaikeyi): Oh Vile woman! Woman of mischievous conduct! Oh Sinful woman! Oh the destroyer of my family What harm has ever been done to you either by me or Raama?

❍ ❍ ❍

८. सदा ते जननीतुल्यां वृत्तिं वहति राघवः ।
तस्यैव त्वमनर्थाय किंनिमित्तमिहोद्यता ॥

8. Raama has always bestowed upon you (service with)* good conduct like (towards) his own mother: Why have you now undertaken (the task of) bringing harm to such a man?

(*Poet uses word-Vriththim vahathi)

❍ ❍ ❍

९. त्वं मयात्मविनाशार्थं भवनं स्वं प्रवेशिता ।
अविज्ञानान्नृपसुता व्याली तीक्ष्णविषा यथा ॥

9. Out of my ignorance, you were allowed by me to 'Enter' (live with me in my abode, in my) palace: You,

a princess, are (indeed) like a poisonous viper, out to destroy me.

❍ ❍ ❍

१०. जीवलोको यदा सर्वो रामस्याह गुणस्तवम् ।
अपराधं कमुद्दिश्य त्यक्ष्यामीष्टमहं सुतम् ॥

10. All living beings have spoken about Raama's noble qualities: When such is the case, on what grounds of misdemeanour, shall I abandon my loving son.

❍ ❍ ❍

११. कौसल्यां वा सुमित्रां वा त्यजेयमपि वा श्रियम् ।
जीवितं वाऽऽत्मनो रामं न त्वेव पितृवत्सलम् ॥

11. (Here Dhascharatha, being a good king, makes a point: None can be exiled without proper grounds of misbehaviour etc.)

I may give up my (wives) Kowsalya and Sumithra, my wealth, or even my life: but never my (son) Raama, who is most affectionate to his father.

❍ ❍ ❍

१२. परा भवति मे प्रीतिर्दृष्ट्वा तनयमग्रजम् ।
अपश्यतस्तु मे रामं नष्टं भवति चेतनम् ॥

12. When I see my eldest son Raama, there is great happiness in me; When I don't see him, my mind is disturbed.

❍ ❍ ❍

१३. तिष्ठेल्लोको विना सूर्यं सस्यं वा सलिलं विना ।
न तु रामं विना देहे तिष्ठेत्तु मम जीवितम् ॥

13. World may perhaps survive without Sun: Crops without water: But without Raama, there will be no life in my body, never.

❍ ❍ ❍

१४.तदलं त्यज्यतामेष निश्चयः पापनिश्चये ।
अपि ते चरणौ मूर्ध्ना स्पृशाम्येष प्रसीद मे ।।

14. Oh malevolent woman! Enough of this: Give up your design: Shall I touch your feet with my head: Show me mercy:
(Dhascharatha uses the Carrot & Stick technique)

❍ ❍ ❍

१५. किमिदं चिन्तितं पापे त्वया परमदारुणम् ।।

15. Oh Vile Woman! How did you ever conceive such a most cruel (idea) in your mind!

❍ ❍ ❍

१६. अथ जिज्ञाससे मां त्वं भरतस्य प्रियाप्रिये ।
अस्तु यत्तत्त्वया पूर्वं व्याहृतं राघवं प्रति ।।

16. Or perhaps you wish to test me about my love for (our son) Bharatha or about my lack of love towards him! Be that as it may,...Previously what was told by you about (Raama the) Raaghava....(that) ......

❍ ❍ ❍

१७. स मे ज्येष्ठःसुतः श्रीमान् धर्मज्येष्ठ इतीव मे ।
तत्त्वया प्रियवादिन्या सेवार्थं कथितं भवेत् ।।

17. ...."to me, this resplendent (Raama) is (like) my eldest son, who is foremost in Dharma'".. May these (words) uttered by you who spoke so sweetly, be ever cherished (by you) .....

❍ ❍ ❍

१८. तच्छ्रुत्वा शोकसन्तप्ता सन्तापयसि मां भृशम् ।
आविष्टाऽसि गृहं शून्यं सा त्वं परवशं गता ।।

18. ...... (but now) hearing, influenced by others, you have fallen into a pit (of grief and) you are torturing yourself, thus causing me anguish greatly.

❍ ❍ ❍

१९. इक्ष्वाकूणां कुले देवि सम्प्राप्तस्सुमहानयम् ।
अनयो नयसम्पन्ने यत्र ते विकृता मतिः ।।

19. Oh lady (Kaikeyi) who (used to) follow right conduct! If your mind is afflicted (like this), then surely a great calamity awaits (our) Ikshwaaku race.

❍ ❍ ❍

२०. न हि किञ्चिदयुक्तं वा विप्रियं वा पुरा मम ।
अकरोस्त्वं विशालाक्षि तेन न श्रद्दधाम्यहम् ।।

20. Oh (Kaikeyi) with large eyes! Till now you have never done anything that was harmful or displeasing to me: That is why I am unable to believe (all this).

❍ ❍ ❍

२१. ननु ते राघवस्तुल्यो भरतेन महात्मना ।
बहुशो हि स्म बाले त्वं कथाः कथयसे मम ।।

21. Oh childish (Kaikeyi)! You yourself have told me many times that Raama is equal to the great soul Bharatha in (various) matters.

❍ ❍ ❍

२२. तस्य धर्मात्मनो देवि वने वासं यशस्विनः ।
कथं रोचयसे भीरु नव वर्षाणि पञ्च च ।।

22. a Oh timid (Kaikeyi)! Oh Lady! How can you take pleasure in a life in forest for 14 years for this great soul (Raama) the most famous.

❍ ❍ ❍

२३. अत्यर्थं सुकुमारस्य तस्य धर्मे धृतात्मनः ।
कथं रोचयसे वासमरण्ये भृशदारुणे ।।

23. How can you take pleasure in a life in the most cruel forest for this (Raama) who is a (delicate) youth, who is absolutely resolute in (practice of) Dharma.

❍ ❍ ❍

२४. रोचयस्त्यभिरामस्य रामस्य शुभदर्शने ।
तव शुश्रूषमाणस्य किमर्थं विप्रवासनम् ।।

24. Oh woman with pleasing looks! What is the reason that you desire exile for Raama who delights (every one) and who serves you with devotion.

❍ ❍ ❍

२५. रामो हि भरताद्भूयस्तव शुश्रूषते सदा ।
विशेषं त्वयि तस्मात्तु भरतस्य न लक्षये ।।

25. It is Raama who serves you more than (even your own son) Bharatha always: And I have not seen any one dearer to your Bharatha than (Raama).

❍ ❍ ❍

२६. शुश्रूषां गौरवं चैव प्रमाणं वचनक्रियाम् ।
कस्ते भूयस्तरं कुर्यादन्यत्र मनुजर्षभात् ।।

26. Who else other than (Raama) the 'bull' amongst men, will offer better service to you, with veneration and fulfill your command with authority, particularly.

❍ ❍ ❍

२७. बहूनां स्त्रीसहस्राणां बहूनां चोपजीविनाम् ।
परिवादोऽपवादो वा राघवे नोपपद्यते ।।

27. With (Raama) the Raaghva (around), there has never been slander or abuse amongst the thousands of women and many (male & female) servants.

❍ ❍ ❍

२८. सान्त्वयन् सर्वभूतानि रामः शुद्धेन चेतसा ।
गृह्णाति मनुजव्याघ्रः प्रियैर्विषयवासिनः ।।

28. Bringing comfort to all living beings with purity of mind, this 'tiger' amongst men, (Raama) the Raaghava, captivates all inhabitants with love.

❍ ❍ ❍

२९. सत्येन लोकाञ्जयति दीनान्दानेन राघवः ।
गुरुञ्छुश्रूषया वीरो धनुषा युधि शात्रवान् ।।

29. This brave (Raama) the Raaghava subjugates enemies by his bow in war: By devoted service, he wins over elders: By charities (he wins over) the weak (and downtrodden): And the world itself, by Truth.

❍ ❍ ❍

३०. सत्यं दानं तपस्त्यागो मित्रता शोचमार्जवम् ।
विद्या च गुरुशुश्रूषा ध्रुवाण्येतानि राघवे ।।

30. Truth, Charity, Friendship (Loyalty), Sacrifices, Rituals, Integrity, Sincerity, Knowledge, Respect for Elders: ... all these firmly abide in (Raama the) Raaghava.

❍ ❍ ❍

३१. तस्मिन्नार्जवसम्पन्ने देवि देवोपमे कथम् ।
पापमाशंससे रामे महर्षिसमतेजसि ।।

31. Oh lady! How can you censure Raama as sinful when he is endowed with such noble qualities, when he is like a celestial and when his brilliance is like those of great sages.

(Dhascharatha has a point: Only a sinful man devoid of any good qualities is exiled from the kingdom.)

❍ ❍ ❍

३२. न स्मराम्यप्रियं वाक्यं लोकस्य प्रियवादिनः ।
स कथं त्वत्कृते रामं वक्ष्यामि प्रियमप्रियम् ।।

32. Talking sweetly to all in this world (as he ever does) I cannot think of saying anything unpleasant to him... Such as I am, how can I say anything bad to Raama on your account.

❍ ❍ ❍

३३. क्षमा यस्मिंस्तपस्त्यागः सत्यं धर्मः कृतज्ञता ।
अविहिंसा च भूतानां तमृते का गतिर्मम ।।

33. Who else can offer me solace than this (Raama, who is a man of) Truth, in whom is (found qualities of) Dharma, gratitude, sacrifice, non violence to all living beings, and forbearance.

❍ ❍ ❍

३४. मम वृद्धस्य कैकेयि गतान्तस्य तपस्विनः ।
दीनं लालप्यमानस्य कारुण्यं कर्तुमर्हसि ॥

34. Oh Kaikeyi! I am an old man at the fag end of my life, weak, tormented: You should show compassion to me who is in lament.

❍ ❍ ❍

३५. पृथिव्यां सागरान्तायां यत्किञ्चिदधिगम्यते ।
तत्सर्वं तव दास्यामि मा च त्वां मन्युराविशेत् ॥

35. Whatever is obtained in the world surrounded by oceans, all these I will offer you: Let there be not (such a) 'temper' in you.

❍ ❍ ❍

३६. अञ्जलिं कुर्मि कैकेयि पादौ चापि स्पृशामि ते ।
शरणं भव रामस्य माऽधर्मो मामिह स्पृशेत् ॥

36. Oh Kaikeyi! I (beg you) with folded arms in Anjali: May I touch your feet: May you give refuge to Raama: Let not A-Dharma (Immorality) afflict me (Which surely will afflict me if I send innocent Raama to exile.)

❍ ❍ ❍

३७. इति दुःखाभिसन्तप्तं विलपन्तमचेतनम् ।
घूर्णमानं महाराजं शोकेन समभिप्लुतम् ॥

37. Overcome and tormented by sorrow, crying, bewildered (numbed), afflicted by grief, rolling over & over, (Such was the state of this) great king ......

❍ ❍ ❍

३८. पारं शोकार्णवस्याशु प्रार्थयन्तं पुनः पुनः ।
प्रत्युवाचाथ कैकेयी रौद्रा रौद्रतरं वचः ।।

38. ...... who could not see the end of the "shores of the ocean of grief", who was begging her again and again, whom this terrible Kaikeyi addressed in reply, with words that were even more terrible (& cruel to hear).

❍ ❍ ❍

३९. यदि दत्त्वा वरौ राजन् पुनः प्रत्यनुतप्यसे ।
धार्मिकत्वं कथं वीर पृथिव्यां कथयिष्यसि ।।

39. Oh brave, Oh (my) king! Having given me two boons, you are repenting now: As such, how are you going to tell the world about your qualities of Dharma! (You are a cheat, says Kaikeyi)

❍ ❍ ❍

४०. यदा समेता बहवस्त्वया राजर्षयः सह ।
कथयिष्यन्ति धर्मज्ञास्तत्र किं प्रतिवक्ष्यसि ।।

40. When persons most knowledgeable in Dharma who are with you in The Assembly and the royal sages & others talk about this, what answer are you going to give them. (How are you going to justify your turning down the boons you had given me, asks Kaikeyi).

❍ ❍ ❍

४१. यस्याः प्रयत्ने जीवामि या च मामभ्यपालयत् ।
तस्याः कृता मया मिथ्या कैकेय्या इति वक्ष्यसि ।।

41. You will have to tell them: = This Kaikeyi by whose efforts I am alive (today) and who protected me (during the Dheva-Asura war), was deceitfully treated by me =!

❍ ❍ ❍

४२. किल्बिषत्वं नरेन्द्राणां करिष्यसि नराधिप ।
यं दत्त्वा वरमद्यैव पुनरन्यानि भाषसे ।।

42. Oh King! Having offered me boons, now you are talking something else: Are you going to establish (new norms) for kings in (matter of) culpable offense?

❍ ❍ ❍

४३. शैब्यः श्येनकपोतीये स्वमांसं पक्षिणे ददौ ।
अलर्कश्चक्षुषी दत्त्वा जगाम गतिमुत्तमाम् ॥

43. (And Kaikeyi quotes precedents: How great kings behaved.)

(Long ago) King Shibhi offered his own flesh to (Indhra) who had come (as a) bird during a (mock fight) between a dove & a falcon. And royal sage Alarka gave his own eyes away, thus obtaining heaven.

❍ ❍ ❍

४४. सागरः समयं कृत्वा न वेलामतिवर्तते ।
समयं माऽनृतं कार्षीः पूर्ववृत्तमनुस्मरन् ॥

44. The Oceans do not cross over the shores having agreed to a treaty (with Dheva-s, not violating the land): And so, remembering your past conduct, do not make your commitment to me false (now)

(A case of Devil quoting scriptures!)

❍ ❍ ❍

४५. सत्यं धर्मं परित्यज्य रामं राज्येऽभिषिच्य च ।
सह कौसल्यया नित्यं रन्तुमिच्छसि दुर्मते ॥

45. Oh wicked man! Casting aside Truth & Dharma, you wish to enjoy life in the kingdom along with Kowsalya after installing Raama.

❍ ❍ ❍

४६. भवत्वधर्मो धर्मो वा सत्यं वा यदि वाऽनृतम् ।
यत्त्वया संश्रुतं मह्यं तस्य नास्ति व्यतिक्रमः ॥

46. (My demands) may be Dharma or non dharma: Truth or non Truth: (whatever it is) As you have promised

me, there should be no transgression (on your part by denying me now).

❍ ❍ ❍

४७. अहं हि विषमद्यैव पीत्वा बहु तवाग्रत: ।
पश्यतस्ते मरिष्यामि रामो यद्यमिषिच्यते ॥

47. If Raama is crowned, I will at once, before your eyes, drink potent poison and die before you: Surely.

❍ ❍ ❍

४८. एकाहमपि पश्येयं यद्यहं राममातरम् ।
अञ्जलिं प्रतिगृह्णन्तीं श्रेयो ननु मृतिर्मम ॥

48. Death to me is better than to see myself obtaining favours (with hands cupped) in Anjali from Raama's mother, even for a single day.

❍ ❍ ❍

४९. भरतेनात्मना चाहं शपे ते मनुजाधिप ।
यथा नान्येन तुष्येयमृते रामविवासनात् ॥

49. I swear by Bharatha & myself: Oh King! I will not be satisfied with anything else than Raama's exile.

❍ ❍ ❍

५०. एतावदुक्त्वा वचनं कैकेयी विरराम ह ।
विलपन्तं च राजानं न प्रतिव्याजहार सा ॥

50. After telling all these words, Kaikeyi rested (became silent) Ah! And she did not 'comfort' the king who was crying (miserably).

❍ ❍ ❍

५१. श्रुत्वा तु राजा कैकेय्या वृत्तं परमदारुणम् ।
रामस्य च वने वासमैश्वर्यं भरतस्य च ॥

51. Hearing Kaikeyi's cruel demand of forest life for Raama and (kingdom and riches) for Bharatha.... the king .....

❍ ❍ ❍

५२. नाभ्यभाषत कैकेयीं मुहूर्तं व्याकुलेन्द्रियः ।
प्रैक्षतानिमिषो देवीं प्रियामप्रियवादिनीम् ।।

52. ...... lost control of his senses for a muhoortha. Staring at his (once) beloved, at this wife Kaikeyi, without blinking his eyes, he spoke not.

❍ ❍ ❍

५३. तां हि वज्रसमां वाचमाकर्ण्य हृदयाप्रियाम् ।
दु:खशोकमयीं श्रुत्वा राजा न सुखितोऽभवत् ।।

53. Having given his ears to such heart rending words which were like thunderbolts, the king was filled with deep anguish and sorrow; And thinking about (all) this, he could not get any solace.

❍ ❍ ❍

५४. स देव्या व्यवसायं च घोरं च शपथं कृतम् ।
ध्यात्वा रामेति निश्वस्य छिन्नस्तरुरिवापतत् ।।

54. Pondering over his wife's determination, (and pondering over the) way she swore gruesomely, he fell down like a tree felled, exclaiming = Oh Raama! =

❍ ❍ ❍

५५. नष्टचित्तो यथोन्मत्तो विपरीतो यथाऽऽतुरः ।
हृततेजा यथा सर्पो बभूव जगतीपतिः ।।

55. And (Dhascharatha) the lord of earth, was like an insane man; like a perverse man having lost control of his senses, like an afflicted (sick) man, like a cobra whose power (teeth) had been taken away.

❍ ❍ ❍

५६. दीनया तु गिरा राजा इति होवाच कैकयीम् ।।

56. The King addressed Kaikeyi in a feeble voice (once again).

❍ ❍ ❍

५७. अनर्थमिममर्थाभं केन त्वमुपदर्शिता ।
भूतोपहतचित्तेव ब्रुवन्ती त्वं न लज्जसे ॥

57. By whom have you been advised this which is harmful, although appearing as good (to you and all); You are not ashamed to speak like one whose mind is seized by a ghost.

❍ ❍ ❍

५८. शीलव्यसनमेतत्ते नाभिजानाम्यहं पुरा ।
बालायास्तत्त्विदानीं ते लक्षये विपरीतवत् ॥

58. I had not known (or seen) such deficiencies before in your moral conduct from your childhood days: I see now a different character in you.

❍ ❍ ❍

५९. कुतो वा ते भयं जातं या त्वमेवंविधं वरम् ।
राष्ट्रे भरतमासीनं वृणीषे राघवं वने ॥

59. I know not why there is fear in you that you should ask for such a boon to send away (Raama the) Raaghava to forest and keep Bharatha in the kingdom.

❍ ❍ ❍

६०. विरमैतेन भावेन त्वमेतेनानृतेन वा ।
यदि भर्तुः प्रियं कार्यं लोकस्य भरतस्य च ॥

60. If you (really) care to do good to your husband, to (your son) Bharatha and to the world, you must abandon this deceitful (demand) and this attitude.

❍ ❍ ❍

६१. नृशंसे पापसङ्कल्पे क्षुद्रे दुष्कृतकारिणि ।
किं नु दुःखमलीकं वा मयि रामे च पश्यसि ॥

61. Yet, Oh evil monger! You vile woman! Oh (Kaikeyi) who is determined to do evil! Oh mischievous woman! What is it that you see so disagreeable or painful in me or Raama.

❍ ❍ ❍

६२. न कथंचिदृते रामाद्भरतो राज्यमावसेत् ।
रामादपि हि तं मन्ये धर्मतो बलवत्तरम् ।।

62. (And remember, your son) Bharatha will never live in the kingdom even for a moment without Raama: Because, I consider him even firmer than Raama in practice of Dharma.

❍ ❍ ❍

६३. कथं द्रक्ष्यामि रामस्य वनं गच्छेति भाषिते ।
मुखवर्णं विवर्णं तं यथैवेन्दुमुपप्लुतम् ।।

63. How can I (face) and see Raama's lustrous face changing colour like the moon afflicted by Raahu, the moment I say =Go To Forest.=

❍ ❍ ❍

६४. तां हि मे सुकृतां बुद्धिं सुहृद्भिः सह निश्चिताम् ।
कथं द्रक्ष्याम्यपावृत्तां परैरिव हतां चमूम् ।।

64. How can I see the decision of mine well taken after being decided along with my friends, go topsy turvy, like an army being (allowed to be) annihilated by enemies.

❍ ❍ ❍

६५. किं मां वक्ष्यन्ति राजानो नानादिग्भ्यः समागताः ।
बालो बतायमैक्ष्वाकश्चिरं राज्यमाकारयत् ।।

65. The kings who have gathered here from all parts (of the world) will taunt me thus:= How come this childish Ikshwaaku (King Dhascharatha) has been able to rule this kingdom for such a long time.=

❍ ❍ ❍

६६. यदा तु बहवो वृद्धा गुणवन्तो बहुश्रुताः ।
परिप्रक्ष्यन्ति काकुत्स्थं वक्ष्यामि किमहं तदा ।।

66. What can I tell when the great elders who are endowed with good qualities and who are well versed

(in shaasthra-s) start enquiring about (Raama) the Kaakuthsa.

❍ ❍ ❍

६७. कैकेय्या क्लिश्यमानेन रामः प्रव्राजितो मया ।
यदि सत्यं ब्रवीम्येतत्तदसत्यं भविष्यति ॥

67. When I tell them this Truth that Raama was sent away by me being tormented by (& under pressure from you) Kaikeyi, this (will make me a man of) Untruth.

❍ ❍ ❍

६८. किं मां वक्ष्यति कौसल्या राघवे वनमास्थिते ।
किं चैनां प्रतिवक्ष्यामि कृत्वा विप्रियमीदृशम् ॥

68. And when Raama goes to forest, what will Kowsalya tell (of me): What sort of reply (or consolation) can I offer her after doing such a perverse deed (of exile upon sinless Raama).

❍ ❍ ❍

६९. यदा यदा हि कौसल्या दासीवच्च सखीव च ।
भार्यावद्भगिनीवच्च मातृवच्चोपतिष्ठति ॥

69. And Kowsalya has been (and has served me) at various times like a servant, like a companion, like a mother, a wife, and like a sister.

(Readers may note: This is the ideal of an Indian wife)

❍ ❍ ❍

७०. सततं प्रियकामा मे प्रियपुत्रा प्रियंवदा ।
न मया सत्कृता देवी सत्कारार्हा कृते तव ॥

70. Well disposed towards me, who ever spoke sweetly to me, this lady (Kowsalya) who is endowed with a loving son, has never been shown any consideration by me all on your account, although she deserved honour and consideration (from me).

(It is well known that Dhascharatha spent most of his time with Kaikeyi who was his favourite wife)

❍ ❍ ❍

७१. इदानीं तत्तपति मां यन्मया सुकृतं त्वयि ।
अपथ्यव्यञ्जनोपेतं भुक्तमन्नमिवातुरम् ।।

71. What love I had for you, that is now tormenting me (hurting me): Just like the food which is unfit & unwholesome, eaten by a sick man.

❍ ❍ ❍

७२. विप्रकारं च रामस्य संप्रयाणं वनस्य च ।
सुमित्रा प्रेक्ष्य वै भीता कथं मे विश्वसिष्यति ।।

72. How will Sumithra have any confidence in me as she would be terribly frightened when she sees the injury caused to Raama by his departure to forest.

❍ ❍ ❍

७३. कृपणं बत वैदेही श्रोष्यति द्वयमप्रियम् ।
मां च पञ्चत्वमापन्नं रामं च वनमाश्रितम् ।।

73. And (Seetha) the Vaidhehi will witness two bad (events): Raama living in forest and (consequently) me obtaining death. Alas! What a pity! (Dhascharatha is sure he will die if Raama is away in forest).

❍ ❍ ❍

७४. वैदेही बत मे प्राणाञ्छोचन्ती क्षपयिष्यति ।
हीना हिमवतः पार्श्वे किन्नरेणेव किन्नरी ।।

74. Fie on me! Like (a female) Kinnara bird abandoned by (male) Kinnara bird in the slopes of Himaalayas, (Seetha the) Vaidhehi will give up her life in grief.

❍ ❍ ❍

७५. न हि राममहं दृष्ट्वा प्रवसन्तं महावने ।
चिरं जीवितुमाशंसे रुदन्तीं चापि मैथिलीम् ।।

75. I do not desire to live then after; after seeing Raama departing to the forest and (Seetha the) Maithili crying (for Raama).

❍ ❍ ❍

७६. सा नूनं विधवा राज्यं सपुत्रा कारयिष्यसि ।
रामे प्रव्राजिते देवि नाहं जीवितुमुत्सहे ॥

76. I cannot bear to live on if Raama goes: Oh lady (Kaikeyi)! You may rule the kingdom as a widow, along with your son.

❍ ❍ ❍

७७. सतीं त्वामहमत्यन्तं व्यवस्याम्यसतीं सतीम् ।
रूपिणीं विषसंयुक्तां पीत्वेव मदिरां नरः ॥

77. Like a man drinking (nectar like) juice, (but realising later), that it is mixed with poison, I now realise that you are a contemptible woman (in the garb) of an exceedingly virtous woman of beauty.

❍ ❍ ❍

७८. अनृतैर्बत मां सान्त्वैः सान्त्वयन्ती स्म भाषसे ।
गीतशब्देन संरुद्ध्य लुब्धो मृगमिवावधीः ॥

78. (All along) You used to speak sweet words of deceit as though you were bringing comfort to me: Like a hunter capturing a deer with sweet sound (of flute or whistle), you have killed me. Ah!

❍ ❍ ❍

७९. अनार्य इति मामार्याः पुत्रविक्रायिकं ध्रुवम् ।
धिक्करिष्यन्ति रथ्यासु सुरापं ब्राह्मणं यथा ॥

79. The noble men will surely reproach me, calling me an Un-Aryan when I barter away my son, just as they (reproach) a drunken braamin in the street.

८०. अहो दु:खमहो कृच्छ्रं यत्र वाच: क्षमे तव ।
दु:खमेवंविधं प्राप्तं पुराकृतमिवाशुभम् ।।

80. Oh, What a suffering! What a misfortune! I have to bear (listening to) your words: This suffering has come by me now because of such shameful deeds done in my previous birth Ah.

(Indians believe in birth & rebirth.: Sins of previous birth follow you)

❍ ❍ ❍

८१. चिरं खलु मया पापे त्वं पापेनाभिरक्षिता ।
अज्ञानाद्धुपसंपन्ना रज्जुरुद्बन्धिनी यथा ।।

81. Oh wicked (Kaikeyi)! Out of my past sins and out of my ignorance, you were protected (and honoured) by me for so long: (But I did not realise) you had come to me like a hangman's rope.

❍ ❍ ❍

८२. रममाणस्त्वया सार्धं मृत्युं त्वां नाभिलक्षये ।
बालो रहसि हस्तेन कृष्णसर्पमिवास्पृशम् ।।

82. Enjoying pleasures with you, I did not realise that you are (verily my) death! Like a child touching a black Viper with its hands when no one is around, I embraced you (all these years).

❍ ❍ ❍

८३. तं तु मां जीवलोकोऽय नूनमाक्रोष्टुमर्हति ।
मया ह्यपितृक: पुत्र: स महात्मा दुरात्मना ।।

८४. बालिशो बत कामात्मा राजा दशरथो भृशम् ।
स्त्रीकृते य: प्रियं पुत्रं वनं प्रस्थापयिष्यति ।।

83 & 84.

Surely, I will stand condemned by all in the world that this great soul son (Raama) was made 'fatherless' by me, an evil minded man.... (and they will say)... This king Dhascharatha who has sent away his beloved son to forest on account of a woman, is a big fool. A man of lust. Ah !

❍ ❍ ❍

८५. व्रतैश्च ब्रह्मचर्यैश्च गुरुभिश्चोपकर्शितः ।
भोगकाले महत्कृच्छ्रं पुनरेव प्रपत्स्यते ॥

85. By (the services to) teachers, by rigorous studies (as a Brammachari), by his vows and abstinence, he has (upto now) suffered (only) hardships. And now, at a time of enjoyment (& marital pleasures), he is going to face great suffering.

❍ ❍ ❍

८६. नालं द्वितीयं वचनं पुत्रो मां प्रतिभाषितुम् ।
स वनं प्रव्रजेत्युक्तो बाढमित्येव वक्ष्यति ॥

86. And this son (Raama) when told = Go to forest =, will look at me and say; =So Be It= : He will never say any other word.

❍ ❍ ❍

८७. यदि मे राघवः कुर्याद्वनं गच्छेति चोदितः ।
प्रतिकूलं प्रियं मे स्यान्न तु वत्सः करिष्यति ॥

87. If (Raama the) Raaghava (hearing) my command = Go to forest= does the opposite (and refuses to go), this will indeed be pleasing to me. Yet my son will not do this (will never disobey me).

(Dhascharatha will indeed be very happy if Raama refuses to go. this is one occasion when Dhascharatha wants Raama to disobey him!)

❍ ❍ ❍

८८. शुद्धभावो हि भावं मे न तु ज्ञास्यति राघवः ।
स वनं प्रव्रजेत्युक्तो बाढमित्येव वक्ष्यति ॥

88. And (Raama the) Raaghava is pure minded; therefore

he will not know my (true) mind: And my son when told = Go to forest = , he will (only) say:= 'Baadam' (So Be It).=

❍ ❍ ❍

८९. राघवे हि वनं प्राप्ते सर्वलोकस्य धिक्कृतम् ।
मृत्युरक्षमणीयं मां नयिष्यति यमक्षयम् ।।

89. When (Raama the) Raaghava goes to forest, the Lord of Death will take me, who incurs the condemnation of all the world and who can never be pardoned, to the world of the dead.

❍ ❍ ❍

९० मृते मयि गते रामे वनं मनुजपुङ्गवे ।
इष्टे मम जने शेषे किं पापं प्रतिपत्स्यसे ।।

90. After (Raama the) 'tiger' of men goes to forest and after I am also dead, what all evil (sins) are you going to inflict on my dear citizens and others.

❍ ❍ ❍

९१. कौसल्यां मां च रामं च पुत्रौ च यदि हास्यति ।
दुःखान्यसहती देवी मामेवानुमरिष्यति ।।

91. Abandoned by me and Raama and unable to bear the suffering caused to Kowsalya and the two sons (Lakshmana & Schathrugna), lady (Sumithra) will follow me in death.

❍ ❍ ❍

९२. कौसल्यां च सुमित्रां च मां च पुत्रैस्त्रिभिः सह ।
प्रक्षिप्य नरके सा त्वं कैकेयि सुखिता भव ।।

92. Oh Kaikeyi! After casting me away now along with Kowsalya, Sumithra and the three sons in Naraka (place of suffering), you may enjoy life.

❍ ❍ ❍

९३. मया रामेण च त्यक्तं शाश्वतं सत्कृतं गुणैः ।
इक्ष्वाकुकुलमक्षोभ्यमाकुलं पालयिष्यसि ॥

93. In utter chaos (& confusion) you will rule this eternal and unshakeable kingdom of Ikshwaaku that was (hitherto) ruled by me (honoured by me) with qualities (of political norms & justice), and (now) abandoned by Raama also.

❍ ❍ ❍

९४. प्रियं चेद्भरतस्यैतद्रामप्रव्राजनं भवेत् ।
मा स्म मे भरतः कार्षित्प्रेतकृत्यं गतायुषः ॥

94. If Raama's exile pleases Bharatha (also), when I die, Bharatha should not do my Last Rites.

(It is duty & honour for son to do father's Last Rites: But Dhascharatha curses Bharatha thus: He disowns Bharatha)

❍ ❍ ❍

९५. हन्ताऽनार्ये ममामित्रे सकामा भव कैकयि ।
मृते मयि गते रामे वनं पुरुषपुङ्गवे ॥

95. Oh Un-Aryan (Ignoble Lady) Kaikeyi! Oh my enemy! After Raama goes to forest, and I am dead, live on, with pleasure! Fie!

❍ ❍ ❍

९६. सेदानीं विधवा राज्यं सपुत्रा कारयिष्यसि ॥

96. As a widow you will rule the kingdom along with your son.

❍ ❍ ❍

९७. त्वं राजपुत्रीवादेन न्यवसेर्मम वेश्मनि ।
अकीर्तिश्चातुला लोके ध्रुवः परिभवश्च मे ॥
सर्वभूतेषु चावज्ञा यथा पापकृतस्तथा ॥

97. As a most disgraceful person in the world, despised by all living beings, you came to live with me, a sinner, in

my palace, in the garb of a princess, to cause me eternal humiliation.

❍ ❍ ❍

९८. कथं रथैर्विभुर्यात्वा गजाश्वैश्च मुहुर्मुहुः ।
पद्भ्यां रामो महारण्ये वत्सो मे विचरिष्यति ॥

98. How can my son Raama who till now, has always ridden gloriously in chariots, horses, elephants, now walk on his feet in great forests.

❍ ❍ ❍

९९. यस्य त्वाहारसमये सूदाः कुण्डलधारिणः ।
अहंपूर्वाः पचन्ति स्म प्रशस्तं पानभोजनम् ॥

99. During meal time, the (Royal) cooks wearing ear rings, cook excellent food & drinks for Raama, (saying)= I Am First =(to serve him); (Cooks will say, I am the best. so will serve Raama first): ......

❍ ❍ ❍

१००. स कथं नु कषायाणि तिक्तानि कटुकानि च ।
भक्षयन्वन्यमाहारं सुतो मे वर्तयिष्यति ॥

100. ...... (When that is so) How can my son live, eating forest food of (tubers & roots) which are bitter, pungent and astringent.

❍ ❍ ❍

१०१. महार्हवस्त्रसंवीतो भूत्वा चिरसुखोषितः ।
काषायपरिधानस्तु कथं भूमौ निवत्स्यति ॥

101. Having worn costly (quality) garments and having lived in comfort for so long, how can he live on earth in a mendicant's garb.

❍ ❍ ❍

१०२. कस्यैतद्दारुणं वाक्यमेवंविधमचिन्तितम् ।
रामस्यारण्यगमनं भरतस्याभिषेचनम् ॥

102. Bharatha's coronation, let it be! But whose words (of advice) was this exile for Raama, most cruel, unimaginable (punishment).

❍ ❍ ❍

१०३. धिगस्तु योषितो नाम शठाः स्वार्थपरायणाः ।
न ब्रवीमि स्त्रियः सर्वा भरतस्यैव मातरम् ।।

103. (It is said) Young women are flippant, deceitful, self seekers; (But it is) wrong to condemn all women. I will say this only of (you, Kaikeyi) the mother of Bharatha.

❍ ❍ ❍

१०४. अनर्थभावेऽर्थपरे नृशंसे
ममानुतापाय निविष्टभावे ।
किमप्रियं पश्यसि मन्निमित्तं
हितानुकारिण्यथवापि रामे ।।

104. Oh worthless woman! Oh avaricious woman! Oh mischievous woman! Oh woman bent on bringing misery to me! (Tell me)! What wrong do you see in me or in Raama who ever do good (to all).

❍ ❍ ❍

१०५. परित्यजेयुः पितरो हि पुत्रान्
भार्याः पतींश्चापि कृतानुरागाः ।
कृत्स्नं हि सर्वं कुपितं जगत्स्यात्
दृष्ट्वैव रामं व्यसने निमग्नम् ।।

105. When they see Raama plunged in suffering, (when they see him going away), the fathers who are deeply attached (to their own sons) will abandon their sons, wives: And wives will abandon their husbands. Surely. All the beings in the entire world will become agitated. (Citizens will leave with Raama to forest, he tells her)

❍ ❍ ❍

१०६.अहं पुनर्देवकुमाररूपं अलंकृतं तं सुतमाव्रजन्तम् ।
नन्दामि पश्यन्नपि दर्शनेन भवामि दृष्ट्वा च पुनर्युवेव ।।

106. When I think of how my son came into my "possession", well (endowed with), decorated, and in the form like a celestial, I rejoice. The moment I see him, I become a young man!

❍ ❍ ❍

१०७.विना हि सूर्येण भवेत्प्रवृत्तिः अवर्षता वज्रधरेण वापि ।
रामं तु गच्छन्तमितः समीक्ष्य जीवेन्न कश्चित्त्विति चेतनामे ।।

107. Active life, may exist even without Sun: Or even if rain does not fall (by grace of) Indhra: But when it is known that Raama has gone away from here, no man will survive (and live on). This is known to me. (By this Dhascharatha says no citizen will have desire to live without Raama).

❍ ❍ ❍

१०८.विनाशकामामहितामिमित्रां आवासयं मृत्युमिवात्मनस्त्वाम् ।
चिरं बताङ्केन धृता हि सर्पी महाविषा तेन हतोऽस्मि मोहात् ।।

108. Out of my passion, you, who are (verily) a most poisonous snake, was supported by me with my body for so long: Oh! I lived with a woman who is my death, my vile enemy who desired my ruin. Ah! Therefore I am ruined (now).

❍ ❍ ❍

१०९.मया तु रामेण सलक्ष्मणेन प्रशास्तु हीनो भरतस्सह त्वया ।
पुरं च राष्ट्रं च निहत्य बान्धवान् ममाहितानां च
भवाभिहर्षिणी ।।

109. Abandoned by me, Raama and Lakshmana, let Bharatha rule this city and kingdom along with you after killing my folks (relatives & friends): Live on, you who gladden my enemies.

❍ ❍ ❍

११०.नृशंसवृत्ते व्यसनप्रहारिणि प्रसह्य वाक्यं यदिहाद्य भाषसे ।
न नाम ते केन मुखात्पतन्त्यधो विशीर्यमाणा दशनाः
सहस्रधा ।।

110. Oh (Kaikeyi) who inflicts pain! Oh mischievous woman! You have uttered such unbearable words, (I am surprised) as to why your teeth has not fallen out of your mouth, broken into thousand pieces.

❍ ❍ ❍

१११.न किञ्चिदाहाहितमप्रियं वचो न वेत्ति रामः परुषाणि भाषितुम् ।
कथं नु रामे ह्यभिरामवादिनि ब्रवीषि दोषान् गुणनित्यसंमते ।।

111. Raama has never uttered a word that is harmful or unpleasant: He does not know how to speak harshly; his talk is very delightful; How can you talk about danger from Raama when he is esteemed for his foremost qualities?

❍ ❍ ❍

११२.प्रताम्य वा प्रज्वल वा प्रणश्य वा
सहस्रशो वा स्फुटिता महीं व्रज ।
न ते करिष्यामि वचः सुदारुणं
ममाहितं केकयराजपांसनि ।।

112. Torment yourself (as much as you like): Burn yourself: Perish: Be cut up into thousand parts: Lie on floor: Oh (Kaikeyi) the wicked woman from Kekeya kingdom: I Will Not Fulfill Your Wishes Which Is Cruel and Harmful To Me.

❍ ❍ ❍

११३.क्षुरोपमां नित्यमसत्प्रियंवदां
प्रदुष्टभावां स्वकुलोपघातिनीम् ।
न जीवतीं त्वां विषहेऽमनोरमां
दिधक्षमाणां हृदयं सबन्धनम् ।।

113. You always speak false (though) sweetly; You are a woman of mischievous conduct. A destroyer of my

family; Like an arrow you (pierced and) burnt away my life entrenched in my heart: Oh disgusting woman! I will not bear to see you alive.

❍ ❍ ❍

११४. न जीवितं मेऽस्ति कुतः पुनःसुखं
विनात्मजेनात्मवतः कुतो रतिः ।
ममाहितं देवि न कर्तुमर्हसि
स्पृशामि पादावपि ते प्रसीद मे ।।

114. Where is happiness for me without my son:? From whom pleasures for me? My life wont last: Oh Lady (Kaikeyi)! Dont ask from me, a prudent man, that, which is most harmful. (I beg and) Touch your feet. Have mercy on me.

❍ ❍ ❍

११५. स भूमिपालो विलपन्ननाथवत्
स्त्रिया गृहीतो हृदयेऽतिमात्रया ।
पपात देव्याश्चरणौ प्रसारिता
वुभावसंस्पृश्य यथाऽऽतुरस्तथा ।।

115. Helpless, his wife (Kaikeyi) having gone beyond all limits (of Norms), (Fear) seizing his heart, sick of mind and body, this king (Dhascharatha) who was crying, fell down without being able to touch his wife's outstretched feet.

(Note: Dhascharatha begs her, coaxes, abuses & curses her. All his arguments fail. Kaikeyi is adamant as we shall see in next chapter. Raama must go on exile and her son Bharatha must be crowned instead.)

❍ ❍ ❍

Chapter 13

(Dhascharatha) Again Tries to Pacify Kaikeyi

(Dhascharatha again tries to change Kaikeyi's mind; but she is firm: Her son Bharatha must be crowned and Raama must go on exile.)

❍ ❍ ❍

१. अतदर्हं महाराजं शयानमतथोचितम् ।
ययातिमिव पुण्यान्ते देवलोकात्परिच्युतम् ।।

1. Like (king) Yayaathi who was thrown out of heaven when he had exhausted the 'fruits' of his meritorious deeds, this king who was not used to (such treatment and) who did not deserve (such treatment), lay on the floor .....

❍ ❍ ❍

२. अनर्थरूपाऽसिद्धार्था ह्यभीता भयदर्शिनी ।
पुनराकारयामास तमेव वरमङ्गना ।।

2. ..... This worthless woman (Kaikeyi) who never did anything good, who was immodest, who was fearsome, once again began (to 'work' upon) this foremost (King Dhascharatha) and said:

   (Referene is to king Yayaathi: Hindoos believe that good done in the world will bring happiness in the other world. But it is like Bank account! You cannot get overdrafts after our credit runs out. We have to come again to the world to 'accumulate' credits !)

❍ ❍ ❍

३. त्वं कथ्यसे महाराज सत्यवादी दृढव्रतः ।
मम चेमं वरं कस्माद्विधारयितुमिच्छसि ।।

3. Oh great King (Dhascharatha)! You are spoken of as a man who speaks truth, resolute in vows and Dharma. Yet how is it you desire now to withhold the boon (you had offered to) me.

❍ ❍ ❍

४. एवमुक्तस्तु कैकेय्या राजा दशरथस्तदा ।
प्रत्युवाच ततः क्रुद्धो मुहूर्तं विह्वलन्निव ॥

4. When told thus by Kaikeyi, king Dhascharatha trembled for a while, then replied in anger (provoked by her again).

❍ ❍ ❍

४. मृते मयि गते रामे वनं मनुजपुङ्गवे ।
हन्तानार्येममामित्रे सकामा सुखिनी भव ॥

4. Oh un-Aryan (Ignoble Kaikeyi)! Oh my enemy! After sending away Raama to forest and I am dead, you may live-in comfort having obtained your wish.

❍ ❍ ❍

६. स्वर्गेऽपि खलु रामस्य कुशलं देवतैरहम् ।
प्रत्यादेशादभिहितं धारयिष्ये कथं बत ॥

6. Even in heaven, when I am asked at the 'command' of Dheva-s about the welfare of Raama, how can I bear (to tell them): Ah! Fie!

❍ ❍ ❍

७. कैकेय्याः प्रियकामेन रामः प्रव्राजितो वनम् ।
यदि सत्यं ब्रवीम्येतत्तदसत्यं भविष्यति ॥

7. If I tell that Raama was sent to forest by me desirous as I was to be truthful to Kaikeyi (to honour my boon to her), then, (it would mean) that (what I told the Assembly that Raama will be crowned), will turn out to be falsehood (spoken by me)

❍ ❍ ❍

८. अपुत्रेण मया पुत्रः श्रमेण महता महान् ।
रामो लब्धो महाबाहुः स कथं त्यज्यते मया ॥

8. The great mighty limbed Raama was 'obtained' by me who was childless (for a very long time), as a son, through great effort (of a mighty Yaaga): How can I forsake him.

❍ ❍ ❍

९. शूरश्च कृतविद्यश्च जितक्रोधः क्षमापरः ।
कथं कमलपत्राक्षो मया रामो विवास्यते ॥

9. His eyes are like lotus petals; he has studied various disciplines; he is brave, yet has conquered anger; he is very patient and forgiving. How can I send Raama away.

❍ ❍ ❍

१०. कथमिन्दीवरश्यामं दीर्घबाहुं महाबलम् ।
अभिराममहं रामं प्रेषयिष्यामि दण्डकान् ॥

10. His complexion is like that of blue lotus: Has long hands: Mightily strong; very handsome; How can I send Raama to Dhandaka forest.

❍ ❍ ❍

११. सुखानामुचितस्यैव दुःखैरनुचितस्य च ।
दुःखं नामानुपश्येयं कथं रामस्य धीमतः ॥

11. How can I 'see' the suffering for this wise Raama who is never used to suffering but deserves only comforts.

❍ ❍ ❍

१२. यदि दुःखमकृत्वाऽद्य मम संक्रमणं भवेत् ।
अदुःखार्हस्य रामस्य ततः सुखमवाप्नुयाम् ॥

12. I will indeed obtain (great) happiness if death comes to me now before.I do such a harm to Raama who does not deseve suffering.

❍ ❍ ❍

१३. नृशंसे पापसङ्कल्पे रामं सत्यपराक्रमम् ।
किं विप्रियेण कैकेयि प्रियं योजयसे मम ॥

13. Oh cruel Kaikeyi who is determined to do evil ! Why are you 'Yoking' my beloved and truly valiant Raama with unpleasantness (and suffering).

❍ ❍ ❍

१४. अकीर्तिरतुला लोके ध्रुवः परिभवश्च मे ॥

14. There will (surely be) great ill fame and disgrace for me in the world eternally (if I banish the sinless Raama).

❍ ❍ ❍

१५. तथा विलपतस्तस्य परिभ्रमितचेतसः ।
अस्तमभ्यागमत्सूर्योरजनी चाभ्यवर्तत ॥

15. Thus, as he was wailing with a disturbed mind, the Sun obtained sunset and night fell.

❍ ❍ ❍

१६. साऽत्रियामा तथार्तस्य चन्द्रमण्डलमण्डिता ।
राज्ञो विलपमानस्य न व्यभासत शर्वरी ॥

16. (but) To the king who was wailing struck by this calamity, the long night (of many 'Yaama-s) which was shining by the halo of moonlight, did not illuminate him.

❍ ❍ ❍

१७. तथैवोष्णं विनिश्वस्य वृद्धो दशरथो नृपः ।
विललापार्तवद्दुःखं गगनासक्तलोचनः ॥

17. Suffering (greatly) and emitting hot breath (breathing hard & deep), the old king Dhascharatha wailed thus in sorrow as his eyes were drawn towards the sky.

❍ ❍ ❍

१८. न प्रभातं तवेच्छामि निशे नक्षत्रभूषणे ।
क्रियतां मे दया भद्रे मयाऽयं रचितोऽञ्जलिः ॥

18. Oh star studded night! I do not desire day break. Oh gracious (Night)! This prayer is done by me; may you show me compassion.

❍ ❍ ❍

१९. अथवा गम्यतां शीघ्रं नाहमिच्छामि निर्घृणाम् ।
नृशंसां कैकयीं द्रष्टुं यत्कृते व्यसनं महत् ॥

19. If not, pass away quickly: I do not desire to see this obnoxious and contemptible woman Kaikeyi by whom this great suffering was caused.

❍ ❍ ❍

२०. एवमुक्त्वा ततो राजा कैकेयीं संयताञ्जलिः ।
प्रसादयामास पुनः कैकेयीं चेदमब्रवीत् ।।

20. After saying thus, the king once again began to seek the favour of Kaikeyi with his hands cupped in Anjali: He said this to Kaikeyi:

❍ ❍ ❍

२१. साधुवृत्तस्य दीनस्य त्वद्गतस्य गतायुषः ।
प्रसादः क्रियतां देवि भद्रे राज्ञो विशेषतः ।।

21. Oh gracious lady! May you show mercy (& consideration) to an honest king who is very old, who is downtrodden, who particularly seeks refuge under you (for favour).

❍ ❍ ❍

२२. शून्ये न खलु सुश्रोणि मयेदं समुदाहृतम् ।
कुरु साधु प्रसादं मे बाले सहृदया ह्यसि ।।

22. Oh child! (Oh Kaikeyi) with good hips! That this (boon) is null & void, has not been uttered by me. Yet, as you would favour me with your grace, you should do (what I want), because you are kind hearted.

❍ ❍ ❍

२३. प्रसीद देवि रामो मे त्वद्दत्तं राज्यमव्ययम् ।
लभतामसितापाङ्गे यशः परमवाप्नुहि ।।

23. Oh lady whose mind is (somewhat) contaminated! Show me mercy. Let Raama obtain the kingdom (as though) offered by you: You will obtain foremost eternal fame.

❍ ❍ ❍

२४. मम रामस्य लोकस्य गुरूणां भरतस्य च ।
प्रियमेतद्गुरुश्रोणि कुरु चारुमुखेक्षणे ।।

24. Oh (Kaikeyi) with pleasant face! Oh one who is endowed with glorious figure! You must do what is good for me, for Bharatha, for elders, for Raama and (indeed) for the world.

❍ ❍ ❍

२५. विशुद्धभावस्य हि दुष्टभावा
ताम्रेक्षणस्याश्रुकलस्य राज्ञः ।
श्रुत्वा विचित्रं करुणं विलापं
भर्तुर्नृशंसा न चकार वाक्यम् ।।

25. (In spite of) hearing the pitiable entreaties from her pure minded husband king (Dhascharatha), whose eyes were red with copious tears, (spoken) in diverse (ways).... this obnoxious and evil minded (Kaikeyi) did not speak any word.

❍ ❍ ❍

२६. ततः स राजा पुनरेव मूर्च्छितः
प्रियामदुष्टां प्रतिकूलभाषिणीम् ।
समीक्ष्य पुत्रस्य विवासनं प्रति
क्षितौ विसंज्ञो निपपात दुःखितः ।।

26. Then when the king observed that his (once) loving and good (wife Kaikeyi) was 'speaking 'against (his wishes) in sending his son (Raama) away to forest, he became very sad: He swooned and fell down on earth unconscious.

❍ ❍ ❍

२७. इतीव राज्ञो व्यथितस्य सा निशा
जगाम घोरं श्वसतो मनस्विनः ।
विबोध्यमानः प्रतिबोधनं तदा
निवारयामास स राजसत्तमः ।।

27. To this king who was (a man of intelligence and) who was of resolute mind, who was breathing hard & deep due to terrible agitation, the night passed away gruesomely. This foremost king restrained the felicitations that were (customarily) being offered to him by (early morning callers) who awaken (the king as per protocol).

❍ ❍ ❍

Chapter 14

(Kaikeyi) Sends for Sumanthra to Fetch Raama

(Kaikeyi is firm: Raama must go & her son Bharatha must rule. She will not give up the boons and she exercises her options only this way, no other way. On her own, she asks Sumanthra to fetch Raama.)

❍ ❍ ❍

१. पुत्रशोकार्दितं पापा विसंज्ञं पतितं भुवि ।
विवेष्टमानमुद्वीक्ष्य सैक्ष्वाकमिदमब्रवीत् ।।

1. The sinful (Kaikeyi), after some deliberation, addressed the Ikshwaaku king (Dhascharatha) who was ying down on floor, crumpled (crouched), senseless, tormented by grief due to (impending suffering for) his son (Raama).

❍ ❍ ❍

२. पापं कृत्वैव किमिदं मम संश्रुत्य संश्रवम् ।
शेषे क्षितितले सन्नः स्थित्यां स्थातुं त्वमर्हसि ।।

2. Having promised to keep your promise, why are you lying down on the floor totally immobile as if you have sinned. What is this! You should be firm in virtous conduct.

❍ ❍ ❍

३. आहुः सत्यं हि परमं धर्मं धर्मविदो जनाः ।
सत्यमाश्रित्य हि मया त्वं च धर्मे प्रचोदितः ।।

3. (Wise) Men knowing Dharma say there is no greater Dharma than Truth. (and so) You are (merely) being asked (& goaded) to uphold Truth by me.

❍ ❍ ❍

४. संश्रुत्य शैब्यः श्येनाय स्वां तनुं जगतीपतिः ।
प्रदाय पक्षिणे राजा जगाम गतिमुत्तमाम् ॥

4. (Kaikeyi repeats same old stories: Precedents: A case of devil quoting scriptures.)

The lord of earth, King Shibhi, gave (flesh) from his own body to Syena bird as per his promise and obtained foremost state of heaven.

❍ ❍ ❍

५. तथा ह्यलर्कस्तेजस्वी ब्राह्मणे वेदपारगे ।
याच्यमानः स्वके नेत्रे उद्धृत्याविमना ददौ ॥

5. Likewise, the brilliant Alarka plucked his own eyes without any (second) thought and offered to a Braamin well versed in Vedha-s when he was begged by him.

❍ ❍ ❍

६. सरितां तु पतिः स्वल्पां मर्यादां सत्यमन्वितः ।
सत्यानुरोधात्समये वेलां स्वां नातिवर्तते ॥

6. (Even) the lord of rivers, (the ocean), following Truth and bound by dictates of Truth, never crosses the coast line even during season, (the coast line that is) its limit.

❍ ❍ ❍

७. सत्यमेकपदं ब्रह्म सत्ये धर्मः प्रतिष्ठितः ।
सत्यमेवाक्षया वेदाः सत्येनावाप्यते परम् ॥

7. Truth is one letter word for the divine Brammam: Dharma rests on Truth: And Truth is eternal Dharma. And only through Truth, you can achieve eternal salvation.

❍ ❍ ❍

८. सत्यं समनुवर्तस्व यदि धर्मे धृता मतिः ।
स वरः सफलो मेऽस्तु वरदो ह्यसि सत्तम ।।

8. Oh virtous (King)! You are (committed to me as) giver of boon: If your mind is firm in Dharma, you must comply and follow Truth. (Therefore) May the boons (you had offered) become fruitful to me.

❍ ❍ ❍

९. स्वधर्मस्याभिकामार्थं मम चैवाभिचोदनात् ।
प्रव्राजय सुतं रामं त्रिः खलु त्वां ब्रवीम्यहम् ।।

9. If you desire to keep up your Dharma, you must send away Raama,(your eldest) son, as per my directive. I Am (Finally) Asking You Thrice.

(Like Three Cheers, this indicates her firmness in her demands.)

❍ ❍ ❍

१०. समयं च ममार्येमं यदि त्वं न करिष्यसि ।
अग्रतस्ते परित्यक्ता परित्यक्ष्यामि जीवितम् ।।

10. Oh Aryan (noble Dhascharatha)! If you do not comply with my stipulation, I will give up .my life in your presence, abandoned (by you in respect of the two boons you had given me).

❍ ❍ ❍

११. एवं प्रचोदितो राजा कैकेय्या निर्विशङ्कया ।
नाशकत्पाशमुन्मोक्तुं बलिरिन्द्रकृतं यथा ।।

11. Like (great king) Bali who was bound by the action of God (Vishnu), so was the king (Dhascharatha) who could not refuse, committed as he was by Kaikeyi who had no qualms or doubt.

(Readers may refer to The First Book Baala Kaanda regarding this history; How the great king Bali was humbled by God Vishnu.)

❍ ❍ ❍

१२. उद्भ्रान्तहृदयश्चापि विवर्णवदनोऽभवत् ।
स धुर्योवै परिस्पन्दन्युगचक्रान्तरं यथा ॥

12. Quivering like a beast of burden yoked to a cross pole, (Dhascharatha) was terribly agitated in mind, distressed, and his face lost all its 'color'.

❍ ❍ ❍

१३. विह्वलाभ्यां च नेत्राभ्यामपश्यन्निव भूमिपः ।
कृच्छ्राद्धैर्येण संस्तभ्य कैकेयीमिदमब्रवीत् ॥

13. Deeply in pain, agitated, unable to see with his eyes (blurred by tears), this king braving himself, addressed Kaikeyi thus, composing himself somewhat.

❍ ❍ ❍

१४. यस्ते मन्त्रकृतः पाणिरग्नौ पापे मया धृतः ।
तं त्यजामि स्वजं चैव तव पुत्रं सह त्वया ॥

14. Oh sinful woman! I Renounce You Whose Hands I Grasped (in marriage) Before the Holy Fire as per (Rituals and) Chants. (I renounce) also my son (Bharatha) born through you.

❍ ❍ ❍

१५. प्रयाता रजनी देवि सूर्यस्योदयनं प्रति ।
अभिषेकं गुरुजनस्त्वरयिष्यति मां ध्रुवम् ॥

15. Oh lady (Kaikeyi)! Night is over. As soon as Sun rises, my family priest (Vasishta) will hurry me up to perform coronation (of Raama) that was firmly (fixed for the day).

❍ ❍ ❍

१६. रामाभिषेकसंभारैस्तदर्थमुपकल्पितैः ।
रामः कारयितव्यो मे मृतस्य सलिलक्रियाम् ॥

16. With all the materials (procured) for Raama's coronation, Raama will now use them for the purpose

of funereal Rites for me when I am dead, as they are (fit and) ready to be used (for this purpose now).

❍ ❍ ❍

१७. सपुत्रया त्वया नैव कर्तव्या सलिलक्रिया ।
व्याहन्तास्यशुभाचारे यदि रामाभिषेचनम् ।।

17. Oh woman of evil conduct! As you have prevented Raama's coronation, you and your son (Bharatha) should have nothing to do with my last Rites.

❍ ❍ ❍

१८. न शक्तोऽद्यास्म्यहं द्रष्टुं दृष्ट्वा पूर्वं तथासुखम् ।
हतहर्षं निरानन्दं पुनर्जनमवाङ्मुखम् ।।

18. Having seen (all these years) my citizens in such comfort, I cannot tolerate to see them bereft of joy, happiness, with their faces downcast. (This is what it will be, with me and Raama gone).

❍ ❍ ❍

१९. तां तथा ब्रुवतस्तस्य भूमिपस्य महात्मनः ।
प्रभाता शर्वरी पुण्या चन्द्रनक्षत्रशालिनी ।।

19. As he was talking to her like this, the star studded moonlight (luckily and) kindly ended for this great soul king (Dhascharatha).

❍ ❍ ❍

२०. ततः पापसमाचारा कैकेयी पार्थिवं पुनः ।
उवाच परुषं वाक्यं वाक्यज्ञा रोषमूर्च्छिता ।।

20. Then the clever speaking woman of bad conduct, this Kaikeyi who was stupefied by wrath, once again addressed these cruel words to the king:

❍ ❍ ❍

२१. किमिदं भाषसे राजन्वाक्यमङ्गरुजोपमम् ।
आनाययितुमक्लिष्टं पुत्रं राममिहार्हसि ।।

21. Oh king! What is this? You (continue to) speak words that shatter my body. You must (at once) fetch your (eldest)son Raama who is never wearied in action, here (and now).

❍ ❍ ❍

२२. स्थाप्य राज्ये मम सुतं कृत्वा रामं वनेचरम् ।
निःसपत्नां च मां कृत्वा कृतकृत्यो भविष्यसि ॥

22. Sending Raama to forest and then installing my son in the kingdom, and thus eliminating all rivals to me, you become a (contented) man having done your task (as per commitment of boon to me).

❍ ❍ ❍

२३. स नुन्न इव तीक्ष्णेन प्रतोदेन हयोत्तमः ।
राजा प्रचोदितोऽभीक्ष्णं कैकेयीमिदमब्रवीत् ॥

23. Like a foremost horse impelled by repeated whippings with a rough goad (whip), this king then addressed Kaikeyi thus:

❍ ❍ ❍

२४. धर्मबन्धेन बद्धोऽस्मि नष्टा च मम चेतना ।
ज्येष्ठं पुत्रं प्रियं रामं द्रष्टुमिच्छामि धार्मिकम् ॥

24. I am bound by "Rope of Dharma": My consciousness is gone; Therefore I desire to see my eldest son, beloved son Raama who is a man of Dharma.

❍ ❍ ❍

२५ ततः प्रभातां रजनीमुदिते च दिवाकरे ।
पुण्ये नक्षत्रयोगे च मुहूर्ते च समागते ॥

25. (Stanzas 25 to 30: The early morning scene at Ayodhya described: Vasishta enters)

When night ended and Sun arose, when auspicious time " aspected" by auspicious stars was nearing .....

❍ ❍ ❍

२६. वसिष्ठो गुणसम्पन्नः शिष्यैः परिसमावृतः ।
उपसंगृह्य संभारान्प्रविवेश पुरोत्तमम् ।।

26. Vasishta who was endowed with (foremost) qualities, accompanied by his disciples, entered the foremost palace taking the materials for the Ceremony ......

❍ ❍ ❍

२७. सिक्तसंमार्जितपथां पताकोत्तमभूषिताम् ।
विचित्रकुसुमाकीर्णां नानास्रग्भिर्विभूषिताम् ।।

27. The roads were cleansed with water and cleaned up; Decorated with foremost banners; Strewn with various flowers: Decorated with various garlands ......

❍ ❍ ❍

२८. संहृष्टमनुजोपेतां समृद्धविपणापणाम् ।
महोत्सवसमाकीर्णां राघवार्थेसमुत्सुकाम् ।।

28. Crowded with happy people; with plenty of shops filled with (various) fine commodities; full with people (like musicians) taking part in the great festivities, everywhere, all looking forward to Raama's coronation with great zeal .....

❍ ❍ ❍

२९. चन्दनागरुधूपैश्च सर्वतः परिधूपिताम् ।
तां पुरीं समतिक्रम्य पुरन्दरपुरोपमाम् ।।

29. With burning incenses, smelling sweetly of sandal & agara: everywhere; This city was like Lord Indhra's (city of Amaravathy); (And Vasishta) passed along (the roads) of such a city... (and entered king's palace) ......

❍ ❍ ❍

३०. ददर्शान्तः पुरं श्रेष्ठं नानाद्विजगणायुतम् ।
पौरजानपदाकीर्णं ब्राह्मणैरुपशोभितम् ।।
यज्ञाविद्भिः सुसंपूर्णं सदस्यैः परमद्विजैः ।।

30. (Vasishta) saw the Inner halls (of the palace) that were foremost (in grandeur), that was full with men of Braamin & Kshathriya caste-s in groups; full with multitude of men from cities and villages; full with Braamin priests; full with eminent Braamins who take part in assembly (of Vedhic scholars): full with priests who conduct Sacrificial ceremonies; (Vasishta saw the palace) shining beautiful.

(Readers may know that Vasishta shoulders great responsibility, being the traditional chief priest of the kings of Ayodhya: But he is not aware of the 'Drama' at night at the palace.)

❍ ❍ ❍

३१. तदन्तः पुरगाराद्य व्यतिचक्राम तं जनम् ।
वसिष्ठः परमप्रीतः परमर्षिर्विवेश च ॥

31. Extremely pleased, the great Rishi Vasishta entered the Hall, 'wading' through the (multitude of) men.

❍ ❍ ❍

३२. स त्वपश्यद्विनिष्क्रान्तं सुमन्त्रं नाम सारथिम् ।
द्वारे मनुजसिंहस्य सचिवं प्रियदर्शनम् ॥

32. At the entrance, he saw the pleasant faced Sumanthra, the minister and charioteer of (Dhascharatha) the 'lion' amongst men.

❍ ❍ ❍

३३. तमुवाच महातेजाः सूतपुत्रं विशारदम् ।
वसिष्ठः क्षिप्रमाचक्ष्व नृपतेर्मामिहागतम् ॥

33. (Stanzas 33 to 41, the arrangements etc. for Raama's coronation)

The most brilliant Vasishta addressed the celebrated son of the charioteer (this Sumanthra): = Inform the king at once that I have come here .....

❍ ❍ ❍

३४. इमे गङ्गोदकघटाः समुद्रेभ्यश्च काञ्चनाः ।
औदुम्बरं भद्रपीठमभिषेकार्थमाहृतम् ।।

34. ..... A splendid throne made of Audumbara wood: for coronation rituals, pots made of gold full with waters from (holy rivers like) Ganges and oceans have been brought ......

❍ ❍ ❍

३५. सर्वबीजानि गन्धाश्च रत्नानि विविधानि च ।
क्षौद्रं दधि घृतं लाजा दर्भाः सुमनसः पयः ।।

35. ...... All varieties of grains: Sweet smelling scents; various gems; honey; curds; melted butter; puffed grains; Dharbha grass; milk; flowers ......

❍ ❍ ❍

३६. अष्टौ च कन्या रुचिरा मत्तश्च वरवारणः ।
चतुरश्वो रथः श्रीमान्निस्त्रिंशो धनुरुत्तमम् ।।

36. ..... Eight lovely young girls; Resplendent and delightful (Exhilarated) foremost elephants; A chariot yoked to four horses; Sword and foremost bow ......

❍ ❍ ❍

३७. वाहनं नरसंयुक्तं छत्रं च शशिसन्निभम् ।
श्वेते च वालव्यजने भृङ्गारश्च हिरण्मयः ।।

37. ...... Palanquins (for carrying ladies, elders) carried by men; An umbrella (white) like the moon; Two white whisk fans; Vases made of gold ......

❍ ❍ ❍

३८. हेमदामपिनद्धश्च ककुद्मान्पाण्डुरो वृषः ।
केसरी च चतुर्दंष्ट्रो हरिश्रेष्ठो महाबलः ।।

38. ...... Cocks decorated in gold; White bull; Mightily strong lion with four gruesome teeth; foremost horse.....

❍ ❍ ❍

३९. सिंहासनं व्याघ्रतनुः समिद्धश्च हुताशनः ।
सर्ववादित्रसङ्घाश्च वेश्याश्चालंकृताः स्त्रियः ।।

39. ...... Royal seats; tiger skins; Holy Fire, Samith-s (twigs); all type of musical instruments; Beautifully dressed up courtesans ......

❍ ❍ ❍

४०. आचार्या ब्राह्मणा गावः पुण्याश्च मृगपक्षिणः ।
पौरजानपदश्रेष्ठा नैगमाश्च गणैः सह ।।

40. ...... Priests and teachers; Braamins; holy cows; deers and birds; Foremost men from city and villages; scholars reciting Vedha-s; men folk accompanying them ......

(All these listed at random: the arrangements were perfect & grand.)

❍ ❍ ❍

४१. एते चान्ये च बहवः प्रीयमाणाः प्रियंवदाः ।
अभिषेकाय रामस्य सह तिष्ठन्ति पार्थिवैः ।।

41. (Tell the king, says Vasishta to Sumanthra)

All others accompanied by kings (from other regions), those who speak sweetly (about the king) and who are very attached and affectionate, and many others are standing here, (awaiting) Raama's coronation.

❍ ❍ ❍

४२. त्वरयस्व महाराजं यथा समुदितेऽहनि ।
पुण्ये नक्षत्रयोगे च रामो राज्यमवाप्नुयात् ।।

42. (Vasishta tells Sumanthra)

As Raama should (be crowned and) 'obtain' the kingdom at the auspicious time chosen that is ** "aspected" by stars, you must hurry the king (to get ready): (**Note:- an astrological expression)

❍ ❍ ❍

४३. इति तस्य वचः श्रुत्वा सूतपुत्रो महात्मनः ।
स्तुवन्नृपतिशार्दूलं प्रविवेश निवेशनम् ।।

43. Hearing the great soul (Vasishta's) words, (Sumanthra) the son of the charioteer, entered the abode (of the king), extolling (Dhascharatha), the 'lion' amongst kings.

❍ ❍ ❍

४४. तं तु पूर्वोदितं वृद्धं द्वारस्था राजसम्मतम् ।
न शेकुरभिसंरोद्धुं राज्ञः प्रियचिकीर्षवः ।।

44. The King's guards who served (their king) lovingly, did not stop the elderly (Sumanthra) who was highly esteemed by the king and who had previous instruction (to be allowed to enter at will).(Sumanthra was so close to Dhascharatha he could enter the palace without appointment).

❍ ❍ ❍

४५. ससमीपस्थितो राज्ञस्तामवस्थामजज्ञिवान् ।
वाग्भिः परमतुष्टाभिरभिष्टोतुं प्रचक्रमे ।।

45. Not aware of the suffering of the king, he stood by and began to extol (the king) with eulogy to please him greatly.

❍ ❍ ❍

४६. ततः सूतो यथाकालं पार्थिवस्य निवेशने ।
सुमन्त्रः प्राञ्जलिर्भूत्वा तुष्टाव जगतीपतिम् ।।

46. Cupping his hands in Anjali, the charioteer Sumanthra (standing) before the king in his abode extolled (Dhascharatha) the lord of earth at proper time (as per protocol).

❍ ❍ ❍

४७. यथा नन्दति तेजस्वी सागरो भास्करोदये ।
प्रीतः प्रीतेन मनसा तथाऽऽनन्दघनः स्वतः ।।

47. (Sumanthra extols): Just as the brilliant ocean rejoices at Sunrise, so are you rejoicing happily with a happy mind.

❍ ❍ ❍

४८. इन्द्रमस्यां तु वेलायामभितुष्टाव मातलिः ।
सोऽजयद्दानवान् सर्वांस्तथा त्वां बोधयाम्यहम् ।।

48. This was the time when Maathali (the charioteer of Indhra) extolled Lord Indhra: And then (Indhra) conquered all the Dhaanava-s. Like wise I am awakening you (at this early morning, Oh King Dhascharatha, says his charioteer Sumanthra).

❍ ❍ ❍

४९. वेदाः सहाङ्गविद्याश्च यथा ह्यात्मभुवं प्रभुम् ।
ब्रह्माणं बोधयन्त्यद्य तथा त्वां बोधयाम्यहम् ।।

49. Just as Vedha-s embracing all parts of Vedha-s awakens lord Bramma, so am I awakening you.

❍ ❍ ❍

५०. आदित्यः सह चन्द्रेण यथा भूतधरां शुभाम् ।
बोधयत्यद्य पृथिवीं तथा त्वां बोधयाम्यहम् ।।

50. The Sun following the Moon wakes up the auspicious (Mother) Earth: I am awakening you up likewise.

❍ ❍ ❍

५१. उत्तिष्ठाशु महाराज कृतकौतुकमङ्गलः ।
विराजमानो वपुषा मेरोरिव दिवाकरः ।।

51. Oh great king! Get up Quick! Like Sun over Meru Mountain, you will be radiant and handsome, after the morning Kowthumangala ceremony.

❍ ❍ ❍

५२. सोमसूर्यौ च काकुत्स्थ शिववैश्रवणावपि ।
वरुणश्चाग्निरिन्द्रश्च विजयं प्रदिशन्तु ते ।।

52. Oh (Dhascharatha) the Kaakuthsa! May Sun, Moon, God Schiva Lord Varuna, (lord of wealth) Kubhaera, and lord of Fire Agni offer you (& bless you with) "Victory."

❍ ❍ ❍

५३. गता भगवती रात्रिरहः शिवमुपस्थितम् ।
प्रतिबुध्यस्व राजर्षेकुरु कार्यमनन्तरम् ।।

53. The night has passed away pleasantly. The auspicious day has arrived: Oh royal sage: Wake up! Do what is to be done further.

(Some critics of Raamaayana wonder how such a close friend and confidante of the king, this Sumanthra could not suspect that something went wrong at night with his friend, king Dhascharatha.)

❍ ❍ ❍

५४. उपतिष्ठति रामस्य समग्रमभिषेचनम् ।
पौरजानपदैश्चापि नैगमैश्च कृतात्मभिः ।।

54. The citizens of cities and villages, the (pure minded &) self disciplined scholars who recite Vedha-s, are all standing by: All arrangements for Raama's coronation are ready.

❍ ❍ ❍

५५. अयं वसिष्ठो भगवान् ब्राह्मणैः सह तिष्ठति ।
क्षिप्रमाज्ञाप्यतां राजन् राघवस्याभिषेचनम् ।।

55. And lord Sage Vasishta, along with Braamins, is standing by (awaiting you): Oh king! Give orders for (commencement of coronation) now.

❍ ❍ ❍

५६. यथा ह्यपालाः पशवो यथा सेना ह्यनायका ।
यथा चन्द्रं विना रात्रिर्यथा गावो विना वृषम् ।।

56. (If action is not taken now) It will be like a cowherd

without a Cow boy; It will be like army without commander; It will be like night without moon; it will be like cow without udder .....

❍ ❍ ❍

५७. एवं हि भविता राष्ट्रं यत्र राजा न दृश्यते ॥

57. ...... it will be like this in a kingdom when the king is not seen (nor present): Surely.

❍ ❍ ❍

५८. इति तस्य वचः श्रुत्वा सान्त्वपूर्वमिवार्थवत् ।
अभ्यकीर्यत शोकेन भूय एव महीपतिः ॥

58. Hearing such soothing and meaningful words, the king became even more stricken with grief (No wonder!)

❍ ❍ ❍

५९. ततः स राजा तं सूतं सन्नहर्षः सुतं प्रति ।
शोकरक्तेक्षणः श्रीमानुद्वीक्ष्योवाच धार्मिकः ॥

59. Pondering over (the future of) his son (Raama), this resplendent king (Dhascharatha) the man of Dharma who had no joy in life, addressed the charioteer thus, his eye becoming red due to grief.

❍ ❍ ❍

६०. वाक्यैस्तु खलु मर्माणि मम भूयो निकृन्तसि ॥

60. By your eulogies, the vitals of my body are even more cut up now. (I am in no condition to receive praises, bemoans Dhascharatha before his friend Sumanthra).

❍ ❍ ❍

६१ सुमन्त्रः करुणं श्रुत्वा दृष्ट्वा दीनं च पार्थिवम् ।
प्रगृहीताञ्जलिः किञ्चित्तस्माद्देशादपाक्रमत् ॥

61. Hearing the pitiable words of the king and seeing that the king was also miserable, Sumanthra moved away

from that place somewhat, stretching his hands that was cupped in Anjali.

❍ ❍ ❍

६२. यदा वक्तुं स्वयं दैन्यान्न शशाक महीपतिः ।
तदा सुमन्त्रं मन्त्रज्ञा कैकेयी प्रत्युवाच ह ॥

62. So afflicted by grief was he, that the king could not speak himself (further). And then, because of this, Kaikeyi who was clever in understanding (and exploiting the situation), addressed Sumanthra thus:

❍ ❍ ❍

६३. सुमन्त्र राजा रजनीं रामहर्षसमुत्सुकः ।
प्रजागरपरिश्रान्तो निद्राया वशमेयिवान् ॥

63. Oh Sumanthra! Fatigued by keeping awake the whole night, longing to see Raama with joy, he is sleepy and subdued.

❍ ❍ ❍

६४. तद्गच्छ त्वरितं सूत राजपुत्रं यशस्विनम् ।
राममानय भद्रं ते नात्र कार्या विचारणा ॥

64. Oh charioteer (Sumanthra)! Therefore you at once bring the famous Raama the son the king. There need be no deliberation in this matter: Welfare to you. You go.

❍ ❍ ❍

६५. स मन्यमानः कल्याणं हृदयेन ननन्द च ।
निर्जगाम च संप्रीत्या त्वरितो राजशासनात् ॥

65. Thinking that this auspicious (message of Kaikeyi) was only on command of the king, he rejoiced; pleased at heart he left without delay.

❍ ❍ ❍

६६. सुमन्त्रश्चिन्तयामास त्वरितं चोदितस्तया ।
व्यक्तं रामाभिषेकार्थमिहायास्यति धर्मभाक् ॥

66. Commanded by her, Sumanthra began to think that the man of Dharma (Raama) was being brought urgently there in view of the coronation of Raama already fixed.

❍ ❍ ❍

६७. इति सूतो मतिं कृत्वा हर्षेण महता वृतः ।
निर्जगाम महाबाहू राघवस्य दिदृक्षया ॥

67. Entertaining such a thought, the mighty limbed (Sumanthra the) charioteer who was in great joy, left, eager to see (Raama) the Raaghava.

❍ ❍ ❍

६८. सागरह्रदसङ्काशात् सुमन्त्रोऽन्तः पुराच्छुभात् ।
निष्क्रम्य जनसंबाधं ददर्श द्वारमग्रतः ॥

68. Coming out of the lovely inner apartments of the palace that was like an island in the ocean, he saw a multitude of people before him at the gate (of the palace).

❍ ❍ ❍

६९. ततः पुरस्तात् सहसा विनिःसृतो
महीपतीन्द्वारगतान् विलोकयन् ।
ददर्श पौरान् विविधान् महाधनान्
उपस्थितान्द्वारमुपेत्य निष्ठितान् ॥

69. Coming out (of the palace), he saw first many rich citizens and famous kings (of other regions), standing in front of the gate smiling. Then walking along, he saw various devoted citizens along the road ......

❍ ❍ ❍

Chapter 15

Sumanthra Enters Raama's Abode

(Sumanthra, Dhascharatha's friend, minister & charioteer, under command of Kaikeyi, goes to Raama's abode to bring him before Kaikeyi & Dhascharatha.)

❍ ❍ ❍

१. ते तु तां रजनीमुष्य ब्राह्मणा वेदपारगाः ।
उपतस्थुरुपस्थानं सहराजपुरोहिताः ॥

1. Scholars well versed in Vedha-s, these braamins who were all priests of the king, reached the (Ceremonial) Hall, after spending the night. (There were scholars who had 'Crossed the shores of the Ocean' of Vedha-s).

❍ ❍ ❍

२. अमात्या बलमुख्याश्च मुख्या ये निगमस्य च ।
राघवस्याभिषेकार्थेप्रीयमाणास्तु सङ्गताः ॥

2. And king's ministers, army commanders, leading citizens of the city, all of them assembled there for (Raama) the Raaghava's coronation, with (great) desire (to witness ceremonies)

❍ ❍ ❍

३. उदिते विमले सूर्ये पुष्ये चाभ्यागतेऽहनि ।
लग्ने कर्कटके जन्म रामस्य समुपस्थिते ॥
अभिषेकाय रामस्य द्विजेन्द्रैरुपकल्पितम् ॥

3. When the pure and bright Sun rose on the day of star Pushya when Raama's Coronation was to take place, as fixed by (learned) Braamins, and the birth Lagna of Raama, the Kataka Lagna was approaching ......

❍ ❍ ❍

४. काञ्चना जलकुम्भाश्च भद्रपीठं स्वलंकृतम् ।
रथश्च सम्यगास्तीर्णोभास्वता व्याघ्रचर्मणा ॥

4. .... (the following) was got readied: Golden pots for waters; well decorated auspicious seat; A chariot carpeted well by tiger skin that was shining (with gloss).

❍ ❍ ❍

५. गङ्गायमुनयोः पुण्यात् सङ्गमादाहृतं जलम् ।
याश्चान्याः सरितः पुण्या ह्रदाः कूपाः सरांसि च ॥

5. Waters from holy river Ganges and Jamuna at their confluence. And from other holy rivers, ponds and lakes: All these waters were brought.

❍ ❍ ❍

६. प्राग्वाहाश्चोर्ध्ववाहाश्च तिर्यग्वाहाश्च सङ्गताः ।
ताभ्यश्चैवाहृतं तोयं समुद्रेभ्यश्च सर्वशः ॥

6. Waters from oceans at the confluence of rivers flowing to east and flowing west; From these (places) they were brought.

❍ ❍ ❍

७. सजलाः क्षीरिभिश्छन्ना घटाः काञ्चनराजताः ।
पद्मोत्पलयुता भान्ति पूर्णाः परमवारिणा ॥

7. Pots of silver and gold filled with (holy) waters, covered with lotus and Uthpala (Nymphae Carulea) leaves; scented waters, Milk etc. (in pots) fully covered (were there) shining.

❍ ❍ ❍

८. क्षौद्रं दधि घृतं लाजा दर्भाः सुमनसः पयः ।
वेश्याश्चैव शुभाचाराः सर्वाभरणभूषिताः ॥

8. ..... Honey, yoghurt: butter oil; puffed grains; Dharbha grass; flowers; milk; Courtesans of impeccable conduct dressed up with all ornaments .....

❍ ❍ ❍

९. चन्द्रांशुविकचप्रख्यं काञ्चनं रत्नभूषितम् ।
सज्जं तिष्ठति रामस्य वालव्यजनमुत्तमम् ।।

9. ..... A foremost whisk fan (A 'Chourie' made of Yak hairs) whose tufts were like rays of the moon, well spread, with handle made of gold and decorated with gems; all these were kept ready for Raama

❍ ❍ ❍

१०. चन्द्रमण्डलसङ्काशमातपत्रं च पाण्डुरम् ।
सज्जं द्युतिकरं श्रीमदभिषेकपुरस्कृतम् ।।

10. A resplendent white umbrella shining like the halo of the moon, (specially) made for Raama's coronation, was got ready.

❍ ❍ ❍

११. पाण्डुरश्च वृषः सज्जः पाण्डुरोऽश्वश्च संस्थितः ।
प्रसृतश्च गजः श्रीमानौपवाह्यः प्रतीक्षते ।।

11. A white bull was fastened: A white stallion was stationed; A composed (well behaved) resplendent royal elephant was (seen) waiting there.

❍ ❍ ❍

१२. अष्टौ च कन्या माङ्गल्याः सर्वाभरणभूषिताः ।
वादित्राणि च सर्वाणि वन्दिनश्च तथाऽपरे ।।

12. Eight young girls, unmarried, ornamented with various jewelleries were there; Many instrumentalists & singers were there.

❍ ❍ ❍

१३. इक्ष्वाकूणां यथा राज्ये संभ्रियेताभिषेचनम् ।
तथाजातीयमादाय राजपुत्राभिषेचनम् ।।

13. Whatever was to be brought (and was to be offered). for the coronation in the kingdom of Ikshwaaku, they were brought (by kings of other regions) for coronation of the prince ......

❍ ❍ ❍

१४. ते राजवचनात्तत्र समवेता महीपतिम् ।
अपश्यन्तोऽब्रुवन् को नु राज्ञो नः प्रतिवेदयेत् ।।

14. ..... They had assembled there by the invitation of (Dhascharatha the) lord of earth and when they did not see the king, they said: =Who Is Going To Inform About Us To The King (Dhascharatha)?

❍ ❍ ❍

१५. न पश्यामश्च राजानमुदितश्च दिवाकरः ।
यौवराज्याभिषेकश्च सज्जो रामस्य धीमतः ।।

15. ...... The King is not even 'seen' by us; Sun has risen and the time of the wise Raama's coronation is fast approaching.

(For once, the protocol is breaking down in Ayodhya)

❍ ❍ ❍

१६. इति तेषु ब्रुवाणेषु सार्वभौमान्महीपतीन् ।
अब्रवीत्तानिदं वाक्यं सुमन्त्रो राजसत्कृतः ।।

16. While they (these invitees) were talking like this, the king's most honoured (minister and charioteer) Sumanthra addressed these kings and other lords, with following words.

❍ ❍ ❍

१७. रामं राज्ञो नियोगेन त्वरया प्रस्थितोऽस्म्यहम् ।
पूज्या राज्ञो भवन्तस्तु रामस्य च विशेषतः ।।

17. On king's command I am going to Raama's (place) in a hurry. (but) You are all (indeed most honoured guests and) deserve to be honoured by Raama and particularly by the king (Dhascharatha).

❍ ❍ ❍

१८. अयं पृच्छामि वचनात् सुखमायुष्मतामहम् ।
राज्ञः संप्रतिबुद्धस्य यच्चागमनकारणम् ।।

18. Therefore, because of the words spoken by you who are all royal personalities, I will, with pleasure, ask the king who is not awake, as to the reason for his not coming (here as yet).

❍ ❍ ❍

१९. इत्युक्त्वाऽन्तः पुरद्धारमाजगाम पुराणवित् ।
सदासक्तं च तद्वेश्म सुमन्त्रः प्रविवेश ह ॥

19. (Sumanthra gets back to Dhascharatha; has disobeyed Kaikeyi's order to fetch Raama.. He was under pressure from the visiting dignitaries who were kept waiting for the presence of Dhascharatha.)

Sumanthra who knew the past (history & heritage), telling them thus, (re) entered the inner apartments of the palace, having free access at all times (as per protocol given to him).

❍ ❍ ❍

२०. तुष्टावास्य तदा वंशं प्रविश्य स विशां पतेः ।
शयनीयं नरेन्द्रस्य तदासाद्य व्यतिष्ठत ॥

20. Then he entered King's bed room, went near but stood (just) outside; then he began to extol about the lineage of the lord of people., (king Dhascharatha).

(As per protocol, the king is always addressed properly, with praises etc. Here Sumanthra extols king's lineage.)

❍ ❍ ❍

२१. सोऽत्यासाद्य तु तद्वेश्म तिरस्करणिमन्तरा ।
आशीर्भिर्गुणयुक्ताभिरभितुष्टाव राघवम् ॥

21. Going further inside the hall and standing near the curtain, he began to felicitate (the king) with greetings that enumerated the qualities of (Dhascharatha) the Raaghava.

❍ ❍ ❍

२२. सोमसूर्यौ च काकुत्स्थ शिववैश्रवणावपि ।
वरुणश्चाग्निरिन्द्रश्च विजयं प्रदिशन्तु ते ॥

22. Oh Kaakuthsa! May Sun, Moon, Schiva, Kubhaera, Varuna, Agni, Indhra, offer (& bless) you: Victory!

❍ ❍ ❍

२३. यथा साङ्गाश्च वेदा वै ब्रह्माणं बोधयन्ति ते ।
तथा त्वां धीर बोध्यामि ह्युत्तिष्ठ पुरुषर्षभ ॥

23. Just as Vedha which embraces all limbs of Vedha, awakens God Bramma, so do I awake you, Oh 'Bull' amongst kings! Oh brave (Dhascharatha)! Wake up!

❍ ❍ ❍

२४. गता भगवती रात्रिरहः शिवमुपस्थितम् ।
बुध्यस्व नरशार्दूल कुरु कार्यमनन्तरम् ॥

24. Night has passed away peacefully. The auspicious day has arrived. Oh 'tiger' of men! Wake up! May you do the work that is to be done further.

❍ ❍ ❍

२५. ब्राह्मणा बलमुख्याश्च नैगमाश्चागता नृपाः ।
दर्शनं तेऽभिकाङ्क्षन्ते प्रतिबुध्यस्व राघव ॥

25. Oh (Dhascharatha the) Raaghava! Kings (from various places), Braamins, Army chiefs, citizens have come and are awaiting to see you. Wake up!

❍ ❍ ❍

२६. संस्तुतन्तं तदा सूतं सुमन्त्रं मन्त्रकोविदम् ।
प्रतिबुध्य ततो राजा इदं वचनमब्रवीत् ॥

26. Then king (Dhascharatha) realising that it was his charioteer, minister and statesman (Sumanthra) who was extolling him, addressed this Sumanthra with these words:

❍ ❍ ❍

२७. राममानय सूतेति यदस्यभिहितो मया ।
किमिदं कारणं येन ममाज्ञा प्रतिहन्यते ।।

27. Oh Charioteer (Sumanthra)! You were commanded by me to bring Raama here; Yet my command was disobeyed (by you). What is the reason for it?

❍ ❍ ❍

२८. न चैव संप्रसुप्तोऽहमानयेहाशु राघवम् ।
इति राजा दशरथः सूतं तत्रान्वशात्पुनः ।।

28. Then the king Dhascharatha addressed the charioteer further thus: Pressed him again: = I am not asleep: Bring Raama here at once =

❍ ❍ ❍

२९. स राजवचनं श्रुत्वा शिरसा प्रतिपूज्य तम् ।
निर्जगाम नृपावासान्मन्यमानः प्रियं महत् ।।

29. Hearing king's words (of command), and thinking (that calling of Raama there) was a happy (task and was) of great (importance), he bowed to the king with his head down and departed from king's place.

(Even at this stage Sumanthra is not aware that something serious had happened during the night and Dhascharatha was miserable.)

❍ ❍ ❍

३०. प्रपन्नो राजमार्गं च पताकाध्वजशोभितम् ।
हृष्टः प्रमुदितः सूतो जगामाशु विलोकयन् ।।

30. When the charioteer (Sumanthra) came to the royal boulevard, he was very happy to see banners and arches; So in great joy he went fast (to Raama's place).

❍ ❍ ❍

३१. स सूतस्तत्र शुश्राव रामाधिकरणाः कथाः ।
अभिषेचनसंयुक्ताः सर्वलोकस्य हृष्टवत् ।।

31. The charioteer heard with great joy, the conversations of all the people about Raama's supreme virtues and about his (forth coming) coronation.

❍ ❍ ❍

३२. ततो ददर्श रुचिरं कैलासशिखरप्रभम् ।
रामवेश्म सुमन्त्रस्तु शक्रवेश्मसमप्रभम् ।।

32. And Sumanthra then saw the beautiful palace of Raama which was (towering) like peaks of Kailash (of Himalayas) and which was like Indhra's abode.

❍ ❍ ❍

३३. महाकवाटविहितं वितर्दिशतशोभितम् ।
काञ्चनप्रतिमैकाग्रं मणिविद्रुमतोरणम् ।।

33. (Stanzas 33 to 41, scene described)

It had mighty doors; hundreds of balconies; arches studded with gems & stones; statues made of gold .....

❍ ❍ ❍

३४. शारदाभ्रघनप्रख्यं दीप्तमेरुगुहोपमम् ।
मणिभिर्वरमाल्यानां सुमहद्भिरलङ्कृतम् ।।

34. ...... it was like spring clouds; (its corridors) like the caves of Meru mountain, bright; Decorated with costly garland of gems ......

❍ ❍ ❍

३५. मुक्तामणिभिराकीर्णं चन्दनागरुधूपितम् ।
गन्धान्मनोज्ञान्विसृजद्दार्दुरं शिखरं यथा ।।

35. ..... full of stones & pearls all over the place; everywhere smelling sweet with incenses and sandal pastes and Agara; The smoke (of incenses) rising high as though tearing up the peaks (of mountain), most agreeable ......

❍ ❍ ❍

३६. सारसैश्च मयूरैश्च विनदद्भिर्विराजितम् ।
सुकृतेहामृगाकीर्णं सुकीर्णं भक्तिभिस्तथा ॥

36. Full of birds cooing sweetly; with lustrous peacocks; (Pillars) beautifully carved with figures of forest animals (like deers, antelopes, lions etc.); likewise, (floors) decorated with decorations (of coloured materials) .....

❍ ❍ ❍

३७. मनश्चक्षुश्च भूतानामाददत्तिग्मतेजसा ।
चन्द्रभास्करसङ्काशं कुबेरभवनोपमम् ॥

37. ...... Piercing the eye and hearts of the people by its sheer brilliance; (Raama's palace) was like Kubhaera's palace, shining like moon and sun ......

❍ ❍ ❍

३८. महेन्द्रधामप्रतिमं नानापक्षिसमाकुलम् ।
मेरुश्रृङ्गसमं सूतो रामवेश्म ददर्श ह ॥

38. ...... it was as though like Indhra's palace; Various birds were there (flying around); It was like peak of Meru mountain; (Such a) palace of Raama the charioteer saw (from a distance) ......

❍ ❍ ❍

३९. उपस्थितैः समाकीर्णं जनैरञ्जलिकारिभिः ।
उपादाय समाक्रान्तैस्तथा जानपदैर्जनैः ॥

39. ...... People who had assembled there (at court-yards of Raama's palace) from villages (& towns) were standing with their arms cupped in Anjali, bringing with them (gifts) ......

❍ ❍ ❍

४०. रामाभिषेकसुमुखैरुन्मुखैः समलंकृतम् ।
महामेघसमप्रख्यमुदग्रं सुविभूषितम् ॥

40. ...... they were dressed well, were eagerly looking

forward to witness Raama's coronation: The beautifully decorated (palace) was like the mighty clouds ......

❍ ❍ ❍

४१. नानारत्नसमाकीर्णं कुब्जकैरातकावृतम् ।।

41. ..... various gems and pearls embedded all over; there were many (servants of) hunchbacks & midgets.

❍ ❍ ❍

४२. स वाजियुक्तेन रथेन सारथिःनराकुलं राजकुलं विराजयन् ।
वरूथिना राजगृहाभिपातिना पुरस्य सर्वस्य मनांसि हर्षयन् ।।

42. Riding on the chariot that was glittering, that offered protection against all weather and which was rushing towards the royal palace (of Raama), that was yoked to (fine) horses, the charioteer cheered up the hearts of all the citizens, and congregation of kings gathered there.

❍ ❍ ❍

४३. ततः समासाद्य महाधनं महत् प्रहृष्टरोमा स बभूव सारथिः ।
मृगैर्मयूरैश्च समाकुलोल्बणं गृहं वरार्हस्य शचीपतेरिव ।।

43. Then the charioteer reached the richly endowed mighty palace of (Raama) the Varaaha, which was like Indhra's palace, which was full of deers, peacocks: He was exhilarated with joy.

❍ ❍ ❍

४४. स तत्र कैलासन्निभाः स्वलंकृताः
प्रविश्य कक्ष्यास्त्रिदशालयोपमाः ।
प्रियान्नरान् राममते स्थितान्बहू -
नपोह्य शुद्धान्तमुपस्थितो रथी ।।

44. Entering through various Enclosures (Segments) of the palace which were like mountain (ranges) of Kailash, which were well decorated and which were comparable to the abodes of celestials, the charioteer (Sumanthra 'pushed' his way through many dear citizens who were

devoted to Raama; He reached the inner (apartments of Raama's palace).

❍ ❍ ❍

४५. स तत्र शुश्राव च हर्षयुक्ता रामाभिषेकार्थकृता जनानाम् ।
नरेन्द्रसूनोरभिमङ्गलार्थाः सर्वस्य लोकस्य गिरः प्रहृष्टः

45. There, (Sumanthra), with great joy, heard the invocations for the welfare and prosperity of (Raama), the son of king, (sung) by men from all parts of the globe, for success of Raama's coronation.

❍ ❍ ❍

४६. महेन्द्रसद्मप्रतिमं तु वेश्म रामस्य रम्यं मृगपक्षिजुष्टम् ।
ददर्श मेरोरिव श्रृङ्गमुच्चं विभ्राजमानं प्रभया सुमन्त्रः ॥

46. And Sumanthra found Raama's palace shining like Indhra's abode towering like peaks of Meru mountain; and shining (brilliantly), very beautiful with deers and (pet) animals around.

❍ ❍ ❍

४७. उपस्थितैरञ्जलिकारकैश्च सोपायनैर्जानपदैश्च मर्त्यैः ।
कोट्या परार्द्धैश्च विमुक्तयानैः समाकुलं द्वारपथं ददर्श ॥

47. And he saw: men standing at the gates (of the palace:) millions countless number of citizens from villages, with their hands cupped in Anjali: Men with gifts: Unyoked chariots: All crowding up.

❍ ❍ ❍

४८. ततो महामेघमहीधराभं प्रभिन्नमत्यङ्कुशमप्रसह्यम् ।
रामौपवाह्यं रुचिरं ददर्श शत्रुंजयं नागमुदग्रकायम् ॥

48. And he saw Schathrunjaya, the elephant (exclusively) ridden by Raama, which was like mighty cloud, which had a large body and tusk, which was irresistible, which needed no goading (with driver's hook), which was incomparable, and radiant.

❍ ❍ ❍

४९. स्वलङ्कृतान्साश्वरथान्सकुञ्जरान्
अमात्यमुख्याञ्शतशश्च वल्लभान् ।
व्यपोह्य सूत: सहितान्समंतत:
समृद्धमन्त: पुरमाविवेश ।।

49. (Pushing through and) Staying clear of the king's citizens who had arrived there from all parts (of kingdom) along with elephants and on chariots yoked to horses, and also hundreds of well wishers who were dressed up, the charioteer (Sumanthra) entered the prosperous inner apartments of the palace.

❍ ❍ ❍

५०. तदद्रिकूटाचलमेघसन्निभं
महाविमानोत्तमवेश्मसङ्घवत् ।
अवार्यमाण: प्रविवेश सारथि:
प्रभूतरत्नं मकरो यथार्णवम् ।।

50. Like Makara fishes in pearl studded ocean, the charioteer moved into the palace, unrestrained, which was like the summit of the mountain (caressed) by clouds, and which was towering like big Airship, with many storeys (and balconies).

❍ ❍ ❍

Chapter 16

Raama Goes (to See His Father)

१. स तदन्त: पुरद्वारं समतीत्य जनाकुलम् ।
प्रविभक्तां तत: कक्ष्यामाससाद पुराणवित् ।।

1. Entering through the gates of the inner segment of the palace where lots of men (were gathered), this (Sumanthra) who knew the past (ancient history of

the Ikshwaaku kings) reached the private chambers (of Raama's abode) .....

❍ ❍ ❍

२. प्रासकार्मुकबिभ्रद्भिर्युवभिर्मृष्टकुण्डलैः ।
अप्रमादिभिरेकाग्रैरनुरक्तैरधिष्ठिताम् ।।

2. ...... which were well guarded by young, devoted and most vigilant (guards) who were wielding swords, bows, and who were wearing dainty ear rings.

❍ ❍ ❍

३. तत्र काषायिणो वृद्धान्वेत्रपाणीन्स्वलंकृतान् ।
ददर्श विष्ठितान्द्वारि स्त्र्यध्यक्षान्सुसमाहितान् ।।

3. At the entrance, (Sumanthra) saw mendicants in ochre robes, staff bearers, matrons, well decorated men and (many) elders of great composure, sitting there.

❍ ❍ ❍

४. ते समीक्ष्य समायान्तं रामप्रियचिकीर्षवः ।
सहसोत्पतिताः सर्वे ह्यासनेभ्यः सुसंभ्रमाः ।।

4. All these people who were devoted (in service of) Raama for his good, and who were (somewhat) flurried, at once got up when they saw him coming before them.

❍ ❍ ❍

५. तानुवाच विनीतात्मा सूतपुत्रः प्रदक्षिणः ।
क्षिप्रमाख्यात रामाय सुमन्त्रो द्वारि तिष्ठति ।।

5. Then the modest and respected son of charioteer, (this Sumanthra who was also a fine charioteer like his father), said to them:= Inform At Once Raama, That Sumanthra Is Awaiting At The Door.=

❍ ❍ ❍

६. ते राममुपसंगम्य भर्तुः प्रियचिकीर्षवः ।
सहभार्याय रामाय क्षिप्रमेवाचचक्षिरे ।।

6. And they who were devoted to do service to him, approached Raama at once who was with his wife Seetha, and informed him.

❍ ❍ ❍

७. प्रतिवेदितमाज्ञाय सूतमभ्यन्तरं पितुः ।
तत्रैवानाययामास राघवः प्रियकाम्यया ॥

7. When (Raama) the Raaghava was informed of the command of this intimate (friend and) charioteer (of his father), he invited him there (at once) out of his affection to his father.

❍ ❍ ❍

८. तं वैश्रवणसङ्काशमुपविष्टं स्वलंकृतम् ।
ददर्श सूतः पर्यङ्के सौवर्णे सोत्तरच्छदे ॥

8. (Stanzas 8 to 10 scene described)

The charioteer (Sumanthra) saw him seated on a beautifully carved golden Sofa, like lord Kubhaera (the lord of wealth) ....

❍ ❍ ❍

९. वराहरुधिराभेण शुचिना च सुगन्धिना ।
अनुलिप्तं परार्ध्येन चन्दनेन परंतपम् ॥

9. ...... this tormentor of enemies (Raama) was besmeared with excellent red coloured sweet smelling pure sandal pastes ......

❍ ❍ ❍

१०. स्थितया पार्श्वतश्चापि वालव्यजनहस्तया ।
उपेतं सीतया भूयश्चित्रया शशिनं यथा ॥

10. ...... and standing by his side, was Seetha as usual with a whisk fan in her hand. (Raama) appeared like moon on the night of Chithra

❍ ❍ ❍

११. तं तपन्तमिवादित्यमुपपन्नं स्वतेजसा ।
ववन्दे वरदं वन्दी विनयज्ञो विनीतवत् ।।

11. (Sumanthra) who was a man of modesty and who venerated (the Ikshwaaku-s) greeted (Raama) the Raaghava, bowing humbly before him, (before this great) benefactor who, by his brilliance, was shining like the brilliant Sun.

❍ ❍ ❍

१२. प्राञ्जलिस्तु सुखं पृष्ट्वा विहारशयनासने ।
राजपुत्रमुवाचेदं सुमन्त्रो राजसत्कृतः ।।

12. Then Sumanthra who commanded the respect of the king, asked this royal prince (Raama) about his mundane pleasures & his welfare; With folded arms in Anjali then said the following to him.

❍ ❍ ❍

१३. कौसल्यासुप्रजा राम पिता त्वां द्रष्टुमिच्छति ।
महिष्या सह कैकेय्या गम्यतां तत्र मा चिरम् ।।

13. Oh the good son of Kowsalya! Oh Raama! Your father who is with queen Kaikeyi, desires to see you: You may go over there: Do not delay.

❍ ❍ ❍

१४. एवमुक्तस्तु संहृष्टो नरसिंहो महाद्युतिः ।
ततः संमानयामास सीतामिदमुवाच ह ।।

14. When told thus, the majestic (Raama) the 'lion' amongst men became exhilarated with joy, felt honoured. Then he said this to Seetha; (Raama, ofcourse is not aware about happenings of the night).

❍ ❍ ❍

१५. देवि देवश्च देवी च समागम्य मदन्तरे ।
मन्त्रयेते ध्रुवं किञ्चिदभिषेचनसंहितम् ।।

15. Oh Lady (Seetha)! The lord (my father) and lady (Kaikeyi, my step mother), together wish (to see me) to counsel me (privately) something about the coronation fixed (for me).

❍ ❍ ❍

१६. लक्षयित्वा ह्यभिप्रायं प्रियकामा सुदक्षिणा ।
सञ्चोदयति राजानं मदर्थं मदिरेक्षणे ॥

16. Oh (Seetha) with captivating eyes! The righteous (Kaikeyi) desirous of doing good for my sake, having expressed her wish, has requested the king.

❍ ❍ ❍

१७. सा प्रहृष्टा महाराजं हितकामाऽनुवर्तिनी ।
जननी चार्थकामा मे केकयाधिपते: सुता ॥

17. She is the daughter of the king of Kekeya: Obeys king (Dhascharatha): And to me she is my 'mother', who is ever joyous, who ever wishes me welfare and who is ever desirous in my ((material and other) prosperity. (Vaalmeeki uses the word = Janani-; Mother; But Kaikeyi is only stepmother of Raama).

❍ ❍ ❍

१८. दिष्ट्या खलु महाराजो महिष्या प्रियया सह ।
सुमन्त्रं प्राहिणोद्दूतमर्थकामकरं मम ॥

18. The great king who is (now) with his beloved queen (Kaikeyi) has sent message to me through Sumanthra who (ever) fulfills tasks to (the king's) satisfaction. My good fortune indeed!

❍ ❍ ❍

१९. यादृशी परिषत्तत्र तादृशो दूत आगत: ।
ध्रुवमद्यैव मां राजा यौवराज्येऽभिषेक्ष्यति ॥

19. Such is the assembly there; such is this man (Sumanthra) who has come here as emissary; Surely king is going to anoint me as crown prince today.

❍ ❍ ❍

२०. हन्त शीघ्रमितो गत्वा द्रक्ष्यामि च महीपतिम् ।
सह त्वं परिवारेण सुखमास्व रमस्व च ॥

20. Going from here immediately, I am going to see (my father) the lord of earth; You remain here comfortably with your folks; Enjoy yourself. Ah! (our) good luck!

❍ ❍ ❍

२१. पतिसंमानिता सीता भर्तारमसितेक्षणा ।
आद्वारमनुवव्राज मङ्गलान्यभिदध्युषी ॥

21. (Stanzas 21 to 24: Leave taking scene etc.)
The dark eyed Seetha who was held in high esteem by her husband (Raama), followed her husband upto the door and meditated with auspicious prayers ......

❍ ❍ ❍

२२. राज्यं द्विजातिभिर्जुष्टं राजसूयाभिषेचनम् ।
कर्तुमर्हति ते राजा वासवस्येव लोककृत् ॥

22. ...... (Seetha prays): Like the creator (God Bramma) towards Vaasava (Indhra), king (Dhascharatha) should offer you the kingdom and crown you as YuvaRaaja, propitiated by (learned) Braamins ......

❍ ❍ ❍

२३. दीक्षितं व्रतसंपन्नं वराजिनधरं शुचिम् ।
कुरङ्गश्रृङ्गपाणिं च पश्यन्ती त्वां भजाम्यहम् ॥

23. ...... (Even if) I see you as pure (mendicant) observing vows and in Dheeksha, wearing dress of foremost deer skin and holding a beautiful stick in your hand, I will (ever) serve you (abide by you) ......

❍ ❍ ❍

२४. पूर्वां दिशं वज्रधरो दक्षिणां पातु ते यमः ।
वरुणः पश्चिमामाशां धनेशस्तूत्तरां दिशम् ॥

24. ...... May the wishes of Vajra (the Lord Indhra, the

wielder of thunder bolt) protect you in the east; May Yama (the lord of Death) protect you in south. May Varuna (Lord of Rain) protect you in west; May (lord of wealth) Kubhaera protect you in north.

(Note: Seetha invokes these celestials for blessings: It is interesting that she has perhaps a premonition that Raama may not after all wear the crown but go out to forest as a mendicant. In fact this is what Raama 'obtains' in just under an hour!)

❍ ❍ ❍

२५. अथ सीतामनुज्ञाप्य कृतकौतुकमङ्गलः ।
निश्चक्राम सुमन्त्रेण सह रामो निवेशनात् ॥

25. After sending back Seetha, Raama who had completed his pre-coronation Rituals & Rites, went out of his palace along with Sumanthra.

❍ ❍ ❍

२६. पर्वतादिव विष्क्रम्य सिंहो गिरिगुहाशयः ।
लक्ष्मणं द्वारि सोऽपश्यत्प्रह्वाञ्जलिपुटं स्थितम् ॥

26. Coming out (of his palace) like a lion living in the cave of mountain coming out of the mountain, he saw (his brother) Lakshmana who was standing at the entrance with his hands cupped in Anjali.

❍ ❍ ❍

२७. अथ मध्यमकक्ष्यायां समागच्छत्सुहृज्जनैः ।
स सर्वानर्थिनो दृष्ट्वा समेत्य प्रतिनन्द्य च ॥

27. At the central halls of the palace, he saw all his well wishers and followers; Approaching them, he 'met' with them and delighted them.

❍ ❍ ❍

२८. ततः पावकसङ्काशमारुरोह रथोत्तमम् ।
वैयाघ्रं पुरुषव्याघ्रो राजन्तं राजनन्दनः ॥

28. The (Raama) the darling of the king and 'tiger' amongst men, got into a chariot that was foremost and which was well carpeted with tiger skins and which was radiant like fire.

❍ ❍ ❍

२९. मेघनादमसंबाधं मणिहेमविभूषितम् ।
मुष्णन्तमिव चक्षूंषि प्रभया सूर्यवर्चसम् ।।

29. (Raama's chariot): The sound was like those of the clouds; Was huge; Decorated with gold and gems; dazzling the eyes, like Sun's rays, with its brilliancy ......

❍ ❍ ❍

३०. करेणुशिशुकल्पैश्च युक्तं परमवाजिभिः ।
हरियुक्तं सहस्राक्षो रथमिन्द्र इवाशुगम् ।।

30. ...... yoked to fine horses that were like young elephants; these fawn coloured horses could go very fast; it was like the chariot of the thousand eyed Indhra ......

❍ ❍ ❍

३१. प्रययौ तूर्णमास्थाय राघवो ज्वलितः श्रिया ।।

31. ...... this resplendent and radiant Raama the Raaghava got into it quickly and left (for his father's place)

❍ ❍ ❍

३२. स पर्जन्य इवाकाशे स्वनवानभिनादयन् ।
निकेतान्निर्ययौ श्रीमान्महाभ्रादिव चन्द्रमाः ।।

32. Like the cloud making thunder in the sky, this resplendent Raama appeared and he came out of his residence like Moon coming out through clouds, (as the chariot) was making reverberating noise.

❍ ❍ ❍

३३. छत्रचामरपाणिस्तु लक्ष्मणो राघवानुजः ।
जुगोप भ्रातरं भ्राता रथमास्थाय पृष्ठतः ।।

33. And Raama's brother Lakshmana who had got into the chariot, held a white umbrella and fan in his hands to protect his brother (against the elements).

❍ ❍ ❍

३४. ततो हलहलाशब्दस्तुमुलः समजायत ।
तस्य निष्क्रममाणस्य जनौघस्य समन्ततः ॥

34. When (Raama) was going out (in chariot), everywhere there was tumultuous and hallowing sounds of (Hala-Hala) from the multitude of men (lining up the roads).

❍ ❍ ❍

३५. ततो हयवरा मुख्या नागाश्च गिरिसन्निभाः ।
अनुजग्मुस्तदा रामं शतशोऽथ सहस्रशः ॥

35. and hundreds and thousands of well bred foremost horses and elephants which resembled hillocks, followed Raama.

❍ ❍ ❍

३६. अग्रतश्चास्य सन्नद्धाश्चन्दनागरुरूषिताः ।
खड्गचापधराः शूरा जग्मुराशंसवो जनाः ॥

36. Many soldiers wielding weapons, many warriors wielding swords, bow etc., many men besmeared with sandal paste and agara scents who were desirous (of witnessing the coronation) went along.

❍ ❍ ❍

३७. ततो वादित्रशब्दाश्च स्तुतिशब्दाश्च वन्दिनाम् ।
सिंहनादाश्च शूराणां तदा शुश्रुविरे पथि ॥

37. At that time, there, on the (Royal) boulevard, instrumental music, invocation songs from bards, and the roaring lion like sounds of the warriors were heard.

❍ ❍ ❍

३८. हर्म्यवातायनस्थाभिर्भूषिताभिः समन्ततः ।
कीर्यमाणः सुपुष्पौघैर्ययौ स्त्रीभिररिंदमः ।।

38. The conqueror of enemies (this Raama) went along as flowers were strewn everywhere in heaps from beautifully dressed women who were standing in the balconies of their house.

❍ ❍ ❍

३९. रामं सर्वानवद्याङ्ग्यो रामप्रियचिकीर्षवः ।
वचोभिरग्र्यैर्हर्म्यस्थाः क्षितिस्थाश्च ववन्दिरे ।।

39. People standing in the roofs of their houses, people standing in the streets, ladies with lovely limbs, and all others who wished Raama well, extolled Raama with foremost words (thus): ......

❍ ❍ ❍

४०. नूनं नन्दति ते माता कौसल्या मातृनन्दन ।
पश्यन्ती सिद्धयात्रं त्वां पित्र्यं राज्यमवस्थितम् ।।

40. Oh (Raama) the darling of your mother! Your mother Kowsalya will now be overjoyed seeing you, (and seeing you) accomplished (crowned and) established in the kingdom of your forefathers.

❍ ❍ ❍

४१. सर्वसीमन्तिनीभ्यश्च सीतां सीमन्तिनीं वराम् ।
अमन्यन्त हि ता नार्यो रामस्य हृदयप्रियाम् ।।

41. Then the women praised Raama's (beloved wife) who was dear to his heart, the foremost woman Seetha, the foremost amongst all women....(thus) ......

❍ ❍ ❍

४२. तया सुचरितं देव्या पुरा नूनं महत्तपः ।
रोहिणीव शशाङ्केन रामसंयोगमाप या ।।

42. ...... Like Rohini to Moon, she who obtained this 'association' with Raama, by this lady Seetha, great

many penance must have been well done by her long ago (in her previous births).

(No one is more fortunate than Seetha, say all the citizens.)

❍ ❍ ❍

४३. इति प्रासादशृङ्गेषु प्रमदाभिर्नरोत्तमः ।
शुश्राव राजमार्गस्थः प्रिया वाच उदाहृताः ॥

43. While this foremost of men (Raama) was going along the royal boulevard, he heard such sweet words uttered by women from the balconies of their houses.

❍ ❍ ❍

४४. स राघवस्तत्र कथाप्रलापान्
शुश्राव लोकस्य समागतस्य ।
आत्माधिकारा विविधाश्च वाचः
प्रहृष्टरूपस्य पुरो जनस्य ॥

44. And (Raama) the Raaghava heard various conversations amongst themselves about himself, from the excited and exhilarated men from cities and from (other) men who had gathered there from villages as well.

❍ ❍ ❍

४५. एष श्रियं गच्छति राघवोऽद्य
राजप्रसादाद्विपुलां गमिष्यन् ।
एते वयं सर्वसमृद्धकामा
एषामरां नो भविता प्रशास्ता ॥

45. (They praised Raama thus): This (Raama) the Raaghava, by blessings of the king, is going to obtain great glory: We, to whom this (Raama) is going to become (Lord and) Ruler, will now (be very happy) with our desires fulfilled.

❍ ❍ ❍

४६. लाभो जनस्यास्य यदेष सर्वं
प्रपत्स्यते राष्ट्रमिदं चिराय ।
न ह्यप्रियं किञ्चन जातु कश्चित्
पश्येन्न दुःखं मनुजाधिपेऽस्मिन् ॥

46. That this (Raama) is going to take over this kingdom for a long time is good fortune for mankind: When he becomes King, none will see any suffering at all: None will be displeased.

❍ ❍ ❍

४७. स घोषवद्भिश्च हयैश्च नागैः
पुरःसरैः स्वस्तिकसूतमागधैः ।
महीयमानः प्रवरैश्च वादकै
रभिष्टुतो वैश्रवणो यथा ययौ ॥

47. Honoured & extolled thus by the salutations of Sootha-s and Magadha-s who were going in front along with horse and chariots that were making sounds, and extolled by foremost singers, he went along like Vaischrawana (Kubhaera).

❍ ❍ ❍

४८. करेणुमातङ्गरथाश्वसंकुलं
महाजनौघप्रतिपूर्णचत्वरम् ।
प्रभूतरत्नं बहुपण्यसञ्चयं
ददर्शरामो रुचिरं महापथम् ॥

48. Raama saw the royal boulevard crowded with young female & male elephants, horses, chariots; crowded in all (the cty) Squares with multitude; Full with gems and stones (exhibited everywhere): (Shops) full with various commodities, heaps of them. Very pleasing (Sight).

(And thus Raama goes to his father in the morning little realising that he is being commanded to go away at once on exile in forest.)

❍ ❍ ❍

Chapter 17

Raama's Arrival (at Dhascharatha's Palace)

(Sumanthra fetches Raama before Dhascharatha and Kaikeyi.)

❍ ❍ ❍

१. स रामो रथमास्थाय संप्रहृष्टसुहृज्जनः ।
पताकाध्वजसंपन्नं महार्हागरुधूपितम् ।
अपश्यन्नगरं श्रीमान्नानाजनसमाकुलम् ।।

1. Going on his chariot, the resplendent Raama who rejoiced in having friendly citizens, saw the city crowded with various people, with various arches and banners, and smelling sweetly with foremost incenses.

❍ ❍ ❍

२. स गृहैरभ्रसङ्काशैः पाण्डुरैरुपशोभितम् ।
राजमार्गं ययौ रामो मध्येनागरुधूपितम् ।।

2. Raama drove through the middle of the royal boulevard with beautiful white mansions resembling clouds (on either side) and sweet smell of Amiris Agalloca incense emanating (from all sides).

❍ ❍ ❍

३ चन्दनानां च मुख्यानामगरूणां च सञ्चयैः ।
उत्तमानां च गन्धानां क्षौमकौशाम्बरस्य च ।।

3. (Scene described as Raama drove. Stanzas 3 to 6)

Quality sandal paste and Agara incenses; foremost scents and perfumes; heaps of dresses made of silk & linen .....

❍ ❍ ❍

४. अविद्धाभिश्च मुक्ताभिरुत्तमैः स्फाटिकैरपि ।
शोभमानमसंबाधं तं राजपथमुत्तमम् ।।

4. ..... Shining with foremost quartz and pearls: uncut gems; The royal boulevard was very wide; And foremost ......

❍ ❍ ❍

५. संवृतं विविधैः पण्यैर्भक्ष्यैरुच्चावचैरपि ।
ददर्श तं राजपथं दिवि देवपथं यथा ।।

5. ...... (lined up) shops filled with diverse commodities and various eats...(Such a) royal boulevard that was like road in heaven treaded by celestials (Raama saw)....

❍ ❍ ❍

६. दध्यक्षतहविर्लाजैर्धूपैरगरुचन्दनैः ।
नानामाल्योपगन्धैश्च सदाऽभ्यर्चितचत्वरम् ।।

6. Plenty of curds (Yoghurt), Akshatha-s (Holy seeds for rituals), butter oil, puffed rice... incenses, Agara, sandal paste and sticks, various flowers and garlands smelling sweetly, decorating the Quadrangles...(All these Raama saw as he drove to his father's place).

❍ ❍ ❍

७. आशीर्वादान्बहूञ्छृण्वन्सुहृद्भिः समुदीरितान् ।
यथार्हं चापि संपूज्य सर्वानेव नरान्ययौ ।।

7. Hearing many laudatory words (blessings) uttered by affectionate citizens, (Raama) saluted all these men as per custom and went along.

❍ ❍ ❍

८. पितामहैराचरितं तथैव प्रपितामहैः ।
अद्योपादाय तं मार्गमभिषिक्तोऽनुपालय ।।

8. (Citizens' laudatory words, blessings: stanzas 8 to 12)

You must rule us in the same way, as your father and forefathers before you conducted themselves, from now on, being crowned (as YuvaRaaja) ......

❍ ❍ ❍

९. यथा स्म लालिताः पित्रा यथा पूर्वैः पितामहैः ।
ततः सुखतरं सर्वे रामे वत्स्याम राजनि ॥

9. ...... just as we were caressed and fondled by his father and by the predecessors before, we will all live even more happily while Raama is on the throne ......

❍ ❍ ❍

१०. अलमद्य हि भुक्तेन परमार्थैरलं च नः ।
यथा पश्याम निर्यान्तं रामं राज्ये प्रतिष्ठितम् ॥

10. ...... we are seeing Raama going out to be duly crowned in the kingdom: (We desire) nothing more (than this): We desire not wealth, nor pleasures, or foods ......

❍ ❍ ❍

११. अतो हि नः प्रियतरं नान्यत्किञ्चिद्भविष्यति ।
यथाऽभिषेको रामस्य राज्येनामिततेजसः ॥

11. ...nothing else is going to give us greater happiness than (seeing) the installation of this most brilliant Raama as crown prince.

❍ ❍ ❍

१२. एताश्चान्याश्च सुहृदामुदासीनः कथाः शुभाः ।
आत्मसंपूजनीः शृण्वन्ययौ रामो महापथम् ॥

12. ...Hearing all this and other pleasant words from the good hearted citizens which extolled him, the *stoic Raama rode along the royal boulevard:(Poet has used*- Udhaaseena-).

❍ ❍ ❍

१३. न हि तस्मान्मनः कश्चिच्चक्षुषी वा नरोत्तमात् ।
नरः शक्नोत्यपाक्रष्टुमतिक्रान्तेऽपि राघवे ॥

13. Even when Raama had gone far away, no man was able to take his eyes or his mind away from this foremost man.

❍ ❍ ❍

१४. यश्च रामं न पश्येत्तु यं च रामो न पश्यति ।
निन्दितः स वसेल्लोके स्वात्माऽप्येनं विगर्हते ॥

14. He who does not see Raama or is not seen by Raama, will live in this world, condemned! His soul will despise him!

❍ ❍ ❍

१५. सर्वेषां हि स धर्मात्मा वर्णानां कुरुते दयाम् ।
चतुर्णां हि वयस्थानां तेन ते तमनुव्रताः ॥

15. This noble soul man of Dharma shows compassion to all; To all the men from the four caste-s and to men of all ages. That is why they are all attached to him.

(Thus they praised Raama)

❍ ❍ ❍

१६. चतुष्पथान्देवपथांश्चैत्यान्यायतनानि च ।
प्रदक्षिणं परिहरञ्जगाम नृपतेः सुतः ॥

16. (Raama) the son of the king, went around in circumbambulation, the Braamins (who were followers of Four Paths-The Vedha-s), (and he went around) Chaithya tree, places of worship, the ceremonial Halls: Then he went (to his father's place).

❍ ❍ ❍

१७. स राजकुलमासाद्य मेघसङ्घोपमैः शुभैः ।
प्रासादश्रृङ्गैर्विविधैः कैलासशिखरोपमैः ॥

17. (Stanzas 17 to 19: Palace again described)

Approaching the royal Palace of his ancestors which was very lovely, which was like cluster of clouds, which, with many storeys & balconies, was like peaks of mount Kailash.

❍ ❍ ❍

१८. आवारयद्भिर्गगनं विमानैरिव पाण्डुरैः ।
वर्धमानगृहैश्चापि रत्नजालपरिष्कृतैः ।।

18. ..... It was white: The prosperous multi storeyed (palace) appeared as if it encompassed the entire sky! Decorated with numerous stone and gems ......

❍ ❍ ❍

१९. तत्पृथिव्यां गृहवरं महेन्द्रसदनोपमम् ।
राजपुत्रः पितुर्वेश्म प्रविवेश श्रिया ज्वलन् ।।

19. ...... The resplendent and radiant (Raama) the son of King (Dhascharatha) entered his father's palace that was like Lord Indhra's abode, and which was foremost mansion on earth.

❍ ❍ ❍

२०. स कक्ष्या धन्विभिर्गुप्तास्तिस्रोऽतिक्रम्य वाजिभिः ।
पदातिरपरे कक्ष्ये द्वे जगाम नरोत्तमः ।।

20. Riding the chariot, (Raama) the foremost of men, covered the three 'Segments' of the palace which were well guarded by armed guards; and then covered the inner segments (of palace) on foot.

❍ ❍ ❍

२१. स सर्वाः समतिक्रम्य कक्ष्या नरवरात्मजः ।
सन्निवर्त्य जनं सर्वं शुद्धान्तःपुरमभ्यगात् ।।

21. This noble son of the king, having covered all the segments of the palace, then entered the fine inner apartments of the queen (Kaikeyi where Dhascharatha

had spent the night in misery). He entered after passing (wading) through the crowd.

❍ ❍ ❍

२२. ततः प्रविष्टे पितुरन्तिकं तदा
जनः स सर्वोमुदितो नृपात्मजे ।
प्रतीक्षते तस्य पुनश्च निर्गमं
यथोदयं चन्द्रमसः सरित्पतिः ।।

22. When (Raama) the son of the king went inside towards his father, all the happy citizens (waiting outside) were eagerly looking for his return (after meeting his father), just like the ocean (awaiting) moon rise.

❍ ❍ ❍

Chapter 18

(Kaikeyi) Orders Raama to go to Forest

(Raama sees his father lying down in pitiable state: Is shocked: Kaikeyi tells him why his father is in such a state; Raama without any second thought, assures Kaikeyi that he will obey the command and go on exile.)

❍ ❍ ❍

१. स ददर्शासने रामो निषण्णं पितरं शुभे ।
कैकेयीसहितं दीनं मुखेन परिशुष्यता ।।

1. This Raama saw his father who was with Kaikeyi lying down on a lovely couch but with his face emaciated, and looking feeble.

❍ ❍ ❍

२. स पितुश्चरणौ पूर्वमभिवाद्य विनीतवान् ।
ततो ववन्दे चरणौ कैकेय्याः सुसमाहितः ।।

2. This well behaved (Raama) composed himself, bowed (& touched) his fathers feet and then bowed to Kaikeyi (touching her) feet.

❍ ❍ ❍

३. रामेत्युवाच वचनं बाष्पपर्याकुलेक्षणः ।
शशाक नृपतिर्दीनो नेक्षितुं नाभिभाषितुम् ।।

3. The downcast king whose eyes were blurred by tears, just uttered (one) word = Oh Raama = He could neither open his eyes nor speak (further).

❍ ❍ ❍

४. तदपूर्वं नरपतेर्दृष्ट्वा रूपं भयावहम् ।
रामोऽपि भयमापन्नः पदा स्पृष्ट्वेव पन्नगम् ।।

4. (Stanzas 4 to 6: The meeting described)

Seeing the strange unprecedented sight of the king whose appearance caused great fear, Raama became terribly seized with fear as though he had trampled upon a snake with his feet .....

❍ ❍ ❍

५. इन्द्रियैरप्रहृष्टैस्तं शोकसंतापकर्शितम् ।
निःश्वसन्तं महाराजं व्यथिताकुलचेतसम् ।।

5. ..... (He saw that) The great king who was breathing hard and deep, was in a state of mind with fear gripping him, was afflicted by grief and torment with his senses (numbed, lacking joy) .....

❍ ❍ ❍

६. ऊर्मिमालिनमक्षोभ्यं क्षुभ्यन्तमिव सागरम् ।
उपप्लुतमिवादित्यमुक्तानृतमृषिं यथा ।।

6. ...... (He saw the king like this):he was like the agitated ocean that is full of waves, which is unshakeable though. He was like the Sun afflicted by Rahu (eclipsed by Raahu): He was like a Rishi who had spoken a lie.

❍ ❍ ❍

७. अचिन्त्यकल्पं हि पितुस्तं शोकमुपधारयन् ।
बभूव संरब्धतरः समुद्र इव पर्वणि ॥

7. Unable to comprehend (the reason for his) father's grief, he reflected upon it and became agitated like ocean during season.

❍ ❍ ❍

८. चिन्तयामास च ततो रामः पितृहिते रतः ।
किं स्विदद्यैव नृपतिर्न मां प्रत्यभिनन्दति ॥

8. The devoted Raama who was ever concerned about his father's welfare, began to ponder:= How is it that the king is not pleased with me today? ......

❍ ❍ ❍

९. अन्यदा मां पिता दृष्ट्वा कुपितोऽपि प्रसीदति ।
तस्य मामद्य संप्रेक्ष्य किमायासः प्रवर्तते ॥

9. ...... Till now, whenever he got angry,(the moment) he saw me,he used to be appeased: (but) Today why is it that (even) after seeing me, weariness still persists (in him) =

❍ ❍ ❍

१०. स दीन इव शोकार्तोविषण्णवदनद्युतिः ।
कैकेयीमभिवाद्यैव रामो वचनमब्रवीत् ॥

10. Feeling dejected, afflicted by grief, his countenance having lost 'color' and brilliance, this Raama looked at Kaikeyi and said these words.

❍ ❍ ❍

११. कच्चिन्मया नापराद्धमज्ञानाद्येन मे पिता ।
कुपितस्तन्ममाचक्ष्व त्वं चैवैनं प्रसादय ॥

11. Why is my father angry? You must enlighten me: I hope I have not done anything wrong in ignorance: Please console him.

१२. अप्रसन्नमनाः किं नु सदा मां प्रति वत्सलः ।
विषण्णवदनो दीनो न हि मामभिभाषते ॥

12. (Raama asks Kaikeyi to console his father little realising that it is because of Kaikeyi that he is reduced to this ghastly state: he bemoans)

He always had deep attachment to me as his son; Why is it he does not speak to me now with his face down cast, his mind totally cheerless.

❍ ❍ ❍

१३. शारीरो मानसो वाऽपि कच्चिदेनं न बाधते ।
सन्तापो वाऽभितापो वा दुर्लभं हि सदासुखम् ॥

13. No illness of body nor affliction of mind, which are both difficult (to bear for mortals), will ever bother this man who is ever endowed with happiness and comfort... I hope! ......

❍ ❍ ❍

१४. कच्चिन्न किञ्चिद्भरते कुमारे प्रियदर्शने ।
शत्रुघ्ने वा महासत्त्वे मातृणां वा ममाशुभम् ॥

14. ...... I hope there is nothing wrong afflicting your pleasant looking son Bharatha (whose mere sight causes joy), or the most pure Schathrugna, (or anything wrong with) mothers (Kowsalya and step mother Sumithra).

❍ ❍ ❍

१५. अतोषयन्महाराजमकुर्वन्वा पितुर्वचः ।
मुहूर्तमपि नेच्छेयं जीवितुं कुपिते नृपे ॥

15. As the king is angry, I do not desire to live even for a muhoortha without fulfilling whatever my father's words (of command) may be and without gratifying the great king (my father).

❍ ❍ ❍

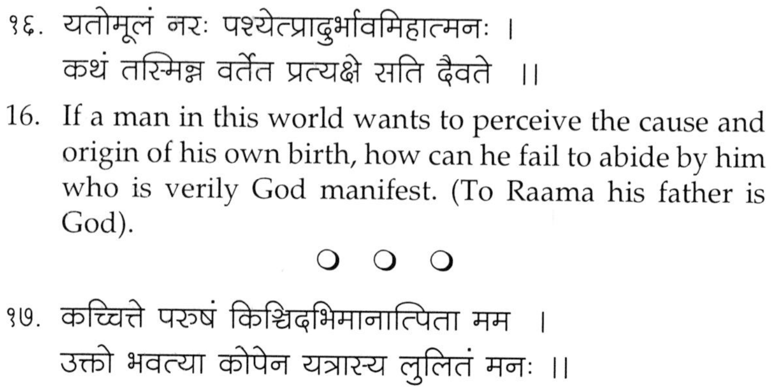

१६. यतोमूलं नरः पश्येत्प्रादुर्भावमिहात्मनः ।
कथं तस्मिन्न वर्तेत प्रत्यक्षे सति दैवते ॥

16. If a man in this world wants to perceive the cause and origin of his own birth, how can he fail to abide by him who is verily God manifest. (To Raama his father is God).

❍ ❍ ❍

१७. कच्चित्ते परुषं किञ्चिदभिमानात्पिता मम ।
उक्तो भवत्या कोपेन यत्रास्य लुलितं मनः ॥

17. Why is his mind agitated? Was my father spoken to harshly by you, either out of passion or in wrath?

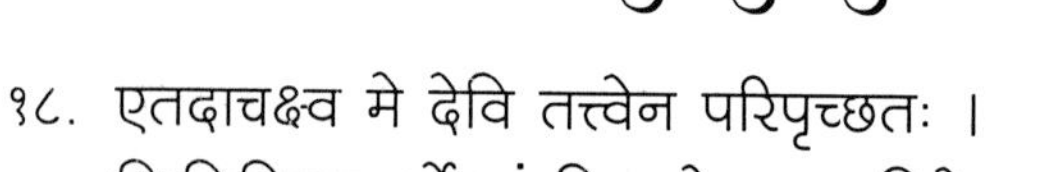

❍ ❍ ❍

१८. एतदाचक्ष्व मे देवि तत्त्वेन परिपृच्छतः ।
किन्निमित्तमपूर्वोऽयं विकारो मनुजाधिपे ॥

18. Oh Lady (Kaikeyi)! What is the cause of this (never seen before) transformation in the king? As I am asking you (please) enlighten me exactly ......

❍ ❍ ❍

१९. एवमुक्ता तु कैकेयी राघवेण महात्मना ।
उवाचेदं सुनिर्लज्जा धृष्टमात्महितं वचः ॥

19. Having heard thus from the noble soul Raama, the shameless Kaikeyi said the following words which indicated her audacity and (utter) selfishness.

❍ ❍ ❍

२०. न राजा कुपितो राम व्यसनं नास्य किञ्चन ।
किञ्चिन्मनोगतं त्वस्य त्वद्भयान्नाभिभाषते ॥

20. Oh Raama! The king (your father) is not angry (with you): He is not in any evil predicament: A matter bothers him in his mind which he does not speak about, due to fear (that may) cause you.

❍ ❍ ❍

२१. प्रियं त्वामप्रियं वक्तुं वाणी नास्योपवर्तते ।
तद्वश्यं त्वया कार्यं यदनेनाश्रुतं मम ।।

21. He has become speechless unable to speak unpleasantly to you who are his beloved; Now what was promised by him to me, must surely be done by you.

❍ ❍ ❍

२२. एष मह्यं वरं दत्त्वा पुरा मामभिपूज्य च ।
स पश्चात्तप्यते राजा यथाऽन्यः प्राकृतस्तथा ।।

22. Long ago, honouring me, (for services rendered by me to him in a war), offering me boons, this King, now, like an ordinary and 'some' person, is repenting.

❍ ❍ ❍

२३. प्रतिश्रुत्य ददामीति वरं मम विशां पतिः ।
स निरर्थं गतजले सेतुं बन्धितुमिच्छति ।।

23. (your father the) Lord of Earth, having promised = I Will Give = now desires to wriggle out of the commitment and make (the boons) worthless, out of his stupidity.

❍ ❍ ❍

२४. धर्ममूलमिदं राम विदितं च सतामपि ।
तत्सत्यं न त्यजेद्राजा कुपितस्त्वत्कृते यथा ।।

24. Oh Raama! This was committed (by him long ago). Truth alone is the root of Dharma for all good men. Therefore the angry king should not abandon this even for your sake.

❍ ❍ ❍

२५. यदि तद्वक्ष्यते राजा शुभं वा यदि वाऽशुभम् ।
करिष्यसि ततः सर्वमाख्यास्यामि पुनस्त्वहम् ।।

25. The king is (holding this back) in his bosom: If you (promise to) do whether it is good or bad for you, then I will tell (in detail) everything.

❍ ❍ ❍

२६. यदि त्वभिहितं राज्ञा त्वयि तन्न विपत्स्यते ।
ततोऽहमभिधास्यामि न ह्येष त्वयि वक्ष्यति ।।

26. This man will not tell you: Therefore, if that which was expressed (and committed) by the king does not come to nought at your hands, then only will I explain.

❍ ❍ ❍

२७. एतत्तु वचनं श्रुत्वा कैकेय्या समुदाहृतम् ।
उवाच व्यथितो रामस्तां देवीं नृपसन्निधौ ।।

27. Hearing these words uttered by Kaikeyi before the king, Raama who was distressed, then addressed the lady thus:

❍ ❍ ❍

२८. अहो धिङ्नार्हसे देवि वक्तुं मामीदृशं वचः ।
अहं हि वचनाद्राज्ञः पतेयमपि पावके ।।
भक्षयेयं विषं तीक्ष्णं मज्जेयमपि चार्णवे ।।

28. (Kaikeyi is a clever woman: First makes Raama promise) By the king's word (of command) I will even jump into fire: I will drink potent poison: I will drown myself in ocean: Therefore, Oh Lady (Kaikeyi)! You should not speak such words to me: Ah! Fie (What a shame that you should think of me as a disobedient son).

❍ ❍ ❍

२९. नियुक्तो गुरुणा पित्रा नृपेण च हितेन च ।।

29. I am bound to my father the king (who is verily my) teacher, ever seeking his welfare and good.

❍ ❍ ❍

३०. तद्ब्रूहि वचनं देवि राज्ञो यदभिकाङ्क्षितम् ।
करिष्ये प्रतिजाने च रामो द्विर्नाभिभाषते ।।

30. Raama Never Speaks In Two Ways; Oh lady (Kaikeyi)! {please) tell me the words (of command) of the king

as desired by him ; And that I will (faithfully) fulfill: I swear.

❍ ❍ ❍

३१. तमार्जवसमायुक्तमनार्या सत्यवादिनम् ।
उवाच रामं कैकेयी वचनं भृशदारुणम् ।।

31. Then this un-Aryan Kaikeyi told these most cruel words to Raama who was a man of Truth (whoever spoke truth) and who was endowed with honesty and sincerity.

❍ ❍ ❍

३२. पुरा देवासुरे युद्धे पित्रा ते मम राघव ।
रक्षितेन वरौ दत्तौ सशल्येन महारणे ।।

32. Oh (Raama the) Raaghava! Long ago, in a
Dheva-Asura war, two Boons were offered to me by your father at the battle field when he was wounded by Asura-s but well protected (and saved by me).

❍ ❍ ❍

३३. तत्र मे याचितो राजा भरतस्याभिषेचनम् ।
गमनं दण्डकारण्ये तव चाद्यैव राघव ।।

33. (Oh (Raama) the Raaghava! As per that, now the king was requested by me (to fulfill the two boons): Exile to Dhandaka forest for you and Crowning (as successor to the throne) for my (son) Bharatha.

❍ ❍ ❍

३४. यदि सत्यप्रतिज्ञं त्वं पितरं कर्तुमिच्छसि ।
आत्मानं च नरश्रेष्ठ मम वाक्यमिदं श्रृणु ।।

34. Oh noble man (Raama)! If you desire to make your father faithful to Truth, (a man of commitment), then you must 'listen' (to and honour) this, my word (of command).

❍ ❍ ❍

३५. सन्निदेशे पितुस्तिष्ठ यथा तेन प्रतिश्रुतम् ।
त्वयाऽरण्यं प्रवेष्टव्यं नव वर्षाणि पञ्च च ॥

35. Stand firm by your father's order: As per his promise, you should live in forest for (9 plus 5), 14 years in forest.

❍ ❍ ❍

३६. भरतश्चाभिषिच्येत यदेतदभिषेचनम् ।
त्वदर्थेविहितं राज्ञा तेन सर्वेण राघव ॥

36. Oh (Raama) the Raaghava! By all and by the very same arrangements (made by your father) for your coronation, this Bharatha should (now) be crowned.

❍ ❍ ❍

३७. सप्त सप्त च वर्षाणि दण्डकारण्यमाश्रितः ।
अभिषेकमिमं त्यक्त्वा जटाजिनधरो वस ॥

37. Renouncing this (your coronation) you should spend your time living in Dhandaka forest for (7 plus 7) 14-years, wearing deer skin and sporting (unkempt) hair locks (of a mendicant).

❍ ❍ ❍

३८. भरतः कोसलपुरे प्रशास्तु वसुधामिमाम् ।
नानारत्नसमाकीर्णां सवाजिरथकुञ्जराम् ॥

38. May Bharatha in Kosala city (of Ayodhya) rule this earth (richly endowed) with various costly gems and stones, and which is full of horses, elephants and chariots.

❍ ❍ ❍

३९. एतेन त्वां नरेन्द्रोऽयं कारुण्येन समाप्लुतः ।
शोकसंक्लिष्टवदनो न शक्नोति निरीक्षितुम् ॥

39. This king, overwhelmed by compassion (to you) with his face down cast by grief, is unable to look at you.

❍ ❍ ❍

४०. एतत्कुरु नरेन्द्रस्य वचनं रघुनन्दन ।
सत्येन महता राम तारयस्व नरेश्वरम् ।।

40. Oh darling of Raghu-s, Oh Raama! You comply with this order of the king. You must protect (& save) the king in this matter of great (honour and) Truth.

❍ ❍ ❍

४१. इतीव तस्यां परुषं वदन्त्यां
न चैव रामः प्रविवेश शोकम् ।
प्रविव्यथे चापि महानुभावो
राजा स पुत्रव्यसनाभितप्तः ।।

41. In spite of hearing such cruel words from (his step mother Kaikeyi), the magnanimous Raama did not allow any grief to enter him (afflict him); But the king was even more distressed, tormented by the (impending) suffering to his son (Raama).

❍ ❍ ❍

Chapter 19

(Raama) Vows to go to Forest

(Raama vows that he will honour his father's commitment to Kaikeyi; Will go to forest on exile.)

❍ ❍ ❍

१. तदप्रियममित्रघ्नो वचनं मरणोपमम् ।
श्रुत्वा न विव्यथे रामः कैकेयीं चेदमब्रवीत् ।।

1. This Raama the destroyer of enemies, hearing these words (of Kaikeyi) which was unpalatable and were like death (to the king) distressed not. And he said these words to Kaikeyi.

❍ ❍ ❍

२. एवमस्तु गमिष्यामि वनं वस्तुमहं त्वित: ।
जटाजिनधरो राज्ञ: प्रतिज्ञामनुपालयन् ।।

2. So Be It! Wearing (mendicant's robe) of deer skin and sporting unkempt hairlocks, honouring king's command, I will now, from here itself, go away to forest to live.

❍ ❍ ❍

३. इदं तु ज्ञातुमिच्छामि किमर्थं मां महिपति: ।
नाभिनन्दति दुर्धर्षो यथापुरमरिंदम: ।।

3. Why does not the conqueror of enemies, this uncrushable lord of Earth (my father) rejoice (seeing me) as is usual with him. This alone I wish to know.

❍ ❍ ❍

४. मन्युर्न च त्वया कार्यो देवि ब्रूमि तवाग्रत: ।
यास्यामि भव सुप्रीता वनं चीरजटाधर: ।।

4. Oh queen (Kaikeyi)! I am going to forest now wearing deer skin and sporting unkempt hair lock: I tell you this before your presence; There should be no (room for) anxiety (doubt) in you. Be happy.

❍ ❍ ❍

५. हितेन गुरुणा पित्रा कृतज्ञेन नृपेण च ।
नियुज्यमानो विस्राब्ध: किं न कुर्यामहं प्रियम् ।।

5. What will I not do with pleasure and in tranquillity when I am commanded by my father, the king, who is my teacher, well wisher and who is a man of gratitude.

❍ ❍ ❍

६. अलीकं मानसं त्वेकं हृदयं दहतीव मे ।
स्वयं यन्नाह मां राजा भरतस्याभिषेचनम् ।।

6. What burns up my heart most disagreeably is this

alone: That (my father the) King did not himself tell me about Bharatha's Coronation that was in his mind.

❍ ❍ ❍

७. अहं हि सीतां राज्यं च प्राणानिष्टान्धनानि च ।
हृष्टो भ्रात्रे स्वयं दद्यां भरतायाप्रचोदितः ॥

7. For my brother, for Bharatha, without anybody's bidding, I myself will give up my kingdom, wealth and even Seetha and my dear citizens.

❍ ❍ ❍

८. किं पुनर्मनुजेन्द्रेण स्वयं पित्रा प्रचोदितः ।
तव च प्रियकामार्थं प्रतिज्ञामनुपालयन् ॥

8. (When that is so) Will I not fulfill my promise for the sake of fulfilling your desire (particularly) when I am commanded by my father, the lord of men.

❍ ❍ ❍

९. तदाश्वासय भीतं त्वं किं न्विदं यन्महीपतिः ।
वसुधासक्तनयनो मन्दमश्रूणि मुञ्चति ॥

9. The King (my father) is shedding tears slowly, looking down on earth with 'detached' eyes, (gripped) by fear: Why should it be so. You please console him now.

❍ ❍ ❍

१०. गच्छन्तु चैवानयितुं दूताः शीघ्रजवैर्हयैः ।
भरतं मातुलकुलादद्यैव नृपशासनात् ॥

10. On king's command, let couriers be sent at once on fast moving horses to fetch Bharatha from his maternal uncle's place now.

❍ ❍ ❍

११. दण्डकारण्यमेषोऽहमितो गच्छामि सत्वरः ।
अविचार्य पितुर्वाक्यं समा वस्तुं चतुर्दश ॥

11. (Obeying) King's Command unhesitatingly (without any deliberation) and losing no time, I will go from here itself to live in Dhandaka forest for 14 years.

❍ ❍ ❍

१२. सा हृष्टा तस्य तद्वाक्यं श्रुत्वा रामस्य कैकयी ।
प्रस्थानं श्रद्दधाना हि त्वरयामास राघवम् ।।

12. (What follows is the unkindest 'Cut' of all-from the cruel Kaikeyi.)

Hearing such words from Raama, this Kaikeyi became very confident and joyous; And she 'hurried (Raama) the Raaghava in the matter of his departure (to forest).

❍ ❍ ❍

१३. एवं भवतु यास्यन्ति दूता: शीघ्रजवैर्हयै: ।
भरतं मातुलकुलादुपावर्तयितुं नरा: ।।

13. (Kaikeyi is firm): The Couriers will (of course) go forth on fast moving horses to fetch Bharatha from his uncle's place: Be that as it may ......

❍ ❍ ❍

१४. तव त्वहं क्षमं मन्ये नोत्सुकस्य विलम्बनम् ।
राम तस्मादित: शीघ्रं वनं त्वं गन्तुमर्हसि ।।

14. ...... Oh Raama! Zealous as you are (in honouring your own commitment), I think it is not necessary for you to delay (your departure and hang around to await Bharatha): Therefore you should go at once to forest from here (itself).

❍ ❍ ❍

१५. व्रीडान्वित: स्वयं यच्च नृपस्त्वां नाभिभाषते ।
नैतत्किञ्चिन्नरश्रेष्ट मन्युरेषोऽपनीयताम् ।।

15. Oh noble (Raama): Out of shame, the king is not able to talk to you himself; There is no other reason (nothing is wrong with him!); Cast away this anxiety (over him).

❍ ❍ ❍

१६. यावत्वं न वनं यातः पुरादस्मादभित्वरन् ।
पिता तावन्न ते राम स्नास्यते भोक्ष्यतेऽपि वा ॥

16. Oh Raama! Unless you leave this city for forest quickly, till then, your father will not take (even) bath nor eat at all.

(This was how the cruel Kaikeyi goaded Raama to make a quick get away from Ayodhya: Dhascharatha is totally submerged in grief.)

❍ ❍ ❍

१७. धिक्कष्टमिति निःश्वस्यः राजा शोकपरिप्लुतः ।
मूर्च्छितो न्यपतत्तस्मिन्पर्यङ्के हेमभूषिते ॥

17. = Oh Fie! What a torture! = The king grieved (thus); Completely engulfed in grief, breathing hard and deep, he became unconscious and fell down on the couch that was decorated in gold.

❍ ❍ ❍

१८. रामोऽप्युत्थाप्य राजानं कैकेय्याऽभिप्रचोदितः ।
कशयेवाहतो वाजी वनं गन्तुं कृतत्वरः ॥

18. Even as Raama was (trying) to lift up the king, he was goaded by Kaikeyi to speed up his departure to the forest, like a horse being whipped up with a whip.

❍ ❍ ❍

१९. तदप्रियमनार्याया वचनं दारुणोदयम् ।
श्रुत्वा गतव्यथो रामः कैकेयीं वाक्यमब्रवीत् ॥

19. (Even) After hearing such most unpalatable and pitilessly cruel words from this un-Aryan (ignoble Kaikeyi), Raama was not perturbed and he addressed Kaikeyi these words;

❍ ❍ ❍

२०. नाहमर्थपरो देवि लोकमावस्तुमुत्सहे ।
विद्धि मामृषिभिस्तुल्यं केवलं धर्ममास्थितम् ॥

20. Oh queen! I do not desire to live in this world (merely) for the sake of seeking material things; You should know me as a man steadfast in Dharma only and like Rishi-s...(and) ......

❍ ❍ ❍

२१. यदत्रभवतः किञ्चिच्छक्यं कर्तुं प्रियं मया ।
प्राणानपि परित्यज्य सर्वथा कृतमेव तत् ।।

21. ..... if there is anything that will please this noble man (this, my father) which could be done, that will be done by me even if life has to be given up by me ......

❍ ❍ ❍

२२. न ह्यतो धर्मचरणं किञ्चिदस्ति महत्तरम् ।
यथा पितरि शुश्रूषा तस्य वा वचनक्रिया ।।

22. Because, there is nothing greater and foremost in practice of Dharma than doing service to a father and fulfilling his words.

❍ ❍ ❍

२३. अनुक्तोऽप्यत्रभवता भवत्या वचनादहम् ।
वने वत्स्यामि निजने वर्षाणीह चतुर्दश ।।

23. Although I am not (directly) told (and commanded) by this noble man here, because it is your words of command, I am going to live for 14 years in the uninhabited forest.

❍ ❍ ❍

२४. न नूनं मयि कैकेयि किञ्चिदाशंसते गुणान् ।
यद्राजानमवोचस्त्वं ममेश्वरतरा सती ।।

24. (Raama says he will even obey his (step) mother Kaikeyi.)

Oh Kaikeyi! (I regret) That you, who are like a Goddess to me, did not expect (or find) even a little of the good qualities in me; That is why you spoke to the king. (I would have gladly gone away to forest to make room for Bharatha, even if you had given such a command).

❍ ❍ ❍

२५. यावन्मातरमापृच्छे सीतां चानुनयाम्यहम् ।
ततोऽद्यैव गमिष्यामि दण्डकानां महद्धनम् ।।

25. I am bidding my mother (Kowsalya) farewell: Then I will (go to) pacify Seetha. Then I will go to the great forest, the Dhandaka.

❍ ❍ ❍

२६. भरतः पालयेद्राज्यं शुश्रुषेच्च पितुर्यथा ।
तथा भवत्या कर्तव्यं स हि धर्मस्सनातनः ।।

26. Let Bharatha serve father (when I am gone): This is the Eternal Dharma. Likewise it should be done by you also. Let him rule the kingdom.

❍ ❍ ❍

२७. स रामस्य वचः श्रुत्वा भृशं दुःखहतः पिता ।
शोकादशक्नुवन् बाष्पं प्ररुरोद महास्वनम् ।।

27. When he heard his words, Raama's father became even more sad. In utter grief, shed tears, unable to control it. He began to cry in loud voice.

❍ ❍ ❍

२८. वन्दित्वा चरणो रामो विसंज्ञस्य पितुस्तदा ।
कैकेय्याश्चाप्यनार्याया निष्पपात महाद्युतिः ।।

28. After bowing and falling at the feet of his father who was unconscious and also (at the feet of this) un-Aryan Kaikeyi, the glorious Raama stepped out.

❍ ❍ ❍

२९. स रामः पितरं कृत्वा कैकेयीं च प्रदक्षिणम् ।
निष्क्रम्यान्तः पुरात्तस्मात्स्वं ददर्श सुहृज्जनम् ।।

29. After going round his father (in circumbambulation) and then round Kaikeyi, Raama came out of the inner apartments of the palace and saw (crowd) of his devoted citizens.

❍ ❍ ❍

३०. तं बाष्पपरिपूर्णाक्षः पृष्ठतोऽनुजगाम ह ।
लक्ष्मणः परमक्रुद्धस्सुमित्रानन्दवर्धनः ॥

30. And Lakshmana the darling of (his mother) Sumithra and who makes her rejoice, was in terrible wrath with tears coming out of his eyes. And he followed (Raama as he came out).

❍ ❍ ❍

३१. अभिषेचनिकं भाण्डं कृत्वा रामः प्रदक्षिणम् ।
शनैर्जगाम सापेक्षो दृष्टिं तत्राविचालयन् ॥

31. Giving this matter serious consideration (to leave quickly to forest) without deviating from his objective Raama slowly circumbambulated the holy ritual mound and then left.

❍ ❍ ❍

३२. न चास्य महतीं लक्ष्मीं राज्यनाशोऽपकर्षति ।
लोककान्तस्य कान्तत्वं शीतरश्मेरिव क्षपा ॥

32. (In spite of) Losing the kingdom, the great resplendency and the charm of this man who charmed the whole world, did not diminish (at all) like the night by the (full) moon.

❍ ❍ ❍

३३. न वनं गन्तु कामस्य त्यजतश्च वसुन्धराम् ।
सर्वलोकातिगस्येव लक्ष्यते वित्तविक्रिया ॥

33. (In spite of) Abandoning the earth (kingdom), and choosing to go to forest, there was no change in his

character, like one who had no 'attachment' in the (material) world.

❍ ❍ ❍

३४. प्रतिषिध्य शुभं छत्रं व्यजने च स्वलङ्कृते ।
विसर्जयित्वा स्वजनं रथं पौरांस्तथा जनान् ।।

३५. धारयन्मनसा दुःखमिन्द्रियाणि निगृह्य च ।
प्रविवेशात्मवान् वेश्म मातुरप्रियशंसिवान् ।।

34 & 35.

Discarding the beautiful umbrella, the well decorated whisk fan, and the chariot, and making way through the citizens and village folks.....this man of composure (this Raama) then entered the palace with a view to tell the unpleasant news, bearing (the thought) in his mind, the misery (that would be caused) to his mother. He restrained his feelings (controlled his senses).

❍ ❍ ❍

३६. सर्वोह्यभिजनः श्रीमाञ्छ्रीमतस्सत्यवादिनः ।
नालक्षयत रामस्य किञ्चिदाकारमानने ।।

36. None, not even a noble resplendent man could see any change nor (weariness) in the face of the resplendent Raama, the man of Truth.

❍ ❍ ❍

३७. उचितं च महाबाहुर्न जहौ हर्षमात्मनः ।
शारदः समुदीर्णांशुश्चन्द्रस्तेज इवात्मजम् ।।

37. Like moon which doesn't lose its lustre of its manifold rays during autumn, so was Raama, this mighty limbed man who did not give up his befitting brilliance (and cheer).

❍ ❍ ❍

३८. वाचा मधुरया रामस्सर्वं सम्मानयञ्जनम् ।
मातुस्समीपं धीरात्मा प्रविवेश महायशाः ।।

38. This famous strong minded Raama entered his mother's palace, honouring (and cheering) all the citizens there with sweet words.

❍ ❍ ❍

३९. तं गुणैस्समतां प्राप्तो भ्राता विपुलविक्रमः ।
सौमित्रिरनुवव्राज धारयन्दुःखमात्मजम् ।।

39. His brother Lakshmana of immense valour, (this son of Sumithra) who by his qualities had the same attainments (like his brother Raama), followed Raama (to the palace), bearing his grief (within himself).

❍ ❍ ❍

४०. प्रविश्य वेश्मातिभृशं मुदाऽन्वितं
समीक्ष्य तां चार्थविपत्तिमागताम् ।
न चैव रामोऽत्र जगाम विक्रियां
सुहृज्जनस्यात्मविपत्तिशङ्कया ।।

40. Entering the most pleasant place, and reflecting upon the failure in the matter (of his coronation) that came about, Raama did not exhibit any change (in his behaviour) as it would cause great suffering (and disappointment) to his beloved citizens.

(Comment is unnecessary; Vaalmeeki has said all that is to be said about Raama. Kingdom or no kingdom, city life or forest life, it is all the same for this unique personality.)

❍ ❍ ❍

Chapter 20

Kowsalya's Bemoaning

(News spreads: Beloved Raama is not to be crowned: Raama informs his mother Kowsalya who is completely shattered hearing that her son has to go on exile for 14 years)

❍ ❍ ❍

१. तस्मिंस्तु पुरुषव्याघ्रे निष्क्रामति कृताञ्जलौ ।
आर्तशब्दो महाञ्जज्ञे स्त्रीणामन्तःपुरे तदा ॥

1. As this 'tiger' of men (Raama) was walking along with his hands cupped in Anjali, loud conversations took place indicating grief of ladies of the inner apartments (of the palace).

❍ ❍ ❍

२. कृत्येष्वचोदितः पित्रा सर्वस्यान्तः पुरस्य च ।
गतिर्यश्शरणं चापि स रामोऽद्य प्रवत्स्यति ॥

2. (The ladies bemoan): He who fulfills the wishes of all the ladies of the royal household, he who is not even commanded by his father (to go on exile), he who is the Refuge for those seeking refuge, such a Raama is going away today ......

❍ ❍ ❍

३. कौसल्यायां यथा युक्तो जनन्यां वर्तते सदा ।
तथैव वर्ततेऽस्मासु जन्मप्रभृति राघवः ॥

3. ...... Right from his birth, always, this (Raama the) Raaghava has been behaving towards us just the same way as he has been devoted to his mother Kowsalya.

❍ ❍ ❍

४. न क्रुध्यत्यभिशप्तोऽपि क्रोधनीयानि वर्जयन् ।
क्रुद्धान्प्रसादयन् सर्वान् स इतोऽद्य प्रवत्स्यति ॥

4. He shuns angry words and deeds: Never gets angry even when reviled (& harshly spoken to): He pacifies one who gets angry; Such (a Raama) is going away from here.

❍ ❍ ❍

५. अबुद्धिर्बत नो राजा जीवलोकं चरत्ययम् ।
यो गतिं सर्वभूतानां परित्यजति राघवम् ।।

5. This, our king (Dhascharatha) who is now abandoning this (Raama) the Raaghava who is the Refuge of all beings, will now live in this world having lost his mind (like a mad man) What a shame!

❍ ❍ ❍

६. इति सर्वा महिष्यस्ता विवत्सा इव धेनवः ।
पतिमाचुक्रुशुश्चैव सस्वरं चापि चुक्रुशुः ।।

6. All the * ladies (of the royal household) were lamenting over (the action of) their lord (Dhascharatha); And they cried aloud like cows bereft of their calves.

(Vaalmeeki uses the word * = Mahishi =: there were 350 wives of Dhascharatha who had no royal status like his 3 queens,)

❍ ❍ ❍

७. स हि चान्तःपुरे घोरमार्तशब्दं महीपतिः ।
पुत्रशोकाभिसन्तप्तः श्रुत्वा व्यालीयतासने ।।

7. Tormented by the grief over his son (Raama), the king who heard the loud, gruesome wailing (of the ladies) in the inner apartments (of the palace), trembled in his seat.

❍ ❍ ❍

८. रामस्तु भृशमायस्तो विश्वसन्निव कुञ्जरः ।
जगाम सहितो भ्रात्रा मातुरन्तः पुरं वशी ।।

8. Raama who subjugated himself (in service of others)

and who (ever) exerted himself greatly, entered his mother's apartment, (firm) like an elephant, breathing freely (like a happy man), followed by his brother (Lakshmana).

❍ ❍ ❍

९. सोऽपश्यत्पुरुषं तत्र वृद्धं परमपूजितम् ।
उपविष्टं गृहद्वारि तिष्ठतश्चापरान्बहून् ।।

9. There, at the entrance of the mansion, he saw the old and most respected man (a guard), sitting and many others who were standing.

❍ ❍ ❍

१०. दृष्ट्वैव तु तदा रामं ते सर्वेसमुपस्थिताः ।
जयेति जयतां श्रेष्ठं वर्धयन्ति स्म राघवम् ।।

10. When all of them saw this foremost amongst the victorious, this Raama the Raaghava, they stood up near him and greeted him = Victory = (This is as per protocol).

❍ ❍ ❍

११. प्रविश्य प्रथमां कक्ष्यां द्वितीयायां ददर्श सः ।
ब्राह्मणान्वेदसम्पन्नान्वृद्धान्राज्ञाऽभिसत्कृतान् ।।

11. Crossing the first segment (of the palace) he saw in the second segment, elderly braamins who were honoured by the king for their erudition in Vedha-s.

❍ ❍ ❍

१२. प्रणम्य रामस्तान्वृद्धांस्तृतीयायां ददर्श सः ।
स्त्रियो वृद्धाश्च बालाश्च द्वाररक्षणतत्पराः ।।

12. After offering his respects to these elders, this Raama saw in the third segment (of the palace), old trustworthy guards and young girls.

❍ ❍ ❍

१३. वर्धयित्वा प्रहृष्टास्ताः प्रविश्य च गृहं स्त्रियः ।
न्यवेदयन्त त्वरिता राममातुः प्रियं तदा ॥

13. These ladies greeted him with joy; And they entered the palace quickly and informed Raama's mother the happy news (of Raama's arrival).

❍ ❍ ❍

१४. कौसल्याऽपि तदा देवी रात्रिं स्थित्वा समाहिता ।
प्रभाते चाकरोत्पूजां विष्णोः पुत्रहितैषिणी ॥

14. Always seeking welfare for her son, the queen Kowsalya who was steadfast in meditation during the whole night, was doing prayers to God Vishnu in the morning.

❍ ❍ ❍

१५. सा क्षौमवसना हृष्टा नित्यं व्रतपरायणा ।
अग्निं जुहोति स्म तदा मन्त्रवत् कृतमङ्गला ॥

15. Ever steadfast in Vows, this propitious (Kowsalya) was happily making offerings to (holy) fire with chants.

❍ ❍ ❍

१६. प्रविश्य तु तदा रामो मातुरन्तःपुरं शुभम् ।
ददर्श मातरं तत्र हावयन्तीं हुताशनम् ॥

16. Entering the inner apartments of the auspicious (palace) of his mother, Raama saw his mother doing fire rituals on (holy) fire.

❍ ❍ ❍

१७. देवकार्यनिमित्तं च तत्रापश्यत्समुद्यतम् ॥

17. And he observed that everything was properly set up for prayers to Deities.

❍ ❍ ❍

१८. दध्यक्षतं घृतं चैव मोदकान् हविषस्तदा ।
लाजान्माल्यानि शुक्लानि पायसं कृसरं तथा ।।
समिधः पूर्णकुम्भांश्च ददर्श रघुनन्दनः ।।

18. (Raama) the darling of Raghu-s, saw there Akshatha (holy seeds), butter oil, sweet cakes. fire, puffed grains, white flower garlands, sweet milk, likewise seed cakes, Samiths (twigs), *and pots full (with holy waters-* Poornakumbha).

❍ ❍ ❍

१९. तां शुक्लक्षौमसंवीतां व्रतयोगेन कर्शिताम् ।
तर्पयन्तीं ददर्शाद्भिर्देवतां वरवर्णिनीम् ।।

19. And (Raama) saw her (who was somewhat) emaciated because of doing vows & rituals. And he saw this lady of lovely complexion who was wearing white silken garments, offering (& pleasing) the Deities with holy waters.

❍ ❍ ❍

२०. सा चिरस्यात्मजं दृष्ट्वा मातृनन्दनमागतम् ।
अभिचक्राम संहृष्टा किशोरं बडबा यथा ।।

20. When she saw her son who ever delighted his mother, come there, she went towards him in great joy, like a female horse (going to its) young one.

❍ ❍ ❍

२१. स मातरमभिक्रान्तामुपसंगृह्य राघवः ।
पर्यष्वजत धर्मात्मा मात्रा चैव परन्तपः ।।
परिष्वक्तश्च बाहुभ्यामुपाघ्रातश्च मूर्धनि ।।

21. The noble soul man of Dharma, this tormentor of enemies, this (Raama) the Raaghava, embraced his mother when she approached him. And he clasped her. And he was hugged by his mother with her hands. He was kissed by her on his forehead.

❍ ❍ ❍

२२. तमुवाच दुराधर्षं राघवं सुतमात्मनः ।
कौसल्या पुत्रवात्सल्यादिदं प्रियहितं वचः ।।

22. Then Kowsalya addressed this (Raama the) Raaghava, her son, who was uncrushable, with following salutary words, out of her deep love for her son.

❍ ❍ ❍

२३. वृद्धानां धर्मशीलानां राजर्षीणां महात्मनाम् ।
प्राप्नुह्यायुश्च कीर्तिं च धर्मं चाप्युचितं कुले ।।

23. May you obtain, (being born) in this family, the long life of royal sages, the fame of men of great soul, the Dharma of those devoted to Dharma and the befitting (conduct) of elders.

❍ ❍ ❍

२४. सत्यप्रतिज्ञं पितरं राजानं पश्य राघव ।
अद्यैव हि त्वां धर्मात्मा यौवराज्येऽभिषेक्ष्यति ।।

24. Oh (Raama the) Raaghava ! The noble soul (king Dhascharatha) is going to crown you as YuvaRaaja. Therefore (seek and) 'behold' your father, the king, who is verily steadfast in Truth.

(Kowsalya does not know the happenings of the night at Kaikeyi's place: She has been awake the whole night in vows, meditation and prayers for her son Raama who was to be crowned.)

❍ ❍ ❍

२५. दत्तमासनमालभ्य भोजनेन निमन्त्रितः ।
मातरं राघवः किञ्चिद्व्रीडात्प्राञ्जलिरब्रवीत् ।।

25. Sitting down somewhat * bashfully on the seat offered, (Raama) the Raaghava who was invited to breakfast (by his mother), then addressed his mother with his hands cupped in Anjali .....

❍ ❍ ❍

२६. स स्वभावविनीतश्च गौरवाच्च तदा नतः ।
प्रस्थितो दण्डकारण्यमाप्रष्टुमुपचक्रमे ॥

26. ...... (Raama conveys the disturbing news)... (this Raama) who by nature was modest, who was preparing to leave for Dhandaka forest, who, out of respect (to his mother), had bowed, began to take leave (of his mother).

(Vaalmeeki uses the word* = Vreeda = bashfulness, because Raama has already discarded the comforts of a prince, feels embarrassed to sit in a royal seat at his mother's place when invited by his mother)

❍ ❍ ❍

२७. देवि नूनं न जानीषे महद्भयमुपस्थितम् ।
इदं तव च दुःखाय वैदेह्या लक्ष्मणस्य च ॥

27. Oh Lady (my mother Kowsalya)! A great dreadful (situation) has now arisen that would cause suffering to you, to (Seetha) the Vaidhehi and to Lakshmana. You are not aware of this.

❍ ❍ ❍

२८. गमिष्ये दण्डकारण्यं किमनेनासनेन मे ।
विष्टरासनयोग्यो हि कालोऽयं मामुपस्थितः ॥

28. I am gong to Dhandaka forest. I am fit (to sit) only on a seat of Vishtara grass. This, is the destiny ordained for me. What is the purpose (in wasting time sitting) in this (lovely) seat for me (now).

❍ ❍ ❍

२९. चतुर्दश हि वर्षाणि वत्स्यामि विजने वने ।
मधुमूलफलैर्जीवन् हित्वा मुनिवदामिषम् ॥

29. Living in the uninhabited forest for 14 years, giving up pleasures (of royal life), sustaining myself on tubers and fruits & honeys, I will live on like a Muni.

❍ ❍ ❍

३०. भरताय महाराजो यौवराज्यं प्रयच्छति ।
मां पुनर्दण्डकारण्ये विवासयति तापसम् ।।

30. The Emperor desires the (Title of) crown prince to Bharatha instead; And he has exiled me to Dhandaka forest as a man of penance.

❍ ❍ ❍

३१. स षट् चाष्टौ च वर्षाणि वत्स्यामि विजने वने ।
आसेवमानो वन्यानि फलमूलैश्च वर्तयन् ।।

31. Such as I am, am going to live in the uninhabited forest for (6 plus 8), 14 years, leading a life of forest, sustaining myself on tubers, fruits.

❍ ❍ ❍

३२. सा निकृत्तेव सालस्य यष्टिः परशुना वने ।
पपात सहसा देवी देवतेव दिवश्च्युता ।।

32. (Some commentators feel that Raama should have been more 'diplomatic' in conveying such a terrible news to his mother. There need not be any reference to royal seat- Seat made of grass in forest, tubers and honeys etc. in the forest. Any mother's heart will bleed hearing what Raama said).

(hearing this) This lady (Kowsalya) suddenly fell down on earth, like a branch of a (big) tree that is cut with an axe, and like a (celestial) thrown out from sky (heaven).

❍ ❍ ❍

३३. तामदुःखोचितां दृष्ट्वा पतितां कदलीमिव ।
रामस्तूत्थापयामास मातरं गतचेतसम् ।।

33. Seeing his mother who had never seen suffering before (nor deserved suffering) fallen down like a Kadali (deer), with her consciousness gone, Raama at once lifted her up.

❍ ❍ ❍

३४. उपावृत्योत्थितां दीनां बडबामिव वाहिताम् ।
पांसुकुण्ठितसर्वाङ्गीं विममर्श च पाणिना ॥

34. (Raama), with his hands, stroked her who was like mother of Ashwinis, who had attained state of misery, who was 'bearing' this news (who was 'hit' by this news), who was besmeared with holy camphor powders & scents: (She got up somehow).

❍ ❍ ❍

३५. सा राघवमुपासीनमदुःखार्हा सुखोचिता ।
उवाच पुरुषव्याघ्रमुपश्रृण्वति लक्ष्मणे ॥

35. She (Lady Kowsalya) who was ever used to comforts, who did not deserve to suffer, addressed (Raama) the Raaghava, the 'tiger' of men, who was standing close by her, even as Lakshmana was listening:

❍ ❍ ❍

३६. यदि पुत्र न जायेथा मम शोकाय राघव ।
न स्म दुःखमतो भूयः पश्येयमहमप्रजाः ॥

36. Oh my son (Raama) the Raaghava! Had you not been born to me and thus made me childless, I would not (now) be 'seeing' such great sorrow caused by grief.

❍ ❍ ❍

३७. एक एव हि वन्ध्यायाश्शोको भवति मानसः ।
अप्रजाऽस्मीति सन्तापो न ह्यन्यः पुत्र विद्यते ॥

37 Oh my son! For a barren woman there is only one grief in her mind that she has no son. There is no other torment in her.

❍ ❍ ❍

३८. न दृष्टपूर्वं कल्याणं सुखं वा पतिपौरुषे ।
अपि पुत्रे विपश्येयमिति रामास्थितं मया ॥

38. Oh Raama! (In spite of) Having the patronage of my

husband, happiness was not enjoyed by me before. The abiding happiness I was looking forward to, was only (through you) my son.

(Here Kowsalya bemoans because Dhascharatha spent most time with his other wife Kaikeyi who was very possessive & demanding.)

❍ ❍ ❍

३९. सा बहून्यमनोज्ञानि वाक्यानि हृदयच्छिदाम् ।
अहं श्रोष्ये सपत्नीनामवराणां वरा सती ।।

39. Eldest (though I am), I am now going to listen to heart breaking, various insulting words from Co-wives (like Kaikeyi).

❍ ❍ ❍

४०. अतो दुःखतरं किं नु प्रमदानां भविष्यति ।
मम शोको विलापश्च यादृशोऽयमनन्तकः ।।

40. This most lamentable grief is (now) endless for me; the like of which (is not seen). Can there be any greater calamity for ladies than this.

❍ ❍ ❍

४१. त्वयि संनिहितेऽप्येवमहमासं निराकृता ।
किं पुनः प्रोषिते तात ध्रुवं मरणमेव मे ।।

41. Oh Lad! Even when you are here, I am spurned: Then how much more when you go away: Death is certain for me (without you).

❍ ❍ ❍

४२. अत्यन्तं निगृहीताऽस्मि भर्तुर्नित्यमसंमता ।
परिवारेण कैकेय्यास्समा वाप्यथवाऽवरा ।।

42. Despised by (my) husband, totally and eternally abandoned, I become like one of Kaikeyi's maids or even lower than that.

४३. यो हि मां सेवते कश्चिदथवाऽप्यनुवर्तते ।
कैकेय्याः पुत्रमन्वीक्ष्य स जनो नाभिभाषते ॥

43. And further, this person who (used to) serve me and gratify me, he also would now not even talk to me out of consideration for the son of Kaikeyi.

(Kowsalya fears that Dhascharatha would not even speak to her when Bharatha takes over.)

❍ ❍ ❍

४४. नित्यक्रोधतया तस्याः कथं नु खरवादि तत् ।
कैकेय्या वदनं द्रष्टुं पुत्र शक्ष्यामि दुर्गता ॥

44. Oh my son (Raama)! Unfortunate as I am, how can I bear to see the face of the ever irritable woman Kaikeyi who has a pungent tongue.

❍ ❍ ❍

४५. दश सप्त च वर्षाणि तव जातस्य राघव ।
आसितानि प्रकाङ्क्षन्त्या मया दुःखपरिक्षयम् ॥

45. Oh (Raama) the Raaghava! All these 17 (and more) years of your birth have been spent away in suffering. I was looking forward (to see better days after you were crowned).

❍ ❍ ❍

४६. तदक्षयं महद्दुःखं नोत्सहे सहितुं चिरम् ।
विप्रकारं सपत्नीनामेवं जीर्णाऽपि राघव ॥

46. Oh (Raama) the Raaghava! Withered with age, I cannot tolerate to bear the cruel and eternal suffering caused by the disrespectful mistresses for long.

❍ ❍ ❍

४७. अपश्यन्ती तव मुखं परिपूर्णशशिप्रभम् ।
कृपणा वर्तयिष्यामि कथं कृपणजीविका ॥

47. Wretched as I am, how can I live a life of servitude without seeing your face which is radiant like full moon.

❍ ❍ ❍

४८. उपवासैश्च योगैश्च बहुभिश्च परिश्रमैः ।
दुःखं संवर्धितो मोघं त्वं हि दुर्गतया मया ॥

48. You were brought up by me (with great care), with (various) fasts (undertaken by me) and with various (tiresome and) strenuous Yoga-s (meditation); All the suffering (in raising you) by me who is most unfortunate, has gone to waste.

❍ ❍ ❍

४९. स्थिरं तु हृदयं मन्ये ममेदं यन्न दीर्यते ।
प्रावृषीव महानद्याः स्पृष्टं कूलं नवाम्भसा ॥

49. This my heart should break like embankments of a great river, (broken up) by the flood of new waters during rainy season; As it is not so, I think (my heart) is a rock. (My heart is stone, says Kowsalya).

❍ ❍ ❍

५०. ममैव नूनं मरणं न विद्यते
न चावकाशोऽस्ति यमक्षये मम ।
यदन्तकोऽद्यैव न मां जिहीर्षति
प्रसह्य सिंहो रुदतीं मृगीमिव ॥

50. (Oh, The lord of Death) Yama is not carrying me away now who is crying like a deer before lion. Therefore, is there no death at all? Is there no place for me even in the abode of death.

❍ ❍ ❍

५१. स्थिरं हि नूनं हृदयं ममायसं
न भिद्यते यद्भुवि नावदीर्यते ।
अनेन दुःखेन च देहमर्पितं
ध्रुवं ह्यकाले मरणं न विद्यते ॥

51. My heart being a stone is not split up although it is afflicted by such sorrow; And my body is not broken up and scattered on earth as if it is steel. Therefore

death can never come by (to anyone) 'Out Of Time'! Surely! (Death decides The Appointment!)

❍ ❍ ❍

५२. इदं तु दुःखं यदनर्थकानि मे
व्रतानि दानानि च संयमाश्च हि ।
तपश्च तप्तं यदपत्यकारणात्
सुनिष्फलं बीजमिवोप्तमूषरे ॥

52. This indeed is grief: Therefore, all my vows, fasting, charities, prayers, that were 'observed' well for the welfare of my son, have become purposeless. All those penance done by me have gone to waste like seeds sown in parched land.

❍ ❍ ❍

५३. यदि ह्यकाले मरणं स्वयेच्छया
लभेत कश्चिद्गुरुदुःखकर्शितः ।
गताऽहमद्यैव परेतसंसदं
विना त्वया धेनुरिवात्मजेन वै ॥

53. If a person who is 'crushed' by terrific (suffering and) sorrow can obtain death before his (appointed) time out of his own volition, then, like a cow without (its calf that) is born to it, I will, now itself, go to the assembly of dead men. (I wish I were dead).

❍ ❍ ❍

५४. अथापि किं जीवितमद्य मे वृथा
त्वया विना चन्द्रनिभाननप्रभ ।
अनुव्रजिष्यामि वनं त्वयैव गौः
सुदुर्बला वत्समिवानुकांक्षया ॥

54. (Oh Raama who is) Bright like the rays of moon! Without you, life to me is a waste now; Weak though I am, ike a cow which longs for its calf, I will come along with you to forest.

❍ ❍ ❍

५५. भृशमसुखममर्षिता तदा
बहु विललाप समीक्ष्य राघवम् ।
व्यसनमुपनिशाम्य सा महत्
सुतमिव बद्धमवेक्ष्य किन्नरी ॥

55. (Thus Kowsalya wailed: She thought only about herself!)

Like a female bird seeing its chick in captivity, she looked at (Raama the) Raaghava; Thinking about the great misery and suffering (to herself) again and again, unable to bear all this, she wailed very much.

❍ ❍ ❍

Chapter 21

(Raama) Swears to Honour his Father's Command

(Kowsalya, like all mothers, is terribly shocked; but she behaves like an ordinary woman, thinking only about herself, unlike Dhascharatha who grieves for his son Raama.: Lakshmana challenges the right of his father to send Raama on exile. But Raama is firm; He will honour his father's commitment to Kaikeyi.)

❍ ❍ ❍

१. तथा तु विलपन्तीं तां कौसल्यां राममातरम् ।
उवाच लक्ष्मणो दीनस्तत्कालसदृशं वचः ॥

1. Then Lakshmanaa addressed Kowsalya the mother of Raama who was wailing thus, with words suited to the occasion, (feeling very) miserable.

❍ ❍ ❍

२. न रोचते ममाप्येतदार्येयद्राघवो वनम् ।
त्यक्त्वा राज्यश्रियं गच्छेत् स्त्रिया वाक्यवशं गतः ॥

2. Oh Aryan (lady Kowsalya)! That (Raama the) Raaghava, abandoning the kingdom just to honour the words of a (mere) woman should go to forest, is not desired (approved) by me also.

❍ ❍ ❍

३. विपरीतश्च वृद्धश्च विषयैश्च प्रधर्षितः ।
नृपः किमिव न ब्रूयाच्चोद्यमानस्समन्मथः ।।

3. The King (my father) is old and is perverse; Therefore, in the affairs (of the State) he transgresses (norms). Enamoured and instigated (by Kaikeyi), what will he not say (or do)!

❍ ❍ ❍

४. नास्यापराधं पश्यामि नापि दोषं तथाविधम् ।
येन निर्वास्यते राष्ट्राद्वनवासाय राघवः ।।

4. By what (reason) (Raama) the Raaghava is being sent out from his kingdom for a life in forest? I do not see (find) any offence in him (for such a treatment): (I do not see) any guilt (in him at all).

❍ ❍ ❍

५. अहं हनिष्ये पितरं वृद्धं कामवशं गतम् ।
स्त्रिया युक्तं च निर्लज्जं धर्मायुक्तं नृपं यथा ।।

5. I will kill this aged father, this king (of ours) as he is consumed by passion, dominated by a woman, has lost (his sense), has no shame, and as he is not devoted to Dharma.

❍ ❍ ❍

६. न तं पश्याम्यहं लोके परोक्षमपि यो नरः ।
स्वमित्रोऽपि निरस्तोऽपि योऽस्य दोषमुदाहरेत् ।।

6. An enemy of his, or any man who is expelled (due to bad conduct), can utter (and find) unseen faults in him; Yet, I have not seen any such a man in this world.

(Lakshmana says, that even Raama's enemy will not find any fault in Raama, dare not speak ill of Raama.)

❍ ❍ ❍

७. देवकल्पमृजुं दान्तं रिपूणामपि वत्सलम् ।
अवेक्षमाणः को धर्मं त्यजेत्पुत्रमकारणात् ।।

7. Will any man who has some regard for Dharma expel, without reason, his own loving son, who is righteous, who is like a celestial and who shows restraint even towards enemies?

❍ ❍ ❍

८. तदिदं वचनं राज्ञः पुनर्बाल्यमुपेयुषः ।
पुत्रः को हृदये कुर्याद्राजवृत्तमनुस्मरन् ।।

8. Who, even if he is a son, will accept heartily this word (of command) of the king who has obtained (the state of) childishness, remembering the (present) conduct of the king.

❍ ❍ ❍

९. यावदेव न जानाति कश्चिदर्थमिमं नरः ।
तावदेव मया सार्धमात्मस्थं कुरु शासनम् ।।

9. Before some man (like Bharatha) considers and takes over the rule of the wealthy (Kingdom), make this yours (oh Raama, assisted by and) along with me .....

❍ ❍ ❍

१०. मया पार्श्वेसधनुषा तवं गुप्तस्य राघव ।
कस्समर्थोऽधिकं कर्तुं कृतान्तस्येव तिष्ठतः ।।

10. ...... Oh (Raama) The Raaghava! When you stand firm and act decisively, who is capable of doing you (harm) later on, (particularly) when you will be protected by me standing by your side, (armed) with bow (in my hand)?

❍ ❍ ❍

११. निर्मनुष्यामिमां सर्वामयोध्यां मनुजर्षभ ।
करिष्यामि शरैस्तीक्ष्णैर्यदि स्थास्यति विप्रिये ॥

11. Oh 'Bull' amongst men (Oh Raama)! If he establishes himself in Ayodhya committing transgression, then I will make the entire (kingdom) without any human being, with my sharp arrows.

❍ ❍ ❍

१२. भरतस्याथ पक्ष्यो वा यो वास्य हितमिच्छति ।
सर्वानेतान्वधिष्यामि मृदुर्हि परिभूयते ॥

12. If a man is (merciful and) soft, he is humiliated: Therefore if 'they' desire the welfare of Bharatha and (joins) his side, I will then kill all those.

❍ ❍ ❍

१३. प्रोत्साहितोऽयं कैकेय्या स दुष्टो यदि नः पिता ।
अमित्रभूतो निस्सङ्गं बध्यतां वध्यतामपि ॥

13. As our father, instigated by Kaikeyi, is evil (and has turned wicked), let him be 'Bound' (Imprisoned)! And if he becomes our enemy, let him be killed without any attachment (as our father).

❍ ❍ ❍

१४. गुरोरप्यवलिप्तस्य कार्याकार्यमजानतः ।
उत्पथं प्रतिपन्नस्य कार्यं भवति शासनम् ॥

14. If a man cannot know (the difference between) right and wrong, and (his mind) is blurred, and if he gets into wrong path, punishment must be meted out to him even if he is a (Guru), father.

❍ ❍ ❍

१५. बलमेष किमाश्रित्य हेतुं वा पुरुषोत्तम ।
दातुमिच्छति कैकेय्यै राज्यं स्फीतमिदं तव ॥

15. Oh noble (Raama)! Based on what power and reason

does he desire to hand over the kingdom, the mighty kingdom of yours, to Kaikeyi (through her son Bharatha).

❍ ❍ ❍

१६. त्वया चैव मया चैव कृत्वा वैरमनुत्तमम् ।
काऽस्य शक्तिः श्रियं दातुं भरतायारिशासन ॥

16. Oh (Raama) the chastisiser of enemies! Exhibiting great animosity to you and me, where is the capacity for him to offer the kingdom to Bharatha.

❍ ❍ ❍

१७. अनुरक्तोऽस्मि भावेन भ्रातरं देवि तत्त्वतः ।
सत्येन धनुषा चैव दत्तेनेष्टेन ते शपे ॥

17. Oh lady (Kowsalya)! I swear to you on Truth, on my bow, On the charities (I had given) and on all that you cherish: I am totally devoted to my brother (Raama); ...... By my true nature.

❍ ❍ ❍

१८. दीप्तमग्निमरण्यं वा यदि रामः प्रवेक्ष्यति ।
प्रविष्टं तत्र मां देवि त्वं पूर्वमवधारय ॥

18. Oh lady! You rest assured. If Raama enters burning fire or foremost forest, I would have also entered even before him.

❍ ❍ ❍

१९. हरामि वीर्याद्दुःखं ते तमः सूर्य इवोदितः ।
देवी पश्यतु मे वीर्यं राघवश्चैव पश्यतु ॥

19. Let (Raama the) Raaghava consider all this: like rising Sun destroying darkness, I will remove your sorrow by my valour; May (you my) lady witness my valour!

❍ ❍ ❍

२०. हनिष्ये पितरं वृद्धं कैकेय्यासक्तमानसम् ।
कृपणं च स्थितं बाल्ये वृद्धभावेन गर्हितम् ।।

20. I will kill this old, senile, childish father who clings to Kaikeyi with heart and soul, and who has become wretched and despicable.

❍ ❍ ❍

२१. एतत्तु वचनं श्रुत्वा लक्ष्मणस्य महात्मनः ।
उवाच रामं कौसल्या रुदन्ती शोकलालसा ।।

21. (So spoke Lakshmana: This is the case of a member of royal family trying to revolt against king. Here Lakshmana expounds Kshathriya Dharma of a true warrior).

Hearing such words from the great soul Lakshmana, Kowsalya who was in deep anguish and was crying, addressed Raama.

❍ ❍ ❍

२२. भ्रातुस्ते वदतः पुत्र लक्ष्मणस्य श्रुतं त्वया ।
यदत्रानन्तरं कार्यं कुरुष्व यदि रोचते ।।

22. Oh son (Raama)! If what you heard from your brother Lakshmana is agreeable, you must act here and now.

❍ ❍ ❍

२३. न चाधर्म्यं वचः श्रुत्वा सपत्न्या मम भाषितम् ।
विहाय शोकसन्तप्तां गन्तुमर्हसि मामितः ।।

23. Abandoning me who is tormented by grief, hearing (and obeying) the unjust words spoken by the co-mistress (Kaikeyi), you should not leave from here.

❍ ❍ ❍

२४ धर्मज्ञ यदि धर्मिष्ठ धर्मं चरितुमिच्छसि ।
शुश्रूष मामिहस्थस्त्वं चर धर्ममनुत्तमम् ।।

24. Oh knower of Dharma! Oh follower of Dharma! Follow

the foremost path of Dharma (The Royal Dharma). If you desire to uphold Dharma, you should serve me (your mother from) here itself.

❍ ❍ ❍

२५. शुश्रूषुर्जननीं पुत्र स्वगृहे नियतो वसन् ।
परेण तपसा युक्तः काश्यपस्त्रिदिवँगतः ।।

25. Oh son! (Long ago) Sage Kaaschyapa, living in his own place, practising vows, served his mother with great devotion and mortification, (and thereby) attained heaven.

❍ ❍ ❍

२६. यथैव राजा पूज्यस्ते गौरवेण तथा ह्यहम् ।
त्वां नाहमनुजानामि न गन्तव्यमितो वनम् ।।

26. Just as the king (your father), because of your veneration, is to be honoured by you, so am I, and I need not go to forest from here (with you to be served by you): I will not give you permission.

(Kowsalya says that like his father, she, as his mother, has a claim on her son. Raama must satisfy her wish, must not leave her.)

❍ ❍ ❍

२७. त्वद्वियोगान्न मे कार्यं जीवितेन सुखेन वा ।
त्वया सह मम श्रेयस्तृणानामपि भक्षणम् ।।

27. If I am separated from you, there is no purpose in life or comforts for me. But with you (in forest), even (mere) sustenance on mere grass, is preferable.

❍ ❍ ❍

२८. यदि त्वं यास्यसि वनं त्यक्त्वा मां शोकलालसाम् ।
अहं प्रायमिहासिष्ये न हि शक्ष्यामि जीवितुम् ।।

28. If abandoning me who is engulfed in grief you go to

forest, I will fast unto death here itself. I wont be alive. Certain.

❍ ❍ ❍

२९. ततस्त्वं प्राप्स्यसे पुत्र निरयं लोकविश्रुतम् ।
ब्रह्महत्यामिवाधर्मात्समुद्रस्सरितां पतिः ॥

29. Oh son! Like lord of all rivers, the ocean, who, out of Adharma, (was afflicted) with (sin of) killing a Braamin, you will also obtain hell that is well known in the world.

(So spoke Kowsalya; she was supported by Lakshmana: Both, for different reasons want Raama to remain in kingdom, take over power. But Raama is firm. His 'Dharma' is very clear. Obey father's command; Will honour his father's promise to Kaikeyi although it causes pain to them. He will go on exile that day itself.)

❍ ❍ ❍

३०. विलपन्तीं तथा दीनां कौसल्यां जननीं ततः ।
उवाच रामो धर्मात्मा वचनं धर्मसंहितम् ॥

30. Then the noble soul man of Dharma, Raama, addressed his mother Kowsalya who was miserable and who was wailing, with (following) words of (wisdom and) Dharma.

❍ ❍ ❍

३१. नास्ति शक्तिः पितुर्वाक्यं समतिक्रमितुं मम ।
प्रसादये त्वां शिरसा गन्तुमिच्छाम्यहं वनम् ॥

31. (Oh mother Kowsalya!) I have no power to transgress the word (of command) of my father. I desire to go to forest; with my head (bowed) I beseech you (for blessings).

❍ ❍ ❍

३२. ऋषिणा च पितुर्वाक्यं कुर्वता व्रतचारिणा ।
गौर्हता जानता धर्मं कण्डुनाऽपि विपश्चिता ॥

32. (Raama quotes precedents: Father's command is supreme.)
(Long ago) At the bidding of his father, even an (innocent) cow was killed by Rishi Kandu who knew Dharma, who was learned, and who practiced vows.

❍ ❍ ❍

३३. अस्माकं च कुले पूर्वं सगरस्याज्ञया पितुः ।
खनद्भिः सागरैर्भूमिमवाप्तस्सुमहान्वधः ॥

33. (And) Long ago, in our own family, under father Sagara's orders, that great killing took place for (all the) sons of Sagara when they dug up the Earth.**
(See Baala Kaanda **)

❍ ❍ ❍

३४. जामदग्न्येन रामेण रेणुका जननी स्वयम् ।
कृत्ता परशुनाऽरण्ये पितुर्वचनकारिणा ॥

34. (And long ago) By ParaschuRaama, the son of Jamadhagni, who ever fulfilled the words of his father (Jamadhagni), his own mother Renuka was axed (to death) in forest.

❍ ❍ ❍

३५. एतैरन्यैश्च बहुभिर्देवि देवसमैः कृतम् ।
पितुर्वचनमक्लीबं करिष्यामि पितुर्हितम् ॥

35. Oh lady (mother Kowsalya)! A father's words have been executed without any blemish by these who were like celestials and also by many other (ordinary) persons. I will do what is salutary to my father.

❍ ❍ ❍

३६. न खल्वेतन्मयैकेन क्रियते पितृशासनम् ।
एतैरपि कृतं देवि ये मया तव कीर्तिताः ॥

36. Oh lady! (It is not as though) A father's command is being done by me alone. You should not think so. As narrated by me, this has been done (before, by many).

❍ ❍ ❍

३७. नाहं धर्ममपूर्वं ते प्रतिकूलं प्रवर्तये ।
पूर्वैरयमभिप्रेतो गतो मार्गोऽनुगम्यते ॥

37. Adverse (and disagreeable though it may be) to you, I am not setting in motion a (new) unprecedented Dharma. This 'path' has been approved by ancient men and followed, accepted (as norms) as such.

❍ ❍ ❍

३८. तदेतत्तु मया कार्यं क्रियते भुवि नान्यथा ।
पितुर्हि वचनं कुर्वन्न कश्चिन्नाम हीयते ॥

38. In this world, one who obeys his father's command, never comes to grief; It has never been otherwise; With certainty, this deed (of going to forest at my father's command) is being done by me.

❍ ❍ ❍

३९. तामेवमुक्त्वा जननीं लक्ष्मणं पुनरब्रवीत् ।
वाक्यं वाक्यविदां श्रेष्ठः श्रेष्ठः सर्वधनुष्मताम् ॥

39. Having spoken thus to his mother, (Raama) who was foremost amongst wielders of bow and who was foremost amongst men of (good) speech, addressed Lakshmana these words.

❍ ❍ ❍

४०. तव लक्ष्मण जानामि मयि स्नेहमनुत्तमम् ।
विक्रमं चैव सत्वं च तेजश्चैव दुरासदम् ॥

40. Oh Lakshmana! (Do I not) know of your unapproachable (unparalleled) valour, your brilliance, your truthfulness, and your foremost affection for me.

❍ ❍ ❍

४१. मम मातुर्महद्दुःखमतुलं शुभलक्षण ।
अभिप्रायमविज्ञाय सत्यरस्य च शमरस्य च ।।

41. Oh (Lakshmana endowed with) Pleasant qualities! Great (indeed) is this grief of my mother who is not able to understand the (essence & true) meaning of Truth and tranquillity: (because her grief) is mighty.

❍ ❍ ❍

४२. धर्मोहि परमो लोके धर्मेसत्यं प्रतिष्ठितम् ।
धर्मसंश्रितमेतच्च पितुर्वचनमुत्तमम् ।।

42. Dharma is supreme in the world: And Truth abides in and is foremost in Dharma. And this my father's words (of command) is based on Dharma.

❍ ❍ ❍

४३. संश्रुत्य च पितुर्वाक्यं मातुर्वा ब्राह्मणस्य वा ।
न कर्तव्यं वृथा वीर धर्ममाश्रित्य तिष्ठता ।।

43. Oh brave (Lakshmana)! Any one who accepts Dharma and abides by it, should not be frivolous after having committed to his father, or mother or to a Braamin.

❍ ❍ ❍

४४. सोऽहं न शक्ष्यामि पितुर्नियोगमतिवर्तितुम् ।
पितुर्हि वचनाद्वीर कैकेय्याऽहं प्रचोदितः ।।

44. Oh brave (Lakshmana)! At the bequest of father, I was ordered by Kaikeyi. I will not repudiate my father's order.

(Raama is very clear; although his father had not spoken as grief was overwhelming him, what Kaikeyi told him was in effect his father's order; No uncertainty in Raama's mind.)

❍ ❍ ❍

४५. तदेतां विसृजानार्यां क्षत्रधर्माश्रितां मतिम् ।
धर्ममाश्रय मा तैक्ष्ण्यं मद्बुद्धिरनुगम्यताम् ।।

45. Therefore you must abandon this idea which is un-Aryan, which exhibits (merely) Kshatriya Dharma (of force and arms): Abide by The Dharma. Give up this severity. Accept my view.

❍ ❍ ❍

४६. तमेवमुक्त्वा सौहार्दाद्भ्रातरं लक्ष्मणाग्रजः ।
उवाच भूयः कौसल्यां प्राञ्जलिश्शिरसा नतः ।।

46. After saying thus to his brother out of his deep affection, (Raama the) elder brother of Lakshmana, then (once again) bowed to Kowsalya with his head and said to her with his hands in Anjali.

❍ ❍ ❍

४७. अनुमन्यस्व मां देवि गमिष्यन्तमितो वनम् ।
शापिताऽसि मम प्राणैः कुरु स्वस्त्ययनानि मे ।।

47. (Oh mother Kowsalya) Oh Lady! Please give me leave who is going away to forest from here; I am swearing on my life (to beg you to allow me to go): Please offer me your Swasthi Blessings.

❍ ❍ ❍

४८. तीर्णप्रतिज्ञश्च वनात्पुनरेष्याम्यहं पुरीम् ।
ययातिरिव राजर्षिः पुरा हित्वा पुनर्दिवम् ।।

48. Long ago (you may recall) the royal sage (king) Yayaathi was sent away to Earth, but came back to heaven. Likewise, I will also come back to the city (Kingdom) again, after fulfilling my commitment.

❍ ❍ ❍

४९. शोकः सन्धार्यतां मातर्हृदये साधु मा शुचः ।
वनवासादिहैष्यामि पुनः कृत्वा पितुर्वचः ।।

49. Oh mother! Enough of grief. No lament in your heart. Restrain yourself. After life in forest, I will come back here again, fulfilling my father's command.

❍ ❍ ❍

५०. त्वया मया च वैदेह्या लक्ष्मणेन सुमित्रया ।
पितुर्नियोगे स्थातव्यमेष धर्मस्सनातनः ।।

50. King's wishes (command) must always be 'abided' by me, by Vaidhehi (Seetha), by Lakshmana, by Sumithra and also by you (my mother).. This is the eternal Dharma.

❍ ❍ ❍

५१. अम्ब संहृत्य संभारान् दुःखं हृदि निगृह्य च ।
वनवासकृता बुद्धिर्मम धर्म्याऽनुवर्त्यताम् ।।

51. Oh dear mother! Holding on to (teachings from) The Collection (of holy Texts) and abandoning grief from your heart, you must (now) give me your assent to my decision of (accepting) forest life, that is based on Dharma.

❍ ❍ ❍

५२. एतद्वचस्तस्य निशम्य माता
सुधर्म्यमव्यग्रमविक्लबं च ।
मृतेव संज्ञां प्रतिलभ्य देवी
समीक्ष्य रामं पुनरित्युवाच ।।

52. (But Kowsalya will have none of it; She pleads with Raama again to reconsider his decision)

Hearing such words of Dharma (spoken by Raama) with firmness and calmness, his mother, the lady (Kowsalya) (lost her bearing) like one dead. Regaining her composure (and consciousness) said to Raama, after some deliberation, (the following):

❍ ❍ ❍

५३. यथैव ते पुत्र पिता तथाऽहं
गुरुः स्वधर्मेण सुहृत्तया च ।
न त्वाऽनुजानामि न मां विहाय
सुदुःखितामर्हसि गन्तुमेवम् ।।

53. Oh (Raama my) Son! Just as your father is a Guru (and venerated) because of your Dharma, affection and devotion, likewise I am also to you: I will not give you leave to go: You should not abandon me who is in deep suffering.

❍ ❍ ❍

५४. किं जीवितेनेह विना त्वया मे
लोकेन वा किं स्वधयाऽमृतेन ।
श्रेयो मुहूर्तं तव सन्निधानं
ममेह कृत्स्नादपि जीवलोकात् ।।

54. In the entire world of living beings, your presence near me is foremost to me. (Only your presence I cherish most): If I am separated from you even for a Muhoortha, what (is it) to me with nectar like tastiest (foods) of the world. What is the use of my living (at all without you).

❍ ❍ ❍

५५. नरैरिवोल्काभिरपोह्यमानो
महागजोऽध्वानमनुप्रविष्टः ।
भूयः प्रजज्वाल विलापमेनं
निशम्य रामः करुणं जनन्याः ।।

55. Just as big elephant proceeds along its (chosen) path although obstructed by stones (thrown at it) by men, Raama remained (steadfast and) bright even as he was listening to the pitiable wailing (and pleadings) of his mother.

❍ ❍ ❍

५६. स मातरं चैव विसंज्ञकल्पां
आर्तं च सौमित्रिमभिप्रतप्तम् ।
धर्मे स्थितो धर्म्यमुवाच वाक्यं
यथा स एवार्हति तत्र वक्तुम् ।।

56. Indeed he (this Raama) had the ability to speak

befittingly to his mother who had lost her composure:: And to (Lakshmana the) son of Sumithra who was in deep anguish and who was tormented greatly, he said the following words of Dharma.

❍ ❍ ❍

५७. अहं हि ते लक्ष्मण नित्यमेव
जानामि भक्तिं च पराक्रमं च ।
मम त्वभिप्रायमसंनिरीक्ष्य
मात्रा सहाभ्यर्दसि मां सुदुःखम् ।।

57. Oh Lakshmana! I know of your eternal devotion to me and your valour: Disregarding my views (and decision), you are also causing (and aggravating) sorrow upon me who is grieving along with my mother.

❍ ❍ ❍

५८. धर्मार्थकामाः किल तात लोके
समीक्षिता धर्मफलोदयेषु ।
ते तत्र सर्वेस्युरसंशयं मे
भार्येव वश्याऽभिमता सुपुत्रा ।।

58. Oh lad! In this world, Dharma, Artha and Kaama are perceived when 'fruits' of Dharma manifests: Indeed so: As such (as a consequence of following Dharma) all these manifests in one, like a wife (blessed) with long desired good son. There is no doubt about this in me.

❍ ❍ ❍

५९. यस्मिंस्तु सर्वेस्युरसंनिविष्टा
धर्मोयतः स्यात्तदुपक्रमेत ।
द्वेष्यो भवत्यर्थपरो हि लोके
कामात्मता खल्वपि न प्रशस्ता ।।

59. When, (in a situation), all (the three, Dharma, Artha, Kaama) are not found together, then one must take recourse to Dharma: (from which the other two Artha

and Kaama follow). Indeed: In this world one who is intent on Artha (alone), becomes despised. And so is one who is ever intent on Kaama, not to be praised (at all).

(Dharma- norms, duty, etc: Artha: Material pursuits etc. situation, the pursuit of Dharma alone will give one everlasting tranquillity: Mundane pleasures, material pursuits should be given up: Even Moksha, spiritual enlightenment follows the first, The Dharma)

❍ ❍ ❍

६0. गुरुश्च राजा च पिता च वृद्धः
क्रोधात्प्रहर्षाद्यदि वाऽपि मोहात् ।
यद्धयादिशेत्कार्यमवेक्ष्य धर्मं
कस्तं न कुर्यादनृशंसवृत्तिः ॥

60. My aged father, my Guru (teacher), this king (Dhascharatha) might have assigned this task (of my going to forest) either out of anger or out of passion, or even out of joy (for his own pleasure): (But) How can one who (follows and) perceives (only) Dharma, fail to do (his command, his task)?

(My father's command is absolute, I dont need to know the reason.)

❍ ❍ ❍

६१. स वै न शक्नोमि पितुः प्रतिज्ञा
मिमामकर्तुं सकलां यथावत् ।
स ह्यावयोस्तात गुरुर्नियोगे
देव्याश्च भर्ता स गतिः स धर्मः ॥

61. I will not fail to do this command of my father completely and properly. Oh Lad (Lakshmana)! (Our father) is our lord who can command us both: And he is the husband and refuge for our mother: He is verily Dharma (for us. all).

❍ ❍ ❍

६२. तस्मिन् पुनर्जीवति धर्मराजे
विशेषतः स्वे पथि वर्तमाने ।
देवी मया सार्धमितोऽपगच्छेत्
कथं स्विदन्या विधवेव नारी ।।

62. When (our father) this (king) who is verily a king practising Dharma, and who particularly follows his own path of Dharma, is alive, why bother about anything at all: And how can lady (Kowsalya who is his queen) go away from here along with me as though she is a widow.

(Duty of a woman is to be by the side of her husband; She is queen as well, says Raama.)

❍ ❍ ❍

६३. सा माऽनुमन्यस्व वनं व्रजन्तं
कुरुष्व नः स्वस्त्ययनानि देवि ।
यथा समाप्ते पुनराव्रजेयं
यथा हि सत्येन पुनर्ययातिः ।।

63. Oh lady (my mother Kowsalya)! Such as you are, must allow me to go to forest; Like king Yayaathi, (after my exile) is completed as per Truth (& commitment), I will come back. Please offer *us Swasthi blessings.

(* The use of = us = instead of = me=, is significant. As events turn out, Lakshmana also follows Raama to forest along with Seetha)

❍ ❍ ❍

६४. यशो ह्यहं केवलराज्यकारणात्
न पृष्ठतः कर्तुमलं महोदयम् ।
अदीर्घकाले न तु देवि जीविते
वृणेऽवरामद्य महीमधर्मतः ।।

64. O lady! I will not ignore fame that will bring prosperity; In this short life of one's existence, for the sake of mere kingdom (and title of YuvaRaaja), I will not chose the 'Earth' (which will offer) only inferior (pleasures) through A-Dharma (non Dharma).

❍ ❍ ❍

६५. प्रसादयन्नरवृषभः स्वमातरं
पराक्रमाज्जिगमिषुरेव दण्डकान् ।
अथानुजं भृशमनुशास्य दर्शनं
चकार तां हृदि जननीं प्रदक्षिणम् ।।

65. Exhibiting his desire to go to Dhandaka forest with zeal. this 'Bull of men' (Raama), thus cheered up his mother: Enlightening her and his brother on the perceptions (of Dharma) which is severe (and difficult to follow & comprehend), he went round his mother (in circumbambulation) in his heart.

(Note: This is a very important chapter because Raama enlightens us all in perceptions of Dharma. A father's command is absolute. And this father is a king who has practised Dharma throughout his long life. A wife's place is always by her husband. And this wife is a queen as well. When Lakshmana threatens a 'Coup' as per Kshatriya Dharma of warriors, Raama rejects this saying that in a tight situation, one should follow The Dharma. It is through Dharma, all others follow, like Artha-material, mundane things, Kaama-Love, pleasures etc. Why, even Moksha, spiritual enlightenment cannot be obtained without following Dharma. And Truth is the basis of Dharma. And Dhascharatha's commitment to Kaikeyi must be honoured, because, if Raama had failed him, it would make his father a man of Untruth, a man of A-Dharma.)

❍ ❍ ❍

Chapter 22

The 'Way' of Fate and Destiny

(Raama again talks to his brother Lakshmana who is not convinced about Raama's acceptance of exile; He is still angry; Raama expounds philosophy of Life.)

❍ ❍ ❍

१. अथ तं व्यथया दीनं सविशेषममर्षितम् ।
श्वसन्तमिव नागेन्द्रं क्रोधविस्फारितेक्षणम् ॥

1. Then, the meritorious (Lakshmana) who was feeling depressed by (terrible) anguish, who was indignant, who was hissing (& breathing) like a king Cobra, whose eyes were dilated due to wrath .....

❍ ❍ ❍

२. आसाद्य रामस्सौमित्रिं सुहृदं भ्रातरं प्रियम् ।
उवाचेदं स धैर्येण धारयन् सत्त्वमात्मवान् ॥

2. ..... (Such a Lakshmana) the son of Sumithra, his brother, who was dear to him, who was good hearted.....this tranquil Raama looked at.... Holding on steadfastly to his true (& natural) character, (Raama) said (the following):

❍ ❍ ❍

३. निगृह्य रोषं शोकं च धैर्येमाश्रित्य केवलम् ।
अवमानं निरस्येमं गृहीत्वा हर्षमुत्तमम् ॥

3. (Raama advises Lakshmana)
Give up this fury! This grief. Take recourse to fortitude only; Drive away (from your mind thoughts) that will bring only contempt: Obtain the foremost happiness (through Dharma).....

❍ ❍ ❍

४. उपक्लृप्तं हि यत्किञ्चिदभिषेकार्थमद्य मे ।
सर्वं विसर्जय क्षिप्रं कुरु कार्यं निरत्ययम् ॥

4. ...... You must discard whatever was procured for my coronation. You must accept with delight this deed (of my Dharma,exile). Now.

❍ ❍ ❍

५. सौमित्रे योऽभिषेकार्थेमम संभारसंभ्रमः ।
अभिषेकनिवृत्त्यर्थे सोऽस्तु संभारसंभ्रमः ॥

5. Oh (Lakshmana) the son of Sumithra! The zeal (exhibited) in procurement of materials for my coronation, (the same) zeal in procurement of materials (for my forest life) may be shown.

❍ ❍ ❍

६. यस्या मदभिषेकार्थेमानसं परितप्यते ।
माता मे सा यथा न स्यात् सविशङ्का तथा कुरु ।।

6. You must act in such a way that my 'mother' (step mother Kaikeyi) whose mind is tormented in the matter of my coronation, will (now) have no fear or doubt.

(Raama warns Lakshmana; He is going for good for 14 years. Kaikeyi should not entertain any doubt that he will not go.)

❍ ❍ ❍

७. तस्याः शङ्कामयं दुःखं मुहूर्तमपि नोत्सहे ।
मनसि प्रतिसञ्जातं सौमित्रेऽहमुपेक्षितुम् ।।

7. Oh (Lakshmana) the son of Sumithra! I cannot tolerate to see even for a moment, any grief in her, caused because of apprehension in her mind (that I will trick her, fail to make room for Bharatha).

❍ ❍ ❍

८. न बुद्धिपूर्वं नाबुद्धं स्मरामीह कदाचन ।
मातॄण वा पितुर्वाऽहं कृतमल्पं च विप्रियम् ।।

8. In this world, never has any transgression been committed upon mothers and fathers (by sons) even thoughtlessly. I will not even think about it in my mind (to disobey my father).

❍ ❍ ❍

९. सत्यः सत्याभिसन्धश्च नित्यं सत्यपराक्रमः ।
परलोकभयाद्भीतो निर्भयोऽस्तु पिता मम ।।

9. My father who ever abides by Truth, who speaks Truth,

who is truly valiant, who is now frightened with fear of (death and) going to the other word, should become freed from fear.

❍ ❍ ❍

१०. तस्यापि हि भवेदस्मिन् कर्मण्यप्रतिसंहृते ।
सत्यं नेति मनस्तापस्तस्य तापस्तपेच्च माम् ।।

10. If this assignment (of going on exile) is restrained, then there will be mental agony for him that there is no Truth. His torment will also burn me up.

❍ ❍ ❍

११. अभिषेकविधानन्तु तस्मात्संहृत्य लक्ष्मण ।
अन्वगेवाहमिच्छामि वनं गन्तुमितः पुनः ।।

11. Oh Lakshmana! Therefore, abandoning my coronation ceremonies, I desire to go to forest instead, in happy disposition, from here. (have decided , as this is my desire).

❍ ❍ ❍

१२. मम प्रव्राजनादद्य कृतकृत्या नृपात्मजा ।
सुतं भरतमव्यग्रमभिषेचयिता ततः ।।

12. Now that I am exiled, this (Kaikeyi) the daughter of king (of Kekeya) will have her wish fulfilled and crown her son Bharatha calmly (without hindrance).

❍ ❍ ❍

१३. मयि चीराजिनधरे जटामण्डलधारिणि ।
गतेऽरण्यं च कैकेय्या भविष्यति मनस्सुखम् ।।

13. Only after I go to forest dressed up in deer skin and sporting tufted hair, Kaikeyi will have peace of mind.

❍ ❍ ❍

१४. बुद्धिः प्रणीता येनेयं मनश्च सुसमाहितम् ।
तं तु नार्हामि संक्लेष्टुं प्रव्रजिष्यामि मा चिरम् ।।

14. In this matter, (the reason) by which I was led into (taking this) decision and making my mind content, that, I will not allow to be tarnished. No (need to) waste time; I am going away (now).

❍ ❍ ❍

१५. कृतान्तस्त्वेव सौमित्रे द्रष्टव्यो मत्प्रवासने ।
राज्यस्य च वितीर्णस्य पुनरेव निवर्तने ॥

15. Oh Lakshmana) the son of Sumithra! You must look at all this as work of fate (My) Losing the kingdom that was offered to me, and my life of exile.

❍ ❍ ❍

१६. कैकेय्याः प्रतिपत्तिर्हि कथं स्यान्मम पीडने ।
यदि भावो न दैवोऽयं कृतान्तविहितो भवेत् ॥

16. If what has happened to me is not destiny, the divine work of Karma, how else would have Kaikeyi conceived this harm for me?

❍ ❍ ❍

१७. जानासि हि यथा सौम्य न मातृषु ममान्तरम् ।
भूतपूर्वं विशेषो वा तस्या मयि सुतेऽपि वा ॥

17. Oh pleasant (Lakshmana): You know (very well) that never before there has been any distinction between my 'mothers' (between my mother Kowsalya and step mothers Sumithra and Kaikeyi) for me. And for her also, (for Kaikeyi also there was never any distinction). between me (her step son) and her own son (Bharatha)

(Yet Kaikeyi gets rid of me, surely work of fate, says Raama.)

❍ ❍ ❍

१८. सोऽभिषेकनिवृत्त्यर्थैः प्रवासार्थैश्च दुर्वचैः ।
उग्रैर्वाक्यैरहं तस्या नान्यद्दैवात्समर्थये ॥

18. Such as I am, I perceive (clearly) that there can be no

other (reason) than Fate, that she should utter cruel words which should never have been spoken, and that she should stop my coronation and banish me.

❍ ❍ ❍

१९. कथं प्रकृतिसम्पन्ना राजपुत्री तथागुणा ।
ब्रूयात्सुप्राकृतेव स्त्री मत्पीडां भर्तृसन्निधौ ।।

19. (Born) as a princess, endowed with such natural (inborn) qualities, endowed with praiseworthy qualities, why (and what other reason could be there) that, like an ordinary woman, she spoke before her husband for causing me injury and harm.

❍ ❍ ❍

२०. यदचिन्त्यं तु तद्दैवं भूतेष्वपि न हन्यते ।
व्यक्तं मयि च तस्यां च पतितो हि विपर्ययः ।।

20. When, unexpectedly (inconceivably), certain occurrences are not hindered, that, is (the work of) divine Fate. This is manifested in me, in her, in (diverse and in) perverse ways (all) occurred (thus).

❍ ❍ ❍

२१. कश्च दैवेन सौमित्रे योद्धुमुत्सहते पुमान् ।
यस्य न ग्रहणं किञ्चित्कर्मणोऽन्यत्र दृश्यते ।।

21. Oh (Lakshmana) the son of Sumithra! Which man can dare to fight with Fate, when, during a course of action, something else (occurs) which cannot be perceived (or comprehended).

❍ ❍ ❍

२२. सुखदुःखे भयक्रोधौ लाभालाभौ भवाभवौ ।
यच्च किञ्चित्तथाभूतं ननु दैवस्य कर्म तत् ।।

22. Happiness or Sorrow: Profit or Loss: Fear or Wrath; Birth or Death (These cannot be comprehended at all): The reason for occurrence of these cannot be known,

even little, this verily (is Karma), the work of divine Fate.

❍ ❍ ❍

२३. ऋषयोऽप्युग्रतपसो दैवेनाभिप्रचोदिताः ।
उत्सृज्य नियमांस्तीव्रान् भ्रश्यन्ते काममन्युभिः ।।

23. Even sages who do rigorous penance, goaded (and afflicted) by destiny, abandon their steadfast rituals and fall down (as victim) of wrath and passion.

(Like Vischwaamithra falling a prey to damsel Menaka!)

❍ ❍ ❍

२४. असङ्कल्पितमेवेह यदकस्मात्प्रवर्तते ।
निवर्त्यारंभमारब्धं ननु दैवस्य कर्म तत् ।।

24. In this world, when a work that is undertaken, takes on a different course inconceivably without rhyme or reason, verily it is the divine work of Fate, nothing else.

❍ ❍ ❍

२५. एतया तत्त्वया बुद्ध्या संस्तभ्यात्मानमात्मना ।
व्याहतेप्यभिषेके मे परितापो न विद्यते ।।

25. In this matter of impediments (denial of) coronation to me, there is (absolutely) no remorse or pain in me, because of the knowledge of these truths (I have enumerated), which are firmly lodged in me.

❍ ❍ ❍

२६. तस्मादपरितापः संस्त्वमप्यनुविधाय माम् ।
प्रातिसहारय क्षिप्रमाभिषेचानिको क्रियाम् ।।

26. Therefore you should also follow me (in this Dharma), remain untormented and at once stop the work pertaining to my coronation.

❍ ❍ ❍

२७. एभिरेव घटैस्सर्वैरभिषेचनसंभृतैः ।
मम लक्ष्मण तापस्ये व्रतस्नानं भविष्यति ।।

27. Oh Lakshmana! With (holy waters) contained in all these pots which were brought for my austerities in connection with my coronation, the (Ritual) bath for my vow (to go on exile) will now take place.

(For Raama forest life is coronation! He wants to do 'Ritual Baths' before going on exile with these waters)

❍ ❍ ❍

२८. अथवा किं ममैतेन राजद्रव्यमयेन तु ।
उद्धृतं मे स्वयं तोयं व्रतादेशं करिष्यति ।।

28. (And Raama entertains doubt over what he said in impulse; perhaps, as a mendicant, he has no right to these holy waters).

With these (Holy) waters prepared for (pre-ritual baths for) royal crown prince, (will it be proper) for me now (to take baths) before going on exile? If it is not (proper), then let waters (specially) meant for my vows be brought. (Vows of a mendicant)

❍ ❍ ❍

२९. मा च लक्ष्मण सन्तापं कार्षीर्लक्ष्म्या विपर्यये ।
राज्यं वा वनवासो वा वनवासो महोदयः ।।

29. Oh Lakshmana! Do not grieve over this reversal in my fortune. Between kingdom and forest Life, (for me) forest life is more eminent.

❍ ❍ ❍

३०. न लक्ष्मणास्मिन् खलु कर्मविघ्ने
माता यवीयस्यतिशङ्कितव्या ।
दैवाभिपन्ना हि वदत्यनिष्टं
जानासि दैवं च तथाप्रभावम् ।।

30. Oh Lakshmana! Let not my young (step) mother (Kaikeyi) have any great apprehension in regard to obstacle in this matter. Seized by Fate, she speaks undesirably. (Dont) You know that such is the power of Fate, indeed!

(Note: In introduction to The Raamaayana, the translator had indicated that Raamaayana is considered as a Vedha, next only to the four unwritten Vedha-s; Here Raama expounds philosophy, Truth Dharma etc. Later on, in The Kishkindha Kaanda, the great Hanumaan also expounds philosophy)

❍ ❍ ❍

Chapter 23

Lakshmana's Wrath

(Lakshmana, Raama's beloved brother and companion, cannot accept Raama's arguments. He is angry.)

❍ ❍ ❍

१. इति ब्रुवति रामे तु लक्ष्मणोऽधश्शिरा मुहुः ।
श्रुत्वा मध्यं जगामेव मनसा दुःखहर्षयोः ।।

1. When Raama was speaking like this, Lakshmana who was hearing (all this) with his head bowed, went into thinking for a while. He was passing through joy and sorrow.

(Joy because Raama was obedient to his father, sorrow because of his total 'surrender' to his father and Kaikeyi and acceptance of exile, forgetting Kshathriya Dharma of a warrior.)

❍ ❍ ❍

२. तदा तु बद्ध्वा भ्रूकुटीं भ्रुवोर्मध्ये नरर्षभः ।
निशश्वास महासर्पोबिलस्थ इव रोषितः ।।

2. This (Lakshmana) the 'Bull' amongst men, became angry like a cobra in a pit; With his eyebrows drawn close on his forehead, was breathing hard and deep (in wrath).

❍ ❍ ❍

३. तस्य दुष्प्रतिवीक्षं तद्भ्रुकुटीसहितं तदा ।
बभौ क्रुद्धस्य सिंहस्य मुखस्य सदृशं मुखम् ॥

3. At that moment as his eye brows were drawn thus, his face was harsh to look at like an angry lion.

❍ ❍ ❍

४. अग्रहस्तं विधुन्वंस्तु हस्तिहस्तमिवात्मनः ।
तिर्यगूर्ध्वं शरीरे च पातयित्वा शिरोधराम् ॥
अग्राक्ष्णा वीक्षमाणास्तु तिर्यग्भ्रातरमब्रवीत् ॥

4. Shaking his forearm like the trunk of an elephant, shaking his neck over body from side to side, and up and down, he addressed his brother (Raama) thus, looking at him obliquely.

❍ ❍ ❍

५. अस्थाने संभ्रमो यस्य जातो वै सुमहानयम् ।
धर्मदोषप्रसङ्गेन लोकस्यानतिशङ्कया ॥

5. Because of your indulgence (and adherence) to this faulty Dharma, and because of fear (that you may) cause to the world at large, this great 'Confusion' has now come about. (This will make the kingdom fall into) wrong hands.

❍ ❍ ❍

६. कथं ह्येतदसंभ्रान्तस्त्वद्विधो वक्तुमर्हति ।
यथा दैवमशौण्डीरं शौण्डीर क्षत्रियर्षभ ॥

6. Oh (Raama) the 'bull' amongst the Kshathriya-s! Oh proud man! Such a composed man like you, how can you talk like this about Fate which (leads to) unmanliness (and takes away self confidence).

❍ ❍ ❍

७. किं नाम कृपणं दैवमशक्तमभिशंससि ।
पापयोस्ते कथं नाम तयोः शङ्का न विद्यते ॥

7. How can you praise this cruel Fate which cannot be

overcome easily. How is it that it has not occurred to you that these two sinners (your father and Kaikeyi) are dreadful.

❍ ❍ ❍

८. सन्ति धर्मोपधाः श्लक्ष्णा धर्मात्मन् किं न बुध्यसे ।
तयोस्सुचरितं स्वार्थं शाठ्यात्परिजिहीर्षतोः ।।

8. Oh noble soul (man of) Dharma! There are many suave slippery (characters in this world) who pretend (to be) men of Dharma. Why dont you realise that this well executed (plan) by these two, by which, that which was due to you, was taken away by fraud?

❍ ❍ ❍

९. यदि नैवं व्यवसितं स्याद्धि प्रागेव राघव ।
तयोः प्रागेव दत्तश्च स्याद्वरः प्रकृतश्च सः ।।

9. (Lakshmana cannot accept that his father had no choice but to abide by Kaikeyi's wishes).

Oh (Raama the) Raaghava! If this was not decided by them thus (connived by them), this boon that was offered long ago (to Kaikeyi by our father) would have been utilised long ago.

❍ ❍ ❍

१०. लोकविद्विष्टमारब्धं त्वदन्यस्याभिषेचनम् ।
नोत्सहे सहितुं वीर तत्र मे क्षन्तुमर्हसि ।।

10. Oh brave (Raama)! I will not tolerate the coronation now (planned and) started for a person other than you, that is detested by all in the world. You should not make me bear this patiently.

❍ ❍ ❍

११. येनेयमागता द्वैधं तव बुद्धिर्महामते ।
स हि धर्मोमम द्वेष्यः प्रसङ्गाद्यस्य मुह्यसि ।।

11. Oh most respected (Raama)! This Dharma (of yours) is repugnant to me. (Because) By this, your decision

is (perverse &) contrary (to Kshathriya Dharma). (So much) attached (are you to this Dharma), that you are stupefied!

❍ ❍ ❍

१२. कथं त्वं कर्मणा शक्तः कैकेयीवशवर्तिनः ।
करिष्यसि पितुर्वाक्यमधर्मिष्ठं विगर्हितम् ।।

12. Why is it that you who are capable (of achieving anything) by your action, are fulfilling the words of your father which are contemptible, which is A-Dharma, and (particularly) when he is under the clutches (influence) of Kaikeyi.

❍ ❍ ❍

१३. यद्ययं किल्बिषाद्भेदः कृतोऽप्येवं न गृह्यते ।
जायते तत्र मे दुःखं धर्मसङ्गश्च गर्हितः ।।
तवायं धर्मसंयोगो लोकस्यास्य विगर्हितः ।।

13. This Dharma of yours that is followed now is despicable to the world. This betrayal that has come about through injustice under garb of Dharma, must be censured. As you dont accept this (as such), grief overwhelms me.

❍ ❍ ❍

१४. मनसाऽपि कथं कामं कुर्यास्त्वं कामवृत्तयोः ।
तयोस्त्वहितयोर्नित्यं शत्र्वोः पित्रभिधानयोः ।।

14. How can you also, with all your mind (& heart) be obliged (to fulfill) the wishes of these two, who are parents only in name, who are (very) harmful, who act as per their passions, and who are hostile (to you).

❍ ❍ ❍

१५. यद्यपि प्रतिपत्तिस्ते दैवी चापि तयोर्मतम् ।
तथाप्युपेक्षणीयं ते न मे तदपि रोचते ।।

15. Your opinion that the action of these two is (work of) Fate, does not please me. In any case this must be investigated by you further.

❍ ❍ ❍

१६. विक्लबो वीर्यहीनो यः स दैवमनुवर्तते ।
वीरास्संभावितात्मानो न दैवं पर्युपासते ॥

16. He who has no bravery, and is confused, (only he) follows (& and accepts) Fate; Brave men with inborn qualities of self reliance do not 'sit around' Fate (and do nothing).

❍ ❍ ❍

१७. दैवं पुरुषकारेण यस्समर्थः प्रबाधितुम् ।
न दैवेन विपन्नार्थः पुरुषस्सोऽवसीदति ॥

17. He, who, by his manly effort is capable of driving away (the impediments caused) by Fate, only that man does not get disheartened at the failure in his affairs caused by Fate.

❍ ❍ ❍

१८. द्रक्ष्यन्ति त्वद्य दैवस्य पौरुषं पुरुषस्य च ।
दैवमानुषयोरद्य व्यक्ता व्यक्तिर्भविष्यति ॥

18. Let (the world) witness now The Power of Man's Effort Over Fate; The true nature of (the power of) Fate and of (the power of) man will now manifest itself. (Lakshmana vows to set this right!)

❍ ❍ ❍

१९. अद्य मत्पौरुषहतं दैवं द्रक्षन्ति वै जनाः ।
यद्दैवादाहतं तेऽद्य दृष्टं राज्याभिषेचनम् ॥

19. People will now witness the knocking down of this (so called) Fate by my manly prowess; the Fate by which your royal coronation that was fixed, was frustrated.

❍ ❍ ❍

२० अत्यङ्कुशमिवोद्दामं गजं मदबलोद्धतम् ।
प्रधावितमहं दैवं पौरुषेण निवर्तये ॥

20. I will 'suppress' this work of Fate (which denied you the crown), by my own manly prowess, just like

(seizing) an unmanageable elephant which is proud of its strength and arrogance, running wild.

❍ ❍ ❍

२१. लोकपालास्समस्तास्ते नाद्य रामाभिषेचनम् ।
न चकुत्स्नास्त्रयो लोका विहन्युः किं पुनः पिता ॥

21. Oh Raama! The Lokpaala-s (the angel guardians of the corners of the Universe) and the entire people from all over the three worlds, will not prevent your coronation; How then will your father (be able to prevent it), now.

❍ ❍ ❍

२२. यैर्विवासस्तवारण्ये मिथो राजन् समर्थितः ।
अरण्ये ते विवत्स्यन्ति चतुर्दश समास्तथा ॥

22. Oh king (Raama)! these (two, your father and Kaikeyi), by whom your exile was determined for you by a mutual (secret pact), shall live in forest for 14 years (instead).

❍ ❍ ❍

२३. अहं तदाशां छेत्स्यामि पितुस्तस्याश्च या तव ।
अभिषेकविघातेन पुत्रराज्याय वर्तते ॥

23. Therefore I will shatter the hopes of my father and hers. (shatter the hopes of Kaikeyi) who wants crown for her son and who frustrated your coronation.

❍ ❍ ❍

२४. मद्बलेन विरुद्धाय न स्याद्दैवबलं तथा ।
प्रभविष्यति दुःखाय यथोग्रं पौरुषं मम ॥

24. The (Suffering) caused by (the so called) Fate, can never be (anything like) the most hateful suffering caused by my formidable manliness drawn from my own power and strength.

❍ ❍ ❍

२५. ऊर्ध्वं वर्षसहस्रान्ते प्रजापाल्यमनन्तरम् ।
आर्यपुत्राः करिष्यन्ति वनवासं गते त्वयि ॥

25. After thousands of years you may take to forest life and then after, (your Aryan) noble sons will take on the rule of the kingdom.

❍ ❍ ❍

२६. पूर्वराजर्षिवृत्त्या हि वनवासो विधीयते ।
प्रजा निक्षिप्य पुत्रेषु पुत्रवत्परिपालने ।।

26. As per tradition of our royal sages, (our Ikshwaaku kings), it is ordained that there is forest life (for a king) only after he hands over (the kingdom) to his sons to rule over the citizens (who are to be treated) like sons.

❍ ❍ ❍

२७. स चेद्राजन्यनेकाग्रे राज्यविभ्रमशङ्कया ।
नैवमिच्छसि धर्मात्मन्राज्यं राम त्वमात्मनि ।।

27. Oh noble soul man of Dharma, Oh Raama! If you do not desire (to accept) the kingdom because the kingdom has become restless and agitated as the king is engaged in other pursuits (and is against you) .....

❍ ❍ ❍

२८. प्रतिजाने च ते वीर मा भूवं वीरलोकभाक् ।
राज्यं च तव रक्षेयमहं वेलेव सागरम् ।।

28. ...... then, Oh brave (Raama) I promise to protect the kingdom of yours like the shores (protecting the) ocean, as I will (then) obtain the world of heroes in heaven.

❍ ❍ ❍

२९. मङ्गलैराभिषेञ्चस्व तत्र त्वं व्यापृतो भव ।
अहमेको महीपालानलं वारयितुं बलात् ।।

29. You should anoint yourself with (baths with) holy waters. Be engaged in this (task). (Because), alone, I am enough to drive away (hostile) kings with my strength.

❍ ❍ ❍

३०. न शोभार्थाविमौ बाहू न धनुर्भूषणाय मे ।
नासिराबन्धनार्थाय न शराः स्तम्भहेतवः ।।

30. My two hands are not for beautification (of my body)! And (my) bow is not for ornamentation. And my sword is not a piece of attachment. My arrows are not (mere) sticks of support ...... For me ......

❍ ❍ ❍

३१. अमित्रदमनार्थं मे सर्वमेतच्चतुष्टयम् ।।

31. ...... all these four are for the purpose of destroying the enemy.

❍ ❍ ❍

३२. न चाहं कामयेत्यर्थं यः स्याच्छत्रुर्मतो मम ।
असिना तीक्ष्णधारेण विद्युच्चलितवर्चसा ।।

32. I will not wish (him to be alive) who is considered (and who becomes) my terrible enemy: With sharp edged sword glittering like lightning ......

❍ ❍ ❍

३३. प्रगृहीतेन वै शत्रुं वज्रिणं वा न कल्पये ।।

33. ...... wielding this in my hand, I will not spare the enemy even if he is (Indhra) the wielder of Vajra (thunderbolt)

❍ ❍ ❍

३४. खड्गनिष्पेषनिष्पिष्टैर्गहना दुश्चरा च मे ।
हस्त्यश्वनरहस्तोरुशिरोभिर्भविता मही ।।

34. Cut and split by my sword, this Earth is going to become dense with hands and heads of elephants, horses, soldiers, difficult to tread.

❍ ❍ ❍

३५. खड्गधाराहता मेऽद्य दीप्यमाना इवाद्रयः ।
पतिष्यन्ति द्विपा भूमौ मेघा इव सविद्युतः ।।

35. The elephants that are radiant, that are like mountain peaks, that are like clouds stricken with lightning, will now fall on earth, felled by the tip of my sword.

❍ ❍ ❍

३६. बद्धगोधाङ्गुलित्राणे प्रगृहीतशरासने ।
कथं पुरुषमानी स्यात्पुरुषाणां मयि स्थिते ॥

36. When I stand (at the battle field) with bow in my hand (duly protected by) wearing finger gloves made of leather, who amongst men will fancy himself as a man (to stand before me)?

❍ ❍ ❍

३७. बहुभिश्चैकमत्यस्यन्नेकेन च बहूञ्जनान् ।
विनियोक्ष्याम्यहं बाणान् नृवाजिगजमर्मसु ॥

37. Shooting my arrows at men, horses, and elephants in their vital parts, I will crush them to pieces, one of them with many arrows and all of them with a single arrow.

❍ ❍ ❍

३८. अद्य मेऽस्त्रप्रभावस्य प्रभावः प्रसरिष्यति ।
राज्ञश्चाप्रभुतां कर्तुं प्रभुत्वं तव च प्रभो ॥

38. Oh Lord (Raama): When I accomplish (the task of) removal of kingship from the king and offer the Kingship (lordship) to you, the glory of the power of my weapons will spread (all over the world).

❍ ❍ ❍

३९. अद्य चन्दनसारस्य केयूरागोक्षणस्य च ।
वसूनां च विमोक्षस्य सुहृदां पालनस्य च ॥

39. Oh Raama! (My two hands) Besmeared with sandalpaste, (fit for) wearing Keyura ornaments, (and which) offered gifts, and was helping friends .....

❍ ❍ ❍

४०. अनुरूपाविमौ बाहू राम कर्म करिष्यताः ।
अभिषेचनविघ्नस्य कर्तृणां ते निवारणे ।।

40. ...... my two hands which were used (to this), will now do the work to suppress the agents (and stooges of the king) who cause harm to your coronation.

❍ ❍ ❍

४१. ब्रवीहि कोऽद्यैव मया वियुज्यतां
तवासुहृत्प्राणयशः सुहृज्जनैः ।
यथा तवेयं वसुधा वशे भवेत्
तथैव मां शाधि तवास्मि किङ्करः ।।

41. I am your servant. Tell me! Which man who is inimical to you must be separated from his fame, friends or even from his life. And you should command me (and me) alone in such a way that this entire Earth will come under your control.

❍ ❍ ❍

४२. विमृज्य बाष्पं परिसान्त्व्य चासकृत्
स लक्ष्मणं राघववंशवर्धनः ।
उवाच पित्र्ये वचने व्यवस्थितं
निबोध मामेव हि सौम्य सत्पथे ।।

42. (This Lakshmana spoke that he will use Force and revolt against the injustice caused to Raama by the king, his father.)

Consoling Lakshmana repeatedly and wiping his tears, Raama who increased the glory of the Raghu dynasty, addressed him:= Oh pleasant (Lakshmana)! You must know me as a man of firm conviction that the righteous path is in (obeying) words (of command) of father.=

(Note: Raama rejects revolt or war. His Dharma is very clear. he must obey his father, the king, without any deliberation.)

❍ ❍ ❍

Chapter 24

(Rama) Enlightens Kowsalya

(Raama consoles his mother Kowsalya. A masterly dissertation.)

❍ ❍ ❍

१. तं समीक्ष्य त्ववहितं पितुर्निर्देशपालने ।
कौसल्या बाष्पसंरुद्धा वचो धर्मिष्ठमब्रवीत् ।।

1. Kowsalya, choked with tears, addressed (Raama), realising that this man of Dharma was bent on protecting (honouring) his father's command.

❍ ❍ ❍

२. अदृष्टदुःखो धर्मात्मा सर्वभूतप्रियंवदः ।
मयि जातो दशरथात्कथमुञ्छेन वर्तयेत् ।।

2. Born to me through Dhascharatha, having never seen suffering before, how will this noble soul man of Dharma, who speaks sweetly to all beings, sustain himself with gleanings and pickings (in forest now)?

❍ ❍ ❍

३. यस्य भृत्याश्च दासाश्च मृष्टान्यन्नानि भुञ्जते ।
कथं स भोक्ष्यते नाथो वने मूलफलान्ययम् ।।

3. When (even) his servants and hirelings eat good food, how can their lord, this, (my son Raama), eat fruits and tubers in forest.

❍ ❍ ❍

४. क एतच्छद्दधेच्छ्रुत्वा कस्य वा न भवेद्भयम् ।
गुणवान्दयितो राज्ञो राघवो यद्विवास्यते ।।

4. Who will believe when they hear this that (Raama the) Raaghava who is dear to the king and who is endowed

with character, is driven away. Who will not be scared (when such a thing is happening in the kingdom)

❍ ❍ ❍

५. नूनं तु बलवांल्लोके कृतान्तस्सर्वमादिशेत् ।
लोके रामाभिरामस्त्वं वनं यत्र गमिष्यसि ॥

5. Oh Raama! That you, who delight every one in the world, should now go to forest (on exile), only indicates that Fate Is Everything In This World.

❍ ❍ ❍

६. अयं तु मामात्मभवस्तवादर्शनमारुतः ।
विलापदुःखसमिधो रुदिताश्रुहुताहुतिः ॥
चिन्ताबाष्पमहाधूमस्तवादर्शनचित्तजः ॥

6. (Poet Vaalmeeki goes poetic when he describes Kowsalya's grief.)

To me this (Grief) has firmly lodged in myself, my mind afflicted. by the denial of your sight (and presence before me in future).

(The fire of grief being stoked) By the unseen wind (by your unseen face).

(The fire of grief) which is fed by wailing that are the Samith-s (the twigs, used in holy fire) (The fire of grief) fed by tears that are the oblations.

(The fire of grief) with hot smoke that are (my) worries ......

❍ ❍ ❍

७. कर्शयित्वाऽधिकं पुत्र निश्वासायाससंभवः ।
त्वया विहीनामिह मां शोकाग्निरतुलो महान् ॥
प्रधक्ष्यति यथा कक्षं चित्रभानुर्हिमात्यये ॥

7. ..... This great unparalleled fire of grief, fanned by pain and torment, will make me terribly emaciated (and finally) burn me up, like forest fire burning up wood

when winter season has gone away, when I am without you, Oh my son!

❍ ❍ ❍

८. कथं हि धेनुः स्वं वत्सं गच्छन्तं नानुगच्छति ।
अहं त्वाऽनुगमिष्यामि यत्र पुत्र गमिष्यसि ॥

8. Oh son! Wherever you go I will follow you: Will not a cow follow its calf that is going in front.

❍ ❍ ❍

९. तथा निगदितं मात्रा तद्वाक्यं पुरुषर्षभः ।
श्रुत्वा रामोऽब्रवीद्वाक्यं मातरं भृशदुःखिताम् ॥

9. (Thus Kowsalya bemoaned: And Raama enlightens her.)

Hearing the words spoken by his mother, Raama, the 'Bull' amongst men, addressed his mother who was in great sorrow, these words.

❍ ❍ ❍

१०. कैकेय्या वञ्चितो राजा मयि चारण्यमाश्रिते ।
भवत्या च परित्यक्तो न नूनं वर्तयिष्यति ॥

10. Cheated by Kaikeyi, (if) he is abandoned by you also, while I also stay in forest, this king will (surely) not live.

❍ ❍ ❍

११. भर्तुः किल परित्यागो नृशंसः केवलं स्त्रियाः ।
स भवत्या न कर्तव्यो मनसाऽपि विगर्हितः ॥

11. For a woman, abandonment of husband is verily most despicable, vile: This should not even be thought of by you.

❍ ❍ ❍

१२. यावज्जीवति काकुत्स्थः पिता मे जगतीपतिः ।
शुश्रूषा क्रियतां तावत्स हि धर्मस्सनातनः ॥

12. Till my father, the Kaakuthsa king is alive, he should be served (by you): This, is the eternal Dharma.

❍ ❍ ❍

१३. एवमुक्ता तु रामेण कौसल्या शुभदर्शना ।
तथेत्युवाच सुप्रीता राममक्लिष्टकारिणम् ।।

13. When told thus by Raama, the auspicious Kowsalya who was (somewhat) satisfied (and consoled), then told Raama who was ever unwearied in action: = Let It Be (as per your wish) =.

❍ ❍ ❍

१४. एवमुक्तस्तु वचनं रामो धर्मभृतां वरः ।
भूयस्तामब्रवीद्वाक्यं मातरं भृशदुःखिताम् ।।

14. Hearing this word (from his mother), this Raama the foremost amongst men of Dharma, (again) addressed his mother who was even more in sorrow, with these words.

❍ ❍ ❍

१५. मया चैव भवत्या च कर्तव्यं वचनं पितुः ।
राजा भर्ता गुरुः श्रेष्ठस्सर्वेषामीश्वरः प्रभुः ।।

15. The king is foremost amongst us all: He is our Guru: He is our protector, our lord; (Like) a God! Therefore my father's words must be acted upon by me and you as well.

❍ ❍ ❍

१६. इमानि तु महारण्ये विहृत्य नव पञ्च च ।
वर्षाणि परमप्रीतः स्थास्यामि वचने तव ।।

16. After "Sporting" away for 14 years in the great forest most happily, then (I will come back and) I will stand by your command (to serve you).

❍ ❍ ❍

१७. एवमुक्ता प्रियं पुत्रं बाष्पपूर्णानना तदा ।
उवाच परमार्ता तु कौसल्या पुत्रवत्सला ॥

17. When told thus, Kowsalya who was very fond of her son, then addressed her beloved son (Raama) in great distress with tears filling her eyes.

❍ ❍ ❍

१८. आसां राम सपत्नीनां मध्ये वस्तुं न मे क्षमम् ।
नय मामपि काकुत्स्थ वनं वन्यां मृगीं यथा ॥
यदि ते गमने बुद्धिः कृता पितुरपेक्षया ॥

18. Oh Raama the Kaakuthsa! I cannot bear to live amidst co-wives of my husband. As you have decided to go to forest respecting (the wishes of) your father, you take me along with you to forest as well, like a female deer.

❍ ❍ ❍

१९. तां तथा रुदतीं रामो रुदन् वचनमब्रवीत् ।
जीवन्त्या हि स्त्रिया भर्ता दैवतं प्रभुरेव च ॥
भवत्या मम चैवाद्य राजा प्रभवति प्रभुः ॥

19. Then Raama addressed her who was in tears even (while he himself) was in tears. Oh (Mother) who has long life! For a woman, her husband is her lord and God. The king is Lord to me and to you,

❍ ❍ ❍

२०. न ह्यनाथा वयं राज्ञा लोकनाथेन धीमता ।
भरतश्चापि धर्मात्मा सर्वभूतप्रियंवदः ॥
भवतीमनुवर्तेत स हि धर्मरतः सदा ॥

20. It should not be that we made the wise king who is the lord of the World "protector less" Further Bharatha is a noble soul man of Dharma. Devoted to Dharma; Speaks sweetly (kindly) to all living being. And he will ever be obedient to you. Indeed!

❍ ❍ ❍

२१. यथा मयि तु निष्क्रान्ते पुत्रशोकेन पार्थिवः ।
श्रमं नावाप्नुयात्किंचिदप्रमत्ता तथा कुरु ।।

21. You should ever be vigilant and remain (in such a way) that when I am expelled (to live in forest), the king will not obtain any suffering, even a little, because of grief over (me), his son.

❍ ❍ ❍

२२. दारुणश्चाप्ययं शोको यथैनं न विनाशयेत् ।
राज्ञो वृद्धस्य सततं हितं चर समाहिता ।।

22. You must always be good to him, devoted (and serve him) in such a way this cruel grief will disappear from this old king.

❍ ❍ ❍

२३. व्रतोपवासनिरता या नारी परमोत्तमा ।
भर्तारं नानुवर्तेत सा च पापगतिभवेत् ।।

23. If a woman (even if) she is noble, performs vows and rituals, but does not follow her husband, she will go the way of sinners.

❍ ❍ ❍

२४. भर्तुः शुश्रूषया नारी लभते स्वर्गमुत्तमम् ।
अपि या निर्नमस्कारा निवृत्ता देवपूजनात् ।।

24. A woman may refrain from doing prayers to Deities; Or may not even pay respects (to elders) Even she, obtains foremost heaven if she serves her husband.

❍ ❍ ❍

२५. शुश्रूषामेव कुर्वीत भर्तुः प्रियहिते रता ।
एष धर्मः पुरा दृष्टो लोके वेदे श्रुतः स्मृतः ।।

25. (you) Must do service to (your) husband, devoted to do him good, please him; This Dharma is a very old

practice in the world. It is enshrined in Vedha-s and Smrithi-s. (Holy Texts and Codes)

❍ ❍ ❍

२६. अग्निकार्येष्ववहितास्सुमनोभिश्च देवताः ।
पूज्यास्ते मत्कृते देवि ब्राह्मणाश्चैव सत्कृताः ।।

26. Oh lady (mother Kowsalya)! For my welfare, the Braamins who are confined to the study of Vedha-s must be honoured and worshipped; The deities in fire rituals and religious rites, (must also be worshipped) with flowers.

❍ ❍ ❍

२७. एवं कालं प्रतीक्षस्व ममागमनकाङ्क्षिणी ।
नियता नियताहारा भर्तृशुश्रूषणे रता ।।

27. Keenly awaiting my return, performing such rituals, devoting yourself in serving your husband, you should look forward (to my safe return), spending your time in restraint.

❍ ❍ ❍

२८. प्राप्स्यसे परमं कामं मयि प्रत्यागते सति ।
यदि धर्मभृतां श्रेष्ठो धारयिष्यति जीवितम् ।।

28. If, when I return, this foremost amongst men devoted to Dharma, (this my father lives) bearing his life (in his old body), then my foremost wish would be fulfilled.

❍ ❍ ❍

२९. एवमुक्ता तु रामेण बाष्पपूर्णायतेक्षणा ।
कौसल्या पुत्रशोकार्ता रामं वचनमब्रवीत् ।।

29. When told thus by Raama, Kowsalya became even more afflicted by grief over his son. With her eyes blurred by tears, she then addressed Raama these words.

❍ ❍ ❍

३०. गमने सुकृतां बुद्धिं न ते शक्नोमि पुत्रक ।
विनिवर्तयितुं वीर नूनं कालो दुरत्ययः ।।

30. Fate is unfathomable. Therefore, Oh my brave son, I am incapable of changing your mind which is 'Fixed' on going to forest.

❍ ❍ ❍

३१. गच्छ पुत्र त्वमेकाग्रो भद्रं तेऽस्तु सदा विभो ।
पुनस्त्वयि निवृत्ते तु भविष्यामि गतक्लमा ।।

31. You may go, Take care! May there be welfare for you. Oh my bright son! Only when you return, I will become free from weariness (grief, sorrow).

❍ ❍ ❍

३२. प्रत्यागते महाभागे कृतार्थे चरितव्रते ।
पितुरानृण्यतां प्राप्ते त्वयि लप्स्ये परं सुखम् ।।

32. When you return after discharging your debt (of honour) of your father and as a most illustrious man having fulfilled your mission and having followed righteous conduct, then only I will obtain great happiness.

❍ ❍ ❍

३३. कृतान्तस्य गतिः पुत्र दुर्विभाव्या सदा भुवि ।
यस्त्वां संचोदयति मे वच आच्छिद्य राघव ।।

33. In this world the work of Fate can never be apprehended: Oh my son! Oh (Raama) the Raaghava! It is this, that impels you to reject my words (my request to you not to go on exile).

❍ ❍ ❍

३४. गच्छेदानीं महाबाहो क्षेमेण पुनरागतः ।
नन्दयिष्यसि मां पुत्र साम्ना श्लक्ष्णेन चारुणा ।।

34. Oh son with mighty limbs! You may go now. Coming back (after 14 years), you will make me rejoice by your

peaceful, tender, loving and tranquilising (presence & speech)

❍ ❍ ❍

३५. अपीदानीं स कालःस्याद्वनात्प्रत्यागतं पुनः ।
येन त्वां पुत्र पश्येयं जटावल्कलधारिणम् ॥

35. Oh my son! (How I wish) That, that day is here and now! (the day) when I would see you again, returning from forest wearing deer skin and sporting (Tufted) knotted unkempt hair locks.

❍ ❍ ❍

३६. तथा हि रामं वनवासनिश्चितं
समीक्ष्य देवी परमेण चेतसा ।
उवाच रामं शुभलक्षणं वचो
बभूव च स्वस्त्ययनाभिकाङ्क्षिणी ॥

36. Realising that Raama was determined to go to forest with all his heart thus, the lady (Kowsalya) longed (for prosperity) and desired Swasthi (blessings) for Raama. And she spoke only pleasant and auspicious words to Raama (from then on).

(Raama is a Vaagmee, master of speech. Although Kowsalya 'refuses' to be convinced due to grief overwhelming her, she accepts Raama's decision because it is very difficult to score over Raama. who ever speaks Truth and speaks sweetly and convincingly.)

❍ ❍ ❍

Chapter 25

(Raama) Receives Mother's Blessings

१. साऽपनीय तमायासमुपस्पृश्य जलं शुचिः ।
चकार माता रामस्य मङ्गलानि मनस्विनी ॥

1. This intelligent mother (Kowsalya) gave up her effort (and weariness) and then sipped waters (as per norms

of rituals). She began to offer her benediction to the pure Raama (her son).

❍ ❍ ❍

२. न शक्यसे वारयितुं गच्छेदानीं रघूत्तम ।
शीघ्रं च विनिवर्तस्व वर्तस्व च सतां पथि ॥

2. Oh Foremost of Raghu-s! You cannot be restrained. Therefore you leave soon. Follow the path of the Righteous. Thus you return (safely after 14 years).

❍ ❍ ❍

३. यं पालयसि धर्मं त्वं धृत्या च नियमेन च ।
स वै राघवशार्दूल धर्मस्त्वामभिरक्षतु ॥

3. Oh 'lion' amongst Raghu-s! This Dharma that you are nourishing (and practising) with resolution and devotion, may that Dharma protect you.

❍ ❍ ❍

४. येभ्यः प्रणमसे पुत्र चैत्येष्वायतनेषु च ।
ते च त्वामभिरक्षन्तु वने सह महर्षिभिः ॥

4. Oh my son! May those whom you worship in temples and sacrificial halls, protect you who will (now) be with great sages in the forest.

❍ ❍ ❍

५. यानि दत्तानि तेऽस्त्राणि विश्वामित्रेण धीमता ।
तानि त्वामभिरक्षन्तु गुणैः समुदितं सदा ॥

5. May the weapons offered by the wise Vischwaamithra to you, always protect you who are endowed with noble qualities.

❍ ❍ ❍

६. पितृशुश्रूषया पुत्र मातृशुश्रूषया तथा ।
सत्येन च महाबाहो चिरं जीवाभिरक्षितः ॥

6. Oh my son, the mighty limbed (Raama)! May you live

long, protected as you are by the services rendered to your father, by the services rendered to your mother likewise, by your (steadfastness in) Truth.

❍ ❍ ❍

७. समित्कुशपवित्राणि वेद्यश्चायतनानि च ।
स्थण्डिलानि पवित्राणि शैला वृक्षाः क्षुपा ह्रदाः ।।
पतङ्गाः पन्नगास्सिंहास्त्वां रक्षन्तु नरोत्तम ।।

7. Oh noble man! May the (sacred ritual materials like) Samith-s, Dharbha grass, the halls of worship, holy fire mounds, sacrificial halls, mountains, trees, plants, ponds, serpents and lions protect you.

❍ ❍ ❍

८. स्वस्ति साध्याश्च विश्वे च मरुतश्च महर्षयः ।
स्वस्ति धाता विधाता च स्वस्ति पूषा भगोऽर्यमा ।।

8. May the celestials, the Saadhya-s, the Vischwa-Dheva-s, the Maruth-s, the great sages offer you Swasthi (blessings). May Dhaatha and Vidhaatha (the two deities) protect you with Swasthi; May Poosha, Bhaga, Aryama, protect you with Swasthi.

❍ ❍ ❍

९. लोकपालाश्च ते सर्वे वासवप्रमुखास्तथा ।
ऋतवश्चैव पक्षाश्च मासास्संवत्सराः क्षपाः ।।

9. May the Lokpaals (guardians of the Universe) and lords like Indhra and all, the Rithu-s (Seasons), the (Hal month period of) new Moon and full Moon, the months, the Samvathsara-s, The (lord of) night ......

❍ ❍ ❍

१०. दिनानि च मुहूर्ताश्च स्वस्ति कुर्वन्तु ते सदा ।
स्मृतिर्धृतिश्च धर्मश्च पान्तु त्वां पुत्र सर्वतः ।।

10. ...... (The lord of) day, and the Muhoortha (the minutes of time), may always bless you with Swasthi. Oh my

son! May Smrithi-s, Dharma, resoluteness, always protect you.

❍ ❍ ❍

११. स्कन्दश्च भगवान्देवस्सोमश्चेन्द्रो बृहस्पतिः ।
सप्तर्षयो नारदश्च ते त्वां रक्षन्तु सर्वतः ।।

11. May God Skandha, Lord Brihaspathi, Lord Indhra, Lord Moon, The Seven Sages, Sage Naaradha, protect you totally.

❍ ❍ ❍

१२. ते चापि सर्वतः सिद्धा दिशश्च सदिग्गीश्वराः ।
स्तुता मया वने तस्मिन्पान्तु त्वां पुत्र सर्वशः ।।

12. Oh son! May the tribes and guardians protecting the corners of earth, and may the Sidhdha-s who are always (worshipped and) extolled by me daily, protect you constantly in forest.

❍ ❍ ❍

१३. शैलास्सर्वेसमुद्राश्च राजा वरुण एव च ।
द्यौरन्तरिक्षं पृथिवी नद्यस्सर्वास्तथैव च ।।

13. May the mountains, oceans, Lord Varuna, king (Kubhaera), all the rivers, earth, heaven and sky ......

❍ ❍ ❍

१४. नक्षत्राणि च सर्वाणि ग्रहाश्च सहदेवताः ।
अहोरात्रे तथा सन्ध्ये पान्तु त्वां वनमाश्रितम् ।।

14. ...... all the stars, lord of twelve (Astrological) houses, Night, Day, Sunrise and Sunset, protect you when you live in forest

❍ ❍ ❍

१५. ऋतवश्चैव षट्पुण्या मासास्संवत्सरास्तथा ।
कलाश्च काष्ठाश्च तथा तव शर्म दिशन्तु ते ।।

15. May the Six Rith-s, the lords of holy months, Months, Samvathsar-s (year), Deities of Time, lords of twelve houses, offer you bliss.

❍ ❍ ❍

१६. महावने विचरतो मुनिवेषस्य धीमतः ।
तवादित्याश्च दैत्याश्च भवन्तु सुखदास्सदा ॥

16. May the Aadhithya-s, Dhaithya-s, always offer you comfort who are wise, as you roam about in great forest in the garb of a Muni.

❍ ❍ ❍

१७. राक्षसानां पिशाचानां दैत्यानां क्रूरकर्मणाम् ।
क्रव्यादानां च सर्वेषां मा भूत्पुत्रक ते भयम् ॥

17. Oh son ! There should be no danger for you from all the Dhaithya-s who are carnivorous, from Demons who do cruel deeds, and from Pischaacha-s.

❍ ❍ ❍

१८. प्लवगा वृश्चिका दंशा मशकाश्चैव कानने ।
सरीसृपाश्च कीटाश्च मा भूवन् गहने तव ॥

18. Let not monkeys, scorpions, Gnats, mosquitoes, pythons, worms, trouble you in dense forest.

❍ ❍ ❍

१९. महाद्विपाश्च सिंहाश्च व्याघ्रा ऋक्षाश्च दंष्ट्रिणः ।
महिषा श्रृङ्गिणो रौद्रा न ते दुह्यन्ति पुत्रक ॥

19. Oh Son! Big elephants, lions, tigers, wild boars, bears, long hoofed terrible buffaloes, should not harm you.

❍ ❍ ❍

२०. नृमांसभोजना रौद्रा ये चान्ये सत्त्वजातयः ।
मा च त्वां हिंसिषुः पुत्र मया संपूजितास्त्विह ॥

20. Oh son ! Cannibals, cruel ghosts, and all others should not harm you, by (the power of) my prayers done here.

❍ ❍ ❍

२१. आगमास्ते शिवास्सन्तु सिध्यन्तु च पराक्रमाः ।
सर्वसम्पत्तये राम स्वस्तिमान् गच्छ पुत्रक ॥

21. Oh son Oh Raama ! May your journey be pleasant. May your valour bring about success in all affairs; May you go with blessings of Swasthi (now).

❍ ❍ ❍

२२. स्वस्ति तेऽस्त्वान्तरिक्षेभ्यः पार्थिवेभ्यः पुनःपुनः ।
सर्वेभ्यश्चैव देवेभ्यो ये च ते परिपन्थिनः ॥

22. Those of your adversaries who are residents in earth and Deities who live upper worlds: From all these, let there be Swasthi for you, more and more.

❍ ❍ ❍

२३. शुक्रस्सोमश्च सूर्यश्च धनदोऽथ यमस्तथा ।
पान्तु त्वामर्चिता राम दण्डकारण्यवासिनम् ॥

23. Oh Raama ! May Venus, Moon, Jupiter, Sun, Kubhaera, Yama, who are now worshipped, protect you who will be living in forest of Dhandaka.

❍ ❍ ❍

२४. अग्निर्वायुस्तथा धूमो मन्त्राश्चर्षिमुखाच्च्युताः ।
उपस्पर्शनकाले तु पान्तु त्वां रघुनन्दन ॥

24. Oh darling of Raghu-s ! May lords of fire, wind, holy Smoke, and the chants which emanate from lips of Sages during oblation, protect you.

❍ ❍ ❍

२५. सर्वलोकप्रभुर्ब्रह्मा भूतभर्ता तथर्षयः ।
ये च शेषास्सुरास्ते त्वां रक्षन्तु वनवासिनम् ॥

25. May (Vishnu) the lord of all the Worlds, May the lord of holy Spirits (Schiva), and God Bramma and all other celestials, Rishi-s, protect you who are (going to be) resident of forest.

❍ ❍ ❍

२६. इति माल्यैस्सुरगणान्गन्धैश्चापि यशस्विनी ।
स्तुतिभिश्चानुकूलाभिरानर्चायतलोचना ॥

26. This (glorious) famous lady (Kowsalya) who had large eyes, invoked the Deities. thus: And she prayed to them suitably, with flowers, incenses and hymns.

❍ ❍ ❍

२७. ज्वलनं समुपादाय ब्राह्मणेन महात्मना ।
हावयामास विधिना राममङ्गलकारणात् ॥

27. With great soul Braamins (priests), she lit fire and performed Homa (Rituals) as per norms, for the welfare of Raama.

❍ ❍ ❍

२८. घृतं श्वेतानि माल्यानि समिधः श्वेतसर्षपान् ।
उपसम्पादयामास कौसल्या परमाङ्गना ॥

28. This foremost woman Kowsalya brought oil of butter, white flowers, Samith-s, white mustard seeds.

❍ ❍ ❍

२९. उपाध्यायस्स विधिना हुत्वा शान्तिमनामयम् ।
हुतहव्यावशेषेण बाह्यं बलिमकल्पयत् ॥

29. These priests performed fire rituals as per norms for peace and good health. And with the balance of fire (remaining in Mound), they offered Sacrifice* outside.

(It was customary those days to offer *animal sacrifices as oblations.)

३०. मधुदध्यक्षतघृतैः स्वस्ति वाच्य द्विजांस्ततः ।
वाचयामास रामस्य वने स्वस्त्ययनक्रियाम् ।।

30. With honey, yogurt, holy seeds, butter oil, she made the Braamins perform Swasthi ceremony (for Raama) with chants. Then she asked them to recite Swasthi blessings for Raama in forest.

❍ ❍ ❍

३१. ततस्तस्मै द्विजेन्द्राय राममाता यशस्विनी ।
दक्षिणां प्रददौ रामं वचनं चेदमब्रवीत् ।।

31. Then the famous (Kowsalya) the mother of Raama, offered gifts to these Braamins. Then she addressed Raama these words.

❍ ❍ ❍

३२. यन्मङ्गलं सहस्राक्षे सर्वदेवनमस्कृते ।
वृत्रनाशे समभवत्तत्ते भवतु मङ्गलम् ।।

32. The felicitation offered to the thousand eyed (Indhra) who was prayed to by all Dheva-s in the matter of the destruction of (Demon) Vrithra... (may) the same blessings and benediction be bestowed on you.

❍ ❍ ❍

३३. यन्मङ्गलं सुपर्णस्य विनताऽकल्पयत्पुरा ।
अमृतं प्रार्थयानस्य तत्ते भवतु मङ्गलम् ।।

33. Long ago, Vinatha (wife of Kaaschyapa) offered benediction to Suparna (son of Vinatha) when he went (& sought) Nectar. (May) the same benediction be bestowed on you.

❍ ❍ ❍

३४. अमृतोत्पादने दैत्यान्घ्नतो वज्रधरस्य यत् ।
अदितिर्मङ्गलं प्रादात्तत्ते भवतु मङ्गलम् ।।

34. (And long long ago) The benediction offered to (Lord

Indhra) the wielder of Vajra by (his mother) Adhithi when Daithya-s were killed (during the churning of Ocean) for getting Nectar... (May) the same benediction be bestowed on you.

❍ ❍ ❍

३५. त्रीन्विक्रमान्प्रक्रमतो विष्णोरमिततेजसः ।
यदासीन्मङ्गलं राम तत्ते भवतु मङ्गलम् ॥

35. Oh Raama! The benediction (and bliss) that came by to God Vishnu of incomparable brilliance when he measured (the Universe) with (just) Three Steps.. (May) the same benediction be there for you.

❍ ❍ ❍

३६. ऋतवस्सागरा द्वीपा वेदा लोका दिशश्च ते ।
मङ्गलानि महाबाहो दिशन्तु तव कानने ॥

36. Oh mighty limbed (Raama): May the Rithu-s, Oceans, Islands, Vedha-s, all the worlds, All the Directions, offer you bliss in forest.

❍ ❍ ❍

३७. मङ्गलं भगवान्विष्णुर्मङ्गलं मधुसूदनः ।
मङ्गलं पुण्डरीकाक्षो मङ्गलं गरुडध्वजः ॥

37. May (Vishnu) who rides in Garuda bestow welfare; May (Vishnu) the destroyer of demon Madhu bestow welfare.

❍ ❍ ❍

३८. इति पुत्रस्य शेषांश्च कृत्वा शिरसि भामिनी ।
उवाचातिप्रहृष्टेव सा दुःखवशवर्तिनी ॥
गन्धैश्चापि समालभ्य राममायतलोचना ॥

38. Thus this (Kowsalya) who was 'passionately' (attached to her son Raama) whose eyes were large, appeared happy in spite of being seized with grief (at the parting of Raama); and showered the flowers remaining there

on the head of Raama and besmeared him with scents, blessed him ......

❍ ❍ ❍

३९. ओषधीं चापि सिद्धार्थां विशल्यकरणीं शुभाम् ।
चकार रक्षां कौसल्या मन्त्रैरभिजजाप च ।।
वाङ्मात्रेण न भावेन वाचाऽसंसज्जमानया ।।

39. ...... (And she besmeared him) With fine herbal called Vischalyakarni that would fulfill one's wishes: Then Kowsalya tied the sacred thread (On Raama's wrist) and prayed, reciting chants, words just coming out, unsteady, in faltering voice, (but) with devotion.

❍ ❍ ❍

४०. आनम्य मूर्ध्नि चाघ्राय परिष्वज्य यशस्विनी ।
अवदत्पुत्र सिद्धार्थोगच्छ राम यथासुखम् ।।

40. The most famous (Kowsalya) kissed his forehead, clasped and hugged him: Then said: Oh my son Raama! You may go as you please, having accomplished (your objective of holding on to Truth).

❍ ❍ ❍

४१. अरोगं सर्वसिद्धार्थमयोध्यां पुनरागतम् ।
द्रक्ष्यामि त्वामहं वत्स सुस्थितं राजवर्त्मनि ।।

41. Oh son! I will see you return back to Ayodhya in health, firmly established (as Ruler) in royal duties, having accomplished all your tasks.

❍ ❍ ❍

४२. प्रनष्टदुःखसङ्कल्पा हर्षविद्योतितानना ।
द्रक्ष्यामि त्वां वनात्प्राप्तं पूर्णचन्द्रमिवोदितम् ।।

42. I will see you return from forest like the rising Moon, with my face glittering with joy and happiness, without sorrow or anxiety in me.

❍ ❍ ❍

४३. भद्रासनगतं राम वनवासादिहागतम् ।
द्रक्ष्यामि त्वामहं वत्स तीर्णवन्तं पितुर्वचः ।।

43. Oh my son Raama! I will see you return from forest having fulfilled your father's words and (I will see you) seated in the auspicious Throne.

❍ ❍ ❍

४४. मङ्गलैरुपसम्पन्नो वनवासादिहागतः ।
वध्वा मम च नित्यं त्वं कामान्संवर्धय प्रभो ।।

44. Oh lord (my son Raama)! After you return here from life in forest, you will fulfill my desires, always, and my daughter-in- law's (as well), endowed with (all the) Bliss.

❍ ❍ ❍

४५. मयाऽर्चिता देवगणाश्शिवादयो
महर्षयो भूतमहासुरोरगाः ।
अभिप्रयातस्य वनं चिराय ते
हितानि काङ्क्षन्तु दिशश्च राघव ।।

45. Oh Raama the Raaghava! May God Schiva and the multitude of Dheva-s who have been worshipped by me, (and may) the great sages, great holy ghosts, Asura-s, Naaga-s, and all the (ten) regions (of Earth) do you good who are going to live in forest for a long time

❍ ❍ ❍

४६. इतीव चाश्रुप्रतिपूर्णलोचना
समाप्य च स्वस्त्ययनं यथाविधि ।
प्रदक्षिणं चैव चकार राघवं
पुनःपुनश्चापि निपीड्य सस्वजे ।।
४७. तथा तु देव्या स कृतप्रदक्षिणो
निपीड्य मातुश्चरणौ पुनःपुनः ।
जगाम सीतानिलयं महायशाः
स राघवः प्रज्वलितः स्वया श्रिया ।।

46 & 47.

Her eyes were full with tears as she (spoke) thus: After blessing him with Swasthi, she did (the tying of thread) from right to left. And again and again she clasped, embraced (Raama) the Raaghava..... With (Sacred thread) tied by the lady, (Raama) the Raaghava fell at his mother's feet and clasped it repeatedly. Then, shining by his own inborn replendency, this most famous (Raama) went to (his wife) Seetha's abode.

❍ ❍ ❍

Chapter 26

Raama Gives Advice to Seetha

१. अभिवाद्य च कौसल्यां रामस्संप्रस्थितो वनम् ।
कृतस्वस्त्ययनो मात्रा धर्मिष्ठे वर्त्मनि स्थितः ॥

1. After bowing to Kowsalya and receiving blessings of Swasthi from his mother (Kowsalya), Raama who was firmly resolved in the path of Dharma, who was setting out to go to forest ......

❍ ❍ ❍

२. विराजयन्राजसुतो राजमार्गं नरैर्वृतम् ।
हृदयान्याममन्थेव जनस्य गुणवत्तया ॥

2. ...... this son of the king, (this Raama) who captivated the hearts of all people by his excellent qualities, illuminated (as it were), the royal boulevard which was full with citizens (as he was going to Seetha's place)

❍ ❍ ❍

३. वैदेही चापि तत्सर्वं न शुश्राव तपस्विनी ।
तुेव हृदि तस्याश्च यौवराज्याभिषेचनम् ॥

3. But the austere Seetha the Vaidhehi, had not heard

about all these (events). Her heart was set only on (Raama's) coronation

❍ ❍ ❍

४. देवकार्यं स्म सा कृत्वा कृतज्ञा हृष्टचेतना ।
अभिज्ञा राजधर्माणां राजपुत्रं प्रतीक्षते ॥

4. (Seetha), a woman of gratitude, conversant with (norms of) royal Dharma (Duties), who had performed prayers to Deities happily, was awaiting the prince (her husband Raama).

❍ ❍ ❍

५. प्रविवेशाथ रामस्तु स्ववेश्म सुविभूषितम् ।
प्रहृष्टजनसम्पूर्णं ह्रिया किञ्चिदवाङ्मुखः ॥

5. Then Raama entered the beautifully decorated palace that was full with happy citizens, with his face drawn downwards, (looking) somewhat anxious.

❍ ❍ ❍

६. अथ सीता समुत्पत्य वेपमाना च तं पतिम् ।
अपश्यच्छोकसन्तप्तं चिन्ताव्याकुलितेन्द्रियम् ॥

6. Then Seetha who had got up, observed that her husband was in torment with grief and was disturbed due to worry; And she was shaken (to see him thus).

❍ ❍ ❍

७. तां दृष्ट्वा स हि धर्मात्मा न शशाक मनोगतम् ।
तं शोकं राघवस्सोढुं ततो विवृततां गतः ॥

7. On seeing her, (Raama) the Raaghava, this man of Dharma, could not conceal his grief that was in his mind; Therefore (his facial expression) underwent a change.

❍ ❍ ❍

८. विवर्णवदनं दृष्ट्वा तं प्रस्विन्नममर्षणम् ।
आह दुःखाभिसन्तप्ता किमिदानीमिदं प्रभो ॥

8. Seeing him perspiring, (seeing) colour gone from his face, and (looking somewhat) indignant, she was tormented by sorrow. And she said to him. = Oh my Lord! What is this now?=

❍ ❍ ❍

९. अद्य बार्हस्पतः श्रीमानुक्तः पुष्यो नु राघव ।
प्रोच्यते ब्राह्मणैः प्राज्ञैः केन त्वमसि दुर्मनाः ।।

9. Oh (Raama) the Raaghava! It has been announced by learned Braamins that today is the day (of coronation) as proclaimed, (the day) that is (holy and) resplendent, (the day) of Pushya star in association with lord sage Brihaspathi. You are in low spirits?

❍ ❍ ❍

१०. न ते शतशलाकेन जलफेननिभेन च ।
आवृतं वदनं वल्गु छत्रेणाभिविराजते ।।

10. And your handsome face does not shine, not having been covered (protected against Sun) by (your usual royal) umbrella that is white like foam of water and which has 100 ribs.

(Readers may note that the moment he accepted his father's/Kaikeyi's, command, he rejected royal comforts.)

❍ ❍ ❍

११. व्यजनाभ्यां च मुख्याभ्यां शतपत्रनिभेक्षणम् ।
चन्द्रहंसप्रकाशाभ्यां वीज्यते न तवाननम् ।।

11. (How is it) Your face (beautified by) your eyes that are (lovely) like (Lotus) with 1000 petals, is not caressed (fanned by) two whisk fans which shine like the moon and swan, and which always is essential to you.

❍ ❍ ❍

१२. वाग्मिनो वन्दिनश्चापि प्रहृष्टास्त्वां नरर्षभ ।
स्तुवन्तो नाद्य दृश्यन्ते मङ्गलैस्सूतमागधाः ॥

12. Oh 'Bull' amongst men! (How is it) Your equerries, and the happy bards who are eloquent and who sing praises and offer felicitations to you, are not seen now?

❍ ❍ ❍

१३. न ते क्षौद्रं च दधि च ब्राह्मणा वेदपारगाः ।
मूर्ध्नि मूर्धाभिषिक्तस्य दधति स्म विधानतः ॥

13. (How is it) Braamins renowned in Vedha-s have not offered, as per norms, holy scented waters on your forehead after you had taken your (coronation) head bath?

❍ ❍ ❍

१४. न त्वा प्रकृतयस्सर्वाः श्रेणीमुख्याश्च भूषिताः ।
अनुव्रजितुमिच्छन्ति पौरजानपदास्तथा ॥

14. (How is it) The well dressed citizens, leading businessmen and other ordinary citizens have not desired to accompany you?

❍ ❍ ❍

१५. चतुर्भिर्वेगसम्पन्नैर्हयैः काञ्चनभूषितैः ।
शशमुख्यः पुष्परथो युक्तः किं न गच्छति तेऽग्रतः ॥

15. (How is it) Your most important chariot, the Pushya Ratha yoked to four horses that are endowed with good speed and are ornamented in gold, have not come in front of you?

❍ ❍ ❍

१६. न हस्ती चाग्रतः श्रीमांस्तव लक्षणपूजितः ।
प्रयाणे लक्ष्यते वीर कृष्णमेघगिरिप्रभः ॥

16. (How is it) Oh Brave (Raama) the resplendent, the distinguished royal elephant that resembles dark cloud

and mountain, is not seen ahead of you (as you came here)?

❍ ❍ ❍

१७. न च काञ्चनचित्रं ते पश्यामि प्रियदर्शन ।
भद्रासनं पुरस्कृत्य यान्तं वीरपुरस्सरम् ।।

17. Oh pleasant looking (Raama)! I do not see the royal seat decorated in gold and which is fit for warriors, which (always) accompanies you..

❍ ❍ ❍

१८. अभिषेको यदा सज्जः किमिदानीमिदं तव ।
अपूर्वोमुखवर्णश्च न प्रहर्षश्च लक्ष्यते ।।

18. Your coronation is fast approaching: (But) Your cheer is not seen. The color of your countenance is not like before (is strange), What is this ?

❍ ❍ ❍

१९. इतीव विलपन्तीं तां प्रोवाच रघुनन्दनः ।
सीते तत्रभवांस्तातः प्रव्राजयति मां वनम् ।।

19. (Raama) the darling of Raghu-s, then replied to (Seetha) who was lamenting thus; = Oh Seetha! Our lord, my father is sending me to forest.=

❍ ❍ ❍

२०. कुले महति संभूते धर्मज्ञे धर्मचारिणि ।
श्रृणु जानकि येनेदं क्रमेणाभ्यागतं मम ।।

20. Oh (Seetha) born in the noble family as daughter of (King) Janaka! Oh (Seetha) who knows Dharma! (Oh Seetha) who practises Dharma! Under what circumstances this has happened to me, (may you) listen .

❍ ❍ ❍

२१. राज्ञा सत्यप्रतिज्ञेन पित्रा दशरथेन मे ।
कैकेय्यै प्रीतमनसा पुरा दत्तौ महावरौ ।।

21. (Raama tells Seetha the drama at night at Kaikeyi's place.)

Long ago, two boons were offered to Kaikeyi in great happiness by my father, king Dhascharatha who is ever most Truthful.

❍ ❍ ❍

२२. तयाऽद्य मम सज्जेऽस्मिन्नभिषेके नृपोद्यते ।
प्रचोदितस्ससमयो धर्मेण प्रतिनिर्जितः ।।

22. While preparations for my coronation at the direction of the king was going on, compelled by Dharma, he (my father Dhascharatha), who was bound by agreement, was *countermanded by her (by Kaikeyi).

(Poet uses word-*PrathiNirjitha:Translator has used countermanded.)

❍ ❍ ❍

२३. चतुर्दश हि वर्षाणि वस्तव्यं दण्डके मया ।
पित्रा मे भरतश्चापि यौवराज्ये नियोजितः ।।

23. (Raama tells Seetha how Kaikeyi pressed his father with the two Boons she had received, how she exercised her options now): Fourteen years must be lived by me in Dhandaka (forest): And by my father, (by his decision), Bharatha also is appointed as crown prince (instead).

❍ ❍ ❍

२४. सोऽहं त्वामागतो द्रष्टुं प्रस्थितो विजनं वनम् ।
भरतस्य समीपे तु नाहं कथ्यः कदाचन ।।

24. Before setting out to the uninhabited forest, I came here to see you (to bid you farewell): (Remember)! Before Bharatha, I should never be extolled (because he is our 'king' now)

❍ ❍ ❍

२५. ऋद्धियुक्ता हि पुरुषा न सहन्ते परस्तवम् ।
तस्मान्न ते कथाः कथ्या भरतस्याग्रतो मम ।।

25. (Because) People who are endowed with prosperity cannot stand others being praised: Therefore, before Bharatha, (in his presence), I should never be praised about my qualities by you.

(Here Raama's love for Bharatha comes out: Seetha should never embarrass his brother Bharatha by praising Raama, thus making Bharatha diffident about his capability to rule.)

❍ ❍ ❍

२६. नापि त्वं तेन भर्तव्या विशेषेण कदाचन ।
अनुकूलतया शक्यं समीपे तस्य वर्तितुम् ।।

26. (It may be that) You may not particularly be cared for by him at all times. You must (however) be well disposed to him.

(Here again, Raama tells Seetha that Bharatha is not just a brother but a 'King' with lots of responsibility, equal in service to all.)

❍ ❍ ❍

२७. तस्मै दत्तं नृपतिना यौवराज्यं सनातनम् ।
स प्रसाद्यस्त्वया सीते नृपतिश्च विशेषतः ।।

27. Under extraordinary circumstances, this traditional (ancient) title of crown prince was offered to him by our king; Oh Seetha! (but) As he is now 'king', he must be propitiated by you.

❍ ❍ ❍

२८. अहं चापि प्रतिज्ञां तां गुरोस्समनुपालयन् ।
वनमद्यैव यास्यामि स्थिरीभव मनस्विनि ।।

28. And I am going alone to Forest to honour this, my father's command; Oh intelligent (Seetha) Be composed (Steadfast, resolute).

❍ ❍ ❍

२९. याते च मयि कल्याणि वनं मुनिनिषेवितम् ।
व्रतोपवासरतया भवितव्यं त्वयाऽनघे ॥

29. Oh sinless (Seetha)! Oh Auspicious Lady! When I am away in forest where Muni-s live, your time should be spent in vows and rituals by you also (here, at Ayodhya).

❍ ❍ ❍

३०. काल्यमुत्थाय देवानां कृत्वा पूजां यथाविधि ।
वन्दितव्यो दशरथः पिता मम जनेश्वरः ॥

30. Getting up early morning after saying prayers to Gods as per norms, my father, the lord of men, king Dhascharatha must be honoured (served by you).

❍ ❍ ❍

३१. माता च मम कौसल्या वृद्धा सन्तापकर्शिता ।
धर्ममेवाग्रतः कृत्वा त्वत्तस्संमानमर्हति ॥

31. Considering it as your utmost in Dharma, my old mother Kowsalya who is tormented by grief, deserves to be honoured (served by you).

❍ ❍ ❍

३२. वन्दितव्यास्त्वया नित्यं याः शेषा मम मातरः ।
स्नेहप्रणयसंभोगैः समा हि मम मातरः ॥

32. My mothers (my mother Kowsalya, step mothers Sumithra and Kaikeyi), are all equal (to me) in affection, confidence, and favour. (They and) my other (step) mothers should always be served by you.

(Readers should not be surprised: Dhascharatha had 350 wives apart from the three queens: Secondly the three qualities for service are:: affection must be shown first; you then build confidence in them; and they will seek favour by right. This is the Dharma of Service.)

❍ ❍ ❍

३३. भ्रातृपुत्रसमौ चापि द्रष्टव्यौ च विशेषतः ।
उभौ भरतशत्रुघ्नौ प्राणैः प्रियतरौ मम ॥

33. (And my brothers) Bharatha and Schathrugna are dearer to me than my life. Therefore they should particularly be perceived by you like your own son and brother.

❍ ❍ ❍

३४. विप्रियं न च कर्तव्यं भरतस्य कदाचन ।
स हि राजा प्रभुश्चैव देशस्य च कुलस्य च ॥

34. You should never do anything that will displease Bharatha: Because he is king, the lord of this kingdom (of ours) and our family.

❍ ❍ ❍

३५. आराधिता हि शीलेन प्रयत्नैश्चोपसेविताः ।
राजानः संप्रसीदन्ति प्रकुप्यन्ति विपर्यये ॥

35. Kings are pleased when they are served diligently and honoured by good conduct. If otherwise, they get angry.

❍ ❍ ❍

३६. औरसानपि पुत्रान् हि त्यजन्त्यहितकारिणः ।
समर्थान् संप्रगृह्णन्ति परानपि नराधिपाः ॥

३७. सा त्वं वसेह कल्याणि राज्ञस्समनुवर्तिनी ।
भरतस्य रता धर्मेसत्यव्रतपरायणा ॥

36 & 37.

Kings will discard their own sons if they indulge in bad acts: And they will accept others (even not related to them) if they are capable (in doing good). Oh auspicious Seetha! Treating king Bharatha with respect, you remain here itself (when I am gone to forest), devoted to Dharma and observing vows & rituals with devotion.

❍ ❍ ❍

३८. अहं गमिष्यामि महावनं प्रिये
त्वया हि वस्तव्यमिहैव भामिनि ।
यथा व्यलीकं कुरुषे न कस्यचित्
तथा त्वया कार्यमिदं वचो मम ।।

38. Oh endearing (passionate) Seetha! Oh my beloved! You have never done anything disagreeable to any one. I am going to the great forest alone. You should remain here only. As this is my word (order), this should be done by you.

(Thus Raama tells Seetha that he is away to forest on 14 years exile and she should remain in Ayodhya to serve his father, mother and others. But Seetha has other ideas. She will and must accompany Raama on his exile.)

❍ ❍ ❍

Chapter 27

Seetha Begs (Raama) to Take Her to Forest with Him

(Seetha is very strong determined person; she must and will go with Raama on exile to forest.)

❍ ❍ ❍

१. एवमुक्ता तु वैदेही प्रियार्हा प्रियवादिनी ।
प्रणयादेव संक्रुद्धा भर्तारमिदमब्रवीत् ।।

1. When she was told thus (by her husband Raama), (Seetha the) Vaidhehi, who ever spoke sweetly and who deserved his love, out of her deep attachment to him, became (somewhat) angry, She addressed him thus.

❍ ❍ ❍

२. किमिदं भाषसे राम वाक्य लघुतया ध्रुवम् ।
त्वया यदपहास्यं मे श्रुतं नरवरोत्तम ।।

2. Oh foremost of men, Oh Raama! It is mockery to me to hear from you about your command, spoken by you in (such a) light hearted way. How is this?

❍ ❍ ❍

३. आर्यपुत्र पिता माता भ्राता पुत्रस्तथा स्नुषा ।
स्वानि पुण्यानि भुंजानाः स्वं स्वं भाग्यमुपासते ।।

3. Oh son of an Aryan! Oh (Raama)! A son, brother, father, mother, a daughter-in-law enjoys ('fruits' of) their own (deeds and) merit. They get their own respective share (of 'fruits') of their own* Merit (and deeds, * Punya).

❍ ❍ ❍

४. भर्तुर्भाग्यन्तु नार्येका प्राप्नोति पुरुषर्षभ ।
अतश्चैवाहमादिष्टा वने वस्तव्यमित्यपि ।।

4. Oh (Raama) the 'Bull' amongst men! (But) A woman alone obtains (and shares) her husband's fortunes. For this reason, it is enjoined that I should also live in forest (to share life with you)
(This is the Sanaathana Dharma of a married woman, like Seetha)

❍ ❍ ❍

५. न पिता नात्मजो नात्मा न माता न सखीजनः ।
इह प्रेत्य च नारीणां पतिरेको गतिस्सदा ।।

5. For a woman her husband alone is ever her refuge in this world and even (in the world) after death. Not father, not mother, not even son born to her. nor friends; nor even (Supreme) soul.

❍ ❍ ❍

६. यदि त्वं प्रस्थितो दुर्गं वनमद्यैव राघव ।
अग्रतस्ते गमिष्यामि मृद्‌गन्ती कुशकण्टकान् ।।

6. Oh (Raama) the Raaghava! When you go to the

impassable forest, I will go along with you now, treading upon grass, thorns, softly.

❍ ❍ ❍

७. ईर्ष्यारोषौ बहिष्कृत्य पतिशेषमिवोदकम् ।
नय मां वीर विस्रब्धः पापं मयि न विद्यते ॥

7. Expelling your impatience and 'anger' (from your mind caused by my speaking thus) (Expelling it) like throwing away water that remains (in glass) after drinking, you must take me (along with you) in full confidence. There is no sin in me (in asking of you thus).

❍ ❍ ❍

८. प्रासादाग्रैर्विमानैर्वा वैहायसगतेन वा ।
सर्वावस्थागता भर्तुः पादच्छाया विशिष्यते ॥

8. (Serving) husband at the shadow of his feet (remaining with him) under all circumstances, is better than living in multi storyed mansion, or in (heavenly) space crafts or (even) in wandering over the Skies. (treaded by Sidhdha-s and celestials).

❍ ❍ ❍

९. अनुशिष्टाऽस्मि मात्रा च पित्रा च विविधाश्रयम् ।
नास्मि संप्रति वक्तव्या वर्तितव्यं यथा मया ॥

9. I have been taught in many ways by my father and mother about (my duties) to be carried out by me; I do not need to be told now by (any one about my duties as a wife).

(Seetha is no timid girl; An Indian wife is not a weak person.)

❍ ❍ ❍

१०. अहं दुर्गं गमिष्यामि वनं पुरुषवर्जितम् ।
नानामृगगणाकीर्णं शार्दूलगणसेवितम् ॥

10. I will go to the dense forest which is uninhabited by men, which is full with various beasts in multitude, and where tigers roam about in packs.

❍ ❍ ❍

११. सुखं वने निवत्स्यामि यथैव भवने पितुः ।
अचिन्तयन्ती त्रीन् लोकांश्चिन्तयन्ती पतिव्रतम् ।।

11. Not caring for even (the comfort of) the three worlds, vowing (only) to serve my husband, I will live in forest as comfortably as in your father's place.

❍ ❍ ❍

१२. शुश्रूषमाणा ते नित्यं नियता ब्रह्मचारिणी ।
सह रंस्ये त्वया वीर वनेषु मधुगन्धिषु ।।

12. Oh brave (Raama)! With great restraint, leading a life of *celibacy in the sweet smelling forests, serving you ever, I will enjoy myself with you (there) (Poet uses word * Brammachaarini)

❍ ❍ ❍

१३. त्वं हि कर्तुं वने शक्तो राम संपरिपालनम् ।
अन्यस्यापि जनस्येह किं पुनर्मम मानद ।।

13. Oh Raama! In the forest you have the capacity to offer protection even to other men (unrelated to you): Oh honourable (Raama)! (When that is so) What to say in my case.

❍ ❍ ❍

१४. सह त्वया गमिष्यामि वनमद्य न संशयः ।
नाहं शक्या महाभाग निवर्तयितुमुद्यता ।।

14. Oh most illustrious (Raama)! I will come with you to forest right away; No doubt about it; As I am intent (on going with you), I will not be 'turned' away (rejected to accompany you to forest).

❍ ❍ ❍

१५. फलमूलाशना नित्यं भविष्यामि न संशयः ।
न ते दुःखं करिष्यामि निवसन्ती सह त्वया ॥

15. Sustaining myself on fruits and tubers, I will ever be with you. I will not cause any suffering to you. No doubt about this.

❍ ❍ ❍

१६. इच्छामि सरितः शैलान्पल्वलानि वनानि च ।
द्रष्टुं सर्वत्र निर्भीता त्वया नाथेन धीमता ॥

16. Along with you, Oh my wise lord, I desire to see there, forests, rivers, mountains, lakes and ponds.

❍ ❍ ❍

१७. हंसकारण्डवाकीर्णाः पद्मिनीस्साधुपुष्पिताः ।
इच्छेयं सुखिनी द्रष्टुं त्वया वीरेण सङ्गता ॥

17. Being with you my brave (husband) with pleasure, I desire to see lotus ponds full of Hamsa, Karanda birds and in full blossom.

❍ ❍ ❍

१८. अभिषेकं करिष्यामि तासु नित्यं यतव्रता ।
सह त्वया विशालाक्ष रंस्ये परमनन्दिनी ॥

18. Oh large eyed (Raama)! (Remaining) with you (close) always, taking on only such vows, will take bath in these, rejoicing greatly; I will enjoy myself (with you in forest).

❍ ❍ ❍

१९. एवं वर्षसहस्राणां शतं वाऽहं त्वया सह ।
व्यतिक्रमं न वेत्स्यामि स्वर्गोऽपि न हि मे मतः ॥

19. When I am with you thus, I would not realise that (even) 1,000 years had passed away. Even heaven for me is not better (than this life in forest with you) Indeed!

❍ ❍ ❍

२०. स्वर्गेऽपि च विना वासो भविता यदि राघव ।
त्वया मम नरव्याघ्र नाहं तमपि रोचये ॥

20. Oh tiger of men! Oh (Raama the) Raaghava! If a stay (is offered and) comes by me in heaven, even this I desire not if I am without you.

❍ ❍ ❍

२१. अहं गमिष्यामि वनं सुदुर्गमं
मृगायुतं वानरवारणैर्युतम् ।
वनेऽपि वत्स्यामि यथा पितुर्गृहे
तवैव पादावुपगृह्य सर्वदा ॥

21. I will come to the forest that is full of beasts, full of monkeys, elephants, and which is difficult to tread. And in forest I will ever touch your feet (serve you). I will live as though I am in your father's mansion.

❍ ❍ ❍

२२. अनन्यभावामनुरक्तचेतसं
त्वया वियुक्तां मरणाय निश्चिताम् ।
नयस्व मां साधु कुरुष्व याचनां
न ते मयाऽतो गुरुता भविष्यति ॥

22. You should take me whose mind is terribly directed (towards you) without thinking about anything else (other than serving you), who is determined to die if I am separated from you. You should fulfill my request righteously. There will be no suffering for you from me.

❍ ❍ ❍

२३. तथा ब्रुवाणामपि धर्मवत्सलो
न च स्म सीतां नृवरो निनीषति ।
उवाच चैनां बहु संनिवर्तने
वने निवासस्य च दुःखितां प्रति ॥

23. (But) Raama the man devoted to Dharma, who was

foremost of men, did not desire to take this Seetha who was speaking thus in sorrow; He talked to her in many ways in the matter of restraining her (to accompany him and to) live in forest.

(Raama uses all arguments to dissuade Seetha: But Seetha has her way as we shall see in subsequent chapters.)

❍ ❍ ❍

Chapter 28

Raama Narrates the Difficulties of Forest Life to Seetha

१. स एवं ब्रुवतीं सीतां धर्मज्ञो धर्मवत्सलः ।
न नेतुं कुरुते बुद्धिं वने दुःखानि चिन्तयन् ॥

1. Considering the difficulties in forest, (Raama) the man of Dharma who knew Dharma, had no intention of taking along Seetha who was talking like this.

❍ ❍ ❍

२. सान्त्वयित्वा ततस्तां तु बाष्पदूषितलोचनाम् ।
निवर्तनार्थेधर्मात्मा वाक्यमेतदुवाच ह ॥

2. This noble soul man of Dharma, then consoled her (who was crying) with eyes full of tears: He addressed the following words so as to restrain her (from coming to forest with him).

❍ ❍ ❍

३. सीते महाकुलीनाऽसि धर्मेच निरता सदा ।
इहाचर स्वधर्मं त्वं मम कृत्वा मनस्सुखम् ॥

3. Oh Seetha! Born in great family, you delight in (being steadfast in) Dharma. Therefore, remaining here you follow your Dharma, doing always what would give me mental satisfaction.

❍ ❍ ❍

४. सीते यथा त्वां वक्ष्यामि तथा कार्यं त्वयाऽबले ।
वने दोषा हि बहवो वदतस्ताञ्निबोध मे ॥

4. Oh timid Seetha! What I am telling, that must be done by you; There are many difficulties (and dangers) in forest; You listen to me as I narrate them.

❍ ❍ ❍

५. सीते विमुच्यतामेषा वनवासकृता मतिः ।
बहुदोषं हि कान्तारं वनमित्यभिधीयते ॥

5. Oh Seetha! Give up this idea of this (your) life in forest (with me): A forest is spoken of as a wilderness, full of dangers.

❍ ❍ ❍

६. हितबुद्ध्या खलु वचो मयैतदभिधीयते ।
सदा सुखं न जानामि दुःखमेव सदा वनम् ॥

6. These words are spoken by me out of consideration for (your) welfare. I have never known that forest life ever gives comfort. It is always suffering (there).

❍ ❍ ❍

७. गिरिनिर्झरसंभूता गिरिकन्दरवासिनाम् ।
सिंहानां निनदा दुःखाः श्रोतुं दुःखमतो वनम् ॥

7. (The thud) from the mountain water falls, the roars of the lions living in the caves of mountains, are frightening to hear. Therefore Forest Life is difficult.** (Dhukka)
(Poet Vaalmeeki uses the word** = Dhukka=, painful, difficult, etc.)

❍ ❍ ❍

८. क्रीडमानाश्च विस्रब्धा मत्ताश्शून्ये महामृगाः ।
दृष्ट्वा समभिवर्तन्ते सीते दुःखमतो वनम् ॥

8. Oh Seetha! In the uninhabited (forest), the great animals

which are fearless and play around exhilarated, charge against one on seeing him; Therefore forest is difficult, (painful, sorrowful).

❍ ❍ ❍

९. सग्रहास्सरितश्चैव पङ्कवत्यश्चदुस्तराः ।
मत्तैरपि गजैर्नित्यं सीते दुःखमतो वनम् ।।

9. Oh Seetha! The rivers are muddy, infested with crocodiles: Even wild elephants cannot cross over them. Therefore forest is always difficult.

❍ ❍ ❍

१०. लताकण्टकसङ्कीर्णाः कृकवाकूपनादिताः ।
निरपाश्च सुदुर्गाश्च मार्गा दुःखमतो वनम् ।।

10. The routes and paths are covered by creepers and thorny bushes; Difficult to tread; Cooing from carnivorous birds are heard; (Some) places, no drinking water: Therefore Forest is painful (cruel).

❍ ❍ ❍

११. सुप्यते पर्णशय्यासु स्वयं भग्नासु भूतले ।
रात्रिषु श्रमखिन्नेन सीते दुःखमतो वनम् ।।

11. Oh Seetha! Monks sleep at nights on bare floor over bed of leaves that fall down by themselves (from trees). Therefore forest is difficult.

❍ ❍ ❍

१२. अहोरात्रं च सन्तोषः कर्तव्यो नियतात्मना ।
फलैर्वृक्षावपतितैः सीते दुःखमतो वनम् ।।

12. Oh Seetha! Day and night, (eating merely) fruits that may fall from trees, satisfaction must be obtained by a person of restraint Therefore forest is painful.

❍ ❍ ❍

१३. उपवासश्च कर्तव्यो यथाप्राणेन मैथिलि ।
जटाभारश्च कर्तव्यो वल्कलाम्बरधारिणा ॥

13. Oh (Seetha the) Maithili! Dressed in (forest garments of) deer skin and bark materials, one should practice abstinence with all his strength (mind). One must sport twisted hair locks (Unkempt hair).

❍ ❍ ❍

१४. देवतानां पितॄणां च कर्तव्यं विधिपूर्वकम् ।
चाप्तानामतिथीनां च नित्यशः प्रतिपूजनम् ॥

14. At all times, as per norms of Shaasthra-s, Salutations must be offered to Deities, forefathers and the guests who come.
(Even in forest one extends hospitality, an arduous task indeed.)

❍ ❍ ❍

१५. कार्यस्त्रिरभिषेकश्च काले काले च नित्यशः ।
चरता नियमेनैव तस्माद्दुःखतरं वनम् ॥

15. Daily, at appropriate time, baths should be taken thrice, by one who practises restraint. Therefore forest is painful.
(There is no Bath room with hot water & privacy.)

❍ ❍ ❍

१६. उपहारश्च कर्तव्यः कुसुमैः स्वयमाहृतैः ।
आर्षेण विधिना वेद्यां बाले दुःखमतो वनम् ॥

16. Oh Child! Worship as per norms ordained by Rishi-s (of forest) must be done on holy Mounds, with flowers procured by himself. Therefore forest is difficult.
(No Royal maids for Seetha there, says Raama, for flowers etc.)

❍ ❍ ❍

१७. यथालब्धेन कर्तव्यः सन्तोषस्तेन मैथिलि ।
यताहारैर्वनचरैर्नित्यं दुःखमतो वनम् ।।

17. Oh (Seetha) the Maithili! With whatever that is obtained, satisfaction must be obtained at all times by a person living in forest, with whatever 'eats' (that come by). Therefore forest is difficult.

❍ ❍ ❍

१८. अतीव वातास्तिमिरं बुभुक्षा चात्र नित्यशः ।
भयानि च महान्त्यत्र ततो दुःखतरं वनम् ।।

18. In this (forest), at all times, wind, darkness, hunger, will all be fierce. Here, (in forest), dangers are many and mighty (gruesome). Therefore forest is difficult.

❍ ❍ ❍

१९. सरीसृपाश्च बहवो बहुरूपाश्च भामिनि ।
चरन्ति पृथिवीं दर्पात्ततो दुःखतरं वनम् ।।

19. Oh endearing (Seetha)! Many pythons with many forms, in sheer arrogance move about on earth. Therefore forest difficult.

❍ ❍ ❍

२०. नदीनिलयनास्सर्पा नदीकुटिलगामिनः ।
तिष्ठन्त्यावृत्य पन्थानं ततो दुःखतरं वनम् ।।

20. Snakes living in the bed (banks) of rivers which sneak through (and move) like rivers, will be staying on the path, blocking the way Therefore forest is totally difficult.

❍ ❍ ❍

२१. पतङ्गा वृश्चिकाः कीटां दंशाश्च मशकैस्सह ।
बाधन्ते नित्यमबले सर्वं दुःखमतो वनम् ।।

21. Insects, scorpions, worms, mosquitoes, will all bother you: Oh girl! Therefore forest is totally difficult.

❍ ❍ ❍

२२. द्रुमाः कण्टकिनश्चैव कुशकाशाश्च भामिनि ।
वने व्याकुलशाखाग्रास्तेन दुःखतरं वनम् ।।

22. Oh Endearing (Seetha)! In the forest, there are thorny trees; thick stalks of Kuscha grass; tips of branches which shake (and are sharp). Therefore forest is difficult.

❍ ❍ ❍

२३. कायक्लेशाश्च बहवो भयानि विविधानि च ।
अरण्यवासे वसतो दुःखमेव सदा वनम् ।।

23. Those dwellers living a forest life, their body ailments are many; (They face) various dangers. Forest Life is always difficult.
(No doctors there, says Raama!!)

❍ ❍ ❍

२४. क्रोधलोभौ विमोक्तव्यौ कर्तव्या तपसे मतिः ।
न भेतव्यं च भेतव्ये नित्यं दुःखमतो वनम् ।।

24. (In forest) Desire and Anger must be given up; Mind should be directed to Thapas (Meditation, vows etc.) Must have no fear from fear. Therefore forest is difficult.

❍ ❍ ❍

२५. तदलं ते वनं गत्वा क्षमं न हि वनं तव ।
विमृशन्निह पश्यामि बहुदोषतरं वनम् ।।

25. As enumerated, I see (clearly) that forest is most cruel: You cannot bear forest (life). Therefore, enough of this to go to forest!

❍ ❍ ❍

२६. वनं तु नेतुं न कृता मतिस्तदा
बभूव रामेण तदा महात्मना ।
न तस्य सीता वचनं चकार तत्
ततोऽब्रवीद्राममिदं सुदुःखिता ।।

26. At that time, Seetha was not considered by great soul Raama to be taken to forest. And she did not relish his words. Therefore she said to Raama just this: = I Am In Great Sorrow.=

❍ ❍ ❍

Chapter 29

(Seetha) Again Begs (Raama) to Take Her Along to Forest

१. एतत्तु वचनं श्रुत्वा सीता रामस्य दुःखिता ।
प्रसक्ताश्रुमुखी मन्दमिदं वचनमब्रवीत् ॥

1. Hearing such words of Raama, Seetha who was in grief (with tears flowing and) making her face full with tears, then said these words gently.

❍ ❍ ❍

२. ये त्वया कीर्तिता दोषा वने वस्तव्यतां प्रति ।
गुणानित्येव तान्मन्ये तव स्नेहपुरस्कृता ॥

2. All these difficulties that are enumerated by you about life in forest, I consider as beneficial! (They were spoken) only because of your attachment and consideration (for me).

❍ ❍ ❍

३. मृगास्सिंहा गजाश्चैव शार्दूलाश्शरभास्तथा ।
पक्षिणस्सृमराश्चैव ये चान्ये वनचारिणः ॥

3. Deers, lions, elephants, tigers, Scharabha-s (Reptiles) birds, antelopes, and other (animals) living in forest .....

❍ ❍ ❍

४. अदृष्टपूर्वरूपत्वात्सर्वेते तव राघव ।
रूपं दृष्ट्वाऽपसर्पेयुर्भये सर्वेहि बिभ्यति ॥

4. .... all these, the moment they see your 'Form', will run

away as they have never seen such a form (like yours)! Oh (Raama) the Raaghava! All the fearsome, will dread (by your very sight).

❍ ❍ ❍

५. त्वया च सह गन्तव्यं मया गुरुजनाज्ञया ।
त्वद्वियोगेन मे राम त्यक्तव्यमिह जीवितम् ।।

5. Oh Raama! Because it is your father's and mother's command, I must also have to go along with you. If I am separated from you, I will give up my life here. (and now)

❍ ❍ ❍

६. न हि मां त्वत्समीपस्थामपि शक्नोति राघव ।
सुराणामीश्वरः शक्रः प्रधर्षयितुमोजसा ।।

6. Oh (Raama the) Raaghava! Even Schakra (Lord Indhra) who is lord of Celestials, will be incapable of harming me with his 'vitality' (power) when I am near you.

❍ ❍ ❍

७. पतिहीना तु या नारी सा न शक्ष्यति जीवितुम् ।
काममेवंविधं राम त्वया मम विदर्शितम् ।।

7. Oh Raama! Surely, I have been taught by you about this, thus: "that a woman will not be able to live without her husband."

❍ ❍ ❍

८. अथवाऽपि महाप्राज्ञ ब्राह्मणानां मया श्रुतम् ।
पुरा पितृगृहे सत्यं वस्तव्यं किल मे वने ।।

8. Oh most intelligent (Raama)! Further; Sometimes back, in my father's place, it had been heard by me that somehow (at some time in my life), I must live in Forest, Surely! These were Braamin's truthful words (Soothsayer's words).

९. लक्षणिभ्यो द्विजातिभ्यः श्रुत्वाऽहं वचनं गृहे ।
वनवासकृतोत्साहा नित्यमेव महाबल ॥

9. Oh mightily strong (Raama)! Having heard such words, (such predictions) of Braamins who can perceive (future), everyday I have been enthusiastic (looking forward) to forest life.

❍ ❍ ❍

१०. आदेशो वनवासस्य प्राप्तव्यः स मया किल ।
सा त्वया सह तत्राहं यास्यामि प्रिय नान्यथा ॥

10. Because it is foretold, this (forest life) must be (obtained and) lived by me, Oh beloved (Raama)! Such as I am, will go with you to live in forest. It cannot be otherwise.

❍ ❍ ❍

११. कृतादेशा भविष्यामि गमिष्यामि सह त्वया ।
कालश्चायं समुत्पन्नः सत्यवाग्भवतु द्विजः ॥

11. I will fulfill what was foretold. The time has come (for this). I will go with you. Let Braamin (ever) be speaker of Truth!

(Let Braamin's prophecy come true as it always does.)

❍ ❍ ❍

१२. वनवासे हि जानामि दुःखानि बहुधा किल ।
प्राप्यन्ते नियतं वीर पुरुषैरकृतात्मभिः ॥

12. I know (very well) that there are many dangers (sufferings) in forest. Oh brave (Raama)! Verily, such restraint, (such fear), is found only in men with unsteady mind.

❍ ❍ ❍

१३. कन्यया च पितुर्गेहे वनवास श्रुतो मया ।
भिक्षिण्यास्साधुवृत्ताया मम मातुरिहाग्रतः ॥

13. (Oh Raama!) In my father's place, in front of my mother,

as a young girl (before marriage) it was heard by me from a beggar woman of virtuous conduct, that there is forest life ......

❍ ❍ ❍

१४. प्रसादितश्च वै पूर्वं त्वं वै बहुविधं प्रभो ।
गमनं वनवासस्य काङ्क्षितं हि सह त्वया ।।

14. ...... long ago:... (so) I am looking forward to go with you for a life in forest. Oh my lord (Raama): Therefore, may you please favour me in every way (and take me with you).

(Indians believe in Astrology-Palmistry This is from ancient days.)

❍ ❍ ❍

१५. कृतक्षणाऽहं भद्रं ते गमनं प्रति राघव ।
वनवासस्य शूरस्य चर्या हि मम रोचते ।।

15. Oh (Raama the) Raaghava! I was awaiting the moment to go (to forest). Service to you alone during your forest life, Oh my brave (husband) is (splendid) for me, desired (by me)... Welfare to you!

❍ ❍ ❍

१६. शुद्धात्मन् प्रेमभावाद्धि भविष्यामि विकल्मषा ।
भर्तारमनुगच्छन्ती भर्ता हि मम दैवतम् ।।

16. Oh pure soul (Raama)! Because of my love for you, without any stain on me, I will be (a woman) who followed her husband. (because) Husband, indeed, is God to me.!

❍ ❍ ❍

१७. प्रेत्यभावेऽपि कल्याणस्सङ्गमो मे सह त्वया ।।

17. Even in life after death, life with you for me is sublime (auspicious).

❍ ❍ ❍

१८. पिता रक्षति कौमारे भर्ता रक्षति यौवने ।
पुत्रा रक्षन्ति वार्धक्ये न स्त्री स्वातन्त्र्यमर्हति ॥

18. A woman cannot have independent (status); She is protected always; When young, her father; In youth, her husband protects her; When old, sons protect her.

❍ ❍ ❍

१९. श्रुतिर्हि श्रूयते पुण्या ब्राह्मणानां यशस्विनाम् ।
इह लोके च पितृभिर्या स्त्री यस्य महामते ॥
अद्भिर्दत्ता स्वधर्मेण प्रेत्यभावेऽपि तस्य सा ॥

19. Oh most honoured (Raama)! It is heard, spoken by famous Braamins that in this world, when one is offered in marriage to a man by her father as per norms of Dharma & ritual of water offerings, she is his wife even in the other world if she is pure (and faithful).

❍ ❍ ❍

२०. एवमस्मात्स्वकां नारीं सुवृत्तां हि पतिव्रताम् ।
नाभिरोचयसे नेतुं त्वं मां केनेह हेतुना ॥

20. As such, what is the reason you do not desire to take me from here who is your wife, who is of good conduct and who is devoted to her husband.

❍ ❍ ❍

२१. भक्तां पतिव्रतां दीनां मां समां सुखदुःखयोः ।
नेतुमर्हसि काकुत्स्थ समानसुखदुःखिनीम् ॥

21. Oh (Raama the) Kaakuthsa! You should take me who is miserable, who worships you, who is devoted, a virtuous wife, who treats joys and sorrows with equanimity, who shares (her husband's) joys and sorrows equally.

❍ ❍ ❍

२२. यदि मां दुःखितामेवं वनं नेतुं न चेच्छसि ।
विषमग्निं जलं वाऽहमास्थास्ये मृत्युकारणात् ।।

22. If you do not desire to take me to forest who is in grief, then I will take recourse to poison, waters, or fire for purpose of my death.

❍ ❍ ❍

२३. एवं बहुविधं तं सा याचते गमनं प्रति ।
नानुमेने महाबाहुस्तां नेतुं विजनं वनम् ।।

23. Thus she begged him in many ways to go to forest; Yet the mighty limbed (Raama) did not assent to take her to the uninhabited forest.

❍ ❍ ❍

२४. एवमुक्ता तु सा चिन्तां मैथिली समुपागता ।
स्नापयन्तीव गामुष्णैरश्रुभिर्नयनच्युतैः ।।

24. Having said thus (Seetha the) Maithili who appeared as though she would be 'bathing' the earth with her hot tears that were flowing out of her eyes, went into deep thought.

❍ ❍ ❍

२५. चिन्तयन्तीं तथा तां तु निवर्तयितुमात्मवान् ।
क्रोधाविष्टां तु वैदेहीं काकुत्स्थो बह्वसान्त्वयत् ।।

25. (Raama the) Kaakuthsa, the man of composure, began to console (Seetha the) Vaidhehi who was seized with wrath, and he tried to change (her mind, by telling her) in so many ways.
(Seetha is firm: She must and will go with Raama to forest.)

❍ ❍ ❍

Chapter 30

(Raama) Consents to Take Along (Seetha) to Forest

(Raama finally agrees: And Raama expounds The Sanaathana Dharma, which is The Religion of India, mistakenly called Hinduism.)

❍ ❍ ❍

१. सान्त्व्यमाना तु रामेण मैथिली जनकात्मजा ।
वनवासनिमित्ताय भर्तारमिदमब्रवीत् ॥

1. Although she was being consoled by Raama, (Seetha the) Maithili who was the daughter of (King) Janaka, addressed her husband (once again) for the sake of going to forest (with him).

❍ ❍ ❍

२. सा तमुत्तमसंविग्ना सीता विपुलवक्षसम् ।
प्रणयाच्चाभिमानाच्च परिचिक्षेप राघवम् ॥

2. This Seetha who was terribly agitated, made this broad chested (Raama the) Raaghava, re-examine (her case of taking her to forest) because of her reverence and deep attachment.

❍ ❍ ❍

३. किं त्वाऽमन्यत वैदेहः पिता मे मिथिलाधिपः ।
राम जामातरं प्राप्य स्त्रियं पुरुषविग्रहम् ॥

3. Oh Raama ! Did my father of Vidheha kingdom and king of Mithila, consider you, his son-in-law, as a woman in the garb of a man, when I obtained you (as my husband)?

(Seetha has sense of humour, although this is severe.)

❍ ❍ ❍

४. अनृतं बत लोकोऽयमज्ञानाद्यद्धि वक्ष्यति ।
तेजो नास्ति परं रामे तपतीव दिवाकरे ॥

4. Oh what a shame that this world, out of ignorance, would now speak falsely (wrongly) that there is no brilliance in Raama like those in the burning Sun! Oh Raama! World will speak falsely about you!
(Seetha is in her elements!)

❍ ❍ ❍

५. किं हि कृत्वा विषण्णस्त्वं कुतो वा भयमस्ति ते ।
यत्परित्यक्तुकामस्त्वं मामनन्यपरायणाम् ॥

5. How do you desire to abandon me (by leaving me here) when I have no other refuge: What makes you despondent; what is the cause of this fear in you?

❍ ❍ ❍

६. द्युमत्सेनसुतं वीर सत्यवन्तमनुव्रताम् ।
सावित्रीमिव मां विद्धि त्वमात्मवशवर्तिनीम् ॥

6. Oh Brave (Raama)! Like Saavithri who was devoted to (her husband) Sathyavaan the son of Dhyumathsena, you must consider me as yours, totally devoted to you.
(Seetha quotes precedents, about some noble women.)

❍ ❍ ❍

७. न त्वहं मनसाऽप्यन्यं द्रष्टास्मि त्वदृतेऽनघ ।
त्वया राघव गच्छेयं यथाऽन्या कुलपांसनी ॥

7. Oh sinless (Raama the) Raaghava! Even in my mind, I have not thought about anything else other than you, like an ordinary (cheap person) who brings disgrace to the family. I will go (with you).

❍ ❍ ❍

८. स्वयं तु भार्यां कौमारीं चिरमध्युषितां सतीम् ।
शैलूष इव मां राम परेभ्यो दातुमिच्छसि ॥

8. Oh Raama! You desire to leave me with my enemies as if I am a street dancer (although) I am your wife who is (ever) your woman, faithful and who has been living with you for some time (long time).

❍ ❍ ❍

९. यस्य पथ्यं च रामात्थ यस्य चार्थेऽवरुध्यसे ।
त्वं तस्य भव वश्यश्च विधेयश्च सदाऽनघ ।।

9. Oh sinless, Oh Raama! You will always remain obedient and submissive to him, for whose sake you have chosen the auspicious path and for whose purpose you are expelled.

(Seetha never questioned Raama's decision, unlike Kowsalya or Lakshmana; She only wants to share everything with her husband.)

❍ ❍ ❍

१०. स मामनादाय वनं न त्वं प्रस्थातुमर्हसि ।
तपो वा यदि वाऽरण्यं स्वर्गोवा स्यात्सह त्वया ।।

10. Yet! Such as you are, should not go to forest without taking me with you; whether it be forest, or land of penance, or heaven.

❍ ❍ ❍

११. न च मे भविता तत्र कश्चित्पथि परिश्रमः ।
पृष्ठतस्तव गच्छन्त्या विहारशयनोष्विह ।।

11. Following the righteous path, playing and relaxing there (with you) there will be no 'weariness' in me when I am by your side.

❍ ❍ ❍

१२. कुशकाशशरेषीका ये च कण्टकिनो द्रुमाः ।
तूलाजिनसमस्पर्शा मार्गेमम सह त्वया ।।

12. (In forest) On the way, the Dharbha grass, the twigs,

the thorny bushes, trees, all these will just 'touch' me like (soft) cotton or deer skin, when I am with you.

❍ ❍ ❍

१३. महावातसमुद्धूतं यन्मामपकरिष्यति ।
रजो रमण तन्मन्ये परार्ध्यमिव चन्दनम् ।।

13. Oh Charming (Raama)! When the dust blown off by strong wind settles on me, I will consider this as if it is foremost sandal powder/paste. (My cosmetic, says Seetha!)

❍ ❍ ❍

१४. शाद्वलेषु यथा शिश्ये वनान्ते वनगोचर ।
कुथास्तरणतल्पेषु किं स्यात्सुखतरं ततः ।।

14. Oh (Raama) whose abode is (now) forest! Will I get more comfort in a bed of painted bed spread than when I sleep on the turf in the middle of forest?

❍ ❍ ❍

१५. पत्रं मूलं फलं यत्त्वमल्पं वा यदि वा बहु ।
दास्यसि स्वयमाहृत्य तन्मेऽमृतरसोपमम् ।।

15. When you bring whatever, leaves, tubers or fruits, yourself and offer me these, they will be like nectar to me greatly.

❍ ❍ ❍

१६. न मातुर्न पितुस्तत्र स्मरिष्यामि न वेश्मनः ।
आर्तवान्युपभुञ्जाना पुष्पाणि च फलानि च ।।

16. Eating fruits, enjoying flowers of seasons, I will not think about palace; nor even my father & mother.

❍ ❍ ❍

१७. न च तत्र गतः किञ्चिद्द्रष्टुमर्हसि विप्रियम् ।
मत्कृते न च ते शोको न भविष्यामि दुर्भरा ।।

17. I will never be a burden; No (cause for) anguish in you; You cannot see in me any transgression (upon you) when we go there.

❍ ❍ ❍

१८. यस्त्वया सह स स्वर्गोनिरयो यस्त्वया विना ।
इति जानन्परां प्रीतिं गच्छ राम मया सह ॥

18. Oh Raama! With you (whatever I have) is heaven (for me); Whatever there is, is hell without you. Knowing this as my foremost desire, you should go (only) with me.

❍ ❍ ❍

१९. अथ मामेवमव्यग्रां वनं नैव नयिष्यसि ।
विषमद्यैव पास्यामि मा गगं द्विषतां वशम् ॥

19. Determined as I am, if you dont take me to forest, I will now itself drink poison. I will not be a slave to hostile elements.

❍ ❍ ❍

२०. पश्चादपि हि दुःखेन मम नैवास्ति जीवितम् ।
उज्झितायास्त्वया नाथ तदैव मरणं वरम् ॥

20. Oh Lord! Discarded by you, in grief, there will be no life for me then after. Therefore it is better to die right away.

❍ ❍ ❍

२१. इगं हि सहितुं शोकं मुहूर्तमपि नोत्सहे ।
किं पुनर्दश वर्षाणि त्रीणि चैकं च दुःखिता ॥

21. I cannot stand this grief (of separation from you) even for a muhoortha: (when that is so), how can I (live) for one year plus three years plus ten years (14 years) in grief?

❍ ❍ ❍

२२. इति सा शोकसन्तप्ता विलप्य करुणं बहु ।
चुक्रोश पतिमायस्ता भृशमालिङ्ग्य सस्वरम् ।।

22. Totally wearied (distressed), she wailed most pitiably thus in many ways; Tormented by grief, she hugged her husband and cried aloud.

❍ ❍ ❍

२३. सा विद्धा बहुभिर्वाक्यैर्दिग्धैरिव गजाङ्गना ।
चिरसंनियतं बाष्पं मुमोचाग्निमिवारणिः ।।

23. Like limbs of an elephant (struck by) poisoned arrows, she was wounded by various words (of Raama who tried to restrain her). And the tears she held back for long time (while she was speaking to Raama), she discharged, like Agni (Fire, flame stoked) with Arani wood.

❍ ❍ ❍

२४. तस्याः स्फटिकसङ्काशं वारि सन्तापसम्भवम् ।
नेत्राभ्यां परिसुस्राव पङ्कजाभ्यामिवोदकम् ।।

24. From her eyes, crystalline tears flowed out like waters from lotus leaves, caused by her torment.

❍ ❍ ❍

२५. तच्चैवामलचन्द्राभं मुखमायतलोचनम् ।
पर्यशुष्यत बाष्पेण जलोद्धृतमिवाम्बुजम् ।।

25. Her face was spotless like the moon, with eyes of hers that were large... (Such a face) was bathed in tears, like lotus flowers plucked out from water pond.

❍ ❍ ❍

२६. तां परिष्वज्य बाहुभ्यां विसंज्ञामिव दुःखिताम् ।
उवाच वचनं रामः परिविश्वासयंस्तदा ।।

26. Comforting her who was suffering like this and who was in a state of (semi) consciousness, Raama then hugged her with his hands and said these words.

❍ ❍ ❍

२७. न देवि तव दुःखेन स्वर्गमप्यभिरोचये ।
न हि मेऽस्ति भयं किञ्चित्स्वयम्भोरिव सर्वतः ॥

27. Oh Lady (Seetha)! If it causes you grief, I will not desire even heaven. Like the Self Born (God Vishnu), there is no fear (in me) whatsoever, in every way.

(Raama is quick to tell Seetha he is no coward)

❍ ❍ ❍

२८. तव सर्वमभिप्रायमविज्ञाय शुभानने ।
वासं न रोचयेऽरण्ये शक्तिमानपि रक्षणे ॥

28. Oh (Seetha) with a pleasant face! Although I am competent to protect you, without knowing your mind (intention) fully, I did not desire to take you to forest.

❍ ❍ ❍

२९. यत्सृष्टाऽसि मया सार्धं वनवासाय मैथिलि ।
न विहातुं मया शक्या प्रीतिरात्मवता यथा ॥

29. Oh (Seetha) the Maithili ! You are born for living in forest along with me (as my better half): Therefore you, who are like Preethi (to Manmatha) are not to be abandoned by me who is ever composed (prudent). (Readers may note that Manmatha is lord of Love).

❍ ❍ ❍

३०. धर्मस्तु गजनासोरु सद्भिराचरितः पुरा ।
तं चाहमनुवर्तेऽद्य यथा सूर्यं सुवर्चला ॥

30. O lady with (beautiful) thighs like those of elephant's tusks! Like Suvarchala (who is ever with her husband the Sun) and like the ancient elders (good folks), this Dharma (of Muni's life in forest) that is practiced by them, I am now following (I am taking to this forest life shortly)

❍ ❍ ❍

३१. न खल्वहं न गच्छेयं वनं जनकनन्दिनि ।
वचनं तन्नयति मां पितुस्सत्योपबृंहितम् ।।

31. Oh Seetha, the darling of Janaka 1 The words (of command) of my father leads me to forest because I cling to Truth: Therefore it will never be that I will not go (to forest).

❍ ❍ ❍

३२. एष धर्मस्तु सुश्रोणि पितुर्मातुश्च वश्यता ।
आज्ञामहं व्यतिक्रम्य नाऽहं जीवितुमुत्सहे ।।

32. Oh (Seetha) with lovely hips! We are bound by father's and (step) mother's command. This, is the Dharma. I will not live transgressing this.

❍ ❍ ❍

३३. अस्वाधीनं कथं दैवं प्रकारैरभिराध्यते ।
स्वाधीनं समतिक्रम्य मातरं पितरं गुरुम् ।।

33. Why is it that a Deity which is not close to (and is invisible) is being propitiated in many ways, (while) transgressing one's mother, father, teacher, who are close to him.

(By this Raama tells the world that one need not 'seek' God elsewhere, when we have 'Gods' at hand in the form of mother, father, teacher, Dharma, truth etc. "Hindu" religion is different from all religions in this concept of God.)

❍ ❍ ❍

३४. यत्र तत्र त्रयो लोकाः पवित्रं तत्समं भुवि ।
नान्यदस्ति शुभापाङ्गे तेनेदमभिराध्यते ।।

34. There is nothing else equal in this world, this means of purification, that which sustains the three worlds; Oh lady with lovely eyes! That is why this is favoured (by me; this obeying my father's command; command of father who is verily God).

❍ ❍ ❍

३५. न सत्यं दानमानौ वा न यज्ञाश्चाप्तदक्षिणाः ।
तथा बलकरास्सीते यथा सेवा पितुर्हिता ॥

35. Oh Seetha! Even (other Dharma-s like observance of) Truth, cannot give same benefits as service to father; not even charities, honour, Sacrificial Rituals made with proper gifts, can give us the same strength.

❍ ❍ ❍

३६. स्वर्गोधनं वा धान्यं वा विद्याः पुत्राः सुखानि च ।
गुरुवृत्त्यनुरोधेन न किञ्चिदपि दुर्लभम् ॥

36. There is nothing that cannot be obtained through devoted service to father: Heavenly bliss, wealth, grains (foods), knowledge, sons, pleasures.

❍ ❍ ❍

३७. देवगन्धर्वगोलोकान् ब्रह्मलोकांस्तथा नराः ।
प्राप्नुवन्ति महात्मानो मातापितृपरायणाः ॥

३८. स मां पिता यथा शास्ति सत्यधर्मपथे स्थितः ।
तथा वर्तितुमिच्छामि स हि धर्मस्सनातनः ॥

37 & 38.

When eminent men take refuge under their father and mother as last resort, they obtain the world of Dheva-s and Ghandharva-s and also the Bramma world (Therefore) I desire to act exactly as my father has commanded me, firmly standing on the path of Truth and Dharma. This is the Eternal Dharma.

❍ ❍ ❍

३९. मम सन्ना मतिस्सीते त्वां नेतुं दण्डकावनम् ।
वसिष्यामीति सा त्वं मामनुयातुं सुनिश्चिता ॥

39. Oh Seetha! *Oh Sa!You have decided = I Will Go To Dhandaka = My mind is made up to take you who are depressed, to follow me (to forest): (* Sa- the bestower of joy to me).

❍ ❍ ❍

४०. सा हि सृष्टाऽनवद्याङ्गि वनाय मदिरेक्षणे ।
अनुगच्छस्व मां भीरु सहधर्मचरी भव ।।

40. Oh (Seetha) with faultless limbs! (Oh Seetha) with intoxicating eyes! Oh timid one! You are indeed 'created' for forest life! Therefore follow me. You will practise Dharma by my side.

❍ ❍ ❍

४१. सर्वथा सदृशं सीते मम स्वस्य कुलस्य च ।
व्यवसायमनुप्राप्ता कान्ते त्वमतिशोभनम् ।।

41. Oh beloved Seetha! You have taken on a strenuous (decision) that is ever splendorous, which befits you, me, and our family.

❍ ❍ ❍

४२. आरभस्व शुभश्रोणि वनवासक्षमाः क्रियाः ।
नेदानीं त्वदृते सीते स्वर्गोऽपि मम रोचते ।।

42. Oh Seetha with lovely hips! Without you, even heaven will not please me. May you begin now the propitiating ceremonies for our forest life.

❍ ❍ ❍

४३. ब्राह्मणेभ्यश्च रत्नानि भिक्षुकेभ्यश्च भोजनम् ।
देहि चाशंसमानेभ्यः संत्वरस्व च मा चिरम् ।।

43. To the needy braamins who seek (charity), and to the Bhikshu-s (mendicants who sustain by alms), you give gems and foods; Hurry up: Dont waste time.

❍ ❍ ❍

४४. भूषणानि महार्हाणि वरवस्त्राणि यानि च ।
रमणीयाश्च ये केचित् क्रीडार्थाश्चाप्युपस्कराः ।।

44. Such costly ornaments, garments, articles you have accumulated, even enjoyable items used for play and relaxation ......

❍ ❍ ❍

४५. शयनीयानि यानानि मम चान्यानि यानि च ।
देहि स्वभृत्यवर्गस्य ब्राह्मणानामनन्तरम् ।।

45. ...... and my various (items whatever, like) beds, vehicles... you give these to Braamins: Then after, you give the large complement of our personal staff (our servants, their needs).

❍ ❍ ❍

४६. अनुकूलन्तु सा भर्तुर्ज्ञात्वा गमनमात्मनः ।
क्षिप्रं प्रमुदिता देवी दातुमेवोपचक्रमे ।।

46. Realising that her going with him was most favourable to her husband, Lady (Seetha) became very pleased and at once began to offer gifts.

❍ ❍ ❍

४७. ततः प्रहृष्टा प्रतिपूर्णमानसा
यशस्विनी भर्तुरवेक्ष्य भाषितम् ।
धनानि रत्नानि च दातुमङ्गना
प्रचक्रमे धर्मभृतां मनस्विनी ।।

47. This intelligent, most famous, beautiful Lady (Seetha) became very happy with her mind fully satisfied. Giving due consideration to what her husband had said, she began to offer (gifts of) wealth, gems etc, to men of Dharma, (then and) there.

❍ ❍ ❍

Chapter 31

(Raama) Agrees to Take Lakshmana Also With Him

(Seetha accompanies Raama on exile. Lakshmana joins them, making it a three some party that goes on exile for 14 years.)

❍ ❍ ❍

१. एवं श्रुत्वा तु संवादं लक्ष्मणः पूर्वमागतः ।
बाष्पपर्याकुलमुखः शोकं सोढुमशक्नुवन् ।।

1. Hearing these discussions (between Raama and Seetha), Lakshmana who had come there earlier, could not bear the grief, his face was flooded by tears.

❍ ❍ ❍

२. स भ्रातुश्चरणौ गाढं निपीड्य रघुनन्दनः ।
सीतामुवाचातियशा राघवं च महाव्रतम् ।।

2. This most famous darling of Raghu-s, held the feet of his brother tightly and addressed the man of vows, this (Raama) the Raaghava, (in presence of) Seetha.

❍ ❍ ❍

३. यदि गन्तुं कृता बुद्धिर्वनं मृगगजायुतम् ।
अहं त्वाऽनुगमिष्यामि वनमग्रे धनुर्धरः ।।

3. As you have decided upon going to forest, I will also go along, in front of you, to the forest that abounds in deers & elephants, wielding my bow.

❍ ❍ ❍

४. मया समेतोऽरण्यानि बहूनि विचरिष्यसि ।
पक्षिभिर्मृगयूथैश्च सङ्घुष्टानि समन्ततः ।।

4. Together with me, you will spend the time in the mighty forest, where, everywhere, it is noisy with hordes of animals and birds.

❍ ❍ ❍

५. न देवलोकाक्रमणं नामरत्वमहं वृणे ।
ऐश्वर्यं वाऽपि लोकानां कामये न त्वया विना ।।

5. Without you, I care not (nor chose a) life in heaven; Nor care for eternal life; I will not desire even (all the wealth and) lordship of the worlds.

❍ ❍ ❍

६. एवं ब्रुवाणः सौमित्रिर्वनवासाय निश्चितः ।
रामेण बहुभिः सान्त्वैर्निषिद्धः पुनरब्रवीत् ।।

6. When (Lakshmana) the son of Sumithra was speaking like this determined on life in forest (with Raama), he was restrained by Raama with conciliatory words; he said further (to Raama).

❍ ❍ ❍

७. अनुज्ञातश्च भवता पूर्वमेव यदस्म्यहम् ।
किमिदानीं पुनरिदं क्रियते मे निवारणम् ।।

7. Even before, I had received permission from you. Therefore why is this restraint upon me at this time?
(Perhaps Lakshmana is referring to his going along with him when Vischwaamithra took Raama to his hermitage. Readers know that Vischwaamithra wanted only Raama, but Lakshmana also accompanies them - The Baala Kaanda.)

❍ ❍ ❍

८. यदर्थं प्रतिषेधो मे क्रियते गन्तुमिच्छतः ।
एतदिच्छामि विज्ञातुं संशयो हि ममानघ ।।

8. For what reason you are preventing me who desires to go. There is doubt in me (that I may have caused some transgression upon you); Oh sinless (Raama) ! I desire to know this.

❍ ❍ ❍

९. ततोऽब्रवीन्महातेजा रामो लक्ष्मणमग्रतः ।
स्थितं प्राग्गामिनं वीरं याचमानं कृताञ्जलिम् ।।

9. The most brilliant Raama, then addressed the brave Lakshmana who was begging him, who was ready to leave (for forest) and who was standing. there before him with his hands cupped in Anjali.

❍ ❍ ❍

१०. स्निग्धो धर्मरतो वीरः सततं सत्पथे स्थितः ।
प्रियः प्राणसमो वश्यो भ्राता चासि सखा च मे ।।

10. You are most attached to me; Steadfast in Dharma: Always stand on the righteous path; very brave; And you are a brother, dear to me as my life (itself); My comrade; My beloved; and most obedient to me.

❍ ❍ ❍

११. मयाऽद्य सह सौमित्रे त्वयि गच्छति तद्वनम् ।
को भरिष्यति कौसल्यां सुमित्रां वा यशस्विनीम् ।।

11. (Oh Lakshmana the) son of Sumithra! If you come along with me now, then who will bear (the burden of protecting) Kowsalya and your famous (mother) Sumithra?

❍ ❍ ❍

१२. अभिवर्षति कामैर्यः पर्जन्यः पृथिवीमिव ।
स कामपाशपर्यस्तो महातेजा महीपतिः ।।

12. And this (our father), the most brilliant lord of Earth who showers upon (every one) with all their 'Desires' just like lord of Rain upon Earth, is now bound by ropes of passion (bound by Kaikeyi).

❍ ❍ ❍

१३. सा हि राज्यमिदं प्राप्य नृपस्याश्वपतेः सुता ।
दुःखितानां सपत्नीनां न करिष्यति शोभनम् ।।

13. And (this Kaikeyi) the daughter of King Aschwapathi, having now obtained the kingdom (for her son Bharatha) will not do good to the co-wives who are suffering in sorrow.

❍ ❍ ❍

१४. न स्मरिष्यति कौसल्यां सुमित्रां च सुदुःखिताम् ।
भरतो राज्यमासाद्य कैकेय्यां पर्यवस्थितः ।।

14. After obtaining the kingdom, Bharatha will be so devoted to (and dominated by) Kaikeyi that he will not even think about (our mothers) Kowsalya and Sumithra, who are in sorrow .....

(Raama knows this not true: His brother Bharatha is a good man, man of Dharma; most endearing brother. But Raama uses this to dissuade Lakshmana from accompanying him!)

❍ ❍ ❍

१५. तामार्यां स्वयमेवेह राजानुग्रहणेन वा ।
सौमित्रे भर कौसल्यामुक्तमर्थमिमं चर ।।

15. Oh (Lakshmana the) son of Sumithra! You must, on your own or with blessings of the king (our father), from here (itself), bear (the burden to protect) this Aryan lady Kowsalya. (when I go away): You must do what is told (by me now, for me).

❍ ❍ ❍

१६. एवं मयि च ते भक्तिर्भविष्यति सुदर्शिता ।
धर्मज्ञ गुरुपूजायां धर्मश्चाप्यतुलो महान् ।।

16. If you do like this, then your loyalty to me will become well known. Oh knower of Dharma! Service to parents is incomparable, a great Dharma.

❍ ❍ ❍

१७. एवं कुरुष्व सौमित्रे मत्कृते रघुनन्दन ।
अस्माभिर्विप्रहीणाया मातुर्नोन भवेत्सुखम् ।।

17. Oh son of Sumithra! (Lakshmana) the darling of Raghu-s! For my sake you should do this: Separated from both of us, our mothers will never have happiness (here).

❍ ❍ ❍

१८. एवमुक्तस्तु रामेण लक्ष्मणः श्लक्ष्णया गिरा ।
प्रत्युवाच तदा रामं वाक्यज्ञो वाक्यकोविदम् ।।

18. When told thus by Raama with words uttered gently, Lakshmana who knew the art of speech, then replied to Raama who was well versed in speech.

❍ ❍ ❍

१९. तवैव तेजसा वीर भरतः पूजयिष्यति ।
कौसल्यां च सुमित्रां च प्रयतो नात्र संशयः ।।

19. Oh .brave (Raama)! By your (grace and) power, Bharatha will honour, (take care of), Kowsalya and Sumithra, piously disposed towards them. No doubt about this.

❍ ❍ ❍

२०. यदि दुष्टो न रक्षेत भरतो राज्यमुत्तमम् ।
प्राप्य दुर्मनसा वीर गर्वेण च विशेषतः ।।

20. Having obtained (our) foremost Kingdom, if he does not protect (them all), particularly due to his arrogance and evil mindedness and becomes wicked ......

❍ ❍ ❍

२१. तमहं दुर्मतिं क्रूरं वधिष्यामि न संशयः ।
तत्पक्ष्यानपि तान् सर्वांस्त्रैलोक्यमपि किं कृतम् ।।

21. ...... then I will kill this evil minded and cruel (Bharatha) and all those on his side: Even (if he has support of) all the worlds. what can (they all) do (to me). No doubt at all.

❍ ❍ ❍

२२. कौसल्या बिभृयादार्या सहस्रमपि मद्विधान् ।
यस्याः सहस्रं ग्रामाणां संप्राप्तमुपजीवनम् ।।

22. This (noble) Aryan lady Kowsalya by whom thousands of villages are sustained with substance (from her) can (easily) support (and protect) thousands like me.

(Lakshmana says that Kowsalya will have the support of citizens who are eternally grateful to her. Raama need not worry about her.)

❍ ❍ ❍

२३. तदात्मभरणे चैव मम मातुस्तथैव च ।
पर्याप्ता मद्विधानां च भरणाय यशस्विनी ।।

23. She is most famous. She is capable of protecting herself. Likewise my mother (Sumithra) also. She can support (protect) people like me. She is enough (and does not need me here).

❍ ❍ ❍

२४. कुरुष्व मामनुचरं वैधर्म्यं नेह विद्यते ।
कृतार्थोऽहं भविष्यामि तव चार्थः प्रकल्पते ॥

24. Allow me to go along with you. In this there is no Non Dharma. I will become an accomplished man (with my desire fulfilled). And your mission will also be successful.

❍ ❍ ❍

२५. धनुरादाय सगुणं खनित्रपिटकाधरः ।
अग्रतस्ते गमिष्यामि पन्थानमनुदर्शयन् ॥

25. Taking with me the strung up bow, carrying a spade and basket (to clear the way), I will go in front of you, showing you the way.

❍ ❍ ❍

२६. आहरिष्यामि ते नित्यं मूलानि च फलानि च ।
वन्यानि यानि चान्यानि स्वाहाराणि तपस्विनाम् ॥
भवांस्तु सह वैदेह्या गिरिसानुषु रंस्यते ॥

26. I will procure for you, daily, such of those forest products that are used as food by men of penance, (foods) like tubers, fruits etc. Therefore you can enjoy yourself in the slopes of hills, along with (Seetha the) Vaidhehi.

❍ ❍ ❍

२७. अहं सर्वं करिष्यामि जाग्रतः स्वपतश्च ते ।
रामस्त्वनेन वाक्येन सुप्रीतः प्रत्युवाच तम् ॥
व्रजापृच्छस्व सौमित्रे सर्वमेव सुहृज्जनम् ॥

27. I will do everything, whether you are awake or asleep.

When Raama was begged (by Lakshmana) with such words, he became pleased and replied to him: = Oh (Lakshmana) the son of Sumithra! Come Along; Take Leave of All Your Friends. (Readers may note the Poet Vaalmeeki has devoted 3 chapters to Seetha in the matter of accompanying Raama on exile; but just this much in the case of Lakshmana. Raama/ Lakshmana are indeed inseparable)❍ ❍ ❍

२८. ये च राज्ञो ददौ दिव्ये महात्मा वरुणः स्वयम् ।
जनकस्य महायज्ञे धनुषी रौद्रदर्शने ।।
अभेद्ये कवचे दिव्ये तूणी चाक्षयसायकौ ।।

28. The great soul Lord Varuna himself gave to king Janaka during a great sacrificial ceremony, a divine, gruesome looking pair of bows and divine (pair of) Armours that can never be pierced through, and quivers that is full with arrows, (never empty of arrows) .....

❍ ❍ ❍

२९. आदित्यविमलौ चोभौ खड्गौ हेमपरिष्कृतौ ।
सत्कृत्य निहितं सर्वमेतदाचार्यसद्मनि ।।
स त्वमायुधमादाय क्षिप्रमाव्रज लक्ष्मण ।।

29. ...... and two swords that glitter like Sun and which are done up in gold. Oh Lakshmana: All these (that are intrusted with our Guru Vasishta), are kept in the mansion of our teacher and worshipped there. Taking all these weapons, you come back soon.
(Readers may note that even in forest, Raama cannot absolve himself of his responsibility of a Kshathriya prince; hence these weapons on his exile. These weapons are divine, worshipped at Vasishta's place).

❍ ❍ ❍

३०. स सुहृज्जनमामन्त्र्य वनवासाय निश्चितः ।
इक्ष्वाकुगुरुमागम्य जग्राहायुधमुत्तमम् ।।

30. His life in forest decided, (Lakshmana) took leave of his

friends and going to (Vasishta) the (Guru), the teacher of Ikshwaaku (kings), he took the foremost weapons (from him)

❍ ❍ ❍

३१. तद्दिव्यं रघुशार्दूलः सत्कृतं माल्यभूषितम् ।
रामाय दर्शयामास सौमित्रिः सर्वमायुधम् ॥

31. This (Lakshmana the) son of Sumithra who was a 'lion' amongst Raghu-s, then (brought) and exhibited to Raama all these divine weapons that were worshipped and which were decorated with garlands.

(These are not conventional weapons, but Divine. They 'appear' 'in form', only when called upon through Chants. So Raama and Lakshmana are not really 'carrying' them.)

❍ ❍ ❍

३२. तमुवाचात्मवान् रामः प्रीत्या लक्ष्मणमागतम् ।
काले त्वमागतः सौम्य काङ्क्षिते मम लक्ष्मण ॥

32. Raama the man of composure, addressed Lakshmana who had (just) returned there, with affection, thus; Oh my pleasant Lakshmana! You have come even as I was awaiting you, on time.

❍ ❍ ❍

३३. अहं प्रदातुमिच्छामि यदिदं मामकं धनम् ।
ब्राह्मणेभ्यस्तपस्विभ्यस्त्वया सह परन्तप ॥

33. I desire to give away all this, my own (private) wealth to Braamins who are men of penance, along with you, (assisted by you). Oh Lakshmana the tormentor of enemies! ......

❍ ❍ ❍

३४. वसन्तीह दृढं भक्त्या गुरुषु द्विजसत्तमाः ।
तेषामपि च मे भूयः सर्वेषां चोपजीविनाम् ॥

34. ...... To these braamins who live here; with total devotion (I wish to give)..And to the teachers, to men of penance also and to all others who seek their livelihood from me..... In plenty....

❍ ❍ ❍

३५. वसिष्ठपुत्रं तु सुयज्ञमार्यं
त्वमानयाशु प्रवरं द्विजानाम् ।
अभिप्रयास्यामि वनं समस्तान्
अभ्यर्च्य शिष्टानपरान्द्विजातीन् ।।

35. Kindly fetch soon Suyagnya who is foremost amongst braamins, who is (our respected) elder, and who is son of Vasishta; and also learned braamins. After paying my respects to all of them, I am going to leave for forest.

❍ ❍ ❍

Chapter 32

Offer of Charities & Gifts Before Going on Exile

(Raama distributes all his private wealth before going on 14 year exile along with wife Seetha and brother Lakshmana.)

❍ ❍ ❍

१. ततः शासनमाज्ञाय भ्रातुः प्रियकरं शुभम् ।
गत्वा स प्रविवेशाशु सुयज्ञस्य निवेशनम् ।।

1. Perceiving that his brother's command was auspicious and will do them good, he went out at once from there and entered Suyagnya's abode.

❍ ❍ ❍

२. तं विप्रमग्न्यगारस्थं वन्दित्वा लक्ष्मणोऽब्रवीत् ।
सखेऽभ्यागच्छ पश्य त्वं वेश्म दुष्करकारिणः ।।

2. And Lakshmana bowed before this Braamin who was

in the Hall of Fire Rituals. And he said to him:= Oh comrade, come to the abode of (Raama) who performs arduous tasks, See (him and learn about other matters from him).=

❍ ❍ ❍

३. ततः सन्ध्यामुपास्याथ गत्वा सौमित्रिणा सह ।
जुष्टं तत्प्राविशल्लक्ष्म्या रम्यं रामनिवेशनम् ।।

3. Then, at this (request), (Suyagnya), after finishing Sandhya rituals, went along with him and entered this Raama's palace which was beautiful, endowed with riches.

❍ ❍ ❍

४. तमागतं वेदविदं प्राञ्जलिः सीतया सह ।
सुयज्ञमभिचक्राम राघवोऽग्निमिवार्चितम् ।।

4. Along with Seetha, (Raama the) Raaghava, with his hands cupped in Anjali, received Suyagnya, the knower of Vedha-s, who was like burning fire, when he came there.

❍ ❍ ❍

५. जातरूपमयैर्मुख्यैरङ्गदैः कुण्डलैः शुभैः ।
सहेमसूत्रैर्मणिभिः केयूरैर्वलयैरपि ।।

5. With golden foremost and beautiful bracelets, bangles, ear drops, girdles, gems, keyura ornaments ......

❍ ❍ ❍

६. अन्यैश्च रत्नैर्बहुभिः काकुत्स्थः प्रत्यपूजयत् ।
सुयज्ञं स तदोवाच रामः सीताप्रचोदितः ।।

6. ...... and many other ornaments, (Raama) honoured him, (presented these to him). At the same time, goaded by Seetha, he said the following:

❍ ❍ ❍

७. हारं च हेमसूत्रं च भार्यायै सौम्य हारय ।
रशनां चाधुना सीता दातुमिच्छति ते सखे ।।

7. Oh pleasant comrade! Seetha desires to give your wife, at this moment, a necklace, a girdle, and a golden chain. (Please) receive.

❍ ❍ ❍

८. अङ्गदानि विचित्राणि केयूराणि शुभानि च ।
प्रयच्छति सखे तुभ्यं भार्यायै गच्छति वनम् ।।

8. Oh friend! She (my wife) who is about to leave for forest, is offering you, for your wife, lovely, wonderful bracelets, Keyura ornaments.

❍ ❍ ❍

९. पर्यङ्कमग्र्यास्तरणं नानारत्नविभूषितम् ।
तमपीच्छति वैदेही प्रतिष्ठापयितुं त्वयि ।।

9. And (Seetha the) Vaidhehi desires to bestow her a cot that is decorated with many gems and which is covered by beautiful bed spreads.

❍ ❍ ❍

१०. नागः शत्रुञ्जयो नाम मातुलो यं ददौ मम ।
तं ते गजसहस्रेण ददामि द्विजपुङ्गव ।।

10. Oh 'tiger' amongst Braamins! The elephant named Schathrunjaya was given to me by my maternal uncle: I am giving this along with 1,000 elephants.

❍ ❍ ❍

११. इत्युक्तः स तु रामेण सुयज्ञः प्रतिगृह्य तत् ।
रामलक्ष्मणसीतानां प्रयुयोजाशिषः शुभाः ।।

11. When told thus by Raama, this Suyagnya received these and offered auspicious blessings to Raama, Lakshmana and Seetha.

❍ ❍ ❍

१२. अथ भ्रातरमव्यग्रं प्रियं रामः प्रियंवदम् ।
सौमित्रिं तमुवाचेदं ब्रह्मेव त्रिदशेश्वरम् ।।

12. Then Raama addressed these (words) to his beloved brother (Lakshmana) the son of Sumithra who always spoke sweetly and who was standing there in attention, like God Bramma addressing (Indhra) the lord of Dheva-s:

❍ ❍ ❍

१३. अगस्त्यं कौशिकं चैव तावुभौ ब्राह्मणोत्तमौ ।
अर्चयाहूय सौमित्रे रत्नैः सस्यमिवांबुभिः ।।

13. Oh (Lakshmana the) son of Sumithra! Invoking the two foremost Braamins, Agasthya and Kowschika, you offer (gifts in plenty) like rain upon crops, (offer) Gems etc ......

❍ ❍ ❍

१४. तर्पयस्व महाबाहो गोसहस्रैश्च मानद ।
सुवर्णैः रजतैश्चैव मणिभिश्च महाधनैः ।।

14. ...... costly ornaments made in gold and silver, thousands of cows.... (and thus) Please them (satisfy them), Oh mighty limbed, the destroyer of pride (Oh Lakshmana)!

❍ ❍ ❍

१५. कौसल्यां च य आशीर्भिर्भक्तः पर्युपतिष्ठति ।
आचार्यस्तैत्तिरीयाणामभिरूपश्च वेदवित् ।।

15. To that Braamin who is teacher to those who recite Thaithrey Upanishad (Holy Text), who is learned, most learned in Vedha-s, who stands in attendance by the side of the devoted Kowsalya, offering her blessings ....

❍ ❍ ❍

१६. तस्य यानं च दासीश्च सौमित्रे सम्प्रदापय ।
कौशेयानि च वस्त्राणि यावत्तुष्यति स द्विजः ।।

16. ..... You must do (all) in such a way that he will be pleased: And you will offer to him a palanquin, slaves, silks, garments.

❍ ❍ ❍

१७. सूतश्चित्रंरथश्चार्यः सचिवः सुचिरोषितः ।
तोषयैनं महार्हैश्च रत्नैर्वस्त्रैर्धनैस्तथा ॥
पशुकाभिश्च सर्वाभिर्गवां दशशतेन च ॥

17. The noble minister Chithraratha has been with us for a long time. He is a charioteer (as well): You should please him with gems, costly garments, wealth and with 10,000 cows with many calves.

❍ ❍ ❍

१८. ये चेमे कठकालापा बहवो दण्डमाणवाः ।
नित्यस्वाध्यायशीलत्वान्नान्यत् कुर्वन्ति किञ्चन ॥

18. The many students who carry sticks in their hands (like mendicants) and who spend their (entire) time in study (of Vedha-s etc) daily, do not do anything else...(but study) ......

❍ ❍ ❍

१९. अलसाः स्वादुकामाश्च महतां चापि सम्मताः ।
तेषामशीतियानानि रत्नपूर्णानि दापय ॥
२०. शालिवाहसहस्रं च द्वे शते भद्रकांस्तथा ।
व्यञ्जनार्थं च सौमित्रे गोसहस्रमुपाकुरु ॥

19. & 20.

...... they get tired... they are fond of delicious foods. They are equal to great men though. To them you give 80 vehicles laden with gems....thousands of oxen, 200 bullocks; and for their food, 100 (milking) cows... you give.. Oh (Lakshmana) the son of Sumithra

❍ ❍ ❍

२१. मेखलीनां महासङ्घः कौसल्यां समुपस्थितः ।
तेषां सहस्रं सौमित्रे प्रत्येकं संप्रदापय ॥

21. Oh (Lakshmana) the son of Sumithra! There is a crowd (of boys) wearing girdles (loin) clothes who depend on Kowsalya (for support) You must give to every one of them in thousands.

❍ ❍ ❍

२२. अम्बा यथा च सा नन्देत् कौसल्या मम दक्षिणाम् ।
तथा द्विजातींस्तान् सर्वांल्लक्ष्मणार्चय सर्वशः ।।

22. Oh Lakshmana! You must honour in every way all these braamins with gifts, so that my mother Kowsalya will rejoice.

❍ ❍ ❍

२३. ततः स पुरुषव्याघ्रस्तद्धनं लक्ष्मणः स्वयम् ।
यथोक्तं ब्राह्मणेन्द्राणामददाद्धनदो यथा ।।

23. Then this 'tiger' of men, this Lakshmana, himself gave gifts appropriately to braamins, like Kubhaera (the lord of wealth).

❍ ❍ ❍

२४. अथाब्रवीद्बाष्पकलांस्तिष्ठतश्चोपजीविनः ।
संप्रदाय बहु द्रव्यमेकैकस्योजीविनः ।।

24. After offering plenty of wealth to every one of these dependents, he then said to these dependents who were all standing there with tears in their eyes.

❍ ❍ ❍

२५. लक्ष्मणस्य च यद्वेश्म गृहं च यदिदं मम ।
अशून्यं कार्यमेकैकं यातदागमनं मम ।।

25. (Raama makes a request): Our own separate houses, (that is) Lakshmana's and my house, should not become dilapidated till we come back (after 14 years of exile).

(Raama is very thoughtful; Monuments must be protected. Their palaces are indeed national monuments.)

❍ ❍ ❍

२६. इत्युक्त्वा दुःखितं सर्वं जनं तमुपजीविनम् ।
उवाचेदं धनाध्यक्षं धनमानीयतामिति ॥

26. After telling these, his dependents, who were in sorrow, thus, he told the keeper of his treasury, May (my chest of) wealth be brought, All (of it).

❍ ❍ ❍

२७. ततोऽस्य धनमाजह्रुः सर्वमेवोपजीविनः ।
स राशिः सुमहांस्तत्र दर्शनीयो ह्यदृश्यत ॥

27. The servants then brought all his (personal) wealth. (coins of gold, silver etc). At that time the Pile appeared huge and grand looking.

❍ ❍ ❍

२८. ततः स पुरुषव्याघ्रस्तद्धनं सहलक्ष्मणः ।
द्विजेभ्यो बालवृद्धेभ्यः कृपणेभ्यो ह्यदापयत् ॥

28. The (Raama) the 'tiger' of men who was (ever) with Lakshmana, gave away wealth to the miserable and poor braamins, old and young.

❍ ❍ ❍

२९. तत्रासीत्पिङ्गलो गार्ग्यस्त्रिजटो नाम वै द्विजः ।
क्षतवृत्तिर्वने नित्यं फालकुद्दाललाङ्गली ॥

29. (Now follows a very interesting episode: With a sense of humour & Jest, Raama brings home a truth: Thrijata episode.)

At that time, in forest (nearby) there was a Braamin named Thrijata, who was of Gaargya family, whose face was yellowish brown, who had no means of subsistence and who carried with him spade and shovel.

❍ ❍ ❍

३०. तं वृद्धं तरुणी भार्या बालानादाय दारकान् ।
अब्रवीद्ब्राह्मणं वाक्यं दारिद्रेणाभिपीडिता ॥

30. His young wife, taking her young children with her addressed this old braamin the following words, tormented by poverty.

❍ ❍ ❍

३१. अपास्य फालं कुद्दालं कुरुष्व वचनं मम ।
रामं दर्शय धर्मज्ञं यदि किञ्चिदवाप्स्यसि ॥

31. Do as I tell you. Casting away your spade & shovel, (go and) see Raama, the knower of Dharma. You may get something from him.

❍ ❍ ❍

३२. स भार्याया वचः श्रुत्वा शाटीमाच्छाद्य दुश्छदाम् ।
स प्रातिष्ठत पन्थानं यत्र रामनिवेशनम् ॥

32. Hearing the words (of request) from his wife, (Thrijata) wearing torn garments, started out on the path leading to Raama's palace.

❍ ❍ ❍

३३. भृग्वङ्गिरस्समं दीप्त्या त्रिजटं जनसंसदि ।
आ पञ्चमायाः कक्ष्याया नैनं कश्चिदवारयत् ॥

33. Shining as he was like (Sages) Bhrighu and Angiras, no one in the vast crowd standing in the five segments (of Raama's Palace) stopped him (from approaching Raama).

(In any case, Raama was most accessible to citizens.)

❍ ❍ ❍

३४. स राजपुत्रमासाद्य त्रिजटो वाक्यमब्रवीत् ।
निर्धनो बहुपुत्रोऽस्मि राजपुत्र महायशः ॥
क्षतवृत्तिर्वने नित्यं प्रत्यवेक्षस्व मामिति ॥

34. Approaching the prince (Raama), this Thrijata said these words: Oh famous royal prince! I am poor. I have many sons. I have no sustenance in the forest (almost) every day. Consider me (for your favour).

❍ ❍ ❍

३५. तमुवाच ततो रामः परिहाससमन्वितम् ॥

35. Then Raama addressed this (Thrijata) who appeared like an object of ridicule.

❍ ❍ ❍

३६. गवां सहस्रमप्येकं न तु विश्राणितं मया ।
परिक्षिपसि दण्डेन यावत्तावदवाप्स्यसि ॥

36. Thousands of Cows have been (already) gifted away by me; Yet, as you have received not even one from me, you can receive as much (that will cover up and are found in the area) thrown over by your rod (Walking stick).

(This was the jest played by Raama, of course with a purpose.)

❍ ❍ ❍

३७. स शाटीं त्वरितः कट्यां संभ्रान्तः परिवेष्ट्य ताम् ।
आविध्य दण्डं विक्षेप सर्वप्राणेन वेगितः ॥

37. Then tying up his garment firmly around his hips, with zeal and haste, he swiftly threw the stick, whirling it around in full breath.

❍ ❍ ❍

३८. स तीर्त्वा सरयूपारं दण्डस्तस्य कराच्च्युतः ।
गोव्रजे बहुसाहस्रे पपातोक्षणसन्निधौ ॥

38. This pole that was 'discharged' from his hand, crossed Saraayu river and fell near a cowshed of 1,000 cows, right in front of an oxen.

(Even Olympic Javelin throwers cannot throw beyond 200 metres.)

❍ ❍ ❍

३९. तं परिष्वज्य धर्मात्मा आ तस्मात्सरयूतटात् ।
आनयामास ता गोपैस्त्रिजटायाश्रमं प्रति ॥

39. (Raama) the man of Dharma, hugged this (Thrijata): Then with the help of cowherds in the hermitage there, collected and gave all those (found around) the banks of Sarayu river.

❍ ❍ ❍

४०. उवाच च ततो रामस्तं गार्ग्यमभिहर्षयन् ।
मन्युर्न खलु कर्तव्यः परिहासो ह्ययं मम ॥

40. Then Raama addressed (Thrijata) of the Gaargya family smilingly: =This Jest of mine (upon you should not be considered as an insult) causing you indignation. Indeed, (I pray).=

❍ ❍ ❍

४१. इदं हि तेजस्तव यद्दुरत्ययं
तदेव जिज्ञासितुमिच्छता मया ।
इमं भवानर्थमभिप्रचोदितो
वृणीष्व किञ्चेदपरं व्यवस्यति ॥

41. You were 'goaded' by me in this matter (and put to test), because I desired (the world) to know this, your power (of penance which is unfathomable. (Please) ask if there is anything else you desire.

❍ ❍ ❍

४२. ब्रवीमि सत्येन न तेऽस्ति यन्त्रणा
धनं हि यद्यन्मम विप्रकारणात् ।
भवत्सु सम्यक् प्रतिपादनेन तन्
मयाऽऽर्जितं प्रीतियशस्करं भवेत् ॥

42. I swear by Truth and tell you. There need be no restraint in you (to ask what you want). There will be happiness and fame for me by giving those things properly that are earned by me (collected by me), for the sake of use by Braamins (like you).

❍ ❍ ❍

४३. ततः सभार्यस्त्रिजटो महामुनिः
गवामनीकं प्रतिगृह्य मोदितः ।
यशोबलप्रीतिसुखोपबृंहिणीः
तदाऽऽशिषः प्रत्यवदन्महात्मनः ॥

43. Then the great sage Thrijata who had (a large family and) a wife (to support) received a herd of cows; Greatly pleased, he recited blessings upon the great soul (Raama) for increasing his fame, strength, affection and pleasure.

❍ ❍ ❍

४४. स चापि रामः परिपूर्णपौरुषो
महद्धनं धर्मबलैरुपार्जितम् ।
नियोजयामास सुहृज्जने चिरात्
यथार्हसंमानवचःप्रचोदितः ॥

44. And finally, this Raama bestowed all his immense wealth he had procured by the use of his power as per Dharma, to all his good friends, to every one, as per their needs and merit, honouring them with words (of eulogy) and with a full happy heart.

❍ ❍ ❍

४५. द्विजः सुहृद्भृत्यजनोऽथ वा तदा
दरिद्रभिक्षाचरणश्च यो भवेत् ।
न तत्र कश्चिन्न बभूव तर्पितो
यथार्हसंमाननदानसंभ्रमैः ॥

45. At that moment, there was none who was not satisfied (with his gifts). Whether he was a braamin beggar seeking alms, or a devoted (affectionate) servant; (All) were honoured with eulogies as they received (their respective share) according to their needs and merit.

(Poet Vaalmeeki brings home a few points: Raama has sense of humour and jest, but uses this to prove the efficacy of power of penance: Secondly, gifts, charity must always be given in good grace.)

❍ ❍ ❍

Chapter 33

Raama goes to Meet Dhascharatha to Bid Farewell

१. दत्त्वा तु सह वैदेह्या ब्राह्मणेभ्यो धनं बहु ।
जग्मतुः पितरं द्रष्टुं सीतया सह राघवौ ।।

1. After the two Raaghava-s (Raama and Lakshmana) along with (Seetha the) Vaidhehi had given away lots of gifts to Braamins (and others), he went to see his father (Dhascharatha) along with his wife.

❍ ❍ ❍

२. ततो गृहीते दुष्प्रेक्षे त्वशोभेतां तदायुधे ।
मालादामभिराबद्धे सीतया समलंकृते ।।

2. The Arms (Bow, arrow, sword etc) that were carried by them which were well tied up with garlands by Seetha and decorated, shone, making these (weapons) difficult to 'look' upon.

(Divinity goes with these Arms, readers may note.)

❍ ❍ ❍

३. ततः प्रासादहर्म्याणि विमानशिखराणि च ।
अधिरुह्य जनः श्रीमाणुदासीनो व्यलोकयत् ।।

3. The prosperous citizens who had got on top of the temple towers and the roof of the multi storied buildings, were looking on, down hearted.

❍ ❍ ❍

४. न हि रथ्याः स्म शक्यन्ते गन्तुं बहुजनाकुलाः ।
आरुह्य तस्मात् प्रासादाद्दीनाः पश्यन्ति राघवम् ।।

4. The roads were crowded with multitude of men. It was difficult to get through. Therefore the distressed citizens got on (top of) the mansions and were looking at (Raama the) Raaghava.

❍ ❍ ❍

५. पदातिं वर्जितच्छत्रं रामं दृष्ट्वा तदा जनाः ।
उचुर्बहुविधा वाचः शोकोपहतचेतसः ।।

5. And when they saw Raama without his umbrella and was going on foot, the citizens became afflicted with grief and talked in so many ways with these words

❍ ❍ ❍

६. यं यान्तमनुयाति स्म चतुरङ्गबलं महत् ।
तमेकं सीतया सार्धमनुयाति स्म लक्ष्मणः ।।

6. (Citizens have never seen such a spectacle: They wail.) A mighty Army drawn from four services, used to follow him! (Now only) Lakshmana is following him who is going alone with (his wife) Seetha.

❍ ❍ ❍

७. ऐश्वर्यस्य रसज्ञः सन् कामिनां चैव कामदः ।
नेच्छत्येवानृतं कर्तुं पितरं धर्मगौरवात् ।।

7. (Raama) who knows the true value of wealth, who satisfies all those who desire, who remains steadfast (in Dharma), does not desire to make his father untruthful, out of his respect for Dharma.

❍ ❍ ❍

८. या न शक्या पुरा द्रष्टुं भूतैराकाशगैरपि ।
तामद्य सीतां पश्यन्ति राजमार्गगता जनाः ।।

8. And one who could never be seen by even celestials roaming in the sky,such a one, such a Seetha, citizens are now seeing, standing in the royal boulevard.!

❍ ❍ ❍

९. अङ्गरागोचितां सीतां रक्तचन्दनसेविनीम् ।
वर्षमुष्णं च शीतं च नेष्यन्त्याशु विवर्णताम् ।।

9. Indeed Seetha who used to (deserves to) be anointed with scents and besmeared with sandal pastes,.... Now, rain, cold and heat, will soon make her lose her complexion.

❍ ❍ ❍

१०. अद्य नूनं दशरथस्सत्त्वमाविश्य भाषते ।
न हि राजा प्रियं पुत्रं विवासयितुमर्हति ।।

10. Now it is certain. King Dhascharatha, having allowed (evil) spirits to enter (him) speaks (differently). Otherwise he would not have agreed to send his beloved son on exile (to forest).

❍ ❍ ❍

११. निर्गुणस्यापि पुत्रस्य कथं स्याद्विप्रवासनम् ।
किं पुनर्यस्य लोकोऽयं जितो वृत्तेन केवलम् ।।

11. Even to a characterless son, exile is not meted out; When that is so, how can it be for this (Raama) who has 'captured' the entire world with his (good) conduct?

❍ ❍ ❍

१२. आनृशंस्यमनुक्रोशः श्रुतं शीलं दमः शमः ।
राघवं शोभयन्त्येते षड्गुणाः पुरुषोत्तमम् ।।

12. Six qualities shine in this noble man (Raama) the Raaghava: Non Injury, Compassion, Knowledge of Schruthi-s (Holy Texts), Good conduct, Restraint, Composure.

❍ ❍ ❍

१३. तस्मात्तस्योपघातेन प्रजाः परमपीडिताः ।
औदकानीव सत्त्वानि ग्रीष्मे सलिलसंक्षयात् ।।

13. Because of the imposition (of exile) upon him, the

citizens are greatly (frustrated), tormented, like living beings in summer when water dries up.

❍ ❍ ❍

१४. पीडया पीडितं सर्वं जगदस्य जगत्पतेः ।
मूलस्येवोपघातेन वृक्षः पुष्पफलोपगः ।।

14. Because of the torment of this lord of Earth (Raama), the entire earth is like a tree offering fruits and flowers, being destroyed at its roots.
(Raama is the root of all that is good in the kingdom.)

❍ ❍ ❍

१५. मूलं ह्येष मनुष्याणां धर्मसारो महाद्युतिः ।
पुष्पं फलं च पत्रं च शाखाश्चास्येतरे जनाः ।।

15. This majestic man who knows the essence of Dharma, is indeed the root for all men; All other men its flowers, fruits, leaves, branches. (Poet Vaalmeeki goes poetic)

❍ ❍ ❍

१६. ते लक्ष्मण इव क्षिप्रं सपत्नीकाः सबान्धवाः ।
गच्छन्तमनुगच्छामो येन गच्छति राघवः ।।

16. Like Lakshmana (going along with him), we, along with our wives & relatives, will follow (Raama) the Raaghava, by the same (way) he goes along.

❍ ❍ ❍

१७. उद्यानानि परित्यज्य क्षेत्राणि च गृहाणि च ।
एकदुःखसुखा राममनुगच्छाम धार्मिकम् ।।

17. (Leaving (our) gardens, homes, temples, we shall follow this man of Dharma, treating sorrows and pleasures the same ......

❍ ❍ ❍

१८. समुद्धृतनिधानानि परिध्वस्ताजिराणि च ।
उपात्तधनधान्यानि हृतसाराणि सर्वशः ।।

18. (In the following stanzas they all curse Kaikeyi.)
With all our treasures tucked away; with all places desolate; with all our substance removed; with grains and other produce appropriated ......

❍ ❍ ❍

१९. रजसाऽभ्यवकीर्णानि परित्यक्तानि दैवतैः ।
मूषिकैः परिधावद्भिरुद्बिलैरावृतानि च ॥

19. ...... (With city) covered by dust; abandoned by deities; infested with rats jumping about; overflowing with rats; ......

❍ ❍ ❍

२०. अपेतोदकधूमानि हीनसंमार्जनानि च ।
प्रनष्टबलिकर्मेज्यामन्त्रहोमजपानि च ॥

20. ...... (the city) not cleaned up with water, without sweet smell; without anything being cleaned up; without sacrificial fire rituals, chants and prayers being performed ......

❍ ❍ ❍

२१. दुष्कालेनैव भग्नानि भिन्नभाजनवन्ति च ।
अस्मत्त्यक्तानि वेश्मानि कैकेयी प्रतिपद्यताम् ॥

21. ...... with broken things, with broken vessels; with all our homes deserted.... Let Kaikeyi, in this evil time (for us all), obtain all this!
(This is what Kaikeyi will get, if Raama is sent away: Citizens will not co-operate nor do their duties).

❍ ❍ ❍

२२. वनं नगरमेवास्तु येन गच्छति राघवः ।
अस्माभिश्च परित्यक्तं पुरं संपद्यतां वनम् ॥

22. When (Raama) the Raaghava goes, may the forest become (our) city! And (our) city, abandoned by us all, may turn into forest

❍ ❍ ❍

२३. बिलानि दंष्ट्रिणः सर्वेसानूनि मृगपक्षिणः ।
त्यजन्त्वस्मद्भयाद्भीता गजाः सिंहा वनान्यपि ।।

23. The biting snakes, animals, elephants, lions, birds, ... may these run away from (and abandon) forest in fear, seeing us all there.

❍ ❍ ❍

२४. अस्मत्त्यक्तं प्रपद्यन्तां सेव्यमानं त्यजन्तु च ।।

24. May they abandon their dwellings: May they inhabit what we have abandoned!

❍ ❍ ❍

२५. तृणमांसफलादानं देशं व्यालमृगद्विजम् ।
प्रपद्यतां हि कैकेय्यी सपुत्रा सहबान्धवैः ।।
राघवेण वने सर्वेसह वत्स्याम निर्वृताः ।।

25. May Kaikeyi and her son (Bharatha), along with her relatives, enjoy the kingdom infested by cruel animals and birds that live on grass, meat and fruits. And we will live in tranquillity in forest with (Raama) the Raaghava.

❍ ❍ ❍

२६. इत्येवं विविधा वाचो नानाजनसमीरिताः ।
शुश्राव रामः श्रुत्वा च न विचक्रेऽस्य मानसम् ।।

26. And Raama heard all these diverse talks from various citizens speaking thus; Yet, there was no change (in his demenour), in his mind. (And of course no change in his decision either!)

❍ ❍ ❍

२७. स तु वेश्म पितुर्दूरात् कैलासशिखरप्रभम् ।
अभिचक्राम धर्मात्मा मत्तमातङ्गविक्रमः ।।

27. This noble soul man of Dharma, (this Raama), who possessed the strides of an exhilarated elephant, walked

towards his father's palace which even from a distance, shone like peak of Kailash (in Himalayas).

❍ ❍ ❍

२८. विनीतधीरपुरुषं प्रविश्य तु नृपालयम् ।
दर्दशावस्थितं दीनं सुमन्त्रमविदूरतः ।।

28. Entering the palace of the king, at the entrance itself, he saw the (normally) composed Sumanthra looking feeble (depressed).

❍ ❍ ❍

२९. प्रतीक्षमाणोऽपि जनं तदाऽऽर्तं
अनार्तरूपः प्रहसन्निवाथ ।
जगाम रामः पितरं दिदृक्षुः
पितुर्निदेश विधिवच्चिकीर्षुः ।।

29. Desirous of fulfilling his father's command properly, desirous of seeing him (to take leave of him), Raama observed that people were in deep sorrow; Yet he went there smiling, with no appearance of any pain in him.

❍ ❍ ❍

३०. तत्पूर्वमैक्ष्वाकसुतो महात्मा
रामो गमिष्यन् वनमार्तरूपम् ।
व्यतिष्ठत प्रेक्ष्य तदा सुमन्त्रं
पितुर्महात्मा प्रतिहारणार्थम् ।।

30. The noble soul man of Dharma, Raama, the son of Ikshwaaku king, wishing to be announced to his great soul father first as he was going away to the forest, looked at Sumanthra who was afflicted by sorrow, and he stood there.

❍ ❍ ❍

३१. पितुर्निदेशेन तु धर्मवत्सलो
वनप्रवेशे कृतबुद्धिनिश्चयः ।
स राघवः प्रेक्ष्य सुमन्त्रमब्रवीत्
निवेदयस्वागमनं नृपाय मे ॥

31. Having resolved with a firm mind to go to forest by the command of his father, this (Raama the) Raaghava who was a devotee of Dharma addressed Sumanthra: = Inform the king about my arrival.=

❍ ❍ ❍

Chapter 34

Dhascharatha Swoons on Seeing His Son

१. ततः कमलपत्राक्षः श्यामो निरुदरो महान् ।
उवाच रामस्तं सूतं पितुराख्याहि मामिति ॥

1. The lotus eyed blue (blooded) great Raama who cannot be 'suppressed', told the charioteer Sumanthra thus = Announce me to (my) father about me.=

❍ ❍ ❍

२. स रामप्रेषितः क्षिप्रं सन्तापकलुषेन्द्रियः ।
प्रविश्य नृपतिं सूतो निश्वसन्तं ददर्श ह ॥

2. Commissioned by Raama, this (Sumanthra) the charioteer whose senses were numbed by torment and grief, at once entered and saw his king breathing hard and deep (due to the imminent separation from Raama).

❍ ❍ ❍

३. उपरक्तमिवादित्यं भस्मच्छन्नमिवानलम् ।
तटाकमिव निस्तोयमपश्यज्जगतीपतिम् ॥

3. He saw (this Dhascharatha) the lord of Earth (looking)

like the Sun eclipsed, like fire reduced to ashes, like a pond without water.

❍ ❍ ❍

४. आलोक्य तु महाप्राज्ञः परमाकुलचेतराग् ।
रामभेवानुशोचन्तं सूतः प्राञ्जलिरासदत् ।।

4. Observing that (Dhascharatha) was deeply worried over Raama and that his mind was terribly agitated, the most intelligent charioteer approached him with his hands cupped in reverence of Anjali.

❍ ❍ ❍

५. तं वर्धयित्वा राजानं सूतः पूर्वं जयाशिषा ।
भयविक्लवया वाचा मन्दया श्लक्ष्णमब्रवीत् ।।

5. The Charioteer first greeted the king with = Victory (To You)=: And then addressed him gently with words indicating his misery.

(Even in difficult / sad moments protocol is observed; Sumanthra addresses the king with victory slogans!)

❍ ❍ ❍

६. अयं स पुरुषव्याघ्रो द्वारि तिष्ठति ते सुतः ।
ब्राह्मणेभ्यो धनं दत्त्वा सर्वं चैवोपजीविनाम् ।।

6. Your son, (this Raama) the 'tiger' of men, after having given away all his wealth to Braamins and to those who live by him, is now standing at the door.

❍ ❍ ❍

७. स त्वा पश्यतु भद्रं ते रामः सत्यपराक्रमः ।
सर्वान् सुहृद आपृच्छ्य त्वामिदानीं दिदृक्षते ।।

7. This truly brave Raama, after taking leave from all his friends, is now desirous of seeing you: Let him meet you. Welfare to you.

❍ ❍ ❍

८. गमिष्यति महारण्यं तं पश्य जगतीपते ।
वृतं राजगुणैः सर्वैरादित्यमिव रश्मिभिः ।।

8. He is going away to the great forest: Oh lord of Earth! May you see (Raama) who is like Sun endowed with 'rays' that are his (various) royal qualities... (Poet Vaalmeeki goes poetic!)

❍ ❍ ❍

९. स सत्यवादी धर्मात्मा गांभीर्यात् सागरोपमः ।
आकाश इव निष्पङ्को नरेन्द्रः प्रत्युवाच तम् ।।

9. (Then) This pure man (Dhascharatha the) lord of men who ever spoke Truth, who ever was a noble man of Dharma, who was profound like the Ocean and Sky (and large hearted), replied:

❍ ❍ ❍

१०. सुमन्त्रानय मे दारान् ये केचिदिह मामकाः ।
दारैः परिवृतः सर्वैर्द्रष्टुमिच्छामि राघवम् ।।

10. Oh Sumanthra! Please fetch my wives, these who are my own, (my well wishers), here. I desire to see the Raaghava, (my Raama), surrounded by (in the company of) all the my wives.

❍ ❍ ❍

११. सोऽन्तःपुरमतीत्यैव स्त्रियस्ता वाक्यमब्रवीत् ।
आर्या ह्वयति वो राजा गम्यतां तत्र मा चिरम् ।।

11. Then (Sumanthra) went to the private chambers and addressed the ladies; = Oh noble ladies! The king summons you all; May you go there; Let there be no delay.=

❍ ❍ ❍

१२. एवमुक्ताः स्त्रियः सर्वाः सुमन्त्रेण नृपाज्ञया ।
प्रचक्रमुस्तद्भवनं भर्तुराज्ञाय शासनम् ।।

12. When they were told thus by Sumanthra about the command of the king, all these ladies started out to his palace, obeying their husband's order.

❍ ❍ ❍

१३. अर्धसप्तशतास्तास्तु प्रमदास्ताम्रलोचनाः ।
कौसल्यां परिवार्याथ शनैर्जग्मुर्धृतव्रताः ।।

13. Steadfast in vows, these wives, (Half of seven hundred), the 350 wives (of Dhascharatha) whose eyes were red (due to crying), then surrounded Kowsalya and came along quietly. (with her).

१४. आगतेषु च दारेषु समवेक्ष्य महीपतिः ।
उवाच राजा तं सूतं सुमन्त्रानय मे सुतम् ।।

14. When his wives had arrived, the lord of earth, this king, looked at the charioteer and said: = Oh Sumanthra! Bring my son here.=

❍ ❍ ❍

१५. स सूतो राममादाय लक्ष्मणं मैथिलीं तदा ।
जगामाभिमुखस्तूर्णं सकाशं जगतीपतेः ।।

15. Then the most friendly disposed (Sumanthra the) charioteer, at once brought Raama and Lakshmana along with (Seetha the) Maithili before (Dhascharatha), the lord of earth.

❍ ❍ ❍

१६. स राजा पुत्रमायान्तं दृष्ट्वा दूरात् कृताञ्जलिम् ।
उत्पपातासनात्तूर्णमार्तः स्त्रीजनसंवृतः ।।

16. Surrounded by his wives, king (Dhascharatha) who was in deep distress, saw from a distance, his son coming towards him with his hands cupped in Anjali: He got up at once from his seat.

❍ ❍ ❍

१७. सोऽभिदुद्राव वेगेन रामं दृष्ट्वा विशां पतिः ।
तमसंप्राप्य दुःखार्तः पपात भुवि मूर्च्छितः ।।

17. The Lord of earth, seeing Raama, ran towards him quickly; (but) overwhelmed by grief, he fell down on floor before reaching him and he swooned.

❍ ❍ ❍

१८. तं रामोऽभ्यपतत् क्षिप्रं लक्ष्मणश्च महारथः ।
विसंज्ञमिव दुःखेन सशोकं नृपतिं तदा ।।

18. Raama and the great charioteer-warrior (Lakshmana), at once ran towards the king who was unconscious due to sorrow, afflicted by grief.

❍ ❍ ❍

१९. स्त्रीसहस्रनिनादश्च सञ्जज्ञे राजवेश्मनि ।
हा हा रामेति सहसा भूषणध्वनिमूर्च्छितः ।।

19. In the royal mansion, (reverberating sounds) sounded forth= Ha:- Ha - Raama:- = sounds from the many ladies there, mixed with (tinkling) sounds of their ornaments.

❍ ❍ ❍

२०. तं परिष्वज्य बाहुभ्यां तावुभौ रामलक्ष्मणौ ।
पर्यङ्के सीतया सार्धं रुदन्तः समवेशयन् ।।

20. Along with Seetha, these two, Raama and Lakshmana, then clasped him with their hands and (lifted and) rested him on his couch, (even as they were) crying.

❍ ❍ ❍

२१. अथ रामो मुहूर्तात्तं लब्धसंज्ञं महीपतिम् ।
उवाच प्राञ्जलिर्भूत्वा शोकार्णवपरिप्लुतम् ।।

21. After some time when emperor had regained his consciousness, Raama addressed him who was engulfed in sorrow, with his hands cupped in Anjali.

❍ ❍ ❍

२२. आपृच्छे त्वां महाराज सर्वेषामीश्वरोऽसि नः ।
प्रस्थितं दण्डकारण्यं पश्य त्वं कुशलेन माम् ।।

22. Oh emperor! You are a living God to us all. Please 'See' me. (Bless me) who is now leaving for Dhandaka forest, with welfare. I am (begging you) for leave (to go).

❍ ❍ ❍

२३. लक्ष्मणं चानुजानीहि सीता चान्वेतु मां वनम् ।
कारणैर्बहुभिस्तथ्यैर्वार्यमाणौ न चेच्छतः ।।

23. Seetha is accompanying me to forest. And you must give permission to Lakshmana. In spite of being restrained (by me) with many reasons, he does not desire (to remain here).

(It is significant that Poet Vaalmeeki differentiates between wife Seetha and brother Lakshmana. Raama merely informs his father that he is taking Seetha along; but with Lakshmana, he seeks the king's permission. After all Lakshmana is royal prince; king must 'release' him for 'other' duties!)

❍ ❍ ❍

२४. अनुजानीहि सर्वान्नः शोकमुत्सृज्य मानद ।
लक्ष्मणं मां च सीतां च प्रजापतिरिव प्रजाः ।।

24. Oh revered (Father!) therefore, giving up (this) your Grief, give permission for me, Lakshmana, and Seetha to leave, just as God Bramma before all his subjects.

❍ ❍ ❍

२५. प्रतीक्षमाणमव्यग्रमनुज्ञां जगतीपतेः ।
उवाच राजा संप्रेक्ष्य वनवासाय राघवम् ।।

25. Then the king addressed (Raama the) Raaghava who was composed, who was awaiting permission from (his father the) lord of earth to go to forest.

❍ ❍ ❍

२६. अहं राघव कैकेय्या वरदानेन मोहितः ।
अयोध्यायास्त्वमेवाद्य भव राजा निगृह्य माम् ।।

26. Oh (Raama the) Raaghava! I am stupefied (and duped) by giving the boons to Kaikeyi. (But ignoring my orders) Restraining me, you become the King of Ayodhya now.

(Readers may note: Dhascharatha in effect begs Raama to ignore his command and take over = I have given my command, but if you ignore and take this kingdom from me, I will be the happiest man =)

❍ ❍ ❍

२७. एवमुक्तो नृपतिना रामो धर्मभृतां वरः ।
प्रत्युवाचाञ्जलिं कृत्वा पितरं वाक्यकोविदः ।।

27. Raama, who was foremost amongst those steadfast in Dharma, who was well versed in speech, when told thus by the king (his father), cupped his hands in Anjali and replied to him:

❍ ❍ ❍

२८. भवान् वर्षसहस्रायुः पृथिव्या नृपते पतिः ।
अहंत्वरण्ये वत्स्यामि न मे कार्यं त्वयाऽनृतम् ।।

28. Oh king ! You should remain the lord of earth for thousand years. Even on my account untruth must never be 'done' by you: I will live in forest.

(Raama tells his father that the boons he had given to Kaikeyi must be honoured by him, Truthfully; even if it means losing his son. And Raama will not be a party to cheat Kaikeyi, thus making his father a liar, a man of untruth, a man who went back on his boons.)

❍ ❍ ❍

२९. नव पञ्च च वर्षाणि वनवासे विहृत्य ते ।
पुनः पादौ ग्रहीष्यामि प्रतिज्ञान्ते नराधिप ।।

29. Oh King! After spending (5 plus 9) 14 years in forest

'playfully', (and after) fulfilling (your) command, I will (surely come back to you and) touch your feet.

❍ ❍ ❍

३०. रुदन्नार्तः प्रियं पुत्रं सत्यपाशेन संयतः ।
कैकेय्या चोद्यमानस्तु मिथो राजा तमब्रवीत् ।।

30. The king who was incited by Kaikeyi who had turned hostile to him, (the king) who was in deep distress bound by the 'Ropes' of (Dharma of) Truth, then addressed his beloved son (Raama) crying.

❍ ❍ ❍

३१. श्रेयसे वृद्धये तात पुनरागमनाय च ।
गच्छस्वारिष्टमव्यग्रः पन्थानमकुतोभयम् ।।

31. Oh Dear (son)! For the sake of your (safe) return, your fame and your prosperity, may you (ever) be composed, tread the righteous path without fear.

❍ ❍ ❍

३२. न हि सत्यात्मनस्तात धर्माभिमनसस्तव ।
विनिवर्तयितुं बुद्धिः शक्यते रघुनन्दन ।।

32. Oh (Raama) the darling of Raghu-s! Oh dear (son)! It is not possible to restrain you, (change your mind), as you are an embodiment of Truth and as your mind is fixed on Dharma. Indeed!

❍ ❍ ❍

३३. अद्य त्विदानीं रजनीं पुत्र मा गच्छ सर्वथा ।
एकाहदर्शनेनापि साधु तावच्चराम्यहम् ।।

33. Oh son! (But, please): In any case, you should not go away this night By your sight of even one day, I will live on, that much with (some) comfort.

❍ ❍ ❍

३४. मातरं मां च संपश्यन्वसेमामद्य शर्वरीम् ।
तर्पितः सर्वकामैस्त्वं श्वः काले साधयिष्यसि ।।

34. Do stay this night atleast, seeing (keeping company with) me and your mother, (enjoying comforts) and be satisfied with all the desirables. Then tomorrow morning you may satisfy (your wish of going away on exile).

(Give me at least one day's satisfaction, begs Dhascharatha; You will have 14 years of 'satisfaction' of exile, after satisfying my wish!)

○ ○ ○

३५. दुष्करं क्रियते पुत्र सर्वथा राघव त्वया ।
मत्प्रियार्थं प्रियांस्त्यक्त्वा यद्यासि विजनं वनम् ।।

35. Oh my son (Raama) the Raaghava! For the sake of doing me good, (to make me a man of Truth), you are going out to the uninhabited forest, leaving your dear (friends, folks) Thereby, a great arduous task is being undertaken by you.

○ ○ ○

३६. न चैतन्मे प्रियं पुत्र शपे सत्येन राघव ।
छन्नया चलितस्त्वस्मि स्त्रिया छन्नाग्निकल्पया ।।

36. Oh son, Oh Raaghava! This, (your going away on exile), is not (at all) pleasing to me; I swear on Truth. I have been shaken up (violently) by this clandestine woman (Kaikeyi) who is like a hidden fire.

○ ○ ○

३७. वञ्चना या तु लब्धा मे तां त्वं निस्तर्तुमिच्छसि ।
अनया वृत्तसादिन्या कैकेय्याऽभिप्रचोदितः ।।

37. The fraud that was perpetrated (by this Kaikeyi on me) against established norms, (That), you are now desirous of fulfilling, impelled by this Kaikeyi.

३८. न चैतदाश्चर्यतमं यस्त्वं ज्येष्ठः सुतो मम ।
अपानृतकथं पुत्र पितरं कर्तुमिच्छसि ।।

38. Oh son! you, my eldest son, desire to see your father, as a man free (from stain of) falsehood. It is no wonder. (you are such).

❍ ❍ ❍

३९. अथ रामस्तथा श्रुत्वा पितुरार्तस्य भाषितम् ।
लक्ष्मणेन सह भ्रात्रा दीनो वचनमब्रवीत् ।।

39. Hearing such words of his father who was in utter grief, Raama who was (ever) with his brother Lakshmana, became depressed and he addressed these words.

❍ ❍ ❍

४०. प्राप्स्यामि यानद्य गुणान् को मे श्वस्तान् प्रदास्यति ।
अपक्रमणमेवातः सर्वकामैरहं वृणे ।।

40. All those *Guna-s, (these good things), who will give me these tomorrow? Therefore I desire to gratify myself, by my going away to forest today itself, with all my heart.

(As per Nyaya shaasthra there are 8 *delightful mundane things in life.)

❍ ❍ ❍

४१. इयं सराष्ट्रां सजना धनधान्यसमाकुला ।
मया विसृष्टा वसुधा भरताय प्रदीयताम् ।।

41. This entire kingdom, along with its citizens, wealth, grains, produce (and all the) earth that has been 'cast' away by me, may (now) be given to (my brother) Bharatha.

❍ ❍ ❍

४२ वनवासकृता बुद्धिर्न च मेऽद्य चलिष्यति ।।

42. My decision to go to forest today, is unshaken!

❍ ❍ ❍

४३. यस्तुष्टेन वरो दत्तः कैकेय्यै वरद त्वया ।
दीयतां निखिलेनैव सत्यस्त्वं भव पार्थिव ॥

43. Oh king (who answers every one's prayers), one who gives (boons and honours them)! What boons were offered in happiness by you to Kaikeyi, let them be given, (fulfilled), without Any Stain. You Must (Ever) Be A Man of Truth.

❍ ❍ ❍

४४. अहं निदेशं भवतो यथोक्तमनुपालयन् ।
चतुर्दश समा वत्स्ये वने वनचरैः सह ॥

44. I will honour your command as per your commitment and so will live in forest for 14 years along with forest dwellers.

❍ ❍ ❍

४५. मा विमर्शोवसुमती भरताय प्रदीयताम् ।
न हि मे काङ्क्षितं राज्यं सुखमात्मनि वा प्रियम् ॥
यथा निदेशं कर्तुं वै तवैव रघुनन्दन ॥

45. Oh (my father the) darling of Raghu-s! Do not deliberate. (Dont think about your decision). I desire not the kingdom, (because) in my heart, I desire to fulfill your command exactly as directed (by Kaikeyi), happily, pleasantly. May this Earth (the kingdom), be given to (my brother) Bharatha.

❍ ❍ ❍

४६. अपगच्छतु ते दुःखं मा भूर्बाष्पपरिप्लुतः ।
न हि क्षुभ्यति दुर्धर्षः समुद्रः सरितां पतिः ॥

46. May your grief vanish: You should not be soaked in tears; The lord of rivers, the ocean, does not get agitated, never crushed.

❍ ❍ ❍

४७. नैवाहं राज्यमिच्छामि न सुखं न च मैथिलीम् ।
नैव सर्वानिमान् कामान्न स्वर्गं नैव जीवितम् ।।

47. I do not desire kingdom: Nor pleasures; or even (Seetha the) Maithili; nor all these desirables; nor heaven; nor even my life.

❍ ❍ ❍

४८. त्वामहं सत्यमिच्छामि नानृतं पुरुषर्षभ ।
प्रत्यक्षं तव सत्येन सुकृतेन च ते शपे ।।

48. Oh (my father the) 'Bull' amongst men! I desire (this only) You should be (man of) Truth. Untruth never (should touch you). This I swear, and on my honour (and good deeds). (I swear) In your presence.

❍ ❍ ❍

४९. न च शक्यं मया तात स्थातुं क्षणमपि प्रभो ।
न शोकं धारयस्वैनं न हि मेऽस्ति विपर्ययः ।।

49. Oh dear Lord! I cannot remain even for a minute (now): You should not suffer this grief (any longer). There is no change (in my decision to go to forest right away).

❍ ❍ ❍

५०. अर्थितो ह्यस्मि कैकेय्या वनं गच्छेति राघव ।
मया चोक्तं व्रजामीति तत्सत्यमनुपालये ।।

50. I was entreated by Kaikeyi: = Oh (Raama) the Raaghava! You go to forest=: And by me also was she told thus: = I am going"– (So) I am honouring that commitment.

❍ ❍ ❍

५१. मा चोत्कण्ठां कृथा देव वने रंस्यामहे वयम् ।
प्रशान्तहरिणाकीर्णेनानाशकुननादिते ।।

51. Oh Lord! You should not raise (shake) your neck (in disagreement nor in sorrow). We will be enjoying

ourselves in the forest which abounds in tranquil deers, which is full of various cooing birds.

❍ ❍ ❍

५२. पिता हि दैवतं तात देवतानामपि स्मृतम् ।
तस्माद्दैवतमित्येव करिष्यामि पितुर्वचः ।।

52. Oh father! The Scriptures (Smrithi-s etc) say father alone is God of Gods. Therefore, as you are my (living) God, I am acting on my father's words (of command).

❍ ❍ ❍

५३. चतुर्दशसु वर्षेषु गतेषु नरसत्तम ।
पुनर्द्रक्ष्यसि मां प्राप्तं सन्तापोऽयं विमुच्यताम् ।।

53. Oh noble man! After 14 years go by, you will again see me on my return. (Therefore) May you give up this torment (of separation).

❍ ❍ ❍

५४. व येन संस्तम्भनीयोऽयं सर्वोबाष्पगलो जनः ।
स त्वं पुरुषशार्दूल किमर्थं विक्रियां गतः ।।

54. Oh 'tiger' of men! (Oh my father)! When the entire tear shedding multitude of men (citizens) can be made to suppress their sorrow by you, how can you (yourself) give way to perplexity and agitation.

(Here Raama has a special point; Raama may be his son, but Dhascharatha should remember that he is a king and think of his citizens and the kingdom. Life in kingdom must go on smoothly.)

❍ ❍ ❍

५५. मया विसृष्टां भरतो महीमिमां
सशैलषण्डां सपुरां सकाननाम् ।
शिवां सुसीमामनुशास्तु केवलं
त्वया यदुक्तं नृपते तथाऽस्तु तत् ।।

55. May Bharatha govern the entire Earth (Kingdom) with all its mountains, cities, forests, pleasant territories and all given up by me: Oh King! What was told by you (as command), may that take place without any blemish and accordingly.

❍ ❍ ❍

५६. पुरं च राष्ट्रं च मही च केवला
मया विसृष्टा भरताय दीयताम् ।
अहं निदेशं भवतोऽनुपालयन्
वनं गमिष्यामि चिराय सेवितुम् ।।

56. The entire earth, city, kingdom which have been turned down by me, may be handed over to Bharatha: I will go to forest to live there for a long time (of 14 years) so as to honour your command.

❍ ❍ ❍

५७. न मे तथा पार्थिव धीयते मनो
महत्सु कामेषु न चात्मनः प्रिये ।
यथा निदेशे तव शिष्टसम्मते
व्यपैतु दुःखं तव मत्कृतेऽनघ ।।

57. Oh sinless king! (The extent to which) My mind desires to fulfill your command that will meet with approval of learned men (also), the same (desire) is not there for me in great pleasures (of the kingdom), nor even in my dear self! May you throw away your grief on my account ......

❍ ❍ ❍

५८. तदद्य नैवानघ राज्यमव्ययं
स सर्वकामान्न सुखं न मैथिलीम् ।
न जीवितं त्वामनृतेन योजयन्
वृणीय सत्यं व्रतमस्तु ते तथा ।।

58. Oh sinless (Father)! I do not cherish this kingdom now

by binding you with Untruth. I do not desire every form of pleasures (of our kingdom): Not even eternal pleasures: Not even (Seetha) the Maithili: Not even my life. Likewise, may your vow ever be True. (May your boons be true).

❍ ❍ ❍

५९. फलानि मूलानि च भक्षयन् वने
गिरींश्च पश्यन् सरितः सरांसि च ।
वनं प्रविश्यैव विचित्रपादपं
सुखी भविष्यामि तवास्तु निर्वृतिः ।।

59. Entering the forest which is full of wonderful trees, eating fruits tubers there, seeing mountains, rivers and ponds and lakes in forest, I will be in comfort: (Therefore) Let there be tranquillity in you:

❍ ❍ ❍

६०. एवं स राजा व्यसनाभिपन्नः
शोकेन दुःखेन च पीड्यमानः ।
आलिङ्ग्य पुत्रं सुविनष्टसंज्ञो
मोहं गतो नैव चिचेष्ट किञ्चित् ।।

60. (So spoke Raama to his father before taking his leave)

Yet, overpowered by sorrow of separation (from Raama), tormented by grief, the king hugged his son in (great) sorrow and he became unconscious, losing control of himself. He could not move (his limbs) even a little.

❍ ❍ ❍

६१. देव्यस्ततः संरुरुदः समेताः
तां वर्जयित्वा नरदेवपत्नीम् ।
रुदन् सुमन्त्रोऽपि जगाम मूर्च्छां
हाहाकृतं तत्र बभूव सर्वम् ।।

61. At that moment, every one of his wives who had come

there excepting (Kaikeyi) the one wife of the king, cried aloud. And Sumanthra also became unconscious as he was crying. Everywhere there were (cries of) Ha, Ha.

(Note: In this leave taking scene, Raama tells his father that no purpose will be served by his staying at Ayodhya any longer as Kaikeyi wants him to leave at once. Let the parting be quick. And he assures his father he will return after serving 14 years banishment to serve him. He will honour the commitment made by his father to Kaikeyi as per the two boons he had offered her long ago.)

❍ ❍ ❍

Chapter 35

Sumanthra Censures Kaikeyi

(Sumanthra, Dhascharatha's friend, charioteer, and minister tries to change Kaikeyi's mind. He fails.)

❍ ❍ ❍

१. ततो निर्धूय सहसा शिरो निश्वस्य चासकृत् ।
पाणिं पाणौ विनिष्पिष्य दन्तान् कटकटाप्य च ॥

1. Then (Sumanthra).... Shaking his head violently, breathing hard and taking deep breaths again and again, squeezing his hand over his other hand, biting his teeth hard making 'kata-kat' (sound) ...

❍ ❍ ❍

२. लोचने कोपसंरक्ते वर्णं पूर्वोचितं जहत् ।
कोपाभिभूतः सहसा सन्तापमशुभं गतः ॥

2. ..... .his eyes red with wrath, his usual lustre gone (from his face, totally stricken with wrath, afflicted & tormented by vicious grief, ...

❍ ❍ ❍

३. मनः समीक्षमाणश्च सूतो दशरथस्य सः ।
कम्पयन्निव कैकेय्या हृदयं वाक्छरैः शितैः ।।

3. ...... (this Sumanthra), the charioteer who knew the mind of Dhascharatha, (spoke) sharp arrow like words, as though he would make the heart (and mind) of Kaikeyi tremble ......

❍ ❍ ❍

४. वाक्यवज्रैरनुपमैर्निर्भिन्दन्निव चाशुगैः ।
कैकेय्याः सर्वमर्माणि सुमन्त्रः प्रत्यभाषत ।।

4. ...... (In such a state was he): This Sumanthra spoke 'cruel' words, unmatched; These vajra (thunder bolt) like words appeared as though they would split up Kaikeyi's vital organs (of her body).

❍ ❍ ❍

५. यस्यास्तव पतिस्त्यक्तो राजा दशरथः स्वयम् ।
भर्ता सर्वस्य जगतः स्थावरस्य चरस्य च ।।
न ह्यकार्यतमं किञ्चित्तव देवीह विद्यते ।।

5. Oh lady (Kaikeyi)! There can be nothing more improper in (this world) here for you, than this Dhascharatha, your husband and king, who is verily protector of all the world of living beings and non beings (Immovable things), being abandoned (by you).

❍ ❍ ❍

६. पतिघ्नीं त्वामहं मन्ये कुलघ्नीमपि चान्ततः ।।

6. I consider you as killer of your husband and ultimately, (killer of) the Ikshwaaku race (itself).

❍ ❍ ❍

७. यन्महेन्द्रमिवाजय्यं दुष्प्रकम्प्यमिवाचलम् ।
महोदधिमिवाक्षोभ्यं सन्तापयसि कर्मभिः ।।

7. Because, by your (evil) deed, you have tortured (your

husband) who is unconquerable like Indhra, who is firm, unshakeable like a rock, and who is like the great ocean, unperturbable.

❍ ❍ ❍

८. माऽवमंस्था दशरथं भर्तारं वरदं पतिम् ।
भर्तुरिच्छा हि नारीणां पुत्रकोट्या विशिष्यते ।।

8. Because, for a woman, acting as per the desires of her husband, is more (noble) than (the glory of having) many sons. You should not 'repudiate' your husband Dhascharatha who is protector, who is a Giver (satisfying every one's wish).

❍ ❍ ❍

९. यथावयो हि राज्यानि प्राप्नुवन्ति नृपक्षये ।
इक्ष्वाकुकुलनाथेऽस्मिंस्तल्लोपयितुमिच्छसि ।।

9. When king dies, as per age (and seniority), one obtains the kingdom; (But) You desire to take away this from (Dhascharatha) the lord of Ikshwaaku-s, even (while he is alive!)

❍ ❍ ❍

१०. राजा भवतु ते पुत्रो भरतः शास्तु मेदिनीम् ।
वयं तत्र गमिष्यामि यत्र रामो गमिष्यति ।।

10. Let your son Bharatha become king: Let him rule the earth; (But) We will all go to wherever Raama goes.

❍ ❍ ❍

११. अयोध्यावासिनः पौरा ये च जानपदा जनाः ।
नूनं सर्वेगमिष्यामो मार्गं रामानिषेवितम् ।।

11. The citizens of Ayodhya, men of town and village, and all of us, will now go away, going the way of Raama.

❍ ❍ ❍

१२. त्यक्ताया बान्धवैः सर्वैर्ब्राह्मणैस्साधुभिः सदा ।
का प्रीती राज्यलाभेन तव देवि भविष्यति ।।

12. Oh lady (Kaikeyi)! Abandoned by the (close) relatives, (and by) good and virtuous braamins, what pleasure can there be for you by obtaining this kingdom (for yourself and Bharatha).

❍ ❍ ❍

१३. न हि ते विषये कश्चिद्ब्राह्मणो वस्तुमर्हति ।
तादृशं त्वममर्यादमद्य कर्म चिकीर्षसि ।।

13. In your kingdom, (when Bharatha takes over), no braamin will like to live; because you have done such an improper (immoral) act now.

❍ ❍ ❍

१४. आश्चर्यमिव पश्यामि यस्यास्ते वृत्तमीदृशम् ।
आचरन्त्या न विवृता सद्यो भवति मेदिनी ।।

14. I see only a miracle that this kingdom of yours has not, at this (very) moment become ruined. Such is the (evil) deed of yours.

❍ ❍ ❍

१५. महाब्रह्मर्षिसृष्टा वा ज्वलन्तो भीमदर्शनाः ।
धिग्वाग्दण्डा न हिंसन्ति रामप्रव्राजने स्थिताम् ।।

15. Are these words of reprimand that can burn up one, that are (like) those emanating from the great Bramma Rishi-s, frightful, ...(are they) not causing any hurt upon you who are standing firm in the matter of Raama's exile.

❍ ❍ ❍

१६. आम्रं छित्वा कुठारेण निम्बं परिचरेत्तु यः ।
यश्चैनं पयसा सिञ्चेन्नैवास्य मधुरो भवेत् ।।

16. (Your deed is like this): Like felling a mango tree with an axe and growing a Nimba (Neem) tree (instead)!

Even if one sprinkles milk upon it (and nurtures it) (Fruits with) sweet juice will never come out of it!

❍ ❍ ❍

१७. अभिजातं हि ते मन्ये यथा मातुस्तथैव च ।
न हि निम्बात्स्रवेत्क्षौद्रं लोके निगदितं वचः ।।

17. Just like in your mother, (this wickedness) is born in you as well. I consider it so! Honey cannot come out of Neem tree! These words are proclaimed in the world (as the saying goes).

❍ ❍ ❍

१८. तव मातुरसद्ग्राहं विद्मः पूर्वं यथा श्रुतम् ।।

18. (And Sumanthra tells Kaikeyi about her mother. Sumanthra is an old man. No one likes to hear anything bad about one's mother. Sumanthra hits Kaikeyi where it will hit hard.)

Long ago, I had heard and came to know about your mother's malignant tricks.

❍ ❍ ❍

१९. पितुस्ते वरदः कश्चिद्ददौ वरमनुत्तमम् ।
सर्वभूतरुतं तस्मात्सञ्जज्ञे वसुधाधिपः ।।
तेन तिर्यग्गतानां च भूतानां विदितं वचः ।।

19. A noble man offered a great foremost boon to your father: By this, the lord of earth, (your father, the king of Kekeya) could understand the sounds (and language) of all living beings. Therefore he could understand the speech of even slow moving species (like ants etc).

❍ ❍ ❍

२०. ततो जृम्भस्य शयने विरुताद्भूरिवर्चसः ।
पितुस्ते विदितो भावः स तत्र बहुधाऽहसत् ।।

20. (And once) When your most glorious father was lying down, a sound from an ant (called) Jirumbha (emanated) and its meaning came to be known (to him

because of the boon). And he laughed in many ways (hearing this from the ant).

❍ ❍ ❍

२१. तत्र ते जननी क्रुद्धो मृत्युपाशमभीप्सती ।
हासं ते नृपते सौम्य जिज्ञासामीति चाब्रवीत् ॥

21. Your mother, not even caring for life, asked him thus in anger: = Oh pleasant king! I desire to know (the cause of) your mirth =

❍ ❍ ❍

२२. नृपश्चोवाच तां देवीं देवि शंसामि ते यदि ।
ततो मे मरणं सद्यो भविष्यति न संशयः ॥

22. And the king (your father) addressed this lady (your mother) thus: = Oh Lady! If I tell you, then there will be death for me at once. No doubt about it.=

(The boon was only for the king: He cannot share the secrets with any one else. If he did, it was death for him. Such was the boon.)

❍ ❍ ❍

२३. माता ते पितरं देवि ततः केकयमब्रवीत् ।
शंस मे जीव वा मा न मामपहसिष्यसि ॥

23. Oh lady (Kaikeyi)! Your mother then addressed your father, the king of Kekeya; = Whether you are alive or not, you must tell me; In this matter (dont be flippant and) laugh at me. =

❍ ❍ ❍

२४. प्रियया च तथोक्तः सन् केकयः पृथिवीपतिः ।
तस्मै तं वरदायार्थं कथयामास तत्त्वतः ॥

24. When told thus by his beloved (wife), the lord of earth, the king of Kekeya, reported the matter in detail to the person who had given him (such a) boon.

२५. ततः स वरदः साधू राजानं प्रत्यभाषत ।
म्रियतां ध्वंसतां चेयं मा कृथास्त्वं महीपते ॥

25. And this virtuous man who had given the boon, then replied to the King: = Oh lord of earth ! Let her die or perish. But you should not (tell her) =

❍ ❍ ❍

२६. स तच्छ्रुत्वा वचस्तस्य प्रसन्नमनसो नृपः ।
मातरं ते निरस्याशु विजहार कुबेरवत् ॥

26. Hearing this, his words, the king whose mind became tranquil, at once banished your mother and lived thenceforth like Kubhaera.

❍ ❍ ❍

२७. तथा त्वमपि राजानं दुर्जनाचरिते पथि ।
असद्ग्राहमिमं मोहात्कुरुषे पापदर्शिनि ॥

27. (Such was the fate of your mother, Oh Kaikeyi, says Sumanthra.)

Oh malevolent (Kaikeyi)! Out of passion, you also (like your mother), have followed the path of persons of evil conduct and playing malicious tricks on the king.

❍ ❍ ❍

२८. सत्यश्चाद्य प्रवादोऽयं लौकिकः प्रतिभाति माम् ।
पितॄन् समनुजायन्ते नरा मातरमङ्गनाः ॥

28. It is common knowledge (ancient Saying) that sons take after father and girls after their mother: This truth dawns on me now.

❍ ❍ ❍

२९. नैवं भव गृहाणेदं यदाह वसुधाधिपः ।
भर्तुरिच्छामुपास्वेह जनस्यास्य गतिर्भव ॥

29. (Oh Kaikeyi)! You should not be like this: What (your husband) the lord of earth tells you, that, you must accept (gracefully). Abide by king's wishes. Give solace to the people. Now.

❍ ❍ ❍

३०. मा त्वं प्रोत्साहिता पापैर्देवराजसमप्रभम् ।
भर्तारं लोकभर्तारमसद्धर्ममुपादधाः ॥

30. Instigated by evil persons, do not (lead and) commit your husband who is like Lord Indhra in prowess, who is protector of the world, to the wrong and evil customs (Adharma).

❍ ❍ ❍

३१. न हि मिथ्या प्रतिज्ञातं करिष्यति तवानघः ।
श्रीमान्दशरथो राजा देवि राजीवलोचनः ॥

31. Oh lady (Kaikeyi)! The lotus eyed resplendent king Dhascharatha, being a sinless man, will never be false to his commitment to you.

(It is you who have to withdraw your cruel demand on him.)

❍ ❍ ❍

३२. ज्येष्ठो वदान्यः कर्मण्यः स्वधर्मस्यापि रक्षिता ।
रक्षिता जीवलोकस्य बली रामोऽभिषिच्यताम् ॥

32. May Raama the eldest son who is strong and accomplished, who is protector of the world of living beings, who protects Dharma be anointed (as crown prince).

❍ ❍ ❍

३३. परिवादो हि ते देवि महान् लोके चरिष्यति ।
यदि रामो वनं याति विहाय पितरं नृपम् ॥

33. Oh lady! If Raama goes to forest leaving the king, great censure will be upon you in the world.

❍ ❍ ❍

३४. स्वराज्यं राघवः पातु भव त्वं विगतज्वरा ।
न हि ते राघवादन्यः क्षमः पुरवरे वसेत् ॥

34. Let (Raama) the Raaghava protect his kingdom; You

become freed from this fever (of passion); Because, in this foremost of cities, (in this our Ayodhya) there is none who lives here who is more indulgent to you than (Raama) the Raaghava.

❍ ❍ ❍

३५. रामे हि यौवराज्यस्थे राजा दशरथो वनम् ।
प्रवेक्ष्यति महेष्वासः पूर्ववृत्तमनुस्मरन् ।।

35. Only when Raama is appointed as YuvaRaaja, this great warrior (and Archer) Dhascharatha, our king, will go to forest, remembering (and following) the custom of our ancestors.

(It is the custom of very old kings to seek retirement in forest after handing over his kingdom to a worthy successor.)

❍ ❍ ❍

३६. इति सान्त्वैश्च तीक्ष्णैश्च कैकेयीं राजसंसदि ।
सुमन्त्रः क्षोभयामास भूय एव कृताञ्जलिः ।।

36. With folded arms (of Anjali), Sumanthra tried to 'shake up' Kaikeyi thus in the king's Hall, with many conciliatory words and also with sharp words.

❍ ❍ ❍

३७. नैव सा क्षुभ्यते देवी न च स्म परिदूयते ।
न चास्या मुखवर्णस्य लक्ष्यते विक्रिया तदा ।।

37. (But) this lady was not (disturbed or) pained: Nor was she 'shaken' up; There was absolutely no change in the color of her countenance.

(Note: As Dhascharatha would never back out of his commitment, repudiate his two boons, it was for Kaikeyi to withdraw her demands and seek fulfillment of the two boons in a different way. Sumanthra begs her, censures her. But Kaikeyi is adamant: Raama must go.)

❍ ❍ ❍

Chapter 36

Sidhaartha's Advice

(Having reconciled to Raama's exile, Dhascharatha suggests that Raama should be provided with all comforts during his stay in forest. But Kaikeyi will have none of this; Raama must live like a mendicant there. It is now the old Sidhaartha's turn to change the mind of Kaikeyi.)

❍ ❍ ❍

१. ततः सुमन्त्रमैक्ष्वाकः पीडितोऽत्र प्रतिज्ञया ।
सबाष्पमतिनिश्वस्य जगादैनं पुनः पुनः ।।

1. Then, (Dhascharatha) the Ikshwaaku (king), being bound (and tormented) by this commitment (to Kaikeyi) wept repeatedly with tears coming out, breathing hard and deep; He then said to Sumanthra.

❍ ❍ ❍

२. सूत रत्नसुसंपूर्णा चतुर्विधबला चमूः ।
राघवस्यानुयात्रार्थं क्षिप्रं प्रतिविधीयताम् ।।

2. Oh Charioteer (Sumanthra)! Make ready at once a Foursome Army to go along with Raama the Raaghava on his journey, full with various supplies (for Raama's needs).

❍ ❍ ❍

३. रूपाजीवाश्च शालिन्यो वणिजश्च महाधनाः ।
शोभयन्तु कुमारस्य वाहिनीं सुप्रसारिताः ।।

3. Let attendants, maid servants, renowned merchants (go along) and embellish my son's Army.

❍ ❍ ❍

४. ये चैनमुपजीवन्ति रमते यैश्च वीर्यतः ।
तेषां बहुविधं दत्त्वा तानप्यत्र नियोजय ।।

4. All those who are dependents (of Raama) and all those in whom (Raama) delights because they are valorous, to them all, various gifts must be given. You must entrust them all (in the task of serving Raama) there (on his exile in forest).

❍ ❍ ❍

५. आयुधानि च मुख्यानि नागराः शकटानि च ।
अनुगच्छन्तु काकुत्स्थं व्याधाश्चारण्यगोचराः ।।

5. Let hunters who know (the topography of) forest, foremost weapons, citizens, and vehicles, accompany (Raama the) Kaakuthsa.

❍ ❍ ❍

६. निघ्नन् मृगान् कुञ्जरांश्च पिबंश्चारण्यकं मधु ।
नदीश्च विविधाः पश्यन्न राज्यस्य स्मरिष्यति ।।

6. Hunting animals and elephants (in forest) and drinking forest honeys, seeing various rivers, (Raama) will not think about the kingdom (and miss city life).

❍ ❍ ❍

७. धान्यकोशश्च यः कश्चिद्धनकोशश्च मामकः ।
तौ राममनुगच्छेतां वसन्तं निर्जने वने ।।

7. The grain silos and the treasury chest, may these two follow Raama who is going to live in the uninhabited forest.

❍ ❍ ❍

८. यजन् पुण्येषु देशेषु विसृजश्चाप्तदक्षिणाः ।
ऋषिभिश्च समागम्य प्रवत्स्यति सुखं वने ।।

8. Living in sacred places along with Rishi-s, offering plenty of gifts, performing (Rituals and) Sacrifices, let him live in forest comfortably.

❍ ❍ ❍

९. भरतश्च महाबाहुरयोध्यां पालयिष्यति ।
सर्वकामैः पुनः श्रीमान्रामः संसाध्यतामिति ॥

9. Thus may the resplendent Raama be furnished with all the desirables. And let the mighty limbed Bharatha rule this Ayodhya.

(Seetha is firm: She must and will go with Raama to forest.)

❍ ❍ ❍

१०. एवं ब्रुवति काकुत्स्थे कैकेय्या भयमागतम् ।
मुखं चास्यागमच्छोषं स्वरश्चापि न्यरुध्यत ॥

10. When (Dhascharatha the) Kaakuthsa spoke thus, fear gripped this Kaikeyi. Her face became 'parched up': Her voice 'dropped'.

❍ ❍ ❍

११. सा विवर्णा सुसंत्रस्ता मुखेन परिशुष्यता ।
राजानमेवाभिमुखी कैकेयी वाक्यमब्रवीत् ॥

11. Trembling, her color gone from her parched up face, Kaikeyi addressed the king these words, facing him.

(Who is the boss now; Already Kaikeyi exercises her authority.)

❍ ❍ ❍

१२. राज्यं गतजनं साधो पीतमण्डां सुरामिव ।
निरास्वाद्यतमं शून्यं भरतो नाभिपत्स्यते ॥

12. Oh virtuous (King)! Bharatha (my son) will not accept the kingdom, barren, desolate without inhabitants. It will be like drinking the slurry* of wine, bereft of taste.

(*Poet Vaalmeeki uses the word= Peetha Manda Sura = for the remains in the glass of wine; Obviously, those days, wine was not clarified!)

❍ ❍ ❍

१३. कैकेय्यां मुक्तलज्जायां वदन्त्यामतिदारुणम् ।
राजा दशरथो वाक्यमुवाचायतलोचनाम् ।।

13. When the king heard (such and) most cruel words from Kaikeyi who had cast away her modesty, king Dhascharatha said to this wide eyed woman.

❍ ❍ ❍

१४. वहन्तं किं तुदसि मां नियुज्य धुरि माऽहिते ।
अनार्येकृत्यमारब्धं किं न पूर्वमुपारुधः ।।

14. Oh my Enemy! Having bound me in misery, why do you wound me (further) who is bearing (all this agony): Oh un-Aryan (Kaikeyi) Why did you not (bind me with and), seek this, even at the beginning, at the commencement of (your evil) deed. Don't be (like this) (Why did you not ask all these as part of your boons?).

❍ ❍ ❍

१५. तस्यैतत्क्रोधसंयुक्तमुक्तं श्रुत्वा वराङ्गना ।
कैकेयी द्विगुणं क्रुद्धा राजानमिदमब्रवीत् ।।

15. Hearing such words spoken in wrath by him, this beautiful lady became twice as angry and he addressed the king thus.

❍ ❍ ❍

१६. तवैव वंशे सगरो ज्येष्ठं पुत्रमुपारुधत् ।
असमञ्ज इति ख्यातं तथाऽयं गन्तुमर्हति ।।

16. (Kaikeyi justifies her stand by quoting wrong precedents.)

In your own family, Sagara drove away his eldest son, the renowned Asamanja: Likewise this (Raama) should go.

❍ ❍ ❍

१७. एवमुक्तो धिगित्येव राजा दशरथोऽब्रवीत् ।
व्रीडितश्च जनः सर्वः सा च तं नावबुध्यते ।।

17. When she told him thus, king Dhascharatha merely said: Fie, Fie. And the entire citizens there became ashamed. But she (alone) was insensitive.

❍ ❍ ❍

१८. तत्र वृद्धो महामात्रः सिद्धार्थोनाम नामतः ।
शुचिर्बहुमतो राज्ञः कैकेयीमिदमब्रवीत् ।।

18. At that moment, the old, pure, most honoured by the king, this Sidhdhaartha by name who was high ranking minister, addressed Kaikeyi with these words:

❍ ❍ ❍

१९. असमञ्जो गृहीत्वा तु क्रीडतः पथि दारकान् ।
सरय्वाः प्रक्षिपन्नप्सु रमते तेन दुर्मतिः ।।

19. (Oh Kaikeyi): This evil minded Asamanja (about whom reference is made by you) was seizing children playing in the streets and he was hurling them into the Sarayu river and enjoyed (sadistic pleasure).

❍ ❍ ❍

२०. तं दृष्ट्वा नागराः सर्वेक्रुद्धा राजानमब्रुवन् ।
असमञ्जं वृणीष्वैकमस्मान् वा राष्ट्रवर्धन ।।

20. Seeing all this, the angry citizens, all of them, addressed their king (Sagara) = Oh glorifier of our kingdom! You must chose between this single Asamanja and us (all)=

❍ ❍ ❍

२१. तानुवाच ततो राजा किन्निमित्तमिदं भयम् ।
ताश्चापि राज्ञा संपृष्टा वाक्यं प्रकृतयोऽब्रुवन् ।।

21. To this, king (Sagara) asked them:= What is the cause for this fear.= When questioned by the king thus, these citizens replied with these words:

२२. क्रीडतस्त्वेष नः पुत्रान् बालानुद्भ्रान्तचेतसः ।
सरय्वां पातयन् मौर्ख्यादतुलां प्रीतिमश्नुते ॥

22. This one (this your son) throws our young children who are playing, who are frightened, in Sarayu river and obtains great 'pleasure' out of this folly (of sadism, stupidity).

❍ ❍ ❍

२३. स तासां वचनं श्रुत्वा प्रकृतीनां नराधिपः ।
तं तत्याजाहितं पुत्रं तासां प्रियचिकीर्षया ॥

23. Hearing the words of his subjects, the king then abandoned his inimical son, desirous of doing good to them all.

❍ ❍ ❍

२४. तं यानं शीघ्रमारोप्य सभार्यं सपरिच्छदम् ।
यावज्जीवं विवास्योऽयमिति स्वानन्वशात् पिता ॥

24. His father at once put him on a chariot along with his wife and with necessities and he commanded his own subjects thus = He is Banished For Life (as long as he is alive)=

❍ ❍ ❍

२५. सफालपिटकं गृह्य गिरिदुर्गाण्यलोकयत् ।
दिशः सर्वास्त्वनुचरन् स यथा पापकर्मकृत् ॥

25. This (Asamanja) who indulged in such sinful deeds, taking on a basket and axe, roamed about in all directions, mountain peaks and forest.

❍ ❍ ❍

२६. इत्येनमत्यजद्राजा सगरो वै सुधार्मिकः ।
रामः किमकरोत् पापं येनैवमुपरुध्यते ॥

26. It was thus that the great man of Dharma, king Sagara, abandoned him. For this reason he was "Shut Up"(in

forest): (But) Raama, what sin has he committed? (Tell me Kaikeyi?)

❍ ❍ ❍

२७. न हि कश्चन पश्यामो राघवस्यागुणं वयम् ।
दुर्लभो ह्यस्य निरयः शशाङ्कस्येव कल्मषम् ।।

27. We fail to see any single bad quality in (Raama) the Raaghava: As there can be no stain (darkness) in Moon, there cannot be any hell for him.

❍ ❍ ❍

२८. अथवा देवि दोषं त्वं कञ्चित् पश्यसि राघवे ।
तमद्य ब्रूहि तत्त्वेन ततो रामो विवास्यताम् ।।

28. Oh lady! But if it is not so and if you see any fault in (Raama the) Raaghava, then tell us in detail: Then Raama can be banished now.

❍ ❍ ❍

२९. अदुष्टस्य हि संत्यागः सत्पथे निरतस्य च ।
अप्राप्तस्य विवासोऽयं वनेषु सुयशस्विनः ।।
निर्दहेदपि शक्रस्य द्युतिं धर्मनिरोधनात् ।।

29. When a most famous man, who delights in righteous path, who is not guilty of any sin, who should not receive (any) punishment and who is abandoned (and sent) to forest, this exile is against all norms of Dharma and (as such) will even burn up the glory of Indhra.

❍ ❍ ❍

३०. तदलं देवि रामस्य श्रिया विहतया त्वया ।
लोकतोऽपि हि ते रक्ष्यः परिवादः शुभानने ।।

30. Oh bright faced lady: Therefore protect yourself against the censure of the world, because of the impediment caused by you to Raama's resplendency (Coronation). (Thus Sidhdhaartha advises Kaikeyi.)

३१. श्रुत्वा तु सिद्धार्थवचो राजा श्रान्ततरस्वनः ।
शोकोपहतया वाचा कैकेयीमिदमब्रवीत् ।।

31. After hearing Sidhdhaartha's words, the king who was in a lethargic state, addressed Kaikeyi thus with words full of anguish.

❍ ❍ ❍

३२. एतद्वचो नेच्छसि पापवृत्ते
हितं न जानासि ममात्मनो वा ।
आस्थाय मार्गं कृपणं कुचेष्टा
चेष्टा हि ते साधुपथादपेता ।।

32. Oh evil monger! Following wretched path, you, a wicked woman, are not accepting these words (of advice); You do not know what is good for you and me. Your conduct has deviated from the path of the good and virtuous.

❍ ❍ ❍

३३. अनुव्रजिष्याम्यहमद्य रामं
राज्यं परित्यज्य सुखं धनं च ।
सहैव राज्ञा भरतेन च त्वं
यथासुखं भुङ्क्ष्व चिराय राज्यम् ।।

33. Leaving this kingdom, my pleasures, my wealth, I am now (going and) following Raama. You may enjoy for a long time this kingdom along with (your son) Bharatha, as you please.

❍ ❍ ❍

Chapter 37

Wearing of (Forest) Garments of Bark Materials

(It is Raama who sets Kaikeyi's mind at rest. His forest life is total. He will not "carry Ayodhya" with him on his exile.)

❍ ❍ ❍

१. महामात्रवचः श्रुत्वा रामो दशरथं तदा ।
अन्वभाषत वाक्यं तु विनयज्ञो विनीतवत् ।।

1. After hearing the words of the most exalted (minister Sidhdhaartha), the well behaved Raama addressed Dhascharatha these words respectfully.

❍ ❍ ❍

२. त्यक्तभोगस्य मे राजन् वने वन्येन जीवतः ।
किं कार्यमनुयात्रेण त्यक्तसङ्गस्य सर्वतः ।।

2. Oh king! Having given up all mundane pleasures, given up all attachment, of what use is it to me with all the retinue when I am going to live in forest sustaining myself with forest products?

❍ ❍ ❍

३. यो हि दत्त्वा द्विपश्रेष्ठं कक्ष्यायां कुरुते मनः ।
रज्जुस्नेहेन किं तस्य त्यजतः कुञ्जरोत्तमम् ।।

3. Having given away a foremost elephant, if one sets his mind on (and desires) the Seat (of the elephant), what is the use for him in holding on to (and being attached to) the rope (that ties the seat), when he has already given away the Elephant itself!

(Raama says, when he has abandoned the mighty kingdom itself for a life in forest, what has he got to do with things like chariots, army.)

❍ ❍ ❍

४. तथा मम सतां श्रेष्ठ किं ध्वजिन्या जगत्पते ।
सर्वाण्येवानुजानामि चीराण्येवानयन्तु मे ॥

4. Oh Lord of earth. Oh foremost amongst the virtuous: (oh my father)! Likewise, what is the use of an army to me; I refuse all this; Only (forest apparel) of bark material be brought for me.

❍ ❍ ❍

५. खनित्रपिटके चोभे ममानयत गच्छतः ।
चतुर्दश वने वासं वर्षाणि वसतो मम ॥

5. Going to the forest to live there for 14 years, may a shovel and spade be brought for me for my stay (there).

❍ ❍ ❍

६. अथ चीराणि कैकेयी स्वयमाहृत्य राघवम् ।
उवाच परिधत्स्वेति जनौघे निरपत्रपा ॥

6. At that moment, before the multitude of men, the shameless Kaikeyi herself brought the bark dress and told (Raama) the Raaghava: = Wear This.=

❍ ❍ ❍

७. स चीरे पुरुषव्याघ्रः कैकेय्याः प्रतिगृह्य ते ।
सूक्ष्मवस्त्रं परिक्षिप्य मुनिवस्त्राण्यवस्त ह ॥

7. This (Raama) the 'tiger' of men, receiving this bark dress from Kaikeyi, threw away his royal garments (he was wearing) and wore the dress (worn) by Muni-s (of forest).

❍ ❍ ❍

८. लक्ष्मणश्चापि तत्रैव विहाय वसने शुभे ।
तापसाच्छादने चैव जग्राह पितुरग्रतः ॥

8. And Lakshmana also cast away his shining garments before his father (and others) and covered himself with this apparel of Muni-s (the men of penance of forest).

❍ ❍ ❍

९. अथात्मपरिधानार्थं सीता कौशेयवासिनी ।
समीक्ष्य चीरं संत्रस्ता पृषती वागुरामिव ।।

9. And Seetha who was dressed up in Silken Apparel, observing that there was (one such) bark garment for her to be worn, trembled like a (female) antelope (caught up) at net.

❍ ❍ ❍

१०. सा व्यपत्रपमाणेव प्रगृह्य च सुदुर्मनाः ।
कैकेय्याः कुशचीरे ते जानकी शुभलक्षमणा ।।

10. Somewhat embarrassed, the most auspicious (Seetha) the Jaanaki, received the bark dress from Kaikeyi, down hearted ......

❍ ❍ ❍

११. अश्रुसंपूर्णनेत्रा च धर्मज्ञा धर्मदर्शिनी ।
गन्धर्वराजप्रतिमं भर्तारमिदमब्रवीत् ।।

11. ...... With tears in her eyes, she, who knew Dharma, who ever practised Dharma, addressed her husband who looked like a celestial king (even in that dress), thus:

❍ ❍ ❍

१२. कथं नु चीरं बध्नन्ति मुनयो वनवासिनः ।
इति ह्यकुशला सीता सा मुमोह मुहुर्मुहुः ।।

12. How do Sages living in forest wear these Bark materials? Saying this, ignorant as she was (about the ways of the forest), Seetha, for a moment, was stunned (stupefied).

❍ ❍ ❍

१३. कृत्वा कण्ठे च सा चीरमेकमादाय पाणिना ।
तस्थौ ह्यकुशला सीता व्रीडिता जनकात्मजा ।।

13. This Seetha the daughter of Janaka, (merely) hung out (one piece of) of the Bark 'cloth' around her neck and

held the other in her hand. Not conversant with (such dresses), she stood there bashfully.

❍ ❍ ❍

१४. तस्यास्तत्क्षिप्रमागम्य रामो धर्मभृतां वरः ।
चीरं बबन्ध सीतायाः कौशेयस्योपरि स्वयम् ।।

14. And Raama the most noble amongst followers of Dharma, at once came near Seetha, and he himself dressed up this bark 'cloth' over her silk petticoat.

❍ ❍ ❍

१५. रामं प्रेक्ष्य तु सीताया बध्नन्तं चीरमुत्तमम् ।
अन्तः पुरगता नार्योमुमुचुर्वारि नेत्रजम् ।।

15. When the ladies of the palace saw the foremost Raama dressing up Seetha with bark materials, they shed tears from their eyes.

❍ ❍ ❍

१६. ऊचुश्च परमायस्ता रामं ज्वलिततेजसम् ।
वत्स नैवं नियुक्तेयं वनवासे मनस्विनी ।।

16. Consumed by grief, they addressed Raama who was shining with brilliance (even in that dress)! Oh son, (Oh Raama)! This praiseworthy girl should not be put away to forest like this.

❍ ❍ ❍

१७. पितुर्वाक्यानुरोधेन गतस्य विजनं वनम् ।
तावद्दर्शनमस्या नः सफलं भवतु प्रभो ।।

17. Oh Lord! As per the command of your father till you go to the uninhabited forest and return, may (Seetha's) presence (here) do us good. (Let Seetha live with us during your exile, say these ladies).

❍ ❍ ❍

१८. लक्ष्मणेन सहायेन वनं गच्छस्व पुत्रक ।
नेयमर्हति कल्याणि वस्तुं तापसवद्वने ॥

18. Oh son! With Lakshmana as companion, you go to forest. This auspicious lady does not deserve to live in forest like a woman of penance (like an ascetic).

❍ ❍ ❍

१९. कुरु नो याचनां पुत्र सीता तिष्ठतु भामिनी ।
धर्मनित्यः स्वयं स्थातुं न हीदानीं त्वमिच्छसि ॥

19. Oh son! You must fulfill our request: This endearing Seetha should stay (with us): And as you are resolute in Dharma, you will not desire to stay on here.

(But Seetha is not commanded by Kaikeyi, so she can stay with us.)

❍ ❍ ❍

२०. तासामेवंविधा वाचः श्रृण्वन् दशरथात्मजः ।
बबन्धैव तदा चीरं सीतया तुल्यशीलया ॥

20. (Even) As he was listening to such words (spoken) by them, (Raama) the son of Dhascharatha, tied the bark garments on Seetha who was indeed equal (to him) in good conduct.

❍ ❍ ❍

२१. चीरे गृहीते तु तया समीक्ष्य नृपतेर्गुरुः ।
निवार्य सीतां कैकेयीं वसिष्ठो वाक्यमब्रवीत् ॥

21. When she was dressed up in Bark, the king's Guru (Chief teacher, Priest) Vasishta looking at Kaikeyi, addressed her, to restrain her.

❍ ❍ ❍

२२. अतिप्रवृत्ते दुर्मेधे कैकेयि कुलपांसनि ।
वञ्चयित्वा तु राजानं न प्रमाणेऽवतिष्ठसे ॥

22. Oh Insolent (Kaikeyi)! Oh foolish woman! Oh Kaikeyi who brings the downfall of the family! Having cheated

(your husband) the king, you do not "Stay" within Norms; (have violated Dharma)

❍ ❍ ❍

२३. न गन्तव्यं वनं देव्या सीतया शीलवर्जिते ।
अधिष्ठास्यति रामस्य सीता प्रकृतमासनम् ॥

23. (Oh Kaikeyi) who has strayed from good conduct! Princess Seetha need not go to forest. Seetha may occupy the seat (on the throne) made for Raama (who alone is asked to go to forest).

(Readers are surprised that Vasishta should suggest this. Seetha need not go to forest; but that does not mean she can take over the kingdom of her husband. For once Vasishta loses his composure.)

❍ ❍ ❍

२४. आत्मा हि दाराः सर्वेषां दारसंग्रहवर्तिनाम् ।
आत्मेयमिति रामस्य पालयिष्यति मेदिनीम् ॥

24. As, for all men who lead a good life with their wives, the wives are their souls, this (Seetha) who is Raama's soul, will rule this Earth.

❍ ❍ ❍

२५. अथ यास्यति वैदेही वनं रामेण संगता ।
वयमत्रानुयास्यामः पुरं चेदं गमिष्यति ॥

25. If (Seetha the) Vaidhehi goes along with Raama to forest, we will all go along with him there. This (forest) will become city then!

❍ ❍ ❍

२६. अन्तपालाश्च यास्यन्ति सदारो यत्र राघवः ।
सहोपजीव्यं राष्ट्रं च पुरं च सपरिच्छदम् ॥

26. Wherever Raama (goes along) with his wife, all the chieftains, vassals, villagers, residents of towns, will go there (taking with them) commodities and necessities.

❍ ❍ ❍

२७. भरतश्च सशत्रुघ्नश्चीरवासा वनेचरः ।
वने वसन्तं काकुत्स्थमनुयास्यति पूर्वजम् ।।

27. (And even your own son) Bharatha, along with Schathrugna, wearing dress of Bark, will follow his eldest brother (Raama), the Kaakuthsa, who will be living in forest as a forest dweller.

❍ ❍ ❍

२८. ततः शून्यां गतजनां वसुधां पादपैः सह ।
त्वमेका शाधि दुर्वृत्ता प्रजानामहिते स्थिता ।।

28. Having resorted to doing harm to citizens, you, who are of evil conduct, will rule all alone: (Rule) this desolate Earth bereft of people, Only with (company of) trees.

❍ ❍ ❍

२९. न हि तद्भविता राष्ट्रं यत्र रामो न भूपतिः ।
तद्वनं भविता राष्ट्रं यत्र रामो निवत्स्यति ।।

29. Where Raama is not a ruler, that place can never be a kingdom. And where Raama resides, that place will be a kingdom, even if it be a forest.

❍ ❍ ❍

३०. न ह्यदत्तां महीं पित्रा भरतः शास्तुमर्हति ।
त्वयि वा पुत्रवद्वस्तुं यदि जातो महीपतेः ।।

30. (Your son) Bharatha is born to the lord of earth (Dhascharatha): As such, he will not accept to rule this kingdom as it was not offered by his father and he will not even live with you as your son.

❍ ❍ ❍

३१. यद्यपि त्वं क्षितितलाद्गगनं चोत्पतिष्यसि ।
पितृवंशचरित्रज्ञः सोऽन्यथा न करिष्यति ।।

31. You may 'fly' up in the sky from earth, but he (this son Bharatha) also, who knows the tradition of his father's family, will not go astray.

❍ ❍ ❍

३२. तत्त्वया पुत्रगर्धिन्या पुत्रस्य कृतमप्रियम् ।
लोके हि न स विद्येत यो न राममनुव्रतः ।।

32. Therefore, because of the greed (and passion) towards your son, this harm was done by you to your son. (Because) There is no one in this world who is not a follower of Raama.(Bharatha included).

❍ ❍ ❍

३३. द्रक्ष्यस्यद्यैव कैकेयि पशुव्यालमृगद्विजान् ।
गच्छतः सह रामेण पादपांश्च तदुन्मुखान् ।।

33. Oh Kaikeyi! You will presently witness sheep, cows, elephants, horses, going along with him: Even trees will 'Bend' towards (the path taken by Raama).

❍ ❍ ❍

३४. अथोत्तमान्याभरणानि देवि
देहि स्नुषायै व्यपनीय चीरम् ।
न चीरमस्याः प्रविधीयतेति
न्यवारयत्तद्वसनं वसिष्ठः ।।

34. Oh lady! The Bark materials was not to be bestowed upon her; Now (therefore), putting aside these Bark garments, you give to this "daughter-in-law" (Seetha), foremost ornaments etc. Thus Vasishta restrained (the use of) such (bark) dress (upon Seetha).

❍ ❍ ❍

३५. एकस्य रामस्य वने निवासः
त्वया वृतः केकयराजपुत्रि ।
विभूषितेयं प्रतिकर्मनित्या
वसत्वरण्ये सह राघवेण ।।

35. Oh daughter of Kekeya king! For Raama alone, this forest life was stipulated by you. And this (Seetha) who is to perform rituals along with Raama in forest, should live (there) well ornamented.

❍ ❍ ❍

३६. यानैश्च मुख्यैः परिचारकैश्च
सुसंवृता गच्छतु राजपुत्री ।
वस्त्रैश्च सर्वैः सहितैर्विधानैः
नेयं वृता ते वरसंप्रदाने ॥

36. May this royal princess who has ever (enjoyed comforts of) fine vehicles, and attended upon by servants surrounding her, go (to forest) with all ornaments, and (good) clothes. . In the boon offered to you, this was not provided for (asked for by you that Seetha should dress up in Bark materials).

❍ ❍ ❍

३७. तस्मिंस्तथा जल्पति विप्रमुख्ये
गुरौ नृपस्याप्रतिमप्रभावे ।
नैव स्म सीता विनिवृत्तभावा
प्रियस्य भर्तुः प्रतिकारकामा ॥

37. When the king's Guru, this foremost Braamin (Vasishta) of incomparable brilliance was discoursing thus, Seetha whose desire was (only) to attend upon her beloved husband, did not exhibit any adverse features in her appearance.
(What is good for Raama is good enough for her. What Raama asks her to wear she will wear. Readers may note that two renowned men tried to dissuade Kaikeyi, Vasishta and Siddhhaartha. But Kaikeyi is firm. Raama must go to forest and her son Bharatha must take over.)

❍ ❍ ❍

Chapter 38

Raama Prays for Welfare of (His Mother) Kowsalya

१. तस्यां चीरं वसानायां नाथवत्यामनाथवत् ।
प्रचुक्रोश जनः सर्वोधिक् त्वां दशरथं त्विति ॥

1. When she (this Seetha) who (considered her husband) as her Lord, was dressed up in bark materials (looking like one) without a protector, all the citizens spoke like this to Dhascharatha, crying aloud: = Fie, (Shame, shame) upon you.=

❍ ❍ ❍

२. तेन तत्र प्रणादेन दुःखितः स महीपतिः ।
चिच्छेद जीविते श्रद्धां धर्मेयशसि चात्मनः ।।

2. At that moment, (Dhascharatha) the lord of earth, became very sad by this loud (wailing) sound. And all his attachment for life, Dharma, Fame etc were 'destroyed' (in him: He lost interest in life).

❍ ❍ ❍

३ स निःश्वस्योष्णमैक्ष्वाकस्तां भार्यामिदमब्रवीत् ।
कैकेयि कुशचीरेण न सीता गन्तुमर्हति ।।

3. Breathing hard and emitting hot breath, this Ikshwaaku (king Dhascharatha) addressed his wife thus. Oh Kaikeyi! Seetha should not go dressed in bark.

❍ ❍ ❍

४. सुकुमारी च बाला च सततं च सुखोचिता ।
नेयं वनस्य योग्येति सत्यमाह गुरुर्मम ।।

4. She is a sweet (young) girl. She is a child, used to comforts, (deserves comforts). My Guru (Vasishta) has also said this truth that this forest (garment) is not proper (on her).

❍ ❍ ❍

५. इयं हि कस्यापकरोति किञ्चित्
तपस्विनी राजवरस्य कन्या ।
या चीरमासाद्य जनस्य मध्ये
स्थिता विसंज्ञा श्रमणीव काचित् ।।

5. And she is the daughter of the most noble amongst kings. Has clear conception and knowledge (of Dharma). An

austere person. And she is now standing dressed up in Bark as though she is some menial person. What harm has she ever done to any one?

❍ ❍ ❍

६. चीराण्यपास्याज्जनकस्य कन्या
नेयं प्रतिज्ञा मम दत्तपूर्वा ।
यथासुखं गच्छतु राजपुत्री
वनं समग्रा सह सर्वरत्नैः ।।

6. This daughter of Janaka, this Seetha, must cast away these bark garments. This stipulation was not contained in the (Boon) offered by me to you before... This royal princess must go to forest fully provided and along with all her ornaments and as she pleases.

❍ ❍ ❍

७. अजीवनार्हेण मया नृशंसा
कृता प्रतिज्ञा नियमेन तावत् ।
त्वया हि बाल्यात् प्रतिपन्नमेतत्
तन्मां दहेद्वेणुमिवात्मपुष्पम् ।।

7. This cruel order was committed to by me because death is nearing me (and as I deserve death); out of your childishness and because of restraint (due to my Dharma), this has been obtained by you. And because of (all) this it is burning me up like a bamboo rubbing against full grown bamboo.

(It is well known forest fires are started by frictional heat of trees).

❍ ❍ ❍

८. रामेण यदि ते पापे किञ्चित् कृतमशोभनम् ।
अपकारः क इह ते वैदेह्या दर्शितोऽथ मे ।।

8. Oh sinful (Kaikeyi)! Even if any impropriety upon you was done by Raama (in any way), what misconduct was done to you by (Seetha) the Vaidhehi which was brought up before me?

❍ ❍ ❍

९. मृगीवोत्फल्लनयना मृदुशीला तपस्विनी ।
अपकारं कमिव ते करोति जनकात्मजा ।।

9. What harm has this (Seetha) the daughter of Janaka who is an austere girl, who is like a (young) female deer, whose eyes blossom (with joy) and who is of soft nature and conduct, done to you.

❍ ❍ ❍

१०. ननु पर्याप्तमेकं ते पापे रामविवासनम् ।
किमेभिः कृपणैर्भूयः पातकैरपि ते कृतैः ।।

10. Oh sinful (Kaikeyi)! Are you not satisfied with this single act of sending away Raama. And more than this, why, why all this wretched sinful acts for you, further (further more).

❍ ❍ ❍

११. प्रतिज्ञातं मया तावत्त्वयोक्तं देवि शृण्वता ।
रामं यदभिषेकाय त्वमिहागतमब्रवीः ।।

11. Oh Lady! What you said, (and asked for) was only in respect of Raama who had come here to be anointed as YuvaRaaja. Committed by me to what was asked by you (through your two boons), (that alone) was promised by me.

(There was nothing in the boons that you asked for about Seetha's exile or her dress etc.)

❍ ❍ ❍

१२. तत्त्वेतत् समतिक्रम्य निरयं गन्तुमिच्छसि ।
मैथिलीमपि या हि त्वमीक्षसे चीरवासिनीम् ।।

12. Transgressing this (and overstepping your limit) now, you are such as to desire to see (Seetha) the Maithili dressed up in bark garments; Therefore, you desire (& deserve) to go to hell.

❍ ❍ ❍

१३. इतीव राजा विलपन् महात्मा
शोकस्य नान्तं स ददर्श किञ्चित् ।
भृशातुरत्वाच्च पपात भूमौ
तेनैव पुत्रव्यसने निमग्नः ॥

13. There was no end to the suffering of this great soul king who was wailing thus; Steeped in sorrow at the (impending) misfortune to his son, he fell down on earth, greatly sick of mind and body.

❍ ❍ ❍

१४. एवं ब्रुवन्तं पितरं रामः सम्प्रस्थितो वनम् ।
अवाक्छिरसमासीनमिदं वचनमब्रवीत् ॥

14. And with his head down, Raama who was getting ready to go to forest, addressed his father who was speaking thus and who was lying down (on bare floor), the following words.

❍ ❍ ❍

१५. इयं धार्मिक कौसल्या मम माता यशस्विनी ।
वृद्धा चाक्षुद्रशीला च न च त्वां देव गर्हते ॥

15. Oh man of Dharma! Oh my lord! My mother, this renowned Kowsalya who is old, whose conduct is never mean, has never behaved reproachfully towards you.

❍ ❍ ❍

१६. मया विहीनां वरद प्रपन्नां शोकसागरम् ।
अदृष्टपूर्वव्यसनां भूयः सम्मन्तुमर्हसि ॥

16. Oh munificent (King)! You should show even greater consideration to her (because) she will be without me, she is submerged in grief and has never seen any suffering before.

❍ ❍ ❍

१७. पुत्रशोकं यथा नर्च्छेत्त्वया पूज्येन पूजिता ।
मां हि सञ्चिन्तयन्तीयमपि जीवेत्तपस्विनी ॥

17. This austere lady who is ever thinking and worrying about me, must be honoured by you who are most worshipful. in such a way that she will not be afflicted (infatuated by) pangs of separation of her son and live on.

❍ ❍ ❍

१८. इमां महेन्द्रोपम जातगर्धिनीं
तथा विधातुं जननीं ममार्हसि ।
यथा वनस्थे मयि शोककर्शिता
न जीवितं न्यस्य यमक्षयं व्रजेत् ।।

18. (Oh my father) who is like Indhra! Agonized by grief (as she is now), this, my mother who brought me into existence (& nurtured me), you must bestow upon her (great attention) in such a way that she may not give up her life and go to abode of death.

❍ ❍ ❍

Chapter 39

(Raama) Takes Leave to Go to Forest

१. रामस्य वचनं श्रुत्वा मुनिवेषधरं च तम् ।
समीक्ष्य सह भार्याभी राजा विगतचेतनः ।।

1. Hearing Raama's words, the king who was surrounded by his wives, stared at him who was dressed up (in 'Bark') as a Muni. And he lost control of himself.

❍ ❍ ❍

२. नैनं दुःखेन सन्तप्तः प्रत्यवैक्षत राघवम् ।
न चैनमभिसंप्रेक्ष्य प्रत्यभाषत दुर्मनाः ।।

2. Tormented by grief, and in very low spirits, he could not look at Raama nor even speak to him.

❍ ❍ ❍

३. स मुहूर्तमिवासंज्ञो दुःखितश्च महीपतिः ।
विललाप महाबाहू राममेवानुचिन्तयन् ।।

3. The mighty limbed (Dhascharatha) the lord of earth, became unconscious for a while; Then thinking about Raama, he wailed in grief.

❍ ❍ ❍

४. मन्ये खलु मया पूर्वं विवत्सा बहवः कृताः ।
प्राणिनो हिंसिता वापि तस्मादिदमुपस्थितम् ।।

4. (And Dhascharatha wailed thus); Perhaps, in my previous births, many lives were harmed by me and made to be separated from their young ones: That is why this has befallen me, I think.

(Readers may note that an Indian always thinks this way in distress.)

❍ ❍ ❍

५. न त्वेवानागते काले देहाच्च्यवति जीवितम् ।
कैकेय्या क्लिश्यमानस्य मृत्युर्मम न विद्यते ।।

5. Life does not depart till his time is up: That is why, Death has not come to me also (now) who am tormented by Kaikeyi.

(Death chooses its time, not ours!)

❍ ❍ ❍

६. योऽहं पावकसङ्काशं पश्यामि पुरतः स्थितम् ।
विहाय वसने सूक्ष्मे तापसाच्छादनात्मजम् ।।

6. Such as I am, am now seeing Raama my son, who is (brilliant) like fire, standing before me dressed up in bark apparel (worn by) men of penance, having discarded fine silken robes.

❍ ❍ ❍

७. एकस्याः खलु कैकेय्याः कृतेऽयं क्लिश्यते जनः ।
स्वार्थेप्रयतमानायाः संश्रित्य निकृतिं त्विमाम् ।।

7. Because of the deed of this one person Kaikeyi who indulged in this trickery intent upon achieving her selfish ends, this entire population is in torment.

❍ ❍ ❍

८. एवमुक्त्वा तु वचनं बाष्पेण पिहितेक्षणः ।
रामेति सकृदेवोक्त्वा व्याहर्तुं न शशाक ह ॥

8. Saying these words, with his eyes covered by tears, he just uttered = Oh Raama = once; but could not speak further.

❍ ❍ ❍

९. संज्ञां तु प्रतिलभ्यैव मुहूर्तात् स महीपतिः ।
नेत्राभ्यामश्रुपूर्णाभ्यां सुमन्त्रमिदमब्रवीत् ॥

9. After sometime, the lord of earth (Dhascharatha), regained his consciousness, then looked at Sumanthra and said, with his eyes filled with tears.

❍ ❍ ❍

१०. औपवाह्यं रथं युक्त्वा त्वमायाहि हयोत्तमैः ।
प्रापयैनं महाभागमितो जनपदात् परम् ॥

10. You bring a royal chariot yoked to fine horse: You take this most illustrious (Raama) from here and lead him beyond the inhabited territory.

❍ ❍ ❍

११. एवं मन्ये गुणवतां गुणानां फलमुच्यते ।
पित्रा मात्रा च यत्साधुर्वीरो निर्वास्यते वनम् ॥

11. It is said that even for the most virtuous, the (fruits) and the consequence of the deeds (done in their previous births) turn out this way (in their present birth). That is why this virtuous and brave (Raama) has been expelled by his father and mother to forest. I think.

(This is the Indian thought. However good a man may be pays for his past sins in this life.)

❍ ❍ ❍

१२. राज्ञो वचनमाज्ञाय सुमन्त्रः शीघ्रविक्रमः ।
योजयित्वाऽऽययौ तत्र रथमश्वैरलंकृतम् ॥

12. Sumanthra who always acted quickly, obeying his

king's words (of command), brought there a well decorated chariot yoked to horses.

❍ ❍ ❍

१३. तं रथं राजपुत्राय सूतः कनकभूषितम् ।
आचचक्षेऽञ्जलिं कृत्वा युक्तं परमवाजिभिः ।।

13. The charioteer (Sumanthra) with his hands cupped in Anjali, announced that a chariot decorated in gold (and yoked to) foremost horses, was ready for (Raama) the son of the king.

❍ ❍ ❍

१४. राजा सत्वरमाहूय व्यापृतं वित्तसञ्चये ।
उवाच देशकालज्ञो निश्चितं सर्वतः शुचिम् ।।

14. King (Dhascharatha) who knew the time and place (for anything), soon called the officer of the Treasury who had sound judgement of Finance and who was pure (and honest), with: treasury funds. And he said to him.

❍ ❍ ❍

१५. वासांसि च महार्हाणि भूषणानि वराणि च ।
वर्षाण्येतानि संख्याय वैदेह्याः क्षिप्रमानय ।।

15. Calculating the needs of (Seetha the) Vaidhehi for these (14) years, you bring at once worthy dresses and foremost ornaments.

❍ ❍ ❍

१६. नरेन्द्रेणैवमुक्तस्तु गत्वा कोशगृहं ततः ।
प्रायच्छत् सर्वमाहृत्य सीतायै सर्वमेव तत् ।।

16. When he was told thus by the king, he at once went over to the treasury house, brought all of them & placed before Seetha, all of it.

❍ ❍ ❍

१७. सा सुजाता सुजातानि वैदेही प्रस्थिता वनम् ।
भूषयामास गात्राणि तैर्विचित्रैर्विभूषणैः ।।

17. Then this (Seetha) the * 'divine' Vaidhehi who was of noble birth and who was leaving for forest, began to ornament herself with wonderful ornaments on her well formed body.

(*Poet uses word -Saa- Translator has used divine.)

❍ ❍ ❍

१८. व्यराजयत वैदेही वेश्म तत्सुविभूषिता ।
उद्यतोंऽशुमतः काले खं प्रभेव विवस्वतः ।।

18. When (Seetha) the Vaidhehi was well ornamented, she made the palace glitter like rays of rising sun in the morning, giving lustre to the sky.

❍ ❍ ❍

१९. तां भुजाभ्यां परिष्वज्य श्वश्रूर्वचनमब्रवीत् ।
अनाचरन्तीं कृपणं मूध्न्र्युपाघ्राय मैथिलीम् ।।

19. Her mother-in-law (Kowsalya), with her two hands, hugged (Seetha) the Maithili who did not give way to her misery & sorrow, She kissed her on her forehead and said these words.

❍ ❍ ❍

२०. असत्यः सर्वलोकेऽस्मिन् सततं सत्कृताः प्रियैः ।
भर्तारं नानुमन्यन्ते विनिपातगतं स्त्रियः ।।

20. In all this world, unfaithful women will not (care for nor) honour their husbands who are 'fallen' down by calamity, although they had always been loved and honoured (by their husbands before).

❍ ❍ ❍

२१. एष स्वभावो नारीणामनुभूय पुरा सुखम् ।
अल्पामप्यापदं प्राप्य दुष्यन्ति प्रजहत्यपि ।।

21. After enjoying all pleasures before, (these women) begin to censure their husbands even though they suffer minor difficulties only. They (even) desert (their husbands). This is the nature of women.

❍ ❍ ❍

२२. असत्यशीला विकृता दुर्ग्राह्यहृदयाः सदा ।
युवत्यः पापसङ्कल्पाः क्षणमात्रविरागिणः ।।

22. Young girls are prone to go astray; they easily change; they easily fall into sinful ways; In just a moment they abandon (their husbands in misfortune).

❍ ❍ ❍

२३. न कुलं न कृतं विद्यां न दत्तं नापि संग्रहम् ।
स्त्रीणां गृह्णाति हृदयमनित्यहृदया हि ताः ।।

23. Their affections are transient: their heart is never set on their (husband's) family; they (never give thought to all the good) done to them (in their husband's place;) they have no wisdom; All this in spite of being offered in marriage (under oath, before holy fire).

❍ ❍ ❍

२४. साध्वीनां तु स्थितानां हि शीले सत्ये श्रुते शमे ।
स्त्रीणां पवित्रं परमं पतिरेको विशिष्यते ।।

24. For women of blemishless character who are steadfast in Truth, moral conduct, in Vedha-s, and in forbearance, etc, husband alone is the supreme means of purification. (Thus it is spoken off) with distinction.

❍ ❍ ❍

२५. स त्वया नावमन्तव्यः पुत्रः प्रव्राजितो मम ।
तव दैवतमस्त्वेष निर्धनः सधनोऽपि वा ।।

25. This my son who is being sent away on exile, must not to be treated with contempt by you. May he be your living God, whether he is with wealth or without wealth.

❍ ❍ ❍

२६. विज्ञाय वचनं सीता तस्या धर्मार्थसंहितम् ।
कृताञ्जलिरुवाचेदं श्वश्रूमभिमुखे स्थिता ।।

26. Understanding (the significance of) her speech, Seetha addressed her mother-in-law, facing her with her hands cupped in Anjali, the following words endowed with (essence of) Dharma.

❍ ❍ ❍

२७. करिष्ये सर्वमेवाहमार्या यदनुशास्ति माम् ।
अभिज्ञाऽस्मि यथा भर्तुर्वर्तितव्यं श्रुतं च मे ॥

27. (Kowsalya need not have taken all this trouble to advise Seetha and enlighten her on the duties of a faithful wife. The very fact that Seetha chooses to go along with her husband to forest should be enough to prove Seetha's qualifications. With all her prayers, worship and faith in Gods, Kowsalya appears as an average person: And Seetha gives dignified reply to Kowsalya thus)

How (a wife) should behave towards her husband, has been heard by me (even before as I have already been enlightened by my parents). Yet I am being enlightened (by you now). What all my noble (mother-in-law) advises me now, I will do that.

❍ ❍ ❍

२८. न मामसज्जनेनार्या समानयितुमर्हति ।
धर्माद्विचलितुं नाहमलं चन्द्रादिव प्रभा ॥

28. (You), my noble (mother-in-law) should not compare me with ordinary vulgar women. Like light following Moon, I will not go astray from Dharma.

❍ ❍ ❍

२९. नातन्त्री वाद्यते वीणा नाचक्रो वर्तते रथः ।
नापतिः सुखमेधेत या स्यादपि शतात्मजा ॥

29. The (musical instrument) Veena will not play without strings; Chariot will not go without wheels; Woman, even if she has 100 sons, cannot obtain happiness without her husband.

❍ ❍ ❍

३०. मितं ददाति हि पिता मितं माता मितं सुतः ।
अमितस्य हि दातारं भर्तारं का न पूजयेत् ।।

30. A father gives in measure (only). A mother gives, in measure. A son also gives only in measure; Who will not then honour a husband who gives limitless (to his wife).

❍ ❍ ❍

३१. साऽहमेवं गता श्रेष्ठा श्रुतधर्मपरावरा ।
आर्येकिमवमन्ये यं स्त्रीणां भर्ताहि दैवतम् ।।

31. For women, husband alone is a (living) God: Oh Aryan (Kowsalya)! Such as I am who has been enlightened about traditional values of Dharma, who follows this path as it is auspicious, how (then) will I disrespect him (dishonour my Raama).

❍ ❍ ❍

३२. सीताया वचनं श्रुत्वा कौसल्या हृदयङ्गमम् ।
शुद्धसत्त्वा मुमोचाश्रु सहसा दुःखहर्षजम् ।।

32. Hearing such heart warming words of Seetha, the pure wise Kowsalya at once shed tears of joy and sorrow. (Joy because Seetha is so steadfast in Dharma; sorrow because she is going away).

❍ ❍ ❍

३३. तां प्राञ्जलिरभिक्रम्य मातृमध्येऽतिसत्कृताम् ।
रामः परमधर्मज्ञो मातरं वाक्यमब्रवीत् ।।

33. Raama the most knowledgeable man of Dharma, then approached his most revered mother who was in the midst of all his 'mothers' and said these words, his hands cupped in Anjali.

❍ ❍ ❍

३४. अम्ब मा दुःखिता भूस्त्वं पश्य त्वं पितरं मम ।
क्षयोऽपि वनवासस्य क्षिप्रमेव भविष्यति ।।

34. Oh mother! You should not be in such a sorrow; You should look after my father. The end of my (14 years) stay in forest will come about quickly.

❍ ❍ ❍

३५. सुप्तायास्ते गमिष्यन्ति नव वर्षाणि पञ्च च ।
सा समग्रमिह प्राप्तं मां द्रक्ष्यसि सुहृद्वृतम् ।।

35. The (9 plus 5) 14 years will pass away just like your (overnight) sleep. You will see me amidst my friends, having returned here (after completing my exile) fully. (Thus Raama consoled his mother Kowsalya.)

❍ ❍ ❍

३६. एतावदभिनीतार्थमुक्त्वा स जननीं वचः ।
त्रयश्शतशतार्धा हि ददर्शाविक्ष्य मातरः ।।

36. Raama's (step) Mothers were 350. After addressing his own mother (Kowsalya) with proper speech thus, he (pondered for a while and) he 'saw' (them all).

❍ ❍ ❍

३७. ताश्चापि स तथैवार्ता मातृर्दशरथात्मजः ।
धर्मयुक्तमिदं वाक्यं निजगाद कृताञ्जलिः ।।

37. (Yet another example of Raama's noble character.)

Then with folded arms (in Anjali), this son of Dhascharatha addressed all these (step) mothers who were afflicted with grief, with these words with content of Dharma.

❍ ❍ ❍

३८. संवासात् परुषं किञ्चिदज्ञानाद्वापि यत्कृतम् ।
तन्मे समनुजानीत सर्वाश्चामन्त्रयामि वः ।।

38. If I had caused any harm to you,, either in my ignorance or out of my attachment, (out of taking liberty with you), that, you must forgive. I am bidding you all farewell. (Give me leave to go, I beg).

❍ ❍ ❍

३९. वचनं राघवस्यैतद्धर्मयुक्तं समाहितम् ।
शुश्रुवुस्ताः स्त्रियः सर्वाः शोकोपहतचेतसः ।।

39. All the ladies (all the 350 wives of his father) who were all downhearted afflicted by grief, heard these words of Raama spoken with deliberation and endowed with Dharma.

❍ ❍ ❍

४०. जज्ञेऽथ तासां संनादः क्रौञ्चीनामिव निस्वनः ।
मानवेन्द्रस्य भार्याणामेवं वदति राघवे ।।

40. While (Raama the) Raaghava was speaking thus, the wailing of these women who were king's wives appeared like cooing of Krauncha birds.

❍ ❍ ❍

४१. मुरजपणवमेघघोषवत्
दशरथवेश्म बभूव यत्पुरा ।
विलपितपरिदेवनाकुलं
व्यसनगतं तदभूत् सुदुःखितम् ।।

41. Where the strains of music from instruments like Murasa and Panava sounding like vibrant clouds were heard before, now, this palace of king Dhascharatha, was full with sounds of wailing and crying. It was fallen into a state of 'calamity' and was in deep sorrow.

(Poet Vaalmeeki brings out the character of Raama and Seetha. This lady of Dharma is not a timid girl. She 'chides' her mother-in-law, by saying that she knows what Dharma of a wife is as she has already been enlightened by her parents. Poet Vaalmeeki's reference in stanza 27 is very significant. And Raama's leave-taking before all his 'mothers' shows his consideration, his character.)

❍ ❍ ❍

Chapter 40

Citizens (Try to) Go Along (With Raama)

(Raama departs with his wife Seetha and brother Lakshmana to forest. The grieving citizens try to go along with him to forest.)

❍ ❍ ❍

१. अथ रामश्च सीता च लक्ष्मणश्च कृताञ्जलिः ।
उपसंगृह्य राजानं चक्रुर्दीनाः प्रदक्षिणम् ।।

1. Feeling depressed, Raama, Seetha and Lakshmana, with their hands cupped in Anjali, prostrated before them and went around them in circumbumbulation.

❍ ❍ ❍

२. तं चापि समनुज्ञाप्य धर्मज्ञः सीतया सह ।
राघवः शोकसम्मूढो जननीमभ्यवादयत् ।।

2. After making them give permission for him to leave, Raama who was (somewhat) perplexed due to grief, this (Raama the) Raaghava the knower of Dharma, along with Seetha, then prostrated before his mother (Kowsalya).

❍ ❍ ❍

३. अन्वक्षं लक्ष्मणो भ्रातुः कौसल्यामभ्यवादयत् ।
अथ मातुः सुमित्राया जग्राह चरणौ पुनः ।।

3. And Lakshmana followed his brother and prostrated before Kowsalya and then after they fell at the feet of (his mother) Sumithra.

❍ ❍ ❍

४. तं वन्दमानं रुदती माता सौमित्रिगब्रवीत् ।
हितकामा महाबाहुं मूर्ध्न्युपाघ्राय लक्ष्मणम् ।।

4. Mother (Sumithra) who was well wisher of everyone and who was crying, kissed the son of Sumithra, the mighty limbed (Lakshmana) on his forehead. And she said to him.

❍ ❍ ❍

५. सृष्टस्त्वं वनवासाय स्वनुरक्तः सुहृज्जने ।
रामे प्रमादं मा कार्षीः पुत्र भ्रातरि गच्छति ॥

5. Oh my son (Lakshmana)! You are indeed (born)*, created for forest life! With great devotion to Raama, your brother who is a friend of all, you should never give room for negligence as he goes out (to forest with Seetha on exile).

(Why poet Vaalmeeki says that Lakshmana is 'Created' for forest life is significant. He uses the word= Srishta=*)

❍ ❍ ❍

६. व्यसनी वा समृद्धो वा गतिरेष तवानघ ।
एष लोके सतां धर्मोयज्जेष्ठवशगो भवेत् ॥

6. In this world, if service to elders (like elder brother) is there, That, is the Dharma of the virtous. Oh sinless (Lakshmana)! He, (your elder brother Raama) is your refuge, whether he is in prosperity or in difficulties.

❍ ❍ ❍

७. इदं हि वृत्तमुचितं कुलस्यास्य सनातनम् ।
दानं दीक्षा च यज्ञेषु तनुत्यागो मृधेषु च ॥
ज्येष्ठस्याप्यनुवृत्तिश्च राजवंशस्य लक्षणम् ॥

7. (One of the most noble characters in Raamaayana, this Sumithra).

This is verily the proper conduct traditionally (eternally) practised by your race. To serve elders and follow them. Sacrifice: Consideration and dedication in Ritual ceremonies: Sacrifice one's own life in war;.... All these are the characteristics of your race.

❍ ❍ ❍

८. लक्ष्मणं त्वेवमुक्त्वा सा संसिद्धं प्रियराघवम् ।
सुमित्रा गच्छ गच्छेति पुनः पुनरुवाच तम् ।।

8. Having said thus to the accomplished Lakshmana who was very dear to (Raama the) Raaghava, Sumithra said again and again:= You Go, You Go.=

❍ ❍ ❍

९. गम्यतामर्थलाभाय क्षेमाय विजयाय च ।
शत्रुपक्षविनाशाय पुनः संदर्शनाय च ।।

9. ...... (and Sumithra said) again.. You May Go.(to forest with Raama): For the sake of wealth (of Dharma): For the sake of welfare and tranquility (of the world): For the sake of victory (of Truth over falsehood): For the destruction of inimical forces; And for consideration of your *friendship (with Raama).

(Poet Vaalmeeki uses the word *= Samdharshana= to be seen together: Readers know Lakshmana is ever with Raama.)

❍ ❍ ❍

१०. रामं दशरथं विद्धि मां विद्धि जनकात्मजाम् ।
अयोध्यामटवीं विद्धि गच्छ तात यथासुखम् ।।

10. Oh dear (son Lakshmana)! Consider Raama as (your father) Dhascharatha. Consider (Seetha) the daughter of Janaka as me, (your mother). Consider forest as Ayodhya. You may go as you please.

(Thus this noble woman of Dharma Sumithra spoke giving leave to her son Lakshmana to go to forest although Lakshmana was .not bound by the two Boons of his step mother Kaikeyi. Sumithra knows that in protecting Raama in forest, her son was protecting Dharma itself.)

❍ ❍ ❍

११. ततः सुमन्त्रः काकुत्स्थं प्राञ्जलिर्वाक्यमब्रवीत् ।
विनीतो विनयज्ञश्च मातलिर्वासवं यथा ।।

11. And the modest Sumanthra who knew the virtue of modesty, with his hands cupped in Anjali, addressed these words to (Raama) the Kaakuthsa, just like (Indhra's charioteer) Maathali addressing Indhra.

❍ ❍ ❍

१२. रथमारोह भद्रं ते राजपुत्र महायशः ।
क्षिप्रं त्वां प्रापयिष्यामि यत्र मां राम वक्ष्यसि ॥

12. Oh most famous royal prince, Oh Raama! You may mount the chariot. Welfare to you. Wherever you tell me to go, I will take you quickly.

❍ ❍ ❍

१३. चतुर्दश हि वर्षाणि वस्तव्यानि वने त्वया ।
तान्युपक्रमितव्यानि यानि देव्याऽसि चोदितः ॥

13. Because, the 14 years that are to be lived by you in forest, is to commence now as you are directed by the lady (Kaikeyi).

❍ ❍ ❍

१४. तं रथं सूर्यसङ्काशं सीता हृष्टेन चेतसा ।
आरुरोह वरारोहा कृत्वाऽलङ्कारमात्मनः ॥

14. The well dressed Seetha who had lovey hips, got into the chariot that was (shining) like the Sun, with a happy mind.

❍ ❍ ❍

१५. अथो ज्वलनसङ्काशं चामीकरविभूषितम् ।
तमारुरुहतुस्तूर्णं भ्रातरौ रामलक्ष्मणौ ॥

15. Then the brothers, Raama and Lakshmana, got in quickly into it that was sparkling like flame and which was ornamented in gold.

❍ ❍ ❍

१६. वनवासं हि संख्याय वासांस्याभरणानि च ।
भर्तारमनुगच्छन्त्यै सीतायै श्वशुरो ददौ ॥
तथैवायुधजातानि भ्रातृभ्यां कवचानि च ॥

16. Calculating the needs for life in forest, her father.in.law offered to Seetha who was following her husband, dresses and ornaments. like wise (he gave) to the brothers, diverse Arms and armours ......

❍ ❍ ❍

१७. रथोपस्थे प्रतिन्यस्य सचर्म कठिनं च तत् ।
सीतातृतीयानारुढान्दृष्ट्वा धृष्टमचोदयत् ।।
सुमन्त्रः संमतानश्वान् वायुवेगसमाञ्जवे ।।

17. ..... And placing the basket that was made of leather in the centre of the Chariot, Sumanthra who saw the three of them including Seetha duly seated on the chariot, then speeded up the esteemed horses which, in speed, could go like the wind, with firmness.

❍ ❍ ❍

१८. प्रयाते तु महारण्यं चिररात्राय राघवे ।
बभूव नगरे मूर्च्छा बलमूर्च्छा जनस्य च ।।

18. As Raama was going to the great forest for a long stay (of 14 years), hallucination and stupefaction seized the citizens of the city.

❍ ❍ ❍

१९. तत्समाकुलसंभ्रान्तं मत्तसङ्कुपितद्विपम् ।
हयशिञ्जितनिर्घोषं पुरमासीन्महास्वनम् ।।

19. The city was bewildered, agitated. Was full of elephants that were mad with anger; Rattling noise from horses (were heard); Humming noises (were heard).

❍ ❍ ❍

२०. ततः सबालवृद्धा सा पुरी परमपीडिता ।
राममेवाभिदुद्राव घर्मार्तः सलिलं यथा ।।

20. (There was an exodus from the city, unable to bear separation from Raama)
The residents of the city, young and old, every one, was

tormented greatly and ran towards Raama, like a man suffering from heat, rushing towards water.

❍ ❍ ❍

२१. पार्श्वतः पृष्ठतश्चापि लंबमानास्तदुन्मुखाः ।
बाष्पपूर्णमुखाः सर्वेतमूचुर्भृशनिस्वनाः ॥

21. Their faces covered by tears; making loud noises; looking at Raama from side and behind; (Following him and trying) to stay close to him; they then said: (to charioteer Sumanthra).

❍ ❍ ❍

२२. संयच्छ वाजिनां रश्मीन् सूत याहि शनैः शनैः ।
मुखं द्रक्ष्याम रामस्य दुर्दर्शं नो भविष्यति ॥

22. Oh Charioteer! Please tighten the leash and go slowly. We (desire to) see Raama's face: (At your speed) it will become impossible to see (Raama).

❍ ❍ ❍

२३. आयसं हृदयं नूनं राममातुरसंशयम् ।
यद्देवगर्भप्रतिमे वनं याति न भिद्यते ॥

23. (They wailed thus): Raama's mother's heart is steel: No doubt! Because, (Even) now when (Raama) who is like a celestial born, is going away, it has not 'split up'.

❍ ❍ ❍

२४. कृतकृत्या हि वैदेही छायेवानुगता पतिम् ।
न जहाति रता धर्मेमेरुमर्कप्रभा यथा ॥

24. (Seetha the) Vaidhehi follows the path of Dharma like rays of Sun over Meru mountain. She follows her husband like a shadow, without abandoning him. She is indeed most dutiful. (accomplished).

❍ ❍ ❍

२५. अहो लक्ष्मण सिद्धार्थः सततं प्रियवादिनम् ।
भ्रातरं देवसङ्काशं यस्त्वं परिचरिष्यसि ॥

25. Oh Lakshmana! Ah! You, who are like a celestial, who ever speaks sweetly (and kindly), are indeed most accomplished as you (ever) serve your brother (Raama).

❍ ❍ ❍

२६. महत्येषा हि ते सिद्धिरेष चाभ्युदयो महान् ।
एष स्वर्गस्य मार्गश्च यदेनमनुगच्छसि ॥

26. You are following him: This indeed is most luminous. This, is the greatest accomplishment. Therefore this is the 'route' to heaven.

❍ ❍ ❍

२७. एवं वदन्तस्ते सोढुं न शेकुर्बाष्पमागतम् ।
नरास्तमनुगच्छन्तः प्रियमिक्ष्वाकुनन्दनम् ॥

27. Thus did the citizens speak about their beloved darlings of Ikshwaaku-s. And following them, they could not control the tears from their eyes.

❍ ❍ ❍

२८. अथ राजा वृतः स्त्रीभिर्दीनाभिर्दीनचेतनः ।
निर्जगाम प्रियं पुत्रं द्रक्ष्यामीति ब्रुवन् गृहात् ॥

28. At that time, the down hearted king (Dhascharatha), surrounded by his wives who were all depressed, came out of his palace, saying; = I Will See My Beloved Son = (even while he is going away).

❍ ❍ ❍

२९. शुश्रुवे चाग्रतः स्त्रीणां रुदन्तीनां महास्वनः ।
यथा नादः करेणूनां बद्धे महति कुञ्जरे ॥

29. The loud wailing of these ladies who were crying, were heard in his presence. It was like the (wailing) sound of female elephant when male elephant is bound (captured).

❍ ❍ ❍

३०. पिता च राजा काकुत्स्थः श्रीमान् सन्नस्तदा बभौ ।
परिपूर्णः शशी काले ग्रहेणोपप्लुतो यथा ॥

30. At that time, (Raama's) father, this resplendent king (Dhascharatha) the Kaakuthsa, became depressed (and dull) like the full moon eclipsed by Raahu during season.

❍ ❍ ❍

३१. स च श्रीमानचिन्त्यामा रामो दशरथात्मजः ।
सूतं संचोदयामास त्वरितं वाह्यतामिति ॥

31. The resplendent (divine like) Raama the son of Dhascharatha whose power was unthinkable (unimaginable), goaded the charioteer (Sumanthra) = May this be driven faster =

(Raama wanted the suffering of separation of his father to end quickly. He wants a quick Get-Away.)

❍ ❍ ❍

३२. रामो याहीति सूतं तं तिष्ठेति स जनस्तदा ।
उभयं नाशकत् सूतः कर्तुमध्वनि चोदितः ॥

32. While Raama was telling his charioteer to go fast, the citizens were saying: = Stop =; The charioteer did not know what to do, as diverse (requests) were made during the journey.

❍ ❍ ❍

३३. निर्गच्छति महाबाहौ रामे पौरजनाश्रुभिः ।
पतितैरभ्यवहितं प्रशशाम महीरजः ॥

33. When the strong limbed Raama was going away, the dust of the earth that was covering (and was rising up), was 'quenched' by the tears that fell from the (eyes of) citizens.(Poet Vaalmeeki goes poetic).

❍ ❍ ❍

३४. रुदिताश्रुपरिक्लिन्नं हाहाकृतमचेतनम् ।
प्रयाणे राघवस्यासीत् पुरं परमपीडितम् ॥

34. During Raama's journey, the city was wet with tears from the crying! It was tormented greatly. Sounds of Ha, Ha were heard. It was bewildered.

❍ ❍ ❍

३५. सुस्राव नयनैः स्त्रीणामास्रमायाससंभवम् ।
मीनसंक्षोभचलितैः सलिलं पङ्कजैरिव ॥

35. The tears from the wearied eyes of the ladies were like waves of water of ponds when the fishes violently shake up the lotuses!

❍ ❍ ❍

३६. दृष्ट्वा तु नृपतिः श्रीमानेकचित्तगतं पुरम् ।
निपपातैव दुःखेन हतमूल इव द्रुमः ॥

36. Seeing the city had one track mind (in that they should go to where Raama was going), the resplendent King became very sad and fell down (on floor) like a tree cut off from root.

❍ ❍ ❍

३७. ततो हलहलाशब्दो जज्ञे रामस्य पृष्ठतः ।
नराणां प्रेक्ष्य राजानं सीदन्तं भृशदुःखितम् ॥

37. When they saw their king sinking down suffering terribly, sounds of** Ah, Ah, Oh Oh from the citizens who were near Raama emanated. (** Sanskrit word is= Halahala=)

❍ ❍ ❍

३८. हा रामेति जनाः केचिद्रामममातेति चापरे ।
अन्तःपुरं समृद्ध च क्रोशन्तः पर्यदेवयन् ॥

38. Some people residing in prosperous mansions cried and lamented. Oh Raama: And some said: Ha! Oh the mother of Raama!

❍ ❍ ❍

३९. अन्वीक्षमाणो रामस्तु विषण्णं भ्रान्तचेतसम् ।
राजानं मातरं चैव ददर्शानुगतौ पथि ॥

39. And Raama whose mind was perplexed (somewhat), who was despondent and who was philosophical, observed that his father and mother were coming along the road (chasing the chariot).

❍ ❍ ❍

४०. स बद्ध इव पाशेन किशोरो मातरं यथा ।
धर्मपाशेन संयुक्तः प्रकाशं नाभ्युदैक्षत ।।

40. Like (the grief of) a mother when its young deer is bound by rope (of the net), so was he, (this Raama), who was bound by 'Ropes' of Dharma. He beheld himself (in such a way as he would be) unseen. (Even for Raama, a man of composure agony of parting was terrible).

❍ ❍ ❍

४१. पदातिनौ च यानार्हावदुःखार्हौ सूखोचितौ ।
दृष्ट्वा संचोदयामास शीघ्रं याहीति सारथिम् ।।

41. And when (Raama) saw (his father and mother) who had never known suffering before, who were used to comforts, who, although, were ever used to go on chariot and vehicle, were now walking (on the road in the direction of his chariot), he, (Raama), goaded charioteer (Sumanthra) = Go Fast =

❍ ❍ ❍

४२. न हि तत् पुरुषव्याघ्रो दुःखजं दर्शनं पितुः ।
मातुश्च सहितुं शक्तस्तोत्रार्दित इव द्विपः ।।

42. (Raama) the 'tiger' amongst men could not tolerate to see his father's and his mother's 'state' caused by such suffering; (he was hurt) like an elephant hurt by a goad (a 'hook' used by a elephant driver).

❍ ❍ ❍

४३. प्रत्यगारमिवायान्ती वत्सला वत्सकारणात् ।
बद्धवत्सा यथा धेनू राममाताऽभ्यधावत ।।

43. And Raama's mother (Kowsalya) who had deep love for her son, ran after him like a cow running towards its calf in cowshed.

❍ ❍ ❍

४४. तथा रुदन्तीं कौसल्यां रथं तमनुधावतीम् ।
क्रोशन्तीं राम रामेति हा सीते लक्ष्मणेति च ॥

44. And the crying Kowsalya ran after the chariot, wailing Oh Raama, Oh Raama, Oh Seetha, Oh Lakshmana ....

❍ ❍ ❍

४५. रामलक्ष्मणसीतार्थं स्रवन्तीं वारि नेत्रजम् ।
असकृत्प्रैक्षत तदा नृत्यन्तीमिव मातरम् ॥

45. ...... and Raama saw his mother (Kowsalya) with tears flowing from her eyes on account of separation (from) Raama, Seetha and Lakshmana. (She was running towards chariot) as though she was dancing (staggering, zig, zag).

❍ ❍ ❍

४६. तिष्ठेति राजा चुक्रोश याहि याहीति राघवः ।
सुमन्त्रस्य बभूवात्मा चक्रयोरिव चान्तरा ॥

46. King (Dhascharatha) cried aloud = Stop = And (Raama the) Raaghava said (to the charioteer) = Go, Go =. And the heart of Sumanthra (the charioteer) was as though it was caught in between the wheels.

❍ ❍ ❍

४७. नाश्रौषमिति राजानमुपालब्धोऽपि वक्ष्यसि ।
चिरं दुःखस्य पापिष्ठमिति रामस्तमब्रवीत् ॥

47. And Raama told him: If you are reprimanded (reproached for disobeying him), tell the king thus (on your return to Ayodhya): = I did not obey because prolonged agony was very cruel.=
(Raama could not stand the sight of his father and

mother running towards chariot on the road like some ordinary street people. So Raama asked Sumanthra to drive fast, make the Get-Away quick.)

❍ ❍ ❍

४८. रामस्य स वचः कुर्वन्ननुज्ञाप्य च तं जनम् ।
व्रजतोऽपि हयाञ्शीघ्रं चोदयामास सारथिः ॥

48. The charioteer (Sumanthra), hearing the words of Raama who was traveling (along), goaded the horses at once, clearing the crowd.

❍ ❍ ❍

४९. न्यवर्तत जनो राज्ञो रामं कृत्वा प्रदक्षिणम् ।
मनसाऽप्यश्रुवेगैश्च न न्यवर्तत मानुषम् ॥

49. The king's citizens went round Raama in circumbumbulation and stopped there. But the gush of tears due to their affection, that, could not be stopped, human as they were.

❍ ❍ ❍

५०. यमिच्छेत्पुनरायान्तं नैनं दूरमनुव्रजेत् ।
इत्यमात्या महाराजमूचुर्दशरथं वचः ॥

50. And the ministers addressed the great king Dhascharatha: It is said that if one desires to see him return (safely home after his long visit abroad), then he should not follow him afar.

(This is the common superstition in India; Elders never give a long send off to their close relatives or friends. Leave taking should stop at the front door of the house.)

❍ ❍ ❍

५१. तेषां वचः सर्वगुणोपपन्नं
प्रस्विन्नगात्रः प्रविषण्णरुपः ।
निशम्य राजा कृपणः सभार्यो
व्यवस्थितस्तं सुतमीक्षमाणः ॥

51. Hearing the words, (the words) endowed with all qualities, from these (his ministers), this miserable King stopped there itself along with his wife; looking towards his son, even as he was sweating profusely with down cast (face).

❍ ❍ ❍

Chapter 41

Description of the City in Turmoil

१. तस्मिंस्तु पुरुषव्याघ्रे विनिर्याति कृताञ्जलौ ।
आर्तशब्दो हि सञ्जज्ञे स्त्रीणामन्तःपुरे महान् ।।

1. When (Raama the) 'tiger' of men was going away with his hands cupped in Anjali, loud wailings of the ladies of the inner apartments of the palace emanated. (they cried thus)

❍ ❍ ❍

२. अनाथस्य जनस्यास्य दुर्बलस्य तपस्विनः ।
यो गतिः शरणं चासीत्स नाथः क्व नु गच्छति ।।

2. Where is this lord going away, who was the resort and refuge to all those weak, helpless and tormented persons?

❍ ❍ ❍

३. न क्रुद्ध्यत्यभिशप्तोऽपि क्रोधनीयानि वर्जयन् ।
क्रुद्धान्प्रसादयन्सर्वान्समदुःखः क्वचिद्गतः ।।

3. He who abhors anything that will hurt people; he who soothes angry man; he who never gets angry even when reviled by them; he, this well known (Raama) who shares suffering of others ......

❍ ❍ ❍

४. कौसल्यायां महातेजा यथा मातरि वर्तते ।
तथा यो वर्ततेऽस्मासु महात्मा क्व नु गच्छति ।।

4. ...... he who treated us like he treated his own mother Kowsalya.... this most brilliant great soul (Raama) is going somewhere!

❍ ❍ ❍

५. कैकेय्या क्लिश्यमानेन राज्ञा सञ्चोदितो वनम् ।
परित्राता जनस्यास्य जगतः क्वनु गच्छति ।।

5. He who is protector of all mankind, is going some where, ordered away to forest by the king who was tormented by Kaikeyi.

❍ ❍ ❍

६. अहो निश्चेतनो राजा जीवलोकस्य संप्रियम् ।
धर्म्यं सत्यव्रतं रामं वनवासे प्रवत्स्यति ।।

6. Ah! Ah! The king having lost his sense, has sent away to a forest life this truthful man Raama who is steadfast in Dharma and who is dear to living beings in this world.

❍ ❍ ❍

७. इति सर्वा महिष्यस्ता विवत्सा इव धेनवः ।
रुरुदश्चैव दुःखार्ताः सस्वरं च विचुक्रुशुः ।।

7. All the wives (of Dhascharatha) wailed thus and cried in same tone* in great sorrow like cow bereft of calf. (* Word used -Sasvara)

❍ ❍ ❍

८. सतमन्तःपुरे घोरमार्तशब्दं महीपतिः ।
पुत्रशोकाभिसंतप्तः श्रुत्वा चासीत्सुदुःखितः ।।

8. And when the king who was tormented by grief of separation from his son heard the gruesome wailings from the inner apartments (of his palace), he became even more distressed.

❍ ❍ ❍

९. नाग्निहोत्राण्यहूयन्त नापचन् गृहमेधिनः ।
अकुर्वन्न प्रजाः कार्यं सूर्यश्चान्तरधीयत ॥

9. There were none (of the usual) fire rituals (in various houses); Housewives did not cook; Citizens did not attend to their work; And (even) the Sun was 'obscure'.

❍ ❍ ❍

१०. व्यसृजन्कबलान्नागा गावो वत्सान्न पाययन् ।
पुत्रं प्रथमजं लब्ध्वा जननी नाभ्यनन्दत ॥

10. The serpents shed their prey; Cows did not milk their calves; Mothers did not take pleasure in their foremost sons even on seeing them.

❍ ❍ ❍

११. त्रिशङ्कुर्लोहिताङ्गश्च बृहस्पतिबुधावपि ।
दारुणाः सोममभ्येत्य ग्रहाः सर्वेव्यवस्थिताः ॥

11. (It appeared as if) Stellar bodies like Thrischanku, Mars, Mercury, Jupiter, Moon all stopped their movements as if to 'hurt' (mankind) dreadfully.

❍ ❍ ❍

१२. नक्षत्राणि गतार्चींषि ग्रहाश्च गततेजसः ।
विशाखाश्च सधूमाश्च नभसि प्रचकाशिरे ॥

12. Stars in the sky were lustreless (no twinkling even): Constellations lost their 'glory'; The Vischaaka (Star) appeared engulfed in smoke.
(This star is the auspicious star of the Ikshwaaku kings)

❍ ❍ ❍

१३. कालिकानिलवेगेन महोदधिरिवोद्धतः ।
रामे वनं प्रव्रजिते नगरं प्रचचाल तत् ॥

13. When Raama went away to forest, the city was agitated and trembled like the turbulent mighty ocean struck by high velocity winds from (rain bearing) clouds.

❍ ❍ ❍

१४. दिशः पर्याकुलाः सर्वास्तिमिरेण समावृताः ।
न ग्रहो नापि नक्षत्रं प्रचकाशे न किश्चन ।।

14. The entire kingdom was engulfed in darkness and confusion (prevailed): The (Nine) stars were not seen. Stars (like) Pole star were not seen at all.

❍ ❍ ❍

१५. अकस्मान्नागरः सर्वोजनो दैन्यमुपागमत् ।
आहारे च विहारे च न कश्चिदकरोन्मनः ।।

15. All of a sudden, all the citizens of the city attained (a state of) feebleness: None directed his mind to take food nor go about.

❍ ❍ ❍

१६. शोकपर्यायसन्तप्तः सततं दीर्घमुच्छ्वसन् ।
अयोध्यायां जनः सर्वः शुशोच जगतीपतिम् ।।

16. In Ayodhya, every man was in torment, afflicted by sorrow; And panting hard for breath, they lamented endlessly, thinking about (Raama) the lord of Earth.

❍ ❍ ❍

१७. बाष्पपर्याकुलमुखो राजमार्गगतो जनः ।
न हृष्टो लक्ष्यते कश्चित्सर्वः शोकपरायणः ।।
न वाति पवनः शीतो न शची सौम्यदर्शनः ।।

17. In the Royal boulevard, all (every man) was submerged in grief with their faces covered by tears; none was seen in joy; and wind did not blow cool; and moon did not give a pleasant sight.

❍ ❍ ❍

१८. न सूर्यस्तपते लोकं सर्वं पर्याकुलं जगत् ।
अनर्थिनः सुताः स्त्रीणां भर्तारो भ्रातरस्तथा ।।
सर्वेसर्वं परित्यज्य राममेवान्वचिन्तयन् ।।

18. The Sun did not illuminate the world; The entire world appeared topsy turvy; Sons, brothers, wives, husbands, all of them, abandoned every thing and (always) thought only about Raama, (were) without (any) interest (in anything else).

❍ ❍ ❍

१९. ये तु रामस्य सुहृदः सर्वेते मूढचेतसः ।
शोकभारेण चाक्रान्ताः शयनं न जहुस्तदा ॥

19. And those Raama's friends, all of them, were overwhelmed by grief, unable to bear (separation). They were so numbed (lethargic) that they did not get up from their beds.

❍ ❍ ❍

२०. ततस्त्वयोध्या रहिता महात्मना
पुरन्दरेणेव मही सपर्वता ।
चचाल घोरं भयशोकपीडिता
सनागयोधाश्वगणा ननाद च ॥

20. The entire mighty city of Ayodhya which (boasted of) mountain like structures, which had a large complement of elephants, warriors, horses,...(such a city) 'quivered' and 'wailed' gruesomely as though abandoned by the great soul Purandhara (God Vishnu).
(Even making allowances for Vaalmeeki's poetic licence, it is obvious that without Raama, Ayodhya was a joyless city.)

❍ ❍ ❍

Chapter 42

Dhascharatha Wails

१. यावत्तु निर्यतस्तस्य रजोरूपमदृश्यत ।
नैवेक्ष्वाकुवरस्तावत्सञ्जहारात्मचक्षुषी ॥

1. The noble Ikshwaaku king (Dhascharatha) did not take his eyes off till he could see (only) the dust raised (by the chariot) as it went along ......

❍ ❍ ❍

२. यावद्राजा प्रियं पुत्रं पश्यत्यत्यन्तधार्मिकम् ।
तावद्व्यवर्धतेवास्य धरण्यां पुत्रदर्शने ॥

2. ...... (and till dust) fell on earth copiously; the king kept on looking out to get a glimpse of his beloved son (Raama) who was foremost man of Dharma

(Poor Dhascharatha, he could not take his eyes off towards Raama who was speeding fast on chariot).

❍ ❍ ❍

३. न पश्यति रजोऽप्यस्य यदा रामस्य भूमिपः ।
तदाऽऽर्तश्च विषण्णश्च पपात धरणीतले ॥

3. When the king could not see even the dust of Raama's (chariot), he was so stricken by grief that he fell down on earth down hearted.

❍ ❍ ❍

४. तस्य दक्षिणमन्वागात्कौसल्या बाहुमङ्गना ।
वामं चास्यान्वगात्पार्श्वं कैकेयी भरतप्रिया ॥

4. And the handsome woman Kowsalya stood by his right; And Bharatha's beloved (mother) Kaikeyi stood by his left.

५. तां नयेन च संपन्नो धर्मेण विनयेन च ।
उवाच राजा कैकेयीं समीक्ष्य व्यथितेन्द्रियः ।।

5. The king who was a man of modesty, who ruled his subjects justly, who ruled with Dharma, who was most accomplished (but) whose senses were (now) afflicted, looked at Kaikeyi and said:

❍ ❍ ❍

६. कैकेयि मा ममाङ्गानि स्प्राक्षीस्त्वं दुष्टचारिणी ।
न हि त्वां द्रष्टुमिच्छामि न भार्या न च बान्धवी ।।

6. Oh Evil mongering Kaikeyi! You are not a relative. Therefore you are not my wife. Do not touch my body. I do not desire to look at you.

❍ ❍ ❍

७. ये च त्वामनुजीवन्ति नाहं तेषां न ते मम ।
केवलार्थपरां हि त्वां त्यक्तधर्मां त्यजाम्यहम् ।।

7. You and all those who live by you, they have nothing to do with me; And I have nothing to do with them. I renounce you because you have abandoned Dharma for paltry (selfish) object (which you value highly).

❍ ❍ ❍

८. अगृह्णां यच्च ते पाणिमग्निं पर्यणयं च यत् ।
अनुजानामि तत्सर्वमस्मिंल्लोके परत्र च ।।

8. I renounce all that, in this world, in the next world; All (that is associated with marriage) like my taking your hand (in mine), and going round in circumbumbulation over fire (mound).

❍ ❍ ❍

९. भरतश्चेत्प्रतीतः स्याद्राज्यं प्राप्येदमव्ययम् ।
यन्मे स दद्यात्प्रीत्यर्थं मां मा तद्दत्तमागमत् ।।

9. If the well known Bharatha accepts this imperishable kingdom and if he should offer Ritual Services for my 'good' (during my funeral). those offerings should not reach me.
(It is Indian tradition that a son performs Last Rites and offers Oblations in Fire that supposedly goes to parents in heaven. Here Dhascharatha says he will not accept 'Offerings' from Bharatha when he goes to the other world.)

❍ ❍ ❍

१०. अथ रेणुसमुध्वस्तं तमुत्थाप्य नराधिपम् ।
न्यवर्तत तदा देवी कौसल्या शोककर्शिता ॥

10. Then, Kowsalya who was tormented by grief, lifted up the king who was besmeared with dust and (just stood) turning her back.

❍ ❍ ❍

११. हत्वेव ब्राह्मणं कामात्स्पृष्ट्वाऽग्निमिव पाणिना ।
अन्वतप्यत धर्मात्मा पुत्रं सञ्चिन्त्य तापसम् ॥

11. Like one who, out of passion (madness) had touched Fire with his hands, this noble soul man of Dharma (Dhascharatha), was like one who had killed a Braamin. He was' burning up' thinking about his son (who had chosen life of forest, and who was) like a man of penance.

❍ ❍ ❍

१२. निवृत्यैव निवृत्यैव सीदतो रथवर्त्मसु ।
राज्ञो नातिबभौ रूपं ग्रस्तस्यांशुमतो यथा ॥

12. As (Raama's) chariot was going away, the 'form' (the face) of the king who kept on turning and turning (in that direction), who was wearied, appeared obscure like the Sun eclipsed by Raahu.

❍ ❍ ❍

१३. विललाप च दुःखार्तः प्रियं पुत्रमनुस्मरन् ।
नगरान्तमनुप्राप्तं बुद्ध्वा पुत्रमथाब्रवीत् ।।

13. Thinking about his beloved son, he wept afflicted by grief; Realising that his son must have crossed (the outskirts of) the city, he said: (He wailed)

❍ ❍ ❍

१४. वाहनानां च मुख्यानां वहतां तं ममात्मजम् ।
पदानि पथि दृश्यन्ते स महात्मा न दृश्यते ।।

14. The foot prints of the foremost horses that carried my son (on chariot) are seen: But the great soul (Raama), is not seen.

❍ ❍ ❍

१५. यः सुखेषूपधानेषु शेते चन्दनरूषितः ।
वीज्यमानो महार्हाभिः स्त्रीभिर्मम सुतोत्तमः ।।

15. My noble son who used to be besmeared with sandal paste and fanned by charming ladies, who used to lie on soft beds ......

❍ ❍ ❍

१६. स नूनं क्वचिदेवाद्य वृक्षमूलमुपाश्रितः ।
काष्ठं वा यदि वाऽश्मानमुपधाय शयिष्यते ।।

16. ...... will now be lying down under some tree, using twigs or stones as bed.

❍ ❍ ❍

१७. उत्थास्यति च मेदिन्याः कृपणः पांसुकुण्ठितः ।
विनिश्वसन्प्रस्रवणात्करेणूनामिवर्षभः ।।

17. He will get up miserably from bare earth, sighing deeply, with his body covered by dust, like a male elephant with female elephants (in the region of) water falls (in forest).

❍ ❍ ❍

१८. द्रक्ष्यन्ति नूनं पुरुषा दीर्घबाहुं वनेचराः ।
रामुत्थाय गच्छन्तं लोकनाथमनाथवत् ।।

18. From now on, the people living in forests will see this lord of the world, this mighty limbed Raama who has got away (from here), going (to forest) helpless, (abandoned by his own father).

❍ ❍ ❍

१९. सा नूनं जनकस्येष्टा सुता सुखसदोचिता ।
कण्टकाक्रमणक्लान्ता वनमद्य गमिष्यति ।।

19. And the beloved of King Janaka, this daughter (Seetha), who deserves to be in comfort only, from now on, will be going along (in forest), wearied, treading on thorns.

❍ ❍ ❍

२०. अनभिज्ञा वनानां सा नूनं भयमुपैष्यति ।
श्वापदानर्दितं श्रुत्वा गम्भीरं रोमहर्षणम् ।।

20. Unaccustomed to the ways of forest (not knowing about forest), she will now be scared and 'bristled' with fear, hearing the loud roar of beasts of prey.

❍ ❍ ❍

२१. सकामा भव कैकेयि विधवा राज्यमावस ।
न हि तं पुरुषव्याघ्रं विना जीवितुमुत्सहे ।।

21. Oh Kaikeyi! I will not live without this (Raama) the 'tiger' of men Therefore you live in the kingdom as my widow: (enjoy yourself) With all your desires (fulfilled).

❍ ❍ ❍

२२. इत्येवं विलपन्राजा जनौघेनाभिसंवृतः ।
अपस्नात इवारिष्टं प्रविवेश गृहोत्तमम् ।।

22. Lamenting thus, the king who was surrounded on all sides by a crowd of citizens, entered his foremost palace which was (now) hit by misfortune, like one (returning from) a funereal bath.

❍ ❍ ❍

२३. शून्यचत्वरवेश्मान्तां संवृतापणदेवताम् ।
क्लान्तदुर्बलदुःखार्तां नात्याकीर्णमहापथाम् ।।

23. All the four segments of the palace was deserted; all shops and places of worship were closed; there were no crowds in the roads; people were emaciated, afflicted by grief ......

❍ ❍ ❍

२४. तामवेक्ष्य पुरीं सर्वां राममेवानुचिन्तयन् ।
विलपन्प्राविशद्राजा गृहं सूर्य इवाम्बुदम् ।।

24. ...... Observing all this in the city, thinking only about Raama, and wailing over him, the king entered his abode like Sun through rainy clouds.

❍ ❍ ❍

२५. महाह्रदमिवाक्षोभ्यं सुपर्णेन हृतोरगम् ।
रामेण रहितं वेश्म वैदेह्या लक्ष्मणेन च ।।

25. ...... Bereft of Raama, Lakshmana, and (Seetha the) Vaidhehi, the palace looked like a still mighty pond, (and gruesome, like) when a snake is seized by Garuda bird.

❍ ❍ ❍

२६. अथ गद्गदशब्दस्तु विलपन्मनुजाधिपः ।
उवाच मृदु मन्दार्थं वचनं दीनमस्वरम् ।।

26. This ruler of men (Dhascharatha) who was wailing, who was feeble, and crestfallen, who had lost all interest, spoke the following words in a low voice, stammering.

❍ ❍ ❍

२७ कौसल्याया गृहं शीघ्रं राममातुर्नयन्तु माम् ।
न ह्यन्यत्र ममाश्वासो हृदयस्य भविष्यति ।।

27. Take me to Raama's mother's house at once, to Kowsalya's: Because, there will be no consolation (comfort) for my heart any where else.

❍ ❍ ❍

२८. इति ब्रुवन्तं राजानमनयन्द्वारदर्शिनः ।
कौसल्याया गृहं तत्र न्यवेश्यत विनीतवत् ।।

28. The guards then led the king who was saying thus, to Kowsalya's palace; There they rested him respectfully.

❍ ❍ ❍

२९. ततस्तस्य प्रविष्टस्य कौसल्याया निवेशनम् ।
अधिरुह्यापि शयनं बभूव लुलितं मनः ।।

29. Although he entered Kowsalya's place and was rested there on a bed, his mind still remained agitated.

❍ ❍ ❍

३०. पुत्रद्वयविहीनं च स्नुषयाऽपि विवर्जितम् ।
अपश्यद्भवनं राजा नष्टचन्द्रमिवाम्बरम् ।।

30. Without his two sons (Raama and Lakshmana) and his daughter.in.law, (Seetha), he observed that the mansion was like sky without Moon.

❍ ❍ ❍

३१. तच्च दृष्ट्वा महाराजो भुजमुद्यम्य वीर्यवान् ।
उच्चैः स्वरेण चुक्रोश हा राघव जहासि माम् ।।

31. Hearing (all this) (and thinking thus), the great brave king lifted his two hands up and in a loud voice, cried. Oh Raama the Raaghava! You have **abandoned me ! Alas!
(Vaalmeeki uses the word ** = Jahaasi= This is from sanskrit root = hus= meaning Ridicule, to mock, deride etc. literally last line should read: You are mocking me, deriding me.)

❍ ❍ ❍

३२. सुखिता बत तं कालं जीविष्यन्ति नरोत्तमाः ।
परिष्वजन्तो ये रामं द्रक्ष्यन्ति पुनरागतम् ।।

32. Alas! Indeed only these noble men are fortunate who will live long enough to see Raama return (from forest) and embrace him.
(Dhascharatha feels he is too old to bear suffering and thinks he will die very soon. As events turn out, he died very soon.)

❍ ❍ ❍

३३. अथ रात्र्यां प्रपन्नायां कालरात्र्यामिवात्मनः ।
अर्धरात्रे दशरथः कौसल्यामिदमब्रवीत् ॥

33. The king whose condition was like that of his last night (in the world) addressed Kowsalya in the middle of the night.

❍ ❍ ❍

३४. रामं मेऽनुगता दृष्टिरद्यापि न निवर्तते ।
न त्वा पश्यामि कौसल्ये साधु मां पाणिना स्पृश ॥

34. My faculty of sight has gone away with Raama; It is not coming back. Oh Kowsalya! I am not able to see you. Touch me softly (stroke me). with your hands.

❍ ❍ ❍

३५. तं राममेवानुविचिन्तयन्तं
समीक्ष्य देवी शयने नरेन्द्रम् ।
उपोपविश्याधिकमार्तरूपा
विनिश्वसन्ती विललाप कृच्छ्रम् ॥

35. Observing that he was constantly thinking about (Raama) the lord of men and was in great pain (sorrow), Lady (Kowsalya) sat down on his bed and wailed in great anguish, breathing hard and deep.

❍ ❍ ❍

Chapter 43

Kowsalya Wails

१. ततः समीक्ष्य शयने सन्नं शोकेन पार्थिवम् ।
कौसल्या पुत्रशोकार्ता तमुवाच महीपतिम् ।।

1. (Raama's mother Kowsalya wails: More so because her husband is losing control of himself.)
Tormented by grief over his son, Kowsalya looked at the mighty lord of earth, king (Dhascharatha) who was motionless in the bed, grief stricken, and she said:

❍ ❍ ❍

२. राघवे नरशार्दूले विषं मुक्त्वा हि जिह्मगा ।
विचरिष्यति कैकेयी निर्मुक्तेव हि पन्नगी ।।

2. Having let lose poison on (Raama) the Raaghava who is a 'lion' amongst men, the crooked Kaikeyi will now go about (causing harm) like a snake let lose (unrestrained).

❍ ❍ ❍

३. विवास्य रामं सुभगा लब्धाकामा समाहिता ।
त्रासयिष्यति मां भूयो दुष्टाहिरिव वेश्मनि ।।

3. Having sent away Raama, thus having achieved her objective, she will now take control: This prosperous (Kaikeyi) will become wicked like a snake, as to make me tremble in palace even more.

❍ ❍ ❍

४. अथ स्म नगरे रामश्चरन्भैक्षं गृहे वसेत् ।
कामकारो वरं दातुमपि दासं ममात्मजम् ।।

4. Raama could have stayed in the palace making a living as a beggar in the city; It would have been better if my son was offered as a slave by you, fulfilling (every one's) desires!

❍ ❍ ❍

५. पातयित्वा तु कैकेय्या रामं स्थानाद्यथेष्टतः ।
प्रदिष्टो रक्षसां भागः पर्वणीवाहिताग्निना ॥

5. It is ordained that Raama should be thrown out of his place (the kingdom), at the pleasure of Kaikeyi. It is just like offering, in a fleeting moment, the Oblations (meant for celestial lords) to the demons, by a person doing Fire Rituals.

❍ ❍ ❍

६. गजराजगतिर्वीरो महाबाहुर्धनुर्धरः ।
वनमाविशते नूनं सभार्यः सहलक्ष्मणः ॥

6. The man whose stride is like those of an elephant, who is mighty limbed, who is brave, (such a Raama) will now have abode in forest along with Lakshmana and his wife (Seetha), wielding his bow.

❍ ❍ ❍

७. वने त्वदृष्टदुःखानां कैकेय्यानुमते त्वया ।
त्यक्तानां वनवासाय का न्ववस्था भविष्यति ॥

7. What is going to be the fate (of these three) in the forest who have been abandoned (sent away) to forest life by you so as to (honour and) favour Kaikeyi. And they have never seen suffering before!

❍ ❍ ❍

८. ते रत्नहीनास्तरुणाः फलकाले विवासिताः ।
कथं वत्स्यन्ति कृपणाः फलमूलैः कृताशनाः ॥

8. At such tender age, at a time when they ought to enjoy "fruits" (various mundane pleasures), how will they live miserably, losing everything *(at Ayodhya), feeding themselves with fruits and tubers, being exiled (* Rathna heena- Without Gem of princely life).

❍ ❍ ❍

९. अपीदानीं स कालः स्यान्मम शोकक्षयः शिवः ।
सभार्यं च सह भ्रात्रा पश्येयमिह राघवम् ।।

9. I must see Raama along with his brother (Lakshmana) and with his wife (Seetha): That time alone will see the end of suffering for me. Will this auspicious (moment) come now!

❍ ❍ ❍

१०. श्रुत्वैवोपस्थितौ वीरौ कदाऽयोध्या भविष्यति ।
यशस्विनी हृष्टजना सूच्छ्रितध्वजमालिनी ।।

10. When will the famous (glorious) Ayodhya, hearing the return of these two brave men, become (joyous) with happy people, and decorated with banners and garlands.

❍ ❍ ❍

११. कदा प्रेक्ष्य नरव्याघ्रावरण्यात्पुनरागतौ ।
नन्दिष्यति पुरी हृष्टा समुद्र इव पर्वणि ।।

11. When will this city see these 'tigers' of men return back from forest and become gay (once again) like ocean during seasons.

❍ ❍ ❍

१२. कदाऽयोध्यां महाबाहुः पुरीं वीरः प्रवेक्ष्यति ।
पुरस्कृत्य रथे सीतां वृषभो गोवधूमिव ।।

12. When will the mighty limbed, strong and brave (Raama) enter the city of Ayodhya on his chariot along with his tender wife Seetha?

❍ ❍ ❍

१३. कदा प्राणिसहस्राणि राजमार्गेममात्मजौ ।
लाजैरवकिरिष्यन्ति प्रविशन्तावरिन्दमौ ।।

13. When will the multitude of citizens shower puffed grains on the two invincible sons of mine when they enter the Royal boulevard.

(Like a ticker-tape welcome in New york; but Indians do not do it with paper bits! Interesting Kowsalya calls Lakshmana also her son)

❍ ❍ ❍

१४. प्रविशन्तौ कदाऽयोध्यां द्रक्ष्यामि शुभकुण्डलौ ।
उदग्रायुधनिस्त्रिंशौ सश्रृङ्गाविव पर्वतौ ।।

14. When will I see (Raama and Lakshmana) who are like mountains with lofty peaks, enter Ayodhya, wearing beautiful ear rings and wielding foremost bows and swords.

❍ ❍ ❍

१५. कदा सुमनसः कन्या द्विजातीनां फलानि च ।
प्रदिशन्त्यः पुरीं हृष्टाः करिष्यन्ति प्रदक्षिणम् ।।

15. When will the happy girls of Braamin families receive them with reverential welcome of circumbumbulation (with lamps) and offer them fruits and garlands.

❍ ❍ ❍

१६. कदा परिणतो बुद्ध्या वयसा चामरप्रभः ।
अभ्युपैष्यति धर्मज्ञः सुवर्ष इव लालयन् ।।

16. When will (my Raama) who is mature in wisdom, who in power, is of imperishable glory, who knows Dharma, who cheers (delights) like rain, serve me (again)?

❍ ❍ ❍

१७. निःसंशयं मया मन्ये पुरा वीर कदर्यया ।
पातुकामेषु वत्सेषु मातॄणां छादिताः स्तनाः ।।

17. Oh Brave king! (Perhaps) before (in my previous birth), out of my avariciousness, the udders of cows must have been "hidden" (covered) by me pitilessly from the calves (thus denying milk for their young ones). I consider (my present misfortune as such).

❍ ❍ ❍

१८. साऽहं गौरिव सिंहेन विवत्सा वत्सला कृता ।
कैकेय्या पुरुषव्याघ्र बालवत्सेव गौर्बलात् ।।

18. Oh 'tiger' of men (Dhascharatha)! Like a cow which has a young calf to which it is deeply attached, like that cow becoming calfless (being seized) forcibly by a lion, I have (now) become (childless) because of Kaikeyi.

❍ ❍ ❍

१९. न हि तावद्गुणैर्जुष्टं सर्वशास्त्रविशारदम् ।
एकपुत्रा विना पुत्रमहं जीवितुमुत्सहे ।।

19. I have but one son who possesses such (noble) qualities, who is (loved) and worshipped by all, who is well versed in all Shaasthra-s, Separated by (such a) son, I cannot live.

❍ ❍ ❍

२०. न हि मे जीविते किञ्चित्सामर्थ्यमिह कल्प्यते ।
अपश्यन्त्याः प्रियं पुत्रं महाबाहुं महाबलम् ।।

20. Without seeing the mighty limbed mightily strong beloved son in this world, no purpose will be served for me to live on.

❍ ❍ ❍

२१. अयं हि मां दीपयते समुत्थितः
तनूजशोकप्रभवो हुताशनः ।
महीमिमां रश्मिभिरुद्धतप्रभो
यथा निदाघे भगवान्दिवाकरः ।।

21. The Fire (that is burning in me) caused by the grief of separation from my son, is burning me up like lord Sun burning the Earth with his rays in summer when he rises up and strikes with violent power.

❍ ❍ ❍

Chapter 44

(Sumithra) Consoles Kowsalya

१. विलपन्तीं तथा तां तु कौसल्यां प्रमदोत्तमाम् ।
इदं धर्म्येस्थिता धर्म्यं सुमित्रा वाक्यमब्रवीत् ।।

1. When this noble lady Kowsalya was wailing thus, Sumithra who was steadfast in Dharma, addressed her with these words of Dharma.

❍ ❍ ❍

२. तवार्येसद्गुणैर्युक्तः पुत्रः स पुरुषोत्तमः ।
किं ते विलपितेनैवं कृपणं रुदितेन वा ।।

2. Oh Aryan! How can you cry and wail thus so pitiably; Your son is endowed with virtuous qualities and is foremost of men.

❍ ❍ ❍

३. यस्तवार्येगतः पुत्रस्त्यक्त्वा राज्यं महाबलः ।
साधु कुर्वन्महात्मानं पितरं सत्यवादिनम् ।।

3. Oh Aryan! This, your mightily strong son, in order to make his great soul father truly a truthful man, has abandoned his kingdom and gone away (on exile).

❍ ❍ ❍

४. शिष्टैराचरिते सम्यक्छश्वत्प्रेत्यफलोदये ।
रामो धर्मेस्थितः श्रेष्ठो न स शोच्यः कदाचन ।।

4. (Your son) Raama always stands firm in Dharma totally, (the Dharma) that is practised by learned and (wise) men, (the Dharma) that offers reward in the world after death. He is a **very superior being. (Such a person) should never be grieved over.
(You should be proud that your son is going to forest to protect your husband's honour and protect his

Dharma, says Sumithra. And poet Vaalmeeki uses word = Shreshta.= A word used for God Vishnu. Sumithra, perhaps, kmows Raama as God Vishnu on earth.)

❍ ❍ ❍

५. वर्तते चोत्तमां वृत्तिं लक्ष्मणोऽस्मिन्सदानघः ।
दयावान्सर्वभूतेषु लाभस्तस्य महात्मनः ।।

5. This Lakshmana who has (always) been compassionate (to all) is now staying with him as a sinless man, always (doing service) in this noble course of action (of going to forest with Raama). To this great soul, this is a (great) Gain..... (Gain of fame in all the worlds).

❍ ❍ ❍

६. अरण्यवासे यद्दुःखं जानती वै सुखोचिता ।
अनुगच्छति वैदेही धर्मात्मानं तवात्मजम् ।।

6. And (Seetha the) Vaidhehi who is used to comforts, has followed your (son the) noble man of Dharma, (to share and) suffer all the sufferings caused by the life of forest. (What about Seetha, who shares this life voluntarily with your son.)

❍ ❍ ❍

७. कीर्तिभूतां पताकां यो लोके भ्रमयति प्रभुः ।
दमसत्यव्रतपरः किं न प्राप्तस्तवात्मजः ।।

7. (Your son) Is a lord in this world: He is foremost in Restraint; in Truth; In Vows; His fame and glory is like (lofty) banner and well spread. How then (can you grieve over him that) your son is not a man of attainment + (+Word used is = Praaptham = accomplish).

❍ ❍ ❍

८. व्यक्तं रामस्य विज्ञाय शौचं माहात्म्यमुत्तमम् ।
न गात्रमंशुभिः सूर्यः संतापयितुमर्हति ।।

8. (Even) The Sun, realising Raama's purity and his foremost eminence and endowments, will not torment his body with his rays.

❍ ❍ ❍

९. शिवः सर्वेषु कालेषु काननेभ्यो विनिःसृतः ।
राघवं युक्तशीतोष्णः सेविष्यति सुखोऽनिलः ।।

9. (Even) Wind blowing across the dense forests, will serve (Raama) the Raaghava favourably and bring comfort at all times by being moderately cool (in summer) and warm (in winter).

❍ ❍ ❍

१०. शयानमनघं रात्रौ पितेवाभिपरिष्वजन् ।
रश्मिभिः संस्पृशञ्छीतैश्चन्द्रमा ह्लादयिष्यति ।।

10. (Even) Moon will gladden the sinless (Raama) when he rests at night, 'caressing' him and 'embracing' him with rays, just like his father (used to do at Ayodhya).

❍ ❍ ❍

११. ददौ चास्त्राणि दिव्यानि यस्मै ब्रह्मा महौजसे ।
दानवेन्द्रं हतं दृष्ट्वा तिमिध्वजसुतं रणे ।।

11. The great Braamin (Vischwaamithra) who saw the lord of demons (Schambara) the son of Thimidhwaja being killed long ago in battle with such weapons....had given mighty celestial weapons ......

❍ ❍ ❍

१२. स शूरः पुरुषव्याघ्रः स्वबाहुबलमाश्रितः ।
असन्त्रस्तोऽप्यरण्यस्थो वेश्मनीव निवत्स्यति ।।

12. ...... (And so with such weapons from Vischwaamithra), this brave (Raama) the 'tiger' of men who is endowed with his own inborn power, will live in forest without any fear as though he is living in his palace (at Ayodhya).

(Readers may note that in the First Book Bala Kanda, a reference has been made that Raama was very fortunate that he was taught all celestial weapons by Vischwaamithra. and Vischwaamithra was a very mighty, powerful warrior. Of course he became a great man of penance, a Bramma Rishi So Sumithra tells Kowsalya that she need not have any fear over Raama.)

❍ ❍ ❍

१३. यस्येषुपथमासाद्य विनाशं यान्ति शत्रवः ।
कथं न पृथिवी तस्य शासने स्थातुमर्हति ॥

13. The enemies when they come within the range of his arrows, get annihilated; When the World (itself) is under his authority.how then will (it not treat him) worthy (enough).

❍ ❍ ❍

१४. या श्रीः शौर्यं च रामस्य या च कल्याणसत्त्वता ।
निवृत्तारण्यवासः स क्षिप्रं राज्यमवाप्स्यति ॥

14. With resplendent (divine) qualities, with his prowess, with his auspicious qualities of Sathva (Righteousness), he will 'soon' complete his forest life and then obtain (take over) the kingdom.

❍ ❍ ❍

१५. सूर्यस्यापि भवेत्सूर्योह्यग्नेरग्निः प्रभोः प्रभुः ।
श्रियः श्रीश्च भवेदग्र्या कीर्त्याः कीर्तिः क्षमाक्षमा ॥

15. He is the Source of Power to Sun; He gives Fire power to Fire; He is Lord of Lords; He gives Splendour to Resplendency; He is The First to give Glory to the most Glorious; He is indulgent to even those who are insufferable....(merciful to even sinners) .....

❍ ❍ ❍

१६. दैवतं दैवतानां च भूतानां भूतसत्तमः ।
तस्य के ह्यगुणा देवि वने वाऽप्यथ वा पुरे ॥

16. ...... He is God of Gods; He is Most noble amongst all creations; Therefore, Oh Lady! Is there any one in the city or in forest who will treat him without merit (and consideration).

(In Raamaayana, Sumithra was one of the few persons who knew that Raama was a divine being. The above stanzas, read with previous observations of hers, brings this out clearly)

❍ ❍ ❍

१७. पृथिव्या स ह वैदेह्या श्रिया च पुरुषर्षभः ।
क्षिप्रं तिसृभिरेताभिः सह रामोऽभिषेक्ष्यते ॥

17. Such a ' Bull' amongst men, such a Raama, will be anointed along with these three, (namely) With the world, with (Seetha) the Vaidhehi and with Resplendancy. (and) very soon!

❍ ❍ ❍

१८. दुःखजं विसृजन्त्यास्रं निष्क्रामन्तमुदीक्ष्य यम् ।
अयोध्यायां जनः सर्वः शोकवेगसमाहताः ॥

18. Seeing him going away, all the citizens of Ayodhya who are afflicted by the fierceness of grief are shedding tears, caused by sorrow .....

❍ ❍ ❍

१९. कुशचीरधरं वीरं गच्छन्तमपराजितम् ।
सीतेवानुगता लक्ष्मीस्तस्य किं नाम दुर्लभम् ॥

19. ...... (When citizens are like this, when all are with him)...Is there anything difficult for him to obtain who is going away dressed up in 'Bark', (particularly) when this Seetha who is (like Goddess) Lakshmi, is following this brave, invincible (Raama).

❍ ❍ ❍

२०. धनुर्ग्रहवरो यस्य बाणखड्गास्त्रभृत्स्वयम् ।
लक्ष्मणो व्रजति ह्यग्रे तस्य किं नाम दुर्लभम् ॥

20. Is there anything difficult for this man, when the foremost amongst the wielders of bow, this Lakshmana is himself going before him, armed with arrows, sword and weapons.

❍ ❍ ❍

२१. निवृत्तवनवासं तं द्रष्टासि पुनरागतम् ।
जहि शोकं च मोहं च देवि सत्यं ब्रवीमि ते ॥

21. I am telling you this Truth; Give up this, your stupefaction and grief; Oh Lady! You will see (Raama) back again returning from forest.

❍ ❍ ❍

२२. शिरसा चरणावेतौ वन्दमानमनिन्दिते ।
पुनर्द्रक्ष्यसि कल्याणि पुत्रं चन्द्रमिवोदितम् ॥

22. Oh blemishless and auspicious (Koswalya)! You are going to see your venerable son bowing at your feet with his head, like rising of the full Moon, again.

❍ ❍ ❍

२३. पुनः प्रविष्टं दृष्ट्वा तमभिषिक्तं महाश्रियम् ।
समुत्स्रक्ष्यसि नेत्राभ्यां क्षिप्रमानन्दजं पयः ॥

23. You will soon see him crowned, taking over the great kingdom; You will shed tears (but) of joy from your eyes.

❍ ❍ ❍

२४. मा शोको देवि दुःखं वा न रामे दृश्यतेऽशिवम् ।
क्षिप्रं द्रक्ष्यसि पुत्रं तं ससीतं सहलक्ष्मणम् ॥

24. Oh Lady! No harm will come by Raama (in forest). There need be no grief or sorrow. You will see your son with Seetha and Lakshmana (after his exile).

❍ ❍ ❍

२५. त्वयाऽशेषो जनश्चायं समाश्वास्यो यदाऽनघे ।
किमिदानीमिदं देवि करोषि हृदि विक्लबम् ।।

25. Oh sinless lady (Kowsalya)! When this is so, what is this, you have given room for confusion in your heart (mind); (As their queen) All these citizens are to be consoled by you. (Remember).

❍ ❍ ❍

२६. नार्हा त्वं शोचितुं देवि यस्यास्ते राघवः सुतः ।
न हि रामात्परो लोके विद्यते सत्पथे स्थितः ।।

26. Oh Lady! This (Raama the) Raaghava is your son. There is none in the world who is more steadfast in the righteous path than Raama; Therefore you ought not to grieve.

❍ ❍ ❍

२७. अभिवादयोत्मानं तं दृष्ट्वा ससुहृदं सुतम् ।
मुदाऽश्रु मोक्ष्यसे क्षिप्रं मेघलेखेव वार्षिकी ।।

27. When you see your son bowing before you soon, affectionately, you will shed tears of joy, like cluster of clouds (shedding) in rainy season.

❍ ❍ ❍

२८. पुत्रस्ते वरदः क्षिप्रमयोध्यां पुनरागतः ।
कराभ्यां मृदुपीनाभ्यां चरणौ पीडयिष्यति ।।

28. Very soon your son who is a (munificent) bestower, will return to Ayodhya back again to caress (press) your feet with his strong (thick but) soft hands.

❍ ❍ ❍

२९. अभिवाद्य नमस्यन्तं शूरं ससुहृदं सुतम् ।
मुदाऽऽस्रैः प्रोक्षसि पुनर्मेघराजिरिवाचलम् ।।

29. You will shower your son, your brave (Raama) when he announces himself (with Abhivaadhana) and

prostrate before you along with his devoted (Seetha and Lakshmana), with tears of joy, like cloud formations (showering rain) upon mountains.

❍ ❍ ❍

३०. आश्वासयन्ती विविधैश्च वाक्यैः
वाक्योपचारे कुशलाऽनवद्या ।
रामस्य तां मातरमेवमुक्त्वा
देवी सुमित्रा विरराम रामा ॥

30. (Thus Sumithra consoled Kowsalya.)
Faultless in word and speech, skilful (in exposition), this lady Sumithra who delighted everyone, talked thus with various (meaningful) words to Raama's mother, and (after) consoling her, rested (became silent).

❍ ❍ ❍

३१. निशम्य तल्लक्ष्मणमातृवाक्यं
रामस्य मातुर्नरदेवपत्न्याः ।
सद्यः शरीरे विननाश शोकः
शरद्गतो मेघ इवाल्पतोयः ॥

31. Hearing the words of (Sumithra the) mother of Lakshmana, the sorrows of (Kowsalya) the mother of Raama, the wife of king (Dhascharatha), at once disappeared, just like water being shed from the 'body' of clouds laden with sparse water during autumn season.

(Note: What a noble woman this Sumithra is. Her own son Lakshmana has also gone away. Yet she consoles Kowsalya as though she alone will be missing her son Raama.. Readers with religious bent of mind consider Sumithra as a 'divine' lady who alone knew that Raama was God Vishnu on earth.)

❍ ❍ ❍

Chapter 45

(Raama) Reaches Banks of Thamasa River

(Raama continues his journey to forest along with wife Seetha and brother Lakshmana in the Chariot driven by Sumanthra. They reach Thamasa river. Large number of the citizens are following him!)

❍ ❍ ❍

१. अनुरक्ता महात्मानं रामं सत्यपराक्रमम् ।
अनुजग्मुः प्रयान्तं तं वनवासाय मानवाः ।।

1. The citizens who were devoted to the great soul Raama who was truly valiant, followed him when he was going away to forest.

❍ ❍ ❍

२. निवर्तितेऽपि च बलात्सुहृद्वर्गेच राजनि ।
नैव ते संन्यवर्तन्त रामस्यानुगता रथम् ।।

2. As the king (Dhascharatha) who was well disposed (towards his citizens) returned (to his palace) under pressure (from his ministers), those who followed Raama's chariot, did not return (but were following him to go to forest).

❍ ❍ ❍

३. अयोध्यानिलयानां हि पुरुषाणां महायशाः ।
बभूव गुणसंपन्नः पूर्णचन्द्र इव प्रियः ।।

3. The most famous (Raama), who was endowed with all noble qualities, shone like moon, loved by men who were residents of Ayodhya.

❍ ❍ ❍

४. स याच्यमानः काकुत्स्थः स्वाभिः प्रकृतिभिस्तदा ।
कुर्वाणः पितरं सत्यं वनमेवान्वपद्यते ।।

4. At that time, this (Raama) the Kakuthsa, although entreated by his citizens (to return to Ayodhya), was determined upon going to forest to make his father, a man of Truth.

❍ ❍ ❍

५. अवेक्षमाणः सस्नेहं चक्षुषा प्रपिबन्निव ।
उवाच रामः सस्नेहं ताः प्रजाः स्वाः प्रजा इव ।।

5. And Raama who was affectionate to his citizens like his own blood relatives, looked at them with pleasing eye and he addressed them with affection.

❍ ❍ ❍

६. या प्रीतिर्बहुमानश्च मय्ययोध्यानिवासिनाम् ।
मत्प्रियार्थं विशेषेण भरते सा निवेश्यताम् ।।

6. The esteem and affection, you, the citizens of Ayodhya have for me, all that must now be bestowed upon (my brother) Bharatha in (even) greater measure for my sake, for pleasing me.

❍ ❍ ❍

७. स हि कल्याणाचारित्रः कैकेय्यानन्दवर्धनः ।
करिष्यति यथावद्वः प्रियाणि च हितानि च ।।

7. He (my brother Bharatha) who delights his mother Kaikeyi and who possesses all auspicious qualities and who acts properly, will (now) serve you all with affection. and do you all good.

❍ ❍ ❍

८. ज्ञानवृद्धो वयोबालो मृदुर्वीर्यगुणान्वितः ।
अनुरूपः स वो भर्ता भविष्यति भयापहः ।।

8. He is young in years, (yet) old in wisdom. Gentle; Endowed with qualities of the brave; Will protect you properly from fear as your lord.

❍ ❍ ❍

९. स हि राजगुणैर्युक्तो युवराजः समीक्षितः ।
अपि चापि मया शिष्टैः कार्यं वो भर्तृशासनम् ।।

9. Endowed with royal qualities, he is now (appointed as) crown prince being considered fit. King's orders must always be obeyed by me and by you, learned men, as well.

❍ ❍ ❍

१०. न सन्तप्येद्यथा चासौ वनवासं गते मयि ।
महाराजस्तथा कार्योमम प्रियचिकीर्षया ।।

10. If you desire to do good by me, then you must act in such a way that the great king (my father Dascharatha) will not be in torment when I am gone far away to forest.

❍ ❍ ❍

११. यथा यथा दाशरथिर्धर्म एव स्थितोऽभवत् ।
तथा तथा प्रकृतयो रामं पतिमकामयन् ।।

11. (Thus Raama tried to keep the crowd from following him).

As this son of Dhascharatha stood firm in the Path of Dharma, so were the citizens (firm) desirous of making Raama their Lord.

❍ ❍ ❍

१२. बाष्पेण पिहितं दीनं रामः सौमित्रिणा सह ।
चकर्षेत गुणैर्बध्वा जनं पुरनिवासिनम् ।।

12. Raama, who was (ever) with Lakshmana, restrained in many ways, (arguments), the citizens living in the city, whose faces were covered by tears and who were depressed. (It appeared as though Raama) 'Bound' them with reasons and 'dragged' them (away from him).

❍ ❍ ❍

१३. ते द्विजास्त्रिविधं वृद्धा ज्ञानेन वयसौजसा ।
वयःप्रकम्पशिरसो दूराद्चुरिदं वचः ।।

13. The Braamins there who were elderly in three ways (namely) in age, in wisdom, and in penance, then said the following words from a distance, their heads shaking due to their old age.

❍ ❍ ❍

१४. वहन्तो जवना रामं भो भो जात्यास्तुरङ्गमाः ।
निवर्तध्वं न गन्तव्यं हिता भवत भर्तरि ।।

14. Oh! Oh! Ye Horses! Well bred and fast moving horses who are carrying away Raama (to forest): Dont Go! Dont Go:! Turn Back: Be (Considerate and) Do Good To Your Master (king Dhascharatha).

❍ ❍ ❍

१५. कर्णवन्ति हि भूतानि विशेषेण तुरङ्गमाः ।
यूयं तस्मान्निवर्तध्वं याचनां प्रतिवेदिताः ।।

15. All living beings have ears (and hearing): And horses have greater (power of hearing). Therefore, Ye (horses) must understand (must listen) to our pleadings and return. (to Ayodhya with Raama).

(Citizens want Raama back so much they cry before the horses which are driving away Raama to forest in chariot.)

❍ ❍ ❍

१६. धर्मतः स विशुद्धात्मा वीरः शुभदृढव्रतः ।
उपवाह्यस्तु वो भर्ता नापवाह्यः पुराद्वनम् ।।

16. Your master (Raama) is a pure soul. Is resolute in doing good. Very brave. Therefore, as per Dharma, must be brought back. He is not to be carried to forest from the city.

❍ ❍ ❍

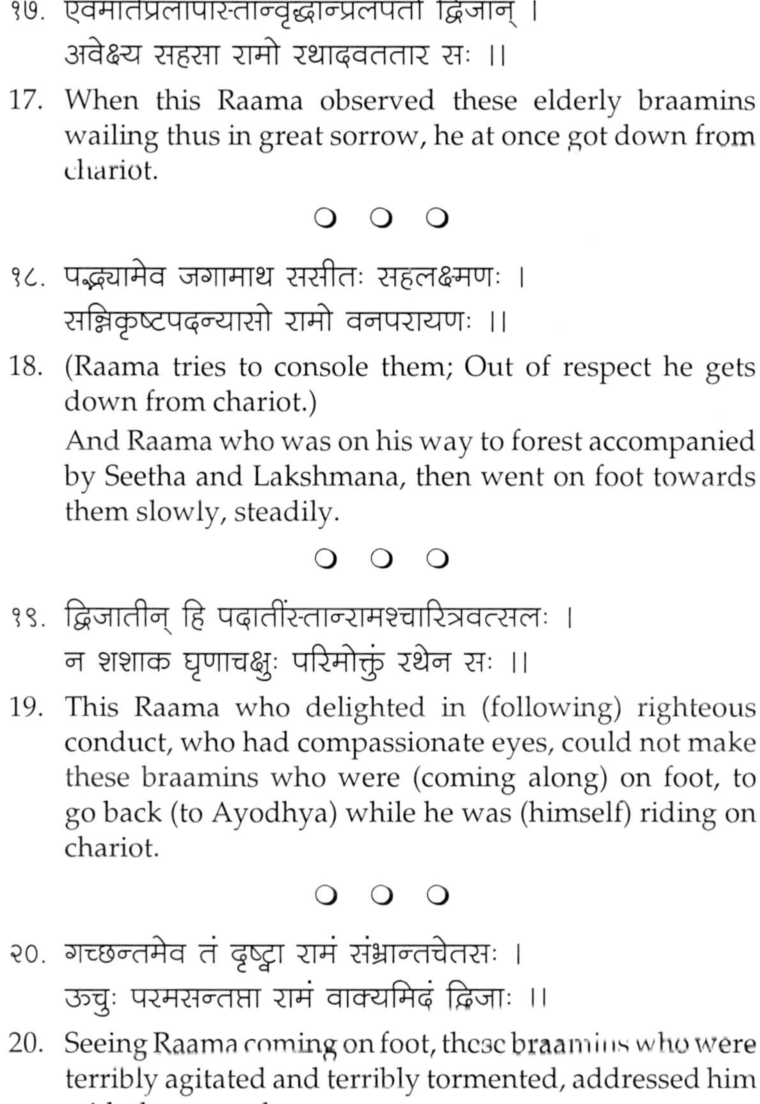

१७. एवमार्तप्रलापांस्तान्वृद्धान्प्रलपतो द्विजान् ।
अवेक्ष्य सहसा रामो रथादवततार सः ॥

17. When this Raama observed these elderly braamins wailing thus in great sorrow, he at once got down from chariot.

❍ ❍ ❍

१८. पद्भ्यामेव जगामाथ ससीतः सहलक्ष्मणः ।
सन्निकृष्टपदन्यासो रामो वनपरायणः ॥

18. (Raama tries to console them; Out of respect he gets down from chariot.)

And Raama who was on his way to forest accompanied by Seetha and Lakshmana, then went on foot towards them slowly, steadily.

❍ ❍ ❍

१९. द्विजातीन् हि पदातींस्तान्रामश्चारित्रवत्सलः ।
न शशाक घृणाचक्षुः परिमोक्तुं रथेन सः ॥

19. This Raama who delighted in (following) righteous conduct, who had compassionate eyes, could not make these braamins who were (coming along) on foot, to go back (to Ayodhya) while he was (himself) riding on chariot.

❍ ❍ ❍

२०. गच्छन्तमेव तं दृष्ट्वा रामं संभ्रान्तचेतसः ।
ऊचुः परमसन्तप्ता रामं वाक्यमिदं द्विजाः ॥

20. Seeing Raama coming on foot, these braamins who were terribly agitated and terribly tormented, addressed him with these words.

❍ ❍ ❍

२१. ब्राह्मण्यं कृत्स्नमेतत्त्वां ब्रह्मण्यमनुगच्छति ।
द्विजस्कन्धाधिरूढास्त्वामग्नयोऽप्यनुयान्त्यमी ॥

21. All these groups of Braamins are following you who are devoted to (Sacred knowledge of) Brammam. All the Ritual Fires are 'following' you, being carried by Braamins on their shoulders.

❍ ❍ ❍

२२. वाजपेयसमुत्थानि छत्राण्येतानि पश्य नः ।
पृष्ठतोऽनुप्रयातानि हंसानिव जलात्यये ॥

22. Behold these umbrellas that were obtained during Vaajapeya Sacrificial ceremonies. These are like swans during dry season and are covering and following us.

❍ ❍ ❍

२३. अनवाप्तातपत्रस्य रश्मिसन्तापितस्य ते ।
एभिश्छायां करिष्यामः स्वैश्छत्रैर्वाजपेयिकैः ॥

23. We are going to give shade to you who are without umbrella, who is tormented by rays of sun, with these umbrellas obtained during Vaajapaayi ceremony.

❍ ❍ ❍

२४. या हि नः सततं बुद्धिर्वेदमन्त्रानुसारिणी ।
त्वत्कृते सा कृता वत्स वनवासानुसारिणी ॥

24. Oh (Raama who is like a) Son! Our mind which is ever bent on following the 'Practice' of Vedha-s and chants, is now (bent on) following you to forest, because of you.

❍ ❍ ❍

२५. हृदयेष्ववतिष्ठन्ते वेदा ये नः परं धनम् ।
वत्स्यन्त्यपि गृहेष्वेव दाराश्चारित्ररक्षिताः ॥

25. You are greater 'wealth' to us than Vedha-s which abide in our hearts: And (our) wives will live in their own homes, protected by their virtue.

❍ ❍ ❍

२६. न पुनर्निश्चयः कार्यस्त्वद्गतौ सुकृता मतिः ।
त्वयि धर्मव्यपेक्षे तु किं स्याद्धर्ममपेक्षितुम् ।।

26. Your decision of going (to forest) must never be acted upon; As you are a man attached to Dharma, this is our rightful prayer. If not, what Dharma is there to look forward to.

❍ ❍ ❍

२७. याचितो नो निवर्तस्व हंसशुक्लशिरोरुहैः ।
शिरोभिर्निभृताचार महीपतनपांसुलैः ।।

27. (Oh Raama) who is resolute in good conduct! Our hair has gone white like the swan (old as we are): We are bowing with our heads down on earth, covered by dust. Begging you as we are, you should return with us (and not go on exile).

❍ ❍ ❍

२८. बहूनां वितता यज्ञा द्विजानां य इहागताः ।
तेषां समाप्तिरायत्ता तव वत्स निवर्तने ।।

28. Oh 'Son'! The successful completion of all those rituals undertaken by elderly braamins, depend on your return (to Ayodhya).

❍ ❍ ❍

२९. भक्तिमन्ति हि भूतानि जङ्गमाजङ्गमानि च ।
याचमानेषु तेषु त्वं भक्तिं भक्तेषु दर्शय ।।

29. All the moving and non moving things, all living beings, are all devoted to you; You must show your 'devotion' (consideration) to those who are devoted to you and who beg you (to return).

❍ ❍ ❍

३०. अनुगन्तुमशक्तास्त्वां गूलैरुद्धतवेगिनः ।
उन्नता वायुवेगेन विक्रोशन्तीव पादपाः ।।

30. The trees, because of their roots, are not able to follow you. (But) They are crying out an agony as if hit by intense fury of wind power, as they stand aloft.

❍ ❍ ❍

३१. निश्चेष्टाहारसञ्चारा वृक्षैकस्थाननिष्ठिताः ।
पक्षिणोऽपि प्रयाचन्ते सर्वभूतानुकम्पिनम् ।।

31. Even birds perched on top of trees are unable to stir out even for food. They are begging you who are compassionate to all living beings.

❍ ❍ ❍

३२. एवं विक्रोशतां तेषां द्विजातीनां निवर्तने ।
ददृशे तमसा तत्र वारयन्तीव राघवम् ।।

32. (Thus the Braamins beg Raama to return to Ayodhya with them.)

When all these braamins were exclaiming thus in the matter of his return, the Thamasa River was sighted, as though it was 'blocking' (Raama the) Raaghava (from proceeding further).

❍ ❍ ❍

३३. ततः सुमन्त्रोऽपि रथाद्विमुच्य
श्रान्तान् हयान् सम्परिवर्त्य शीघ्रम् ।
पीतोदकांस्तोयपरिप्लुताङ्गान्
अचारयद्वै तमसाविदूरे ।।

33. Then (Charioteer) Sumantra unyoked the horses which were tired and soon turned them lose; Making them drink waters (of the river) and bathing their bodies, he allowed them to roam around (the banks of Thamasa river).

❍ ❍ ❍

Chapter 46

(Raama) Tricks the Citizens

(Unable to prevent large number of citizens following him to forest, Raama plays a trick on them so that he can escape into forest without them all.. Raama is very keen that they should get back to Ayodhya.)

❍ ❍ ❍

१. ततस्तु तमसातीरं रम्यमाश्रित्य राघवः ।
सीतामुद्वीक्ष्य सौमित्रिमिदं वचनमब्रवीत् ।।

1. And Raama having reached the beautiful banks of the river Thamasa, looked at Seetha; Then he addressed (Lakshmana) the son of Sumithra, these words.

❍ ❍ ❍

२. इयमद्य निशा पूर्वा सौमित्रे प्रस्थिता वनम् ।
वनवासस्य भद्रं ते न चोत्कण्ठितुमर्हसि ।।

2. Oh (Lakshmana) the son of Sumithra! The first night of our forest life has now come. Welfare to you. Do not give room for regret.

❍ ❍ ❍

३. पश्य शून्यान्यरण्यानि रुदन्तीव समन्ततः ।
यथानिलयमायद्भिर्निलीनानि मृगद्विजैः ।।

3. See this: The creatures of forest, having returned to their nests are hiding themselves from animals and (big) birds; they are crying out in this wilderness everywhere.

❍ ❍ ❍

४. अद्यायोध्या तु नगरी राजधानी पितुर्मम ।
सस्त्रीपुंसाऽऽगतानस्माञ्छोचिष्यति न संशयः ।।

4. Our father's capital of Ayodhya, along with its men and womenfolk, will now be grieving over us who have gone away here; No doubt in me about this.

❍ ❍ ❍

५. अनुरक्ता हि मनुजा राजानं बहुभिर्गुणैः ।
त्वां च मां च नरव्याघ्र शत्रुघ्नभरतौ तथा ॥

5. Oh (Lakshmana) the 'tiger' of men! The citizens are all attached to (our father, the) King, to me and to you and likewise, to Bharatha and Schathrugna because of our various qualities.

❍ ❍ ❍

६. छितरं चानुशोचामि मातरं च यशस्विनीम् ।
अपि वाऽन्धौ भवेतां तु रुदन्तो तावभीक्ष्णशः ॥

6. I grieve for my father and most famous mother. What if they become blind by continuous crying!

❍ ❍ ❍

७. भरतः खलु धर्मात्मा पितरं मातरं च मे ।
धर्मार्थकामसहितैर्वाक्यैराश्वासयिष्यति ॥

7. Yet, (I am sure) the noble soul man of Dharma, Bharatha, will console my father and mother with (soothing) words enjoined with Dharma, Artha and Kaama.

❍ ❍ ❍

८. भरतस्यानृशंसत्वं सञ्चिन्त्याहं पुनः पुनः ।
नानुशोचामि पितरं मातरं चापि लक्ष्मण ॥

8. Oh Lakshmana! Yet I do not grieve (much) over my father ad mother, as I have noticed in Bharatha, qualities of non injury, many, many times (before).
(Bharatha will be very kind, considerate to my mother, says Raama.)

❍ ❍ ❍

९. त्वया कार्यं नरव्याघ्र मामनुव्रजता कृतम् ।
अन्वेष्टव्या हि वैदेह्या रक्षणार्थेसहायता ॥

9. Oh (Lakshmana) 'the tiger' of men! You must offer assistance and 'investigate' in the matter of protection to (Seetha the) Vaidhehi: As you have (chosen to) come along with me, this (I dare say) is the duty to be done by you.

❍ ❍ ❍

१०. अद्भिरेव तु सोमित्रे वत्स्याम्यद्य निशामिमाम् ।
एतद्धि रोचते मह्यं वन्येऽपि विविधे सति ॥

10. Oh (Lakshmana) the son of Sumithra! Although forest is full with various fruits and tubers, I am going to 'live' upon mere water tonight atleast. (Only this) is desired by me.

(Perhaps Raama has no appetite being the first night of separation)

❍ ❍ ❍

११. एवमुक्त्वा तु सौमित्रिं सुमन्त्रमपि राघवः ।
अप्रमत्तस्त्वमश्वेषु भव सौम्येत्युवाच ह ॥

11. Saying thus to (Lakshmana the) son of Sumithra, (Raama) the Raaghava addressed Sumanthra: Oh pleasant man! Be vigilant with your horses.

❍ ❍ ❍

१२. सोऽश्वान्सुमन्त्रः संयम्य सूर्येऽस्तं समुपागते ।
प्रभूतयवसान्कृत्वा बभूव प्रत्यनन्तरः ॥

12. After Sun had set, Sumanthra tied the horses and kept plenty of feeds; he (then) attended to other work.

❍ ❍ ❍

१३. उपास्य तु शिवां सन्ध्यां दृष्ट्वा रात्रिमुपागताम् ।
रामस्य शयनं चक्रे सूतः सौमित्रिणा सह ॥

13. The charioteer (Sumanthra) then performed holy Sandhya rituals and seeing that night was falling,

prepared a bed for Raama, along with (Lakshmana the) son of Sumithra.

❍ ❍ ❍

१४. तां शय्यां तमसातीरे वीक्ष्य वृक्षदलैः कृताम् ।
रामः सौमित्रिणा सार्धं सभार्यः संविवेश ह ।।

14. Observing that a bed of tree leaves were made up with assistance of Lakshmana, on the banks of the river Thamasa, Raama then went to sleep along with his wife.

❍ ❍ ❍

१५. सभार्यं संप्रसुप्तं तं भ्रातरं प्रेक्ष्य लक्ष्मणः ।
कथयामास सूताय रामस्य विविधान्गुणान् ।।

15. And Lakshmana, seeing his brother (Raama) who was fast asleep with his wife, began to narrate about Raama's diverse qualities, to charioteer (Sumanthra).

(Readers may note that Lakshmana does not sleep; Infact during 14 years of exile he rarely slept. Kept vigil, ever.)

❍ ❍ ❍

१६. जाग्रतोरेव सा रात्रिस्तयोः सौमित्रिसूतयोः ।
जगाम तमसातीरे रामस्य ब्रुवतोर्गुणान् ।।

16. As they were conversing about Raama's qualities on the banks of river Thamasa, the night passed away for Lakshmana and the charioteer who were awake. (the whole night).

❍ ❍ ❍

१७. गोकुलाकुलतीरायास्तमसायाऽविदूरतः ।
अवसत्तत्र तां रात्रिं रामः प्रकृतिभिः सह ।।

17. And Raama, along with the citizens (who had come along), spent the night not far from the river Thamasa where there were many cowpens near the banks.

❍ ❍ ❍

१८. उत्थाय तु महातेजाः प्रकृतीस्ता निशाम्य च ।
अब्रवीद्भ्रातरं रामो लक्ष्मणं पुण्यलक्षणम् ।।

18. When this most brilliant Raama got up, he thought about these citizens; He addressed his brother Lakshmana who was endowed with noble qualities.

❍ ❍ ❍

१९. अस्मद्व्यपेक्षान्सौमित्रे निरपेक्षान्गृहेष्विमान् ।
वृक्षमूलेषु संसुप्तान्पश्य लक्ष्मण सांप्रतम् ।।

19. Oh (Lakshman the) son of Sumithra! See these (men) who are most attached to me, lying down, fast asleep under trees without caring for their homes (at Ayodhya).

❍ ❍ ❍

२०. यथैते नियमं पौराः कुर्वन्त्यस्मन्निवर्तने ।
अपि प्राणानसिष्यन्ति न तु त्यक्ष्यन्ति निश्चयम् ।।

20. These citizens are determined on our return (to Ayodhya); Therefore they dont even care for their lives; They will not give up their resolve.

❍ ❍ ❍

२१. यावदेव तु संसुप्तास्तावदेव वयं लघु ।
रथमारुह्य गच्छाम पन्थानमकुतोभयम् ।।

21. While they are fast asleep (and still sleeping), let us get into our chariots and go on our way soon without fear (of being followed by them)

❍ ❍ ❍

२२. अतो भूयोऽपि नेदानीमिक्ष्वाकुपुरवासिनः ।
स्वपेयूरनूरक्ता मां वृक्षमूलानि संश्रिताः ।।

22. The citizens of our Ikshwaaku city (and kingdom) are very much attached to me; They are now sleeping under trees and will soon wake up.

❍ ❍ ❍

२३. पौरा ह्यात्मकृताद्दुःखाद्विप्रमोक्ष्या नृपात्मजैः ।
न ते खल्वात्मना योज्या दुःखेन पुरवासिनः ।।

23. These citizens who are suffering (voluntarily and) without reason, must be relieved (of suffering) by us who are princes. The citizens should not be 'yoked' to (& share with us in) our suffering.

❍ ❍ ❍

२४. अब्रवील्लक्ष्मणो रामं साक्षाद्धर्ममिव स्थितम् ।
रोचते मे महाप्राज्ञ क्षिप्रमारुह्यतामिति ।।

24. Lakshmana at once addressed Raama who was like an embodiment of Dharma Oh must intelligent (Raama)! This (idea) pleases me; (Let us) Mount (the chariot).

❍ ❍ ❍

२५. अथ रामोऽब्रवीच्छ्रीमान्सुमन्त्रं युज्यतां रथः ।
गमिष्यति ततोऽरण्यं गच्छ शीघ्रमिति प्रभुः ।।

25. Then the resplendent Lord, Raama, addressed Sumanthra with these words.= I am going to forest now: Go and make ready the chariot.=

❍ ❍ ❍

२६. सूतस्ततः संत्वरितः स्यन्दनं तैर्हयोत्तमैः ।
योजयित्वाऽथ रामाय प्राञ्जलिः प्रत्यवेदयत् ।।

26. Then charioteer Sumanthra) who was prompt in action, yoked the chariot with these fine horses and informed Raama with Anjali.

❍ ❍ ❍

२७. अयं युक्तो महाबाहो रथस्ते रथिनां वर ।
त्वमारोह सुभद्रं ते ससीतः सहलक्ष्मणः ।।

27. Oh master charioteer (Raama)! Oh man of mighty limbs! Your chariot is ready. You may mount along with Lakshmana and Seetha. Welfare to you.

❍ ❍ ❍

२८. तं स्यन्दनमधिष्ठाय राघवः सपरिच्छदः ।
शीघ्रगामाकुलावर्तां तमसामतरन्नदीम् ।।

28. (Raama the) Raaghava, along with (two) persons accompanying him, got into it, then crossed over the river Thamasa which was fast flowing, turbulent.

२९. स सन्तीर्य महाबाहुः श्रीमाञ्छिवमकण्टकम् ।
प्रापद्यत महामार्गमभयं भयदर्शिनाम् ।।

29. (After going to the other side of river, Raama plans a strategy.)

Getting down from the chariot, the resplendent strong limbed Raama, evolved a great strategy that would be good for these distressed (citizens), that would free them from predicament (suffering) and give them (some) peace and security (at their homes in Ayodhya).

३०. मोहनार्थं तु पौराणां सुतं रामोऽब्रवीद्वचः ।
उदङ्मुखः प्रयाहि त्वं रथमास्थाय सारथे ।।

30. To make the (sleeping) citizens bewildered (about Raama's escape and whereabouts), Raama addressed his charioteer: Oh Charioteer! You take the chariot and go towards north. (alone).

३१. मुहूर्तं त्वरितं गत्वा निवर्तय रथं पुनः ।
यथा न विद्युः पौरा गां तथा कुरु समाहितः ।।

31. (Raama's strategy unfolds): Going away fast for one Muhoortha (of 48 minutes), you come back: Citizens should not know (about this ruse, through chariot markings). You follow me carefully in this. (as I have planned). Do exactly.

३२. रामस्य तु वचः श्रुत्वा तथा चक्रे स सारथिः ।
प्रत्यागम्य च रामस्य स्यन्दनं प्रत्यवेदयत् ।।

32. And the charioteer hearing Raama's words (of order), did this exactly. And returning back, he stationed the chariot before Raama.

❍ ❍ ❍

३३. तौ संप्रयुक्तं तु रथं समास्थितौ
तदा ससीतौ रघुवंशवर्धनौ ।
प्रचोदयामास ततस्तुरङ्गमान्
ससारथिर्येन पथा तपोवनम् ।।

33. And then these two (Raama and Lakshmana) who increased joy and prosperity of Raghu family, sat on the chariot that was ready, along with Seetha. And the charioteer hurried the horses towards the route to forest.

❍ ❍ ❍

३४. ततः समास्थाय रथं महारथः
ससारथिर्दाशरथिर्वनं ययौ ।
उदङ्मुखं तं तु रथं चकार सः
प्रयाणमाङ्गल्यनिमित्तदर्शनात् ।।

34. The great charioteer (Raama the) son of Dhascharatha, having got into the chariot, looked up towards North to seek blessings for his (onward) journey and for his welfare which was customary. Then they all went (drove) to the forest in the chariot (driven) by charioteer. (Sumanthra).

❍ ❍ ❍

Chapter 47

Citizens Return to Ayodhya

१. प्रभातायां तु शर्वर्यां पौरास्ते राघवं विना ।
शोकोपहतनिश्चेष्टा बभूवुर्गतचेतसः ।।

1. When darkness had gone away and it became day, these citizens, not finding (Raama the) Raghava, became helpless overcome by grief and lost their composure.

❍ ❍ ❍

२. शोकजाश्रुपरिद्यूना वीक्षमाणास्ततस्ततः ।
आलोकमपि रामस्य न पश्यन्ति स्म दुःखिताः ।।

2. Looking (all around) there, they could not see any clue (about) Raama's (disappearance): They suffered, shedding tears that came out of their grief.

❍ ❍ ❍

३. ते विषादार्तवदना रहितास्तेन धीमता ।
कृपणाः करुणा वाचो वदन्ति स्म मनस्विनः ।।

3. Abandoned by the wise Raama, the faces of these noble miserable men became down cast and depressed with grief; They began to speak these words that indicated their misery.

❍ ❍ ❍

४. धिगस्तु खलु निद्रां तांययाऽपहृतचेतसः ।
नाद्य पश्यामहे रामं पृथूरस्कं महाभुजम् ।।

4. Fie on that sleep, because of which we lost our senses and are now unable to see the broad chested mighty limbed Raama.

❍ ❍ ❍

५. कथं नाम महाबाहुः स तथाऽवितथक्रियः ।
भक्तं जनमभित्यज्य प्रवासं राघवो गतः ।।

5. How can this mighty limbed Raama whose work never goes in vain, leaving his devoted people, obtain (a life of) exile.

❍ ❍ ❍

६. यो नः सदा पालयति पिता पुत्रानिवौरसान् ।
कथं रघूणां स ज्येष्ठस्त्यक्त्वा नो विपिनं गतः ।।

6. How can this foremost of Raghu-s who protected us always like a father (towards) his own sons, abandon us all and go away to forest.

❍ ❍ ❍

७. इहैव निधनं यामो महाप्रस्थानमेव वा ।
रामेण रहितानां हि किमर्थं जीवितं हि नः ।।

7. Giving up all our wealth, we will go on our 'Last' journey of death here itself; Because, abandoned by Raama, what is the purpose in living.

❍ ❍ ❍

८. सन्ति शुष्काणि काष्ठानि प्रभूतानि महान्ति च ।
तैः प्रज्वाल्य चितां सर्वेप्रविशामोऽथ पावकम् ।।

8. There are lots of dry wood here: We shall alight a Fire over mound and enter (and cremate ourselves alive).

❍ ❍ ❍

९. किं वक्ष्यामो महाबाहुरनसूयः प्रियंवदः ।
नीतः स राघवोऽस्माभिरिति वक्तुं कथं क्षमम् ।।

9. (Raama) the Raaghava is mighty limbed; Never spiteful; Speaks sweetly (kindly); How can we (bear to) say that he was led away (by us) for a short distance (only). What can we tell them.(back home).

❍ ❍ ❍

१०. सा नूनं नगरी दीना दृष्ट्वाऽस्मान्राघवं विना ।
भविष्यति निरानन्दा सस्त्रीबालवयोधिका ।।

10. When this city sees us without Raama (on our return), it will become cheerless with miserable boys, girls and elderly folks.

❍ ❍ ❍

११. निर्यातास्तेन वीरेण सह नित्यं धृतात्मना ।
विहीनास्तेन च पुनः कथं द्रक्ष्याम तां पुरीम् ।।

11. How can we see this city again, having gone away with this brave (Raama) who is ever strong willed (only to be) abandoned by him.

❍ ❍ ❍

१२. इतीव बहुधा वाचो बाहुमुद्यम्य ते जनाः ।
विलपन्ति स्म दुःखार्ता विवत्सा इव धेनवः ।।

12. These people becoming like cows without calves, and engulfed in grief, wailed with various words (of lament), with their hands lifted up.

❍ ❍ ❍

१३. ततो मार्गानुसारेण गत्वा किञ्चित्क्षणं पुनः ।
मार्गनाशाद्विषादेन महता समभिप्लुताः ।।

13. Again, at that moment, following (and going) along the tracks (made by the horses * chariot) for a short (distance) they were overwhelmed by 'madness' because of disappearance of tracks (further on).

❍ ❍ ❍

१४. रथस्य मार्गनाशेन न्यवर्तन्त मनास्विनः ।
किमिदं किं करिष्यामो देवेनोपहता इति ।।

14. When these noble men could not see the tracks of chariot, (they exclaimed): What is this? What will we do now! we are seized by fate. They returned (back to Ayodhya).

❍ ❍ ❍

१५. ततो यथागतेनैव मार्गेण क्लान्तचेतसः ।
अयोध्यामगमन्सर्वेपुरीं व्यथितसज्जनाम् ।।

15. Their minds (totally) shaken up, all these citizens went back to Ayodhya where its good citizens were all restless; By the same route they went back (the route by which they had accompanied Raama).

❍ ❍ ❍

१६. आलोक्य नगरीं तां च क्षयव्याकुलमानसाः ।
अवर्तयन्त तेऽश्रूणि नयनैः शोकपीडितैः ।।

16. Seeing (the citizens of the) city wearied and with perplexed mind, they (who had returned after having failed to go with Raama), shed tears from their eyes, tormented by grief.

❍ ❍ ❍

१७. एषा रामेण नगरी रहिता नातिशोभते ।
आपगा गरुडेनेव ह्रदादुद्धृतपन्नगा ।।

17. Bereft of Raama, this city did not shine; it was like a river (of dead snakes) when snakes are pulled out from pits by Garuda bird.

❍ ❍ ❍

१८. चन्द्रहीनमिवाकाशं तोयहीनमिवार्णवम् ।
अपश्यन्निहतानन्दं नगरं ते विचेतसः ।।

18. The citizens whose senses were numbed, observed that this city was bereft of joy, and was like sky without moon, like ocean without waters.

❍ ❍ ❍

१९. ते तानि वेश्मानि महाधनानि
दुःखेन दुःखेपहता विशन्तः ।
नैव प्रजज्ञुः स्वजनं जनं वा
निरीक्षमाणाः प्रविनष्टहर्षाः ।।

19. Overwhelmed by grief, their joy gone, they entered their wealthy mansions, (only to find) that their folks and others were in great distress, (unconcerned and) without any sense perception (and without interest in anything).

(Note: *Some of the citizens who had chosen to go along with Raama and had followed Raama upto Thamasa river get back to Ayodhya very much disappointed as Raama had played a 'Trick' on them when they were all asleep on the banks of the river. Raama did not want any citizen of Ayodhya to come along wth him to forest, Raama tricked them by this strategy of false Track markings made by the Chariot when Raama asked Sumanthra to drive the empty chariot up North for an hour and get back. On waking up the citizens follow the track of the chariot going towards north, but it leads them nowhere and Raama was 'lost' to them.)

❍ ❍ ❍

Chapter 48

The Womenfolk of Ayodhya wail

१. तेषामेवं विषण्णानां पीडितानामतीव च ।
बाष्पविप्लुतनेत्राणां सशोकानां मुमूर्षया ।।

1. They were all totally downcast and despondent, being in great torment; their eyes were blurred by tears; they were in such a grief that they desired death ......

❍ ❍ ❍

२. अनुगम्य निवृत्तानां रामं नगरवासिनाम् ।
उद्धतानीव सत्त्वानि बभूवुरमनस्विनाम् ।।

2. ...... And to those citizens who had gone along with Raama and returned (without Raama), it appeared as if

the 'Soul' of these citizens (of Ayodhya) had departed (from their body).

❍ ❍ ❍

३. स्वं स्वं निलयमागम्य पुत्रदारैः समावृताः ।
अश्रूणि मुमुचुः सर्वेबाष्पेण पिहिताननाः ।।

3. All of them were inside their homes; they shed tears; their faces covered by tears; they were not (seeking company) with their sons and wives.

❍ ❍ ❍

४. न चाहृष्यन्न चामोदन्वणिजो न प्रसारयन् ।
न चाशोभन्त पण्यानि चापचन्गृहमेधिनः ।।

4. There was no laughter; No rejoicing; Traders did not open shops; No trading activity; Housewives did not cook.

❍ ❍ ❍

५. नष्टं दृष्ट्वा नाभ्यनन्दन्विपुलं वा धनागमम् ।
पुत्रं प्रथमजं लब्ध्वा जननी नाभ्यनन्दत ।।

5. They did not rejoice even on seeing vast moneys (due to them) being returned. Mothers did not rejoice when they received their eldest born son.

❍ ❍ ❍

६. गृहे गृहे रुदन्त्यश्च भर्तारं गृहमागतम् ।
व्यगर्हयन्त दुःखार्ता वाग्भिस्तोत्रैरिव द्विपान् ।।

6. In every household, the grieving and crying (wives) teased their husbands who had returned (without Raama) with these words, like elephants (being goaded, tormented) by goad (elephant hooks).

❍ ❍ ❍

७. किं नु तेषां गृहैः कार्यं किं दारैः किं धनेन वा ।
पुत्रैर्वा किं सुखैर्वापि ये न पश्यन्ति राघवम् ।।

7. Of what use is a house or a wife or wealth or sons or pleasures for these men who cannot see (Raama the) Raaghava.

❍ ❍ ❍

८. एकः सत्पुरुषो लोके लक्ष्मणः सह सीतया ।
योऽनुगच्छति काकुत्स्थं रामं परिचरन्वने ॥

8. (Indeed) In this world it is only Lakshmana who is good (and fortunate) person as he has followed Raama the Kaakuthsa to forest along with Seetha, serving him.

❍ ❍ ❍

९. आपगाः कृतपुण्यास्ताः पद्मिन्यश्च सरांसि च ।
येषु पास्यति काकुत्स्थो विगाह्य सलिलं शुचि ॥

9. And as this (Raama) the Kaakuthsa approaches the pure waters and beholds, (verily) it is these rivers, lotus ponds and lakes that are meritorious.

❍ ❍ ❍

१०. शोभयिष्यन्ति काकुत्स्थमटव्यो रम्यकाननाः ।
आपगाश्च महानूपाः सानुमन्तश्च पर्वताः ॥

10. Beautiful groves, dense forests, mighty ponds, rivers, mountains, hillocks will bring lustre to Raama.

❍ ❍ ❍

११. काननं वाऽपि शैलं वा यं रामोऽनुगमिष्यति ।
प्रियातिथिमिव प्राप्तं नैनं शक्ष्यन्त्यनर्चितुम् ॥

11. To any forest or mountain, if Raama goes, they will not but honour him in everyway as a beloved guest who has come (to them).

❍ ❍ ❍

१२. विचित्रकुसुमापीडा बहुमञ्जरिधारिणः ।
राघवं दर्शयिष्यन्ति नगाभ्रमरशालिनः ॥

12. The trees adorned with strange (exotic) flowers and dense with cluster of flowers and (humming) with black bees, will offer (Raama the) Raaghava delightful sight.

❍ ❍ ❍

१३. अकाले चापि मुख्यानि पुष्पाणि च फलानि च ।
दर्शयिष्यन्त्यनुक्रोशाद्गिरयो राममागतम् ।।

13. Even in off season, the mountains also, will, out of consideration to Raama who has gone there, exhibit foremost flowers and fruits.

❍ ❍ ❍

१४. प्रस्रविष्यन्ति तोयानि विमलानि महीधराः ।
विदर्शयन्तो विविधान्भूयश्चित्रांश्च निर्झरान् ।।
पादपाः पर्वताग्रेषु रमयिष्यन्ति राघवम् ।।

14. And great mountains will make pure waters gush forth from various wonderful waterfalls, exhibiting (to Raama) And trees in mountain top, will delight (Raama the) Raaghava.

❍ ❍ ❍

१५. यत्र रामो भयं नात्र नास्ति तत्र पराभवः ।
स हि शूरो महाबाहुः पुत्रो दशरथस्य च ।।

15. Wherever Raama is, there will be (no injury) or harm: No fear; Truly he is brave and mighty limbed, this son of Dhascharatha.

❍ ❍ ❍

१६. पुरा भवति नो दूरादनुगच्छाम राघवम् ।।

16. He will soon be gone far away; (therefore) we will follow him (now itself).

❍ ❍ ❍

१७. पादच्छाया सुखोदर्का तादृशस्य महात्मनः ।
स हि नाथो जनस्यास्य स गतिः स परायणम् ।।

17. Such as he is, the shadow of the feet of this great soul (Raama) alone can bring comfort; He is indeed the Lord of the worlds. He is our Refuge. He is the last Resort.

❍ ❍ ❍

१८. वयं परिचरिष्यामः सीतां यूयं तु राघवम् ।
इति पौरस्त्रियो भर्तॄन्दुःखार्तास्तत्तदब्रुवन् ।।

18. You serve (Raama) the Raaghava while we (ladies) will serve Seetha respectively. Thus the ladies of the city who were in great grief, talked to their husbands.

❍ ❍ ❍

१९ युष्माकं राघवोऽरण्ये योगक्षेमं विधास्यति ।
सीता नारीजनस्यास्य योगक्षेमं करिष्यति ।।

19. (And they continued)

And in this forest, (Raama) the Raaghava will bestow you all, substance and security; And Seetha will offer substance and security for women folk.

❍ ❍ ❍

२०. को न्वनेनाप्रतीतेन सोत्कण्ठितजनेन च ।
संप्रीयेतामनोज्ञेन वासेन हृतचेतसा ।।

20. Who can take pleasure in (such a) life which is uncommon (strange), which is disagreeable, which has taken away sense of understanding, which (sees) citizens sorrowing (for Raama).

❍ ❍ ❍

२१. कैकेय्या यदि चेद्राज्यं स्यादधर्म्यमनाथवत् ।
न हि नो जीवितेनार्थः कुतः पुत्रैः कुतो धनैः ।।

21. If the kingdom becomes Kaikeyi's, then it will become protector less and will be (steeped in) "Non Dharma".

No purpose in living; When that is so, of what (use to us) with our sons or wealth?

○ ○ ○

२२. यया पुत्रश्च भर्ता च त्यक्तावैश्वर्यकारणात् ।
कं सा परिहरेदन्यं कैकेयी कुलपांसनी ॥

22. When her husband and (step) son have been abandoned by her all for the sake of (mere) wealth (and kingdom), ... this disgrace of her family, ... this Kaikeyi, whom will she not abandon ?

○ ○ ○

२३. कैकेय्या न वयं राज्ये भृतकामा वसेमहि ।
जीवन्त्या जातु जीवन्त्यः पुत्रैरपि शपामहे ॥

23. We shall never live with our lives in this kingdom as hired servants of Kaikeyi (as long as) she is alive; We swear this on our sons.

○ ○ ○

२४. या पुत्रं पार्थिवेन्द्रस्य प्रवासयति निर्घृणा ।
कस्तां प्राप्य सुखं जीवेदधर्म्यां दुष्टचारिणीम् ॥

24. Who can live happily under this evil mongering (Kaikeyi) who is a woman of Adharma, who has sent away the son of our king (to forest) mercilessly.

○ ○ ○

२५. उपद्रुतमिदं सर्वमनालम्बमनायकम् ।
कैकेय्या हि कृते सर्वं विनाशमुपयास्यति ॥

25. Because of this Kaikeyi, everything will become oppressive, despondent (without any support for citizens), everything in total disorder. And (finally) there will be destruction totally.

२६. न हि प्रव्राजिते रामे जीविष्यति महीपतिः ।
मृते दशरथे व्यक्तं विलोपस्तदनन्तरम् ।।

26. And this lord of earth (our king Dhascharatha), will not live when Raama is in exile; And after Dhascharatha dies, ruin will manifest itself.

❍ ❍ ❍

२७. ते विषं पिबतालोड्य क्षीणपुण्याः स्म दुर्गताः ।
राघवं वाऽनुगच्छध्वमश्रुतिं वाऽपि गच्छत ।।

27. Having lost all your merit, all of you who are in misery, may drink poison after deliberation; or go to (Raama) the Raaghava. Or else, go to oblivion (go to hell!).

❍ ❍ ❍

२८. मिथ्या प्रव्राजितो रामः सभार्यः सहलक्ष्मणः ।
भरते संनिविष्टाः स्मः सौनिके पशवो यथा ।।

28. Falsely Raama has been driven away along with his wife and Lakshmana. And we are going to dwell under Bharatha like goats under butcher.

❍ ❍ ❍

२९. पूर्णचन्द्राननः श्यामो गूढजत्रुररिंदमः ।
आजानुबाहुः पद्माक्षो रामो लक्ष्मणपूर्वजः ।।

29. Raama the elder brother of Lakshmana has face like that of the Moon (pleasant). His complexion is royal blue; Has well concealed bones (he is not bony). Is destroyer of enemies. Has long hands.(reaching up to knees) His eyes like lotus.

❍ ❍ ❍

३०. पूर्वाभिभाषी मधुरः सत्यवादी महाबलः ।
सौम्यश्च सर्वलोकस्य चन्द्रवत्प्रियदर्शनः ।।

30. He is first amongst conversationalists. (He initiates discussion); He is sweet; Speaks ever Truth; Mightily

strong: Very pleasant; He is pleasant to all the world like the Moon.

❍ ❍ ❍

३१. नूनं पुरुषशार्दूलो मत्तमातङ्गविक्रमः ।
शोभयिष्यत्यरण्यानि विचरन्स महारथः ॥

31. He is 'tiger' amongst men! Has strides like those of an exhilarated elephant. A great charioteer (warrior): Wandering in forest now he will shine (as ever).

❍ ❍ ❍

३२. तास्तथा विलपन्त्यस्तु नगरे नागराः स्त्रियः ।
चुक्रुशुर्दुःखसंतप्ता मृत्योरिव भयागमे ॥

32. In the city, the ladies of the city were wailing thus and cried aloud afflicted by grief as though they were in fear, awaiting Yama (the lord of Death).

❍ ❍ ❍

३३. इत्येवं विलपन्तीनां स्त्रीणां वेश्मसु राघवम् ।
जगामास्तं दिनकरो रजनी चाभ्यवर्तत ॥

33. When ladies were wailing thus in their homes over (Raama the) Raaghava, the sun obtained sunset. Night fell.

❍ ❍ ❍

३४. नष्टज्वलनसम्पाता प्रशान्ताध्यायसत्कथा ।
तिमिरैघानुलिप्तेव सा तदा नगरी बभौ ॥

34. At that time, none lit fires in the city; No recitations of holy Texts; Every where there was total darkness.

❍ ❍ ❍

३५. उपशान्तवणिक्पण्या नष्टहर्षा निराश्रया ।
अयोध्या नगरी चासीन्नष्टतारमिवाम्बरम् ॥

35. The city of Ayodhya was unsettled; joyless; shops closed with merchandise 'resting' inside. It was like sky without stars.

❍ ❍ ❍

३६. तथा स्त्रियो रामनिमित्तमातुरा
    यथा सुते भ्रातरि वा विवासिते ।
विलप्य दीना रुरुदुर्विचेतसः
    सुतैर्हि तासामधिको हि सोऽभवत् ।।

36. As though their own sons and brothers had been sent away, these ladies who were sick on account of (exile of) Raama, wailed and cried, being miserable, their understanding and perceptions gone. Indeed for them, (Raama) alone was more than their own sons.

❍ ❍ ❍

३७. प्रशान्तगीतोत्सवनृत्तवादिनी
    व्यपास्तहर्षा पिहितापणोदया ।
तदा ह्ययोध्या नगरी बभूव सा
    महार्णवः संक्षुभितोदको यथा ।।

37. The city was like an Ocean with its waters turbulent and violent. All happiness gone. Everything silent, with no music, nor dance, nor (group) singing; Doors of shops were all closed.

❍ ❍ ❍

Chapter 49

(Rama) Crosses River Like Gomathi

१. रामोऽपि रात्रिशेषेण तेनैव महदन्तरम् ।
जगाम पुरुषव्याघ्रः पितुराज्ञामनुस्मरन् ।।

1. Always keeping in mind his father's command, the 'tiger' of men Raama went far away even before balance of night ended.

❍ ❍ ❍

२. तथैव गच्छतस्तस्य व्यपायाद्रजनी शिवा ।
उपास्य तु शिवां सन्ध्यां विषयान्तं व्यगाहत ।।

2. The night passed off pleasantly to him as he was going on his journey: He crossed the border (of the kingdom); There he performed the holy morning Sandhya water ritual.

❍ ❍ ❍

३. ग्रामान्विकृष्टसीमान्तान् पुष्पितानि वनानि च ।
पश्यन्नतिययौ शीघ्रं शनैरिव हयोत्तमैः ।।
श्रृण्वन्वाचो मनुष्याणां ग्रामसंवासवासिनाम् ।।

3. Seeing (and enjoying the sights of) villages where fertile fields were ploughed, and seeing forests where flowers were in blossom, he heard words (conversations) of the men residing in the homes of these villages; Moving away quickly and quietly, he went away with these foremost horses (pulling the chariot).

❍ ❍ ❍

४. विगर्हितां हि कैकेयीं क्रूरं क्रूरेण कर्मणा ।
राजानं धिग्दशरथं कामस्य वशमागतम् ।।

4. (Villagers were talking about Raama); Fie... because of the cruelty by this act of the king Dhascharatha when

he came under the spell and passion of this cruel and despicable Kaikeyi.

❍ ❍ ❍

५. हा नृशंसाऽद्य कैकेयी पापा पापानुबन्धिनी ।
तीक्ष्णा संभिन्नमर्यादा तीक्ष्णे कर्मणि वर्तते ॥

5. This fiery mischievous Kaikeyi, as a consequence (of all this) is now indulging in pungent acts as a sinful woman, breaking away from all norms of propriety. Ah! (What a shame).

❍ ❍ ❍

६. या पुत्रमीदृशं राज्ञः प्रवासयति धार्मिकम् ।
वनवासे महाप्राज्ञं सानुक्रोशं जितेन्द्रियम् ॥

6. She has sent away to the forest such a son of the king, (Sent away Raama) who is a man of Dharma, who is most intelligent, who is a man of compassion, who has conquered 'senses': (very composed man of restraint).

❍ ❍ ❍

७. कथं नाम महाभागा सीता जनकनन्दिनी ।
सदा सुखेष्वभिरता दुःखान्यनुभविष्यति ॥

7. How can Seetha, the daughter of Janaka, who is most illustrious, who is always used to comfort till now, experience suffering now?

❍ ❍ ❍

८. अहो दशरथो राजा निःस्नेहः स्वसुतं प्रियम् ।
प्रजानामनघं रामं परित्यक्तुमिहेच्छति ॥

8. Without any attachment, king Dhascharatha desires to abandon now, his sinless son Raama who is beloved of all citizens.

९. एता वाचो मनुष्याणां ग्रामसंवासवासिनाम् ।
श्रृण्वन्नतिययौ वीरः कोसलान्कोसलेश्वरः ।।

9. (Such words were spoken by villagers): Hearing the words of the residents of villages, (Raama) the brave lord of Kosala, crossed the villages of Kosala.

❍ ❍ ❍

१०. ततो वेदश्रुतिं नाम शीततोयवहां नदीम् ।
उत्तीर्याभिमुखः प्रायादगस्त्याध्युषितां दिशम् ।।

10. Crossing the cool waters of river Vedhaschruthi, (Raama) went in the direction inhabited by Sage Agasthya.

❍ ❍ ❍

११. गत्वा तु सुचिरं कालं ततः शीतजलां नदीम् ।
गोमतीं गोयुतानूपामतरत्सागरङ्गमाम् ।।

11. After going for sometime, he crossed the river Gomathi whose waters were cool and which was flowing towars the Sea, and in whose banks there were lots of cows.

❍ ❍ ❍

१२. गोमतीं चाप्यतिक्रम्य राघवः शीघ्रगैर्हयैः ।
मयूरहंसाभिरुतामतरत्स्यन्दिकां नदीम् ।।

12. Having crossed the river Gomathi, Raama crossed river Syandhika on fast moving horse. (This region) was filled with cooing peacocks and swans.

❍ ❍ ❍

१३. स महीं मनुना राज्ञा दत्तामिक्ष्वाकवे पुरा ।
स्फीतां राष्ट्रावृतां रामो वैदेहीमन्वदर्शयत् ।।

13. And Raama pointed to (Seetha the) Vaidhehi, how these various prosperous 'kingdoms' were given to Ikshwaaku (kings) by king Manu (himself) long ago.

❍ ❍ ❍

१४. सूत इत्येवमाभाष्य सारथिं तमभीक्ष्णशः ।
हंसमत्तस्वरः श्रीमानुवाच पुरुषर्षभः ।।

14. Conversing with his charioteer constantly in tender voice like that of a swan (Raama) the 'Bull' amongst men, this resplendent (Raama) addressed the charioteer thus.

❍ ❍ ❍

१५. कदाऽहं पुनरागम्य सरय्वाः पुष्पिते वने ।
मृगयां पर्यटिष्यामि मात्रा पित्रा च सङ्गतः ।।

15. When will I ever be with my mother and father; when will I go to the full blossomed forest of Sarayu river for hunting!

❍ ❍ ❍

१६. राजर्षीणां हि लोकेऽस्मिन्रत्यर्थं मृगया वने ।
काले वृतां तां मनुजैर्धन्विनामभिकाङ्क्षिताम् ।।

16. In this world hunting in forest for amusement for royal sages (kings) who are wielders of bow, is accepted (as proper only) at proper times, by all men. ...they all look forward to this.. (to hunting) ......

❍ ❍ ❍

१७. अत्यर्थमभिकाङ्क्षामि मृगयां सरयूवने ।
रतिर्ह्येषाऽतुला लोके राजर्षिगणसंमता ।।

17. ...... I desire very much, am greatly looking forward to this hunting in the forest of Sarayu river which is unequalled in this world, which is accepted by multitude of royal sages.

(Readers may note that those days, there was never indiscriminate hunting or devastation of forest.)

❍ ❍ ❍

१८. स तमध्वानमैक्ष्वाकः सूतं मधुरया गिरा ।
तं तमर्थमभिप्रेत्य ययौ वाक्यमुदीरयन् ।।

18. Making conversation with sweet words and expounding various subjects to the charioteer Sumanthra, (Raama) of the Ikshwaaku family, went along the journey.

❍ ❍ ❍

Chapter 50

(Raama) Meets Guha on Banks of River Ganges

१. विशालान् कोसलान्रम्यान्यात्वा लक्ष्मणपूर्वजः ।
अयोध्याभिमुखो धीमान् प्राञ्जलिर्वाक्यमब्रवीत् ।।

1. (Raama) the wise elder brother of Lakshmana, crossed the extensive beautiful Kosala territory: And facing towards Ayodhya, addressed these words with his hands cupped in Anjali.

❍ ❍ ❍

२. आपृच्छे त्वां पुरि श्रेष्ठे काकुत्स्थपरिपालिते ।
दैवतानि च यानि त्वां पालयन्त्यावसन्ति ।।

2. Oh Foremost City That Is Ruled By Ikshwaaku-s,the Kaakuthsas! Farewell To You and To Those Deities That Abide and Protect You.

❍ ❍ ❍

३. निवृत्तवनवासस्त्वामनृणो जगतीपतेः ।
पुनर्द्रक्ष्यामि मात्रा च पित्रा च सह सङ्गतः ।।

3. Discharging my debt to my (father Dhascharatha) the lord of the world, I will see you again (living) along with my father and mother, after I return from my forest life.

❍ ❍ ❍

४. ततो रुचिरताम्राक्षो भुजमुद्यम्य दक्षिणम् ।
अश्रुपूर्णमुखो दीनोऽब्रवीज्जानपदं जनम् ।।

4. Raising his right hand before the village folks, his face full with tears, his lovely eyes turning red (due to sadness), Raama , who was very sad, said to them.

❍ ❍ ❍

५. अनुक्रोशो दया चैव यथार्हं मयि वः कृतः ।
चिरं दुःखस्य पापीयो गम्यतामर्थसिद्धये ।।

5. (I appreciate and) I accept your compassionate and tender feelings towards me: Permit me to go for fulfilling my obligations. It is sinful to grieve for long.

❍ ❍ ❍

६. तेऽभिवाद्य महात्मानं कृत्वा चापि प्रदक्षिणम् ।
विलपन्तो नरा घोरं व्यतिष्ठन्त क्वचित्क्वचित् ।।

6. Then these folks bowed and went round the great soul (Raama) in circumbumbulation: Wailing bitterly, they spread out here and there.

❍ ❍ ❍

७. तथा विलपतां तेषामतृप्तानां च राघवः ।
अचक्षुर्विषयं प्रायाद्यथार्कः क्षणदामुखे ।।

7. Even as they were wailing and were unsatisfied (with Raama's resolve to go to forest), (Raama the) Raaghava went away beyond their sight like Sun before nightfall.

❍ ❍ ❍

८. ततो धान्यधनोपेतान्दानशीलजनाञ्छिवान् ।
अकुतश्चिद्भयान्रम्यांश्चैत्ययूपसमावृतान् ।।

8. (Poet Vaalmeeki describes Kosala territories): Plenty of grains and riches endowed (this Kosala region); Peopled by men of charitable disposition: Everything auspicious: No fear from any quarter: Full of beautiful ritual places with (Fire) mounds ......

❍ ❍ ❍

९. उद्यानाम्रवणोपेतान् सम्पन्नसलिलाशयान् ।
तुष्टपुष्टजनाकीर्णान् गोपगोकुलसेवितान् ।।

9. ..... Gardens, mango groves, ponds, pools, well maintained with plenty of waters: Citizens well nourished and healthy; With plenty of cowherds and shepherds .....

❍ ❍ ❍

१०. रक्षणीयान्नरेन्द्राणां ब्रह्मघोषाभिनादितान् ।
रथेन पुरुषव्याघ्रः कोसलानत्यवर्तत ।।

10. ...... Well protected against (other) rulers (chieftains): Sounds of recitations of holy scriptures always heard: (Such a) Kosala kingdom (Raama) the 'tiger' of men left behind, riding on chariot.

❍ ❍ ❍

११. मध्येन मुदितं स्फीतं रम्योद्यानसमाकुलम् ।
राज्यं भोग्यं नरेन्द्राणां ययौ धृतिमतां वरः ।।

11. The foremost amongst those steadfast in doing things, (this Raama) reached at mid day, the territory which was rich, which had lovely gardens, which gave pleasure to kings.

❍ ❍ ❍

१२. ततस्त्रिपथगां दिव्यां शीततोयामशैवलाम् ।
ददर्श राघवो गङ्गां पुण्यामृषिनिषेविताम् ।।

12. There (Raama) the Raaghava saw the divine and auspicious river Ganges which flows out in 'Three Ways'. whose waters are cool, free from weeds and moss, which is honoured by Sages.

❍ ❍ ❍

१३. आश्रमैरविदूरस्थैः श्रीमद्भिः समलंकृताम् ।
कालेऽप्सरोभिर्हृष्टाभिः सेविताम्भोहृदां शिवाम् ।।

१४. देवदानवगन्धर्वैः किन्नरैरुपशोभिताम् ।
नानागन्धर्वपत्नीभिः सेवितां सततं शिवाम् ।।

१५. देवक्रीडाशताकीर्णां देवोद्यानयुतां नदीम् ।
देवार्थमाकाशगमां विख्यातां देवपद्मिनीम् ।।

१६. जलाघाताट्टहासोग्रां क्वचिदावर्तशोभिताम् ।
क्वचिद्वेणीकृतजलां क्वचिदावर्तशोभिताम् ।।

१७. क्वचित्स्तिमितगम्भीरां क्वचिद्वेगजलाकुलाम् ।
क्वचिद्गम्भीरनिर्घोषां क्वचिद्भैरवनिस्वनाम् ।।

१८. देवसङ्घाप्लुतजलां निर्मलोत्पलसंकुलाम् ।
क्वचिदाभोगपुलिनां क्वचिन्निर्मलवालुकाम् ।।

१९. हंससारससंघुष्टां चक्रवाकोपकूजिताम् ।
सदा मत्तैश्च विहगैरभिसंनादितान्तराम् ।।
क्वचित्तीररुहैर्वृक्षैर्मालाभिरुपशोभिताम् ।।

२०. क्वचित्फुल्लोत्पलच्छन्नां क्वचित्पद्मवनाकुलाम् ।
क्वचित्कुमुदषण्डैश्च कुड्मलैरुपशोभिताम् ।।

२१. नानापुष्परजोध्वस्तां समदामिव च क्वचित् ।
व्यपेतमलसंघातां मणिनिर्मलदर्शनाम् ।।

२२. दिशागजैर्वनगजैर्मत्तैश्च वरवारणैः ।
देवोपवाह्यैश्च मुहुः संनादितवनान्तराम् ।।

२३. प्रमदामिव यत्नेन भूषितां भूषणोत्तमैः ।
फलैः पुष्पैः किसलयैर्वृतां गुल्मैर्द्विजैस्तथा ।।

२४. शिशुमारैश्च नक्रैश्च भुजङ्गैश्च निषेविताम् ।
विष्णुपादच्युतां दिव्यामपापां पापनाशिनीम् ।।

२५. तां शङ्करजटाजूटाद्भ्रष्टां सागरतेजसा ।
समुद्रमहिषीं गङ्गां सारसक्रौञ्चनादिताम् ।।
आससाद महाबाहुः शृङ्गवेरपुरं प्रति ।।

13 to 25:

(Poet Vaalmeeki describes Ganges and basin at this place; Stanzas 13 to 25: readers may refer to Baala Kaanda also.)

Nor far from there, there were beautiful holy hermitages around the territory: And where during seasons, the (Ganga) waters are enjoyed by Apsara maidens... Ever auspicious, it is frequented ("ornamented') by Dheva-s, Dhaanava-s, Kinnaras, and many wives of Ghandharvass......Full of celestials sporting (in the waters): studded with gardens that are heavenly: River which is famous and which went over the sky for the sake of celestials; full of lotus befitting celestials......... Waves of the river making terrible sounds; its foam (white) and spotless like a smile (with white teeth); the river which at some place is confluenced by Waters (of rivers like Yamuna, Saraswathi etc); At some places where there are whirlpools....... Where at some places it flows in tranquility and in some places where it is deep; in some places it flows rapidly with surging waters; where in some places it makes deep sounds; where in some places the sounds are terrible......Its waters are bathed by multitude of Dheva-s: Full with pure lotuses in abundance; in some places where there are wide sand banks. In some places where lots of pebbles (line up the banks).... Abundant in swans and Sarasa birds; where cooing of Chakravaaka birds are heard; where intermittent sounds are heard from joyous birds; where in some places, the banks are beautified, lined up with row of trees....

Where in some places it is densely covered with Nilothpala flowers; where in some places it is dense with clusters of lotus; where in some places there are plenty of water lillies: beautified by flowers in full bloom......... where in some places, heaps of secretions of intoxicated (birds) are spread and covered by pollens from various flowers; Where (in some places) it glitters like pure

Gem.......where the forests (around the river at some places) reverberate continuously with sounds of wild elephants of forest with foremost of elephants, (like) the Dischagaja-s (The eight Mythological elephants 'Bearing' The Earth: namely, Eyeraawatha, Vaamana, Pundareeka, Kumudha, Anjana, Pushpadhantha, Sarvabhowma, Soopradhika).......(River) Looking like a lovely maiden ornamented with foremost ornaments with great effort; With its fruits, flowers, tender plants; with fine wharfs (for bathing), fine fishes ...... (River) abundant in Simsumaara fishes, crocodiles, river snakes: This sinless divine (River) that originated from the feet of God Vishnu: (The river) that removes Sin.....(the River) That flowed out through Hair locks of God Schiva; (thus released on earth) by the power of Sagara's (great,great grandson Bhageeratha): Sarasa birds and Krauncha birds making cooing sounds; To this Ganges which is consort of king of the oceans, the mighty limbed (Raama) came (at a town called) Schringabhaerapura.

(Schringabhaerapura, according to some, is near Mirzapur in UP.)

❍ ❍ ❍

२६. तामूर्मिकलिलावर्तामन्ववेक्ष्य महारथः ।
सुमन्त्रमब्रवीत्सूतमिहैवाद्य वसामहे ॥

26. The great charioteer (warrior Raama) looked at this (Ganges) which was surging with waves. And he addressed his charioteer Sumanthra:= We Shall Stay Here = (for a while).

❍ ❍ ❍

२७. अविदूरादयं नद्या बहुपुष्पप्रवालवान् ।
सुमहानिङ्गुदीवृक्षो वसामोऽत्रैव सारथे ॥

27. Oh charioteer! Near the river there is a big Ingu tree

in full blossom: We shall stay there (under tree= Terminaali Catappa=)

❍ ❍ ❍

२८. द्रक्ष्यामः सरितां श्रेष्ठां संमान्यसलिलां शिवाम् ।
देवदानवगन्धर्वमृगमानुषपक्षिणाम् ।।

28. We shall behold (and worship) this auspicious and foremost of rivers, (this Ganges) whose waters are 'honoured' by Dheva-s, Dhaanava-s, Ghandharva-s, animals and men.

❍ ❍ ❍

२९. लक्ष्मणश्च सुमन्त्रश्च बाढमित्येव राघवम् ।
उक्त्वा तमिङ्गुदीवृक्षं तदोपययतुर्हयैः ।।

29. And Lakshmana and Sumanthra told Raama: =So Be It:= Then they went to the Ingudha tree with their horses.

❍ ❍ ❍

३०. रामोऽभियाय तं रम्यं वृक्षमिक्ष्वाकुनन्दनः ।
रथादवातरत्तस्मात्सभार्यः सहलक्ष्मणः ।।

30. The darlings of Ikshwaaku race, this Raama, approaching the beautiful tree, then got down from the chariot along with his wife and Lakshmana.

❍ ❍ ❍

३१. सुमन्त्रोऽप्यवतीर्यास्मान्मोचयित्वा हयोत्तमान् ।
वृक्षमूलगतं राममुपतस्थे कृताञ्जलिः ।।

31. And Sumanthra also got down, set free the foremost horses (unyoked them from chariot), and came near Raama who was under the tree, with his hands cupped in Anjali.

❍ ❍ ❍

३२. तत्र राजा गुहो नाम रामस्यात्मसमः सखा ।
निषादजात्यो बलवान् स्थपतिश्चेति विश्रुतः ।।

32. There lived there a chieftain ruling that place, a strong man born in the family of hunters, Guha by name, who was well known as a friend of Raama, (dear to him as) his own life.

❍ ❍ ❍

३३. स श्रुत्वा पुरुषव्याघ्रं रामं विषयमागतम् ।
वृद्धैः परिवृतोऽमात्यैर्ज्ञातिभिश्चाप्युपागतः ।।

33. Hearing that this Raama the 'tiger' of men had come to the region, he came accompanied by his ministers, relatives and other elders.

❍ ❍ ❍

३४. ततो निषादाधिपतिं दृष्ट्वा दूरादवस्थितम् ।
सह सौमित्रिणा रामः समागच्छद्गुहेन सः ।

34. Raama saw this lord of hunters (his friend Guha) who was long resident (of these parts) and he (got together), conversed with Guha along with Lakshmana.

❍ ❍ ❍

३५. तमार्तः संपरिष्वज्य गुहो राघवमब्रवीत् ।
यथाऽयोध्या तथेदं ते राम किं करवाणि ते ।।

35. And Guha who was distressed (seeing Raama in that state) hugged (Raama the) Raaghava and said this to him: Oh Raama! This (place) is like Ayodhya for you. What should be done for you (by me).

❍ ❍ ❍

३६. ईदृशं हि महाबाहो कः प्राप्स्यत्यतिथिं प्रियम् ।।

36. Oh mighty limbed Raama! Who can (have the good fortune to) obtain (and receive) such a beloved guest!

❍ ❍ ❍

३७. ततो गुणवदन्नाद्यमुपादाय पृथग्विधम् ।
अर्घ्यं चोपानयत्क्षिप्र वाक्यं चेदमुवाच ह ।।

37. After placing (before him) wonderful and various types of foods, he offered Arghya at once. And then said:

❍ ❍ ❍

३८. स्वागतं ते महाबाहो तवेयमखिला मही ।
वयं प्रेष्या भवान् भर्ता साधु राज्यं प्रशाधि नः ।।

38. Oh mighty limbed (Raama)! Welcome to you! All this Earth (including my territory) is yours. We are your 'servants'. As you are lord to the kingdom and to us, you command (me as you wish).

❍ ❍ ❍

३९. भक्ष्यं भोज्यं च पेयं च लेह्यं चोष्यमुपस्थितम् ।
शयनानि च मुख्यानि वाजिनां खादनं च ते ।।

39. All these have been brought for you; Foods, eats, drinks, syrupy (sweet things); fried things, and foremost beds, feeds for horses.

❍ ❍ ❍

४०. गुहमेवं ब्रुवाणं तु राघवः प्रत्युवाच ह ।
अर्चिताश्च प्रहृष्टाश्च भवता सर्वथा वयम् ।।
पद्भ्यामभिगमाच्चैव स्नेहसंदर्शनेन च ।।

40. Guha the lord of hunters wants to treat his dear friend Raama with some hospitality; but alas, Raama declines. He is no longer a prince but a common mendicant.

And Raama replied to Guha when he had spoken thus. We are (deeply) honoured by you in every way by your deep exhibition of your friendship for us and by (your rushing to us) coming on foot. We are delighted.

❍ ❍ ❍

४१. भुजाभ्यां साधु वृत्ताभ्यां पीडयन्वाक्यमब्रवीत् ।।

41. Hugging him happily with his well rounded arms (his bones well concealed by flesh), he said:

❍ ❍ ❍

४२. दिष्ट्या त्वां गुह पश्यामि ह्यरोगं सह बान्धवैः ।
अपि ते कुशलं राष्ट्रे मित्रेषु च धनेषु च ॥

42. Oh Guha! I am seeing you in good health along with your folks: By my good fortune (indeed)! Is everything well with you, with your citizens, friends and substance (of wealth etc).

❍ ❍ ❍

४३. यत्त्विदं भवता किञ्चित्प्रीत्या समुपकल्पितम् ।
सर्वं तदनुजानामि न हि वर्तेप्रतिग्रहे ॥

43. (But) I am in no position to receive (these) whatsoever: Therefore all that have been offered by you out of your affection for me, I am leaving (without enjoying them).

❍ ❍ ❍

४४. कुशचीराजिनधरं फलमूलाशिनं च माम् ।
विद्धि प्रणिहितं धर्मेतापसं वनगोचरम् ॥

44. Know me (and consider me) as a mendicant living in forest, donning (forest dress of) 'Bark' and deer skin, totally bent towards Dharma, sustaining myself (only) on tubers and fruits.

❍ ❍ ❍

४५. अश्वानां खादनेनाहमर्थी नान्येन केनचित् ।
एतावताऽत्रभवता भविष्यामि सुपूजितः ॥

45. I will be satisfied with (just offer of) food for (my) horses: Nothing else, (I want) not; At this time, by this alone I become well honoured (by you)

(Raama's acceptance of forest life is total; He honours Kaikeyi's command in letter and spirit.)

❍ ❍ ❍

४६. एते हि दयिता राज्ञः पितुर्दशरथस्य मे ।
एतैः सुसुखितैरश्वैर्भविष्याम्यहमर्चितः ॥

46. These (horses) are most cherished by my father Dhascharatha: I become honoured by these horses when they are in comfort. Indeed.

❍ ❍ ❍

४७. अश्वानां प्रतिपानं च खादनं चैव सोऽन्वशात् ।
गुहस्तत्रैव पुरुषांस्त्वरितं दीयतामिति ॥

47. Therefore, this Guha then commanded his men thus:= At once, may feeds and water be brought for the horses.=

❍ ❍ ❍

४८. तश्चीरोत्तरासङ्गः सन्ध्यामन्वास्य पश्चिमाम् ।
जलमेवाददे भोज्यं लक्ष्मणेनाहृतं स्वयम् ॥

48. Then after performing evening rituals of Sandhya, Raama who was dressed in forest robes of bark and deer skin, partook water only that was brought by Lakshmana as his food (for the night).

❍ ❍ ❍

४९. तस्य भूमौ शयानस्य पादौ प्रक्षाल्य लक्ष्मणः ।
सभार्यस्य ततोऽभ्येत्य तस्थौ वृक्षमुपाश्रितः ॥

49. And Lakshmana washed the feet of (Raama) who was lying down on bare earth along with his wife (Seetha) and then he stood by the side of the tree, holding (resting) on it.

❍ ❍ ❍

५०. गुहोऽपि सह सूतेन सौमित्रिमनुभाषयन् ।
अन्वजाग्रत्ततो राममप्रमत्तो धनुर्धरः ॥

50. There, Guha conversed with (Lakshmana the) son of Sumatra along with charioteer (Sumanthra) about Raama. And spent the night in vigil, awake, wielding bow (in hand)

❍ ❍ ❍

५१. तथा शयानस्य ततोऽस्य धीमतो
यशस्विनो दाशरथेर्महात्मनः ।
अदृष्टदुःखस्य सुखोचितस्य सा
तदा व्यतीयाय चिरेण शर्वरी ॥

51. To this great soul, wise and famous (Raama) the son of Dhasciharatha who was ever used to comforts, who had never seen suffering before, (but) who was then sleeping there like that (on bare earth), that night passed away after a long time (as though) ......

❍ ❍ ❍

Chapter 51

Lakshmana and Guha Converse

१. तं जाग्रतमदम्भेन भ्रातुरर्थाय लक्ष्मणम् ।
गुहः सन्तापसन्तप्तो राघवं वाक्यमब्रवीत् ॥

1. Guha who was most straight forward (free from deceit), addressed Lakshmana the Raaghava who was awake for the sake of (safety of) his brother (Raama who was sleeping along with Seetha), he was tormented (by Lakshmana's self mortification and) suffering (for the sake of his brother).

❍ ❍ ❍

२. इयं तात सूखा शय्या त्वदर्थमुपकल्पिता ।
प्रत्याश्वसिहि साध्वस्यां राजपुत्र यथासुखम् ॥

2. Oh dear (Lakshmana)! Oh royal prince! This, a comfortable bed has been set up for you here; please refresh yourself as you please.

❍ ❍ ❍

३. उचितोऽयं जनः सर्वः क्लेशानां त्वं सुखोचितः ।
गुप्त्यर्थं जागरिष्यामः काकुत्स्थस्य वयं निशाम् ॥

3. All these people (of mine) are used to discomforts (and 'suffering'): (But) You are used to comforts. We shall keep vigil (right) through the night for safety of (Raama) the Kaakuthsa.

❍ ❍ ❍

४. न हि रामात्प्रियतमो ममास्ति भुवि कश्चन ।
ब्रवीम्येतदहं सत्यं सत्येनैव च ते शपे ।।

4. In this world, there is none dearer to me than Raama: I am telling this in Truth: I am swearing on Truth.

❍ ❍ ❍

५. अस्य प्रसादादाशंसे लोकेऽस्मिन्सुमहद्यशः ।
धर्मावाप्तिं च विपुलामर्थावाप्तिं च केवलाम् ।।

5. In this world, all the great fame, acquisition of knowledge of Dharma, acquisition of mundane wealth, are all due to his munificence. (to his grace), I affirm!

❍ ❍ ❍

६. सोऽहं प्रियसखं रामं शयानं सह सीतया ।
रक्षिष्यामि धनुष्पाणिः सर्वतो ज्ञातिभिः सह ।।

6. Such as I am, along with my folks, bearing bow in my arm, will protect my dear comrade Raama who is sleeping along with Seetha.

❍ ❍ ❍

७. न हि मेऽविदितं किञ्चिद्वनेऽस्मिंश्चरतः सदा ।
चतुरङ्गं ह्यपि बलं सुमहत्प्रसहेमहि ।।

7. As I am constantly wandering in these forests, there is nothing that is not known to me; (Why!) We can even conquer a mighty army drawn from Four Services.

❍ ❍ ❍

८. लक्ष्मणस्तं तदोवाच रक्ष्यमाणास्त्वयाऽनघ ।
नात्र भीता वयं सर्वेधर्ममेवानुपश्यता ।।

8. And Lakshmana then said to him: Oh sinless (Guha) ! As we are protected by you who sees Dharma only (who follows Dharma), we are in no fear (at all here).

❍ ❍ ❍

९. कथं दाशरथौ भूमौ शयाने सह सीतया ।
शक्या निद्रा मया लब्धुं जीवितं वा सुखानि ॥

9. (But) When (this Raama the) son of Dhascharatha is lying down on bare earth along with Seetha, how will it be possible for me to obtain (or seek) comforts, sleep or (even seek) livelihood.

❍ ❍ ❍

१०. यो न देवासुरैः सर्वैः शक्यः प्रसहितुं युधि ।
तं पश्य सुखसंसुप्तं तृणेषु सह सीतया ॥

10. You are seeing. (see such a man) who cannot be overpowered even by Dheva-s or Asura-s in war, lying down along with Seetha, sleeping happily on grass.

❍ ❍ ❍

११. यो मन्त्रतपसा लब्धो विविधैश्चपरिश्रमैः ।
एको दशरथस्येष्टः पुत्रः सदृशलक्षणः ॥

11. He is unique: He is beloved (of all): He is born as a son to Dhascharatha obtained by him through various Sacrifices and rigorous prayers (exertions). His (noble) qualities befit him.

❍ ❍ ❍

१२. अस्मिन्प्रव्राजिते राजा न चिरं वर्तयिष्यति ।
विधवा मेदिनी नूनं क्षिप्रमेव भविष्यति ॥

12. And as he is on exile, King (Dhascharatha) will not live long (pining away in grief): And so the Earth will soon become widowed.

❍ ❍ ❍

१३. अनुरक्तजनाकीर्णा सुखालोकप्रियावहा ।
राजव्यसनसंसृष्टा सा पुरी विनशिष्यति ॥

13. The City (Ayodhya) which is full with people who are devoted to him, which looks beautiful, which delights (citizens), will now (wither away) and be destroyed, grieving over the loss of the king.

❍ ❍ ❍

१४. विनद्य सुमहानादं श्रमेणोपरताः स्त्रियः ।
निर्घोषोपरतं तात मन्ये रामनिवेशनम् ॥

14. Oh dear (Guha)! I should imagine that Raama's palace will be stilled by silence after the ladies cry out in loud voice and stop (crying) due to fatigue.

❍ ❍ ❍

१५. कौसल्या चैव राजा च तथैव जननी मम ।
नाशंसे यदि जीवन्ति सर्वेते शर्वरीमिमाम् ॥

15. I suspect that the king, Kowsalya and my mother (Sumithra) may not live through this night (this first night of separation from us).

❍ ❍ ❍

१६. जीवेदपि हि मे माता शत्रुघ्नस्यान्ववेक्षया ।
तद्दुःखं यत्तु कौसल्या वीरसूर्विनशिष्यति ॥

16. Perhaps my mother (Sumithra), out of consideration for (my brother) Schathrugna may be alive. But Kowsalya, the mother of the brave son (Raama) will die, by all this grief.
(As readers know Sumithra had two sons, Lakshmana and Schathrugna. So she may live for atleast Schathrugna's sake.)

❍ ❍ ❍

१७. कथं पुत्रं महात्मानं ज्येष्ठं सन्तमपश्यतः ।
शरीरं धारयिष्यन्ति प्राणा राज्ञो महात्मनः ॥

17. How can life be sustained in the body of this great soul king when he cannot see his eldest, virtuous great soul son.(Raama)?

❍ ❍ ❍

१८. विनष्टे नृपतौ पश्चात्कौसल्या विनशिष्यति ।
अनन्तरं च माताऽपि मम नाशमुपैष्यति ॥

18. After the king dies, Kowsalya will die. Then my mother will also attain death.

❍ ❍ ❍

१९. अतिक्रान्तमतिक्रान्तमनवाप्य मनोरथम् ।
राज्ये राममनिक्षिप्य पिता मे विनशिष्यति ॥

19. My father will die unable to fulfill his wish of appointing his son Raama in the kingdom. (as Yuva raaja). Oh What a transgression, What a transgression!

❍ ❍ ❍

२०. सिद्धार्थाः पितरं वृत्तं तस्मिन्कालेऽप्युपस्थिते ।
प्रेतकार्येषु सर्वेषु संस्करिष्यन्ति भूमिपम् ॥

20. When that time comes, only those who are blessed (accomplished) will perform The Last Rites of my dead father, the lord of earth.

❍ ❍ ❍

२१. रम्यचत्वरसंस्थानां सुविभक्तमहापथाम् ।
हर्म्यप्रासादसम्पन्नां गणिकावरशोभिताम् ॥
२२. रथाश्वगजसंबाधां तूर्यनादविनादिताम् ।
सर्वकल्याणसम्पूर्णां हृष्टपुष्टजनाकुलाम् ॥
२३. आरामोद्यानसंपन्नां समाजोत्सवशालिनीम् ।
सुखिता विचरिष्यन्ति राजधानीं पितुर्मम ॥

21. to 23.

(Once again poet describes Ayodhya through lips of Lakshmana.)

The city boasts of beautiful well laid out (Royal) boulevards and quadrangles; Captivating mansions plenty (in the city); Shining lovely with wonderful Ganika flowers (Premna Spinosa)....... Full of chariots and elephants and horses; Strains from musical instruments of Thoorya, reverberating (the city); Auspicious festivities (all over the city); Full with people who suffer no disease nor wants......Endowed with gardens, orchards: public meetings and festival (Congregations galore); Only fortunate people will move about in my father's capital city (of his kingdom).

❍ ❍ ❍

२४. अपि जीवेद्दशरथो वनवासात्पुनर्वयम् ।
प्रत्यागम्य महात्मानमपि पश्याम सुव्रतम् ।।

24. Will Dhascharatha live (at all)! After we return back again from exile of forest life, will we see this great soul (my father) who is most pious.

❍ ❍ ❍

२५. अपि सत्यप्रतिज्ञेन सार्धं कुशलिना वयम् ।
निवृत्तवनवासेऽस्मिन्नयोध्यां प्रविशेमहि ।।

25. Fulfilling his word of honour and truth, when he completes his forest life (of 14 years) will we (return and) enter Ayodhya in good state?

❍ ❍ ❍

२६. परिदेवयमानस्य दुःखार्तस्य महात्मनः ।
तिष्ठतो राजपुत्रस्य शर्वरी साऽत्यवर्तत ।।

26. The night was spent away (thus) by this great soul (Lakshmana) the son of the king, who was lamenting in deep sorrow and who was standing there (keeping vigil over Raama).

❍ ❍ ❍

२७. तथा हि सत्यं ब्रुवति प्रजाहिते
नरेन्द्रपुत्रे गुरुसौहृदाद्गुहः ।
मुमोच बाष्पं व्यसनाभिपीडितो
ज्वरातुरो नाग इव व्यथातुरः ।।

27. While the son of the king (this Lakshmana) who was ever (concerned with) welfare of the people, was speaking thus with such truthful words coming out of his mouth out of his affection for his Guru (and brother Raama), Guha became tormented and shed tears like an elephant that is suffering from pain and high fever.

❍ ❍ ❍

Chapter 52

Raama and Others Cross Ganges

१. प्रभातायां तु शर्वर्यां पृथुवक्षा महायशाः ।
उवाच रामः सौमित्रिं लक्ष्मणं शुभलक्षमणम् ।।

1. When night ended and it dawned, the broad chested and most famous Raama addressed Lakshmana, the son of Sumithra who was endowed with auspicious qualities.

❍ ❍ ❍

२. भास्करोदयकालोऽयं गता भगवती निशा ।
असौ सुकृष्णो विहगः कोकिलस्तात कूजति ।।

2. Oh dear (Lakshmana)1 It is sunrise: Night passed away happily; And the bird Srikrishna and Kokila are cooing.

❍ ❍ ❍

३. बर्हिणानां च निर्घोषः श्रूयते नदतां वने ।
तराम जाह्नवी सौम्य शीघ्रगां सागरङ्गमाम् ।।
गच्छामः सन्ध्युपासार्थं त्वरयस्व महारथ ।।

3. Oh pleasant (Lakshmana) the great charioteer (and warrior)! The cooing of the cooing peacocks are heard in the forest. We will go (to perform) Sandhya rituals; And we shall cross the river Jaahnavi (Ganges) that flows out rapidly towards the ocean; Make haste.

❍ ❍ ❍

४. विज्ञाय रामस्य वचः सौमित्रिर्मित्रनन्दनः ।
गुहमामन्त्र्य सूतं च सोऽतिष्ठद्भ्रातुरग्रतः ।।

4. Hearing the words of Raama, this Lakshmana the darling of his friends, taking leave of Guha and Sumanthra, stood before his brother (Raama).

❍ ❍ ❍

५. स तु रामस्य वचनं निशम्य प्रतिगृह्य च ।
स्थपतिस्तूर्णमाहूय सचिवानिदमब्रवीत् ।।

5. Hearing the words of Raama, this (Guha) the chief of the place, accepting (the words of Raama as command) at once invited his ministers and said these words:

❍ ❍ ❍

६. अस्य वाहनसंयुक्तां कर्णग्राहवतीं शुभाम् ।
सुप्रतारां दृढां तीर्थेशीघ्रं नावमुपाहर ।।

6. (Guha wants to offer all assistance to Raama: He commands.)

Bring at once to the waters (on banks of the river), a strong boat for (Raama) which will be comfortable, easy to cross over with, endowed with accessories for journey (like oars and sails). along with oarsmen:

❍ ❍ ❍

७. तं निशम्य गुहादेशं गुहामात्यगणो महान् ।
उपोह्य रुचिरां नावं गुहाय प्रत्यवेदयत् ।।

7. Hearing the command of Guha, these great ministers of Guha pulled in a lovely boat and informed Guha.

❍ ❍ ❍

८. ततः स प्राञ्जलिर्भूत्वा गुहो राघवमब्रवीत् ।
उपस्थितेयं नौर्देव भूयः किं करवाणि ते ॥

8. Then Guha addressed Raama the Raaghava with his hands cupped in Anjali: oh Lord! This boat is kept (ready) for you. What else is to be done for you.

❍ ❍ ❍

९. तवामरसुतप्रख्य तर्तुं सागरगां नदीम् ।
नौरियं पुरुषव्याघ्र तां त्वमारोह सुव्रत ॥

9. Oh Raama the 'tiger' amongst men! One who is comparable to son of celestial! Oh man of austerities! This boat is yours. You may get in and cross the river (Ganges) that flows out into ocean.

❍ ❍ ❍

१०. अथोवाच महातेजा रामो गुहमिदं वचः ।
कृतकार्योऽस्मि भवता शीघ्रमारोप्यतामिति ॥

10. Then this most brilliant Raama addressed Guha these words: I have become (fully) satisfied by you; Therefore let (the boat) be fixed up soon (ready for sail).

❍ ❍ ❍

११. ततः कलापान्संनह्य खङ्गौ बद्ध्वा च धन्विनौ ।
जग्मतुर्येन तौ गङ्गां सीतया सह राघवौ ॥

11. Then the two Raaghava-s (Raama and Lakshmana) bearing arms and carrying swords and taking bundles duly tied up, went towards the (river) Ganges, along with Seetha.

❍ ❍ ❍

१२. राममेव तु धर्मज्ञमुपगम्य विनीतवत् ।
किमहं करवाणीति सूतः प्राञ्जलिरब्रवीत् ॥

12. And the charioteer (Sumanthra) who was modest, approached Raama the knower of Dharma and

addressed him with his hands cupped in Anjali: (Pray) What should I do now?

❍ ❍ ❍

१३. ततोऽब्रवीद्दाशरथिः सुमन्त्रं
स्पृशन्करेणोत्तम दक्षिणेन ।
सुमन्त्र शीघ्रं पुनरेव याहि
राज्ञः सकाशे भव चाप्रमत्तः ।।

13. Then (Raama) the son of Dhascharatha, stroked Sumanthra with his right hand and said this: Oh foremost Sumanthra! You may (please) go back (to Ayodhya): Being near the king (my father), you be vigilant as ever.(You serve my father as always, says Raama.)

(Raama bids goodbye to Sumanthra: No more comforts for Raama)

❍ ❍ ❍

१४. निवर्तस्वेत्युवाचैनमेतावद्धि कृतं मम ।
रथं विहाय पद्भ्यां तु गमिष्यामो महावनम् ।।

14. All this (done for me) is enough: Discharging the chariot, we shall (from now on) tread this mighty forest on foot. You may return (to Ayodhya with chariot): Thus he spoke to him.

❍ ❍ ❍

१५. आत्मानं त्वभ्यनुज्ञातमवेक्ष्यार्तः स सारथिः ।
सुमन्त्रः पुरुषव्याघ्रमैक्ष्वाकमिदमब्रवीत् ।।

15. When he beheld that he was given leave to go, this charioteer Sumanthra became very sad and addressed (Raama) the 'tiger' of men, this Ikshwaaki (Raama):

❍ ❍ ❍

१६. नातिक्रान्तमिदं लोके पुरुषेणेह केनचित् ।
तव सभ्रातृभार्यस्य वासः प्राकृतवद्वने ।।

16. (Sumanthra is very sad he is asked to go back; he speaks to Raama with some feelings).

To live in forest with brother and wife is indeed very *ordinary (for a prince like you): In this world such transgression has never happened on any man. (Word * Praakrithavath is used by Vaalmeeki).

❍ ❍ ❍

१७. न मन्ये ब्रह्मचर्येऽस्ति स्वधीते वा फलोदयः ।
मार्दवार्जवयोर्वापि त्वां चेद्व्यसनमागतम् ॥

17. I consider nothing else as of any value to me; (like) practising leniency, propriety, abstinence and celibacy or (even) study of Vedha-s, separated from you, (very much attached to you as I am).

❍ ❍ ❍

१८. सह राघव वैदेह्या भ्रात्रा चैव वने वसन् ।
त्वं गतिं प्राप्स्यसे वीर त्रीन्लोकांस्तु जयन्निव ॥

18. Oh brave (Raama the) Raaghava! As you have chosen to live in forest with (Seetha the) Vaidhehi and your brother(Lakshmana) you are like one who has conquered the three worlds. You will (like God Vishnu), offer refuge (to all).

❍ ❍ ❍

१९. वयं खलु हता राम यत्त्वयाऽप्युपवञ्चिताः ।
कैकेय्याः वशमेष्यामः पापाया दुःखभागिनः ॥

19. "Deceived" * (and discarded) by you, we are going to come under the hold of the sinful Kaikeyi and will (eventually) be destroyed, after suffering (terribly). Indeed!

(Sumanthra feels that Raama had 'deceived' them all by refusing the Crown*: Word used is-Upavanchitha.)

❍ ❍ ❍

२०. इति ब्रुवन्नात्मसमं सुमन्त्रः सारथिस्तदा ।
दृष्ट्वा दूरगतं रामं दुःखार्तोरुरुदे चिरम् ।।

20. So saying, the charioteer Sumanthra, realising that Raama who was like himself (in affection) was going away (from him to forest) began to cry afflicted by grief, having been long with him (having served the royalty of Ikshwaaku-s so long).

❍ ❍ ❍

२१. ततस्तु विगते बाष्पे सूतं स्पृष्टोदकं शुचिम् ।
रामस्तु मधुरं वाक्यं पुनःपुनरुवाच तम् ।।

21. At that moment Raama addressed the virtuous charioteer even while he was wiping off his tears that came out with water; With very sweet words, he said.

❍ ❍ ❍

२२. इक्ष्वाकूणां त्वया तुल्यं सुहृदं नोपलक्षये ।
यथा दशरथो राजा मां न शोचेत्तथा कुरु ।।

22. I cannot perceive a good friend equal to you (in friendship) towards the members of Ikshwaaku family; You must do all that in such a way that king Dhascharatha will not grieve over me.

❍ ❍ ❍

२३. शोकोपहतचेतास्तु वृद्धश्च जगतीपतिः ।
कामभारावसन्नश्च तस्मादेतद्ब्रवीमि ते ।।

23. The old (king the) lord of the world, is engulfed in sorrow as he is carrying the burden of his unfulfilled desire (of not crowning me). That is why I am telling you now the following.

❍ ❍ ❍

२४. यद्यदाज्ञापयेत्किंचित्स महात्मा महीपतिः ।
कैकेय्याः प्रियकामार्थंकार्यं तदविकाङ्क्षया ।।

24. Whatever the task this great soul king commands (me to do) to fulfill the desires of Kaikeyi, that must be done (by me) favourably disposed.

❍ ❍ ❍

२५. एतदर्थं हि राज्यानि प्रशासति नराधिपाः ।
यदेषां सर्वकृत्येषु मनो न प्रतिहन्यते ।।

25. Kings adminster their kingdoms with a view to remove hindrances to every one of the actions conceived by them.

❍ ❍ ❍

२६. यद्यथा स महाराजो नालीकमधिगच्छति ।
न च ताम्यति दुःखेन सुमन्त्र कुरु तत्तथा ।।

26. Oh Sumanthra! This being so, the king should not suffer anything disagreeable. Should not pine away in grief. You must (therefore) do (all for him) in such a way it would be like this.

❍ ❍ ❍

२७. अदृष्टदुःखं राजानं वृद्धमार्यं जितेन्द्रियम् ।
ब्रूयास्त्वमभिवाद्यैव मम हेतोरिदं वचः ।।

27. You convey these words, for my sake, respectfully to the old, most noble king (my father) who has never seen suffering, who has controlled his senses (till now)......

❍ ❍ ❍

२८. नैवाहमनुशोचामि लक्ष्मणो न च मैथिली ।
अयोध्यायाश्च्युताश्चेति वने वत्स्यामहेति वा ।।

28. ...... I do not grieve either on account of having left Ayodhya or because we are living in Forest; likewise Lakshmana nor (Seetha the) the Maithili, (We grieve not.) ......

❍ ❍ ❍

२९. चतुर्दशसु वर्षेषु निवृत्तेषु पुनःपुनः ।
लक्ष्मणं मां च सीतां च द्रक्ष्यसि क्षिप्रमागतान् ।।

29. ...... After completing 14 years (which will pass away) quickly, you will see me, Seetha and Lakshmana again when we return.

❍ ❍ ❍

३०. एवमुक्त्वा तु राजानं मातरं च सुमन्त्र मे ।
अन्याश्च देवीः सहिताः कैकेयीं च पुनः पुनः ।।

30. Oh Sumanthra! After telling this repeatedly to the king thus, and to other ladies there and also to Kaikeyi and to my mother ......

❍ ❍ ❍

३१. आरोग्यं ब्रूहि कौसल्यामथ पादाभिवन्दनम् ।
सीताया मम चार्यस्य वचनाल्लक्ष्मणस्य च ।।

31. ...... Kowsalya; You may also tell that we are well and by these words of Seetha, Aryan (noble) Lakshmana and mine, we are paying our respects (to all, "falling") at their feet: (Convey our respects).

❍ ❍ ❍

३२. ब्रूयाश्च हि महाराजं भरतं क्षिप्रमानय ।
आगतश्चापि भरतः स्थाप्यो नृपमते पदे ।।

32. And you must at once fetch Bharatha (from his holiday at his uncle's place) to be with the king. And Bharatha, when he gets back, must be told that he should ever be steadfast (in acting as per) king's mind at every step.

❍ ❍ ❍

३३. भरतं च परिष्वज्य यौवराज्येऽभिषिच्य च ।
अस्मत्सन्तापजं दुःखं न त्वामभिभविष्यति ।।

33. When Bharatha is crowned and installed as crown prince and (warmly) embraced, there will not be much

sorrow for you on account of torment over us (who are away from you in forest).

❍ ❍ ❍

३४. भरतश्चापि वक्तव्यो यथा राजनि वर्तसे ।
तथा मातृषु वर्तेथाः सर्वास्वेवाविशेषतः ।।

34. (And Bharatha must be told).... that he must behave exactly as he behaves towards the king, towards all the mothers, without any discrimination .....

❍ ❍ ❍

३५. यथा च तव कैकेयी सुमित्रा च विशेषतः ।
तथैव देवी कौसल्या मम माता विशेषतः ।।

35. ...... (and Bharatha must be told).... As Kaikeyi is particularly (honoured) by you, so should Sumithra and my mother Kowsalya deserve (to be treated with) distinction.

❍ ❍ ❍

३६. तातस्य प्रियकामेन यौवराज्यमवेक्षता ।
लोकयोरुभयोः शक्यं नित्यदा सुखमेधितुम् ।।

36. ...... (and Bharatha must be told)...By serving his father lovingly, looking after the kingdom properly as Yuvaraaja, it will be possible for him to obtain eternal happiness in both the two worlds (of heaven and earth).

❍ ❍ ❍

३७. निवर्त्यमानो रामेण सुमन्त्रः शोककर्शितः ।
तत्सर्वं वचनं श्रुत्वा स्नेहात्काकुत्स्थमब्रवीत् ।।

37. When Sumanthra was asked to get back (to Ayodhya), he was agonised by grief. (Even) after hearing all his (Raama's) words, he (again) addressed him out of his deep attachment to him.

❍ ❍ ❍

३८. यदहं नोपचारेण ब्रूयां स्नेहादविक्लबः ।
भक्तिमानिति तत्तावद्वाक्यं त्वं क्षन्तुमर्हसि ॥

38. (Sumanthra refuses to give up; wants to accompany Raama.)

As I am your devotee, you must pardon me because of my reverence and friendship to you, for speaking these words (of request) firmly, without timidity (nor perturbation).

❍ ❍ ❍

३९. कथं हि त्वद्विहीनोऽहं प्रतियास्यामि तां पुरीम् ।
तव तात वियोगेन पुत्रशोकाकुलामिव ॥

39. Oh dear (Raama)! Separated from you, how can I alone go back to the -city, which, being deprived of you, is like (a mother) in grief over loss of her son.

❍ ❍ ❍

४०. सराममपि तावन्मे रथं दृष्ट्वा तदा जनः ।
विना रामं रथं दृष्ट्वा विदीर्येतापि सा पुरी ॥

40. Will not that city whose citizens have always seen Raama on my chariot, be torn apart when it sees this chariot (return to Ayodhya) without Raama?

❍ ❍ ❍

४१. दैन्यं हि नगरी गच्छेद्दृष्ट्वा शुन्यमिमं रथम् ।
सूतावशेषं स्वं सैन्यं हतवीरमिवाहवे ॥

41. When the city sees the chariot empty with only (me as its) charioteer, it will feel miserable like the army having lost its brave (commander) in battle.

❍ ❍ ❍

४२. दूरेऽपि निवसन्तं त्वां मानसेनाग्रतः स्थितम् ।
चिन्तयन्त्योऽद्य नूनं त्वां निराहाराः कृताः प्रजाः ॥

42. The citizens will be thinking about you (even) while

you are living far away as though you are standing before them, with their mind (ever on you). They will now be made to go without food.

❍ ❍ ❍

४३. दृष्टं तद्धि त्वया राम यादृशं त्वत्प्रवासने ।
प्रजानां सङ्कुलं वृत्तं त्वच्छोकक्लान्तचेतसाम् ।।

43. Oh Raama ! What sort of confusion, disorder there was in the citizens whose minds were agitated by grief over you when you left on exile, all that, was seen by yourself; (Is it not).

❍ ❍ ❍

४४. आर्तनादो हि यः पौरैर्मुक्तस्त्वद्विप्रवासने ।
सरथं मां निशाम्यैव कुर्युः शतगुणं ततः ।।

44. Seeing me alone in the chariot (on my return to Ayodhya) they will cry out hundred times (louder) than the wailing sounds released by the citizens when you went away (from Ayodhya) on exile.

❍ ❍ ❍

४५. अहं किं चापि वक्ष्यामि देवीं तव सुतो मया ।
नीतोऽसौ मातुलकुलं सन्तापस्त्यज्यतामिति ।।

45. What can I say to the lady (your mother Kowsalya)? = Oh Lady! Your son (Raama) has been left by me in his uncle's place! (Therefore) May you give up your torment!=

❍ ❍ ❍

४६. असत्यमपि नैवाहं ब्रूयां वचनमीदृशम् ।
कथमप्रियमेवाहं ब्रूयां सत्यमिदं वचः ।।

46. (True), such a lie, I should never speak. (but then) how can I tell this detestable truth (that I abandoned you in forest): What am I going to tell her?

(Poet Vaalmeeki at his usual best)

❍ ❍ ❍

४७. मम तावन्नियोगस्थास्त्वद्बन्धुजनवाहिनः ।
कथं रथं त्वया हीनं प्रवाह्यन्ति हयोत्तमाः ।।

47. Will these foremost horses that are obedient to my command, which have always carried you and your folks, pull the chariot now without you (on the chariot)?

❍ ❍ ❍

४८. तन्न शक्ष्याम्यहं गन्तुमयोध्यां त्वदृतेऽनघ ।
वनवासानुयानाय मामनुज्ञातुमर्हसि ।।

48. Oh sinless Raama! I Cannot Go Back To Ayodhya Without You; You Must Give Me Permission To Follow You In Forest life.

❍ ❍ ❍

४९. यदि मे याचमानस्य त्यागमेव करिष्यसि ।
सरथोऽग्निं प्रवेक्ष्यामि त्यक्तमात्र इह त्वया ।।

49. Begging you as I am, if you abandon me, then I will enter Fire along with this chariot, the moment you abandon me; here itself!

❍ ❍ ❍

५०. भविष्यन्ति वने यानि तपोविघ्नकराणि ते ।
रथेन प्रतिबाधिष्ये तानि सत्त्वानि राघव ।।

50. Oh (Raama the) Raaghava! If there is any living being which causes harm to your 'penance' (or rituals) in the forest, I will drive them away from chariot. (I will be the charioteer for you, Raama).

❍ ❍ ❍

५१. त्वत्कृते न मयाऽवाप्तं रथचर्याकृतं सुखम् ।
आशंसे त्वत्कृतेनाहं वनवासकृतं सुखम् ।।

51. That (good fortune and) happiness was not obtained by me as a charioteer for your sake (during your

coronation that did not take place) ..... (now therefore) I wish for that happiness that will come by me in forest life for your sake.

(Again a beautiful stanza by Vaalmeeki: Sumanthra says he will get the same pleasure as charioteer for Raama in forest as when he drives in royal boulevard, for Raama the Yuvaraaaja.)

❍ ❍ ❍

५२. प्रसीदेच्छामि तेऽरण्ये भवितुं प्रत्यनन्तरः ।
प्रीत्याऽभिहितमिच्छामि भव मे प्रत्यनन्तरः ।।

52. I desire to be by your side in forest. I desire that you declare: = Stay By My Side=. (Oh Raama) Have mercy on me.

❍ ❍ ❍

५३. इमे चापि हया वीर यदि ते वनवासिनः ।
परिचर्यां करिष्यन्ति प्राप्स्यन्ति परमां गतिम् ।।

53. Oh Brave (Raama)! May these horses also do service to you, living in forest (with you): And by this, may they attain foremost state.

❍ ❍ ❍

५४. तव शुश्रूषणं मूर्ध्ना करिष्यामि वने वसन् ।
अयोध्यां देवलोकं वा सर्वथा प्रजहाम्यहम् ।।

54. Living in forest, I will serve you in all ways. Head (and foot). I renounce Ayodhya, even heaven (for you).

❍ ❍ ❍

५५. न हि शक्या प्रवेष्टुं सा मयाऽयोध्या त्वया विना ।
राजधानी महेन्द्रस्य यथा दुष्कृतकर्मणा ।।

55. Just as Lord Indhra's capital cannot be entered by a man of evil deeds, this Ayodhya cannot be entered by me without you.

❍ ❍ ❍

५६. वनवासे क्षयं प्राप्ते ममैष हि मनोरथः ।
यदनेन रथेनैव त्वां वहेयं पुरीं पुनः ।।

56. This is my heartfelt desire that I should carry you back again to the city in this very chariot at the end of your forest life.

❍ ❍ ❍

५७. चतुर्दश हि वर्षाणि सहितस्य त्वया वने ।
क्षणभूतानि यास्यन्ति शतसंख्यान्यतोऽन्यथा ।।

57. When I stay with you in forest, 14 years will pass away in a trice; But, if not, it will be hundred times: (like living for 1400 years in suffering when I am without you at Ayodhya).

❍ ❍ ❍

५८. भृत्यवत्सल तिष्ठन्तं भर्तृपुत्रगते पथि ।
भक्तं भृत्यं स्थितं स्थित्यां त्वं न मां हातुमर्हसि ।।

58. Oh (Raama) the devoted son of the king! Oh (Raama) who is devoted to those who serve you! You should not (abandon me), sending me back, who is steadfast in the path (of service to you), who is steadfast in righteousness, and who is your worshipful servant.

(Thus Sumanthra pleads with Raama that he should accompany Raama to forest during his 14 years exile)

❍ ❍ ❍

५९. एवं बहुविधं दीनं याचमानं पुनः पुनः ।
रामो भृत्यानुकम्पी तु सुमन्त्रमिदमब्रवीत् ।।

59. And Raama who was most compassionate to his servants, then addressed this Sumanthra who was 'begging' him thus in many ways repeatedly, pitiably,...... with these words:

❍ ❍ ❍

६०. जानामि परमां भक्तिं मयि ते भर्तृवत्सल ।
श्रृणु चापि यदर्थं त्वां प्रेषयामि पुरीमितः ।।

60. Oh (Sumanthra) who is most devoted to (your) master (the king)! I know of your great devotion to me. Yet: (Please) listen to the reasons why I press you to go back to the city from here.

❍ ❍ ❍

६१. नगरं त्वां गतं दृष्ट्वा जननी मे यवीयसी ।
कैकेयी प्रत्ययं गच्छेदिति रामो वनं गतः ।।

61. Seeing you return to the city, my youngest (step) mother Kaikeyi will believe Raama has gone away to forest.

❍ ❍ ❍

६२. परितुष्टा तु सा देवी वनवासं गते मयि ।
राजानं नातिशङ्केत मिथ्यावादीति धार्मिकम् ।।

62. (Only) When I (reach and) get forest life, this Lady (Kaikeyi) will become satisfied and will not entertain doubts that the king who is a man of Dharma is a man of falsehood.

❍ ❍ ❍

६३. एष मे प्रथमः कामो यदम्बा मे यवीयसी ।
भरतारक्षितं स्फीतं पुत्रराज्यमवाप्नुयात् ।।

63. My young (step) mother will flourish in his son's kingdom, ruled by Bharatha: This indeed is my first (and foremost) wish.

❍ ❍ ❍

६४. मम प्रियार्थं राज्ञश्च सरथस्त्वं पुरीं व्रज ।
संदिष्टश्चापि यानर्थांस्तांस्तान्ब्रूयास्तथा तथा ।।

64. For my sake and for happiness of the king (my father), you go (back) to the city along with chariot. As a messenger, you must convey all the news to all those exactly as (conveyed by me)

❍ ❍ ❍

६५. इत्युक्त्वा वचनं सूतं सान्त्वयित्वा पुनःपुनः ।
गुहं वचनमक्लीबं रामो हेतुमदब्रवीत् ।।

65. (Thus Raama asked Sumanthra to get back.)
Raama repeatedly consoled him with these words with reasoning: After saying (this to Sumanthra) he addressed the *energetic Guha.
(*Word used is Akleebha= Translator has used energetic.)

❍ ❍ ❍

६६. नेदानी गुह योग्योऽयं वासो मे सजने वने ।
अवश्यं ह्याश्रमे वासः कर्तव्यस्तद्गतो विधिः ।।

66. Oh Guha! It is not proper for me to live in the forest inhabited by men. Surely life in hermitage must be accepted (by me): In this matter, the established norms are like this.
(Raama says he wants to be a true mendicant, away from crowd)

❍ ❍ ❍

६७. सोऽहं गृहीत्वा नियमं तपस्विजनभूषणम् ।
हितकामः पितुर्भूयः सीताया लक्ष्मणस्य च ।।
जटाः कृत्वा गमिष्यामि न्यग्रोधक्षीरमानय ।।

67. Seeking welfare of my father, Seetha and Lakshmana, such as I am, will now adorn (myself) in the proper way the mendicants adorn themselves. So I will take on (and sport) my hair with braided hair locks. (Therefore) Bring me the (resinous) milk from the Nyagrodha tree (Ficus Indica).

❍ ❍ ❍

६८. तत्क्षीरं राजपुत्राय गुहः क्षिप्रमुपाहरत् ।
लक्ष्मणस्यात्मनश्चैव रामस्तेनाकरोज्जटाः ।।

68. (And this resinous milk was used as Cosmetic hair dresser for making 'hair permanent'; no need for combs!)

And Guha at once brought the milk to the prince (Raama): With this Raama did Hair:"lock" for himself and for Lakshmana.

❍ ❍ ❍

६९. दीर्घबाहुर्नरव्याघ्रो जटिलत्वमधारयत् ॥

69. The 'tiger' of men (Raama) whose hands were long, then sported twisted (braided) "Hair Lock" (like a mendicant).

❍ ❍ ❍

७०. तौ तदा चीरवसनौ जटामण्डलधारिणौ ।
अशोभेतामृषिसमौ भ्रातरौ रामलक्ष्मणौ ॥

70. The two brothers Raama and Lakshman who were wearing (forest dress) of bark (and deer skin) and sporting braided twisted hair lock, appeared like hermits.

❍ ❍ ❍

७१. ततो वैखानसं मार्गमास्थितः सहलक्ष्मणः ।
व्रतमादिष्टवान्रामः सहायं गुहमब्रवीत् ॥

71. Assigning to himsef to vows (and rigour of forest life), Raama who took to the ways of life of a hermit along with Lakshmana, then addressed his comrade Guha;

❍ ❍ ❍

७२. अप्रमत्तो बले कोशे दुर्गेजनपदे तथा ।
भवेथा गुह राज्यं हि दुरारक्षतमं मतम् ॥

72. Oh Guha! You must ever remain vigilant in the matter of (Defence and) army, finance and over the inhabited and uninhabited (impassable) territories. It is well (known and) accepted (as a fact) that protecting a kingdom is arduous.

(Readers may note that here Raama advises his comrade Guha partly because he is his friend but mainly because he is also a royal prince of Ikshwaaku. He has obligation to advise his 'vassal'.)

❍ ❍ ❍

७३. ततस्तं समनुज्ञाप्य गुहमिक्ष्वाकुनन्दनः ।
जगाम तूर्णमव्यग्रः सहभार्यः सलक्ष्मणः ।।

73. The darling of Ikshwaaku-s, this steady and 'cool' Raama, gave leave to Guha and started out along with his wife Seetha and Lakshmana at once.

❍ ❍ ❍

७४. स तु दृष्ट्वा नदीतीरे नावमिक्ष्वाकुनन्दनः ।
तितीर्षुः शीघ्रगां गङ्गामिदं लक्ष्मणमब्रवीत् ।।

74. The darling son of Ikshwaaku, (this Raama), seeing the boat on the banks of the river addressed Lakshmana these words, (desirous of) crossing the fast flowing Ganges.

❍ ❍ ❍

७५. आरोह त्वं नरव्याघ्र स्थितां नावमिमां शनैः ।
सीतां चारोपयान्वक्षं परिगृह्य मनस्विनीम् ।।

75. Oh (Lakshmana) the 'tiger' of men! Holding (firmly) on to the boat that is stationed, assist the high spirited Seetha to mount the boat carefully. Then you get in.

❍ ❍ ❍

७६. स भ्रातुः शासनं श्रुत्वा सर्वमप्रतिकूलयन् ।
आरोप्य मैथिलीं पूर्वमारुरोहात्मवांस्ततः ।।

76. The obedient and composed (Lakshmana), hearing all these words (of command) of his brother, got in after (helping Seetha the) Maithili to mount (the boat).

❍ ❍ ❍

७७. अथारुरोह तेजस्वी स्वयं लक्ष्मणपूर्वजः ।
ततो निषादाधिपतिर्गुहो ज्ञातीनचोदयत् ।।

77. Then the brilliant (Raama) the elder brother of Lakshmana, got into (the boat) himself. Then the chief of hunters, Guha goaded his folks.

❍ ❍ ❍

७८. राघवोऽपि महातेजा नावमारुह्य तां ततः ।
ब्रह्मवत्क्षत्रवच्चैव जजाप हितमात्मनः ॥

78. Then the most brilliant (Raama) the Raaghava, who had got into the boat, prayed for his welfare, with princely dignity, according to sacred Texts.

❍ ❍ ❍

७९. आचम्य च यथाशास्त्रं नदीं तां सह सीतया ।
प्राणमत्प्रीतिसंहृष्टो लक्ष्मणश्चामितप्रभः ॥

79. And Lakshmana who had immense brilliance, bristled with joy and love, took sips of waters as per Shaasthra. He bowed to the (holy) River (Ganges) along with Seetha.

❍ ❍ ❍

८०. अनुज्ञाय सुमन्त्रं च सबलं चैव तं गुहम् ।
आस्थाय नावं रामस्तु चोदयामास नाविकान् ॥

80. When Raama had got into the boat, he gave leave to Sumanthra and to Guha who was with his henchmen; He then goaded the oarsmen (to sail across river).

❍ ❍ ❍

८१. ततस्तैश्चोदिता सा नौः कर्णधारसमाहिता ।
शुभस्फ्यवेगाभिहता गङ्गासलिलमत्यगात् ॥

81. This boat (with complement of) pilot and oarsmen, was 'goaded' by them with fine strong oars. It sailed across the waters of Ganges.

❍ ❍ ❍

८२. मध्यं तु समनुप्राप्य भागीरथ्यास्त्वनिन्दिता ।
वैदेही प्राञ्जलिर्भूत्वा तां नदीमिदमब्रवीत् ।।

82. When the blemishless (Seetha) the Vaidhehi had reached the middle (of river Ganges the) Bhaageerathi (along with Raama and Lakshmana in the boat), she cupped her hands in Anjali and addressed the (holy) River.

❍ ❍ ❍

८३. पुत्रो दशरथस्यायं महाराजस्य धीमतः ।
निदेशं पारयत्वेष गङ्गे त्वदभिरक्षितः ।।

83. Oh Ganga! Blessed and protected by you, may this wise son of the great king Dhascharatha, cross you over to the other side.

❍ ❍ ❍

८४. चतुर्दश हि वर्षाणि समग्राण्युष्य कानने ।
भ्रात्रा सह मया चैव पुनः प्रत्यागमिष्यति ।।

84. After (completing) 14 years of stay in forest, he should come back again along with me and his brother (Lakshmana) fully (accomplished).

❍ ❍ ❍

८५. ततस्त्वां देवि सुभगे क्षेमेण पुनरागता ।
यक्ष्ये प्रमुदिता गङ्गे सर्वकामप्रसाधिनि ।।

85. Oh Ganga, the most illustrious (river) who bestows all desires on all! When I return safely I will (again) worship you in happiness.

❍ ❍ ❍

८६. त्वं हि त्रिपथगा देवि ब्रह्मलोकं समीक्षसे ।
भार्या चोदधिराजस्य लोकेऽस्मिन्संप्रदृश्यसे ।।

86. Oh Lady (Ganges)! You flow in Three regions (heaven,earth and underworlds): You even 'look' at the

world of Bramma. And in this world, you are looked upon, (honoured) as wife of the lord of oceans.

❍ ❍ ❍

८७. तत्त्वां देवि नमस्यामि प्रशंसामि च शोभने ।
प्राप्तराज्ये नरव्याघ्रे शिवेन पुनरागते ॥

87. Oh bright (Ganges)! Oh Lady! I extol you: I bow to you. When (my husband Raama) the tiger of men, on returning , takes over the kingdom auspiciously....

❍ ❍ ❍

८८. गवां शतसहस्रं च वस्त्राण्यन्नं च पेशलम् ।
ब्राह्मणेभ्यः प्रदास्यामि तव प्रियचिकीर्षया ॥

88. ..... I shall offer gifts of 100,000 cows, garments, delicious foods to Braamins, desirous of pleasing you.

❍ ❍ ❍

८९. सुराघटसहस्रेण मांसभूतौदनेन च ।
यक्ष्ये त्वां प्रयता देवि पुरीं पुनरुपागता ॥

89. Oh Lady! Getting back to (our capital) city again, I shall worship you with devotion, with 100 pots (of holy waters) and *with food delicacies. (*Maamsa-Bhootha: Usually Meats with rice).

❍ ❍ ❍

९०. यानि त्वत्तीरवासीनि दैवतानि वसन्ति हि ।
तानि सर्वाणि यक्ष्यामि तीर्थान्यायतनानि च ॥

90. I will worship sacred waters, holy places-temples, and all the deities that live on your banks and nearby.

❍ ❍ ❍

९१. पुनरेव महाबाहुर्मया भ्रात्रा च सङ्गतः ।
अयोध्यां वनवासात्तु प्रविशत्वनघोऽनघे ॥

91 Oh sinless (Pure) Ganges! This sinless mighty limbed

(Raama) should enter Ayodhya again after completing forest life along with me and brother (Lakshmana).

❍ ❍ ❍

९२. तथा संभाषमाणा सा सीता गङ्गामनिन्दिता ।
दक्षिणा दक्षिणं तीरं क्षिप्रमेवाभ्युपागमत् ।।

92. (Praying) Thus to the river Ganges, this blemishless and very able* Seetha who was "conversing' (with this holy river), reached the southern banks soon. (* Word is Dhakshina- Many meanings).

❍ ❍ ❍

९३. तीरं हि समनुप्राप्य नावं हित्वा नरर्षभः ।
प्रातिष्ठत सह भ्रात्रा वैदेह्या च परन्तपः ।।

93. (Raama) the Tormentor of enemies who was a 'bull' amongst men, on reaching the banks, discharged the boat, and then walked down with brother (Lakshmana) and (wife Seetha the) Vaidhehi.

❍ ❍ ❍

९४. अथाब्रवीन्महाबाहुः सुमित्रानन्दवर्धनम् ।
भव संरक्षणार्थाय सजने विजनेऽपि वा ।।

94. The mighty limbed (Raama) then addressed (Lakshmana the) darling son of Sumithra who ever increased the joy of Sumithra,: You must (ever be on guard) for the sake of protection (for us all), whether (the place) is inhabited or uninhabited.

❍ ❍ ❍

९५. अवश्यं रक्षणं कार्यमदृष्टे विजने वने ।
अग्रतो गच्छ सौमित्रे सीता त्वामनुगच्छतु ।।

95. Oh (Lakshmana) the son of Sumithra! It is (our duty and) task to be on guard, in every way, in the uninhabited (forest) which we have not seen before. You go first. Seetha will follow you (behind you).

❍ ❍ ❍

९६. पृष्ठतोऽनुगमिष्यामि त्वां च सीतां च पालयन् ।
अन्योन्यस्य हि नो रक्षा कर्तव्या पुरुषर्षभ ॥

96. Oh (Lakshmana) the 'bull amongst men'! Guarding you and Seetha, I will follow you (both) from behind. We should guard mutually. (This is our duty) that must be done by us all.

❍ ❍ ❍

९७. न हि तावदतिक्रान्ता सुकरा काचन क्रिया ।
अद्य दुःखं तु वैदेही वनवासस्य वेत्स्यति ॥

97. If any transgression takes place (and gets out of hand), it cannot be (remedied, corrected easily). Only now (Seetha) the Vaidhehi will (appreciate and) understand the difficulties of forest Life!

(Raama takes a dig at Seetha!)

❍ ❍ ❍

९८. प्रनष्टजनसंबाधं क्षेत्रारामविवर्जितम् ।
विषमं च प्रपातं च वनं ह्यद्य प्रवेक्ष्यति ॥

98. Because, now she is going to enter the undulated, rugged forest which is without any human beings (without activity), without any houses nor gardens.

❍ ❍ ❍

९९. श्रुत्वा रामस्य वचनं प्रतस्थे लक्ष्मणोऽग्रतः ।
अनन्तरं च सीताया राघवो रघुनन्दनः ॥

99. Hearing Raama's words, Lakshmana went in front of Seetha. And (Raama) the Raaghava, the darling son of Raghu-s, went behind them.

❍ ❍ ❍

१००. गतं तु गङ्गापरपारमाशु
रामं सुमन्त्रः प्रततं निरीक्ष्य ।
अध्वप्रकर्षाद्विनिवृत्तदृष्टि
र्मुमोच बाष्पं व्यथितस्तपस्वी ॥

100. (Sumanthra and Guha have been watching all this from the other side of river.)

The austere Sumanthra, observing that Raama had crossed over to the other bank of river Ganges, was "burning' within in (great) distress. As (Raama) had gone far (away) from him he turned his eyes back and shed tears.

❍ ❍ ❍

१०१. स लोकपालप्रतिमप्रभावां
स्तीर्त्वा महात्मा वरदो महानदीम् ।
ततः समृद्धाञ्छुभसस्यमालिनः
क्षणेन वत्सान्मुदितानुपागमत् ।।

101. The benefactor who was as glorious and equal to the protector of the worlds, this great soul (Raama) having crossed the great river, soon reached the territory called Vathsa which was lush with corn and paddy fields and it was joyous.

❍ ❍ ❍

१०२. तौ तत्र हत्वा चतुरो महामृगान्
वराहमृश्यं पृषतं महारुरुम् ।
आदाय मेध्यं त्वरितं बुभुक्षितौ
वासाय काले ययतुर्वनस्पतिम् ।।

102. Hungry as they were, these two killed four animals, wild boars, a deer of Rish family, and a deer from foremost Ruru family and a deer from Prishtatha. Taking these, they (walked along) quickly and came to a blemishless tree in the evening to spend the night.

(Readers may observe that although Raama and the two are going to sustain themselves only on tubers and fruits during their 14 year exile in forest, here they kill 4 animals. Perhaps Raama wants to give a 'Last meal' for Seetha and Lakshmana.)

❍ ❍ ❍

Chapter 53

Raama and Lakshmana Converse

१. स तं वृक्षं समासाद्य सन्ध्यामन्वास्य पश्चिमाम् ।
रामो रमयतां श्रेष्ठ इति होवाच लक्ष्मणम् ।।

1. This Raama who was foremost in pleasing (every one's heart), performed the evening Sandhya rituals on reaching this tree; then he said to Lakshmana thus.

❍ ❍ ❍

२. अद्येयं प्रथमा रात्रिर्याता जनपदाद्बहिः ।
या सुमन्त्रेण रहिता तां नोत्कण्ठितुमर्हसि ।।

2. (Oh Lakshmana): This is our first night away from inhabitation and without Sumanthra. You should have no regrets.

❍ ❍ ❍

३. जागर्तव्यमतन्द्रिभ्यामद्यप्रभृति रात्रिषु ।
योगक्षेमो हि सीताया वर्तते लक्ष्मणावयोः ।।

3. Oh Lakshmana! Protection and welfare of Seetha rests with us now: Therefore from now on, during the nights (particularly) we have to be careful and be awake and be alert (free from lassitude).

❍ ❍ ❍

४. रात्रिं कथञ्चिदेवेमां सौमित्रे वर्तयामहे ।
उपावर्तामहे भूमावास्तीर्य स्वयमार्जितैः ।।

4. Oh (Lakshmana) the son of Sumithra! We shall somehow spend this night ourselves, (spreading) on the floor with (whatever) we have gathered.

❍ ❍ ❍

५. स तु संविश्य मेदिन्यां महार्हशयनोचितः ।
इमाः सौमित्रये रामो व्याजहार कथाः शुभाः ।।

5. And Raama who was used to sleeping in costly beds, lay on bare earth; He ventilated (his feelings) to (Lakshmana) the son of Sumithra about matters, agreeably.

❍ ❍ ❍

६. ध्रुवमद्य महाराजो दुःखं स्वपिति लक्ष्मण ।
कृतकामा हि कैकेयी तुष्टा भवितुमर्हति ।।

6. Oh Lakshmana! It is certain that the great king will be lulled by grief (at Ayodhya). And perhaps Kaikeyi may be happy having fulfilled her desire.

❍ ❍ ❍

७. सा हि देवी महाराजं कैकेयी राज्यकारणात् ।
अपि न च्यावयेत्प्राणान्दृष्ट्वा भरतमागतम् ।।

7. Seeing (her son) Bharatha return, will lady Kaikeyi spare at least the life of the great king (our father), having taken over the kingdom.
(By reason of taking over kingdom all for herself through her son.)

❍ ❍ ❍

८. अनाथश्चैव वृद्धश्च मया चैव विनाकृतः ।
किं करिष्यति कामात्मा कैकेयीवशमागतः ।।

8. Separated from me, what will he, the old (king, our father) who is sensuous, do now, having come under the clutches of Kaikeyi.

❍ ❍ ❍

९. इदं व्यसनमालोक्य राज्ञश्च मतिविभ्रमम् ।
काम एवार्थधर्माभ्यां गरीयानिति मे मतिः ।।

9. Now, when I observe the king's mental aberration and

grief,it appears to me that, between Dharma and Artha, it is Kaama (passion, love etc) that is more precious ! (Readers know Dharma, Artha, Kaama and Moksha constitute four aspects of Indian life.)

❍ ❍ ❍

१०. को ह्यविद्वानपि पुमान्पमदायाः कृते त्यजेत् ।
छन्दानुवर्तिनं पुत्रं तातो मामिव लक्ष्मण ॥

10. For the sake of a pleasure seeking woman, will any man (even) an uneducated man, who is a father, abandon a son like me who ever complies with his will and pleasure.

❍ ❍ ❍

११. सुखी बत सभार्यश्च भरतः केकयीसुतः ।
मुदितान्कोसलानेको यो भोक्ष्यत्यधिराजवत् ॥

11. This Bharatha, Kaikeyi's son, who has been in comfort, may (perhaps) enjoy the happy Kosala kingdom as a ruler, all alone, along with his wife.

❍ ❍ ❍

१२. स हि राज्यस्य सर्वस्य मुखमेकं भविष्यति ।
ताते च वयसाऽतीते मयि चारण्यमाश्रिते ॥

12. If father passes away due to old age and while I am living in forest, alone, he will have (to look after) all (the affairs of) the kingdom and become its chief.

❍ ❍ ❍

१३. अर्थधर्मौ परित्यज्य यः काममनुवर्तते ।
एवमापद्यते क्षिप्रं राजा दशरथो यथा ॥

13. As king Dhascharatha, having abandoned Dharma and Artha thus but follows Kaama (Sensuality, pleasures), he will soon obtain (even greater) misfortune.

❍ ❍ ❍

१४. मन्ये दशरथान्ताय मम प्रव्राजनाय च ।
कैकेयी सौम्य संप्राप्ता राज्याय भरतस्य च ।।

14. Oh pleasant (Lakshmana)! I think Kaikeyi has accomplished all this: Kingdom for (her son) Bharatha; Exile for me; Death for Dhascharatha.

❍ ❍ ❍

१५. अपीदानीं न कैकेयी सौभाग्यमदमोहिता ।
कौसल्यां च सुमित्रां च सा प्रबाधेत मत्कृते ।।

15. Will this Kaikeyi, infatuated by all this good fortune, drive away Kowsalya and Sumithra on my account, now!

❍ ❍ ❍

१६. मा स्म मत्कारणाद्देवी सुमित्रा दुःखमावसेत् ।
अयोध्यामित एव त्वं काल्ये प्रविश लक्ष्मण ।।

16. Oh Lakshmana: (Your mother) Sumithra should not suffer hardships on my account. (Therefore) you go back to Ayodhya in the morning.

❍ ❍ ❍

१७. अहमेको गमिष्यामि सीतया सह दण्डकान् ।
अनाथाया हि नाथस्त्वं कौसल्याया भविष्यसि ।।

17. All alone, I will go to Dhandaka forest (to live out 14 years) with Seetha. And you will be the protector for the helpless Kowsalya.

❍ ❍ ❍

१८. क्षुद्रकर्मा हि कैकेयी द्वेषादन्यायमाचरेत् ।
परिदद्या हि धर्मज्ञे भरते मम मातरम् ।।

18. Out of enmity, if Kaikeyi becomes vile and commits atrocities, then you may entrust my mother (Kowsalya to the care of) Bharatha, the knower of Dharma.

❍ ❍ ❍

१९. नूनं जात्यन्तरे कस्मिंस्त्रियः पुत्रैर्वियोजिताः ।
जनन्या मम सौमित्रे तस्मादेतदुपस्थितम् ।।

19. Oh (Lakshmana) the son of Sumithra! Perhaps in previous birth, mothers would have been separated from their sons by my mother (Kowsalya, forcibly). That is why this has happened (to her) now.

❍ ❍ ❍

२०. मया हि चिरपुष्टेन दुःखसंवर्धितेन च ।
विप्रायुज्यत कौसल्या फलकाले धिगस्तु माम् ।।

(As already mentioned, this is typically Indian view)

20. Having nourished me for so long and having reared me (from birth) with (her personal) suffering, at a time when she should enjoy only the "fruits" (of her labours over me), this Kowsalya was separated (from me). Shame on me.

(Every mother thinks that her son will serve her during her later and last years of life: This again is typical Indian Dharma.)

❍ ❍ ❍

२१. मा स्म सीमन्तिनी काचिज्जनयेत्पुत्रमीदृशम् ।
सौमित्रे योऽहमम्बाया दद्मि शोकमनन्तकम् ।।

21. Oh (Lakshmana) the son of Sumithra! Such as I am, am causing endless grief to my mother. No mother should beget a son like me!

❍ ❍ ❍

२२. मन्ये प्रीतिविशिष्टा सा मत्तो लक्ष्मण शारिका ।
यस्यास्तच्छ्रूयते वाक्यं शुक पादमरेर्दश ।।

22. Oh! I consider her pet parrot more useful to her than myself (now); whose cooing =** Schuka-Arey, Paadam Dhascha – will be heard (by her). (Parrot talk ;** these are some sounds from her pet).

❍ ❍ ❍

२३. शोचन्त्या अल्पभाग्याया न किञ्चिदुपकुर्वता ।
पुत्रेण किमपुत्राया मया कार्यमरिन्दम ।।

23. Oh invincible (Lakshmana)! What is the use for her from me, her son, who has not done any service at all to her who is now of feeble fortune, who is without (me), her son, and who is in lament.

❍ ❍ ❍

२४. अल्पभाग्या हि मे माता कौसल्या रहिता मया ।
शेते परमदुःखार्ता पतिता शोकसागरे ।।

24. Being abandoned by me, my most unfortunate mother Kowsalya will be lying down, suffering terribly, engulfed in ocean of grief.

❍ ❍ ❍

२५. एको ह्यहमयोध्यां च पृथिवीं चापि लक्ष्मण ।
तरेयमिषुभिः क्रुद्धो ननु वीर्यमकारणम् ।।

25. Oh Lakshmana! If I get angry, I can single handedly conquer Ayodhya and Earth with arrows; But (then) one should not exhibit his bravery without reason. Is it not!

(Using force for taking away the kingdom from Kaikeyi & Bharatha, cannot be reason at all, says Raama.)

❍ ❍ ❍

२६. अधर्मभयभीतश्च परलोकस्य चानघ ।
तेन लक्ष्मण नाद्याहमात्मानमभिषेचये ।।

26. Oh sinless Lakshmana! Out of fear (of consequence) of Non Dharma (that may befall me) in the other world (of heaven), for this reason alone, I did not crown myself.

(It is great sin to dishonour father's command or make one's father a liar and a man who is untrue to his commitment.)

❍ ❍ ❍

२७. एतदन्यच्च करुणं विलप्य विजने बहु ।
अश्रुपूर्णमुखो रामो निशि तूष्णीमुपाविशत् ।।

27. (Thus Raama wailed; Afterall, even Raama is human.) With tears over his face, Raama wailed thus during the night in the uninhabited (forest) in many ways, pitiably: Then he became silent.

❍ ❍ ❍

२८. विलापोपरतं रामं गतार्चिषमिवानलम् ।
समुद्रमिव निर्वेगमाश्वासयत लक्ष्मणः ।।

28. Lakshmana then consoled Raama who was like fire with its lustre gone, who was like a stilled Ocean, at the end of his wailings.

❍ ❍ ❍

२९. ध्रुवमद्य पुरी राम अयोध्याऽऽयुधिनां वर ।
निष्प्रभा त्वयि निष्क्रान्ते गतचन्द्रेव शर्वरी ।।

29. Oh master of weapons! oh Raama! After you got out, the city of Ayodhya will now be like night without moon; Surely lustre less.

❍ ❍ ❍

३०. नैतदौपयिकं राम यदिदं परितप्यसे ।
विषादयसि सीतां च मां चैव पुरुषर्षभ ।।

30. Oh Raama! 'the bull' amongst men! You are tormenting yourself. Now all this is not proper (does not befit you;) You are making Seetha and me despondent.

❍ ❍ ❍

३१. न च सीता त्वया हीना न चाहमपि राघव ।
मुहूर्तमपि जीवावो जलान्मत्स्याविवोद्धृतौ ।।

31. Oh (Raama the) Raaghava! Seetha will not be without you; So will I not; We will be like fishes pulled out

of water; We will not live even for a muhoortha, (a moment without you).

❍ ❍ ❍

३२. न हि तातं न शत्रुघ्नं न सुमित्रां परन्तप ।
द्रष्टुमिच्छेयमद्याहं स्वर्गं वाऽपि त्वया विना ॥

32. Oh (Raama the) tormentor of enemies! Without you, I do not desire to see my father, (even) my mother. Nor (care for) heaven; Nor even (my brother) Schathrughna.

❍ ❍ ❍

३३. ततस्तत्र सुखासीनौ नातिदूरे निरीक्ष्य ताम् ।
न्यग्रोधे सुकृतां शय्यां भेजाते धर्मवत्सलौ ॥

33. (Thus Lakshmana rejects Raama's suggestion that he should go back to Ayodhya and not follow him on exile.)

Seeing (Seetha) in sound sleep, these two (Raama and Lakshmana) who were devotees of Dharma, then spent the night pleasantly, sitting under Nyagrodha tree, not far away from (where she was sleeping).

❍ ❍ ❍

३४. स लक्ष्मणस्योत्तमपुष्कलं वचो
निशम्य चैवं वनवासमादरात् ।
समाः समस्ता विदधे परन्तपः
प्रपद्य धर्मं सुचिराय राघवः ॥

34. This tormentor of enemies (Raama the) Raaghava, heard thus such numerous noble words of Lakshmana with *respect (and consideration). He decided to complete the entire (stay of 14 Annual) Seasons in forest, in a state of Dharma, for a long time.

(*Word used is Aadhara- Raama had great respect for Lakshmana.)

❍ ❍ ❍

३५. ततस्तु तस्मिन्विजने वने तदा
महाबलौ राघववंशवर्धनौ ।
न तौ भयं संभ्रममभ्युपेयतुः
यथैव सिंहौ गिरिसानुगोचरौ ॥

35. At that time, these two mightily strong men who brought glory to the Ikshwaaku race were like lions in mountain caves and they did not get agitated in the uninhabited forest.

❍ ❍ ❍

Chapter 54

Raama Goes to Bharadhwaaja's Hermitage

(Raama begins his exile; Visits the great sage Bharadhwaaja.)

❍ ❍ ❍

१. ते तु तस्मिन्महावृक्ष उषित्वा रजनीं शिवाम् ।
विमलेऽभ्युदिते सूर्येतस्माद्देशात्प्रतस्थिरे ॥

1. After spending the night away pleasantly under the big tree, they all left the place when the blemishless Sun arose.

❍ ❍ ❍

२. यत्र भागीरथी गङ्गा यमुनामभिवर्तते ।
जग्मूस्तं देशमुद्देश्य विगाह्य सुमहद्वनम् ॥

2. They went towards the territory where (Ganges) Bhaageerathi 'confluenced' with Yamuna.... Entering the mighty forest .....

❍ ❍ ❍

३. ते भूमिभागान्विविधान्देशांश्चापि मनोरमान् ।
अदृष्टपूर्वान्पश्यन्तस्तत्र तत्र यशस्विनः ॥

3. ..... these famous (brothers) who had never seen such sights before, saw many captivating places here and there, many (different) regions.

❍ ❍ ❍

४. यथाक्षेमेण गच्छन्स पश्यंश्च विविधान्द्रुमान् ।
निवृत्तमात्रे दिवसे रामः सौमित्रिमब्रवीत् ।।

4. Going along without hindrance and seeing various tress, he addressed (Lakshmana) the son of Sumithra, when day passed over.

❍ ❍ ❍

५. प्रयागमभितः पश्य सौमित्रे धूममुन्नतम् ।
अग्नेर्भगवतः केतुं मन्ये संनिहितो मुनिः ।।

5. Oh (Lakshmana) the son of Sumithra! (Do you) notice an abode from where smoke from the 'lord of' Fire is coming, near Prayaag. I think some sage is around (This most sacred place Prayaag is perhaps modern Allahabad!)

❍ ❍ ❍

६. नूनं प्राप्ताः स्म संभेदं गङ्गायमुनयोर्वयम् ।
तथा हि श्रूयते शब्दो वारिणो वारिघट्टजः ।।

6. I think we have come to the confluence of Ganges and Yamuna rivers; Because, the sounds of waters 'rubbing' against waters are heard.

❍ ❍ ❍

७. दारूणि परिभिन्नानि वनजैरुपजीविभिः ।
भरद्वाजाश्रमे चैते दृश्यन्ते विविधा द्रुमाः ।।

7. At the hermitage of Bhardhwaaja, these various trees and logs of wood cut up from forest grown (trees) by the inhabitants here, are seen.

❍ ❍ ❍

८. धन्विनौ तौ सुखं गत्वा लम्बमाने दिवाकरे ।
गङ्गायमुनयोर्मध्ये प्रापतुर्निलयं मुनेः ।।

8. Armed with bow, these two (along with Seetha), walked along pleasantly and reached the abode of the sage. near the confluence of Ganges and Yamuna, when sun was setting.

❍ ❍ ❍

९. रामस्त्वाश्रममासाद्य त्रासयन्मृगपक्षिणः ।
गत्वा मुहूर्तमध्वानं भरद्वाजमुपागमत् ।।

9. Approaching the hermitage, they stayed at a distance, causing fear to the birds and deers for a moment: They awaited (the great sage) Bharadhwaaja.

❍ ❍ ❍

१०. ततस्त्वाश्रममासाद्य मुनेर्दर्शनकाङ्क्षिणौ ।
सीतयाऽनुगतौ वीरौ दूरादेवावतस्थतुः ।।

10. Followed by Seetha, these two brave (brothers) approached the hermitage desirous of seeing (and meeting) the sage, (but) stood at a distance from there,

❍ ❍ ❍

११. संप्रविश्य महात्मानमृषिं शिष्यगणैर्वृतम् ।
संशितव्रतमेकाग्रं तपसा लब्धचक्षुषम् ।।

11. Entering (the hermitage) of the great soul Rishi (Bharadhwaaja) who was surrounded by lots of disciples and who was totally devoted and who had attained spiritual 'vision' through penance completing his vows diligently .....

❍ ❍ ❍

१२. हुताग्निहोत्रं दृष्ट्वैव महाभागं कृताञ्जलिः ।
रामः सौमित्रिणा सार्धं सीतया चाभ्यवादयत् ।।

12. ...... Raama, accompanied by Seetha and (Lakshmana)

the son of Sumithra, saw this most illustrious (Sage) and prostrated before him, his hands cupped in Anjali (in total reverence).

❍ ❍ ❍

१३. न्यवेदयत चात्मानं तस्मै लक्ष्मणपूर्वजः ।
पुत्रौ दशरथस्यावां भगवन्रामलक्ष्मणौ ।।

13. (Raama) the elder brother of Lakshmana, then announced himself thus: Oh Lord (Bharadhwaaja)! We are, Raama and Lakshmana, the sons of Dhascharatha.

❍ ❍ ❍

१४. भार्या ममेयं वैदेही कल्याणी जनकात्मजा ।
मां चानुयाता विजनं तपोवनमनिन्दिता ।।

14. And she is my wife, (Seetha the) Vaidhehi: A blameless woman. Auspicious; daughter of king Janaka; she has accompanied me to the uninhabited forest.

❍ ❍ ❍

१५. पित्रा प्रव्राज्यमानं मां सौमित्रिरनुजः प्रियः ।
अयमन्वगमद्भ्राता वनमेव दृढव्रतः ।।

15. This is my younger brother, son of Sumithra: A man of firm resolution. He who loves me is following me when (I was) sent away to forest by my father.

❍ ❍ ❍

१६. पित्रा नियुक्ता भगवन्प्रवेक्ष्यामस्तपोवनम् ।
धर्ममेव चरिष्यामस्तत्र मूलफलाशनाः ।।

16. Oh Lord (Bharadhwaaja)! We are going to forest under the directive of our father. Sustaining ourselves on fruits and tubers, we are going (to live there to) follow Dharma, (and Dharma) alone.

१७. तस्य तद्वचनं श्रुत्वा राजपुत्रस्य धीमतः ।
उपानयत धर्मात्मा गामर्घ्यमुदकं ततः ।।

17. Hearing the words of the wise (Raama) the son of king (Dhascharatha), this noble soul man of Dharma (Bharadhwaaja), at once offered drinks, and waters of Arghya (as per norms).

❍ ❍ ❍

१८. नानाविधानन्नरसान्वन्यमूलफलाश्रयान् ।
तेभ्यो ददौ तप्ततपा वासं चैवान्वकल्पयत् ।।

18. (Bharadhwaaja) who had performed many penance, gave then various forest products of Tubers and fruits and also foods and gravies; he directed them to their seats.

❍ ❍ ❍

१९. मृगपक्षिभिरासीनो मुनिभिश्च समन्ततः ।
राममागतमभ्यर्च्य स्वागतेनाह तं मुनिः ।।

19. Surrounded by deers and birds all around and by hermits, the Muni (Bharadhwaaja) extolled Raama who had come to him, with a (hearty) welcome: Ah!

❍ ❍ ❍

२०. प्रतिगृह्य च तामर्चामुपविष्टं स राघवम् ।
भरद्वाजोऽब्रवीद्वाक्यं धर्मयुक्तमिदं तदा ।।

20. And this Bharadhwaaj addressed (Raama the) Raaghava who was sitting there having received welcome and honour, with the following words full of Dharma.

❍ ❍ ❍

२१. चिरस्य खलु काकुत्स्थ पश्यामि त्वामिहागतम् ।
श्रुतं तव मया चेदं विवासनमकारणम् ।।

21. Oh (Raama the) Kaakuthsa! I am seeing you here, coming here after a long time. That your, this your

exile, is without any reason (or blemish on your part) is well known to me. (Readers may note that this Bharadhwaaja was one of the greatest of sages. He has the 'Inward' eye through which he can see even the future)

❍ ❍ ❍

२२. अवकाशो विविक्तोऽयं महानद्योः समागमे ।
पुण्यश्च रमणीयश्च वसत्विह भवान्सुखम् ।।

22. This place (situated) at the confluence of the great rivers (Yamuna and Ganges) is very (auspicious), holy: Very delightful; You can stay here in comfort and in solitude.

❍ ❍ ❍

२३. एवमुक्तस्तु वचनं भरद्वाजेन राघवः ।
प्रत्युवाच शुभं वाक्यं रामः सर्वहिते रतः ।।

23. Hearing the words spoken by Bharadhwaaja, (Raama) the Raaghava who desired the welfare of everyone, replied with these pleasant words:

❍ ❍ ❍

२४. भगवन्नित आसन्नः पौरजानपदो जनः ।
सुदर्शमिह मां प्रेक्ष्य मन्येऽहमिममाश्रमम् ।।

24. Oh Lord The village and city folks settled down near these parts, would easily see me here in this hermitage, I should think.

❍ ❍ ❍

२५. आगमिष्यति वैदेहीं मां चापि प्रेक्षको जनः ।
अनेन कारणेनाहमिह वासं न रोचये ।।

25. People would come here to take a 'look' at me and (Seetha the) Vaidhehi also; By this reason alone, living here I do not desire.

(Raama feels he will 'disturb' the peace and tranquillity of the hermitage if the three lived there. Wants to stay in isolated place.)

❍ ❍ ❍

२६. एकान्ते पश्य भगवन्नाश्रमस्थानमुत्तमम् ।
रमते यत्र वैदेही सुखार्हा जनकात्मजा ॥

26. Oh Lord! (Please) Find a fine hermitage (for us) where this (Seetha the) Vaidhehi, the daughter of Janaka who is used to comforts, can delight in solitude.

❍ ❍ ❍

२७. एतच्छ्रुत्वा शुभं वाक्यं भरद्वाजो महामुनिः ।
राघवस्य ततो वाक्यमर्थग्राहकमब्रवीत् ॥

27. Hearing the auspicious words of substance and reasoning, the great Muni Bharadhwaaja addressed him thus:

❍ ❍ ❍

२८. दशक्रोश इतस्तात गिरिर्यस्मिन्निवत्स्यसि ।
महर्षिसेवितः पुण्यः सर्वतः सुखदर्शनः ॥

28. Oh 'son' (Raama)! At a distance of 10 Kroscha (about 45 miles) from here, there is a hill where everything around is beautiful, auspicious and which is inhabited by great sages. You may live there.

❍ ❍ ❍

२९. गोलाङ्गूलानुचरितो वानरर्क्षनिषेवितः ।
चित्रकूट इति ख्यातो गन्धमादनसन्निभः ॥

29. It is known as Chithrakoot: A species of monkeys called Golaankula inhabits the place: (Ordinary) monkeys and bears also live there; It is comparable to the mountain Ghandhamaadhana.

❍ ❍ ❍

३०. यावता चित्रकूटस्य नरः श्रृङ्गाण्यवेक्षते ।
कल्याणानि समाधत्ते न पापे कुरुते मनः ।।

30. When any man sets his eyes on Chithrakoot (just takes a look at) the peaks of Chithrakoot, he obtains prosperity. None directs his mind on (anything) sinful.

❍ ❍ ❍

३१. ऋषयस्तत्र बहवो विहृत्य शरदां शतम् ।
तपसा दिवमारूढाः कपालशिरसा सह ।।

31. Many sages having spent many autumn seasons there, have ascended to heaven (to be with) **God Schiva and the Lord of Fire.
(**God Schiva is also Kapaala Schiras: Vaalmeeki uses this name.)

❍ ❍ ❍

३२. प्रविविक्तमहं मन्ये तं वासं भवतः सुखम् ।
इह वा वनवासाय वस राम मया सह ।।

32. I consider this isolated place comfortable for your stay in forest; Or, Stay with me here itself, Oh Raama.

❍ ❍ ❍

३३. स रामं सर्वकामैस्तं भरद्वाजः प्रियातिथिम् ।
सभार्यं सह च भ्रात्रा प्रतिजग्राह धर्मवित् ।।

33. This sage Bharadhwaaja who was well versed in Dharma, entertained his beloved guest Raama who was with brother (Lakshmana) and his wife (Seetha), with all the desirables.

❍ ❍ ❍

३४. तस्य प्रयागे रामस्य तं महर्षिमुपेयुषः ।
प्रपन्ना रजनी पुण्या चित्राः कथयतः कथाः ।।

34. For this Raama who was near the sage and was

conversing.with him at Prayaag with wonderful conversations, the holy night fell.

❍ ❍ ❍

३५. सीतातृतीयः काकुत्स्थः परिश्रान्तः सुखोचितः ।
भरद्वाजाश्रमे रम्ये तां रात्रिमवसत्सुखम् ।।

35. (Raama the) Kaakuthsa who was used to comforts, and who was now there as Three-some along with Seetha, spent the night happily at the delightful hermitage of Bharadhwaaja, exhausted (by long journey).

❍ ❍ ❍

३६. प्रभातायां रजन्यां तु भरद्वाजमुपागमत् ।
उवाच नरशार्दूलो मुनिं ज्वलिततेजसम् ।।

36: When the day dawned after night had ended, (Raama)'the tiger' of men approached Bharadhwaaja; And he addressed this Muni whose brilliance was like flame.

❍ ❍ ❍

३७. शर्वरीं भगवन्नद्य सत्यशील तवाश्रमे ।
उषिताः स्मेह वसतिमनुजानातु नो भवान् ।।

37. Oh Lord! Oh devotee of Truth! Staying in your hermitage, night was spent away (in comfort); You should now give us permission to leave.

❍ ❍ ❍

३८. रात्र्यां तु तस्यां व्युष्टायां भरद्वाजोऽब्रवीदिदम् ।
मधुमूलफलोपेतं चित्रकूटं व्रजेति ह ।।

38. When the night had passed away, Bharadhwaaja said this thus: =You Go To Chithrakoot Which Abounds In Honey, Fruits and Tubers =

❍ ❍ ❍

३९. वासमौपयिकं मन्ये तव राम महाबल ॥

39. Oh mightily strong Raama! I consider the stay (there) fit for you.

❍ ❍ ❍

४०. नानामृगगणोपेतः किन्नरोरगसेवितः ।
मयूरनादाभिरुतो गजराजनिषेवितः ॥

40. (At Chithrakoot) there are numerous and different species of animals. Inhabited by Kinnara-s and Uraga-s; sounds from peacocks reverberate; 'Royal' elephants roam about .....

❍ ❍ ❍

४१. गम्यतां भवता शैलश्चित्रकूटः स विश्रुतः ।
पुण्यश्च रमणीयश्च बहुमूलफलायुतः ॥

41. ..... this Chithrakoot mountain is renowned. Holy. Lovely. Full with many (types of) tubers and fruits. May you go there.

❍ ❍ ❍

४२. तत्र कुञ्जरयूथानि मृगयूथानि चाभितः ।
विचरन्ति वनान्तेषु तानि द्रक्ष्यति राघव ॥

42. Oh (Raama) the Raaghava: Everywhere, in the forest region, there, flocks of deers roam about: You will see these (and enjoy).

❍ ❍ ❍

४३. सरित्प्रस्रवणप्रस्थान्दरीकन्दरनिर्झरान् ।
चरतः सीतया सार्धं नन्दिष्यति मनस्तव ॥

43. When you spend your time along with Seetha there (amidst) rivers, rivulets, mountain peaks, caves, waterfalls, mountain ridges and plateu, your mind will rejoice.

❍ ❍ ❍

४४. प्रहृष्टकोयष्टिककोकिलस्वनैः
विनादितं तं वसुधाधरं शिवम् ।
मृगैश्च मत्तैर्बहुभिश्च कुञ्जरैः
सुरम्यमासाद्य समावसाश्रमम् ।।

44. Going to the beautiful and auspicious mountain (the bearer of Earth), which is (inhabited by) exhilarated elephants, many deers, and which reverberates with cooing of joyous cranes and kokila birds, you make your hermitage (there).

❍ ❍ ❍

Chapter 55

They Cross Yamuna River

१. उषित्वा रजनीं तत्र राजपुत्रावरिन्दमौ ।
महर्षिमभिवाद्याथ जग्मतुस्तं गिरिं प्रति ।।

1. The destroyers of enemies, these two princes, (Raama and Lakshmana), after spending the night there, left towards the mountain after bowing to the great Rishi (Bharadwaaja).

❍ ❍ ❍

२. तेषां स्वस्त्ययनं चैव महर्षिः स चकार ह ।
प्रस्थितांश्चैव तान्प्रेक्ष्य पिता पुत्रानिवान्वगात् ।।

2. And the great sage blessed them with Swasthi: When they were going, he followed them (to a distance) like a father (following his sons when they depart), looking (at them)

(Bharadhwaaja, although a sage is human, so fond of Raama that he follows them a distance when they depart, never taking his eyes off.)

❍ ❍ ❍

३. ततः प्रचक्रमे वक्तुं वचनं स महामुनिः ।
भरद्वाजो महातेजा रामं सत्यपराक्रमम् ।।

3. Then this most brilliant and great Muni Bharadhwaaja began to say these words to the truly valiant Raama:

❍ ❍ ❍

४. गङ्गायमुनयोः संधिमासाद्य मनुजर्षभौ ।
कालिन्दीमनुगच्छेतां नदीं पश्चान्मुखाश्रिताम् ।।

4. Oh (Raama and Lakshmana the) 'bulls' amongst men! Going up to the confluence of rivers Ganges and Yamuna, you go towards Kaalindhi river that flows from west to east.

❍ .❍ ❍

५. अथासाद्य तु कालिन्दीं शीघ्रस्रोतसमापगाम् ।
तस्यास्तीर्थं प्रचरितं पुराणं प्रेक्ष्य राघवौ ।।

5. Oh the two Raaghava-s! Going along with the fast flowing river Kaalindhi (the Yamuna river), you will observe a Bank that has been frequented from time immemorial: Taking a boat from there you go across (this Yamuna the) Amshumathi

(Yamuna is called by Amschumathi and Kaalindhi.)

❍ ❍ ❍

६. तत्र यूयं प्लवं कृत्वा तरतांशुमतीं नदीम् ।
ततो न्यग्रोधमासाद्य महान्तं हरितच्छदम् ।।

6. Reaching a Big Banyan tree (Nyagrodha- Ficus India tree) whose leaves are green ......

❍ ❍ ❍

७. विवृद्धं बहुभिर्वृक्षैः श्यामं सिद्धोपसेवितम् ।
तस्मै सीताऽञ्जलिं कृत्वा प्रयुञ्जीताशिषः शिवाः ।।

7. ...... (and which is called) Schyaama and which is standing amidst cluster of trees and which is honoured

by Sidhdha-s, may Seetha, with her hands cupped in Anjali, pray for holy blessings.

❍ ❍ ❍

८. समासाद्य तु तं वृक्षं वसेद्वाऽतिक्रमेत् वा ॥

8. After approaching (and making prayers to) the tree, you may stay (for a while) or leave.

❍ ❍ ❍

९. क्रोशमात्रं ततो गत्वा नीलं द्रक्ष्यथ काननम् ।
पलाशबदरीमिश्रं राम वंशैश्च यामुनैः ॥

9. From there, going a distance of 2 ½ Kroscha-s, you will see a forest, dark with trees of Palasa (Butea frondosa), berry trees and bamboo trees.

❍ ❍ ❍

१०. स पन्थाश्चित्रकूटस्य गतः सुबहुशो मया ।
रम्यो मार्दवयुक्तश्च वनदावैर्विवर्जितः ॥

10. This route to Chithrakoot is pleasant and soft (to tread): Without any impediments of forest (path): Many times (this route has been) gone by me.

❍ ❍ ❍

११. इति पन्थानमावेद्य महर्षिः संन्यवर्तत ।
अभिवाद्य तथेत्युक्त्वा रामेण विनिवर्तितः ॥

11. After making this route known (to Raama and Lakshmana), the great sage was told by Raama: (We will take this route) as directed; he (Bhardhwaaja), returned (to his hermitage) having taken leave and having been bowed to by them.

(Readers may note that although Bhardhwaaja has abandoned mundane life for a life of penance in forest, he takes great pains to guide Raama. A great sage does not cease to be a sage because he takes interest in mundane affairs of people).

❍ ❍ ❍

१२. उपावृत्ते मुनौ तस्मिन् रामो लक्ष्मणमब्रवीत् ।
कृतपुण्याः स्म सौमित्रे मुनिर्यन्नोऽनुकम्पते ।।

12. When this muni returned (to his hermitage), Raama addressed (Lakshmana the) son of Sumithra: The Muni (Bharadhwaaja) is most compassionate to us: We are indeed most fortunate.

❍ ❍ ❍

१३. इति तौ पुरुषव्याघ्रौ मन्त्रयित्वा मनस्विनौ ।
सीतामेवाग्रतः कृत्वा कालिन्दीं जग्मतुर्नदीम् ।।

13. These high spirited men (Raama and Lakshmana) who were 'tigers' of men, having discussed thus, walked along towards (Yamuna the) Kaalindhi river, with Seetha going in front of them.

❍ ❍ ❍

१४. अथासाद्य तु कालिन्दीं शीघ्रस्रोतोवहां नदीम् ।
चिन्तामापेदिरे सर्वेनदीजलतितीर्षवः ।।

14. They reached the fast flowing river Kaalindhi and they all directed their minds to cross the waters of the river.

❍ ❍ ❍

१५. तौ काष्ठसङ्घाटमथो चक्रतुः सुमहाप्लवम् ।
शुष्कैर्वंशैः समाकीर्णमुशीरैश्च समावृतम् ।।

15. These two then made a big and beautiful Raft out of well laid out dry logs of wood and bamboo (poles) and covered it with grass.

(Readers may note that Raama and Lakshmana are also experts in fabricating a make shift 'boat'.)

❍ ❍ ❍

१६. ततो वेतसशाखाश्च जम्बूशाखाश्च वीर्यवान् ।
चकार लक्ष्मणश्छित्वा सीतायाः सुखमासनम् ।।

16. Then the brave Lakshmana cut sticks of Ratan (Calassus

Rotung) from Jambu tree (Eugenia Jambolana) and made a comfortable seat for Seetha (on the raft).

❍ ❍ ❍

१७. तत्र श्रियमिवाचिन्त्यां रामो दाशरथिः प्रियाम् ।
ईषत्संलज्जमानां तामध्यारोपयत प्लवम् ।।

17. Then Raama the son of Dhascharatha, helped his dear and most resplendent (wife Seetha) who was of unwavering mind, (but) who was somewhat shy, to get into the raft.

❍ ❍ ❍

१८. पार्श्वेच तत्र वैदेह्या वसने भूषणानि च ।
प्लवे कठिनवाजं च रामश्चक्रे सहायुधैः ।।

18. Then Raama placed his weapons, spades and shovels, ornaments etc by the side of (Seetha the) Vaidhehi, on the raft.

❍ ❍ ❍

१९. आरोप्य सीतां प्रथमं संघाटं परिगृह्य तौ ।
ततः प्रतेरतुर्यत्तौ वीरौ दशरथात्मजौ ।।

19. Holding her and helping her to mount the raft first, these two brave sons of Dhascharatha prepared to move (the raft).

❍ ❍ ❍

२०. कालिन्दीमध्यमायाता सीता त्वेनामवन्दत ।
स्वस्ति देवि तरामि त्वां पारयेन्मे पतिर्व्रतम् ।।

20. When they were in the middle of the river Kaalindhi, Seetha saluted this (river) thus:= Oh Lady! Swasthi (Bless us)! I am crossing you; May my lord (Raama) fulfill his vow (of exile) ......

❍ ❍ ❍

२१. यक्ष्ये त्वां गोसहस्रेण सुराघटशतेन च ।
स्वस्ति प्रत्यागते रामे पुरीमिक्ष्वाकुपालिताम् ।।

21. When Raama, blessed with Swasthi, returns to the city (of Ayodhya) ruled by Ikshwaaku (kings), I will worship you with offering of thousand cows and with vessels containing holy waters.=

❍ ❍ ❍

२२. कालिन्दीमथ सीता तु याचमाना कृताञ्जलिः ।
तीरमेवाभिसंप्राप्ता दक्षिणं वरवर्णिनी ।।

22. The beautiful Seetha kept on begging (praying) to Yamuna River with her hands cupped in Anjali even as the southern banks were nearing.

❍ ❍ ❍

२३. ततः प्लवेनांशुमतीं शीघ्रगामूर्मिमालिनीम् ।
तीरजैर्बहुभिर्वृक्षैः संतेरुर्यमुनां नदीम् ।।

23. They (thus) crossed on the raft the Yamuna river considered as daughter of Sun. It was swift and its waves picked up many trees standing near the embankments.

❍ ❍ ❍

२४. ते तीर्णाः प्लवमुत्सृज्य प्रस्थाय यमुनावनात् ।
श्यामं न्यग्रोधमासेदुः शीतलं हरितच्छदम् ।।

24. They who had crossed (river Yamuna), discharged the raft and going along the abutting forest around the river Yamuna, (saw) and approached the Nyagrodha tree called Schyaama which was full with green leaves and (which gave) cool (shade).

❍ ❍ ❍

२५. न्यग्रोधं तमुपास्थाय वैदेही वाक्यमब्रवीत् ।
नमस्तेऽस्तु महावृक्ष पारयेन्मे पतिर्व्रतम् ।।

25. Approaching the Banyan tree, (Seetha the) Vaidhehi

addressed thus: = Oh Great Tree ! I am bowing to you. May my lord fulfill his vows ......

❍ ❍ ❍

२६. कौसल्यां चैव पश्येयं सुमित्रां च यशस्विनीम् ।
इति सीताऽञ्जलिं कृत्वा पर्यगच्छद्वनस्पतिम् ॥

26. I should see (again) Kowsalya and the famous Sumithra:= Saying thus, Seetha went round the tree with her hands cupped in Anjali.

❍ ❍ ❍

२७. अवलोक्य ततः सीतामायाचन्तीमनिन्दिताम् ।
दयितां च विधेयां च रामो लक्ष्मणमब्रवीत् ॥

27. And Raama saw his obedient and most cherished wife Seetha who was blemishless, worshipping: He then addressed Lakshmana.

❍ ❍ ❍

२८. सीतामादाय गच्छ त्वमग्रतो भरताग्रज ।
पृष्ठतोऽहं गमिष्यामि सायुधो द्विपदां वर ॥

28. Oh (Lakshmana) the foremost of men! Oh the elder brother of Bharatha! You go in front with Seetha behind you; Wielding arms, I shall follow (you both).

❍ ❍ ❍

२९. यद्यत्फलं प्रार्थयते पुष्पं वा जनकात्मजा ।
तत्तत्प्रदद्या वैदेह्या यत्रास्या रमते मनः ॥

29. Whatever fruits or flowers this (Seetha) the daughter of Janaka requests and in which Seetha's mind will rejoice, all these must be brought to her.

❍ ❍ ❍

३०. गच्छतोस्तु तयोर्मध्ये बभूव जनकात्मजा ।
मातङ्गयोर्मध्यगता शुभा नागवधूरिव ॥

30. When she walked between these two in the middle, this auspicious (Seetha) the daughter of Janaka appeared like a female elephant going along between two male elephants.

❍ ❍ ❍

३१. एकैकं पादपं गुल्मं लतां वा पुष्पशालिनीम् ।
अदृष्टपूर्वां पश्यन्ती रामं पप्रच्छ साऽबला ॥

31. The docile (Seetha) who had not seen before such creepers laden with flowers and who had not seen such trees and crotons, asked Raama about every one of them as she saw these.

❍ ❍ ❍

३२. रमणीयान्बहुविधान्पादपान्कुसुमोत्कटान् ।
सीतावचनसंरब्ध आनयामास लक्ष्मणः ॥

32. And Lakshmana thrilled by Seetha's words (her enquiries about trees and plants), brought various beautiful stalks and (branches of) trees that were full with flowers.

❍ ❍ ❍

३३. विचित्रवालुकजलां हंससारसनादिताम् ।
रेमे जनकराजस्य तदा प्रेक्ष्य सुता नदीम् ॥

33. (Seetha) the daughter of Janaka saw the river full with water and with lovely sand embankments; sounds from swans and Sarasa birds reverberating (the place): And she rejoiced.

❍ ❍ ❍

३४. क्रोशमात्रं ततो गत्वा भ्रातरौ रामलक्ष्मणौ ।
बहून्मेध्यान्मृगान्हत्वा चेरतुर्यमुनावने ॥

34. The two brothers, Raama and Lakshmana, after driving away many (wild) tough animals, walked along, going

a distance of one Kroscha (about 2 to 3 miles) in the forest around Yamuna.

❍ ❍ ❍

३५. विहृत्य ते बर्हिणपूगनादिते
शुभे वने वानरवारणायुते ।
समं नदीवप्रमुपेत्य सम्मतं
निवासमाजग्मुरदीनदर्शनाः ॥

35. The tireless (Raama and Lakshmana) wandered around the delightful forest which was full of monkeys, elephants; cooing from multitude of peacocks reverberated: Seeing a place near the river, they decided to stay (for the night) there.

(Readers may note that for an Indian, worship of mountains, trees, rivers, holy cities, great sages, was more important than even worship of Gods in temples.)

❍ ❍ ❍

Chapter 56

(Raama) Goes To Chithrakoot

१. अथ रात्र्यां व्यतीतायामवसुप्तमनन्तरम् ।
प्रबोधयामास शनैर्लक्ष्मणं रघुनन्दनः ॥

1. When night had passed away, (Raama) the darling of Raghu-s, gently awakened Lakshmana who was sleepy (and said the following) about further (action).

❍ ❍ ❍

२. सौमित्रे श्रृणु वन्यानां वल्गु व्याहरतां स्वनम् ।
संप्रतिष्ठामहे कालः प्रस्थानस्य परन्तप ॥

2. Oh (Lakshmana the) son of Sumithra! Oh the tormentor of enemies! Listen to the sweet sounds of cooing forest

(birds): It is time for journey; We will continue (to move on).

❍ ❍ ❍

३. स सुप्तः समये भ्रात्राः लक्ष्मणः प्रतिबोधितः ।
जहौ निद्रां च तन्द्रीं च प्रसक्तं च पथि श्रमम् ।।

3. Lakshmana got rid of his sleepishness, sluggishness and weariness caused by travel; he was woken up by his brother when he was (somewhat) sleepy.

❍ ❍ ❍

४. तत उत्थाय ते सर्वेस्पृष्ट्वा नद्याः शिवं जलम् ।
पन्थानमृषिणोद्दिष्टं चित्रकूटस्य तं ययुः ।।

4. They all got up and "touched' (bathed) in the auspicious waters of the river and went on the path indicated by the Rishi (Bharadhwaaja), to Chithrakoot.

❍ ❍ ❍

५. ततः संप्रस्थितः काले रामः सौमित्रिणा सह ।
सीतां कमलपत्राक्षीमिदं वचनमब्रवीत् ।।

5. And Raama who, along with (Lakshmana) the son of Sumithra, had started out, addressed Seetha whose eyes were like lotus leaves.

❍ ❍ ❍

६. आदीप्तानिव वैदेहि सर्वतः पुष्पिताञ्नगान् ।
स्वैः पुष्पैः किंशुकान्पश्य मालिनः शिशिरात्यये ।।

6. Oh (Seetha the) Vaidhehi! Being spring (at the end of cool season), the trees (Butea Fondosa etc) are in full blossom and blaze (with colors of) their flowers everywhere: See (and enjoy) the 'gardens'.

❍ ❍ ❍

७. पश्य भल्लातकान्बिल्वाञ्नरैरनुपसेवितान् ।
फलपत्रैरवनताञ्नूनं शक्ष्यामि जीवितुम् ।।

7. See: The Nut Trees (Carpus Anacardus, that are so tall) they cannot be 'reached' by men. And Plants (Ficus Heterophylla) and trees of (Aegele Marmosa)that are bent: From now on, I insist (that the trees are sufficient for us) to live upon.

(No meats, No grains for Raama and Seetha and Lakshmana.)

❍ ❍ ❍

८. छश्य द्रोणप्रमाणानि लम्बमानानि लक्ष्मण ।
मधूनि मधुकारीभिः संभृतानि नगे नगे ।।

8. Oh Lakshmana! See the honeys gathered by honey bees on tree by tree, hanging down like a trough. (on trees).

❍ ❍ ❍

९. एष क्रोशति नत्यूहस्तं शिखी प्रतिकूजति ।
रमणीये वनोद्देशे पुष्पसंस्तरसङ्कटे ।।

9. In this beautiful forest with well spread out extensive flowers (with trees so close together), this bird is cooing; And the peacock is cooing back

❍ ❍ ❍

१०. मातङ्गयूथानुसृतं पक्षिसङ्घानुनादितम् ।
चित्रकूटमिमं पश्य प्रवृद्धशिखरं गिरिम् ।।

10. See the Chithrakoot mountain with its lofty peaks, with sounds from flock of birds and inhabited by scores of elephants.

❍ ❍ ❍

११. समभूमितले रम्ये द्रुमैर्बहुभिरावृते ।
पुण्ये रंस्यामहे तात चित्रकूटस्य कानने ।।

11. Oh dear (Lakshmana)! In this forest around Chithrakoot, we shall (stay and) enjoy (life) on flat, even beautiful spot, surrounded by many trees.

❍ ❍ ❍

१२. ततस्तौ पादचारेण गच्छन्तौ सह सीतया ।
रम्यमासेदतुः शैलं चित्रकूटं मनोरमम् ।।

12. Going along on foot with Seetha, they reached the captivating and lovely Chithrakoot mountain.

❍ ❍ ❍

१३. तं तु पर्वतमासाद्य नानापक्षिगणायुतम् ।
बहुमूलफलं रम्यं संपन्नसरसोदकम् ।।

13. Reaching the mountain which was abundant in various types of birds, and which was full with fruits and tubers, which was lovely and which had plenty of streams with pure waters ......

❍ ❍ ❍

१४. चित्रकूटं हि संपश्यन् रामो लक्ष्मणमब्रवीत् ।।

14. ..... Seeing (such a mountain) Chithrakoot, Raama addressed Lakshmana:

❍ ❍ ❍

१५. मनोज्ञोऽयं गिरिः सौम्य नानाद्रुमलतायुतः ।
बहुमूलफलो रम्य स्वाजीवः प्रतिभाति मे ।।

15. Oh Pleasant (Lakshmana)! This mountain is captivating and appears to me very beautiful with various trees and plants and has many fruits and tubers for our easy living.

❍ ❍ ❍

१६. मुनयश्च महात्मानो वसन्त्यस्मिञ्छिलोच्चये ।
अयं वासो भवेत्तावदत्र सौम्य रमेमहि ।।

16. Oh Pleasant (Lakshmana)! In this hill live great soul Rishi-s. Let this be our abode for now: We will (live and) enjoy here.

❍ ❍ ❍

१७. इति सीता च रामश्च लक्ष्मणश्च कृताञ्जलिः ।
अभिगम्याश्रमं सर्वेवाल्मीकिमभिवादयन् ।।

17. (Saying) thus, all of them, Raama, Seetha and Lakshmana, went over to and bowed before Vaalmeeki with their hands cupped in Anjali, in his abode.

(Sage Vaalmeeki the would be author of Raamaayana stayed here.)

❍ ❍ ❍

१८. तान्महर्षिः प्रमुदितः पूजयामास धर्मवित् ।
आस्यतामिति चोवाच स्वागतं तं निवेद्य च ।।

18. The great sage who was well versed in Dharma honoured them with joy; After offering welcome, he said:= May You Be Seated.=

❍ ❍ ❍

१९. राघवं प्रीतिसंयुक्तमिदं वचनमब्रवीत् ।
ज्ञातं मया रघुश्रेष्ठ त्वदागमनकारणम् ।।
अत्र वासमृषीणां च सकाशे रोचय प्रभो ।।

19. He then addressed (Raama the) Raaghava with these words indicating his affection:= Oh Lord (Raama) the foremost of Raghu-s! The purpose of your coming here is known to me; Be pleased to make your abode here near the Rishi-s. =

(Like Bharadhwaaja Vaalmeeki had an invisible eye through which he could 'perceive' things)

❍ ❍ ❍

२०. इति तेज समाज्ञप्तः प्रीयमाणो महारथः ।
तथेति प्रतिजग्राह ऋषिणोक्तं कृताञ्जलिः ।।

20. Commanded thus by the sage, the great (warrior and) charioteer (Raama) became pleased and with his hands cupped in Anjali, accepted what was told by the Rishi to him and said:= I Will. Do Likewise.=

❍ ❍ ❍

२१. ततोऽब्रवीन्महाबाहुर्लक्ष्मणं लक्ष्मणाग्रजः ।
संनिवेद्य यथान्यायमात्मानमृषये प्रभुः ।।

21. After informing him, (after informing) properly to Rishi (Vaalmeeki), Lord (Raama) the mighty limbed elder brother of Lakshmana, then told Lakshmana:

❍ ❍ ❍

२२. लक्ष्मणानय दारूणि दृढानि च वराणि च ।
कुरुष्वावसथं सौम्य वासे मेऽभिरतं मनः ।।

22. Oh pleasant Lakshmana! Bring strong logs from choicest of woods; Build a cottage. My mind delights in living (here).

❍ ❍ ❍

२३. तस्य तद्वचनं श्रुत्वा सौमित्रिर्विविधान्द्रुमान् ।
आजहार ततश्चक्रे पर्णशालामरिंदमः ।।

23. (Lakshmana) the son of Sumithra, the destroyer of enemies, hearing his words, brought various 'trees' And he built a hermitage (Parnasaala) there.

❍ ❍ ❍

२४. तां निष्ठितां बद्धकटां दृष्ट्वा रामः सुदर्शनाम् ।
शुश्रूषमाणमेकाग्रमिदं वचनमब्रवीत् ।।

24. And when Raama saw that this (cottage) was beautiful and firmly (put up), tied with twisted hemps, he addressed these words to (Lakshmana) who served him with single minded devotion.

❍ ❍ ❍

२५. ऐणेयं मांसमाहृत्य शालां यक्ष्यामहे वयम् ।
कर्तव्यं वास्तुशमनं सौमित्रे चिरजीविभिः ।।

25. Oh (Lakshmana) the son of Sumithra! House warming (Vaasthu) Ceremony must be done by those who are going to live long (in a house): And (so) we shall

perform Rituals (of Vaasthu-Homa) with deer meat, for our hermitage (where we are to live long).

❍ ❍ ❍

२६. मृगं हत्वाऽऽनय क्षिप्रं लक्ष्मणेह शुभेक्षण ।
कर्तव्यः शास्त्रदृष्टो हि विधिर्धर्ममनुस्मर ॥

26. Oh Lakshmana with pleasing eyes! Follow (and remember) Dharma; The norms as seen in our Shaasthra-s must be followed: Therefore you bring a deer after killing it, soon.

❍ ❍ ❍

२७. भ्रातुर्वचनमाज्ञाय लक्ष्मणः परवीरहा ।
चकार च यथोक्तं स तं रामः पुनरब्रवीत् ॥

27. Accepting his brother's words (of command) Lakshmana the destroyer of hostile elements, did as directed: And this Raama again said to him:

❍ ❍ ❍

२८. ऐणेयं श्रपयस्वैतच्छालां यक्ष्यामहे वयम् ।
त्वर सौम्यमुहूर्तोऽयं ध्रुवश्च दिवसो ह्ययम् ॥

28. Cook this meat: Make haste: Today is (holy and will give) eternal (happiness to the master of the house): It is auspicious time (as well). Therefore we shall perform (Vaasthu ceremony) for our hermitage.

❍ ❍ ❍

२९. स लक्ष्मणः कृष्णमृगं हत्वा मेध्यं प्रतापवान् ।
अथ चिक्षेप सौमित्रिः समिद्धे जातवेदसि ॥

29. Then the glorious son of Sumithra, this Lakshmana, offered a killed fat black deer as Oblation to Fire (the Jaathvedhas).

❍ ❍ ❍

३०. तं तु पक्वं समाज्ञाय निष्टप्तं छिन्नशोणितम् ।
लक्ष्मणः पुरुषव्याघ्रमथ राघवमब्रवीत् ।।

30. Then, seeing it completely cooked and well roasted with blood gone, Lakshmana addressed Raama the 'tiger of men'.

❍ ❍ ❍

३१. अयं कृष्णः समाप्ताङ्गः श्रृतः कृष्णमृगो यथा ।
देवता देवसङ्काश यजस्व कुशलो ह्यसि ।।

31. Oh (Raama) who is comparable to a celestial! This black deer is as dark (as before) and well cooked on all parts of the body: You are conversant (with all these rituals): Therefore you (begin rituals and) worship the deities. (the yaaga).

❍ ❍ ❍

३२. रामः स्नात्वा तु नियतो गुणवाञ्जप्यकोविदः ।
सङ्ग्रहेणाकरोत्सर्वान्मन्त्रान्सत्रावसानिकान् ।।

32. Then Raama who was endowed with such qualities and who was well versed in chants and prayers, took bath, and went into meditation. He performed the house warming (Vasthu) ceremonies, propitiating (deities) with all the chants.

❍ ❍ ❍

३३. इष्ट्वा देवगणान्सर्वान्विवेशावसथं शुचिः ।
बभूवः च मनोह्लादो रामस्यामिततेजसः ।।

33. After praying to all deities and (thus) becoming 'pure', he entered the cottage: There was (great) mental happiness for this Raama of incomparable brilliance.

❍ ❍ ❍

३४. वैश्वदेवबलिं कृत्वा रौद्रं वैष्णवमेव च ।
वास्तुसंशमनीयानि मङ्गलानि प्रवर्तयन् ।।

34. After offering oblations to Vischwadheva-s, the Rudhra, and Vishnu, he began auspicious prayers for tranquillity and peace (in their life) in the abode ......

❍ ❍ ❍

३५. जपं च न्यायतः कृत्वा स्नात्वा नद्यां यथाविधि ।
पापसंशमनं रामश्चकार बलिमुत्तमम् ।।

35. ...... as per norms; Raama prayed with chants and took baths as per norms, and he offered supreme Oblations for driving away sins.

❍ ❍ ❍

३६. वेदिस्थलविधानानि चैत्यान्यायतनानि च ।
आश्रमस्यानुरूपाणि स्थापयामास राघवः ।।

36. nd (Raama the) Raaghava established in the hermitage, suitable prayer hall with raised platform for doing prayers, and also rest rooms.

❍ ❍ ❍

३७. वन्यैर्माल्यैः फलैर्मूलैः पक्वैर्मांसैर्यथाविधि ।
अद्भिर्जपैश्च वेदोक्तैर्दर्भैश्च ससमित्कुशैः ।।

37. With wild forest flowers, fruits, tubers, flowers, cooked meats, waters, with Dharbha grass and Samith-s (sticks for fire), with renderings of Vedha-s ......

❍ ❍ ❍

३८. तौ तर्पयित्वा भूतानि राघवौ सह सीतया ।
तदा विविशतुः शालां सुशुभां शुभलक्षणौ ।।

38. ...... the two Raaghava-s who possessed good qualities, (prayed thus) pleased the Bhootha-s and entered the auspicious abode, (having performed all the ceremonies) as per custom, along with Seetha.

❍ ❍ ❍

३९. तां वृक्षपर्णच्छदनां मनोज्ञां
यथाप्रदेशं सुकृतां निवाताम् ।
वासाय सर्वेविविशुः समेताः
सभां यथा देवगणाः सुधर्माम् ।।

39. It was like abode of celestials, Sudharma, as they all entered their hermitage to live there together: Well constructed, Airy, covered by (shade of) trees and creepers, most captivating and well laid out (where everything was in its place).

❍ ❍ ❍

४०. अनेकनानामृगपक्षिसङ्कुले
विचित्रपुष्पस्तबकैर्द्रुमैर्युते ।
वनोत्तमे व्यालमृगानुनादिते
तदा विजहुः सुसुखं जितेन्द्रियाः ।।

40. At that time, in this foremost forest which was full of various animals and birds, which was full of trees and which was full of strange (wonderful) cluster of flowers, these men (Raama and Lakshmana) who had conquered their senses and passions, lived comfortably (even as they were hearing) the roar of wild animals.

❍ ❍ ❍

४१. सुरम्यमासाद्य तु चित्रकूटं
नदीं च तां माल्यवतीं सुतीर्थाम् ।
ननन्द रामो मृगपक्षिजुष्टां
जहौ च दुःखं पुरविप्रवासात् ।।

41. Raama (approaching and) seeing the most lovely Chithrakoot and the river Maalyavathi which had pure waters and which was full of birds and animals (around it), rejoiced. Sadness did not seize him although he was living far away from his city (of Ayodhya).

(Note: One of the remarkable feature of these Royal princes of Ikshwaaku family is their versatality: They are masters of Vedha-s; Norms, prayers; Warriors with exceptional ability to wield diverse weapons; they are lovers of fine arts; And they can build a cottage or a raft with same felicity as they can discharge arrows.)

❍ ❍ ❍

Chapter 57

Sumanthra Enters Ayodhya

१. कथयित्वा सुदुःखार्तः सुमन्त्रेण चिरं सह ।
रामे दक्षिणकूलस्थे जगाम स्वगृहं गुहः ॥

1. (The scene shifts to Ayodhya: Sumanthra the charioteer returns.)

When Raama had crossed over to the southern banks (of river Ganges and when Raama had bid him good bye), Guha spent some time conversing with Sumanthra; and in great sorrow he then went back to his place.

❍ ❍ ❍

२. भरद्वाजाभिगमनं प्रयागे च सहासनम् ।
आ गिरेर्गमनं तेषां तत्रस्थैरभिलक्षितम् ॥

2. They came to know about (Raama's) meeting with sage Bharadwaaja, their stay together at Prayaag and their going to (Chithrakoot) mountain for stay.

❍ ❍ ❍

३. अनुज्ञातः सुमन्त्रोऽथ योजयित्वा हयोत्तमान् ।
अयोध्यामेव नगरीं प्रययौ गाढदुर्मनाः ॥

3. Taking leave (of Guha), Sumanthra whose mind was depressed, yoked his foremost horses and left for the city of Ayodhya.

❍ ❍ ❍

४. स वनानि सुगन्धीनि सरितश्च सरांसि च ।
पश्यन्नतिययौ शीघ्रं ग्रामाणि नगराणि च ॥

4. Seeing (and passing through) pleasant smelling forests, rivers lakes, villages, towns, he went along fast.

❍ ❍ ❍

५. ततः सायाह्न समये तृतीयेऽहनि सारथिः ।
अयोध्यां समनुप्राप्य निरानन्दां ददर्श ह ॥

5. The charioteer (Sumanthra) reached Ayodhya in the evening on the third day from there and found (the city) bereft of joy.

❍ ❍ ❍

६. स शून्यामिव निःशब्दां दृष्ट्वा परमदुर्मनाः ।
सुमन्त्रश्चिन्तयामास शोकवेगसमाहतः ॥

6. Observing (the city) stilled by silence and as though empty, this Sumanthra became terribly upset and began to ponder, stricken greatly by grief.

❍ ❍ ❍

७. कच्चिन्न सगजा साश्वा सजना सजनाधिपा ।
रामसन्तापदुःखेन दग्धा शोकाग्निना पुरी ॥

7. I hope the city, along with elephants, horses, people including their king, are not 'Burnt' up by 'Fire of Grief'.

❍ ❍ ❍

८. इति चिन्तापरः सूतो वाजिभिः शीघ्रपातिभिः ।
नगरद्वारमासाद्य त्वरितः प्रविवेश ह ॥

8. Thus this charioteer (Sumanthra) was lost in thought: Riding on fast moving horses (pulling his chariot), he reached the gates of the city and entered quickly.

❍ ❍ ❍

९. सुमन्त्रमभियान्तं तं शतशोऽथ सहस्रशः ।
क्व राम इति पृच्छन्तः सूतमभ्यद्रवन्नराः ।।

9. And men, hundreds, nay in thousands, ran after the charioteer as he was returning, asking Sumanthra:= Where Is Raama? =

❍ ❍ ❍

१०. तेषां शशंस गङ्गायामहमापृच्छ्य राघवम् ।
अनुज्ञातो निवृत्तोऽस्मि धार्मिकेण महात्मना ।।

10. (Sumanthra) told them: = I bid farewell to Raama at Ganges and have come back, being asked to return by the great soul (Raama) the man of Dharma.–

❍ ❍ ❍

११. ते तीर्णा इति विज्ञाय बाष्पपूर्णमुखा जनाः ।
अहो धिगिति निश्वस्य हा रामेति च चुक्रुशुः ।।

11. Realising that (Raama) had crossed (the river) the citizens sighed deeply with tears covering their faces and they cried:= Ah Raama ! What a shame. Ah! =

❍ ❍ ❍

१२. शुश्राव च वचस्तेषां बृन्दं बृन्दं च तिष्ठताम् ।
हताः स्म खलु ये नेह पश्याम इति राघवम् ।।

12. And he heard the words of these (citizens) who were standing there in groups and groups. = As we cannot see (Raama the Raaghava, we are surely ruined.

❍ ❍ ❍

१३. दानयज्ञविवाहेषु समाजेषु महत्सु च ।
न द्रक्ष्यामः पुनर्जातु धार्मिकं राममन्तरा ।।

13. We can never again see another man of Dharma like Raama in charity, in performance of Sacrificial ceremonies, in (help during) marriages, and (equal to him) before an assembly of great men.

❍ ❍ ❍

१४. किं समर्थं जनस्यास्य किं प्रियं किं सुखावहम् ।
इति रामेण नगरं पित्रेव परिपालितम् ।।

14. The city was protected by Raama like a father; So what purpose is served for the citizens (who are) without him; Is there anything dear or anything which can bring happiness. = ...

❍ ❍ ❍

१५. वातायनगतानां च स्त्रीणामन्वन्तरापणम् ।
रामशोकाभितप्तानां शुश्राव परिदेवनम् ।।

15. (Sumanthra) heard the wailings of the ladies who were standing by the windows of their houses and who were tormented by grief over Raama; (and heard wailings) from market place.

❍ ❍ ❍

१६. स राजमार्गमध्येन सुमन्त्रः पिहिताननः ।
यत्र राजा दशरथस्तदेवोपययौ गृहम् ।।

16. His face covered (by tears), this Sumanthra went along the royal boulevard towards the palace where Dhascharatha was.

❍ ❍ ❍

१७. सोऽवतीर्य रथाच्छीघ्रं राजवेश्म प्रविश्य च ।
कक्ष्याः सप्तातिचक्राम महाजनसमाकुलाः ।।

17. Getting down from his chariot, he entered King's palace and quickly crossed over (and passed through) the 7 bastions (segments of the palace) which was full with citizens.

❍ ❍ ❍

१८. हर्म्यैर्विमानैः प्रासादैरवेक्ष्याथ समागतम् ।
हाहाकारकृता नार्योरामादर्शनकर्शिताः ।।

18. Ladies standing in their mansions, in their homes, in

the palaces, looked at him who was returning (without Raama) cried aloud with HA- HAA, emaciated, because of not seeing Raama.

❍ ❍ ❍

१९. आयतैर्विमलैर्नेत्रैरश्रुवेगपरिप्लुतैः ।
अन्योन्यमभिवीक्षन्तेऽव्यक्तमार्ततराः स्त्रियः ।।

19. Engulfed in grief, their spotless eyes blurred by force of tears, the ladies saw one another indistinctively, with some effort.

❍ ❍ ❍

२०. ततो दशरथस्त्रीणा प्रासादेभ्यस्ततस्ततः ।
रामशोकाभितप्तानां मन्दं शुश्राव जल्पितम् ।।

20. At that time he heard subdued chatter of the wives of Dhascharatha who were all tormented by grief over separation from Raama, from all these palaces. (They said).

❍ ❍ ❍

२१. सह रामेण निर्यातो विना राममिहागतः ।
सूतः किं नाम कौसल्यां शोचन्तीं प्रतिवक्ष्यति ।।

21. What answer will charioteer (Sumanthra) give the lamenting Kowsalya when he has come back without Raama, having gone out with Raama?

❍ ❍ ❍

२२. यथा च मन्ये दुर्जीवमेवं न सुकरं ध्रुवम् ।
आच्छिद्य पुत्रे निर्याते कौसल्या यत्र जीवति ।।

22. When her son has gone away and cut off from her thus, Kowsalya (still) lives on: I consider therefore, it is not easy to give up one's wretched life, (a life that seems) everlasting.

❍ ❍ ❍

२३. सत्यरूपं तु तद्वाक्यं राजस्त्रीणां निशामयन् ।
प्रदीप्त इव शोकेन विवेश सहसा गृहम् ।।

23. Hearing these words of the royal ladies indicating their true feelings, (Sumanthra) who appeared as though he was burning by grief, at once entered the palace.

❍ ❍ ❍

२४. स प्रविश्याष्टमीं कक्ष्यां राजानं दीनमातुरम् ।
पुत्रशोपरिद्यूनमपश्यत्पाण्डुरे गृहे ।।

24. Entering the eighth bastion of this white palace, he saw that the king was in distress, miserable and wailing in grief over his son.

❍ ❍ ❍

२५. अभिगम्य तमासीनं नरेन्द्रमभिवाद्य च ।
सुमन्त्रो रामवचनं यथोक्तं प्रत्यवेदयत् ।।

25. Approaching the king who was seated he bowed to him and conveyed Raama's words (Raama's message) exactly as (Raama had) told (Sumanthra during leave taking in forest).

❍ ❍ ❍

२६. स तूष्णीमेव तच्छ्रुत्वा राजा विभ्रान्तचेतनः ।
मूर्च्छितो न्यपतद्भूमौ रामशोकाभिपीडितः ।।

26. Hearing this (message of Raama) the lord of men (king Dhascharatha) became silent; His mind became bewildered; he then fell down on earth, unconscious, tormented terribly by grief over Raama.

❍ ❍ ❍

२७. ततोऽन्तः पुरमाविद्धं मूर्च्छिते पृथिवीपतौ ।
उद्धृत्य बाहू चुक्रोश नृपतौ पतिते क्षितौ ।।

27. When king (Dhascharatha the) ruler of earth fell down on earth unconscious, the ladies of the palace raised

their hands and cried piercing (the heart of every one as though).

❍ ❍ ❍

२८. सुमित्रया तु सहिता कौसल्या पतितं पतिम् ।
उत्थापयामास तदा वचनं चेदमब्रवीत् ।।

28. Kowsalya, along with Sumithra, lifted up their husband who had fallen down. And she said these words.

❍ ❍ ❍

२९. इमं तस्य महाभाग दूतं दुष्करकारिणः ।
वनवासादनुप्राप्तं कस्मान्न प्रतिभाषसे ।।

29. Oh most illustrious (Dhascharatha)! Why are you not replying to (Sumanthra) who has come here bringing news of this (Raama) who does arduous tasks and (brings news about Raama about) his life in forest.

❍ ❍ ❍

३०. अद्येममनयं कृत्वा व्यपत्रपसि राघव ।
उत्तिष्ठ सुकृतं तेऽस्तु शोके न स्यात्सहायता ।।

30. Oh Raaghava (my husband)! It is shameful to turn (your face) considering this now as misfortune; Arise: May this be benevolent to you. Help rarely comes by grief!

❍ ❍ ❍

३१. देव यस्या भयाद्रामं नानुपृच्छसि सारथिम् ।
नेह तिष्ठति कैकेयी विस्रब्धं प्रतिभाष्यताम् ।।

31. Oh Lord (Dhascharatha)! Fearing whom you have not (dared to) ask charioteer (Sumanthra) about Raama, that (woman) Kaikeyi is not here. You may (therefore) talk to him in confidence.

❍ ❍ ❍

३२. सा तथोक्त्वा महाराजं कौसल्या शोकलालसा ।
धरण्यां निपपाताशु बाष्पविप्लुतभाषिणी ॥

32. Surrendering totally to grief, her speech blurred by tears flowing, this Kowsalya fell down on earth suddenly after saying thus to the emperor.

❍ ❍ ❍

३३. एवं विलपतीं दृष्ट्वा कौसल्यां पतितां भुवि ।
पतिं चावेक्ष्य ताः सर्वाः सुस्वरं रुरुदुः स्त्रियः ॥

33. All the ladies seeing that Kowsalya had fallen down on earth wailing and also looking over their husband, cried aloud harmoniously (together).

❍ ❍ ❍

३४. ततस्तमन्तःपुरनादमुत्थितं
समीक्ष्य वृद्धास्तरुणाश्च मानवाः ।
स्त्रियश्च सर्वा रुरुदुः समन्ततः
पुरं तदाऽऽसीत्पुनरेव विह्वलम् ॥

34. Noticing (and affected by) the wailings emanating from the inner apartments of the palace, all others, old and young, ladies (all) cried: At that moment, the city 'trembled' even more, totally.

❍ ❍ ❍

Chapter 58

(Sumanthra) Conveys Raama's Message (to Dhascharatha)

१. प्रत्याश्वस्तो यदा राजा मोहात्प्रत्यागतः पुनः ।
अथाजुहाव तं सूतं रामवृत्तान्तकारणात् ॥

1. Consoled, the king, on recovering from his unconsciousness, called the charioteer (Sumanthra), to have the tidings about Raama.

❍ ❍ ❍

२. अथ सूतो महाराजं कृताञ्जलिरुपस्थितः ।
रामेवानुशोचन्तं दुःखशोकसमन्वितम् ॥

३. वृद्धं परमसंतप्तं नवग्रहमिव द्विपम् ।
विनिश्वसन्तं ध्यायन्तमस्वस्थमिव कुञ्जरम् ॥

2 & 3.

With hands cupped in Anjali, the charioteer stood before the great king who was afflicted by grief and sorrow, grieving over Raama, ever....This old (Dhascharatha) who was terribly tormented like an elephant just captured, and like a sick elephant, was breathing hard and deep.

❍ ❍ ❍

४. राजा तु रजसा धूतं ध्वस्ताङ्गं समुपस्थितम् ।
अश्रुपूर्णमुखं दीनमुवाच परमार्तवत् ॥

4. The king who was emaciated, agitated, whose body was besmeared with dust, whose face was full with tears, then said to (Sumanthra) who was standing before him, in great anguish.

❍ ❍ ❍

५. क्व नु वत्स्यति धर्मात्मा वृक्षमूलमुपाश्रितः ।
सोऽत्यन्तसुखितः सूत किमशिष्यति राघवः ॥

5. Oh Charioteer! Where does the noble soul man of Dharma (my son Raama) live, having reached the foot of the tree? What does this (my son) Raaghava eat who has ever been in comfort?

❍ ❍ ❍

६. दुःखस्यानुचितो दुःखं सुमन्त्र शयनोचितः ।
भूमिपालात्मजो भूमौ शेते कथमनाथवत् ॥

6. Oh Sumanthra! How can this son of a great ruler of earth lie on earth like a helpless man in discomfort,

when he does not deserve to be in discomfort and when he deserves only good beds.

❍ ❍ ❍

७. यं यान्तमनुयान्ति स्म पदातिरथकुञ्जराः ।
स वत्स्यति कथं रामो विजनं वनमाश्रितः ।।

7. How can this Raama, whom, whenever he stepped out, footmen, chariots, elephants used to follow, now live, staying in the uninhabited forest?

❍ ❍ ❍

८. व्यालैर्मृगैराचरितं कृष्णसर्पनिषेवितम् ।
कथं कुमारौ वैदेह्या सार्धं वनमुपस्थितौ ।।

8. How did the two young (sons of mine) along with (Seetha) the Vaidhehi, reach the forest which is roamed about by wicked animals and infested with dark venomous snakes?

❍ ❍ ❍

९. सुकुमार्या तपस्विन्या सुमन्त्र सह सीतया ।
राजपुत्रौ कथं पादैरवरुह्य रथाद्गतौ ।।

9. Oh Charioteer! How did (my) two royal princes along with the young girl Seetha who must (surely) be miserable, walk along on foot having got down from the chariot?

❍ ❍ ❍

१०. सिद्धार्थः खलु सूत त्वं येन दृष्टौ ममात्मजौ ।
वनान्तं प्रविशन्तौ तावश्विनाविव मन्दरम् ।।

10. Oh Charioteer! The two sons of mine who are like Ashwini-s, were seen by you entering the dense (forest): For this (and because of this), you are indeed accomplished (and most fortunate).

❍ ❍ ❍

११. किमुवाच वचो रामः किमुवाच च लक्ष्मणः ।
सुमन्त्र वनमासाद्य किमुवाच च मैथिली ॥

11. Oh Sumanthra! When he reached forest, what words did Raama say (as message to me)? What did Lakshmana say? And what did (Seetha) the Maithili also say?

❍ ❍ ❍

१२. आसितं शयितं भुक्तं सूत रामस्य कीर्तय ॥

12. Oh charioteer! Enlighten me about Raama's abode, his resting place, his food etc.!

❍ ❍ ❍

१३. जीविष्याम्यहमेतेन ययातिरिव साधुषु ॥

13. Like (king) Yayaathi before holy men, I will live along, by (hearing) this (Readers may note Yayaathi was a great king of yore).

❍ ❍ ❍

१४. इति सूतो नरेन्द्रेण चोदितः सज्जमानया ।
उवाच वाचा राजानं स बाष्पपरिरब्धया ॥

14. Commanded thus by the lord of men (king Dhascharatha), this charioteer (Sumanthra), preparing himself (to convey everything about Raama at forest), said to the king, with words choked by tears.

❍ ❍ ❍

१५. अब्रवीन्मां महाराज धर्ममेवानुपालयन् ।
अञ्जलिं राघवः कृत्वा शिरसाऽभिप्रणम्य च ॥

15. Oh great King! (Raama) the Raaghava, being steadfast in Dharma only, addressed me with his hands cupped in Anjalii, bowing with his head down.

❍ ❍ ❍

१६. सूत मद्वचनात्तस्य देवस्य विदितात्मनः ।
शिरसा वन्दनीयस्य वन्द्यौ पादौ पुनः पुनः ॥

16. (Oh king Dhascharatha, this is what Raama told me to convey.)
Oh charioteer! As my message (please convey this to my father): The feet of this renowned and most honoured Lord (my father), must be repeatedly bowed to by me with my head.

❍ ❍ ❍

१७. सर्वमन्तःपुरं वाच्यं सूत मद्वचनात्त्वया ।
आरोग्यमविशेषेण यथार्हमभिवादनम् ।।

17. Oh Charioteer: As my message, the ladies of the inner apartments (of royal palace), all of them, without discrimination, must be told by you about my respects, befitting them, and about my (concern) for their well being and health.

❍ ❍ ❍

१८. माता च मम कौसल्या कुशलं चाभिवादनम् ।
अप्रमादं च वक्तव्या ब्रुयाश्चैनामिदं वचः ।।

18. And my mother Kowsalya must be told about my welfare and my respects (to her). These words (of mine) must particularly be spoken to her carefully (by you).

❍ ❍ ❍

१९. धर्मनित्या यथाकालमग्न्यगारपरा भव ।
देवि देवस्य पादौ च देववत्परिपालय ।।

19. (Tell my mother, this, Oh Sumanthra): Oh Lady (Kowsalya)! You must ever be (steadfast) in Dharma: At proper times, take care of (holy Fire in) fire ritual place: Foster and nourish the feet of (my) father (as though he is) God.

❍ ❍ ❍

२०. अभिमानं च मानं च त्यक्त्वा वर्तस्व मातृषु ।
अनु राजानमार्यां च कैकेयीमम्ब कारय ।।

20. Oh mother (Kowsalya)! You should live, abandoning excessive pride and haughtiness before (my step) mothers: You should make the noble Kaikeyi follow the King (make her obedient to my father).

❍ ❍ ❍

२१. कुमारे भरते वृत्तिर्वर्तितव्या च राजवत् ।
अर्थज्येष्ठा हि राजानो राजधर्ममनुस्मर ॥

21. (And tell my mother): Her behaviour towards young Bharatha should be like towards a King. Because kings are foremost in (many) matters. Remember this Royal Dharma.

(Do not treat Bharatha as a child, he is now our YuvaRaaja)

❍ ❍ ❍

२२. भरतः कुशलं वाच्यो वाच्यो मद्वचनेन च ।
सर्वास्वेव यथान्यायं वृत्तिं वर्तस्व मातृषु ॥

22. And Bharatha (my brother and Yuvaraaja), must be told about (my concern for his) welfare; He must be told as my words (of advice): In his behaviour, he should conduct himself properly before all his mothers (his mother and step mothers).

❍ ❍ ❍

२३. वक्तव्यश्च महाबाहुरिक्ष्वाकुकुलनन्दनः ।
पितरं यौवराज्यस्थो राज्यस्थमनुपालय ॥

23. And he must be told that he, this mighty limbed darling of Ikshwaaku race, should cherish his father living in the kingdom, (even though) he is appointed as crown prince.

❍ ❍ ❍

२४. अतिक्रान्तवया राजा मा स्मैनं त्वमुपारुधः ।
कुमारराज्ये जीव त्व तस्यैवाज्ञा प्रवर्तताम् ॥

24. The king (our father), has gone through long years (is old); Do not 'molest' him. You be the crown prince: (but) let his will prevail. (Always consult father advises Raama to Bharatha).

❍ ❍ ❍

२५. अब्रवीच्चापि मां भूयो भृशमश्रूणि वर्तयन् ।
मातेव मम माता ते द्रष्टव्या पुत्रगर्धिनी ॥

25. (Such was the message of Raama to Bharatha that was conveyed through me, says Sumanthra) Shedding tears greatly, (Raama) told me further: My mother (Kowsalya) who is extremely fond of her son, should be 'seen' (and treated) like your own mother (Kaikeyi).

❍ ❍ ❍

२६. इत्येवं मां महाराज ब्रुवन्नेव महायशाः ।
रामो राजीवताम्राक्षो भृशमश्रूण्यवर्तयत् ॥

26. Oh great king! Thus did the most famous lotus eyed Raama tell me: And he shed tears greatly.

❍ ❍ ❍

२७. लक्ष्मणस्तु सुसंक्रुद्धो निश्वसन्वाक्यमब्रवीत् ।
केनायमपराधेन राजपुत्रो विवासितः ॥

27. (Now Sumanthra conveys to Dhascharatha, Lakshmana's words, the words of anger.)

And Lakshmana also told me these words, in anger, sighing (and breathing hard and deep): This (Raama) the son of the king, For what crime was he sent out (on exile)?

❍ ❍ ❍

२८. राज्ञा तु खलु कैकेय्या लघु त्वाश्रित्य शासनम् ।
कृतं कार्यमकार्यं वा वयं येनाभिपीडिताः ॥

28. Having taken a decision in a light (flippant) manner, the rule of the kingdom was offered to Kaikeyi (and her

son Bharatha) by the king. Whether this was proper or not proper, as a consequence, we are indeed in torment (and suffering this forest life now).

❍ ❍ ❍

२९. यदि प्रव्राजितो रामो लोभकारणकारितम् ।
वरदाननिमित्तं वा सर्वथा दुष्कृतं कृतम् ।।

29. In this matter of Raama being exiled, whether it was done because of a boon (to Kaikkeyi) or whether it was done out of passion and greed, (the fact remains) that this (act) is unjust in everyway.

❍ ❍ ❍

३०. इदं तावद्यथाकाममीश्वरस्य कृते कृतम् ।
रामस्य तु परित्यागे न हेतुमुपलक्षये ।।

30. I cannot perceive any reason in the conferment of exile upon this most capable Raama: This deed was done (by my father) at his will and pleasure and nothing else.

❍ ❍ ❍

३१. असमीक्ष्य समारब्धं विरुद्धं बुद्धिलाघवात् ।
जनयिष्यति संक्रोशं राघवस्य विवासनम् ।।

31. This exile of (Raama the) Raaghava undertaken (in haste) with levity of mind, without ascertaining (considering) the opposition (to it from every one), will lead to indignation (universal condemnation).

❍ ❍ ❍

३२. अहं तावन्महाराजे पितृत्वं नोपलक्षये ।
भ्राता भर्ता च बन्धुश्च पिता च मम राघवः ।।

32. Therefore I fail to perceive (any virtue of a) father in this great king. And (so, Raama) the Raaghava is father, master, brother, kinsman to me.

(Lakshmana practically renounces his father king Dhascharatha.)

❍ ❍ ❍

३३. सर्वलोकप्रियं त्यक्त्वा सर्वलोकहिते रतम् ।
सर्वलोकोऽनुरज्येत कथं त्वाऽनेन कर्मणा ॥

33. (And tell my father, Laakshmana says to Sumanthra): How will any one in the world be devoted to you, when, by this deed (of yours), you have abandoned (your son Raama) who is ever concerned with welfare of all in the world and who is beloved of all in the world.

❍ ❍ ❍

३४. सर्वप्रजाभिरामं हि रामं प्रव्राज्य धार्मिकम् ।
सर्वलोकं विरुद्ध्येमं कथं राजा भविष्यति ॥

34. How can you remain king when you have sent away (on exile) this man of Dharma, this Raama who delights every one in the world, having incurred the enmity of every one in the world.

❍ ❍ ❍

३५. जानकी तु महाराज निश्वसन्ती मनस्विनी ।
भूतोपहतचित्तेव विस्मिता विस्मृता स्थिता ॥

35. (And now Sumanthra talks about Seetha to king Dhascharatha.)
Oh great king! And this noble and wise (Seetha) the daughter of Janaka, stood there, perplexed, sighing deeply, forgetting herself, as though her senses were numbed, hit by (some) evil spirit.

❍ ❍ ❍

३६. अदृष्टपूर्वव्यसना राजपुत्री यशस्विनी ।
तेन दुःखेन रुदती नैव मां किञ्चिदब्रवीत् ॥

36. But this famous princess (Seetha) who had never seen suffering before, did not tell me anything (although) she was crying by all the suffering (caused to her husband Raama and Laakshmana).

❍ ❍ ❍

३७. उद्वीक्षमाणा भर्तारं मुखेन परिशुष्यता ।
मुमोच सहसा बाष्पं मां प्रयान्तमुदीक्ष्य सा ।।

37. Seeing me departing, she (wept) without restraint and shed tears, (even) as she was staring at her husband with a withered face.

❍ ❍ ❍

३८. तथैव रामोऽश्रुमुखःकृताञ्जलिः
स्थितोऽभवल्लक्ष्मणबाहुपालितः ।
तथैव सीता रुदती तपस्विनी
निरीक्षते राजरथं तथैव माम् ।।

38. Raama who is well served by Lakshmana, stood there itself with his hands cupped in Anjali, his face full with tears; And the suffering Seetha who was crying, kept on looking at me and the royal chariot.

❍ ❍ ❍

Chapter 59

Dhascharatha Wails

१. इति ब्रुवन्तं सन्देशं सुमन्त्रं मन्त्रिसत्तमम् ।
ब्रूह्यशेषं पुनरिति राजा वचनमब्रवीत् ।।

1. And king (Dhascharatha) told (the charioteer and) his foremost minister Sumanthra who had (brought and) was conveying the message, thus: = Tell me more:, without leaving out anything of the news (about Raama) =

❍ ❍ ❍

२. तस्य तद्वचनं श्रुत्वा सुमन्त्रो बाष्पविक्लबः ।
कथयामास भूयोऽपि रामसन्देशविस्तारम् ।।

2. Hearing his words, Sumanthra began to narrate once again the entire news about Raama, with tears choking him.

❍ ❍ ❍

३. जटाः कृत्वा महाराज चीरवल्कलधारिणौ ॥

3. Oh great king! (Your sons Raama and Lakshmana) sported braided hair locks and wore dresses of bark (like hermits).

❍ ❍ ❍

४. अग्रतो लक्ष्मणो यातः पालयन् रघुनन्दनम् ।
अनन्तरं च सीताऽथ राघवो रघुनन्दनम् ॥
तास्तथा गच्छतो दृष्ट्वा निवृत्तोऽस्म्यवशस्तदा ॥

4. Guarding (Raama the) darling of Raghu-s, Lakshmana went first: Then Seetha (followed): Then after, Raama the Raaghava, the darling of Raghu-s went. Seeing them going away like this, I then returned (back to Ayodhya in chariot) unwillingly. (under duress).

❍ ❍ ❍

५. मम त्वश्वा निवृत्तस्य न प्रावर्तन्त वर्त्मनि ।
उष्णमश्रु विमुञ्चन्तो रामे सम्प्रस्थिते वनम् ॥

5. When Raama went away to forest, the horses which were shedding hot tears, would not move on in my return path. (in my return journey to Ayodhya).

❍ ❍ ❍

६. उभाभ्यां राजपुत्राभ्यामथ कृत्वाऽहमञ्जलिम् ।
प्रस्थितो रथमास्थाय तद्दुःखमपि धारयन् ॥

6. Then, after (bowing) with my hands cupped in Anjali towards these two Royal princes, I mounted the chariot and started, bearing all this suffering (of separation from Raama).

❍ ❍ ❍

७. गुहेन सार्धं तत्रैव स्थितोऽस्मि दिवसान्बहून् ।
आशया यदि मां रामः पुनः शब्दापयेदिति ॥

7. Hoping that perhaps Raama might call out for me again, I stayed on there itself for a few days along with Guha.

❍ ❍ ❍

८. विषये ते महाराज रामव्यसनकर्शिताः ।
अपि वृक्षाः परिम्लानाः सपुष्पाङ्कुरकोरकाः ॥

8. Oh great king! Unable to bear the suffering over Raama, all the trees in your land have become withered, along with its flowers, buds, leaves and stalks.

❍ ❍ ❍

९. उपतप्तोदका नद्यः पल्वलानि सरांसि च ।
परिशुष्कपलाशानि वनान्युपवनानि च ॥

9. Rivers, pools, tanks etc are drying up; forest and gardens are found with leaves parched up.

❍ ❍ ❍

१०. न च सर्पन्ति सत्त्वानि व्याला न प्रचरन्ति च ।
रामशोकाभिभूतं तन्निष्कूजमभवद्वनम् ॥

10. No living being came out; even animals did not roam about; And the forest became still, seized by grief over Raama.

❍ ❍ ❍

११. लीनपुष्करपत्राश्च नरेन्द्र कलुषोदकाः ।
संतप्तपद्माः पद्मिन्यो लीनमीनविहङ्गमाः ॥

11. Oh Lord of men! The lotus ponds are muddy, with lotuses and leaves strewn around, submerged (in waters), withered, 'burnt' up, bereft of water birds, fishes.

❍ ❍ ❍

१२. जलजानि च पुष्पाणि माल्यानि स्थलजानि च ।
नाद्य भान्त्यल्पगन्धीनि फलानि च यथापुरम् ।।

12. The flowers of creepers on earth and water flowers are without any fragrance: Fruits are not (tasty) as before.

❍ ❍ ❍

१३. अत्रोद्यानानि शून्यानि प्रलीनविहगानि च ।
न चाभिरामानारामान् पश्यामि मनुजर्षभ ।।

13. Oh (Dhascharatha) The 'Bull' amongst men! The gardens are deserted; bereft of birds; Groves, I did not see (find) any beauty in them.

❍ ❍ ❍

१४. प्रविशन्तमयोध्यां मां न कश्चिदभिनन्दति ।
नरा राममपश्यन्तो निश्वसन्ति मुहुर्मुहुः ।।

14. No one rejoiced (nor greeted me) as I was entering Ayodhya. All citizens were panting for breath, again and again, not seeing Raama.

❍ ❍ ❍

१५. देव राजरथं दृष्ट्वा विना राममिहागतम् ।
दुःखादश्रुमुखः सर्वोराजमार्गगतो जनः ।।

15. Oh Lord (Dhascharatha)! Men standing on the royal boulevard, every one of them, seeing the royal chariot return without Raama, (shed tears) in grief and their faces were (full) with tears.

❍ ❍ ❍

१६. हर्म्यैर्विमानैः प्रासादैरवेक्ष्य रथमागतम् ।
हाहाकारकृता नार्योरामादर्शनकर्शिताः ।।

16. Seeing the chariot return, the ladies residing in palaces, mansions and multi storeyed buildings, (wailed) with cries of Ha-Ha, deeply pained in not seeing Raama.

१७. आयतैर्विमलैर्नेत्रैरश्रुवेगपरिप्लुतैः ।
अन्योन्यमभिवीक्षन्ते व्यक्तमार्ततराः स्त्रियः ॥

17. Deeply afflicted, their spotless eyes bathed in tears, the ladies stared at one another, with their eyes wide open.

❍ ❍ ❍

१८. नामित्राणां न मित्राणामुदासीनजनस्य च ।
अहमार्ततया किञ्चिद्विशेषसमुपलक्षये ॥

18. In the matter of the state (and degree of) their affliction, I perceive no distinction (difference) at all, either in the common man, or in a friend or even in a foe. (Every one misses Raama).

❍ ❍ ❍

१९. अप्रहृष्टमनुष्या च दीननागतुरङ्गमा ।
आर्तस्वरपरिम्लाना विनिश्वसितनिस्वना ॥

19. The horses and elephants have become feeble; Men are joy- less; Withering away with wailing sounds; Only sounds of sighing and of deep, hard breathing (are heard).

❍ ❍ ❍

२०. निरानन्दा महाराज रामप्रव्राजनातुरा ।
कौसल्या पुत्रहीनेव अयोध्या प्रतिभाति मे ॥

20. Oh great king! I see Ayodhya bereft of joy. Like Kowsalya (grieving) without her son, (all because) of grief due to Raama being sent away.

❍ ❍ ❍

२१. सूतस्य वचनं श्रुत्वा वाचा परमदीनया ।
बाष्पोपहतया राजा तं सूतमिदमब्रवीत् ॥

21. Hearing charioteer (Sumanthra's) words, the king addressed the charioteer with words choked by tears, deeply afflicted (by pain).

❍ ❍ ❍

२२. कैकेय्या विनियुक्तेन पापाभिजनभावया ।
मया न मन्त्रकुशलैर्वृद्धैः सह समर्थितम् ॥

22. (Dhascharatha bemoans to Sumanthra, his friend and minister) Bound as I was by Kaikeyi who has imbibed the evil qualities from her ancestors, (this decision of sending Raama on exile) was not even considered (nor discussed) with elders who are experts in (giving) counsel.

❍ ❍ ❍

२३. न सुहृद्भिर्न चामात्यैर्मन्त्रयित्वा न नैगमैः ।
मयाऽयमर्थः सम्मोहात्स्त्रीहेतोः सहसा कृतः ॥

23. This action was not even discussed with my friends by me; Nor even with my ministers; Nor even with my citizens; Out of passion to my wife, this was done in haste (without premeditation).

❍ ❍ ❍

२४. भवितव्यतया नूनमिदं वा व्यसनं महत् ।
कुलस्यास्य विनाशाय प्राप्तं सूत यदृच्छया ॥

24. Oh Charioteer! This great calamity has now befallen by fate and accident for the sake of destruction of my race.

❍ ❍ ❍

२५. सूत यद्यस्ति ते किञ्चिन्मयाऽपि सुकृतं कृतम् ।
त्वं प्रापयाशु मां रामं प्राणाः सन्त्वरयन्ति माम् ॥

25. Oh Charioteer! (If you consider and) if at all any little good has been done for you by me, then you should at once enjoin me with Raama at once. My breath (of life) hastens me.

❍ ❍ ❍

२६. यद्यद्यापि ममैवाज्ञा निवर्तयतु राघवम् ।
न शक्ष्याभि विना रामं मुहूर्तमपि जीवितुम् ॥

26. Even now, if my* command (can prevail) may (Raama) the Raaghava be brought back. I cannot be alive even for a muhoortha without Raama.

(*But that will be against his commitment/Dharma.)

❍ ❍ ❍

२७. अथवाऽपि महाबाहुर्गतो दूरं भविष्यति ।
मामेव रथमारोप्य शीघ्रं रामाय दर्शय ।।

27. Alternatively if the mighty limbed (Raama) has gone away far, then you put me on to a chariot at once and show me (take me to) Raama.

❍ ❍ ❍

२८. वृत्तदंष्ट्रो महेष्वासः क्वासौ लक्ष्मणपूर्वजः ।
यदि जीवामि साध्वेनं पश्येयं सीतया सह ।।

28. Where is this (my beloved Raama) who possesses strong teeth, who is a great archer (warrior), and who is elder brother of Lakshmana: If I am alive, I will surely see him along with Seetha (who has gone with him).

❍ ❍ ❍

२९. लोहिताक्षं महाबाहुमामुक्तमणिकुण्डलम् ।
रामं यदि न पश्यामि गमिष्यामि यमक्षयम् ।।

29. If I do not see Raama who has long hands, who is red eyed, and who sports ear drops made of gems, I will go to the abode of Yama (Death).

❍ ❍ ❍

३०. अतो नु किं दुःखतरं योऽहमिक्ष्वाकुनन्दनम् ।
इमामवस्थामापन्नो नेह पश्यामि राघवम् ।।

30. In this state, afflicted as I am, I am not seeing (Raama) the Raaghava, the darling of the Ikshwaaku-s. Can there be greater sorrow than this!

❍ ❍ ❍

३१. हा राम रामानुज हा हा वैदेहि तपस्विनि ।
न मां जानीत दुःखेन म्रियमाणमनाथवत् ।।

31. Ha Raama! Ha Lakshmana the brother of Raama! Ah the austere (Seetha) the Vaidhehi! You do not know that I am dying in grief, helpless.

❍ ❍ ❍

३२. स तेन राजा दुखेन भृशमर्पितचेतनः ।
अवगाढः सुदुष्पारं शोकसागरमब्रवीत् ।।

32. Submerged by the uncrossable "Ocean of Grief", his mind completely fixed (seized) by this sorrow, this King said further.

❍ ❍ ❍

३३. रामशोकमहावेगः सीताविरहपारगः ।
श्वसितोर्मिमहावर्तोबाष्पफेनजलाविलः ।।

33. (Poet Vaalmeeki goes poetic: Stanzas 33 to 36: The Ocean of Grief of Dhascharatha due to separation from Raama described.)

The grief (of separation) from Raama was turbulent (like waves);

The abandonment of Seetha like crossing over the shores of ocean

The deep sighing and breathing are the whirlpools and waves

The tears are the froth and foam of water waves

❍ ❍ ❍

३४. बाहुविक्षेपमीनौघो विक्रन्दितमहास्वनः ।
प्रकीर्णकिशशैवालः कैकेयीबडबानलः ।।

34. ...... The movements of hands are the multitude of fishes

The wailings are the sounds (of the roar of waves of ocean of grief)

The stretched (unkempt and untied) hair (of ladies), the moss ......

The mystical Fire is this Kaikeyi (the Badabha Fire).

❍ ❍ ❍

३५. ममाश्रुवेगप्रभवः कुब्जावाक्यमहाग्रहः ।
वरवेलो नृशंसाया रामप्रव्राजनायतः ।।

35. ...... The waves and waters caused by the flood of my tears ......

The evil words of hunchback, are the sharks (of the Ocean).

The boon of the cruel (Kaikeyi) is this side of the shore (of the uncrossable) ocean.

Raama's exile as vast (and long drawn) as the (deep ocean).

❍ ❍ ❍

३६. यस्मिन्बत निमग्नोऽहं कौसल्ये राघवं विना ।
दुस्तरो जीवता देवि मयाऽयं शोकसागरः ।।

36. Oh Kowsalya! Submerged as I am in such a ocean of grief, it is impossible for me to live on without this Raama, the Raaghava.

❍ ❍ ❍

३७. अशोभनं योऽहमिहाद्य राघवं
दिदृक्षमाणो न लभे सलक्ष्मणम् ।
इतीव राजा विलपन्महायशाः
पपात तूर्णं शयने स मूर्च्छितः ।।

37. Such as I am, am longing to see Raama along with Lakshmana now; (yet) this (sight is denied), not obtained (by me); Wailing thus, the famous king (Dhascharatha) became unconscious and suddenly fell off fom his couch losing (all) his grace (majesty).

❍ ❍ ❍

३८. इति विलपति पार्थिव प्रनष्टे
करुणतरं द्विगुणं च रामहेतोः ।
वचनमनुनिशम्य तस्य देवी
भयमगमत्पुनरेव राममाता ।।

38. When the king who was wailing pitiably over Raama thus and lost (control of himself), the lady (Kowsalya) the mother of Raama, who had listened to his words, became even more stricken with fear.

❍ ❍ ❍

Chapter 60

Sumanthra Consoles Kowsalya

१. ततो भूतोपसृष्टेव वेपमाना पुनः पुनः ।
धरण्यां गतसत्त्वेव कौसल्या सूतमब्रवीत् ।।

1. Looking as if she was possessed by some evil spirit, and as though life had gone out of her, Kowsalya lay on the floor, trembling, quivering even more; And she addressed charioteer (Sumanthra).

❍ ❍ ❍

२. नय मां यत्र काकुत्स्थः सीता यत्र च लक्ष्मणः ।
तान्विना क्षणमप्यत्र जीवितुं नोत्सहे ह्यहम् ।।

2. Take me to where Raama, and where Seetha and Lakshmana are: Without them I cannot bear to live even for a moment.

❍ ❍ ❍

३. नवर्तय रथं शीघ्रं दण्डकान्नय मामपि ।
अथ तान्नानुगच्छामि गमिष्यामि यमक्षयम् ।।

3. Turn back the chariot at once; Take me also to Dhandaka forest; I will follow them; Or else I will go to the abode of Yama (Death).

❍ ❍ ❍

४. बाष्पवेगोपहतया स वाचा सज्जमानया ।
इदमाश्वासयन्देवीं सूतः प्राञ्जलिरब्रवीत् ।।

4. Cupping his hands in Anjali, this charioteer (Sumanthra) facing the lady (Kowsalya), addressed her with words choked by flow of tears, (trying) to console her.

❍ ❍ ❍

५. त्यज शोकं च मोहं च संभ्रमं दुःखजं तथा ।
व्यवधूय च संतापं वने वत्स्यति राघवः ।।

5. Give up this grief and passion and bewilderment caused by your sorrow: (Because Raama the) Raaghava, is living in forest, having discarded torment (totally).

(Raama is quite happy in the forest, so dont grieve, says Sumanthra.)

❍ ❍ ❍

६. लक्ष्मणश्चापि रामस्य पादौ परिचरन्वने ।
आराधयति धर्मज्ञः परलोकं जितेन्द्रियः ।।

6. And the knower of Dharma, this Lakshmana who has conquered his passion and senses is serving Raama's feet in the forest, (thereby) (seeking) merit in the other world (of heaven).

❍ ❍ ❍

७. वजनेऽपि वने सीता वासं प्राप्य गृहेष्विव ।
विस्रम्भं लभतेऽभीता रामे सन्यस्तमानसा ।।

7. And Seetha, although (living) in the uninhabited forest, has resigned herself (totally in service) to Raama and has obtained life there without any fear, as though (she

is living) in her own palace and (further) has obtained (great) confidence.(and is relaxed).

❍ ❍ ❍

८. नास्या दैन्यं कृतं किञ्चित्सुसूक्ष्ममपि लक्षये ।
उचितेव प्रवासानां वैदेही प्रतिभाति मे ॥

8. I did not see even a little of depression overcoming her, although (I observed her) closely: (Indeed) it appears to me that (Seetha) the Vaidhehi is used to forest life!

❍ ❍ ❍

९. नगरोपवनं गत्वा यथा स्म रमते पुरा ।
तथैव रमते सीता निर्जनेषु वनेष्वपि ॥

9. In the uninhabited forest also, Seetha enjoys (life) as much as she used to enjoy going to gardens of the city before.

❍ ❍ ❍

१०. बालेव रमते सीताऽबालचन्द्रनिभानना ।
रामा रामे ह्यधीनात्मा विजनेऽपि वने सती ॥

10. Lovely Seetha whose face is like full moon, is living in the uninhabited forest happily like child resting herself (with her body and soul) with Raama.

❍ ❍ ❍

११. तद्गतं हृदयं ह्यस्यास्तदधीनं च जीवितम् ।
अयोध्याऽपि भवेदस्या रामहीना तथा वनम् ॥

11. Her heart belongs to him; Her life rests on him; without Raama, even Ayodhya will become forest for her.

❍ ❍ ❍

१२. पथि पृच्छति वैदेही ग्रामांश्च नगराणि च ।
गतिं दृष्ट्वा नदीनां च पादपान्विविधानपि ॥

12. Enroute, this (Seetha the) Vaidhehi, seeing villages,

towns and the course of rivers, various trees, asks (Raama about their history).

❍ ❍ ❍

१३. रामं वा लक्ष्मणं वाऽपि पृष्ट्वा जानाति जानकी ।
अयोध्याक्रोशमात्रे तु विहारमिव संश्रिता ।।

13. And (Seetha) the Jaanaki asks and learns, either from Raama or from Lakshmana as though she is staying in a nursery which is just one Kroscha (distance) from Ayodhya.

❍ ❍ ❍

१४. इदमेव स्मराम्यस्याः सहसैवोपजल्पितम् ।
कैकेयीसंश्रितं वाक्यं नेदानीं प्रतिभाति मे ।।

14. (Suddenly Sumanthra remembers something about Kaikeyi, but checks himself, because any mention of Kaikeyi will make Kowsalya flare up in wrath).

A talk about Kaikeyi has just entered (my mind): I am remembering these words (about Kaikeyi now): (Yet) these words should not be told now (made known, particularly to Kowsalya) ......

❍ ❍ ❍

१५. ध्वंसयित्वा तु तद्वाक्यं प्रमादात्पर्युपस्थितम् ।
ह्लादनं वचनं सूतो देव्या मधुरमब्रवीत् ।।

15. Destroying (that is, hiding this thought that crossed his mind about Kaikeyi), the charioteer said these words that were sweet and which would bring (only) joy to this lady (Kowsalya).

❍ ❍ ❍

१६. अध्वना वातवेगेन संभ्रमेणातपेन च ।
न हि गच्छति वैदेह्याश्चन्द्रांशुसदृशी प्रभा ।।

16. (Seetha) the Vaidhehi's moon like brilliance did not vanish either due to heat or by the long walks, or by the fierce winds, or by (any) agitation.

❍ ❍ ❍

१७. सदृशं शतपत्रस्य पूर्णचन्द्रोपमप्रभम् ।
वदनं तद्वदान्याया वैदेह्या न प्रकम्पते ॥

17. There was no tremor (or change) in the face of this sweet tongued (Seetha) the Vaidhehi which is comparable to lotus flowers, which is like full moon in luminescence.

❍ ❍ ❍

१८. अलक्तरससरक्ताभावलक्तरसवर्जितौ ।
अद्यापि चरणौ तस्याः पद्मकोशसमप्रभौ ॥

18. Her two feet, although not touched up (besmeared with) red cosmetics of Alaktha resin, is even now red like the red cosmetic and shines like the petals of lotus.

❍ ❍ ❍

१९. नूपुरोद्घुष्टहेलेव खेलं गच्छति भामिनी ।
इदानीमपि वैदेही तद्रागान्न्यस्तभूषणा ॥

19. The charming (Seetha) the Vaidhehi goes along playfully even now, (although) without her ornaments, without sounds from the (tinkling) Noopura (foot) ornaments, delighting with him.

❍ ❍ ❍

२०. गजं वा वीक्ष्य सिंहं वा व्याघ्रं वा वनमाश्रिता ।
नाहारयति संत्रासं बाहू रामस्य संश्रिता ॥

20. She who is in forest, does not get scared by an elephant or a lion or seeing a tiger, as she has taken refuge under (the strong) arms of Raama.

❍ ❍ ❍

२१. करसम्मितमध्याङ्गी पीनोन्नतपयोधरा ।
राजहंसीव रामस्य पादमालोक्य गच्छति ।।

21. She who is like a royal swan, whose waist is (small and) as much as (the size of) palm of both hands (cupped), whose breast is firm and round, goes along looking at (and following) Raama's feet.

❍ ❍ ❍

२२. न शोच्यास्ते न चात्मानः शोच्यो नापि जनाधिपः ।
इदं हि चरितं लोके प्रतिष्ठास्यति शाश्वतम् ।।

22. (Therefore) They, (these three) are not to be grieved over by us. Nor are we (to be grieved over by them); Nor should the king (grieve or grieved over) Because, in this world this event is going to stand eternally (for mankind**).

(** Reference is to the future: Raama's 14 years life in exile is going to be of great service for the world: Raama is going to destroy the evil in various territories and finally kill Raavana as well. Sumanthra being a great seer, sees Raama's exile as a divine dispensation)

❍ ❍ ❍

२३. विधूय शोकं परिहृष्टमानसा
महर्षियाते पथि सुव्यवस्थिताः ।
वने रता वन्यफलाशनाः पितुः
शुभां प्रतिज्ञां परिपालयन्ति ते ।।

23. Discarding grief, their mind very joyous, steadfast in the path followed by great sages, enjoying (life in) forest, eating forest products of fruits, they are (thus) fulfilling a father's command gloriously.

❍ ❍ ❍

२४. तथाऽपि सूतेन सुयुक्तवादिना
निवार्यमाणा सुतशोककर्शिता ।
न चैव देवी विरराम कूजितात्
प्रियेति पुत्रेति च राघवेति च ।।

24. Although lady (Kowsalya) was restrained (consoled) thus by the charioteer who spoke appropriately, she, afflicted by grief over (separation of) son (Raama), did not stop from bemoaning (and crying): Oh My Beloved! Oh My Son, Oh My (Raama) Raaghava!

❍ ❍ ❍

Chapter 61

(Kowsalya) Rebukes Dhascharatha

१. वनं गते धर्मपरे रामे रमयतां वरे ।
कौसल्या रुदती स्वार्ता भर्तारमिदमब्रवीत् ।।

1. On hearing that Raama who was steadfast in Dharma and who was foremost in delighting (every one) had reached the forest, Kowsalya who was in distress, addressed her husband thus, crying.

❍ ❍ ❍

२. यद्यपि त्रिषु लोकेषु प्रथितं ते महद्यशः ।
सानुक्रोशो वदान्यश्च प्रियवादी च राघवः ।।

2. When you are a Raaghava, munificent, most compassionate and when your fame is well spread in all the three worlds, when you are one who speaks sweetly......

❍ ❍ ❍

३. कथं नरवरश्रेष्ठ पुत्रौ तौ सह सीतया ।
दुःखितौ सुखसंवृद्धौ वने दुःखं सहिष्यतः ।।

3. ...... (When you are such) Oh foremost of men, why should your two sons who (are used to and) have been raised in comfort, bear the suffering in forest along with Seetha, stricken with sorrow ?

❍ ❍ ❍

४. सा नूनं तरुणी श्यामा सुकुमारी सुखोचिता ।
कथमुष्णं च शीतं च मैथिली विसहिष्यति ॥

4. Why should the young girl (Seetha the) Maithili, who is delicate, who is used to (and deserves) comforts, suffer now the heat and cold, (making her face) dark ......

❍ ❍ ❍

५. भुक्त्वाऽशनं विशालाक्षी सूपदंशान्वितं शुभम् ।
वन्यं नैवारमाहारं कथं सीतोपभोक्ष्यते ॥

5. Why should this wide eyed Seetha (who is used to) and has consumed good foods with soups and (fried foods and eats) that are 'Bitten', now eat (only) forest grown things as her food.

(Sanskrit word for Soups and the like, is Soopa!)

❍ ❍ ❍

६. गीतवादित्रनिर्घोषं श्रुत्वा शुभमनिन्दिता ।
कथं क्रव्यादसिंहानां शब्दं श्रोष्यत्यशोभनम् ॥

6. Why should this blameless (Seetha) who has heard (till now) only pleasant music and strains from instruments, hear (from now on) unpleasant roars of lions which eat raw meat.

❍ ❍ ❍

७. महेन्द्रध्वजसङ्काशः क्व नु शेते महाभुजः ।
भुजं परिघसङ्काशमुपधाय महाबलः ॥

7. Where does this mightily strong, mighty limbed (Raama) who is comparable to Lord Indhra, sleep,

placing (and resting his head) upon his arm that is like a steel mace.

❍ ❍ ❍

८. पद्मवर्णं सुकेशान्तं पद्मनिश्वासमुत्तमम् ।
कदा द्रक्ष्यामि रामस्य वदनं पुष्करेक्षणम् ।।

8. When am I going to see the foremost countenance of this Raama, which is the colour of lotus, which is beautified by lovely locks of hair, and whose breath is sweet like (the fragrance of) lotus, which sports eyes that are like lotus.

❍ ❍ ❍

९. वज्रसारमिदं नूनं हृदयं मे न संशयः ।
अपश्यन्त्या न तं यद्वै फलतीदं सहस्रधा ।।

9. There is no doubt, because this, my heart, has not split up into thousand parts (in spite of) not seeing him, it is verily like a Vajra (thunderbolt).
(I am made of stone without heart and feelings, bemoans Kowsalya.)

❍ ❍ ❍

१०. यत्त्वया दारुणं कर्म व्यपोह्य मम बान्धवाः ।
निरस्ताः परिधावन्ति सुखार्हाः कृपणा वने ।।

10. My close folks (Raama, Seetha and Lakshmana) have been banished, driven away (to forest): Used to comforts, they are wandering in the forest in misery. This deed is most cruel (done by you).

❍ ❍ ❍

११. यदि पञ्चदशे वर्षेराघवः पुनरेष्यति ।
जह्याद्राज्यं च कोशं च भरतेनोपभोक्ष्यते ।।

11. Even if Raama returns on the 15th. year, he will not care for the kingdom nor its wealth: These will be enjoyed by Bharatha only.

❍ ❍ ❍

१२. भोजयन्ति किल श्राद्धे केचित्स्वानेव बान्धवान् ।
ततः पश्चात्समीक्षन्ते कृतकार्या द्विजर्षभान् ।।

12. During Shraadha ceremonies, some feed only their own folks; After accomplishing this (satisfying their own folks), later they (pretend and) look at the foremost Braamins (whether they have enjoyed food).

❍ ❍ ❍

१३. तत्र ये गुणवन्तश्च विद्वांसश्च द्विजातयः ।
न पश्चात्तेऽभिमन्यन्ते सुधामपि सुरोपमाः ।।

13. Therefore the Braamins who are men of character, who are learned and who are comparable to celestials, do not even care to (drink) water (from them !)

(Readers may note that every Indian performs Shraadha ceremony for their forefathers with offerings of foods, gifts etc.)

❍ ❍ ❍

१४. ब्राह्मणेष्वपि तृप्तेषु पश्चाद्भोक्तुं द्विजर्षभाः ।
नाभ्युपैतुमलं प्राज्ञाः शृङ्गच्छेदमिवर्षभाः ।।

14. Even when braamins are satisfied, the foremost and wise Braamins will not approach them (for gifts) and will be like Bulls rejecting to eat the (remains of) grass whose top has been grazed upon (by other cows earlier).

❍ ❍ ❍

१५. एवं कनीयसा भ्रात्रा भुक्तं राज्यं विशां पते ।
भ्राता ज्येष्ठो वरिष्ठश्च किमर्थं नावमंस्यते ।।

15. Oh Lord of earth (my husband Dhascharatha)! By what reason will this foremost (Raama) the elder brother (of Bharatha) not treat this kingdom with anything but contempt when (this kingdom) has been "Enjoyed" by his younger brother (Bharatha before), thus

❍ ❍ ❍

१६. न परेणाहृतं भक्ष्यं व्याघ्रः खादितुमिच्छति ।
एवमेव नरव्याघ्रः परलीढं न मंस्यते ॥

16. Even a tiger will not desire to take a bite on the (meat) eaten by some other (animal): Likewise, this (Raama) the 'Tiger' of men, will not care for (the kingdom) tasted by another!

❍ ❍ ❍

१७. हविराज्यं पुरोडाशः कुशा यूपाश्च खादिराः ।
नैतानि यातयामानि कुर्वन्ति पुनरध्वरे ॥

17. (It is well known) that fire, ghee, rice cakes, Dharbha grass, twigs, wooden masts, pillars, all these, once used (during holy Fire Rituals) ... they will not use them again in sacrificial ceremonies.
(Only fresh materials are used in ritual ceremonies)

❍ ❍ ❍

१८. तथा ह्यात्तमिदं राज्यं हृतसारां सुरामिव ।
नाभिमन्तुमलं रामो नष्टसोममिवाध्वरम् ॥

18. Raama will not care for this kingdom enjoyed (by another); It will be like (drinking) wine after 'essence' (of it) has been taken away (and only sediments remain). It will be like the remnants of a sacrificial ceremony.
(It is obvious that those days wines were not clarified so well!)

❍ ❍ ❍

१९. नैवंविधमसत्कारं राघवो मर्षयिष्यति ।
बलवानिव शार्दूलो वालधेरभिमर्शनम् ॥

19. (Raama) the Raaghava will not tolerate such an injury; like a strong lion (which will not tolerate) when its tail is touched.

❍ ❍ ❍

२०. नैतस्य सहिता लोका भयं कुर्युर्महामृधे ।
अधर्मं त्विह धर्मात्मा लोकं धर्मेण योजयेत् ॥

20. Even if the whole world gets together (to attack him) in a great war, it will not cause any fear in him. Being a noble soul man of Dharma, he will harness (and restrain) the A-Dharma world with his Dharma. (Evil will ever be destroyed by Raama, says his mother).

❍ ❍ ❍

२१. नन्वसौ काञ्चनैर्बाणैर्महावीर्योमहाभुजः ।
युगान्त इव भूतानि सागरानपि निर्दहेत् ॥

21. Indeed, this mightily brave, mighty limbed (Raama) can 'Burn' up with his golden arrows, even oceans and living beings (like) at Pralaya. (at the end of the Universe).

❍ ❍ ❍

२२. स तादृशः सिंहबलो वृषभाक्षो नरर्षभः ।
स्वयमेव हतः पित्रा जलजेनात्मजो यथा ॥

22. Such a man, such a noble (Raama) the 'bull ' mongst men who has the strength of a lion, whose eyes are like those of bulls, has destroyed himself, (thanks to) his father, like a fish swallowing its own young (small fish).

❍ ❍ ❍

२३. द्विजातिचरितो धर्मः शास्त्रदृष्टः सनातनः ।
यदि ते धर्मनिरते त्वया पुत्रे विवासिते ॥

23. As your son who is totally devoted to Dharma is sent away by you, do you possess (at all anything of) the eternal Dharma as seen in our Shaasthra-s which is practised by Kshathriya-s?

❍ ❍ ❍

२४. गतिरेका पतिर्नार्या द्वितीया गतिरात्मजः ।
तृतीया ज्ञातयो राजंश्चतुर्थी नेह विद्यते ॥

24. Oh King! For a woman, a husband is her first Refuge: The son is her second Refuge. Her relatives are the third. In this (world) here, there is no fourth (for a woman).

❍ ❍ ❍

२५. तत्र त्वं चैव मे नास्ति रामश्च वनमाश्रितः ।
न वनं गन्तुमिच्छामि सर्वथा हि हता त्वया ॥

25. Raama has gone to forest: I did not desire him to go to forest; As such you are also nothing to me. I am ruined in every way by you.

❍ ❍ ❍

२६. हतं त्वया राज्यमिदं सराष्ट्रं
हतस्तथाऽऽत्मा सह मन्त्रिभिश्च ।
हता सपुत्राऽस्मि हताश्च पौराः
सुतश्च भार्या च तव प्रहृष्टौ ॥

26. This land and kingdom is ruined by you; Along with ministers, you are also ruined. And I am ruined with my son (gone): Citizens are ruined. Your (other) wife (Kaikeyi) along with her son, (alone) will be happy.

❍ ❍ ❍

२७. इमां गिरं दारुणशब्दसंश्रितां
निशम्य राजाऽपि मुमोह दुःखितः ।
ततः स शोकं प्रविवेश पार्थिवः
स्वदुष्कृतं चापि पुनस्तदा स्मरन् ॥

27. Hearing (Kowsalya's) 'address' which contained such cruel words, King (Dhascharatha) became very sad and became unconscious. And this king, thinking (again and) again about his own wrong action, entered (into a state of total) grief.

❍ ❍ ❍

Chapter 62

Dhascharatha Consoles Kowsalya

१. एवं तु क्रुद्धया राजा राममात्रा सशोकया ।
श्रावितः परुषं वाक्यं चिन्तयामास दुःखितः ।।

1. When the king was spoken to with such cruel words thus by the mother of Raama (Kowsalya) who was angry and who was in great sorrow, he began to ponder in distress.

❍ ❍ ❍

२. चिन्तयित्वा स च नृपो मुमोह व्याकुलेन्द्रियः ।
अतिदीर्घेण कालेन संज्ञामाप परन्तपः ।।

2. His mind (and senses) confused, this tormentor of enemies pondered and became stupefied: After a long time, he regained his consciousness, this king (Dhascharatha).

❍ ❍ ❍

३. स संज्ञामुपलभ्यैव दीर्घमुष्णं च निश्वसन् ।
कौसल्यां पार्श्वतो दृष्ट्वा पुनश्चिन्तामुपागमत् ।।

3. Breathing hard and deep with hot (breath), when he obtained consciousness, he looked at Kowsalya and once again went into (a state of deep) thinking.

❍ ❍ ❍

४. तस्य चिन्तयमानस्य प्रत्यभात्कर्म दुष्कृतम् ।
यदनेन कृतं पूर्वमज्ञानाच्छब्दवेधिना ।।

4. Engrossed in thought, stung by her words (as he was), an evil deed that was done by him long, long ago (when quite young), in ignorance, appeared before him in his mind.

(Dhascharatha recollects an incident, when he was very young.)

❍ ❍ ❍

५. अमनास्तेन शोकेन रामशोकेन च प्रभुः ।
द्वाभ्यामपि महाराजः शोकाभ्यामन्वतप्यत ।।

5. And the lord, this great king was lost in thought and was tormented by the two fold grief: By this grief over Raama and by this grief (caused by the recollection of his deed done long ago)

❍ ❍ ❍

६. दह्यमानस्तु शोकाभ्यां कौसल्यामाह भूपतिः ।
वेपमानोऽञ्जलिं कृत्वा प्रसादार्थमवाङ्मुखः ।।

6. The lord of earth (Dhascharatha) who was being 'burnt' up by these two (fold) griefs, addressed Kowsalya so as to console her, with his hands in Anjali, his face looking down.

❍ ❍ ❍

७. प्रसादये त्वां कौसल्ये रचितोऽयं मयाऽञ्जलिः ।
वत्सला चाऽनृशंसा च त्वं हि नित्यं परेष्वपि ।।

7. Oh Kowsalya! (I beg) You (to) be gracious: This Anjali (Salutations) is being made by me: (I know) You are always kind and gentle even to enemies.

❍ ❍ ❍

८. भर्ता तु खलु नारीणां गुणवान्निर्गुणोऽपि वा ।
धर्मं विमृशमानानां प्रत्यक्षं देवि दैवतम् ।।

8. Oh Lady! For women who can deliberate (dispassionately) husband is indeed a living 'God' for them, whether he be a man of character or not a man of character.

❍ ❍ ❍

९. सा त्वं धर्मपरा नित्यं दृष्टलोकपरावरा ।
नार्हसे विप्रियं वक्तुं दुःखिताऽपि सुदुःखितम् ।।

9. Such as you are who are ever devoted to Dharma, who knows ** (good and bad in the world due to), Cause and Effect in the world, should never speak adversely to me who am in distress, (even making allowances for the fact that) you are also in distress.

(Poet Vaalmeeki uses the word **= Loka-Paraa- Vara =: This has highly philosophical content; The Cause-Effect equation- Fate.)

❍ ❍ ❍

१०. तद्वाक्यं करुणं राज्ञः श्रुत्वा दीनस्य भाषितम् ।
कौसल्या व्यसृजद्बाष्पं प्रणालीव नवोदकम् ॥

10. Hearing the pitiable words spoken by the depressed (feeble) King, Kowsalya shed tears like fresh waters of channel (waterfall).

❍ ❍ ❍

११. सा मूर्ध्नि बद्ध्वा रुदती राज्ञः पद्ममिवाञ्जलिम् ।
संभ्रमादब्रवीत्त्रस्ता त्वरमाणाऽक्षरं वचः ॥

11. Trembling and crying, making haste, being bewildered (by the pitiable sight of her husband), she replied with (proper) austere words, placing the cupped (Anjali) hands of the king on her head as though they were (a pair of) lotus flowers.

❍ ❍ ❍

१२. प्रसीद शिरसा याचे भूमौ निपतिताऽस्मि ते ।
याचिताऽस्मि हता देव हन्तव्याऽहं न हि त्वया ॥

12. (Kowsalya begs her husband for his forgiveness; If Raama is her son, he is also her husband's son!)

Oh Lord! Have mercy. I beg you, prostrating myself upon the floor with my head. I stand condemned (in as much as) I am beng begged by you. (But) I am not (I wish not) to be condemned.*

(Vaalmeeki uses word* =Han= Hath=; The extreme

meaning of this word is = To kill: Dont 'kill' me by bowing to me!)

❍ ❍ ❍

१३. नैषा हि सा स्त्री भवति श्लाघनीयेन धीमता ।
उभयोर्लोकयोर्वीर पत्या या संप्रसाद्यते ॥

13. Oh brave (husband)! Because, if one is favoured (with an apology) from a wise praiseworthy husband, then that lady will have no place in both the worlds (of heaven and earth).

(A Indian woman never demands an apology from her husband!)

❍ ❍ ❍

१४. जानामि धर्मं धर्मज्ञ त्वां जाने सत्यवादिनम् ।
पुत्रशोकार्तया तत्तु मया किमपि भाषितम् ॥

14. Oh (my husband who is) knower of Dharma! I know Dharma. I know you are a man of Truth (a speaker of truth only). But somehow as I was stricken with pangs of separation from my son, (all) this was spoken by me (like this).

❍ ❍ ❍

१५. शोको नाशयते धैर्यं शोको नाशयते श्रुतम् ।
शोको नाशयते सर्वं नास्ति शोकसमो रिपुः ॥

15. Grief Destroys Courage: Grief Destroys Understanding: Grief Destroys Every thing. There is No Enemy Greater than Grief.

❍ ❍ ❍

१६. शक्य आपतितः सोढुं प्रहारो रिपुहस्ततः ।
सोढुमापतितः शोकः सुसूक्ष्मोऽपि न शक्यते ॥

16. The blows falling from the hands of the enemy is possible to be borne; But (blows struck) by grief, cannot be borne even if trivial.

१७. वनवासाय रामस्य पञ्चरात्रोऽत्र गण्यते ।
यः शोकहतहर्षायाः पञ्चवर्षोपमो मम ।।

17. It is reckoned that five nights have gone by in Raama's forest life. (But) To me who is bereft of joy due to grief (of separation from him), it is like five years.

❍ ❍ ❍

१८. तं हि चिन्तयमानायाः शोकोऽयं हृदि वर्धते ।
नदीनामिव वेगेन समुद्रसलिलं महत् ।।

18. Like ocean 'Swelling' by the inflow of flood of rivers (at estuary), this grief in my heart is increasing thinking about Raama.

❍ ❍ ❍

१९. एवं हि कथयन्त्यास्तु कौसल्यायाः शुभं वचः ।
मन्दरश्मिरभूत्सूर्योरजनी चाभ्यवर्तत ।।

19. While Kowsalya was telling like this with such (auspicious) pleasant words, the Sun (set) with his rays getting dull. Night fell.

❍ ❍ ❍

२०. अथ प्रह्लादितो वाक्यैर्देव्या कौसल्यया नृपः ।
शोकेन च समाक्रान्तो निद्राया वशमेयिवान् ।।

20. The King (although) overwhelmed by grief, was (somewhat) pleased (consoled) by lady Kowsalya's words. (but) he got into a state of slumber

❍ ❍ ❍

Chapter 63

(Dhascharatha's Anecdote) His Killing of a Son of a Muni

(Grief stricken Dhascharatha remembers an event that happened long long ago; He recollects this- A curse upon him, which he narrates to Kowsalya. He realises that his death is imminent.)

❍ ❍ ❍

१. प्रतिबुद्धो मुहूर्तेन शोकोपहतचेतनः ।
अथ राजा दशरथः स चिन्तामभ्यपद्यत ॥

1. After a muhoortha, king Dhascharatha was awake and was engrossed in (deep) thought, his mind stricken with grief.

❍ ❍ ❍

२. रामलक्ष्मणयोश्चैव विवासाद्वासवोपमम् ।
आविवेशोपसर्गस्तं तमः सूर्यमिवासुरम् ॥

2. Like (demon) Star (Raahu) the Thamasa (the malefic), covering the Sun (during eclipse), the misfortune (and grief) caused by the exile of Raama and Lakshmana, gripped him who was comparable to Vaasava (lord Indhra).

❍ ❍ ❍

३. सभार्येहि गते रामे कौसल्यां कोसलेश्वरः ।
विवक्षुरसितापाङ्गां स्मृत्वा दुष्कृतमात्मनः ॥

3. Now that Raama had gone away, the lord of Kowsalya (king Dhascharatha) who was with his wife (Kowsalya) thought about the evil deed (that he had committed long ago when he was young) and he desired to speak about this to Kowsalya whose eye lashes were dark.

❍ ❍ ❍

४. स राजा रजनीं षष्ठीं रामे प्रव्राजिते वनम् ।
अर्धरात्रे दशरथः संस्मरन्दुष्कृतं कृतम् ॥

4. On this sixth night after Raama had gone away to forest, king Dhascharatha remembered this evil deed in the middle of the night.

❍ ❍ ❍

५. स राजा पुत्रशोकार्तः स्मृत्वा दुष्कृतमात्मनः ।
कौसल्यां पुत्रशोकार्तामिदं वचनमब्रवीत् ।।

5. The king who was afflicted by grief over his son, remembering his own evil deed, said these words to Kowsalya who was stricken with grief over her son.

❍ ❍ ❍

६. यदाचरति कल्याणि शुभं वा यदि वाऽशुभम् ।
तदेव लभते भद्रे कर्ता कर्मजमात्मनः ।।

6. Oh blessed and auspicious (Kowsalya)! A man who does (a deed), good or bad, he reaps only the consequences of his own deed.

❍ ❍ ❍

७. गुरुलाघवमर्थानामारम्भे कर्मणां सुखम् ।
दोषं वा यो न जानाति स बाल इति होच्यते ।।

7. He is indeed a fool (and childish) when he, at the commencement of his action, does not comprehend whether it will be good or bad, or whether its value will be great or of little importance.

❍ ❍ ❍

८. कश्चिदाम्रवणं छित्वा पलाशांश्च निषिञ्चति ।
पुष्पं दृष्ट्वा फले गृध्नुः स शोचति फलागमे ।।

8 Seeing flowers on a tree, if a man desirous of fruits, cuts of mangoe (tree) and grows only Palasa tree, surely he will grieve during the (Fruit season) when fruits come up (No mangos for him!)

❍ ❍ ❍

९. अविज्ञाय फलं यो हि कर्म त्वेवानुधावति ।
स शोचेत्फलवेलायां यथा किंशुकसेचकः ।।

9. Without understanding the 'Fruits' (of his actions), if one jumps into action, he will indeed suffer like the man growing Palaasa tree at the time of reaping fruits (from mangoe tree).

❍ ❍ ❍

१०. सोऽहमाम्रवणं छित्त्वा पलाशांश्च न्यषेचयम् ।
रामं फलागमे त्यक्त्वा पश्चाच्छोचामि दुर्मतिः ।।

10. Such a fool as I am, having cut off mangoe grove, I grew (instead) Palasa tree. Having abandoned Raama, afterwards, at the time of reaping 'fruits' (of Raama's service in my old age), I am grieving.

(Dhascharatha, readers may note wanted a life of retirement and he was looking forward to Raama taking over the kingdom. Raama the Mangoe tree was cut off; instead Kaikeyi the Palaasa tree was grown.)

❍ ❍ ❍

११. लब्धशब्देन कौसल्ये कुमारेण धनुष्मता ।
कुमारः शब्दवेधीति मया पापमिदं कृतम् ।।

11. Oh Kowsalya! This sin (I am about to narrate to you) was committed by me, when I was young and while wielding a bow; (They used to say about me): "This young prince (Dhascharatha) is renowned for his sense of sound."

(Dhascharatha can hit and kill a target by mere sound of the target: The target need not be seen by him!)

❍ ❍ ❍

१२. तदिदं मेऽनुसम्प्राप्तं देवि दुःखं स्वयं कृतम् ।
सम्मोहादिह बाल्येन यथा स्याद्भक्षितं विषम् ।।

12. Oh Lady! Out of my childishness, this suffering due to my own (previous) action has now come by me. Like the drinking of poison out of ignorance!

❍ ❍ ❍

१३. यथान्यः पुरुषः कश्चित्पलाशैर्मोहितो भवेत् ।
एवं ममाप्यविज्ञातं शब्दवेध्यमयं फलम् ।।

13. Like an ordinary man confounded by Palaasa tree's flowers, for me also the 'fruits' (the consequence of my action in hitting a target) by mere sound, was not realised.

❍ ❍ ❍

१४. देव्यनूढा त्वमभवो युवराजो भवाम्यहम् ।
ततः प्रावृडनुप्राप्ता मदकामविवर्धनी ।।

14. Oh Lady! You were young (at that time): And I was crown prince: It was the time of rainy season which exhilarated every one's passion and desire.

❍ ❍ ❍

१५. उपास्य हि रसान्भौमांस्तप्त्वा च जगदंशुभिः ।
परेताचरितां भीमां रविराविशते दिशम् ।।

15. The Sun having burnt up the earth and having 'drunk' up the waters of (surface of) earth, entered the terrible region, the home of the dead, (The south: Tropic of Cancer).

(Indians believe the Lord of death lives in South Pole area: The Rainy season starts on mid june when the Sun heads back towards South via the equator. After rains, you have autumn and winter.)

❍ ❍ ❍

१६. उष्णमन्तर्दधे सद्यः स्निग्धा ददृशिरे घनाः ।
ततो जहृषिरे सर्वेभेकसारङ्गबर्हिणः ।।

16. Heat subsided soon: Clouds were seen sticking together; frogs, birds and peacocks rejoiced, all of them.

❍ ❍ ❍

१७. क्लिन्नपक्षोत्तराः स्नाताः कृच्छ्रादिव पतत्रिणः ।
वृष्टिवातावधूताग्रान्पादपानभिपेदिरे ।।

17. Birds whose feathers were wet as if they had their baths, reached (and were perched on) trees with some difficulty, whose (stalk) ends were fanned by cool wet winds.

❍ ❍ ❍

१८. पतितेनाम्भसा छन्नः पतमानेन चासकृत् ।
आबभौ मत्तसारङ्गस्तोयराशिरिवाचलः ।।

18. The mountains were covered by waters due to fall of incessant rain and appeared like an ocean; there were full of exhilarated elephants.

❍ ❍ ❍

१९. पाण्डुरारुणवर्णानि स्रोतांसि विमलान्यपि ।
सुस्रुवुर्गिरिधातुभ्यः सभस्मानि भुजङ्गवत् ।।

19. Although the streams were pure (through pure waterfalls), due to (presence and spillage of) 'Elements' of mountains, they were coloured red and white and also mixed with ashes (of trees parched up by preceding summer); they flowed (looking) like serpents.

❍ ❍ ❍

२०. तस्मिन्नतिसुखे काले धनुष्मानिषुमान्रथी ।
व्यायामकृतसङ्कल्पः सरयूमन्वगां नदीम् ।।

20. During this most pleasant season, having decided on sport and (hunting) exercises, I went to (the banks of) river Sarayu on a chariot, (armed) with bow and arrow.

❍ ❍ ❍

२१. निपाने महिषं रात्रौ गजं वाभ्यागतं नदीम् ।
अन्यं वा श्वापदं कश्चिज्जिघांसुरजितेन्द्रियः ।।

21. Without restraint (without controlling my passion and senses), I was desirous of killing any beast, or a wild buffalo or an elephant that may come to the river at night for water .....

❍ ❍ ❍

२२. अथान्धकारे त्वश्रौषं जले कुम्भस्य पूर्यतः ।
अचक्षुर्विषये घोषं वारणस्येव नर्दतः ।।

22. ...... Then hiding myself in a place in this total darkness, I heard a sound from a pitcher being filled with water (in the river, which I thought) was sound of an elephant.

❍ ❍ ❍

२३. ततोऽहं शरमुद्धृत्य दीप्तमाशीविषोपमम् ।
शब्दं प्रति गजप्रेप्सुरभिलक्ष्य त्वपातयम् ।।

23. At once, desirous of obtaining the elephant (with my arrow), I took an arrow that was fiery, that was like a cobra and I took aim and discharged it in the (direction of) sound.

(Dhascharatha was so dexterous that he could aim perfectly at the 'Kill' by its mere sound without its sight.)

❍ ❍ ❍

२४. अमुञ्चं निशितं बाणमहमाशीविषोपमम् ।
तत्र वागुषसि व्यक्ता प्रादुरासीद्वनौकसः ।।

24. I discharged the snake like sharp arrow: At that moment, a clear voice of an inhabitant of forest (was heard and) fell on my ears.

❍ ❍ ❍

२५. हा हेति पततस्तोये बाणाभिहतमर्मणः ।।

२६. तस्मिन्निपतिते बाणे वागभूत्तत्र मानुषी ।
कथमस्मद्विधे शस्त्रं निपतेत्तु तपस्विनि ।।

25 & 26.

(From one) who was falling into the waters being hit by my weapon in his vital organs, (sounds of) Ha, Ha, Ha (were heard) ......

...... when my arrow fell (on him), this sound from a man emanated forth (from) there. = Why should a weapon fall upon a man of penance (like me) = (Such words I heard, says Dhascharatha.)

❍ ❍ ❍

२७. प्रविविक्तां नदीं रात्रावुदाहारोऽहमागतः ।
इषुणाऽभिहतः केन कस्य वाऽपकृतं मया ॥

27. (Further I heard, Oh Kowsalya!):= By whom have I been hit with a weapon in this night when I had come to this uninhabited river for taking water. What harm has been done to any one by me=

❍ ❍ ❍

२८. ऋषेर्हि न्यस्तदण्डस्य वने वन्येन जीवतः ।
कथं नु शस्त्रेण वधो मद्विधस्य विधीयते ॥

28. (Further I heard)...= How is this killing by a weapon come about for a sage like me who has discarded even a stick (abandoned violence) and am in forest sustaining myself with forest products=

❍ ❍ ❍

२९. जटाभारधरस्यैव वल्कलाजिनवाससः ।
को वधेन ममार्थी स्यात्किं वाऽस्यापकृतं मया ॥

29. (Further I heard, Oh Kowsalya): = Who will benefit by my death who dresses up with bark and deer skin materials and sports twisted hair locks. What injury has been done to him by me (that he should kill me like this with an arrow) =

❍ ❍ ❍

३०. एवं निष्फलमारब्धं केवलानर्थसंहितम् ।
न किञ्चित्साधु मन्येत यथैव गुरुतल्पगम् ॥

30. (I heard further, Kowsalya): = This (act of killing), this deed is fruitless: Like (a sinner) who violates a teacher's wife, no one will consider him a good man as his deed is entirely purposeless ......

❍ ❍ ❍

३१. नेमं तथाऽनुशोचामि जीवितक्षयमात्मनः ।
मातरं पितरं चोभावनुशोचामि मद्वधे ॥

31. ..... I grieve not, that, this, my life, is coming to an end; (but) I am grieving for my father and mother, these two.in this, my killing ......

❍ ❍ ❍

३२. तदेतन्मिथुनं वृद्धं चिरकालभृतं मया ।
मयि पञ्चत्वमापन्ने कां वृत्तिं वर्तयिष्यति ॥

32. ...... After my attainment of death, what kind of life will they lead, when these two old (parents of mine) have been nourished by me for such a long time ......

❍ ❍ ❍

३३. वृद्धौ च मातापितरावहं चैकेषुणा हतः ।
केन स्म निहताः सर्वेसुबालेनाकृतात्मना ॥

33. ...... My mother and father are very old. and (now) I am killed by a single arrow: By which childish evil doer, have all of us been destroyed? = .

(Thus Dhascharatha heard all these at the dead of the night from the river front from a voice that he had not 'seen' but had unwittingly 'killed'. He narrates all this to Kowsalya.)

❍ ❍ ❍

३४. तां गिरं करुणां श्रुत्वा मम धर्मानुकाङ्क्षिणः ।
कराभ्यां सशरं चापं व्यथितस्यापतद्भुवि ॥

34. When I, who ever desire (to uphold) Dharma, heard this pitiable utterances, my bow and arrow fell off from my hands on to earth, (even) as I was in great distress.

❍ ❍ ❍

३५. तस्याहं करुणं श्रुत्वा बहु लालपतो निशि ।
संभ्रान्तः शोकवेगेन भृशमासं विचेतनः ॥

35. Hearing his pitiable, many wailings at night, I was

terribly bewildered by the fierceness of my grief and I lost my sense (of understanding).

❍ ❍ ❍

३६. तं देशमहमागम्य दीनसत्त्वः सुदुर्मनाः ।
अपश्यमिषुणा तीरे सरय्वास्तापसं हतम् ।।

३७. अवकीर्णजटाभारं प्रविद्धकलशोदकम् ।
पांसुशोणितदिग्धाङ्गं शयानं शल्यपीडितम् ।।

36 & 37.

Downhearted, depressed, I came to the place near the banks of the Sarayu river and saw the sage who had been hit by (my) arrow (unwittingly)..... His trusses were scattered, his pitcher tossed away without water, his body besmeared with blood and dust; He was lying down, hit by the arrow (from my bow).

❍ ❍ ❍

३८. स मामुद्वीक्ष्य नेत्राभ्यां त्रस्तमस्वस्थचेतसम् ।
इत्युवाच वचः क्रूरं दिधक्षन्निव तेजसा ।।

38. Staring at me who was trembling, whose mind was restless, (staring) with his eyes as though .he would burn me up by the power (of penance), he addressed me with these cruel words.

❍ ❍ ❍

३९. किं तवापकृतं राजन्वने निवसता मया ।
जिहीर्षुरम्भो गुर्वर्थं यदहं ताडितस्त्वया ।।

39. (Listen, Oh Kowsalya, this is what this dying sage said to me):

Oh King! When I came to fetch water for my parents, I was hit by you. What harm has been done to you by me who is living in forest?

❍ ❍ ❍

४०. एकेन खलु बाणेन मर्मण्यभिहते मयि ।
द्वावन्धौ निहतौ वृद्धौ माता जनयिता च मे ।।

40. When with one arrow my vital (life giving) organs were hit (my life being taken away), indeed my blind old mother and father, these two were also 'killed'.

❍ ❍ ❍

४१. तौ नूनं दुर्बलावन्धौ मत्प्रतीक्षौ पिपासितौ ।
चिरमाशाकृतां कष्टां तृष्णां संधारयिष्यतः ।।

41. These two weak old (parents of mine) who were awaiting me (for water) to quench thirst, will now have to bear this (unfulfilled) desire of quenching thirst for a very long time!

❍ ❍ ❍

४२. न नूनं तपसो वास्ति फलयोगः श्रुतस्य वा ।
पिता यन्मां न जानीते शयानं पतितं भुवि ।।

42. My father does not know me as having fallen down on earth (hit by your arrow): Thus there is no merit or fruits for penance nor for Vedhic rites.

❍ ❍ ❍

४३. जानन्नपि च किं कुर्यादशक्तिरपरिक्रमः ।
भिद्यमानमिवाशक्तस्त्रातुमन्यो नगो नगम् ।।

43. And even if he knows what can he do, weak as he is and unable to walk; (He will be) like a nearby tree unable to save a tree that is being axed.

❍ ❍ ❍

४४. पितुस्त्वमेव मे गत्वा शीघ्रमाचक्ष्व राघव ।
न त्वामनुदहेत्क्रुद्धो वनं वह्निरिवेधितः ।।

44. Oh (Dhascharatha the) Raaghava! You yourself go at once and inform my father. (But) Let not my angry father 'burn' you up like a (spreading) forest fire burning a tree.

❍ ❍ ❍

४५. इयमेकपदी राजन्यतो मे पितुराश्रमः ।
तं प्रसादय गत्वा त्वं न त्वां सङ्कुपितः शपेत् ।।

45. Oh king! My father's hermitage is there, where this single track (will lead you to). You go to him, console him; (I pray) that he may not curse you.

❍ ❍ ❍

४६. विशल्यं कुरु मां राजन्मर्म मे निशितः शरः ।
रुणद्धि मृदु सोत्सेधं तीरमम्बुरयो यथा ।।

46. Oh king! The sharp arrow is slowly squeezing out life from my (vital) organs, like the waters (of a river) jerking the banks (of a river): (So) Make me "arrowless" (by pulling out this, your arrow from my body).

❍ ❍ ❍

४७. सशल्यः क्लिश्यते प्राणैर्विशल्यो विनशिष्यति ।
इति मामविशच्चिन्ता तस्य शल्यापकर्षणे ।।

47. (Oh Kowsalya, this is what the dying sage requested me as he was in terrific pain.)

Such (a diverse conflicting) thought entered me in the matter of pulling out the arrow (from his body): With arrow in body, he is suffering with his life; Without arrow, he will lose his life (at once).

(Dhascharatha was in two minds: He wants this man to live for sometime so that his parents may see him; But he is in terrific pain and wants to die. If he pulled the arrow he will die quickly sparing himself long agony).

❍ ❍ ❍

४८. दुःखितस्य च दीनस्य मम शोकातुरस्य च ।
लक्षयामास हृदये चिन्तां मुनिसुतस्तदा ।।

48. And this son of Rishi perceived about the worry in my heart as I was (terribly) depressed and afflicted by grief and was in sorrow.

(He knew I was in two minds; to pull or not to pull the arrow in his body.)

❍ ❍ ❍

४९. ताम्यमानः स मां कृच्छ्राद्दुवाच परमार्तवत् ।
सीदमानो विवृत्ताङ्गो वेष्टमानो गतः क्षयम् ।।

49. And he, anxious as he was as his end was nearing, addressed me with difficulty in great distress, with despondency, even as he changed (the position of his) body (frequently by) rolling the body.

❍ ❍ ❍

५०. संस्तभ्य शोकं धैर्येण स्थिरचित्तो भवानघ ।
ब्रह्महत्याकृतं पापं हृदयादपनीयताम् ।।

50. Oh sinless (Dhascharatha)! Be firm in mind, controlling your grief with courage: Cast away from your heart the (fear of) Sin (that may afflict you) caused by the killing of a Braamin.

(Readers may note that killing a poor braamin is a great crime: Further it is one thing for Dhascharatha to have hit this man unwittingly by a deadly arrow; but if he does not attempt to save life of this braamin and pulls out the arrow from his body it may amount to killing, even if it is mercy killing.)

❍ ❍ ❍

५१. न द्विजातिरहं राजन्मा भूत्ते मनसो व्यथा ।
शूद्रायामस्मि वैश्येन जातो जनपदाधिप ।।

51. Oh king! (In any case) I am not a Braamin; (Therefore) there need be no (fear and) suffering in your mind: Oh lord of citizens! I am born to Schoodhra woman through a Vaischya.

❍ ❍ ❍

५२. इतीव वदतः कृच्छ्राद्बाणाभिहतमर्मणः ।
विघूर्णतो विचेष्टस्य वेपमानस्य भूतले ।।

52. (Oh Kowsalya!) Thus he was speaking with great difficulty, hit by my weapon on his vital organs, rolling on earth, trembling (quivering with life), unable to do anything ......

❍ ❍ ❍

५३. तस्य त्वाताम्यमानस्य तं बाणमहमुद्धरम् ।
स मामुद्वीक्ष्य संत्रस्तो जहौ प्राणांस्तपोधनः ।।

53. ...... I drew out (this) his arrow (from the body of this man) who was (senseless and) stiff: And this man of penance (whose wealth was penance) gave up his life, staring at me, his body quivering.

❍ ❍ ❍

५४. जलार्द्रगात्रं तु विलप्य कृच्छ्रा
न्मर्मव्रणं सन्ततमुच्छ्वसन्तम् ।
ततः सरय्वां तमहं शयानं
समीक्ष्य भद्रे सुभृशं विषण्णः ।।

54. Oh noble Kowsalya! Seeing him with his body still wet, his vital organs wounded and life ebbing out), wailing with great difficulty, breathing deep and hard ever, lying down on Sarayu river, (Seeing all this), I became totally down cast.

❍ ❍ ❍

Chapter 64

King Dhascharatha Dies

(Dhascharatha continues the narration to Kowsalya how he was cursed long ago when unwitttingly he had killed the son of a Muni. The curse comes true. He dies.)

❍ ❍ ❍

१. वधमप्रतिरूपं तु महर्षेस्तस्य राघवः ।
विलपन्नेव धर्मात्मा कौसल्यां पुनरब्रवीत् ।।

1. The noble soul man of Dharma (Dhascharatha the) Raaghava, wailing over this Muni's repulsive killing (unwittingly by him), told Kowsalya further (about what happened there at Sarayu river).

❍ ❍ ❍

२. तदज्ञानान्महत्पापं कृत्वाऽहं सङ्कुलेन्द्रियः ।
एकस्त्वचिन्तयं बुद्ध्यां कथं नु सुकृतं भवेत् ।।

2. Having done this great sin in ignorance, with mingled feelings I began to ponder in my mind alone, what (should be done by me) that would do (some) good (to his family).

❍ ❍ ❍

३. ततस्तं घटमादाय पूर्णं परमवारिणा ।
आश्रमं तमहं प्राप्य यथाख्यातपथं गतः ।।

3. Then taking the pitcher full with pure water, I reached the hermitage (of this man whom I had killed), taking the path indicated to me.

❍ ❍ ❍

४. तत्राहं दुर्बलावन्धौ वृद्धावपरिणायकौ ।
अपश्यं तस्य पितरौ लूनपक्षाविव द्विजौ ।।

4. There, I saw his two parents, blind, weak, very old, like two birds stripped out of feather, without a guide ......

❍ ❍ ❍

५. तन्निमित्ताभिरासीनौ कथाभिरपरिक्रमौ ।
तामाशां मत्कृते हीनावुदासीनावनाथवत् ।।

5. ...... and they were sitting there unable to walk, talking only about him (about their son), indifferent (to anything else).

❍ ❍ ❍

६. शोकोपहतचित्तश्च भयसंत्रस्तचेतनः ।
तच्चाश्रमपदं गत्वा भूयः शोकमहं गतः ।।

6. My mind afflicted by grief, my mind overwhelmed by fear, I went (inside) the hermitage and became even more seized by grief.

❍ ❍ ❍

७. पदशब्दं तु मे श्रुत्वा मुनिर्वाक्यमभाषत ।
किं चिरायसि मे पुत्र पानीयं क्षिप्रमानय ॥

7. And the (old) Muni (this dead man's father), hearing the sound of my foot steps, spoke these words (thinking I was his son come back): = Oh my son! Why are you delaying: Bring water at once.

❍ ❍ ❍

८. यन्निमित्तमिदं तात सलिले क्रीडितं त्वया ।
उत्कण्ठिता ते मातेयं प्रविश क्षिप्रमाश्रमम् ॥

8. Oh son! Why were you playing (sporting) in water (of the river). Your mother is also longing for you. Enter the hermitage at once.

❍ ❍ ❍

९. यद्व्यलीकं कृतं पुत्र मात्रा ते यदि वा मया ।
न तन्मनसि कर्तव्यं त्वया तात तपस्विना ॥

9. Oh my son! If anything painful (or disagreeable) was done to you by me, or by your mother, that should not be taken to heart by you who are a man of penance.

❍ ❍ ❍

१०. त्वं गतिस्त्वगतीनां च चक्षुस्त्वं हीनचक्षुषाम् ।
समासक्तास्त्वयि प्राणाः किञ्चिन्नो नाभिभाषसे ॥

10. Helpless as we are, you are our Refuge: Having lost our eyes, you are indeed our eyes! Our life depends on you. Why are you not speaking anything at all to us.=

❍ ❍ ❍

११. मुनिमव्यक्तया वाचा तमहं सज्जमानया ।
हीनव्यञ्जनया प्रेक्ष्य भीतो भीत इवाब्रुवम् ॥

11. Seeing this Muni, totally in fear and (more) fear, I prepared (myself for this ordeal) and announced with

indistinctive words, (words) deficient in consonants... (I just mumbled).

❍ ❍ ❍

१२. मनसः कर्मचेष्टाभिरभिसंस्तभ्य वाग्बलम् ।
आचचक्षे त्वहं तस्मै पुत्रव्यसनजं भयम् ।।

12. Exerting my mind to strengthen the power of my speech, I enlightened him about the calamity to him because of the loss of his son (through the discharge of my arrow on him at Sarayu river).

❍ ❍ ❍

१३. क्षत्रियोऽहं दशरथो नाहं पुत्रो महात्मनः ।
सज्जनावमतं दुःखमिदं प्राप्तं स्वकर्मजम् ।।

13. (I told this Muni some how like this): I am a Kshathriya, Dhascharatha (by name) (I am) not the great soul's son. (am not your son): This calamity (to you) that will be condemned by good men has (now) befallen (all because of and) by my action.

❍ ❍ ❍

१४. भगवंश्चापहस्तोऽहं सरयूतीरमागतः ।
जिघांसुः श्वापदं कश्चिन्निपाने चागतं गजम् ।।

14. Oh Lord! Wielding bow in my hand, I went to Sarayu river desirous of (hunting and) killing some animal or an elephant that may come to drink water (in the river).

❍ ❍ ❍

१५. ततः श्रुतो मया शब्दो जले कुम्भस्य पूर्यतः ।
द्विपोऽयमिति मत्वाऽयं बाणेनाभिहतो मया ।।

15. There, at that time, a sound of pot being filled with water was heard by me. Thinking that this was an elephant (drinking water), this was hit by me with my arrow.

❍ ❍ ❍

१६. गत्वा नद्यास्ततस्तीरमपश्यमिषुणा हृदि ।
विनिर्भिन्नं गतप्राणं शयानं भुवि तापसम् ।।

16. Then, going to the banks of the river, I saw a saintly man, lying down on earth, in a state of dying, hit by (my) arrow on his chest.

❍ ❍ ❍

१७. भगवञ्छब्दमालक्ष्य मया गजजिघांसुना ।
विसृष्टोऽम्भसि नाराचस्तेन ते निहतः सुतः ।।

17. Oh Lord! Intending to kill an elephant by aiming at mere sound, this steel arrow was discharged by me. (But) By this, your son was felled (alas).

❍ ❍ ❍

१८. ततस्तस्यैव वचनादुपेत्य परितप्यतः ।
स मया सहसा बाण उद्धृतो मर्मतस्तदा ।।

18. When I reached there, then, by the words (of request of your dying son) who was in torment, this arrow (of mine) was at once pulled out by me from his vital part (of his body).

❍ ❍ ❍

१९. स चोद्धृतेन बाणेन तत्रैव स्वर्गमास्थितः ।
भगवन्तावुभौ शोचन् वृद्धाविति विलप्य च ।।

19. And he also, when the arrow was pulled out, grieved, wailed over you two lords, (saying) that you were very old: And then he (died) and went over to heaven.

❍ ❍ ❍

२०. अज्ञानाद्भवतः पुत्रः सहसाऽभिहतो मया ।
शेषमेवं गते यत्स्यात्तत्प्रसीदतु मे मुनिः ।।

20. Your son was unexpectedly killed by me in ignorance (thus); At this juncture, whatever remains to be

done, that (you, my lord) the Muni may favour me. (Command me what I should do).

❍ ❍ ❍

२१. स तच्छ्रुत्वा वचः क्रूरं मयोक्तमघशंसिना ।
नाशकत्तीव्रमायासमकर्तुं भगवानृषिः ।।

21. (Oh Kowsalya! Listen further to what happened next.) Hearing the cruel words told by me as confession of my sin, this lord, this Rishi, could not prevent the fierce torment (weariness) 'touching' him (striking him).

❍ ❍ ❍

२२. स बाष्पपूर्णवदनो निश्वसञ्छोककर्शितः ।
मामुवाच महातेजाः कृताञ्जलिमुपस्थितम् ।।

22. The most brilliant (sage) addressed me who was standing there with my hands in Anjali and with tears covering my face, afflicted by grief, breathing hard and deep.

❍ ❍ ❍

२३. यद्येतदशुभं कर्म न स्म मे कथयेः स्वयम् ।
फलेन्मूर्धा स्म ते राजन्सद्यः शतसहस्रधा ।।

23. (Oh Kowsalya this is what this old Sage said to me then.)

Oh king! If you had not voluntarily told me about this most unfortunate deed (of killing), then (at once), there itself, your head would have split up into hundred thousand bits.

❍ ❍ ❍

२४. क्षत्रियेण वधो राजन्वानप्रस्थे विशेषतः ।
ज्ञानपूर्वं कृतः स्थानाच्च्यावयेदपि वज्रिणम् ।।

24. Oh King! And act of deliberate killing of a man leading an ascetic life in forest, will remove even (Lord Indhra) the wielder of the Vajra (the thunderbolt), from his

position (as lord of celestials of heaven). And if done by a Kshathriya, it will particularly be so (will even be worse).

(A kshathriya is a man of valour: He never kills the weak and unarmed.)

❍ ❍ ❍

२५. सप्तधा तु भवेन्मूर्धा मुनौ तपसि तिष्ठति ।
ज्ञानाद्विसृजतः शस्त्रं तादृशे ब्रह्मचारिणि ॥

25. And the head of a man, who, with full knowledge, hurls a weapon on a Muni who practises celibacy doing penance, will become split into 7 bits.

❍ ❍ ❍

२६. अज्ञानाद्धि कृतं यस्मादिदं तेनैव जीवसि ।
अपि ह्यद्यं कुलं न स्याद्राघवाणां कुतो भवान् ॥

26. When that is so, when your entire Raghu race would have ceased (to exist), how can you live (and are still alive). This is because it was done in ignorance that you are alive (now).

❍ ❍ ❍

२७. नय नौ नृप तं देशमिति मां चाभ्यभाषत ।
अद्य तं द्रष्टुमिच्छावः पुत्रं पश्चिमदर्शनम् ॥

27. Oh King! We now wish to see our son for the last time. Please take us to that place. Thus he told me (Oh Kowsalya).

❍ ❍ ❍

२८. रुधिरेणवसिक्ताङ्गं प्रकीर्णाजिनवाससम् ।
शयानं भुवि निःसंज्ञं धर्मराजवशं गतम् ॥

28. His body was besmeared with blood: His deer skin dress dishevelled; he was lying down on earth; unconscious; had reached the state of death: (such was the state of their son when they saw him).

❍ ❍ ❍

२९. अथाहमेकरस्तं देशं नीत्वा तौ भृशदुःखितौ ।
अस्पर्शयमहं पुत्रं तं मुनिं सह भार्यया ॥

29: ...... All by myself, I took them both to this place who were in terrible distress: And along with his wife, I made this Muni touch his son. (as both of them were totally blind).

❍ ❍ ❍

३०. तौ पुत्रमात्मनः स्पृष्ट्वा तमासाद्य तपस्विनौ ।
निपेततुः शरीरेऽस्य पिता चास्येदमब्रवीत् ॥

30. When these two saintly persons touched their son approaching him, they fell on his body. And the father told this even as he wailed.

❍ ❍ ❍

३१. नाभिवादयसे माऽद्य न च मामभिभाषसे ।
किं नु शेषेऽद्य भूमौ त्वं वत्स किं कुपितो ह्यसि ॥

31. Oh my son! You are not bowing to me now. You are not talking to me. Why are you lying down on earth. Perhaps you are angry (with me)!

❍ ❍ ❍

३२. नन्वहं ते प्रियः पुत्र मातरं पश्य धार्मिक ।
किं च नालिङ्गसे पुत्र सुकुमारवचो वद ॥

32. Oh my son! Am I not your beloved. Oh my son who is a man of Dharma. Why are you not embracing your mother: Look (at us): Say something with sweet words.

❍ ❍ ❍

३३. कस्य वाऽपररात्रेऽह श्रोष्यामि हृदयङ्गमम् ।
अधीयानस्य सततं शास्त्रं वाऽन्यद्विशेषतः ॥

33. How will I now, gladly, with all my heart, listen to him who (used to) read out with devotion, Shaasthra-s or

some other (Holy Texts) in the middle of the night, always, (for us who are blind).

❍ ❍ ❍

३४. को मां सन्ध्यामुपास्यैव स्नात्वा हुतहुताशनः ।
श्लाघयिष्यत्युपासीनः पुत्रशोकभयार्दितम् ॥

34. After (making me) take bath, and (helping me) do Sandhya and perform Homa-fire rituals, who will (now) stand by me and comfort me, who is now suffering due to pangs of separation from his son.

❍ ❍ ❍

३५. कन्दमूलफलं हृत्वा को मां प्रियमिवातिथिम् ।
भोजयिष्यत्यकर्मण्यमप्रग्रहमनायकम् ॥

35. Incapacitated to do any work, unable to hold on (for support), unprotected as I am, who will feed me as a beloved (welcome) guest, bringing fruits and tubers.

❍ ❍ ❍

३६. इमामन्धां च वृद्धां च मातरं ते तपस्विनीम् ।
कथं वत्स भरिष्यामि कृपणां पुत्रगर्धिनीम् ॥

36. Oh my son! How will I now support this old, blind, saintly, pitiable mother (of yours) who dotes on her son.

❍ ❍ ❍

३७. तिष्ठ मां मा गमः पुत्र यमस्य सदनं प्रति ।
श्वो मया सह गन्तासि जनन्या च समेधितः ॥

37. Oh son! Do not go to the abode of Yama! (Dont die): Stay here with me. And you will go with me and your mother tomorrow.

(Take me also with you:We will go together in death,says the Muni)

३८. उभावपि च शोकार्तावनाथौ कृपणौ वने ।
क्षिप्रमेव गमिष्यावस्त्वया सह यमक्षयम् ।।

38. Afflicted by grief, without any protector in forest, being miserable, both of us will go along with you and soon reach the abode of Yama (death).

❍ ❍ ❍

३९. ततो वैवस्वतं दृष्ट्वा तं प्रवक्ष्यामि भारतीम् ।
क्षमतां धर्मराजो मे बिभृयात्पितरावयम् ।।

39. May lord of death (Yama, the king of Dharma) permit this for my sake. And I will tell this (lord of death) Vaivaswatha on seeing him: "Let him bring his parents (along): With (such a) speech (I will beg)."

❍ ❍ ❍

४०. दातुमर्हति धर्मात्मा लोकपालो महायशाः ।
ईदृशस्य ममाक्षय्यामेकामभयदक्षिणाम् ।।

40. This (Yama) the guardian of the world, the most famous noble soul (lord of death), may offer me who is in such a state, a gift of protection, without fail. (The gift of protection of a son).

❍ ❍ ❍

४१. अपापोऽसि यदा पुत्र निहतः पापकर्मणा ।
तेन सत्येन गच्छाशु ये लोकाः शस्त्रयोधिनाम् ।।

41. Oh son! Killed by an evil action, you are (however) sinless; By this Truth, you go on straight to the world of warriors (in heaven).

❍ ❍ ❍

४२. यान्ति शूरा गतिं यां च संग्रामेष्वनिवर्तिनः ।
हतास्त्वभिमुखाः पुत्र गतिं तां परमां व्रज ।।

42. Oh son! You will attain the most supreme state, (the

state) attained by warriors who never turn back in wars and get killed, facing (enemies).

❍ ❍ ❍

४३. यां गतिं सगरः शैब्यो दिलीपो जनमेजयः ।
नहुषो धुन्धुमारश्च प्राप्तास्तां गच्छ पुत्रक ।।

43. Oh son! You will attain status attained by Sagara, Schaibhya, Dhileepa Janamejaya, Nahusha, Dhundhumaara.

❍ ❍ ❍

४४. या गतिः सर्वसाधूनां स्वाध्यायात्तपसश्च या ।
भूमिदस्याहिताग्नेश्च एकपत्नीव्रतस्य च ।।

44. Oh my son! The status of men who are good in everyway (obtained) through study of holy Texts and through penance, (that status attained by) men who gift away land, who do fire rituals, who have vowed to have only one wife (and devoted to her) ......

❍ ❍ ❍

४५. गोसहस्रप्रदातॄणां या या गुरुभृतामपि ।
देहन्यासकृतां या च तां गतिं गच्छ पुत्रक ।।

45. ...... (that status enjoyed by) men who offer thousands of cows (in charity); (the status enjoyed by) those who serve their elders; (the status enjoyed by) those who sacrifice their bodies in penance to the deities, such a status you will obtain.

❍ ❍ ❍

४६. न हि त्वस्मिन्कुले जातो गच्छत्यकुशलां गतिम् ।
स तु यास्यति येन त्वं निहतो मम बान्धवः ।।

46. None who was born in your family has obtained a status of ignominy; (but) he, by whom, you, my close relative (as my son) are killed, will obtain this (status of ignominy).

(Thus he lamented, Oh Kowsalya and further he cursed me also.)

❍ ❍ ❍

४७. एवं स कृपणं तत्र पर्यदेवयतासकृत् ।
स तस्मै कर्तुमुदकं प्रवृत्तः सह भार्यया ॥

47. Thus he lamented pitiably, continuously (cried). Then he performed the last Rites (for his dead son) along with his wife.

❍ ❍ ❍

४८. ददौ तिलोदकं तस्मै स पुत्राय यथाविधि ॥

48. As per norms of Shaasthra-s, he offered Thilodhaka to his dead son. (Water offerings with seeds- a Ritual).

❍ ❍ ❍

४९. स तु दिव्येन रूपेण मुनिपुत्रः स्वकर्मभिः ।
स्वगर्गमध्यारुहत्क्षिप्रं शक्रेण सह धर्मवित् ॥

49. The (dead) son of this Muni who was a man of Dharma, by his own good deeds, at once went to heaven along with lord Indhra, in a celestial form.

❍ ❍ ❍

५०. आबभाषे च तौ वृद्धौ सह शक्रेण तापसः ।
आश्वास्य च मुहूर्तं तौ पितरौ वाक्यमब्रवीत् ॥

50. And this (dead son) who was man of penance, then spoke to the old (parents) along with Indhra. After consoling his parents for a muhoortha (after a few minutes), he said these words (as he was going away to heaven, discarding his mortal body, along with Indhra, the lord of heaven).

❍ ❍ ❍

५१. स्थानमस्मि महत्प्राप्तो भवतोः परिचारणात् ।
भवन्तावपि च क्षिप्रं मम मूलमुपैष्यतः ॥

51. Because of service to you both, this great status I have obtained: And soon, You will also obtain my status.

(It is Indian belief that highest service is service to elders and the infirm; And no wonder this son of the Muni goes to heaven because he had served his elderly blind weak parents with devotion.)

❍ ❍ ❍

५२. एवमुक्त्वा तु दिव्येन विमानेन वपुष्मता ।
आरुरोह दिवं क्षिप्रं मुनिपुत्रो जितेन्द्रियः ॥

52. Having said thus, the son of the Muni who had conquered his senses and passions, at once went up to heaven in a divine wonderful Aircraft (thanks to Lord Indhra).

❍ ❍ ❍

५३. स कृत्वा तूदकं तूर्णं तापसः सह भार्यया ।
मामुवाच महातेजाः कृताञ्जलिमुपस्थितम् ॥

53. And this most brilliant man of penance, after completing quickly the last rites (for his son who went to heaven) along with his wife, then addressed me who was standing there with hands cupped in Anjali (in reverence).

❍ ❍ ❍

५४. अद्यैव जहि मां राजन्मरणे नास्ति मे व्यथा ।
यच्छरेणैकपुत्रं मां त्वमकार्षीरपुत्रकम् ॥

54. (Oh Kowsalya. listen to what this Muni said to me then.)

Oh king! Kill me now itself (You took away my only son) and made me who had just one son, "sonless", with a single arrow. Therefore there will be no grief in my death (at your hands).

❍ ❍ ❍

५५. त्वया तु यदविज्ञानान्निहतो मे सुतः शुचिः ।
तेन त्वामभिशप्स्यामि सुदुःखमतिदारुणम् ।।

55. My pure son was killed by you in ignorance or otherwise; Therefore I Am Now Cursing You Cruelly And Pitilessly.

❍ ❍ ❍

५६. पुत्रव्यसनजं दुःखं यदेतन्मम सांप्रतम् ।
एवं त्वं पुत्रशोकेन राजन्कालं गमिष्यसि ।।

56. Oh king! This suffering of mine that has come about to us is caused by separation from my son. Therefore, You Will Go To Your Death Due To Grief Over (separation from your) Son.

❍ ❍ ❍

५७. अज्ञानात्तु हतो यस्मात्क्षत्रियेण त्वया मुनिः ।
तस्मात्त्वां नाविशत्याशु ब्रह्महत्या नराधिप ।।

57. Oh Lord of men! By you, a Kshathriya, (my son) a Muni was killed in ignorance. Therefore, in this matter, the sin of killing a Braamin will not approach , (afflict) you.

❍ ❍ ❍

५८. त्वामप्येतादृशो भावः क्षिप्रमेव गमिष्यति ।
जीवितान्तकरो घोरो दातारमिव दक्षिणा ।।

58. Such a gruesome (horrible) state which will take away your life, will soon overtake you, like (benefits reaped by one) who gives gifts.

❍ ❍ ❍

५९. एवं शापं मयि न्यस्य विलप्य करुणं बहु ।
चितामारोप्य देहं तन्मिथुनं स्वर्गमभ्ययात् ।।

59. (Oh Kowsalya; thus I was cursed long ago; I remember this now.)

Having inflicted such a curse on me, these two went to

heaven after wailing pitiably in many ways and after they put their bodies on (fire) mound (Self immolation).

❍ ❍ ❍

६०. तदेतच्चिन्तयानेन स्मृतं पापं मया स्वयम् ।
तदा बाल्यात्कृतं देवि शब्दवेध्यनुकर्षिणा ।।

60. Oh Lady (kowsalya)! Reminiscing about all this, the "crime" done by me then out of my childishness in discharging a weapon by mere sound, came back to memory by itself. (short while ago).

❍ ❍ ❍

६१. तस्यायं कर्मणो देवि विपाकः समुपस्थितः ।
अपथ्यैः सह संयुक्ते व्याधिरन्नरसे यथा ।।

61. Oh lady (Kowsalya)! The result of that deed (of mine) happened to me like a disease when one (consumes) fine foods mixed with putrefied foods.

❍ ❍ ❍

६२. तस्मान्मामागतं भद्रे तस्योदारस्य तद्वचः ।
इत्युक्त्वा स रुदंस्त्रस्तो भार्यामाह च भूमिपः ।।

62. Oh noble (Kowsalya)! Therefore, the words (of curse) of this lofty (Muni) has befallen me (now). Saying thus, this lord of earth (Dhascharatha) spoke (further) to his wife, crying, (his body) shaking.

❍ ❍ ❍

६३. यदहं पुत्रशोकेन संत्यक्ष्याम्यद्य जीवितम् ।
चक्षुर्भ्यां त्वां न पश्यामि कौसल्ये साधु मा स्पृश ।।

63. Oh Kowsalya! I am now giving up my life by the (very same) grief of (separation from) son. I am not able to see you with my eyes: Please touch me (stroke me).

❍ ❍ ❍

६४. यमक्षयमनुप्राप्ताः प्रेक्ष्यन्ते न हि मानवाः ।
यदि मां संस्पृशेद्रामः सकृदप्यालपेत वा ॥
धनं वा यौवराज्यं वा जहेयमिति मे मतिः ॥

64. Men who reach the abode of death (Yama), are not seen. If Raama should touch me at least once (and caress me) or talk to me, it will be my (last) wish to offer him wealth and (the title of) crown prince ......

❍ ❍ ❍

६५. तन्मे न सदृशं देवि यन्मया राघवे कृतम् ।
सदृशं तत्तु तस्यैव यदनेन कृतं मयि ॥

65. Oh Lady! What was done by me to (Raama) the Raaghava is not befitting me. (But) what was done by him, that is befitting him.

(Vaalmeeki's master piece: My son is so worthy even as I am not so, bemoans Dhascharatha to wife Kowsalya.)

❍ ❍ ❍

६६. दुर्वृत्तमपि कः पुत्रं त्यजेद्भुवि विचक्षणः ।
कश्च प्रव्राज्यमानो वा नासूयेत्पितरं सुतः ॥

66. Which sagacious man in this world will abandon his son even if he is very bad; And which son who is driven away (by his father) will not but be displeased with his father.

❍ ❍ ❍

६७. चक्षुषा त्वां न पश्यामि स्मृतिर्मम विलुप्यते ।
दूता वैवस्वतस्यैते कौसल्ये त्वरयन्ति माम् ॥

67. Oh Kowsalya! I am not able to see you with my eyes; My memory is failing me; And (Death) Vaivaswatha's messengers are 'hurrying' me up.

❍ ❍ ❍

६८. अतस्तु किं दुःखतरं यदहं जीवितक्षये ।
न हि पश्यामि धर्मज्ञं रामं सत्यपराक्रमम् ॥

68. Can there be anything more miserable than that I am not seeing (my beloved son) Raama who is knower of Dharma, who is truly valiant, (particularly) at the time of my life's end.

❍ ❍ ❍

६९. तस्यादर्शनजः शोकः सुतस्याप्रतिकर्मणः ।
उच्छोषयति मे प्राणान्वारि स्तोकमिवतपः ।।

69. The grief caused by my inability to see this son (Raama) whose deeds are incomparable, is sucking my life out, like heat (drying up) small quantities of water.

❍ ❍ ❍

७०. न ते मनुष्या देवास्ते ये चारुशुभकुण्डलम् ।
मुखं द्रक्ष्यन्ति रामस्य वर्षेपञ्चदशे पुनः ।।

70. Those, who, on the 15th. year, once again see Raama's face (beautified) by lovely ear drops (on him), are not men at all. (They are) but divine celestials!

❍ ❍ ❍

७१. पद्मपत्रेक्षणं सुभ्रु सुदंष्ट्रं चारुनासिकम् ।
धन्यां द्रक्ष्यन्ति रामस्य ताराधिपनिभं मुखम् ।।

71. Oh (Kowsalya) with lovely brows! Only the most fortunate men will see Raama's face which is comparable to that of the Moon (who is lord of stars); (the face) which has eyes beautiful like lotus, teeth (which are all) well set, the nose beautiful (and sharp).

❍ ❍ ❍

७२. सदृशं शारदस्येन्दोः फुल्लस्य कमलस्य च ।
सुगन्धि मम नाथस्य धन्या द्रक्ष्यन्ति तन्मुखम् ।।

72. Only the most lucky ones are going to see my* Lord's (my beloved son's) face which is like the autumn Moon and like full blossom lotus and which smells sweet.

(It is interesting to note that Dhascharatha calls his

son, * My Lord: No wonder Dhascharatha realises that Raama is no ordinary mortal as his death approaches- Naatha- Lord)

❍ ❍ ❍

७३. निवृत्तवनवासं तमयोध्यां पुनरागतम् ।
द्रक्ष्यन्ति सुखिनो रामं शुक्रं मार्गगतं यथा ॥

73. The happy people will see Raama return back to Ayodhya after completing his exile in forest, like Star Schukra returning to his own house.

❍ ❍ ❍

७४. कौसल्ये चित्तमोहेन हृदयं सीदतीव मे ।
वेदये न च संयुक्ताञ्छब्दस्पर्शरसानहम् ॥

74. Oh Kowsalya! My heart aches by confusion of my mind. I do not have perception of sound, touch, taste (now).

(All my senses are deserting me, wails Dhscharatha.)

❍ ❍ ❍

७५. चित्तनाशाद्विपद्यन्ते सर्वाण्येवेन्द्रियाणि मे ।
क्षीणस्नेहस्य दीपस्य संसक्ता रश्मयो यथा ॥

75. The sense organs (of my body), all of them, are failing by the loss of my thinking faculty, just like rays from a lamp without oil.

❍ ❍ ❍

७६. अयमात्मभवः शोको मामनाथमचेतनम् ।
संसादयति वेगेन यथा कूलं नदीरयः ॥

76. This grief caused by my own action to make me helpless and lose my mind, is sinking me (sweeping me away) fiercely, like force of a river (breaking) embankments.

❍ ❍ ❍

७७. हा राघव महाबाहो हा ममायासनाशन ।
हा पितृप्रिय मे नाथ हा ममासि गतः सुत ।।

77. Ah (Raama) the mighty limbed Raaghava! Oh the beloved of your father! Ah! One who destroys my weariness! Oh my Lord! Ah! My Son! You have gone away (from me)!

❍ ❍ ❍

७८. हा कौसल्ये विनश्यामि हा सुमित्रे तपस्विनि ।
हा नृशंसे ममामित्रे कैकेयि कुलपांसनि ।।

78. Oh Kowsalya! Ah the saintly Sumithra! Oh my Enemy Kaikeyi, the heartless destroyer of my family: I Am Dying.

❍ ❍ ❍

७९. इति मातुश्च रामस्य सुमित्रायाश्च सन्निधौ ।
राजा दशरथः शोचञ्जीवितान्तमुपागमत् ।।

79. Wailing thus before Raama's mother (Kowsalya) and before Lakshmana's mother (Sumithra), king Dhascharatha reached the End of His Life.

❍ ❍ ❍

८०. तथा तु दीनं कथयन्नराधिपः
प्रियस्य पुत्रस्य विवासनातुरः ।
गतेऽर्धरात्रे भृशदुःखपीडिता
स्तदा जहौ प्राणमुदारदर्शनः ।।

80. The lofty lord of men (this king Dhascharatha) gave up his life in the middle of the night because of the suffering due to separation from his beloved son (Raama), tormented greatly and wailing pitiably like this.

(Note: King Dhascharatha dies: unable to bear separation from his son Raama. The Curse upon him by an old Braamin sage takes effect. But some commentators are of the view, that when his son Raama who was the embodiment of Dharma left him, Dhascharatha who was a man of Dharma, had neither the strength nor desire to live. With "DHARMA" gone 'away', He Was Gone Too!)

❍ ❍ ❍

Chapter 65

The Royal Ladies Cry

१. अथ रात्र्यां व्यतीतायां प्रातरेवापरेऽहनि ।
वन्दिनः पर्युपातिष्ठंस्तत्पार्थिवनिवेशनम् ।।

1. Then, when night had passed away, on the morning of the next day, the (royal) bards came to the same place, at king's palace.

(They did not know the king had died at night: Royal custom, the king is always woken up with music and salutations.)

❍ ❍ ❍

२. सूताः परमसंस्कारा मागधाश्चोत्तमश्रुताः ।
गायकाः स्तुतिशीलाश्च निगदन्तः पृथक्पृथक् ।।

2. Well adorned bards, most renowned Maaghada-s (Poets adorning the Court): Singers well versed in invocational singing, sang one after the other.

❍ ❍ ❍

३. राजानां स्तुवतां तेषामुदात्ताभिहिताशिषाम् ।
प्रासादाभोगविस्तीर्णः स्तुतिशब्दो व्यवर्धत ।।

3. Offering benediction in loud clear voice, the sound of invocation from (all those) who were extolling (their king), reverberated the entire palace.

❍ ❍ ❍

४. ततस्तु स्तुवतां तेषां सूतानां पाणिवादकाः ।
अपदानान्युदाहृत्य पाणिवादानवादयन् ॥

4. At that time, the hand clappers kept beat with their palms to these singers who were extolling (the king and his rule) with quotations from legends.

❍ ❍ ❍

५. तेन शब्देन विहगाः प्रतिबुद्धा विसस्वनुः ।
शाखास्थाः पञ्जरस्थाश्च ये राजकुलगोचराः ॥

5. The birds perched on the branches of trees and in their nests and in the palace, they all were awakened by these sounds and they cooed.

❍ ❍ ❍

६. व्याहृताः पुण्यशब्दाश्च वीणानां चापि निस्वनाः ।
आशीर्गेयं च गाथानां पूरयामास वेश्म तत् ॥

6. The entire palace was filled with (sounds of) devotional songs that were sung to the strains from instruments (like) Veena and with songs of benediction from singers.

❍ ❍ ❍

७. ततः शुचिसमाचाराः पर्युपस्थानकोविदाः ।
स्त्रीवर्षवरभूयिष्ठा उपतस्थुर्यथापुरम् ॥

7. Then, the men who follow 'pure practises' (like rituals and so on), men of learning in service of the king, and eunuchs, all came there as usual.

❍ ❍ ❍

८. हरिचन्दनसंपृक्तमुदकं काञ्चनैर्घटैः ।
आनिन्युः स्नानशिक्षाज्ञा यथाकालं यथाविधि ॥

8. Those who were well versed in the art of (giving) baths, brought water in golden pots, mixed with sandal paste/ scents, as per norms. and at the appropriate time (of the early morning).

❍ ❍ ❍

९. मङ्गलालम्भनीयानि प्राशनीयान्युपस्करान् ।
उपनिन्युस्तथाऽप्यन्याः कुमारीबहुलाः स्त्रियः ॥

9. And likewise, young maidens and other ladies brought sweet smelling bath materials, *short eats, **spiced condiments.

(*Praaschaneeyani= short eats: ** Upaskaraan, like betel nuts etc.)

❍ ❍ ❍

१०. सर्वलक्षणसम्पन्नं सर्वं विधिवदर्चितम् ।
सर्वं सुगुणलक्ष्मीवत्तद्बभूवाभिहारिकम् ॥

10. All the things brought up there were (choicest and) were well endowed with all fine qualities and were well served as per norms.They presented a grand spectacle. (they were well served) .

❍ ❍ ❍

११. तत्तु सूर्योदयं यावत्सर्वं परिसमुत्सुकम् ।
तस्थावनुपसंप्राप्तं किंस्विदित्युपशङ्कि तम् ॥

11. All of them awaited sunrise with great zeal: (but) they stood there with some suspicion saying: = What Is This!=

(They all realised something was wrong in the palace.)

❍ ❍ ❍

१२. अथ याः कोसलेन्द्रस्य शयनं प्रत्यनन्तराः ।
ताः स्त्रियस्तू समागम्य भर्तारं प्रत्यबोधयन् ॥

12. Then the wives who were near the bed of the Kosala king (Dhascharatha), all of them, came (close to bed) and (tried to) awake their husband.

❍ ❍ ❍

१३ तथाऽप्युचितवृत्तास्ता विनयेन नयेन च ।
न ह्यस्य शयनं स्पृष्ट्वा किञ्चिदप्युपलेभिरे ॥

13. These wives of proper conduct, touched his bed with respect and properly; but they did not perceive (anything wrong particularly).

❍ ❍ ❍

१४. ताः स्त्रियः स्वप्नशीलज्ञाश्चेष्टासञ्चलनादिषु ।
ता वेपथुपरीताश्च राज्ञः प्राणेषु शमिताः ।।

14. (But) From the movements and placement of the limbs, the ladies who knew about their (husband's) mode of sleep, began to entertain doubts about king's life; They shuddered.

❍ ❍ ❍

१५. अतिस्रोतस्तृणाग्राणां समं ताः सञ्चकम्पिरे ।।

15. They trembled like the tip of grass against torrential current of water.

❍ ❍ ❍

१६. अथ संवेपमानानां स्त्रीणां दृष्ट्वा च पार्थिवम् ।
यत्तदा शङ्कितं पापं तस्य जज्ञे विनिश्चयः ।।

16. Then seeing the king (in that state), what misfortune they suspected became confirmed to these ladies who were trembling.

❍ ❍ ❍

१७. कौसल्या च सुमित्रा च पुत्रशोकपराजिते ।
प्रसुप्ते न प्रबुध्येते यथा कालसमन्विते ।।

17. Kowsalya and Sumithra who were completely consumed by grief over (separation from) son, were sleeping as though they were seized by death. They did not awake.

❍ ❍ ❍

१८. निष्प्रभा च विवर्णा च सन्ना शोकेन सन्नता ।
न व्यराजत कौसल्या तारेव तिमिरावृता ।।

18. Kowsalya was lying down afflicted by grief, her (face) colorless, without (her usual) lustre, did not shine, like a diminishing (dying) star covered by darkness.

❍ ❍ ❍

१९. कौसल्यानन्तरं राज्ञः सुमित्रा तदनन्तरम् ।
न स्म विभ्राजते देवी शोकाश्रुलुलितानना ॥

19. Next to the king was Kowsalya and next to her was lady Sumithra whose face did not 'shine', agitated by tears of grief.

❍ ❍ ❍

२०. ते च दृष्ट्वा तथा सुप्ते उभौ देव्यौ च तं नृपम् ।
सुप्तमेवोद्गतप्राणमन्तःपुरमतप्यत ॥

20. The ladies of the palace seeing the king losing his life while sleeping and also seeing these two ladies sleeping like this, became tormented (greatly by grief).

❍ ❍ ❍

२१. ततः प्रचुक्रुशुर्दीनाः सस्वरं ता वराङ्गनाः ।
करेणव इवारण्ये स्थानप्रच्युतयूथपाः ॥

21. Then these miserable foremost ladies cried aloud like female elephants when (their) male elephants are gone away from their place in forest (leaving them alone).

❍ ❍ ❍

२२. तासामाक्रन्दशब्देन सहसोद्गतचेतने ।
कौसल्या च सुमित्रा च व्यक्तनिद्रे बभूवतुः ॥

22. (Hearing and) By the wailing sound from them, Kowsalya and Sumithra at once became awakened out of their sleep, regaining consciousness (as well).

❍ ❍ ❍

२३. कौसल्या च सुमित्रा च दृष्ट्वा स्पृष्ट्वा च पार्थिवम् ।
हा नाथेति परिक्रुश्य पेततुर्धरणीतले ॥

23. Kowsalya and Sumithra saw and touched the King: And they cried: Ho! Lord! And they fell down on earth.

❍ ❍ ❍

२४. सा कोसलेन्द्रदुहिता वेष्टमाना महीतले ।
न बभ्राज रजोध्वस्ता तारेव गगनाच्च्युता ॥

24. (This kowsalya) The daughter of Kosala (king), who was besmeared with dust (as she lay) on the floor, who was turning (and twisting) her body, did not 'shine' like a star falling down from the sky.

❍ ❍ ❍

२५. नृपे शान्तगुणे जाते कौसल्यां पतितां भुवि ।
अपश्यंस्ताः स्त्रियः सर्वा हतां नागवधूमिव ॥

25. And when the ladies saw this Kowsalya fallen down on the floor like a female elephant, and when the king was (dead and) in a state of tranquillity, they all considered (Kowsalya, totally) destroyed.

❍ ❍ ❍

२६. ततः सर्वा नरेन्द्रस्य कैकेयीप्रमुखाः स्त्रियः ।
रुदन्त्यः शोकसन्तप्ता निपेतुर्गतचेतनाः ॥

26. Then Kaikeyi and the ladies with her, all of them, fell down crying, tormented by grief, losing their composure.

❍ ❍ ❍

२७. ताभिः स बलवान्नादः क्रोशन्तीभिरनुद्रुतः ।
येन स्फीतीकृतं भूयस्तद्गृहं समनादयत् ॥

27. The loud sounds from these crying ladies reverberated; Because of this (it shook up) this large, well spread (extensive) palace, making it reverberate with sounds.

❍ ❍ ❍

२८. तत्समुत्प्रस्तसंभ्रान्तं पर्युत्सुकजनाकुलम् ।
सर्वतस्तुमुलाक्रन्दं परितापार्तबान्धवम् ।।

28. There was wide spread agitation; Tumultuous crying; All the folks were in a state of restlessness: All the relatives were tormented by grief .....

❍ ❍ ❍

२९. सद्यो निपतितानन्दं दीनं विक्लबदर्शनम् ।
बभूव नरदेवस्य सद्म दिष्टान्मीयुषः ।।

29. ...... On this (fateful) day the entire palace of the king who had (just) died, was bereft of joy; It presented an appearance of confusion and bewilderment. Most miserable.

❍ ❍ ❍

३०. अतीतामाज्ञाय तु पार्थिवर्षभं
यशस्विनं सम्परिवार्य पत्नयः ।
भृशं रुदन्त्यः करुणं सुदुःखिताः
प्रगृह्य बाहू व्यलपन्ननाथवत् ।।

30. All the wives, when they realised that the most noble king (Dhascharatha) who was 'bull' amongst kings, had died, surrounded him, helpless. They began to wail most pitiably, crying out in great grief, squeezing their hands (palms).

❍ ❍ ❍

Chapter 66

Preserving the Body of Dhascharatha in Herbal Oil

(King Dhascharatha is dead: As all his four sons are away, the body is preserved for Bharatha and Schathrugna to come from their holiday to perform the Last Rites.)

❍ ❍ ❍

१. तमग्निमिव संशान्तमम्बुहीनमिवार्णवम् ।
हतप्रभमिवादित्यं स्वर्गस्थं प्रेक्ष्य भूमिपम् ।।

1. Seeing this lord of earth who had gone to heaven (after death), who was like the Sun whose brilliance had gone, who was like fire extinquished, who was like the ocean without water .....

❍ ❍ ❍

२. कौसल्या बाष्पपूर्णाक्षी विविधं शोककर्शिता ।
उपगृह्य शिरो राज्ञः कैकेयीं प्रत्यभाषत ।।

2. ...... Kowsalya who was afflicted by grief in every way, addressed Kaikeyi, with her eyes full with tears, taking the king's head (on to her lap).

❍ ❍ ❍

३. सकामा भव कैकेयि भुङ्क्ष्व राज्यमकण्टकम् ।
त्यक्त्वा राजानमेकाग्रा नृशंसे दुष्टचारिणि ।।

3. Oh Kaikeyi! You will now remain with your desires fulfilled: Oh cruel and mischievous woman! Having abandoned ('killed') the king, you enjoy this kingdom, free from troubles, undisturbed.

❍ ❍ ❍

४. विहाय मां गतो रामो भर्ता च स्वर्गतो मम ।
विपथे सार्थहीनेव नाहं जीवितुमुत्सहे ।।

4. Raama has gone away leaving me; And my husband has gone away to heaven (is dead); Under such a calamity, I have no desire to live without any purpose (in life).

❍ ❍ ❍

५. भर्तारं तं परित्यज्य का स्त्री दैवतमात्मनः ।
इच्छेज्जीवितुमन्यत्र कैकेय्यास्त्यक्तधर्मणः ।।

5. Which woman other than you Kaikeyi who have

abandoned Dharma, will desire to live, having given up her divine husband.

❍ ❍ ❍

६. न लब्धो बुध्यते दोषान्किंपाकमिव भक्षयन् ।
कुब्जानिमित्तं कैकेय्या राघवाणां कुलं हतम् ।।

6. A greedy (hungry) man cannot perceive the 'flaws' in bad food as he eats; So it is that the entire Raghu race is destroyed by Kaikeyi because (of the evil advice of) the hunchback (Manthara).

(The consequence of eating bad food is felt only a little later)!

❍ ❍ ❍

७. अनियोगे नियुक्तेन राज्ञा रामं विवासितम् ।
सभार्यं जनकः श्रुत्वा परितप्स्यत्यहं यथा ।।

7. Hearing that Raama along with his wife was exiled by the king who was bound (and forced) to act wrongly, King Janaka (Seetha's father) will (now) be tormented just as I am.

❍ ❍ ❍

८. स मामनाथां विधवां नाद्य जानाति धार्मिकः ।
रामः कमलपत्राक्षो जीवनाशमितो गतः ।।

8. Now this man of Dharma, this Raama whose eyes are like lotus petals, who has already lost his life (of comfort and kingdom), does not know me as a helpless widow here (at Ayodhya).

❍ ❍ ❍

९. विदेहराजस्य सुता तथा सीता तपस्विनी ।
दुःखस्यानुचिता दुःखं वने पर्युद्विजिष्यति ।।

9. And likewise, the austere Seetha the daughter of the king of Vidheha, who does not deserve this suffering will tremble in forest in suffering.

❍ ❍ ❍

१०. नदतां भीमघोषाणां निशासु मृगपक्षिणाम् ।
निशम्य नादं संत्रस्ता राघवं संश्रयिष्यति ।।

10. At night, hearing the sounds of birds and beasts that roar with terrible sounds, she, in fear, will cling to (Raama the) Raaghava.

❍ ❍ ❍

११. वृद्धश्चैवाल्पपुत्रश्च वैदेहीमनुचिन्तयन् ।
सोऽपि शोकसमाविष्टो ननु त्यक्ष्यति जीवितम् ।।

11. Old as he is, and without any son, this (Janaka) also will surely give up his life, overwhelmed by grief, always thinking about (his daughter) Seetha the Vaidhehi.

❍ ❍ ❍

१२. साऽहमद्यैव दिष्टान्तं गमिष्यामि पतिव्रता ।
इदं शरीरमालिङ्ग्य प्रवेक्ष्यामि हुताशनम् ।।

12. As I am devoted to my husband (loyal to him), I am now itself going to 'obtain' Death; Hugging this (my husband's) body, I am going to enter fire (to be cremated with him).

❍ ❍ ❍

१३. तां ततः संपरिष्वज्य विलपन्तीं तपस्विनीम् ।
व्यपनिन्युः सुदुःखार्तां कौसल्यां व्यावहारिकाः ।।

13. Then the ladies in waiting (at the palace), clasped this austere Kowsalya who was wailing in great sorrow and led her away.

❍ ❍ ❍

१४. तैलद्रोण्यामथामात्याः संवेश्य जगतीपतिम् ।
राज्ञः सर्वाण्यथादिष्टाश्चक्रुः कर्माण्यनन्तरम् ।।

14. Then the appointed ministers placed the lord of the world (Dhascharatha) in a Vat of (Herbal) Oil. Then

they (made necessary preparations and), did all the duties to be done further.

❍ ❍ ❍

१५. न तु सङ्कलनं राज्ञो विना पुत्रेण मन्त्रिणः ।
सर्वज्ञाः कर्तुमीषुस्ते ततो रक्षन्ति भूमिपम् ।।

15. These ministers who knew all (formalities, norms, customs etc), did not accept the Funereal Rites to be performed without (any) son. Therefore they 'protected' (the body of Dhascharatha) the king.

(Readers may note that those days they even knew the art of preserving, embalming the dead body: They were awaiting Bharatha.)

❍ ❍ ❍

१६. तैलद्रोण्यां तु सचिवैः शायितं तं नराधिपम् ।
हा मृतोऽयमिति ज्ञात्वा स्त्रियस्ताः पर्यवारयन् ।।

16. When these ladies (and wives) came to know that this king was kept (lying down) in a vat of oil, they surrounded (and wailed) = Ha! He Is Dead!=

❍ ❍ ❍

१७. बाहूनुद्धृत्य कृपणा नेत्रप्रस्रवणैर्मुखैः ।
रुदन्त्यः शोकसंतप्ताः कृपणं पर्यदेवयन् ।।

17. Feeling miserable, lifting up their hands, crying, their faces with tears flowing, they wailed pitiably, tormented by grief.

❍ ❍ ❍

१८. हा महाराज रामेण सततं प्रियवादिना ।
विहीनाः सत्यसन्धेन किमर्थं विजहासि नः ।।

18. Ha! Oh great king! Why have you abandoned us who are now deprived of that man of Truth, Raama, who ever speaks sweetly.

❍ ❍ ❍

१९. कैकेय्या दुष्टभावाया राघवेण वियोजिताः ।
कथं परिघ्न्या वत्स्यामः समीपे विधवा वयम् ।।

19. Abandoned by (Raama the) Raaghava (also), how can we, as widows, live on by the side of Kaikeyi who has (virtually) 'killed' her husband and whose (conduct and) nature is bad. (To remind readers, Dhascharatha had 350 wives apart from three queens, Kowsalya, Sumithra and Kaikeyi).

❍ ❍ ❍

२०. स हि नाथः सदाऽस्माकं तव च प्रभुरात्मवान् ।
वनं रामो गतः श्रीमान्विहाय नृपतिश्रियम् ।।

20. The resplendent Raama who was (ever) composed (self reliant), who at all times was our protector and lord to us and to you, has gone away to forest, giving up the kingship.

❍ ❍ ❍

२१. त्वया तेन च वीरेण विना व्यसनमोहिताः ।
कथं वयं निवत्स्यामः कैकेय्या च विदूषिताः ।।

21. (Separated) from you and without this brave (Raama), how can we live on, stupefied by sorrow, and disgraced by Kaikeyi (as well).

❍ ❍ ❍

२२. यया तु राजा रामश्च लक्ष्मणश्च महाबलः ।
सीतया सह संत्यक्ताः सा कमन्यं न हास्यति ।।

22. Whom will she not ridicule, when this king, Raama, and the mightily strong Lakshmana and Seetha, were (all) got rid off by her.

❍ ❍ ❍

२३. ता बाष्पेण च संवीताः शोकेन विपुलेन च ।
व्यवेष्टन्त निरानन्दा राघवस्य वरस्त्रियः ।।

23. The noble wives of this (Dhascharatha the) Raaghava, engulfed by grief and excessive tears, were 'wrapped' up without any joy.

❍ ❍ ❍

२४. निशा नक्षत्रहीनेव स्त्रीव भर्तृविवर्जिता ।
पुरी नाराजतायोध्या हीना राज्ञा महात्मना ।।

24. Without the great soul king, the city of Ayodhya (was gloomy and) did not shine, like night without stars and like woman without husband.

❍ ❍ ❍

२५. बाष्पपर्याकुलजना हाहाभूतकुलाङ्गना ।
शून्यचत्वरवेश्मान्ता न बभ्राज यथापुरम् ।।

25. The citizens were all confused, with the tears (shed copiously): The ladies were wailing Ha, Ha! The quadrangles were deserted and the interiors (of many) houses were deserted; (the city) did not 'shine' like before.

❍ ❍ ❍

२६. गते तु शोकात्त्रिदिवं नराधिपे
महीतलस्थासु नृपाङ्गनासु च ।
निवृत्तचारः सहसा गतो रविः
प्रवृत्तचारा रजनी ह्युपस्थिता ।।

26. When this (Dhascharatha) the lord of men went to heaven in grief and when the royal ladies were lying down on the floor, the sun having completed his movement, at once went (out of sight). Night also began its journey and appeared.

❍ ❍ ❍

२७. ऋते तु पुत्राद्दहनं महीपतेः
न रोचयन्ते सुहृदः समागताः ।
इतीव तस्मिञ्शयने न्यवेशयन्
विचिन्त्य राजानमचिन्त्यदर्शनम् ।।

27. Friends (and well wishers) got together and decided that the cremation of the king without his son (or sons) will not be desired (by one and all). (Therefore), they rested this king of inconceivable appearance, in that resting (position in vat of oil)

❍ ❍ ❍

२८. गतप्रभा द्यौरिव भास्करं विना
व्यपेतनक्षत्रगणेव शर्वरी ।
पुरी बभासे रहिता महात्मना
न चास्रकण्ठाकुलमार्गचत्वरा ॥

28. Deprived of the great soul (Dhascharatha), this city (of Ayodhya) was like lustrous sky without the Sun; like night without galaxy of stars; It was lustreless; (with citizens) suffering with tears; with roads and quadrangles in confusion.

❍ ❍ ❍

२९. नराश्च नार्यश्च समेत्य संघशो
विगर्हमाणा भरतस्य मातरम् ।
तदा नगर्यां नरदेवसंक्षये
बभूवुरार्ता न च शर्म लेभिरे ॥

29. At that time, in this city, crowds of men and women got together and were in great distress, reproaching Bharatha's mother (Kaikeyi) for the death of lord of men (Dhascharatha). They did not obtain any solace. (with King dead and Raama gone away on exile).

❍ ❍ ❍

Chapter 67

The Suffering of a Kingless Kingdom

(King is dead: But all the four princes are away: Ayodhya is without king. An impossible situation.)

❍ ❍ ❍

१. आक्रन्दितनिरानन्दा सास्रकण्ठजनाकुला ।
अयोध्यायामवतता सा व्यतीयाय शर्वरी ॥

1. That night at Ayodhya passed away as a long drawn (night), joyless, with wailing by citizens whose voices were choked by tears.

❍ ❍ ❍

२. व्यतीतायां तु शर्वर्यामादित्यस्योदये ततः ।
समेत्य राजकर्तारः सभामीयुर्द्विजातयः ॥

2. Then, when night passed away and sun arose, officers of the Government met with Braamins and they (all) reached (Council) Hall.

❍ ❍ ❍

३. मार्कण्डेयोऽथ मौद्गल्यो वामदेवश्च काश्यपः ।
कात्यायनो गौतमश्च जाबालिश्च महायशाः ॥

3. (There were): Maarkandeya, Moudgalya, Vaamadheva, Kaathyaayana, Gauthama, Jaabaali... most famous .....

❍ ❍ ❍

४. एते द्विजाः सहामात्यैः पृथग्वाचमुदीरयन् ।
वसिष्ठमेवाभिमुखा. श्रेष्ठं राजपुरोहितम् ॥

4. ...... all these learned braamins along with ministers looked up to Vasishta, the foremost royal priest and said these words individually.

❍ ❍ ❍

५. अतीता शर्वरी दुःखं या नो वर्षशतोपमा ।
अस्मिन्पञ्चत्वमापन्ने पुत्रशोकेन पार्थिवे ॥

5. Because of the death of our king due to pangs of separation from his son (Raama), this night passed away in sorrow like hundred years.

❍ ❍ ❍

६. स्वर्गतश्च महाराजो रामश्चारण्यमाश्रितः ।
लक्ष्मणश्चापि तेजस्वी रामेणैव गतः सह ॥

6. The great king (Dhascharatha) has gone to heaven: And Raama has reached the forest: Along with Raama, the brilliant Lakshmana has gone (away too).

❍ ❍ ❍

७. उभौ भरतशत्रुघ्नौ केकयेषु परन्तपौ ।
पुरे राजगृहे रम्ये मातामहनिवेशने ॥

7. And the tormentors of the enemy, the two (brothers) Bharatha and Schathrugna are now in the lovely palace of their uncle in the city of Rajagriha in the land of Kekeya.

❍ ❍ ❍

८. इक्ष्वाकूणामिहाद्यैव कश्चिद्राजा विधीयताम् ।
अराजकं हि नो राष्ट्रं न विनाशमवाप्नुयात् ॥

8. Any one from amongst the Ikshwaaku-s may be appointed as king here and now; Because our kingdom should not wither away without a king (even for a moment).

❍ ❍ ❍

९. नाराजके जनपदे विद्युन्माली महास्वनः ।
अभिवर्षति पर्जन्यो महीं दिव्येन वारिणा ॥

9. (Poet Vaalmeeki brings out a Truth: No kingdom can survive without a king, a leader.)

In a kingless kingdom, (even) thundering clouds with lightning will not rain over earth with wonderful water.

❍ ❍ ❍

१०. नाराजके जनपदे बीजमुष्टिः प्रकीर्यते ।
नाराजके पितुः पुत्रो भार्या वा वर्तते वशे ॥

10. In a kingless kingdom, even a handful of seeds will not be sown: In a kingless kingdom men will never be obedient towards a father. So will a wife (towards a husband).

❍ ❍ ❍

११. नाराजके धनं चास्ति नास्ति भार्याऽप्यराजके ।
इदमत्याहितं चान्यत्कुतः सौख्यमराजके ॥

11. Not only this, there is more danger in a kingless kingdom; There will be no wealth: In a kingless kingdom, there will be no (true) wife. In a kingless kingdom how can there be any comfort.

❍ ❍ ❍

१२. नाराजके जनपदे कारयन्ति सभां नराः ।
उद्यानानि च रम्याणि हृष्टाः पुण्यगृहाणि च ॥

12. In a kingless kingdom, the citizens will not happily establish assemblies, beautiful gardens and holy places (of worship).

❍ ❍ ❍

१३. नाराजके जनपदे यज्ञशीला द्विजातयः ।
सत्राण्यन्वासते दान्ता ब्राह्मणाः संशितव्रताः ॥

13. In the kingless kingdom, the Braamins knowing Brammam, who are devoted in doing sacrificial ceremonies, who practise vows and austerities, and men who are men of restraint, will not perform Homa rituals.

❍ ❍ ❍

१४. नाराजके जनपदे महायज्ञेषु यज्वनः ।
ब्राह्मणा वसुसम्पूर्णा विसृजन्त्याप्तदक्षिणाः ।।

14. In the kingdom without .ruler, the Braamins will not offer sufficient moneys as fees and gold coins to priests who perform at ritual (Ceremonies).

❍ ❍ ❍

१५. नाराजके जनपदे प्रभूतनटनर्तकाः ।
उत्सवाश्च समाजाश्च वर्धन्ते राष्ट्रवर्धनाः ।।

15. In the kingless kingdom, dancers, actors do not perform in Festivities; No Assembly that brings glory to kingdom.

❍ ❍ ❍

१६. नाराजके जनपदे सिद्धार्था व्यवहारिणः ।
कथाभिरनुरज्यन्ते कथाशीलाः कथाप्रियैः ।।

16. In the kingless kingdom, men customarily interested in history, will not be fulfilled (of their desire of listening to) history, rendered sweetly by historians and thus made happy.

❍ ❍ ❍

१७. नाराजके जनपदे चोद्यानानि समागताः ।
सायाह्ने क्रीडितुं यान्ति कुमार्यौहेमभूषिताः ।।

17. In the kingless kingdom, the young ones wearing golden ornaments will not spend time together in sport (and play) in the gardens in the evening.

❍ ❍ ❍

१८. नाराजके जनपदे वाहनैः शीघ्रगामिभिः ।
नरा निर्यान्त्यरण्यानि नारीभिः सह कामिनः ।।

18. In the kingless kingdom, romantic men will not go to forest along with their women in their speeding chariots.

❍ ❍ ❍

१९. नाराजके जनपदे धनवन्तः सुरक्षिताः ।
शेरते विवृतद्वाराः कृषिगोरक्षजीविनः ।।

19. In the rulerless kingdom, the wealthy men who live by farming and dairying will not feel safe to open their doors and sleep.

❍ ❍ ❍

२०. नाराजके जनपदे बद्धघण्टा विषाणिनः ।
अटन्ति राजमार्गेषु कुञ्जराः षष्टिहायनाः ।।

20. In the kingless kingdom, sixty year old Tuskers, the elephants, will not roam about in royal boulevards with bells tied (on them).

❍ ❍ ❍

२१. नाराजके जनपदे शरान् सततमस्यताम् ।
श्रूयते तलनिर्घोष इष्वस्त्राणामुपासने ।।

21. In the ruler less kingdom, the 'Base' (Twang) sounds (from strings of bows from) archers practising (Archery), who 'throw' arrows, are not heard.

❍ ❍ ❍

२२. नाराजके जनपदे वणिजो दूरगाभिनः ।
गच्छन्ति क्षेममध्वानं बहुपण्यसमाचिताः ।।

22. In the kingless kingdom, merchants carrying excellent merchandise, will not be able to go far on the road in safety.

❍ ❍ ❍

२३. नाराजके जनपदे चरत्येकचरो वशी ।
भावयन्नात्मनाऽऽत्मानं यत्र सायंगृहो मुनिः ।।

23. In the kingless kingdom, a man of self control; a man who is in solitude thinking about the Supreme Soul with his mind; a Muni who looks forward to the evenings as their (rest) 'homes', (all these men) are not found.

❍ ❍ ❍

२४. नाराजके जनपदे योगक्षेमं प्रवर्तते ।
न चाप्यराजके सेना शत्रून्विषहते युधि ।।

24. In the kingless kingdom, there is no security nor welfare: In the rulerless kingdom, even the Army in war will not (face nor) subdue the enemy.

❍ ❍ ❍

२५. नाराजके जनपदे हृष्टैः परमवाजिभिः ।
नराः संयान्ति सहसा रथैश्च प्रतिमण्डिताः ।।

25. In the ruler less kingdom, citizens themselves will not go out laughing (happily) on chariots drawn by cheerful horses.

❍ ❍ ❍

२६. नाराजके जनपदे नराः शास्त्रविशारदाः ।
संवदन्तोऽवतिष्ठन्ते वनेषूपवनेषु च ।।

26. In the rulerless kingdom, citizens well versed in holy Texts will not discuss (or discourse), either in gardens or in forests.

❍ ❍ ❍

२७. नाराजके जनपदे माल्यमोदकदक्षिणाः ।
देवताभ्यर्चनार्थाय कल्प्यन्ते नियतैर्जनैः ।।

27. In the kingless kingdom, devoted citizens will not make preparations of flowers, foods, offerings, for prayers to the deities.

❍ ❍ ❍

२८. नाराजके जनपदे चन्दनागरुरूषिताः ।
राजपुत्रा विराजन्ते वसन्त इव शाखिनः ।।

28. In the ruler less kingdom, the royal princes will not shine like trees in spring season, besmearing themselves with sandal paste and scents.

❍ ❍ ❍

२९. यथा ह्यनुदका नद्यो यथा वाऽप्यतृणं वनम् ।
अगोपाला यथा गावस्तथा राष्ट्रमराजकम् ।।

29. The ruler less kingdom will be like river without water; Forest without grass; Cows without cowherd.

❍ ❍ ❍

३०. ध्वजो रथस्य प्रज्ञानं धूमो ज्ञानं विभावसोः ।
तेषां यो नो ध्वजो राजा स देवत्वमितो गतः ।।

30. The Mast is the distinctive mark of a chariot: Fire is spotted by smoke: And he who is our mast (Standard Bearer), our king, has gone to heaven from here.

❍ ❍ ❍

३१. नाराजके जनपदे स्वकं भवति कस्यचित् ।
मत्स्या इव नरा नित्यं भक्षयन्ति परस्परम् ।।

31. In the ruler less kingdom, nothing belongs to any one; Like fishes, men will devour each other, daily.

❍ ❍ ❍

३२. ये हि संभिन्नमर्यादा नास्तिकाश्छिन्नसंशयाः ।
तेऽपि भावाय कल्पन्ते राजदण्डनिपीडिताः ।।

32. Men who break all norms of propriety, men who used to fear punishment at the hands of their king, Non believers,(atheists), all these men will establish themselves without (fear nor) hesitancy.

❍ ❍ ❍

३३. यथा दृष्टिः शरीरस्य नित्यमेव प्रवर्तते ।
तथा नरेन्द्रो राष्ट्रस्य प्रभवः सत्यधर्मयोः ।।

33. Like sight to a body, the king always is the source (and inspiration) of Truth and Dharma in a kingdom.

❍ ❍ ❍

३४. राजा सत्यं च धर्मश्च राजा कुलवतां कुलम् ।
राजा माता पिता चैव राजा हितकरो नृणाम् ।।

34. The king is the mother and father to all; King is benefactor of the people; King is Truth and Dharma: The king is head of the family (of his citizens).

❍ ❍ ❍

३५. यमो वैश्रवणः शक्रो वरुणश्च महाबलः ।
विशेष्यन्ते नरेन्द्रेण वृत्तेन महता ततः ।।

35. Therefore, the king, by his great conduct is considered more distinguished than (celestial) Lords Yama, Kubhaera, Indhra and the mightily strong Varuna.

❍ ❍ ❍

३६. अहो तम इवेदं स्याान्न प्रज्ञायेत किंचन ।
राजा चेन्न भवेल्लोके विभजन्साध्वसाधुनी ।।

36. In this world, if there is no king to isolate good from bad, everything will become 'Dark': Nothing will be discernible.

❍ ❍ ❍

३७. जीवत्यपि महाराजे तवैव वचनं वयम् ।
नातिक्रमामहे सर्वेवेलां प्राप्येव सागरः ।।

37. When the great king was alive, all of us did not transgress your words (of command) like ocean not transgressing the shores.

❍ ❍ ❍

३८. स नः समीक्ष्य द्विजवर्य वृत्तं
नृपं विना राज्यमरण्यभूतम् ।
कुमारमिक्ष्वाकुसुतं वदान्यं
त्वमेव राजानमिहाभिषिञ्च ।।

38. oh noble Braamin (Vasishta): Such (a noble man) as you are, may you please crown a son from the noble

Ikshwaaku family now, taking note, that, without our king who is dead, our kingdom will become a jungle.

❍ ❍ ❍

Chapter 68

Messengers Sent to Fetch Bharatha

१. तेषां तद्वचनं श्रुत्वा वसिष्ठः प्रत्युवाच ह ।
मित्रामात्यगणान्सर्वान्ब्राह्मणांस्तानिदं वचः ।।

1. Hearing such words from them, Vasishta replied with these words to the Braamins, friends and ministers.

❍ ❍ ❍

२. यदसौ मातुलकुले पुरे राजगृहे सुखी ।
भरतो वसति भ्रात्रा शत्रुघ्नेन समन्वितः ।।

2. This Bharatha is now staying in comfort in his maternal uncle's place in the city of Rajagriha along with his brother Schathrugna ......

❍ ❍ ❍

३. तच्छीघ्रं जवना दूता गच्छन्तु त्वरितं हयैः ।
आनेतुं भ्रातरौ वीरौ किं समीक्षामहे वयम् ।।

3. ..... Therefore let couriers going fast mounting horses, go at once and fetch the two brave brothers: Why should we consider (anything else)

❍ ❍ ❍

४ गच्छन्त्विति ततः सर्वेवसिष्ठं वाक्यमब्रुवन् ।
तेषा तु वचनं श्रुत्वा वसिष्ठो वाक्यमब्रवीत् ।।

4. Then all of them said to Vasishta, these words:= May they go =: Hearing their words, Vasishta said these words.

❍ ❍ ❍

५. एहि सिद्धार्थ विजय जयन्ताशोक नन्दन ।
श्रूयतामितिकर्तव्यं सर्वानेव ब्रवीमि वः ।।

5. Oh Sidhaartha! Come here. Oh Vijaya, Asoka, Jayantha, Nandhana! I will tell you all as to what should be done. Listen.

❍ ❍ ❍

६. पुरं राजगृहं गत्वा शीघ्रं शीघ्रजवैर्हयैः ।
त्यक्तशोकैरिदं वाच्यः शासनाद्भरतो मम ।।

6. Giving up grief (not exhibiting your sorrow), you go to the city of Raajagriha on fast moving horses. And (there) Bharatha must be told these words as my command.

❍ ❍ ❍

७. पुरोहितस्त्वां कुशलं प्राह सर्वेच मन्त्रिणः ।
त्वरमाणश्च निर्याहि कृत्यमात्ययिकं त्वया ।।

7. (You tell Bharatha thus, says Vasishta to the messengers.)

The Purohith (Vasishta) enquired about your welfare: And like wise, all the ministers (enquired about you); Without Wasting Time, You Come Back. The Work To Be Done By You (at Ayodhya) is Urgent.

❍ ❍ ❍

८. मा चास्मै प्रोषितं रामं मा चास्मै पितरं मृतम् ।
भवन्तः शंसिषुर्गत्वा राघवणामिमं क्षयम् ।।

8. Going there, you should not report to him about Raama's exile or about his father's death. Nor (should you talk) about this calamity to the Raghu family.

❍ ❍ ❍

९. कौशेयानि च वस्त्राणि भूषणानि वराणि च ।
क्षिप्रमादाय राज्ञश्च भरतस्य च गच्छत ।।

9. Taking with you silken dresses and foremost ornaments for the king of Kekeya and to (our) Bharatha, you go at once.

(Vasishta's orders are very clear. As Bharatha who is holidaying at his maternal grandfather's house is unaware of all the happenings at Ayodhya, Vasishta is firm that Bharatha should learn about his father's death, and Raama's exile, only at Ayodhya.)

❍ ❍ ❍

१०. दत्तपथ्यशना दूता जग्मुः स्वं स्वं निवेशनम् ।
केकयांस्ते गमिष्यन्तो हयानारुह्य सम्मतान् ।।

10. Taking necessities for journey, these couriers who were going to Kekeya kingdom, rode on proper horses and left (first) for their respective homes (to take leave of their families).

❍ ❍ ❍

११. ततः प्रास्थानिकं कृत्वा कार्यशेषमनन्तरम् ।
वसिष्ठेनाभ्यनुज्ञाता दूताः संत्वरिता ययुः ।।

11. Given permission to leave by Vasishta, the couriers finished their unfinished work for their journey and then after left in hurry.

❍ ❍ ❍

१२. न्यन्तेनापरतालस्य प्रलम्बस्योत्तरं प्रति ।
निषेवमाणास्ते जग्मुर्नदीं मध्येन मालिनीम् ।।

12. Going close to Aparathaala hills, then towards north of (mountain) Pralamba, sighting Maalini river, they went along.

❍ ❍ ❍

१३. ते हस्तिनापुरे गङ्गां तीर्त्वा प्रत्यङ्मुखा ययुः ।
पाञ्चालदेशमासाद्य मध्येन कुरुजाङ्गलम् ।।

13. Crossing Ganges at Hasthinaapura, going towards west, passing by route to Kurujangala, they reached Paanchaala territory and went along.

❍ ❍ ❍

१४. सरांसि च सुफुल्लानि नदीश्च विमलोदकाः ।
निरीक्षमाणास्ते जग्मुर्दूताः कार्यवशाद्द्रुतम् ।।

14. These couriers went along fast owing to the (urgency of their) mission, looking at ponds and lakes, full blossomed (trees around), rivers with pure waters.

❍ ❍ ❍

१५. ते प्रसन्नोदकां दिव्यां नानाविहगसेविताम् ।
उपातिजग्मुर्वेगेन शरदण्डां जनाकुलाम् ।।

15. They crossed over quickly the wonderful Scharadhanda river whose waters were clear, which was inhabited by many birds (and around which) there were lot of inhabitation.

❍ ❍ ❍

१६. निकूलवृक्षमासाद्य दिव्यं सत्योपयाचनम् ।
अभिगम्याभिवाद्यं तं कुलिङ्गां प्राविशन्पुरीम् ।।

16. Approaching the holy tree of Sathyopayachana on its bank, they passed by this venerable tree and entered city of Kulinga.

❍ ❍ ❍

१७. अभिकालं ततः प्राप्य ते बोधिभवनाच्च्युताम् ।
पितृपैतामहीं पुण्यां तेरुरिक्षुमतीं नदीम् ।।

17. From there, they reached Adhikaala. Then they crossed the holy river Ikshumathi, which originates from (mountain) Bodhibavana, most honoured by forefathers.

❍ ❍ ❍

१८. अवेक्ष्याञ्जलिपानांश्च ब्राह्मणान्वेदपारगान् ।
ययुर्मध्येन बाह्लीकान्सुदामानं च पर्वतम् ।।

18. They met (on the way) Braamins who were well versed in Vedha-s and who (sustain themselves) with just

handful of water.(water cupful of an Anjali). Passing through Baahleeka territory, they reached mountain Sudhaama.

❍ ❍ ❍

१९. विष्णोः पदं प्रेक्षमाणा विपाशां चापि शाल्मलीम् ।
नदीर्वापीस्तटाकानि पल्वलानि सरांसि च ।।

19. Looking at (and meditating upon) the feet of God Vishnu (and passing along) river Vipaascha and (other) rivers, streams, ponds, small tanks, pools ......

❍ ❍ ❍

२०. पश्यन्तो विविधांश्चापि सिंहव्याघ्रमृगद्विपान् ।
ययुः पथाऽतिमहता शासनं भर्तुरीप्सवः ।।

20. ...... and seeing various (animals like) lions, tigers and deer, elephants etc., they went along on the long route, desirous of (obeying) their master (Vasishta's) command.

❍ ❍ ❍

२१. ते श्रान्तवाहना दूता विकृष्टेन सता पथा ।
गिरिव्रजं पुरवरं शीघ्रमासेदुरञ्जसा ।।

21. Although the horses were tired, these couriers went along vast (extended) territories and went straight to the foremost city of Girivraja quickly.

❍ ❍ ❍

२२. भर्तुः प्रियार्थं कुलरक्षणार्थं
भर्तुश्च वशंस्य परिग्रहार्थम् ।
अहेडमानास्त्वरया स्म दूता
रात्र्यां तु ते तत्पुरमेव याताः ।।

22. Out of their regard for their master and for the protection of their race and for the honour of their master's family, the couriers, in great hurry, reached the very city (of Raajagriha) that night (itself) in earnestness.

❍ ❍ ❍

Chapter 69

Bharatha's Bad Dreams

(Scene shifts to Raajagriha where Bharatha has been holidaying in his maternal grandfather's capital. But he is tormented by some bad dreams, even as messengers from Ayodhya come there to take him back to Ayodhya on urgent summons from Vasishta, the chief priest).

१. यामेव रात्रिं ते दूताः प्रविशन्ति स्म तां पुरीम् ।
भरतेनापि तां रात्रिं स्वप्नो दृष्टोऽयमप्रियः ॥

1. The messengers entered the city at night. And on that very night, this bad dream also was seen by Bharatha.

❍ ❍ ❍

२. व्युष्टामेव तु तां रात्रिं दृष्ट्वा तं स्वप्नमप्रियम् ।
पुत्रो राजाधिराजस्य सुभृशं पर्यतप्यत ॥

2. Seeing this bad dream at that night, at day break, this (Bharatha) the son of the king of kings, (this son of Dhascharatha), was very much tormented.

❍ ❍ ❍

३. तप्यमानं समाज्ञाय वयस्याः प्रियवादिनः ।
आयासं विनयिष्यन्तः सभायां चक्रिरे कथाः ॥

3. And his friends who (ever) speak sweetly to him, seeing him in torment, desirous of removing his worries, began to narrate stories in the hall. (to take his mind off, to cheer him up).

❍ ❍ ❍

४. वापयन्ति तथा शान्तिं लोलयन्त्यपरे तथा ।
नाटकान्यपरे प्राहुर्हास्यानि विविधानि च ॥

4. They likewise counselled him to be in tranquillity; some inverted his mind; likewise some told various jokes and (dramatic) plays.

❍ ❍ ❍

५. स तैर्महात्मा भरतः सखिभिः प्रियवादिभिः ।
गोष्ठीहास्यानि कुर्वद्भिर्न प्राहृष्यत राघवः ॥

5. (Yet): This great soul Bharatha the Raaghava was not cheered up by his friends who spoke sweetly to him with jokes.

❍ ❍ ❍

६. तमब्रवीत्प्रियसखो भरतं सखिभिर्वृतम् ।
सुहृद्भिः पर्युपासीनः किं सखे नानुमोदसे ॥

6. One of his friends close to him who was surrounded by his friends and companions, addressed this Bharatha: =Oh friend! Why are you not cheerful? =

❍ ❍ ❍

७. एवं ब्रुवाणं संहृष्टं भरतः प्रत्युवाच ह ।
श्रृणु त्वं यन्निमित्तं मे दैन्यमेतदुपस्थितम् ॥

7. And Bharatha replied to him who was speaking cheerfully: =You listen as to the reason why this affliction has befallen me.=

❍ ❍ ❍

८. स्वप्ने पितरमद्राक्षं मलिनं मुक्तमूर्धजम् ।
पतन्तमाद्रिशिखरात्कलुषे गोमयह्रदे ॥

8. (Bharatha narrates a dreadful dream he dreamt; Portends.)

In (my) dream, I saw my father, dirty, his hair disheveled and he was falling down from a cliff of mountain into an impure pond filled with cow dung.

❍ ❍ ❍

९. प्लवमानश्च मे दृष्टः स तस्मिन्गोमयहृदे ।
पिबन्नञ्जलिना तैलं हसन्निव मुहुर्मुहुः ।।

9. He appeared 'swimming' in the cow dung filled pond and drinking oil with his hands cupped. He was seen laughing intermittently.

❍ ❍ ❍

१०. ततस्तिलौदनं भुक्त्वा पुनः पुनरधःशिराः ।
तैलेनाभ्यक्तसर्वाङ्गस्तैलमेवावगाहत ।।

10. Eating balls of oil seed (cakes), his head tilted downwards, again and again, he was plunged in oil, his body entirely besmeared with oil.

❍ ❍ ❍

११. स्वप्नेऽपि सागरं शुष्कं चन्द्रं च पतितं भुवि ।
उपरुद्धां च जगतीं तमसेव समावृताम् ।।

11. In the dream, ocean was dried up. Moon had fallen on earth. World covered by darkness; as though it was altered (in shape) .....

❍ ❍ ❍

१२. औपवाह्यस्य नागस्य विषाणं शकलीकृतम् ।
सहसा चापि संशान्तं ज्वलितं जातवेदसम् ।।

12. ...... The tusk of royal elephant was broken; Earth was burning, suddenly put out, consumed by fire ......

❍ ❍ ❍

१३. अवतीर्णां च पृथिवीं शुष्कांश्च विविधान्द्रुमान् ।
अहं पश्यामि विध्वस्तान्सधूमांश्चैव पर्वतान् ।।

13. ...... Various trees dried up mountains cracking up to pieces: smoke coming out; all these I saw (in my dream).

❍ ❍ ❍

१४. पीठे कार्ष्णायसे चैनं निषण्णं कृष्णवाससम् ।
प्रहसन्ति स्म राजानं प्रमदाः कृष्णपिङ्गलाः ।।

14. ...... Ladies with yellow and black teased the king who was seated in a black throne, wearing black dress ......

❍ ❍ ❍

१५. त्वरमाणश्च धर्मात्मा रक्तमाल्यानुलेपनः ।
रथेन खरयुक्तेन प्रयातो दक्षिणामुखः ।।

15. ...... (And I dreamt) ...... The noble soul man of Dharma (my father) wearing a red garland and besmeared in sandal paste and riding a chariot yoked to donkeys was going fast towards South.

(South is Lord Yama's place: The Lord of Death)

❍ ❍ ❍

१६. प्रहसन्तीव राजानं प्रमदा रक्तवासिनी ।
प्रकर्षन्ती मया दृष्टा राक्षसी विकृतानना ।।

16. And a woman demon with a disfigured face, wearing a red dress, was dragging the king (my father), laughing (mockingly) at him. This was seen by me (in dream)

❍ ❍ ❍

१७. एवमेतन्मया दृष्टमिमां रात्रिं भयावहाम् ।
अहं रामोऽथ वा राजा लक्ष्मणो वा मरिष्यति ।।

17. Thus all this was seen by me at night (in my dream), causing fear in me. The King (my father), or (my brothers) Raama or Lakshmana will die; If not, I will die!

❍ ❍ ❍

१८. नरो यानेन यः स्वप्ने खरयुक्तेन याति हि ।
अचिरात्तस्य धूमाग्रं चितायां संप्रदृश्यते ।।

18. When a man in dream (is seen) to go in a vehicle drawn

by donkeys, very soon great smoke is seen coming from his funereal mound.

❍ ❍ ❍

१९. एतन्निमित्तं दीनोऽहं न च वः प्रतिपूजये ।
शुष्यतीव च मे कण्ठो न स्वस्थमिव मे मनः ।।

19. For this reason, I did not salute you. because I was miserable. My throat is parched up. My mind is not at rest (in peace)

❍ ❍ ❍

२०. न पश्यामि भयस्थानं भयं चैवोपधारये ।
भ्रष्टश्च स्वरयोगो मे छाया चोपहता मम ।।

20. I do not see the cause of this fear (this dream causing fear). But I am seized by fear: My voice is also 'dropping' (getting feeble). The lustre (in my face) is gone. (has taken a beating).

❍ ❍ ❍

२१. जुगुप्सन्निव चात्मानं न च पश्यामि कारणम् ।।

21. I censure myself as I cannot see the reason (for all this).

❍ ❍ ❍

२२. इमां हि दुःस्वप्नगतिं निशाम्य ता
मनेकरूपामवितर्कितां पुरा ।
भयं महत् हृदयान्न याति मे
विचिन्त्य राजानमचिन्त्यदर्शनम् ।।

22. Seeing the course of this bad sorrowful dream of many facets, (the dream) which has never been (seen nor) comprehended before, and thinking about the king of unthinkable appearance, this great fear has not left my heart.

(Note: Indian belief: When a good man gets a bad dream it portends to some calamity. No wonder Bharatha is terribly upset.)

❍ ❍ ❍

Chapter 70

Bharatha Rushes Back to Ayodhya

१. भरते ब्रुवति स्वप्नं दूतास्ते क्लान्तवाहनाः ।
प्रविश्यासह्यपरिघं रम्यं राजगृहं पुरम् ।।

२. समागम्य तु राज्ञा च राजपुत्रेण चार्चिताः ।
राज्ञः पादौ गृहीत्वा तु तमूचुर्भरतं वचः ।।

1. & 2.
While Bharatha was narrating his dream (to his friends at Rajagriha), the messengers (from Ayodhya) on their fatigued horses entered the beautiful city of Rajagriha whose gates were (well guarded and) impossible to get through...Honoured by the king (of Kekeya) and the prince (of Kekeya, Yudhajith), they (bowed) and touched the feet of the king. then they approached Bharatha and said these words to him:

❍ ❍ ❍

३. पुरोहितस्त्वां कुशलं प्राह सर्वेच मन्त्रिणः ।
त्वरमाणश्च निर्याहि कृत्यमात्ययिकं त्वया ।।

3. The Purohith (Vasishta) enquires about your welfare; And all the ministers (at Ayodhya) also enquire (about you). Get started without delay: The work to be done (at Ayodhya) is very urgent.

❍ ❍ ❍

४. इमानि च महार्हाणि वस्त्राण्याभरणानि च ।
प्रतिगृह्य विशालाक्ष मातुलस्य च दापय ।।

4. Oh (Bharatha) with large eyes! Please take these choicest ornaments and dresses and give them to your uncle.

❍ ❍ ❍

५. अत्र विंशतिकोट्यस्तु नृपतेर्मातुलस्य ते ।
दश कोट्यस्तु सम्पूर्णास्तथैव च नृपात्मज ।।

5. Oh (Bharatha) the son of king! There are two hundred millions for (your grandfather the) King and likewise hundred millions for your maternal uncle, full up in this.

(Poet Vaalmeeki has indulged in poetic license: It is customary for a great king to offer plenty of gifts to another king, particularly as the king of Kekaya is father-in-law of King Dhascharatha.)

❍ ❍ ❍

६. प्रतिगृह्य तु तत्सर्वं स्वनुरक्तः सुहृज्जने ।
दूतानुवाच भरतः कामैः सम्प्रतिपूज्य तान् ॥

6. After receiving all this and honouring them with all the desirables, Bharatha who was very much attached to his friends, addressed these messengers (who had come from his Ayodhya to take him back).

❍ ❍ ❍

७. कच्चित्सुकुशली राजा पिता दशरथो मम ।
कच्चिच्चारोगता रामे लक्ष्मणे च महात्मनि ॥

7. I trust my father the king Dhascharatha is well: I trust that the great soul Raama and Lakshmana also are in good state of health.

❍ ❍ ❍

८. आर्या च धर्मनिरता धर्मज्ञा धर्मदर्शिनी ।
अरोगा चापि कौसल्या माता रामस्य धीमतः ॥

8. And the wise Aryan (noble) mother of Raama, Kowsalya, who knows Dharma, who is devoted to Dharma, who practises Dharma is also well, I hope.

❍ ❍ ❍

९. कच्चित्सुमित्रा धर्मज्ञा जननी लक्ष्मणस्य या ।
शत्रुघ्नस्य च वीरस्य साऽरोगा चापि मध्यमा ॥

9. The mother of brave Lakshmana and Schathrugna,

this Sumithra the knower of Dharma who is most **impartial is in good health, I hope.

(** The word used by Vaalmeeki is =Madhyama=. Your translator has used the expression= Impartial=; But it can also be interpreted as = The middle one =. Sumithra is the middle one between the first queen Kowsalya and the third queen Kaikeyi.)

❍ ❍ ❍

१०. आत्मकामा सदा चण्डी क्रोधना प्राज्ञमानिनी ।
अरोगा चापि कैकेयी माता मे किमुवाच ह ।।

10. And my mother, the selfish (self centered), impetuous Kaikeyi who is (easily) provoked, who thinks she is very clever, is also well, I hope. And (pray) what has she said (to be conveyed to me)?

❍ ❍ ❍

११. एवमुक्तास्तु ते दूता भरतेन महात्मना ।
ऊचुः संप्रश्रितं वाक्यमिदं तं भरतं तदा ।।

11. When told thus by the great soul Bharatha, these messengers replied to this man of modesty, Bharatha, thus:

❍ ❍ ❍

१२. कुशलास्ते नरव्याघ्र येषां कुशलमिच्छसि ।
श्रीश्च त्वां वृणुते पद्मा युज्यतां चापि ते रथः ।।

12. Oh 'tiger' of men (Oh Bharatha)! These people whose welfare you desire, are all well. The lotus Goddess (of prosperity, Lakshmi) beckons you: (Bestows glory upon you): May your chariot be got readied (to go back with us to Ayodhya immediately).

(Readers may note this; Poet Vaalmeeki has deliberately put lies in the mouth of these messengers as Vasishta's instructions were quite clear. Bharatha should be told of the calamity only at Ayodhya. And this great Vasishta who has never spoken a lie, now connives at this lie. All are well at Ayodhya, the messengers tell Bharatha under instructions from Vasishta. Of course Dhascharatha is not 'well' but quite dead! And Raama and Lakshmana, far away in forest)

❍ ❍ ❍

१३. भरतश्चापि तान्दूतानेवमुक्तोऽभ्याभाषत ।
आपृच्छेऽहं महाराजं दूताः संत्वरयन्ति माम् ।।

13. When told thus, Bharatha told these messengers:= I will (first) take leave (of my grandfather) the great king (of Kekeya) telling him that the messengers are 'hurrying' me (to get back to my Ayodhya)=

❍ ❍ ❍

१४. एवमुक्त्वा तु तान्दूतान् भरतः पार्थिवात्मजः ।
दूतैः सञ्चोदितो वाक्यं मातामहमुवाच ह ।।

14. Saying thus to the messengers, this son of emperor, this Bharatha who was goaded by these messengers, addressed his maternal grandfather these words.

❍ ❍ ❍

१५. राजन्पितुर्गमिष्यामि सकाशं दूतचोदितः ।
पुनरप्यहमेष्यामि यदा मे त्वं स्मरिष्यसि ।।

15. Oh king (my grand father)! Goaded by messengers, I am going to my father's place. When you again 'remember' me (and want me), I will come back.

❍ ❍ ❍

१६. भरतेनैवमुक्तस्तु नृपो मातामहस्तदा ।
तमुवाच शुभं वाक्यं शिरस्याघ्राय राघवम् ।।

16. When told thus by Bharatha, the maternal grandfather, this king, kissed Bharatha on forehead and then said these pleasant words.

❍ ❍ ❍

१७. गच्छ तातानुजाने त्वां कैकेयी सुप्रजास्त्वया ।
मातरं कुशलं ब्रूयाः पितरं च परन्तप ॥

17. Oh lad! I give you leave (to go back to Ayodhya): Go: (My daughter) Kaikeyi (is indeed) blessed with a good son because of you. Oh (Bharatha) the tormentor of enemies! (Please convey): Tell your father and mother about (my enquiries of their) welfare.

❍ ❍ ❍

१८. पुरोहितं च कुशलं ये चान्ये द्विजसत्तमाः ।
तौ च तात महेष्वासौ भ्रातरौ रामलक्ष्मणौ ॥

18. Oh Lad! To the Purohith (Vasishta) and other braamins and to the two great wielders of bow, Raama and Lakshmana also (convey my enquiries) about (their) welfare.

❍ ❍ ❍

१९. तस्मै हस्त्युत्तमांश्चित्रान्कम्बलानजिनानि च ।
अभिसत्कृत्य कैकेयो भरताय धनं ददौ ॥

19. The Kekeya (king) then honoured and gave to this (grandson) Bharatha, foremost elephants, wonderful woollen blankets, (Deer tiger) skins as gift.

❍ ❍ ❍

२०. रुक्मनिष्कसहस्रे द्वे षोडशाश्वशतानि च ।
सत्कृत्य कैकयीपुत्रं केकयो धनमादिशत् ॥

20. The king of Kekeya honoured him and directed that two thousand gold coins, sixteen hundred horses to be given to (Bharatha) the son of Kaikeyi.

❍ ❍ ❍

२१. तथाऽमात्यानभिप्रेतान्विश्वास्यांश्च गुणान्वितान् ।
ददावश्वपतिः शीघ्रं भरतायानुयायिनः ॥

21. This (King) Aschwapathi then offered (services of his)

ministers who were his friends and men of trust and who were endowed with good qualities, to go along with Bharatha (on his journey back to Ayodhya), then.

❍ ❍ ❍

२२. ऐरावतानैन्द्रशिराञ्नागान्वै प्रियदर्शनान् ।
खराञ्छीघ्रान्सुसंयुक्तान्मातुलोऽस्मै धनं ददौ ।।

22. And his (maternal) uncle gave as gifts to (Bharatha), elephants that were lovely to look at, that were pedigreed from Eyeraawatha, and born in mountain of Indhraschiras: And fast moving stallions (cross bred horses) fit to be well yoked (to fine chariots).

❍ ❍ ❍

२३. अन्तःपुरेऽतिसंवृद्धान्व्याघ्रवीर्यबलोपमान् ।
दंष्ट्रायुधान्महाकायाञ्शुनश्चोपायनं ददौ ।।

23. He also offered as gifts, strong bodied (robust) dogs that were well reared in his* palace. These were like tigers in bravery and used their teeth as weapons. (In *Anthapura- Ladies'apartment of palace).

❍ ❍ ❍

२४. स दत्तं केकयेन्द्रेण धनं तन्नाभ्यनन्दत ।
भरतः कैकयीपुत्रो गमनत्वरया तदा ।।

24. (But) Due to urgency of travel, at that time, this Bharatha the son of Kaikeyi did not delight in (nor was enamoured of) these gifts offered by king of Kekeya (and his uncle).

❍ ❍ ❍

२५. बभूव ह्यस्य हृदये चिन्ता सुमहती तदा ।
त्वरया चापि दूतानां स्वप्नस्यापि च दर्शनात् ।।

25. Because of the bad dream, and because of his being hurried by these messengers, only great worry prevailed in his heart.

❍ ❍ ❍

२६. स स्ववेश्माभ्यतिक्रम्य नरनागाश्वसंवृतम् ।
प्रपेदे सुमहच्छ्रीमान्राजमार्गमनुत्तमम् ।।

26. The resplendent (Bharatha) getting out of this place (of his stay at Raajagriha) reached the grand royal boulevard that was wide and which was full with men, horses and elephants.

❍ ❍ ❍

२७. अभ्यतीत्य ततोऽपश्यदन्तःपुरमनुत्तमम् ।
ततस्तद्भरतः श्रीमानाविवेशानिवारितः ।।

27. Then the resplendent Bharatha, going over this, saw the foremost palace. He entered (the inner apartments) unhindered and unchecked.

❍ ❍ ❍

२८. स मातामहमापृच्छ्य मातुलं च युधाजितम् ।
रथमारुह्य भरतः शत्रुघ्नसहितो ययौ ।।

28. Taking leave of his maternal grandmother and maternal uncle Yudhaajith, he got into his chariot along with (his brother) Schathrugna and started (back to Ayodhya).

❍ ❍ ❍

२९. रथान्मण्डलचक्रांश्च योजयित्वा परःशतम् ।
उष्ट्रगोऽश्वखरैर्भृत्या भरतं यान्तमन्वयुः ।।

29. The attendants followed this Bharatha as he was leaving, on thousands of chariots whose wheels were perfectly round, and which were yoked to horses, donkeys and bulls.

❍ ❍ ❍

३०. बलेन गुप्तो भरतो महात्मा
सहार्यकरस्यात्मसमैरमात्यैः ।
आदाय शत्रुघ्नमपेतशत्रुः
गृहाद्ययौ सिद्ध इवेन्द्रलोकात् ।।

30. Protected by this army, the great soul Bharatha who had no enemies, taking with him Schathrugna, accompanied by ministers who were equal to the noble (king, his grandfather), rode away from the place, like a Sidhdha from the celestial world of Lord Indhra.

❍ ❍ ❍

Chapter 71

(Bharatha Returns) Enters Ayodhya

१. स प्राङ्मुखो राजगृहादभिनिर्याय वीर्यवान् ।
ततः सुदामां द्युतिमान्संतीर्यावेक्ष्य तां नदीम् ।।
२. ह्लादिनीं दूरपारां च प्रत्यक्स्रोतस्तरङ्गिणीम् ।
शतद्रूमतरच्छ्रीमान्नदीमिक्ष्वाकुनन्दनः ।।

1 & 2.
Leaving the city of Rajagriha and going towards easterly direction, the brave and majestical (Bharatha) saw river Sudhaama and then crossed it...This resplendent darling of the Ikshwaaku-s then crossed the wide river Hlaadhini and river Schathadhri and another river that flowed towards west.

❍ ❍ ❍

३. ऐलधाने नदीं तीर्त्वा प्राप्य चापरपर्पटान् ।
शिलामाकुर्वतीं तीर्त्वा ह्याग्नेयं शल्यकर्तनम् ।।
४. अत्यसन्धः शुचिः श्रीमान्प्रेक्षमाणः शिलावहाम् ।
अत्ययात्स महाशैलान्वनं चैत्ररथं प्रति ।।

3 & 4.
At (town) Ailaadhana he crossed a river; And reaching Aparaparpatana (then passing by), he crossed river Schilaavana that rolled away stones (from embankments)...And looking (and passing by) the territory of Schalyakartha near Agni (mountain)

this resplendent and pure (Bharatha) who was (ever) devoted to Truth, crossed over mountains, going towards forest of Chaithyaratha.

❍ ❍ ❍

५. सरस्वतीं च गङ्गां च युग्मेन प्रत्यपद्यत ।
उत्तरं वीरमत्स्यानां भारुण्डं प्राविशद्वनम् ॥

5. And he reached the confluence of rivers Saraswathi and Ganges: And he entered the forest of Baarunda in the north of Veeramathsya.

❍ ❍ ❍

६. वेगिनीं च कुलिङ्गाख्यां ह्लादिनीं पर्वतावृताम् ।
यमुनां प्राप्य संतीर्णोबलमाश्वासयत्तदा ॥

6. Then he reached and crossed the Yamuna river called by the (name of) Kulinga that flowed out fast, that delighted (every one) and which was surrounded there by mountains. Then he rested the entourage.

❍ ❍ ❍

७. शीतीकृत्य तु गात्राणि क्लान्तानाश्वास्य वाजिनः ।
तत्र स्नात्वा च पीत्वा च प्रायादादाय चोदकम् ॥

7. There, he rested the tired horses and cooled their bodies with bathing and drinking water: He started out taking waters (for further journey).

❍ ❍ ❍

८. राजपुत्रो महारण्यमनभीक्ष्णोपसेवितम् ।
भद्रो भद्रेण यानेन मारुतः खमिवात्यगात् ॥

8. Like wind in the sky, this good (and gracious) son of king, this Bharatha, crossed over the great forest on his safe chariot; this forest was totally uninhabited.

❍ ❍ ❍

९. भागीरथीं दुष्प्रतरां सोंशुधाने महानदीम् ।
उपायाद्राघवस्तूर्णं प्राग्वटे विश्रुते पुरे ॥

9. Near Amshudhaana this (Bharatha) the Raaghava, reached the great river Bhaageerathi (Ganges) quickly, at the famous town Praagvat.

❍ ❍ ❍

१०. स गङ्गां प्राग्वटे तीर्त्वा समायात्कुटिकोष्टिकाम् ।
सबलस्तां स तीर्त्वाऽथ समायाद्धर्मवर्धनम् ॥

10. Crossing Ganges at Praagvat along with the army, he reached Kutikoshtaka. Then crossing it he reached town Dharmavardhana.

❍ ❍ ❍

११. तोरणं दक्षिणार्धेन जम्बूप्रस्थमुपागमत् ।
वरूथं च ययौ रम्यं ग्रामं दशरथात्मजः ॥

11. (This Bharatha) the son of Dhascharatha, going along the southern side of village Thorana, reached Ambooprastha. Then reached beautiful village Varootha.

❍ ❍ ❍

१२. तत्र रम्ये वने वासं कृत्वाऽसौ प्राङ्मुखो ययौ ।
उद्यानमुज्जिहानायाः प्रियका यत्र पादपाः ॥

12. After spending some time in the beautiful forest, going towards East, he reached Ujjihaana and the forest (around it) where there were Priyaka trees (Nauclea Cadamba, Terminalia Tormentosa).

❍ ❍ ❍

१३. सालास्तु प्रियकान्प्राप्य शीघ्रानास्थाय वाजिनः ।
अनुज्ञाप्याथ भरतो वाहिनीं त्वरितो ययौ ॥

13. Then Bharatha, after going around the Priyaka trees, (spending some time there) yoked his fast moving

horses (on his chariot), went along fast after dismissing the Army (that had accompanied him from Rajagriha) (Customarily, A royal Army escort is provided by a king to a prince or a king of another territory. Here Bharatha happens to be grandson of Kekeya king as well.)

❍ ❍ ❍

१४. वासं कृत्वा सर्वतीर्थेतीर्त्वा चोत्तानिकां नदीम् ।
अन्या नदीश्च विविधाः पार्वतीयैस्तुरङ्गमैः ।।

१५. हस्तिपृष्ठकमासाद्य कुटिकामत्यवर्तत ।
ततार च नरव्याघ्रो लौहित्ये स कपीवतीम् ।।

14 & 15.

After spending (night) at Sarvatheertha, after crossing river Uthaanika and other rivers and crossing over mountain regions with horses....(Bharatha) the 'tiger' of men, reached Hasthiprishaka after crossing river Kutika; And at Louhithya, he crossed Kapeevathi.

❍ ❍ ❍

१६. एकसाले स्थाणुमतीं विनते गोमतीं नदीम् ।।

१७. कलिङ्गनगरे चापि प्राप्य सालवनं तथा ।
भरतः क्षिप्रमागच्छत्सुपरिश्रान्तवाहनः ।।

16 & 17.

At (village) Ekasaala (he crossed successively) Sthaanumathi, Vinatha and Gomathi rivers...With his horses very tired, Bharatha came to forest of Saala trees in the city of Kalinga quickly.

❍ ❍ ❍

१८. वनं च समतीत्याशु शर्वर्यामरुणोदये ।
अयोध्यां मनुना राज्ञा निर्मितां संददर्श ह ।।

18. Spending the night in this forest, in the (early) morning (he left) and saw Ayodhya soon, that was founded by emperor Manu.

❍ ❍ ❍

१९. तां पुरीं पुरुषव्याघ्रः सप्तरात्रोषितः पथि ।
अयोध्यामग्रतो दृष्ट्वा रथे सारथिमब्रवीत् ।।

19. Thus (this Bharatha) the tiger of men, having spent Seven nights (on journey) saw before him this (his) city of Ayodhya: He addressed the charioteer from the chariot.

❍ ❍ ❍

२०. एषा नातिप्रतीता मे पुण्योद्याना यशस्विनी ।
अयोध्या दृश्यते दूरात्सारथे पाण्डुमृत्तिका ।।

20. (Bharatha does not like the "Look" of his city Ayodhya: Something is wrong for sure, Bharatha feels): .....

Oh charioteer! This famous Ayodhya with its holy (lovely) gardens, with its earth (and roads) sandy white, now appears cheerless even from a distance ......

❍ ❍ ❍

२१. यज्वभिर्गुणसंपन्नैब्राह्मणैर्वेदपारगैः ।
भूयिष्ठमृद्धैराकीर्णा राजर्षिवरपालिता ।।

21. (This Ayodhya was ever) Endowed with fine qualities (of a city) with sacrificial ceremonies (taking place:) Full of Braamins well versed in Vedha-s; Full with prosperous people: Is ruled by a Sage King (Raaja Rishi, my father Dhascharatha).

❍ ❍ ❍

२२. अयोध्यायां पुरा शब्दः श्रूयते तुमुलो महान् ।
समन्तान्नरनारीणां तमद्य न श्रृणोम्यहम् ।।

22. Hitherto, from every corner of Ayodhya, great tumultuous sounds (from conversations of) men and women used to be heard. But now I am not hearing this. (City is silent, Why, asks Bharatha).

❍ ❍ ❍

२३. उद्यानानि च सायो क्रीडित्वोपरतैर्नरैः ।
समन्ताद्विप्रधावद्भिः प्रकाशन्ते ममान्यथा ॥
तान्यद्यानुरुदन्तीव परित्यक्तानि कामिभिः ॥

23. It is abandoned by romantic men who, after playing in the (pleasure) gardens in the evenings, would spread out all over the city. It appears now that these (gardens) are 'Crying' it appears different to me.

❍ ❍ ❍

२४. अरण्यभूतेव पुरी सारथे प्रतिभाति मे ।
न ह्यत्र यानैर्दृश्यन्ते न गजैर्न च वाजिभिः ॥
निर्यान्तो वाऽभियान्तो वा नरमुख्या यथापुरम् ॥

24. Oh charioteer! Like before, (here in Ayodhya) the well known citizens (VIP-s) are not seen either going out or coming in, riding on chariots; nor on elephants, nor on horseback. Therefore it appears to me that the city has turned into a forest (deserted place).

❍ ❍ ❍

२५. उद्यानानि पुरा भान्ति मत्तप्रमुदितानि च ।
जनानां रतिसंयोगेष्वत्यन्तगुणवन्ति च ॥

25. Hitherto this city shone with its parks and gardens delightful for making love; It possessed all the qualities for citizen's sport and amusement.

❍ ❍ ❍

२६. तान्येतान्यद्य पश्यामि निरानन्दानि सर्वशः ।
स्रस्तपर्णैरनुपथं विक्रोशद्भिरिव द्रुमैः ॥

26. But now, I see these (gardens) as though wailing and without any joy all around. The paths are strewn with withered leaves from trees (and plants).

❍ ❍ ❍

२७. नाद्यापि श्रूयते शब्दो मत्तानां मृगपक्षिणाम् ।
संरक्तां मधुरां वाणीं कलं व्याहरतां बहु ।।

27. The sounds of passionate birds and animals which coo indistinctively (but) with sound that is sweet and that which charms, are not heard now (as before).

❍ ❍ ❍

२८. चन्दनागरुसंपृक्तो धूमसंमूर्छितोऽतुलः ।
प्रवाति पवनः श्रीमान्किं नु नाद्य यथापुरम् ।।

28. Why is it the glorious wind that smells of sandal paste and Agara, that 'stupefies' with its fine aroma, which is unequalled (in giving comfort) is not blowing (sweet air) now as before?

❍ ❍ ❍

२९. भेरीमृदङ्गवीणानां कोणसंघट्टितः पुनः ।
किमद्य शब्दो विरतः सदाऽदीनगतिः पुरा ।।

29. Why has the sound of (musical instruments) of Bheri, Mridunga, Veena that are struck up and which used to be always loud (and clear), stopped now?

❍ ❍ ❍

३०. अनिष्टानि च पापानि पश्यामि विविधानि च ।
निमित्तान्यमनोज्ञानि तेन सीदति मे मनः ।।

30. I see evil; unfavourable and most disagreeable omens now; Therefore my mind is distressed.

❍ ❍ ❍

३१. सर्वथा कुशलं सूत दुर्लभं मम बन्धुषु ।
तथा ह्यसति संमोहे हृदयं सीदतीव मे ।।

31. Oh charioteer! (I fear) In every way, the welfare of my relatives will be hard to find (now): And so my heart aches by all this unreal stupefaction.

❍ ❍ ❍

३२. विषण्णः श्रान्तहृदयस्त्रस्तः संलुलितेन्द्रियः ।
भरतः प्रविवेशाशु पुरीमिक्ष्वाकुपालिताम् ।।

32. Bharatha entered (the capital) city ruled by Ikshwaaku (kings) quickly, despondent, down hearted, trembling with fear, his senses (composure) shaken up.

❍ ❍ ❍

३३. द्वारेण वैजयन्तेन प्राविशच्छ्रान्तवाहनः ।
द्वारस्थैरुत्थाय विजयमुक्तस्तैः सहितो ययौ ।।

33. He entered (Ayodhya) through the Gates of Vaijayantha (on his chariot drawn by) tired horses. The officers protecting the Gate got up (and greeted him with Victory slogans). When told (and greeted with) 'Victory', he went along with them.

❍ ❍ ❍

३४. स त्वनेकाग्रहृदयो द्वारस्थं प्रत्यर्च्य तं जनम् ।
सूतमश्वपतेः क्लान्तमब्रवीत्तत्र राघवः ।।

34. His mind (seized) with many (thoughts), this (Bharatha) the Raaghava, greeted the men standing at the Gate and then addressed the tired charioteer (of his grand grandfather) Aschwapathi.

❍ ❍ ❍

३५. किमहं त्वरयाऽनीतः कारणानि विनाऽनघ ।
अशुभाशङ्कि हृदयं शीलं च पततीव मे ।।

35. Oh sinless (charioteer)! Without any reason why was I brought (back) here in a hurry? My mind thinks only of bad things. My natural disposition (and character) is falling apart.

❍ ❍ ❍

३६. श्रुता नो यादृशाः पूर्वं नृपतीनां विनाशने ।
आकारांस्तानहं सर्वानिह पश्यामि सारथे ।।

36. Oh charioteer! Such as those that are usually seen (and heard) by us before when kings pass away, I now see here, all these (the very same) appearances.

❍ ❍ ❍

३७. संमार्जनविहीनानि परुषाण्युपलक्षये ।
अरसंयतकवाटानि श्रीविहीनानि सर्वशः ।।

37. I observe all around, (everything) bereft of any grandeur, without anything being cleaned up, with doors not shut, (everything) severe (in the city).

❍ ❍ ❍

३८. बलिकर्मविहीनानि धूपसंमोदनेन च ।
अनाशितकुटुम्बानि प्रभाहीनजनानि च ।।
अलक्ष्मीकानि पश्यामि कुटुम्बिभवनान्यहम् ।।

38. I am seeing everything inauspicious; With no prayers or family; Oblations performed in households. Without sweet smell emanating (from houses); With none taking food in thewith citizens lacking in lustre (none looking bright)

❍ ❍ ❍

३९. अपेतमाल्यशोभानि ह्यसंमृष्टाजिराणि च ।
देवागाराणि शून्यानि न च भान्ति यथापुरम् ।।

39. The temples do not shine bereft of flowers and garlands; The courtyards are not cleaned up; Everything deserted there; They do not shine like before.

❍ ❍ ❍

४०. देवतार्चाः प्रविद्धाश्च यज्ञगोष्ठ्यस्तथाविधाः ।
माल्यापणेषु राजन्ते नाद्य पण्यानि वै तथा ।।

40. Daily Worship has stopped; Groups doing Sacrificial ceremonies, likewise, (are not to be seen now); And like before, in the Flower Shops, (flowers for Sale) are not (there) to delight.

❍ ❍ ❍

४१. दृश्यन्ते वणिजोऽप्यत्र न यथापूर्वमद्य वै ।
ध्यानसंविग्नहृदया नष्टव्यापारयन्त्रिताः ।।

41. And merchants are not to be seen like before, due to suffering caused by loss of business, their minds seized by worry.

❍ ❍ ❍

४२. देवायतनचैत्येषु दीनाः पक्षिमृगाः स्थिताः ।।

42. In the temples and sacrificial halls birds and animals are resting miserably.

❍ ❍ ❍

४३. मलिनं चाश्रुपूर्णाक्षं दीनं ध्यानपरं कृशम् ।
सस्त्रीपुंसं च पश्यामि जनमुत्कण्ठितं पुरे ।।

43. In the city, all the citizens, men and women, are dirty, their eyes filled with tears, feeling feeble, in deep thought, emaciated; I see (every one) in terrible sorrow.

❍ ❍ ❍

४४. इत्येवमुक्त्वा भरतः सूतं तं दीनमानसः ।
तान्यरिष्टान्ययोध्यायां प्रेक्ष्य राजगृहं ययौ ।।

44. Seeing these ill omens in Ayodhya, Bharatha whose mind was depressed, went to the Royal palace after telling the charioteer (all this) thus.

❍ ❍ ❍

४५. तां शून्यशृङ्गाटकवेश्मरथ्यां
रजोऽरुणद्वारकपाटयन्त्राम् ।
दृष्ट्वा पुरीमिन्द्रपुरप्रकाशां
दुःखेन संपूर्णतरो बभूव ।।

45. Seeing this city (of Ayodhya) that used to shine like Indhra's City, (but now) with its roads and quadrangles and houses deserted, with doors at entrances covered

by dust and looking reddish, he was totally consumed by sorrow.

❍ ❍ ❍

४६. बहूनि पश्यन्मनसोऽप्रियाणि
यान्यन्यदा नास्य पुरे बभूवुः ।
अवाक्शिरा दीनमना नहृष्टः
पितुर्महात्मा प्रविवेश वेश्म ॥

46. Seeing various such things (in his city), where, before, in the city, such (occurrences) which were disquieting to the mind, had never happened, the great soul (Bharatha) entered his father's palace without joy, his mind depressed, his head bowed.

❍ ❍ ❍

Chapter 72

Bharatha Wails

१. अपश्यंस्तु ततस्तत्र पितरं पितुरालये ।
जगाम भरतो द्रष्टुं मातरं मातुरालये ॥

1. Then, there, unable to find his father at his father's palace, Bharatha went to his mother's palace to meet his mother (Kaikeyi).

❍ ❍ ❍

२. अनुप्राप्तं तु तं दृष्ट्वा कैकेयी प्रोषितं सुतम् ।
उत्पपात तदा हृष्टा त्यक्त्वा सौवर्णमासनम् ॥

2. Then, seeing her son having come back from 'abroad', (from her father's place of Rajagriha), Kaikeyi left her golden seat and 'jumped' up in joy (to receive him).

❍ ❍ ❍

३. स प्रविश्यैव धर्मात्मा स्वगृहं श्रीविवर्जितम् ।
भरतः प्रेक्ष्य जग्राह जनन्याश्चरणौ शुभौ ।।

3. Entering his home and observing that it was bereft of any lustre, this noble soul man of Dharma, this Bharatha, fell at the auspicious feet of his mother.

❍ ❍ ❍

४. सा तं मूर्धन्युपाघ्राय परिष्वज्य यशस्विनम् ।
अङ्के भरतमारोप्य प्रष्टुं समुपचक्रमे ।।

4. (Of course readers know that Bharatha is ignorant of all that had happened during his holiday in his grandfather's place of Rajagriha) She hugged the famous Bharatha, lifted him up on to her body, kissed his forehead and began to ask him:

❍ ❍ ❍

५. अद्य ते कतिचिद्रात्र्यश्च्युतस्यार्यकवेश्मनः ।
अपि नाध्वश्रमः शीघ्रं रथेनापततस्तव ।।

5. How many nights now, since you left the Aryan's Palace (at Rajagriha)? Returning back so quickly on chariot, was not the journey tiring?

❍ ❍ ❍

६. आर्यकस्ते सुकुशली युधाजिन्मातुलस्तव ।
प्रवासाच्च सुखं पुत्र सर्वं मे वक्तुमर्हसि ।।

6. Oh (my) Son! Is your noble (grandfather) in good health? Your uncle Yudhajith, like wise, Is he well? Your stay 'abroad' (at Rajagriha), was it comfortable? You must tell all about these.

❍ ❍ ❍

७. एवं पृष्ठस्तु कैकेय्या प्रियं पार्थिवनन्दनः ।
आचष्ट भरतः सर्वं मात्रे राजीवलोचनः ।।

7. When he was asked sweetly by Kaikeyi, the darling

of the king, this Bharatha whose eyes were like lotus, informed all to his mother.

❍ ❍ ❍

८. अद्य मे सप्तमी रात्रिश्च्युतस्यार्यकवेश्मनः ।
अम्बायाः कुशली तातो युधाजिन्मातुलश्च मे ।।

8. It is now 7 nights since I started out from the place of the Aryan (king, my grandfather): My mother's father (your father), is well and likewise my uncle Yudhajith (your brother), is also well

❍ ❍ ❍

९. यन्मे धनं च रत्नं च ददौ राजा परंतपः ।
परिश्रान्तं पथ्यभवत्ततोऽहं पूर्वमागतः ।।

9. (My grandfather the king of Kekeya), The tormentor of enemies, offered me gems and (other) Gifts: (But) these were "tiresome" to me while on my route (back home): I came before all this (came quickly without enjoying the sights nor the gifts: I came earlier than the consignment of gifts!)

❍ ❍ ❍

१०. राजवाक्यहरैर्दूतैस्त्वर्यमाणोऽहमागतः ।
यदहं प्रष्टुमिच्छामि तदम्बा वक्तुमर्हति ।।

10. Hurried by the messengers who had brought the words (of command) of the king, I came (back) here. What I desire to ask you, (you, my) mother should tell me.

❍ ❍ ❍

११. शून्योऽयं शयनीयस्ते पर्यङ्को हेमभूषितः ।
न चायमिक्ष्वाकुजनः प्रहृष्टः प्रतिभाति मे ।।

11. (Bharatha asks his mother why Ayodhya is engulfed in gloom) This gold decorated cot, this bed is empty (unused): And the citizens of Ikshwaaku do not appear to be happy now.

❍ ❍ ❍

१२. राजा भवति भूयिष्ठमिहाम्बाया निवेशने ।
तमहं नाद्य पश्यामि द्रष्टुमिच्छन्निहागतः ।।

12. Mostly, at this time, the king (my father) will be at my mother's palace. I came here desirous of seeing him. But I do not see him now. (Why?) (Dhascharatha used to spend more time with Kaikeyi).

❍ ❍ ❍

१३. पतुर्गृहीष्ये पादौ च तं ममाख्याहि पृच्छतः ।
आहोस्विदम्ब ज्येष्ठायाः कौसल्याया निवेशने ।।

13. Oh mother! I must touch (and prostrate before him) at the feet of my father. Perhaps he is at the eldest (Queen) Kowsalya's palace. As I am asking you, (Please) tell me.

❍ ❍ ❍

१४. तं प्रत्युवाच कैकेयी प्रियवद्धोरमप्रियम् ।
अजानन्तं प्रजानन्ती राज्यलोभेन मोहिता ।।

14. Consumed by greed to obtain the kingdom, thinking that her gruesome and most unkind act was good, this Kaikeyi replied to (her son Bharatha) who was (totally) unaware (of all the happenings).

❍ ❍ ❍

१५. या गतिः सर्वभूतानां तां गतिं ते पिता गतः ।
राजा महात्मा तेजस्वी यायजूकः सतां गतिः ।।

15. Your brilliant father, the great soul king, who performed Yaagas and who was the Refuge for all good men, has gone the way of all living beings. (Dhascharatha is dead, informs Kaikeyi to Bharatha) (To all living beings one thing is certain, Death).

❍ ❍ ❍

१६. तच्छ्रुत्वा भरतो वाक्यं धर्माभिजनवाञ्छुचि. ।
पपात सहसा भूमौ पितृशोकबलार्दितः ।।

16. Hearing these words (from his mother) the pure Bharatha who followed the family traditions as per Dharma, at once fell down on earth, terribly stricken with grief over loss of his father.

❍ ❍ ❍

१७. हा हतोऽस्मीति कृपणां दीनां वाचमुदीरयन् ।
निपपात महाबाहुर्बाहू विक्षिप्य वीर्यवान् ।।

17. This brave mighty limbed Bharatha, lifting up his hands, fell down, saying "Ha! I am destroyed"!.... these pitiable, most depressing words.

❍ ❍ ❍

१८. ततः शोकेन संवीतः पितुर्मरणदुःखितः ।
विललाप महातेजा भ्रान्ताकुलितचेतनः ।।

18. At that moment, the most brilliant (Bharatha), overwhelmed by grief, terribly saddened by the death of his father, wailed, with his senses (and thinking power) confused.(He lost his usual composure).

❍ ❍ ❍

१९. एतत्सुरुचिरं भाति पितुर्मेशयनं पुरा ।
शशिनेवामलं रात्रौ गगनं तोयदात्यये ।।

19. (When my father rested), this bed of my father used to shine brilliantly before, like the moon in a clear sky during autumn night.

❍ ❍ ❍

२०. तदिदं न विभात्यद्य विहीनं तेन धीमता ।
व्योमेव शशिना हीनमप्छुष्क इव सागरः ।।

20. Now, (such a bed), this, does not shine without the wise man (It is) Like the sky without moon, like ocean (without water), dried up.

❍ ❍ ❍

२१. बाष्पमुत्सृज्य कण्ठेन स्वार्तः परमपीडितः ।
प्रच्छाद्य वदनं श्रीमद्वस्त्रेण जयतां वरः ।।

21. The foremost amongst the victorious, (this Bharatha) who was terribly tormented, covered up his resplendent face with his (upper) garment and shed tears, cried aloud in full throat.

❍ ❍ ❍

२२. तमार्तं देवसङ्काशं समीक्ष्य पतितं भुवि ।
निकृत्तमिव सालस्य स्कन्धं परशुना वने ।।

22. (Kaikeyi) saw this celestial like (Bharatha) in very great sorrow, lying down on floor like a trunk of Saala tree cut off by an axe in the forest.

❍ ❍ ❍

२३. मत्तमातङ्गसङ्काशं चन्द्रार्कसदृशं भुवः ।
उत्थापयित्वा शोकार्तं वचनं चेदमब्रवीत् ।।

23. Then lifting him up from the floor who was like a mad elephant, who was comparable to Sun and Moon, (but) who was (now) afflicted by grief, she said these words.

❍ ❍ ❍

२४. उत्तिष्ठोत्तिष्ठ किं शेषे राजन्नत्र महायशः ।
त्वद्विधा न हि शोचन्ति सन्तः सदसि संमताः ।।

24. Oh most famous King! (Oh my son)! Get up! Get up! Why are you lying down; Good men like you who are honoured in Assembly, do not grieve (thus) in this (situation) .... (It is interesting to note Kaikeyi addresses Bharatha as "King")

❍ ❍ ❍

२५. दानयज्ञाधिकारा हि शीलश्रुतितपोनुगा ।
बुद्धिस्ते बुद्धिसंपन्न प्रभेवार्कस्य मन्दिरे ।।

25. Oh (Bharatha who is) Endowed with intelligence! Like

the brilliance around the Ark of the Sun, your mind (and attention should be directed to and) be fit for (offering) charities and (doing) sacrifices and rituals, fit for doing penance, for study of Vedhas and for following Norms. (Good conduct).

❍ ❍ ❍

२६. स रुदित्वा चिरं कालं भूमौ विपरिवृत्य च ।
जननीं प्रत्युवाचेदं शोकैर्बहुभिरावृतः ॥

26. Engulfed by grief, rolling and turning over (his body on the floor) for a long time, crying, he then replied to his mother with these words.

❍ ❍ ❍

२७. अभिषेक्ष्यति रामं नु राजा यज्ञं नु यक्ष्यते ।
इत्यहं कृतसङ्कल्पो हृष्टो यात्रामयासिषम् ॥

27. Thinking that the King was going to anoint Raama (as Yuvaraja) and perform the (great) ceremony, I came back on my journey in joy.... (Bharatha does not know how his father died).

❍ ❍ ❍

२८. तदिदं ह्यन्यथा भूतं व्यवदीर्णं मनो मम ।
पितरं यो न पश्यामि नित्यं प्रियहिते रतम् ॥

28. But this which has happened, is (entirely) different (to what I was looking forward to): Therefore my mind is broken; I am not seeing my father who loved doing good ever (to me, to all).

❍ ❍ ❍

२९. अम्ब केनात्यगाद्राजा व्याधिना मय्यनागते ।
धन्या रामादयः सर्वैर्यैः पिता संस्कृतः स्वयम् ॥

29. Oh mother ! Before I came, the king (my father), by what disease did he die: And Raama and those by

whom alone my father was cremated, they are (indeed) most fortunate.

(In India it is considered a great privilege for a father and son, when the last Rites for a father is done by his son.:Ofcourse, Bhaatha did not know as yet that his father was still to be cremated)

❍ ❍ ❍

३०. न नूनं मां महाराजः प्राप्तं जानाति कीर्तिमान् ।
उपजिघ्रेत्तु मां मूर्ध्नि तातः सन्नम्य सत्वरम् ।।

30. The renowned king does not know me as having returned (from my holiday, to him). Father would have at once kissed me on my forehead, bending (his head down).

❍ ❍ ❍

३१. क्व स पाणिः सुखस्पर्शस्तातस्याक्लिष्टकर्मणः ।
येन मां रजसा ध्वस्तमभीक्ष्णं परिमार्जति ।।

31. Where are the hands with soft touch of my father who is never wearied in (doing good) actions, (the hands) with which he used to wipe off the dust covering (my face and body).

❍ ❍ ❍

३२. यो मे भ्राता पिता बन्धुर्यस्य दासोऽस्मि धीमतः ।
तस्य मां शीघ्रमाख्याहि रामस्याक्लिष्टकर्मणः ।।

32. (Please) Inform at once (of my arrival to) Raama, who is never wearied in (good) service, who is my brother, father and friend. To this wise man, I am (but) a (devoted) servant.

❍ ❍ ❍

३३. पिता हि भवति ज्येष्ठो धर्ममार्यस्य जानतः ।
तस्य पादौ ग्रहीष्यामि स हीदानीं गतिर्मम ।।

33. To one who understands Dharma, his elder brother becomes a father (to him); I will (fall and) 'catch' the feet of this Aryan (my noble brother Raama). (With my father gone) Indeed he is now my refuge.

❍ ❍ ❍

३४. धर्मविद्धर्मनित्यश्च महाभागो दृढव्रतः ।
आर्येकिमब्रवीद्राजा पिता मे सत्यविक्रमः ।।

34. Oh Aryan lady (Oh my mother)! What did my father, the king who was truly valiant, who was knower of Dharma, who was ever steadfast in Dharma, who was a man of vows, say (on his death bed).

❍ ❍ ❍

३५. पश्चिमं साधु संदेशमिच्छामि श्रोतुमात्मनः ।
इति पृष्टा यथातत्त्वं कैकेयी वाक्यमब्रवीत् ।।

35. I desire to hear his last (wish and) command to me, clearly. When asked thus, Kaikeyi said these words, just as it happened.

❍ ❍ ❍

३६. रामेति राजा विलपन्हा सीते लक्ष्मणेति च ।
स महात्मा परं लोकं गतो गतिमतां वरः ।।

36. The foremost amongst men of conduct, this great soul king went to the other world (of heaven) wailing: Ha Raama! Ha Seetha! Ha Lakshmana!

❍ ❍ ❍

३७. इमां तु पश्चिमां वाचं व्याजहार पिता तव ।
कालधर्मपरिक्षिप्तः पाशैरिव महागजः ।।

37. Like a great elephant bound by ropes, your father who was bound by the eternal law of time, (Death), said these words finally (as his last words).

❍ ❍ ❍

३८. सिद्धार्थास्तु नरा राममागतं सीतया सह ।
लक्ष्मणं च महाबाहुं द्रक्ष्यन्ति पुनरागतम् ॥

38. Only accomplished (and fortunate) men will see Raama again, returning with Seetha and also the mighty limbed Lakshmana returning (back).

❍ ❍ ❍

३९. तच्छ्रुत्वा विषसादैव द्वितीयाप्रियशंसनात् ।
विषण्णवदनो भूत्वा भूयः पप्रच्छ मातरम् ॥

39. As soon as he heard this (from his mother Kaikeyi), (Bharatha) sank down; Hearing this second disquieting announcement, he asked his mother again, his face became (totally) downcast.

❍ ❍ ❍

४०. क्व चेदानीं स धर्मात्मा कौसल्यानन्दवर्धनः ।
लक्ष्मणेन सह भ्रात्रा सीतया च समागतः ॥

40. Where is this noble soul man of Dharma, (this, my brother Raama) who increases the joy of (his mother) Kowsalya, now? Accompanied by brother Lakshmana and Seetha where (have they gone)?

❍ ❍ ❍

४१. तथा पृष्टा यथातत्त्वमाख्यातुमुपचक्रमे ।
माताऽस्य सुमहद्वाक्यं विप्रियं प्रियशङ्कया ॥

41. Being asked thus, his mother (Kaikeyi) began to narrate all that happened, exactly, considering the most unpleasant news as though it was good (for her son Bharatha).

❍ ❍ ❍

४२. स हि राजसुतः पुत्र चीरवासा महावनम् ।
दण्डकान्सह वैदेह्या लक्ष्मणानुचरो गतः ॥

42. Oh (Bharatha my) Son! (Raama) the son of the king has

gone away to the forest of Dhandaka along with (Seetha the) Vaidhehi, followed by Lakshmana, wearing dress of bark.

❍ ❍ ❍

४३. तच्छ्रुत्वा भरतस्त्रस्तो भ्रातुश्चारित्रशङ्कया ।
स्वस्य वंशस्य माहात्म्यात्प्रष्टुं समुपचक्रमे ॥

43. When he heard this, Bharatha entertaining fear about the conduct of his brother (Raama) shuddered and began to ask her (further) for the sake of honour and greatness of his family.

(Bharatha is shocked that Raama had gone away to forest. Only great sinners are offered punishment of exile. Bharatha's first reaction to this news, is one of bewilderment. For what crime Raama had to go.)

❍ ❍ ❍

४४. कच्चिन्न ब्राह्मणधनं हृतं रामेण कस्यचित् ।
कच्चिन्नाढ्यो दरिद्रो वा तेनापापो विहिंसितः ॥

44. (Bharatha questions his mother Kaikeyi as to why Raama had to go)... I trust some Braamin's wealth was not snatched away by Raama. I hope no sinless man, poor or rich, was harmed by (Raama) in any way.

❍ ❍ ❍

४५. कच्चिन्न परदारान्वा राजपुत्रोऽभिमन्यते ।
कस्मात्स दण्डकारण्ये भ्रूणहेव विवासितः ॥

45. Or perhaps, this (Raama) the son of the king, has not desired (considered in his mind) another's wife. I hope. For what reason has he been exiled to Dhandaka forest like one who kills an embryo (of an expectant mother).

❍ ❍ ❍

४६. अथास्य चपला माता तत्स्वकर्म यथातथम् ।
तेनैव स्त्रीस्वभावेन व्याहर्तुमुपचक्रमे ॥

46. (Bharatha wonders: I hope Raama has not committed such sins) Then, his thoughtless mother (Kaikeyi), with the typical nature of a (ordinary) woman, began to tell about her own deed, exactly.

❍ ❍ ❍

४७. एवमुक्ता तु कैकेयीं भरतेन महात्मना ।
उवाच वचनं हृष्टा मूढा पण्डितमानिनी ॥

47. When told thus by the great soul Bharatha, (this Kaikeyi) who considered herself a Pundit ("Know all"), this foolish Kaikeyi said these words happily:

❍ ❍ ❍

४८. न ब्राह्मणधनं किञ्चिद्हृत्वं रामेण कस्यचित् ।
कश्चिन्नाढ्यो दरिद्रो वा तेनापापो विहिंसितः ॥

48. No Braamin's wealth was snatched away by Raama: Nor any sinless man, poor or rich, was harmed by him.

❍ ❍ ❍

४९. न रामः परदारान् स्म चक्षुर्भ्यामपि पश्यति ॥

49. And Raama never cast his eye on any (other) woman.

❍ ❍ ❍

५०. मया तु पुत्र श्रुत्वैव रामस्यैवाभिषेचनम् ।
याचितस्ते पिता राज्यं रामस्य च विवासनम् ॥

50. Oh (my) son! Hearing about Raama's (forthcoming) coronation, your father was begged by me, for (the offer of) Kingdom to you and exile for Raama.

❍ ❍ ❍

५१. स स्ववृत्तिं समास्थाय पिता ते तत्तथाऽकरोत् ।
रामश्च सहसौमित्रिः प्रोषितः सह सीतया ॥

51. To fulfill his own commitment (of the boons offered to me long ago), this, your father, did this (as per my

demands). And (so) Raama along with Seetha and (Lakshmana) the son of Sumithra was exiled.

❍ ❍ ❍

५२. तमपश्यन्प्रियं पुत्रं महीपालो महायशाः ।
पुत्रशोकपरिद्यूनः पञ्चत्वमुपपेदिवान् ।।

52. The most famous ruler of earth, (your father Dhascharatha), unable to see (and live without) his beloved son (Raama), obtained death due to pangs of separation from his son.

❍ ❍ ❍

५३. त्वया त्विदानीं धर्मज्ञ राजत्वमवलम्ब्यताम् ।
त्वत्कृते हि मया सर्वमिदमेवंविधं कृतम् ।।

53. Oh (my son Bharatha the) Knower of Dharma ! May the rule of kingdom be "Held" (taken over), by you now. All this was done by me for your sake, and in such a way.

❍ ❍ ❍

५४. मा शोकं मा च सन्तापं धैर्यमाश्रय पुत्रक ।
त्वदधीना हि नगरी राज्यं चैतदनामयम् ।।

54. Oh son! Do not grieve; Do not torment yourself; Take on courage; The city is yours; Likewise this salubrious kingdom.

❍ ❍ ❍

५५. तत्पुत्र शीघ्रं विधिना विधिज्ञै
र्वसिष्ठमुख्यैः सहितो द्विजेन्द्रैः ।
सङ्काल्य राजानमदीनसत्त्व
मात्मानमुर्व्यामभिषेचयस्व ।।

55. Oh (my) son! Therefore, (assisted by and) along with foremost braamins, with Vasishta as their chief, and along with men who are experts in norms (of rituals), after enjoining (your dead father) the King (with his

forefathers) as per custom (by doing all, the last rites etc.), then you soon crown yourself over this extensive (kingdom). You are most noble, possessing unimpaired goodness.

❍ ❍ ❍

Chapter 73

Bharatha Censures his Mother Kaikeyi

१. कैकेय्याऽप्येवमुक्तस्तु भरतो राघवानुजः ।
कर्णौ कराभ्यां प्रच्छाद्य पपात धरणीतले ॥

1. Although told by Kaikeyi thus, Bharatha the brother of (Raama) the Raaghava, at once, closed his ears with (palm of his) hands and fell down on earth, (Unable to 'swallow' this gruesome deed of his mother Kaikeyi).

❍ ❍ ❍

२. हा राम नाथेति तदा विलप्य करुणं बहु ।
मुहूर्तमिव निस्संज्ञस्संज्ञावानिदमब्रवीत् ॥

2. For one full Muhoortha (48 minutes), he was unconscious; Regaining consciousness, he wailed most pitiably: Ha Raama! Oh my lord! Then (after some time) he said these (words).

❍ ❍ ❍

३. हतोऽस्मि राजा निहतो हतो लोकश्च दुर्मते ।
किमिदं शिक्षितं येन कस्य कार्यं त्वया कृतम् ॥

3. I am ruined; The King is 'killed'; The World is destroyed. Oh wicked (woman)! What is all this! By whom were you advised. Whose 'work' was done by you. (Who instigated you).

❍ ❍ ❍

४. राजानं प्रेतभावस्थं कृत्वा रामं च तापसम् ।
राज्यमात्रफलं भोक्तुमनुतिष्ठसि दुर्मते ॥

4. Oh wicked woman! You have carried out (all this) for mere enjoyment of fruits of the kingdom by making the king a dead body and making Raama, a man of penance (in forest).

❍ ❍ ❍

५. रामप्रस्थापिकायाश्च पतिघ्न्याश्च तवोदरे ।
दश मासा मया नीता हा लोके निन्दितोऽस्म्यहम् ॥

5. Ah! (Shame upon me that) Ten months was spent by me in your womb; (In you) who sent away Raama on exile and who killed her husband. Ha! I stand condemned in the world.

❍ ❍ ❍

६. कण्ठेऽवसज्य वा पाशं विषं पीत्वाऽथवाऽधमे ।
त्यज प्राणांश्च दुर्मेधे जलमग्निं प्रविश्य वा ॥

6. Oh sinful stupid woman! Give up your life. Either by tying a rope around your neck or by drinking poison or enter fire or water.

❍ ❍ ❍

७. त्वामद्य निहनिष्यामि नो चेद्द्रुह्यामि च स्वयम् ।
राघवस्यानुजो भ्राता भरतो मातृहा इति ॥

7. I would kill you (myself) right now, if I do not cause harm to Raama (as then people will talk about Raama thus), that his younger brother Bharatha is a killer of his own mother!

❍ ❍ ❍

८. एवं परुषमुक्त्वा तु निर्दहन्निव चक्षुषा ।
निरीक्षमाणे भरते कैकेयी वाक्यमब्रवीत् ॥

8. After saying such cruel words, (and appearing) as if he

would 'burn' her up with his eyes, Bharatha stared at her; And Kaikeyi addressed these words.

❍ ❍ ❍

९. किं मयाऽपकृतं तेऽद्य गर्हसे मां मुहुर्मुहुः ।
प्रसूय वर्धयित्वा त्वां राज्यस्थं द्रष्टुमुत्सुकाम् ।।

9. Having given birth to you and brought you up, you are constantly reproaching me who desires to see you king: What harm has been done by me to you?

❍ ❍ ❍

१०. ते पिता स्वर्गतो राजा भ्रातरौ च विवासितौ ।
बहुना किं प्रलापेन कुरु राज्यं यथासुखम् ।।

10. Your father the king has gone to heaven; Your two brothers (Raama and Lakshmana) are exiled. What is the use of all this great prattle You must take over the kingdom with pleasure, (agreeably).

❍ ❍ ❍

११. श्रुत्वा तु पितरं वृत्तं भ्रातरौ च विवासितौ ।
भरतो दुःखसन्तप्त इदं वचनमब्रवीत् ।।

11. And Bharatha who heard of his father's death and of his brother's exile, said these words, being terribly tormented by sorrow.

❍ ❍ ❍

१२. किं नु कार्यं हतस्येह मम राज्येन शोचतः ।
विहीनस्याथ पित्रा च भ्रात्रा पितृसमेन च ।।

12. What purpose will be served for me with this kingdom in this world, when I am in grief, with my father 'killed' and with my brother (Raama) who is equal to my father, abandoned.

❍ ❍ ❍

१३. दुःखे मे दुःखमकरोर्व्रणे क्षारमिवादधाः ।।

13. You (heaped) sorrow upon sorrow. You put salt on my wound.

❍ ❍ ❍

१४. कुलस्य त्वमभावाय कालरात्रिरिवागता ॥

14. You came (into this world) for the destruction of the family of Ikshwaaku family, like night before deluge (Pralaya).

❍ ❍ ❍

१५. अङ्गारमुपगूह्य स्म पिता मे नावबुद्धवान् ॥

15. My father did not realise that he was "hugging" hot charcoal.

❍ ❍ ❍

१६. मृत्युमापादितो राजा त्वया मे पापदर्शिनि ।
सुखं परिहृतं मोहात्कुलेऽस्मिन्कुलपांसिनि ॥

16. Oh malevolent (woman)! The king was led to his death by you. Oh destroyer of the race! Because of (your greed and) passion, all happiness was taken out of the family.

❍ ❍ ❍

१७. त्वां प्राप्य हि पिता मेऽद्य सत्यसंधो महायशाः ।
तीव्रदुःखाभिसंतप्तो वृत्तो दशरथो नृपः ॥

17. My father, the most famous king Dhascharatha the man of Truth, died, tormented by terrific suffering, having accepted you (as his wife).

❍ ❍ ❍

१८. विनाशितो महाराजः पिता मे धर्मवत्सलः ।
कस्मात्प्रव्राजितो रामः कस्मादेव वनं गतः ॥

18. How come (why is it) my father the great king who was a devotee of Dharma was destroyed (by you). On what account this Raama also was exiled and gone away to forest.

❍ ❍ ❍

१९. कौसल्या च सुमित्रा च पुत्रशोकाभिपीडिते ।
दुष्करं यदि जीवेतां प्राप्य त्वां जननीं मम ।।

19. It will indeed be extraordinary if Kowsalya and Sumithra live on with you, my mother, when they are tormented by grief over their sons (Raama and Lakshmana).

❍ ❍ ❍

२०. ननु त्वार्योऽपि धर्मात्मा त्वयि वृत्तिमनुत्तमाम् ।
वर्तते गुरुवृत्तिज्ञो यथा मातरि वर्तते ।।

20. (Is it not a fact) that the great soul man of Dharma, (this Raama) who knows how to conduct himself before elders, who is an Aryan (noble), behaves himself with foremost conduct towards you, just like he behaves to his (own) mother (Kowsalya).

❍ ❍ ❍

२१. यथा ज्येष्ठा हि मे माता कौसल्या दीर्घदर्शिनी ।
त्वयि धर्मं समास्थाय भगिन्यामिव वर्तते ।।

21. Indeed, like wise, my elder (step) mother Kowsalya who has foresight (and is sagacious), has (always) behaved towards you like a sister, reposing in Dharma.

❍ ❍ ❍

२२. तस्याः पुत्रं कृतात्मानं चीरवल्कलवाससम् ।
प्रस्थाप्य वनवासाय कथं पापे न शोचसि ।।

22. Oh evil monger! How come you are not lamenting (burning inside) after sending her most disciplined son to the forest dressed up in (forest attire of) bark (material) and deer skin.

❍ ❍ ❍

२३. अपापदर्शनं शूरं कृतात्मानं यशस्विनम् ।
प्रव्राज्य चीरवसनं किं नु पश्यसि कारणम् ।।

23. What possible reason do you see (and what excuse you have) in sending (Raama) whose very sight removes sin, who is brave, who is most famous, who is self disciplined, dressed up in bark.

❍ ❍ ❍

२४. लुब्धाया विदितो मन्ये न तेऽहं राघवं प्रति ।
तथा ह्यनर्थोराज्यार्थं त्वयाऽऽनीतो महानयम् ।।

24. Greedy as you are, I think, I have not been understood by you properly (as to my relationship) with (Raama the) Raaghava. Therefore, this great purposeless (evil) was caused by you for (mere) sake of (snatching) the kingdom (for yourself through me).

❍ ❍ ❍

२५. अहं हि पुरुषव्याघ्रावपश्यन्रामलक्ष्मणौ ।
केन शक्तिप्रभावेण राज्यं रक्षितुमुत्सहे ।।

25. Without seeing (without support of) Raama and Lakshmana the two 'tigers' amongst men, with what strength of power can I bear to rule and protect this kingdom.

❍ ❍ ❍

२६. तं हि नित्यं महाराजो बलवन्तं महाबलः ।
अपाश्रितोऽभूद्धर्मात्मा मेरुर्मेरुवनं यथा ।।

26. (Even) the mightily strong king, the noble soul man of Dharma, (my father) depended upon this strong (Raama) always, like Meru mountain resting with Meru forests.

❍ ❍ ❍

२७. सोऽहं कथमिमं भारं महाधुर्यसमुद्धृतम् ।
दम्यो धुरमिवासाद्य वहेयं केन चौजसा ।।

27. Taking over this burden, this great burden (of the kingdom) held by great men of stature, with what

strength, will I conduct (the administration), timid as I am.

○ ○ ○

२८. अथवा मे भवेच्छक्तिर्योगैर्बुद्धिबलेन वा ।
सकामां न करिष्यामि त्वामहं पुत्रगर्द्धिनीम् ।।

28. If perchance, there is found in me that strength by (some) method and power of judgement, I will not see you, who are greedy for the sake of your son, fulfilling your desire (of taking over)........ (Bharatha tells his mother that even if he is as capable as his brother Raama, he will not take over the kingdom and satisfy her lust for power).

○ ○ ○

२९. न मे विकाङ्क्षा जायेत त्यक्तुं त्वां पापनिश्चयाम् ।
यदि रामस्य नावेक्षा त्वयि स्यान्मातृवत्सदा ।।

29. If, for Raama, such (affection, regard and) consideration has not been there (for you) like towards his own mother, then (let me tell you) that there would be no lack of desire in me to (totally) abandon you who have determined to do evil.

(Bharatha says; because Raama treats you, my mother, as if you are his own, I have to have some regard for you. Otherwise I would have rejected you as my mother although you have given birth to me.)

○ ○ ○

३०. उत्पन्ना तु कथं बुद्धिस्तवेयं पापदर्शिनि ।
साधुचारित्रविभ्रष्टे पूर्वेषां नो विगर्हिता ।।

30. Oh (woman) who has strayed from the conduct of the good! Oh (woman) who sees and does evil! How has this (evil) thought that causes censure by our elders, arisen?

३१. अस्मिन्कुले हि पूर्वेषां ज्येष्ठो राज्येऽभिषिच्यते ।
अपरे भ्रातरस्तस्मिन्प्रवर्तन्ते समाहिताः ।।

31. (Customarily), In our race (of Ikshwaaku-s), only the eldest is anointed in our forefather's kingdom (of ours) And other brothers serve him with devotion.

❍ ❍ ❍

३२. न हि मन्ये नृशंसे त्वं राजधर्ममवेक्षसे ।
गतिं वा न विजानासि राजवृत्तस्य शाश्वतीम् ।।

32. Oh mischievous woman! You do not respect royal Dharma. And I think you do not understand the royal norms and eternal practices.

❍ ❍ ❍

३३. सततं राजवृत्ते हि ज्येष्ठो राज्येऽभिषिच्यते ।
राज्ञामेतत्समं तत्स्यादिक्ष्वाकूणां विशेषतः ।।

33. As per royal norms, the eldest alone is anointed (to succeed throne): This is common (practice).amongst kings. And for (us) the Ikshwaaku-s, it is particularly so.

❍ ❍ ❍

३४. तेषां धर्मैकरक्षाणां कुलचारित्रशोभिनाम् ।
अद्य चारित्रशौण्डीर्यं त्वां प्राप्य विनिवर्तितम् ।।

34. (Alas): The pride and glory by the conduct of those whose sole aim was in protecting Dharma, (of those) who shone by noble conduct of their race* (of Ikshwaaku-s),... all that has gone topsy turvy at your hands.

❍ ❍ ❍

३५. तवापि सुमहाभागा जनेन्द्राः कुलपूर्वगाः ।
बुद्धेर्मोहः कथमयं संभूतस्त्वयि गर्हितः ।।

35. And the forefathers of your (own) family were also

most illustrious kings: Then, how come this (stupidity and) infatuation that will cause revulsion in mind, has come about (in you)?

❍ ❍ ❍

३६. न तु कामं करिष्यामि तवाहं पापनिश्चये ।
यया व्यसनमारब्धं जीवितान्तकरं मम ॥

36. Oh (woman) who is determined to do evil! I will never fulfill the desire of yours by whom all this suffering that will take away (even) my life was caused.

❍ ❍ ❍

३७. एष त्विदानीमेवाहमप्रियार्थं तवानघम् ।
निवर्तयिष्यामि वनाद्भ्रातरं स्वजनप्रियम् ॥

37. I will now itself bring back this sinless brother (Raama) who is beloved of all his folks, from the forest, disagreeable though it may be to you.

❍ ❍ ❍

३८. निवर्तयित्वा रामं च तस्याहं दीप्ततेजसः ।
दासभूतो भविष्यामि सुस्थितेनान्तरात्मना ॥

38. Bringing back Raama, I will become the devoted servant of this (Raama) who possesses 'burning' brilliance, fully resolved with all my heart.

❍ ❍ ❍

३९. इत्येवमुक्त्वा भरतो महात्मा
प्रियेतरैर्वाक्यगणैस्तुदंस्ताम् ।
शोकातुरश्चापि जनाद भूयः
सिंहो यथा पर्वतगह्वरस्थः ॥

39. Saying thus and vexing her with many unpalatable words, this great soul Bharatha, roared like a lion from the cave of mountain, although he was very much afflicted by grief.

❍ ❍ ❍

Chapter 74

(Bharatha) Condemns (His Mother) Kaikeyi

(Bharatha cannot contain himself: He is overpowered by grief and wrath. He abuses his mother Kaikeyi for her dastardly deed.)

❍ ❍ ❍

१. तां तथा गर्हयित्वा तु मातरं भरतस्तदा ।
रोषेण महताऽऽविष्टः पुनरेवाब्रवीद्वचः ॥

1. Censuring his mother thus, Bharatha who became seized with even greater wrath, spoke again, with these words.

❍ ❍ ❍

२. राज्याद्भ्रंशस्व कैकेयि नृशंसे दुष्टचारिणि ।
परित्यक्ता च धर्मेण मा मृतं रुदती भव ॥

2. Oh mischievous, evil mongering Kaikeyi! (Get Lost): Disappear from the kingdom! Consider me as dead. Abandoned by Dharma, you remain in (lament) crying (always).

❍ ❍ ❍

३. किंनु तेऽदूषयद्राजा रामो वा भृशधार्मिकः ।
ययोर्मृत्युर्विवासश्च त्वत्कृते तुल्यमागतौ ॥

3. What wrong has this great man of Dharma or the king done to you? By you (and by your cruel action), Death and Exile happened simultaneously.

❍ ❍ ❍

४. भ्रूणहत्यामसि प्राप्ता कुलस्यास्य विनाशनात् ।
कैकेयि नरकं गच्छ मा च भर्तुः सलोकताम् ॥

4. Oh Kaikeyi! Because of the harm done to this family

(by you), you have obtained 'the sin of killing a pregnant woman'.Go to hell! You will never be with your husband (in heaven).

(Two sins of killing are committed when a pregnant woman is killed; likewise, two sins were committed by Kaikeyi.)

❍ ❍ ❍

५. यत्त्वया हीदृशं पापं कृतं घोरेण कर्मणा ।
सर्वलोकप्रियं हित्वा ममाप्यापादितं भयम् ।।

5. Because of your gruesome deed, such a sin was committed by you. that you have lost the goodwill of all the world and fear was generated in me also.

❍ ❍ ❍

६. त्वत्कृते मे पिता वृत्तो रामश्चारण्यमाश्रितः ।
अयशो जीवलोके च त्वयाऽहं प्रतिपादितः ।।

6. By your action, my father died: And Raama has gone to forest. And I also have been disgraced in this world of living beings by you.

❍ ❍ ❍

७. मातृरूपे ममामित्रे नृशंसे राज्यकामुके ।
न तेऽहमभिभाष्योऽस्मि दुर्वृत्ते पतिघातिनि ।।

7. Oh mischievous enemy who has 'come' as my mother! Oh woman of evil conduct, obsessed with possession of kingdom! Oh killer of your husband! I will not speak to you (I will have nothing to do with you henceforth)

❍ ❍ ❍

८. कौसल्या च सुमित्रा च याश्चान्या मम मातरः ।
दुःखेन महताऽऽविष्टास्त्वां प्राप्य कुलदूषिणीम् ।।

8. My (step) mothers Kowsalya and Sumithra and all others are engulfed by great sorrow at your hands who has defiled, and who is a contaminator of our race.

❍ ❍ ❍

९. न त्वमश्वपतेः कन्या धर्मराजस्य धीमतः ।
राक्षसी तत्र जाताऽसि कुलप्रध्वंसिनी पितुः ।।

9. You are not the daughter of the wise king Aschwapathi, a king of Dharma. (Verily)You were born there (in your father's family) as a demoness to your father, to destroy his family (as well).

❍ ❍ ❍

१०. यत्त्वया धार्मिको रामो नित्यं सत्यपराक्रमः ।
वनं प्रस्थापितो दुःखात्पिता च त्रिदिवं गतः ।।

10. (I say this) Because, this man of Dharma, Raama, who is ever truly most valiant, was sent away to forest by you. and in (utter) sorrow, my father went to heaven.

❍ ❍ ❍

११. यत्प्रधानाऽसि तत्पापं मयि पित्रा विनाकृते ।
भ्रातृभ्यां च परित्यक्ते सर्वलोकस्य चाप्रिये ।।

11. As you are the originator, this sin of being separated from my father and the (sin of) abandonment of my brothers (Raama and Lakshmana) has befallen on me who is hated by all the world.

❍ ❍ ❍

१२. कौसल्यां धर्मसंयुक्तां वियुक्तां पापनिश्चये ।
कृत्वा कं प्राप्स्यसे त्वद्य लोकं निरयगामिनि ।।

12. Oh woman who is determined to do evil and who is (surely) going to hell! Making this Kowsalya who is endowed with Dharma (and devoted to Dharma), destitute, what world are you now going to obtain (for yourself)?

❍ ❍ ❍

१३. किं नावबुध्यसे क्रूरे नियतं बन्धुसंश्रयम् ।
ज्येष्ठं पितृसमं रामं कौसल्यायात्मसंभवम् ।।

13. Oh cruel (Kaikeyi)! Why have you not realised as an established fact that this Raama, the son born to Kowsalya, is Refuge for all the relatives and is as eminent as his father (equal to him).

❍ ❍ ❍

१४. अङ्गप्रत्यङ्गजः पुत्रो हृदयाच्चापि जायते ।
तस्मात्प्रियतमो मातुः प्रियत्वान्न तु बान्धवः ।।

14. A son born out of body and womb, is also born out of a (woman's) heart: Therefore he is most beloved of his mother. Merely being loved, one does not become a relative (or a son)!

(Poet Vaalmeeki remembers the old saying= Blood is thicker than water. However much I may love my step mother Kowsalya, as I am not born in her womb and only Raama was born in her womb, it is Raama that Kowsalya will miss most, not me, says Bharatha.)

❍ ❍ ❍

१५. अन्यदा किल धर्मज्ञा सुरभिः सुरसंमता ।
वहमानौ ददर्शोर्व्यां पुत्रौ विगतचेतसौ ।।

15. (Bharatha narrates an old story to his mother Kaikeyi, how, even for a celestial being, a 'Son' is dear to her heart and she cannot see the 'son' suffering. When that is so, how can Kowsalya bear Raama's suffering).

Indeed, there is this another (story of old); (The holy cow) Surabhi which knows Dharma and which is honoured by celestials, saw (from heaven), her two 'sons' (two bullocks) carrying (very heavy load) in the world, (burdened to such an extent, that they almost) lost their consciousness.

(Surabhi, as readers know from Baala Kaanda, is the First Cow. All the Cows, bullocks etc. in the world are her 'sons' and 'daughters'.)

❍ ❍ ❍

१६. तावर्धदिवसं श्रान्तौ पुत्रौ दृष्ट्वा महीतले ।
रुरोद पुत्रशोकेन बाष्पपर्याकुलेक्षणा ॥

16. Seeing these two 'sons' very tired at mid day on the earth (unable to bear the load), (this Surabhi, the holy cow) wept out grief over these 'sons', its eyes blurred by tears.

❍ ❍ ❍

१७. अधस्ताद्व्रजतस्तस्याः सुरराज्ञो महात्मनः ।
बिन्दवः पतिता गात्रे सूक्ष्माः सुरभिगन्धिनः ॥

17. Minute (tear) drops that were smelling sweet fell on the body of the great soul, Lord Indhra, when he was going along underneath this (holy cow in the sky).
(Surabhi is so holy that its tears are sweet smelling!)

❍ ❍ ❍

१८. इन्द्रोऽप्यश्रुनिपातं तं स्वगात्रे पुण्यगन्धिनम् ।
सुरभिं मन्यते दृष्ट्वा भूयसीं तां सुरेश्वरः ॥

18. When the lord of celestials Indhra saw this fall of tears on his body sweet smelling, he considered this (as falling from) the munificent Surabhi.

❍ ❍ ❍

१९. निरीक्षमाणः शक्रस्तां ददर्श सुरभिं स्थिताम् ।
आकाशे विष्ठितां दीनां रुदन्तीं भृशदुःखिताम् ॥

19. Looking up, this Schakra (Lord Indhra), saw this Surabhi, standing in the sky, immobile, crying miserably in sorrow.

❍ ❍ ❍

२०. तां दृष्ट्वा शोकसन्तप्तां वज्रपाणिर्यशस्विनीम् ।
इन्द्रः प्राञ्जलिरुद्विग्नः सुरराजोऽब्रवीद्वचः ॥

20. And seeing this most famous (Cow) tormented by grief, Indhra the wielder of the Vajra (thunderbolt), this

celestial lord, addressed her with his hands cupped in Anjali, somewhat frightened.

❍ ❍ ❍

२१. भयं कच्चिन्न चास्मासु कुतश्चिद्विद्यते महत् ।
कुतोनिमित्तः शोकस्ते ब्रूहि सर्वहितैषिणि ॥

21. Oh (Surabhi) who bestows good on every one! I hope there is no great fear (or danger), for 'us' (all) from anywhere. Therefore on what account this grief for you? Tell me.

❍ ❍ ❍

२२. एवमुक्ता तु सुरभिः सुरराजेन धीमता ।
प्रत्युवाच ततो धीरा वाक्यं वाक्यविशारदम् ॥

22. When told thus by this wise Lord Indhra, the gentle (cow) Surabhi replied with following proficient speech.

❍ ❍ ❍

२३. शान्तं पापं न वः किञ्चित्कुतश्चिदमराधिप ।
अहं तु मग्नौ शोचामि स्वपुत्रौ विषमे स्थितौ ॥

23. Oh lord of Amara (Oh celestial lord)! Nothing from any where for you. (There cannot be fear for you from anywhere). Sin is tranquilized (at your hands). (But) It is about my two 'sons' who are in a state submerged by suffering, that I am grieving about.

❍ ❍ ❍

२४. एतौ दृष्ट्वा कृशौ दीनौ सूर्यरश्मिप्रतापितौ ।
वध्यमानौ बलीवर्दौ कर्षकेण सुराधिप ॥

24. Oh lord of celestials! I observed (from heaven) these two bullocks being tortured by the farmer (the ploughman), and being 'burnt' up by the rays of the sun, emaciated, feeble.

❍ ❍ ❍

२५. मम कायात्प्रसूतौ हि दुःखितौ भारपीडितौ ।
यौ दृष्ट्वा परितप्येऽहं नास्ति पुत्रसमः प्रियः ।।

25. None is equal to a son in (the matter of) Love (and affection): Therefore, seeing these two 'Born' out of my body, tormented by the (heavy) load and suffering (heat and thirst), I am tormented.

❍ ❍ ❍

२६. यस्याः पुत्रसहस्रैस्तु कृत्स्नं व्याप्तमिदं जगत् ।
तां दृष्ट्वा रुदतीं शक्रो न सुतान्मन्यते परम् ।।

26. Seeing her by whom the entire world is pervaded (and filled) with thousands and (thousands of) her own 'sons' (these creations) crying, (Indhra the) Schakra thought (and realised) that None Is Dearer Than One's Own Son.

(Mythologically, Surabhi the holy cow is the "creator' of all quadrupeds So these two Bullocks are her 'sons and Surabhi grieves.)

❍ ❍ ❍

२७. सदाऽप्रतिमवृत्ताया लोकधारणकाम्यया ।
श्रीमत्या गुणनित्यायाः स्वभावपरिवेषया ।।

२८. यस्याः पुत्रसहस्राणि साऽपि शोचति कामधुक् ।
किं पुनर्या विना रामं कौसल्या वर्तयिष्यति ।।

27 & 28.

(Bharatha, by this story tells how cruel Kaikeyi is to Kowsalya) Always of impeccable conduct; most resplendent; possessing eternal (noble) virtues; always desirous of sustaining the world; possessing natural disposition to serve and protect ....(Such a celestial Cow) the Kaamadhenu (which fulfills desires) Grieves (in spite of having) thousands of 'sons'. How can this Kowsalya survive without (her only son) Raama?

❍ ❍ ❍

२९. एकपुत्रा च साध्वी च विवत्सेयं त्वया कृता ।
तस्मात्त्वं सततं दुःखं प्रेत्य चेह च लप्स्यसे ॥

29. (Such an) Impeccable (lady Kowsalya) who has just one son, was made son-less by you (when you exiled Raama). Therefore, whether you remain here or die, you will always obtain suffering only. (You are a cursed woman)

❍ ❍ ❍

३०. अहं ह्यपचितिं भ्रातुः पितुश्च सकलामिमाम् ।
वर्धनं यशसश्चापि करिष्यामि न संशयः ॥

30. (But) I am going to do all these honours for my father and (do all) for increasing the glory and fame of my brother (Raama, by bringing him back at once). No doubt about it.

❍ ❍ ❍

३१. आनाययित्वा तनयं कौसल्याया महाद्युतिम् ।
स्वयमेव प्रवेक्ष्यामि वनं मुनिनिषेवितम् ॥

31. After bringing back the most majestic son of Kowsalya, I myself will enter (and go to) the forest inhabited by great sages.

❍ ❍ ❍

३२. न ह्यहं पापसङ्कल्पे पापे पापं त्वया कृतम् ।
शक्तो धारयितुं पौरैरश्रुकण्ठैर्निरीक्षितः ॥

32. Oh sinful (Kaikeyi) who has decided on doing evil! I cannot bear to be seen by citizens whose throats are choked by tears because of the sin committed by you.

❍ ❍ ❍

३३. सा त्वमग्निं प्रविश वा स्वयं वा विश दण्डकान् ।
रज्जुं बद्ध्वाऽथवा कण्ठे न हि तेऽन्यत्परायणम् ॥

33. Such as you are, Jump Into Fire: Or (Die) By Tightening

a Rope Around Your Neck: Or Enter the Dhandaka Forest on your own. There is no other fate for you (No other resort for you).

❍ ❍ ❍

३४. अहमप्यवनिं प्राप्ते रामे सत्यपराक्रमे ।
कृतकृत्यो भविष्यामि विप्रवासितकल्मषः ।।

34. When the truly valiant Raama accepts this 'Earth' (Rule of kingdom), then (only) I will become accomplished with moral stain and sin gone (from me).

❍ ❍ ❍

३५. इति नाग इवारण्ये तोमराङ्कुशचोदितः ।
पपात भुवि संक्रुद्धो निःश्वसन्निव पन्नगः ।।

35. Thus (saying), he fell down on the floor, hissing like an angry cobra, like an elephant in the forest goaded and pierced by a lance and by (elephant driver's) hook.

❍ ❍ ❍

३६. संरक्तनेत्रः शिथिलाम्बरस्तदा
विधूतसर्वाभरणः परन्तपः ।
बभूव भूमौ पतितो नृपात्मजः
शचीपतेः केतुरिवोत्सवक्षये ।।

36. Falling down on earth, this (Bharatha) the son of king and tormentor of enemies, appeared like the mast of (Indhra) the husband of Sachi, at the end of a Jubilee celebration. His eyes were red; His dress slackened and crumpled; All his ornaments were scattered (on the floor).

❍ ❍ ❍

Chapter 75

Bharatha Vows (to Bring Back Raama)

(Bharatha will not accept the kingdom: Will bring back Raama from forest. Kaikeyi's plans to install her son misfires.)

❍ ❍ ❍

१. दीर्घकालात्समुत्थाय संज्ञां लब्ध्वा च वीर्यवान् ।
नेत्राभ्यामश्रुपूर्णाभ्यां दीनामुद्वीक्ष्य मातरम् ।।
सोऽमात्यमध्ये भरतो जननीमभ्यकुत्सयत् ।।

1. Regaining his consciousness after quite sometime, the brave Bharatha got up and looked at his down cast mother with his eyes that were full with tears. He reviled his mother (again) in front of ministers.

❍ ❍ ❍

२. राज्यं न कामये जातु मन्त्रये नापि मातरम् ।
अभिषेकं न जानामि योऽभूद्राज्ञा समीक्षितः ।।

2. I never desired the kingdom. Nor did I talk about this with my mother. I did not (even) know about the coronation (of Raama) contemplated by the king.

❍ ❍ ❍

३. विप्रकृष्टे ह्यहं देशे शत्रुघ्नसहितोऽवसम् ।।

3. (As you are aware) I was living in far away land along with Schathrugna.

❍ ❍ ❍

४. वनवासं न जानामि रामस्याहं महात्मनः ।
विवासनं च सौमित्रेः सीतायाश्च यथाऽभवत् ।।

4. I was not aware of the exile of Raama, (Lakshmana) the

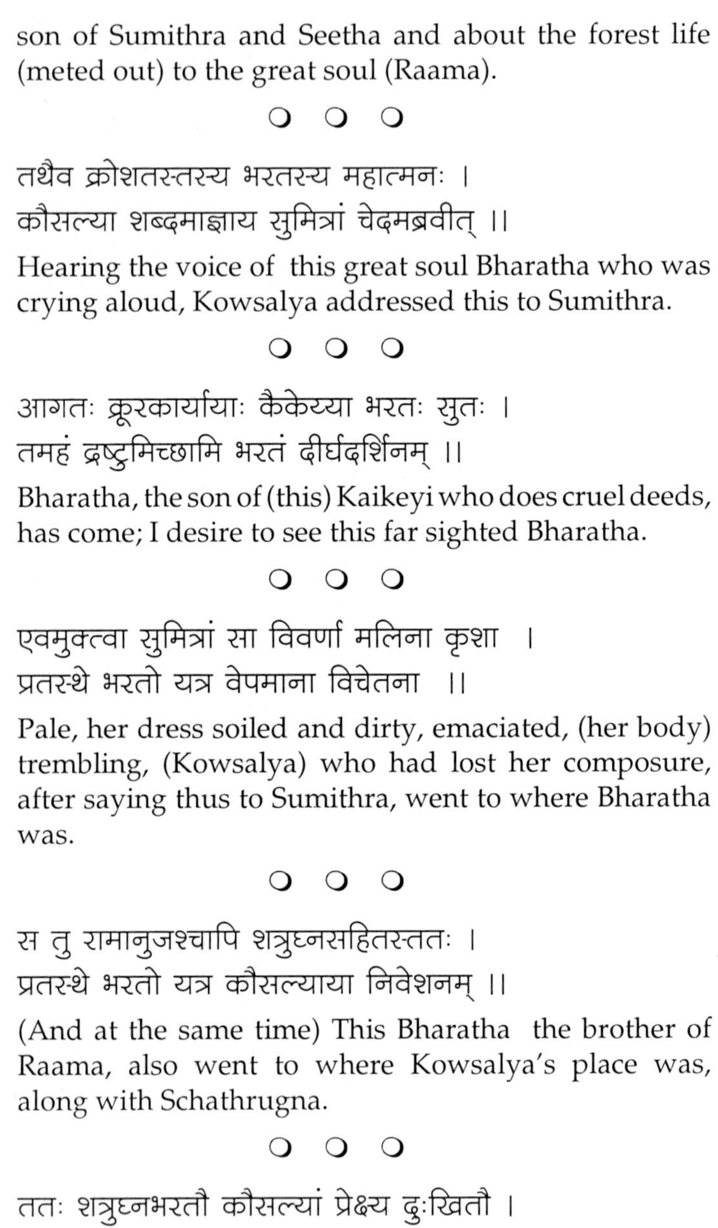

son of Sumithra and Seetha and about the forest life (meted out) to the great soul (Raama).

❍ ❍ ❍

५. तथैव क्रोशतस्तस्य भरतस्य महात्मनः ।
कौसल्या शब्दमाज्ञाय सुमित्रां चेदमब्रवीत् ।।

5. Hearing the voice of this great soul Bharatha who was crying aloud, Kowsalya addressed this to Sumithra.

❍ ❍ ❍

६. आगतः क्रूरकार्यायाः कैकेय्या भरतः सुतः ।
तमहं द्रष्टुमिच्छामि भरतं दीर्घदर्शिनम् ।।

6. Bharatha, the son of (this) Kaikeyi who does cruel deeds, has come; I desire to see this far sighted Bharatha.

❍ ❍ ❍

७. एवमुक्त्वा सुमित्रां सा विवर्णा मलिना कृशा ।
प्रतस्थे भरतो यत्र वेपमाना विचेतना ।।

7. Pale, her dress soiled and dirty, emaciated, (her body) trembling, (Kowsalya) who had lost her composure, after saying thus to Sumithra, went to where Bharatha was.

❍ ❍ ❍

८. स तु रामानुजश्चापि शत्रुघ्नसहितस्ततः ।
प्रतस्थे भरतो यत्र कौसल्याया निवेशनम् ।।

8. (And at the same time) This Bharatha the brother of Raama, also went to where Kowsalya's place was, along with Schathrugna.

❍ ❍ ❍

९. ततः शत्रुघ्नभरतौ कौसल्यां प्रेक्ष्य दुःखितौ ।
पर्यष्वजेतां दुःखार्तां पतितां नष्टचेतनाम् ।।
रुदन्तौ रुदतीं दुःखात्समेत्यार्यां मनस्विनीम् ।।

9. Then Bharatha and Schathrugna who were crying in great sorrow, met and saw the Aryan lady (Kowsalya) who was noble and intelligent, who was crying, and who had lost her senses (composure) They hugged her.

❍ ❍ ❍

१०. भरतं प्रत्युवाचेदं कौसल्या भृशदुःखिता ॥

10. Kowsalya who was in great anguish, addressed this Bharatha thus: (Kowsalya is rather cruel on the sinless Bharatha).

❍ ❍ ❍

११. इदं ते राज्यकामस्य राज्यं प्राप्तमकण्टकम् ।
संप्राप्तं बत कैकेय्या शीघ्रं क्रूरेण कर्मणा ॥

11. By the cruel (scheming) deed of Kaikeyi, this kingdom was given to you who was greedy to possess this kingdom. And it was obtained by you very quickly, without any hindrance to you. Ah!

❍ ❍ ❍

१२. प्रस्थाप्य चीरवसनं पुत्रं मे वनवासिनम् ।
कैकेयी कं गुणं तत्र पश्यति क्रूरदर्शिनी ॥

12. What virtue does this evil eyed Kaikeyi see in this, in sending away my son (Raama) to forest in (forest attire of) bark.

❍ ❍ ❍

१३. क्षिप्रं मामपि कैकेयी प्रस्थापयितुमर्हति ।
हिरण्यनाभो यत्रास्ते सुतो मे सुमहायशाः ॥

13. Kaikeyi should at once send me also to where my most famous son whose countenance shines like pure gold, is ......

❍ ❍ ❍

१४. अथवा स्वयमेवाहं सुमित्रानुचरा सुखम् ।
अग्निहोत्रं पुरस्कृत्य प्रस्थास्ये यत्र राघवः ।।

14. If not, I myself, along with Sumithra, will willingly (happily) go to where Raama is, taking with me fire (Ritual materials).

(Kowsalya is a very religious woman!)

❍ ❍ ❍

१५. कामं वा स्वयमेवाद्य तत्र मां नेतुमर्हसि ।
यत्रासौ पुरुषव्याघ्रः पुत्रो मे तप्यते तपः ।।

15. Or rather, You yourself should take me now to where my son, this (Raama) the 'tiger' of men is doing penance (in forest).

❍ ❍ ❍

१६. इदं हि तव विस्तीर्णं धनधान्यसमाचितम् ।
हस्त्यश्वरथसंपूर्णं राज्यं निर्यातितं तया ।।

16. This extensive (mighty) kingdom which is abundant with wealth, grains, and full with horses, elephants, chariots, was handed out to you by her (by your mother in a platter!)

❍ ❍ ❍

१७. इत्यादि बहुभिर्वाक्यैः क्रूरैः संभर्त्सितोऽनघः ।
विव्यथे भरतोऽतीव व्रणे तुद्येव सूचिना ।।

17. (Thus Kowsalya spoke to Bharatha with such cruel words) Like needle on one's wound, this sinless Bharatha was terribly distressed as he was reviled thus with many cruel words.

❍ ❍ ❍

१८. पपात चरणौ तस्यास्तदा संभ्रान्तचेतनः ।
विलप्य बहुधाऽसंज्ञो लब्धसंज्ञस्ततः स्थितः ।।

18. With his mind agitated, wailing in many ways, he fell

down at her feet, (almost) unconscious; Then regaining his consciousness, he (got up and) stood there.

❍ ❍ ❍

१९. एवं विलपमानां तां प्राञ्जलिर्भरतस्तदा ।
कौसल्यां प्रत्युवाचेदं शोकैर्बहुभिरावृताम् ।।

19. With folded arms in Anjali, Bharatha addressed Kowsalya who was lamenting thus being engulfed by grief greatly.

❍ ❍ ❍

२०. आर्येकस्मादजानन्तं गर्हसे मामकिल्बिषम् ।
विपुला च मम प्रीतिं स्थिरां जानासि राघवे ।।

20. Oh Aryan (Lady Kowsalya) ! Why do you censure me who is sinless (in this matter), ignorant as I am: You know (very well) of my great strong attachment (and love) towards (Raama the) Raaghava.

❍ ❍ ❍

(From stanzas 21 to 57, Poet Vaalmeeki, through the lips of Bharatha enumerates Sins that are accursed.. When his step mother suspects Bharatha's hand in the Exile of Raama, the innocent Bharatha is so dejected that he tells Kowsalya = Let the basest of sins afflict me = . And he enumerates what he considers vilest of sins: That is, if I had connived with my mother Kaikeyi to get kingdom and sending Raama away, let these sins afflict me)

२१. कृता शास्त्रानुगा बुद्धिर्मा भूत्तस्य कदाचन ।
सत्यसन्धः सतां श्रेष्ठो यस्यार्योऽनुमते गतः ।।

21. By whose approbation this noble (Aryan), this truthful and foremost amongst the good, (this Raama) went away, may that man's (mind and) perceptions never be (considered proper), conforming to norms of Shaasthra-s.

❍ ❍ ❍

२२. प्रेष्यं पापीयसां यातु सूर्यं च प्रति मेहतु ।
हन्तु पादेन गां सुप्तां यस्यार्योऽनुमते गतः ।।

22. By whose approbation, this Aryan (noble Raama) went away, may he obtain slavery of the sinners; May he urinate before the Sun. May he kick a sleeping cow with his feet.

(Defecating in public is an offense; Abusing the docile cow is sin.)

❍ ❍ ❍

२३. परिपालयमानस्य राज्ञो भूतानि पुत्रवत् ।
ततस्तं द्रुह्यतां पापं यस्यार्योऽनुमते गतः ।।

23. By whose approbation this Aryan (noble Raama) went away, may a king who rules and protects his subjects like his own sons, be harmed by him viciously. (Harming a good king is a crime).

❍ ❍ ❍

२४. कारयित्वा महत्कर्म भर्ता भृत्यमनर्थकम् ।
अधर्मोयोऽस्य सोऽस्यास्तु यस्यायोऽनुमते गतः ।।

24. By whose approbation, this Aryan (noble Raama) went away, may such a sin which befalls on a master who, having extracted hard labour from his servants, refuses to pay him, afflict him.

(A worker is not a slave; Not settling his dues is great sin).

❍ ❍ ❍

२५. बलिषड्भागमुद्धृत्य नृपस्यारक्षतः प्रजाः ।
अधर्मोयोऽस्य सोऽस्यास्तु यस्यार्योऽनुमते गतः ।।

25. By whose approbation this noble (Aryan Raama) went away, may such a sin that befalls a king, who, having collected a sixth as Tax, does not protect his subjects, befall him.

(One must pay proper wages. and a king should not take more than a Sixth as Taxes. And he must govern well with this money.)

❍ ❍ ❍

२६. संश्रुत्य च तपस्विभ्यः सत्रे वै यज्ञदक्षिणाम् ।
तां विप्रलपतां पापं यस्यार्योऽनुमते गतः ।।

26. By whose approbation the noble (Raama) went away, may he (reap the consequence of) one who, sinfully, ('debates') and cheats to pay the promised Fees (for services rendered) in a Yaaga ceremony to the priests, in (such) sacrificial ceremonies.

(Breach of contract is a sin: Refusing to pay the agreed fees to priests under some pretext is a great sin).

❍ ❍ ❍

२७. हस्त्यश्वरथसंबाधे युद्धे शस्त्रसमाकुले ।
मा स्म कार्षीत्सतां धर्मं यस्यार्योऽनुमते गतः ।।

27. By whose approbation, the noble (Raama) went away, may he never attain the Dharma (the status) of the good (Warriors) during war (fought with full complement) of horses, elephants, chariots, armaments, weaponry.

❍ ❍ ❍

२८. उपदिष्टं सुसूक्ष्मार्थं शास्त्रं यत्नेन धीमता ।
स नाशयतु दुष्टात्मा यस्यार्योऽनुमते गतः ।।

28. By whose approbation, the noble (Raama) went away, may that wicked man deny the subtle meaning of the holy Texts expounded by wise men with great effort (and diligence).

(An Indian can deny God: But he cannot deny holy Texts.: This is the basic difference between Religion of India-Bhaarath and other religions : Sanaathana Dharma is the religion of India.)

❍ ❍ ❍

२९. मा च तं व्यूढबाहृंसं चन्द्रभास्करतेजसम् ।
द्राक्षीद्राज्यस्थमासीनं यस्यार्योऽनुमते गतः ।।

29. By whose approbation this noble (Raama) went away, may he not see (and enjoy the sight) of this (Raama) who has the brilliancy of the Sun and Moon and who has large chest and hands.

(As Raama is incarnation of God Vishnu, one who is denied the sight of Raama, is verily a man of sin, says Bharatha, although he does not know that Raama is really Vishnu incarnate.)

❍ ❍ ❍

३०. पायसं कृसरं छागं वृथा सोऽश्नातु निर्घृणः ।
गुरूंश्चाप्यवजानातु यस्यार्योऽनुमते गतः ।।

30. By whose approbation this noble (Raama) has gone away, may he frivolously, voraciously, and shamefully 'devour' oil cakes, sweet milk, and goat's meat: May he insult elders!

(Gluttony is sin; Insulting elders is a very great sin)

❍ ❍ ❍

३१. गाश्च स्पृशतु पादेन गुरून् परिवदेत् च ।
मित्रे द्रुह्येत सोऽत्यन्तं यस्यार्योऽनुमते गतः ।।

31. By whose approbation, the noble (Raama) went away, may he 'Touch' (and kick) cows with his feet; May he abuse elders; May he cheat his own friends (Harm friends).

❍ ❍ ❍

३२. विश्वसात्कथितं किञ्चित्परिवादं मिथः क्वचित् ।
विवृणोतु स दुष्टात्मा यस्यार्योऽनुमते गतः ।।

32. By whose approbation this noble (Raama) went away, may this wicked soul (man) spread accusations that are told to him in secrecy and in confidence and which are divulged only partially, everywhere.

(Rumour mongering is sin; particularly when only partial facts are known. And that too when told in secrecy and confidence.)

❍ ❍ ❍

३३. अकर्ता चाकृतज्ञश्च त्यक्तात्मा निरपत्रपः ।
लोके भवतु विद्विष्टो यस्यार्योऽनुमते गतः ।।

33. By whose approbation this noble (Raama) went away, may this man in the world be ungrateful, lose his self respect, shameless, lazy and most hated (by all).

❍ ❍ ❍

३४. पुत्रदारैश्च भृत्यैश्च स्वगृहे परिवारितः ।
स एको मृष्टमश्नातु यस्यार्योऽनुमते गतः ।।

34. By whose approbation this noble (Raama) went away, may this man eat up all the food by himself in his own house, before his wife, children and (the dependent) servants.

(Food must be shared by all, including servants of the household.)

❍ ❍ ❍

३५. अप्राप्य सदृशान्दारानवपत्यः प्रमीयताम् ।
अनवाप्य क्रियां धर्म्यां यस्यार्योऽनुमते गतः ।।

35. By whose approbation the noble (Raama) went away, may that man perish without a suitable wife and without sons to do his Last Rites as per Dharma.

❍ ❍ ❍

३६. माऽऽत्मनः सन्ततिं द्राक्षीत्स्वेषु दारेषु दुःखितः ।
आयुः समग्रमप्राप्य यस्यार्योऽनुमते गतः ।।

36. By whose approbation this noble (Raama) went away, may his life be short and may he be in sorrow without seeing any progeny through his wife.

❍ ❍ ❍

३७. राजस्त्रीबालवृद्धानां वधे यत्पापमुच्यते ।
भृत्यत्यागे च यत्पापं तत्पापं प्रतिपद्यताम् ।।

37. (Such a person who sent away Raama) May he obtain that Sin, the sin that is spoken of in the killing of a king, a woman, a child, or an old man and the sin in abandoning those who serve him.

❍ ❍ ❍

३८. लाक्षया मधुमांसेन लोहेन च विषेण च ।
सदैव बिभृताद्भृत्यान् यस्यार्योऽनुमते गतः ।।

38. By whose approbation this noble (Raama) went away, may he bestow his servants who should ever be (offered) gold (for services rendered), poison, resin, liquor and (putrefied) meat.

❍ ❍ ❍

३९. संग्रामे समुपोढे तु शत्रुपक्षे भयङ्करे ।
पलायमानो वध्येत यस्यार्योऽनुमते गतः ।।

39. By whose approbation this noble (Raama) was sent away, may he be slain as he flees from the cruel enemy forces when battle is raging. (No warrior turns his back; It is a great sin).

❍ ❍ ❍

४०. कपालपाणिः पृथिवीमटतां चीरसंवृतः ।
भिक्षमाणो यथोन्मत्तो यस्यार्योऽनुमते गतः ।।

40. By whose approbation, the noble (Raama) went away, may he wander on earth in rags, like a beggar with a begging bowl, as though he is mad.

❍ ❍ ❍

४१. मद्ये प्रसक्तो भवतु स्त्रीष्वक्षेषु च नित्यशः ।
कामक्रोधाभिभूतश्च यस्यार्योऽनुमते गतः ।।

41. By whose approbation this noble (Raama) went away,

may he be overwhelmed by wrath and passion, always indulge in liquor, women and gambling.

❍ ❍ ❍

४२. मा स्म धर्मेमनो भूयादधर्मं सुनिषेविताम् ।
अपात्रवर्षी भवतु यस्यार्योऽनुमते गतः ॥

42. By whose approbation this noble (Raama) went away, may his mind never be on Dharma. May A-Dharma abide in him. (Like rain in unwanted place) May (his pursuits) be worthless.

❍ ❍ ❍

४३. संचितान्यस्य वित्तानि विविधानि सहस्रशः ।
दस्युभिर्विप्रलुप्यन्तां यस्यार्योऽनुमते गतः ॥

43. By whose approbation the noble (Raama) went away, may all his various accumulations of wealth and thousands of possessions, be plundered by robbers.

❍ ❍ ❍

४४. उभे सन्ध्ये शयानस्य यत्पापं परिकल्प्यते ।
तच्च पापं भवेत्तस्य यस्यार्योऽनुमते गतः ॥

44. By whose approbation this noble (Raama) was sent away, may the sin afflict him, (the sin) that befalls one who sleeps in the early morning and late evening (of the) two Sandhya-s.

(Early to bed and early to rise; No one should sleep during sunlight.)

❍ ❍ ❍

४५. यदग्निदायके पापं यत्पापं गुरुतल्पगे ।
मित्रद्रोहे च यत्पापं तत्पापं प्रतिपद्यताम् ॥

45. May he obtain the sin, the sin of setting Fire (Arson): May he obtain the sin, the sin of one who violates his teacher's wife; May he obtain the sin, the sin of one who commits treachery on his friend.

❍ ❍ ❍

४६. देवतानां पितॄणां च मातापित्रोस्तथैव च ।
मा स्म कार्षीत्स शुश्रूषां यस्यार्योऽनुमते गतः ।।

46. By whose approbation this noble (Raama) went away, may he not serve the Deities, forefathers (with prayers and offerings) and likewise (may he not serve) his own mother and father.

❍ ❍ ❍

४७. सतां लोकात्सतां कीर्त्याः संजुष्टात्कर्मणस्तथा ।
भ्रश्यतु क्षिप्रमद्यैव यस्यार्योऽनुमते गतः ।।

47. By whose approbation this noble (Raama) went away, may he at once, be thrown out from the world of good men, from the glory of the good and likewise, from traditional practices and deeds .....

❍ ❍ ❍

४८. अपास्य मातृशुश्रूषामनर्थेसोऽवतिष्ठताम् ।
दीर्घबाहुर्महावक्षा यस्यार्योऽनुमते गतः ।।

48. By whose approbation this noble broad chested and long limbed (Raama) went away, may he be worthless without (even) serving (his own) mother.

❍ ❍ ❍

४९. बहुपुत्रो दरिद्रश्च ज्वररोगसमन्वितः ।
स भूयात्सततं क्लेशी यस्यार्योऽनुमते गतः ।।

49. By whose approbation this noble (Raama) went away, may he be a poor man with innumerous children, always suffering, stricken with fever and disease.
(Even those days having too many children was a sin)

❍ ❍ ❍

५०. आशामाशंसमानानां दीनानामूर्ध्वचक्षुषाम् ।
अर्थिनां वितथां कुर्याद्यस्यार्योऽनुमते गतः ।।

50. By whose approbation this noble (Raama) went away, may he be false to the expectations (of promised

assistance) to those who seek him, to those who are feeble, who extol him and look up (to him for help) with their eyes raised up.

(Insincere and false promise is a sin)

❍ ❍ ❍

५१. मायया रमतां नित्यं परुषः पिशुनोऽशुचिः ।
राज्ञो भीतस्त्वधर्मात्मा यस्यार्योऽनुमते गतः ।।

51. By whose approbation the noble (Raama) went away, may this cruel man live by fraud and deceit, in Adharma, in filth, in calumny, always in fear of the king (and the laws of the land)

❍ ❍ ❍

५२. ऋतुस्नातां सतीं भार्यामृतुकालानुरोधिनीम् ।
अतिवर्तेत दुष्टात्मा यस्यार्योऽनुमते गतः ।।

52. By whose approbation the noble (Raama) went away, may this wicked soul, violate his virtuous wife after she had just completed (her monthly periods) and taken menstrual bath and when she observes abstinence during her monthly periods.

(Forcing a wife is sin, a Rape, particularly during certain times.)

❍ ❍ ❍

५३. धर्मदारान्परित्यज्य परदारान्निषेवताम् ।
त्यक्तधर्मरतिर्मूढो यस्यार्योऽनुमते गतः ।।

53. By whose approbation the noble (Raama) went away, may this fool who has abandoned Dharma, abandon (his own) lawful (wedded) wife and have intercourse with another's wife.

❍ ❍ ❍

५४. विप्रलुप्तप्रजातस्य दुष्कृतं ब्राह्मणस्य यत् ।
तदेव प्रतिपद्येत यस्यार्योऽनुमते गतः ।।

54. By whose approbation the noble (Raama) went away, may he obtain that evil that befalls a braamin who has no progeny.

❍ ❍ ❍

५५. पानीयदूषके पापं तथैव विषदायके ।
यत्तदेकः स लभतां यस्यार्योऽनुमते गतः ।।

55. By whose approbation the noble (Raama) was sent away, may he, all by himself, obtain (and bear) that Sin (that befalls on) one who makes drinking water dirty, and likewise, who offers poison

(Protecting water supply is every body's business!)

❍ ❍ ❍

५६. ब्राह्मणायोद्यतां पूजां विहन्तु कलुषेन्द्रियः ।
बालवत्सां च गां दोग्धु यस्यार्योऽनुमते गतः ।।

56. By whose approbation the noble (Raama) went away, may he, with a dirty mind, disturb (the prayers and) worship set up for a Braamin. And may he milk a Cow which has just given birth to its calf.

❍ ❍ ❍

५७. तृष्णार्तं सति पानीये विप्रलम्भेन योजयेत् ।
यत्पापं लभते तत्स्याद्यस्यार्योऽनुमते गतः ।।

57. By whose approbation the noble (Raama) went away, may he indulge in deceit (and refuse) water to a thirsty man when water is available. May he obtain this Sin.

(It is custom in India, even in Rajasthan which is "dry" area, to offer drinking water to guests and others first,even in waterless summer.)

❍ ❍ ❍

५८. भक्त्या विवदमानेषु मार्गमाश्रित्य पश्यतः ।
तस्य पापेन युज्येत यस्यार्योऽनुमते गतः ।।

58. By whose approbation this noble (Raama) went away,

may he be 'yoked' with Sin of one, who, during a debate, although he 'sees' the path (of righteousness in other's arguments) still, steadfastly 'Sees' (and sticks to) his own (arguments and wrong views).

(Bharatha thus condemns himself that if what Kowsalya says is true about his integrity or lack of it, then let all these sins he had listed above, fall upon him and devour him. Bharatha is of course sinless.)

❍ ❍ ❍

५९. विहीनां पतिपुत्राभ्यां कौसल्यां पार्थिवात्मजः ।
एवमाश्वासयन्नेव दुःखार्तोनिपपात ह ॥

59. After consoling Kowsalya who was without her husband, (Bharatha) the son of king, fell down on earth in great distress.

❍ ❍ ❍

६०. तथा तु शपथैः कष्टैः शपमानमचेतनम् ।
भरतं शोकसंतप्तं कौसल्या वाक्यमब्रवीत् ॥

60. Kowsalya then addressed Bharatha who had vowed thus with such painful curses (upon himself) and who had lost his composure (sense perceptions), being tormented by grief.

❍ ❍ ❍

६१. मम दुःखमिदं पुत्र भूयः समुपजायते ।
शपथैः शपमानो हि प्राणानुपरुणत्सि मे ॥

61. Oh * Son! At this moment, my sorrow (and grief) is even more aroused; Vowing thus with such (cruel) curses (upon yourself) you are tormenting my (very breath of) Life.

(*It is interesting that Kowsalya addressees Bharatha as= Puthra=)

❍ ❍ ❍

६२ दिष्ट्या न चलितो धर्मादात्मा ते शुभलक्षण ।
वत्स सत्यप्रतिज्ञो मे सतां लोकानवाप्स्यसि ॥

62. Oh my Son** (Bharatha) who is endowed with noble qualities ! Blessed with divinity as you are, your soul does not swerve away from Dharma. As a man true to your words and promise, you will attain the world of good men.

(**Here again she uses the word= Vathsa= meaning 'darling' child, a term of endearment for a son; but not "Puthra", born of womb.)

❍ ❍ ❍

६३. इत्युक्त्वा चाङ्कमानीय भरतं भ्रातृवत्सलम् ।
परिष्वज्य महाबाहुं रुरोद भृशदुःखिता ॥

63. Saying thus to the mighty limbed Bharatha who was (ever) devoted to his brother (Raama), she (this Kowsalya) 'placed' him on her lap, hugged him, and wept in great distress.

❍ ❍ ❍

६४. एवं विलपमानस्य दुःखार्तस्य महात्मनः ।
मोहाच्च शोकसंरोधाद्बभूव लुलितं मनः ॥

64. In great distress (and grieving) and wailing thus, the great soul (Bharatha's) mind became unsteady due to bewilderment, and by the vehemence of his grief.

❍ ❍ ❍

६५. लालप्यमानस्य विचेतनस्य
प्रणष्टबुद्धेः पतितस्य भूमौ ।
मुहुर्मुहुर्निश्वसतश्च धर्मं
सा तस्य शोकेन जगाम रात्रिः ॥

65. Chattering and wailing, breathing hard and deep again and again, this night passed away in grief for him as he lay on earth, without sense of understanding, 'senseless'..

❍ ❍ ❍

Chapter 76

Last Rites of Dhascharatha Performed

१. तमेवं शोकसन्तप्तं भरतं कैकयीसुताम् ।
उवाच वदतां श्रेष्ठो वसिष्ठः श्रेष्ठवागृषिः ।।

1. Sage Vasishta who was foremost amongst speakers and who was pre-eminent in speech, addressed the son of Kaikeyi, this Bharatha who was tormented by grief.

❍ ❍ ❍

२. अलं शोकेन भद्रं ते राजपुत्र महायशः ।
प्राप्तकालं नरपतेः कुरु संयानमुत्तमम् ।।

2. Oh most famous prince! Enough of this grieving! You (must) do the foremost Last Rites for the king at proper time. Welfare to you.

❍ ❍ ❍

३. वसिष्ठस्य वचः श्रुत्वा भरतो धारणां गतः ।
प्रेतकृत्यानि सर्वाणि कारयामास धर्मवित् ।।

3. Hearing Vasishta's words, (Bharatha) the knower of Dharma, composed himself and began to perform all the Last Rites (for his father).

❍ ❍ ❍

४. उद्धृतं तैलसंक्लेदात्स तु भूमौ निवेशितम् ।
आपीतवर्णवदनं प्रसुप्तमिव भूमिपम् ।।

५. संवेश्य शयने चाग्र्ये नानारत्नपरिष्कृते ।
ततो दशरथं पुत्रो विललाप सुदुःखितः ।।

4. & 5.

Washing (the dead body) which was soaked in (herbal) Oil, the body kept on the floor, the (dead) king appeared as though he was sleeping; his face was (somewhat) of yellow colour...When the (body of) Dhascharatha was placed on a bed which was embedded with foremost and various gems, this son (Bharatha) began to wail in great sorrow.

❍ ❍ ❍

६. किं ते व्यवसितं राजन्प्रोषिते मय्यनागते ।
विवास्य रामं धर्मज्ञं लक्ष्मणं च महाबलम् ।।

6. Oh king! What was lodged (in your mind when you resolved) to send away Raama, the knower of Dharma and the mightily strong Lakshmana, (even) before I returned from abroad?

❍ ❍ ❍

७. क्व यास्यसि महाराज हित्वेमं दुःखितं जनम् ।
हीनं पुरुषसिंहेन रामेणाक्लिष्टकर्मणा ।।

7. Oh Emperor! Without Raama who is a 'lion' amongst men and who is never wearied in (good) actions, where are you going, leaving these distressed people (here).

❍ ❍ ❍

८. योगक्षेमं तु ते राजन्कोऽस्मिन्कल्पयिता पुरे ।
त्वयि प्रयाते स्वस्तात रामे च वनमाश्रिते ।।

8. Oh king! Oh dear (father)! With you going to heaven and Raama going to forest, who is going to offer (and establish) security and welfare in this, your city?

❍ ❍ ❍

९. विधवा पृथिवी राजंस्त्वया हीना न राजते ।
हीनचन्द्रेव रजनी नगरी प्रतिभाति मे ।।

9. Oh king! Without you, this world, does it not appear like a widow? And to me, the city appears like a night without moon.
(Vasishta, the family priest and friend of Ikshwaaku-s rebukes Bharatha for not giving attention to the matter that brooks no delay).

❍ ❍ ❍

१०. एवं विलपमानं तं भरतं दीनमानसम् ।
अब्रवीद्वचनं भूयो वसिष्ठस्तु महामुनिः ।।

10. The great sage Vasishta once again addressed these words to this Bharatha who was down hearted and wailing thus.

❍ ❍ ❍

११. प्रेतकार्याणि यान्यस्य कर्तव्यानि विशांपतेः ।
तान्यव्यग्रं महाबाहो क्रियन्तामविचारितम् ।।

11. Oh (Bharatha) of mighty limbs! (Bear in mind): Such of those Last Rites for the king that are to be done, must be done calmly and clearly (by you). (So this is not the time to exhibit this grief).

❍ ❍ ❍

१२. तथेति भरतो वाक्यं वसिष्ठस्याभिपूज्य तत् ।
ऋत्विक्पुरोहिताचार्यांस्त्वरयामास सर्वशः ।।

12. Accepting and honouring such words (of advice) of Vasishta, Bharatha (said): = So Be It:= Then he 'hurried' up from all over, Rithviks, Purohiths, Teachers (for performance of his father's Rites).

❍ ❍ ❍

१३. ये त्वग्नयो नरेन्द्रस्य ह्यग्न्यागाराद्बहिष्कृता ।
ऋत्विग्भिर्याजकैश्चैव ते हूयन्ते यथाविधि ।।

13. (Last Rites Described): The royal fires, all these were taken out from the hall of Fire; And (Homa)fire Rituals were done as per norms, by the Rithviks, priests doing sacrificial ceremonies.

❍ ❍ ❍

१४. शिबिकायामथारोप्य राजानं गतचेतसम् ।
बाष्पकण्ठा विमनसस्तमूहुः परिचारकाः ।।

14. Then mounting the (body of) dead king on a Bier, the (Pall) bearers carried him with tears choking their throats; they were dejected.

❍ ❍ ❍

१५. हिरण्यं च सुवर्णं च वासांसि विविधानि च ।
प्रकिरन्तो जना मार्गं नृपतेरग्रतो ययुः ।।

15. And the citizens went before their king, scattering gold, coins, various robes, on the path (of funereal procession).

❍ ❍ ❍

१६. चन्दनागरुनिर्यासान् सरलं पद्मकं तथा ।
देवदारूणि चाहृत्य चितां चक्रुस्तथापरे ।।

16. Likewise, some fetched sandal wood and pastes, Agara incenses, Sarala logs, Padmaka and Dhevadhaaru wood; And some prepared the Mound.

❍ ❍ ❍

१७. गन्धानुच्चावचांश्चान्यांस्तत्र दत्त्वाऽथ भूमिपम् ।
ततः संवेशयामासुश्चितामध्ये तमृत्विजः ।।

17. Then the Rithviks placed upon it many other variety of scented (materials) and then laid the king in the middle of the Mound.

❍ ❍ ❍

१८. तुा हुताशनं हुत्वा जेपुस्तस्य तमृत्विजः ।।

18. The Rithviks lit his fire, likewise recited prayers.

❍ ❍ ❍

१९. जगुश्च ते यथाशास्त्रं तत्र सामानि सामगाः ।।

19. The Singers of Saama Vedha then sang Saama Texts as per norms of Shaasthra.

❍ ❍ ❍

२०. शिबिकाभिश्च यानैश्च यथार्हं तस्य योषितः ।
नगरान्निर्ययुस्तत्र वृद्धैः परिवृतास्तदा ॥

20. The (King's) wives surrounded by elders, went there from the city in their respective palanquins and vehicles.

❍ ❍ ❍

२१. प्रसव्यं चापि तं चक्रुर्ऋत्विजोऽग्निचितं नृपम् ।
स्त्रियश्च शोकसन्तप्ताः कौसल्याप्रमुखास्तदा ॥

21. Then the Rithviks and the ladies like Kowsalya and others who were all tormented by grief, did all those favourable (rituals) for the king who had performed (many) Homa Fire rituals, in the Fire mound (for peace and tranquillity).

❍ ❍ ❍

२२. क्रौञ्चीनामिव नारीणां निनादस्तत्र शुश्रुवे ।
आर्तानां करुणं काले क्रोशन्तीनां सहस्रशः ॥

22. At that time, the wailing of thousands of ladies there who were all crying pitiably in distress were heard like (shrieks of) Krauncha birds.

❍ ❍ ❍

२३. ततो रुदन्त्यो विवशा विलप्य च पुनः पुनः ।
यानेभ्यः सरयूतीरमवतेरुर्वराङ्गनाः ॥

23. Then the foremost ladies who were crying without any (self) control, wailed again and again, and they (went and) got down from their vehicles on the banks of Sarayu river.

❍ ❍ ❍

२४. कृत्वोदकं ते भरतेन सार्धं
नृपाङ्गना मन्त्रिपुरोहिताश्च ।
पुरं प्रविश्याश्रुपरीतनेत्रा
भूमौ दशाहं व्यनयन्त दुःखम् ॥

24. The noble royal ladies, the ministers and purohiths, along with Bharatha took their baths with tears in their eyes; Then went back to the city and spent 10 days in mourning, lying on (bare) floor.

❍ ❍ ❍

Chapter 77

Bharatha and Schathrugna Lament

१. ततो दशाहेऽतिगते कृतशौचो नृपात्मजः ।
द्वादशेऽहनि संप्राप्ते श्राद्धकर्माण्यकारयत् ।।

1. After 10 days (of mourning) had gone by, (Bharatha) the son of (the late) king (Dhascharatha) performed the Purification ceremony; And on the Twelfth day, he performed the Shraadha ceremony.

❍ ❍ ❍

२. ब्राह्मणेभ्यो ददौ रत्नं धनमन्नं च पुष्कलम् ।
वासांसि च महार्हाणि रत्नानि विविधानि च ।।

2. They gave abundantly to the Braamins: moneys, gems, food, costly garments, various objects.

❍ ❍ ❍

३. बास्तिकं बहु शुक्लं च गाश्चापि शतशस्तदा ।
दासीर्दासांश्च यानानि वेश्मानि सुमहान्ति च ।।
ब्राह्मणेभ्यो ददौ पुत्रौ राज्ञस्तस्यौर्ध्वदैहिकम् ।।

3. This (Bharatha) the son of the (late) King performing Obsequies, offered Altars to Holy men, big cottages to braamins, and also vehicles, butter, goat's milk and thousands of cows.

❍ ❍ ❍

४. ततः प्रभातसमये दिवसेऽथ त्रयोदशे ।
विललाप महाबाहुर्भरतः शोकमूर्च्छितः ।।
शब्दापिहितकण्ठश्च शोधनार्थमुपागतः ।।

4. Then on the Thirteenth day, in the early morning, the mighty limbed Bharatha who had come for the Schodhana (Purification) ceremony, wailed, overwhelmed by grief, his voice stilled in his throat.

❍ ❍ ❍

५. चितामूले पितुर्वाक्यमिदमाह सुदुःखितः ।।

5. Standing near the mound (where his father had been cremated) he said these words in great sorrow.

❍ ❍ ❍

६. तात यस्मिन्निसृष्टोऽहं त्वया भ्रातरि राघवे ।
तस्मिन्वनं प्रव्रजिते शून्ये त्यक्तोऽस्म्यहं त्वया ।।

6. Oh father! I have been abandoned by you and made a destitute. My brother (Raama) the Raaghava (under whose care) I was to be entrusted by you, has been sent away to forest.

❍ ❍ ❍

७. यस्या गतिरनाथायाः पुत्रः प्रव्राजितो वनम् ।
तामम्बां तात कौसल्यां त्यक्त्वा त्वं क्व गतो नृप ।।

7. Oh dad! Oh King! Where have you gone away leaving and abandoning my (step) mother Kowsalya who is helpless (without protector), with her son who was her refuge, sent away to forest?

❍ ❍ ❍

८. दृष्ट्वा भस्मारुणं तच्च दग्धास्थिस्थानमण्डलम् ।
पितुः शरीरं निर्वाणं निष्टनन्विषसाद सः ।।

8. Seeing his father's body annihilated and reduced to red

ashes and strewn with heaps of burnt bones, he cried aloud in distress.

❍ ❍ ❍

९. स तु दृष्ट्वा रुदन्नार्तः पपात धरणीतले ।
उत्थाप्यमानः शक्रस्य यन्त्रध्वज इव च्युतः ।।

9. Seeing (all this), crying in deep distress, he fell down on earth like Lord Indhra's mast falling down as it was being raised up.

❍ ❍ ❍

१०. अभिपेतुस्ततः सर्वेतस्यामात्याः शुचिव्रतम् ।
अन्तकाले निपतितं ययातिमृषयो यथा ।।

10. At that moment, all his ministers approached (Bharatha) who was virtuous in conduct, like sages approaching the fallen king Yayaathi during his last moments.

❍ ❍ ❍

११. शत्रुघ्नश्चापि भरतं दृष्ट्वा शोकपरिप्लुतम् ।
विसंज्ञो न्यपतद्भूमौ भूमिपालमनुस्मरन् ।।

11. And Schathrugna also, thinking about (his dead father the) King, fell down on earth, unconscious, even as he saw Bharatha so engulfed in grief.

❍ ❍ ❍

१२. उन्मत्ता इव निश्चेता विललाप सुदुःखितः ।
स्मृत्वा पितुर्गुणाङ्गानि तानि तानि तदा तदा ।।

12. Remembering all such qualities of their father (which he exhibited) at appropriate times, they wailed like insane men, in great distress, (forgetting themselves that they were royal princes).

❍ ❍ ❍

१३. मन्थराप्रभवस्तीव्रः कैकेयीग्राहसङ्कुलः ।
उरदानमयोऽक्षोभ्योऽमज्जयच्छोकसागरः ।।

13. (Poet Vaalmeeki goes poetic as he describes the events leading to all this). This Imperishable severe ocean of grief shaken up by Kaikeyi the crocodile, that originated from (the evil adviser of Kaikeyi, this) Manthara, submerged every one (with its) harmful (effects) that were (the two) boons offered (to the Crocodile).

❍ ❍ ❍

१४. सुकुमारं च बालं च सततं लालितं त्वया ।
क्व तात भरतं हित्वा विलपन्तं गतो भवान् ।।

14. Oh Father! Where have you gone away, leaving your young and delicate wailing son Bharatha who was ever fondled by you.

❍ ❍ ❍

१५. ननु भोज्येषु पानेषु वस्त्रेष्वाभरणेषु च ।
प्रवारयसि नः सर्वांस्तन्नः कोऽद्य करिष्यति ।।

15. You used to satisfy us with (good) foods, drinks, garments and jewelleries; Who will now do all these for us.

❍ ❍ ❍

१६. अवदारणकाले तु पृथिवी नावदीर्यते ।
विहीना या त्वया राज्ञा धर्मज्ञेन महात्मना ।।

16. (It is a wonder) that at this time when this Earth should have burst being without you who are a knower of Dharma, who are a great soul and king, has not burst!

❍ ❍ ❍

१७. पितरि स्वर्गमापन्ने रामे चारण्यमाश्रिते ।
किं मे जीवितसामर्थ्यं प्रवेक्ष्यामि हुताशनम् ।।

17. Where is my ability to (survive) and) live on after my father has attained heaven and Raama had reached the forest. I will enter fire (and immolate myself).

❍ ❍ ❍

१८. हीनो भ्रात्रा च पित्रा च शून्यामिक्ष्वाकुपालिताम् ।
अयोध्यां न प्रवेक्ष्यामि प्रवेक्ष्यामि तपोवनम् ॥

18. I will not enter the desolate Ayodhya that is ruled by Ikshwaaku-s, without father and brother (Raama). I will enter forest of penance.

❍ ❍ ❍

१९. तयोर्विलपितं श्रुत्वा व्यसनं चान्ववेक्ष्य तत् ।
भृशमार्ततरा भूयः सर्व एवानुगामिनः ॥

19. Seeing their plight, and hearing their wail, all those who had come there, were even more distressed.

❍ ❍ ❍

२०. ततो विषण्णौ विश्रान्तौ शत्रुघ्नभरतावुभौ ।
धरायां संव्यवेष्टेतां भग्नश्रृङ्गाविवर्षभौ ॥

20. Tired and despondent, these (two brothers), Bharatha and Schathrugna, rolled on earth like bulls whose horns were chipped off.

❍ ❍ ❍

२१. ततः प्रकृतिमान्वैद्यः पितुरेषां पुरोहितः ।
वसिष्ठो भरतं वाक्यमुत्थाप्य तमुवाच ह ॥

21. At that moment, Vasishta who had inborn (great) qualities and who was an authority on Vedha-s and who was the Purohith (of the Ikshwaaku-s) lifted up Bharatha and said:

❍ ❍ ❍

२२. त्रयोदशोऽयं दिवसः पितुर्वृत्तस्य ते विभो ।
सावशेषास्थिनिचये किमिह त्वं विलम्बसे ॥

22. Oh (Bharatha the most) capable man! Today is the Thirteenth day of your father's Death. Why are you delaying in collecting the remains of bones (of your father) for libations, now?

❍ ❍ ❍

२३. त्रीणि द्वन्द्वानि भूतेषु प्रवृत्तान्यविशेषतः ।
तेषु चापरिहार्येषु नैवं भवितुमर्हसि ॥

23. (Vasishta is a man of few words; Again he is severe on Bharatha who should do his duty... Vasishta expounds philosophy) ......

In all living beings, there exists without discrimination, Three Laws of Duality = Male- Female; Happiness and Sorrow; Birth and Death =. Inevitable as these are, you should not behave like this (and pine away in grief; This is The Universal Law.)

❍ ❍ ❍

२४. सुमन्त्रश्चापि शत्रुघ्नमुत्थाप्याभिप्रसाद्य च ।
श्रावयामास तत्त्वज्ञः सर्वभूतभवाभवौ ॥

24. And the philosophical Sumanthra, lifted up Schathrugna, consoled him and expounded (about the) Duality of Life and Death in all living beings.

❍ ❍ ❍

२५. उत्थितौ च नरव्याघ्रौ प्रकाशेते यशस्विनौ ।
वर्षातपपरिक्लिन्नौ पृथगिन्द्रध्वजाविव ॥

25. These two famous "tigers amongst men", then stood up and they appeared like two separate masts of Lord Indhra when Sun strikes upon them after rain.

❍ ❍ ❍

२६. अश्रूणि परिमृद्गन्तौ रक्ताक्षौ दीनभाषिणौ ।
अमात्यास्त्वरयन्ति स्म तनयौ चापराः क्रियाः ॥

26. Wiping off their tears, the ministers hastened the two brothers whose eyes were red (due to crying) and who were speaking with feeble voice, (to complete) other remaining Rituals (for their dead father).

❍ ❍ ❍

Chapter 78

Schathrugna Attacks Manthara

१. अथ यात्रां समीहन्तं शत्रुघ्नो लक्ष्मणानुजः ।
भरतं शोकसन्तप्तमिदं वचनमब्रवीत् ।।

1. Then Schathrugna, the younger brother of Lakshmana addressed Bharatha who was tormented by grief, with his *customary earnestness (eagerness in Dharma).

(*Poet uses words- Yaathraam-Sameehantham: Normal meaning for Yaathra is journey: Translator has used customary earnestness.)

❍ ❍ ❍

२. गतिर्यः सर्वभूतानां दुःखे किं पुनरात्मनः ।
स रामः सत्त्वसंपन्नः स्त्रिया प्रव्राजितो वनम् ।।

2. When he (our Raama) is Refuge to all living beings in distress, need (I say) what he is to you! And this Raama endowed with all natural good qualities has been sent away to forest by a woman.

❍ ❍ ❍

३. बलवान्वीर्यसम्पन्नो लक्ष्मणो नाम योऽप्यसौ ।
किं न मोचयते रामं कृत्वाऽपि पितृनिग्रहम् ।।

3. This strong one, endowed with bravery and who goes by the name of Lakshmana, why did he not release Raama (from this suffering of separation from all of us) after restraining our father?

❍ ❍ ❍

४. पूर्वमेव तु निग्राह्यः समवेक्ष्य नयानयौ ।
उत्पथं यः समारूढो नार्या राजा वशं गतः ।।

4. When a king is under the clutches of a woman and goes

on the wrong path, he must be restrained earlier, after taking into consideration (what is) right or wrong.

❍ ❍ ❍

५. इति संभाषमाणे तु शत्रुघ्ने लक्ष्मणानुजे ।
प्राग्द्वारेऽभूत्तदा कुब्जा सर्वाभरणभूषिता ।।

5. While Schathrugna the brother of Lakshmana was talking like this, at that time the hunchback (Manthara) was standing at the door, well ornamented herself with all jewels.

❍ ❍ ❍

६. लिप्ता चन्दनसारेण राजवस्त्राणि बिभ्रती ।
विविधं विविधैस्तैस्तैर्भूषणैश्च विभूषिता ।।

6. Besmeared with sandal paste and dressed up in royal attire, she was bedecking herself with various ornaments.

❍ ❍ ❍

७. मेखलादामभिश्चित्रैरन्यैश्च शुभभूषणैः ।
बभासे बहुभिर्बद्धा रज्जुबद्धेव वानरी ।।

7. Wearing various girdles, and tying upon herself with various other lovely ornaments, she appeared like a female monkey, sporting braided hair!

❍ ❍ ❍

८. तां समीक्ष्य तदा द्वारस्थो भृशं पापस्य कारिणीम् ।
गृहीत्वाऽकरुण कुब्जा शत्रुघ्नाय न्यवेदयत् ।।

8. Then the door keeper seeing this hunch back who relentlessly indulged in cruel (sinful) deeds, caught her and presented her before Schathrugna. (And announced her thus).

❍ ❍ ❍

९. यस्याः कृते वने रामो न्यस्तदेहश्च वः पिता ।
सेयं पापा नृशंसा च तस्याः कुरु यथामति ।।

9. This is the vile woman. The sinful: By whose actions Raama is in forest (now) and father left his body. Teach her a lesson!

❍ ❍ ❍

१०. शत्रुघ्नश्च तदाज्ञाय वचनं भृशदुःखितः ।
अन्तःपुरचरान्सर्वानित्युवाच धृतव्रतः ।।

10. Realising this, the resolute (man of vows) Schathrugna said these words before all the ladies of the palace house hold who were in deep sorrow.

❍ ❍ ❍

११. तीव्रमुत्पादितं दुःखं भ्रातॄणां मे तथा पितुः ।
यथा चेयं नृशंसस्य कर्मणः फलमश्नुताम् ।।

11. May she reap the fruits befitting her cruel deed, as she has brought immense suffering to me, to my brothers, to my father.

❍ ❍ ❍

१२. एवमुक्ता च तेनाशु सखीजनसमावृता ।
गृहीता बलवत्कुब्जा सा तद्गृहमनादयत् ।।

12. After being told thus by him, this hunch back who was with her companions shrieked loudly in that palace when she was dragged fiercely (by Schathrugna)

❍ ❍ ❍

१३. ततः सुभृशसंतप्तस्तस्याः सर्वः सखीजनः ।
क्रुद्धमाज्ञाय शत्रुघ्नं विपलायत सर्वशः ।।

13. Then, all her companions, realising that Schathrugna was in wrath, ran away in all directions, terribly tormented (by fear).

❍ ❍ ❍

१४. अमन्त्रयत कृत्स्नश्च तस्याः सर्वः सखीजनः ।
यथाऽयं समुपक्रान्तो निःशेषं नः करिष्यति ।।

14. Then all her companions opined thus: "He (this Schathrugna) is totally committed to punish without leaving out any one of us."

❍ ❍ ❍

१५. सानुक्रोशां वदान्यां च धर्मज्ञां च यशस्विनीम् ।
कौसल्यां शरणं याम सा हि नोऽस्तु ध्रुवा गतिः ।।

15. Let us all take refuge under the famous Kowsalya who is compassionate, who is munificent, who is knower of Dharma; Indeed she is the eternal refuge for us all.

❍ ❍ ❍

१६. स च रोषेण ताम्राक्षः शत्रुघ्नः शत्रुतापनः ।
विचकर्ष तदा कुब्जां क्रोशन्तीं पृथिवीतले ।।

16. His eyes red with anger, this Schathrugna the tormentor of enemies, then dragged this crying Hunchback on the floor.

❍ ❍ ❍

१७. तस्यां ह्याकृष्यमाणायां मन्थरायामितस्ततः ।
चित्रं बहुविधं भाण्डं पृथिव्यां तद्व्यशीर्यत ।।

17. While this Manthara was being dragged, all the wonderful ornaments (worn by her) scattered here and there on the floor.

❍ ❍ ❍

१८. तेन भाण्डेन सङ्कीर्णं श्रीमद्राजनिवेशनम् ।
अशोभत तदा भूयः शारदं गगनं यथा ।।

18. At that moment, the resplendent palace shone like sky in autumn, with these ornaments spread extensively (on the floor).

❍ ❍ ❍

१९. स बली बलवत्क्रोधाद्गृहीत्वा पुरुषर्षभः ।
कैकेयीमभि निर्भर्त्स्य बभाषे परुषं वचः ।।

19. This strong (Schathrugna) the 'bull' amongst men, in mighty wrath, dragging her (who was) near Kaikeyi, reviled her and spoke harsh words.

❍ ❍ ❍

२०. तैर्वाक्यैः परुषैर्दुःखैः कैकेयी भृशदुःखिता ।
शत्रुघ्नभयसंत्रस्ता पुत्रं शरणमागता ।।

20. Kaikeyi who was in deep distress at these cruel and painful words (of Schathrugna) took shelter by the side of her son (Bharatha), shivering with fear from Schathrugna.

❍ ❍ ❍

२१. तं प्रेक्ष्य भरतः क्रुद्धं शत्रुघ्नमिदमब्रवीत् ।
अवध्याः सर्वभूतानां प्रमदाः क्षम्यतामिति ।।

21. And Bharatha, observing that Schathrugna was in wrath, said these words: = A female amongst all living beings should never be harassed. Therefore, may (this Manthara) be forgiven =

(Schathrugna -the Nithya Schathrugna- is a man, as his name suggests, conqueror of eternal enemies of wrath and passion: Yet it is Bharatha who advises him not to take on his wrath on this evil woman Manthara The Kshathriyam in Bharatha asserts itself- Chivalry: A woman is never harmed by a Kshathriya- soldier.)

❍ ❍ ❍

२२. हन्यामहमिमां पापां कैकेयीं दुष्टचारिणीम् ।
यदि मां धार्मिको रामो नासूयेन्मातृघातकम् ।।

22. If the man of Dharma, (our brother) Raama will not be annoyed with me as a Mother Killer, then I would have killed this sinful, evil mongering Kaikeyi (who, alas, is my mother).

❍ ❍ ❍

२३. इमामपि हतां कुब्जां यदि जानाति राघवः ।
त्वां च मां चैव धर्मात्मा नाभिभाषिष्यते ध्रुवम् ।।

23. If the noble soul Raama comes to know about the harassment to this Hunchback (Manthara), he will not talk to you (ever) surely.

❍ ❍ ❍

२४. भरतस्य वचः श्रुत्वा शत्रुघ्नो लक्ष्मणानुजः ।
न्यवर्तत ततो रोषात्तां मुमोच च मन्थराम् ।।

24. Hearing the words of Bharatha, Schathrugna the brother of Lakshmana, gave up his wrath and released Manthara (from his grip).

❍ ❍ ❍

२५. सा पादमूले कैकेय्या मन्थरा निपपात ह ।
निश्वसन्ती सुदुःखार्ता कृपणं विललाप च ।।

25. And Manthara fell at the feet of Kaikeyi; breathing hard and deep, she cried pitiably in great anguish.

❍ ❍ ❍

२६. शत्रुघ्नविक्षेपविमूढसंज्ञां
समीक्ष्य कुब्जां भरतस्य माता ।
शनैः समाश्वासयदार्तरूपां
क्रौञ्चीं विलग्नामिव वीक्षमाणाम् ।।

26. Seeing the Hunch back in distress and bewildered, shaken up by Schathrugna, clinging to her like a (terrified) Krauncha bird, (Kaikeyi the) mother of Bharatha consoled her.

❍ ❍ ❍

Chapter 79

(Bharatha Orders Preparation for Journey)

(Ministers request Bharatha to take over the kingdom: Bharatha refuses the crown. Instead he prepares to take a large Army with him to go to forest, crown Raama there and bring him back to Ayodhya.)

१. ततः प्रभातसमये दिवसे च चतुर्दशे ।
समेत्य राजकर्तारो भरतं वाक्यमब्रुवन् ॥

1. Then on the fourteenth day (after Dhascharatha's cremation), in the early morning, the ministers of the realm came together and addressed Bharatha these words.

❍ ❍ ❍

२. गतो दशरथः स्वर्गं यो नो गुरुतरो गुरुः ।
रामं प्रव्राज्य वै ज्येष्ठं लक्ष्मणं च महाबलम् ॥

2. Sending away (on exile) the eldest (son) Raama and the mightily strong (second son) Lakshmana, the venerable amongst most venerable men, this Dhascharatha went away to heaven.

❍ ❍ ❍

३. त्वमद्य भव नो राजा राजपुत्र महायशः ।
सङ्गत्या नापराध्नोति राज्यमेतदनायकम् ॥

3. Oh royal prince, Oh most famous (Bharatha)! You be our King Now. appropriately, this (our) Kingdom has never transgressed by being without a lord… (King is Dead, Long live The King).

४. आभिषेचनिकं सर्वमिदमादाय राघव ।
प्रतीक्षते त्वां स्वजनः श्रेणयश्च नृपात्मज ॥

4. Oh Prince, Oh (Bharatha the) Raaghava! Your citizens are awaiting you with all the (necessary) coronation materials brought; The entire multitude (is looking forward to your being crowned).

❍ ❍ ❍

५. राज्यं गृहाण भरत पितृपैतामहं ध्रुवम् ।
अभिषेचय चात्मानं पाहि चास्मान्नरर्षभ ॥

5. Oh (Bharatha) 'the bull' amongst men! Accept the kingdom of your forefathers; Anoint yourself (as king): Rule over us eternally.

❍ ❍ ❍

६. आभिषेचनिकं भाण्डं कृत्वा सर्वं प्रदक्षिणम् ।
भरतस्तं जनं सर्वं प्रत्युवाच धृतव्रतः ॥

6. Bharatha who was resolute in vows, went round in Circumbumbulation over all the materials for the Coronation ceremony and then replied to all these citizens.

❍ ❍ ❍

७. ज्येष्ठस्य राजता नित्यमुचिता हि कुलस्य नः ।
नैवं भवन्तो मां वक्तुमर्हन्ति कुशला जनाः ॥

7. Men like you who are all well versed (and conversant in norms), should not talk to me like this. Because, this kingdom for the eldest (son), is custom in our family: Traditionally.

❍ ❍ ❍

८. रामः पूर्वोहि नो भ्राता भविष्यति महीपतिः ।
अह त्वरण्ये वत्स्यामि वर्षाणि नव पञ्च च ॥

8. And Raama is the eldest brother (of mine): Therefore

he (alone) should become our King. And I will live in forest for 14 years instead.

(Some commentators are critical of Bharatha's point on his going away to forest on exile for 14 years. Obviously Bharatha wishes to atone for the sins of his mother Kaikeyi.)

❍ ❍ ❍

९. युज्यतां महती सेना चतुरङ्गमहाबला ।
आनयिष्याम्यहं ज्येष्ठं भ्रातरं राघवं वनात् ।।

9. I am going to bring my eldest brother (Raama) the Raaghava from forest. May the Army drawn from the Four Strong Services be got ready: And mighty (may the army of ours be!)

❍ ❍ ❍

१०. आभिषेचनिकं चैव सर्वमेतदुपस्कृतम् ।
पुरस्कृत्य गमिष्यामि रामहेतोर्वनं प्रति ।।

10. With all these materials for Coronation (you have brought here for me), I am going to forest for honouring Raama (and crown him)

❍ ❍ ❍

११. तत्रैव तं नरव्याघ्रमभिषिच्य पुरस्कृतम् ।
आनेष्यामि तु वै रामं हव्यवाहमिवाध्वरात् ।।

11. I will crown Raama, 'the tiger' of men there itself. Honouring him thus, I will bring him back, like (bringing) holy Fire from Soma Sacrifice.

❍ ❍ ❍

१२. न सकामां करिष्यामि स्वामिमां मातृगन्धिनीम् ।
वने वत्स्याम्यहं दुर्गेरामो राजा भविष्यति ।।

12. Raama is going to be (our) king. I will not fulfill her wishes who calls herself my mother! And I am going to live in the impenetrable forest (instead of Raama).

❍ ❍ ❍

१३. क्रियतां शिल्पिभिः पन्थाः समानि विषमाणि च ।
रक्षिणश्चानुसंयान्तु पथि दुर्गविचारकाः ॥

13. Let workers prepare the way: Paths difficult to traverse may be levelled up: Let guides knowing these difficult territories come along enroute.

❍ ❍ ❍

१४. एवं संभाषमाणं तं रामहेतोर्नृपात्मजम् ।
प्रत्युवाच जनः सर्वः श्रीमद्वाक्यमनुत्तमम् ॥

14. All the citizens replied to this (Bharatha) the son of king who was speaking thus for the sake of Raama, (for the sake of bringing him back to take over), with these foremost resplendent words.

❍ ❍ ❍

१५. एवं ते भाषमाणस्य पद्मा श्रीरुपतिष्ठताम् ।
यस्त्वं ज्येष्ठे नृपसुते पृथिवीं दातुमिच्छसि ॥

15. May Goddess Padhma abide in you (and ever protect you) who speak thus and who desires to offer The Earth (our kingdom) to the eldest son of the king.

❍ ❍ ❍

१६. अनुत्तमं तद्वचनं नृपात्मज
प्रभाषितं संश्रवणे निशम्य च ।
प्रहर्षजास्तं प्रति बाष्पबिन्दवो
निपेतुरार्याननेत्रसंभवाः ॥

16. Hearing such foremost words spoken by (Bharatha) the son of the king, and learning (about the decision to bring back Raama), tears of joy fell from their faces of these noble men because of this noble Bharatha (and his decision).

❍ ❍ ❍

१७. ऊचुस्ते वचनमिदं निशम्य हृष्टाः
सामात्याः सपरिषदो वियातशोकाः ।
पन्थानं नरवर भक्तिमाञ्जनश्च
व्यादिष्टास्तव वचनाच्च शिल्पिवर्गः ।।

17. Hearing such words, the men in The Assembly who were with ministers and who had been directed regarding the route (of journey and arrangements), spoke in joy, with their grief gone away: Oh foremost of men = (Oh Bharatha) ! By your words (of command) men are loyally standing at your service.=

(Note: Some commentators have questioned Bharatha's right to perform The Last Rites of his father, king Dhascharatha, when he had virtually 'disowned' him. But as Bharatha never accepted, nor even had an iota of desire to take over the kingdom, it must have pleased the late king that the sinless Bharatha performed his Last Rites. The very wise Sage Vasishta would never have approved this if he was not sure that it would please the late king immensely.)

❍ ❍ ❍

Chapter 80

Preparation of the Route (Towards Forest)

(As Bharatha is taking a huge Army and also because many citizens are following him to forest to fetch Raama, the route is cleared.)

❍ ❍ ❍

१. अथ भूमिप्रदेशज्ञाः सूत्रकर्मविशारदाः ।
स्वकर्माभिरताः शूराः खनका यन्त्रकास्तथा ।।

२. कर्मान्तिकाः स्थपतयःपुरुषा यन्त्रकोविदाः ।
तथा वर्धकयश्चैव मार्गिणो वृक्षतक्षकाः ।।

३. कूपकाराः सुधाकारा वंशकर्मकरास्तथा ।
समर्था ये च द्रष्टारः पुरतस्ते प्रतस्थिरे ॥

1. to 3. (The advance party described)

The men who knew the topography of the land; Experts in taking measurements with tape (Land surveyors): experts in respective fields; Brave workers; Diggers and excavators; Machine operators .Porters; Carpenters; Builders; Experts handling movers; Vehicles; Wood fellers; Guides showing the route... Many men... Well diggers; Masons, house painters; Cane furniture makers; All these capable men with experience, went ahead.

❍ ❍ ❍

४. स तु हर्षात्तमुद्देशं जनौघो विपुलः प्रयान् ।
अशोभत महावेगः समुद्र इव पर्वणि ॥

4. With all these mighty crowd of men going ahead to that place, it was like the swelling ocean during the joyous Monsoon (rainy) season.

❍ ❍ ❍

५. ते स्ववारं समास्थाय वर्त्मकर्मणि कोविदाः ।
करणैर्विविधोपेतैः पुरस्तात्संप्रतस्थिरे ॥

5. Experts in road work, each one taking on to himself (work load), went ahead, carrying their various implements.

❍ ❍ ❍

६. लता वल्लीश्च गुल्मांश्च स्थाणूनश्मन एव च ।
जनास्ते चक्रिरे मार्गं छिन्दन्तो विविधान्द्रुमान् ॥

6. Cutting creepers, branches and stalks (of trees), bushes, roots, rocks and many trees, these men paved the way (making it easy for the retinue of Bharatha)

❍ ❍ ❍

७. अवृक्षेषु च देशेषु केचिद्वृक्षानरोपयन् ॥

7. Some planted trees where there were no trees.

❍ ❍ ❍

८. केचित्कुठारैष्टङ्कैश्च दात्रैश्छिन्दन्क्वचित्क्वचित् ॥

8. Some cut with axes, sickles, swords, here and there.

❍ ❍ ❍

९. अपरे वीरणस्तम्बान्बलिनो बलवत्तराः ॥

9. Some others who were very strong, cut bunch of thick grass.

❍ ❍ ❍

१०. विधमन्ति स्म दुर्गाणि स्थलानि च ततस्ततः ॥

10. Some destroyed places that were difficult to get through, here and there.

❍ ❍ ❍

११. अपरेऽपूरयन्कूपान्पांसुभिः श्वभ्रमायतम् ॥

11. Some filled up pot holes and deep crevices with sand.

❍ ❍ ❍

१२. निम्नभागांस्ततः केचित्समांश्चक्रुस्ततस्ततः ॥

12. Some levelled up deep (uneven) surfaces, here and there.

❍ ❍ ❍

१३. बबन्धुर्बन्धनीयांश्च क्षोद्यन्संचुक्षुदुस्तदा ॥

13. Likewise, some constructed constructions (like embankments): Some demolished those that were to be demolished.

❍ ❍ ❍

१४. बिभिदुर्भेदनीयांश्च तांस्तान्देशांस्तथाऽपरे ॥

14. Some chiselled out (Rocks) that were to be cut away, at various place.

❍ ❍ ❍

१५. अचिरेणैव कालेन परिवाहान्बहूदकान् ।
चक्रुर्बहुविधाकारान्सागरप्रतिमान्बहून् ।।

15. Places with plenty of water, looking like ocean, were quickly made into canals. (Flood control!).

❍ ❍ ❍

१६. निर्जलेषु च देशेषु खानयामासुरुत्तमान् ।
उदपानान्बहुविधान्वेदिकापरिमण्डितान् ।।

16. In places where there was no water, they dug wells, erected circular pavilions (around them).

❍ ❍ ❍

१७. ससुधाकुट्टिमतलः प्रपुष्पितमहीरुहः ।
मत्तोद्घुष्टद्विजगणः पताकाभिरलंकृतः ।।

17. The dwellings in villages were white washed; (Route was) lined with trees in blossom; plenty of exhilarated cooing birds; Decorated with lots of banners.

❍ ❍ ❍

१८. चन्दनोदकसंसिक्तो नानाकुसुमभूषितः ।
बह्वशोभत सेनायाः पन्थाः सुरपथोपमः ।।

18. The path treaded by the Army was sprinkled with sandal scented waters; strewn with various flowers; It shone like celestial pathways.

❍ ❍ ❍

१९. आज्ञाप्याथ यथाज्ञप्ति युक्तास्तेऽधिकृता नराः ।
रमणीयेषु देशेषु बहुस्वादुफलेषु च ।।

19. The Supervisors gave necessary instructions in these

lovely territories which was full with many sweet fruits; They were devoted (in their work).

❍ ❍ ❍

२०. यो निवेशस्त्वभिप्रेतो भरतस्य महात्मनः ।
भूयस्तं शोभयामासुर्भूषाभिस्त्रिदिवोपमम् ।।

20. The place of stay proposed for the most eminent (this great soul) Bharatha (during his journey) was well decorated, it appeared like heaven (heavenly abode).

❍ ❍ ❍

२१. नक्षत्रेषु प्रशस्तेषु मुहूर्तेषु च तद्विदः ।
निवेशान्स्थापयामासुर्भरतस्य महात्मनः ।।

21. These men who were well versed in such matters (as choosing) right Muhoortha of auspicious time, day and stars, established dwelling places for the great soul Bharatha.

❍ ❍ ❍

२२. बहुपांसुचयाश्चापि परिखापरिवारिताः ।
तत्रेन्द्रनीलप्रतिमाः प्रतोलीवरशोभिताः ।।

22. (Levelling up) and filling up with plenty of sand that were like pearls of Indhraneela; Canals dug up for rain fed water ways; shining like principal roads of towns......

❍ ❍ ❍

२३. प्रासादमालासंयुक्ताः सौधप्राकारसंवृताः ।
पताकाशोभिताः सर्वेसुनिर्मितमहापथाः ।।

23. With raised platforms erected (for people to have clear view): Walls of abodes well (white) washed and plastered: All these well constructed roads were beautified by masts and banners.

❍ ❍ ❍

२४. विसर्पद्भिरिवाकाशे विटङ्काग्रविमानकैः ।
समुच्छ्रितैर्निवेशास्ते बभुः शक्रपुरोपमाः ।।

24. These dwelling places were so lofty with towers on them that they appeared to touch the sky! Appeared like Indhra's abode.

❍ ❍ ❍

२५. जाह्नवीं तु समासाद्य विविधद्रुमकाननाम् ।
शीतलामलपानीयां महामीनसमाकुलाम् ।।

25. Extending up to river Jahnavi (Ganges) which is full of mighty fishes, whose waters are clear and pure and cool, which is lined up with various plants and gardens......

❍ ❍ ❍

२६. सचन्द्रताराागणमण्डितं यथा
नभः क्षपायाममलं विराजते ।
नरेन्द्रमार्गः स तथा व्यराजत
क्रमेण रम्यः शुभशिल्पिनिर्मितः ।।

26. The beautiful royal route well laid by fine workmen, shone like pure sky studded by stars, galaxies, over Moon.

(Note: As usual there is exaggeration in this description: But the point to remember is that Bharatha is carrying a huge Army with multitude of citizens to the forest where Raama resides. As Bharatha wants to crown him there, the route on the way is cleared and beautified for Raama's glorious return as well. Kings of Ikshwaaku lineage have always 'nursed' their territory. No wonder they plant trees where there were none. They dig canals etc. Alas Raama refuses to come back till he completes his exile of 14 years as we will see later).

❍ ❍ ❍

Chapter 81

Bharatha Goes to the Royal Assembly Hall

१. ततो नान्दीमुखीं रात्रिं भरतं सूतमागधाः ।
तुष्टुवुर्वाग्विशेषज्ञाः स्तवैर्मङ्गलसंहितैः ।।

1. On the first auspicious* night (after the mourning period was over), Bards and Singers, (the Sootha-s and Maagadha-s, men of distinction) who knew merits (of good) speech, praised Bharatha with various auspicious renderings. (*The first night of- Naandhi).

❍ ❍ ❍

२. सुवर्णकोणाभिहतः प्राणदद्यामदुन्दुभिः ।
दध्मुः शङ्खांश्च शतशो नादांश्चोच्चावचस्वरान् ।।

2. Drum beats with golden and foremost (Drum) sticks sounded. They blew hundreds of conches of varying 'pitch' high and low.

❍ ❍ ❍

३. स तूर्यघोषः सुमहान्दिवमापूरयन्निव ।
भरतं शोकसन्तप्तं भूयः शोकैररन्ध्रयत् ।।

3. The loud musical sounds of Thoorya that appeared as though reverberating (filling up) the entire sky, made Bharatha who was tormented by grief, even more tormented by grief.

❍ ❍ ❍

४. ततः प्रबुद्धो भरतस्तं घोषं संनिवर्त्य च ।
नाहं राजेति चाप्युक्त्वा शत्रुघ्नमिदमब्रवीत् ।।

4. Bharatha who woke up (from slumber), stopped this tumult saying:= King, I Am Not! =Then addressed Schathrugna.

(Customarily a king is woken up by music and singing. But Bharatha will have none of it. He is not king, only Raama is according to him)

❍ ❍ ❍

५. पश्य शत्रुघ्न कैकेय्या लोकस्यापकृतं महत् ।
विसृज्य मयि दुःखानि राजा दशरथो गतः ।।

5. Oh Schathrugna! (Do you) See how great the harm is to the world (done) by Kaikeyi? King Dhascharatha has gone (to heaven) handing over (problems and) grief to me.

❍ ❍ ❍

६. तस्यैषा धर्मराजस्य धर्ममूला महात्मनः ।
परिभ्रमति राजश्रीर्नौरिवाकर्णिका जले ।।

6. This glorious kingdom of the great soul (Dhascharatha) the king of Dharma, (our) resplendent kingdom which is rooted in Dharma, is tottering like a boat without a rudder.

❍ ❍ ❍

७. यो हि नः सुमहान्नाथः सोऽपि प्रव्राजितो वनम् ।
अनया धर्ममुत्सृज्य मात्रा मे राघवः स्वयम् ।।

7. And our great protector (and lord), this (Raama) the Raaghava has been sent away to forest by this mother (of mine) who had abandoned her Dharma.

❍ ❍ ❍

८. इत्येवं भरतं प्रेक्ष्य विलपन्तमचेतनम् ।
कृपणं रुरुदुः सर्वाः सुस्वरं योषितस्तदा ।।

8. At that moment (when Bharatha was talking like this), all the ladies, seeing Bharatha wailing thus without restraint, cried pitiably in loud voice

९. तथा तस्मिन्विलपति वसिष्ठो राजधर्मवित् ।
सभामिक्ष्वाकुनाथस्य प्रविवेश महायशाः ।।

9. When they were wailing thus, the most famous Vasishta who was expert in royal Dharma (laws of kingdom), entered the Assembly Hall of the king of Ikshwaaku-s.

❍ ❍ ❍

१०. शातकुम्भमयीं रम्यां मणिरत्नसमाकुलाम् ।
सुधर्मामिव धर्मात्मा सगणः प्रत्यपद्यत ।।

10. Along with his entourage, this noble soul man of Dharma reached the Hall which was like the golden Sudharma and which was decorated with beautiful stones and gems.

❍ ❍ ❍

११. स काञ्चनमयं पीठं परार्ध्यास्तरणावृतम् ।
अध्यास्ते सर्ववेदज्ञो दूताननुशशास ह ।।

11. He knew all Vedha-s (a master of Vedha). He sat down on a golden chair with an excellent well spread out furnishing. He commanded the messengers.

❍ ❍ ❍

१२. ब्राह्मणान्क्षत्रियान्वैश्यानमात्यान् गणवल्लभान् ।
क्षिप्रमानयताव्यग्राः कृत्यमात्ययिकं हि नः ।।

12. With diligence, (go and) fetch at once, Braamins, Kshathriya-s, Vaisya-s and ministers and other well wishers: Because, our work is urgent (and brooks no delay).

❍ ❍ ❍

१३. सराजपुत्रं शत्रुघ्नं भरतं च यशस्विनम् ।
युधाजितं सुमन्त्रं च ये च तत्र हिता जनाः ।।

13. All those well disposed men (who are important) for this (occasion): the famous Bharatha, along with

the royal prince Schathrugna, minister Yudhaajith, Sumanthra, etc. (must also come).

❍ ❍ ❍

१४. ततो हलहलाशब्दो महान्समुदपद्यत ।
रथैरश्वैर्गजैश्चापि जनानामुपगच्छताम् ॥

14. At that moment, the rattling sounds of chariots, horses, elephants and of other visiting personalities arose loudly.

❍ ❍ ❍

१५. ततो भरतमायान्तं शतक्रतुमिवामराः ।
प्रत्यनन्दनप्रकृतयो यथा दशरथं तथा ॥

15. The citizens rejoiced as Bharatha was coming along at that time, just like they (used to) when Dhascharatha (appeared before them) and just like celestials (rejoicing before) Lord Indhra the Schakra.

❍ ❍ ❍

१६. ह्रद इव तिमिनागसंवृतः
स्तिमितजलो मणिशङ्खशर्करः ।
दशरथसुतशोभिता सभा
सदशरथेव बभूव सा पुरा ॥

16. Like it used to be when Dhascharatha (was in .the Hall), this Hall that shone by (the presence of) Dhascharatha's son (Bharatha) was like a big lake (of men), inhabited by fishes and sea lions, whose waters were calm and still and whose bed was of (pure) sand,, with shells and pearls
(Poet Vaalmeeki goes Poetic!)

❍ ❍ ❍

Chapter 82

Army Gets Ready (To go to Forest)

(Inspite of Vasishta's advice that Bharatha should take over the kingdom, Bharatha is firm that only Raama is successor to the throne. He is determined to get back Raama from forest.)

❍ ❍ ❍

१. तामार्यगणसंपूर्णां भरतः प्रग्रहां सभाम् ।
दद‍र्श बुद्धिसंपन्नः पूर्णचन्द्रो निशामिव ॥

1. Bharatha who was endowed with wisdom, viewed this Assembly that was filled with noble men, like moon over the star studded sky.

❍ ❍ ❍

२. आसनानि यथान्यायमार्याणां विशतां तदा ।
वस्त्राङ्गरागप्रभया द्योतिता सा सभोत्तमा ॥

2. The great assembly of these noble men who were all seated in their respective seats (as per protocol), shone by the lustre of their scented garments.

❍ ❍ ❍

३. सा विद्वज्जनसंपूर्णा सभा सुरुचिरा तदा ।
अदृश्यत घनापाये पूर्णचन्द्रेव शर्वरी ॥

3. At that time, this assembly which was full with most learned men, shone splendidly and was seen like night with full moon in autumn.

❍ ❍ ❍

४. राज्ञस्तु प्रकृतीः सर्वाः समग्राः प्रेक्ष्य धर्मवित् ।
इदं पुरोहितो वाक्यं भरतं मृदु चाब्रवीत् ॥

4. The King's Purohith, this (Vasishta) who knew Dharma,

took a look at all the men (gathered there) entirely, and then addressed Bharatha softly with these words.

५. तात राजा दशरथः स्वर्गतो धर्ममाचरन् ।
धनधान्यवतीं स्फीतां प्रदाय पृथिवीं तव ॥

5. Oh Lad! King Dhascharatha having (ever) followed Dharma, has gone to heaven offering this fertile land full with wealth and grains, to you (to rule the kingdom).

६. रामस्तथा सत्यधृतिः सतां धर्ममनुस्मरन् ।
नाजहात्पितुरादेशं शशी ज्योत्स्नामिवोदितः ॥

6. Likewise, remembering (and following) the Dharma of the Good, Raama who is steadfast in Truth, did not abandon his father's command (and went away on exile); Like light following the rising moon (Raama followed Dharma).

७. पित्रा भ्रात्रा च ते दत्तं राज्यं निहतकण्टकम् ।
तद्भुङ्क्ष्व मुदितामात्यः क्षिप्रमेवाभिषेचय ॥

7. (Therefore) You must take on this kingdom that is offered to you by your father and brother (Raama) without any hindrance: Anoint yourself (as king) before your happy ministers.

८. उदीच्याश्च प्रतीच्याश्च दाक्षिणात्याश्च केवलाः ।
कोट्याऽपरान्ताः सामुद्रा रत्नान्युपहरन्तु ते ॥

8. May (vassals) from north, west, and south and also islanders and others offer you gems in millions (as Tribute).

९. तच्छ्रुत्वा भरतो वाक्यं शोकेनाभिपरिप्लुतः ।
जगाम मनसा रामं धर्मज्ञो धर्मकाङ्क्षया ।।

9. Hearing these words (of Vasishta), the knower of Dharma, this Bharatha, out of his reverence to Dharma, thought about Raama (for a while), afflicted by grief .

❍ ❍ ❍

१०. स बाष्पकलया वाचा कलहंसस्वरो युवा ।
विललाप सभामध्ये जगर्हेच पुरोहितम् ।।

10. (Bharatha) who was of tender age, wailed before the Assembly with a feeble voice like that of a Hansa bird, words choked by tears. He was seized by anxiety over Purohith (Vasishta and his advice to take over the kingdom himself).

❍ ❍ ❍

११. चरितब्रह्मचर्यस्य विद्यास्नातस्य धीमतः ।
धर्मेप्रयतमानस्य को राज्यं मद्विधो हरेत् ।।

11. (Bharatha rejects Vasishta's advice): How can a man like me snatch away the kingdom from (Raama) who has practised Brammachaarya (Total celibacy in youth), who has 'Bathed' in knowledge of Vedha-s and who is wise and who is a keen follower of Dharma?

❍ ❍ ❍

१२. कथं दशरथाज्जातो भवेद्राज्यापहारकः ।
राज्यं चाहं च रामस्य धर्मं वक्तुमिहार्हसि ।।

12. How can I who am born as son of Dhascharatha, steal away the kingdom? The Kingdom and I are Raama's: You must talk about (and appreciate) the Dharma (and morality) in this matter.

❍ ❍ ❍

१३. ज्येष्ठः श्रेष्ठश्च धर्मात्मा दिलीपनहुषोपमः ।
लब्धुमर्हति काकुत्स्थो राज्यं दशरथो यथा ।।

13. Like (my forefathers) Dhileepa, Nahusha and (my father) the noble soul man of Dharma Dhascharatha, this foremost (Raama) the Kaakuthsa who is foremost (of men) and (also) the eldest, should obtain this kingdom.

❍ ❍ ❍

१४. अनार्यजुष्टमस्वर्ग्यं कुर्यां पापमहं यदि ।
इक्ष्वाकूणामहं लोके भवेयं कुलपांसनः ॥

14. If I commit this sin that will not lead me to heaven, (the sin) 'practised' by ignoble men, then I would become destroyer of my race of the Ikshwaaku-s in this world.

❍ ❍ ❍

१५. यद्धि मात्रा कृतं पापं नाहं तदपि रोचये ।
इहस्थो वनदुर्गस्थं नमस्यामि कृताञ्जलिः ॥

15. I do not desire 'that' Sin committed by my mother; With my hands cupped in Anjali, from here itself I bow to (Raama) who is (now) in the impenetrable forest.

❍ ❍ ❍

१६. राममेवानुगच्छामि स राजा द्विपदां वरः ।
त्रयाणामपि लोकानां राघवो राज्यमर्हति ॥

16. I will follow (and go after) Raama: The foremost of men (Raama) the Raaghava alone is King. He is fit to rule over the kingdoms of all the three worlds (of Heaven, Earth and Underworld).

❍ ❍ ❍

१७. तद्वाक्यं धर्मसंयुक्तं श्रुत्वा सर्वसभासदः ।
हर्षान्मुमुचुरश्रूणि रामे निहितचेतसः ॥

17. Hearing these words which contained Dharma, all the men in assembly who had surrendered their (heart) and mind to Raama, shed tears of joy.

❍ ❍ ❍

१८. यदि त्वार्यं न शक्ष्यामि विनिवर्तयितुं वनात् ।
वने तत्रैव वत्स्यामि यथाऽऽर्योलक्ष्मणस्तथा ॥

18. (Bharatha continued): If I am unable to bring back the noble (Aryan) Raama, from forest, then like the noble Lakshmana, I will (also) live in that forest (with them).

❍ ❍ ❍

१९. सर्वोपायं तु वर्तिष्ये विनिवर्तयितुं वनात् ।
समक्षमार्यमिश्राणां साधूनां गुणवर्तिनाम् ॥

19. In the presence of the good and most noble men who are endowed with good qualities, I am going to put in all my efforts to bring him back from forest.

❍ ❍ ❍

२०. विष्टिकर्मान्तिकाः सर्वेमार्गशोधकतक्षकाः ।
प्रस्थापिता मया पूर्वं यात्राऽपि मम रोचते ॥

20. (In fact) Already all have been sent out; workers and slaves and guides conversant with the Route, wielders of axes (an advance party).** Tradition alone satisfies me.

(** Poet Vaalmeeki uses the word =Yaathra= which has two meanings. Conventional meaning is Journey. The other meaning is even more appropriate, Tradition, Custom etc. Readers are welcome to chose any one of these two.)

❍ ❍ ❍

२१. एवमुक्त्वा तु धर्मात्मा भरतो भ्रातृवत्सलः ।
समीपस्थमुवाचेदं सुमन्त्रं मन्त्रकोविदम् ॥

21. Having said this, the noble soul man of Dharma, Bharatha, who was (deeply) attached to his brother (Raama) addressed this to Sumanthra who was expert in (offering) counsel, who was (standing very) near him.

❍ ❍ ❍

२२. तूर्णमुत्थाय गच्छ त्वं सुमन्त्र मम शासनात् ।
यात्रामाज्ञापय क्षिप्रं बलं चैव समानय ॥

22. Oh Sumanthra! You 'get up' and go soon. By my command, order the Journey. Bring the Army Soon. (Get started).

❍ ❍ ❍

२३. एवमुक्तः सुमन्त्रस्तु भरतेन महात्मना ।
प्रदिष्टस्सोऽदिशत्सर्वं यथासंदिष्टमिष्टवत् ॥

23. When told thus by the great soul Bharatha, this Sumanthra, receiving his order with pleasure, executed the order (of Bharatha) as per his command.

(Readers may note; Bharatha does not accept Vasishta's counsel. He does not talk to Vasishta the senior most adviser to the Ikshwaaku kings. He makes his intention very clear and orders Sumanthra. Bharatha is not crowned king; yet as the senior most prince, he exercises his right to command the Army to get ready.)

❍ ❍ ❍

२४. ताः प्रहृष्टाः प्रकृतयो बलाध्यक्षा बलस्य च ।
श्रुत्वा यात्रां समाज्ञप्तां राघवस्य निवर्तने ॥

24. When the citizens and the Army leaders heard about the command for journey of the Army to bring back Raama, they became very glad.

❍ ❍ ❍

२५. ततो योधाङ्गनाः सर्वा भर्तॄन्सर्वान्गृहे गृहे ।
यात्रागमनमाज्ञाय त्वरयन्ति स्म हर्षिताः ॥

25. At that time, the wives of warriors (soldiers), hearing about the journey, became very joyous and in house after house, they 'hurried' up their husbands (Wives were very glad to give a quick send off to their husbands who were members of the King's Army)

❍ ❍ ❍

२६. ते हयैर्गोरथैः शीघ्रैः स्यन्दनैश्च महाजवैः ।
सह योधैर्बलाध्यक्षा बलं सर्वमचोदयन् ।।

26. The Chiefs of the Army, (some riding) on horses, some on fast moving vehicles drawn by bulls, some on fast moving chariots, goaded the soldiers and all the army. (To get started quickly).

❍ ❍ ❍

२७. सज्जं तु तद्बलं दृष्ट्वा भरतो गुरुसन्निधौ ।
रथं मे त्वरयस्वेति सुमन्त्रं पार्श्वतोऽब्रवीत् ।।

27. Seeing the army ready (and well commissioned), Bharatha addressed Sumanthra who was standing by the side of the Guru (Vasishta): = Get Ready Soon (with) My Chariot.=

❍ ❍ ❍

२८. भरतस्य तु तस्याज्ञां प्रतिगृह्य च हर्षितः ।
रथं गृहीत्वा प्रययौ युक्तं परमवाजिभिः ।।

28. Receiving Bharatha's command, (Sumanthra), with great joy, at once brought and 'placed' (before Bharatha) a chariot yoked to fast moving horses.

❍ ❍ ❍

२९. स राघवः सत्यधृतिः प्रतापवान्
ब्रुवन्सुयुक्तं दृढसत्यविक्रमः ।
गुरुं महारण्यगतं यशस्विनं
प्रसादयिष्यन्भरतोऽब्रवीत्तदा ।।

29. The truly valiant, most majestic, most truthful, this Bharatha the Raaghava (looking forward to see and) honour his famous Guru (brother Raama) who was in the great forest, then said (this), speaking suitably (for the occasion).

❍ ❍ ❍

३०. तूर्णं समुत्थाय सुमन्त्र गच्छ
बलस्य योगाय बलप्रधानान् ।
आनेतुमिच्छामि हि तं वनस्थं
प्रसाद्य रामं जगतो हिताय ॥

30. Oh Sumanthra! Getting out quickly, go (at once) to the Army chiefs for the sake of welfare (and needs of) the army. I desire to honour this Raama who is in forest (now) and bring him back for the good of the world.

(The Army as ever gets first priority: No wonder Bharatha asks his senior minister Sumanthra to see that Army is well provided.)

❍ ❍ ❍

३१. स सूतपुत्रो भरतेन सम्य
गाज्ञापितः संपरिपूर्णकामः ।
शशास सर्वान्प्रकृतिप्रधानान्
बलस्य मुख्यांश्च सुहृज्जनं च ॥

31. Properly commanded by Bharatha, (this charioteer Sumanthra) this son of a charioteer whose desire (of getting Raama back) was (now being) fulfilled, commanded all the foremost men, all the chiefs of the Army, friends etc.

❍ ❍ ❍

३२. ततः समुत्थाय कुले कुले ते
राजन्यवैश्या वृषलाश्च विप्राः ।
अयूयुजन्नुष्ट्रखरान् रथांश्च
नागान्हयांश्चैव कुलप्रसूतान् ॥

32. The Kshathriya-s, the Vaischya-s, the Schoodhra-s, the Braamins (citizens from all communities) got ready from house to house; And they got really well bred camels, chariots, elephants, horses.

(Note: As Raama is going to be king, Bharatha takes with him such a huge Army along with thousands of citizens; Wants to convert forest into Ayodhya! Alas, Bharatha's mission fails. Raama refuses to return till 14 years exile is over, as we shall see later.)

❍ ❍ ❍

Chapter 83

Bharatha Starts (from Ayodhya to Fetch Raama)

१. ततः समुत्थितः काल्यमास्थाय स्यन्दनोत्तमम् ।
प्रययौ भरतः शीघ्रं रामदर्शनकाङ्क्षया ॥

1. Keenly looking forward to see Raama, then Bharatha got up in the early morning and started out, riding on a foremost chariot.

❍ ❍ ❍

२. अग्रतः प्रययुस्तस्य सर्वेमन्त्रिपुरोधसः ।
अधिरुह्य हयैर्युक्तान्रथान्सूर्यरथोपमान् ॥

2. All the ministers, purohiths (priests etc) got into chariots which resembled the chariot of Sun (God) and which were yoked to horses. They left before him.

❍ ❍ ❍

३. नवनागसहस्राणि कल्पितानि यथाविधि ।
अन्वयुर्भरतं यान्तमिक्ष्वाकुकुलनन्दनम् ॥

3. Nine thousand well behaved elephants followed Bharatha, the darling of the Ikshwaaku race as he was going along, as per custom.

❍ ❍ ❍

४. षष्टी रथसहस्राणि धन्विनो विविधायुधाः ।
अन्वयुर्भरतं यान्तं राजपुत्रं यशस्विनम् ॥

4. Sixty thousand chariots, (Soldiers) wielding various

weapons, Bow men, followed the famous Royal Prince (Bharatha) as he went along.

❍ ❍ ❍

५. शतं सहस्राण्यश्वानां समारूढानि राघवम् ।
अन्वयुर्भरतं यान्तं सत्यसन्धं जितेन्द्रियम् ।।

5. Ten thousand Riders on horse back followed this most truthful Bharatha the Raaghava who was a man of composure, (who had conquered his senses and passions), as he went along.

❍ ❍ ❍

६. कैकेयी च सुमित्रा च कौसल्या च यशस्विनी ।
रामानयनसंहृष्टा ययुर्यानेन भास्वता ।।

6. Happy to bring back Raama, the famous Kowsalya, Sumithra and Kaikeyi went on a chariot that was glorious.

(It is interesting to note that in his effort to bring back Raama from forest, Bharatha takes along with him his mother Kaikeyi also, who, by now, has reconciled to the fact that her son Bharatha does not want to become King.)

❍ ❍ ❍

७. प्रयाताश्चार्यसङ्घाता रामं द्रष्टुं सलक्ष्मणम् ।
तस्यैव च कथाश्चित्राः कुर्वाणा हृष्टमानसाः ।।

7. The multitude of noble men whose minds were exhilarated in order to see Raama who was (ever) with Lakshmana, went along, talking about (Raama's) wonderful qualities.

❍ ❍ ❍

८. मेघश्यामं महाबाहुं स्थिरसत्त्वं दृढव्रतम् ।
कदा द्रक्ष्यामहे रामं जगतः शोकनाशनम् ।।

8. (The citizens were talking like this as they went along to

forest) When will we see (our) Raama whose complexion is royal blue like that of sky, who is absolutely good, who is resolute in vows, who is mighty limbed and who destroys sorrow of the world.

❍ ❍ ❍

९. दृष्ट एव हि नः शोकमपनेष्यति राघवः ।
तमः सर्वस्य लोकस्य समुद्यन्निव भास्करः ।।

9. The moment (Raama) the Raaghava is seen (by us), he will remove our grief (and suffering) like the rising sun removing darkness of the entire world.

❍ ❍ ❍

१०. इत्येवं कथयन्तस्ते संप्रहृष्टाः कथाः शुभाः ।
परिष्वजानाश्चान्योन्यं ययुर्नागरिकास्तदा ।।

10. The happy citizens narrating such auspicious (and glorious) stories, went along, clasping one another (by hand).

❍ ❍ ❍

११. ये च तत्रापरे सर्वेसंमता ये च नैगमाः ।
रामं प्रति ययुर्हृष्टाः सर्वाः प्रकृतयस्तथा ।।

11. The scholars who are renowned in Vedhic studies, all of them, and also other citizens and accomplished men, went along happily 'towards' Raama (to meet Raama in forest)

❍ ❍ ❍

१२. मणिकाराश्च ये केचित्कुम्भकाराश्च शोभनाः ।
सूत्रकर्मकृतश्चैव ये च शस्त्रोपजीविनः ।।
१३. मायूरकाः क्राकचिका रोचका वेधकास्तथा ।
दन्तकाराः सुधाकारा ये च गन्धोपजीविनः ।।
१४. सुवर्णकाराः प्रख्यातास्तथा कम्बलधावकाः ।
स्नापकोच्छादका वैद्या धूपकाः शौण्डिकास्तथा ।।

१५. रजकारस्तुन्नवायाश्च ग्रामघोषमहत्तराः ।
शैलूषाश्च सह स्त्रीभिर्ययुः कैवर्तकास्तथा ॥
१६. समाहिता वेदविदो ब्राह्मणा वृत्तसंमताः ।
गोरथैर्भरतं यान्तमनुजग्मुः राहस्रशः ॥

12. to 16.

(Poet Vaalmeeki describes Bharatha's entourage)
Jewellers and gem cutters, potters, weavers, skilled yarn spinners, soldiers, Artisans using Peacock feathers, Sawyers (working on wood), glass blowers, excavators, diggers, masons, white washers, merchants dealing in perfumes... expert goldsmiths, likewise carpet makers, Masseurs giving oil baths, doctors, wine makers, & merchants. Washermen, Dairy men, Men from villages and hamlets, Actors (and entertainers): Likewise fishermen; Some accompanied their wives, went along....Religious men, scholars of Vedha-s, Braamins who were honoured for their conduct, all went along in thousands of vehicles drawn by bullocks and they followed Bharatha who was going along.

❍ ❍ ❍

१७. सुवेषाः शुद्धवसनास्ताम्रमृष्टानुलेपनाः ।
सर्वेते विविधैर्यानैः शनैर्भरतमन्वयुः ॥

17. All of them were well dressed, well ornamented, besmeared with sandal paste and (other unguents) (Riding) on various vehicles in rows (in formations) they followed Bharatha.

❍ ❍ ❍

१८. प्रहृष्टमुदिता सेना साऽन्वयात्कैकयीसुतम् ।
भ्रातुरानयने यान्तं भरतं भ्रातृवत्सलम् ॥

18. Exhilarated with joy, this Army followed Bharatha the son of Kaikeyi who was most attached to his brother (Raama), who was going to bring back his brother (Raama from forest)

❍ ❍ ❍

१९. ते गत्वा दूरमध्वानं रथयानाश्वकुञ्जरैः ।
समासेदुस्ततो गङ्गां शृङ्गिबेरपुरं प्रति ॥

19. Going far away in chariot, vehicles, on horse backs and on elephants, they then reached Ganges near Schringabhaerapura.

❍ ❍ ❍

२०. यत्र रामसखो वीरो गुहो ज्ञातिगणैर्वृतः ।
निवसत्यप्रमादेन देशं तं परिपालयन् ॥

20. This is the territory where Raama's, 'Comrade', the brave Guha, surrounded (and served by) multitude of his folks, lives, protecting it with vigilance.

(Poet Vaalmeeki occasionally uses present tense; as in this case, he says Guha lives here.)

❍ ❍ ❍

२१. उपेत्य तीरं गङ्गायाश्चक्रवाकैरलंकृतम् ।
व्यवातिष्ठत सा सेना भरतस्यानुयायिनी ॥

21. This Army that was following Bharatha reached the banks of Ganges that was beautified by (the presence of a large number of) Chakravaka birds.

❍ ❍ ❍

२२. निरीक्ष्य सुस्थितां सेनां तां च गङ्गां शिवोदकाम् ।
भरतः सचिवान्सर्वानब्रवीद्वाक्यकोविदः ॥

22. Bharatha, the master of speech (and conversation), observing that his Army was resting there and (seeing) the auspicious river as well, addressed all his ministers.

❍ ❍ ❍

२३. निवेशयत मे सैन्यमभिप्रायेण सर्वतः ।
विश्रान्ताः प्रतरिष्यामः श्व इदानीं महानदीम् ॥

23. As per their desire, let my Army now be made to rest

around all these places. After taking rest, we shall cross the river tomorrow.

❍ ❍ ❍

२४. दातुं च तावदिच्छामि स्वर्गतस्य महीपतेः ।
और्ध्वदेहनिमित्तार्थमवतीर्योदकं नदीम् ॥

24. At this time, I desire to get down in the river and offer waters' for the King (my late father) who has gone to heaven, for his welfare in the other world.

(It is customary to perform water Rituals for forefathers. Of course waters of the Ganges is about the holiest in the world.)

❍ ❍ ❍

२५. तस्यैवं ब्रुवतोऽमात्यास्तथेत्युक्त्वा समाहिताः ।
न्यवेशयंस्तांश्छन्देन स्वेन स्वेन पृथक् पृथक् ॥

25. When he was speaking thus, the ministers who accepted this, told; = So Be It:= They then stationed (Army and others) at their pleasure, there and there.

❍ ❍ ❍

२६. निवेश्य गङ्गामनु तां महानदीं
चमूं विधानैः परिबर्हशोभिनीम् ।
उवास रामस्य तदा महात्मनो
विचिन्तयानो भरतो निवर्तनम् ॥

26. After making arrangements and resting this (vast) Army that was shining with its retinue (of citizens and all) near the banks of the great river Ganges, Bharatha stayed there thinking about the return of the great soul Raama.

Chapter 84

Bharatha and Guha Meet (Near Schringabhaerapura)

१. ततो निविष्टां ध्वजिनीं गङ्गामन्वाश्रितां नदीम् ।
निषादराजो दृष्टैव ज्ञातीन्संत्वरितोऽब्रवीत् ।।

1. When the king of hunters (Guha) saw the stationed Army that had reached river Ganges, in great hurry he addressed his kinsmen.

❍ ❍ ❍

२. महतीयमितः सेना सागराभा प्रदृश्यते ।
नास्यान्तमवगच्छामि मनसाऽपि विचिन्तयन् ।।

2. This Army is mighty and is seen (to appear) like an ocean. I cannot even conceive in my mind its extent.

❍ ❍ ❍

३. यथा तु खलु दुर्बुद्धिर्भरतः स्वयमागतः ।
स एष हि महाकायः कोविदारध्वजो रथे ।।

3. There is a mighty bodied (lofty) mast (made of wood) that is difficult to split up, on (top of) the chariot. Therefore (I think) the wicked minded Bharatha has himself come (to harm Raama)

(A King's army is recognised by the mast and banner. Guha sees this and has suspicion that Bharatha has come with his Army to do harm to his dear friend Raama in forest.)

❍ ❍ ❍

४. बन्धयिष्यति वा दाशानथवाऽस्मान्वधिष्यति ।
अथ दाशरथिं रामं पित्रा राज्याद्विवासितम् ।।

५. संपन्नां श्रियमिच्छन् स तस्य राज्ञोऽतिदुर्लभाम् ।
भरतः कैकयीपुत्रो हन्तुं समधिगच्छति ।।

4. & 5.

He is going to enslave us all or kill us who are fishermen; now that Raama has been sent away by his father Dhascharatha. .....To kill (Raama), this Bharatha the son of Kaikeyi, has come here now, desirous of accomplishing (his objective of taking full control) over this resplendent kingdom that is difficult to obtain.

(Guha being a very dear friend of Raama suspects that Bharatha has brought the huge Army to forest to destroy his brother Raama and rule the kingdom without hindrance!)

❍ ❍ ❍

६. भर्ता चैव सखा चैव रामो दाशरथिर्मम ।
तस्यार्थकामाः सन्नद्धा गङ्गानूपेऽत्र तिष्ठत ॥

6. Raama the son of Dhascharatha is my master (and besides) my friend. (And so) all of you be prepared (for war) and stay near Ganges river for this purpose (of warding off attack from Bharatha).

❍ ❍ ❍

७. तिष्ठन्तु सर्वदाशाश्च गङ्गामन्वाश्रिता नदीम् ।
बलयुक्ता नदीरक्षा मांसमूलफलाशनाः ॥

7. All the fishermen, along with (our) Army and with (rations of) meats, fruits, and tubers for sustenance, stay near Ganges river and stand on guard over the river... Saying thus, he goaded them further.

(Here is a case of friendship blinding a person. Guha is almost certain that Bharatha has come to destroy Raama and so 'prepares' for war. He does not want Bharatha to cross the river!)

❍ ❍ ❍

८. नावां शतानां पञ्चानां कैवर्तानां शतं शतम् ।
सन्नद्धानां तथा यूनां तिष्ठत्वित्यभ्यचोदयत् ॥

8. Fishermen with 500 well harnessed boats and "nets' etc stand (in readiness). Saying thus, he 'goaded' them (further).

❍ ❍ ❍

९. यदा दुष्टस्तु भरतो रामस्येह भविष्यति ।
नेयं स्वस्तिमती सेना गङ्गामद्य तरिष्यति ॥

9. If this Bharatha now becomes wicked (and intends harm) to Raama, then this (his) Army should not cross Ganges in safety.

❍ ❍ ❍

१०. इत्युक्त्वोपायनं गृह्य मत्स्यमांसमधूनि च ।
अभिचक्राम भरतं निषादाधिपतिर्गुहः ॥

10. Having said thus, the chief of hunters, this Guha, then went out to meet Bharatha, taking with him fish, meats and wines.

❍ ❍ ❍

११. तमायान्तं तु संप्रेक्ष्य सूतपुत्रः प्रतापवान् ।
भरतायाचचक्षेऽथ विनयज्ञो विनीतवत् ॥

11. The glorious (Sumanthra) the son of charioteer who knew the protocol and the laws (of the realm), seeing (this Guha) coming (towards them), enlightened Bharatha about him with reverence, thus.

❍ ❍ ❍

१२. एष ज्ञातिसहस्रेण स्थपतिः परिवारितः ।
कुशलो दण्डकारण्ये वृद्धो भ्रातुश्च ते सखा ॥

12. (Of course Sumanthra knows all about Guha and he tells Bharatha about Guha and his friendship and devotion to Raama). This eminent man is the chief (of this territory).He is surrounded (and served) by thousands of his kinsmen. Well conversant about Dhandaka forest. And besides he is your brother (Raama's) friend.

❍ ❍ ❍

१३. तस्मात्पश्यतु काकुत्स्थ त्वां निषादाधिपो गुहः ।
असंशयं विजानीते यत्र तौ रामलक्ष्मणौ ।।

13. Oh (Bharatha the Kaakuthsa! He will, without any doubt, know where Raama and Lakshmana are. Therefore, you should see (meet) this Guha, the chief of hunters.

❍ ❍ ❍

१४. एतत्तु वचनं श्रुत्वा सुमन्त्राद्भरतः शुभम् ।
उवाच वचनं शीघ्रं गुहः पश्यतु मामिति ।।

14. Hearing these pleasing words of Sumanthra, Bharatha at once said these words: = May Guha see me now =

❍ ❍ ❍

१५. लब्ध्वा ह्यनुज्ञां संहृष्टो ज्ञातिभिः परिवारितः ।
आगम्य भरतं प्रह्वो गुहो वचनमब्रवीत् ।।

15. Having received permission, Guha, who was very happy, approached Bharatha, accompanied by his retinue. He addressed these words humbly.

❍ ❍ ❍

१६. निष्कुटश्चैव देशोऽयं वञ्चिताश्चापि ते वयम् ।
निवेदयामस्ते सर्वेस्वके दासकुले वस ।।

16. This territory is your pleasure garden. We are all cheated (by you, because we were denied the pleasure of meeting you earlier). Yet, we proclaim (and request) that you should stay (here) in your Vassal's territory.

❍ ❍ ❍

१७. अस्ति मूलं फलं चैव निषादैः समुपार्जितम् ।
आर्द्रमांसं च संशुष्कं वन्यं चोच्चावचं महत् ।।

17. Tubers, fruits, dry meats and fresh (meats) all brought by hunters, are plenty, procured from forest here (for you all).

❍ ❍ ❍

१८. आशंसे स्वाशिता सेना वत्स्यतीमां विभावरीम् ।
अर्चितो विविधैः कामैः श्वः ससैन्यो गमिष्यसि ॥

18. Let your Army stay here this night, well fed: I beg you to go only tomorrow with your Army (only) after being honoured with various desirables (offered by us).

❍ ❍ ❍

Chapter 85

Bharatha and Guha Converse

१. एवमुक्तस्तु भरतो निषाधिपतिं गुहम् ।
प्रत्युवाच महाप्राज्ञो वाक्यं हेत्वर्थसंहितम् ॥

1. When told thus (by Guha), the most intelligent Bharatha replied to Guha, the lord of hunters, with words of content and reasoning.

❍ ❍ ❍

२. ऊर्जितः खलु ते कामः कृतो मम गुरोः सखे ।
यो मे त्वमीदृशीं सेनामेकोऽभ्यर्चितुमिच्छसि ॥

2. Oh (Guha) my Guru (Raama's) friend! Indeed, all by yourself, you desire to honour (and extend hospitality) to such an army (of mine): Your strong desire is indeed (welcome and) fulfilled.

❍ ❍ ❍

३. इत्युक्त्वा तु महातेजा गुहं वचनमुत्तमम् ।
अब्रवीद्भरतः श्रीमान्निषादाधिपतिं पुनः ॥

3. Saying foremost words thus, this resplendent, most brilliant Bharatha, again addressed Guha, the chief of hunters, further.

❍ ❍ ❍

४. कतरेण गमिष्यामि भरद्वाजाश्रमं गुह ।
गहनोऽयं भृशं देशो गङ्गानूपो दुरत्ययः ॥

4. Oh Guha! By which route should we go to the hermitage of Sage Bharadhwaja: This territory is very impenetrable; And Ganges is difficult to cross.

❍ ❍ ❍

५. तस्य तद्वचनं श्रुत्वा राजपुत्रस्य धीमतः ।
अब्रवीत्प्राञ्जलिर्वाक्यं गुहो गहनगोचरः ॥

5. Hearing the words of the wise son of the king, this Guha the resident of forest, addressed him with his hands cupped in Anjali.

(Bharatha does not disclose the purpose of his visit with his huge army and Guha comes out with his fear about Bharatha's intentions.)

❍ ❍ ❍

६. दाशास्त्वाऽनुगमिष्यन्ति धन्विनः सुसमाहिताः ।
अहं चानुगमिष्यामि राजपुत्र महायशः ॥

6. Oh most famous Prince (Bharatha)! Devoted fishermen wielding bow will come along with you. I will also accompany you.

❍ ❍ ❍

७. कच्चिन्न दुष्टो व्रजसि रामस्याक्लिष्टकर्मणः ।
इयं ते महती सेना शड्कां जनयतीव मे ॥

7 I trust you are going on this journey without (intention of doing) harm to Raama, who (ever) does tasks without weariness: (But) This mighty Army (of yours) raises some fear and doubt in me.

❍ ❍ ❍

८. तमेवमभिभाषन्तमाकाश इव निर्मलः ।
भरतः श्लक्ष्णया वाचा गुहं वचनमब्रवीत् ॥

8. And Bharatha who was (pure) and spotless like (the clear) sky, addressed this Guha who was talking like this, with words of sincerity.

❍ ❍ ❍

९. मा भूत्स कालो यत्कष्टं न मां शङ्कितुमर्हसि ।
राघवः स हि मे भ्राता ज्येष्ठः पितृसमो मतः ।।

9. You should not entertain doubts about me; This is cruel (for me to hear); Such a situation should never arise; Because, this (Raama) the Raaghava, my elder brother, is equal to my father in (my) esteem.

❍ ❍ ❍

१०. तं निवर्तयितुं यामि काकुत्स्थं वनवासिनम् ।
बुद्धिरन्या न ते कार्या गुह सत्यं ब्रवीमि ते ।।

10. Oh Guha! I am going (on journey), to bring back this (Raama the) Kaakuthsa who is (now) resident of forest (here). There should be no other thought in you. I am telling you truthfully.

❍ ❍ ❍

११. स तु संहृष्टवदनः श्रुत्वा भरतभाषितम् ।
पुनरेवाब्रवीद्वाक्यं भरतं प्रति हर्षितः ।।

11. Hearing Bharatha's speech, (Guha) became delighted and once again addressed Bharatha these words with a happy face.

❍ ❍ ❍

१२. धन्यस्त्वं न त्वया तुल्यं पश्यामि जगतीतले ।
अयत्नादागतं राज्यं यस्त्वं त्यक्तुमिहेच्छसि ।।

12. (Oh Bharatha): I do not see any one in this world equal to you, as you desire to (voluntarily) relinquish the kingdom that came by you without any exertion. You are most virtuous.

❍ ❍ ❍

१३. शाश्वती खलु ते कीर्तिर्लोकाननुचरिष्यति ।
यस्त्वं कृच्छ्रगतं रामं प्रत्यानयितुमिच्छसि ।।

13. Your fame will follow (and stand) in this world eternally as you desire to bring back Raama who is in 'hardship' (in forest). (Raama is not in hardship, Raama can never be any where; but Guha's friendship makes him say that Raama is suffering in forest!)

❍ ❍ ❍

१४. एवं संभाषमाणस्य गुहस्य भरतं तदा ।
बभौ नष्टप्रभः सूर्योरजनी चाभ्यवर्तत ।।

14. While Guha was talking to Bharatha like this, the Sun was 'losing' its lustre: Night fell.

❍ ❍ ❍

१५. संनिवेश्य सतां सेनां गुहेन परितोषितः ।
शत्रुघ्नेन सह श्रीमाञ्छयनं समुपागमत् ।।

15. Pleased (and extolled) thus by Guha, this resplendent (Bharatha), along with Schathrugna, rested his Army and then went to (the place of) sleep

❍ ❍ ❍

१६. रामचिन्तामयः शोको भरतस्य महात्मनः ।
उपस्थितो ह्यनर्हस्य धर्मप्रेक्षस्य तादृशः ।।

16. The grief caused by worrying about Raama who did not deserve such (treatment meted out to him), afflicted this great soul Bharatha who (always) looked up to Dharma.

❍ ❍ ❍

१७. अन्तर्दाहेन दहनः संतापयति राघवम् ।
वनदाहाभिसन्तप्तं गूढोऽग्निरिव पादपम् ।।

17. Like the hidden (forest) Fire (burning up) in

conflagration dried up trees of forest, this burning (of his grief) burnt (Bharatha) the Raaghava, from inside.

❍ ❍ ❍

१८. प्रसृतः सर्वगात्रेभ्यः स्वेदं शोकाग्निसंभवम् ।
यथा सूर्यांशुसन्तप्तो हिमवान्प्रसृतो हिमम् ।।

18. Like Himaalaya-s shedding its snow by the heat of Sun's rays, the sweat caused by the heat of his grief issued forth from all parts of his body.

❍ ❍ ❍

१९. ध्याननिर्दरशैलेन विनिश्वसितधातुना ।
दैन्यपादपसङ्घेन शोकायासाधिश्रृङ्गिणा ।।
२०. प्रमोहानन्तसत्त्वेन सन्तापौषधिवेणुना ।
आक्रान्तो दुःखशैलेन मज्जता कैकयीसुतः ।।

19 & 20.

(Poet Vaalmeeki goes poetic! Mountain with its caves, trees, medicinal plants, minerals. etc = The mountain of suffering.)

Like rocks in the 'caves' of meditation; Like (Mineral) elements (The Daathu-s of mountain) that is the deep hard breath; Like stilled trees of (mental) depression; Like sharp peaks of mountain that is pain and grief.... Like bewilderment (and uncertainty) of a pregnant woman; Like the bitter medicinal plants that are his 'Anguish'; ...This (Bharatha) the son of Kaikeyi was overcome (by torment), depressed (and pressed down) by the mountain of grief.

❍ ❍ ❍

२१. विनिश्वसन्वै भृशदुर्मनास्ततः
प्रमूढसंज्ञः परमापदं गतः ।
शमं न लेभे हृदयज्वरार्दितो
नरर्षभो यूथहतो यथर्षभः ।।

21. Being in a state of affliction, in deep melancholy, his heart 'burning' with 'fever' (of grief), this (Bharatha) the 'bull' amongst men, having lost his sense of understanding, did not obtain any sleep, and he was breathing hard and deep. He was like a goat that strayed from its herd.

❍ ❍ ❍

२२. गुहेन सार्धं भरतः समागतो
महानुभावः सजनः समाहितः ।
सुदुर्मनास्तं भरतं तदा पुनः
गुहःसमाश्वासयदग्रजं प्रति ॥

22. Man of experience and understanding, man of composure, this Bharatha kept company with Guha along with his men. At that time Guha, although he (himself) was depressed, consoled Bharatha regarding his brother (Raama).

❍ ❍ ❍

Chapter 86

Guha Talks About Lakshmana (to Bharatha)

१. आचचक्षेऽथ सद्भावं लक्ष्मणस्य महात्मनः ।
भरतायाप्रमेयाय गुहो गहनगोचरः ॥

1. This Guha who was resident of the forest, enlightened about the good nature of the great soul Lakshmana, to Bharatha (of) unfathomable (prowess).

❍ ❍ ❍

२. तं जाग्रतं गुणैर्युक्तं वरचापेषुधारिणम् ।
भ्रातृगुप्त्यर्थमत्यन्तमहं लक्ष्मणमब्रवम् ॥

2. (Oh Bharatha, listen): I told this Lakshmana who is endowed with (noble) qualities, who wielded his bow,

who was completely awake (at night in order) to keep guard over his brother

❍ ❍ ❍

३. इयं तात सुखा शय्या त्वदर्थमुपकल्पिता ।
प्रत्याश्वसिहि शेष्वास्यां सुखं राघवनन्दन ।।

3. (Oh Bharatha! I said to him): Oh dear (Lakshmana)! A pleasant bed is kept here for you. (Oh Lakshmana the) darling of Raghu-s! You lie down comfortably on this. Take (some) rest.

❍ ❍ ❍

४. उचितोऽयं जनः सर्वो दुःखानां त्वं सुखोचितः ।
धर्मात्मंस्तव गुप्त्यर्थं जागरिष्यामहे वयम् ।।

4. Oh noble soul man of Dharma,(Oh Lakshmana)! All these (my) men are accustomed to hardships; (But) You are used to comforts; We will (all) be awake for your protection (and also for Raama's).

❍ ❍ ❍

५. न हि रामात्प्रियतरो ममास्ति भुवि कश्चन ।
सोत्सुकोऽभूर्ब्रवीम्येतदप्यसत्यं तवाग्रतः ।।

5. (And I told Lakshmana further, Oh Bharatha): In this world, there is no one dearer to me than Raama. So do not be uneasy: Will I (dare to) speak untruth before you?

❍ ❍ ❍

६. अस्य प्रसादादाशंसे लोकेऽस्मिन्सुमहद्यशः ।
धर्मावाप्तिं च विपुलामर्थावाप्तिं च केवलाम् ।।

6. I swear, that, in this world, the great fame, the attainment of extensive (fruits of) Dharma, and also the gathering of mundane wealth, all these are due to his grace. (Raama's grace upon me).

❍ ❍ ❍

७. सोऽहं प्रियसखं रामं शयानं सह सीतया ।
रक्षिष्यामि धनुष्पाणिः सर्वैः स्वैर्ज्ञातिभिः सह ।।

7. (And I told Lakshmana): Such as I am, wielding my bow, I will guard and protect my beloved Raama who is sleeping along with Seetha, (and will guard them both) along with all my kinsmen.

❍ ❍ ❍

८. न हि मेऽविदितं किंचिद्वनेऽस्मिंश्चरतः सदा ।
चतुरङ्गं ह्यपि बलं प्रसहेम वयं युधि ।।

8. (And I told Lakshmana): In this forest, as I am always moving about, there is nothing that is not known to me: And besides, we can match even a (mighty) Army drawn from Four Services.

❍ ❍ ❍

९. एवमस्माभिरुक्तेन लक्ष्मणेन महात्मना ।
अनुनीता वयं सर्वेधर्ममेवानुपश्यता ।।

9. (Oh Bharatha, listen): When thus told by us, by this great soul Lakshmana who can see only Dharma, we were all (humbly) entreated thus.

❍ ❍ ❍

१०. कथं दाशरथौ भूमौ शयाने सह सीतया ।
शक्या निद्रा मया लब्धुं जीवितं वा सुखानि च ।।

10. (And this is what Lakshmana said to me, Oh Bharatha): How can I tolerate to (seek and) obtain comfort and sleep (for myself) or even (making a) living, when (Raama) the son of Dhascharatha is lying down on bare earth along with Seetha?

❍ ❍ ❍

११. यो न देवासुरैः सर्वैः शक्यः प्रसहितुं युधि ।
तं पश्य गुह संविष्टं तृणेषु सह सीतया ।।

11. (And Lakshmana continued): Oh Guha! You are seeing a man whom, even Dheva-s and Asura-s (of celestial world), cannot face in a war, now lying down on the floor on (a bed of) grass, by the side of Seetha!

❍ ❍ ❍

१२. महता तपसा लब्धो विविधैश्च परिश्रमैः ।
एको दशरथस्येष्टः पुत्रः सदृशलक्षणः ।।

12. (And Lakshmana told me further, Oh Bharatha): He is unique: Possesses (all) qualities befitting him. He was born as a son by (virtue of) many sacrifices and great penance, to Dhascharatha.

❍ ❍ ❍

१३. अस्मिन्प्रव्राजिते राजा न चिरं वर्तयिष्यति ।
विधवा मेदिनी नूनं क्षिप्रमेव भविष्यति ।।

13. (And Lakshmana said further): As he is in exile, king (Dhascharatha) will not live long. Soon the entire Earth will become a 'widow'.

(Readers know that, what Lakshmana feared and told Guha, came true. His father passed away when Lakshmana and Raama were away on exile. Of course Lakshmana was not aware of his father's death.)

❍ ❍ ❍

१४. विनद्य सुमहानादं श्रमेणोपरताः स्त्रियः ।
निर्घोषोपरतं तात मन्ये रामनिवेशनम् ।।

14. (And Lakshmana said to me further, Oh Bharatha): Oh dear (friend Guha) 1 I think Raama's palace (at Ayodhya) will now be still and silent and the ladies there, after crying aloud, would have stopped (crying) by sheer tiresomeness.

❍ ❍ ❍

१५. कौसल्या चैव राजा च तथैव जननी मम ।
नाशंसे यदि जीवेयुः सर्वेते शर्वरीमिमाम् ।।

15. And I suspect that the king, Kowsalya, and my mother (Sumithra), all of them, will not be alive even (before) this night.

(Lakshmana was wrong here: These two were very much alive!)

❍ ❍ ❍

१६. जीवेदपि हि मे माता शत्रुघ्नस्यान्ववेक्षया ।
दुःखिता या तु कौसल्या वीरसूर्विनशिष्यति ।।

16. Perhaps, my mother (Sumithra) may be alive, out of consideration (and) for (the sake of her other son) Schathrugna: But Kowsalya the mother of the brave son (Raama) will perish in sorrow.

(Readers know Sumithra had two sons, Lakshmana & Schathrugna.)

❍ ❍ ❍

१७. अतिक्रान्तमतिक्रान्तमनवाप्य मनोरथम् ।
राज्ये राममनिक्षिप्य पिता मे विनशिष्यति ।।

17. My father unable to install Raama in the kingdom, will perish, unable to fulfill his desire. Oh what a transgression, what a transgression!

❍ ❍ ❍

१८. सिद्धार्थाः पितरं वृत्तं तस्मिन्काले ह्युपस्थिते ।
प्रेतकार्येषु सर्वेषु संस्करिष्यन्ति भूमिपम् ।।

18. When that time comes, (when my father dies) only accomplished (and fortunate ones) will perform all the Funereal Rites for my father, the lord of Earth.

❍ ❍ ❍

१९. रम्यचत्वरसंस्थानां सुविभक्तमहापथाम् ।
हर्म्यप्रासादसंपन्नां सर्वरत्नविभूषिताम् ।।

19. (And Lakshmana described to me about Ayodhya, Oh Bharatha) Beautiful, well segmented royal roads with lovely quadrangles well designed; full of mansions and houses; endowed with all riches ......

❍ ❍ ❍

२०. गजाश्वरथसंबाधां तूर्यनादविनादिताम् ।
सर्वकल्याणसंपूर्णां हृष्टपुष्टजनाकुलाम् ।।

20. Plenty of horses, elephants, reverberating with sounds of (Musical instruments of) Thoorya etc: Happy and well fed citizens; Endowed with all auspicious events (taking place all the time) .....

❍ ❍ ❍

२१. आरामोद्यानसंपन्नां समाजोत्सवशालिनीम् ।
सुखिता विचरिष्यन्ति राजधानीं पितुर्मम ।।

21. With delightful gardens and parks: People getting together (to celebrate) Festivities: Only fortunate people will now go about in my father's city of Ayodhya.

❍ ❍ ❍

२२. अपि सत्यप्रतिज्ञेन सार्धं कुशलिना वयम् ।
निवृत्ते समये ह्यस्मिन्सुखिताः प्रविशेमहि ।।

22. (And Lakshmana said further, Oh Bharatha): Will we (ever) return (to that Ayodhya) in comfort and in good health after completing the time (of Exile), having kept our promise (of spending 14 years in forest).
(This is what your brother Lakshmana told me that night, Bharatha.)

❍ ❍ ❍

२३. परिदेवयमानस्य तस्यैवं सुमहात्मनः ।
तिष्ठतो राजपुत्रस्य शर्वरी साऽत्यवर्तत ।।

23. Wailing and lamenting thus, that night passed away thus for (your brother) the royal prince, for this great

soul (Lakshmana) who was standing (there on guard over his Raama who was sleeping).

❍ ❍ ❍

२४. प्रभाते विमले सूर्येकारयित्वा जटा उभौ ।
अस्मिन्भागीरथीतीरे सुखं संतारितौ मया ॥

24. When Sun arose bright, these two (brothers of yours) who had done up their Hair style into "Twisted and Braided Hair", were (then) safely taken across from this (side of) the banks of river (Ganges, the) Bhaageerathi, (by us).

❍ ❍ ❍

२५. जटाधरौ तौ द्रुमचीरवाससौ
महाबलौ कुञ्जरयूथपोपमौ ।
वरेषुचापासिधरौ परंतपौ
व्यपेक्षमाणौ सह सीतया गतौ ॥

25. (And Oh Bharatha): These two (Your brothers Raama and Lakshmana) who are very strong like royal elephants and who were wearing dresses of bark and deer skins and sporting braided tufted hair (style) and who were carrying bow, arrows, swords, went along with Seetha, looking after each other mutually.

(Note: Thus Guha describes to Bharatha how his brother Lakshmana refused to accept any of the comforts like a bed from him, and how he was awake the whole night guarding over Raama.)

❍ ❍ ❍

Chapter 87

And Guha Talks About Raama

१. गुहस्य वचनं श्रुत्वा भरतो भृशमप्रियम् ।
ध्यानं जगाम तत्रैव यत्र तच्छ्रुतमप्रियम् ॥

1. Hearing most disagreeable (unbearable) words of Guha (about Raama and his 'hardships'), Bharatha went into deep thought then and there, at the very place where he heard (such disturbing and) unpleasant news.

❍ ❍ ❍

२. सुकुमारो महासत्त्वः सिंहस्कन्धो महाभुजः ।
पुण्डरीकविशालाक्षस्तरुणः प्रियदर्शनः ।।

३. प्रत्याश्वस्य मुहूर्तं तु कालं परमदुर्मनाः ।
पपात सहसा तोत्रैर्हृदि विद्ध इव द्विपः ।।

2 & 3.

This delicate youth (Bharatha) who was endowed with great (natural) virtues, whose chest was (firm) like those of a lion, whose hands were long, whose eyes were wide and lovely like lotus, who was very young, who was handsome......and who was, for a short while (trying) to compose himself, became terribly depressed and fell down suddenly, like an elephant pierced by a spike through its heart.

❍ ❍ ❍

४. तदवस्थं तु भरतं शत्रुघ्नोऽनन्तरस्थितः ।
परिष्वज्य रुरोदोच्चैर्विसंज्ञः शोककर्शितः ।।

4. And Schathrugna who was by his side, hugged this Bharatha who was in that state and he cried aloud, bewildered, tormented by grief.

❍ ❍ ❍

५. ततः सर्वाः समापेतुर्मातरो भरतस्य ताः ।
उपवासकृशा दीना भर्तुर्व्यसनकर्शिताः ।।

5. All those (step) mothers who were in feeble state thinned down by abstinence, and who were emaciated by grief (over separation from) their husband, gathered there.

❍ ❍ ❍

६. ताश्च तं पतितं भूमौ रुदन्त्यः पर्यवारयन् ।
कौसल्या त्वनुसृत्यैनं दुर्मनाः परिषस्वजे ॥

6. And they surrounded him who had fallen down on earth, crying (all the while). The low spirited Kowsalya approached (Bharatha) and hugged him.

❍ ❍ ❍

७. वत्सला स्वं यथा वत्समुपगूह्य तपस्विनी ।
परिपप्रच्छ भरतं रुदन्ती शोकलालसा ॥

7. This austere lady who was crying, was engulfed in grief. This child loving (Kowsalya) hugged Bharatha as if he was her own son and she asked him thus.

❍ ❍ ❍

८. पुत्र व्याधिर्न ते कच्चिच्छरीरं परिबाधते ।
अस्य राजकुलस्याद्य त्वदधीनं हि जीवितम् ॥

8. Oh 'Son' (Bharatha)! I hope (and pray), that fever and disease is not molesting your body. The very life (and welfare) of our Royal family rests with you.

❍ ❍ ❍

९. त्वां दृष्ट्वा पुत्र जीवामि रामे सभ्रातृके गते ।
वृत्ते दशरथे राज्ञि नाथ एकस्त्वमद्य नः ॥

9. As Raama has gone away (on exile) with his brother (Lakshmana), and as king Dhascharatha is (also) dead, now you alone are our protector. Oh Son! I am alive (only because) I am beholding you.

❍ ❍ ❍

१०. कच्चिन्न लक्ष्मणे पुत्र श्रुतं ते किञ्चदप्रियम् ।
पुत्रे वाऽप्येकपुत्रायाः सहभार्येवनं गते ॥

10. Oh 'Son'! Nothing unpleasant about my son, my only son (Raama) who has gone to forest with Seetha, or

about Lakshmana, has been heard by you. (So why do you grieve thus, says Kowsalya endearingly).

❍ ❍ ❍

११. स मुहूर्तात्समाश्वस्य रुदन्नेव महायशाः ।
कौसल्यां परिसान्त्व्येदं गुहं वचनमब्रवीत् ।।

11. Reviving after sometime, this famous (Bharatha) consoled Kowsalya, crying (all the while). And he (then) addressed Guha with these (words).

❍ ❍ ❍

१२. भ्राता मे क्वावसद्रात्रिं क्व सीता क्व च लक्ष्मणः ।
अस्वपच्छयने कस्मिन्किं भुक्त्वा गुह शंस मे ।।

12. Oh Guha! That night, eating what, did my brother (Raama sustain himself)? Where did he stay? In what bed did he lie? Where was Seetha? and where was Lakshmana. Tell me.

❍ ❍ ❍

१३. सोऽब्रवीद्भरतं हृष्टो निषादाधिपतिर्गुहः ।
यद्विधं प्रतिपेदे च रामे प्रियहितेऽतिथौ ।।

13. This Guha the chief of hunters, then told Bharatha how he behaved (and treated) his guest Raama who was benefactor to his dear (citizens and friends) (Oh Bharatha, Listen!).

❍ ❍ ❍

१४. अन्नमुच्चावचं भक्षाः फलानि विविधानि च ।
रामायाभ्यवहरार्थं बहु चोपहृतं मया ।।

14. As food for Raama, many cereal foods and eats and various fruits were brought by me (and placed before him).

❍ ❍ ❍

१५. तत्सर्वं समनुज्ञासीद्रामः सत्यपराक्रमः ।
न हि तत्प्रत्यगृह्णात्स क्षत्रधर्ममनुस्मरन् ।।

15. But this truly valiant Raama did not accept any of this, remembering the (Norms and) code of the Kshathriya Dharma. He did not accept and 'returned' all of them (untouched).

❍ ❍ ❍

१६. न ह्यस्माभिः प्रतिग्राह्यं सखे देयं तु सर्वदा ।
इति तेन वयं राजन्ननुनीता महात्मना ।।

16. (And this was the reason Raama did not accept my hospitality) "Oh Comrade (Guha)! (As Kshathriya-belonging to royal family), Always, things are to be given by us; never to be received (from others)." ..... Oh King (Bharatha, Listen)! We were humbly entreated by this great soul (Raama) like this.

❍ ❍ ❍

१७. लक्ष्मणेन यदानीतं पीत्वा वारि महायशाः ।
औपवास्यं तदाऽकार्षीद्राघवः सह सीतया ।।

17. The most famous (Raama) the Raaghava drank only the water that was brought by Lakshmana, and along with Seetha, he fasted.

❍ ❍ ❍

१८. ततस्तु जलशेषेण लक्ष्मणोऽप्यकरोत्तदा ।
वाग्यतास्ते त्रयः सन्ध्यामुपासत समाहिताः ।।

18. And the Lakshmana too did likewise, with the balance of water. And all the three performed Sandhya Rituals with devotion, (chanting in) low voice.

(Interesting to note that even Seetha joins them in Sandhya Ritual.)

❍ ❍ ❍

१९. सौमित्रिस्तु ततः पश्चादकरोत्स्वास्तरं शुभम् ।
स्वयमानीय बर्हींषि क्षिप्रं राघवकारणात् ।।

19. The after, (Lakshmana) the son of Sumithra brought (dried) feathers (and grass) and soon prepared a lovely bed himself, for Raama's sake.

❍ ❍ ❍

२०. तस्मिन्समाविशद्रामः स्वास्तरे सह सीतया ।
प्रक्षाल्य च तयोः पादौ व्यपाक्रामत्स लक्ष्मणः ।।

20. And Raama along with Seetha sat down on this bed: And Lakshmana rinsed the feet (of Raama) with water and came away.

❍ ❍ ❍

२१. एतत्तदिङ्गुदीमूलमिदमेव च तत्तृणम् ।
यस्मिन्रामश्च सीता च रात्रिं तां शयितावुभौ ।।

21. This is the Inguda tree under which these two, Raama and Seetha, lay that night. These are the (remains of) the grass (of the grass bed).

❍ ❍ ❍

२२. नियम्य पृष्ठे तु तलाङ्गुलित्रवा
श्च्छरैः सुपूर्णाविषुधी परन्तपः ।
महद्धनुः सज्यमुपोह्य लक्ष्मणो
निशामतिष्ठत्परितोऽस्य केवलम् ।।

22. Lakshmana, the tormentor of enemies, stood there the whole night near them, stringing up the mighty bow of his, carrying a quiver full of arrows on his back (and protecting his fingers) with leather thimbles on his fingers and hand.

❍ ❍ ❍

२३. ततस्त्वहं चोत्तमचापबाणधृक्
स्थितोऽभवं तत्र स यत्र लक्ष्मणः ।
अतन्द्रिभिर्ज्ञातिभिरात्तकार्मुकैः
महेन्द्रकल्पं परिपालयंस्तदा ॥

23. Then, I also stood, guarding (this Raama) who was comparable to Indhra, along with my alert kinsmen who were with their strung up bows (at the place nearby) where Lakshmana was wielding his foremost bow with arrows.

❍ ❍ ❍

Chapter 88

Bharatha's Vow (To Bring Back Raama)

१. तच्छ्रुत्वा निपुणं सर्वं भरतः सह मन्त्रिभिः ।
इङ्गुदीमूलमागम्य रामशय्यामवेक्ष्य ताम् ॥
२. अब्रवीज्जननीः सर्वा इह तेन महात्मना ।
शर्वरी शयिता भूमाविदमस्य विमर्दितम् ॥

1. & 2.

Hearing all this along with his ministers, and approaching the base of the Ingudha Tree (Terminalia catapa) and observing this Raama's 'bed', (remnants of the grass bed), very carefully... Bharatha.....addressed all his 'mothers' = On this floor, One Night was slept by that great soul (Raama); These are the marks ......

❍ ❍ ❍

३. महाभागकुलीनेन महाभागेन धीमता ।
जातो दशरथेनोर्व्यां न रामः स्वप्तुमर्हति ॥

3. Coming as he does from the most illustrious race, this wise most illustrious Raama who is born to Dhascharatha, does not deserve to lie on bare earth.=

(And Bharatha talks about Raama's life at Ayodhya: Stanzas 4 to 9):

❍ ❍ ❍

४. अजिनोत्तरसंस्तीर्णेवरास्तरणसञ्चये ।
शयित्वा पुरुषव्याघ्रः कथं शेते महीतले ।।
५. प्रासादाग्रविमानेषु वलभीषु च सर्वदा ।
हैमराजतभौमेषु वरास्तरणशालिषु ।।
६. पुष्पसञ्चयचित्रेषु चन्दनागरुगन्धिषु ।
पाण्डुराभ्रप्रकाशेषु शुकसङ्घरुतेषु च ।।
७. प्रासादवरवर्येषु गीतवत्सु सुगन्धिषु ।
उषित्वा मेरुकल्पेषु कृतकाञ्चनभित्तिषु ।।
८. गीतवादित्रनिर्घोषैर्वराभरणनिस्वनैः ।
मृदङ्गवरशब्दैश्च सततं प्रतिबोधितः ।।
९. वन्दिभिर्वन्दितः काले बहुभिः सूतमागधैः ।
गाथाभिरनुरूपाभिः स्तुतिभिश्च परन्तपः ।।

4. to 9.

How can this (Raama) the 'tiger' of men, sleep on bare earth (after being used to and having) slept always on fine beds with well spread deer skin (as bed spreads).... In foremost huge palace with huge towers and multi storeyed: (palaces) Decorated in gold and silver: With well carpetted foremost (furnishings)... (The palaces).... Lined up with wonderful cluster of flowers: Smelling sweetly with sandal paste and Agar: (Palace) that shine like white clouds: where cooing of parrots are heard......And having lived in foremost towering palaces (how can Raama lie like this)....Where music is heard: Ever smelling sweet; (Palaces huge) like Meru mountain: Walls decorated in gold....Sound of music from instruments and vocalists: Sounds from drums like Mridunga, sounds from foremost ornaments very pleasant: (And Raama) was ever woken up..... in early morning by (morning) callers, by many Sootha-s and Magadha-s (poets and bards); This (Raama the) tormentor of enemies was (ever) extolled (in such palaces) with befitting songs and praises.

❍ ❍ ❍

१०. अश्रद्धेयमिदं लोके न सत्यं प्रतिभाति मे ।
मुह्यते खलु मे भावः स्वप्नोऽयमिति मे मतिः ॥

10. This is unbelievable in this world! (Raama sleeping like this): I cant believe this to be true! My mind is shaken up; I think this is all a dream!

❍ ❍ ❍

११. न नूनं दैवतं किञ्चित्कालेन बलवत्तरम् ।
यत्र दाशरथी रामो भूमावेव शयीत सः ॥

11. If Raama the son of Dhascharatha should lie on bare Earth (it only means) that Gods are not stronger than Fate!

(This is a very important stanza: Expresses Indian philosophy.)

❍ ❍ ❍

१२. विदेहराजस्य सुता सीता च प्रियदर्शना ।
दयिता शयिता भूमौ स्नुषा दशरथस्य च ॥

12. The beloved daughter of King of Vidheha, this Seetha, who looks at every one with kindness, this (beloved) daughter-in-law of Dhascharatha slept on bare earth. (Unbelievable).

❍ ❍ ❍

१३. इयं शय्या मम भ्रातुरिदं हि परिवर्तितम् ।
स्थण्डिले कठिने सर्वं गात्रैर्विमृदितं तृणम् ॥

13. This was my brother (Raama's) 'Bed' (of grass). All the grass have been crushed and pressed under his body over the rough earth (as he slept here that night).

❍ ❍ ❍

१४. मन्ये साभरणा सुप्ता सीताऽस्मिञ्छयने शुभे ।
तत्र तत्र हि दृश्यन्ते सक्ताः कनकबिन्दवः ।।

14. I think Seetha slept on this 'Holy' 'Bed' with her ornaments: Because, the imprints of her ornaments are seen here and there.

❍ ❍ ❍

१५. उत्तरीयमिहासक्तं सुव्यक्तं सीतया तया ।
तथा ह्येते प्रकाशन्ते सक्ताः कौशेयतन्तवः ।।

15. Upper garments have been well spread out by Seetha at this place; Because, threads of the silken cloth are seen lodged on this.

❍ ❍ ❍

१६. मन्ये भर्तुः सुखा शय्या येन बाला तपस्विनी ।
सुकुमारी सती दुःखं न विजानाति मैथिली ।।

16. I hope her husband's bed was comfortable; That is why this very young tender girl (Seetha) the Maithily who is virtuous and austere, did not feel the suffering.

❍ ❍ ❍

१७. हा हतोऽस्मि नृशंसोऽहं यत्सभार्यः कृते मम ।
ईदृशीं राघवः शय्यामधिशेते ह्यनाथवत् ।।

17. Ha! Vile as I am, am destroyed! Because it is for my sake (Raama) the Raaghava, along with his wife has slept in such a bed like a vagabond (without protector).

❍ ❍ ❍

१८. सार्वभौमकुले जातः सर्वलोकसुखावहः ।
सर्वलोकप्रियस्त्यक्त्वा राज्यं सुखमनुत्तमम् ।।

१९. कथमिन्दीवरश्यामो रक्ताक्षः प्रियदर्शनः ।
सुखभागी नदुःखार्ह शयितो भुवि राघवः ।।

18. & 19.

Born in family of great rulers, bringing prosperity and

comfort to all in the world, beloved of all in the world, abandoning comforts and the foremost kingdom .... How can this (Raama) the Raaghava whose complexion is like those of Nilothpala flowers, whose eyes are red, who is handsome, lie down on bare earth when he has never seen suffering before, having enjoyed (only) comforts (all his life).

❍ ❍ ❍

२०. धन्यः खलु महाभागो लक्ष्मणः शुभलक्षणः ।
भ्रातरं विषमे काले यो राममनुवर्तते ॥

20. Lakshmana is indeed most illustrious (and fortunate) as he serves his brother Raama during his difficult times; He, who possesses (only noble and) auspicious qualities, is indeed lucky.

❍ ❍ ❍

२१. सिद्धार्था खलु वैदेही पतिं याऽनु गता वनम् ।
वयं संशयिताः सर्वेहीनास्तेन महात्मना ॥

21. (Seetha the) Vaidhehi, is indeed accomplished (and fortunate) as she has followed her husband to the forest: (But) all of us who have been left out by this great soul (Raama) are 'dubious' and suspect!

❍ ❍ ❍

२२. अकर्णधारा पृथिवी शून्येव प्रतिभाति मे ।
गते दशथो स्वर्गं रामे चारण्यमाश्रिते ॥

22. It appears to me that this world is desolate and without a pilot, now that Dhascharatha has gone to heaven and Raama is staying in forest.

❍ ❍ ❍

२३ न च प्रार्थयते कश्चिन्मनसाऽपि वसुंधराम् ।
वनेऽपि वसतस्तस्य बाहुवीर्याभिरक्षिताम् ॥

23. Even though he lives in forest, none will (dare to) desire

this kingdom even in his mind, as this is protected by the power of his arm. (Kings dare not go near Raama's kingdom even when he is away, says his brother Bharatha).

❍ ❍ ❍

२४. शून्यसंवरणारक्षामयन्त्रितहयद्विपाम् ।
अपावृतपुरद्वारां राजधानीमरक्षिताम् ।।

२५. अप्रहृष्टबलां न्यूनां विषमस्थामनावृताम् ।
शत्रवो नाभिमन्यन्ते भक्षान् विषकृतानिव ।।

24. & 25.

Fortress is desolate (unprotected), horses and elephants unleashed. The Gates (of city) not closed (wide open): Capital unprotected...... Army (disgruntled and) unhappy; (City and kingdom) Destitute, topsy turvy; And in great danger: (But) enemies do not consider (and desire this kingdom) like poisoned food.

❍ ❍ ❍

२६. अद्यप्रभृति भूमौ तु शयिष्येऽहं तृणेषु वा ।
फलमूलाशनो नित्यं जटाचीराणि धारयन् ।।

26. From now on, I am going to lie on (bare) Earth over grass, sustaining myself only on fruits and tubers always, sporting tufted braided hair (like a mendicant).

❍ ❍ ❍

२७. तस्यार्थमुत्तरं कालं निवत्स्यामि सुखं वने ।
तं प्रतिश्रवमामुच्य नास्य मिथ्या भविष्यति ।।

27. Keeping up this promise, I will live in the forest in comfort for a long time for his sake. I will not be contrary to this (vow).

❍ ❍ ❍

२८. वसन्तं भ्रातुरर्थाय शत्रुघ्नो माऽनुवत्स्यति ।
लक्ष्मणेन सह त्वार्योह्ययोध्यां पालयिष्यति ।।

28. And Schathrugna who lives for (my) sake, for (me) his brother, will (also) live with me (like this in forest); And the Aryan (Raama) will rule over Ayodhya along with (brother) Lakshmana.

❍ ❍ ❍

२९. अभिषेक्ष्यन्ति काकुत्स्थमयोध्यायां द्विजोत्तमाः ।
अपि मे देवताः कुर्युरिमं सत्यं मनोरथम् ।।

29. Braamins will anoint (Raama) the Kaakuthsa at Ayodhya (as king). Will the Gods fulfill this hearty wish (of mine): (Will The Gods make this true).

❍ ❍ ❍

३०. प्रसाद्यमानः शिरसा मया स्वयं
बहुप्रकारं यदि न प्रपत्स्यते ।
ततोऽनुवत्स्यामि चिराय राघवं
वने वसन्नार्हति मामुपेक्षितुम् ।।

30. If he (this Raama) who will be begged by me in many ways with my head bowed to him, does not accept, I will live in forest and live along with (Raama the) Raaghava for a long time. (But) he will not deny me (he will fulfill my desire of his becoming king, and return to Ayodhya with me because he loves me so).

❍ ❍ ❍

Chapter 89

Bharatha Crosses River Ganges

१. व्युष्य रात्रिं तु तत्रैव गङ्गाकूले स राघवः ।
भरतः काल्यमुत्थाय शत्रुघ्नमिदमब्रवीत् ।।

1. After spending the night on the banks of Ganges at that place, Bharatha the Raaghava, got up early morning and told Schathrugna.

❍ ❍ ❍

२. शत्रुघ्नोत्तिष्ठ किं शेषे निषादाधिपतिं गुहम् ।
शीघ्रमानय भद्रं ते तारयिष्यति वाहिनीम् ।।

2. Oh Schathrugna! Get up; Welfare to you! Why are you (still) sleeping? Fetch Guha, the chief of hunters soon; He will take our army across (Ganges).

❍ ❍ ❍

३. जागर्मि नाहं स्वपिमि तथैवार्यं विचिन्तयन् ।
इत्येवमब्रवीद्भ्रात्रा शत्रुघ्नोऽपि प्रचोदितः ।।

3. Having goaded thus by his brother, Schathrugna said this:= I was also not sleeping. I was awake thinking about the Aryan (our brother Raama) =

❍ ❍ ❍

४. इति संवदतोरेवमन्योन्यं नरसिंहयोः ।
आगम्य प्राञ्जलिः काले गुहो भरतमब्रवीत् ।।

4. While these 'Lions' amongst men were conversing thus, Guha came along in the early morning and addressed Bharatha with his hands cupped in Anjali (in reverence).

❍ ❍ ❍

५. कच्चित्सुखं नदीतिरेऽवात्सीः काकुत्स्थ शर्वरीम् ।
कच्चित्ते सह सैन्यस्य तव सर्वमनामयम् ।।

5. Oh (Bharatha) the Kaakuthsa! You spent the night at the river banks. I trust it was comfortable. I hope you and your Army are in good health.

❍ ❍ ❍

६. गुहस्य तत्तु वचनं श्रुत्वा स्नेहादुदीरितम् ।
रामस्यानुवशो वाक्यं भरतोऽपीदमब्रवीत् ।।

6. Hearing the words of Guha uttered in friendship, Raama's obedient (brother) Bharatha said these words.

७. सुखा नः शर्वरी राजन्पूजिताश्चापि ते वयम् ।
गङ्गां तु नौभिर्बह्वीभिर्दाशाः संतारयन्तु नः ।।

7. Oh King (Oh Guha, the lord of hunters)! Night was pleasant for us; We are honoured (by your hospitality). Let fishermen carry us across (the river) Ganges in many boats.

❍ ❍ ❍

८. ततो गुहः संत्वरितः श्रुत्वा भरतशासनम् ।
प्रतिप्रविश्य नगरं तं ज्ञातिजनमब्रवीत् ।।

8. Then, hearing the command of Bharatha, Guha, without delay, went to the town (nearby) and he addressed his kinsmen there.

❍ ❍ ❍

९. उत्तिष्ठत प्रबुध्यध्वं भद्रमस्तु हि वः सदा ।
नावः समनुकर्षध्वं तारयिष्याम वाहिनीम् ।।

9. Wake up! Get up! Drag (bring up) the boats; Let us carry the Army across. By this (service), may there be welfare to you all, always.

❍ ❍ ❍

१०. ते तथोक्ताः समुत्थाय त्वरिता राजशासनात् ।
पञ्च नावां शतान्येव समानिन्युः समन्ततः ।।

10. When told thus, they got up and as per their king's command, they brought 500 boats quickly from all over.

❍ ❍ ❍

११. अन्याः स्वस्तिकविज्ञेया महाघण्टाधरा वराः ।
शोभमानाः पताकिन्यो युक्तवाहाः सुसंहताः ।।

11. A beautiful (Boat) named Swasthika, decorated with banners and bells was brought along with excellent crew.

❍ ❍ ❍

१२. ततः स्वस्तिकविज्ञेयां पाण्डुकम्बलसंवृताम् ।
सनन्दिघोषां कल्याणीं गुहो नावमुपाहरत् ।।

12. Guha then stationed the auspicious boat named Swasthika which was carpeted with white rugs, with music and drum (beatings).

❍ ❍ ❍

१३. तामारुरोह भरतः शत्रुघ्नश्च महाबलः ।।

13. The mightily strong Bharatha, got into (the boat); So did Schathrugna.

❍ ❍ ❍

१४. कौसल्या च सुमित्रा च याश्चान्या राजयोषितः ।
पुरोहितश्च तत्पूर्वं गुरवो ब्राह्मणाश्च ये ।।
अनन्तरं राजदारास्तथैव शकटापणाः ।।

14. Then, first, Kowsalya, Sumithra and then after other royal wives and other ladies, then Purohith (Chief priest Vasishta), respected Braamins, with cartloads of merchandise.

❍ ❍ ❍

१५. आवासमादीपयतां तीर्थं चाप्यवगाहताम् ।
भाण्डानि चाददानानां घोषस्त्रिदिवमस्पृशत् ।।

15. The sounds from those who set fire (to the Garbage at the place where they stayed (that night) and (the sounds) from those who took plunge in the waters (of Ganges) and (the sound) from those who carried merchandise, 'reached up to sky'!

❍ ❍ ❍

१६. पताकिन्यस्तु ता नावः स्वयं दाशैरधिष्ठिताः ।
वहन्त्यो जनमारूढं तदा संपेतुराशुगाः ।।

16. Carrying the (multitude of) men who had got into them, these boats that could go fast, that were full

with banners and masts, and which were brought by fishermen, went along (sailed across Ganges).

❍ ❍ ❍

१७. नारीणामभिपूर्णास्तु काश्चित्काश्चित्तु वाजिनाम् ।
काश्चित्तत्र वहन्ति स्म यानयुग्यं महाधनम् ।।

17. (Filled up) With women, some (filled up) with horses, some with great merchandise and vehicles and chariots, (these boats) carried (the entire entourage across).

❍ ❍ ❍

१८. ताः स्म गत्वा परं तीरमवरोप्य च तं जनम् ।
निवृत्ताः काण्डचित्राणि क्रियन्ते दाशबन्धुभिः ।।

18. Reaching the other banks (of the river Ganges), discharging all the men (of Bharatha), these Boats, when they were returning (back to their side) were (playfully) stroked with bright coloured oars by the fishermen, the kinsmen (of Guha).

❍ ❍ ❍

१९. सवैजयन्तास्तु गजा गजारोहैः प्रचोदिताः ।
तरन्तः स्म प्रकाशन्ते सध्वजा इव पर्वताः ।।

19. As the elephants with banners over them were goaded by elephant riders and were crossing (the river), they appeared like mountains lined up with banners on them.

❍ ❍ ❍

२०. नावश्चारुरुहुस्त्वन्ये प्लवैस्तेरुस्तथा परे ।
अन्ये कुम्भघटैस्तेरुरन्ये तेरुश्च बाहुभिः ।।

20. Some got into rafts; some on flotillas; likewise, some others crossed the river with hollow pots (on their hands, like safety belts!) Some (simply) swam across, stroking (easily) with their hands.

❍ ❍ ❍

२१. सा पुण्या ध्वजिनी गङ्गां दाशैः संतारिता स्वयम् ।
मैत्रे मुहूर्तेप्रययौ प्रयागवनमुत्तमम् ।।

21. The fine Army that was carried across Ganges by the fishermen themselves in the early time of "Maithra", reached the foremost Prayaag forest (Prayaag is around modern Allahabad).

❍ ❍ ❍

२२. आश्वासयित्वा च चमूं महात्मा
निवेशयित्वा च यथोपजोषम् ।
द्रष्टुं भरद्वाजमृषिप्रवर्यं
ऋत्विग्वृतः सन्भरतः प्रतस्थे ।।

22. (Resting and) Comforting his Army, the great soul Bharatha who was accompanied by the Rithvik, then started out to 'See' the eminent Sage Bharadhwaaja as he had desired (and planned to meet).

❍ ❍ ❍

२३. स ब्राह्मणस्याश्रममभ्युपेत्य
महात्मनो देवपुरोहितस्य ।
ददर्श रम्योटजवृक्षषण्डं
महद्वनं प्रीतिकरं सुरम्यम् ।।

23. Approaching the lovely hermitage of the great soul (Bharadhwaaja) the Braamin who was priest of (even the) celestials, he saw a row of cottages and the very lovely and large forest (around them).

❍ ❍ ❍

Chapter 90

Bharadhwaaja-Bharatha Meeting

१. भरद्वाजाश्रमं दृष्ट्वा क्रोशादेव नरर्षभः ।
बलं सर्वमवस्थाप्य जगाम सह मन्त्रिभिः ।।

२. पद्भ्यामेव हि धर्मज्ञो न्यस्तशस्त्रपरिच्छदः ।
वसानो वाससी क्षौमे पुरोधाय पुरोहितम् ।।

1. & 2.

On sighting the hermitage of Bharadhwaaja, (Bharatha) the 'Bull amongst men', halted all his (vast) Army at a distance of a Kroscha (about 2-3 miles) and went along with his ministers (towards hermitage) ...... Casting away his Arms and ornaments, this (Bharatha the) knower of Dharma, wearing dress of silk and linen, went on foot along with Purohith (Vasishta).

(Readers may note that Bharatha does not want to disturb peace and tranquillity of the Hermitage. He follows the Protocol.)

❍ ❍ ❍

३. ततः संदर्शने तस्य भरद्वाजस्य राघवः ।
मन्त्रिणस्तानवस्थाप्य जगामानुपुरोहितम् ।।

3. Then on 'seeing' Bharadhwaaja, (Bharatha) the Raaghava stopped his ministers and then went along with Purohith (Vasishta).

(Here again Protocol is observed by Bharatha; takes with him only sage Vasishta to the hermitage.)

❍ ❍ ❍

४. वसिष्ठमथ दृष्ट्वैव भरद्वाजो महातपाः ।
संचचालासनात्तूर्णं शिष्यानर्घ्यमिति ब्रुवन् ।।

4. And when the man of great penance Bharadhwaaja saw Vasishta, he told his disciples:= Get Arghya (Waters) quickly = , getting up from his seat.

❍ ❍ ❍

५. समागम्य वसिष्ठेन भरतेनाभिवादितः ।
अबुध्यत महातेजाः सुतं दशरथस्य तम् ।।

5. As he was being met by Vasishta, this most brilliant

(Bharadhwaaja) was greeted with reverence by Bharatha whom he recognised as son of Dhascharatha.

❍ ❍ ❍

६. ताभ्यामर्घ्यं च पाद्यं च दत्वा पश्चात्फलानि च ।
आनुपूर्व्याच्च धर्मज्ञः पप्रच्छ कुशलं कुले ॥
७. अयोध्यायां बले कोशे मित्रेष्वपि च मन्त्रिषु ।
जानन्दशरथं वृत्तं न राजानमुदाहरत् ॥

6. & 7.

The Knower of Dharma (Bharadhwaaja), after offering Arghya, Paadhya, and fruits etc., asked about the welfare of his family, and Ayodhya, in successive order...about Army, about (State of) Finance, about friends there and about his ministers: (But) Knowing about Dhascharatha's death, he did not talk about the king.

❍ ❍ ❍

८. वसिष्ठो भरतश्चैनं पप्रच्छतुरनामयम् ।
शरीरेऽग्निषु शिष्येषु वृक्षेषु मृगपक्षिषु ॥

8. And (in turn) Vasishta and Bharatha asked him about his health (fitness of body), welfare, about his Fire Rituals, about his disciples, about trees, birds and animals (of his hermitage).

❍ ❍ ❍

९. स तथेति प्रतिज्ञाय भरद्वाजो महायशाः ।
भरतं प्रत्युवाचेदं राघवस्नेहबन्धनात् ॥

9. Saying: =It it so = (All is well with me), the most famous Bharadhwaaja then addressed Bharatha thus, due to his affection and attachment to Raama.

❍ ❍ ❍

१०. किमिहागमने कार्यं तव राज्यं प्रशासतः ।
एतदाचक्ष्व मे सर्वं न हि मे शुध्यते मनः ॥

10. (Bharadhwaaja asks Bharatha as to why he has come there at all) What is the business of coming here when you have a kingdom to rule? Enlighten me, all about this; Because my mind is not clear.

❍ ❍ ❍

११. सुषुवे यममित्रघ्नं कौसल्याऽऽनन्दवर्धनम् ।
भ्रात्रा सह सभार्योयश्चिरं प्रव्राजितो वनम् ॥
१२. नियुक्ताः स्त्रीनियुक्तेन पित्रा योऽसौ महायशाः ।
वनवासी भवेतीह समाः किल चतुर्दश ॥
१३. कच्चिन्न तस्यापापस्य पापं कर्तुमिहेच्छसि ।
अकण्टकं भोक्तुमना राज्यं तस्यानुजस्य च ॥

11. to 13.

(Bharadhwaaja expresses his concern further: Stanzas 11 to 13) He who was begotten by Kowsalya: he who destroys the enemies; he who increases every one's joy; he, who along with his wife and brother (Lakshmana) was sent out to forest for a long time.......he, the most famous one commanded by his father who was bound by his wife Kaikeyi, was told = You live here for full 14 years as resident of forest=....(Oh Bharatha)... I trust that you do not desire to bring harm (to such a man), to such a sinless (man, Raama) and (bring harm) to his brother (Lakshmana), in order to enjoy his kingdom without any hindrance (to yourself).

❍ ❍ ❍

१४. एवमुक्तो भरद्वाज भरतः प्रत्यूवाच ह ।
पर्यश्रुनयनो दुःखाद्वाचा संसज्जमानया ॥

14. When told thus, Bharatha replied to Bharadhwaaja with tears rolling down his eyes, stricken by sorrow, words coming out haltingly.

❍ ❍ ❍

१५. हतोऽस्मि यदि मामेवं भगवानपि मन्यते ।
मत्तो न दोषमाशङ्के नैवं मामनुशाधि हि ।।

15. I have no apprehensions that (any) sin is in me. (But you my) Lord, if you think like this about me, (if you suspect me), then I am done for! You should not chastise me thus!

❍ ❍ ❍

१६. न चैतदिष्टं माता मे यदवोचन्मदन्तरे ।
नाहमेतेन तुष्टश्च न तद्वचनमाददे ।।

16. What my mother (Kaikeyi) said (and did) when I was not there (at Ayodhya), those words (that I should become king), was not accepted (by me). Nor was this desired (by me).

❍ ❍ ❍

१७. अहं तु तं नरव्याघ्रमुपयातः प्रसादकः ।
प्रतिनेतुमयोध्यां च पादौ तस्याभिवन्दितुम् ।।

17. That is why I am not pleased (by all this): Wishing to win back favour (of Raama) the 'tiger' of men, I have come here to take him back to Ayodhya, worshipping his feet (to serve him).

❍ ❍ ❍

१८. त्वं मामेवं गतं मत्वा प्रसादं कर्तुमर्हसि ।
शंस मे भगवन्रामः क्व संप्रति महीपतिः ।।

18. You must believe that I am man of such conduct and should favour (and bless) me. Oh Lord (Bharadhwaaja)! Where is Raama the lord of earth now? Please tell me.

❍ ❍ ❍

१९. वसिष्ठादिभिर्ऋत्विग्भिर्याचितो भगवांस्ततः ।
उवाच तं भरद्वाजः प्रसादाद्भरतं वचः ।।

19. Then, when he was begged by Rithvik Vasishta and

others, Lord (sage Bharadhwaaja) addressed Bharatha with these words.

❍ ❍ ❍

२०. त्वय्येतत्पुरुषव्याघ्र युक्तं राघववंशजे ।
गुरुवृत्तिर्दमश्चैव साधूनां चानुयायिता ॥

20. Oh(Bharatha)'The tiger of men'! Born in the family of Raghus (as you are), good conduct towards Guru-s (Elders and teachers), restraint, practice of the conduct of the good, all these abide in you.

❍ ❍ ❍

२१. जाने चैतन्मनःस्थं ते दृढीकरणमस्त्विति ।
अपृच्छं त्वां तवात्यर्थं कीर्तिं समभिवर्धयन् ॥

21. I know this, the nature of your mind: (But) I asked you because of the reason that your great fame should spread (and surpass every one) and be firmly established.

(Readers may note that Sage Bharadhwaaja is a Great 'Seer': He knows everything of the world; He acted as though he entertained some doubt about Bharatha's intention in coming here with a mighty army. He wants the world to know for sure about Bharatha.)

❍ ❍ ❍

२२. जाने च रामं धर्मज्ञं ससीतं सहलक्ष्मणम् ।
असौ वसति ते भ्राता चित्रकूटे महागिरौ ॥

22. I know (the whereabouts of) the knower of Dharma, Raama, who is with Lakshmana and Seetha: Your brother is living in the great mountain Chithrakoot.

❍ ❍ ❍

२३. श्वस्तु गन्तासि तं देशं वसाद्य सह मन्त्रिभिः ।
एतं मे कुरु सुप्राज्ञ कामं कामार्थकोविद ॥

23. Oh most intelligent (Bharatha) who knows about passion (and mundane) matters! You stay here tonight

along with your ministers; Tomorrow morning you may go to that place (where Raama is); Fulfill this, my desire (my wish).

❍ ❍ ❍

२४. ततस्तथेत्येवमुदारदर्शनः
प्रतीतरूपो भरतोऽब्रवीद्वचः ।
चकार बुद्धिं च तदा तदाश्रमे
निशानिवासाय नराधिपात्मजः ॥

24. Then, the son of emperor, this Bharatha who had graceful countenance, whose handsomeness was well recognised, decided to stay that night in the hermitage (of Bharadhwaaja): Therefore he said these words at once:= So Be It.= (I will accept your hospitality).

❍ ❍ ❍

Chapter 91

Bharadhwaaja Extends Lavish Hospitality

१. कृतबुद्धिं निवासाय तत्रैव स मुनिस्तदा ।
भरतं कैकयीपुत्रमातिथ्येन न्यमन्त्रयत् ॥

1. The Muni (Sage Bharadhwaaja) extended his hospitality to (Bharatha) the son of Kaikeyi, who had decided to spend (the night) there itself.

❍ ❍ ❍

२. अब्रवीद्भरतस्त्वेनं नन्विदं भवता कृतम् ।
पाद्यमर्घ्यं तथाऽऽतिथ्यं वने यदुपपद्यते ॥

2. Bharatha addressed him thus:= In this forest (at this place) Paadhya and Arghya and likewise hospitality (befitting a resident of forest) has been extended by you (to us). This (further hospitality) that is (going to be) extended, (pray) what may that be! =

(Bharatha cannot imagine what hospitality this sage living in forest can possibly offer him and his army. He is in for a great surprise.)

❍ ❍ ❍

३. अथोवाच भरद्वाजो भरतं प्रहसन्निव ।
जाने त्वां प्रीतिसंयुक्तं तुष्येस्त्वं येन केनचित् ।।

3. Then, with a smile, Bharadhwaaja told Bharatha: I know you are already satisfied: Because, you are satisfied with a even a little!

❍ ❍ ❍

४. सेनायास्तु तवैतस्याः कर्तुमिच्छामि भोजनम् ।
मम प्रीतिर्यथारूपा त्वमर्होमनुजर्षभ ।।

4. Oh (Bharatha) 'the Bull' amongst men! (But) I desire to feed your, this (vast), Army: You should satisfy my desire in such a manner I have planned (for them all).

❍ ❍ ❍

५. किमर्थं चापि निक्षिप्य दूरे बलमिहागतः ।
कस्मान्नेहोपयातोऽसि सबलः पुरुषर्षभ ।।

5. Oh (Bharatha) 'the Bull' amongst men! Why did you station your Army far away? Why did you not come here with your army?

❍ ❍ ❍

६. भरतः प्रत्युवाचेदं प्राञ्जलिस्तं तपोधनम् ।
ससैन्यो नोपयातोऽस्मि भगवन्भगवद्भयात् ।।

6. With his arms cupped in Anjali, Bharatha then replied to this man of penance (Bharadhwaaja) whose wealth was penance: =Oh Lord! Out of Fear (and respect) for you, I did not come here with my Army.

❍ ❍ ❍

७. राज्ञा हि भगवन्नित्यं राजपुत्रेण वा सदा ।
यत्नतः परिहर्तव्या विषयेषु तपस्विनः ।।

7. Oh Lord! Sages (men of penance), should be zealously kept away always from (and guarded against) kings and princes, in matters (pertaining to) their daily Rituals (vows etc.)

(In effect, Bharatha says that a Forest or a Hermitage is a zone of peace; and kings and their soldiers should not disturb the area.)

❍ ❍ ❍

८. वाजिमुख्या मनुष्याश्च मत्ताश्च वरवारणाः ।
प्रच्छाद्य महतीं भूमिं भगवन्ननुयान्ति माम् ।।

8. Oh Lord (Bharadhwaaja)! Foremost horses, exhilarated elephants, and men all spreading out on earth extensively, are following me.

❍ ❍ ❍

९. ते वृक्षानुदकं भूमिमाश्रमेषूटजांस्तथा ।
न हिंस्युरिति तेनाहमेक एवागतस्ततः ।।

9. I came alone (to your abode) because they (this vast army of mine) should not cause harm to the trees, waters etc. around your hermitage and likewise, other hermitages (and the region nearby) =

❍ ❍ ❍

१०. आनीयतामितः सेनेत्याज्ञप्तः परमर्षिणा ।
तथा स चक्रे भरतः सेनायाः समुपागमम् ।।

10. Then, when commanded by the great Rishi (Bharadhwaaja who said)= Let The Army Be Brought (here) =, Bharatha brought his army accordingly

(Readers are in for a miracle: Bharadhwaaja organises a great Feast for this multitude by sheer power of his Penance. Bharadhwaaja is no ordinary sage; He can even command services of God's servants.)

❍ ❍ ❍

११. अग्निशालां प्रविश्याथ पीत्वाऽपः परिमृज्य च ।
आतिथ्यसत्क्रियाहेतोर्विश्वकर्माणमाह्वयत् ।।

11. Then entering the hall of ritual Fire ceremonies (of his abode), he took sips of water (as per norms), cleansed himself, and then invoked (the divine architect) Vischwakarma: for the sake of extending hospitality:

❍ ❍ ❍

१२. आह्वये विश्वकर्माणमहं त्वष्टारमेव च ।
आतिथ्यं कर्तुमिच्छामि तत्र मे संविधीयताम् ।।

12. I Invoke The Divine Architect Vischwakarma. I Desire To Extend Hospitality (to my guest Bharatha): (Therefore) May Preparations Be Made For Me (on my behalf).

❍ ❍ ❍

१३. आह्वये लोकपालांस्त्रीन्देवाञ्छक्रमुखांस्तथा ।
आतिथ्यं कर्तुमिच्छामि तत्र मे संविधीयताम् ।।

13. Likewise, I Invoke The Three Protectors of The World, the (three) Deities (Lord of Fire, Lord of Wind and Lord Varuna) whose chief is (Indhra the) Schakra. I Desire to Extend Hospitality. May Arrangements Be Made (for my sake).

❍ ❍ ❍

१४. प्राक्स्रोतसश्च या नद्यः प्रत्यक्स्रोतस एव च ।
पृथिव्यामन्तरिक्षे च समायान्त्वद्य सर्वशः ।।

14 All those rivers, from all over, whether on earth or in sky, whether they flow towards east or west, they should all come here together, from everywhere, now.

❍ ❍ ❍

१५. अन्याः स्रवन्तु मैरेयं सुरामन्याः सुनिष्ठिताः ।
अपराश्चोदकं शीतमिक्षुकाण्डरसोपमम् ।।

15. And let some (rivers) stream forth Maireya wines, some Sura liquors, (and let some rivers) stream forth cool sugar cane juice.

❍ ❍ ❍

१६. आह्वये देवगन्धर्वान्विश्वावसुहहाहुहून् ।
तथैवाप्सरसो देवीर्गन्धर्वीश्चापि सर्वशः ।।

16. I invite from every where the ladies from Ghandharva clan, the Dheva Ghandharva-s, Vischwaasu and Haahaahuu and likewise Apsara maidens.

❍ ❍ ❍

१७. घृताचीमथ विश्वाचीं मिश्रकेशीमलम्बुसाम् ।
नागदन्तां च हेमां च हिममाद्रिकृतस्थलाम् ।।

१८. एकं याश्चोपतिष्ठन्ति ब्रह्माणं याश्च भामिनीः ।
सर्वास्तुम्बुरुणा सार्धमाह्वये सपरिच्छदाः ।।

17. & 18.

Dhrithaaschee, Vishaaschee, Mishrakaaschi, Alambusa,Hema and Hima who live in mountains, Naagadhantha... All the lovely (passionate) ladies, all those who serve (Indhra the) Schakra and God Bramma; I invite (all of them) along with their attendants (the Thumbura-s) and their folks.

(Bharadhwaaja is such a powerful sage he can requisition service of people who serve the celestial Lords!)

❍ ❍ ❍

१९. नं कुरुषु यद्दिव्यं वासोभूषणपत्रवत् ।
दिव्यनारीफलं शश्वत्तत्कौबेरमिहैतु च ।।

19. Let that foremost forest of Kubhaera which is the region of Kuru, where ornaments and dresses are the divine leaves and where, at all times, fruits are divine ladies... (Let this forest) come here now.

(The Region Kuru is celestial region beyond Himaalaya-s.)

❍ ❍ ❍

२०. इह मे भगवान्सोमो विधत्तामन्नमुत्तमम् ।
भक्ष्यं भोज्यं च चोष्यं च लेह्यं च विविधं बहु ।।
२१. विचित्राणि च माल्यानि पादपप्रच्युतानि च ।
सुरादीनि च पेयानि मांसानि विविधानि च ।।

20. & 21.

May the Lord Moon offer me here, various types of foremost cereal foods, eats, small eats, sweets, Syrupy dishes.... in plenty...various types of flowers, liquors like Sura, various meats, drinks.

❍ ❍ ❍

२२. एवं समाधिना युक्तस्तेजसाऽप्रतिमेन च ।
शीक्षास्वरसमायुक्तं तपसा चाब्रवीन्मुनिः ।।

22. By (the power of his penance), By this utter devotion to The Ultimate (Soul), this Muni (Bharadhwaaja) who was endowed with incomparable brilliance (and power) said (his prayers from holy Texts) in a voice (and manner) as contained in (holy scriptures of) Scheeksha.

❍ ❍ ❍

२३. मनसा ध्यायतस्तस्य प्राङ्मुखस्य कृताञ्जलेः ।
आजग्मुस्तानि सर्वाणि दैवतानि पृथक् पृथक् ।।

23. Facing east, his hands cupped in Anjali, as (Bharadhwaaja) was meditating with his mind (transfixed in The Supreme), all those Deities came there one after the other.

❍ ❍ ❍

२४. मलयं दर्दुरं चैव ततः स्वेदनुदोऽनिलः ।
उपस्पृश्य ववौ युक्तस्सुप्रियात्मा सुखः शिवः ।।

24. At that moment, sweeping across Malaya and Dhurdhura mountains, Wind that removed sweat, blew sweetly, pleasantly and comfortably.

(The Entire Area Air conditioned:Humidity, temparature control.)

❍ ❍ ❍

२५. ततोऽभ्यवर्तन्त घना दिव्याः कुसुमवृष्टयः ।
देवदुन्दुभिनिर्घोषो दिक्षु सर्वासु शुश्रुवे ॥

25. Then Divine flowers rained (flowers) in abundance; And sounds from Dhundhubi drums were heard from all directions.

❍ ❍ ❍

२६. प्रववुश्चोत्तमा वाता ननृतुश्चाप्सरोगणाः ।
प्रजगुर्देवगन्धर्वा वीणाः प्रमुमुचुः स्वरान् ॥

26. Air blew (from all sides): Foremost Apsara maidens danced: The Dheva- Ghandharvas sang. (And musical Instrument) Veena issued forth sweet strains, (No need for Veena artists to play!)

❍ ❍ ❍

२७. स शब्दो द्यां च भूमिं च प्राणिनां श्रवणानि च ।
विवेशोच्चारितः श्लक्ष्णः समो लयगुणान्वितः ॥

27. The sounds (of music) was loud and clear, tender and soft, endowed with proper rhythm and they entered the ears of all living beings on earth and sky.

❍ ❍ ❍

२८. तस्मिन्नुपरते शब्दे दिव्ये श्रोत्रसुखे नृणाम् ।
ददर्श भारतं सैन्यं विधानं विश्वकर्मणः ॥

28. And when these divine sounds which were sweet upon the ears of men stopped, Bharatha's Army saw Vischwakarma's creations (for their hospitality).

२९. बभूव हि समा भूमिः समन्तात्पञ्चयोजना ।
शाद्वलैर्बहुभिश्छन्ना नीलवैडूर्यसंनिभैः ॥

29. The entire territory covering 5 yojana-s (about 45 miles) on all sides equally was covered with fresh grass which resembled blue diamonds.

❍ ❍ ❍

३०. तस्मिन्बिल्वाः कपित्थाश्च पनसा बीजपूरकाः ।
आमलक्यो बभूवुश्च चूताश्च फलभूषणाः ॥

30. There were there trees full with flowers Kapith (Feronia Elephantum), Aegle (Agele Marmalosa): Panasa (Artocarpus Intergrifolia); Bheejapuraka (Citrus medica) Amalakaya (Embric myrobala); Chootha (Mango).

❍ ❍ ❍

३१. उत्तरेभ्यः कुरुभ्यश्च वनं दिव्योपभोगवत् ।
आजगाम नदी दिव्या कूलजैर्बहुभिर्वृता ॥

31. From northern region of Kuru, came the divine forest. And divine rivers. And many fine species of trees shone there.

❍ ❍ ❍

३२. चतुश्शालानि शुभ्राणि शालाश्च गजवाजिनाम् ।
हर्म्यप्रासादसंबाधास्तोरणानि शुभानि च ॥

32. Beautiful homes with verandah-s on four sides Resting places for horses, elephants; palaces and mansions, arches; all (shone) lovely

❍ ❍ ❍

३३ सितमेघनिभं चापि राजवेश्म सुतोरणम् ।
शुक्लमाल्यकृताकारं दिव्यगन्धसमुक्षितम् ॥

३४. चतुरश्रमसंबाधं शयनासनयानवत् ।
दिव्यैः सर्वरसैर्युक्तं दिव्यभोजनवस्त्रवत् ॥

३५. उपकल्पितसर्वान्नं धौतनिर्मलभाजनम् ।।

33. to 35.

The Royal palace had lovely arches; was like white clouds; well decorated with white flowers; was scented with sweet wonderful unguents .... Was large with four sides symmetrical; furnished with cots, beds and sofa-s; well stocked with wonderful foods, and dresses; endowed with all comforts....with well prepared foods (cooked rice preparations etc), with (Crockery and) utensils made of pure silver.

❍ ❍ ❍

३६. क्लृप्तसर्वासनं श्रीमत्स्तीर्णशयनोत्तमम् ।
प्रविवेश महाबाहुरनुज्ञातो महर्षिणा ।।
वेश्म तद्रत्नसंपूर्णं भरतः कैकयीसुतः ।।

36. Commanded (and 'invited') by the great sage, the mighty limbed Bharatha the son of Kaikeyi, entered the resplendent palace which was full with gems, which had delightful couches, lovely beds with good furnishings.

❍ ❍ ❍

३७. अनुजग्मुश्च तं सर्वेमन्त्रिणः सपुरोहिताः ।
बभूवुश्च मुदायुक्तास्तं दृष्ट्वा वेश्मसंविधिम् ।।

37. All his ministers along with priests, followed him. (The moment) they saw the structure of the palace, they became seized with joy.

❍ ❍ ❍

३८. तत्र राजासनं दिव्यं व्यजनं छत्रमेव च ।
भरतो मन्त्रिभिः सार्धमभ्यवर्तत राजवत् ।।

38. And there (in this palace got ready by sage Bharadhwaaja), Bharatha turned towards the wonderful royal seat (like a throne) and the (royal like) umbrella

and the whisk (fan), along with his ministers and (he worshipped them) as though before king (Raama).

❍ ❍ ❍

३९. आसनं पूजयामास रामायाभिप्रणम्य च ।
वालव्यजनमादाय न्यषीदत्सचिवासने ॥

39. Bowing to "Raama" (as though Raama was occupying The Throne), he took the whisk fan and honoured (the empty) throne (fanning it with the whisk fan): And (Bharatha) occupied a seat meant for ministers.

(Bharatha's devotion to Raama is total; As far as he is concerned, it is Raama and Raama alone who is king of Ikshwaaku-s. Here he does not even occupy the Royal Seat but sits along with his ministers, although the Sage had "created" all this for him.)

❍ ❍ ❍

४०. आनुपूर्व्यान्निषेदुश्च सर्वेमन्त्रिपुरोहिताः ।
ततः सेनापतिः पश्चात्प्रशास्ता च निषेदतुः ॥

40. The ministers and priests occupied their respective seats in succession (as per protocol). Then the Army chief and then after other chiefs and officers.

❍ ❍ ❍

४१. ततस्तत्र मुहूर्तेन नद्यः पायसकर्दमाः ।
उपातिष्ठन्त भरतं भरद्वाजस्य शासनात् ॥

41. Then, there, in a Muhoortha, by the command of Bhardhwaaja, the rivers (flowing) with sweet milk preparations awaited Bharatha (to satisfy his entourage).

❍ ❍ ❍

४२. तासामुभयतः कूलं पाण्डुमृत्तिकलेपनाः ।
रम्याश्चावसथा दिव्या ब्रह्मणस्तु प्रसादजाः ॥

42. On either side of the Banks of these rivers, lovely

wonderful mansions, well plastered in white, appeared by the grace of this Braamin (Bharadhwaaja).

❍ ❍ ❍

४३. तेनैव च मुहूर्तेन दिव्याभरणभूषिताः ।
आगुर्विंशतिसाहस्रा ब्रह्मणा प्रहिताः स्त्रियः ।।

43. At the same time, twenty thousand ladies ornamented with wonderful jewellery, came there, sent by God Bramma.

❍ ❍ ❍

४४. सुवर्णमणिमुक्तेन प्रवालेन च भूषिताः ।
आगुर्विंशतिसाहस्राः कुबेरप्रहिताः स्त्रियः ।।

44. And twenty thousand ladies ornamented with (jewelleries made of gold, gems, stones, pearls, and corals came there sent by Kubhaera.(the lord of wealth).

❍ ❍ ❍

४५. याभिर्गृहीतः पुरुषः सोन्माद इव लक्ष्यते ।
आगुर्विंशतिसाहस्राः नन्दनादप्सरोगणाः ।।

45. A group of twenty thousand Apsara maidens, came from Nandhana (the celestial garden of Indhra): (These were so ravishing) that if any man is 'seized' (looked at) by these (ladies even for a second), he is seen to become mad (with passion).

❍ ❍ ❍

४६. नारदस्तुम्बुरुर्गोपः प्रवराः सूर्यवर्चसः ।
एते गन्धर्वराजानो भरतस्याग्रतो जगुः ।।

46. The Ghandharva kings like Naaradha, Thumburu, Gopa who were foremost and who shone with brilliancy of the Sun, sang before Bharatha.

❍ ❍ ❍

४७. अलम्बुसा मिश्रकेशी पुण्डरीकाऽथ वामना ।
उपानृत्यंस्तु भरतं भरद्वाजस्य शासनात् ।।

47. And by the command of Bharadhwaaja, then Alambusa, Mischrakeshi, Pundarika, and Vaamana. danced before Bharatha.

❍ ❍ ❍

४८. यानि माल्यानि देवेषु यानि चैत्ररथे वने ।
प्रयागे तान्यदृश्यन्त भरद्वाजस्य तेजसा ।।

48. Whatever flowers that were in the (celestial) gardens of Chaithyaratha, the flowers (used by) Dheva-s, were now seen at Prayaag, by the power of Bharadhwaaja. (around his hermitage).

❍ ❍ ❍

४९. बिल्वा मार्दङ्गिका आसञ्छम्यग्राहा विभीतकाः ।
अश्वत्था नर्तकाश्चासन्भरद्वाजस्य तेजसा ।।

49. By the power of Bharadhwaaja, trees like Bhilva, produced Rhythmic sounds and Vibhheshaka produced beats. And Ashwatha trees danced!

❍ ❍ ❍

५०. ततः सरलतालाश्च तिलका नक्तमालकाः ।
प्रहृष्टास्तत्र संपेतुः कुब्जा भूत्वाऽथ वामनाः ।।

50. Then the (tall) Sarala, Thaala, Thilaka, Nakthamaalaka tress shrunk themselves and became joyous.

❍ ❍ ❍

५१. शिंशुपामलकीजम्ब्वो याश्चान्याः कानने लताः ।
मल्लिका मालती जातिर्याश्चान्याः कानने लताः ।
प्रमदाविग्रहं कृत्वा भरद्वाजाश्रमेऽवदन् ।।

५२. सुराः सुरापाः पिबत पायसं च बुभुक्षिताः ।
मांसानि च सुमेध्यानि भक्ष्यन्तां यावदिच्छथ ।।

51. & 52.

Trees (like) Schimshupa, Amala, Jambu, other creepers in the forest, (like) Maalathi, Mallika, Jaathi and other plants of forest took on the form of (pretty) maidens in the hermitage of Bharadhwaaja!... And they spoke: ..= Oh men who desire Liquors! Drink wine and sweet milk preparations as much as you desire: oh men who are hungry! May you eat nourishing meats.=

❍ ❍ ❍

५३. उच्छाद्य स्नापयन्ति स्म नदीतीरेषु वल्गुषु ।
अप्येकमेकं पुरुषं प्रमदाः सप्त चाष्ट च ॥

53. Every man was (massaged) with oil and bathed in the beautiful banks (of rivers) by 7 or 8 maidens.

❍ ❍ ❍

५४. संवाहन्त्यः समापेतुर्नार्योरुचिरलोचनाः ।
परिमृज्य तथाऽन्योऽन्यं पाययन्ति वराङ्गनाः ॥

54. These beautiful eyed ladies who had lovely body, rushed to massage their bodies one after the other: They dried them up and made them drink (liquors and juices).

❍ ❍ ❍

५५. हयान्गजान्खरानुष्ट्रांस्तथैव सुरभेः सुतान् ।
अभोजयन्वाहनपास्तेषां भोज्यं यथाविधि ॥

55. The men in charge of transport, fed foods for horses, elephants, camels, and donkeys and for oxen, as per their requirements.

❍ ❍ ❍

५६. इक्षूंश्च मधु लाजांश्च भोजयन्ति स्म वाहनान् ।
इक्ष्वाकुरयोधानां चोदयन्तो महाबलाः ॥

56. The mightily strong foremost warriors of the Ikshwaaku (Army of Bharatha), goaded and fed the animals (that

pulled the vehicles), with sugar cane and sweet cakes (like molasses)

❍ ❍ ❍

५७. नाश्वबन्धोऽश्वमाजानान्न गजं कुञ्जरग्रहः ।
मत्तप्रमत्तमुदिता चमूः सा तत्र संबभौ ॥

57. The horsemen did not worry about their horses: The elephant riders (Mahouts) did not (worry about their elephants). At that time this Army (of Bharatha) was captivated with joy, was very happy.

❍ ❍ ❍

५८. तर्पिताः सर्वकामैस्ते रक्तचन्दनरूषिताः ।
अप्सरोगणसंयुक्ताः सैन्या वाचमुदैरयन् ॥

58. Being served by multitude of Apsara maidens, being satisfied with all the desirables, the men of the Army who were all besmeared with red sandal paste, uttered these words.

❍ ❍ ❍

५९. नैवायोध्यां गमिष्यामो न गमिष्याम दण्डकान् ।
कुशलं भरतस्यास्तु रामस्यास्तु तथा सुखम् ॥

59. (The Army of Bharatha was treated to such a lavish hospitality that Bharadhwaaja's Hermitage is Heaven on earth and they all say). We will not get back to Ayodhya: We will not go to Dhandaka forest. May there be welfare for Bharatha; May there be happiness for Raama.

❍ ❍ ❍

६०. इति पादापयोधाश्च हस्त्यश्वारोहबन्धकाः ।
अनाथास्तं विधिं लब्ध्वा वाचमेतामुदैरयन् ॥

60. The Infantry, the men on horse back, the elephant riders, seeing all this, uttered these words: We have no master (here. None can restrain us from merriment).

❍ ❍ ❍

६१. संप्रहृष्टा विनेदुस्ते नरास्तत्र सहस्रशः ।
भरतस्यानुयातारः स्वर्गोऽयमिति चाब्रुवन् ।।

61. The thousands of men who followed Bharatha, then rejoiced and shouted (in merriment): They said; = This Is Indeed Heaven.=

❍ ❍ ❍

६२. नृत्यन्ति स्म हसन्ति स्म गायन्ति स्म च सैनिकाः ।
समन्तात्परिधावन्ति माल्योपेताः सहस्रशः ।।

62. Thousands of soldiers danced: They sang; They Laughed: Wearing garlands they jumped all over the place (exhilarated)

❍ ❍ ❍

६३. ततो भुक्तवतां तेषां तदन्नममृतोपमम् ।
दिव्यानुद्वीक्ष्य भक्ष्यांस्तानभवद्भक्षणे मतिः ।।

63. Having eaten such foods that were like nectar, they had desire to eat (more and) further, as they saw these divine foods (heaped up).

❍ ❍ ❍

६४. प्रेष्याश्चेट्यश्च वध्वश्च बलस्थाश्चापि सर्वशः ।
बभूवुस्ते भृशं दृप्ताः सर्वेचाहतवाससः ।।

64. Attendants, servants, maids, soldiers, all of them wearing new clothes, became wild and proud in every way.

❍ ❍ ❍

६५. कुञ्जराश्च खरोष्ट्राश्च गोऽश्वाश्च मृगपक्षिणः ।
बभूवुः सुभृतास्तत्र नान्यो ह्यन्यमकल्पयत् ।।

65. There, elephants, asses, cows, horses, animals, birds were all fully satisfied: No one wished for anything.

❍ ❍ ❍

६६. नाशुक्लवासास्तत्रासीत्क्षुधितो मलिनोऽपि वा ।
रजसा ध्वस्तकेशो वा नरः कश्चिददृश्यत ।।

66. There, no person was hungry; nor seen wearing dirty dress; nor dirty; (every one) was with his hair, strewn with pollens of flowers.

❍ ❍ ❍

६७. आजैश्चापि च वाराहैर्निष्ठानवरसंचयैः ।
फलनिर्व्यूहसंसिद्धैः सूपैर्गन्धरसान्वितैः ।।

६८. पुष्पध्वजवतीः पूर्णाः शुक्लस्यान्नस्य चाभितः ।
ददृशुर्विस्मितास्तत्र नरा लौहीः सहस्रशः ।।

67. & 68.

Meats of goats: (Wild boars and) pigs; Limitless: Choicest fruit juices and squashes emitting fine aroma, well prepared: Soups which were endowed with fine taste (spiced).......Thousands of copper vessels decorated with flowers and full with white rice preparations; (All these) men saw there with wonder.

❍ ❍ ❍

६९. बभूवुर्वनपार्श्वेषु कूपाः पायसकर्दमाः ।
ताश्च कामदुघा गावो द्रुमाश्चासन्मधुस्रुतः ।।

69. The wells in these forests were filled with sweet milk (and milk preparations); And the cows there became Kaamadhenu (the holy cow that satisfies all desires). And trees oozed out honeys and liquors.

❍ ❍ ❍

७०. वाप्यो मैरेयपूर्णाश्च मृष्टमांसचयैर्वृताः ।
प्रतप्तपिठरैश्चापि मार्गमायूरकौक्कुटैः ।।

70. Ponds were full with Maireya liquors: (The embankments) were full with meats of deer and peacocks and birds. In heaps: meats well cooked, (seasoned in wines).

❍ ❍ ❍

७१. पात्रीणां च सहस्राणि स्थालीनां नियुतानि च ।
न्यर्बुदानि च पात्राणि शातकुम्भमयानि च ।।
७२. स्थाल्यः कुम्भ्यः करम्भ्यश्च दधिपूर्णाः सुसंस्कृताः ।
यौवनस्थस्य गौरस्य कपित्थस्य सुगन्धिनः ।।
७३. ह्रदाः पूर्णा रसालस्य दध्नः श्वेतस्य चापरे ।
बभूवुः पयसश्चान्ये शर्करायाश्च सञ्चयाः ।।

71. to 73.

Vessels in hundred thousands; Millions of (Water) mugs. Hundred million of golden pots and vessels; Beautiful (cups etc.) ......Vessels filled with (foods like) Oatmeal; Some beautiful vessels full of sweet smelling pure unsour Curds (and butter milk), smelling of Kapitsa fruit ...... (even) Some ponds full with fluids mixed with essences. There were heaps of sugar, some with plenty of sweet milk.

❍ ❍ ❍

७४. कल्कांश्चूर्णकषायांश्च स्नानानि विविधानि च ।
ददृशुर्भाजनस्थानि तीर्थेषु सरितां नराः ।।

74. The men (of Bharatha's entourage) saw on the banks of the river, vessels full of Kalka Oil (for bathing), aromatic powders, various items for bathing... (Kalka oil Terminalia Bellarica) .....

❍ ❍ ❍

७५. शुक्लानंशुमतश्चापि दन्तधावनसंचयान् ।
शुक्लाश्चन्दनकल्कांश्च समुद्गेष्ववतिष्ठतः ।।
७६. दर्पणान्परिमृष्टांश्च वाससां चापि संचयान् ।
पादुकोपानहां चैव युग्मान्यत्र सहस्रशः ।।
७७. आञ्जनीः कङ्कतान्कूर्चाञ्छत्राणि च धनूंषि च ।
मर्मत्राणानि चित्राणि शयनान्यासनानि च ।।
७८. प्रतिपानह्रदान्पूर्णान्खरोष्ट्रगजवाजिनाम् ।
अवगाह्यसुतीर्थांश्च ह्रदान्सोत्पलपुष्करान् ।।

७९. आकाशवर्णप्रतिमान्स्वच्छतोयान्सुखप्लवान् ।
नीलवैडूर्यवर्णांश्च मृदून्यवससञ्चयान् ॥
८०. निर्वापार्थान्पशूनां ते ददृशुस्तत्र सर्वशः ॥

75. to 80.

Hundreds of sharp white (Neem) twigs (to be used as tooth brush) for cleaning teeth; White sandal paste and oil ointments etc. (kept) in containers......Well cleaned (polished) Mirrors: Numerous dresses; Thousands of pairs of sandals; Cosmetics for Eye; Combs; Brushes; Umbrellas, Bows, wonderful jackets; beds and couches, Sofa-s ...... Plenty of water pools for asses, camels, horses and elephants; Ponds fit for taking plunge (for baths) in the waters; Ponds with pure waters, full with Nilothpala flowers, colour of water like the (blue) of the sky: Where one can take a plunge in comfort... Soft grass lands with lots of grass that were like blue diamond, which can be grazed by animals. They saw every where all these.

❍ ❍ ❍

८१. व्यस्मयन्त मनुष्यास्ते स्वप्नकल्पं तदद्भुतम् ।
दृष्ट्वाऽऽतिथ्यं कृतं तादृग्भरतस्य महर्षिणा ॥

81. This wonderful hospitality extended to Bharatha by the great sage Bharadhwaaja..... These men (of Bharatha), thinking that all this was a dream, became astounded.

❍ ❍ ❍

८२. इत्येषां रममाणानां देवानामिव नन्दने ।
भरद्वाजाश्रमे रम्ये सा रात्रिर्व्यत्यवर्तत ॥

82. The night passed away thus at Bharadhwaja's hermitage as they were enjoying themselves like celestials in (the celestial garden of) Nandhana.

❍ ❍ ❍

८३. प्रतिजग्मुश्च ता नद्यो गन्धर्वाश्च यथागतम् ।
भरद्वाजमनुज्ञाप्य ताश्च सर्वा वराङ्गनाः ।।

83. (After hospitality was done)... All these (divine) rivers and Ghandharva-s and the foremost (divine maidens, went back as they came, having obtained leave from Bharadhwaaja.

❍ ❍ ❍

८४. तथैव मत्ता मदिरोत्कटा नरा
स्तथैव दिव्यागरुचन्दनोक्षिताः ।
तथैव दिव्या विविधाः स्रगुत्तमाः
पृथक्प्रकीर्णा मनुजैः प्रमर्दिताः ।।

84. The men (of Bharatha) were intoxicated with joy; and further they were in a state of inebriation; and likewise they were besmeared with wonderful scents and sandal paste; The various wonderful foremost garlands which were cast aside by men separately, lay crushed there (after their rest).

(Note: Poet Vaalmeeki describes how Sage Bharadhwaaja the austere man of great penance and vows, entertained the Royal Prince Bharatha and his army. The peaceful hermitage was transformed into a place of merriment, with Wine, Women and Song! "Hindoo" Chauvinists will be aghast reading this. but the point to remember is that a sage does not cease to be a sage because he treats a Royal guest as he is used to be treated. Bharadhwaaja of course has nothing to do with wine, women and song)

❍ ❍ ❍

Chapter 92

(Bharatha) Leaves for Chithrakoot

१. ततस्तां रजनीं व्युष्य भरतः सपरिच्छदः ।
कृतातिथ्यो भरद्वाजं कामादभिजगाम ह ॥

1. After spending the night having enjoyed the hospitality (of sage Bharadhwaaja), Bharatha called on Bhardhwaaja with (great) endearment.

❍ ❍ ❍

२. तमृषिः पुरुषव्याघ्रं प्रेक्ष्य प्राञ्जलिमागतम् ।
हुताग्निहोत्रः भरतं भरद्वाजोऽभ्यभाषत ॥

2. Seeing him standing before him with his hands cupped in Anjali, Sage Bharadhwaaja who had finished his fire rituals, spoke to Bharatha, the 'tiger' of men.

❍ ❍ ❍

३. कच्चिदत्र सुखा रात्रिस्तवास्मद्विषये गता ।
समग्रस्ते जनः कच्चिदातिथ्ये शंस मेऽनघ ॥

3. Oh sinless (Bharatha)! I trust that the night spent away in my hermitage was comfortable to you; Your entourage, I hope, was satisfied with (my) hospitality. Tell me.

❍ ❍ ❍

४. तमुवाचाञ्जलिं कृत्वा भरतोऽभिप्रणम्य च ।
आश्रमादुपनिष्क्रान्तमृषिमुत्तमतेजसम् ॥

4. Bowing to this foremost and brilliant sage (Bharadhwaaja) who had come out of his hermitage, Bharatha then said this to him with his hands cupped in Anjali.

❍ ❍ ❍

५. सुखोषितोऽस्मि भगवन्समग्रबलवाहनः ।
तर्पितः सर्वकामैश्च सामात्यो बलवत्त्वया ॥

5. Oh Lord! I spent (the night) comfortably. Along with my ministers and with my Army and my retinue, I was satisfied by you, with all that is desirable, mightily (satisfied we are).

❍ ❍ ❍

६. अपेतक्लमसन्तापाः सुभिक्षाः सुप्रतिश्रयाः ।
अपि प्रेष्यानुपादाय सर्वेस्म सुसुखोषिताः ॥

6. Including even my servants, all of them were well fed, well taken care of and they spent (the night) in comfort, with their fatigue and pain (of journey) gone away.

❍ ❍ ❍

७. आमन्त्रये त्वां भगवन्कामं त्वमृषिसत्तम ।
समीपं प्रस्थितं भ्रातुर्मैत्रेणेक्षस्व चक्षुषा ॥

7. Oh Lord! Oh foremost Rishi! I beg you to please give me leave who has started (on this journey) to go and meet my brother (Raama). You (please) 'Look' at me with your friendly eyes.

❍ ❍ ❍

८. आश्रमं तस्य धर्मज्ञ धार्मिकस्य महात्मनः ।
आचक्ष्व कतमो मार्गः कियानिति च शंस मे ॥

8. Oh Knower of Dharma! Enlighten me about the great soul (Raama's) hermitage, (about this Raama) who is a man of Dharma. (Please) tell me how far it is and the route to be taken.

❍ ❍ ❍

९. इति पृष्टस्तु भरतं भ्रातृदर्शनलालसम् ।
प्रत्युवाच महातेजा भरद्वाजे महातपाः ॥

9. When asked thus, the most brilliant Bharadhwaaja who

was a man of mighty penance, replied to Bharatha who was eager to meet his brother.

❍ ❍ ❍

१०. भरतार्धतृतीयेषु योजनेष्वजने वने ।
चित्रकूटगिरिस्तत्र रम्यनिर्दरकाननः ।।

10. Oh Bharatha! About *55 miles from here, in the uninhabited forest, there is a mountain called Chithrakoot where there are caves and a garden of forests. (* Half of thirteen yojanas).

❍ ❍ ❍

११. उत्तरं पार्श्वमासाद्य तस्य मन्दाकिनी नदी ।
पुष्पितद्रुमसंछन्ना रम्यपुष्पितकानना ।।

11. On the northern side close (to the mountain) there is a river called Mandaakini, around which, there is a garden of flowers, and which is completely covered by trees in bloom.

❍ ❍ ❍

१२. अनन्तरं तत्सरितश्चित्रकूटश्च पर्वतः ।
तयोः पर्णकुटी तात तत्र तौ वसतो ध्रुवम् ।।

12. Very near the river, is Chithrakoot mountain and the hermitage of these two;. Oh lad! These two (your brothers Raama and Lakshmana) are well settled there.

❍ ❍ ❍

१३. दक्षिणेनैव मार्गेण सव्यदक्षिणमेव च ।
गजवाजिरथाकीर्णां वाहिनीं वाहिनीपते ।।

13. Oh (Bharatha) the leader of Army! Taking the southern route, lead your Army that is full with elephants, horses, chariots, towards south west.

❍ ❍ ❍

१४. वाहयस्व महाभाग ततो द्रक्ष्यसि राघवम् ।।

14. Oh most illustrious (Bharatha)! Then you will see (and meet) Raama, the Raaghava.

❍ ❍ ❍

१५. प्रयाणमिति च श्रुत्वा राजराजस्य योषितः ।
हित्वा यानानि यानार्हा ब्राह्मणं पर्यवारयन् ।।

15. And the wives of (Dhascharatha) the king of kings who were all in (various) chariots, got down from their chariots when they heard that journey was to commence and they surrounded this Braamin (Bharadhwaaja to pay their respects).

❍ ❍ ❍

१६. वेपमाना कृशा दीना सह देव्या सुमित्रया ।
कौसल्या तस्य जग्राह कराभ्यां चरणौ मुनेः ।।

16. The emaciated and miserable Kowsalya, along with lady Sumithra, touched the feet of Muni (Bharadhwaaja) with her hands, trembling.

❍ ❍ ❍

१७. असमृद्धेन कामेन सर्वलोकस्य गर्हिता ।
कैकेयी तस्य जग्राह चरणौ सव्यपत्रपा ।।

17. And Kaikeyi whose wishes (of making her son Bharatha king of Ayodhya) were not fulfilled and who was censured by all the world, fell and touched the feet of (Bharadhwaaja), ashamed of herself (for having driven away her step son Raama to make room for her son).

❍ ❍ ❍

१८. तं प्रदक्षिणमागम्य भगवन्तं महामुनिम् ।
अदूराद्भरतस्यैव तस्थौ दीनमनास्तदा ।।

18. Down hearted, she then went around the great Muni, this lord Sage (Bharadhwaaja) in circumbumbulation and stood there, not far from (her son) Bharatha.

❍ ❍ ❍

१९. ततः पप्रच्छ भरतं भरद्वाजो दृढव्रतः ।
विशेषं ज्ञातुमिच्छामि मातॄणां तव राघव ॥

19. Then, Bharadhwaaja the resolute man of vows (and penance) asked Bharatha: Oh Bharatha the Raaghava! I desire to know (and be introduced to) your mothers, particularly (as to who is who).

❍ ❍ ❍

२०. एवमुक्तस्तु भरतो भरद्वाजेन धार्मिकः ।
उवाच प्राञ्जलिर्भूत्वा वाक्यं वचनकोविदः ॥

20. When told thus by Bharadhwaaja, this man of Dharma, this Bharatha who was well versed in speech, addressed these words with his hands cupped in Anjali.

❍ ❍ ❍

२१. यामिमां भगवन्दीनां शोकानशनकर्शिताम् ।
पितुर्हि महिषीं देवीं देवतामिव पश्यसि ॥

21. Oh Lord! Here, whom you see appearing like a deity, who is my father's first lady (and queen), who is emaciated due to abstinence caused by grief, who is miserable ......

❍ ❍ ❍

२२. एषा तं पुरुषव्याघ्रं सिंहविक्रान्तगामिनम् ।
कौसल्या सुषुवे रामं धातारमदितिर्यथा ॥

22. ...... is indeed Kowsalya: Like Adhithi (begetting son) Indhra, she begot the 'tiger of men' Raama whose strides are like those of a lion.

❍ ❍ ❍

२३. अस्या वामभुजं श्लिष्टा यैषा तिष्ठति दुर्मनाः ।
कर्णिकारस्य शाखेव शीर्णपुष्पा वनान्तरे ॥

२४. एतस्यास्तु सुतौ देव्याः कुमारौ देववर्णिनौ ।
उभौ लक्ष्मणशत्रुघ्नौ वीरौ सत्यपराक्रमौ ॥

23. & 24.

And she who clings and clutches her left hand and stands (by the side of Kowsalya) like the branches of Karnikara tree in the forest with all flowers fallen down, who is in low spirits, (is the) lady to whom two sons Lakshmana and Schathrugna who are brave, who possess brilliance of celestials, who are truly valiant, were born.

❍ ❍ ❍

२५. यस्याःकृते नरव्याघ्रो जीवनाशमितो गतौ ।
राजा पुत्रविहीनश्च स्वर्गं दशरथो गतः ।।
२६. क्रोधनामकृतप्रज्ञां दृप्तां सुभगमानिनीम् ।
ऐश्वर्यकामां कैकेयीमनार्यामार्यरूपिणीम् ।।
२७. ममैतां मातरं विद्धि नृशंसां पापनिश्चयाम् ।
यतोमूलं हि पश्यामि व्यसनं महदात्मनः ।।

25. to 27.

(Bharatha introduces his mother Kaikeyi rather harshly) And she by whose (immoral) deed king Dhascharatha (died and) went to heaven because of (grief of) separation from his son (Raama), and on whose account this (Raama) the 'tiger of men' is wasting away his life (in the forest)...... She, who is wrathful, obstinate, proud of her beauty, arrogant, lover of wealth and power, an Un-Aryan woman appearing like an Aryan woman is Kaikeyi....You should know her as my mother: A cruel woman, 'accustomed' to sin: Great calamity I see (falling upon) me because of her.

❍ ❍ ❍

२८. इत्युक्त्वा नरशार्दूलो बाष्पगद्गदया गिरा ।
स निशश्वास ताम्राक्षः क्रुद्धो नाग इवासकृत् ।।

28. Eyes turning red due to wrath, this (Bharatha) the 'tiger' of men, having said these utterances coming

out haltingly due to tears, breathed hard and deep intermittently, like a cobra.

❍ ❍ ❍

२९. भरद्वाजो महर्षिस्तं ब्रुवन्तं भरतं तदा ।
प्रत्युवाच महाबुद्धिरिदं वचनमर्थवत् ।।

29. The great Rishi (Sage) Bharadhwaaja who was a man of great wisdom, replied to this Bharatha with these words with 'meaning'.

❍ ❍ ❍

३०. न दोषेणावगन्तव्या कैकेयी भरत त्वया ।
रामप्रव्राजनं ह्येतत्सुखोदर्कं भविष्यति ।।

30. Oh Bharatha! (Your mother) Kaikeyi should not be considered (or viewed) wicked by you; Because, this Raama's exile is going to result in good (for the world).

❍ ❍ ❍

३१. देवानां दानवानां च ऋषीणां भावितात्मनाम् ।
हितमेव भविष्यद्धि रामप्रव्राजनादिह ।।

31. By this exile of Raama, there is going to be welfare for Dheva-s, Dhaanava-s and for Rishi-s who meditate upon the universal soul, in this world.

(As readers know, everything has a divine sanction. Raama as incarnation of God Vishnu on earth. is going to destroy evil forces, particularly demon King Raavana of Lanka. Bharadhwaaja is such a great sage and 'Seer, he 'knows' why Raama is on 14 year exile)

❍ ❍ ❍

३२. अभिवाद्य तु संसिद्धः कृत्वा चैनं प्रदक्षिणम् ।
आमन्त्र्य भरतः सैन्यं युज्यतामित्यचोदयत् ।।

32. The most accomplished man Bharatha went round this (Bharadhwaaja) in circumbumbulation, bowed to him

and then took leave of him; And he goaded (his men):= May The Army Get Ready=.

❍ ❍ ❍

३३. ततो वाजिरथान्युक्तान् दिव्यान्हेमपरिष्कृतान् ।
अध्यारोहत्प्रयाणार्थी बहून्बहुविधो जनः ।।

33. Then the various men who were getting ready for journey, got into chariots which were decorated in gold, which looked divine, which carried many things and which were yoked to horses.

❍ ❍ ❍

३४. गजकन्या गजाश्चैव हेमकक्ष्याः पताकिनः ।
जीमूता इव घर्मान्ते सघोषाः संप्रतस्थिरे ।।

34. The elephants and the female young elephants wearing golden girdles carrying (huge) banners, started out with a roar, like those of clouds during rainy (hot monsoon) season.

❍ ❍ ❍

३५. विविधान्यपि यानानि महान्ति च लघूनि च ।
प्रययुः सुमहार्हाणि पादैरेव पदातयः ।।

35. They went on various chariots, big and small, and some on various costly chariots: The Infantry went on foot.

❍ ❍ ❍

३६. अथ यानप्रवेकैस्तु कौसल्याप्रमुखाः स्त्रियः ।
रामदर्शनकाङ्क्षिण्यः प्रययुर्मुदितास्तदा ।।

36. Keenly looking forward to see Raama, the ladies with Kowsalya as their chief, then went along, getting on to chariots happily.

❍ ❍ ❍

३७. स चार्कतरुणाभासां नियुक्तां शिबिकां शुभाम् ।
आस्थाय प्रययौ श्रीमान्भरतः सपरिच्छदः ।।

37. And the resplendent Bharatha got into a glorious palanquin chosen for him which shone like tender rays of the morning sun; He went along with his retinue.

❍ ❍ ❍

३८. सा प्रयाता महासेना गजवाजिरथाकुला ।
दक्षिणां दिशमावृत्य महामेघ इवोत्थितः ।।

38. The mighty Army that consisted of horses, elephants, chariots etc., went along the southern direction, covering (the distance), like mighty cloud sweeping (the sky).

❍ ❍ ❍

३९. वनानि तु व्यतिक्रम्य जुष्टानि मृगपक्षिभिः ।
गङ्गायाः परवेलायां गिरिष्वपि नदीषु च ।।

39. Passing through forests full of beasts and birds, passing by mountains and (passing by) rivers around the banks of river Ganges.

❍ ❍ ❍

४०. सा संप्रहृष्टद्विजवाजियोधा
वित्रासयन्ती मृगपक्षिसङ्घान् ।
महद्वनं तत्प्रतिगाहमाना
रराज सेना भरतस्य तत्र ।।

40. ...... Bharatha's happy Army consisting of exhilarated elephants, horses, and warriors, went ahead through the great forest, frightening away multitude of birds and beasts.

❍ ❍ ❍

Chapter 93

(Bharatha's) Search of Raama's Hermitage

१. तया महत्या यायिन्या ध्वजिन्या वनवासिनः ।
अर्दिता यूथपा मत्ताः सयूथाः संप्रदुद्रुवुः ।।

1. Scared away by the great Army (of Bharatha) that was going along, the huge elephants living in forest there, ran away with their herd (here and there, in fear).

❍ ❍ ❍

२. ऋक्षाः पृषतसङ्घाश्च रुरवश्च समन्ततः ।
दृश्यन्ते वनराजीषु गिरिष्वपि नदीषु च ।।

2. All along the path in the forest and on all sides of the rivers and mountains, bears, dears and spotted dears, were seen in multitude.

❍ ❍ ❍

३. स संप्रतस्थे धर्मात्मा प्रीतो दशरथात्मजः ।
वृतो महत्या यायिन्या सेनया चतुरङ्गया ।।

3. The noble soul man of Dharma (Bharatha) the beloved son of Dhascharatha went along, surrounded (and accompanied by) the great foursome Army that was going along,

❍ ❍ ❍

४. सागरौघनिभा सेना भरतस्य महात्मनः ।
महीं संछादयामास प्रावृषि द्यामिवाम्बुदः ।।

4. The great soul Bharatha's Army that was like ocean, engulfed the entire region like cloud covering the sky during rainy season.

❍ ❍ ❍

५. तुरङ्गौघैरवतता वारणैश्च महाजवैः ।
अनालक्ष्या चिरं कालं तस्मिन्काले बभूव भूः ।।

5. At that time, the territory being covered by elephants and fast moving horses, the 'earth' was not visible for a long time.

❍ ❍ ❍

६. स यात्वा दूरमध्वानं सुपरिश्रान्तवाहनः ।
उवाच भरतः श्रीमान्वसिष्ठं मन्त्रिणां वरम् ॥

6. After leading his tired Army for a long distance, the resplendent Bharatha said to Sage Vasishta who was foremost amongst ministers.

❍ ❍ ❍

७. तादृशं लक्ष्यते रूपं यथा चैव श्रुतं मया ।
व्यक्तं प्राप्ताः स्म तं देशं भरद्वाजो यमब्रवीत् ॥

7. Such a spot is seen. Surely we have reached that place as 'understood' by me from what Bharadhwaaja told (me).

❍ ❍ ❍

८. अयं गिरिश्चित्रकूट इयं मन्दाकिनी नदी ।
एतत्प्रकाशते दूरान्नीलमेघनिभं वनम् ॥

8. This mountain is Chithrakoota: This river (surely) is Mandhaakini. this forest which is like the dark big cloud (and dense) is seen from a distance.

❍ ❍ ❍

९. गिरेः सानूनि रम्याणि चित्रकूटस्य संप्रति ।
वारणैरवमृद्यन्ते मामकैः पर्वतोपमैः ॥

9. At this very moment, the beautiful table lands of Chithrakoot hills, is being trampled by our elephants that are like mountains.

❍ ❍ ❍

१०. मुञ्चन्ति कुसुमान्येते नगाः पर्वतसानुषु ।
नीला इवातपापाये तोयं तोयधरा घनाः ॥

10. These trees are shedding flowers on the foot of the hills like water from dark water bearing clouds.

❍ ❍ ❍

११. किन्नराचरितोद्देशं पश्य शत्रुघ्न पर्वतम् ।
हयैः समन्तादाकीर्णं मकरैरिव सागरम् ।।

11. Oh Schathrugna! See this. All around the mountain, it is full of horses; Inhabited by Kinnara-s, like an ocean full of fishes.

❍ ❍ ❍

१२. एते मृगगणा भान्ति शीघ्रवेगाः प्रचोदिताः ।
वायुप्रविद्धाः शरदि मेघजाला इवाम्बरे ।।

12. And it appears that these flocks of deers are running away wildly, in excitement, like cluster of clouds driven away by wind during autumn season.

❍ ❍ ❍

१३. कुर्वन्ति कुसुमापीडाञ्छिरःसु सुरभीनमी ।
मेघप्रकाशैः फलकैर्दाक्षिणात्या यथा नराः ।।

13. These men here, sport 'Chaplets' of sweet smelling flowers on their heads like men of south, with their tufts looking like clouds.

❍ ❍ ❍

१४. निष्कूजमिव भूत्वेदं वनं घोरप्रदर्शनम् ।
अयोध्येव जनाकीर्णा संप्रति प्रतिभाति मे ।।

14. This forest which was still and silent and appeared gruesome before, is now appearing like populous Ayodhya to me.

❍ ❍ ❍

१५. खुरैरुदीरितो रेणुर्दिवं प्रच्छाद्य तिष्ठति ।
तं वहत्यनिलः शीघ्रं कुर्वन्निव मम प्रियम् ।।

15. The dust kicked up by the hoofs of horses, rises and stands (upto) the sky! And the wind, as though doing good by me (and favouring me), quickly drives away (the dust to clear the way).

❍ ❍ ❍

१६. स्यन्दनांस्तुरगोपेतान्सूतमुख्यैरधिष्ठितान् ।
एतान्संपततः शीघ्रं पश्य शत्रुघ्न कानने ॥

16. Oh Schathrugna! Observe how even in forest, these chariots yoked to (fine) horses are going so fast, driven by (our) expert charioteers ......

❍ ❍ ❍

१७. एतान्वित्रासितान्पश्य बर्हिणः प्रियदर्शनान् ।
एनमाविशतः शैलमधिवासं पतत्रिणाम् ॥

17. (Do you) See how the beautiful looking peacocks are going away to their nests in the mountain, frightened (by our Army)

❍ ❍ ❍

१८. अतिमात्रमयं देशो मनोज्ञः प्रतिभाति मे ।
तापसानां निवासोऽयं व्यक्तं स्वर्गपथो यथा ॥

18. This place appears to me like 'Heaven', captivating my mind beyond measure. This is proper place for men of penance.

❍ ❍ ❍

१९. मृगा मृगीभिः सहिता बहवः पृषता वने ।
मनोज्ञरूपा दृश्यन्ते कुसुमैरिव चित्रिताः ॥

19. In this forest, the many spotted deers along with female deers are seen as though they are decorated with flowers: Their form is bewitching.

❍ ❍ ❍

२०. साधुः सैन्याः प्रतिष्ठन्तां विचिन्वन्तु च काननम् ।
यथा तौ पुरुषव्याघ्रौ दृश्येते रामलक्ष्मणौ ।।

20. Let expert Army men go along first in the forest: And let them search till the 'tigers of men' Raama and Lakshmana are sighted.

❍ ❍ ❍

२१. भरतस्य वचः श्रुत्वा पुरुषाः शस्त्रपाणयः ।
विविशुस्तद्वनं शूरा धूमं च ददृशुस्ततः ।।

21. Hearing Bharatha's words (of command), the brave men who were wielding weapons, entered the forest: And there they saw smoke (coming out).

❍ ❍ ❍

२२. ते समालोक्य धूमाग्रमूचुर्भरतमागताः ।
नामनुष्ये भवत्यग्निर्व्यक्तमत्रैव राघवौ ।।

22. Observing the tip of the smoke, they came back to Bharatha and said: =There will be no Fire in an uninhabited place: It is there that the two Raaghava-s (Raama and Lakshmana) must be.

❍ ❍ ❍

२३. अथ नात्र नरव्याघ्रौ राजपुत्रौ परन्तपौ ।
अन्ये रामोपमाः सन्ति व्यक्तमत्र तपस्विनः ।।

23. (But) If the tormentors of enemy, these two princes (Raama and Lakshmana) who are 'tigers' of men are not there, then in that place, surely some other men of penance like Raama must be there.=

❍ ❍ ❍

२४. तच्छ्रुत्वा भरतस्तेषां वचनं साधुसम्मतम् ।
सैन्यानुवाच सर्वांतानमित्रबलमर्दनः ।।

24. Hearing their words, concurring with them, Bharatha the destroyer of enemy forces, addressed all the Army.

❍ ❍ ❍

२५. यत्ता भवन्तस्तिष्ठन्तु नेतो गन्तव्यमग्रतः ।
अहमेव गमिष्यामि सुमन्त्रो धृतिरेव च ॥

25. You should not go beyond this: Stay on guard here. I alone will go: Sumanthra and Dhrithi also (will come along with me).

❍ ❍ ❍

२६. एवमुक्तास्ततः सर्वेतत्र तस्थुः समन्ततः ।
भरतो यत्र धूमाग्रं तत्र दृष्टिं समादधात् ॥

26. When told thus, all of them stood there on all sides. Bharatha directed his sight to the place (where) smoke was (coming from).

❍ ❍ ❍

२७. व्यवस्थिता या भरतेन सा चमू
निरीक्षमाणाऽपि च धूममग्रतः ।
बभूव हृष्टा नचिरेण जानती
प्रियस्य रामस्य समागमं तदा ॥

27. And the Army which was stationed there by Bharatha, observing the smoke before them, became very happy, realising that their meeting with their beloved Raama will (now) be not long.

❍ ❍ ❍

Chapter 94

Raama Describes Chithrakoota

१. दीर्घकालोषितस्तस्मिन्गिरौ गिरिवनप्रियः ।
वैदेह्याः प्रियमाकाङ्क्षन्स्वं च चित्तं विलोभयन् ॥

२. अथ दाशरथिश्चित्रं चित्रकूटमदर्शयत् ।
भार्याममरसंकाशः शचीमिव पुरन्दरः ॥

1. & 2.

Having lived for some time in this mountain (region) (Raama) the lover of forests and mountains, endeavoring to please (Seetha) the Vaidhehi, ...his mind allured.... this (Raama) the son of, Dhascharatha who was like a celestial, began to describe (the beauty of) wonderful Chithrakoot to his wife (Seetha).

❍ ❍ ❍

३. न राज्याद्भ्रंशनं भद्रे न सुहृद्भिर्विनाभवः ।
मनो मे बाधते दृष्ट्वा रमणीयमिमं गिरिम् ।।

3. Oh blessed (Seetha)! Seeing this beautiful mountain, my mind does not grieve over my exile from kingdom: Nor even separation from friends.

❍ ❍ ❍

४. पश्येममचलं भद्रे नानाद्विजगणायुतम् ।
शिखरैः खमिवोद्विद्धैर्धातुमद्भिर्विभूषितम् ।।

4. Oh blessed (Seetha)! Observe this beautiful mountain full of various flocks of birds; its peaks full of elements and are (so lofty) that they appear to touch the sky.

❍ ❍ ❍

५. केचिद्रजतसङ्काशाः केचित्क्षतजसन्निभाः ।
पीतमाञ्जिष्ठवर्णाश्च केचिन्मणिवरप्रभाः ।।

६. पुष्पार्ककेतकाभाश्च केचिज्ज्योतीरसप्रभाः ।
विराजन्तेऽचलेन्द्रस्य देशा धातुविभूषिताः ।।

5. & 6.

(Some places) are silvery: Some are of reddish hue like (colour of) blood; some coloured reddish yellow; some bluish like blue diamonds....some places in the mountain abound in trees of Arka (Calatropic-Gigantea); of Kethaka (Odoratis-Simus): Some places glitter like stars.

❍ ❍ ❍

७. नानामृगगणद्वीपितरक्ष्वृक्षगणैर्वृतः ।
अदुष्टैर्भात्ययं शैलो बहुपक्षिसमाकुलः ।।

7. This mountain 'shines' with hordes of harmless animals like deer, bears, and tigers, leopard, roaming about ; Is full of various birds.

❍ ❍ ❍

८. आम्रजम्बूसनैर्लोध्रैः प्रियालैः पनसैर्धवैः ।
अङ्कोलैर्भव्यतिनिशैर्बिल्वतिन्दुकवेणुभिः ।।

९. काश्मर्यरिष्टवरुणैर्मधूकैस्तिलकैस्तथा ।
बदर्यामलकैर्नीपैर्वेत्रधन्वनबीजकैः ।।

१०. पुष्पवद्भिः फलोपेतैश्छायावद्भिर्मनोरमैः ।
एवमादिभिराकीर्णः श्रियं पुष्यत्ययं गिरिः ।।

8. to 10.

(Various trees found in mountain- mountain slopes).. Amra (Mangefera Indica); Jamba (Eugenia Jambula); Loudhra (Symplocus Reacemos); Priyaala (Bean creepers); Panasa (Artocarpus Integrifolia); Dhava (Grislea Tormentosa): Angkola (Alanguim Hexapetula); Bhavya (Dilinea Indica); Thinisa (Dalbergia Ujjainesis); Bhilva (Aegle Marmelosa)..... Kaashmaari (Gemeli Arborer) Arishta (Azedirachea Indica); Varuna (Crataeva Roxburghi): Madhuak (Jonesia Asoka); Thilaka (Symplocos Racesmos); Bhaadharya (Eyezephus jujora); Amalaka (Embelica Officinalis); Neepa (Ixora banduca): Vethra (Calamus Rotung); Dhanvana (Alhagi Maurorum). Bheejaka (Fig tree)...Fruit bearing trees; Flower bearing trees; Shade giving trees; all captivating the mind. So many trees filling up (the mountain slopes and region) that they all enhance the beauty.

❍ ❍ ❍

११. शैलप्रस्थेषु रम्येषु पश्येमान् रोमहर्षणान् ।
किन्नरान्द्वन्द्वशो भद्रे रममाणान्मनस्विनः ।।

11. Oh blessed (Seetha)! Observe the most loved and desired Kinnara-s, playing about in high spirits, in pairs, on the slopes of mountain.

❍ ❍ ❍

१२. शाखावसक्तान्खड्गांच प्रवराण्यम्बराणि च ।
पश्य विद्याधरस्त्रीणां क्रीडोद्देशान्मनोरमान् ।।

12. Observe in the beautiful play ground, the foremost dresses, swords of the Vidhyaadhara-s and their wives, hung up on branches of trees.

❍ ❍ ❍

१३. जलप्रपातैरुद्भेदैर्निष्यन्दैश्च क्वचित्क्वचित् ।
स्रवद्भिर्भात्ययं शैलः स्रवन्मद इव द्विपः ।।

13. This mountain shines with water gushing forth from water falls and many streams, here and there....like wild elephants (running about here and there) ......

❍ ❍ ❍

१४. गुहासमीरणो गन्धान्नानापुष्पभवान्वहन् ।
घ्राणतर्पणमभ्येत्य कं नरं न प्रहर्षयेत् ।।

14. Which man, will it not delight, when this wind, coming through the caves bearing the sweet smell of various flowers, reaches him to 'satisfy' his breath (nose)!

❍ ❍ ❍

१५. यदीह शरदोऽनेकास्त्वया सार्धमनिन्दिते ।
लक्ष्मणेन च वत्स्यामि न मां शोकः प्रधक्ष्यति ।।

15. Oh blameless (Seetha)! Even if I live for many autumns here with you and Lakshmana, grief will not afflict me (grief of separation from my folks at Ayodhya).

❍ ❍ ❍

१६. बहुपुष्पफले रम्ये नानाद्विजगणायुते ।
विचित्रशिखरे ह्यस्मिन्रतवानस्मि भामिनि ।।

16. Oh endearing (Seetha)! I am indeed delighted in this beautiful (Place) whose mountain peaks are so beautiful, where there are many fruits and flowers and which is full of various flocks of birds.

❍ ❍ ❍

१७. अनेन वनवासेन मया प्राप्तं फलद्वयम् ।
पितुश्चानृणता धर्मेभरतस्य प्रियं तथा ॥

17. By this forest life, Two 'Fruits' (objectives) have been obtained (by me): (fulfilling) My debt to my father in the matter of his Dharma; likewise, .the good for Bharatha (in making him king).

(Raama's greatness comes out again through this stanza.)

❍ ❍ ❍

१८. वैदेहि रमसे कच्चिच्चित्रकूटे मया सह ।
पश्यन्ती विविधान्भावान्मनोवाक्कायसंयतान् ॥

18. Oh (Seetha the) Vaidhehi! Seeing various settings (sights) which soothe the mind, body and speech along with me, I trust you are delighted.

❍ ❍ ❍

१९. इदमेवामृतं प्राहू राज्ञि राजर्षयः परे ।
वनवासं भवार्थाय प्रेत्य मे प्रपितामहाः ॥

19. Oh queen (Seetha)! My forefathers, the sage kings (of Ikshwaaku-s), have said, that, for life after death and for welfare in the world, this forest life is like nectar.

❍ ❍ ❍

२०. शिलाः शैलस्य शोभन्ते विशालाः शतशोऽभितः ।
बहुला बहुलैर्वर्णैर्नीलपीतसितारुणैः ॥

20. On all sides, the rocks of mountain shine, with thousands of stones in various colours of blue, yellow and white and red in various (shapes), large (and small).

❍ ❍ ❍

२१. निशि भान्त्यचलेन्द्रस्य हुताशनशिखा इव ।
ओषध्यः स्वप्रभालक्ष्या भ्राजमानाः सहस्रशः ।।

21. The thousands of medicinal plants of the mountain, glow brilliantly by their own radiance at night, like flames of fire.

❍ ❍ ❍

२२. केचित्क्षयनिभा देशाः केचिदुद्यानसन्निभाः ।
केचिदेकशिला भान्ति पर्वतस्यास्य भामिनि ।।

22. Oh endearing (Seetha)! At some places in mountains, it appears like dwelling places; in some places like gardens, and in some places like a single rock.

❍ ❍ ❍

२३. भित्त्वेव वसुधां भाति चित्रकूटः समुत्थितः ।
चित्रकूटस्य कूटोऽसौ दृश्यते सर्वतः शुभः ।।

23. The Chithrakoot appears as though having ploughed through earth and risen high! The plateau of Chithrakoot is lovely at all places.

❍ ❍ ❍

२४. कुष्ठपुन्नागस्थगरभूर्जपत्रोत्तरच्छदान् ।
कामिनां स्वास्तरान्पश्य कुशेशयदलायुतान् ।।

24. See the 'Bed' (like spread), fit for lovers, (of strewn) lotus leaves covered with flowers of Kushta, Punnaga and leaves of Bhoorja.

❍ ❍ ❍

२५. मृदिताश्चापविद्धाश्च दृश्यन्ते कमलस्रजः ।
कामिभिर्वनिते पश्य फलानि विविधानि च ।।

25. Most desirable (Seetha) ! The (remnants of) various fruits, lotus garlands that are crushed and thrown away by lovers, are seen. See this.

❍ ❍ ❍

२६. वस्वोकसारां नलिनीमतीत्यैवोत्तरान्कुरून् ।
पर्वतश्चित्रकूटोऽसौ बहुमूलफलोदकः ।।

26. The Chithrakoota mountain with its various fruits and tubers, surpasses (Indhra's) Nalini, Kubhaera's city, and the northern Kuru region.

❍ ❍ ❍

२७. इमं तु कालं वनिते विजह्रिवां
स्त्वया च सीते सह लक्ष्मणेन च ।
रतिं प्रपत्स्ये कुलधर्मवर्धिनीं
सतां पथि स्वैर्नियमैः परैः स्थितः ।।

27. Oh most desirable (Seetha)! Living with you and Lakshmana till the time of (my exile) with supreme self restraint, abiding in the path of the Good, I will obtain the pleasure of increasing (fostering) the Dharma of our family.

(Raama is so happy and well settled at Chithrakoota that he is totally unaware that his brother (Bharatha) is coming there with a huge army and VIP-s to force him to cut short his exile and get back to Ayodhya with him).

❍ ❍ ❍

Chapter 95

(Raama) Describes Mandhaakini

१. अथ शैलाद्विनिष्क्रम्य मैथिलीं कोसलेश्वरः ।
अदर्शयच्छुभजलां रम्यां मन्दाकिनीं नदीम् ।।

1 Then (Raama) the lord of Kosala, getting away from the mountain, pointed out the beautiful river Mandhaakini, whose waters were pure, to (Seetha the) Maithili.

❍ ❍ ❍

२. अब्रवीच्च वरारोहां चारुचन्द्रनिभाननाम् ।
विदेहराजस्य सुतां रामो राजीवलोचनः ।।

2. The Lotus eyed Raama addressed (Seetha) the daughter of Vidheha king, this worthy lady whose face was lovely like the moon.

❍ ❍ ❍

३. विचित्रपुलिनां रम्यां हंससारससेविताम् ।
कुसुमैरुपसम्पन्नां पश्य मन्दाकिनीं नदीम् ।।

3. See (and enjoy the sight of) Mandhaakini river which is beautiful, which has wonderful banks, which is inhabited by flock of Hamsa birds, which is studded with flowers ......

❍ ❍ ❍

४. नानाविधैस्तीररुहैर्वृतां पुष्पफलद्रुमैः ।
राजन्तीं राजराजस्य नलिनीमिव सर्वतः ।।

4. ...... which is full of various trees with fruits and flowers covering its banks, which is like Nalini (Lotus) of the king of kings, (Kubhaera)

❍ ❍ ❍

५. मृगयूथनिपीतानि कलुषाम्भांसि साम्प्रतम् ।
तीर्थानि रमणीयानि रतिं सञ्जनयन्ति मे ।।

5. The beautiful dark waters (somewhat) muddy, gladden me as they are being drunk by herd of deers.

❍ ❍ ❍

६. जटाजिनधराः काले वल्कलोत्तरवाससः ।
ऋषयस्त्ववगाहन्ते नदीं मन्दाकिनीं प्रिये ।।

6. Oh my beloved (Seetha)! At proper times (and seasons), sages who sport locks of tufted hair and wear deer skins, take their baths in this Mandhaakini river.

❍ ❍ ❍

७. आदित्यमुपतिष्ठन्ते नियमादूर्ध्वबाहवः ।
एते परे विशालाक्षि मुनयः संशितव्रताः ।।

7. Oh large eyed (Seetha)! Other Muni-s, after performing rituals, raise their hands towards the sun and stand in devotion.

❍ ❍ ❍

८. मारुतोद्धूतशिखरैः प्रनृत्त इव पर्वतः ।
पादपैः पत्रपुष्पाणि सृजद्भिरभितो नदीम् ।।

8. When the top of trees are shaken up by wind and they shed leaves and flowers, it appears as though the mountain (itself) is dancing across the river.

❍ ❍ ❍

९. क्वचिन्मणिनिकाशोदां क्वचित्पुलिनशालिनीम् ।
क्वचित्सिद्धजनाकीर्णां पश्य मन्दाकिनीं नदीम् ।।

9. See this Mandhaakini river! In some places its water glitters like blue diamond. In some places it has wide banks. In some places it is inhabited by men of enlightenment (sages and the like).

❍ ❍ ❍

१०. निर्धूतान्वायुना पश्य विततान्पुष्पसञ्चयान् ।।

10. See the well spread out cluster of flowers strewn by the wind.

❍ ❍ ❍

११. पोप्लूयमानानपरान्पश्य त्वं जलमध्यगान् ।।

11. You see objects floating in the middle of the river.

❍ ❍ ❍

१२. तांश्चातिवल्गुवचसो रथाङ्गाह्वयना द्विजाः ।
अधिरोहन्ति कल्याणि निकूजन्तः शुभा गिरः ।।

12. Oh auspicious (Seetha)! Wild goose birds are perched

on top of these. In very sweet voice, they are cooing, emitting nice sounds,

❍ ❍ ❍

१३. दर्शनं चित्रकुटस्य मन्दाकिन्याश्च शोभने ।
अधिकं पुरवासाच्च मन्ये तव च दर्शनात् ।।

13. Oh bright (Seetha)! Because of your presence, I consider the sight of Chithrakoot and Mandhaakini river more (satisfying) than life in the city (of Ayodhya).

❍ ❍ ❍

१४. विधूतकलुषैः सिद्धैस्तपोदमशमान्वितैः ।
नित्यं विक्षोभितजलां विगाहस्व मया सह ।।

14. You take bath with me in these waters, bathed daily by holy men who have abandoned evil (who are delivered from sin), and who are endowed with (many) penance and mental tranquillity.

❍ ❍ ❍

१५. सखीवच्च विगाहस्व सीते मन्दाकिनीं नदीम् ।
कमलान्यवमज्जन्ती पुष्कराणि च भामिनी ।।

15. Oh endearing (Seetha)! Immersing Kampala and Pucker (lotuses), you will come along with me to Mandhaakini river as my companion.

❍ ❍ ❍

१६. त्वं पौरजनवद्व्यालानयोध्यामिव पर्वतम् ।
मन्यस्व वनिते नित्यं सरयूवदिमां नदीम् ।।

16. Oh most desirable (Seetha)! (From now on) You must always consider the dangerous animals as (our) citizens; and consider the mountains as though it is Ayodhya and this river (as our river) Sarayu

❍ ❍ ❍

१७. लक्ष्मणश्चैव धर्मात्मा मन्निदेशे व्यवस्थितः ।
त्वं चानुकूला वैदेहि प्रीतिं जनयती मम ॥

17. Oh (Seetha) the Vaidhehi! The noble soul man of Dharma Lakshmana who is ever obedient to my command and you, who are ever favorably disposed to me, cause me (immense) happiness.

❍ ❍ ❍

१८. उपस्पृशंस्त्रिषवणं मधुमूलफलाशनः ।
नायोध्यायै न राज्याय स्पृहयामि त्वया सह ॥

18. Bathing (in Mandhaakini) three times a day, eating fruits, tubers and honey (products), I will not envy (nor care for) Ayodhya nor the rule of kingdom.

❍ ❍ ❍

१९. इमां हि रम्यां मृगयूथशालिनीं
निपीततोयां गजसिंहवानरैः ।
सुपुष्पितैः पुष्पधरैरलङ्कृतां
न सोऽस्ति यः स्यादगतक्लमः सुखी ॥

19. There is no one whose weariness will not disappear if he enjoys the comfort in this delightful (river) which is (surrounded) by well blossomed flower bearing trees, whose waters are drunk by elephants, lions, monkeys and where there are herds of deers.

❍ ❍ ❍

२०. इतीव रामो बहु सङ्गतं वचः
प्रियहायः सरितं प्रति ब्रुवन् ।
चचार रम्यं नयनाञ्जनप्रभं
स चित्रकूटं रघुवंशवर्धनः ॥

20. Speaking many such touching words about the river, this Raama the glorifier of his race of Raghu-s, (enjoyed life and) roamed about in this Chithrakoot (region)

which was beautiful like eye brows (of lovely maidens), along with his beloved companion (Seetha).

❍ ❍ ❍

Chapter 96

Lakshmana's Agitation

१. तां तथा दर्शयित्वा तु मैथिलीं गिरिनिम्नगाम् ।
निषसाद गिरिप्रस्थे सीतां मांसेन छन्दयन् ।।

1. After showing Seetha the Maithili this river that was flowing around the mountains, he rested on the foothills, delighting himself with the flesh of these fruits.

❍ ❍ ❍

२. इदं मेध्यामिदं स्वादु निष्टप्तमिदमग्निना ।
एवमास्ते स धर्मात्मा सीतया सह राघवः ।।

2. The noble soul man of Dharma (Raama the) Raaghava saying=This place is burnt by (performance of) holy ritual fires; This place is lovely: This place is clean= then sat down along with Seetha.

❍ ❍ ❍

३. तथा तत्रासतस्तस्य भरतस्यानुयायिनः ।
सैन्यरेणुश्च शब्दश्च प्रादुरास्तां नभस्पृशौ ।।

3. As he was resting thus (with Seetha), The 'Dust of the Army' and the loud noise of Bharatha's entourage manifested as though touching the sky.

❍ ❍ ❍

४. एतस्मिन्नन्तरे त्रस्ताः शब्देन महता ततः ।
अर्दिताः यूथपा मत्ताः सयूथा दुद्रुवुर्दिशः ।।

4. Fat elephants (of the forest) along with herds of

elephants being tormented and scared by the loud noise (of Bharatha's huge Army), ran away in all directions from there at that time.

❍ ❍ ❍

५. स तं सैन्यसमुद्धूतं शब्दं शुश्राव राघवः ।
तांश्च विप्रद्रुतान्सर्वान्यूथपानन्ववैक्षत ॥

5. And this (Raama the) Raaghava heard the intense sound of the Army: And he saw (the forest) elephants, all of them, fleeing.

❍ ❍ ❍

६. तांश्च विद्रवतो दृष्ट्वा तं च श्रुत्वा च निस्स्वनम् ।
उवाच रामः सौमित्रिं लक्ष्मणं दीप्ततेजसम् ॥

6. Seeing them running away and hearing the noise, Raama addressed Lakshmana the son of Sumithra who had fiery brilliance.

❍ ❍ ❍

७. हन्त लक्ष्मण पश्येह सुमित्रा सुप्रजास्त्वया ।
महीस्तनितगम्भीरस्तुमुलः श्रूयते स्वनः ॥

7. Oh dear Lakshmana! (Your mother) Sumithra has begotten a good son in you! A tumultuous noise with intensity (of sound during) earthquake is heard now. Observe this now.

❍ ❍ ❍

८. गजयूथानि वाऽरण्ये माहिषा वा महावने ।
वित्रासिता मृगाः सिंहैः सहसा प्रद्रुता दिशः ॥

8. In this forest, the great forest, lions along with herds of elephants and buffaloes and deers, are suddenly running away in all directions, scared.

❍ ❍ ❍

९. राजा वा राजमात्रो वा मृगयामटते वने ।
अन्यद्वा श्वपदं किंचित्सौमित्रे ज्ञातुमर्हसि ॥

9. Oh (Lakshmana the) son of Sumithra ! You should find out whether a king or a king's son has come for hunting wild beasts in the forest or else for any other purpose.

❍ ❍ ❍

१०. सुदुश्चरो गिरिश्चायं पक्षिणामपि लक्ष्मण ।
सर्वमेतद्यथातत्त्वमचिराज्ज्ञातुमर्हसि ॥

10. Oh Lakshmana! This mountain (is so dense with trees etc.) that even arrows cannot get through; Without delay, you should find out all this, exactly.

❍ ❍ ❍

११. स लक्ष्मणः संत्वरितः सालमारुह्यः पुष्पितम् ।
प्रेक्षमाणो दिशः सर्वाः पूर्वां दिशमुदैक्षत ॥

11. This Lakshmana quickly climbed up a Saala tree in blossom: Looking from there in all directions, observed the eastern direction.

❍ ❍ ❍

१२. उदङ्मुखः प्रेक्षमाणो ददर्श महतीं चमूम् ।
गजाश्वरथसंबाधां यानैर्युक्तां पदातिभिः ॥

12. Looking around with his face lifted up, he saw a big Army, full with vehicles, foot soldiers, elephants, horses, chariots etc.

❍ ❍ ❍

१३. तामश्वगजसंपूर्णां रथध्वजविभूषिताम् ।
शशंस सेनां रामाय वचनं चेदमब्रवीत् ॥

13. He announced to Raama (about his sighting of) an Army full of horses and elephants, shining with a chariot, a banner on it He said these words.

❍ ❍ ❍

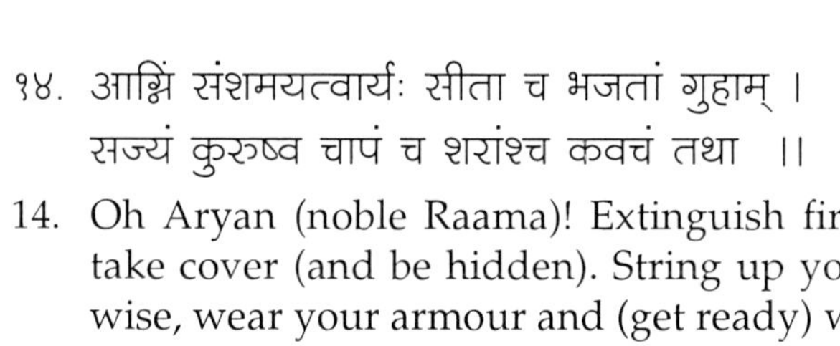

१४. आग्निं संशमयत्वार्यः सीता च भजतां गुहाम् ।
सज्यं कुरुष्व चापं च शरांश्च कवचं तथा ॥

14. Oh Aryan (noble Raama)! Extinguish fire: Let Seetha take cover (and be hidden). String up your bow; Like wise, wear your armour and (get ready) with arrows.

❍ ❍ ❍

१५. तं रामः पुरुषव्याघ्रो लक्ष्मणं प्रत्युवाच ह ।
अङ्गावेक्षस्व सौमित्रे कस्येमां मन्यसे चमूम् ॥

15. Raama the 'tiger of men' replied to this Lakshmana. Oh (Lakshmana) the son of Sumithra! Whose Army is this you think? Observe (carefully). Indeed!

❍ ❍ ❍

१६. एवमुक्तस्तु रामेण लक्ष्मणो वाक्यमब्रवीत् ।
दिधक्षन्निव तां सेनां रुषितः पावको यथा ॥

16. When he was asked thus by Raama, Lakshmana, as though he would 'burn' up this Army that was like Fire, said these words in wrath.

❍ ❍ ❍

१७. सम्पन्नं राज्यमिच्छंस्तु व्यक्तं प्राप्यभिषेचनम् ।
आवां हन्तुं समभ्येति कैकेय्या भरतः सुतः ॥

17. It is quite obvious that this Bharatha the son of Kaikeyi, having been anointed (as crown prince), has come here to kill us both, desirous of making the kingdom absolute.

❍ ❍ ❍

१८. एष वै सुमहाञ्छ्रीमान्विटपी संप्रकाशते ।
विराजत्युद्गतस्कन्धः कोविदारध्वजो रथे ॥

18. There shines the mighty resplendent banner Vitapi (of Fig tree): Raised high over the chariot, the (mighty) mast that cannot be split up, shines

❍ ❍ ❍

१९. भजन्त्येते यथाकाममश्वानारुह्य शीघ्रगान् ।
एते भ्राजन्ति संहृष्टा गजानारुह्य सादिनः ।।

19. These (men) riding on fast moving horses are pursuing us at their (will and) pleasure The Mahouts, riding on elephants gleam (with joy).

❍ ❍ ❍

२०. गृहीतधनुषौ चावां गिरिं वीर श्रयावहे ।
अथवेहैव तिष्ठावः संनद्धावुद्यतायुधौ ।।

20. Oh brave (Raama)! Bearing our Arms, we two will proceed to mountain; Or, with our weapons in readiness, we will stay here itself.

❍ ❍ ❍

२१. अपि नौ वशमागच्छेत्कोविदारध्वजो रणे ।।

21. In battle, this Mast (of Bharatha) that cannot be split up, will fall into our hands, will it not? (We will easily conquer Bharatha).

❍ ❍ ❍

२२. अपि द्रक्ष्यामि भरतं यत्कृते व्यसनं महत् ।
त्वया राघव संप्राप्तं सीतया च मया तथा ।।

22. Oh (Raama) the Raaghava! Will I see this Bharatha because of whom this great suffering has befallen upon you, me and Seetha!

(I have a score to settle with this Bharatha says Lakshmana, little realising that Bharatha has come to take them back to Ayodhya)

❍ ❍ ❍

२३. यन्निमित्तं भवान्राज्याच्च्युतो राघव शाश्वतात् ।
संप्राप्तोऽयमरिर्वीर भरतो वध्य एव मे ।।

23. Oh Brave (Raama the) Raaghava! He, on whose account you were expelled from your traditional kingdom,

this Bharatha, this enemy, who has come (here), must surely be killed.

❍ ❍ ❍

२४. भरतस्य वधे दोषं नाहं पश्यामि राघव ।
पूर्वापकारिणां त्यागे न ह्यधर्मोविधीयते ।।

24. Oh (Raama the) Raaghava! I see no sin in killing this Bharatha! Because, in eliminating one who has done harm first, no A-Dharma is bestowed (on the killer).

❍ ❍ ❍

२५. पूर्वापकारी भरतस्त्यक्तधर्मश्च राघव ।
एतस्मिन्निहते कृत्स्नामनुशाधि वसुन्धराम् ।।

25. Oh (Raama the) Raaghava! Bharatha sinned first: Has abandoned Dharma; After he is killed, you rule over the entire earth.

❍ ❍ ❍

२६. अद्य पुत्रं हतं संख्ये कैकेयी राज्यकामुका ।
मया पश्येत्सुदुःखार्ता हस्तिभग्नमिव द्रुमम् ।।

26. This Kaikeyi whose passion is (rule of) kingdom, will now see her son (Bharatha) killed by me in battle, like a tree felled by an elephant; She will (then) be in great sorrow.

❍ ❍ ❍

२७. कैकेयीं च वधिष्यामि सानुबन्धां सबान्धवाम् ।
कलुषेणाद्य महता मेदिनी परिमुच्यताम् ।।

27. I will kill this Kaikeyi along with her relatives and folks; May this Earth be freed from the great sin, now!

❍ ❍ ❍

२८. अद्येम सयतं क्रोधमसत्कारं च मानद ।
मोक्ष्यामि शत्रुसैन्येषु कक्षेष्विव हुताशनम् ।।

28. Oh Raama who commands respect! The suppressed wrath and disgrace (we received at Ayodhya)... All

that in me, I am now going to 'discharge' on the hostile Army (of Bharatha) like fire on dry wood.

❍ ❍ ❍

२९. अद्यैतच्चित्रकूटस्य काननं निशितैः शरैः ।
भिन्दञ्छत्रुशरीराणि करिष्ये शोणितोक्षितम् ।।

29. With my sharp arrows, I will cut up the bodies of my enemies and will make this entire forest of Chithrakoot blood stained.

❍ ❍ ❍

३०. शरैर्निर्भिन्नहृदयान्कुञ्जरांस्तुरगांस्तथा ।
श्वापदाः परिकर्षन्तु नरांश्च निहतान्मया ।।

30. And let wild animals drag the (bodies of) men killed by my arrows and (also the bodies of) elephants and horses whose chest will be split up.

❍ ❍ ❍

३१. शराणां धनुषश्चाहमनृणोऽस्मि महामृधे ।
ससैन्यं भरतं हत्वा भविष्यामि न संशयः ।।

31. I Will Discharge My Debt To My Bow and Arrow! I will remain so (even) after killing Bharatha and his Army in great war. No doubt about this

(Note: For once Lakshmana loses his "bearing"! His thoughts turn amuck. Cannot believe that Bharatha could be visiting Raama for any other purpose than to do 'good' to them. But being a Kshthariya warrior, Lakshmana, on seeing the vast army considers only evil at the hands of his brother Bharatha.. It is this vast army that has "Disturbed " him. He can be condoned!)

❍ ❍ ❍

Chapter 97

Raama Pacifies Lakshmana

(Bharatha's Huge army at the outskirts of Raama's hermitage: Lakshmana is certain Bharatha has come there to kill them. Raama knows that his sinless brother Bharatha has come there to take him back to Ayodhya. Raama tells Lakshmana not to entertain such horrible thoughts about his brother Bharatha)

१. सुसंरब्धं तु सौमित्रिं लक्ष्मणं क्रोधमूर्च्छितम् ।
रामस्तु परिसान्त्व्याथ वचनं चेदमब्रवीत् ।।

1. Then Raama consoled (calmed) Lakshmana the son of Sumithra who was agitated and overcome by wrath: He said these words.

❍ ❍ ❍

२. किमत्र धनुषा कार्यमसिना वा सचर्मणा ।
महेष्वासे महाप्राज्ञे भरते स्वयमागते ।।

2. As the most intelligent Bharatha who is great wielder of bow himself has come here now, what purpose would be served by a bow or sword with leather handle.(for me or you)?

❍ ❍ ❍

३. पितुः सत्यं प्रतिश्रुत्य हत्वा भरतमागतम् ।
किं करिष्यामि राज्येन सापवादेन लक्ष्मण ।।

3. Oh Lakshmana! Having promised my father truthfully, what will I do with the 'ill gotten' kingdom after killing Bharatha who is coming here.

❍ ❍ ❍

४. यद्द्रव्यं बान्धवानां वा मित्राणां वा क्षये भवेत् ।
नाहं तत्प्रतिगृह्णीयां भक्षान्विषकृतानिव ।।

4. Like poisonous food, I will not accept any wealth that comes through killing of either relatives or friends.

❍ ❍ ❍

५. धर्ममर्थं च कामं च पृथिवीं चापि लक्ष्मण ।
इच्छामि भवतामर्थेएतत्प्रतिश्रृणोमि ते ॥

5. Oh Lakshmana! Dharma, Artha, Kaama, Earth (all these) I desire only for your sake. I assure you.

❍ ❍ ❍

६. भ्रातॄणां संग्रहार्थं च सुखार्थं चापि लक्ष्मण ।
राज्यमप्यहमिच्छामि सत्येनायुधमालभे ॥

6. Oh Lakshmana! (If at all), it is (only) for the good and pleasure of my brothers that I desire this kingdom. I swear on my Arms truly.

(Raama's love for all his brothers is well known; Any brother of his can become king and enjoy all the pleasures.)

❍ ❍ ❍

७. नेयं मम मही सौम्य दुर्लभा सागराम्बरा ।
न हीच्छेयमधर्मेण शक्रत्वमपि लक्ष्मण ॥

7. Oh pleasant Lakshmana! The entire earth surrounded by oceans is not difficult for me (to obtain, if I chose to): Yet, I do not desire even the post of (the Lord of Heaven) Indhra, if it is through Non Dharma.(Adharma)

(Ends cannot justify means; Only through Dharma one should obtain whatever in this world. Raama will not resort to A-Dharma.)

❍ ❍ ❍

८. यद्विना भरतं त्वां च शत्रुघ्नं चापि मानद ।
भवेन्मम सुखं किंचिद्भस्म तत्कुरुतां शिखी ॥

8. Oh respected (Lakshmana)! If there is any happiness at all for me without Bharatha, you and Schathrugna (sharing it), then may fire reduce this to ashes.

❍ ❍ ❍

९. मन्येऽहमागतोऽयोध्यां भरतो भ्रातृवत्सलः ।
मम प्राणात्प्रियतरः कुलधर्ममनुस्मरन् ।।

१०. श्रुत्वा प्रव्राजितं मां हि जटावल्कलधारिणम् ।
जानक्या सहितं वीर त्वया च पुरुषोत्तम ।।

११. स्नेहेनाक्रान्तहृदयः शोकेनाकुलितेन्द्रियः ।
द्रष्टुमभ्यागतो ह्येष भरतो नान्यथाऽऽगतः ।।

9. to 11.

Oh brave (Lakshmana)! I consider (there cannot be any happiness without my brothers).: Bharatha is very much attached to his brothers: He is dearer to me than my life. He ever remembers the Dharma of our Race. On his return to Ayodhya (from his holiday)... Bharatha, when he heard about my exile to forest with you and (Seetha) the Jaanaki, (and when he heard about me) being dressed up in (forest costume of) bark and sporting tufted hair locks, (Bharatha) has now come here to see me, his heart stricken (with grief) due to his affection for me, his mind deeply perturbed by grief (of separation from me) Oh (Lakshmana) the foremost of men! He has come for no other (reason than to meet me).

❍ ❍ ❍

१२. अम्बां च कैकयीं रुष्य भरतश्चाप्रियं वदन् ।
प्रसाद्य पितरं श्रीमान्राज्यं मे दातुमागतः ।।

12. The resplendent Bharatha, after (scolding) his mother Kaikeyi, in wrath against her and after speaking unpleasantly to her, has now come here after asking his father to give (back) the kingdom to me.

(Raama of course is quite sure as to why Bharatha has come with Army. And Raama doesn't know that his father is dead and gone.)

❍ ❍ ❍

१३. प्राप्तकालं यदेषोऽस्मान्भरतो द्रष्टुमिच्छति ।।

13. That this Bharatha desires to see us is but proper (and it is right time as well).

❍ ❍ ❍

१४. अस्मासु मनसाऽप्येष नाहितं किञ्चिदाचरेत् ।।

14. He would not even think in his mind of (doing) harm to us both, not even little.

❍ ❍ ❍

१५. विप्रियं कृतपूर्वं ते भरतेन कदा नु किम् ।
ईदृशं वा भयं तेऽद्य भरतं योऽत्र शङ्कसे ।।

15. (Oh Lakshmana, tell me): Has any wrong ever been done to you by Bharatha before. Then how come you have such a fear and doubt about Bharatha?

❍ ❍ ❍

१६. न हि ते निष्ठुरं वाच्यो भरतो नाप्रियं वचः ।
अहं ह्यप्रियमुक्तः स्यां भरतस्याप्रिये कृते ।।

16. Bharatha is not to be spoken off so harshly by you. Nor (even) with unpleasant words. If Bharatha is displeased by you, then (it would mean) that I am spoken to harmfully (by you).
(If you hurt Bharatha, you are in effect hurting me, says Raama.)

❍ ❍ ❍

१७. कथं नु पुत्राः पितरं हन्युः कस्यांचिदापदि ।
भ्राता वा भ्रातरं हन्यात्सौमित्रे प्राणमात्मनः ।।

17. Oh (Lakshmana the) son of Sumithra! When some misfortune befalls, will sons kill their father: How will a brother (like Bharatha) kill a brother who is dear to him as his life.

❍ ❍ ❍

१८. यदि राज्यस्य हेतोस्त्वमिमां वाचं प्रभाषसे ।
वक्ष्यामि भरतं दृष्ट्वा राज्यमस्मै प्रदीयताम् ।।

18. (Oh Lakshmana): If you are uttering these words for the sake of obtaining the kingdom (for yourself), then I will tell Bharatha on seeing him: = May (this Kingdom) Be Given (to Lakshmana)=

❍ ❍ ❍

१९. उच्यमानो हि भरतो मया लक्ष्मण तत्त्वतः ।
राज्यमस्मै प्रयच्छेति बाढमित्येव वक्ष्यति ।।

19. Oh Lakshmana! When told thus (by me)= Give The Kingdom To Him= Bharatha will truthfully say only this:= So Be It =

❍ ❍ ❍

२०. तथोक्तो धर्मशीलेन भ्रात्रा तस्य हिते रतः ।
लक्ष्मणः प्रविवेशेव स्वाणि गात्राणि लज्जया ।।

20. When told thus by brother (Raama) who was steadfast in Dharma, Lakshmana who was devoted to him in his welfare, became (so) ashamed (that he appeared) as though he had 'entered'(shrunk himself) under his body.

❍ ❍ ❍

२१. तद्वाक्यं लक्ष्मणः श्रुत्वा व्रीडितः प्रत्युवाच ह ।
त्वां मन्ये द्रष्टुमायातः पिता दशरथः स्वयम् ।।

21. Hearing (Raama's) words, Lakshmana replied bashfully: (Perhaps) Our father Dhascharatha himself has come to see you, I think.

❍ ❍ ❍

२२. व्रीडितं लक्ष्मणं दृष्ट्वा राघवः प्रत्युवाच ह ।
एष मन्ये महाबाहुरिहास्मान्द्रष्टुमागतः ।।

22. Seeing Lakshmana so ashamed, (Raama the) Raaghava replied: The mighty limbed this (father of ours) has come to see us, I think.

❍ ❍ ❍

२३. अथवा नौ ध्रुवं मन्ये मन्यमानः सुखोचितौ ।
वनवासमनुध्याय गृहाय प्रतिनेष्यति ।।

23. Perhaps, considering that we are used to comforts, and contemplating about (our) firm life in forest, (our father) will (try to) take us back to our house (at Ayodhya). I (should) imagine!

❍ ❍ ❍

२४. इमां वाऽप्येष वैदेहीमत्यन्तसुखसेविनीम् ।
पिता दशरथः श्रीमान्वनादादाय यास्यति ।।

24. Perhaps, the resplendent Dhascharatha, this our father, will take along with him and go (back to Ayodhya) with Seetha, this Vaidhehi who has lived in great comfort (till now), from this forest.

❍ ❍ ❍

२५. एतौ तौ संप्रकाशेते गोत्रवन्तौ मनोरमौ ।
वायुवेगसमौ वीरौ जवनौ तुरगोत्तमौ ।।

25. There, is seen! The two fierce well bred fast moving pleasing horses that can go with speed of wind.

❍ ❍ ❍

२६. स एष सुमहाकायः कम्पते वाहिनीमुखे ।
नागः शत्रुंजयो नाम वृद्धस्तातस्य धीमतः ।।

26. Our wise father's very old mighty bodied elephant Schathrunjaya is (coming), swinging along before the Army.

❍ ❍ ❍

२७. न तु पश्यामि तच्छत्रं पाण्डुरं लोकसत्कृतम् ।
पितुर्दिव्यं महाबाहो संशयो भवतीह ये ।।

27. Oh mighty limbed (Lakshmana)! (But) I do not see father's divine (royal) white Umbrella revered by all

the world. Doubt arises in me. (Raama suspects that something is wrong at Ayodhya).

❍ ❍ ❍

२८. इतीव रामो धर्मात्मा सौमित्रिं तमुवाच ह ।
वृक्षाग्राद्‌दवरोह त्वं कुरु लक्ष्मण मद्वचः ॥

28. The noble soul man of Dharma Raama spoke thus to this (Lakshmana), the son of Sumithra. And said (further): Oh Lakshmana! Do what I tell you. Get down from the top of tree.

❍ ❍ ❍

२९. अवतीर्य तु सालाग्रात्तस्मात्स समितिंजयः ।
लक्ष्मणः प्राञ्जलिर्भूत्वा तस्थौ रामस्य पार्श्वतः ॥

29. The (ever) victorious Lakshmana got down from the Saala tree and stood before Raama with his hands cupped in Anjali.

❍ ❍ ❍

३०. भरतेनापि संदिष्टा संमर्दो न भवेदिति ।
समन्तात्तस्य शैलस्य सेना वासमकल्पयत् ॥

30. (Scene shifts to Bharatha's Army: Bharatha's search.)

Ordered by Bharatha that (Army) should not trample (over the Hermitage of Raama), the Army (of Bharatha) was stationed around the mountain (at a distance from Raama's place).

❍ ❍ ❍

३१. अध्यर्धमिक्ष्वाकुचमूर्योजनं पर्वतस्य सा ।
पार्श्वेन्यविशदावृत्य गजवाजिरथाकुला ॥

31. This Ikshwaaku Army, full with elephants, horses, chariots, etc. stayed, strolling around near mountain, about 1 1/2 Yojana-s (from there (about 12 miles or so).

❍ ❍ ❍

३२. सा चित्रकूटे भरतेन सेना
धर्मं पुरस्कृत्य विधूय दर्पम् ।
प्रसादनार्थं रघुनन्दनस्य
विराजते नीतिमता प्रणीता ।।

32. This Army shone in Chithrakoot, having been thus ordered by Bharatha, the man of justice, observing Dharma, giving up its arrogance (its might and power), for the sake of receiving favour from (Raama) the darling of Raghu-s.

❍ ❍ ❍

Chapter 98

(Bharatha's) Search For Raama's Hermitage

१. निवेश्य सेनां तु विभुः पद्भ्यां पादवतां वरः ।
अभिगन्तुं स काकुत्स्थमियेष गुरुवर्तकम् ।।

1. This foremost of men, the most able man (Bharatha), after encamping his Army, decided to go on foot to meet (Raama the) Kaakuthsa who had great respect for elders.

❍ ❍ ❍

२. निविष्टमात्रे सैन्ये तु यथोद्देशं विनीतवत् ।
भरतो भ्रातरं वाक्यं शत्रुघ्नमिदमब्रवीत् ।।

2. When the Army stationed itself respectfully at the place indicated by Bharatha, he then addressed his brother Schathrugna with following words:

❍ ❍ ❍

३. क्षिप्रं वनमिदं सौम्य नरसङ्घैः समन्ततः ।
लुब्धैश्च सहितैरेभिस्त्वमन्वेषितुमर्हसि ।।

3. Oh pleasant (Schathrugna)! You, along with men who have come with us and along with hunters, must

quickly search this forest on all sides (for our brother Raama's hermitage).

❍ ❍ ❍

४. गुहो ज्ञातिसहस्रेण शरचापासिपाणिना ।
समन्वेषतु काकुत्स्थावस्मिन्परिवृतः स्वयम् ।।

4. And wielding bow, arrows, sword etc., Guha, accompanied by thousands of his folks, should search for the two Kaakuthsa-s (Raama and Lakshmana) in this region, by himself (independently).

❍ ❍ ❍

५. अमात्यैः सह पौरैश्च गुरुभिश्च द्विजातिभिः ।
सह सर्वं चरिष्यामि पद्भ्यां परिवृतः स्वयम् ।।

5. I myself, accompanied by my ministers, citizens, elders and Braamins, will go on foot everywhere and wander (in search of Raama).

❍ ❍ ❍

६. यावन्न रामं द्रक्ष्यामि लक्ष्मणं वा महाबलम् ।
वैदेहीं वा महाभागां न मे शान्तिर्भविष्यति ।।

6. Till I see either Raama or the mightily strong Lakshmana or the most illustrious (Seetha the) Vaidhehi, there will be no peace for me.

❍ ❍ ❍

७. यावन्न चन्द्रसंकाशं द्रक्ष्यामि शुभमाननम् ।
भ्रातुः पद्मपलाशाक्षं न मे शान्तिर्भविष्यति ।।

7. Till I see the auspicious face of my brother (Raama) which is like the moon, with his eyes like lotus, there will be no peace for me.

❍ ❍ ❍

८. यावन्न राज्ये राज्यार्हः पितृपैतामहे स्थितः ।
अभिषेकजलक्लिन्नो न मे शान्तिर्भविष्यति ।।

8. Till this (Raama) who deserves (to rule over) kingdom, after being anointed and bathed in Ritual waters is (firmly) established in the kingdom of his forefathers, there will be no peace for me.

❍ ❍ ❍

९. यावन्न चरणौ भ्रातुः पार्थिवव्यञ्जनान्वितौ ।
शिरसा धारयिष्यामि न मे शान्तिर्भविष्यति ॥

9. Till I 'Bear' my brother's feet which are endowed with royal character, with my head, there will be no peace for me.

❍ ❍ ❍

१०. सिद्धार्थः खलु सौमित्रिर्यश्चन्द्रविमलोपमम् ।
मुखं पश्यति रामस्य राजीवाक्षं महाद्युति ॥

10. He, this (Lakshmana the) son of Sumithra is indeed fortunate (and accomplished) as he sees Raama's most brilliant face which is like the spotless moon, (the face) with eyes that are like lotus.

❍ ❍ ❍

११. कृतकृत्या महाभागा वैदेही जनकात्मजा ।
भर्तारं सागरान्तायाः पृथिव्या याऽनुगच्छति ॥

11. The most illustrious daughter of Janaka, this (Seetha the) Vaidhehi, is indeed fortunate as she follows (Raama) who is protector of the entire earth upto ocean.

❍ ❍ ❍

१२. शुभगश्चित्रकूटोऽसौ गिरिराजोपमो गिरिः ।
यस्मिन्वसति काकुत्स्थः कुबेर इव नन्दने ॥

12. This Chithrakoot mountain is (indeed) fortunate like (Himaalyas) which is the king of mountains, as (Raama the) Kaakuthsa lives here like Kubhaera in his Nandhana.

❍ ❍ ❍

१३. कृतकार्यमिदं दुर्गं वनं व्यालनिषेवितम् ।
यदध्यास्ते महातेजा रामः शस्त्रभृतां वरः ।।

13. Where this most brilliant Raama the foremost amongst wielders of bow lives, this impenetrable forest inhabited by wild beasts is indeed fortunate.

❍ ❍ ❍

१४. एवमुक्त्वा महाबाहुर्भरतः पुरुषर्षभः ।
पद्भ्यामेव महातेजाः प्रविवेश महद्वनम् ।।

14. Speaking thus, the most brilliant and mighty limbed Bharatha the 'bull' amongst men, entered the great forest on foot.

❍ ❍ ❍

१५. स तानि द्रुमजालानि जातानि गिरिसानुषु ।
पुष्पिताग्राणि मध्येन जगाम वदतां वरः ।।

15. (Bharatha) the foremost amongst men of (good) speech, went along through the gaps between rows of full blossomed trees around mountain slopes.

❍ ❍ ❍

१६. स गिरेश्चित्रकूटस्य सालमासाद्य पुष्पितम् ।
रामाश्रमगतस्याग्नेर्ददर्श ध्वजमुच्छ्रितम् ।।

16. Then, getting on top of a full blossomed Saala tree in Chithrakoot hill, he saw the smoke; coming from fire in Raama's hermitage.

❍ ❍ ❍

१७. तं दृष्ट्वा भरतः श्रीमान्मुमोद सह बान्धवैः ।
अत्र राम इति ज्ञात्वा गतः पारमिवाम्भसः ।।

17. Seeing this, the resplendent Bharatha, realising that Raama must be there, rejoiced along with his folks, like as though he had reached the other shore of the ocean.

❍ ❍ ❍

१८. स चित्रकूटे तु गिरौ निशम्य
रामाश्रमं पुण्यजनोपपन्नम् ।
गुहेन सार्धं त्वरितो जगाम
पुनर्निवेश्यैव चमूं महात्मा ॥

18. Perceiving that this was Raama's hermitage in Chithrakoot hill where holy men lived, the great soul (Bharatha) walked along with Guha quickly, after making Army to station itself there, once again (making sure Army did not move from there).

❍ ❍ ❍

Chapter 99

Bharatha Meets Raama

१. निविष्टायां तु सेनायामुत्सुको भरतस्ततः ।
जगाम भ्रातरं द्रष्टुं शत्रुघ्नमनुदर्शयन् ॥

1. His Army stationed (about 10 miles away), Bharatha who was very eager to meet his brother (Raama) went along with Schathrugna, indicating (and surveying the area near Raama's hermitage)

❍ ❍ ❍

२. ऋषिं वसिष्ठं संदिश्य मातॄर्मेशीघ्रमानय ।
इति त्वरितमग्रे स जगाम गुरुवत्सलः ॥

2. (Bharatha) who was devoted to his Guru (Raama), informed sage Vasishta:: = Bring My Mothers At Once = and he went along fast.

❍ ❍ ❍

३. सुमन्त्रस्त्वपि शत्रुघ्नमदूरादन्वपद्यत ।
रामदर्शनजस्तर्षोभरतस्येव तस्य च ॥

3. And Sumanthra also went along by the side of

Schathrugna: Like Bharatha, he also was 'thirsty' to meet Raama.

❍ ❍ ❍

४. गच्छन्नेवाथ भरतस्तापसालयसंस्थिताम् ।
भ्रातुः पर्णकुटीं श्रीमानुटजं च ददर्श ह ।।

4. Then, the resplendent Bharatha, as he was going along, saw his brother's 'Hut' and the hermitage which was well constructed, a good place for (doing penance by) men of penance.

❍ ❍ ❍

५. शालायास्त्वग्रतस्तस्या ददर्श भरतस्तदा ।
काष्ठानि चावभग्नानि पुष्पाण्यपचितानि च ।।

5. Then Bharatha saw logs of wood cut up and (also) the plucked flowers in front of hermitage,

❍ ❍ ❍

६. लक्ष्मणस्य च रामस्य ददर्शाश्रममीयुषः ।
कृतं वृक्षेष्वभिज्ञानं कुशचीरैः क्वचित्क्वचित् ।।

6. He saw in trees here and there around hermitage of Raama and Lakshmana, the signs (the markings) made by ropes that tied up (bundles of) Dharbha grass (used for Rituals)

❍ ❍ ❍

७. ददर्श च वने तस्मिन्महतः सञ्चयान्कृतान् ।
मृगाणा महिषाणां च करीषैः शीतकारणात् ।।

7. He saw huge collection of Dung (refuse of) buffaloes and deers of the forest for heating and warming purposes.

(Even today poor villagers use cow dung as heating material.)

❍ ❍ ❍

८. गच्छन्नेव महाबाहुर्द्युतिमान्भरतस्तदा ।
शत्रुघ्नं चाब्रवदहृष्टस्तानमात्यांश्च सर्वशः ॥

8. Going along, this mighty limbed majestic Bharatha then addressed Schathrugna and the ministers, happily.

❍ ❍ ❍

९. मन्ये प्राप्ताः स्म तं देशं भरद्वाजो यमब्रवीत् ।
नातिदूरे हि मन्येऽहं नदीं मन्दाकिनीमितः ॥

9. I think we have come to the place as described by Bharadhwaaja: And I think river Mandhaakini is not far from this place.

❍ ❍ ❍

१०. उच्चैर्बद्धानि चीराणि लक्ष्मणेन भवेदयम् ।
अभिज्ञानकृतः पन्था विकाले गन्तुमिच्छता ॥

10. The markings (made by ropes) on trees are well embedded. Perhaps, these marking might have been made by Lakshmana (to guide him) in his path when he desired to go at odd times (at night).

❍ ❍ ❍

११. इदं चोदात्तदन्तानां कुञ्जराणां तरस्विनाम् ।
शैलपार्श्वेपरिक्रान्तमन्योन्यमभिगर्जताम् ॥

11. Here, near the foot of the hills (you see) the energetic elephants with long tusks, roaming about, making roaring noise against one another.

❍ ❍ ❍

१२. यमेवाधातुमिच्छन्ति तापसाः सततं वने ।
तस्यासौ दृश्यते धूमः सङ्कुलः कृष्णवर्त्मनः ॥

12. Here is seen black smoke coming out copiously (from fire of rituals) which men of penance desire to see that it is never extinguished at all times.

❍ ❍ ❍

१३. अत्राहं पुरुषव्याघ्रं गुरुसत्कारकारिणम् ।
आर्यं द्रक्ष्यामि संहृष्टो महर्षिमिव राघवम् ।।

13. In this place I am going to see happily the 'tiger' of men, this noble (Aryan Raama) the Raaghava who ever honours Guru-s (father and teachers). (I am going) as though (I am going to see) a great sage! (Bharatha compares his brother Raama to a Sage).

❍ ❍ ❍

१४. अथ गत्वा मुहूर्तं तु चित्रकूटं स राघवः ।
मन्दाकिनीमनुप्राप्तस्तं जनं चेदमब्रवीत् ।।

14. After walking along Mandhakini river for a Muhoortha (of 48 minutes), then (Bharatha) the Raaghava who had reached Chithrakoota hill, said this before the men (who had accompanied him on foot).

❍ ❍ ❍

१५. जगत्यां पुरुषव्याघ्रं आस्ते वीरासने रतः ।
जनेन्द्रो निर्जनं प्राप्य धिङ्मे जन्म सजीवितम् ।।

15. This lord of men in the world, this 'tiger of men' (Raama), having reached this uninhabited (forest without men), is delighting himself, staying in the open (living in wilderness).Ah! Fie On My Birth and Life!

❍ ❍ ❍

१६. मत्कृते व्यसनं प्राप्तो लोकनाथो महाद्युतिः ।
सर्वान्कामान्परित्यज्य वने वसति राघवः ।।

16. This lord of the world (Raama) the Raaghava who is most brilliant, has obtained (all this) suffering on my account and is living in forest, having given up all pleasures.

❍ ❍ ❍

१७ इति लोकसमाक्रुष्टः पादेष्वद्य प्रसादयन् ।
रामस्य निपतिष्यामि सीतायाश्च पुनः पुनः ।।

17. Seeking his favour, and saying = I Am Reviled By The World = I will now, again and again, fall at the feet of Raama and Seetha:

(Hermitage of Raama described as seen by Bharatha: 18 to 23.)

❍ ❍ ❍

१८. एवं स विलपंस्तस्मिन्वने दशरथात्मजः ।
ददर्श महतीं पुण्यां पर्णशालां मनोरमाम् ।।
१९. सालतालाश्वकर्णानां पर्णैर्बहुभिरावृताम् ।
विशालां मृदुभिः स्तीर्णां कुशैर्वेदिमिवाध्वरे ।।
२०. शक्रायुधनिकाशैश्च कार्मुकैर्भारसाधनैः ।
रुक्मपृष्ठैर्महासारैः शोभितां शत्रुबाधकैः ।।
२१. अर्करश्मिप्रतीकाशैर्घोरैस्तूणीगतैः शरैः ।
शोभितां दीप्तवदनैः सर्पैर्भोगवतीमिव ।।
२२. महारजतवासोभ्यामसिभ्यां च विराजिताम् ।
रुक्मबिन्दुविचित्राभ्यां चर्मभ्यां चापि शोभिताम् ।।
२३. गोधाङ्गुलित्रैरासक्तैश्चित्रैः काञ्चनभूषितैः ।
अरिसङ्घैरनाधृष्यां मृगैः सिंहगुहामिव ।।

18. to 23.

Wailing thus in forest, (Bharatha) the son of Dhascharatha, saw the most holy, captivating hermitage (of Raama).....

.....Constructed with numerous leaves of trees (like) Saala Thaala and Ashwakarna; Very large; Appearing like mound in ritual. hall...... Shining with bows like those of Lord Indhra: (Bows) that are most efficacious, that can destroy enemies, covered (decorated) in gold... very strong...Shining with gruesome arrows kept in quivers; (Arrows) like the rays of the sun, like the inflamed cobra-s of Bhogavathi (of the underworlds)..... Shining with swords kept in fine golden caskets, encased in leather jackets embroidered in gold... wonderful... Leather gloves decorated in gold (work): Like deers that cannot enter the caves of lions (this hermitage) could not be entered by enemies (even when they attack) in multitude.

❍ ❍ ❍

२४. प्रागुदक्प्रवणां वेदिं विशालां दीप्तपावकाम् ।
दद्दर्श भरतस्तत्र पुण्यां रामनिवेशने ॥

24. There, in Raama's abode, in the north-eastern side, he saw the sacred fire mound, a large one, with fire burning.

❍ ❍ ❍

२५. निरीक्ष्य स मुहूर्तं तु दद्दर्श भरतो गुरुम् ।
उटजे राममासीनं जटामण्डलधारिणम् ॥

25. After gazing for sometime, this Bharatha then saw his Guru (brother Raama) in the 'Hut', wearing (forest dress of) bark and sporting twisted knotted hair (like a sage), sitting there.

(Bharatha sees Raama at the hermitage: Scene described: 26 to 28.)

❍ ❍ ❍

२६. तं तु कृष्णाजिनधरं चीरवल्कलवाससम् ।
दद्दर्श राममासीनमभितः पावकोपमम् ॥

२७. सिंहस्कन्धं महाबाहुं पुण्डरीकनिभेक्षणम् ।
पृथिव्याः सागरान्ताया भर्तारं धर्मचारिणम् ॥

२८. उपविष्टं महाबाहुं ब्रह्माणमिव शाश्वतम् ।
स्थण्डिले दर्भसंस्तीर्णे सीतया लक्ष्मणेन च ॥

26. to 28.

He saw Raama sitting there; Radiant like fire; Wearing dress of deer skin; wearing bark dress....His chest was like those of a lion; His limbs were mighty (very strong), His eyes like lotus; He was protector of the earth upto the oceans; he was follower of Dharma...(He appeared) like the mighty limbed God Bramma., the eternal; Was sitting on the floor spread with Dharbha grass and attended by Seetha and Lakshmana.

❍ ❍ ❍

२९. तं दृष्ट्वा भरतः श्रीमान्दुःखशोकपरिप्लुतः ।
अभ्यधावत धर्मात्मा भरतः कैकयीसुतः ।।

29. The resplendent Bharatha, seeing him, was overcome by grief and sorrow: And this noble soul man of Dharma, Bharatha, the son of Kaikeyi, rushed towards him.

❍ ❍ ❍

३०. दृष्ट्वैव विललापार्तोबाष्पसन्दिग्धया गिरा ।
अशक्नुवन्धारयितुं धैर्याद्वचनमब्रवीत् ।।

30. On seeing him, he, who was in deep distress, wailed. Could not bear (the sight of his brother Raama in that dress and hair style). (Picking up some) courage (and composure), he said these words, utterance coming haltingly through tears.

(Bharatha addresses Raama when he saw him like this: 31 to 36.)

❍ ❍ ❍

३१. यः संसदि प्रकृतिभिर्भवेद्युक्त उपासितुम् ।
वन्यैर्मृगैरुपासीनः सोऽयमास्ते ममाग्रजः ।।

31. My elder brother who used to be honoured by (eminent) men in the Assembly Hall, such a man is now sitting here "honoured" by animals of forest!

❍ ❍ ❍

३२. वासोभिर्बहुसाहस्रैर्योमहात्मा सदोचितः ।
मृगाजिने सोऽयमिह प्रवस्ते धर्ममाचरन् ।।

32. This great soul (Raama) who was always befittingly dressed up with many thousands of (diverse) garments,

such a one is now dressed up in deer skin, following the Dharma (of forest)

❍ ❍ ❍

३३. अधारयद्यो विविधाश्चित्राः सुमनसस्सदा ।
सोऽयं जटाभारमिमं वहते राघवः कथम् ।।

33. How come this (Raama) the Raaghava who used to wear the wonderful various garlands of sweet smelling flowers, is now able to 'bear' this braided tufted hair (like a sage).

❍ ❍ ❍

३४. यस्य यज्ञैर्यथोद्दिष्टैर्युक्तो धर्मस्य सञ्चयः ।
शरीरक्लेशसंभूतं स धर्मं परिमार्गते ।।

34. He who deserves to accumulate Dharma by the Sacrifices done as per Shaasthra-s (before), such a one is seeking to obtain Dharma by mortification of body now!

(Bharatha says Raama need not go to forest and become a Sage to 'accumulate' Dharma.. He is Dharma personified, even at Ayodhya.)

❍ ❍ ❍

३५. चन्दनेन महार्हेण यस्याङ्गमुपसेवितम् ।
मलेन तस्याङ्गमिदं कथमार्यस्य सेव्यते ।।

35. How is it, he, whose body used to be 'served' upon by superb sandal pastes, such a man's body is now 'served' (besmeared with) dust?

❍ ❍ ❍

३६. मन्निमित्तमिदं दुःखं प्राप्तो रामः सुखोचितः ।
धिग्जीवितं नृशंसस्य मम लोकविगर्हितम् ।।

36. Raama who is ever used to comfort, is now suffering all on my account; Cruel as I am, fie on my life that is censured by the world.

❍ ❍ ❍

३७. इत्येवं विलपन् दीनः प्रस्विन्नमुखपङ्कजः ।
पादावप्राप्य रामस्य पपात भरतो रुदन् ॥

37. The downcast Bharatha whose face was covered by perspiration, wailed and cried; and before he 'reached' the feet of Raama, fell down (near Raama).

❍ ❍ ❍

३८. दुःखाभितप्तो भरतो राजपुत्रो महाबलः ।
उक्त्वार्येति सकृद्दीनं पुनर्नोवाच किञ्चन ॥

38. This mightily strong Royal prince Bharatha who was tormented by grief, just said feebly = Oh Noble (Aryan) = But he could not say anything further.

❍ ❍ ❍

३९. बाष्पापिहितकण्ठश्च प्रेक्ष्य रामं यशस्विनम् ।
आर्येत्येवाथ संक्रुश्च व्याहर्तुं नाशकत्ततः ॥

39. And again approaching Raama, (Bharatha) whose throat was choked by tears then cried = Oh Aryan = Then he could not utter (anything) further.

❍ ❍ ❍

४०. शत्रुघ्नश्चापि रामस्य ववन्दे चरणौ रुदन् ।
तावुभौ स समालिङ्ग्य रामोऽप्यश्रूण्यवर्तयत् ॥

40. And Schathrugna too, fell at Raama's feet, crying : And this Raama hugged them both; And he shed tears.

❍ ❍ ❍

४१. तः सुमन्त्रेण गुहेन चैव
समीयतू राजसुतावरण्ये ।
दिवाकरश्चैव निशाकरश्च
यथाम्बरे शुक्रबृहस्पतिभ्याम् ॥

41. Just as Sun and Moon in the sky are (honoured and 'visited') by Stars Venus and Jupiter, the two princes

Raama and Lakshmana were met by Sumanthra and Guha.

❍ ❍ ❍

४२. तान्पार्थिवान्वारणयूथपाभान्
समागतांस्तत्र महत्यरण्ये ।
वनौकसस्तेऽभिसमीक्ष्य सर्वे
त्वश्रूण्यमुञ्चन्प्रविहाय हर्षम् ।।

42. At that moment, in this mighty forest, all the hermits there shed tears, abandoning their (natural) Joy (of restraint and composure of sages), as they saw the princes who had gathered there, who were like royal elephants.

(Note: It is significant that all the four sons of the late king Dhascharatha are away from their capital Ayodhya. King is dead, Long live the king. But who will 'Be'? Crisis develops as we will see.)

❍ ❍ ❍

Chapter 100

Raama Asks About Welfare (of Every One at Ayodhya)

(This is an important chapter. Bharatha's meeting Raama in the forest. Raama, after asking about welfare of every one at Ayodhya, lists the qualities of a good Ruler. Raama is still not aware that his father king Dhascharatha is dead as Bharatha has not told him about the calamity as yet: Raama thinks Bharatha is Yuva Raaja.)

❍ ❍ ❍

१. जटिलं चीरवसनं प्राञ्जलिं पतितं भुवि ।
ददर्श रामो दुर्दर्शं युगान्ते भास्करं यथा ।।

1. And Raama saw this (Bharatha) wearing bark dress

and sporting twisted locks of hair (like a hermit, like himself): (Saw Bharatha) whose hands were cupped in Anjali, who was like the Sun that falls down on earth after 'Deluge' (at the final end of The Universe).

❍ ❍ ❍

२. कथञ्चिदभिविज्ञाय विवर्णवदनं कृशम् ।
भ्रातरं भरतं रामः परिजग्राह पाणिना ॥

2. Recognising his brother Bharatha somehow as his face had lost its colour and as he was so much emaciated, Raama hugged him with his hands.

❍ ❍ ❍

३. आघ्राय रामस्तं मूर्ध्नि परिष्वज्य च राघवः ।
अङ्के भरतमारोप्य पर्यपृच्छत्समाहितः ॥

3. Taking Bharatha on to his lap, hugging him and kissing his forehead, Raama the Raaghava then asked him in a composed manner.

❍ ❍ ❍

४. क्व नु तेऽभूत्पिता तात यदरण्यं त्वमागतः ।
न हि त्वं जीवतस्तस्य वनमागन्तुमर्हसि ॥

4. Oh Lad! As you have come away to this forest, your father, how will he be? Because, when he is alive, you should not come away to forest (leaving an old man alone).

❍ ❍ ❍

५. चिरस्य बत पश्यामि दूराद्भरतमागतम् ।
दुष्प्रतीकमरण्येऽस्मिन्किं तात वनमागतः ॥

5. Oh Lad, Oh Bharatha! I am seeing you after a long time, coming from a long distance, in this forest, (appearing before me) with an unusual face (with different dress and hair style). I regret seeing (you like this). Why have you come to the forest?

❍ ❍ ❍

६. कच्चिद्धारयते तात राजा यत्त्वमिहागतः ।
कच्चिन्न दीनः सहसा राजा लोकान्तरं गतः ।।

6. Oh Lad! As you have come here, I hope king bears himself (well); I hope king has not gone away to the other world quickly, being emaciated (by grief of separation from me).

❍ ❍ ❍

७. कच्चित्सौम्य न ते राज्यं भ्रष्टं बालस्य शाश्वतम् ।
कच्चिच्छुश्रूषसे तात पितुस्सत्यपराक्रम ।।

7. Oh Pleasant (Bharatha)! Oh Lad! Oh truly most valiant! Young as you are, I hope you do not let all our eternal kingdom from 'slipping' away (from your hands). I hope you serve your father well.

❍ ❍ ❍

८. कच्चिद्दशरथो राजा कुशली सत्यसङ्गरः ।
राजसूयाश्वमेधानामाहर्ता धर्मनिश्चयः ।।

8. I hope (your father) King Dhascharatha who has performed Sacrificial ceremonies of Raajasooya and Aschwamedha, who is a man of Truth and who is steadfast in Dharma, is well.

❍ ❍ ❍

९. स कच्चिद्ब्राह्मणो विद्वान् धर्मनित्यो महाद्युतिः ।
इक्ष्वाकूणामुपाध्यायो यथावत्तात पूज्यते ।।

9. Oh Lad! I trust the most learned braamin, the teacher of (our) Ikshwaaku-s, the most brilliant (Vasishta) who is firmly rooted in Dharma, is duly honoured by you.

❍ ❍ ❍

१०. तात कच्चिच्च कौसल्या सुमित्रा सुप्रजावती ।
सुखिनी कच्चिदार्या च देवी नन्दति कैकयी ।।

10. Oh Lad! I trust Kowsalya and Sumithra are well; I hope

the noble queen Kaikeyi who has borne a fine son (in you) is happy.

❍ ❍ ❍

११. कच्चिद्विनयसम्पन्नः कुलपुत्रो बहुश्रुतः ।
अनसूयुरनुद्रष्टा सत्कृतस्ते पुरोहितः ॥

11. I trust your Purohith, (adviser Suyagnya), who is endowed with modesty, who is born in a noble family, who is well versed in many Shaasthra-s, who is free from jealousy, is treated with respect and consideration.

❍ ❍ ❍

१२. कच्चिदग्निषु ते युक्तो विधिज्ञो मतिमानृजुः ।
हुतं च होष्यमाणं च काले वेदयते सदा ॥

12. Does your wise and upright (Suyagnya) who is expert in Fire Rituals, who knows norms, make known to you, from time to time, about fire rituals performed and fire rituals to be performed, always?

❍ ❍ ❍

१३. कच्चिद्देवान्पितृन्मातृर्गुरूऩ्पितृसमानपि ।
वृद्धांश्च तात वैद्यांश्च ब्राह्मणांश्चाभिमन्यसे ॥

13. Oh Lad! I hope you honour the Deities, our fore-fathers, our mothers, our elders who are like our parents, our Guru-s, Braamins and men learned in Vedha-s.

❍ ❍ ❍

१४. इष्वस्त्रवरसम्पन्नमर्थशास्त्रविशारदम् ।
सुधन्वानमुपाध्यायं कच्चित्त्वं तात मन्यसे ॥

14. Oh Lad! I hope you honour teacher Sudhanva who is master of the science of archery, who is an expert in science of Artha Shaasthra*.

(* Social and political and mundane subjects).

❍ ❍ ❍

१५. कच्चिदात्मसमाः शूराः श्रुतवन्तो जितेन्द्रियाः ।
कुलीनाश्चेङ्गितज्ञाश्च कृतास्ते तात मन्त्रिणः ।।

15. I hope you have appointed your ministers who are unequalled in bravery, who have knowledge of Shaasthra-s, who have controlled their senses (men of composure who overcome passion), who are from noble family, (men who can understand feelings of others) by their mere gestures.

❍ ❍ ❍

१६. मन्त्रो विजयमूलं हि राज्ञां भवति राघव ।
सुसंवृतो मन्त्रधरैरमात्यैः शास्त्रकोविदैः ।।

16. Oh (Bharatha) the Raaghava! The Advice given under (oath of) secrecy by ministers who are expert counsellors, who are well versed in Shaasthra-s, is the very foundation of victory for a king.

❍ ❍ ❍

१७. कच्चिन्निद्रावशं नैषीः कच्चित्काले प्रबुध्यसे ।
कच्चिच्चापररात्रेषु चिन्तयस्यर्थनैपुणम् ।।

17. I hope you do not go after 'sleep' and slumber! I hope you awake at proper time. And at midnight, do you contemplate about utility of your actions (ARTHA NAIPUNA).

❍ ❍ ❍

१८. कच्चिन्मन्त्रयसे नैकः कच्चिन्न बहुभिः सह ।
कच्चित्ते मन्त्रितो मन्त्रो राष्ट्रं न परिधावति ।।

18. I hope you take counsel all by yourself. I hope you seek counsel along with others as well. And I hope that decisions arrived at after deliberation is not allowed to be spread across the kingdom.

❍ ❍ ❍

१९. कच्चिदर्थं विनिश्चित्य लघुमूलं महोदयम् ।
क्षिप्रमारभसे कर्तुं न दीर्घयसि राघव ।।

19. Oh (Bharatha) the Raaghava! Having considered and decided upon an action that can be done with ease and which will bring great prosperity, do you begin to act quickly. I hope you do not procrastinate.

❍ ❍ ❍

२०. कच्चित्तु सुकृतान्येव कृतरूपाणि वा पुनः ।
विदुस्ते सर्वकार्याणि न कर्तव्यानि पार्थिवाः ।।

20. I hope (other) kings know only about your well executed actions in all your endeavour; But never about actions decided upon or to be acted upon. I hope!

❍ ❍ ❍

२१. कच्चिन्न तर्कैर्युक्त्या वा ये चाप्यपरिकीर्तिताः ।
त्वया वा तव वाऽमात्यैर्बुध्यते तात मन्त्रितम् ।।

21. Oh Lad! I hope all (Political and other) decisions taken by you and along with your ministers, either by enquiry or out of sheer expediency which are not announced, are not known (to public and others).

❍ ❍ ❍

२२. कच्चित्सहस्रान्मूर्खाणामेकमिच्छसि पण्डितम् ।
पण्डितो ह्यर्थकृच्छ्रेषु कुर्यान्निःश्रेयसं महत् ।।

22. I trust that you desire (and prefer) to have one learned man rather than 1,000 fools; Because, in difficult situations, this learned man will be most resourceful.

❍ ❍ ❍

२३. सहस्राण्यपि मूर्खाणां यद्युपास्ते महीपतिः ।
अथवाऽप्ययुतान्येव नास्ति तेषु सहायता ।।

23. A king, if he appoints 1000 fools, nay 10,000 fools, cannot get any assistance from them at all.

❍ ❍ ❍

२४. एकोऽप्यमात्यो मेधावी शूरो दक्षो विचक्षणः ।
राजानं राजपुत्रं वा प्रापयेन्महतीं श्रियम् ।।

24. Only a learned, brave, experienced, astute minister can bring great prosperity to a king or a prince.

❍ ❍ ❍

२५. कच्चिन्मुख्या महत्स्वेव मध्यमेषु च मध्यमाः ।
जघन्यास्तु जघन्येषु भृत्यास्ते तात योजिताः ।।

25. Oh Lad! I hope you have entrusted men of great ability in great jobs: Average men in average jobs; And ordinary men in ordinary (routine) jobs.
(Raama must have been an MBA from HARVARD.)

❍ ❍ ❍

२६. अमात्यानुपधातीतान्पितृपैतामहाञ्छुचीन् ।
श्रेष्ठाञ्छ्रेष्ठेषु कच्चित्त्वं नियोजयसि कर्मसु ।।

26. Do you entrust, in great jobs, noble ministers who are pure, who are men of tradition, and who share communication (with whom you have rapport).

❍ ❍ ❍

२७. कच्चिन्नोग्रेण दण्डेन भृशमुद्वेजिताः प्रजाः ।
राष्ट्रं तवानुजानन्ति मन्त्रिणः कैकयीसुत ।।

27. Oh (Bharatha) the son of Kaikeyi! I hope, in the kingdom, your ministers do not direct you to inflict harsh punishment on citizens that will intimidate (and frighten them) terribly.

❍ ❍ ❍

२८. कच्चित्त्वां नावजानन्ति याजकाः पतितं यथा ।
उग्रप्रतिग्रहीतारं कामयानमिव स्त्रियः ।।

28. I hope you are not treated with contempt as one who seizes wealth (as taxes etc.) excessively: as one who

desires another's woman; as one who offers Sacrifices-Rituals (but) insults the Lords .

❍ ❍ ❍

२९. उपायकुशलं वैद्यं भृत्यसंदूषणे रतम् ।
शूरमैश्वर्यकामं च यो न हन्ति स वध्यते ।।

29. (If a ruler) does not destroy those clever (power seeking) men whose sole passion is to acquire wealth by skilfully indulging in corruption through hirelings, then he (himself) gets destroyed (eventually).

❍ ❍ ❍

३०. कच्चिद्दृष्टश्च शूरश्च मतिमान्धृतिमाञ्छुचिः ।
कुलीनश्चानुरक्तश्च दक्षः सेनापतिः कृतः ।।

30. Have you appointed a Commander-in-chief who is brave, intelligent, resolute, dexterous, pure, born in a noble family and one who is devoted and bristles (with joy).

❍ ❍ ❍

३१. बलवन्तश्च कच्चित्ते मुख्या युद्धविशारदाः ।
दृष्टापदाना विक्रान्तास्त्वया सत्कृत्य मानिताः ।।

31. Are your (Army) Chiefs who are well versed in science of war, who are strong, who (ever) seek victory, who learn by (experience and) mistakes, honoured by you.

❍ ❍ ❍

३२. कच्चिद्बलस्य भक्तं च वेतनं च यथोचितम् ।
संप्राप्तकालं दातव्यं ददासि न विलम्बसे ।।

32. I hope you do not delay to pay salaries fixed as per norms, that are to be given to the Army, at proper time.

❍ ❍ ❍

३३. कालातिक्रमणाच्चैव भक्तवेतनयोर्भृताः ।
भर्तुः कुप्यन्ति दुष्यन्ति सोऽनर्थः सुमहान्स्मृतः ।।

33. Servants supported by food and moneys get angry with their masters if there is delay (in their payments): They (may) even turn hostile. It is said that this wrong (leads to) great (problems).

❍ ❍ ❍

३४. कच्चित्सर्वेऽनुरक्तास्त्वां कुलपुत्राः प्रधानतः ।
कच्चित्प्राणांस्तवार्थेषु संत्यजन्ति समाहिताः ।।

34. Are men of good families well disposed towards you; Will they (even) give up their lives (for your welfare and) in your tasks being totally devoted to you.

❍ ❍ ❍

३५. कच्चिज्जानपदो विद्वान्दक्षिणः प्रतिभानवान् ।
यथोक्तवादी दूतस्ते कृतो भरत पण्डितः ।।

35. Oh Bharatha! Have you appointed as ambassador, one who is (first of all) a* citizen, who is clever, learned, scholarly, quick witted and one who can communicate clearly. (*Word used-Jaanapada-).

❍ ❍ ❍

३६. कच्चिदष्टादशान्येषु स्वपक्षे दश पञ्च च ।
त्रिभिस्त्रिभिरविज्ञातैर्वेत्सि तीर्थानि चारकैः ।।

36. With the aid of three, three spies on every one of the 18 Administrators (of various departments) in other (kingdoms) and, in the case of your own kingdom, (with the aid of three spies), on every one of the 15 administrators, do you find out about them without their knowledge (as to what is going on).

(Various departments are; Office of Army Chief; City Protection; Prisons: Treasury for Civil; treasury for Army; Publicity: Civil Justice; Central bureau of Investigation: Criminal justice; Defense: Public works: Protocol: Speaker of assembly: Ecology: River etc.: Property, Taxes etc.)

❍ ❍ ❍

३७. कच्चिद्व्यपास्तानहितान्प्रतियातांश्च सर्वदा ।
दुर्बलाननवज्ञाय वर्तसे रिपुसूदन ।।

37. Oh (Bharatha) the destroyer of enemies I hope you keep a check at all times, on your enemies driven away by you but who return: I hope you do not treat them with indifference as though they are weak. (Once an enemy, always an enemy).

❍ ❍ ❍

३८. कच्चिन्न लोकायतिकान्ब्राह्मणांस्तात सेवसे ।
अनर्थकुशला ह्येते बालाः पण्डितमानिनः ।।

38. Oh Lad! I hope you do not honour Braamins who are totally materialistic. These childish men who consider themselves pundits (as though learned), are experts in (causing) misfortune.

❍ ❍ ❍

३९. धर्मशास्त्रेषु मुख्येषु विद्यमानेषु दुर्बुधाः ।
बुद्धिमान्वीक्षिकीं प्राप्य निरर्थं प्रवदन्ति ते ।।

39. When there is lot to learn from foremost DharmaShaasthra-s, these silly minded men direct their mind to "Vain Enquiry" and talk uselessly.

❍ ❍ ❍

४०. वीरैरध्युषितां पूर्वमस्माकं तात पूर्वकैः ।
सत्यनामां दृढद्वारां हस्त्यश्वरथसंकुलाम् ।।

40. (Raama talks about protection of Ayodhya: Stanzas 40 to 46) Oh Lad! Ever before (our Ayodhya), true to its name, inhabited before by our brave forefathers, with its gates well protected (fortified), with multitude of horses, elephants, chariots ......

❍ ❍ ❍

४१. ब्राह्मणैः क्षत्रियैर्वैश्यैः स्वकर्मनिरतैः सदा ।
जितेन्द्रियैर्महोत्साहैर्वृतामार्यैः सहस्रशः ।।

41. ...... (Where) Noble men, Braamins, Kshathriya-s, Vaischya-s in thousands are all devoted to their profession and work at all times, and are all men of restraint (but) ever enthusiastic (in service) ......

❍ ❍ ❍

४२. प्रासादैर्विविधाकारैर्वृतां वैद्यजनाकुलाम् ।
कच्चित्सुमुदितां स्फीतामयोध्यां परिरक्षसि ॥

42. Where there are thousands of temples of various denominations, where there are great many scholars, where every one is happy...I trust that such a vast city of Ayodhya is protected (by you).

❍ ❍ ❍

४३. कच्चिच्चैत्यशतैर्जुष्टः सुनिविष्टजनाकुलः ।
देवस्थानैः प्रपाभिश्च तटाकैश्चोपशोभितः ॥

43. Inhabited by well behaved men and women, with hundreds of temples and ceremonial halls, water sheds, ponds, I hope (such a city of ours) shines and thrives.

❍ ❍ ❍

४४. प्रहृष्टनरनारीकः समाजोत्सवशोभितः ।
सुकृष्टसीमा पशुमान्हिंसाभिरभिवर्जितः ॥
४५. अदेवमातृको रम्यः श्वापदैः परिवर्जितः ।
परित्यक्तो भयैः सर्वैः खनिभिश्चोपशोभितः ॥
४६. विवर्जितो नरैः पापैर्मम पूर्वैः सुरक्षितः ।
कच्चिज्जनपदः स्फीतः सुखं वसति राघवः ॥

44 to 46.

Inhabited by (common) men and women who are (ever) happy: With festivities, people thronging; with the soil well ploughed; full of cows; Devoid of mischief and injury...With beautiful canals (**its water not dependent on mercy of Lords) city without any harmful animals: city without fear: With plenty of caves (underground passages)... Inhabited by sinless people: ...I hope such a vast land of Raghu-s which was protected and ruled by my forefathers before is happy and in comfort.

(** Vaalmeeki uses the word =A-Dheva Maathrika = for Rainless Waters:: Not by lord of rain)

❍ ❍ ❍

४७. कच्चित्ते दयिताः सर्वेकृषिगोरक्षजीविनः ।
वार्तायां संश्रितस्तात लोको हि सुखमेधते ॥

47. Oh Lad! I hope all the farmers and cowherds cherish you: I trust members of business community are happy and prosperous.

❍ ❍ ❍

४८. तेषां गुप्तिपरीहारैः कच्चित्ते भरणं कृतम् ।
रक्ष्या हि राज्ञा धर्मेण सर्वेविषयवासिनः ॥

48. All the citizens are to be protected as per laws of Dharma by a king. Do you nourish and support them, protecting them against excessive (taxes and the like).

❍ ❍ ❍

४९. कच्चित्स्त्रियः सान्त्वयसि कच्चित्ताश्च सुरक्षिताः ।
कच्चिन्न श्रद्धधास्यासां कच्चिद्गुह्यं न भाषसे ॥

49. Do you console (and respect) women. Are they well protected; I trust you do not repose confidence in them. I hope you do not spell out (your) secrets (to them).

❍ ❍ ❍

५०. कच्चिन्नागवनं गुप्तं कच्चित्ते सन्ति धेनुकाः ।
कच्चिन्न गणिकाश्वानां कुञ्जराणां च तृप्यसि ॥

50. Are the forests abounding in elephants well protected: There should be no (feeling of) satisfaction in regard (to accumulation of) horses, elephants and female elephants. (Enough is not enough).

❍ ❍ ❍

५१. कच्चिद्दर्शयसे नित्यं मनुष्याणां विभूषितम् ।
उत्थायोत्थाय पूर्वाह्णे राजपुत्र महापथे ॥

51. Oh Prince (Bharatha)! Every morning do you present yourself before all citizens, fully decorated, in the Royal Boulevard, getting up (from your chariot).

❍ ❍ ❍

५२. कच्चिन्न सर्वेकर्मान्ताः प्रत्यक्षास्तेऽविशङ्कया ।
सर्वेवा पुनरुत्सृष्टा मध्यमेवात्र कारणम् ॥

52. I hope your officers do not present themselves before you because they have no fear for you (nor fearing consequence): Nor do they all run away (in fear from you). In this matter the middle course is most agreeable.

❍ ❍ ❍

५३. कच्चित्सर्वाणि दुर्गाणि धनधान्यायुधोदकैः ।
यन्त्रैश्च परिपूर्णानि तथा शिल्पिधनुर्धरैः ॥

53. Are all the fortresses filled up with materials, grains, waters, armaments and equipments: I hope they are full, (manned by) craftsmen, warriors (wielders of bow and arms).

❍ ❍ ❍

५४. आयस्ते विपुलः कच्चित्कच्चिदल्पतरो व्ययः ।
अपात्रेषु न ते कच्चित्कोशो गच्छतिराघव ॥

54. Oh (Bharatha the) Raaghava! Is your income (sufficiently) large Is your expenditure less than this? I hope the Treasury has not fallen into wrong hands.

❍ ❍ ❍

५५. देवतार्थेच पित्रर्थेब्राह्मणेष्वागतेषु च ।
योधेषु मित्रवर्गेषु कच्चिद्गच्छति ते व्ययः ॥

55 I hope your expenditure goes to worship of Deities, worship of forefathers, Braamins who come (as guests), and to warriors and friends.

❍ ❍ ❍

५६. कच्चिदार्योविशुद्धात्मा क्षारितश्चोरकर्मणा ।
अपृष्टः शास्त्रकुशलैर्न लोभाद्बध्यते शुचिः ।।

56. I hope you do not punish a sinless, pure, noble man who is (falsely) accused, out of greed, by men who live by theft, without (proper) investigation (as per law), by experts in law

❍ ❍ ❍

५७. गृहीतश्चैव पृष्टश्च काले दृष्टः सकारणः ।
कच्चिन्न मुच्यते चोरो धनलोभान्नरर्षभ ।।

57. Oh (Bharatha) 'The bull amongst men'! I hope when a thief is (quickly) apprehended at (right) time after questioned with proper proofs (evidence), he is not let off by lure of money. (let off through corruption!)

❍ ❍ ❍

५८. व्यसने कच्चिदाढ्यस्य दुर्गतस्य च राघव ।
अर्थं विरागाः पश्यन्ति तवामात्या बहुश्रुताः ।।

58. Oh (Bharatha) the Raaghava! I hope your learned ministers who are interested in your welfare do not see any difference between an affluent man and a poor man, when calamity* strikes.

(Vaalmeeki uses = Vyasana=; There should be no discrimination between rich and poor, when there is suffering or when calamity hits the kingdom.)

❍ ❍ ❍

५९. यानि मिथ्याभिशस्तानां पतन्त्यस्राणि राघव ।
तानि पुत्रपशून्घ्नन्ति प्रीत्यर्थमनुशासतः ।।

59. Oh (Bharatha) the Raaghava! When those tears fall from those who are falsely accused, it will destroy the sons and cows of (a ruler) who rules out of love (towards his citizens)

(Hundred criminals may be let off for insufficient evidence: but no innocent man should ever be punished)

❍ ❍ ❍

६०. कच्चिद्वृद्धांश्च बालांश्च वैद्यमुख्यांश्च राघव ।
दानेन मनसा वाचा त्रिभिरेतैर्बुभूषसे ।।

60. Oh (Bharatha) the Raaghava! Do you 'adorn' elders, children, foremost scholars with these three, (namely), with gifts, affection and conversation (respectively).

❍ ❍ ❍

६१. कच्चिद्गुरूंश्च वृद्धांश्च तापसान्देवतातिथीन् ।
चैत्यांश्च सर्वान्सिद्धार्थान्ब्राह्मणांश्च नमस्यसि ।।

61. Do you bow (and respect) elders, Guru-s, men of penance who have attained (enlightenment), all the (noble) Braamins, Deities, guests and (holy trees like) Chaithya.

❍ ❍ ❍

६२. कच्चिदर्थेन वा धर्ममर्थं धर्मेण वा पुनः ।
उभौ वा प्रीतिलोभेन कामेन न विबाधसे ।।

62. I hope you do not destroy Dharma by Dharma: Wealth by wealth;; Nor do you destroy these two by passion due to greed and gratification.

("Laws " of Dharma must be judiciously used; Wealth must be put to good use; And greed and self gratification should not destroy Dharma and wealth)

❍ ❍ ❍

६३. कच्चिदर्थं च धर्मं च कामं च जयतां वर ।
विभज्य काले कालज्ञ सर्वान् भरत सेवसे ।।

63. Oh (Bharatha) the foremost amongst those who are victorious! Oh (Bharatha) who knows proper time (and place for any action)! Do you (assign to yourself and)

divide your time for pursuit of Dharma, Artha and Kaama, all these.

(Dharma is duty, justice, administration, defense etc. for a king. Artha is procurement of wealth and substance both for himself and his citizens. And Kaama is mundane pleasures like hunting, sport, arts etc. No king's life is complete if he does not enjoy all these)

❍ ❍ ❍

६४. कच्चित्ते ब्राह्मणाः शर्म सर्वशास्त्रार्थकोविदाः ।
आशंसन्ते महाप्राज्ञ पौरजानपदैः सह ॥

64. Oh most intelligent (Bharatha)! Do Braamins well versed in all Shaasthra-s and in the inner meaning of Shaasthras, along with ordinary citizens, extol you with blessings.

(Raama lists 14 Evils that are to be avoided, particularly by kings.)

❍ ❍ ❍

६५. नास्तिक्यमनृतं क्रोधं प्रमादं दीर्घसूत्रताम् ।
अदर्शनं ज्ञानवतामालस्यं पञ्चवृत्तिताम् ॥

६६. एकचिन्तनमर्थानामनर्थज्ञैश्च मन्त्रणम् ।
निश्चितानामनारम्भं मन्त्रस्यापरिरक्षणम् ॥

६७. मङ्गलस्याप्रयोगं च प्रत्युत्थानं च सर्वतः ।
कच्चित्त्वं वर्जयस्येतान्राजदोषांश्चतुर्दश ॥

67. Atheism: Untruth: Anger: Carelessness: Procrastination: Not 'Seeing' (meeting) wise men: Laziness: (Total) Subjugation to all the five sense organs...Thinking alone (one track mind) in (important) matters (of state): Taking counsel from fools: Inaction after taking decision: Not protecting secrets....Not doing that which is auspicious: Not offering respectful salutations totally.... I hope you have discarded all these 14 Evil qualities of a (bad) king.

(Now Raama lists various aspects of king's life: stanzas 68 to 70)

❍ ❍ ❍

६८. दश पञ्च चतुर्वर्गान्सप्तवर्गांश्च तत्त्वतः ।
अष्टवर्गं त्रिवर्गं च विद्यास्तिस्रश्च राघव ॥

68. Oh (Bharatha) the Raaghava! The Ten aspects of Life (namely Hunting, Gambling, Mid day slumber, Gossip, Company with mistresses; Drink: Dance: Singing: Playing, Music).... The Five aspects (of life, namely: Evil by women, wealth, enemies, wrong speech and sinful deed).... The Four aspects (namely Saama-Peace talks; Dhaana-settlement through gifts, bribery, ceding of territory etc.: Bhedha- Threats and arguments, intimidation: Dhanda-the stick, war etc.)....... The Seven Aspects (Pertaining to :King, Ministers of kingdom, Fortress- Defense, Substance, Army and Friends;) The Eight aspects (pertaining to: Talking ill of others, Obstinacy, Revenge, Hatred, Envy: Wrath: Seeking other's Wealth; Cruelty in punishment.).......And Three aspects: (Acting Impetuously; Inaction when quick action is called for; Taking action after times has elapsed.)...... And Three Subjects: (Agriculture, Commerce, Industry and Law).

❍ ❍ ❍

६९. इन्द्रियाणां जयं बुद्ध्वा षाड्गुण्यं दैवमानुषम् ।
कृत्यं विंशतिवर्गं च तथा प्रकृतिमण्डलम् ॥

69. .... The Control of Sense organs (Passions); The Six qualities (pertaining to politics: Treaty and alliance; Breaking up of alliance; War: Bring enmity amongst enemies; Achieving victory without war over the enemy; Forming alliance with your enemy's enemy; Seducing and bribing one from enemy's camp: Natural calamities (like Fire, floods etc.)....... The Twenty aspects (Namely): Politics, Women (and their welfare); City:

Kingdom at large; Relatives and henchmen; Seizure of wealth; Religion; Self respect; Insolvency; Loss of place; Loss of strength; Loss of character; Loss of faith (in Worship); Lack of compassion; Killing one's own folks; Obstinacy; One track mind; Losing friends ..... Likewise Five subjects of kings: Ministers, Kingdom, Fortress, Treasury, Law /Punishment ......

❍ ❍ ❍

७०. यात्रादण्डविधानं च द्वियोनी सन्धिविग्रहौ ।
कच्चिदेतान्महाप्राज्ञ यथावदनुमन्यसे ॥

70. The (Five) Methods of taking .leave and going away: Going away in enmity; Going away making friendship; Going away accompanied by friends; Going away after cheating and sowing seeds of mischief; Going away after (being and treating) with contempt.... Two aspects: Alliance and break of alliance..... .... I hope (Oh Bharatha), You understand the true significance of all these (that I have narrated to you as above) and act accordingly.

❍ ❍ ❍

७१. मन्त्रिभिस्त्वं यथोद्दिष्टैश्चतुर्भिस्त्रिभिरेव वा ।
कच्चित्समस्तैर्व्यस्तैश्च मन्त्रं मन्त्रयसे मिथः ॥

71. I hope you seek counsel jointly with three or four ministers. And you (also seek counsel) separately from every one of them, as prescribed by our Shaasthra-s.

❍ ❍ ❍

७२. कच्चित्ते सफला वेदाः कच्चित्ते सफलाः क्रियाः ।
कच्चित्ते सफला दारा कच्चित्ते सफलं श्रुतम् ॥

72. Is (the study of) Vedha fruitful (and meaningful) to you? Do your actions result in success. Your wife, Is she ever helpful to you? Does (your study of) holy Texts nourish you?

❍ ❍ ❍

७३. कच्चिदेषैव ते बुद्धिर्यथोक्ता मम राघव ।
आयुष्या च यशस्या च धर्मकामार्थसंहिता ।।

73. Oh (Bharatha) the Raaghava! As elucidated by me, is your mind directed to all these, so as to give you long life and fame, befitting Dharma, Artha, Kaama.

❍ ❍ ❍

७४. यां वृत्तिं वर्तते तातो यां च नः प्रपितामहाः ।
तां वृत्तिं वर्तसे कच्चिद्या च सत्पथगा शुभा ।।

74. Are you abiding in that auspicious path that does good, that which our forefathers (followed) and which our father (also) followed.

❍ ❍ ❍

७५. कच्चित्स्वादुकृतं भोज्यमेको नाश्नासि राघव ।
कच्चिदाशंसमानेभ्यो मित्रेभ्यः संप्रयच्छसि ।।

75. Oh (Bharatha) the Raaghava! I hope you do not consume delicious foods all by yourself (selfishly): I hope you (share it with and) offer these to friends who desire.

❍ ❍ ❍

७६. राजा तु धर्मेण हि पालयित्वा
महामतिर्दण्डधरः प्रजानाम् ।
अवाप्य कृत्स्नां वसुधां यथाव
दितश्च्युतः स्वर्गमुपैति विद्वान् ।।

76. (It is said): If a king having obtained the entire earth (to rule), rules over (the kingdom) by Dharma, as a wise and learned man, offering justice to citizens, he duly goes to heaven when he leaves (this world).

❍ ❍ ❍

Chapter 101

(Bharatha Tells Raama About) Dhascharatha's Death

१. रामस्य वचनं श्रुत्वा भरतः प्रत्युवाच ह ।
किं मे धर्माद्विहीनस्य राजधर्मः करिष्यति ॥

1. Hearing Raama's words (of advice) Bharatha replied: =What will this royal Dharma (you just spoke about) do for me. who has strayed away from Dharma (itself).=

❍ ❍ ❍

२. शाश्वतोऽयं सदा धर्मः स्थितोऽस्मासु नरर्षभ ।
ज्येष्ठपुत्रे स्थिते राजन्न कनीयान्नृपो भवेत् ॥

2. Oh King! (Oh Raama) 'the bull'amongst men! When the eldest son is there, the younger (son) does not become king. Amongst us (of Ikshwaaku-s), this Dharma is rooted firmly.

❍ ❍ ❍

३. स समृद्धां मया सार्धमयोध्यां गच्छ राघव ।
अभिषेचय चात्मानं कुलस्यास्य भवाय नः ॥

3. Oh (Raama) the Raaghava! (Therefore) You should come along with me to our prosperous Ayodhya: For your family's sake, for welfare (of the world) you should crown yourself.

❍ ❍ ❍

४. राजानं मानुषं प्राहुर्देवत्वे स मतो मम ।
यस्य धर्मार्थसहितं वृत्तमाहुरमानुषम् ॥

4. They, who talk about his conduct as enjoined with Dharma and Artha and as a divine being, (also) talk about this king as an ordinary man. (But as far as I am concerned), he is to be honoured (and considered) by me (only) as Divinity.

(How can people say Raama is a man endowed with

great qualities when I know he is a Divine being on earth, says Bharatha.)

❍ ❍ ❍

५. केकयस्थे तु च मयि त्वयि चारण्यमाश्रिते ।
दिवमार्योगतो राजा यायजूकः सतां मतः ।।

5. When I was away in Kekeya (kingdom on holiday) and when you went away to forest (on exile), in presence of good men, the noble (Aryan) King (our father Dhascharatha) who was esteemed for (his performance of many) Sacrificial ceremonies, passed away.

❍ ❍ ❍

६. अपेतक्लमसन्तापाः सुभिक्षाः सुप्रतिश्रयाः ।
अपि प्रेष्यानुपादाय सर्वेस्म सुसुखोषिताः ।।

6. The King, the moment you had gone away (to forest) along with Seetha and Lakshmana, went to heaven, overwhelmed by grief and sorrow.

❍ ❍ ❍

७. आमन्त्रये त्वां भगवन्कामं त्वमृषिसत्तम ।
समीपं प्रस्थितं भ्रातुर्मैत्रेणेक्षस्व चक्षुषा ।।

7. (Therefore): Arise, you the 'tiger' of men! May you offer water rituals to (our dead) father: Along with Schathrugna, I have already performed water rituals (for father).

❍ ❍ ❍

८. आश्रमं तस्य धर्मज्ञ धार्मिकस्य महात्मनः ।
आचक्ष्व कतमो मार्गः कियानिति च शंस मे ।।

8. Oh (Raama the) Raaghava! They say that in the world of forefathers, only those offered by their dear ones become eternal (doing them eternal good in heaven). And indeed you alone are the most beloved of our father.

(Customarily, Indians offer, at least once a year, as a Ritual, offerings of foods, meats etc. for their departed parents and elders. Here Bharatha says, in as much as Raama was the most beloved amongst the four sons of Dhascharatha, his, will be most acceptable and welcome for Dhascharatha in heaven)

❍ ❍ ❍

९. इति पृष्टस्तु भरतं भ्रातृदर्शनलालसम् ।
प्रत्युवाच महातेजा भरद्वाजे महातपाः ।।

9. Your father ended his life thinking (only) about you: Grieving over you, desirous of seeing you, abandoned by you, his mind fixed only upon you, unable to take (his mind) off you, was shattered by grief.

❍ ❍ ❍

Chapter 102

Performance of Rituals (by Raama and Lakshmana)

१. तां श्रुत्वा करुणां वाचं पितुर्मरणसंहिताम् ।
राघवो भरतेनोक्तां बभूव गतचेतनः ।।

1. Hearing the pitiable (miserable) words told by Bharatha about their father's death, (Raama) the Raaghava lost his consciousness.

❍ ❍ ❍

२. तं तु वज्रमिवोत्सृष्टमाहवे दानवारिणा ।
वाग्वज्रं भरतेनोक्तममनोज्ञं परन्तपः ।।

2. Hearing such horrible news which was like thunderbolt (of Vajra) hurled by Indhra during war, the tormentor of enemies ......

❍ ❍ ❍

३. प्रगृह्य रामो बाहू वै पुष्पिताग्रो यथा द्रुमः ।
वने परशुना कृत्तस्तथा भुवि पपात ह ॥

3. ...... Raama, clinching his fists, fell down on earth like full blossomed tree in the forest felled by an axe.

❍ ❍ ❍

४. तथा निपतितं रामं जगत्यां जगतीपतिम् ।
कूलघातपरिश्रान्तं प्रसुप्तमिव कुञ्जरम् ॥

4. Like a sleeping tired elephant which had devastated the banks of a river, this Raama this Lord of earth who had fallen down (on earth like this) ......

❍ ❍ ❍

५. भ्रातरस्ते महेष्वासं सर्वतः शोककर्शितम् ।
रुदन्तः सह वैदेह्या सिषिचुः सलिलेन वै ॥

5. ...... this mighty wielder of bow (Raama) who was crushed by grief.... The brothers (Bharatha, Schathrugna and Lakshmana) along with (Seetha the) Vaidhehi, sprinkled water (to revive Raama), all of them crying.

❍ ❍ ❍

६. स तु संज्ञां पुनर्लब्ध्वा नेत्राभ्यामास्रमुत्सृजन् ।
उपाक्रामत काकुत्स्थः कृपणं बहु भाषितुम् ॥

6. Regaining his consciousness, this (Raama) the Kaakuthsa, with tears flowing from his eyes, began to 'blabber' in may ways pitiably.

❍ ❍ ❍

७. स रामः स्वर्गतं श्रुत्वा पितरं पृथिवीपतिम् ।
उवाच भरतं वाक्यं धर्मात्मा धर्मसंहितम् ॥

7. The noble soul man of Dharma, this Raama, having heard that his father the lord of earth had gone away to heaven, addressed Bharatha with these words of Dharma.

❍ ❍ ❍

८. किं करिष्याम्ययोध्यायां ताते दिष्टां गतिं गते ॥

8. As father has obtained the state of death, what is it I am going to do in Ayodhya?

❍ ❍ ❍

९. कस्तां राजवराद्धीनामयोध्यां पालयिष्यति ॥

9. Abandoned by this illustrious king who will rule Ayodhya? (who is worthy to take his place!).

❍ ❍ ❍

१०. किं नु तस्य मया कार्यं दुर्जातेन महात्मनः ।
यो मृतो मम शोकेन मया चापि न संस्कृतः ॥

10. Born as a worthless son, what use was there from me, for that great soul man, when even his Last Rites were not done by me to him who died in grief over me.

❍ ❍ ❍

११. अहो भरत सिद्धार्थोयेन राजा त्वयाऽनघ ।
शत्रुघ्नेन च सर्वेषु प्रेतकृत्येषु संस्कृतः ॥

11. Oh sinless Bharatha! You are indeed most fortunate (accomplished): Because, the king (our father), was hallowed by you and Schathrugna in all the funereal rites (for him).

❍ ❍ ❍

१२. निष्प्रधानामनेकाग्रां नरेन्द्रेण विनाकृताम् ।
निवृत्तवनवासोऽपि नायोध्यां गन्तुमुत्सहे ॥

12. After completing my forest life (of exile), I cannot bear to return to Ayodhya which has been abandoned by (Dhascharatha) the lord of men, which has lost its most eminent personality, (lost) a man of many pursuits.

❍ ❍ ❍

१३. समाप्तवनवासं मामयोध्यायां परन्तप ।
को नु शासिष्यति पुनस्ताते लोकान्तरं गते ॥

13. Oh (Bharatha) the tormentor of enemies! With father having gone away to the other world, who is going to offer me counsel again at Ayodhya when I return, (when I return) completing my forest life.

❍ ❍ ❍

१४. पुरा प्रेक्ष्य सुवृत्तं मां पिता यान्याह सान्त्वयन् ।
वाक्यानि तानि श्रोष्यामि कुतः श्रोत्रसुखान्यहम् ।।

14. From whom am I going to hear, like before, such words pleasant on my ears, those soothing words (of advice) my father used to tell, looking at me who was living such a good life (under his care).

❍ ❍ ❍

१५. एवमुक्त्वा स भरतं भार्यामभ्येत्य राघवः ।
उवाच शोकसन्तप्तः पूर्णचन्द्रनिभाननाम् ।।

15. Saying thus to Bharatha this (Raama the) Raaghava, looked at his wife whose face was like the full moon and he addressed her, tormented by grief.

❍ ❍ ❍

१६. सीते मृतस्ते श्वशुरः पित्रा हीनोऽसि लक्ष्मण ।
भरतो दुःखमाचष्टे स्वर्गतं पृथिवीपतिम् ।।

16. Oh Seetha! Bharatha has spoken about the sad news of the Lord of earth.(Dhascharatha's) departure to heaven. Your father-in-law is dead. Oh Lakshmana, you are (now) without father

❍ ❍ ❍

१७. ततो बहुगुणं तेषां बाष्पं नेत्रेष्वजायत ।
तथा ब्रुवति काकुत्स्थे कुमाराणां यशस्विनाम् ।।

17. At that moment, while (Raama) the Kaakuthsa was saying this, tears from the eyes of the famous princes flowed copiously.

❍ ❍ ❍

१८. ततस्ते भ्रातरः सर्वेभृशमाश्वास्य राघवम् ।
अब्रुवञ्जगतीभर्तुः क्रियतामुदकं पितुः ।।

18. Then all his brothers consoled (Raama) the Raaghava greatly and they said:= May (Rituals with) Waters be offered to (our) father, the master of the world.=

❍ ❍ ❍

१९. सा सीता श्वशुरं श्रुत्वा स्वर्गलोकगतं नृपम् ।
नेत्राभ्यामश्रुपूर्णाभ्यामशकन्नेक्षितुं पतिम् ।।

19. And this Seetha, hearing the passing away of her father-in-law to heaven, could not 'see' her husband as her eyes were covered by tears.

❍ ❍ ❍

२०. सान्त्वयित्वा तु तां रामो रुदन्ती जनकात्मजाम् ।
उवाच लक्ष्मणं तत्र दुःखितो दुःखितं वचः ।।

20. And Raama consoled (Seetha) this daughter of Janaka who was crying; Then after, he, who was in distress, addressed Lakshmana who was (equally) in distress, these words.

❍ ❍ ❍

२१. आनयेङ्गुदिपिण्याकं चीरमाहर चोत्तरम् ।
जलक्रियार्थं तातस्य गमिष्यामि महात्मनः ।।

21. I am going (now) in order to perform Water Rituals for the great soul father; Bring my upper garments of deer skin. Also bring sesame seed cakes (etc. for rituals).

❍ ❍ ❍

२२. सीता पुरस्ताद्व्रजतु त्वमेनामभितो व्रज ।
अहं पश्चाद्गमिष्यामि गतिर्ह्येषा सुदारुणा ।।

22. Let Seetha go first: You then follow her: I will go last (behind you both): (Because) This is the cruel custom.

❍ ❍ ❍

२३. ततो नित्यानुगस्तेषां विदितात्मा महामतिः ।
मृदुर्दान्तश्च शान्तश्च रामे च दृढभक्तिमान् ।।
२४. सुमन्त्रस्तैर्नृपसुतैः सार्धमाश्वास्य राघवम् ।
अवातारयदालम्ब्य नदीं मन्दाकिनीं शिवाम् ।।

23. & 24.

At that moment, the constant (well wisher and) devotee of their (Ikshwaaku family), the most intelligent man who had perception of The "Self- Soul", who was gentle, who was a man of restraint, who was tranquil, who was firmly devoted to Raama...(Such a person) this Sumanthra, along with the princes, consoled (Raama the) Raaghava; Clasping him, he 'made' him (helped him) to get into the pure Mandhaakini river.

❍ ❍ ❍

२५. ते सुतीर्थां ततः कृच्छ्रादुपागम्य यशस्विनः ।
नदीं मन्दाकिनीं रम्यां तथा पुष्पितकाननाम् ।।
२६. शीघ्रस्रोतसमासाद्य तीर्थं शिवमकर्दमम् ।
सिषिचुस्तूदकं राज्ञे तत एतद्भवत्विति ।।

25. & 26.

Then the famous princes, with great difficulty (and sorrow), got into the beautiful Mandhaakini river whose waters are ever pleasant, which had forest of full blossomed trees (around its banks)..... which was flowing fast. They took pure and holy waters from (the river) and offered these waters (as per Rituals) saying: = Let These Be For The King =

❍ ❍ ❍

२७. प्रगृह्य च महीपालो जलपूरितमञ्जलिम् ।
दिशं याम्यामभिमुखो रुदन्वचनमब्रवीत् ।।

27. (Raama) the lord of earth, cupping his hands in Anjali with waters, and raising (his hands) said these words,

facing southern direction (which is Lord of Death, Yaama's region), crying.

❍ ❍ ❍

२८. एतत्ते राजशार्दूल विमलं तोयमक्षयम् ।
पितृलोकगतस्याद्य मद्दत्तमुपतिष्ठतु ॥

28. Oh 'Tiger' of men (Oh father)! May these pure waters offered by me, now serve you, eternally who has gone away to the world of our forefathers.

❍ ❍ ❍

२९. ततो मन्दाकिनीतीरात्प्रत्युत्तीर्य स राघवः ।
पितुश्चकार तेजस्वी निवापं भ्रातृभिः सह ॥

29. The brilliant (Raama the) Raaghava, after crossing over to the banks of Mandhaakini river, then offered sacrificial gifts to (his dead) father along with his brothers.

❍ ❍ ❍

३०. ऐङ्गुदं बदरीमिश्रं पिण्याकं दर्भसंस्तरे ।
न्यस्य रामः सुदुःखार्तोरुदन्वचनमब्रवीत् ॥

30. Spreading a bed of dharbha grass, Raama placed sesame seed cakes mixed with Jujuba fruits and addressed these words crying, afflicted by grief.

❍ ❍ ❍

३१. इदं भुङ्क्ष्व महाराज प्रीतो यदशना वयम् ।
यदन्नं पुरुषोऽश्नाति तदन्नास्तस्य देवताः ॥

31. Oh great king! (Oh father)! The food that a man eats, his deities consume (and are satisfied by) the same food: This, what we are eating, (Please) partake happily.

(It is the belief in India that Gods are pleased by whatever is offered in reverence.)

❍ ❍ ❍

३२. ततस्तेनैव मार्गेण प्रत्युत्तीर्य नदीतटात् ।
आरुरोह नरव्याघ्रो रम्यसानुं महीधरम् ।।

32. Then, (Raama) the 'tiger' of men, coming back by the same route and coming away from the banks of the river, climbed up the mountain that had fine ridges.

❍ ❍ ❍

३३. ततः पर्णकुटीद्वारमासाद्य जगतीपतिः ।
परिजग्राह बाहुभ्यामुभौ भरतलक्ष्मणौ ।।

33. (Raama) the lord of the world, reached the entrance of his hermitage, and then he hugged (the two brothers) Bharatha and Lakshmana with his two hands.

❍ ❍ ❍

३४. तेषां तु रुदतां शब्दात्प्रतिश्रुत्कोऽभवद्गिरौ ।
भ्रातॄणां सह वैदेह्या सिंहानां नर्दतामिव ।।

34. The echo of the mountain caused by the sound of crying of the brothers along with Seetha, was like the roar of lions.

❍ ❍ ❍

३५. महाबलानां रुदतां कुर्वतामुदकं पितुः ।
विज्ञाय तुमुलं शब्दं त्रस्ता भरतसैनिकाः ।।

35. Realising that the tumultuous sounds were from wailing of these mightily strong (Raama and his brothers) after they had performed water Rituals for their father, Bharatha's Army (that was stationed away from hermitage) grieved.

❍ ❍ ❍

३६. अब्रवंश्चापि रामेण भरतः सङ्गतो ध्रुवम् ।
तेषामेव महाञ्छब्दः शोचतां पितरं मृतम् ।।

36. They all talked (amongst themselves)= The mighty sound is from them only who are grieving over their

dead father. (So) It is certain they have (found and) met Raama.=

❍ ❍ ❍

३७. अथ वासान्परित्यज्य तं सर्वेऽभिमुखाः स्वनम् ।
अप्येकमनसो जग्मुर्यथास्थानं प्रधाविताः ।।

37. All of them left their places and walked in the direction of the place from where sound was emanating, with one track mind (to see Raama).

❍ ❍ ❍

३८. हयैरन्य गजैरन्ये रथैरन्ये स्वलङ्कृतैः ।
सुकुमारास्तथैवान्ये पद्भिरेव नरा ययुः ।।

38. The young ones on horse backs; some on elephants; some on well decorated chariots; likewise, some on foot, went along (to see Raama).

❍ ❍ ❍

३९. अचिरप्रोषितं रामं चिरविप्रोषितं यथा ।
द्रष्टुकामो जनः सर्वोजगाम सहसाऽऽश्रमम् ।।

39. All these men went fast towards the hermitage desirous of seeing (Raama) as if he had been exiled for a long time although Raama had not gone away for a long time (from Ayodhya).

(It is interesting to note that there is no evidence that the Army got permission to move on towards Raama's hermitage. Here is a case of Army taking its own decision)

❍ ❍ ❍

४०. भ्रातृणां त्वरितास्ते तु द्रष्टुकामाः समागमम् ।
ययुर्बहुविधैर्यानैः खुरनेमिसमाकुलैः ।।

40. Mounting various vehicles (that were well supported by) wheels and axles, they all went fast, desirous of

witnessing the meeting of the four brothers (Raama, Lakshmana, Bharatha and Schathrugna)

❍ ❍ ❍

४१. सा भूमिर्बहुभिर्यानैः खुरनेमिसमाहता ।
मुमोच तुमुलं शब्दं द्यौरिवाभ्रसमागमे ।।

41. The earth let lose a tumultuous sound like when clouds clash in sky, because of the (sound) of wheels and horses' hoof of various vehicles.

❍ ❍ ❍

४२. तेन वित्रासिता नागाः करेणुपरिवारिताः ।
आवासयन्तो गन्धेन जग्मुरन्यद्वनं ततः ।।

42. By these movements, the elephants (of forest) which were scared, went over to another forest to make their stay there, along with the female elephants.

❍ ❍ ❍

४३. वराहमृगसङ्घाश्च महिषाः सर्पवानराः ।
व्याघ्रगोकर्णगवया वित्रेसुः पृषतैः सह ।।

43. The Bears, deers, buffaloes, reptiles, monkeys, tigers, donkeys, all ran away, scared.

❍ ❍ ❍

४४. रथाङ्गसाह्वा नत्यूहा हंसाः कारण्डवाः प्लवाः ।
तथा पुंस्कोकिला क्रौञ्चा विसंज्ञा भेजिरे दिशः ।।

44. Flocks of goose birds, water birds, swans, scarecrows, peacocks, parrots, Krauncha, flew away in different directions without comprehension.

❍ ❍ ❍

४५. तेन शब्देन वित्रस्तैराकाशं पक्षिभिर्वृतम् ।
मनुष्यैरावृता भूमिरुभयं प्रबभौ तदा ।।

45. The sky was full of birds scared by this sound: the

territory (earth) was full of men (of forest who came into open); Thus the two regions shone!

❍ ❍ ❍

४६. ततस्तं पुरुषव्याघ्रं यशस्विनमकल्मषम् ।
आसीनं स्थण्डिले रामं ददर्श सहसा जनः ।।

46. Then the citizens saw (with sorrow) the famous and stainless Raama the 'tiger' of men at once, who was sitting on (bare) earth.

❍ ❍ ❍

४७. विगर्हमाणः कैकेयीं सहितो मन्थरामपि ।
अभिगम्य जनो रामं बाष्पपूर्णमुखोऽभवत् ।।

47. Cursing Kaikeyi and Manthara also, the citizens gathered there, approached Raama and their faces were covered by tears.

❍ ❍ ❍

४८. तान्नरान्बाष्पपूर्णाक्षान्समीक्ष्याथ सुदुःखितान् ।
पर्यष्वजत धर्मज्ञः पितृवन्मातृवच्च सः ।।

48. At that time (Raama) the knower of Dharma,. comforted these citizens who were in great sorrow, whose eyes were full with tears: He hugged them as though he was like a father and mother to them .

❍ ❍ ❍

४९. स तत्र कांश्चित्परिषस्वजे नरा न्नराश्च केचित्तु तमभ्यवादयन् ।
चकार सर्वान्सवयस्यबान्धवा न्यथार्हमासाद्य तु नृपात्मजः ।।

49. This (Raama the) son of king, then hugged some men there; some men were prostrated before him; Approaching them, his friends and relatives and all, he greeted them as per norms.

❍ ❍ ❍

५०. ततः स तेषां रुदतां महात्मनां
भुवं च खं चानुनिनादयन्स्वनः ।
गुहा गिरीणां च दिशश्च सन्ततं
मृदङ्गघोषप्रतिमो विशुश्रुवे ।।

50. The sound of the crying of these most eminent men, reverberated (beating) sky and earth and was heard continuously through mountain caves and regions, as though it was like rhythmic Mridunga drum beats.

❍ ❍ ❍

Chapter 103

(Raama and Lakshmana) Meet Their Mothers

१. वसिष्ठः पुरतः कृत्वा दारान्दशरथस्य च ।
अभिचक्राम तं देशं रामदर्शनहर्षितः ।।

1. Exhilarated to see Raama, Vasishta walked along in front of the wives of the (late) Dhascharatha to that place .

❍ ❍ ❍

२. राजपत्न्यस्तु गच्छन्त्यो मन्द मन्दाकिनीं प्रति ।
ददृशुस्तत्र तत्तीर्थं रामलक्ष्मणसेवितम् ।।

2. These royal ladies who were walking along slowly towards Mandhaakini river, saw there the sacred place (where water Rituals and sesame cakes) were offered by Raama and Lakshmana (to their dead father).

❍ ❍ ❍

३. कौसल्या बाष्पपूर्णेन मुखेन परिशुष्यता ।
सुमित्रामब्रवीद्दीनां याश्चान्या राजयोषितः ।।

3. With her face downcast, with tears covering it,

Kowsalya addressed the depressed Sumithra and other royal ladies (who all had come with Bharatha to forest).

❍ ❍ ❍

४. इदं तेषामनाथानां क्लिष्टमक्लिष्टकर्मणाम् ।
वने प्राक्केवलं तीर्थं ये ते निर्विषयीकृताः ।।

4. This is the obscure bathing place in the forest for those fatherless (brothers, Raama and Lakshmana) who are ever un wearied in action (but) who have already been exiled (by Kaikeyi).

❍ ❍ ❍

५. इतः सुमित्रे पुत्रस्ते सदा जलमतन्द्रितः ।
स्वयं हरति सौमित्रिर्मम पुत्रस्य कारणात् ।।

5. Oh Sumithra! Your son (Lakshmana) the son of Sumithra, is carrying water by himself for my son (Raama) from here, ever unwearied (in service to him).

❍ ❍ ❍

६. जघन्यमपि ते पुत्रः कृतवान्न तु गर्हितः ।
भ्रातुर्यदर्थसहितं सर्वं तद्विहितं गुणैः ।।

6. Your son will never be censured even if he indulges in mean acts; because, it is decreed, that all the good service done to a brother, is meritorious.

❍ ❍ ❍

७. अद्यायमपि ते पुत्रः क्लेशानामतथोचितः ।
नीचानर्थसमाचारं सज्जं कर्म प्रमुञ्चतु ।।

7. At least now, this, your son (Lakshmana) who is not used to such suffering, will he give up this inferior and worthless (menial) tasks he is doing (as service to his brother Raama)?

(Prince Lakshmana, a water 'Carrier'! Ah! :Bemoans Kowsalya.)

❍ ❍ ❍

८. दक्षिणाग्रेषु दर्भेषु सा ददर्श महीतले ।
पितुरिङ्गुदिपिण्याकं न्यस्तमायतलोचना ॥

8. This wide eyed lady Kowsalya noticed the (Ritual offerings of) sesame seed cakes for their (dead) father, kept on earth over Dharbha grass whose tips were pointed towards South.

❍ ❍ ❍

९. तं भूमौ पितुरार्तेन न्यस्तं रामेण वीक्ष्य सा ।
उवाच देवी कौसल्या सर्वा दशरथस्त्रियः ॥

9. Taking a look at this which had been kept on the floor by the grieving Raama for his (late) father, this Kowsalya addressed all the wives of Dhascharatha.

❍ ❍ ❍

१०. इदमिक्ष्वाकुनाथस्य राघवस्य महात्मनः ।
राघवेण पितुर्दत्तं पश्यतैतद्यथाविधि ॥

10. Observe this! this (is the ritual offering of sesame cakes etc.) offered as per custom to their (late) father, the great soul (Dhascharatha the) Raaghava, the lord of Ikshwaaku-s, by (Raama) the Raaghava.

❍ ❍ ❍

११. तस्य देवसमानस्य पार्थिवस्य महात्मनः ।
नैतदौपयिकं मन्ये भुक्तभोगस्य भोजनम् ॥

11. I cannot consider this as proper food for (my late husband) the great soul king, who is like a celestial, who has enjoyed only comforts (and choicest foods).

❍ ❍ ❍

१२. चतुरन्तां महीं भुक्त्वा महेन्द्रसदृशो भुवि ।
कथमिङ्गुदिपिण्याकं च भुङ्क्ते वसुधाधिपः ॥

12. How can this lord of earth who, in this world, is

comparable to Lord Indhra (of heaven), eat (mere) sesame cakes?

❍ ❍ ❍

१३. अतो दुःखतरं लोके न किंचित्प्रतिभाति मे ।
यत्र रामः पितुर्दद्यादिङ्गुदीक्षोदमृद्धिमान् ।।

13. It appears to me that, in this world, there is nothing more cruel than, that this prosperous Raama offering sesame cakes to his (late) father ...... (All this of course is wailing by Kowsalya. Indians offer only Sesame seeds, cakes etc. as ritualistic offering to the dead).

❍ ❍ ❍

१४. रामेणेङ्गुदिपिण्याकं पितुर्दत्तं समीक्ष्य मे ।
कथं दुःखेन हृदयं न स्फोटति सहस्रधा ।।

14. How is it that my heart has not burst into thousand pieces in sorrow on seeing this sesame cakes offered to (their late) father by Raama.

❍ ❍ ❍

१५. श्रुतिस्तु खल्वियं सत्या लौकिकी प्रतिभाति मे ।
यदन्नं पुरुषोऽश्नाति तदन्नास्तस्य देवताः ।।

15. What foods man eats, that is the food (taken) by Deities: This worldly saying is quite true, so it appears to me. (Kowsalya thus grieves for her son Raama who is not a prince now but a poor mendicant in forest eating tubers and leaves!)

❍ ❍ ❍

१६. एवमार्ता सपत्न्यस्ता जग्मुराश्वास्य तां तदा ।
ददृशुश्चाश्रमे रामं स्वर्गच्युतमिवामरम् ।।

16. As she was wailing thus, (the royal ladies walked along), the co- wives walked along with her, consoling her. And then they saw in hermitage, Raama who was like a celestial come down from heaven.

❍ ❍ ❍

१७. तं भोगैः संपरित्यक्तं रामं संप्रेक्ष्य मातरः ।
आर्ता मुमुचुरश्रूणि सस्वरं शोककर्शिताः ।।

17. On seeing Raama who had abandoned all pleasures and comforts (in forest), his (step) mothers cried, shedding tears of sorrow, crushed by grief.

❍ ❍ ❍

१८. तासां रामः समुत्थाय जग्राह चरणाञ्छुभान् ।
मातॄणां मनुजव्याघ्रः सर्वासां सत्यसङ्गरः ।।

18. And Raama the 'tiger' of men who was ever true to a promise, got up and then fell down (prostrated) and caught hold of the auspicious feet of all these (step) mothers (in reverence).

❍ ❍ ❍

१९. ताः पाणिभिः सुखस्पर्शैर्मृद्वङ्गुलितलैः शुभैः ।
प्रममार्जू रजःपृष्ठाद्रामस्यायतलोचनाः ।।

19. These ladies whose eyes were large, whose palms and fingers were soft, then stroked the dust ridden back of Raama with their lovely hands that had soft 'touch'.

❍ ❍ ❍

२०. सौमित्रिरपि ताः सर्वा मातॄः संप्रेक्ष्य दुःखितः ।
अभ्यवादयतासक्तं शनै रामादनन्तरम् ।।

20. And (Lakshmana) the son of Sumithra also, seeing these (step) mothers, prostrated before them respectfully, one after another, in sorrow, after Raama (had bowed to them all).

❍ ❍ ❍

२१. यथा रामे तथा तस्मिन्सर्वा ववृतिरे स्त्रियः ।
वृत्तिं दशरथाज्जाते लक्ष्मणे शुभलक्षणे ।।

21. And all these ladies, stroked this Lakshmana who was

born to Dhascharatha and who possessed auspicious qualities, exactly as they did in the case of Raama.

❍ ❍ ❍

२२. सीताऽपि चरणांस्तासामुपसंगृह्य दुःखिता ।
श्वश्रूणामश्रुपूर्णाक्षी सा बभूवाग्रतः स्थिता ।।

22. And Seetha too, clasped their feet in sorrow and stood before these mothers-in-law, her eyes full with tears.

❍ ❍ ❍

२३. तां परिष्वज्य दुःखार्तां माता दुहितरं यथा ।
वनवासकृशां दीनां कौसल्या वाक्यमब्रवीत् ।।

23. And Kowsalya hugged (Seetha) who was in sorrow and who was emaciated due to life in forest, like a mother (hugging) her own daughter: She addressed her these words.

❍ ❍ ❍

२४. विदेहराजस्य सुता स्नुषा दशरथस्य च ।
रामपत्नी कथं दुःखं संप्राप्ता निर्जने वने ।।

24. How is it (Seetha the) daughter of king of Vidheha and daughter-in-law of Dhascharatha and the wife of Raama undergoes so much suffering in the uninhabited forest?

❍ ❍ ❍

२५. पद्ममातपसंतप्तं परिक्लिष्टमिवोत्पलम् ।
काञ्चनं रजसा ध्वस्तं क्लिष्टं चन्द्रमिवाम्बुदैः ।।

२६. मुखं ते प्रेक्ष्य मां शोका दहत्यग्निरिवाश्रयम् ।
भृशं मनसि वैदेहि व्यसनारणिसंभवः ।।

25. & 26.

Like a lotus withered by heat of the Sun, like an afflicted Uthpala flower, like dust covering (and darkening) gold, like (dense water bearing) cloud covering moon....... Oh, Seetha the Vaidhehi! On seeing your face (which is like all this), the grief (caused by the) "Fire wood of Grief" is burning my heart like fire burning one's place.

❍ ❍ ❍

२७. ब्रुवन्त्यामेवमार्तायां जनन्यां भरताग्रजः ।
पादावासाद्य जग्राह वसिष्ठस्य च राघवः ॥

27. While mother (Kowsalya) was talking like this in sorrow, (Raama) the Raaghava, the elder brother of Bharatha, approached Vasishta's feet and caught them in reverence.

❍ ❍ ❍

२८. पुरोहितस्याग्निसमस्य वै तदा
बृहस्पतेरिन्द्र इवामराधिपः ।
प्रगृह्य पादौ सुसमृद्धतेजसः
सहैव तेनोपविवेश राघवः ॥

28. Like lord of heaven Indhra, (bowing) before Brihaspathi, (Raama) the Raaghava fell (and caught the) feet of Purohith (Vasishta) who was most brilliant, who was like fire. He then sat down by his side.

❍ ❍ ❍

२९. ततो जघन्यं सहितैः समन्त्रिभिः
पुरप्रधानैश्च सहैव सैनिकैः ।
जनेन धर्मज्ञतमेन धर्मवा
नुपोपविष्टो भरतस्तदाग्रजम् ॥

29. Then, along with ministers, along with important citizens and army chiefs, and along with most learned men of Dharma, Bharatha the man of Dharma, sat behind his brother (Raama).

❍ ❍ ❍

३०. उपोपविष्टस्तु तदा स वीर्यवांस्त
परिस्ववेषेण समीक्ष्य राघवम् ।
श्रिया ज्वलन्तं भरतः कृताञ्जलि
र्यथामहेन्द्रः प्रयतः प्रजापतिम् ॥

30. Like Lord Indhra before God Bramma, the brave devoted Bharatha, looked at (Raama) the Raaghava who was resplendent in the dress of a man of penance, shining with lustre. He sat there with his hands cupped in Anjali.

❍ ❍ ❍

३१. किमेष वाक्यं भरतोऽद्य राघवं
प्रणम्य सत्कृत्य च साधु वक्ष्यति ।
इतीव तस्यार्यजनस्य तत्त्वतो
बभूव कौतूहलमुत्तमं तदा ॥

31. At that moment a great curiosity truly arose in those noble men there: (They were talking like this)= What Is This Bharatha Who Has Prostrated Before (Raama the) Raaghava and (who has) Honoured Him, Going To Tell Him Now: What Befitting Words! =

❍ ❍ ❍

३२. स राघवः सत्यधृतिश्च लक्ष्मणो
महानुभावो भरतश्च धार्मिकः ।
वृताः सुहृद्भिस्तु विरेजुरध्वरे
यथासदस्यैः सहितास्त्रयोऽग्नयः ॥

32. And in the midst of their friends, this (Raama) the Raaghava, this Lakshmana who was steadfast in truth, and this man of Dharma Bharatha who was most generous, shone like Three Holy Fires In A Sacrificial Ceremony.

(Note: Why is there no mention at all about the fourth brother Schathrugna? Commentators may study this.)

❍ ❍ ❍

Chapter 104

Raama- Bharatha Conversation

१. तं तु रामः समाश्वास्य भ्रातरं गुरुवत्सलम् ।
लक्ष्मणेन सह भ्रात्रा प्रष्टुं समुपचक्रमे ।।

4. Raama who was (ever) with his brother Lakshmana, then consoled his brother (Bharatha) who was devoted to elders: He began to question him. (Raama asks his brother Bharatha).

❍ ❍ ❍

२. किमेतदिच्छेयमहं श्रोतुं प्रव्याहृतं त्वया ।
यस्मात्त्वमागतो देशमिमं चीरजटाजिनी ।।

2. I desire to hear from you, to be told by you, as to why you have come to this place, dressed up in bark and deer skin (like a mendicant).

❍ ❍ ❍

३. यन्निमित्तमिमं देशं कृष्णाजिनजटाधरः ।
हित्वा राज्यं प्रविष्टस्त्वं तत्सर्वं वक्तुमर्हसि ।।

3. You must tell me all: Why you entered this place leaving the kingdom and wearing deer skin, sporting tufted hair locks.

❍ ❍ ❍

४. इत्युक्तः कैकयीपुत्रः काकुत्स्थेन महात्मना ।
प्रगृह्य बलवद्भूयः प्राञ्जलिर्वाक्यमब्रवीत् ।।

4. When told thus by the great soul (Raama) the Kaakuthsa, (Bharatha) the son of Kaikeyi, cupped his hands in Anjali, clasped (Raama's) feet even more forcefully, and said these words.

५. आर्यं तातः परित्यज्य कृत्वा कर्म सुदुष्करम् ।
गतः स्वर्गं महाबाहुः पुत्रशोकाभिपीडितः ।।

5. Our mighty limbed father, having done a deed that should never have been done, went to heaven, tormented by separation from his son (you, Raama), abandoning (you) the noble (Aryan).

❍ ❍ ❍

६. स्त्रिया नियुक्तः कैकेय्या मम मात्रा परन्तप ।
चकार सुमहत्पापमिदमात्मयशोहरम् ।।

6. Oh (Raama) the tormentor of enemies! Bound by my mother, this lady Kaikeyi, he committed this great sin which has destroyed his glory.

❍ ❍ ❍

७. सा राज्यफलमप्राप्य विधवा शोककर्शिता ।
पतिष्यति महाघोरे निरये जननी मम ।।

7. (But) this, my mother (Kaikeyi) who is a widow (now), is tormented by grief without obtaining the fruits of the kingdom (as I have refused the kingdom): She is going to fall into gruesome hell.

❍ ❍ ❍

८. तस्य मे दासभूतस्य प्रसादं कर्तुमर्हसि ।
अभिषिञ्चस्व चाद्यैव राज्येन मघवानिव ।।

8. As I am your humble servant (and devotee), you should do me this favour. Now Itself You Should Be Anointed (as king) In (our) Kingdom, like Indhra (the king of Celestial world).

❍ ❍ ❍

९. इमाः प्रकृतयः सर्वा विधवा मातरश्च याः ।
त्वत्सकाशमनुप्राप्ताः प्रसादं कर्तुमर्हसि ।।

9. You should do favour to all these citizens (of Ayodhya)

who have come here (with me) and also the mothers, (your mother and all the step mothers) who have become widows.

❍ ❍ ❍

१०. तदानुपूर्व्या युक्तं च युक्तं चात्मनि मानद ।
राज्यं प्राप्नुहि धर्मेण सकामान्सुहृदः कुरु ॥

10. Oh (Raama) who honours (one who beseeches you)! Therefore, as per Dharma, you must receive this kingdom (which is yours by right) and heredity and (whose citizens) are devoted to you. You should make your friends (and well wishers) obtain their wish (which is, that you should return to Ayodhya as king).

❍ ❍ ❍

११. भवत्वविधवा भूमिः समग्रा पतिना त्वया ।
शशिना विमलेनेव शारदी रजनी यथा ॥

11. Like autumn night (beautified) by the spotless moon, let the world become totally (brightened) without being "widowed", (ruled) by you, their lord.

❍ ❍ ❍

१२. एभिश्च सचिवैः सार्धं शिरसा याचितो मया ।
भ्रातुः शिष्यस्य दासस्य प्रसादं कर्तुमर्हसि ॥

12. Brother, servant and disciple as I am to you, you must favour me as I am begging you with my head down. (I am begging you) along with my ministers.

❍ ❍ ❍

१३. तदिदं शाश्वतं पित्र्यं सर्वं सचिवमण्डलम् ।
पूजितं पुरुषव्याघ्र नातिक्रमितुमर्हसि ॥

13. Oh (Raama) the 'tiger of men'! Therefore you should not neglect this eternal traditional (kingdom of ours). You should not also transgress the honoured ministers and all (the beloved citizens).

❍ ❍ ❍

१४. एवमुक्त्वा महाबाहुः सबाष्पः कैकयीसुतः ।
रामस्य शिरसा पादौ जग्राह भरतः पुनः ।।

14. With tears in his eyes, the mighty limbed Bharatha the son of Kaikeyi, having said thus (to Raama), once again fell at Raama's feet, touching it with his head.

❍ ❍ ❍

१५. तं मत्तमिव मातङ्गं निश्वसन्तं पुनः पुनः ।
भ्रातरं भरतं रामः परिष्वज्येदमब्रवीत् ।।

15. Raama hugged his brother Bharatha who was like a mad elephant, who was breathing hard and deep again and again: He said.

❍ ❍ ❍

१६. कुलीनः सत्त्वसंपन्नस्तेजस्वी चरितव्रतः ।
राज्यहेतोः कथं पापमाचरेत्त्वद्विधो जनः ।।

16. You are born in a noble family, endowed with divine qualities, most brilliant, steadfast in righteous conduct. Such a man like you, how will you (ever) commit transgression for the sake of (obtaining) the kingdom?

❍ ❍ ❍

१७. न दोषं त्वयि पश्यामि सूक्ष्ममप्यरिसूदन ।
न चापि जननीं बाल्यात्त्वं विगर्हितुमर्हसि ।।

17. Oh (Bharatha) the destroyer of enemies! I (cannot and) do not see in you any sin, even a trifle: (But) you also, out of your childishness, should not revile your mother (Kaikeyi).

❍ ❍ ❍

१८. कामकारो महाप्राज्ञ गुरूणां सर्वदाऽनघ ।
उपपन्नेषु दारेषु पुत्रेषु च विधीयते ।।

18. Oh sinless and most intelligent (Bharatha)! It is well established, that, at all times, there is (absolute right)

for fathers to do as they please over his sons or his own wives.

❍ ❍ ❍

१९. वयमस्य यथा लोके संख्याताः सौम्य साधुभिः ।
भार्याः पुत्राश्च शिष्याश्च त्वमनुज्ञातुमर्हसि ॥

19. Oh pleasant Bharatha)! In this world, all of us, sons, wives and disciples are counted upon by good men (and looked up to): Likewise, you also (must honour him), making allowances for him.

❍ ❍ ❍

२०. वने वा चीरवसनं सौम्य कृष्णाजिनाम्बरम् ।
राज्ये वाऽपि महाराजो मां वासयितुमीश्वरः ॥

20. Oh pleasant (Bharatha)! (Our father the) great king is our lord who can make me live in kingdom or make me live in forest wearing deer skin and bark (dress).

❍ ❍ ❍

२१. यावत्पितरि धर्मज्ञे गौरवं लोकसत्कृते ।
तावद्धर्मभृतां श्रेष्ठ जनन्यामपि गौरवम् ॥

21. Oh foremost (of men, Bharatha)! For those who are attached to Dharma, the honour and respect (as shown) by people of the world to our father the knower of Dharma, the same respect must be shown (by us) to our mothers (as well).

(You should not condemn your mother, says Raama to Bharatha.)

❍ ❍ ❍

२२. एताभ्यां धर्मशीलाभ्यां वनं गच्छेति राघव ।
मातापितृभ्यामुक्तोऽहं कथमन्यत्समाचरे ॥

22. Oh (Bharatha the) Raaghava 1 When I was told by these two, by my father and my (step) mother who

are devoted to Dharma = Go To Forest = how can I act otherwise?

❍ ❍ ❍

२३. त्वया राज्यमयोध्यायां प्राप्तव्यं लोकसत्कृतम् ।
वस्तव्यं दण्डकारण्ये मया वल्कलवाससा ॥

23. (Therefore) You should obtain (and rule) the kingdom honoured by the world, (living) in Ayodhya: And (as a mendicant) wearing bark dress in forest of Dhandaka, must I live ... (for 14 years).

❍ ❍ ❍

२४. एवं कृत्वा महाराजो विभागं लोकसन्निधौ ।
व्यादिश्य च महातेजा दिवं दशरथो गतः ॥

24. The most brilliant Dhascharatha the great king, having apportioned (such duties) to us in The Assembly of men, then went away to heaven, having ordered us thus.

❍ ❍ ❍

२५. स च प्रमाणं धर्मात्मा राजा लोकगुरुस्तव ।
पित्रा दत्तं यथा भागमुपभोक्तुं त्वमर्हसि ॥

25. This Lord of earth, this great soul king is your Standard (Your authority): The share (of duties assigned to you as king to rule Ayodhya) offered by our father...... that, you should (receive and) enjoy as such.

❍ ❍ ❍

२६. चतुर्दश समाः सौम्य दण्डकारण्यमाश्रितः ।
उपभोक्ष्ये त्वहं दत्तं भागं पित्रा महात्मना ॥

26. Oh pleasant (Bharatha): (and likewise) Accepting the share (of responsibility) given to me by the great soul father, I shall enjoy stay of Dhandaka forest for 14 years.

❍ ❍ ❍

२७. यदब्रवीन्मां नरलोकसत्कृतः
पिता महात्मा विबुधाधिपोपमः ।
तदेव मन्ये परमात्मनो हितं
न सर्वलोकेश्वरभावमप्यहम् ॥

27. I will consider only that as foremost good for me which the great soul father who is like Lord Indhra and who is honoured by men of the world, tells me (to do). I care not for the glory of being lord of all the world (if it is against the wishes of my father).

(Note: Raama is very clear: The King has absolute right. His father king Dhascharatha had ordered him to go on exile for 14 years. And Bharatha should rule over the kingdom instead. Question as to why and how, does not arise. These commands must be acted upon.)

❍ ❍ ❍

Chapter 105

Raama Affirms to Honour His Father's Command

(Yet another important chapter: Raama expounds the Dharma, the philosophy of Life. There is no question of his cutting short his exile.)

❍ ❍ ❍

१. ततः पुरुषसिंहानां वृतानां तैः सुहृद्गणैः ।
शोचतामेव रजनी दुःखेन व्यत्यवर्तत ॥

1. That night passed away in great sorrow (in Raama's hermitage) for these (brothers), the 'Tigers' of men who were all grieving, who were with friends.

❍ ❍ ❍

२. रजन्यां सुप्रभातायां भ्रातरस्ते सुहृद्वृताः ।
मन्दाकिन्यां हुतं जप्यं कृत्वा राममुपागमन् ॥

2. When night ended and day dawned, the brothers performed morning rituals and prayers in (river) Mandhaakini. They (then) assembled before Raama along with their friends.

❍ ❍ ❍

३. तूष्णीं ते समुपासीना न कश्चित्किञ्चिदब्रवीत् ।
भरतस्तु सुहृन्मध्ये रामं वचनमब्रवीत् ।।

3. And no one spoke anything at all: They all sat in silence. (But after sometime), Bharatha addressed Raama these words before their friends there.

❍ ❍ ❍

४. सान्त्विता मामिका माता दत्तं राज्यमिदं मम ।
तद्ददामि तवैवाहं भुङ्क्ष्व राज्यमकण्टकम् ।।

4. (Bharatha uses a different strategy to coax Raama to return to Ayodhya with him, cutting short his exile: He says).

My mother (Kaikeyi) is consoled (is reconciled to the situation). This kingdom was offered to me (as per her wish): (But by my right) I am giving you (back my kingdom)! (Therefore) Enjoy this kingdom without hindrance.

❍ ❍ ❍

५. महतेवाम्बुवेगेन भिन्नः सेतुर्जलागमे ।
दुरावारं त्वदन्येन राज्यखण्डमिदं महत् ।।

5. No one else than you can restrain (and take control over) this mighty country which is (at the moment) like a breached dam hit by mighty flood of waters during rainy season.

❍ ❍ ❍

६. गतिं खर इवाश्वस्य तार्क्ष्यस्येव पतत्रिणः ।
अनुगन्तुं न शक्तिर्मेगतिं तव महीपते ।।

6. Oh (Raama) the Lord of earth! Like a donkey (trying to emulate) a horse in strides: Like an ordinary bird (trying to emulate) a garuda bird in flying (power): I am not worthy enough to follow (emulate) you.

❍ ❍ ❍

७. सुजीवं नित्यशस्तस्य यः परैरुपजीव्यते ।
राम तस्य तु दुर्जीवं यः परानुपजीवति ।।

7. Oh Raama! When one is sustained by elders there will be eternal good life for him; And he who (goes after) and sustains ordinary man it will be a miserable life for him.

(It will be miserable for every citizen if they are 'protected' by me; but with you, sustaining and protecting him, it will be excellent life for him and for every citizen.)

❍ ❍ ❍

८. यथा चारोपितो वृक्षः पुरुषेण विवर्धितः ।
ह्रस्वकेन दुरारोहो रूढस्कन्धो महाद्रुमः ।।

8. Just like a sapling planted by a man which, when grows up into a tall tree with strong stem, cannot be climbed by a short (midget of a) man ......

❍ ❍ ❍

९. स यथा पुष्पितो भूत्वा फलानि न विदर्शयेत् ।
स तां नानुभवेत्प्रीतिं यस्य हेतोः प्ररोपितः ।।

9. ...... Like one having grown a big tree and having seen it blossom with flowers but without yielding fruits for which purpose this was grown by him, denying him that pleasure (of fruits) ......

❍ ❍ ❍

१०. एषोपगा महाबाहो तमर्थं वेत्तुमर्हसि ।
यदि त्वमस्मान्वृषभो भर्ता भृत्यान्न शाधि हि ।।

10. ...... Such is the comparison (in this case by your action of giving up the kingdom). Oh mighty limbed (Raama) You are 'Bull amongst men' You do not realise the consequences (of your action), if you, as Lord, do not protect us who are your subjects.

(I cannot climb a tall tree, midget as I am; Nor know how to get fruits from that tree. Only you, Oh Raama can do this, says Bharatha, poetically)

❍ ❍ ❍

११. श्रेणयस्त्वां महाराज पश्यन्त्वग्र्याश्च सर्वशः ।
प्रतपन्तमिवादित्यं राज्यस्थितमरिन्दमम् ॥

11. Oh (Raama) the great king! May all the foremost citizens see you as destroyer of enemies, firmly established in the kingdom (as their ruler) and (looking) like the burning sun.

❍ ❍ ❍

१२. तवानुयाने काकुत्स्थ मत्ता नर्दन्तु कुञ्जराः ।
अन्तःपुरगता नार्योनन्दन्तु सुसमाहिताः ॥

12. Oh (Raama) the Kaakuthsa! May exhilarated elephants that follow you, roar (and rejoice): Let ladies of the royal household rejoice, fully pleased.

❍ ❍ ❍

१३. तस्य साध्वित्यमन्यन्त नागरा विविधा जनाः ।
भरतस्य वचः श्रुत्वा रामं प्रत्यनुयाचतः ॥

13. The various citizens hearing this Bharatha's words and pleadings before Raama, approved (& rejoiced saying) = Excellent =

❍ ❍ ❍

१४. तमेवं दुःखितं प्रेक्ष्य विलपन्तं यशस्विनम् ।
रामः कृतात्मा भरतं समाश्वासयदात्मवान् ॥

14. The pure soul and composed Raama, seeing this famous Bharatha wailing thus and in deep distress, consoled him.

❍ ❍ ❍

१५. नात्मनः कामकारोऽस्ति पुरुषोऽयमनीश्वरः ।
इतश्चेतरतश्चैनं कृतान्तः परिकर्षति ।।

15. (Raama consoles Bharatha: Expounds philosophy of life.)

Things don't happen as per his wish for (any) man: Man is not God: Fate Drags Him Here and There.

❍ ❍ ❍

१६. सर्वेक्षयान्ता निचयाः पतनान्ताः समुच्छ्रयाः ।
संयोगा विप्रयोगान्ता मरणान्तं च जीवितम् ।।

16. All acquisitions perish; All lofty positions fall down finally; All associations are terminated (eventually: Life itself ends in Death.

❍ ❍ ❍

१७. यथा फलानां पक्वानां नान्यत्र पतनाद्भयम् ।
एवं नरस्य जातस्य नान्यत्र मरणाद्भयम् ।।

17. There is no fear for a ripe fruit than its (decay and) fall. Likewise, for a man born, there is no fear other than death.

❍ ❍ ❍

१८. यथागारं दृढस्थूणं जीर्णं भूत्वाऽवसीदति ।
तथैव सीदन्ति नरा जरामृत्युवशं गताः ।।

18. Even a house supported by strong columns sinks down becoming old; likewise, men afflicted by old age and 'death', perish.

❍ ❍ ❍

१९. अत्येति रजनी या तु सा न प्रतिनिवर्तते ।
यात्येव यमुना पूर्णा समुद्रमुदकाकुलम् ।।

19. This night that passes away, never comes back; (The waters) of the full (flowing) Jamuna river, goes to ocean, the abode of waters.

❍ ❍ ❍

२०. अहोरात्राणि गच्छन्ति सर्वेषां प्राणिनामिह ।
आयूंषि क्षपयन्त्याशु ग्रीष्मे जलमिवांशवः ।।

20. In this world. the lives of all living beings diminish, like the rays of the sun that wanders day and night (drying up) waters in summer.

❍ ❍ ❍

२१. आत्मानमनुशोच त्वं किमन्यमनुशोचसि ।
आयुस्ते हीयते नित्यं स्थितस्य च गतस्य च ।।

21. Your life is diminishing; You think about Aathma (Soul and the ultimate Reality). Why do you worry about another person, about men here or about men gone away?

❍ ❍ ❍

२२. सहैव मृत्युर्व्रजति सह मृत्युर्निषीदति ।
गत्वा सुदीर्घमध्वानं सह मृत्युर्निवर्तते ।।

22. Death Always Comes Along With You! Death Lives By Your Side! Death May Go Far Away, But Is Always Back!

(Yaama the lord of death is The Dharma Raja- King of Dharma-Lord of Time: And "Death" never takes a holiday!)

❍ ❍ ❍

२३. गात्रेषु वलयः प्राप्ताः श्वेताश्चैव शिरोरुहाः ।
जरया पुरुषो जीर्णः किं हि कृत्वा प्रभावयेत् ।।

23. Wrinkles have appeared in body; Hairs have turned white; What can a man withered by old age do to control (all this).

❍ ❍ ❍

२४. नन्दन्त्युदित आदित्ये नन्दन्त्यस्तमिते रवौ ।
आत्मनो नावबुध्यन्ते मनुष्या जीवितक्षयम् ।।

24. Men rejoice when sun rises: They rejoice when sun sets. (But) they do not (seem to) realise their own life is waning.

❍ ❍ ❍

२५. हृष्यन्त्यृतुमुखं दृष्ट्वा नवं नवमिहागतम् ।
ऋतूनां परिवर्तेन प्राणिनां प्राणसंक्षयः ।।

25. In this world, seeing every new season arriving, they rejoice; (But) Change of season causes reduction of the lives of living beings

(Time ever flows; man cannot control time.)

❍ ❍ ❍

२६. यथा काष्ठं च काष्ठं च समेयातां महार्णवे ।
समेत्य च व्यपेयातां कालमासाद्य कंचन ।।

२७. एवं भार्याश्च पुत्राश्च ज्ञातयश्च वसूनि च ।
समेत्य व्यवधावन्ति ध्रुवो ह्येषां विनाभवः ।।

26. & 27.

In the Ocean, two logs of wood get together: After (floating) together for a while, they get separated: Likewise... wives, sons, relatives, property (and wealth) are enjoined and get separated. Their separation is certain.

❍ ❍ ❍

२८. नात्र कश्चिद्यथाभावं प्राणी समभिवर्तते ।
तेन तस्मिन्न सामर्थ्यं प्रेतस्यास्त्यनुशोचतः ।।

28. In this world, no living being can change Destiny: Therefore no purpose is served by grieving over the dead.

❍ ❍ ❍

२९. यथा हि सार्थं गच्छन्तं ब्रूयात्कश्चित्पथि स्थितः ।
अहमप्यागमिष्यामि पृष्ठतो भवतामिति ।।
३०. एवं पूर्वैर्गतो मार्गः पितृपैतामहो ध्रुवः ।
तमापन्नः कथं शोचेद्यस्य नास्ति व्यतिक्रमः ।।

29. & 30.

Just as a man standing on way side, who, when he has seen a caravan moving along, says; = I am also coming along with you = ...

likewise, the traditional Path followed by forefathers is eternal (and to be followed): How can one come to grief if he follows that which cannot be transgressed.

(Caravan always takes you on the right path and to destination.)

❍ ❍ ❍

३१. वयसः पतमानस्य स्रोतसो वाऽनिवर्तिनः ।
आत्मा सुखे नियोक्तव्यः सुखभाजः प्रजा स्मृताः ।।

31. As our life is 'flowing' away like flow of waters that do not return, (it is) Soul that should be directed to (with our mind) in (bliss and) happiness.. It is said (such) people venerate (and seek only eternal) happiness.

❍ ❍ ❍

३२. धर्मात्मा स शुभैः कृत्स्नैः क्रतुभिश्चाप्तदक्षिणैः ।
धूतपापो गतः स्वर्गं पिता नः पृथिवीपतिः ।।

32. The noble soul man of Dharma, our father (Dhascharatha) the lord of earth, having performed all auspicious sacrificial ceremonies with plenty of gifts, has gone away to heaven rid of his sins.

❍ ❍ ❍

३३. भृत्यानां भरणात्सम्यक्प्रजानां परिपालनात् ।
अर्थदानाच्च धर्मेण पिता नस्त्रिदिवं गतः ।।

33. Our father, by nourishing his dependents well, by ruling over his citizens (well), by offering charities, gifts, has gone to heaven as per norms of Dharma.

❍ ❍ ❍

३४. कर्मभिस्सुशुभैरिष्टैः क्रतुभिश्चाप्तदक्षिणैः ।
स्वर्गं दशरथः प्राप्तः पिता नः पृथिवीपतिः ।।

34. Our father king Dhascharatha the lord of earth, has gone to heaven by performing sacrificial ceremonies with plenty of gifts and by auspicious good deeds.

❍ ❍ ❍

३५. इष्ट्वा बहुविधैर्यज्ञैर्भोगांश्चावाप्य पुष्कलान् ।
उत्तमं चायुरासाद्य स्वर्गतः पृथिवीपतिः ।।

35. Having performed many Yaaga-s, having obtained numerous comforts and pleasures and having attained long life, has gone to heaven.

❍ ❍ ❍

३६. आयुरुत्तममासाद्य भोगानपि च राघवः ।
स न शोच्यः पिता तात स्वर्गतः सत्कृतः सताम् ।।

36. Oh Lad (Bharatha)! Our father the Raaghava, having attained long years of life and also pleasures (of life), is now honoured by the Good (celestials) living in heaven. Therefore he should not be grieved over (by us all).

❍ ❍ ❍

३७. स जीर्णं मानुषं देहं परित्यज्य पिता हि नः ।
दैवीं वृत्तिमनुप्राप्तो ब्रह्मलोकविहारिणीम् ।।

37. Our father, having discarded the decaying human body, is delighting himself in the Bramma world and had obtained the status of divinity, Indeed!

❍ ❍ ❍

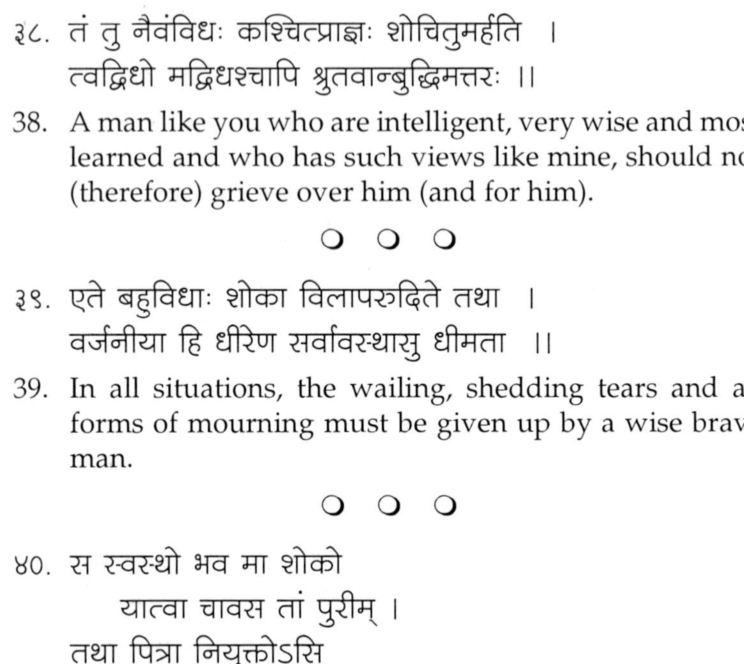

३८. तं तु नैवंविधः कश्चित्प्राज्ञः शोचितुमर्हति ।
त्वद्विधो मद्विधश्चापि श्रुतवान्बुद्धिमत्तरः ॥

38. A man like you who are intelligent, very wise and most learned and who has such views like mine, should not (therefore) grieve over him (and for him).

❍ ❍ ❍

३९. एते बहुविधाः शोका विलापरुदिते तथा ।
वर्जनीया हि धीरेण सर्वावस्थासु धीमता ॥

39. In all situations, the wailing, shedding tears and all forms of mourning must be given up by a wise brave man.

❍ ❍ ❍

४०. स स्वस्थो भव मा शोको
यात्वा चावस तां पुरीम् ।
तथा पित्रा नियुक्तोऽसि
वशिना वदतां वर ॥

40. Oh (Bharatha) the foremost man of speech! You must go to that city (of ours, Ayodhya) and live there. (Remember) You are so commanded by our father, the lord of the world. Give up grief. Be composed. (be at peace with yourself).

❍ ❍ ❍

४१. यत्राहमपि तेनैव नियुक्तः पुण्यकर्मणा ।
तत्रैवाहं करिष्यामि पितुरार्यस्य शासनम् ॥

41. (And likewise) I will also act upon the noble father's command exactly as I was commanded by this virtuous man.

❍ ❍ ❍

४२. न मया शासनं तस्य त्यक्तुं न्याय्यमरिंदम ।
तत्त्वयाऽपि सदा मान्यः स वै बन्धुः स नः पिता ॥

42. Oh (Bharatha) the destroyer of enemies! He is our honoured father; He is our (closest) kinsman; It will therefore be not proper to abandon (transgress) his command at all times, either by you or by me.

❍ ❍ ❍

४३. तद्वचः पितुरेवाहं सम्मतं धर्मचारिणः ।
कर्मणा पालयिष्यामि वनवासेन राघव ॥

43. Oh (Bharatha)! Those words (of command) that are 'esteemed' by my father the follower of Dharma, I will fulfill by (this) deed of life in forest (for 14 years).

❍ ❍ ❍

४४. धार्मिकेणानृशंसेन नरेण गुरुवर्तिना ।
भवितव्यं नरव्याघ्र परलोकं जिगीषता ॥

44. Oh (Bharatha) 'the tiger of men'! A man who is desirous of heaven, must be a man of Dharma, a man of Non Injury, and he must respect elders.

❍ ❍ ❍

४५. आत्मानमनुतिष्ठ त्वं स्वभावेन नरर्षभ ।
निशाम्य तु शुभं वृत्तं पितुर्दशरथस्य नः ॥

45. Oh (Bharatha) the 'Bull' amongst men! Perceiving (and following) the noble conduct (the auspicious conduct) of our (late) father Dhascharatha, you also abide by your own natural behaviour.

❍ ❍ ❍

४६. इत्येवमुक्त्वा वचनं महात्मा
पितुर्निर्देशप्रतिपालनार्थम् ।
यवीयसं भ्रातरमर्थवच्च
प्रभुर्मुहूर्ताद्विरराम रामः ॥

46. After saying such meaningful words to his younger brother (Bharatha) all for the sake of honouring the

command of their father, the great soul Lord Raama became silent for one full muhoortha

❍ ❍ ❍

Chapter 106

Bharatha Begs Raama to Take Over Kingdom

१. एवमुक्त्वा तु विरते रामे वचनमर्थवत् ।
ततो मन्दाकिनीतीरे रामं प्रकृतिवत्सलम् ।।
उवाच भरतश्चित्रं धार्मिको धार्मिकं वचः ।।

1. When Raama rested after saying such meaningful words, Bharatha, the man of Dharma addressed (Raama) the man of Dharma who was most devoted to people, with these distinguished words, on the banks of river Mandhaakini.

❍ ❍ ❍

२. को हि स्यादीदृशो लोके यादृशस्त्वमरिंदम ।
न त्वां प्रव्यथयेद्दुःखं प्रीतिर्वा न प्रहर्षयेत् ।।

2. Oh Raama the) destroyer of enemies: Such a man as you are, who can be like you in this world? Sorrow will not agitate you; Nor pleasures exult you.

❍ ❍ ❍

३. सम्मतश्चासि वृद्धानां तांश्च पृच्छसि संशयान् ।।

3. You are honoured by (and are equal to) elders: (Yet) you ask them doubts (as though you know not!)

❍ ❍ ❍

४. यथा मृतस्तथा जीवन्यथाऽसति तथा सति ।
यस्यैष बुद्धिलाभः स्यात्परितप्येत केन सः ।।

4. How will a man (like you) be in torment when he has such a perception of mind in considering 'Being' as

'Un-Being' (And treating) Living as being Non Living (dead)

❍ ❍ ❍

५. परावरज्ञो यश्च स्याद्यथा त्वं मनुजाधिप ।
स एवं व्यसनं प्राप्य न विषीदितुमर्हति ।।

5. Oh (Raama) the king of men ! If a man is like you knowing Cause and Effect* (in life), he will not grieve (even) when such misfortunes hit him. (* For the word -Paraavara- we have used Cause-Effect).

❍ ❍ ❍

६. अमरोपमसत्त्वस्त्वं महात्मा सत्यसङ्गरः ।
सर्वज्ञः सर्वदर्शी च बुद्धिमांश्चासि राघव ।।

6. Oh (Raama) the Raaghava! You possess qualities of a celestial: You are a great soul; Most truthful, a wise man who knows All and who can "See" All.

❍ ❍ ❍

७. न त्वामेवं गुणैर्युक्तं प्रभावभवकोविदम् ।
अविषह्यतमं दुःखमासादयितुमर्हति ।।

7. Possessing such noble qualities and most learned in understanding the very creation (of Life) you should not meet with such unbearable suffering.

❍ ❍ ❍

८. एवमुक्त्वा तु भरतो रामं पुनरथाब्रवीत् ।।

8. Saying thus to Raama, Bharatha said further (thus)

❍ ❍ ❍

९. प्रोषिते मयि यत्पापं मात्रा मत्कारणात्कृतम् ।
क्षुद्रया तदनिष्टं मे प्रसीदतु भवान्मम ।।

9. You must favour me (by undoing) the most despicable sin committed by my avaricious mother for my sake

when I was away (from Ayodhya on holiday at my maternal uncle's place)

❍ ❍ ❍

१०. धर्मबन्धेन बद्धोऽस्मि तेनेमां नेह मातरम् ।
हन्मि तीव्रेण दण्डेन दण्डार्हां पापकारिणीम् ।।

10. I am bound by bond of Dharma: That is why I do not kill this evil mongering mother of mine who deserves the cruel punishment of death.

❍ ❍ ❍

११. कथं दशरथाज्जातः शुद्धाभिजनकर्मणः ।
जानन्धर्ममधर्मिष्ठं कुर्यां कर्म जुगुप्सितम् ।।

11. How can I, born as son of Dhacharatha who is (descendent of) the righteous forefathers of (great) deeds and accomplishments, do disgusting immoral acts when I know (what) Dharma (is).

❍ ❍ ❍

१२. गुरुः क्रियावान्वृद्धश्च राजा प्रेतः पितेति च ।
तातं न परिगर्हेयं दैवतं चेति संसदि ।।

12. Our father is teacher: An elder: Has done many ceremonies. Is (now) dead; Has become a 'Deity'. (Because of all) these (reasons), I did not censure my father in The Assembly.

❍ ❍ ❍

१३. को हि धर्मार्थयोर्हीनमीदृशं कर्म किल्बिषम् ।
स्त्रियाः प्रियं चिकीर्षुः सन् कुर्याद्धर्मज्ञ धर्मवित् ।।

13. Oh (Raama) the knower of Dharma! How can a man knowing Dharma commit such an evil deed which is against norms of Dharma and Artha, desirous of fulfilling the pleasures of a woman.

❍ ❍ ❍

१४. अन्तकाले हि भूतानि मुह्यन्तीति पुराश्रुतिः ।
राज्ञैवं कुर्वता लोके प्रत्यक्षं सा श्रुतिः कृता ।।

14. There is an old saying: = Living Beings Become Stupefied When Their End Is near = This saying has been made to manifest itself in (the eyes of) the world by (our father) the king who acted in this way.

(There is yet another saying similar to this: = Vinaascha Kaalay Vipareetha Bhudhi = meaning, the first casualty for a 'sinking' person is his sanity, and straight and clean thinking:)

❍ ❍ ❍

१५. साध्वर्थमभिसन्धाय क्रोधान्मोहाच्च साहसात् ।
तातस्य यदतिक्रान्तं प्रत्याहरतु तद्भवान् ।।

15. (Taking note of and) Viewing well the consequence of father's transgression which might have been due to anger, impulse or passion, you must restore (justice and retrieve the situation).

❍ ❍ ❍

१६. पितुर्हि समतिक्रान्तं पुत्रो यः साधु मन्यते ।
तुपत्यं मतं लोके विपरीतमतोऽन्यथा ।।

16. A son who truly considers (setting right) father's transgression, only he is esteemed as a good man in this world. If otherwise, it is perverse.

(Allow me to undo the injustice to you, Oh Raama by giving this kingdom back to you, says Bharatha.)

❍ ❍ ❍

१७. तदपत्यं भवानस्तु मा भवान्दुष्कृतं पितुः ।
अभिपत्ता कृतं कर्म लोके धीर विगर्हितम् ।।

17. Therefore you must be a true son: Oh resolute (Raama): You should not gloat over the evil action of father that is despised in the world..

❍ ❍ ❍

१८. कैकेयीं मां च तातं च सुहृदो बान्धवांश्च नः ।
पौरजानपदानेतांस्त्रातु सर्वमिदं भवान् ।।

18. You must save (and protect) us all: the people of villages, cities, relatives, our (late) father, Kaikeyi, and me (from ignominy).

❍ ❍ ❍

१९. क्व चारण्यं क्व च क्षात्रं क्व जटाः क्व च पालनम् ।
ईदृशं व्याहतं कर्म न भवान्कर्तुमर्हति ।।

19. Where is Forest and where is Kshathriya (life)! Where is matted hair (of a mendicant) and where is rule (of kingdom): You should not indulge in topsy turvy actions.(You are of Royalty, remember).

❍ ❍ ❍

२०. एष हि प्रथमो धर्मः क्षत्रियस्याभिषेचनम् ।
येन शक्यं महाप्राज्ञ प्रजानां परिपालनम् ।।

20. Oh most intelligent (Raama)! It is but proper to anoint (yourself as king now): Because, ruling over people is The First and Foremost Dharma of a Kshathriya.

❍ ❍ ❍

२१. कश्च प्रत्यक्षमुत्सृज्य संशयस्थमलक्षणम् ।
आयतिस्थं चरेद्धर्मं क्षत्रबन्धुरनिश्चितम् ।।

21. Casting aside the (accepted and) visible Dharma, will any one born in a royal (Kshathriya) family, follow doubtful, inauspicious, uncertain path. (that may or may not bring good) in the long run.

❍ ❍ ❍

२२. अथ क्लेशजमेव त्वं धर्मं चरितुमिच्छसि ।
धर्मेण चतुरो वर्णान्पालयन्क्लेशमाप्नुहि ।।

22. If, on the other hand, you desire to follow The path of Dharma through (mortification of body and) suffering,

then you may obtain that suffering by protecting and ruling over the (men of) four castes through Dharma.

(Bharatha tells Raama that ruling of a mighty kingdom is also suffering, as much if not more than the suffering of forest life)

❍ ❍ ❍

२३. चतुर्णामाश्रमाणां हि गार्हस्थ्यं श्रेष्ठमाश्रमम् ।
प्राहुर्धर्मज्ञ धर्मज्ञास्तं कथं त्यक्तुमर्हसि ॥

23. Oh (Raama) the knower of Dharma! Men knowing Dharma acclaim that amongst the four stages of life, life as a man of family is foremost. Therefore how can you abandon this (life of a man of Royal family).

(The four Stages of Man: Boyhood & studentship: Married life-family life: Finally renunciation, retirement and spiritual life.)

❍ ❍ ❍

२४. श्रुतेन बालः स्थानेन जन्मना भवतो ह्यहम् ।
स कथं पालयिष्यामि भूमिं भवति तिष्ठति ॥

24. I am younger to you in age, learning: Therefore when you are there, how can I rule over the kingdom. (in your place).

❍ ❍ ❍

२५. हीनबुद्धिगुणो बालो हीनः स्थानेन चाप्यहम् ।
भवता च विनाभूतो न वर्तयितुमुत्सहे ॥

25. Young, without status, without wisdom and qualities, (such as I am), without you, I cannot bear to live on.

❍ ❍ ❍

२६. इदं निखिलमव्यग्रं पित्र्यं राज्यमकण्टकम् ।
अनुशाधि स्वधर्मेण धर्मज्ञ सह बान्धवैः ॥

26. Oh (Raama) the knower of Dharma! You must rule over the entire kingdom of our father which is free

(from danger at the moment), along with your relatives(and brothers), unhindered. (And rule) as per your (Kshathriya) Dharma.

❍ ❍ ❍

२७. इहैव त्वाऽभिषिञ्चन्तु सर्वाः प्रकृतयः सह ।
ऋत्विजः सवसिष्ठश्च मन्त्रवन्मन्त्रकोविदाः ॥

27: Let all citizens (gathered here) along with Vasishta who is master of Rituals and Prayers, and along with Rithviks, anoint you here itself now, as per norms.

(That is why Bharatha brought the large Army and VIP-s from Ayodhya to the forest, to crown Raama befittingly, in forest.)

❍ ❍ ❍

२८. अभिषिक्तस्त्वमस्माभिरयोध्यां पालने व्रज ।
विजित्य तरसा लोकान्मरुद्भिरिव वासवः ॥

28. Like Vaasava (Lord Indhra) before Maruths, assisted by us, you go back to Ayodhya to rule there, conquering the worlds by your vitality (and strength).

❍ ❍ ❍

२९. ऋणानि त्रीण्यपाकुर्वन्दुर्हृदः साधु निर्दहन् ।
सुहृदस्तर्पयन्कामैस्त्वमेवात्रानुशाधि माम् ॥

29. Discharging the three 'Debts' (the debts to Deities, Rishi-s and forefathers), and burning away evil doers, pleasing the good folks with all the desirables, you command me here itself (as to what I should do now).

❍ ❍ ❍

३०. अद्यार्य मुदिताः सन्तु सुहृदस्तेऽभिषेचने ।
अद्य भीताः पलायन्तां दुर्हृदस्ते दिशो दश ॥

30. Oh (Raama) the noble (Aryan)! Let the good folks

become happy now by your coronation. Let bad folks run away in all the ten directions in fear of you.

❍ ❍ ❍

३१. आक्रोशं मम मातुश्च प्रमृज्य पुरुषर्षभ ।
अद्य तत्रभवन्तं च पितरं रक्ष किल्बिषात् ॥

31. Oh (Raama) the 'Bull' amongst men! Wiping off the stain of abuses upon my mother, at least now you save your father from sin.

❍ ❍ ❍

३२. शिरसा त्वाऽभियाचेऽहं कुरुष्व करुणां मयि ।
बान्धवेषु च सर्वेषु भूतेष्विव महेश्वरः ॥

32. I am bowing to you with my head: Like God (Maheschwara) towards all the living beings who are devoted, may you show your compassion upon me (by coming back with me to Ayodhya to rule).

❍ ❍ ❍

३३. अथवा पृष्ठतः कृत्वा वनमेव भवानितः ।
गमिष्यति गमिष्यामि भवता सार्धमप्यहम् ॥

33. If you stand firm and go back to forest only, I will also go along with you.

❍ ❍ ❍

३४. तथा हि रामो भरतेन ताम्यता
प्रसाद्यमानः शिरसा महीपतिः ।
न चैव चक्रे गमनाय सत्त्ववा
न्मतिं पितुस्तद्वचने व्यवस्थितः ॥

34. In spite of being rendered gracious thus by the distressed Bharatha with his head (bowed), the lord of Earth, Raama who was endowed with noble qualities had no intention of going back (to Ayodhya nor crown himself as king): He was standing firm by the words (of command) of his father (king Dhascharatha)

❍ ❍ ❍

३५. तदद्भुतं स्थैर्यमवेक्ष्य राघवे
समं जनो हर्षमवाप दुःखितः ।
न यात्ययोध्यामिति दुःखितोऽभव
त्स्थिरप्रतिज्ञत्वमवेक्ष्य हर्षितः ॥

35. At that moment, the citizens attained (a state of mingled feelings of) sorrow and joy towards (Raama) the Raaghava. They were distressed he was not coming back to Ayodhya: They were joyous noticing his wonderful steadfastness in being faithful to his promise.

❍ ❍ ❍

३६. तमृत्विजो नैगमयूथवल्लभा
स्तथा विसंज्ञाश्रुकलाश्च मातरः ।
तथा ब्रुवाणं भरतं च तुष्टुवुः
प्रणम्य रामं च ययाचिरे सह ॥

36. The Rithviks, the leading citizens, and the mothers shed copious tears, losing their composure. They extolled Bharatha who had spoken (to Raama) thus, bowing before him with his head (down). And they also begged Raama (to return with them to Ayodhya as king).

❍ ❍ ❍

Chapter 107

(Bharatha) Commanded by Raama to Rule Kingdom

१. पुनरेवं ब्रुवाणं तु भरतं लक्ष्मणाग्रजः ।
प्रत्युवाच ततः श्रीमान् ज्ञातिमध्येऽभिसत्कृतः ॥

1. Then the resplendent (Raama) the brother of Lakshmana who was honoured (thus) before his folks, replied to Bharatha who was again and again saying thus (begging him to return).

❍ ❍ ❍

२. उपपन्नमिदं वाक्यं यत्त्वमेवमभाषथाः ।
जातः पुत्रो दशरथात्कैकेय्यां राजसत्तमात् ॥

2. Son as you are, born to Dhascharatha the most noble king and to Kaikeyi, this speech and what all you said, is indeed adequate!

❍ ❍ ❍

३. पुरा भ्रातः पिता नः स मातरं ते समुद्वहम् ।
मातामहे समाश्रौषीद्राज्यशुल्कमनुत्तमम् ॥

3. (Raama says, Enough is enough: Wont come back. Will complete his 14 years Exile. And Bharatha must rule for 14 years).

Oh Brother! This, our father, after he had married your mother, has heard your maternal grandfather saying about the benefits (one derives as a king) in kingdom, as being foremost and incomparable, long ago.

❍ ❍ ❍

४. दैवासुरे च संग्रामे जनन्यै तव पार्थिवः ।
संप्रहृष्टो ददौ राजा वरमाराधितः प्रभुः ॥

4. (Our) Lord, the lord of earth and king (your father) had given Boons to your mother in great joy during a war between Dheva-s and Asura-s, being honoured (by the service rendered by your mother).

❍ ❍ ❍

५. ततः सा संप्रतिश्राव्य तव माता यशस्विनी ।
अयाचत नरव्याघ्रं द्वौ वरौ वरवर्णिनी ॥

5. Your famous and beautiful mother, having received this promise (of Boons) asked (our father) 'the tiger of men'…two boons ......

❍ ❍ ❍

६. तव राज्यं नरव्याघ्र मम प्रव्राजनं तथा ।
तौ च राजा तथा तस्यै नियुक्तः प्रददौ वरौ ॥

6. ...... (Namely) Kingship for you and exile for me. Oh 'Tiger of men' (Bharatha)! The king (our father), being bound thus, gave her these two boons ....

❍ ❍ ❍

७. तेन पित्राऽहमप्यत्र नियुक्तः पुरुषर्षभ ।
चतुर्दश वने वासं वर्षाणि वरदानिकम् ।।

7. Oh (Bharatha) the 'Bull' amongst men! By this offer of boons, this 14 years of life in forest for me, was ordered by (our) father.

❍ ❍ ❍

८. सोऽहं वनमिदं प्राप्तो निर्जनं लक्ष्मणान्वितः ।
सीतया चाप्रतिद्वन्द्वस्तस्य वाक्ये स्थितः पितुः ।।

8. Such as I am, firmly bound by this command of father, reached this uninhabited forest along with Lakshmana and Seetha without opposition and resistance (to the order).

❍ ❍ ❍

९. भवानपि तथेत्येव पितरं सत्यवादिनम् ।
कर्तुमर्हति राजेन्द्रं क्षिप्रमेवाभिषेचनात् ।।

9. And you too should say: = I will Do Like Wise = and at once crown yourself. Then only you can make your father, the king, a man of truth.

(Both of us are equally bound to obey our father's command, although the 'substance' of the command is different.)

❍ ❍ ❍

१०. ऋणान्मोचय राजानं मत्कृते भरत प्रभुम् ।।

10. Oh Bharatha! For my sake (please) release (and discharge) our Lord the king, from his debt (of fulfilling the two boons he had given your mother).

❍ ❍ ❍

११. पितरं चापि धर्मज्ञं मातरं चाभिनन्दय ॥

11. And make your (late) father the knower of Dharma and your mother, rejoice.

❍ ❍ ❍

१२. श्रूयते हि पुरा तात श्रुतिर्गीता यशस्विना ।
गयेन यजमानेन गयेष्वेव पितृन्प्रति ॥

12. O lad! Long ago a doctrine (a Schruthi) was pronounced by the famous Gaya who performed (Shraadha) ceremonies for his forefathers, at Gaya. This (Doctrine) became famous.

(Readers may note that the holy city Gaya in NE India is named after this Gaya. Indians from all over India do Rituals for their forefathers even now; at least -try to- do once in their lifetime.)

❍ ❍ ❍

१३. पुंनाम्नो नरकाद्यस्मात्पितरं त्रायते सुतः ।
तस्मात्पुत्र इति प्रोक्तः पितृन्यत्पाति वा सुतः ॥

13. (Raama tells about 'The Gaya Doctrine" to Bharatha.)

A man resurrects his father from hell called =Puth= (the pit); Thus the son protects and saves the forefathers: that is how he is called The Puthra (the Son who saves from pit of sins).

❍ ❍ ❍

१४. एष्टव्या बहवः पुत्रा गुणवन्तो बहुश्रुताः ।
तेषां वै समवेतानामपि कश्चिद्गयां व्रजेत् ॥

14. Many sons who are well versed in (Schruthi-s) and endowed with noble qualities are to be cherished. And from amongst them, at least one of them should go to Gaya (to perform Shraadha for forefathers).

❍ ❍ ❍

१५. एवं राजर्षयः सर्वेप्रतीता राजनन्दन ।
तस्मात्त्राहि नरश्रेष्ठ पितरं नरकात्प्रभो ॥

15. (Oh Bharatha) The darling of the lord of kings! The royal sages, all of them have acknowledged this, Oh foremost of men! Therefore you save our (late) father from hell.

(Raama wants Bharatha do all rituals for his father as per norms, including Shraadha at Gaya.)

❍ ❍ ❍

१६. अयोध्यां गच्छ भरत प्रकृतीरनुरञ्जय ।
शत्रुघ्नसहितो वीर सह सर्वैर्द्विजातिभिः ॥

16. Oh brave Bharatha. You go back to Ayodhya along with Braamins and* all others. Along with Schathrugna you make citizens rejoice there.

(*The word used by poet is Dvija= Twice born= Normally, Braamin,Kshathriya and Vyschya are the twice born castes.)

❍ ❍ ❍

१७. प्रवेक्ष्ये दण्डकारण्यमहमप्यविलम्बयन् ।
आभ्यां तु सहितो राजन्वैदेह्या लक्ष्मणेन च ॥

17. Oh King (Bharatha)! Without delay, along with this (Seetha the) Vaidhehi and along with Lakshmana, I too will enter Dhandaka forest.

❍ ❍ ❍

१८. त्वं राजा भव भरत स्वयं नराणां
वन्यानामहमपि राजराण्मृगाणाम् ।
गच्छ त्वं पुरवरमद्य संप्रहृष्टः
संहृष्टस्त्वहमपि दण्डकान्प्रवेक्ष्ये ॥

18. Oh Bharatha! You go back to the foremost city of Ayodhya happily: You yourself be King for these

citizens; And I also with joy will enter Dhandaka forest. I will be the king of animals of forest!

❍ ❍ ❍

१९. छायां ते दिनकरभाः प्रबाधमानां
वर्षत्रं भरत करोतु मूर्ध्नि शीताम् ।
एतेषामहमपि काननद्रुमाणां
छायां तामतिशयिनीं सुखी श्रयिष्ये ॥

19. Oh Bharatha I Let the (Royal) umbrella repel the heat of the sun and give cool shade on your head. And I also will enjoy the (cool) shade of forest trees, the extensive shade, in comfort.

❍ ❍ ❍

२०. शत्रुघ्नः कुशलमतिस्तु ते सहायः
सौमित्रिर्मम विदितः प्रधानमित्रम् ।
चत्वारस्तनयवरा वयं नरेन्द्रं
सत्यस्थं भरत चराम मा विषादम् ॥

20. It is well known that (Lakshmana) the son of Sumithra is foremost of friends (in companionship) to me. And for you too, this wise Schathrugna is your support (and constant companion). we, the four of us, will make our father steadfast in Truth. Do not be dejected.

(Note: Raama tells Bharatha that both of them have almost parallel assignments, similar advantages, equal 'comforts', and a brother each, as support!)

❍ ❍ ❍

Chapter 108

Jaabaali Enunciates Atheistic Philosophy

१. आश्वासयन्तं भरतं जाबालिर्ब्राह्मणोत्तमः ।
उवाच रामं धर्मज्ञं धर्मापेतमिदं वचः ॥

1. The noble Braamin Jaabaali addressed the knower of Dharma, Raama, who was consoling Bharatha, with these words that were bereft of Dharma.

(Jaabaali was a renowned, respected minister of king Dhascharatha: he is an atheist / an agnostic.)

❍ ❍ ❍

२. साधु राघव मा भूत्ते बुद्धिरेवं निरर्थिका ।
प्राकृतस्य नरस्येव ह्यार्यबुद्धेस्तपस्विनः ।।

2. Oh (Raama) the Raaghava! It is not proper for (a man like you who are) enlightened with ways of nobility and who are steadfast, to indulge thus in useless (and purposeless) thinking (and resolutions) worthy only of ordinary men.

❍ ❍ ❍

३. कः कस्य पुरुषो बन्धुः किमाप्यं कस्य केनचित् ।
यदेको जायते जन्तुरेक एव विनश्यति ।।

3. (Jaabali expounds his philosophy thus)

Who is related to whom? Who should obtain what from whom ? Life begins alone. And departs alone.

(Atheist Jaabaali cannot stand talk of "visit" to Gaya for Shraadha etc for their dead father. He chides Raama and more!)

❍ ❍ ❍

४. तस्मान्माता पिता चेति राम सज्जेत यो नरः ।
उन्मत्त इव ज्ञेयो नास्ति कश्चिद्धि कस्यचित् ।।

4. Therefore, Oh Raama, if a man clings to 'father' and 'mother', then he should be considered a fool ! Because, no one is any one to him.(in this world).

❍ ❍ ❍

५. यथा ग्रामान्तरं गच्छन्नरः कश्चित्क्वचिद्वसेत् ।
उत्सृज्य च तमावासं प्रतिष्ठेतापरेऽहनि ।।

5. A man going out of town spends (a night) at some place; Next morning he leaves that place .....

❍ ❍ ❍

६. एवमेव मनुष्याणां पिता माता गृहं वसु ।
आवासमात्रं काकुत्स्थ सज्जन्ते नात्र सज्जनाः ।।

6. ...... it is just like this; father, mother, house, property are mere (temporary) meeting place for men. Oh (Raama the) Kaakuthsa. In this matter (of relationships), wise men do not cling (have attachment, duties etc).

❍ ❍ ❍

७. पित्र्यं राज्यं परित्यज्य स नार्हसि नरोत्तम ।
आस्थातुं कापथं दुःखं विषमं बहुकण्टकम् ।।

7. Oh foremost of men (Raama)! Such as you are, abandoning your father's kingdom (that was your right), you should not resort to the poisonous wrong path strewn with pin pricks of suffering.

❍ ❍ ❍

८. समृद्धायामयोध्यायामात्मानमभिषेचय ।
एकवेणीधरा हि त्वां नगरी संप्रतीक्षते ।।

8. The City Goddess (of Ayodhya) sporting a single long braided hair is awaiting you, only you.; (Therefore) anoint yourself at this prosperous Ayodhya.

(Poet Vaalmeeki is poetic. The Goddess is sporting lovely braided hair while you are wearing a mendicant's hair style! The Ayodhya kingdom is the Goddess!)

❍ ❍ ❍

९. राजभोगाननुभवन्महार्हान्पार्थिवात्मज ।
विहर त्वमयोध्यायां यथा शक्रस्त्रिविष्टपे ।।

9. Oh (Raama) the son of Kaikeyi! You must live-in Ayodhya enjoying all the foremost royal comforts and pleasures like Schakra (Lord Indhra) of heaven.

❍ ❍ ❍

१०. न ते कश्चिद्दशरथस्त्वं च तस्य न कश्चन ।
अन्यो राजा त्वमन्यश्च तस्मात्कुरु यदुच्यते ।।

10. Dhascharatha is no one to you! You are also no one to him! The king is another person. You are also another person. Therefore do as I tell you.

(Who are you to worry about sins etc. for your father when he is nobody to you, says Jaabaali Forget father's command.)

❍ ❍ ❍

११. बीजमात्रं पिता जन्तोः शुक्लं रुधिरमेव च ।
संयुक्तमृतुमन्मात्रा पुरुषस्येह जन्म तत् ।।

11. In this world, a father is just a 'Trifle' for a living being. For a man (or woman) birth is merely connected with his (or her) mother's seasonal periods (caused by) genital white Mucus and red (cells).

(Birth is an accident!)

❍ ❍ ❍

१२. गतः स नृपतिस्तत्र गन्तव्यं यत्र तेन वै ।
प्रवृत्तिरेषा मर्त्यानां त्वं तु मिथ्या विहन्यसे ।।

12. The king has gone to heaven where he should go! This is the destiny of mortals. But you are grieving falsely (not accepting reality).

❍ ❍ ❍

१३. अर्थधर्मपरा ये ये तांस्ताञ्छोचामि नेतरान् ।
ते हि दुःखमिह प्राप्य विनाशं प्रेत्य भेजिरे ।।

13. (And Jaabaali says further to Raama.)

I grieve for such of those who (giving up what they have) are devoted to (and seek) Dharma (that is not perceptible). I do not grieve for others (who are materialistic); These men (of so called Dharma) undergo suffering, (eventually) die and obtain destruction.

❍ ❍ ❍

१४. अष्टकापितृदैवत्यमित्ययं प्रसृतो जनः ।
अन्नस्योपद्रवं पश्य मृतो हि किमशिष्यति ॥

14. These people observe Ceremonies of Ashtaka and Pithrus (Shraadha for their dead). Waste of food, you see! Because, will any dead man eat?

❍ ❍ ❍

१५. यदि भुक्तमिहान्येन देहमन्यस्य गच्छति ।
दद्यात्प्रवसतः श्राद्धं न तत्पथ्यशनं भवेत् ॥

15. If what is eaten by one can enter the body (stomach) of another one then you may (as well) offer Shraadha (offerings) from here itself for one going away; There is no need for food packets for the Road!

❍ ❍ ❍

१६. दानसंवनना ह्येते ग्रन्था मेधाविभिः कृताः ।
यजस्व देहि दीक्षस्व तपस्तप्यस्व संत्यज ॥

16. Perform Yaga! Give (liberally) take to (deeksha) - Abstinence & penance. Give up. All these teachings are conceived by clever men for the sake of money.

(Jaabaali criticizes Shraadha ceremonies for the dead as practised universally by Indians: The foods and offering kept during ceremonies cannot reach them! Waste of food! Secondly, no need to go to Gaya to perform Shraadha. And tauntingly he says, that if your guest leaves on a long journey don't honour him with packets of food for his journey. You eat your fill and lo, by miracle of chants your guest would have eaten on the road, their stomach full!)

❍ ❍ ❍

१७. स नास्ति परमित्येव कुरु बुद्धिं महामते ।
प्रत्यक्षं यत्तदातिष्ठ परोक्ष पृष्ठतः कुरु ॥

17. Oh wise (Raama)! Such as you are, realise in your mind

that there is no other (World): Hold on to what you perceive; Reject what is not visible (nor perceived)

❍ ❍ ❍

१८. स तां बुद्धिं पुरस्कृत्य सर्वलोकनिदर्शिनीम् ।
राज्यं त्वं प्रतिगृह्णीष्व भरतेन प्रसादितः ।।

18. As your favour is sought by Bharatha, you must accept this decision that is acceptable to all the citizens of the world. And so, accept the kingdom (and become king) (Note: Readers may note that, in Dhascharatha's Cabinet they had in Jaabaali a renowned minister who was an atheist. Indians were very liberal those days. Kings did not issue a "fatwa" to have the head of a person who denied God and Religion and Norms).

❍ ❍ ❍

Chapter 109

Raama Condemns Atheism

१. जाबालेस्तु वचः श्रुत्वा रामः सत्यात्मनां वरः ।
उवाच परया भक्त्या स्वबुद्ध्या चाविपन्नया ।।

1. The foremost amongst men of Truth, Raama, hearing the words of Jaabaali, then said thus with foremost respect and deliberation.

❍ ❍ ❍

२. भवान्मे प्रियकामार्थं वचनं यदिहोक्तवान् ।
अकार्यं कार्यसङ्काशमपथ्यं पथ्यसंमितम् ।।

2. These words that were spoken by you desirous of showing your kindness to me, cannot be acted upon, although they may appear to be proper to be acted upon. They may appear to be salutary but they are not salutary.

❍ ❍ ❍

३. निर्मर्यादस्तु पुरुषः पापाचारसमन्वितः ।
मानं न लभते सत्सु भिन्नचारित्रदर्शनः ।।

3. A man who does not know the limits of propriety and is endowed with bad conduct and (expounds and) follows perverse conduct (against norms of Dharma), will never command respect of the Good.

❍ ❍ ❍

४. कुलीनमकुलीनं वा वीरं पुरुषमानिनम् ।
चारित्रमेव व्याख्याति शुचिं वा यदि वाऽशुचिम् ।।

4. It is good conduct alone that describes a man; whether from noble or low family; or whether he is brave or fancies himself as a (brave) man; or whether he is pure or impure person.

❍ ❍ ❍

५. अनार्यस्त्वार्यसङ्काशः शौचाद्धीनस्तथा शुचिः ।
लक्षण्यवदलक्षण्यो दुःशीलः शीलवानिव ।।

5. An ignoble (Un-Aryan) will appear as an Aryan (noble one): An impure man like a pure man. A man of bad qualities will appear as a man of good qualities. A man of bad conduct will appear as a man of good conduct.

❍ ❍ ❍

६. अधर्मं धर्मवेषेण यदीमं लोकसङ्करम् ।
अभिपत्स्ये शुभं हित्वा क्रियाविधिविवर्जितम् ।।

6. Abandoning what is (virtuous and) good, if I pursue (your, this) Non Dharma that is "dressed' up as (true) Dharma and which is against norms of the code, practices and tradition and which would lead to strife in the world ......

❍ ❍ ❍

७. कश्चेतयानः पुरुषः कार्याकार्यविचक्षणः ।
बहुमंस्यति मां लोके दुर्वृत्तं लोकदूषणम् ।।

7. ...... then, in this world, which man of discernment who has the perception to see (and differentiate between) right and wrong, will have any esteem for me, a man of wrong conduct, a corrupter of the world.

❍ ❍ ❍

८. कस्य यास्याम्यहं वृत्तं केन वा स्वर्गमाप्नुयाम् ।
अनया वर्तमानोऽहं वृत्त्या हीनप्रतिज्ञया ॥

8. If I abide by this conduct of forsaking my promise (to my father, tell me Jaabaali), whose traditional practices will I follow? How will I obtain heaven.

❍ ❍ ❍

९. कामवृत्तस्त्वयं लोकः कृत्स्नः समुपवर्तते ॥

9. (If your advice is right) The entire world will be stricken with Licentiousness. (Topsy turvy, without any law and order).

❍ ❍ ❍

१०. यद्वृत्ताः सन्ति राजानस्तद्वृत्तास्सन्ति हि प्रजाः ॥

10. And what conduct kings abide by, the same conduct citizens take to; (Like age old saying= Yathaa Raaja Thathaa Praja= Like king likewise people).

❍ ❍ ❍

११. सत्यमेवानृशंसं च राजवृत्तं सनातनम् ।
तस्मात्सत्यात्मकं राज्यं सत्ये लोकः प्रतिष्ठितः ॥

11. Truth is the harmless royal conduct, the Eternal, (practised by good kings): World rests on Truth: Therefore kingdom is sustained by Truth.

❍ ❍ ❍

१२. ऋषयश्चैव देवाश्च सत्यमेव हि मेनिरे ।
सत्यवादी हि लोकेऽस्मिन्परमं गच्छति क्षयम् ॥

12. (Even) Rishi-s and celestial consider Truth only (as

the root): Therefore, in this world only a man of Truth obtains eternity.

❍ ❍ ❍

१३. उद्विजन्ते यथा सर्पान्नरादनृतवादिनः ।
धर्मः सत्यं परो लोके मूलं स्वर्गस्य चोच्यते ॥

13. In his world, (every one) trembles before men who speak untruth, like (one fearing a) snake; The foremost foundation of heaven, it is said, is the Dharma of Truth.

❍ ❍ ❍

१४. सत्यमेवेश्वरो लोके सत्यं पद्मा समाश्रिता ।
सत्यमूलानि सर्वाणि सत्यान्नास्ति परं पदम् ॥

14. In the world, Truth is God: Padhma (Goddess of prosperity) rests on Truth; Everything is rooted in Truth. There is nothing greater than Truth.

(Readers may know that Mahaathma Gaandhi considered Truth supreme.)

❍ ❍ ❍

१५. दत्तमिष्टं हुतं चैव तप्तानि च तपांसि च ।
वेदाः सत्यप्रतिष्ठानास्तस्मात्सत्यपरो भवेत् ॥

15. Charity (Gifts), Yaaga (and ceremonies), Homa (fire rituals) performance of penance, Vedha, all abide by Truth. Therefore one must give himself upto Truth.

❍ ❍ ❍

१६. एकः पालयते लोकमेकः पालयते कुलम् ।
मज्जत्येको हि निरये एकः स्वर्गेमहीयते ॥

16. One protects the world; One protects his family; One is submerged in (Pit of) hell: One also delights in Heaven.

❍ ❍ ❍

१७. सोऽहं पितुर्नियोगं तु किमर्थं नानुपालये ।
सत्यप्रतिश्रवः सत्यं सत्येन समयीकृतः ॥

17. Having truthfully sworn and truthfully committed, how will I (and for what purpose) not follow my father's command truthfully.

❍ ❍ ❍

१८. नैव लोभान्न मोहाद्वा न ह्यज्ञानात्तमोऽन्वितः ।
सेतुं सत्यस्य भेत्स्यामि गुरोः सत्यप्रतिश्रवः ।।

18. Having truthfully committed to my father, I will not give up my bond with Truth in ignorance (darkness), (lured) by greed or by passion.

❍ ❍ ❍

१९. असत्यसन्धस्य सतश्चलस्यास्थिरचेतसः ।
नैव देवा न पितरः प्रतीच्छन्तीति नः श्रुतम् ।।

19. We are taught thus; The Dheva-s do not look at one who is untruthful, who is of unsteady mind, who is of wavering disposition. Even one's forefathers (treat him with contempt).

❍ ❍ ❍

२०. प्रत्यगात्ममिमं धर्मं सत्यं पश्याम्यहं स्वयम् ।
भारः सत्पुरुषाचीर्णस्तदर्थमभिनन्द्यते ।।

20. I see this Dharma of Truth as concerning itself with 'Personal Soul:' Only for this reason, the burden (and suffering) of good men performing vows (and rituals) is hailed.

❍ ❍ ❍

२१. क्षात्रं धर्ममहं त्यक्ष्ये ह्यधर्मं धर्मसंहितम् ।
क्षुद्रैर्नृशंसैलुब्धैश्च सेवितं पापकर्मभिः ।।

21. I reject the royal Dharma (if) that is immoral, the Dharma that is associated with the Dharma practised by low minded men, cruel men, avaricious men, evil mongers; Surely.

❍ ❍ ❍

२२. कायेन कुरुते पापं मनसा संप्रधारयन् ।
अनृतं जिह्वया चाह त्रिविधं कर्म पातकम् ।।

22. Man conceives evil in his mind; Commits (evil) with body; Speaks falsehood with tongue. Thus act of sin is Threefold.

❍ ❍ ❍

२३. भूमिः कीर्तिर्यशो लक्ष्मीः पुरुषं प्रार्थयन्ति हि ।
स्वर्गस्थं चानुपश्यन्ति सत्यमेव भजेत् ततः ।।

23. Earth, Fame, Glory, Wealth solicit only (noble) men; He is considered as deserving for stay in heaven; Therefore (must and) will pursue Truth.

❍ ❍ ❍

२४. श्रेष्ठं ह्यनार्यमेव स्याद्यद्भवानवधार्य माम् ।
आह युक्तिकरैर्वाक्यैरिदं भद्रं कुरुष्व ह ।।

24. Considering it as beneficial to me, you spoke with suitable words (cleverly), saying: = Do This Which Is Good = (But) what you said is Un-Aryan (ignoble).

❍ ❍ ❍

२५. कथं ह्यहं प्रतिज्ञाय वनवासमिमं गुरोः ।

25. How can I fulfill Bharatha's words (and pleadings that I should not go through with my exile), after having promised to my father this forest life and (thus) disobey my father's words (of command)?

❍ ❍ ❍

२६. स्थिरा मया प्रतिज्ञाता प्रतिज्ञा गुरुसंनिधौ ।
प्रहृष्टमानसा देवी कैकेयी चाभवत्तदा ।।

26. Before my father, this vow was firmly committed by me; And queen Kaikeyi was also pleased at heart by this.

❍ ❍ ❍

२७. वनवासं वसन्नेवं शुचिर्नियतभोजनः ।
मूलपुष्पफलैः पुण्यैः पितृन्देवांश्च तर्पयन् ।।

27. As a pure man, eating with restraint, living a life of forest thus, I will please my forefathers and Deities with (holy) delightful (forest) flowers, fruits and tubers.

❍ ❍ ❍

२८. संतुष्टपञ्चवर्गोऽहं लोकयात्रां प्रवर्तये ।
अकुहः श्रद्दधानः सन्कार्याकार्यविचक्षणः ।।

28. I will go on my life's journey without false pretense, with clear perception as to what should be done and should not be done, with my five senses happy and content, in utter faith.

❍ ❍ ❍

२९. कर्मभूमिमिमां प्राप्य कर्तव्यं कर्म यच्छुभम् ।
अग्निर्वायुश्च सोमश्च कर्मणां फलभागिनः ।।

29. Having been born (attained life in) this world of service, only that must be done, (namely), good deeds: (Even Lords of) Fire, Wind, Moon are enjoying only the fruits of service (and deeds).

(Readers may note that this India that is Bhaarath, is a Karma bhoomi, land of service unlike other countries: Pleasures are incidental, are fringe benefits in India that is Karma Bhoomi.)

❍ ❍ ❍

३०. शतं क्रतुनामाहृत्य देवराट् त्रिदिवं गतः ।
तपांस्युग्राणि चास्थाय दिवं याता महर्षयः ।।

30. (Even) the Lord of Dheva-s (Indhra), obtained heaven only after 100 sacrifices (service, ceremonies); Great Rishi-s go to heaven after rigorous penance.

❍ ❍ ❍

३१. अमृष्यमाणः पुनरुग्रतेजा
निशम्य तन्नास्तिकवाक्यहेतुम् ।
अथाब्रवीत्तं नृपतेस्तनूजो
विगर्हमाणो वचनानि तस्य ॥

31. (And Raama could not contain himself: Becomes angry with Jaabaali, the 'infidel'.)
Then (Raama) the king's son who had heard (Jaabaali) and his atheistic arguments, became angry, unable to bear (his words) and he said to him further, condemning his words (arguments).

❍ ❍ ❍

३२. सत्यं च धर्मं च पराक्रमं च
भूतानुकम्पां प्रियवादितां च ।
द्विजातिदेवातिथिपूजनं च
पन्थानमाहुस्त्रिदिवस्य सन्तः ॥

32. Our elders have said that the path to heaven lies in Truth, Dharma, and valour (before enemy), compassion to living beings, speaking sweetly, honouring braamins, guests and deities.

❍ ❍ ❍

३३. तेनैवमाज्ञाय यथावदर्थ
मेकोदयं संप्रतिपद्य विप्राः ।
धर्मं चरन्तः सकलं यथावत्
काङ्क्षन्ति लोकागममप्रमत्ताः ॥

33. That is why, Braamins, perceiving this true significance of Dharma and Artha, have come to this one conclusion to follow all this diligently as per norms (of Truthful conduct) and (thus) look forward to salvation.

❍ ❍ ❍

३४. निन्दाम्यहं कर्म पितुः कृतंत

घस्त्वामगृह्णाद्विषमस्थबुद्धिम् ।

बुद्ध्याऽनयैवंविधया चरन्तं

सुनास्तिकं धर्मपथादपेतम् ॥

34. (And Raama is so 'worked' up and angry with Jaabaali, he says.)

I despise the action of my father (late king Dhascharatha) in having accepted you (as Cabinet minister) who practises Atheism totally, who in this manner, with an evil mind, has strayed away from path of Dharma, whose mind is unsteady.

❍ ❍ ❍

३५. यथा हि चोरः स तथा हि बुद्ध

स्तथागतं नास्तिकमत्र विद्धि ।

तस्माद्धि यः शङ्कचतमः च्जानां

न नास्तिकेनाभिमुखो बुधः स्यात् ॥

35. This "Budhdha' (the clever man) is just like a 'Thief': Please understand that this kind of thinking is Atheism, in the world. That is why, a wise man does not look at a man in the community who is to be doubted because of atheistic logic.

❍ ❍ ❍

३६. त्वत्तो जनाः पूर्वतरे वराश्च

शुभानि कर्माणि बहूनि चक्रुः ।

जित्वा सदेमं च परं च लोकं

तस्माद्द्विजाः स्वस्ति हुतं कृतं च ॥

36. Therefore, elders ('wiser') than you, these foremost Braamins performed always many holy Rituals, performed Yaaga-s, obtained bliss here and in the other world.

❍ ❍ ❍

३७. धर्मेरताः सत्पुरुषैस्समेता
स्तेजस्विनो दानगुणप्रधानाः ।
अहिंसका वीतमलाश्च लोके
भवन्ति पूज्या मुनयः प्रधानाः ॥

37. In this world, men of nobility and (spiritual) brilliance, men devoted to Dharma, men who are (associated and) in company with good men, men whose foremost quality is 'giving away', men of non violence, sages freed from (Spiritual) darkness, become worthy of honour.

❍ ❍ ❍

३८. इति ब्रुवन्तं वचनं सरोषं
रामं महात्मानमदीनसत्त्वम् ।
उवाच तथ्यं पुनरास्तिकं च
सत्यं वचः सानुनयं च विप्रः ॥

38. With courtesy, (Jaabaali) the Braamin, addressed again the great soul Raama who was personification of goodness, who had spoken truthful words, (although) in wrath: (He spoke to Raama) words of Truth with faith. (Truth, as he saw it!)

❍ ❍ ❍

३९. न नास्तिकानां वचनं ब्रवीम्यहं
न नास्तिकोऽहं न च नास्ति किञ्चन ।
समीक्ष्य कालं पुनरास्तिकोऽभवं
भवेय काले पुनरेव नास्तिकः ॥

39. (Jaabaali says he is only a practical man; Does not bother about 'Truth' etc.: He is only interested in what is good for the kingdom.)

I did not talk (nor preach) Atheism; I am not an Atheist; There is nothing that is not (for me)! Taking note of circumstances, I will be an Asthika also (A man of faith, if need be!) (But) To suit this occasion, I became an atheist (and advised you thus).

❍ ❍ ❍

४०. स चापि कालोऽयमुपागतः शनै
र्यथा मया नास्तिकवागुदीरिता ।
निवर्तनार्थं तव राम कारणात्
प्रसादनार्थं तु मयैतदीरितम् ।।

40. Oh Raama! This and that time, (various events) followed one after another: Therefore Atheism was spoken by me; All this was spoken by me to honour you and to take you back (to Ayodhya as king).

❍ ❍ ❍

Chapter 110

Description of Lineage: From Manu Onwards

१. क्रुद्धमाज्ञाय रामं तु वसिष्ठः प्रत्युवाच ह ।
जाबालिरपि जानीते लोकस्यास्य गतागतिम् ।।

1. Realising Raama was (still) in wrath, Vasishta spoke thus: (Oh Raama!) Jaabaali knows the origin of this world as well.

(Vasishta is so shocked at Raama's attack on the aged, renowned minister Jaabaali, he tells Raama that Jaabaali is no ordinary man.)

❍ ❍ ❍

२. निवर्तयितुकामस्तु त्वामेतद्वाक्यमुक्तवान् ।
इमां लोकसमुत्पत्तिं लोकनाथ निबोध मे ।।

2. Oh Lord of the world (Raama)! He had said all these desirous of taking you back (to Ayodhya as king): Now you shall be enlightened about the creation of this world (and about your ancestors.)

❍ ❍ ❍

३. सर्वं सलिलमेवासीत्पृथिवी यत्र निर्मिता ।
ततः समभवद्ब्रह्मा स्वयंभूर्दैवतैः सह ॥

3. Everything was 'Water': And from this, earth was established (reclaimed): Then The Self Born God Bramma appeared with Deities.

❍ ❍ ❍

४. स वराहस्ततो भूत्वा प्रोज्जहार वसुन्धराम् ।
असृजच्च जगत्सर्वं सह पुत्रैः कृतात्मभिः ॥

4. Then "The Boar" appeared and lifted up the Earth. Then (God Bramma) created the entire world along with his disciplined sons.

❍ ❍ ❍

५. आकाशप्रभवो ब्रह्मा शाश्वतो नित्य अव्ययः ।
तस्मान्मरीचिः संजज्ञे मरीचेः कश्यपः सुतः ॥

5. Bramma appears in Sky: He is Eternal: Immanent: Unaffected (by changes): From Him, Mareechi was created: Mareechi's son was Kaschyapa.

❍ ❍ ❍

६. विवस्वान्कश्यपाज्जज्ञे मनुर्वैवस्वतः स्मृतः ।
स तु प्रजापतिः पूर्वमिक्ष्वाकुस्तु मनोः सुतः ॥

6. From Kaschyapa was born Vivaswaan (Sun): And Manu is said to be Sun's son And he (Manu) is the first of your ancestors: Manu's son is Ikshwaaku. (Raama belongs to Solar race).

❍ ❍ ❍

७. यस्येयं प्रथमं दत्ता समृद्धा मनुना मही ।
तमिक्ष्वाकुमयोध्यायां राजानं विद्धि पूर्वकम् ॥

7. You should know that Ikshwaaku was the first king of Ayodhya when the entire vast earth was handed over to him.

❍ ❍ ❍

८. इक्ष्वाकोस्तु सुतः श्रीमान्कुक्षिरेवेति विश्रुतः ।
कुक्षेरथात्मजो वीरो विकुक्षिरुदपद्यत ॥

8. Ikshwaaaku's son is Kukshi, renowned and resplendent: Then as Kukshi's son was born the brave Vikukshi.

❍ ❍ ❍

९. विकुक्षेस्तु महातेजा बाणः पुत्रः प्रतापवान् ।
बाणस्य तु महाबाहुरनरण्यो महायशाः ॥

9. And Vikukshi's son was the brilliant and powerful Bhaana: And the mighty limbed most virtuous Anaaranya was Bhaana's son.

❍ ❍ ❍

१०. नानावृष्टिर्बभूवास्मिन्न दुर्भिक्षं सतां वरे ।
अनरण्ये महाराजे तस्करो नापि कश्चन ॥

10. And when the most virtuous Anaaranya was king there was no drought nor famine, nor were there any thieves.

❍ ❍ ❍

११. अनरण्यान्महाबाहुः पृथू राजा बभूव ह ।
तस्मात्पृथोर्महाराजस्त्रिशङ्कुरुदपद्यत ॥

11. After Anaaranya, the mighty limbed king Prithu appeared: After Prithu, the great king Thrischanku was born.

❍ ❍ ❍

१२. स सत्यवचनाद्वीरः सशरीरो दिवं गतः ॥

12. This brave (Thrischanku) went to heaven in his own mortal body by a truthful commitment (made by Vischwaamithra).

❍ ❍ ❍

१३. त्रिशङ्कोरस्त्वभवत्सूनुर्धुन्धुमारो महायशाः ।
धुन्धुमारान्महातेजा युवनाश्वो व्यजायत ॥

13. And the most Dhundhumaara was born to Thrischanku as son; And the most brilliant Yuvaascha was born through Dhundhumaara.

❍ ❍ ❍

१४. युवनाश्वसुतः श्रीमान्मान्धाता समपद्यत ।
मान्धातुस्तु महातेजाः सुसन्धिरुदपद्यत ॥

14. The auspicious Maandhaatha was born to Yuvanaascha as son; And to Maandhaatha was born the brilliant Susandhi.

❍ ❍ ❍

१५. सुसन्धेरपि पुत्रौ द्वौ ध्रुवसन्धिः प्रसेनजित् ।
यशस्वी ध्रुवसन्धेस्तु भरतो रिपुसूदनः ॥

15. And Dhruvasandhi and Prasenajith were the two sons of Susandhi, the famous destroyer of enemies Bharatha, was Dhruvasandhi's son. (Bharatha not to be confused with Raama' brother).

❍ ❍ ❍

१६. भरतात्तु महाबाहोरसितो नामतोऽभवत् ।
यस्यैते प्रतिराजान उदपद्यन्त शत्रवः ॥
हैहयास्तालजङ्घाश्च शूराश्च शशिबिन्दवः ॥

16. From the mighty limbed Bharatha, Asitha was born. (But) the brave Haihaya-s, Thaalajanga-s and Shashibhindu came as enemies to his throne.

❍ ❍ ❍

१७. तांस्तु सर्वान्प्रतिव्यूह्य युद्धे राजा प्रवासितः ।
स च शैलवरे रम्ये बभूवाभिरतो मुनिः ॥

17. This king being drawn out in battle with all of them, was driven away in war and became a devoted sage in the lovely Himaalya-s (the foremost of mountains).

❍ ❍ ❍

१८. द्वे चास्य भार्येगर्भिण्यौ बभूवतुरिति श्रुतिः ।।

18. It was said that his two wives were in the family way.

❍ ❍ ❍

१९. एका गर्भविनाशाय सपत्न्यै तु गरं ददौ ।।

19. One of them gave poison to the other co-wife to abort her pregnancy.

❍ ❍ ❍

२०. भार्गवश्च्यवनो नाम हिमवन्तमुपाश्रितः ।
तमृषिं साऽभ्युपागम्य कालिन्दी चाभ्यवादयत् ।।

20. There lived in Himaalya-s, Bhrigu-s son Chyaavana: This lady Kaalindhi approached this Rishi (Chyaavana) and bowed to him: (She told him how she was poisoned to kill the foetus).

❍ ❍ ❍

२१. स तामभ्यवदद्विप्रो वरेप्सुं पुत्रजन्मनि ।
पुत्रस्ते भविता देवि महात्मा लोकविश्रुतः ।।
धार्मिकश्च सुशीलश्च वंशकर्ताऽरिसूदनः ।।

21. Then this Braamin told her who was seeking him for boon for begetting this son; = Oh Lady! A son will be born to you who will be most eminent and renowned in the world, who will be a man of Dharma, a man of good conduct, who will destroy enemies and who will have descendants.=

❍ ❍ ❍

२२. कृत्वा प्रदक्षिणं हृष्टा मुनिं तमभिवाद्य च ।
पद्मपत्रविशालाक्षी पद्मगर्भसमप्रभम् ।।
ततः सा गृहमागम्य देवी पुत्रं व्यजायत ।।

22. This Lady (Kaalindhi) whose eyes were like lotus petals was very happy, went home after saluting him and making circumbumbulation. She begot a son who shone with radiance of the stalk of the lotus.

❍ ❍ ❍

२३. सपत्न्या तु गरस्तस्यै दत्तो गर्भजिघांसया ।
गरेण सह तेनैव जातः स सगरोऽभवत् ।।

23. (It may be recalled) That poison was given to her by the co-wife who was desirous of killing the child in womb, (But with blessings of Sage Chyavana) it was born (but) with 'poison' in its body. That is why he was called Sagara (Sa- Gara - means with poison).

❍ ❍ ❍

२४. स राजा सगरो नाम यः समुद्रमखानयत् ।
इष्ट्वा पर्वणि वेगेन त्रासयन्तमिमाः प्रजाः ।।

24. It was this king named Sagara who performed Yaaga-s and who made these citizens frightened, digging up the ocean, 'flooded' up with waters in season.

❍ ❍ ❍

२५. असमञ्जस्तु पुत्रोऽभूत्सगरस्येति नः श्रुतम् ।
जीवन्नेव स पित्रा तु निरस्तः पापकर्मकृत् ।।

25. Asamanja was a son born to Sagara, so we have heard. As he was indulging in evil acts, he was driven away (from kingdom) by his father even when he was alive.

❍ ❍ ❍

२६. अंशुमानिति पुत्रोऽभूदसमञ्जस्य वीर्यवान् ।
दिलीपोंऽशुमतः पुत्रो दिलीपस्य भगीरथः ।।

26. And to Asamanja the brave Amschumaan was born: And Dhileepa was Amschumaan's son. And Bhageeratha was Dhileepa's son.

❍ ❍ ❍

२७. भगीरथात्ककुत्स्थस्तु काकुत्स्था येन विश्रुताः ।
ककुत्स्थस्य च पुत्रोऽभूद्रघुर्येन तु राघवाः ।।

27. And to Bhageeratha was born Kaakuthsa: And to him

Raghu: And thus (you are all) called Raaghava-s and well known as Kaakuthsas.

❍ ❍ ❍

२८. रघोस्तु पुत्रस्तेजस्वी प्रवृद्धः पुरुषादकः ।
कल्माषपादः सौदास इत्येवं प्रथितो भुवि ॥

28. And Raghu's son is the brilliant Sowdhas: He is famously known in the world as father of Purushaadhala, Kalmaashapaadha, and Purshaadhaka.

❍ ❍ ❍

२९. कल्माषपादपुत्रोऽभूच्छङ्खणस्त्विति विश्रुतः ।
यस्तु तद्वीर्यमासाद्य सहसेनो व्यनीनशत् ॥

29. And Kalmaashapaadha's son is renowned Schankana: (although he obtained Army with) power, he very soon became ruined.

❍ ❍ ❍

३०. शङ्कणस्य च पुत्रोऽभूच्छूरः श्रीमान्सुदर्शनः ।
सुदर्शनस्याग्निवर्ण अग्निवर्णस्य शीघ्रगः ॥

30. And To Schankana was born auspicious Sudharshana. And to Sudharshana Agnivarna. And to Agnivarna , Scheegraga.

❍ ❍ ❍

३१. शीघ्रगस्य मरुः पुत्रो मरोः पुत्रः प्रशुश्रुकः ।
प्रशुश्रुकस्य पुत्रोऽभूदम्बरीषो महाद्युतिः ॥

31. Scheegraga's son was Maru: Maru's son was Praschuschruka: And to him the most majestic son Ambareesha was born.

❍ ❍ ❍

३२. अम्बरीषस्य पुत्रोऽभून्नहुषः सत्यविक्रमः ।
नहुषस्य न नाभागः पुत्रः परमधार्मिकः ॥

32. And the truly valiant Nahusha was born as son to Ambareesha. And Nahusha's son was the foremost man of Dharma, Naabhaaga.

❍ ❍ ❍

३३. अजश्च सुव्रतश्चैव नाभागस्य सुतावुभौ ।
अजस्य चैव धर्मात्मा राजा दशरथः सुतः ।।

33. And Naabhaga's two sons were Aja and Suvratha. The noble man of Dharma, Dhascharatha the king, was Aja's son.

❍ ❍ ❍

३४. तस्य ज्येष्ठोऽसि दायादो राम इत्यभिविश्रुतः ।
तद्गृहाण स्वकं राज्यमवेक्षस्व जनं नृप ।।

34. And you (Raama) are his eldest son and the heir (to throne) You are called Raama. Most renowned. Therefore accept this kingdom of yours. Oh (Raama the) King! look after your citizens.

❍ ❍ ❍

३५. इक्ष्वाकूणां हि सर्वेषां राजा भवति पूर्वजः ।
पूर्वजे नावरः पुत्रो ज्येष्ठो राज्येऽभिषिच्यते ।।

35. Because amongst all the Ikshwaaku-s, eldest born becomes king: When the eldest is around, other sons born after are not anointed in kingdom.

❍ ❍ ❍

३६. स राघवाणां कुलधर्ममात्मनः
सनातनं नाद्य विहातुमर्हसि ।
प्रभूतरत्नामनुशाधि मेदिनीं
प्रभूतराष्ट्रां पितृवन्महायशः ।।

36. Oh most famous (Raama)! Such as you are, you should not abandon now your family Dharma (norms) that was followed eternally by the Raaghava-s (before you). Like your father, you should rule this earth that is

extensive (encompassing many kingdoms) and which is immensely rich.

❍ ❍ ❍

Chapter 111

Raama Consoles Bharatha

१. वसिष्ठस्तु तदा राममुक्त्वा राजपुरोहितः ।
अब्रवीद्धर्मसंयुक्तं पुनरेवापरं वचः ॥

1. Having said thus (having narrated Raama's glorious heritage), the royal priest Vasishta addressed Raama once again, with more words with content of Dharma.

❍ ❍ ❍

२. पुरुषस्येह जातस्य भवन्ति गुरवस्त्रयः ।
आचार्यश्चैव काकुत्स्थ पिता माता च राघव ॥

2. Oh (Raama) the Raaghava! Oh the Kaakuthsa! In this world, for a man born, there are three teachers (Guru-s): Father, Mother and Teacher.

❍ ❍ ❍

३. पिता ह्येनं जनयति पुरुषं पुरुषर्षभ ।
प्रज्ञां ददाति चाचार्यस्तस्मात्स गुरुरुच्यते ॥

3. Oh (Raama the) 'Bull' amongst men! The father creates the man. The teacher imparts knowledge; That is why he is called Guru.

❍ ❍ ❍

४. सोऽहं ते पितुराचार्यस्तव चैव परन्तप ।
मम त्वं वचनं कुर्वन्नातिवर्तेः सतां गतिम् ॥

4. Oh (Raama) The tormentor of enemies! Such as I am, am teacher to you and was also to your (late) father:

8\. Acting as per my words (of advice), you should not transgress the path of the good.

❍ ❍ ❍

५. इमा हि ते परिषदः श्रेणयश्च द्विजास्तथा ।
एषु तात चरन्धर्मं नातिवर्तेः सतां गतिम् ।।

5\. This community of Dhvija-s (Braamins, Kshathriyas, Vyschya-s) are all your folks; Oh lad! Following Dharma in their matter (of welfare), you should not transgress the path of the good.

❍ ❍ ❍

६. वृद्धाया धर्मशीलाया मातुर्नार्हस्यवर्तितुम् ।
अस्यारतु वचनं कुर्वन्नातिवर्तेः सतां गतिम् ।।

6\. You should not go against (wishes) of your old mother (Kowsalya) who is attached to Dharma. You must act as per her words; you should not transgress the path of the good.

❍ ❍ ❍

७. भरतस्य वचः कुर्वन्याचमानस्य राघव ।
आत्मानं नातिवर्तेस्त्वं सत्यधर्मपराक्रम ।।

7\. Oh (Raama) the Raaghava who is steadfast in Dharma, Truth and Valour! You must heed the words of (your brother) Bharatha who is begging you (to return and take over as king): You should not go against your (own) natural (character of fulfilling the wishes of those who beseech you).

❍ ❍ ❍

८. एवं मधुरमुक्तः सन् गुरुणा राघवः स्वयम् ।
प्रत्युवाच समासीनं वसिष्ठं पुरुषर्षभः ।।

8\. After hearing such sweet words spoken by the teacher (Vasishta) the 'bull amongst men' (Raama) the

Raaghava, replied to Vasishta who was sitting close to him.

❍ ❍ ❍

९. यन्मातापितरौ वृत्तं तनये कुरुतः सदा ।
न सुप्रतिकरं तत्तु मात्रा पित्रा च यत्कृतम् ।।
१०. यथाशक्तिप्रदानेन स्नापनाच्छादनेन च ।
नित्यं च प्रियवादेन तथा संवर्धनेन च ।।

9. & 10.

What conduct (and vows) mother and father observe (for begetting son) towards propagating family, (for this, and for all that was done subsequently for the son), by mother and father, there cannot be sufficient requital... at all times.......(because) they bring up sons, offer them things according to their capacity, they bathe them, clothe them and (ever) speak to them sweetly.

(Raama brings home a well known Truth. No one can repay parents)!

❍ ❍ ❍

११. स हि राजा जनयिता पिता दशरथो मम ।
आज्ञातं यन्मया तस्य न तन्मिथ्या भविष्यति ।।

11. This king Dhascharatha my father, begot me; Therefore, whatever be his command, that, cannot be made false by me.

❍ ❍ ❍

१२. एवमुक्ते तु रामेण भरतः प्रत्यनन्तरम् ।
उवाच परमोदारः सूतं परमदुर्मनाः ।।

12. When told thus by Raama, the most illustrious Bharatha became greatly down hearted and spoke to charioteer (Sumanthra) who was sitting behind him.

❍ ❍ ❍

१३. इह मे स्थण्डिले शीघ्रं कुशानास्तर सारथे ।
आर्यं प्रत्युपवेक्ष्यामि यावन्मे न प्रसीदति ।।

13. (Now Bharatha resorts to "Sathyagraha'- a method which Mahaathma Gandhi used against the British- Non Violent Protest) Oh Charioteer (Sumanthra)! On this earth, spread at once a bed of Dharbha Grass for me: Till (Raama) favours me (by going back with me to Ayodhya) I am going to "Besiege" this Aryan (my noble brother, by lying down unto my death).

❍ ❍ ❍

१४. अनाहारो निरालोको धनहीनो यथा द्विजः ।
शेष्ये पुरस्ताच्छालाया यावन्न प्रतियास्यति ।।

14. Till he (agrees to) return, I will lie down, without food, oblivious of the world, in front of his hermitage, as a poor Twice Born ** Kshathriya, bereft of wealth#.

(Poet Vaalmeeki uses ** Dvi-ja which is normally used for a Braamin.A Braamin has two births. when he is born and when he is initiated into study of Vedha-s. And again poet uses ## Dhana-heena. As Raama is 'wealth' for Bharatha, without this wealth-that is Raama-Bharatha wont return to Ayodhya).

❍ ❍ ❍

१५. स तु राममवेक्षन्तं सुमन्त्रं प्रेक्ष्य दुर्मनाः ।
कुशोत्तरमुपस्थाप्य भूमावेवास्तरत्स्वयम् ।।

15. When (Bharatha) saw that Sumanthra was looking up to Raama (for his permission as though), he (this Bharatha) himself brought the bed of grass and spread on the floor.

❍ ❍ ❍

१६. तमुवाच महातेजा रामो राजर्षिसत्तमः ।
किं मां भरत कुर्वाणं तात प्रत्युपवेक्ष्यसि ।।

16. (Raama is upset by Bharatha's obstinacy: He talks to him).
Raama the most brilliant and noble amongst royal sages said to him; Oh Dear Bharatha 1 = What Do You Want Me To Do To Yield To You = (Raama said in exasperation)

❍ ❍ ❍

१७. ब्राह्मणो ह्येकपार्श्वेन नरान्रोद्धुमिहार्हति ।
न तु मूर्धाभिषिक्तानां विधिः प्रत्युपवेशने ॥

17. In this world, only a braamin has the right to confine a man by lying down on one side. There is no justification for one who is to be anointed and crowned (as king) for indulging in such 'coercion' to yield to him.
(A Kshathriya warrior should not use this Instrument of Non Violent Coercion to make others yield to him: Bharatha forgets he is a soldier, a Kshathriya warrior of the famous solar race)

❍ ❍ ❍

१८. उत्तिष्ठ नरशार्दूल हित्वैतद्दारुणं व्रतम् ।
पुरवर्यामितः क्षिप्रमयोध्यां याहि राघव ॥

18. (Oh Bharatha) The 'lion' amongst men! Give up this cruel vow Get up! Oh (Bharatha the) Raaghava! Go at once from here to the foremost city of Ayodhya.

❍ ❍ ❍

१९. आसीनस्त्वेव भरतः पौरजानपदं जनम् ।
उवाच सर्वतः प्रेक्ष्य किमार्यं नानुशासथ ॥

19. (And Bharatha appeals to the .citizens to make Raama return) And lying down, Bharatha looked at all the citizens of the town and cities and said= Why are you not directing this Aryan (Raama to return to Ayodhya; why are you all silent?) = ...

❍ ❍ ❍

२०. ते तमूचुर्महात्मानं पौरजानपदा जनाः ।
काकुत्स्थमभिजानीमः सम्यग्वदति राघवः ।।

20. And the citizens from villages and cities (who had gathered there along with Bharatha) addressed the great soul (Bharatha); = We know (our Raama) the Kaakuthsa! (Raama) the Raaghava speaks correctly. (We justify his decision to continue his exile).

❍ ❍ ❍

२१. एषोऽपि हि महाबाहुः पितुर्वचसि तिष्ठति ।
अत एव न शक्ताः स्मो व्यावर्तयितुमञ्जसा ।।

21. This mighty limbed (Raama) stands by the words (of command) of his father. Therefore we are unable to make him return (to Ayodhya as king), justifiably.=

❍ ❍ ❍

२२. तेषामाज्ञाय वचनं रामो वचनमब्रवीत् ।
एवं निबोध वचनं सुहृदां धर्मचक्षुषाम् ।।

22. Perceiving (and appreciating) their words, Raama said these words: (Oh Bharatha): You listen to the words of these well wishers whose eyes are directed towards Dharma.

❍ ❍ ❍

२३. एतच्चैवोभयं श्रुत्वा सम्यक्संपश्य राघव ।
उत्तिष्ठ त्वं महाबाहो मां च स्पृश तथोदकम् ।।

23. Oh (Bharatha) the Raaghava! Having heard these two (views), you must discern clearly. Oh mighty limbed (Bharatha)! You Get Up: Touch Me: And Like Wise (touch) Waters (to confirm acceptance of your going back to Ayodhya to rule and allow me to go on exile).

❍ ❍ ❍

२४. अथोत्थाय जलं स्पृष्ट्वा भरतो वाक्यमब्रवीत् ।
श्रृण्वन्तु मे परिषदो मन्त्रिणः श्रेणयस्तथा ।।

24. Then Bharatha got up (from the Grass bed). He "Touched' Water; And said these words: = Hear Me, Oh Ministers, Citizens=!

❍ ❍ ❍

२५. न याचे पितरं राज्यं नानुशासामि मातरम् ।
आर्यं परमधर्मज्ञं नानुजानामि राघवम् ।।

25. I Did Not seek Kingdom From Father: Nor Instigate My Mother: (therefore) I Will Not Permit The Noble Foremost Knower of Dharma (our Raama) The Raaghava (to go on exile).

❍ ❍ ❍

२६. यदि त्ववश्यं वस्तव्यं कर्तव्यं च पितुर्वचः ।
अहमेव निवत्स्यामि चतुर्दश समा वने ।।

26. (And Bharatha strangely suggests another option.)
If father's command (on the question of) stay and (exile in forest) must be honoured surely, then I myself will live for 14 years in the forest in (Raama's) place!

❍ ❍ ❍

२७. धर्मात्मा तस्य तथ्येन भ्रातुर्वाक्येन विस्मितः ।
उवाच रामः संप्रेक्ष्य पौरजानपदं जनम् ।।

27. (then) The noble soul man of Dharma Raama who was astounded by these words of his brother (spoken) truthfully, addressed the gathering of the citizens, facing them.

❍ ❍ ❍

२८. विक्रीतमाहितं क्रीतं यत्पित्रा जीवता मम ।
न तल्लोपयितुं शक्यं मया वा भरतेन वा ।।

28. Whatever was conceived by my father when he was alive, whatever was "Bought" or "Sold" (by him), that ('transaction' of my father) cannot be violated by me nor by Bharatha.

(Poet Vaalmeeki has used words of Commerce like =Vikreetha, Kreetha= Selling buying-Barter. Father's orders are not to be "Traded" as commodities of exchange. His orders were specific: Who should get what and do what)

❍ ❍ ❍

२९. उपधिर्न मया कार्योवनवासे जुगुप्सितः ।
युक्तमुक्तं च कैकेय्या पित्रा मे सुकृतं कृतम् ।।

29. In the matter of my exile to forest, what was said by Kaikeyi that, the fraud that is detested by the world, should not be committed by me (by cheating her and her boon and staying on at Ayodhya), was proper. And what was done by my father, was also proper.

(Raama says; His father had every right to send him away on exile as per Kaikeyi's wish: And Kaikeyi's warning that I should not some how circumvent and cheat her, was quite proper: So I will live in exile for 14 years without any second thought whatsoever)

❍ ❍ ❍

३०. जानामि भरतं क्षान्तं गुरुसत्कारकारिणम् ।
सर्वमेवात्र कल्याणं सत्यसन्धे महात्मनि ।।

30. I know Bharatha as very indulgent, as one who reveres elders. . He is true to his promise. Most eminent (a great soul): Everything will be auspicious with him (at Ayodhya).

❍ ❍ ❍

३१. अनेन धर्मशीलेन वनात्प्रत्यागतः पुनः ।
भ्रात्रा सह भविष्यामि पृथिव्याः पतिरुत्तमः ।।

31. When I return (after completing 14 years exile) from forest back again (to Ayodhya) along with this brother (Lakshmana) who is devoted to Dharma, I will become (king), the foremost lord of the earth.

❍ ❍ ❍

३२. वृतो राजा हि कैकेय्या मया तद्वचनं कृतम् ।
अनृतान्मोचयानेन पितरं तं महीपतिम् ।।

32. The King was bound by Kaikeyi: This word of command was accepted by me; You must therefore release our father (the lord of earth) from (sin of) untruth by doing this. (Namely, obey his order by taking over the kingdom and allow me to go on exile as he has stipulated).

❍ ❍ ❍

Chapter 112

The Bestowal of (Raama's) Sandals

(As Bharatha and all others have not been able to persuade Raama to return to Ayodhya, Bharatha requests Raama to offer his Golden Sandals to be The Token of Authority while he "Rules" the kingdom of Ayodhya during Raama's 14 years exile: Bharatha will draw inspiration from Raama's sandals during his entire 14 year Rule.)

१. तमप्रतिमतेजोभ्यां भ्रातृभ्यां रोमहर्षणम् ।
विस्मिताः सङ्गमं प्रेक्ष्य समवेता महर्षयः ।।

1. Listening to the exhilarating (hair raising) intercourse between these two brothers whose brilliance was incomparable, the great sages who had assembled there were amazed.

❍ ❍ ❍

२. अन्तर्हितास्त्वृषिगणाः सिद्धाश्च परमर्षयः ।
तौ भ्रातरौ महात्मानौ काकुत्स्थौ प्रशशंसिरे ।।

2. The multitude of Rishi-s, the invisible Sidhdha-s, great (celestial) Rishi-s, extolled these two most eminent

brothers, these two Kaakuthsa-s (Raama and Bharatha) thus:

❍ ❍ ❍

३. स धन्यो यस्य पुत्रौ द्वौ धर्मज्ञौ धर्मविक्रमौ ।
श्रुत्वा वयं हि संभाषामुभयोः स्पृहयामहे ॥

3. He is indeed most fortunate whose sons are these two, who are both men who know Dharma, who practise Dharma. We are delighted to hear the conversation between these two.

❍ ❍ ❍

४. ततस्त्वृषिगणाः क्षिप्रं दशग्रीववधैषिणः ।
भरतं राजशार्दूलमित्यूचुः सङ्गता वचः ॥

4. The multitude of (celestial) Rishi-s who were looking forward to the destruction of the ten headed (demon Raavana), then said the following words to the 'tiger' of men Bharatha, having gathered (there in the sky, but invisible to them).

(Readers may note that these celestials are watching from sky unseen and unobserved by the brothers. They have a vested interest in Raama being away from Ayodhya as Raama is to kill all demons of the land. Raama has greater purpose than just ruling the kingdom of Ayodhya. He is ultimately going to kill Raavana the Demon king of Lanka. And he should do it within the 14 years of his exile from Ayodhya: Ofcourse very few knew about this at that time.)

❍ ❍ ❍

५. कुलेजात महाप्राज्ञ महावृत्त महायशः ।
ग्राह्यं रामस्य वाक्यं ते पितरं यद्यवेक्षसे ॥

5. (Celestials advise Bharatha from the sky; They can be heard, though although unseen by ordinary citizens.)

Oh (Bharatha), Born in a noble family! Oh the most Intelligent! Oh most famous one! Oh man of great vows! If you want to honour your father (by fulfilling his command), then you must accept Raama's words (of advice and decision).

❍ ❍ ❍

६. सदाऽनृणमिमं रामं वयमिच्छामहे पितुः ।
अनृणत्वाच्च कैकेय्या स्वर्गं दशरथो गतः ।।

6. By discharging his debt to Kaikeyi, Dhascharatha has (now) gone to heaven: And we always desire that this Raama should make his father discharge (that) debt. (of boon to Kaikeyi).

❍ ❍ ❍

७. एतावदुक्त्वा वचनं गन्धर्वाः समहर्षयः ।
राजर्षयश्चैव तथा सर्वेस्वां स्वां गतिं गताः ।।

7. The Ghandharva-s, the great Rishi-s, along with royal sages, saying these words went away as they came to their own respective abodes (in heaven).

❍ ❍ ❍

८. ह्लादितस्तेन वाक्येन शुभेन शुभदर्शनः ।
रामः संहृष्टवदनस्तानृषीनभ्यपूजयत् ।।

8. The auspicious Raama who rejoiced by these auspicious words, honoured these Rishi-s (and worshipped them silently), his face beaming with joy.

❍ ❍ ❍

९. स्रस्तगात्रस्तु भरतः स वाचा सज्जमानया ।
कृताञ्जलिरिदं वाक्यं राघवं पुनरब्रवीत् ।।

9. And this Bharatha too, addressed (Raama) the Raaghava these words, with his hands cupped in Anjali , his limbs languid, with a well prepared (thought out) speech.

❍ ❍ ❍

१०. राजधर्ममनुप्रेक्ष्य कुलधर्मानुसन्ततिम् ।
कर्तुमर्हसि काकुत्स्थ मम मातुश्च याचनाम् ।।

10. Oh (Raama) the Kaakuthsa! For the sake of (our) royal Dharma, for sake of maintaining the continuity of our family (tradition and) Dharma, considering all this, you should (now) do what is my mother's desire as well.

(Readers may note that Kaikeyi is totally changed; Greed has disappeared from her heart now.)

❍ ❍ ❍

११. रक्षितुं सुमहद्राज्यमहमेकस्तु नोत्सहे ।
पौरजानपदांश्चापि रक्तान्रञ्जयितुं तथा ।।

11. By myself, all alone, I do not have the ability to (rule over and) protect the vast kingdom; likewise (I do not have ability) to cheer up the citizens from villages and towns who are devoted to you.

❍ ❍ ❍

१२. ज्ञातयश्च हि योधाश्च मित्राणि सुहृदश्च नः ।
त्वामेव प्रतिकाङ्क्षन्ते पर्जन्यमिव कर्षकाः ।।

12. Because, like farmers (awaiting) rain, our folks, warriors, friends, well wishers are all looking forward only to you.

❍ ❍ ❍

१३. इदं राज्यं महाप्राज्ञ स्थापय प्रतिपद्य हि ।
शक्तिमानसि काकुत्स्थ लोकस्य परिपालने ।।

13. Oh most intelligent (Raama) the Kaakuthsa! In ruling over the world, you are most capable. Therefore you should accept this kingdom and establish (your rule).

❍ ❍ ❍

१४. इत्युक्त्वा न्यपतद्भ्रातुः पादयोर्भरतस्तदा ।
भृशं संप्रार्थयामास राममेव प्रियंवदः ।।

14. The sweet tongued Bharatha having said thus, fell at his brother (Raama's) feet; And he begged Raama in many ways further.

❍ ❍ ❍

१५. तमङ्के भरतं कृत्वा रामो वचनमब्रवीत् ।
श्यामं नलिनपत्राक्षं मत्तहंसस्वरं स्वयम् ।।

15. Placing this Bharatha, whose eyes were dark like the blue lotus, on to his lap, Raama addressed these words in his usual (voice) that sounded like an exhilarated swan.

❍ ❍ ❍

१६. आगता त्वामियं बुद्धिः स्वजा वैनयिकी च या ।
भृशमुत्सहसे तात रक्षितुं पृथिवीमपि ।।

16. Oh Lad! The (faculty of) mind that is associated with character and good moral conduct is (verily) inborn in you. You have the capability to (rule and) protect the (entire) Earth.

❍ ❍ ❍

१७. अमात्यैश्च सुहृद्भिश्च बुद्धिमद्भिश्च मन्त्रिभिः ।
सर्वकार्याणि संमन्त्र्य सुमहान्त्यपि कारय ।।

17. In all great and important) matters, you must take counsel from ministers, wise men, friends, expert counsellors and (then) act.

❍ ❍ ❍

१८. लक्ष्मीश्चन्द्रादपेयाद्वा हिमवान्वा हिमं त्यजेत् ।
अतीयात्सागरो वेलां न प्रतिज्ञामहं पितुः ।।

18. Loveliness may go away from moon; Himaalya-s may 'give' up snow; ocean may cross the shores; (But) I will not (disobey) my father's command.

❍ ❍ ❍

१९. कामाद्वा तात लोभाद्वा मात्रा तुभ्यमिदं कृतम् ।
न तन्मनसि कर्तव्यं वर्तितव्यं च मातृवत् ।।

19. h Lad! What your mother did on your account either by her affection (to you) or for (her) greed, that, you should never take to heart (and curse her for it). You should abide by her as (son) to a mother.

❍ ❍ ❍

२०. एवं ब्रुवाणं भरतः कौसल्यासुतमब्रवीत् ।
तेजसाऽऽदित्यसङ्काशं प्रतिपच्चन्द्रदर्शनम् ।।

20. Bharatha (then) addressed the son of Kowsalya (Raama) who was like the sun in brilliance, whose countenance was like the face of the moon, and who was talking like this.

❍ ❍ ❍

२१. अधिरोहार्य पादाभ्यां पादुके हेमभूषिते ।
एते हि सर्वलोकस्य योगक्षेमं विधास्यतः ।।

21. Oh Aryan (Oh noble Raama)! Please Put On The Gold Decorated Sandals On Your Feet: Because, These Are Going To Bestow Welfare Upon All The World.

(These are the Sandals that Bharatha had brought with him from Ayodhya for Raama to wear during his coronation in the forest as planned by Bharatha. Alas, Raama will not come back nor crown himself. So Bharatha's reverence to Raama inspires him with a great, auspicious thought. He will take Raama's Sandals and 'crown' these in the kingdom. And drawing inspiration from Raama's sandals on throne he will rule Ayodhya for 14 years as regent.)

❍ ❍ ❍

२२. सोऽधिरुह्य नरव्याघ्रः पादुके ह्यवरुह्य च ।
प्रायच्छत्सुमहातेजा भरताय महात्मने ।।

22. Then the most brilliant (Raama) the 'tiger' of men, put on (The Sandals) on his feet and then removed them: He (then) gave (The Sandals) to the great soul Bharatha.

❍ ❍ ❍

२३. स पादुके संप्रणम्य रामं वचनमब्रवीत् ।
चतुर्दश हि वर्षाणि जटाचीरधरो ह्यहम् ।।

23. Then (Bharatha) addressed Raama after paying his respects to The Sandals: = I Will Also Sport Twisted Hair Style (like you Raama)! And Wear (only) Bark Dresses For 14 years .....

❍ ❍ ❍

२४. फलमूलाशनो वीर भवेयं रघुनन्दन ।
तवागमनमाकाङ्क्षन्वसन्वै नगराद्बहिः ।।

24. Oh brave (Raama) the darling of Raghu-s! Awaiting your return (after 14 years of exile), I will stay on, outside the city (of Ayodhya), sustaining myself with (only) fruits and tubers (like you) ......

❍ ❍ ❍

२५. तव पादुकयोर्न्यस्य राज्यतन्त्रं परंतप ।
चतुर्दशे हि संपूर्णेवर्षेऽहनि रघूत्तम ।।
न द्रक्ष्यामि यदि त्वां तु प्रवेक्ष्यामि हुताशनम् ।।

25. Oh foremost (Raama) the Raaghava! Oh the tormentor of enemies! Having invested the governance of the kingdom in your Sandals, if after completion of 14 years, I do not see .you (return), then, that very moment I will enter fire (give up my life)=

❍ ❍ ❍

२६. तथेति च प्रतिज्ञाय संपरिष्वज्य सादरम् ।
शत्रुघ्नं च परिष्वज्य भरतं चेदमब्रवीत् ।।

26. And (Raama) assuring (Bharatha by saying) = So

Be It = , hugged him with affection. Then he hugged Schathrugna. And said this to Bharatha.

❍ ❍ ❍

२७. मातरं रक्ष कैकेय्यीं मा रोषं कुरु तां प्रति ।
मया च सीतया चैव शप्तोऽसि रघुनन्दन ॥

27. Oh (Bharatha) the darling of Raghu-s! (take proper care and) protect mother Kaikeyi. You should never exhibit wrath on your mother (Kaikeyi). You are under oath to me and Seetha!

❍ ❍ ❍

२८. इत्युक्त्वाऽश्रुपरीताक्षो भ्रातरं विससर्ज ह ॥

28. Saying this, (Raama) whose eyes were full with tears, gave leave to his brother (Bharatha and Schathrugna to get back to Ayodhya).

❍ ❍ ❍

२९. स पादुके ते भरतः प्रतापवान्
स्वलंकृते संपरिगृह्य धर्मवित् ।
प्रदक्षिणं चैव चकार राघवं
चकार चैवोत्तमनागमूर्धनि ॥

29. The glorious man of Dharma, this Bharatha, taking the well decorated Sandals, placed them on top of his head. And he went round Raama in circumbumbulation.

❍ ❍ ❍

३०. अथानुपूर्व्यात्प्रतिनन्द्य तं जनं
गुरूंश्च मन्त्रीन्प्रकृतीस्तथाऽनुजौ ।
व्यसर्जयद्राघववंशवर्धनः
स्थितः स्वधर्मेहिमवानिवाचलः ॥

30. Then (Raama) who, like Himaalya-s, was firm and unshaken in his own Dharma and who glorified the race of Raghu-s, gave leave to all the citizens, teachers

(elders), his ministers, likewise the common folks and his two brothers, bidding them all farewell successively (as per protocol).

❍ ❍ ❍

३१. तं मातरो बाष्पगृहीतकण्ठ्यो
दुःखेन नामन्त्रयितुं हि शेकुः ।
स त्वेव मातृरभिवाद्य सर्वा
रुदन्कुटीं स्वां प्रविवेश रामः ॥

31. (But) his mothers (mother Kowsalya and step mother Sumithra and Kaikeyi) could not take leave of him because of their distress, their throats choked by tears. And Raama then entered his hermitage, crying, after paying his obeisance to all his mothers.

❍ ❍ ❍

Chapter 113

Bharatha Returns to Ayodhya

१. ततः शिरसि कृत्वा तु पादुके भरतस्तदा ।
आरुरोह रथं हृष्टः शत्रुघ्नेन समन्वितः ॥

1. Then carrying Raama's (Royal) Sandals on his head, Bharatha who was pleased, got into the chariot along with Schathrugna.

❍ ❍ ❍

२. वसिष्ठो वामदेवश्च जाबालिश्च दृढव्रतः ।
अग्रतः प्रययुः सर्वेमन्त्रिणो मन्त्रपूजिताः ॥

2. Vasishta, Vaamadheva, the austere Jaabaali (the man of firm vows), honoured statesmen, ministers, all went along in front.

❍ ❍ ❍

३. मन्दाकिनीं नदीं रम्यां प्राङ्मुखास्ते ययुस्तदा ।
प्रदक्षिणं च कुर्वाणाश्चित्रकूटं महागिरिम् ।।

3. Going round the lovely Mandhaakini river and the great hills of Chithrakoot, they went towards east.

❍ ❍ ❍

४. पश्यन्सानुसहस्राणि रम्याणि विविधानि च ।
प्रययौ तस्य पार्श्वेन ससैन्यो भरतस्तदा ।।

4. And along with his army, Bharatha went along close by, seeing various beautiful table lands of many mountains.

❍ ❍ ❍

५. अदूराच्चित्रकूटस्य ददर्श भरतस्तदा ।
आश्रमं यत्र स मुनिर्भरद्वाजः कृतालयः ।।

5. Then Bharatha saw the hermitage where Sage Bharadhwaaja had his abode, not far away from Chithrakoot.

❍ ❍ ❍

६. स तामश्रममासाद्य भरतद्वाजस्य बुद्धिमान् ।
अवतीर्य रथात्पादौ ववन्दे भरतस्तदा ।।

6. Then the wise Bharatha, on reaching Sage Bhardhwaaja's hermitage, got down from his chariot, and bowed at his feet.

❍ ❍ ❍

७. ततो हृष्टो भरद्वाजो भरतं वाक्यमब्रवीत् ।
अपि कृत्यं कृतं तात रामेण च समागतः ।।

7. And Sage Bharadhwaaja who was very happy, asked Bharatha these words; = Oh Lad! Was mission successful. Were you 'received' by Raama?=

❍ ❍ ❍

८. एवमुक्तः स तु ततो भरद्वाजेन धीमता ।
प्रत्युवाच भरद्वाजं भरतो भ्रातृवत्सलः ।।

8. When asked thus by the wise Bharadhwaaja, this Bharatha who was most devoted to his brother (Raama) then replied to Bharadhwaaja.

❍ ❍ ❍

९. स याच्यमानो गुरुणा मया च दृढविक्रमः ।
राघवः परमप्रीतो वसिष्ठं वाक्यमब्रवीत् ।।

9. (Bharatha narrates to Bharadhwaaja all that happened at Raama's hermitage: How his mission was not entirely a failure.)

(Raama) the Raaghava, the man with powerful strides who was begged by me and by the Guru (Vasishta), told these words to Vasishta with great joy.

❍ ❍ ❍

१०. पितुः प्रतिज्ञां तामेव पालयिष्यामि तत्त्वतः ।
चतुर्दश हि वर्षाणि या प्रतिज्ञा पितुर्मम ।।

10. (Oh Bharadhwaaja, this is what Raama told Vasishta and me) Whatever be the command of my father, that command I will abide by truly, during the 14 years (I will not cut short my exile).

❍ ❍ ❍

११. एवमुक्तो महाप्राज्ञो वसिष्ठः प्रत्युवाच ह ।
वाक्यज्ञो वाक्यकुशलं राघवं वचनं महत् ।।

11. (And Oh Bharadhwaaja! This is what Vasishta said to Raama.)

When told thus (by Raama) the most intelligent Vasishta who knew the art of speech, replied with these great words.

❍ ❍ ❍

१२. एते प्रयच्छ संहृष्टः पादुके हेमभूषिते ।
अयोध्यायां महाप्राज्ञ योगक्षेमकरे तव ॥

12. Oh most intelligent (Raama)! You bestow your, these Gold Decorated Sandals Happily (and hand over to Bharatha) For The Welfare and Prosperity at Ayodhya. (There is no evidence that Vasishta requested Raama to offer Sandals. Yet, out of his deep regard and respect for Sage Vasishta, Bharatha tells Bharadhwaaja as though Vasishta had requested Raama to offer his Royal Sandals so that under its Token of Authority, Bharatha can rule Ayodhya.)

❍ ❍ ❍

१३. एवमुक्तो वसिष्ठेन राघवः प्राङ्मुखः स्थितः ।
पादुके अधिरुह्यैते मम राज्याय वै ददौ ॥

13. (Oh Bharadhwaaja): When (Raama) was told thus by Vasishta, (Raama) the Raaghava stood up facing east, put on his (royal) Sandals and then gave me these for rule over the kingdom (as a symbol and authority and inspiration of Raama's rule in his absence).

❍ ❍ ❍

१४. निवृत्तोऽहमनुज्ञातो रामेण सुमहात्मना ।
अयोध्यामेव गच्छामि गृहीत्वा पादुके शुभे ॥

14. (Oh Bharadhwaaja): Given leave by the great soul Raama and taking with me the auspicious (royal) Sandals, I returned and am going back to Ayodhya.

❍ ❍ ❍

१५. एतच्छ्रुत्वा शुभं वाक्यं भरतस्य महात्मनः ।
भरद्वाजः शुभतरं मुनिर्वाक्यमुवाच ह ॥

15. (Bharadhwaaja is very happy hearing all this from Bharatha) Hearing such (good) auspicious news of the great soul Bharatha, Sage Bharadhwaaja said these most.

❍ ❍ ❍

१६. नैतच्चित्रं नरव्याघ्र शीलवृत्तवतां वर ।
यदार्यं त्वयि तिष्ठेत्तु निम्ने सृष्टमिवोदकम् ।।

16. Oh (Bharatha) 'the tiger' of men! Oh foremost amongst men of good conduct! Like water (held) in deep crevice, the character of an Aryan (character of nobility), abides in you: (Therefore) All this is not strange.

❍ ❍ ❍

१७. अमृतः स महाबाहुः पिता दशरथस्तव ।
यस्य त्वमीदृशः पुत्रो धर्मज्ञो धर्मवत्सलः ।।

17. Your father, the mighty limbed Dhascharatha is indeed immortal when he has such a son in you, who is a knower of Dharma, who is devoted to Dharma.

❍ ❍ ❍

१८. तमृषिं तु महात्मानमुक्तवाक्यं कृताञ्जलिः ।
आमन्त्रयितुमारेभे चरणावुपगृह्य च ।।

18. Clasping the feet of this Sage, of the great soul (Bharadhwaaja) who had spoken thus, (Bharatha) sought leave from him to depart, with his hands cupped in Anjali.

❍ ❍ ❍

१९. ततः प्रदक्षिणं कृत्वा भरद्वाजं पुनः पुनः ।
भरतस्तु ययौ श्रीमानयोध्यां सह मन्त्रिभिः ।।

19. The resplendent Bharatha went round Bharadhwaaja in circmbumbulation again and again. And from there, along with his ministers (and entourage) left for Ayodhya.

❍ ❍ ❍

२०. यानैश्च शकटैश्चैव हयैर्नागैश्च सा चमूः ।
पुनर्निवृत्ता विस्तीर्णा भरतस्यानुयायिनी ।।

20. Bharatha's Army that comprised chariots, vehicles,

horses, elephants, following him, also returned (with Bharatha to Ayodhya).

❍ ❍ ❍

२१. ततस्ते यमुनां दिव्यां नदीं तीर्त्वोर्मिमालिनीम् ।
ददृशुस्तां पुनः सर्वेगङ्गां शुभजलां नदीम् ।।

21. Then all of them crossed the holy Yamuna river, (the river) with garland of waves; Then they saw the holy waters of Ganges again.

❍ ❍ ❍

२२. तां पुण्यजलसंपूर्णां संतीर्य सहबान्धवः ।
श्रृङ्गिबेरपुरं रम्यं प्रविवेश ससैनिकः ।।

22. Along with relatives and folks and along with his Army, he crossed (Ganges) which was full with holy waters: And they entered the beautiful Schringabhaera pura (town).

❍ ❍ ❍

२३. श्रृङ्गिबेरपुराद्भूयस्त्वयोध्यां संददर्श ह ।।

23. From Schringabhaera pura, they (went along and) saw Ayodhya.

❍ ❍ ❍

२४. अयोध्यां च ततो दृष्ट्वा पित्रा भ्रात्रा विनाकृताम् ।
भरतो दुःखसंतप्तः सारथिं वाक्यमब्रवीत् ।।

24. Tormented by grief on seeing this Ayodhya bereft of his father (Dhascharatha) or brother (Raama), Bharatha addressed his charioteer (Sumanthra).

❍ ❍ ❍

२५. सारथे पश्य विध्वस्ता साऽयोध्या न प्रकाशते ।
निराकारा निरानन्दा दीना प्रतिहतस्वना ।।

25. Oh Charioteer! See this: This (our) Ayodhya appears feeble, formless, bereft of joy, with dull sounds. It appears ruined!

❍ ❍ ❍

Chapter 114

(Bharatha Returns) Enters Ayodhya

(When Bharatha returns to Ayodhya with Raama's Sandals as token of Raama's authority, he finds the city totally dejected. Poet Vaalmeeki describes the scene: Stanzas 2 to 20.)

❍ ❍ ❍

१. स्निग्धगम्भीरघोषेण स्यन्दनेनोपयान्प्रभुः ।
अयोध्यां भरतः क्षिप्रं प्रविवेश महायशाः ।।

1. The most famous Lord Bharatha who was coming in his beautiful chariot that was making loud but pleasant sounds, quickly entered Ayodhya. (And he saw Ayodhya appearing like this) ......

❍ ❍ ❍

२. बिडालोलूकचरितामालीननरवारणाम् ।
तिमिरेणाहतां कालीमप्रकाशां निशामिव ।।

2. ...... Cats and owls were moving about; Deserted by men; Was dark, covered by darkness; Appeared like black night ......

❍ ❍ ❍

३. राहुशत्रोः प्रियां पत्नीं श्रिया प्रज्वलितप्रभाम् ।
ग्रहेणाभ्युत्थितेनैकां रोहिणीमिव पीडिताम् ।।

3. ...... Like (Raahu's enemy) the moon's beloved wife Rohini who (normally) shines with resplendent

brilliancy (but) who is (now) alone, tormented by the rising (of evil) Star (during season) ......

❍ ❍ ❍

४. अल्पोष्णक्षुब्धसलिलां धर्मोत्तप्तविहंगमाम् ।
लीनमीनझषग्राहां कृशां गिरिनदीमिव ॥

4. .... Like a sparse mountain river whose waters are turbid, lukewarm, bereft of small and large fishes, with birds (hovering) being tormented by heat ....

❍ ❍ ❍

५. विधूमामिव हेमाभामध्वराग्नेः समुत्थिताम् ।
हविरभ्युक्षितां पश्चाच्छिखां विप्रलयं गताम् ॥

5. ..... Like fire rising high during Fire Rituals when oblations are offered, appearing golden without any smoke, but later on put out ....

❍ ❍ ❍

६. विध्वस्तकवचां रुग्णगजवाजिरथध्वजाम् ।
हतप्रवीरामापन्नां चमूमिव महाहवे ॥

6. .... Like a broken down Army during a great war with various warriors killed, with armours strewn, with wounded horses, elephants, and broken chariots ....

❍ ❍ ❍

७. सफेनां सस्वनां भूत्वा सागरस्य समुत्थिताम् ।
प्रशान्तमारुतोद्धूतां जलोर्मिमिव निःस्वनाम् ॥

7. Like the waves of the ocean that rise up with foam and loud roar but die out (stilled) by wind and become stilled ......

❍ ❍ ❍

८. त्यक्तां यज्ञायुधैः सर्वैरभिरूपैश्च याजकैः ।
सुत्याकाले विनिर्वृत्ते वेदिं गतरवामिव ॥

8. ...... Like (the stillness) after the stoppage of (recitation of) holy Texts at the end of performance of Rituals by worthy priests, with the materials for the Yaaga Ceremony abandoned (in the Hall)

❍ ❍ ❍

९. गोष्ठमध्ये स्थितामार्तामचरन्तीं नवं तृणम् ।
गोवृषेण परित्यक्तां गवां पत्नीमिवोत्सुकाम् ।।

9. Like cow standing in the middle of a Cow-Pen, refusing to eat fresh grass, grieving over the bull that has abandoned it ....

❍ ❍ ❍

१०. प्रभाकराद्यैः सुस्निग्धैः प्रज्वलद्भिरिवोत्तमैः ।
वियुक्तां मणिभिर्जात्यैर्नवां मुक्तावलीमिव ।।

10. Like a new pearl necklace strung up without sparkling, polished gems of Prabhaakara-s of foremost origin and cuts ....

❍ ❍ ❍

११. सहसा चलितां स्थानान्महीं पुण्यक्षयाद्गताम् ।
संहृतद्युतिविस्तारां तारामिव दिवश्च्युताम् ।।

11. ...... Like star falling down on earth from the sky suddenly, moving out of its place having lost its 'merit' and having lost its extensive (sparkle and) brilliance.

❍ ❍ ❍

१२. पुष्पनद्धां वसन्तान्ते मत्तभ्रमरनादिताम् ।
द्रुतदावाग्निविप्लुष्टां क्लान्तां वनलतामिव ।।

12. ...... Like a black forest tree which was once in full bloom with bees humming around (but now) being ruined by forest fire conflagration during summer ......

१३. संमूढनिगमां स्तब्धां संक्षिप्तविपणापणाम् ।
प्रच्छन्नशशिनक्षत्रां द्यामिवाम्बुधरैर्वृताम् ।।

13. ...... Everything stilled: Population bewildered: Total stoppage of business activity: (appearing) Like a sky with moon and stars covered by clouds ....

❍ ❍ ❍

१४. क्षीणपानोत्तमैर्भिन्नैः शरावैरभिसंवृताम् ।
हतशौण्डामिवाकाशे पानभूमिमसंस्कृताम् ।।

14. ...... Without fine drinks: Full of broken (water and liquor) mugs, cups etc.: Like an open place of drinking deserted by men; disorderly ......

❍ ❍ ❍

१५. वृक्णभूमितलां निम्नां वृक्णपात्रैः समावृताम् ।
उपयुक्तोदकां भग्नां प्रपां निपतितामिव ।।

15. ..... Surface of earth broken up, with lots of cleavages; Earth covered with broken utensils; Was like a dilapidated broken down water shed ......

❍ ❍ ❍

१६. विपुलां विततां चैव युक्तपाशां तरस्विनाम् ।
भूमौ बाणैर्विनिष्कृत्तां पतितां ज्यामिवायुधात् ।।

16. ...... Like the strings of the bow that has fallen on earth being cut away by (constant discharge of) arrows of warriors after (these strings) had been stretched (in the bow.)

❍ ❍ ❍

१७. सहसा युद्धशौण्डेन हयारोहेण वाहिताम् ।
निक्षिप्तभाण्डामुत्सृष्टां किशोरीमिव दुर्बलाम् ।।

17. ...... Like a war horse after its harness is cut off by the horse rider and driven way fiercely but (later on appearing) like a weak female horse ....

❍ ❍ ❍

१८. शुष्कतोयां महामत्स्यैः कूर्मैश्च बहुभिर्वृताम् ।
प्रभिन्नतटविस्तीर्णां वापीमिव हृतोत्पलाम् ।।

18. ...... Like a pond which once was full of many large fishes, tortoises, but now without water nor lotus flowers, its banks broken and shattered ......

❍ ❍ ❍

१९. पुरुषस्याप्रहृष्टस्य प्रतिषिद्धानुलेपनाम् ।
सन्तप्तामिव शोकेन गात्रयष्टिमभूषणाम् ।।

19. ...... like the body of an unhappy man who is tormented by grief, who had not been anointed with sandal pastes nor decorated himself with ornaments ......

❍ ❍ ❍

२०. प्रावृषि प्रविगाढायां प्रविष्टस्याभ्रमण्डलम् ।
प्रच्छन्नां नीलजीमूतैर्भास्करस्य प्रभामिव ।।

20. ...... Like the brightness of the Sun when it enters the cloud region (of the sky) and is covered by blue clouds during fierce rainy season ......

(Such was the state of Ayodhya as Vaalmeeki poetically describes it.)

❍ ❍ ❍

२१. भरतस्तु रथस्थः सञ्श्रीमान्दशरथात्मजः ।
वाहयन्तं रथश्रेष्ठं सारथिं वाक्यमब्रवीत् ।।

21. The resplendent son of Dhascharatha, this Bharatha, spoke to his charioteer (Sumanthra) who was driving this foremost chariot, (standing) on his chariot.

❍ ❍ ❍

२२. किं नु खल्वद्य गम्भीरो मूर्च्छितो न निशम्यते ।
यथापुरमयोध्यायां गीतवादित्रनिःस्वनः ।।

22. Now, in Ayodhya, loud melodies of vocal music and

instrumental strains are not heard as before; How come? Indeed.

❍ ❍ ❍

२३. वारुणीमदगन्धश्च माल्यगन्धश्च मूर्च्छितः ।
धूपितागरुगन्धश्च न प्रवाति समन्ततः ।।

23. The stupefying and permeating smell of liquors, smell of flowers, smell of incenses and Agara, are not blowing forth (now).

❍ ❍ ❍

२४. यानप्रवरघोषश्च स्निग्धश्च हयनिःस्वनः ।
प्रमत्तगजनादश्च महांश्च रथनिःस्वनः ।।
नेदानीं श्रूयते पुर्यामस्यां रामे विवासिते ।।

24. Now that Raama is on exile, in this city, the sounds of (moving) vehicles, the neighing of horses, sounds from exhilarated elephants and the loud roaring sounds of chariots are not heard.

❍ ❍ ❍

२५. चन्दनागरुगन्धांश्च महार्हाश्च नवस्रजः ।
गते हि रामे तरुणाः सन्तप्ता नोपभुञ्जते ।।

25. When Raama left, (since then), youths have not put on costly new garlands nor (anointed themselves) with sandal, agara pastes & scents, being tormented (by grief over Raama).

❍ ❍ ❍

२६. बहिर्यात्रां न गच्छन्ति चित्रमाल्यधरा नराः ।
नोत्सवाः संप्रवर्तन्ते रामशोकार्दिते पुरे ।।

26. In this city that is stricken with grief over Raama, men are not going out on journey wearing wonderful garlands; And (there are) no festivities now.

२७. सा हि नूनं मम भ्रात्रा पुरस्यास्य द्युतिर्गता ।
न हि राजत्ययोध्येयं सासारेवार्जुनो क्षपा ।।

27. Gone is the glory of the city now with my brother (Raama gone): Because this city, the colorful Ayodhya is not shining. It is like the (dark) night with rain and thunder.

❍ ❍ ❍

२८. कदा नु खलु मे भ्राता महोत्सव इवागतः ।
जनयिष्यत्ययोध्यायां हर्षं ग्रीष्म इवाम्बुदः ।।

28. When will my brother (Raama) return (to Ayodhya) like cloud coming back during hot season and bring joy to Ayodhya, (like joy) during festivities.

❍ ❍ ❍

२९. तरुणैश्चारुवेषैश्च नरैरुन्नतगामिभिः ।
संपतद्भिरयोध्यायां नातिभान्ति महापथाः ।।

29. The (royal) boulevards of Ayodhya do not shine with youthful men wearing lovely dresses (and ornaments) roaming about, and walking along gracefully.

❍ ❍ ❍

३०. एवं बहुविधं जल्पन्विवेश वसतिं पितुः ।
तेन हीनां नरेन्द्रेण सिंहहीनां गुहामिव ।।

30. Wailing thus in many ways, (Bharatha) entered father's abode that was (now) without (his father Dhascharatha) the lord of men, which was like a cave without a lion.

❍ ❍ ❍

३१. तदा तदन्तःपुरमुज्झितप्रभं
सुरैरिवोत्सृष्टमभास्करं दिनम् ।
निरीक्ष्य सर्वत्र विभक्तमात्मवान्
मुमोच बाष्पं भरतः सुदुःखितः ।।

31. Then, observing that his (father's) Inner apartments (of his palace) was desolate totally, and its colour (and liveliness gone) like the day without sun, abandoned (and cursed by) Dheva-s, the (usually) composed Bharatha became very sad and shed tears.

❍ ❍ ❍

Chapter 115

(Bharatha) Crowns (Raama's) Sandals

१. ततो निक्षिप्य मातृः स अयोध्यायां दृढव्रतः ।
भरतः शोकसन्तप्तो गुरूनिदमथाब्रवीत् ॥

1. After settling his mothers at Ayodhya, tormented by grief, Bharatha who was resolute in vows, then addressed the elders, thus.

(Bharatha decides to establish a temporary capital; As far as he is concerned only Raama is entitled to the throne at Ayodhya.. Not only that, he crowns Raama's Sandals as though he is only an Agent of Raama during the 14 years of Raama's exile.)

❍ ❍ ❍

२. नन्दिग्रामं गमिष्यामि सर्वानामन्त्रयेऽद्य वः ।
तत्र दुःखमिदं सर्वं सहिष्ये राघवं विना ॥

2. I am now going to Nandhigram. I am taking leave of you all. I will bear all this suffering caused by separation from Raama, there. (I am going to rule Ayodhya kingdom from temporary capital Nandhigram).

❍ ❍ ❍

३. गतश्च हि दिवं राजा वनस्थश्च गुरुर्मम ।
रामं प्रतीक्षे राज्याय स हि राजा महायशाः ॥

3. The king (my father) has gone away to heaven; My Guru (brother Raama) is staying in forest. The most

famous (Raama) is indeed the King! I look up to Raama only! (look up to) for ruling his kingdom.

❍ ❍ ❍

४. एतच्छ्रुत्वा शुभं वाक्यं भरतस्य महात्मनः ।
अब्रुवन्मन्त्रिणः सर्वे वसिष्टश्च पुरोहितः ।।

4. Hearing such noble words of the great soul Bharatha, Purohith Vasishta and all other ministers said:

❍ ❍ ❍

५. सुभृशं श्लाघनीयं च यदुक्तं भरत त्वया ।
वचनं भ्रातृवात्सल्यादनुरूपं तवैव तत् ।।

5. Oh Bharatha! What you said out of affection to your brother (Raama) is very much praise worthy; It befits you.

❍ ❍ ❍

६. नित्यं ते बन्धुलुब्धस्य तिष्टतो भ्रातृसौहृदे ।
आर्यमार्गं प्रपन्नस्य नानुमन्येत कः पुमान् ।।

6. Which person will not respect and honour you who are ever firmly devoted to your brother, who chose the path of a true Aryan, who longs for his (close) relative (brother Raama).

❍ ❍ ❍

७. मन्त्रिणां वचनं श्रुत्वा यथाभिलषितं प्रियम् ।
अब्रवीत्सारथिं वाक्यं रथो मे युज्यतामिति ।।

7. Hearing the words of the ministers spoken so affectionately, (Bharatha) told charioteer (Sumanthra)= May my chariot be got ready =

❍ ❍ ❍

८. प्रहृष्टवदनः सर्वा मातृः समभिवाद्य सः ।
आरुरोह रथं श्रीमाञ्छत्रुघ्नेन समन्वितः ।।

8. With a cheerful face, this resplendent (Bharatha) bowed before all his mothers and got into the chariot with (brother) Schathrugna.

❍ ❍ ❍

९. आरुह्य च रथं शीघ्रं शत्रुघ्नभरतावुभौ ।
ययतुः परमप्रीतौ वृतौ मन्त्रिपुरोहितैः ॥

9. Getting into the chariot, these two, Bharatha and Schathrugna who were accompanied by ministers and purohiths, went along, very pleased.

❍ ❍ ❍

१०. अग्रतो गुरवस्तस्य वसिष्ठप्रमुखा द्विजाः ।
प्रययुः प्राङ्मुखाः सर्वेनन्दिग्रामो यतोऽभवत् ॥

10. The elders, Braamins, along with Vasishta and others, went along before them, towards the direction of east, where Nandhigram was.

❍ ❍ ❍

११. बलं च तदानाहूतं रथाश्वगजसंकुलम् ।
प्रययौ भरते याते सर्वेच पुरवासिनः ॥

11. (But) When Bharatha left, the Army full of chariots, elephants and horses went along uninvited. Likewise, all the citizens.

❍ ❍ ❍

१२. रथस्थः स तु धर्मात्मा भरतो भ्रातृवत्सलः ।
नन्दिग्रामं ययौ तूर्णं शिरस्याधाय पादुके ॥

12. Riding the chariot, placing the (Royal) Sandals (of Raama) on his head, the noble soul man of Dharma, this Bharatha who was devoted to his brother (Raama) reached Nandhigraamam, quickly.

❍ ❍ ❍

१३. ततस्तु भरतः क्षिप्रं नन्दिग्रामं प्रविश्य सः ।
अवतीर्य रथात्तूर्णं गुरुनिदमुवाच ह ॥

13. Entering Nandhigraamam soon, this Bharatha then got down quickly from chariot, and addressed the Guru-s (all the VIP-s and elders).

❍ ❍ ❍

१४. एतद्राज्यं मम भ्रात्रा दत्तं संन्यासवत्स्वयम् ।
योगक्षेमवहे चेमे पादुके हेमभूषिते ॥

14. This Kingdom was given and thrust upon me by my brother (Raama) himself. And these gold decorated (royal) Sandals (of Raama) Will Guide and Offer Security and Welfare.

❍ ❍ ❍

१५. भरतः शिरसा कृत्वा संन्यासं पादुके ततः ।
अब्रवीद्दुःखसन्तप्तः सर्वं प्रकृतिमण्डलम् ॥

15. Then, with his head down, bowing to The Sandals that was intrusted to him, Bharatha addressed the vast multitude of men, tormented by grief.

❍ ❍ ❍

१६. छत्रं धारयत क्षिप्रमार्यपादाविमौ मतौ ।
आभ्यां राज्ये स्थितो धर्मः पादुकाभ्यां गुरोर्मम ॥

16. As these are to be considered (and treated with respect) as Aryan (Raama's) Sandals, hold umbrella over it quickly: With these Sandals of my Guru (Raama), Dharma will be steadfast in our kingdom.

❍ ❍ ❍

१७. क्षिप्रं संयोजयित्वा तु राघवस्य पुनः स्वयम् ।
चरणौ तौ तु रामस्य द्रक्ष्यामि सहपादुकौ ॥

17. These that were entrusted to me by my brother, is the

Trust. I will protect this till (Raama) the Raaghava returns (from his exile).

❍ ❍ ❍

१८. भ्रात्रा तु मयि संन्यासो निक्षिप्तः सौहृदादयम् ।
तमिमं पालयिष्यामि राघवागमनं प्रति ॥

18. When once again I put these (Sandals) on the feet of (Raama) the Raaghava, I will soon "See" and enjoy his feet with these Sandals (on him).

❍ ❍ ❍

१९. ततो निक्षिप्तभारोऽहं राघवेण समागतः ।
निवेद्य गुरवे राज्यं भजिष्ये गुरुवृत्तिताम् ॥

19. When I meet (Raama) the Raaghava and hand over the kingdom back to my Guru (Raama), I will serve my lord (Raama) (but) without burden (of responsibility of ruling the kingdom).

❍ ❍ ❍

२०. राघवाय च संन्यासं दत्त्वेमे वरपादुके ।
राज्यं चेदमयोध्यां च धूतपापो भवामि च ॥

20. (After his exile, after) Handing over to Raama the Raaghava these worshipful Sandals that are The Trust and (thus handing over) also Ayodhya and the rule of kingdom, I will be relieved of my sin (only then).

❍ ❍ ❍

२१. अभिषिक्ते तु काकुत्स्थे प्रहृष्टे मुदिते जने ।
प्रीतिर्मम यशश्चैव भवेद्राज्याच्चतुर्गुणम् ॥

21. When (Raama) the Kaakuthsa is happily anointed (as king) and when citizens become happy (with him as king), my happiness and my fame will be *four times greater than (what I obtain) by rule of kingdom.

(* Four times: No wonder: All four brothers will be there!)

❍ ❍ ❍

२२. एवं तु विलपन्दीनो भरतः स महायशाः ।
नन्दिग्रामेऽकरोद्राज्यं दुःखितो मन्त्रिभिः सह ।।

22. Wailing and grieving thus miserably, the famous Bharatha established rule over kingdom at Nandhigraamam, along with his ministers.

❍ ❍ ❍

२३. स वल्कलजटाधारी मुनिवेषधरः प्रभुः ।
नन्दिग्रामेऽवसद्वीरः ससैन्यो भरतस्तदा ।।

23. The brave lord Bharatha, wearing dress of a Muni by wearing bark and sporting twisted hairlocks (like a mendicant), then lived in Nandhigraamam along with his Army.

❍ ❍ ❍

२४. रामागमनमाकाङ्क्षन्भरतो भ्रातृवत्सलः ।
भ्रातुर्वचनकारी च प्रतिज्ञापारगस्तथा ।।

24. Looking forward to the return of Raama (after his exile), Bharatha was devoted to his brother (Raama): And he acted as per brother (Raama's Diktat and) words; Ever kept his word.

❍ ❍ ❍

२५. पादुके त्वभिषिच्याथ नन्दिग्रामेऽवसत्तदा ।
भरतः शासनं सर्वं पादुकाभ्यां न्यवेदयत् ।।

25. Consecrating The Sandals, Bharatha then lived in Nandhigraamam: He placed all his acts (all his governance at the feet of Raama which, in this case are) the pair of his Sandals!

❍ ❍ ❍

२६. ततस्तु भरतः श्रीमानभिषिच्यार्यपादुके ।
तदधीनस्तदा राज्यं कारयामास सर्वदा ।।

26. After anointing Aryan (Raama's) Sandals, the

resplendent Bharatha, from then on, ruled over the kingdom, always as its subject!

❍ ❍ ❍

२७. तु हि यत्कार्यमुपैति किंचि
द्रुपायनं चोपहृतं महार्हम् ।
स पादुकाभ्यां प्रथमं निवेद्य
चकार पश्चाद्भरतो यथावत् ।।

27. Even if it was a small event that happened or a costly (gift) was brought up (to him from his vassals), this Bharatha first placed them before The Sandals and then only acted suitably.

(Note: Bharatha rules for 14 years as an Agent of Raama from the temporary capital Nandhigram. He treats Raama's sandals honoured in The Throne as his authority to administer the kingdom with Dharma: From now on Raamaayana is all about Raama.We take leave of Bharatha and Ayodhya.)

❍ ❍ ❍

Chapter 116

Sages Narrate About Suffering Caused by Demons like Khara

(Poet Vaalmeeki takes leave of Bharatha who, as Raama's agent, rules over Ayodhya during 14 years of Raama's Exile. The scene shifts to Raama and his forest life. In fact, from now on, it is all about Raama and his service to humanity: No more about Ayodhya.)

❍ ❍ ❍

१. प्रतिप्रयाते भरते वसन्रामस्तपोवने ।
लक्षयामास सोद्वेगमथौत्सुक्यं तपस्विनाम् ।।

1. After Bharatha had gone back (to Ayodhya), Raama who was living in forest, (forest of penance), observed the anxiety and agitation of the sages (living there).

❍ ❍ ❍

२. ये तत्र चित्रकूटस्य पुरस्तात्तापसाश्रमे ।
रामामाश्रित्य निरतास्तानलक्षयदुत्सुकान् ।।

2. In the hermitage of the sages doing penance in Chithrakoot, Raama observed those who before (and till then) sought refuge and were delighted in him (and in his presence), were (now) in a state of anxiety.

❍ ❍ ❍

३. नयनैर्भ्रुकुटीभिश्च राममुद्दिश्य शङ्किताः ।
अन्योन्यमुपजल्पन्तः शनैश्चक्रुर्मिथः कथाः ।।

3. Worrying about Raama, they were silently speaking to each other, talking in secrecy, (twitching) their eyes and eye brows.

❍ ❍ ❍

४. तेषामौत्सुक्यमालक्ष्य रामस्त्वात्मनि शङ्कितः ।
कृताञ्जलिरुवाचेदमृषिं कुलपतिं तदा ।।

4. Then Raama, observing their anxiety, became apprehensive within himself: Cupping his hands in Anjali, he addressed (a sage called) Kulapathi.

❍ ❍ ❍

५. न कच्चिद्भगवन्किञ्चित्पूर्ववृत्तमिदं मयि ।
दृश्यते विकृतं येन विक्रियन्ते तपस्विनः ।।

5. Oh Lord (Kulapathi)! There is change in these men of penance: I hope you do not find change in my (usual proper) conduct now.

❍ ❍ ❍

६. प्रमादाच्चरितं किंचित्कच्चिन्नावरजस्य मे ।
लक्ष्मणस्यर्षिभिर्दृष्टं नानुरूपमिवात्मनः ।।

6. I trust nothing unbecoming, not even a trifle, is seen by these sages in the conduct of my brother Lakshmana towards you all, due to negligence.

❍ ❍ ❍

७. कच्चिच्छुश्रूषमाणा वः शुश्रूषणपरा मयि ।
प्रमादाभ्युचितां वृत्तिं सीता युक्तां न वर्तते ।।

7. I trust Seetha who reveres me in service, has not, during service to you all, committed an act, associated with common negligence.

❍ ❍ ❍

८. अथर्षिर्जरया वृद्धस्तपसा च जरां गतः ।
वेपमान इवोवाच रामं भूतदयापरम् ।।

8. Old in age and penance, the old sage (Kulapathi) addressed Raama who was considerate to all living beings: His body was trembling (as he told Raama thus).

❍ ❍ ❍

९. कुतः कल्याणसत्त्वायाः कल्याणाभिरतेस्तथा ।
चलनं तात वैदेह्यास्तपस्विषु विशेषतः ।।

9. Oh Lad (Oh Raama)! How can there be any change (or deviation in the behaviour of) Seetha the Vaidhehi, who is of noble auspicious character, who delights in doing good service particularly towards sages doing penance!

❍ ❍ ❍

१०. त्वन्निमित्तमिदं तात तापसान्प्रति वर्तते ।
रक्षोभ्यस्तेन संविग्नाः कथयन्ति मिथः कथाः ।।

10. Oh Lad! This (change you have noticed) in these sages

has come about (out of fear) from Demons on your account (and for your sake); therefore they are talking in whispers. (in secrecy).

❍ ❍ ❍

११. रावणावरजः कश्चित्खरो नामेह राक्षसः ।
उत्पाट्य तापसान्सर्वाञ्जनस्थाननिकेतनान् ।।

11. A cruel Raakshasa (Demon) named Khara, the 'brother' of (demon king) Raavana, is 'destroying' all the sages living in Janashthana.

❍ ❍ ❍

१२. धृष्टश्च जितकाशी च नृशंसः पुरुषादकः ।
अवलिप्तश्च पापश्च त्वां च तात न मृष्यते ।।

12. Oh lad! This (Khara) is Impudent; A cannibal; most cruel; steeped in sin; powerful (double fisted); He cannot stand you (Is jealous of you and of your strength).

❍ ❍ ❍

१३. त्वं यदाप्रभृति ह्यस्मिन्नाश्रमे तात वर्तसे ।
तदाप्रभृति रक्षांसि विप्रकुर्वन्ति तापसान् ।।

13. Oh lad! From the moment you stayed in the hermitage here, the demons have started oppressing men of penance here.

❍ ❍ ❍

१४. दर्शयन्ति हि बीभत्सैः क्रूरैर्भीषणकैरपि ।
नानारूपैर्विरूपैश्च रूपैरसुखदर्शनैः ।।

14. These terrible, disgusting, ugly and horrible to look at, (these demons) are now appearing here in different gruesome forms.

❍ ❍ ❍

१५. अप्रशस्तैरशुचिभिः संप्रयोज्य च तापसान् ।
प्रतिघ्नन्त्यपरान्क्षिप्रमनार्याः पुरतः स्थिताः ।।

15. These ignoble (demons) stand before these men of penance who are totally different from them, surround them and at once cause harm to them, (polluting the place) with rotten unworthy things.

❍ ❍ ❍

१६. तेषु तेष्वाश्रमस्थानेष्वबुद्धमवलीय च ।
रमन्ते तापसांस्तत्र नाक्षयन्तोऽल्पचेतसः ॥

16. Petty minded, they delight in destroying the sages in their respective hermitages, hiding themselves, unseen.

❍ ❍ ❍

१७. अपक्षिपन्ति स्रुग्भाण्डानग्नीन्सिञ्चन्ति वारिणा ।
कलशांश्च प्रमृद्नन्ति हवने समुपस्थिते ॥

17. When holy fire rituals are going on, they throw away the holy vessels (from the place of worship). They drop water on the holy Fire. they break vessels.

❍ ❍ ❍

१८. तैर्दुरात्मभिरामृष्टानाश्रमान्प्रजिहासवः ।
गमनायान्यदेशस्य चोदयन्त्यृषयोऽद्य माम् ॥

18. Now (therefore) these Rishi-s are goading me to go away to some other place (of safety), abandoning their (present) hermitages that are being wiped out by these wicked (demons).

❍ ❍ ❍

१९. तत्पुरा राम शारीरीमुपहिंसां तपस्विषु ।
दर्शयन्ति हि दुष्टास्ते त्यक्ष्याम इममाश्रमम् ॥

19. Oh Raama! These demons even maim the bodies of the men of penance. Therefore we are abandoning this place before (more calamity hits us).

❍ ❍ ❍

२०. बहुमूलफलं चित्रमविदूरादितो वनम् ।
कण्वस्याश्रममेवाहं श्रयिष्ये सगणः पुनः ।।

20. Along with my folks here, I am going to live in a place not very far from here, in the forest where Kanva's hermitage is and where there are lots of wonderful fruits and tubers.

❍ ❍ ❍

२१. खरस्त्वय्यपि चायुक्तं पुरा तात प्रवर्तते ।
सहास्माभिरितो गच्छ यदि बुद्धिः प्रवर्तते ।।

21. Oh Lad! (Demon) Khara will harm you also! Before that, if you desire, you may come along with us from here.

❍ ❍ ❍

२२. सकलत्रस्य संदेहो नित्यं यत्तस्य राघव ।
समर्थस्यापि हि सतो वासो दुःखमिहाद्य ते ।।

22. Oh (Raama the) Raaghava! Although you are capable and a watchful man, as you are living with your wife, life here will be dangerous for you. always; uncertain.

❍ ❍ ❍

२३. इत्युक्तवन्तं रामस्तं राजपुत्रस्तपस्विनम् ।
न शशाकोत्तरैर्वाक्यैरवरोद्धुं समुत्सुकम् ।।

23. This Raama the son of king (Dhascharatha), did not prevent (nor offer counter suggestions) with words of reply to this man of penance (Kulapathi) who spoke with anxiety.

❍ ❍ ❍

२४. अभिनन्द्य समापृच्छ्य समाधाय च राघवम् ।
स जगामाश्रमं त्यक्त्वा कुलैः कुलपतिः सह ।।

24. This Kulapathi, after greeting (Raama the) Raaghava and taking his leave, left his hermitage and went along

with his kinsmen, ('permitting' Raama to stay on if he chose to)

❍ ❍ ❍

२५. रामः संसाध्य त्वृषिगणमनुगमना
देशात्तस्मात्कुलपतिमभिवाद्य ऋषिम् ।
सम्यक्प्रीतैस्तैरनुमत उपदिष्टार्थः
पुण्यं वासाय स्वनिलयमुपसंपेदे ॥

25. Raama bowed before the accomplished rishi Kulapathi who was following the multitude of Rishi-s (leaving) from that place; Then honoured and well counselled by these dear (Rishi-s) he (Raama) went back to his own holy abode to live there.

❍ ❍ ❍

२६. आश्रमं त्वृषिविरहितं प्रभुः
क्षणमपि न विजहौ स राघवः ।
राघवं हि सततमनुगता
स्तापसाश्चार्षचरितधृतगुणाः ॥

26. These men of penance who were steadfast in penance and Rituals, these Rishi-s, always thought about (Raama the) Raaghava: And Lord (Raama) the Raaghava did not stir out of the hermitage which was without any Rishi (around), even for a moment.

❍ ❍ ❍

Chapter 117

Anasooya's Righteousness and Virtue

१. राघवस्त्वपयातेषु तपस्विषु विचिन्तयन् ।
न तत्रारोचयद्वासं कारणैर्बहुभिस्तदा ॥

1. When those men of penance had gone away, (Raama

the) Raaghava pondered over the matter and did not desire to live there for various reasons.

❍ ❍ ❍

२. इह मे भरतो दृष्टो मातरश्च सनागराः ।
सा च मे स्मृतिरन्वेति तान्नित्यमनुशोचतः ।।

2. (Raama thought): It was here that Bharatha was seen by me; So were the citizens and my 'mothers': the memory of these who are ever grieving (over me) will follow me (and haunt me if I continue my stay here).

❍ ❍ ❍

३. स्कन्धावारनिवेशेन तेन तस्य महात्मनः ।
हयहस्तिकरीषैश्च उपमर्दः कृतो भृशम् ।।

3. Because of the stationing of the Army of the great soul (Bharatha) and because of the 'refuse' of the elephants and horses etc., this place is 'devastated'.

❍ ❍ ❍

४. तस्मादन्यत्र गच्छाम इति संचिन्त्य राघवः ।
प्रातिष्ठत स वैदेह्या लक्ष्मणेन च सङ्गतः ।।

4. Therefore we shall go to another place: Thinking thus, this (Raama) the Raaghava, along with Lakshmana and (Seetha the) Vaidhehi, started out.

❍ ❍ ❍

५. सोऽत्रेराश्रममासाद्य तं ववन्दे महायशाः ।
तं चापि भगवानत्रिः पुत्रवत्प्रत्यपद्यत ।।

5. Reaching the hermitage of the most famous Sage Athri, he bowed. And the Lord Sage Athri received him just like (a father receiving) a son.

❍ ❍ ❍

६. स्वयमातिथ्यमादिश्य सर्वमस्य सुसत्कृतम् ।
सौमित्रिं च महाभागां सीतां च समसान्त्वयत् ।।

6. Extending hospitality with due honours to (Raama) personally, he comforted (and extended hospitality) to (Lakshmana) the son of Sumithra and to the most illustrious Seetha.

❍ ❍ ❍

७. पत्नीं च समनुप्राप्तां वृद्धामामन्त्र्य सत्कृताम् ।
सान्त्वयामास धर्मज्ञः सर्वभूतहिते रतः ॥

7. The knower of Dharma (Athri) who delighted in doing good to all living beings, then called upon his distinguished old wife and addressed her gently (and kindly).

❍ ❍ ❍

८. अनसूयां महाभागां तापसीं धर्मचारिणीम् ।
प्रतिगृह्णीष्व वैदेहीमब्रवीदृषिसत्तमः ॥

8. This foremost Rishi (Athri) said to the woman of penance, (his wife) Anasooya who practised Dharma = You receive (with due hospitality) the most illustrious (Seetha the) Vaidhehi.=

❍ ❍ ❍

९. रामाय चाचचक्षे तां तापसीं धर्मचारिणीम् ॥

9. He introduced this austere woman who practised Dharma to (Raama) the Raaghava. (like this).

❍ ❍ ❍

१०. दश वर्षाण्यनावृष्ट्या दग्धे लोके निरन्तरम् ।
यया मूलफले सृष्टे जाह्नवी च प्रवर्तिता ॥

10. = (Once) When the world was continuously without rain for 10 years, Fruits and Tubers were created by her! And even (Ganges) river Jaahnavi was 'swelled' (by her penance).

❍ ❍ ❍

११. उग्रेण तपसा युक्ता नियमैश्चाप्यलङ्कृता ।
दश वर्षसहस्राणि यया तप्तं महत्तपः ॥

11. Great penance was performed by her for 10,000 years; She can observe even the most rigorous of penance: She is endowed with restraint and abstinence (totally).

❍ ❍ ❍

१२. अनसूया व्रतैः स्नाता प्रत्यूहाश्च निबर्हिताः ।
देवकार्यनिमित्तं च यया संत्वरमाणया ॥
१३. दशरात्रं कृता रात्रिः सेयं मातेव तेऽनघ ॥

12. & 13.

Anasooya is "bathed" in vows! As a divine (celestial) Duty (and task) with great alacrity, warding off obstacles..............Ten nights were made (to pass off as) one night by her: She is (such a woman): Is sinless: She is like a mother (to you).

❍ ❍ ❍

१४. तामिमां सर्वभूतानां नमस्कार्यां यशस्विनीम् ।
अभिगच्छतु वैदेही वृद्धामक्रोधनां सदा ॥

14. May (Seetha the) Vaidhehi go to (and meet with) this old (Anasooya) who is ever without anger, who is most famous and who deserves to be revered by all living beings.=

❍ ❍ ❍

१५. एवं ब्रुवाणं तमृषिं तथेत्युक्त्वा स राघवः ।
सीतामुवाच धर्मज्ञामिदं वचनमुत्तमम् ॥

15. Saying= So Be It = to the Rishi (Athri) who was talking thus, this (Raama) the Raaghava, addressed the knower of Dharma, (Seetha), with these noble words.

❍ ❍ ❍

१६. राजपुत्रि श्रुतं त्वेतन्मुनेरस्य समीरितम् ।
श्रेयोऽर्थमात्मनः शीघ्रमभिगच्छ तपस्विनीम् ॥

16. Oh royal princess! You have heard this utterance of the Muni (Athri); For the sake of your welfare, go soon to this woman of penance.

❍ ❍ ❍

१७. अनसूयेति या लोके कर्मभिः ख्यातिमागता ।
तां शीघ्रमभिगच्छ त्वमभिगम्यां तपस्विनीम् ।।

17. Go quickly to her who should be approached, who, as Anasooya, has attained renown in the world by her (spiritual) deeds.

❍ ❍ ❍

१८. सीता त्वेतद्वचः श्रुत्वा राघवस्य हितैषिणः ।
तामत्रिपत्नीं धर्मज्ञामभिचक्राम मैथिली ।।

18. Hearing (Raama the) Raaghava's (beneficial) words who desired her welfare, (Seetha) the Maithili, at once went to Athri's wife who was knower of Dharma: (Athri's wife Anasooya was like this).

❍ ❍ ❍

१९. शिथिलां वलितां वृद्धां जरापाण्डुरमूर्धजाम् ।
सततं वेपमानाङ्गीं प्रवाते कदलीं यथा ।।
२०. तां तु सीता महाभागामनसूयां पतिव्रताम् ।
अभ्यवादयदव्यग्रा स्वनाम समुदाहरत् ।।

19. & 20.

She was old; her body bent, tremulous; her white hair decaying with age; all parts of her body trembling; like banana stalks hit by wind.... this most illustrious, most virtuous Anasooya, this Seetha bowed to in reverence; And she (Seetha) uttered her name.

❍ ❍ ❍

२१. अभिवाद्य च वैदेही तापसीं तामनिन्दिताम् ।
बद्धाञ्जलिपुटा हृष्टा पर्यपृच्छदनामयम् ।।

21. After bowing to this sinless woman of penance, (Seetha) the Vaidhehi who had cupped her hands in Anjali, happily enquired about her health.

❍ ❍ ❍

२२. ततः सीतां महाभागां दृष्ट्वा तां धर्मचारिणी ।
सान्त्वयन्त्यब्रवीद्धृष्टा दिष्ट्या धर्ममवेक्षसे ।।

22. On seeing this most illustrious Seetha, (Anasooya) who followed the path of Dharma, became delighted and addressed her kindly; = By Divine (grace) you (always) behold Dharma.

❍ ❍ ❍

२३. त्यक्त्वा ज्ञातिजनं सीते मानमृद्धिं न भामिनि ।
अवरुद्धं वने रामं दिष्ट्या त्वमनुगच्छसि ।।

23. Oh endearing Seetha! It is indeed divine grace that you have abandoned your relatives (and folks), your pride and status, your wealth, (in order) to follow Raama who is in seclusion in forest.

❍ ❍ ❍

२४. नगरस्थो वनस्थो वा पापो वा यदि वा शुभः ।
यासां स्त्रीणां प्रियो भर्ता तासां लोका महोदयाः ।।

24. For those for whom a husband, whether he lives in forest or in city, whether he is a sinner or good man, is the beloved, foremost worlds (after death) are there for them.

❍ ❍ ❍

२५. दुःशीलः कामवृत्तो वा धनैर्वा परिवर्जितः ।
स्त्रीणामार्यस्वभावानां परमं दैवतम पतिः ।।

25. For women who have inborn qualities of an Aryan, husband alone is foremost God, whether he is of evil conduct or of immoral conduct, whether he is in wealth or bereft of wealth.

❍ ❍ ❍

२६. नातो विशिष्टं पश्यामि बान्धवं विमृशन्त्यहम् ।
सर्वत्र योग्यं वैदेहि तपः कृतमिवाव्ययम् ॥

26. Oh (Seetha) the Vaidhehi! I, who am given to (some) deliberation, have not seen greater relative (than my husband) who is worthy in every respect, who is like eternal penance done.

❍ ❍ ❍

२७. न त्वेनमवगच्छन्ति गुणदोषमसत्स्त्रियः ।
कामवक्तव्यहृदया भर्तृनाथाश्चरन्ति याः ॥

27. Bad women who control their husband, whose heart is set on sensuality (and pleasures), do not realise the sinful aspect in this.

❍ ❍ ❍

२८. प्राप्नुवन्त्ययशश्चैव धर्मभ्रंशं च मैथिलि ।
अकार्यवशमापन्नाः स्त्रियो याः खलु तद्विधाः ॥

28. Oh (Seetha) the Maithili! Such women indulge in wrongful acts and obtain disgrace and stray away from Dharma; Surely

❍ ❍ ❍

२९. त्वद्विधास्तु गुणैर्युक्ता दृष्टलोकपरावराः ।
स्त्रियः स्वर्गेचरिष्यन्ति यथा पुण्यकृतस्तथा ॥

29. Women like you possessing such (noble) qualities and following well known traditional ways (norms) in the world, go to heaven just like those who have obtained "Merit" (through vows and penance).

❍ ❍ ❍

३०. तदेवमेनं त्वमनुव्रता सती
पतिव्रतानां समयानुवर्तिनी ।
भव स्वभर्तुः सहधर्मचारिणी
यशश्च धर्मं च ततः समाप्स्यसि ॥

30. Therefore, following (your husband Raama) thus, complying with him with the devotion of women of virtue, you must follow Dharma as practised by your husband, along with him. By this, you will obtain fame and renown.=

(Note: Anasooya need not have wasted her counsel on Seetha: World knows that Seetha was the most virtuous woman on earth.)

❍ ❍ ❍

Chapter 118

Anasooya Offers her Ornaments to Seetha

१. सा त्वेवमुक्ता वैदेही ह्यनसूयाऽनसूयया ।
प्रतिपूज्य वचो मन्दं प्रवक्तुमुपचक्रमे ॥

1. When told thus by Anasooya, this (Seetha) the Vaidhehi who was herself an "Anasooya" (a lady free from jealousy), began to speak gently in reply to her.

(Poet Vaalmeeki uses the word= an- Anasooya=, which means free from jealousy. Amongst many virtues, Seetha was a lady free from jealousy. So here we have two "Anasooya-s!)

❍ ❍ ❍

२. नैतदाश्चर्यमार्याया यन्मां त्वमभिभाषसे ।
विदितं तु ममाप्येतद्यथा नार्याः पतिर्गुरुः ॥

2. For a woman, her husband is her Guru (teacher, Lord): This is (well) known to me. Yet, that a noble (Aryan lady like) you spoke to me (about it, should not cause me) surprise.

(This is not the first time Seetha takes a "dig' at people who preach to her. Readers may know that Seetha " chided" her mother-in-law Kowsalya when she started sermonising about a dutiful wife.)

❍ ❍ ❍

३. यद्यप्येषं भवेद्भर्ता ममार्येवृत्तवर्जितः ।
अद्वैधमुपचर्तव्यस्तथाऽप्येष मया भवेत् ।।

3. Oh Aryan (lady Anasooya)! Even if my husband is devoid of moral conduct, he should be served by me without duplicity.

❍ ❍ ❍

४. किं पुनर्योगुणश्लाघ्यः सानुक्रोशो जितेन्द्रियः ।
स्थिरानुरागो धर्मात्मा मातृवर्ती पितृप्रियः ।।

4. (But) he, (my Raama) possesses laudable qualities; Is compassionate: has control over his senses (and passions): Faithful in love and affection: A noble soul man of Dharma: Obeys mother: Beloved of his father. What more (can I want in a husband).

❍ ❍ ❍

५. यां वृत्तिं वर्तते रामः कौसल्यायां महायशाः ।
तामेव नृपनारीणामन्यासामपि वर्तते ।।

5. What treatment he bestows upon (his own mother) Kowsalya, this famous Raama bestows the very same treatment upon all other wives of (his father, the great) king.

❍ ❍ ❍

६. सकृद्दृष्टास्वपि स्त्रीषु नृपेण नृपवत्सलः ।
मातृवद्वर्तते वीरो मानमुत्सृज्य धर्मवित् ।।

6. When a woman is looked upon even once by the king (his father Dhascharatha), this brave (Raama) the knower of Dharma, as a man devoted to the king, will treat the lady like his own mother, without indignation (that his father had taken on another woman)

(Readers may know that Dhascharatha had 350 wives apart from three queens, Kowsalya, Sumithra and Kaikeyi.)

❍ ❍ ❍

७. आगच्छन्त्याश्च विजनं वनमेवं भयावहम् ।
समाहितं मे श्वश्र्वा च हृदयेऽवस्थितं महत् ।।

7. The Advice, likewise given by my mother-in-law to me when I started out to the uninhabited forest (with Raama), firmly resides in my heart greatly.

❍ ❍ ❍

८. पाणिप्रदानकाले च यत्पुरा त्वग्निसन्निधौ ।
अनुशिष्टा जनन्याऽस्मि वाक्यं तदपि मे धृतम् ।।

8. Long ago, at the time of my marriage, before holy fire, I am taught (instructed about duties of a wife) by my mother. Such words (of counsel) is very solemn to me.

❍ ❍ ❍

९. नवीकृतं च तत्सर्वं वाक्यैस्ते धर्मचारिणि ।
पतिशुश्रूषणान्नार्यास्तपो नान्यद्विधीयते ।।

9. That there is no other penance prescribed for a woman other than devoted service to her husband and all that, are now being reminded (by you) with these words (of advice) from you; Oh (Anasooya), the follower of Dharma!

❍ ❍ ❍

१०. सावित्री पतिशुश्रूषां कृत्वा स्वर्गेमहीयते ।
तथावृत्तिश्च याता त्वं पतिशुश्रूषया दिवम् ।।

10. Saavithri, having done devoted service to her husband, is greatly honoured in heaven. And you too will go to heaven as you have the same conduct, by serving your husband, (Athri)!

❍ ❍ ❍

११. वरिष्ठा सर्वनारीणामेषा च दिवि देवता ।
रोहिणी न विना चन्द्रं मुहूर्तमपि दृश्यते ।।

11. This celestial (woman) who is foremost amongst all

ladies, this Rohini is not seen without (her Lord) the Moon even for a minute in the sky. (Mythologically Rohini is wife of Moon)

❍ ❍ ❍

१२. एवंविधांश्च प्रवराः स्त्रियो भर्तृदृढव्रताः ।
देवलोके महीयन्ते पुण्येन स्वेन कर्मणा ॥

12. Such noble ladies who are firm in service to their husbands are honoured in the world of celestials by their own auspicious deeds.

❍ ❍ ❍

१३. ततोऽनसूया संहृष्टा श्रुत्वोक्तं सीतया वचः ।
शिरस्याघ्राय चोवाच मैथिलीं हर्षयन्त्युत ॥

13. Hearing such words spoken by Seetha, Anasooya became very pleased and kissed (Seetha the) Maithili on her forehead and spoke to her, to gladden her even more.

❍ ❍ ❍

१४. नियमैर्विविधैराप्तं तपो हि महदस्ति मे ।
तत्संश्रित्य बलं सीते छन्दये त्वां शुचिस्मिते ॥

14. Oh Seetha! (by performance of) various Rites, there is in me (power of) mighty penance: Oh Seetha of winsome smile! Possessing such a power (as I have), I (wish) to gratify you.

❍ ❍ ❍

१५. उपपन्नं च युक्तं च वचनं तव मैथिलि ।
प्रीता चास्म्युचितं किं ते करवाणि ब्रवीहि मे ॥

15. Oh (Seetha the) Maithili! Your words are proper and appropriate: I am pleased: What delights you, that I will do: Tell me (what you desire).

❍ ❍ ❍

१६. तस्यास्तद्वचनं श्रुत्वा विस्मिता मन्दविस्मया ।
कृतमित्यब्रवीत्सीता तपोबलसमन्विताम् ।।

16. Hearing such words of hers, Seetha who was wonderstruck, (sporting) a gentle smile, told this (Anasooya) who was endowed with power of penance:= (All that I needed from you is) already done (by you for me)! = (I want only blessings!).

❍ ❍ ❍

१७. इत्येवमुक्ता धर्मज्ञा तया प्रीततराऽभवत् ।
सफलं च प्रहर्षं ते हन्त सीते करोम्यहम् ।।

17. When told thus by her, (this Anasooya) the knower of Dharma was even more pleased: (with her): (And she said): Oh Seetha! Welfare to you. I will (at least) gladden myself and fulfill (my desire) (Readers must remember that this old woman of great penance was like a mother to Seetha. And like all women, wants to please this young girl Seetha although Seetha wants nothing at all).

❍ ❍ ❍

१८. इदं दिव्यं वरं माल्यं वस्त्रमाभरणानि च ।
अङ्गरागं च वैदेहि महार्हं चानुलेपनम् ।।

18. Oh (Seetha) the Vaidhehi! This wonderful divine Garland, this dress and ornaments, the unguents and scents, the costly sandal paste.

❍ ❍ ❍

१९. मया दत्तमिदं सीते तव गात्राणि शोभयेत् ।
अनुरूपसंक्लिष्टं नित्यमेव भविष्यति ।।

19. ...... (all these) which are offered by me, Oh Seetha, will beautify your body. They will suit you and ever remain unsoiled and untarnished.

(By Anasooya's divine power this Seetha gets "Beauty Permanent")

❍ ❍ ❍

२०. अङ्गरागेण दिव्येन लिप्ताङ्गी जनकात्मजे ।
शोभयिष्यसि भर्तारं यथा श्रीर्विष्णुमव्ययम् ।।

20. Oh (Seetha the) daughter of Janaka! Like Goddess Lakshmi before eternal God Vishnu, you will bring lustre to your husband, anointing your body with these divine body unguents and scents.

❍ ❍ ❍

२१. सा वस्त्रमङ्गरागं च भूषणानि स्रजस्तथा ।
मैथिली प्रतिजग्राह प्रीतिदानमनुत्तमम् ।।

21. (Seetha the) Maithili thus accepted the garments, body unguents, ornaments, garland, foremost gifts offered in affection.

❍ ❍ ❍

२२. प्रतिगृह्य च तत्सीता प्रीतिदानं यशस्विनी ।
श्लिष्टाञ्जलिपुटा धीरा समुपास्ते तपोधनाम् ।।

22. Accepting these gifts given in affection, the famous Seetha cupped her hands in Anjali and with composure (and grace): She then sat by the side of (Anasooya) the woman whose wealth was penance.

❍ ❍ ❍

२३. तथा सीतामुपासीनामनसूया दृढव्रता ।
वचनं प्रष्टुमारेभे कथां कांचिदनुप्रियाम् ।।

23. And this Anasooya who was resolute in vows and rituals, began to say (some) words to Seetha who was sitting thus (by her side), to ask her in respect of some story that was (ever) pleasing (to hear).

❍ ❍ ❍

२४. स्वयंवरे किल प्राप्ता त्वमनेन यशस्विना ।
राघवेणेति मे सीते कथा श्रुतिमुपागता ।।

24. Oh Seetha! The story that you were 'obtained' by

this famous (Raama the) Raaghava only through *Swayamvara, has reached my ears.

(*Swayamvara is the mode of selection of bride/ bridegroom in marriage by a contest at a Hall before public.)

❍ ❍ ❍

२५. तां कथां श्रोतुमिच्छामि विस्तरेण च मैथिलि ।
यथाऽनुभूतं कात्स्न्र्येन तन्मे त्वं वक्तुमर्हसि ।।

25. Oh (Seetha) the Maithili! I desire to hear this story in detail; You should tell me all that happened fully.

❍ ❍ ❍

२६. एवमुक्ता तु सा सीता तां ततो धर्मचारिणीम् ।
श्रूयतामिति चोक्त्वाऽथ कथयामास तां कथाम् ।।

26. (Seetha narrates her story to Anasooya; It is interesting that this very old woman of many penance and vows, is still a woman at heart. Curiosity never leaves her! And she even desires to see Seetha well ornamented! Contrary to popular belief, Sages in India were very human, but without any "Attachment".)

When asked thus, this Seetha then told this woman of Dharma:= May You Listen = And she began to narrate the story (of her life).

❍ ❍ ❍

२७. मिथिलाधिपतिर्वीरो जनको नाम धर्मवित् ।
क्षत्रधर्मेह्यभिरतो न्यायतः शास्ति मेदिनीम् ।।

27. A man of Dharma, totally devoted in practising the Dharma of a Kshathriya, the brave (king) named Janaka, as lord of Mithila, rules over the earth (his kingdom) justly.

२८. तस्य लाङ्गलहस्तस्य कर्षतः क्षेत्रमण्डलम् ।
अहं किलोत्थिता भित्त्वा जगतीं नृपतेः सुता ॥

28. When king (Janaka) wielding a plough, was ploughing the (surface of) earth for (preparing a) site for Yaaga, indeed I was the girl who came up, splitting through the earth (that was being ploughed).

❍ ❍ ❍

२९. स मां दृष्ट्वा नरपतिर्मुष्टिविक्षेपतत्परः ।
पांसुकुण्ठितसर्वाङ्गीं जनको विस्मितोऽभवत् ॥

29. And this king Janaka who 'threw' away gifts by handful, became wonderstruck on seeing me who was covered with dust on my body.

❍ ❍ ❍

३०. अनपत्येन च स्नेहादङ्कमारोप्य च स्वयम् ।
ममेयं तनयेत्युक्त्वा स्नेहो मयि निपातितः ॥

30. Childless (as he was then), with great affection he himself took me on his lap and said:= She is my child= (From that time) Love was bestowed upon me.

❍ ❍ ❍

३१. अन्तरिक्षे च वागुक्ता प्रति माऽमानुषी किल ।
एवमेतन्नरपते धर्मेण तनया तव ॥

31. From the (unseen) sky, from a divine being =: Oh King! it is so As per Dharma, she is your daughter.= :(such) words were uttered!

❍ ❍ ❍

३२. ततः प्रहृष्टो धर्मात्मा पिता मे मिथिलाधिपः ।
अवाप्तो विपुलामृद्धिं मामवाप्य नराधिपः ॥

32. Because of this (affirmation by the divine), this noble soul man of Dharma, this king of Mithila became

very happy, took me along, became father to me, and obtained great prosperity.

❍ ❍ ❍

३३. दत्ता चास्मीष्टवद्देव्यै ज्येष्ठायै पुण्यकर्मणा ।
तया संभाविता चास्मि स्निग्धया मातृसौहृदात् ।।

33. I was handed over to his beloved eldest queen by this man who did auspicious deeds: With mother's love (and care) I came to be treated by her, who was very attached (and fond of) me, with great esteem.

❍ ❍ ❍

३४. पतिसंयोगसुलभं वयो दृष्ट्वा तु मे पिता ।
चिन्तामभ्यगमद्दीनो वित्तनाशादिवाधनः ।।

34. Seeing me (coming) of age fit for union with a husband, my father (king Janaka) became downcast and began to worry like a destitute (worrying) by loss of wealth.

❍ ❍ ❍

३५. सदृशाच्चापकृष्टाच्च लोके कन्यापिता जनात् ।
प्रधर्षणामवाप्नोति शक्रेणापि समो भुवि ।।

35. (Seetha tells Anasooya why her father worried about her.)

In the world, even if a man is equal to Lord Indhra, if one is a father of a young girl (of marriageable age), he suffers harassment (and derision) from men whether they are equal to him (in status) or inferior to him (in status).

❍ ❍ ❍

३६. तां धर्षणामदूरस्थां दृष्ट्वा चात्मनि पार्थिवः ।
चिन्तार्णवगतः पारं नाससादाप्लवो यथा ।।

36. Realising that such frayed situation was developing soon even in his case, king (Janaka) was submerged in the 'ocean of worry' and like one immersed (and

struggling in) water, could not reach the Shore (of the ocean of worry).

❍ ❍ ❍

३७. अयोनिजां हि मां ज्ञात्वा नाध्यगच्छद्विचिन्तयन् ।
सदृशं चानुरूपं च महीपालः पतिं मम ॥

37. Considering my (unusual birth of) not being born out of womb, king (Janaka) pondered to find out a husband suitable to me, equal to me (in qualities): Yet he could not find one.

❍ ❍ ❍

३८. तस्य बुद्धिरियं जाता चिन्तयानस्य सन्ततम् ।
स्वयंवरं तनूजायाः करिष्यामीति धीमतः ॥

38. Constantly thinking (worrying) over this, a thought occurred to this wise man; "I Will Conduct A Swayamvara For My Daughter".

❍ ❍ ❍

३९. महायज्ञे तदा तस्य वरुणेन महात्मना ।
दत्तं धनुर्वरं प्रीत्या तूणी चाक्षयसायकौ ॥

39. (Long ago) When a great Yaaga was performed, Two undecaying quivers full with arrows along with foremost Bow was gifted to him by the great soul Varuna with affection.

❍ ❍ ❍

४०. असञ्चाल्यं मनुष्यैश्च यत्नेनापि च गौरवात् ।
तन्न शक्ता नमयितुं स्वप्नेष्वपि नराधिपाः ॥

40. In spite of great effort, because of its (divine) power, it could not even be moved by men! Even in their dreams, kings could not (think of) bending (nor string up the Bow).

❍ ❍ ❍

४१. तद्धनुः प्राप्य मे पित्रा व्याहृतं सत्यवादिना ।
समवाये नरेन्द्राणां पूर्वमामन्त्र्य पार्थिवान् ।।

41. When he had obtained this bow long ago, kings were invited and before an Assembly of the kings, the (following) was told by my father who ever speaks Truth.

❍ ❍ ❍

४२. इदं च धनुरुद्यम्य सज्यं यः कुरुते नरः ।
तस्य मे दुहिता भार्या भविष्यति न संशयः ।।

42. A man who lifts up the bow and strings it up, To That Man My Daughter Will Become Wife: No Doubt (about my resolve).

❍ ❍ ❍

४३. तच्च दृष्ट्वा धनुः श्रेष्ठं गौरवाद्गिरिसन्निभम् ।
अभिवाद्य नृपा जग्मुरशक्तास्तस्य तोलने ।।

43. The kings, when they took a look at this foremost bow that was like a mountain, merely bowed before (the Bow) and went away, unable to even lift this up because of its (divine) power.

❍ ❍ ❍

४४. सुदीर्घस्य तु कालस्य राघवोऽयं महाद्युतिः ।
विश्वामित्रेण सहितो यज्ञं द्रष्टुं समागतः ।।
लक्ष्मणेन सह भ्रात्रा रामः सत्यपराक्रमः ।।

44. After quite some time, the truly brave and most majestic Raaghava, this Raama, came there along with his brother Lakshmana and (Sage) Vischwaamithra to witness a Yaaga (performed at Mithila by my father).

❍ ❍ ❍

४५. विश्वामित्रस्तु धर्मात्मा मम पित्रा सुपूजितः ।
प्रोवाच पितरं तत्र राघवौ रामलक्ष्मणौ ।।

45. The noble soul man of Dharma Vischwaamithra, who was most honoured by my father, then spoke about the two Raaghava-s, Raama and Lakshmana to my father.

❍ ❍ ❍

४६. सुतौ दशरथस्येमौ धनुर्दर्शनकाङ्क्षिणौ ।
धनुर्दर्शय रामाय राजपुत्राय दैविकम् ।।

46. (Vischwaamithra said this to my father, Oh Anasooya): = These two are sons of Dhascharatha: They desire to "See" the Bow: Show the divine Bow to the royal prince.=

❍ ❍ ❍

४७. इत्युक्तस्तेन विप्रेण तद्धनूः समूपानयत् ।।

47. Addressed thus by this Braamin (Vischwaamithra), he (my father), brought out the Bow.

❍ ❍ ❍

४८. निमेषान्तरमात्रेण तदानम्य स वीर्यवान् ।
ज्यां समारोप्य झटिति पूरयामास वीर्यवत् ।।

48. Within a minute, this brave (Raama) bent the Bow: With great power strung it up and filled (the place) with (sounds of) Twang (of the strings), at once.

❍ ❍ ❍

४९. तेन पूरयता वेगान्मध्ये भग्नं द्विधा धनुः ।
तस्य शब्दोऽभवद्भीमः पतितस्याशनेरिव ।।

49. As pressure was applied by him, the Bow broke into two in the middle; The sound of its fall was terrible, like thunder.

❍ ❍ ❍

५०. ततोऽहं तत्र रामाय पित्रा सत्याभिसन्धिना ।
निश्चिता दातुमुद्यम्य जलभाजनमुत्तमम् ।।

50. There, at that moment, it was decided that I should

be given (in marriage) to Raama by my most truthful father, who took (on his hand) a foremost Water vessel (for formal ritual of acceptance of Raama for me).

❍ ❍ ❍

५१. दीयमानां न तु तदा प्रतिजग्राह राघवः ।
अविज्ञाय पितुश्छन्दमयोध्याधिपतेः प्रभोः ।।

51. Then (Raama) the Raaghava did not (straightway) accept me, who was offered (to him) in marriage without knowing the will (and mind) of his father (Dhascharatha), the lord and king at Ayodhya.

❍ ❍ ❍

५२. ततः श्वशुरमामन्त्र्य वृद्धं दशरथं नृपम् ।
मम पित्रा त्वहं दत्ता रामाय विदितात्मने ।।

52. Only after inviting my old father-in-law king Dhascharatha, I was given (in marriage) to the most learned Raama by my father (Janaka).

❍ ❍ ❍

५३. मम चैवानुजा साध्वी ऊर्मिला प्रियदर्शना ।
भार्यार्थेलक्ष्मणस्यापि पित्रा दत्ता मम स्वयम् ।।

53. And my sister, the beautiful looking virtuous Oormila also, was offered to Lakshmana by my father himself, to be his wife.

❍ ❍ ❍

५४. एवं दत्ताऽस्मि रामाय तदा तत्र स्वयंवरे ।
अनुरक्तास्मि धर्मेण पतिं वीर्यवतां वरम् ।।

54. Thus, in this Swayamvara, I was offered (in marriage) to Raama then: As per Dharma, I am totally devoted to my lord (husband Raama) who is foremost amongst brave.

(Note: Like all old ladies, this Anasooya although a very renowned woman of penance and vows, is curious to know all about it! And Seetha of course describes how she met Raama and married him)

❍ ❍ ❍

Chapter 119

Raama Goes to Dhandaka Forest

१. अनसूया तु धर्मज्ञा श्रुत्वा तां महतीं कथाम् ।
पर्यष्वजत बाहुभ्यां शिरस्याघ्राय मैथिलीम् ।।

1. Hearing this magnificent story (of Seetha's wedding) the knower of Dharma Anasooya, kissed (Seetha) the Maithili on her forehead and hugged her with her hands.

❍ ❍ ❍

२. व्यक्ताक्षरपदं चित्रं भाषितं मधुरं त्वया ।
यथा स्वयंवरं वृत्तं तत्सर्वं च श्रुतं मया ।।

2. The story of your Swayamvara as it happened, was narrated sweetly and wonderfully by you, embellished with choice words: All this has been heard by me (now).

❍ ❍ ❍

३. रमेऽहं कथया ते तु दृढं मधुरभाषिणि ।।

3. Oh (Seetha) who talks so sweetly! I am immensely delighted by your story.

❍ ❍ ❍

४. रविरस्तं गतः श्रीमानुपोह्य रजनीं शिवाम् ।
दिवसं प्रतिकीर्णानामाहारार्थं पतत्रिणाम् ।।
सन्ध्याकाले निलीनानां निद्रार्थं श्रूयते ध्वनिः ।।

4. Impelling the auspicious night (to stay), the resplendent sun has set! The sounds from birds that has scattered themselves during the day (in search of) food, are

heard, as they take cover (in trees) in the (late) evening to sleep.

❍ ❍ ❍

५. एते चाप्यभिषेकार्द्रा मुनयः कलशोद्यताः ।
सहिता उपवर्तन्ते सलिलाप्लुतवल्कलाः ।।

5. And the sages also having taken their baths together are returning with their bark dress (still) wet, carrying water mugs.

❍ ❍ ❍

६. ऋषीणामग्निहोत्रेषु हुतेषु विधिपूर्वकम् ।
कपोताङ्गारुणो धूमो दृश्यते पवनोद्धतः ।।

6. Fanned by wind, the smoke emanating from the fire rituals of the Rishi-s (who perform) as per norms, appear red like the belly of a pigeon.

❍ ❍ ❍

७. अल्पपर्णा हि तरवो घनीभूताः समन्ततः ।
विप्रकृष्टेऽपि देशेऽस्मिन्न प्रकाशन्ति वै दिशः ।।

7. In the remote part of forest, in this region, the 'Directions' are not visible: Even trees with very few leaves, appear dense and thick everywhere.

❍ ❍ ❍

८. रजनीचरसत्त्वानि प्रचरन्ति सन्ततः ।
तपोवनमृगा ह्येते वेदितीर्थेषु शेरते ।।

8. (Oh Seetha)! The beasts that roam about at night are roaming everywhere: And animals of forest (of this forest of penance) are resting in these hermitages.

❍ ❍ ❍

९. संप्रवृत्ता निशा सीते नक्षत्रसमलङ्कृता ।
ज्योत्स्नाप्रावरणश्चन्द्रो दृश्यतेऽभ्युदितोऽम्बरे ।।

9. Oh Seetha! The night embellished by stars, has fallen; The moon has risen in the sky and is seen with glorious moonlight.

❍ ❍ ❍

१०. गम्यतामनुजानामि रामस्यानुचरी भव ।
कथयन्त्या हि मधुरं त्वयाऽहं परितोषिता ॥

10. I am immensely delighted by you who narrated the story so beautifully. May you always follow (and abide by) Raama. You may go. I give you leave.

❍ ❍ ❍

११. अलङ्कुरु च तावत्त्वं प्रत्यक्षं मम मैथिलि ।
प्रीतिं जनय मे वत्से दिव्यालङ्कारशोभिनी ॥

11. Oh (Seetha the Maithili! Before me (in my presence), you decorate yourself now. Oh Child! You bring joy to me by decorating yourself wonderfully.

❍ ❍ ❍

१२. सा तदा समलङ्कृत्य सीता सुरसुतोपमा ।
प्रणम्य शिरसा तस्यै रामं त्वभिमुखी ययौ ॥

12. Then this Seetha who was like a celestial lady, dressed herself (with these offered by Anasooya) and bowed to her with her head. Then she went back to Raama.

❍ ❍ ❍

१३. तथा तु भूषितां सीतां ददर्श वदतां वरः ।
राघवः प्रीतिदानेन तपस्विन्या जहर्ष च ॥

13. And the foremost of men of speech, this (Raama) the Raaghava observed Seetha dressed up (and ornamented): And because, all this was offered by a (great) woman of penance, he rejoiced.

(Raama would normally not want Seetha to dress like a princess in forest; he himself has chosen to live like a mendicant during exile.)

❍ ❍ ❍

१४. न्यवेदयत्ततः सर्वं सीता रामाय मैथिली ।
प्रीतिदान तपस्विन्या वसनाभरणस्रजाम् ।।

14. Seetha the Maithili, informed Raama at that moment, that all the dresses and ornaments and garland as being offered by this woman of penance (Anasooya).

❍ ❍ ❍

१५. प्रहृष्टस्त्वभवद्रामो लक्ष्मणश्च महारथः ।
मैथिल्याः सत्क्रियां दृष्ट्वा मानुषेष्वतिदुर्लभाम् ।।

15. Observing that such an honour done to (Seetha the) Maithili, was rarely done upon common human beings, the mighty charioteer (warrior) Raama became very delighted. And so was Lakshmana.

❍ ❍ ❍

१६. ततस्तां शर्वरीं प्रीतः पुण्यां शशिनिभाननः ।
अर्चितस्तापसैः सिद्धैरुवास रघुनन्दनः ।।

16. Then, honoured by the men of penance there and also the Sidhdhas, (Raama) the darling of Raghu-s whose countenance was like that of the moon, spent the auspicious night there, very pleased.

❍ ❍ ❍

१७. तस्यां रात्र्यां व्यतीतयामभिषिच्य हुताग्निकान् ।
आपृच्छेतां नरव्याघ्रौ तापसान्वनगोचरान् ।।

17. After night had passed away, and after taking bath, (Raama the) 'tiger' of men who had completed the Homa Fire Ritual, begged leave to go from these men of penance living in that forest.

❍ ❍ ❍

१८. तावूचुस्ते वनचरास्तापसा धर्मचारिणः ।
वनस्य तस्य सञ्चारं राक्षसैः समभिप्लुतम् ।।

18. These men of penance living in the forest and practising

Dharma, told these two about the difficulties afflicting this forest because of the demons.

❍ ❍ ❍

१९. रक्षांसि पुरुषादानि नानारूपाणि राघव ।
वसन्त्यस्मिन्महारण्ये व्यालाश्च रुधिराशनाः ।।

19. Oh (Raama) the Raaghava! In this mighty forest live many types of demons who seize (and devour) men: They are mischievous and suck blood.

❍ ❍ ❍

२०. उच्छिष्टं वा प्रमत्तं वा तापसं धर्मचारिणम् ।
अदन्त्यस्मिन्महारण्ये तान्निवारय राघव ।।

20. Oh (Raama) the Raaghava! In this mighty forest, (the demons) devour these men of penance and followers of Dharma., if they are careless or 'Impure': You Must Restrain Them (put a stop to this).

❍ ❍ ❍

२१. एष पन्था महर्षीणां फलान्याहरतां वने ।
अनेन तु वनं दुर्गं गन्तुं राघव ते क्षमम् ।।

21. Oh (Raama) the Raaghava! This is the path in the forest of the great sages to bring fruits etc. It will be safe for you to go along (this path) in the dense forest.

❍ ❍ ❍

२२. इतीव तैः प्राञ्जलिभिस्तपस्विभि
द्विजैः कृतस्वस्त्ययनः परन्तपः ।
वनं सभार्यः प्रविवेश राघवः
सलक्ष्मणः सूर्य इवाभ्रमण्डलम् ।।

22. When they told thus, the tormentor of enemies, (this Raama) the Raaghava, along with Lakshmana and wife (Seetha) entered the forest like sun from (behind) cluster of clouds, after receiving Swasthi blessings from

these braamins who were men of penance and who had cupped their hands in Anjali.

(We Come to The End Of Ayodhya Kaanda. From now on it is all about Raama and his forest life and finally his war with Raavana.)